Database
Models, Languages, Design

Database

Models, Languages, Design

James L. Johnson

Western Washington University

New York   Oxford
OXFORD UNIVERSITY PRESS
1997

Oxford University Press

Oxford   New York
Athens   Auckland   Bangkok   Bogota   Bombay
Buenos Aires   Calcutta   Cape Town   Dar es Salaam
Delhi   Florence   Hong Kong   Istanbul   Karachi
Kuala Lumpur   Madras   Madrid   Melbourne
Mexico City   Nairobi   Paris   Singapore
Taipei   Tokyo   Toronto   Warsaw

and associated companies in
Berlin   Ibadan

Published by Oxford University Press, Inc.,
198 Madison Avenue, New York, New York 10016
http://www.oup-usa.org
1-800-334-4249

Oxford is a registered trademark of Oxford University Press

Library of Congress Cataloging-in-Publication Data

Johnson, James L. (James Lee), 1942–
    Database : models, languages, design / James L. Johnson.
        p.   cm.
    ISBN 0-19-510783-7 (cloth)
    1. Database management.   I. Title.
QA76.9.D3J58   1997   96-18198
005.74—dc20   CIP

9 8 7 6 5 4 3 2

Printed in the United States of America
on acid-free paper

To my mother

Contents

Preface

THIS TEXT PRESENTS THE TRADITIONAL TOPICS OF A FIRST undergraduate computer science course in database theory. I make no claim to originality because most of the ideas are well known. My contribution lies in organizing the material and in explaining the concepts to convey a clearer introduction to database theory than competing textbooks. I don't cover database implementation techniques or distributed database matters, nor do I discuss performance issues beyond a one-chapter epilogue. Proper treatment of these topics occurs in a second course, after the student is familiar with the models, languages, and design issues discussed here.

Part I covers five database models. These models represent the present (the relational model), the future (the object-oriented and deductive models), and the past (the network and hierarchical models). In keeping with its current importance, the relational model receives the most attention, including relational representation (data, relationships, and constraints), relational algebra and calculus, and complete coverage of the Structured Query Language (SQL). I make no attempt to adhere to the particular details of any commercial database product. Rather, I emphasize the concepts common to all these products. You should be well prepared to implement applications in any SQL-compliant relational database after mastering this material. I cover the object-oriented and deductive approaches in two chapters each. In each case, the first chapter describes the model itself: the techniques for representing data items with their relationships and constraints. The second chapter then shows how to compose queries against the databases. Finally, I devote one chapter each to the database models of the past, limiting the coverage because both the network and hierarchical models have been superseded by the relational model. Nevertheless, these models deserve some attention, both as an historical development and as further evidence of the similarity that links all five models. Finally, Part I closes with an explicit comparison of the five database models.

Part II takes up physical data storage issues, which I include to make the text self-contained. Because my students have already studied file and index structures, I omit this material from my database course. However, many curriculums do cover file topics in the database course, particularly concepts that deal with the packing of related records, and so this text should accommodate those needs.

Part III deals with application design issues. The first chapter presents entity-relationship (ER) diagrams and Object Modeling Technique (OMT) as examples of semantic modeling tools, which help application designers identify and structure the application entities and their relationships. I use simple ER diagrams early in Part I to illustrate application examples across the various database models. However, the student is better prepared to appreciate the more advanced ER features, such as class hierarchies and related issues, after exposure to all of the database models. Therefore these topics appear in Part III. I then devote two chapters to functional dependency and join dependency analysis. These techniques show how the choice of relational tables can enforce certain constraints.

Because I attempt to provide extensive explanations, buttressed with many examples, Parts I through III exhaust the page count, and the class lecture opportunities, of a one-term textbook. Nevertheless, I include a final one-chapter Part IV, which groups selected advanced topics under the general heading of performance issues. The chapter provides a brief introduction to concurrency, recovery, security, and query optimization.

For most illustrations throughout the text, I use a single, simple example. So when you study a new database model, you refer to the same familiar application. From the oldest to the newest, these models simply represent different approaches to organizing relationships and constraints among data elements. The common application example emphasizes this similarity theme across the five models. I further reinforce the theme by calling attention to certain recurring patterns that account for most database queries.

Goals, uses, and prerequisites of the text

I envision this book primarily as the supporting text for a first undergraduate database course. The book provides more than enough material for an upper division course, either in the format of four lectures per week for an academic quarter or three lectures per week for a semester. Prerequisites for the text are:

- Programming: data structures and algorithm expression in a procedural language. I present algorithms in C, but without supporting routines for the usual operations on stacks, lists, queues, and the like. If you understand a block-structured procedural language, even if it's not C, you should be able to read these algorithms, even if you couldn't write them.

- Predicate calculus. You should have some previous exposure to this topic although I provide a brief review.

- Set theoretic arguments and certain discrete mathematics topics: boolean algebra, relations, and induction proofs.

- Assertions and loop invariants: I use these methods to prove the correctness of algorithms.

- Elementary combinatorics and probability theory: I use both sparingly in hash-table arguments in Part II.

The text can support a database course in a variety of ways. Because my students have already covered the file topics of Part II, I spend about 60% of the term on the models and languages of Part I, skip Part II, and then take up as much of Part III as is possible in the remaining 40% of the course. I first cover the introduction and the material on the relational model, including the more complex SQL topics, in the lectures. I then take up the object-oriented and deductive models. Because I emphasize the generic features of databases, the students learn how to draw their own parallels between the relational model and the newer models, allowing more abbreviated lectures. I leave the historical models as a reading assignment, requiring a short report contrasting either the network or hierarchical approach with the models discussed in class. In Part II, I cover all the features of the entity-relationship notation in lectures before delving into the more mathematical treatment of functional and join dependencies. The pace slows at this point because the mathematics is more demanding. I present the major results, and I do enough derivations to convey the flavor of such developments. Working through the material in this manner, I usually finish the term somewhere in the chapter on join dependencies.

Even using this selected subset of chapters, the instructor must not try to mention all the details in the lectures. Although I have never tried to cover the material in complete detail, I estimate that working through the entire book in lectures would require a full academic year. A successful approach first selects the appropriate chapters and then further selects, for the lectures, the chapters' conceptual high points and supporting examples. Students are instructed to read the selected chapters completely to flesh out their understanding.

If the curriculum requires the file concepts of Part II in the database course, I recommend covering the models in much the same manner as above but necessarily including less of database design topics in Part III. If the course calls for hands-on experience with a commercial database product, this project can be started about one-third through the term, just after the chapter on basic SQL. I ask my students to create a small five-table relational database, similar to the common application example of the text, and to formulate queries against it.

Finally, the text is appropriate for the database practitioner who is familiar with the relational technology and wants to learn about the object-oriented and deductive models. Chapters 1-6 provide a thorough review of relational databases, explaining the features in a manner that invites extension to other models. Chapters 7-10 then continue with the post-relational models, discussing deductive and object-oriented databases.

Presentation style

My presentation differs from most database textbooks. First, I provide more explanation and examples. Second, I emphasize generic concepts, rather than the specific details of existing commercial products. I recognize the value of a survey of existing products, but there isn't space for adequate explanation of concepts and attention to the varying details of commercial systems. Another feature, which I share with some other authors, is the choice of the C language to describe algorithms. A programming language allows precise and concise statements of the algorithms. I also use C code segments to illustrate certain non-algorithmic material, such as embedded SQL and network queries. Most students are somewhat familiar with C by the time they enroll in a database course. In any case, the examples used are short excerpts, rather than full programs, and they should be sufficiently readable to demonstrate the concepts. Finally, bibliographical references appear at the end of the book, rather than at the end of each chapter. I have listed all references that I have consulted on this subject. Because each chapter draws on a large subset of these references, it would be redundant to list sources after each reference. When I know the original reference for a idea, I include it in the bibliography. In any case, the ideas belong to the original researchers. I claim only the organization, explanations, and mistakes of this particular presentation.

Acknowledgments

I am pleased to acknowledge the assistance and encouragement of several persons in the preparation of this work. I am indebted to my editor at Oxford University Press, Mr. Bill Zobrist, who believed in the manuscript when it was still in very rough form. Bill's suggestions have led to a much more readable book. I appreciate the patience of my wife, Ms. Shelley Hoeck, who tolerated the many evenings when I danced with my word processor rather than with her. Shelley also sketched the first drafts of the figures that appear in the text. I am especially grateful to Ms. Julie Schlifske for suggesting how to transform my sometimes convoluted prose into a more readable format. After indulging for years in the unsavory habit of correcting my friends' grammar, I found myself on the other side of the fence. It was, however, an enjoyable experience. I learned a lot from Julie about how to phrase an argument and how to write a book. Finally, I want to thank the technical reviewers for their criticism and comments on the book's content. Just as it takes a village to raise a child, it takes more than an author to make a book. Thanks everybody.

DATABASE MODELS AND ACCESS METHODS

P ART I SURVEYS FIVE DATABASE MODELS: relational, object-oriented, deductive, network, and hierarchical. The systematic development of databases started with the hierarchical and network models, which were popular in the 1960s and 1970s. The relational model is the current favorite, while the object-oriented and deductive models point the way to the future. Regardless of the underlying model, a specific database manages information from some real-world application, such as a hospital management or airline reservation. From the application viewpoint these models all share a common goal: to facilitate the storage and retrieval of information. As you study the details of the five models, you will see that their primary differences lie in the methods for expressing relationships and constraints among the application data elements.

I devote the most detailed exposition to the relational model because of its current popularity, its power as a data organizational took, and its many robust commercial implementations. When the relational model appeared on the scene, its superiority over the existing hierarchical and network models was striking. After certain performance improvements, the relational model essentially rendered its predecessors obsolete. The newer object-oriented and deductive models do offer some advantages over the relational model, but their evolution has not been as dramatic. It seems unlikely that these newer models will quickly overshadow the relational approach, especially because extended relational products continue to appear.

In a sense, Part I emphasizes mental models, that is, application-friendly environments in which you can imagine database responses purely in application terms. These mental models allow you to think in terms of certain generic activities among the application entities, such as a hospital checking in a patient or an airline clerk selling a seat on a flight. The database management system is obligated to project such an application-level illusion, although the internal software routines will rely on computer science mechanisms, such as hashing functions and index trees. These lower level activities serve only to support an overall conceptual model of the database organization. At the higher level, you find the tables and relationships, objects and messages, or axioms and inference rules of the application. Part I investigates how each of the five database models approaches a conceptual organization of information. Later, Part II will consider the data structures, access routines, and disk storage techniques that ultimately implement the concepts.

Part I also emphasizes the features of the various query languages associated with the database models. This emphasis is well-deserved because it is not the data elements themselves that are particularly informative, but rather the rich relationships among them. I use query languages to illustrate these relationships and to compare information retrieval capabilities across the models. The queries are often complex, but they all exemplify relationship patterns that are typical of many applications.

Introduction to Databases

A PROGRAMMER SOON LEARNS THAT WELL-ORGANIZED DATA STRUCTURES simplify a programming task. In a similar manner, an application designer needs organizing principles to handle the large data sets that must be coordinated across a collection of programs. The application designer confronts numerous problems, including data volumes beyond memory capacity, slow performance from unstructured searches, special-purpose code customized for certain storage devices, and varying mechanisms for representing relationships among data elements. These problems arise from computer involvement, not from the intricacies of the application. Normally the application is challenging enough without the added problems of computerized solutions.

A **database management system** (DBMS) provides the needed organizational approach to flexible storage and retrieval of large amounts of data. The DBMS does not eliminate the problems mentioned above. Rather, it isolates them in a generic package that deals with such headaches, presenting the designer with a clean interface. With simple commands, the application dispatches items to be stored in the database, leaving it to the DBMS to find proper physical storage, to guarantee future access through a variety of pathways, and to integrate the data into meaningful relationships with other elements. Moreover, the DBMS handles these difficult tasks in a generic manner so that the same DBMS can serve many applications. For example, suppose one application deals with buildings and their rooms while a second deals with tanks of fish. The same DBMS can run both applications. It must store the various attributes of the buildings and rooms (or tanks and fish), and it must keep track of which building contains which rooms (or of which tank contains which fish). In other words, the DBMS must handle general "container" relationships.

A DBMS can take several approaches to the responsibilities outlined above. Each approach constitutes a database model, and the first part of this book is a systematic study of five such models. A **database model** is an organizing principle that specifies particular mechanisms for data storage and retrieval. The model explains, in terms of the services available to an interfacing application, how to access a data element when other related data elements are known. It also specifies the precise meaning of the term *related data*, and it provides mappings from particular relationships in an application to the more generic types maintained by the DBMS. In the example above, a relationship exists between each room and the building that houses it, or between each fish and the tank that contains it. The DBMS provides a more general type of relationship in which a container object includes component objects. A database model must allow the representation of a specific building-rooms relationship within the more general container-components framework.

The software implementation of each model involves several levels, from the physical structures on disk storage devices through the abstractions (e.g., tables, objects) that describe an application. This text does not develop such implementations although it gives sufficient detail on each model for an implementation to begin. Actual DBMS implementations are very complicated software systems, easily among the most intricate ever written. The models described here all have commercially available implementations, and as is to be expected, these implementations vary considerably. Variations occur both in the expression of the model structures and in the extra features that distinguish a product from its competitors. This text will explore database models in a generic manner, without concern for the minor differences of syntax or capability encountered in real products. The treatment here will provide you with the background needed to use any of today's many database systems.

Motivation for database systems

Database systems separate data storage and retrieval details from application-specific complexities. You can better appreciate the need for this separation by studying some problems of pre-database systems. In each of the following situations, assume that an application consists of a collection of programs, each requiring certain input files and producing output files used by other programs of the collection.

- Without databases, data and the programs are heavily dependent on each other. Data elements depend on a program to give them meaning. Of course, a program requires its input files in order to execute, but a dependency also exists in the reverse direction. Examining an input file in isolation, you might find it totally unreadable, consisting only of ones and zeros. Only inside a program does the data line up in structures that reveal its meaning. If the file is a sequence of ASCII codes, then you can dump it to display the record structure. A record may appear as: 008 11 2 14 JONES 45601 AT7Y 0000 45. The word, JONES, leads you to suspect that this is a personnel record, but the rest of the record doesn't supply much more information. Obviously the data are *not* self-describing. Perhaps there is documentation that describes the fields of the file. Perhaps the programmer remembers the layout. When the program reads the file, the characters fill certain variables and record structures, and perhaps the program contains comments about the meaning of these variables. The point is that the data are meaningful only in the context of the program. In a manner of speaking, the program *owns* the data. Because you need the owning program to understand the data's meaning, you are not likely to use that data file for a new program, even if the file contains exactly the information that the new program requires.

    Data should not depend on a program to render it understandable and useful. That is, data should be self-describing. Coded as follows, the data above is much more useful. Of course, the annotations more than double the length of the file, and their repetition in each record is wasteful. As you will see, more efficient mechanisms are available to implement data self-description.

newRecordFlag = 0, class = 08, age = 11, rank = 2, prevRank = 14, name = JONES, zipCode = 45601, accessCode = AT7Y, padding = 0000, discount = 45

- Outside a database environment, the same data element often appears in many files. Each programmer sets up a file structure to match the input needs of a particular program. Because the programmer is reluctant to search out and interpret files associated with other programs, he creates a new file structure, which may duplicate existing data elements. For example, many programs process personnel records, all from different files, all containing such data elements as employee name, address, city, and phone. While the wasted storage space is an issue, a more important problem is data integrity. If an employee changes residence, will the update reach all the files containing the address data? With the address scattered across many files, certain files might contain the new address, while others would keep the old version. From the application standpoint, this condition is inconsistent because an employee should have a well-defined address.

- Without a central database repository, programs must frequently access data from separate files. For example, suppose you need a report giving certain details about the employees working on various projects. The personnel file and the projects-in-progress file each supply part of the required information. You could write a preliminary procedure to extract the desired fields from each file, thereby producing a special file for this program, but this would only add to the data replication problem. Ideally, you should be able to recover the relationships among the data elements from the raw data without such preprocessing. Since workers and projects are naturally related in the application, you should be able to assemble the fields required by the new program as the need arises. In other words, a flexible storage and retrieval mechanism should maintain relationships on an equal footing with the individual data elements.

- In a non-database context, each programmer "owns" the data files associated with his program, making these filed is less accessible to others. Even if the owner is willing to share, the programmer might use coding conventions or format layouts that are unfamiliar to others. Moreover, a user might question the quality of data from a remote proprietary file. For example, how often is the file updated? By contrast, a database provides more uniform availability of data.

- Without a centralized database, the security policy must deal with a dispersed collection of files of varying formats. Certain security issues arise with any data collection: Who is permitted to view the data? Who is allowed to change it? A database handles security more effectively by concentrating the effort on the database itself. Because all the data is vulnerable to an attack at one point, management can justify a larger cost to secure the centralized site. Database systems feature an elaborate range of security measures, allowing various sorts of access privileges (read, write, delete) at different structural resolutions (data element, record, table, file). Admittedly, the centralized approach has one uncomfortable security disadvantage: if the central facility is compromised, all the data are exposed.

- Without databases, programs can interfere with one another. The effects of transactions in one program are not isolated from those in other programs. For example, suppose that you need to enforce the constraint that no employee should live in a blue house. One program and its associated files maintain the employee's address while a separate program handles house descriptions, including color. If you paint a house blue and use the second program to update its description, will you remember that an employee might live there? If there is such an employee, the data are now inconsistent from the application standpoint. With a database, the constraint between employees and blue houses becomes part of the centralized data service. The DBMS would not allow a change in house color that would violate the constraint.

- Data deletions or updates can produce inconsistencies, which are difficult to control in a non-database system. For example, suppose you demolish an employee's house. The address field of many files may now refer to a nonexistent house. Should the application programs deal with keeping such data alignments current? If so, which application program carries which responsibilities? A database can coordinate deletion activities, ensuring that no dangling references remain after a deletion.

- Without databases, data sharing is more difficult. Although operating systems can provide simultaneous read-only access to files, they normally limit read-write access to one process. A particular data file can then serve only one general-purpose user at any given time. This coarse level of lockout is inefficient because the program might be using only a small portion of the file, and another program might want access to an unrelated portion. A database can coordinate simultaneous access to the data elements. It allows data sharing at a finer resolution, locking only individual data elements during write operations.

- Without database oversight, data inconsistencies can arise when a long process terminates with an error. A process may modify part of the data but abort before installing all the intended changes. For example, suppose a banking transaction is to transfer money from Account X to Account Y. The transaction subtracts the amount from the balance of Account X, and then a power failure interrupts the process before it can add the amount to Account Y. You could recover the affected files from backup copies, but this is an ad hoc approach to the general problem of recovery from failures. By contrast, a database system readily handles such recovery. The DBMS rejects a transaction that does not complete, with the state of the database remaining as though the transaction had never started. Because the DBMS handles recovery, individual applications need not deal with failed transactions.

- Finally, without databases, variations in the physical data representation can cause many problems. If the data storage medium changes from magnetic disk to optical disk, for example, certain applications may become invalid because they have hardcoded references to the first device, such as cylinder and track numbers. Another problem can arise when file records acquire a new field. Old programs could ignore the new field, but will they? It depends on how closely the programmer has coupled read-write activity to the details of the storage structures. Finally, suppose that extra memory becomes available for processing. Will the programs exploit the resource by caching data records, thereby reducing time-consuming disk access cycles? They probably won't, and rightfully so. Programs should be concerned with manipulating the application objects (e.g., persons, tasks, hours, accounts), not with storage details.

 Deficiencies of pre-database information processing include encoded data, interdependence between programs and data files, data repetition and associated inconsistencies, ad hoc representation of relationships among data items, lack of coordination across programs using common data, restricted simultaneous access to data, and non-uniform error recovery methods.

During the late 1950s and early 1960s these problems prompted the development of the first database systems. In Part I of this text, you'll find five approaches to the general problem of data storage and retrieval, each of which addresses the deficiencies of pre-database systems.

Definition of a database system

A **database** is a self-describing collection of data elements, together with relationships among those elements, that presents a uniform service interface. A **database management system** (DBMS) is a software product that supports the reliable storage of the database, implements the structures for maintaining relationships and constraints, and offers storage and retrieval services to users. Additional features address other issues, such as simultaneous access, security, backup, and recovery.

This definition is general in order to include all aspects of database techniques, models, and services. The definition will become more focused as the following chapters investigate specific approaches to these features. For now, a brief look at the relational database model will help you interpret this general definition in more concrete terms.

To describe an application object, you can use a collection of data values. For example, if the application deals with cats, you may describe a particular cat by giving values for color, weight, and napTime. A cat then may appear as: color = black, weight = 17, and napTime = 4:00 am. Different cats will have different attribute values. The isolated bits of data (black, 17, 4:00 am) become informative only when they exist in the context of some application entity. When divorced from context, isolated data values are meaningless.

The above definition requires that the data elements reside in a self-describing structure, which confers meaning on them. The most obvious such structure is a table, as illustrated below, but you'll encounter other interesting possibilities later.

Cat				
name	color	weight	napTime	idNumber
vixen	black	17	4:00 am	110
⋮	⋮	⋮	⋮	⋮

Student				
name	class	eyeColor	cat	idNumber
joe	sophomore	blue	vixen	24
:	:	:	:	:

The definition also states that a database must store relationships among the data elements. What constitutes a relationship? Generally speaking, a relationship is a sense of togetherness that exists among certain data elements. For example, suppose the application deals not only with cats but also with students. Using the table as the organizing structure, you then create separate tabulations of cats and students, as shown above. However, note that an attribute within a student description specifies the name of the cat belonging to that student. This connection declares a certain "closeness" between the set of data values representing the student joe and the set representing the cat vixen. In this case, the database stores this association by embedding some identifying portion of one entity in the description for the other. The basis of each relationship is an abstract principle that groups data elements in a manner that is meaningful for the application. Although attribute embedding is not the only alternative, every DBMS must be able to support relationship groupings. Therefore, your first encounter with a new database model should provoke the question: How are the data elements organized, and what mechanism is used to group data elements into relationships?

Finally, the definition requires a database to present a uniform interface to users. Uniformity means that there should be a standard simple structure for storing or retrieving related data. For example, in the context of students and their cats, you could ask many questions that request certain data elements associated with other known elements. What are the names of cats owned by student X? Among what class of students is the ownership of a cat the most popular? The relational model provides an access language, called **Structured Query Language** (SQL), which expresses such questions in the following syntax.

```
select name                    select roomSize
from Cat                       from Room
where ...                      where ...
```

Details of the unspecified where-clause will come later; the emphasis here is on the standard form of the expression. Although the query on the right above comes from a different application, dealing with buildings and their rooms, it expresses a retrieval query in the same form. Only the names of the attributes vary. These expressions do not involve computer-specific details, such as character-position offsets and record numbers, which frequently characterize data retrieval operations from program-specific files. Nor do they require preprocessing to extract the fields that indicate relationships. By leaving these operational matters to the DBMS, the user can concentrate on the application complexities. Because each database model must provide a flexible storage-retrieval interface, a new model should always provoke the question: What types of expressions are used to provide user services?

To summarize, a DBMS must provide for the organization of the data elements, the representation of relationships among the elements, and the uniform interface for users. These aspects are the most important, and once they are defined, the rest of the features normally associated with a database system fall into place. For example, if the database model uses tables to organize the data, then security mechanisms must deal with read-write privileges on rows, columns, individual cells, or entire tables. Likewise, a constraint specification policy must check entries in different tables for inconsistencies.

 A database is a self-describing collection of data elements and their relationships, which presents a uniform interface to users. A database management system (DBMS) supports the reliable storage of the database, implements the relationship structures, and offers uniform storage/retrieval services to users.

Overview of database models

The above definition helps to formulate some basic similarities and distinctions among the five database models.

Relational database model

The relational model uses tables to organize the data elements. Each table corresponds to an application entity, and each row represents an instance of that entity. For example, the cat entity in the application corresponds to the Cat table in the database. Each table row represents a different cat. Relationships link rows from two tables by embedding row identifiers from one table as attribute values in another table. For example, the identifier of a cat row (the cat name) appears in a student row, thereby establishing the student as the owner of the cat. Despite complications that arise from relationships involving many rows from many tables, this simple mechanism supports relationships without resorting to auxiliary structures, such as linked lists or indexes. Structured Query Language (SQL) serves as the uniform interface for users, providing a collection of standard expressions for storing and retrieving data.

Object-oriented database model

Although the relational model now dominates the field, two aggressive competitors claim to provide more flexible data representation, at least for specialized applications. The literature refers to these newcomers as post-relational models. Each offers an alternative to tabular embeddings for maintaining relationships.

The first post-relational model, the object-oriented model, represents an application entity as a class. A class captures both the attributes and the behavior of the entity. For example, a Cat class possesses not only cat attributes, such as color, weight, and napTime, but also procedures that imitate actions expected of a cat, such as destroyFurniture("sofa"). Instances of the class, called objects, correspond to individual cats. Within an object, the class attributes take specific values, which distinguish, for example, one cat from another. However, the behavior patterns are shared by all cat objects. The object-oriented model does not restrict attribute values to the small set of native data types usually associated with databases and programming languages, such as integer, float, real, decimal, and string. Instead, the values can be other objects. One of the attributes of a cat can be owner, and the value of that attribute can be a student object, corresponding to the student that owns the cat in the application.

The object-oriented model maintains relationships through "logical containment." Consider the cat-student example. You find the student owner of a particular cat *within* the cat, as the value of one of the cat attributes. Since that student is an object in its own right, you can recursively examine its attributes. In particular, the student can have a pet attribute, the value of which is a cat object. Of course, that cat object is the same cat in which you originally found the student. In a manner of speaking, cat X contains student Y which contains cat X! Because physical containment is obviously out of the question, the term *logical containment* is more appropriate. By using pointers you can construct a data structure that can indeed contain itself in a logical sense.

Deductive database model

The second post-relational database model is the deductive model, also known as the inferential model. This model stores as little data as possible but compensates by maintaining rules that allow new data combinations to be created as needed. Suppose that the database stores facts of the form stuOwnsCat (S, C), meaning that student S owns cat C. For example, the fact stuOwnsCat (joe, vixen) may appear in the database. Assume that a student can own many cats, and that a cat can be owned by many students. You could then imagine another relationship in which two students are related if they own the same cat. This relationship would appear in the format catMates (S, T), meaning that students S and T share ownership of a cat. Although the database explicitly stores the stuOwnsCat (S, C) facts, it does not store the catMates (S, T) facts. Instead, it stores a rule stating that some particular fact, say catMates (joe, jim), can be deduced from existing facts, say stuOwnsCat (joe, vixen) and stuOwnsCat (jim, vixen). Such inference rules indirectly capture relationship groupings. The database thus stores certain elementary facts, called axioms, from which other facts can be derived when needed.

Hierarchical database model

In contrast to the object-oriented and deductive models, the hierarchical model is relatively old, dating from the late 1950s. The hierarchical model assumes that a tree structure, such as the company organizational chart of Figure 1.1, is the most frequently occurring relationship. This assumption is recognized today as misleading. In fact, many of the hierarchical model's shortcomings result from this overly restrictive view of relationships. However, for the moment, assume that only hierarchical relationships are important.

Consider, for example, a corporate hierarchy. As Figure 1.1 demonstrates, the president is at the top, over a reporting structure that branches into vice-presidents, departments, and employees. The chart shows only the entity type (e.g., president, vice-president) and suppresses the attributes (e.g., name, social security number, address, phone). Several vice-presidents report to the president, and several departments report to each vice-president. At the lowest level, each department contains many employees. A key feature of this organization is that you can translate it into a linear list, as illustrated below.

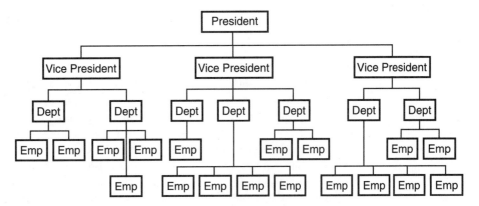

Figure 1.1 A hierarchical organization

```
President (name = jones, phone = 111-222-3333, etc.)
    Vice-President (name = able, ...)
        Department (name = Electrical, ...)
            Employee (name = doyle, ...)
            Employee (name = erikson, ...)
            Employee (name = ferris, ...)
        Department (name = Mechanical, ...)
            Employee (name = gilbert, ...)
            Employee (name = hansen, ...)
    Vice-President (name = baker, ...)
        Department (name = Finance, ...)
            Employee (name = jarbo, ...)
            Employee (name = karlstrom, ...)
        Department (name = Marketing, ...)
        Department (name = Accounting, ...)
            Employee (name = marchand, ...)
```

The hierarchical model organizes data elements as tabular rows, one for each instance of an application entity. In this example, a separate row represents the President, each vice-president, each department, and each employee. The row position implies a relationship to other rows. That is, a given employee belongs to the department that is closest above it in the list; a given department reports to the vice-president immediately above it in the list. The hierarchical model represents relationships with the notion of logical adjacency, or more accurately, with logical proximity, in the linearized tree. You can isolate the set of employees working for departments under Vice-President X by first locating Vice-President X and then including every employee in the list after X and before the next occurrence of a vice-president (or the end of the list). Because the linearized tree is an abstraction, the term *logical proximity* is more appropriate. An actual implementation may scatter the data items across various structures and materialize the linearized tree as needed with hashing schemes or linked lists. Logical proximity describes the organization but doesn't imply physical proximity.

Network database model

The network model replaces the hierarchical tree with a graph, allowing more general connections among the nodes. Suppose in the previous example that an employee works for two departments. Then the strict hierarchical arrangement breaks down, and the tree of Figure 1.1 becomes a more general graph, or network. Logical proximity fails, because you can't place a data item simultaneously in two locations in the list. Although the hierarchical model contains more complicated methods to handle these situations, the syntax becomes difficult to follow. The network database model evolved specifically to handle non-hierarchical relationships. The network model maintains relationships with a system of intersecting chains, as illustrated in Figure 1.2. The solid chain extending from employee charlie contains one circle for each department in which charlie works. Similarly, the dashed chain extending from the electrical department contains one circle for each employee of that department. When a circle is on both chains, then the employee originating the solid chain works for the department owning the dashed chain. The incomplete dashed chains through other circles on charlie's chain belong to other departments. Similarly, the incomplete solid chains through other circles on the electrical department's chain belong to other employees.

Other comparisons

Figure 1.3 summarizes the characteristics of the five database models discussed above. The last two columns outline two further distinctions. First, each model uses a particular style of access language to manipulate the database contents. Some models employ a procedural language, prescribing a sequence of operations to compute the desired results. Others use a non-procedural language, stating only the desired results and leaving the specific computation to the database system. The relational and deductive models use non-procedural languages; the object-oriented, hierarchical, and network systems use procedural syntax.

A second distinction concerns the identity of the data elements. Within a database, an application object or relationship appears as a data element or grouping of data elements. For example, suppose that a fat black cat weighing 20 pounds exists as the collection (black, fat, 20). How is the identity of the application cat tied to the data elements? For example, if the cat loses some weight, the data structure changes to (black, lean, 15). The real-world cat is the same object as before, and therefore the data structure has not changed identity, only value. How many attributes can change before a new creature emerges? Suppose the fat black cat shrinks to one-tenth its size, acquires a rodent-like tail, abandons its regal indifference to the world at large, and exhibits definite mouse-like behavior, such as scurrying shamelessly after tidbits of cheese. Is it still a cat? From the standpoint of the database system, the question is simpler: If all the attributes of the data structure change, has a new entity been created?

The object-oriented, network, and hierarchical models assume that the object survives changes of all its attributes. These systems are **record-based**. A record of the real-world item appears in the database, and even though the record's contents may change completely,

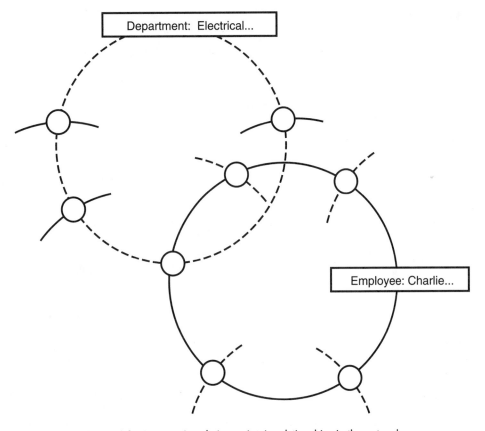

Figure 1.2   Intersecting chains maintain relationships in the network

the record itself represents the application item. As long as the record remains in the database, the object's identity has not changed.

By contrast, the relational and deductive models are **value-based**. They assume real-world item has no identity independent of its attribute values. If a cat changes its attributes sufficiently to represent a mouse, then it *is* a mouse. With this interpretation, the content of the database record, rather than its existence, determines the identity of the object represented.

 A database model is an abstract approach for organizing data elements and their relationships. The relational model is currently the most popular. The object-oriented and deductive models are post-relational technologies; the hierarchical and network models represent pre-relational technologies.

Model	Data element organization	Relationship organization	Identity	Access language
Relational	Tables	Identifiers for rows of one table are embedded as attribute values in another table	value-based	non-procedural
Object-Oriented	Objects—logically encapsulating both attributes and behavior	Logical containment, related objects are found within a given object by recursively examining attributes of an object that are themselves objects	record-based	procedural
Deductive	Base facts that can be arranged in tables	Inference rules that permit related facts to be generated on demand	value-based	non-procedural
Hierarchical	Files, records	Logical proximity in a linearized tree	record-based	procedural
Network	Files, records	Intersecting chains	record-based	procedural

Figure 1.3   Characteristics of the five database models

Components of a database system

Figure 1.4 shows a simplified architectural arrangement of a typical DBMS. At the lowest level, the data elements appear on disk storage. To meet the self-describing requirement, the DBMS must also store metadata, that is, data about the data. In the cats and students example, the database must store attributes values, such as vixen, black, 4:00 am, joe, sophomore. The database must also store the metadata that Cat is the name of one of the storage tables and that it contains attribute headings color, weight, and napTime.

Because the DBMS is generic software, intended to support a wide variety of database applications, it customizes copies of the general storage structure (e.g., tables) to reflect the application needs. The application designer provides the names of entities and their attributes and relationships in a machine-readable script, called a **conceptual schema**. For example, the conceptual schema for the student-cat application describes the Student table and the Cat table, and it notes how student rows relate to cat rows. The DBMS compiles the schema into a compact form, suitable for reference by other parts of the system, and archives it in permanent storage. This data dictionary is then available to resolve references to table and attribute names that arise when database users request services.

Database users can be individuals dealing with an interactive interface, or other computer programs requesting services with calls to subprocedures provided by the DBMS. Although some differences distinguish these two modes of service, the DBMS should provide as much uniformity as possible to its users. The user interface module of the DBMS responds to service requests, using the data dictionary to confirm the existence and compatibility of data elements mentioned in the requests. A second module processes storage-retrieval requests, performs optimizations necessary to reduce execution time, and carries out the data operations needed to respond. The DBMS passes the requested data items and any error messages back to the interface module for relay to the user.

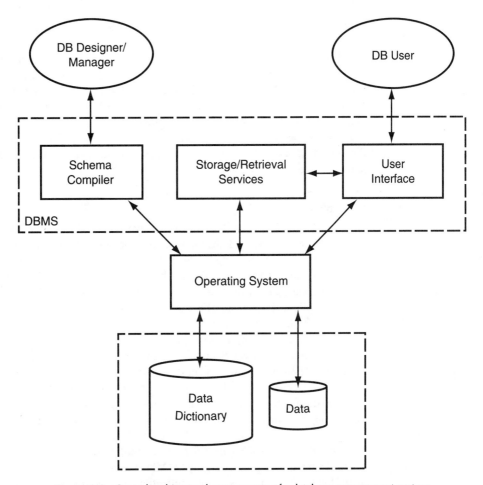

Figure 1.4 Central architectural components of a database management system

The components of Figure 1.4 implement their functions in different ways, depending on the database model involved. However, in all cases, the DBMS projects the illusion that the stored items are application objects. The DBMS tailors the illusion to the application at hand, using the stored conceptual schema. For example, the user might formulate a request in terms of cats, students, and their attributes. The DBMS would translate the request to refer to internal data structures, compute the correct response, and deliver it to the interface in terms of cats and students.

Physical level

There are three levels of database services. At the lowest level, farthest removed from the application entities (e.g., cats, students), certain physical components organize and store the raw data. In addition to the hardware, these components include control structures that track which data elements reside on which disks and in which format. Other structures appear here also to accelerate performance, such as buffers for holding frequently used data and information for conducting rapid searches. The physical layer typically has parameters that can be tuned for optimal performance under the access patterns of a particular application. Therefore, the database designer may want to specify these parameters. However, the later models (i.e., relational, object-oriented, deductive) typically leave the tuning task to the DBMS. If the database designer does have access to these structures, he specifies appropriate values in a **physical schema**. The physical schema is a second machine-readable script, which addresses such issues as what data elements to store in close physical proximity (on the same disk track or cylinder, for example), how to distribute the data across multiple files and storage devices, and which files to index.

Conceptual level

Isolating these storage details in the lowest level of the DBMS provides a comfortable buffer for the next higher layer of abstraction, the conceptual level. The application objects exist at this level. If the underlying hardware or operating system changes, the consequences are confined to the interface between the physical layer and the conceptual layer immediately above it. If the database designer is controlling the physical schema, he may need to modify and recompile it. In any case, he must retune the DBMS to function efficiently in the new environment. In the worst case, this may involve purchasing a new version of the DBMS. For example, if the platform changes from VAX VMS to UNIX (two operating systems), a new version of the DBMS would probably be necessary. The important point is that all applications constructed over the objects in the conceptual layer remain valid. A potentially large investment in application programs that use the database is not affected. The term **physical data independence** describes this decoupling of the application programs from the underlying hardware and data structures. The three-level diagram of Figure 1.5 illustrates the point.

The center layer of Figure 1.5 describes the complete application environment in terms of the abstractions supported by the DBMS, such as tables, objects, or inference rules. Here reside the entities of interest in the application, together with their relationships, constraints, and security measures. Just as this layer can remain stable in the face of changes in the physical support layer below it, modifications to this conceptual picture can often be hidden from the next higher level.

External level

The highest level of Figure 1.5 presents varying external tailored views of the application to different users. For example, one program may consider cat attributes to be simply name and weight, while another program may expect a more complete definition, including eye color, fur color, and associated student owners. Differing external views can use the same conceptual description to satisfy these differing expectations. Moreover, if a program expects an entity to contain certain attributes, it should be unaffected if the conceptual schema changes to add more attributes to the corresponding database object. Of course, certain DBMS parameters may require adjustment to materialize the old external view from a modified conceptual schema. However, the program that uses that old view remains insulated from the change.

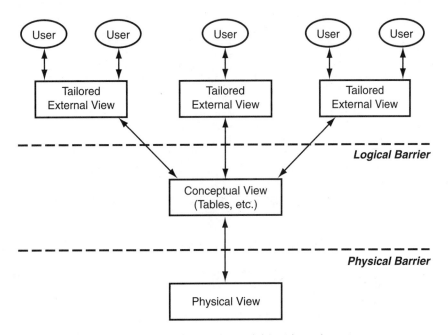

Figure 1.5   Physical and logical data independence

Unfortunately, you can't confine the consequences of all changes in this manner. For example, if an attribute of an entity is deleted from the conceptual view, then unless it was a redundant property in the first place, the DBMS can hardly materialize it for the benefit of an existing program. In this case the program requires rewriting. Despite their limitations, external views can compensate to large extent for changes in the conceptual schema. This decoupling is called **logical data independence**.

DBMS components include the user interface, data and meta-data storage, and a coordinator for storage-retrieval requests. Physical data independence buffers the conceptual view of the application from underlying hardware or data structure changes. Logical data independence similarly buffers particular users from certain conceptual changes.

The database administrator

Besides the hardware and software components described above, a functioning DBMS also involves certain human roles. Because the DBMS provides a global view of the application data, any changes to the structure must be carefully coordinated, taking into account widely dispersed users who will be affected by a change. A **database administrator** (DBA) is a person with these responsibilities:

Application Entity	Attributes
fish	fname—the name of a fish fcolor—the color of a fish fweight—the weight of a fish
species	sname—the name of a species sfood—the dietary preference of a species
tank	tname—the name of a tank tcolor—the color of a tank tvolume—the volume of a tank
event	edate—the date when the event happened to a fish enote—commentary on the event

Relationships
species-fish
tank-fish
fish-events
species-tanks

Figure 1.6   Entities and relationships in the aquarium database example

- Maintaining the conceptual schema

- Tuning performance parameters, including maintaining the physical schema, if such a description is part of the database model

- Establishing valid user accounts and access privileges

- Supervising backup and recovery operations

- Arbitrating conflicting user suggestions for changes in the database structure or access privileges

For a large database, a staff of DBAs may be necessary to handle these functions, particularly if the conceptual view of the application changes over time.

A continuing example

A single application example should help to integrate the various discussions of the database models. For this reason, the text relies on an aquarium database example, in which the entities of interest are species, tanks, fish, and events. Figure 1.6 lists the attributes of these entities. The aquarium maintains many tanks, of varying names, colors, and volumes, and each tank contains a variety of fish. Each fish has a name, color, and weight, and each represents one of many species. For each species the database maintains the name and dietary preference. During its lifetime at the aquarium, each fish experiences many events, such as birth, death, feedings, and militant encounters with other fish. Each event belongs to a particular fish, and the database contains the date of the event and a textual comment on the nature of the event.

Relationships include the grouping of certain fish with the tank they inhabit, the grouping of fish with the species they represent, and the grouping of events with the fish that experienced the events. A more distant relationship links a species with the tanks in which it appears. As the text expands on this example for each of the five database models, many more relationships will become apparent. Admittedly, our example is a small one, involving only four entities. By contrast, a commercial database application can contain hundreds of entities. Nevertheless, the aquarium example has all the complexity needed to illustrate the full range of concepts encountered in the five models.

SUMMARY

A database is a self-describing collection of data elements, together with relationships and constraints among those elements, that presents a uniform interface to users. A database management system (DBMS) is a software product that supports these functions. A DBMS must provide some structure for storing the data elements, and it must present some mechanism for linking these elements into relationships. A database model is a particular technique for attaining these goals.

A database system isolates the computer-related problems of large-volume data storage and retrieval from application-oriented issues. It simplifies software development efforts by providing generic services adaptable to varying applications. It also contributes to the efficiency of many interfacing programs dealing with the same data environment by providing self-describing, consistent data to all users. Moreover, a database system provides a general approach for maintaining relationships among data elements.

Separating data storage and retrieval details into a self-sufficient module represents sound software engineering practice in itself. Still, database systems overcome other deficiencies in the pre-database mode of operation, which use individual programs with their own tailored input/output files. The development of databases helped to avoid the older systems' (1) unhealthy dependence between data and programs, (2) repetition of data elements, (3) opportunities for inconsistencies, (4) unorganized scattering of related data across many files, (5) distributed ownership of data, (6) decentralized security, (7) unregulated interactions between programs using the same data, (8) inadequate multiuser access, (9) ad hoc approach to error recovery, and (10) overdependence on physical considerations, such as disk track and sector addresses.

The five models examined in this text are: hierarchical and network (past), relational (present), and object-oriented and deductive (future). The models differ primarily in the way they represent relationships. The hierarchical model uses a tree format to relate application entities. The tree can be expressed as a linear list, and logical proximity in that linear form implies relations among data elements. The network model provides auxiliary structures, best envisioned as intersecting chains. Navigating along these chains recovers related data elements. The relational model uses common attributes between disjoint tables to relate rows. In one table the attribute serves to identify the row in question; in the other table the same attribute serves as an embedded reference back to that row. The object-oriented model uses logical containment. Since object attributes can be other objects, related data elements can be found through a recursive search within the attributes of a given data element. Finally, the deductive model uses inference rules to derive related elements.

A DBMS contains a module for processing the database schema, which is a script describing the application environment in terms of the structures provided by the model, that is, in terms of tables, objects, inference rules, hierarchical trees, or network chains. The DBMS stores this description as a data dictionary, which it uses to resolve references to application entities that appear in service requests. Another component provides a clean interface to users, hiding the computer structures. The user never faces indices, hash tables, file buffers, and the like. Rather, he deals with the tables, objects, axioms, and rules that model the application environment.

The database provides three layers of abstraction, each buffered to a certain extent from changes in the layers below. At the bottom of the hierarchy is the physical layer, which deals with storage structures. This layer contains low-level data structures (e.g., files, control blocks, search accelerators), and it accommodates the hardware capabilities. The physical layer provides support services for the conceptual layer, which projects the illusion of tables and objects, from which the user fashions the application environment. The DBMS can protect the conceptual layer from certain changes to the physical layer, a feature known as physical data independence. The top layer represents tailored views of the conceptual layer that are suitable for different users. The DBMS can protect the top layer from limited changes to the conceptual schema, a feature known as logical data independence.

The database administrator (DBA) is a person who is responsible for the conceptual and physical schemas, periodic backup, recovery as necessary, and performance and security issues. The DBA is the primary contact person for users who have suggestions for modifying the database structure.

2 Relational Databases

ADATABASE MODEL DESCRIBES A STRUCTURE FOR STORING AND manipulating information in a database. The relational database model uses a particularly simple structure when compared with its network and hierarchical predecessors. In the relational model, a database is a collection of tables, each structurally similar to a file of fixed-length records. Because of this familiar format, the relational model is accessible to a wide range of non-technical users. The relational model also enjoys the distinction of a rigorous mathematical base for its operations. Starting with a set-theoretic description of the basic elements, many characteristics of the relational model follow as mathematical derivations. By contrast, earlier models proceed from behavioral descriptions of the database operations.

Besides describing the relational database model, this chapter introduces concepts that are applicable to all database systems. For example, it discusses the general nature of relationships among data elements and introduces the entity-relationship diagram as a standard tool for describing relationships. The objective is to understand each database model as a particular approach to more general problems of information storage and retrieval.

An informal illustration of a relational database

In our aquarium example, the entities of interest are tanks, fish, and species, together with the events that mark the life of a given fish, such as birth, feedings, and illnesses. Each instance of an entity exhibits a certain set of features. For example, each tank has a particular tank number, name, volume, and color. The application requires three relationships. The first associates each fish with precisely one tank, that in which it lives. The second relationship groups each fish with exactly one species, that which it represents, and the third associates each event with precisely one fish. Using appropriate abbreviations for the features, the four tables of Figure 2.1 model the aquarium as a relational database.

No two rows in the tank table have the same value in the tno column. The same is true of sno in Species, fno in Fish, and eno in Event. Of course, these feature names are abbreviations for fish-number, tank-number, and so forth. The tno value's uniqueness

Species		
sno	sname	sfood
17	dolphin	herring
22	shark	anything
74	guppy	worm
93	shark	peanut butter

Tank			
tno	tname	tcolor	tvolume
55	puddle	green	200
42	cesspool	blue	100
35	lagoon	red	400
85	cesspool	blue	100
38	beach	blue	200
44	lagoon	green	200

Fish					
fno	fname	fcolor	fweight	tno	sno
164	charlie	orange	12	42	74
347	flipper	black	25	35	17
228	killer	white	32	42	22
281	charlie	orange	27	85	22
483	albert	red	45	55	17
119	bonnie	blue	51	42	22
388	cory	purple	12	35	93
654	darron	white	84	42	93
765	elsie	white	73	42	22
438	fran	black	61	55	74
277	george	red	33	42	93
911	helen	blue	48	44	74
104	indira	black	19	42	17
302	jill	red	28	38	17
419	kilroy	red	49	55	74
650	laura	blue	55	85	17
700	maureen	white	71	44	17

Event			
eno	fno	edate	enote
3456	164	01/26	Hatched
6653	347	05/14	Born
5644	347	05/15	Swimming
5645	347	05/30	Takes fish from trainer
6789	228	04/30	Hatched
5211	281	05/23	Hatched
6719	483	06/25	Born
6720	483	06/30	Doubled in length
9874	119	07/22	Hatched
9875	119	08/05	Monopolized food
2176	388	02/04	Hatched
2285	654	02/08	Hatched
2874	765	04/19	Hatched
3116	438	09/25	Hatched
3651	277	10/02	Hatched
3884	911	11/12	Hatched
3992	104	12/25	Born
4004	302	06/04	Born
5118	419	01/11	Hatched
6233	650	04/23	Born
7555	700	05/09	Born

Figure 2.1 The aquarium database under the relational model

allows it to serve as a shorthand identifier of its row, and by extension, of the particular tank corresponding to the row. Similarly, a sno value uniquely identifies a species, and a fno value determines a particular fish. Thus the tank whose features are tno = 42, tname = cesspool, tcolor = blue, tvolume = 100 is precisely the same tank identified simply by tno = 42. No other feature in the tank table has this identifying power. There are several tanks with tname = cesspool, several with tcolor = blue, and several with tvolume = 100. Indeed, no combination of features, excluding tno, has the power to identify a unique tank because several blue cesspools have a volume of 100. When the value of a feature determines a unique row in a table, the feature is a **key** to the table. Sometimes it's necessary to specify the values for a group of features in order to determine a unique table row. In that case, the group of features is the key.

The tables capture all the relevant information about the aquarium application. Using the tables to answer questions about the aquarium demonstrates this point. The simplest questions concern a single table, and you can answer them by scanning that table. For example, what are the colors of tanks named lagoon? How many blue tanks have a volume of 200? For more complicated questions, you must consider how information correlates across several tables.

The tables hold information relating fish and their tanks. Although each fish swims in only one tank, a given tank houses many fish. To express this one-to-many relationship, the tno of the home tank appears as a feature in each fish row. Recall that tno uniquely specifies a particular tank. When the key from a remote table participates as a feature of another table, it is a **foreign key** in the hosting table. Note that tno is not a key of the fish table because it does not have identification powers; several rows have the same tno value in the fish table. Rather, tno is a foreign key in the fish table that refers back to the tno key in the tank table. Similarly, the foreign key sno in the fish table refers to the key sno of the species table, thereby maintaining the relationship between each fish and its species. Finally, a row in the event table connects with precisely one fish row through the foreign key fno in the event table.

By understanding how common features lace the tables together, you can retrieve information across several tables. For example, how many fish in the tank with tno = 42 belong to a species named shark? Simply note the fish rows that have tno = 42 and copy out the corresponding sno values. The species table indicates that there are two species named shark, one with a diet of anything and another with a preference for peanut butter. The corresponding sno values are 22 and 93. Of the sno values isolated in the previous step, three of them are 22 and two are 93, giving a total of five fish that belong to a species named shark. As a quick exercise, determine the names of species represented in *all* tanks in the database. As you study the details of the relational model, you'll see that there is a very systematic process for answering these queries.

The aquarium example reveals the truly simple structure of a relational database. Besides offering an intuitively obvious scheme for storing relationships, tables resemble familiar files of fixed-length records. That is, each row corresponds to a record in the file, and each feature corresponds to a field within the record. Because the organizing principles are so simple, you can easily imagine adapting other applications to this format, say, an expense ledger, an inventory scheme, a personnel accounting project, an audio collection, a graphical display interface, or an election campaign. Also, although there might be some question about the exact form of efficient algorithms, you can envision concrete data structures (files, for example) for maintaining the tables on disk and programs for scanning the tables to respond to queries such as those illustrated above. Not wanting to write a separate program for each query, you might then attempt to organize the queries into groups with certain common properties, or you might impose a language syntax on the query expressions to reduce the variability. In short, you would proceed to organize the consequences of the relational method of data representation. Of course, this investigation of the relational model is a large undertaking, and researchers have been studying it for many years. As you'll see, this simple data model supports very powerful data manipulation functions.

Relational terminology

The most basic component of a relational database is a **domain**, which is simply a set of values. Four simple examples of domains are:

$D_1 = \{$jake, jerry, jill, joe, julie$\}$ $D_3 = \{\alpha \mid \alpha$ is a string and $|\alpha| \le 10\}$

$D_2 =$ all strings of printable characters $D_4 = \{x \mid x$ is an integer and $10000 \le x \le 99999\}$.

Some domains are finite, such as D_1; others are infinite, such as D_2. In either case, membership of a candidate expression in a domain must be testable. You can easily test that jim is not a member of D_1, while jill is a member. D_1 is an enumerated domain, which explicitly lists all its members. However, D_2, D_3 and D_4 are not enumerated. Instead they use predicates to test membership. A **predicate** is a boolean function that evaluates as true or false.

Domains provide the data elements to populate the table cells. Domain names must be distinct within a given relational database. Frequently used domains are the set of all non-negative integers, denoted by $\mathcal{Z}$; the set of all strings of alphanumeric characters, denoted by $\mathcal{S}$; the set of monetary values, denoted by $\mathcal{M}$; and the set of dates, denoted by $\mathcal{D}$. Examples in this book will use these common domains, along with others that arise from the example applications.

An **attribute** is an ordered pair, (N, D), where N is the name of the attribute, and D is a domain. Attributes correspond to the column headings in tables. The string, N, is the actual column heading, while D indicates the pool of values available for the column cells. In the aquarium example, a tank attribute is (tcolor, {red, blue, green, yellow}). This attribute not only names a tank feature but also specifies the set of legal values for that feature. In particular, the tcolor feature of a given tank will always be red, blue, green, or yellow.

The precise term for a table is a relation, a fact that accounts for the name of the relational database model. A relation contains two parts: the shell of the empty table and the body of data that inhabits the shell. The **schema** of a relation is a named collection of attributes, (R, C), where R is the name of the relation, and $C = \{(N_1, D_1), (N_2, D_2), \ldots, (N_n, D_n)\}$ is the finite collection of attributes. The attributes constitute the column headings of the table, and they contain no duplicates: $N_1, N_2, \ldots, N_n$ must all be distinct names. However, the corresponding domains need not be distinct. Note that the definition places no fixed order on the attributes of a schema. Representing a relation as a table is slightly misleading because it implies a left-to-right ordering of the attributes. For convenience, the term *table* will be synonymous with relation, but the attributes are actually an unordered set.

 A domain is a set of values specified by enumeration or by a predicate. An attribute is an ordered pair, (N, D), where N is the name of the attribute and D is a domain. A relational schema is an ordered pair (R, C), where R is the name of the relation (table) to which the schema refers, and C is a collection of attributes with distinct names.

You can now formally define the tank schema for the aquarium example. First, certain domains are necessary. Recalling the standard domains, $\mathcal{S}$, $\mathcal{Z}$, and so forth, you proceed left to right as shown below to define domains, tank attributes, and finally the tank relation.

Domains	Attributes	Attribute collection	Tank Relation
$TC = \{$red, blue, green, yellow$\}$ $TV = \{100, 200, 300, 400\}$	$A_1 = (\text{tno}, \mathcal{Z})$ $A_2 = (\text{tname}, \mathcal{S})$ $A_3 = (\text{tcolor}, TC)$ $A_4 = (\text{tvolume}, TV)$	$C = \{A_1, A_2, A_3, A_4\}$	(tank, C)

An **association** based on the attribute (N, D) is an ordered pair (N, x), where $x \in D$. For example, (tcolor, blue) is an association, as are (tno, 42), (tname, cesspool), and (tvolume, 400). In terms of tables, an association is the value under a certain column heading. Although a table cell normally shows only the value, that is, the x of the (N, x) pair, you can imagine that the column heading repeats along with each value.

For a given relational schema, with attributes $\{(A_1, D_1), (A_2, D_2), \ldots, (A_n, D_n)\}$, a **tuple** under that relational schema is a collection of associations, $\{(A_1, x_1), (A_2, x_2), \ldots, (A_n, x_n)\}$, where each $x_i \in D_i$. If the schema for a relation has n attributes, then every tuple in the relation contains exactly n associations, one based on each attribute. For example, a tuple under the tank schema is: {(tno, 42), (tname, cesspool), (tcolor, blue), (tvolume, 100)}. Informally, a tuple corresponds to a table row. However, the definition preserves the unordered nature of the data values. Instead of neatly lining up under a fixed column headings, each data value is packaged with its attribute name. Within the tuple, the associations can appear in any order without losing track of the data's meaning.

Figure 2.2 more accurately portrays the tank relation according to this formal definition. The upper portion shows the schema while the lower part shows the tuples. The unordered appearance of the various attributes within the schema emphasizes the lack of any particular order. Therefore, the previous sketch, Figure 2.1, was somewhat inaccurate because it neatly arranged the attributes in a left-to-right order. However, as long as you don't use the order implied by the tabular representation, you can continue to think of relations as tables. For example, you couldn't ask to find the third feature of the tank whose tno = 42. Such a request makes no sense in the relational model because the concept of "the third feature" is not defined, even though the table representation might lead you to think that it is. Instead, you should rephrase the query to request the tcolor value of the tank with tno = 42.

A collection of associations forms a tuple, which corresponds to a row in the table. However, Figure 2.2 shows that such a row is actually an unordered bag of values with no particular left-to-right ordering. For this reason, the name of the column heading must be carried along with the value. Because attributes follow no fixed order, a relational schema is a *set* of attributes in the strict mathematical sense. Similarly, a tuple is a set of associations. Because of these definitions, all the well-developed mathematics of set theory is available to study relations. This viewpoint will be very helpful in the development of the relations' properties. However, when the question of order isn't relevant, the table representation allows simpler diagrams.

The schema for a relation is sometimes called the **shell** or the **intension** of the relation. The other part of a relation is the **body**, which is a finite collection of tuples under the corresponding relational schema. Think of the schema as being fairly permanent. The database designer constructs the table, its attributes, and their domains to represent some stable application entity. On the other hand, the body of the relation is transient data. Tuples come and go as the real-world situation changes. For example, if the aquarium buys a new tank, the body of the tank relation must acquire a new tuple to represent it. If the aquarium removes a tank from service, the corresponding tuple must be deleted. Of course, the schema might also require modification. For example, the designer might realize, sometime after implementation of the database, that he must add an attribute to record the salinity of the tank water. However, in the normal course of operations, changes to the schema are much less frequent than changes to the body.

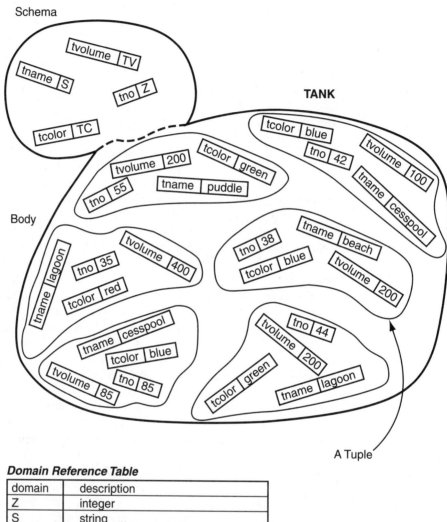

Figure 2.2 More accurate portrayal of the tank relation under the relational model

Domain Reference Table

domain	description
Z	integer
S	string
TC	(red, blue, green, yellow)
TV	(100, 200, 300, 400)

The lower portion of Figure 2.2 shows the tuples that inhabit the relational body. Note that there is no inherent ordering among the tuples of a relation. This definition of the body of a relation as a mathematical set is consistent with the earlier definitions of schema and tuple. Unordered set representations pervade all levels of the relational model. A relational schema is a *set* of attributes. A tuple is a *set* of associations. A relational body is a *set* of tuples. You will see also that a relational database is a *set* of relations.

The **degree** of a relation is the number of attributes in its schema. The **cardinality** of a relation is the number of tuples in its body. Looking at the relation as a table, you see that the degree is the number of column headings and that the cardinality is the number of rows.

An association based on the attribute (N, D) is an ordered pair (N, x) where $x \in D$. A tuple under a relational schema is a collection of associations, one for each attribute of the schema. The body of a relation is a finite collection of tuples under the schema.

An abbreviated notation will be used when there is no possibility of confusion. When the domain is either irrelevant or clearly understood from context, attribute N will replace the name-domain pair, (N, D). Likewise, a tuple is a collection of associations of the form (N, x). The text, however, will say that a tuple has N value x rather than using the more formal notation. For example, when a fish tuple has fcolor value blue, or fcolor blue, or value blue in the attribute fcolor, it means that the association (fcolor, blue) belongs to the tuple.

A **relational database** is a finite set of relational schemas, $\{(R_1, C_1), (R_2, C_2), \ldots, (R_m, C_m)\}$, together with the bodies of the relations. The collection of schemas for the constituent relations is called the **database schema**. The names of the relations, $R_1, R_2, \ldots, R_m$, must be distinct.

Note that attributes in *different* relations can have the same name. The table representation in Figure 2.1 shows an attribute named tno in both the fish and tank relations. On those occasions where confusion might result from overlapping names, you can clarify the situation by using the qualified name of an attribute. That is, Fish.tno refers unambiguously to the attribute within the fish relation. The **qualified** name of an attribute is the name of its host relation, followed by a period, followed by the simple attribute name. Of course, this convention is the same as that used to distinguish among record fields in many programming languages. For example, the following C excerpt uses the dot notation to specify fields within two instances of the same type of record structure.

```
typedef struct {int hpos, vpos;} position;
position p, q;
    .
    .
    .
p.hpos = q.hpos;
```

The major difference between a relational database and a collection of tables is that the tables present an ordered arrangement of rows. Moreover, in each row an ordered display of data appears under particular column headings. In a database the tuples (rows) are unordered, and the attributes (columns) are unordered. Figure 2.3 summarizes the correspondence between the database concepts and their table counterparts.

Relational Database Terminology	Tabular Terminology
relational database	collection of tables
relation	a single table
attribute	column heading of a table
tuple	row of data in a table
cardinality	number of rows in a table
degree	number of columns in a table
domain	set of legal values for the data in a column

Figure 2.3　Correspondence between relational database and tabular terminology

 A relational database is a finite set of relations, each containing a relational schema and a corresponding body. The names of the relations must be distinct, and within each relation the names of the attributes must be distinct.

The definition of a relational database as a set of relations is very simple. The database consists of various kinds of sets. Because it is a mathematical set, a relational database can't have duplicate relations. Moreover, the body of each relation is a set of tuples. It follows from the basic properties of a set that there can be no duplicate tuples within a relational body. This observation guarantees that each relation possesses a **key**, some collection of attributes that unambiguously identifies a tuple. In the extreme case, you can choose the set of all attributes from the relation as the key. Specifying values for all attributes must determine a unique tuple because the alternative, two or more identical tuples, isn't possible.

Remarkably, the relational database definition does *not* specify any structure to express the relationships among the various tables in the database. Earlier models used auxiliary structures, such as linked lists, to maintain connections between data items in separate tables. One of the relational model's strengths is that there are no such peripheral structures from the viewpoint of the database user. In the aquarium example, a connection exists between a tank and the fish that swim in it. The connection occurs because the host tank number appears as an attribute in the fish table. However, the definition of the relational database makes no mention of this convention. The connection between the tank number in the fish relation and the tank number in the tank relation remains in the user's mind, that is, in the user's *interpretation* of these attributes. Without mentioning relationships, Figure 2.4 gives a complete definition of the aquarium relational database.

Because the database setup phase does not specifically define relationships, a certain flexibility remains for new interpretations of the data. Initially, the aquarium database design envisioned only three relationships: between a fish and the tank inhabited, between a fish and the species represented, and between a fish and the events experienced. A user can recover the home tank of a fish from the value of the tno attribute in the fish tuple. Similarly, the representative species of a fish can be obtained from the value in the sno attribute of the fish tuple. Now, suppose a user develops the idea of a "compatible fish" for a given tank. A compatible fish is one whose color matches the color of the tank. The fish associated with a given tank under this new notion of compatibility are not the fish swimming in the tank, but rather those with a matching color. This condition specifies a new relationship between the fish and tank entities. Without any new structures, the model automatically

Aquarium	
Relation	Attributes
tank	tno, tname, tcolor, tvolume
species	sno, sname, sfood
fish	fno, fname, fcolor, fweight, tno, sno
event	eno, fno, edate, enote

Domains of attributes			
Attribute	Domain	Attribute	Domain
tno	$\mathcal{Z}$	tname	$\mathcal{S}$
tcolor	{blue, red, green}	tvolume	$\{100, 200, 300, 400\}$
sno	$\mathcal{Z}$	sname	$\mathcal{S}$
sfood	$\mathcal{S}$	fno	$\mathcal{Z}$
fname	$\mathcal{S}$	fcolor	{blue, red, orange, black, white, purple}
eno	$\mathcal{Z}$	fweight	$\mathcal{Z}$
enote	$\mathcal{S}$	edate	$\mathcal{D}$

Figure 2.4   Definition of the aquarium relational database

supports the new relationship. Note how easy it is to answer a query based on the new relationship. For example, find the names of fish that are compatible with tanks named cesspool. For each tank tuple with tname cesspool, record the tcolor value in a temporary list. Then scan through the fish tuples. The fname value of a tuple under scan becomes part of the answer, if the fcolor value appears in the temporary list. You have connected tanks with their compatible fish by matching the tcolor value in the tank relation with the fcolor value in the fish relation. This flexibility contrasts with earlier database models, in which *all* relationships had to be included in the database description.

Binary relationships

From the standpoint of the aquarium application, the schema of the tank relation captures the essential characteristics of the tank entity. The tuples within the body of the tank relation correspond to particular instances of tanks in the aquarium. From the tank schema you can see that the database designer thinks of a tank as an object whose important features are tno, name, tcolor, and tvolume. Furthermore, the values for each attribute come from a specified domain. From the body of the tank relation, Figure 2.1, you can see that the aquarium contains a tank with tno = 42, tname = cesspool, tcolor = blue, and tvolume = 100. In other words, the schema of a relation represents a generic entity from the application while the body of the relation contains specific instances of that entity. The body of a relation changes as the real-world situation of the aquarium changes. The schema changes only if the designer decides that the current description of the generic entity is not sufficient for the required data manipulations. Because a relation is a representation within the model of an external application entity, I will use the terms synonymously. For example, I may refer to the tank entity or to the tank relation. This convention will be particularly useful in the discussion of relationships. "Relationships among relations" sounds somewhat circular, although it is accurate since relations are now well-defined objects. "Relationships among entities" is more appealing, and it is also accurate because application entities are modeled by database relations.

A relation captures two aspects of an application entity: a generic description through the schema and specific instances in the body. Similarly, a relationship has a general pattern and specific instances. The relationship pattern between the fish and tank entities is that each fish has a home tank. An instance of this relationship is a grouping of a tank with all the fish that inhabit the tank. As the aquarium adds or removes particular fish, the relationship instance changes. However, the general pattern remains fixed as the concept of habitation. The term *relationship* refers to the pattern, and the term *relationship instance* refers to particular grouping that conforms to the pattern. Within the database, these groupings consist of tuples, as illustrated in Figure 2.5 for the tank-fish relationship. Each grouping contains one tank tuple, plus zero, one, or more fish tuples. Within a grouping, the tno attribute of each fish tuple contain the same value as the tno attribute of the tank. Matching values in this common attribute mark the members of the group. The group needs no further structure to store the fact that these particular fish are related to this particular tank in the sense of "fish inhabits tank."

You can describe all relationships in this manner. A **relationship** is an application-defined connection among several entities. A **relationship instance** is a meaningful grouping of tuples taken from those entities. Of course, you must interpret "meaningful" in terms of the application. Figure 2.5 also shows an instance of the species-fish relationship, in which the general pattern is "fish represents species." All fish tuples within an instance grouping belong to the same species, that is, to the single species tuple in the group. The common sno value among all the tuples holds the group together. Notice that instance groupings of *different* relationships can overlap. In Figure 2.5 this overlap simply means that some of the fish in tank number 42 are of species number 22. That is, some fish swimming in one of the cesspool tanks are a variety of shark. However, two instance groupings of the *same* relationship can't intersect. A fish tuple in the intersection of two species-fish groupings would mean that the fish represents two species at the same time, which is not possible.

 A relationship is an application-specific connection among several entities. A relationship instance is a meaningful grouping of tuples from the participating entities that exemplifies that connection.

One-to-many relationships

The relationship examples considered above are binary, one-to-many relationships. A relationship is binary when it connects precisely two entities. A binary relationship is one-to-many when each instance grouping contains a single tuple from one of the entities, together with a multitude of tuples from the other. Defining a relationship instance as a meaningful grouping of tuples from several entities (relations) allows other possibilities. However, before exploring these possibilities, consider another example to illustrate how one-to-many relationships can cascade across several relations.

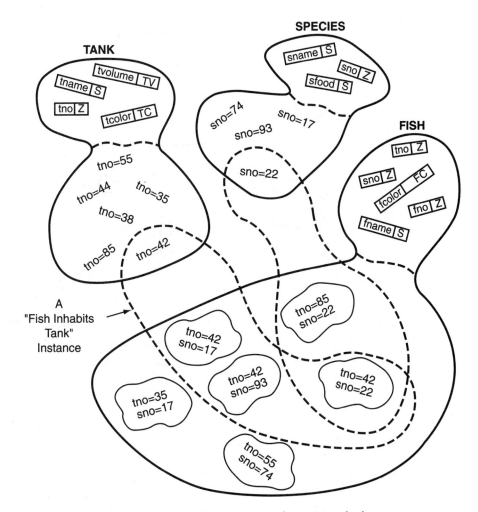

Figure 2.5   Relationship instances in the aquarium database

Each tank associates with many fish, in the sense of "fish inhabits tank," and each fish associates with many events, in the sense of "fish experiences event." Figure 2.6 shows how a tank acts as the "parent" of many fish, each of which serves as the parent of many events. Just as a common tno value unites a grouping at the upper level, a common fno value holds together a lower-level grouping. Notice that fish f1 in tank t1 has no events registered. Therefore, the fish-event instance for this fish contains no event tuples, only the single fish tuple. This boundary case is a legal instance of the relationship. However, the converse situation, where the instance contains only event tuples, is not legal.

An implied relationship connects tanks and events. A particular event associates with precisely one tank, the one that houses the fish that experienced the event. This relationship does not have an explicit representation with common attributes because tno does not

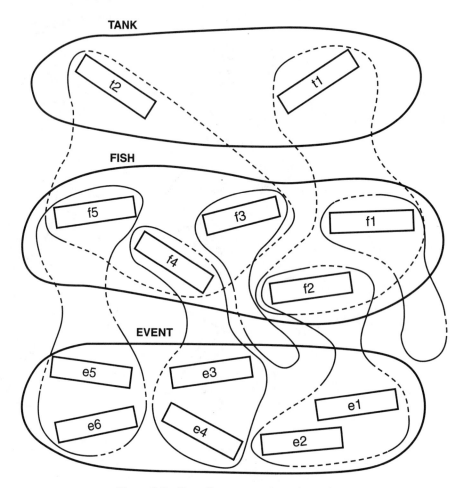

Figure 2.6   Cascading one-to-many relationships

appear in the event tuples. However, the relationship groupings can be recovered, in either direction, by processing the intermediate fish. For example, you can obtain the dates of all events occurring in tno = 42 by using the fish-tank relationship to visit each fish in the tank. You pause at each fish to take an excursion along the fish-event grouping of that fish, accumulating edate values from the events.

In summary, a relationship is a connection among entities, expressed in terms of the application. The fish-tank relationship is the notion: "fish inhabits tank." The fish-event relationship is the notion: "fish experiences event." The fish-species relationship is the concept: "fish represents species." The nature of the connection among the entities varies with the application at hand. An **instance of a relationship** is a grouping of tuples from the involved entities such that the group as a whole conforms to the relationship pattern. The details of the grouping mechanism also vary with the nature of the relationship. In the examples to this point, an instance is a group containing one tuple from one of the entities and a multitude of tuples from the other. A fish-tank relationship instance is a group containing one tank tuple and many fish tuples with the constraint that the fish inhabit the tank.

A **binary** relationship is a relationship that involves two entities. A **many-to-one** relationship is a binary relationship, in which there is a distinguished **dominant** entity. The other entity is the **non-dominant** or **dependent** entity. A tuple from the dominant entity is called a dominant tuple, and a tuple from the non-dominant entity is called a non-dominant tuple. Each relationship instance groups exactly one dominant tuple with zero, one, or more non-dominant tuples. Within each instance, the dominant tuple owns the non-dominant tuples in some application-defined sense. Exactly one relationship instance exists for each tuple of the dominant entity. Each non-dominant tuple appears in at most one instance and therefore associates with at most one dominant tuple. A non-dominant tuple might not participate in any relationship grouping. However, if it does participate, it must appear in only one grouping. By contrast, a dominant tuple associates with a multitude of non-dominant tuples, namely all non-dominant tuples in its group. These rules force all relationship groupings to be disjoint. One-to-many and many-to-one are used synonymously.

 A one-to-many relationship (1) designates one of the participating entities as dominant, (2) has instance groups each containing exactly one dominant tuple and zero, one, or more non-dominant tuples, and (3) allows no overlap between distinct instance groups.

Designers often use the notation of Figure 2.7 to show a one-to-many relationship between two entities. The entities appear as ovals, with all detail suppressed except the name of the relation. A two-ended arrow connects the ovals, with a single arrowhead pointing to the dominant entity and a double arrowhead pointing to the non-dominant entity. Such sketches are called **Bachman diagrams**. As illustrated in Figure 2.7, these diagrams provide a quick summary of the relationships among various entities in a database.

Position yourself on the "many" end of an arrow in a Bachman diagram. That is, position yourself at the non-dominant entity near the double arrowhead. If you look toward the other entity, you see a single arrowhead, which reminds you that each tuple of the non-dominant entity associates with exactly one tuple of the entity on the other end of the arrow. In Figure 2.7, a fish tuple associates with exactly one tank tuple, namely the tank that the fish inhabits. Similarly, each event tuple associates with exactly one fish tuple, namely the fish that experienced the event. However, if you position yourself at the "one" end of the arrow, that is, at the dominant entity near the single arrowhead, and if you look toward the other entity, you see a double arrowhead. This double arrowhead reminds you that each tuple of the dominant entity associates with potentially many tuples of the entity on the other end of the arrow. From the standpoint of a particular tank tuple, there are potentially many fish tuples in its relationship grouping, namely all those fish that live in the tank. This possibility includes zero fish, exactly one fish, and more than one fish. Similarly, a particular fish owns zero, one, or more events.

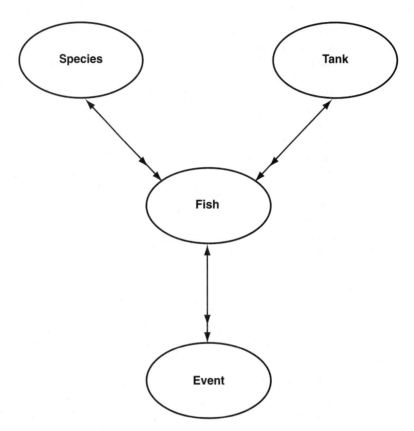

Figure 2.7 Illustrations of relationships with Bachman diagrams

Many-to-many relationships

Suppose you have a binary relationship but with neither entity constrained to supply exactly one tuple to an instance grouping. In other words, there is no dominant entity. Such a relationship holds between species and tanks through the application pattern, "species is represented in tank." A particular tank can house many species, and a particular species appears in many tanks via a multitude of fish. Neither entity plays the dominant role as defined in the one-to-many case. Because a species associates with many tanks and a tank associates with many species, this relationship is called many-to-many. Note that the species-tank relationship is already indirectly represented in the aquarium database through the existing one-to-many fish-species and fish-tank relationships. To identify the tanks housing a particular species, you first use the fish-species relationship instance to visit each of the fish representing the species. From each of these fish, you collect the tno value specifying its home tank. Finally, this collection of tno values identifies the tanks associated with the fixed species in the sense of "species is represented in tank."

Consider another example, where an indirect representation is not present. Suppose a yacht club involves only boats and sailors. The relationship between boats and sailors is "sailor has sailed on boat." It is intrinsically a many-to-many relationship: each boat associates with many sailors, and each sailor associates with many boats. An instance of this boat-sailor relationship is a meaningful grouping of boat tuples and sailor tuples, a grouping that clearly indicates which sailors have sailed which boats and vice versa.

Now try to construct such a grouping. Imitating the grouping patterns of a one-to-many relationship, you start with a boat tuple and then add all the sailors who have sailed on that boat. Now, choosing one of these sailor tuples, you note that this sailor has sailed on other boats. So you extend the grouping to include all the boats on which this sailor has sailed. However, the construction fails at this point because a newly added boat isn't necessarily related to the *other* sailors that you added in the first step. This possibility allows a boat in the same instance grouping with a sailor who didn't sail on it. Figure 2.8 illustrates the process and its potential failure. The boat sea sprite starts the grouping, which you extend to include sailors alfred and bernice. You then add the boat calypso because alfred sails it. But, bernice doesn't sail calypso. Therefore calypso must be excluded from the group. This results in the contradictory situation that calypso should be in the group for one reason but should be excluded for another.

From this failed attempt, you realize you must accommodate the situation where any arrangement of sailors and boats is possible, including such extreme cases as a boat associating with just one sailor or all boats associating with all sailors. The only grouping that can handle all these conditions is a pairwise correspondence, which lists all related boat-sailor pairs. Therefore, the instance groupings of a many-to-many relationship are pairs, with each pair containing a tuple from each entity. As Figure 2.9 illustrates, there is a great deal of tuple sharing among the pairs. Note that certain tuples don't participate in the pairs. This situation is permissible because certain boats may have never sailed with a crew, and certain sailors may have never sailed on a boat.

 A many-to-many relationship is a binary relationship for which instances are pairs of tuples. Each pair contains two tuples, one from each participating entity.

But how do you express the relationship pairs in the database? In the boat-sailor example, you might consider embedding a reference within a given sailor tuple to the related boats. This method doesn't work, however, because the sailor may associate with more than one boat. Suppose the embedded reference is bno. Now recall that the content of a sailor tuple is a set of associations, one association for each attribute. Each association provides for the attribute name and *exactly one* value from the attribute domain. There is no provision for multiple values, so the embedded bno attribute in the sailor relation can accommodate only a single boat per sailor tuple. Therefore, this approach can't express the situation where the sailor is related to many boats.

Alfred sails Calypso and Sea Sprite.

Bernice sails Sea Sprite and Tempest.

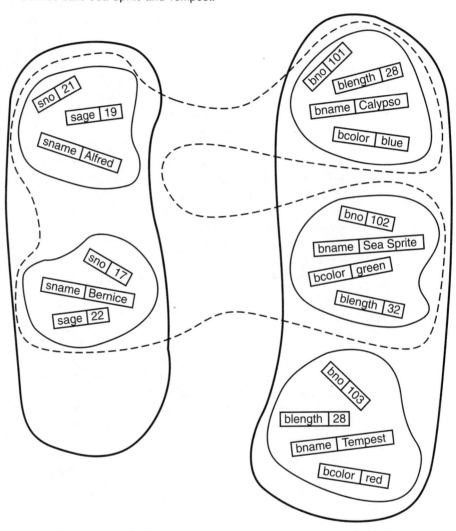

Figure 2.8   Some difficulties constructing an instance of a many-to-many relationship

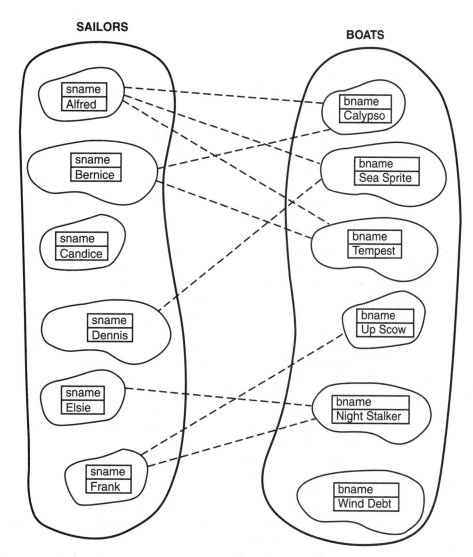

Figure 2.9 Representing a many-to-many relationship

Why did this reference embedding work in the one-to-many case? Consider again the fish-tank relationship of Figure 2.5. Each fish instance contains a tno, an attribute that refers to its host tank. This reference presents no difficulty because there can be only one tank associated with a given fish. The tank is on the "one" end of the relationship. In the tank relation, you make no attempt to embed a reference to the fish that live in the tank. Such references aren't necessary because the tno inside the fish tuples provides sufficient information to recover the relationship groupings. So, on the tank side, where there would be a problem with multiple references, you don't need to make the attempt.

Atomicity is the constraint that requires each association within a tuple to contain exactly one domain value. In terms of tables, atomicity states that each cell's entry must be a single value from the domain of the attribute at the column head.

Because of atomicity, the many-to-many relationship between boats and sailors in Figure 2.9 can't show any common attributes between the participating tuples. Since the common attribute feature provides the "glue" that groups the tuples in a relationship instance, how does the relational model represent many-to-many relationships? Unfortunately, the relational model cannot *directly* represent many-to-many relationships. Although this constraint appears to be a serious deficiency, in fact, it isn't. A standard technique can decompose a many-to-many relationship into an equivalent situation containing two one-to-many relationships.

Factoring many-to-many relationships

Figure 2.10 provides a more suggestive picture of the boat-sailor relationship. Because the relationship groupings are pairs containing a boat and a sailor, you can express the relationship by tabulating those pairs and including the resulting table in the database. This approach is perfectly legal within the definition of a relational database because it introduces no new structural types, only a new table. A minor technicality arises because the tuples in the new table contain boat-sailor pairs. In other words, there are two attributes, the first intended to hold a boat and the second a sailor. But attribute values must be drawn from certain specified domains, such as $\mathcal{Z}, \mathcal{S}, \mathcal{M}$, and therefore they can't be boats or sailors, which are whole tuples in themselves. However, you can use a key value to represent each tuple. Recall that a key is an attribute whose value uniquely identifies a tuple. Assuming that bno and sno are keys of the boat and sailor relations respectively, you can express instances of the boat-sailor relationship by tabulating (bno, sno) pairs.

The new table is the **intersection** relation. It is the result of **factoring** the boat-sailor many-to-many relationship into two one-to-many relationships. Instances of the one-to-many relationships in the decomposed form appear in Figure 2.10. A tuple from the boat relation associates with the intersection tuples bearing the same bno value, thereby constituting an instance of the derived one-to-many relationship between boat and the intersection. Likewise a tuple from the sailor relation associates with the intersection tuples having the same sno value, giving an instance of the derived one-to-many relationship between sailor and the intersection. The bno and sno common attributes maintain the relationships. The process loses no information. For example, to determine all the sailors connected to a particular boat, you locate the pairs in the intersection table with the given boat number as the first half of the pair. The corresponding sno values in the second half of those selected pairs then identify the sailor tuples. A similar procedure finds the boats connected to a particular sailor.

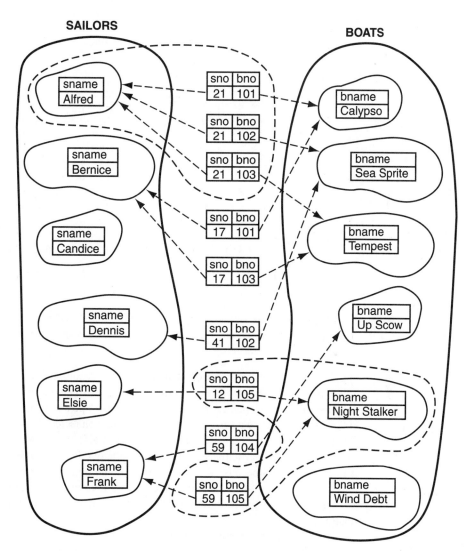

Figure 2.10   Factoring the boat-sailor relationship into one-to-many relationships

Sailor		
sno	sname	sage
21	alfred	19
17	bernice	22
36	candice	25
41	dennis	20
12	elsie	24
59	frank	22

Boat			
bno	bname	bcolor	blength
101	calypso	blue	28
102	sea sprite	green	32
103	tempest	red	28
104	up scow	blue	24
105	night stalker	red	28
106	wind debt	blue	28

Race				
raceDate	raceDistance	seaConditions	sno	bno
June 22	25	calm	21	101
June 28	32	light breeze	21	102
June 29	50	storm	21	103
June 23	25	calm	17	101
July 2	32	stiff breeze	17	103
July 2	32	stiff breeze	41	102
July 8	25	storm	12	105
July 9	32	calm	59	104
July 10	50	light breeze	59	105

Figure 2.11 Discovery of the race entity in the boat-sailor database

 A relational database represents a many-to-many relationship with a third table, the intersection relation, and with two new one-to-many relationships between the original entities and the new table.

The intersection relation created during this decomposition frequently leads to the "discovery" of a new application entity. Usually this new entity should have been in the database in the first place. In the boat-sailor example, the intersection relation can be called "race" because a sailor and a boat become connected through such a sailing event. The pair that connects a sailor and a boat serves also to represent the race in which the sailor and the boat participated. The many-to-many relationship between boats and sailors isn't compromised because there is no limit on the number of times a particular boat can appear in the table. Nor is there a limit on the number of appearances of a particular sailor. So, the renamed intersection entity, "race," participates in the boat-race and sailor-race relationships.

Now that the intersection relation corresponds to an entity in the real-world application, you can add other attributes to describe a race more completely. Figure 2.11 shows new attributes: raceDate, raceDistance, and seaConditions. The value of any of these attributes is a property of a particular boat-sailor combination. For example, the seaConditions value is a descriptive property of a race. It is *not* a property of a sailor or of a boat. A particular boat-sailor pair can now occur repeatedly in the race table, corresponding to different raceDates. Although such multiple occurrences add no new information to the relationship grouping, they do provide further data on the overall application.

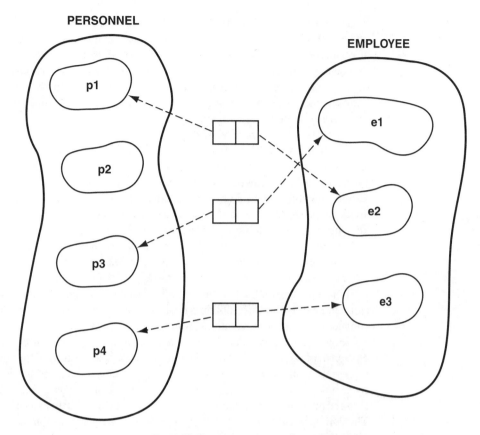

Figure 2.12 A one-to-one relationship

In hindsight, the two, one-to-many relationships of the aquarium example are seen as a factoring of the many-to-many relationship between tank and species. Initially, the fish entity appeared as a natural part of the application, and there was no reason to omit it. However, if you had omitted it, then you would have rediscovered it as the intersection entity necessary to mediate the many-to-many relationship between tank and species.

One-to-one relationships

If you impose the additional constraint that a tuple can appear in no more than one pair, you obtain a one-to-one relationship. A pair in the relationship grouping associates exactly one tuple from each of the participating entities, and these tuples are then excluded from any other pairs. Figure 2.12 illustrates a one-to-one relationship between two entities: personnel and employee. Some tuples don't participate in any relationship pairs: some personnel aren't employees.

Because of the one-to-one coupling between instances of the participating entities, the two entities sometimes represent a single concept in the application domain. In Figure 2.12, an employee is actually a special kind of personnel. As another example, assume that the boat-sailor relationship is one-to-one. Then each sailor is connected to at most one boat, and each boat is connected to at most one sailor. In this case, you might consider the boat attributes (e.g., bno, blength) as sailor attributes, since these features characterize the boat that belongs to a given sailor and to no other sailor. Because the boat can't associate with other sailors, there is little reason to maintain it in the database as a separate tuple. The boat becomes one of the distinguishing characteristics of the sailor, in the same manner as his address or telephone number.

However, this point of view does have certain disadvantages. For example, if a sailor has no boat, then all boat features are null within the tuple representing that sailor. If sailors are commonly without boats, then this representation contains many unused fields. Moreover, a boat without a sailor can't enter the database because it can exist only as attributes within some sailor. The final decision to merge the entities rests with the given application. Combining entities connected by a one-to-one relationship may be better, or keeping them separate may be better. If you keep them separate, you can still avoid the creating an intersection entity. Although the one-to-one relationship is a special case of the many-to-many relationship, it is also a special case of a one-to-many relationship. In the latter context, you can simply embed the key of one entity into the other to maintain the relationship between the two tables. For example, you can include bno as an attribute in sailor to identify the corresponding boat. You don't need to embed sno in boat because you can recover the proper groupings from the other direction.

Figure 2.13 shows the spatial arrangement of the entities in the aquarium and yacht club examples. Note that two of the one-to-many relationships in the aquarium application represent an implicit many-to-many relationship between tank and species. The triad formed by two dominant entities sharing a non-dominant partner is a characteristic feature of a factored many-to-many relationship. In this case, tank and species share the fish intersection. The dominant entity is frequently called the **parent**; the non-dominant entity is called the **child**. In this terminology, a factored many-to-many relationship always appears as a child entity with two parents. Note that the yacht club application exhibits a similar triad.

The situation is fundamentally different in the arrangement of tank, fish, and event within the aquarium diagram. In this case, the two, one-to-many relationships do not consist of a single child shared by two parents. Fish is a child of tank, and event is a child of fish. This arrangement doesn't represent an implicit many-to-many relationship between tank and event. Actually, the relationship between tank and event is one-to-many because each event belongs to at most one fish, and that fish belongs to at most one tank. Figure 2.13 shows this situation as a hierarchical configuration, with the child entity in one relationship serving as the parent entity in a second relationship. Certain variations on these two topologies—the triad and the cascade—account for all possible binary relationships in applications.

You can visualize a one-to-many relationship as a collection of pairs, with the constraint that a tuple from the non-dominant entity can appear in at most one pair. Using the keys of the tuples, you can tabulate these pairs in a separate intersection table. However, this is unnecessary because the embedded foreign key approach is more convenient. Nevertheless, the viewpoint is valuable because it shows that you can represent all binary relationship instances as pairs. This idea then generalizes to relationships that are not binary.

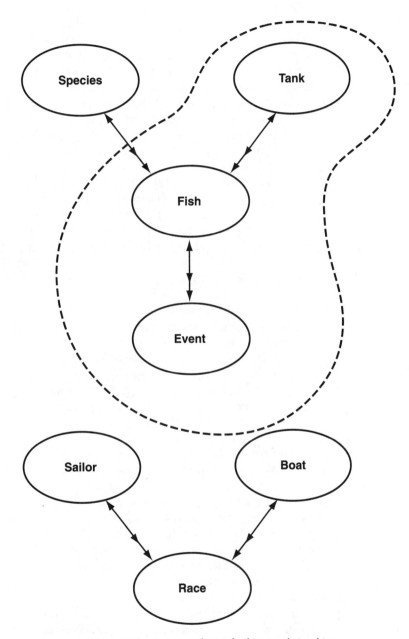

Figure 2.13   Basic topologies for binary relationships

Higher-degree relationships

The **degree** of a relationship is the number of participating entities. Most relationships encountered in database applications are binary, that is, of degree two. However, you may occasionally find a higher-degree relationship. In theory, there is no limit to the degree of a relationship. But in practice most relationships are of degree two. You will rarely encounter a relationship of degree higher than three. The shipping company application of Figure 2.14 is an example of a ternary (i.e., degree three) relationship. A ternary relationship relies on triplets rather than pairs. So, in the shipping application, a relationship grouping is a triplet, with one tuple from each of the participating entities—ship, cargo, and port—contributing a key value. A grouping of ship X with cargo Y and port Z means that ship X carried cargo Y to port Z. A given tuple can enter into such triplets an unlimited number of times. The mutual association between the three tuples is the significant connection. Such a three-way connection is *not* equivalent to pairwise connections among the entities.

Because ship, cargo, and port each have a unique key — say sno, cno, and pno respectively — you can tabulate the triplets in an intersection entity. Recall that the degree of a relation is the number of attributes, whereas the degree of a relationship is the number of participating entities. The degree of a relationship influences the degree of the intersection relation that tabulates the connections. If a ternary relationship involves three entities, each with a single-attribute key, then the intersection entity must contain three attributes. However, once the database designer creates the intersection, he normally recognizes it as some real-world entity in the application. He then adds further attributes to flesh out the description of that entity. Therefore, the degree of the relationship gives the *minimal* degree of the corresponding intersection relation.

In the shipping example, the intersection entity is "mission." A particular mission is the dispatching of Ship X carrying Cargo Y to Port Z. You can then decompose the ternary relationship among ship, cargo, and port into three one-to-many relationships: ship-mission, cargo-mission, and port-mission. Figure 2.15 shows this decomposition, and the corresponding Bachman diagram of Figure 2.16 shows the characteristic appearance of a factored higher-order relationship.

An instance of the ship-mission relationship is a particular ship tuple grouped with all the mission tuples that share the same sno value. Similar interpretations apply to the cargo-mission and port-mission relationships. Note that the transformation preserves the exact meaning of the original relationship. You can recover all the ship-cargo-port triplets and not create any extra triplets by mistake. This equivalence holds because the intersection entity preserves the original relationship as a collection of triplets. Did the ship Enterprise carry beans to Boston? Using the original three entities, you determine that sno = 25, cno = 82, and pno = 91 identify Enterprise, beans, and Boston respectively. The answer to the query is "yes" if and only if some tuple in the mission relation contains sno = 25, cno = 82, pno = 91.

The meaning of the relationship resides in the three-way connection among ship, cargo, and port. Instance groupings are triplets, containing one key from each entity. You might feel that the same meaning resides in three many-to-many binary relationships: ship-cargo, cargo-port, and port-ship. However, this isn't so. Suppose you decompose the ternary relationship as in Figure 2.17, identifying three intersection entities. A ship-cargo pair is a shipment, a cargo-port pair is an arrival, and a port-ship pair is a docking. The shipment

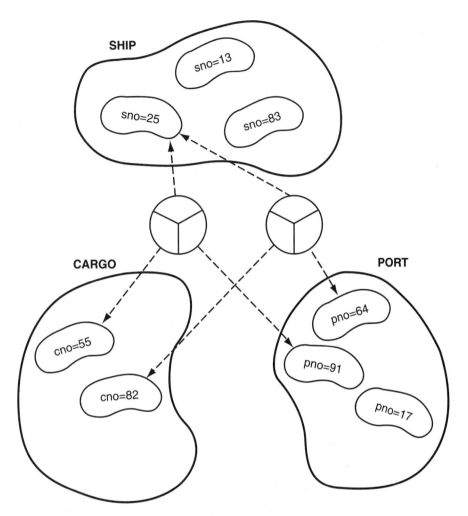

Figure 2.14   A ternary relationship among the entities of a shipping company

entity serves as an intersection between ship and cargo, and it contains all (sno, cno) pairs such that the sno and cno values appear in some triplet from the original ternary relationship, regardless of the corresponding pno. An entry (sno = x, cno = y) in the shipment table means that the ship with sno = x carried the cargo with cno = y to some unspecified port. Similarly, an entry (cno = y, pno = z) in the arrival table means that Cargo y arrived at Port z on some unspecified ship. Finally, an entry (pno = z, sno = x) in the docking table means that Ship x docked at Port z carrying some unspecified cargo.

Now suppose that the ship Enterprise never carried beans to Boston. Accordingly, the triplet corresponding to (Enterprise, beans, Boston) does not appear as a relationship grouping. However, the Enterprise has carried beans somewhere, just not to Boston. So (Enterprise, beans) appears in the shipment table. More precisely, the corresponding key

Ship	
sno	sname
13	Galaxy
25	Enterprise
83	Vega

Port	
pno	pname
91	Boston
17	Tampa
64	Seattle

Cargo	
cno	cname
55	oil
82	beans

Mission		
sno	pno	cno
13	91	82
25	91	55
25	64	82
83	17	82

Figure 2.15 Decomposing a ternary relationship into several one-to-many binary relationships

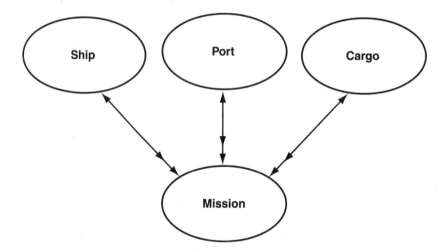

Figure 2.16 Bachman diagram of a factored ternary relationship

values for Enterprise and beans appear, but that detail is not important for the example. Furthermore, some ship has carried beans to Boston, just not the good ship Enterprise. So (beans, Boston) appears in the arrival table. Finally, the Enterprise has delivered some cargo to Boston, just not beans. Therefore, (Boston, Enterprise) appears in the docking table. The data of Figure 2.15 illustrate these circumstances, and the decomposition of Figure 2.17 produces the intersection data of Figure 2.18.

Now, if the Enterprise had delivered beans to Boston, then these three intersection tables (shipment, arrival, docking) would contain exactly the same data! Try it for yourself. If (sno = 25, pno = 91, cno = 82) becomes a relationship triplet, that is, if you add it to the mission table of Figure 2.15, then you must insert (sno = 25, pno = 91) into the docking table. But it is already there! Similar analysis shows that the arrival and shipment tables also remain unchanged. Because the state of the database is the same under either

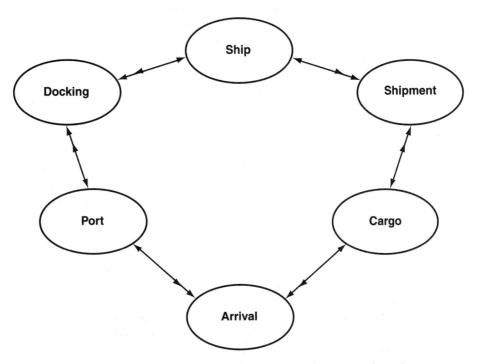

Figure 2.17   An erroneous pairwise decomposition of a ternary relationship

Docking	
sno	pno
13 (Galaxy)	91 (Boston)
25 (Enterprise)	91 (Boston)
25 (Enterprise)	64 (Seattle)
83 (Vega)	17 (Tampa)

Shipment	
sno	cno
13 (Galaxy)	82 (beans)
25 (Enterprise)	55 (oil)
25 (Enterprise)	82 (beans)
83 (Vega)	82 (beans)

Arrival	
pno	cno
91 (Boston)	82 (beans)
91 (Boston)	55 (oil)
64 (Seattle)	82 (beans)
17 (Tampa)	82 (beans)

Figure 2.18   Intersections from the pairwise decompositions of the ship-port-cargo relationship

circumstance, there is no way to answer a query: Did the Enterprise carry beans to Boston? If the Enterprise hadn't carried beans to Boston, you might still incorrectly answer "yes" because you can determine that the Enterprise has carried beans somewhere, that beans have been delivered to Boston, and that the Enterprise has docked at Boston. This situation is sometimes called a "connection trap" because a collection of pairwise associations hints at three-way connection, even though the three-way connection doesn't exist.

The example illustrates that a true ternary is not equivalent to pairwise binary relationships among the three entities. In a ternary relationship, each meaningful grouping involves *three* tuples, one from each of the participating entities. Three tuples—one from ship, one from cargo, and one from port—must come together to make a meaningful mission. This same principle applies for all higher degree relationships. The groupings of an n-degree relationship each contain n tuples, one from each of the n participating entities. If each of the participants has a single attribute key, the relationship becomes an intersection table of degree n. The resulting n one-to-many relationships between each original entity and the intersection presents an equivalent arrangement, which maintains all the meaning from the original relationship. On a diagram this decomposition appears as n dominant parents sharing a common child, as exemplified by Figure 2.16. The arrangement also satisfies the requirement that only common attributes among tables are used to maintain relationships.

The degree of a relationship is the number of participating entities. In general, an n-degree relationship is not equivalent to an arrangement of pairwise connections among the n entities. Rather, its expression uses an additional intersection table to which n one-to-many relationships attach.

Recursive relationships

In a **recursive** binary relationship, the two participating entities coincide. Both one-to-many and many-to-many situations are possible.

One-to-many recursive relationships

Consider the many-to-one relationship between the employee entity and itself, as shown in Figure 2.19. A relationship instance groups a supervisor with zero, one, or more workers. The relationship is many-to-one because a supervisor, who is also an employee, can have many employees working for him, but each employee reports to at most one supervisor. The left portion of Figure 2.19 shows the relationship as a Bachman diagram while the right part uses a table format. In the role of supervisor, the employee entity serves as the dominant entity in the relationship. In the role of worker, it also serves as the non-dominant entity.

A recursive relationship is one in which an entity participates more than once, assuming a different role upon each entry into the relationship.

As in the non-recursive case, you maintain the one-to-many relationship by embedding the key attribute of the dominant entity into the non-dominant partner. In this case, eno is a key for the employee relation because each employee tuple contains a distinct eno value.

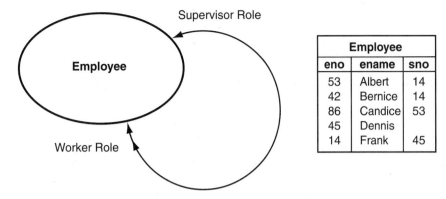

Employee		
eno	ename	sno
53	Albert	14
42	Bernice	14
86	Candice	53
45	Dennis	
14	Frank	45

Figure 2.19   A one-to-many recursive binary relationship

The foreign key sno (supervisor number) refers to the eno of the individual for whom the employee works. Because both attributes occur in the same table, you must depart from the convention of assigning the same name to the linking attributes between two tables. However, the meaning of the foreign key is unchanged. The sno value in a given tuple refers to the supervisor of that employee.

Assume for this example that there are no cycles in the chain of command. Starting from a given employee X, you can determine all his workers, and then all their workers, and so forth. However, you do not expect to encounter employee X a second time in the expanding tree. In the absence of cycles, at least one employee will have no supervisor. Starting from any employee, you can recover his supervisor from the sno value. You can then locate the supervisor of that supervisor in the same manner. Because there are no cycles, and because there are only finitely many tuples in the relation, this progression must terminate with an employee who has no supervisor. In Figure 2.19, such an eno chain is 86, 53, 14, 45.

You can easily handle certain obvious queries about the supervisory situation and not experience any complications from the recursion. For example, who works for employee X? Who is the supervisor of employee Y? Find the employees who are farther down the chain of command from employee Z. To answer the last query, you first locate employee Z and note the eno, say z_1. You then find all employees with sno = z_1. These employees work directly for Z and are therefore part of the answer set. You now note the eno values of these workers, producing the set A_2. All employees with sno value in A_2 work indirectly for Z through some intermediate supervisor, so they are also part of the answer. Continuing in this manner, you will eventually accumulate all the workers under supervisor Z at any level. The number of generations depends on the data. You might have to proceed through two levels or perhaps even ten levels to exhaust the fanout of employees under supervisor Z. It depends on the content of the employee table.

Many-to-many recursive relationships
As a second example, consider the bill of materials database shown in the upper portion of Figure 2.20. The main entity here is a "part," typically a component of some mechanical

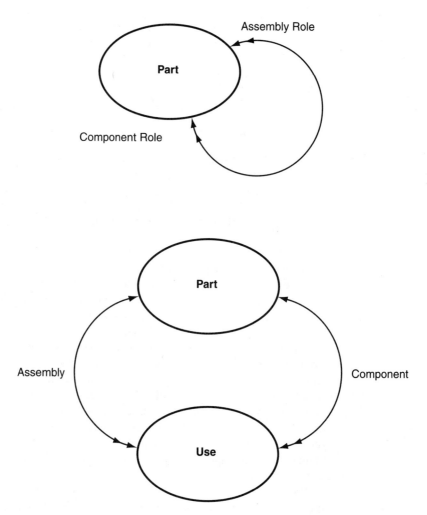

Figure 2.20   Bill of materials database illustrating a recursive many-to-many relationship

assembly. The recursive relationship arises because a given part contains constituent parts. For example, an engine consists of pistons, valves, cams, and so forth. Each of these components, in turn, contains more elementary parts. Eventually, the process reaches indivisible parts, such as nuts and bolts.

Unlike the previous example, this relationship is many-to-many. In addition to containing sub-parts, a given part can appear in many super-parts. For example, a wheel comprises a rim, a tire, and six lug nuts. A wheel also appears as a component of the front axle assembly, the rear axle assembly, and the trunk package (as a spare tire). Since wheels appear as components of three parts, a one-to-many grouping is out of the question because the wheel would be in the intersection of all three groupings.

Use		
pno$_1$	pno$_2$	quantity
35	16	1
35	10	1
35	11	1
35	98	1
35	24	1
10	90	1
10	15	2
10	24	1
10	44	1
10	92	2
11	90	1
11	15	2
11	24	2
11	44	1
11	92	2
15	51	1
15	52	1
15	61	1
15	72	8

Part	
pno	pname
35	wagon
51	tire
52	hub
44	axle
92	cotter pin
72	ball bearing
61	bearing race
90	axle bracket
98	steering tongue
24	bolt
10	front suspension
11	rear suspension
15	wheel
16	carriage

Figure 2.21   Decomposition of the recursive bill of materials relationship

The standard decomposition technique produces an intersection entity between part and itself. As in the employee relation, the part entity now plays two roles. One role is "assembly," and the other is "component." As an assembly, a wheel contains the constituents mentioned above. As a component, it contributes to the makeup of other parts, such as a front axle assembly. Assuming that pno is a key of the part relation, you can tabulate the intersection entity as all pairs of pno values, (pno$_1 = x$, pno$_2 = y$), where part x contains part y. For the constituents of a wagon, this decomposition appears in Figure 2.21.

To recover the components of part x, scan the intersection table for all pairs with pno$_1 = x$. The corresponding pno$_2$ values identify the components. To determine the assemblies that contain part y, scan the intersection table for all pairs with pno$_2 = y$. The corresponding pno$_1$ values identify the containing assemblies. Figure 2.21 shows a wheel (part 15) composed of a tire (part 51), a hub (part 52), a bearing race (part 61) and ball bearings (part 72). Furthermore, a wheel (part 15) appears in the front suspension (part 10) and in the rear suspension (part 11). The lower portion of Figure 2.20 shows the individual one-to-many relationships that result from the decomposition. The appropriate role of the part entity is noted beside each relationship. That is, the leftmost one-to-many relationship groups a part instance as an assembly with all the parts that it contains. As usual, you can identify the intersection entity with a real-world counterpart, namely, the part's use. The leftmost one-to-many relationship between part and use then views the intersection entity as a sub-part, and it groups a given part with all its sub-parts. The rightmost relationship views the intersection as a super-part, and it groups a given part with all the super-assemblies that contain it.

Because the intersection now corresponds to an application concept (use), the use table provides a convenient location for the number of times a given sub-part appears within a given assembly. The quantity attribute adds this information. Continuing with the example of Figure 2.21, a wheel (part 15) contains one tire (part 51), one hub (part 52), one bearing race (part 61), and eight ball bearings (part 72). Reading in the reverse direction, a wheel (part 15) appears twice in the front suspension (part 10) and twice in the rear suspension (part 11).

A frequent query against this type of database is the "parts explosion" request. This asks, given a part X, to produce all its components and then all their components and so on, recursively, down to the basic, indivisible parts. Although this query presents no great difficulty, you should again note that the number of generations from the top part to the basic parts depends on the table data.

You can construct higher-order recursive relationships as an academic exercise, but they seldom occur in practical applications. For example, consider a pool of persons, from which three-member teams are formed. Each team has a captain, left guard, and right guard. Suppose that any person is eligible for any position. A relationship grouping is a triplet, with a tuple (key) from the person entity filling each slot. The first slot is the captain, the second is the left guard, and the third is the right guard. The situation decomposes into three one-to-many relationships between person and the intersection entity, which you could call "team." Each involves the person entity in a different role. For example, one role groups a person with all teams of which he is captain.

Constraints

A **database constraint** restricts the data that can appear in the bodies of relations. The body of a relation contains tuples, and the attribute value in a tuple must come from some specified domain. So the definition to this point already imposes some discipline on the tables' content. For example, from the definition of the aquarium database, repeated here as Figure 2.22, the tank relation can never contain the tuple (tno = 45, tname = cesspool, tcolor = yellow, tvolume = 100). This tuple is disallowed because the tcolor value must come from a particular domain, which does not include yellow.

 A database constraint restricts the data appearing in the bodies of relations.

However, an application often demands restrictions beyond domain constraints. Perhaps last names in a personnel database are restricted to alphabetic characters or to a maximum of twenty characters. Perhaps there must never be more than a hundred fish in any tank in the aquarium database. Perhaps all tanks with tvolume < 1000 are to have tcolor = blue. In other words, constraints arise from the given application. The database designer can instruct the DBMS to enforce application constraints and, therefore, render the database model a more accurate reflection of reality.

A violation occurs if any relational body contains data that does not satisfy a constraint. Because the data in the bodies changes as the corresponding real-world situation evolves, the database content can pass from a consistent state (no violations) to an inconsistent state

Aquarium	
Relation	Attributes
tank	tno, tname, tcolor, tvolume
species	sno, sname, sfood
fish	fno, fname, fcolor, fweight, tno, sno
event	eno, fno, edate, enote

Domains of attributes			
Attribute	Domain	Attribute	Domain
tno	$\mathcal{Z}$	tname	$\mathcal{S}$
tcolor	{blue, red, green}	tvolume	$\{100, 200, 300, 400\}$
sno	$\mathcal{Z}$	sname	$\mathcal{S}$
sfood	$\mathcal{S}$	fno	$\mathcal{Z}$
fname	$\mathcal{S}$	fcolor	{blue, red, orange, black, white, purple}
eno	$\mathcal{Z}$	fweight	$\mathcal{Z}$
enote	$\mathcal{S}$	edate	$\mathcal{D}$

Figure 2.22   Repeated definition of the aquarium relational database

(one or more violations). The **state** of the database at a specified time is the content of the relational bodies at that time. A **consistent state**, with respect to some set of constraints $\mathcal{F}$, is a state with no constraint violations. The database designer must identify the application constraints and then ensure that the database state remains consistent with respect to these constraints.

 The database state at a particular time is the content of the relational bodies at that time. A consistent state, with respect to a set of constraints $\mathcal{F}$, is a state in which no constraint of $\mathcal{F}$ is violated.

Just how does the database maintain a consistent state? The database shell is in place when the definitions of the various relations are complete. Users then manipulate the table contents by adding, modifying, and deleting tuples. You could continuously monitors the database state with the interface routines, which may be either software programs or interactive users. These routines could reject any transaction that would lead to an inconsistent state. Because there may be numerous interacting agents, this requirement places a heavy burden on developing the corresponding software. Moreover, much of the error detection apparatus will be duplicated across a large collection of access programs.

A more efficient approach includes the constraints in the database definition, The DBMS then assumes the chore of continually maintaining a consistent state. The difficulty is that the DBMS supports general-purpose database operations, such as inserting, modifying, and deleting tuples, whereas constraints can vary widely with applications. In the aquarium example, suppose a non-shark fish is never to occupy a tank with a shark, unless that species of shark has already proved harmless through peaceful cohabitation with a guppy. Verifying such application-specific constraints can be very computationally expensive in large databases. It appears that the most general solution must allow the DBMS to invoke application-specific code segments to check for such specialized constraints. However, short of invoking application-dependent code, the DBMS can handle certain generic constraints in a simpler fashion. This section will examine these generic constraints.

Key constraints

For brevity, this text will use the name of a relation synonymously with its collection of attributes and will suppress the domains. For example, Tank = {tno, tname, tcolor, tvolume} under this convention. Then $A \in R$ means A is an attribute of R, and $\mathcal{A} \subset R$ means $\mathcal{A}$ is a subset of the attributes of R. Also, $r(R)$ will denote the body of R. For $A \in R$, two tuples in $r(R)$ **agree on** A if their corresponding A values are equal. For example, the tuples (tno = 45, tname = cesspool, tcolor = blue, tvolume = 100) and (tno = 71, tname = lagoon, tcolor = blue, tvolume = 200) agree on tcolor. If $\{A_1, A_2, \ldots, A_m\} \subset R$, then two tuples in $r(R)$ agree on $\{A_1, A_2, \ldots, A_m\}$ if they agree on each attribute in the subset.

A **superkey** of a relation R is a subset $\mathcal{SK} \subset R$, together with the constraint that $r(R)$ must never contain two distinct tuples that agree on $\mathcal{SK}$. Two important properties follow immediately from this definition. First, a value for a superkey of R uniquely identifies a tuple in $r(R)$. Given the superkey values, you can unambiguously locate the corresponding tuple, if it exists in the table. It might happen that no such tuple exists in the table, but it will never be the case that two or more tuples have those same superkey values. Second, every relation R must possess at least one superkey. Because $r(R)$ is a mathematical set, there are no duplicate tuples. So in the extreme case, you can obtain a superkey by specifying $\mathcal{SK} = R$. Then, the only way two distinct tuples could agree on $\mathcal{SK}$ would be to agree on all the attributes, giving a pair of duplicate tuples.

A **key** for a relation is a minimal superkey for that relation. A key is a superkey with the property that if any attribute is removed, the remaining subset will no longer be a superkey. Clearly any single-attribute superkey is a key because discarding an attribute leaves the empty set. The empty set can't, in general, be a superkey because all tuples agree on the empty set. If the empty set were a superkey, the relation could never contain more than one tuple.

 A subset $\mathcal{SK} \subset R$ is a superkey of R if and only if $r(R)$ obeys the constraint: no two distinct tuples in $r(R)$ can ever agree on $\mathcal{SK}$. A key is a minimal superkey.

For the tank relation, the subset (tno, tcolor) is a superkey. Once the tno value is specified, there can be at most one tuple with that tno value. It follows that there can be at most one tuple with the (tno, tcolor) values specified. However, (tno, tcolor) is not a key because the attribute tcolor is superfluous. You can discard tcolor, leaving tno alone, which is still a superkey. Because you can't discard further attributes, without losing superkey status, tno is a key. The difference between a key and a superkey is that a key is the *smallest* set of attributes that retains the authority to identify a tuple.

The statement that a particular set of attributes constitutes a key (or superkey) of a relation is a constraint on the data that can appear in the body of the relation. Naturally enough, it's called a key constraint (or a superkey constraint). Just as with other constraints, a key constraint must arise from the application. For example, you may suspect that tno is a key of the tank relation because you have watched the body of the tank relation a long time, and you have never observed two tuples agreeing on tno. However, your observation doesn't rule out the possibility that some future state of the database might exhibit two such tuples. In other words, you can never know that a particular set of attributes is a key from watching the data. The key status of an attribute must come from an analysis of the application. In the aquarium application, you decide that all tanks will bear a unique serial number, which you call tno. At this point, tno becomes a superkey of the tank table.

Key constraints are common in applications, and the DBMS can easily enforce them in a general manner. For example, the DBMS can execute on top of an operating system that supports indexed sequential files with unique keys. By maintaining the relations as indexed sequential files, the DBMS can rely on the operating system to report any attempt to insert a tuple that duplicates an existing key.

Functional dependency constraints

A second form of generic constraint is a generalization of the key concept, called a functional dependency. Let R be a relation, and let $X \subset R$ and $Y \subset R$. The **functional dependency**, $X \longrightarrow Y$, is the constraint on $r(R)$: if two tuples agree on X, then they also agree on Y. You should read the notation $X \longrightarrow Y$ as X **determines** Y.

Functional dependency is weaker than a key constraint. Two distinct tuples can indeed have the same X value and still remain in the table body. However, if they do, they must also have the same Y values. For example, in the aquarium database of Figure 2.22, you can constrain the tank relation by insisting that tvolume $\longrightarrow$ tcolor. Small tanks, of volume 100 or 200, must be blue. Medium tanks, of volume 300, must be red, and large tanks, of volume 400 or more, must be green. A relation may still have two tanks of volume 300. But if two or more such tuples are present, they must all have tcolor red.

A key constraint is an extreme form of a functional dependency. That is, if X is a key of R, then $X \longrightarrow Y$ holds, for *all* subsets $Y \subset R$. Suppose that X is a key for R and that two tuples agree on X. Because X is a key, then these two tuples *must coincide*. What was presented as two tuples must in reality be just one. Of course, the two tuples then clearly agree on all attributes. Consider an alternative argument. Since no two distinct tuples will ever agree on X, there will never be a violation of $X \longrightarrow Y$, regardless of the choice of Y. The only way to violate a functional dependency $X \longrightarrow Y$ is to find two distinct tuples that agree on X and disagree on Y. Because no tuples can be found to agree on X, there can be no violation.

A functional dependency, $X \longrightarrow Y$, is a constraint that requires any two tuples in $r(R)$ agreeing on the attributes X to also agree on the attributes Y. If K is a key of R, then $K \longrightarrow X$ holds, for any subset $X \subset R$.

Many application constraints take the form of a functional dependency. The DBMS can enforce such constraints, if they are part of the database definition. However, such enforcement is not as simple as for key constraints, and many commercial database products provide no facilities for enforcing functional dependencies in the general sense. In that case, the data manipulation routines provided for the users must contain the appropriate checks. However, even if the eventual implementation doesn't efficiently enforce functional dependency constraints, these concepts still provide significant insight into the database design process.

Entity and referential integrity

Key values identify tuples and maintain relationships. Both functions entail two further constraints. The phrase tno is a key to the tank relation means that a particular tno value can stand for the corresponding tank in references where it's inconvenient or wasteful to include the entire tank tuple. For example, tno appears in a fish tuple as a foreign key, identifying the tank in which the fish swims. A foreign key is not necessarily a single attribute. Like a key or superkey, it can be a subset of attributes, provided that it serves to identify a unique tuple in the related table. Formally, a **foreign key** of a relation R is a subset of the attributes of R, whose values match a superkey in some other relation and, therefore, establish a relationship between the two tables.

Frequently a foreign key has the same name as the superkey in the table to which it refers. However, this convenience isn't always possible, particularly in recursive relationships. In Figure 2.19, for example, sno is a foreign key referring to eno in the same table.

 A foreign key in a relation is an attribute subset referring to a superkey in another relation. Normally, the foreign key and its matching superkey share a common name. In recursive cases, the foreign key and the superkey appear in the same table, and they must have distinct names.

Because a key value is a fundamental substitute for a tuple, it's reasonable to insist that key values never be null. In other words, you should not insert a tuple into a table unless you specify the key values. This constraint is called **entity integrity**. Admittedly, it's common in large databases for certain data to be missing. For example, a new tank arrives at the aquarium, and the data clerk enters it into the database before giving it a name. The clerk can specify null for the tname value, with the understanding that a later operation will install the correct value. As this example illustrates, nonkey attributes can be null without too much inconvenience. However, you don't want to specify the tno value as null because you might never be able to locate that tank tuple again! Many tank tuples can have the same tname, tcolor, and tvolume values. If they all have a null tno value, which one is the new tank? In a manner of speaking, the tno value *is* the tank instance within the model. By enforcing the entity integrity constraint, you can always locate each tuple individually.

Referential integrity is a constraint requiring that a foreign key value must either (1) be null or (2) contain a value that actually exists in the referenced table. Recall that tno is a foreign key in the fish relation, and its purpose is to refer to the tank in which a fish swims. Suppose a new fish arrives on the receiving dock, but the staff have not yet assigned it to a tank. It is currently living in a plastic bag full of water awaiting a home. Now the data clerk enters the new fish into the aquarium database, dutifully recording its name, color, weight, and especially, a unique fno value to preserve the entity integrity constraint.

However, he specifies null for the tno foreign key attribute. The resulting tuple enters the fish table without violating referential integrity. However, when he later modifies the tuple to provide a tno value, that value must match the tno value of an existing tank.

Referential integrity is important because foreign keys are the only mechanism for maintaining relationships. Therefore referential integrity guards against errors that can disrupt legitimate relationships or create invalid groupings. For example, a one-to-many relationship grouping contains exactly one dominant parent and zero or more non-dominant children. If a nonexistent foreign key value appears in a child tuple, that tuple becomes part of a grouping without a dominant parent, which is an illegal condition.

 Entity integrity requires that a tuple must never contain null values in its key attributes. Referential integrity requires a foreign key to contain either a null value or the key of an existing dominant tuple from the referenced entity.

Elementary entity-relationship diagrams

A relational application uses two distinct notations to describe tables, relationships, and constraints. The first notation serves the needs of database designers while they are developing the application entities and their relationships. Entity-relationship (ER) diagrams are the most popular notation for this purpose, and they are the topic of this section. The second notation is a machine-readable script that presents the final design (tables, relationships, constraints) to the DBMS. The next section on database schemas discusses this second notation.

 ER diagrams provide a notation for documenting a tentative database design. Analysts use them to facilitate the design process. An ER diagram, together with other documentation, captures the important features of the application, but its machine-readable translation, the database schema, actually conveys the information to the DBMS.

Entities and their attributes in ER diagrams

An ER diagram shows an application entity as a rectangle, with the attributes in surrounding ovals, each connected to the rectangle with a line. The rectangle contains the name of the entity. For the aquarium example, a fish entity appears in the upper part of Figure 2.23. A primary goal of ER diagrams is to convey as much information as possible in a concise format. Accordingly, the attribute ovals can take a variety of alternate forms, each of which provides further context for the attribute. An underlined attribute is a key attribute, so fno is underlined in the upper part of Figure 2.23. A dashed oval indicates a **derived** attribute, an attribute that is not explicitly stored because it can be calculated from the values of other attributes. A multivalued attribute appears in a doubled oval, and a composite attribute exhibits sub-ovals for its components.

The lower part of Figure 2.23 expands the fish entity to include examples of these other kinds of attributes. Here, fname is a composite attribute, consisting of a title, a first name,

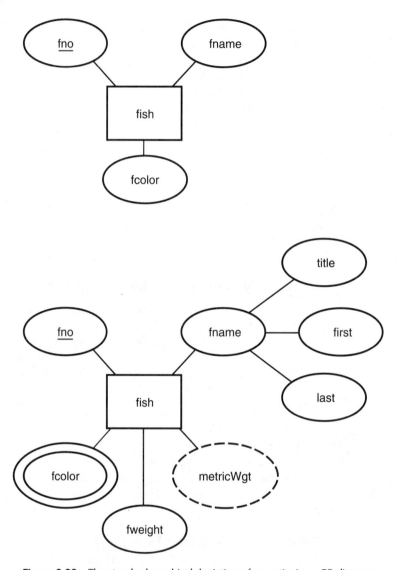

Figure 2.23   The standard graphical depiction of an entity in an ER diagram

and a last name. A particular fish, for example, might have the fname, Doctor Fried Flipper. The fcolor attribute is multivalued, allowing the possibility of a fish with fcolor = (red, white, blue). A derived attribute is metricWgt. There is no need to store the fish's metric weight (in kilograms) because the DBMS can compute the value on demand by dividing the fweight (in pounds) by 2.2.

Of course, relational databases don't allow composite or multivalued attributes. However, ER diagrams are intended for human use, and these additional features allow you to capture more of the application's meaning. ER diagrams are not associated with any partic-

Fish
<u>fno</u>
fweight
fname
title
first
last
fcolor . . .
metricWgt *

Figure 2.24 An alternative notation for entities

ular database model. After an ER diagram captures the application, the designer converts it into a database schema for the available system, which could be relational, object-oriented, deductive, network, or hierarchical.

A more concise format appears in Figure 2.24. A single rectangle holds the entity name and its attributes, and notational devices distinguish the various attribute types. The underline convention marks the key, just as in the full format, and an asterisk indicates a derived attribute. A trailing ellipsis denotes multivalued attributes, and the indentation scheme elaborates composite attributes.

 ER diagrams represent entities as rectangles, either with the attributes in surrounding ovals or with the attributes listed in the rectangle. Specialized notation marks key, multivalued, derived, and composite attributes.

Binary relationships in ER diagrams

In an ER diagram, a relationship appears as a diamond containing the relationship name. Lines connect the relationship diamond to the participating entities. The lines normally emanate from the vertices of the diamond, which might seem to limit the notation to relationships of degree 4 or less. However, no rule states that the lines must originate at a vertex, and therefore, relationships of degree 5 or higher are possible. Most relationships are binary; occasionally a ternary relationship appears. Because higher degree relationships are rare, the four vertices of the diamond are usually more than sufficient.

Figure 2.25 shows the Represents relationship between Species and Fish. Recall that you can tabulate any kind of binary relationships (one-to-many, many-to-many, or one-to-one) as a collection of pairs. The Represents relationship is one-to-many, and each instance is a pair, (species, fish). Of course, a given fish appears in at most one pair, indicating a grouping with a unique species. A single line connecting an entity with a relationship denotes **partial participation**: certain objects of the entity class might not appear in any pair. In Figure 2.25, the Species entity partially participates in the Represents relationship. This means there can be a species that does not group with any fish. The aquarium may have registered a species in the database but not yet have any fish of that species. By contrast, the Fish entity uses a double line to connect with the relationship diamond. The double connection indicates **total participation**, meaning that every object of the entity must

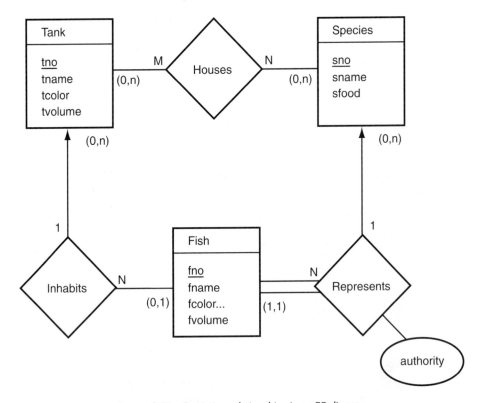

Figure 2.25   Depicting relationships in an ER diagram

appear in at least one pair. A fish must belong to a species, or it can't exist in the database. This example shows how the notation can capture certain nuances of an application. In this context, an ER diagram constitutes a **semantic modeling tool**. A designer uses it to capture the semantics (meaning) of an application.

 An ER diagram shows a relationship as a diamond, with lines connecting it to its participating entities. A single line denotes partial participation; a double line signifies total participation.

An arrowhead appears on the end of the line connecting the relationship diamond to the dominant relation of a one-to-many relationship, as illustrated in Figure 2.25. The absence of an arrowhead marks the other entity as the non-dominant partner. Also, you can annotate one-to-many relationships with a "1" or an "N" where the line leaves the relationship diamond to join the dominant or the non-dominant entity respectively. A "1" on both sides indicates a one-to-one relationship, and the letters M and N represent a many-to-many relationship. Arrowheads on the ends of both lines connect entities in a one-to-one relationship, and no arrowheads at all show a many-to-many relationship. The designations 1:1, 1:N, and M:N are called **multiplicity ratios**.

Participation limits are placed near a connecting line where it joins an entity. A participation limit contains two numbers (x, y), where x gives the minimum number of pairs in which a given entity object can participate, and y gives the maximum number. The letter n signifies "many," when the exact number is not relevant. That is, n means 0, 1, or more. In Figure 2.25, the participation limit $(0, n)$ occurs near the Species entity. The minimum limit of zero means that a given species need not participate in any relationship pair. Its species-fish grouping can contain only the species and no fish. A minimum limit of zero carries the same meaning as the partial participation denoted by the single connecting line.

The maximum limit of n means that there is no specific limit on the number of pairs in which a given species object appears. This limit is consistent with the dominant status of Species in the one-to-many relationship with Fish. Because a species can associate with many fish, repetitive species entries are expected. Such repetitions as $(s_1, f_1), (s_1, f_2), (s_1, f_3), \ldots, (s_1, f_n)$, link a species s_1 to many fish. Note that participation limits allow the model to conform more closely to the particular application. For example, if an egalitarian aquarium has a rule that a species can't have more than 10 representative fish, then the participation limit $(0, 10)$ expresses this constraint in the diagram. However, there is a limit to the notation's flexibility. It can't, for example, express the constraint that some particular species, say, shark, be limited to 10 representatives while other species are limited to 100.

The participation limit $(1, 1)$ appears near the Fish entity in Figure 2.25. A lower limit of 1 carries the same meaning as the total participation denoted by the double connecting line. So, there is some redundancy in the notation, and, unfortunately, a chance to enter conflicting conditions. For example, if the lower limit specifies zero, but a doubled connecting line appears, these two constraints contradict one another. A lower limit of zero means that a fish can fail to appear in any relationship pair, which is precisely the condition forbidden by the double connecting line. Therefore, you must be careful to provide compatible notation when there is a chance for conflict. In particular, a lower participation limit of zero is compatible with a single connecting line, and a lower participation limit of 1 or more is compatible with a double connecting line. Furthermore, an upper participation limit of 1 should appear on the "many" side of a one-to-many relationship.

The Inhabits relationship between Tank and Fish also appears in Figure 2.25. This relationship is one-to-many, but the participation of Fish is partial, leading to a lower participation limit of zero. The upper participation limit of Fish must be 1 because the entity is the non-dominant side of a one-to-many relationship. Finally, the relationship Houses of Figure 2.25 illustrates a typical many-to-many relationship. These examples show the need for compatible notation. The following rules should help you construct consistent ER diagrams.

- In representing a binary one-to-X relationship, where X can be either one or many, the maximum participation limit for the entity on the X side must be 1.

- In representing a binary one-to-X relationship, where X can be either one or many, the connection to the entity on the "one" side must terminate in an arrowhead.

- If a binary relationship involves an upper participation limit of 1 on one of the entities, then the *other* entity is to receive an arrowhead at the end of its connecting line.

- When total participation is indicated by a double line connecting an entity with a relationship, then the lower participation limit of the entity must be 1 or more.

- When partial participation is indicated by a single line connecting an entity with a relationship, then the lower participation limit of the entity must be 0.

When constructing ER diagrams with all the trimmings, be careful to avoid conflicts among notations with overlapping meanings. It's not unusual to find ER diagrams that omit some of the features described here, retaining only those that are crucial for the application. For example, many diagrams omit participation limits, which reduces the opportunity for conflict with multiplicity ratios and double or single connecting lines.

Relationship attributes in ER diagrams

Attributes normally describe entity (rectangle) features. However, Figure 2.25 shows an "authority" attribute attached to the Represents relationship. A **relationship attribute** is an extension of the relationship groupings. With this addition, the Represents relationship is now a collection of triplets of the form (species, fish, authority). The authority portion holds the name of the person or agency that classified the given fish into the given species. Such an attribute does not properly belong to either of the participating entities. Instead, it describes some aspect of the relationship between the two entities.

However, this shared nature of "authority" is an application viewpoint. By exploiting the one-to-many format of the Represents relationship, you can treat authority as an attribute of Fish without losing information. Because the one-to-many relationship always uniquely determines the species associated with a given fish, you can reconstruct the (species, fish, authority) grouping from the fish tuple, using its embedded sno and its authority attribute.

Regardless of whether you move the authority attribute into Fish on the ER diagram, when you map the final design into relational tables, you will have to place it in the fish table. However, this convenience introduces a bias into the representation, suggesting that authority is more closely associated with fish than with species. If the aquarium application views authority as a descriptive feature of a (species, fish) pair, you should not place it inside the fish entity in the ER diagram, even though you will eventually move it there when you construct the relational schema. In terms of the aquarium application, you can argue that authority should be a joint feature of a (species, fish) pair. For example, you might make a classification mistake because you were careless in examining the fish or because you were unclear about the defining characteristics of the species. In other words, both fish and species are equally suspect. Furthermore, the other fish attributes, except for the artificial key, directly describe a fish. The name, color, and weight attributes serve to distinguish a particular fish from other fish. By contrast, the authority attribute is an external judgment. So while crafting the database design with ER diagrams, you should attach the authority attribute to the Represents relationship because that placement more closely represents the application's intent. When you convert the result to a relational database, you have to deal with the shortcoming of the relational model that does not allow relationship attributes. At that point, you must move the authority attribute to the Fish table.

Actually, you encountered relationship attributes earlier, when you studied the standard decomposition technique for factoring a many-to-many relationship into two one-to-many relationships. This process creates an intersection entity, which becomes the common child of the new one-to-many relationships. However, you often discover that the intersection entity corresponds to some application entity in its own right, and you can add further attributes to complete the description of the newly discovered entity. These additional attributes correspond to relationship attributes of the original many-to-many relationship.

For example, an ER diagram of the boat-sailor application appears in the upper portion of Figure 2.26. You envision Crew instances as (boat, sailor) pairs, and you can specify other attributes to flesh out the interaction between a boat and a sailor, such as sailingDate. . ., seaCondition. . ., and so forth. Understand that sailingDate applies to a (boat, sailor) pair in the sense that these dates say when the given boat sailed with the given sailor on board. Therefore, sailingDate is not a descriptive attribute of either Boat or Sailor. The same applies to the seaConditions attribute. When you decompose Crew, as shown in the lower part of the figure, you transfer the relationship attributes to the intersection entity.

Higher-degree relationships in ER diagrams

Figure 2.27 illustrates a ternary relationship with the ship-cargo-port example. Although multiplicity ratios aren't appropriate for non-binary relationships, participation limits remain significant. These values specify the minimum and maximum number of relationship groupings in which a given entity tuple can participate. In this example, all the participation limits are $(0, n)$, reflecting, for example, that a given ship can appear in many ship-cargo-port triplets. The SCP ternary relationship is not equivalent to a collection of pairwise relationships among the entities. Rather it is equivalent to three one-to-many binary relationships between the original entities and an intersection entity (mission). This decomposition appears in the bottom portion of Figure 2.27. Note that the participation of mission must be total in all three derived relationships. A mission comes into existence specifically to represent an SCM relationship grouping of the form (ship, cargo, port). Therefore, each mission object must participate in a relationship pair via each of SM, CM, PM. For example, mission m_1 appears in an SM pair (s_i, m_1) because m_1 is some triplet (s_i, c_j, p_k) of the SCP relationship.

Recursive relationships in ER diagrams

The prototypical one-to-many recursive relationship between supervisors and workers appears in Figure 2.28. Here, the arms of a relationship have certain roles names, although normally such annotation does not contribute to the diagram's information content. For example, in Figure 2.25, you can tag the arms of the Inhabits relationship with the roles "tank" and "fish." However, because the relationship involves two distinct entities, these roles are simply the names of the participating entities. You could use the roles "home" and "resident" instead of "tank" and "fish," leading to a tabulation of the Inhabits relationship as shown on the left below. Clearly, there is little purpose in explicitly assigning roles to the Tank and Fish arms of the relationship because both tank and fish objects serve in the expected roles.

The situation is less clear when an entity enters into a relationship more than once. The Supervises relationship of Figure 2.28 makes good use of the role assignments to determine which employee is the supervisor in a relationship grouping. You can envision the Supervises relationship as the table in the center below.

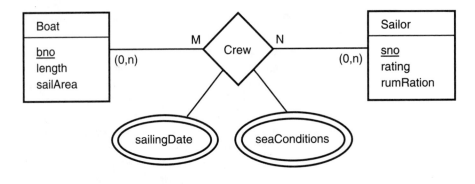

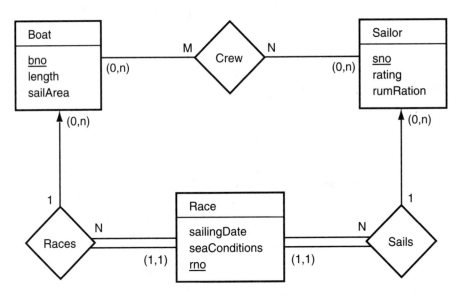

Figure 2.26   Relationship attributes leading to the discovery of a new entity

t_1 (home)	f_1 (resident)
t_1 (home)	f_2 (resident)
t_2 (home)	f_3 (resident)
⋮	⋮

e_1 (supervisor)	e_2 (worker)
e_1 (supervisor)	e_3 (worker)
e_2 (supervisor)	e_4 (worker)
⋮	⋮

p_1 (assembly)	p_2 (component)
p_1 (assembly)	p_3 (component)
p_4 (assembly)	p_2 (component)
⋮	⋮

The parts database provides a recursive many-to-many example, as shown in the lower part of Figure 2.28. The assembly and component roles allow you to visualize the Use

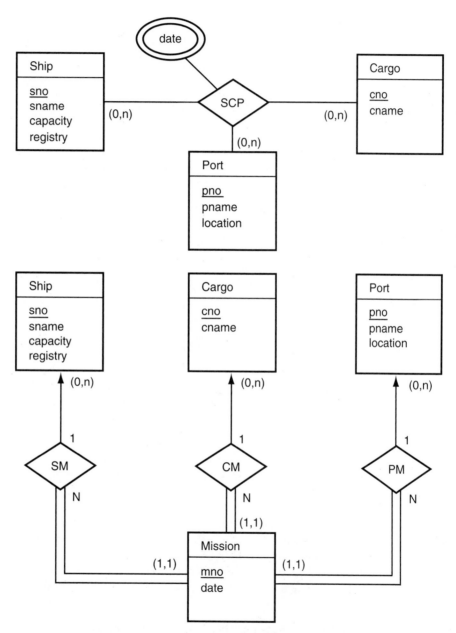

Figure 2.27   A ternary relationship in the ER notation

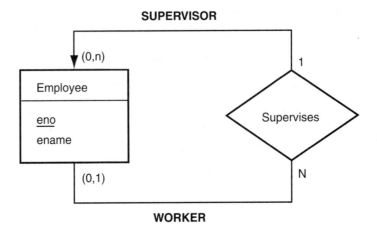

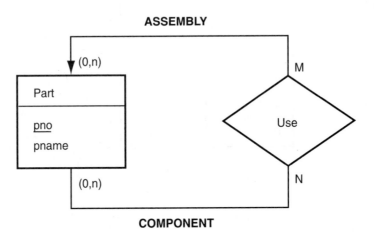

Figure 2.28   Recursive relationships in an ER diagram

relationship as shown to the right above. A parts explosion for a root part, p_i, locates all relationship pairs with p_i in the assembly role and reports all the component parts. The process then recursively repeats for each of these components. A parts implosion for a root part, p_i, searches for relationship pairs with p_i in the component role and reports the corresponding assemblies. The process then recursively repeats for each of these assemblies.

 Annotations on the arms of a relationship symbol can specify the role played by the participating entity at the end of the arm. Such notation is usually unnecessary because the entities play the expected roles. However the convention is helpful in recursive relationships.

Schema specification

You implement a particular application as a relational database in three steps. First, you analyze the application to determine the entities of interest, the relationships among them, and the necessary constraints. This stage results in a design documentation, typically with ER diagrams. Second, you present the design configuration to the DBMS as a relational schema, which create the empty shells of the various tables. This section deals with this second stage by explaining the **Data Definition Language** (DDL). In the final stage, you construct data manipulation routines to enable the user to work with the information in the table bodies, that is, to insert, modify, and delete tuples. This phase also uses a special language, the **Data Manipulation Language** (DML).

The designer specifies the database schema with the Data Definition Language (DDL). The user then inserts, retrieves, modifies, and deletes tuples with the Data Manipulation Language (DML).

Each database model uses a particular kind of DDL, and each commercial implementation involves some variation. Our concern here is with the general characteristics of the relational DDL. The left portion of Figure 2.29 shows a hypothetical DDL description of the aquarium database. Certain attribute descriptions contain key and foreign-key clauses, which express entity and referential integrity constraints. You describe the available domains early in the schema and then use domain constraints to associate each attribute with a particular domain. You assume that the system provides the elementary domains of integer, string, date, and so forth. Finally, functional dependency constraints for the database as a whole appear in a separate section following the table definitions.

No commercial relational database package supports all the schema description features illustrated in the left part of Figure 2.29. The right portion of the figure shows the aquarium schema as it would appear in a typical commercial DBMS. Note that there are no application-specific domain descriptions, so the designer can use only the native domains of the DDL—typically integer, float, fixed-length character strings, and special types for date and currency values. Although you can specify entity integrity with the "not null" notation, there is no provision for indicating referential integrity nor for specifying functional dependencies. Such constraints become the responsibility of the data manipulation procedures associated with the application.

Regardless of the description language's richness, the database schema elaborates a conceptual view of the application. Recall the three levels of a database system. At the bottom, the physical layer handles the disk data structures. The middle layer gives a conceptual view of the tables, keys, domains, and constraints, which the user needs to form a mental image of the application. The database designer specifies this middle level through the schema, but in most relational products, the DBMS automatically generates the lower physical level.

The uppermost level presents tailored versions of the conceptual view, customized for particular users. For example, a particular user may have been long accustomed to working with tank instances as tno, tname, tvolume, without ever making a reference to a tank color. This user doesn't even know that tanks have colors. You can tailor a customized schema

```
database aquarium {                                      create database aquarium
    domain keyvalue integer                                  create table tank (
    domain tankcolor {blue, red, green}                          tno integer not null,
    domain fishcolor {blue, red, orange, black, white, purple}   tname char(20),
    domain namestring string                                     tcolor char(10),
    domain volvalue {100, 200, 300, 400}                         tvolume integer
    relation tank {                                          )
        attribute tno keyvalue key                           create table species (
        attribute tname namestring                               sno integer not null,
        attribute tcolor tankcolor                               sname char(20),
        attribute tvolume volvalue                               sfood char(20)
        }                                                    )
    relation species {                                       create table fish (
        attribute sno keyvalue key                               fno integer not null,
        attribute sname namestring                               fname char(20),
        attribute sfood namestring                               fcolor char(10),
        }                                                        fweight integer,
    relation fish {                                              tno integer,
        attribute fno keyvalue key                               sno integer
        attribute fname namestring                           )
        attribute fcolor fishcolor                           create table event (
        attribute fweight integer                                eno integer not null,
        attribute tno keyvalue foreign key − > tank.tno          edate date,
        attribute sno keyvalue foreign key − > species.sno       enote char(100),
        }                                                        fno integer
    relation event {                                         )
        attribute eno keyvalue key
        attribute edate date
        attribute enote namestring
        attribute fno keyvalue foreign key − > fish.fno
        }
    constraints {
        tank.tvolume − > tank.tcolor
        }
    }
```

Figure 2.29   Specification of the schema for the aquarium relational database

for this user in which tanks appear in the desired form without the tcolor attribute. When this user retrieves a tank, the delivered tuple does not contain the tcolor value. If this user inserts a new tank, it receives a tcolor value of null. This idea has many variations. For example, one user prefers tvolume in cubic feet while another prefers gallons. Or, a user could take the parochial view that the aquarium consists only of tanks, excluding any mention of species or fish.

In all the above examples, the user needs a customized partial view of the complete conceptual schema. Such tailored views are important because many existing programs might rely on a particular format for some application entity, and it could be very expensive to rewrite all that software. Moreover, for security reasons, the full conceptual view of the database should not be accessible to every user. In any case, a particular tailored view of the database is called, reasonably enough, a **view**. Each DBMS provides the capability within its DDL for defining such views. Because the database schema gives a full conceptual view of the application, you could specify customized external views as subschemas, using a similar syntax with references back to the full schema. However, the relational model doesn't use that approach. Instead, it uses a data retrieval approach to specify views. Details of view specification appear in Chapter 6.

 A view is a partial conceptual picture of the application, which uses selected relations, attributes, constraints, and relationships of the schema.

Physical data independence characterizes the boundary between the physical and conceptual layers: it isolates the application's conceptual from changes in the physical access devices or the low-level data structures. For example, an optical storage device might replace a magnetic disk. Although such a change requires modifications in the internal DBMS routines that interface with the hardware, the applications are not affected. The applications are built on the tables, attributes, relationships, domains, keys, and constraints, without explicit reference to the physical details. The database schema provides both a conceptual view of the entire application and also a set of abstract building blocks (e.g., tables, domains, relationships, attributes), which are buffered from changes in the hardware or disk storage structures. This barrier, however, does not offer complete protection from hardware change. For example, if the hardware is simply removed, the virtual world of tables and relationships collapses.

Metadata and the system catalog

One of the shortcomings of a conventional file processing environment is that a typical data file is not self-describing. By contrast, a database is self-describing. A description of the data—data about the data—is called **metadata**. In the relational model, metadata receives the same treatment as the application data. It is stored in a collection of tables, called the **system catalog**. When the DBMS processes the schema description, it establishes tables to hold the names of the relations, their attributes, domains, and constraints, and information about the user who created the database shell. As users insert, modify, and delete tuples, the DBMS maintains update timestamps for each entity, and it collects statistics on the

Table	Contents
systables	table name table id (a key used in references from other tables) number of rows (tuples) number of columns (attributes) owner (user who created the table)
syscolumns	column (attribute) name table id (foreign key referencing systables) column number (a key) column domain (a code distinguishing integer, float, etc.) column size (number of bytes for character strings)
sysusers	user user priority user password (encrypted)
sysviews	view name view number (a key) view creation criteria

Figure 2.30   Partial contents of the system catalog of a typical commercial DBMS

frequency of certain operations. The user can retrieve information from these tables in the same manner as from tables directly concerned with the application.

Figure 2.30 shows some of the more important tables of the system catalog. In truth, the system catalog contains many additional tables, dealing with more advanced features, such as security and performance. Nevertheless, Figure 2.30 provides an illustration of the capacity of the database to describe itself to a user, who might be unaware of table and attribute names, domains, available views, and the like.

The contents of the systables and syscolumns tables for the aquarium application appear in Figure 2.31. If a user needs to know the tank attributes, he inspects systables to obtain the tabid value for the table named tank, that is, 2. He then consults the syscolumns table, looking for those rows that contain the foreign key tabid value of 2. The corresponding colname values (tno, tname, tcolor, tvolume) are the tank entity's attributes. Notice that systables and syscolumns appear as rows in the systables relation because they are indeed tables in the database, equal in every respect to the tables directly associated with the application. Because it contains metadata on every attribute in the database, the syscolumns table even contains references to its own attributes.

Certain entries are not as self-describing as might be desired. For example, the coltype value within syscolumns lists the domain of the attribute (column) described on that row. A code is used: 1 for integer and 2 for character string, with the length of the string given under the colsize heading. The DBMS documentation explains how to interpret such encodings. Even without the documentation, you can examine the application tables once you know the table and column names, and you can then deduce the data types from the data itself.

Finally, if a DBMS supports more of the features of the complete schema on the left of Figure 2.29, such as tailored domains, foreign-key designations, and functional dependency specifications, then these items also appear in appropriate system tables. As the database evolves, the DBMS continually maintains the system tables to reflect an accurate description of the database.

Systables				
tabname	tabid	nrows	ncols	owner
species	1	25	3	jones
tank	2	10	4	jones
fish	3	100	6	jones
event	4	942	4	jones
systables	10	6	5	jones
syscolumns	11	27	5	jones

Syscolumns				
colname	tabid	colno	coltype	colsize
tno	2	1	1	null
tname	2	2	2	20
tcolor	2	3	2	10
tvolume	2	4	1	null
sno	1	5	1	null
sname	1	6	2	20
sfood	1	7	2	10
fno	3	8	1	null
fname	3	9	2	20
fcolor	3	10	2	10
fweight	3	11	1	null
tno	3	12	1	null
sno	3	13	1	null
eno	4	14	1	null
edate	4	15	2	6
enote	4	16	2	100
fno	4	17	1	null
tabname	10	18	2	20
tabid	10	19	1	null
nrows	10	20	1	null
ncols	10	21	1	null
owner	10	22	2	20
colname	11	23	2	20
tabid	11	24	1	null
colno	11	25	1	null
coltype	11	26	1	null
colsize	11	27	1	null

Figure 2.31   Systables and syscolumns for the aquarium database

The next chapter will investigate methods for manipulating the data in the table bodies. The DML syntax can freely use table and attribute names because the DBMS can resolve these references through the system catalog. So the system catalog not only serves as a source of information about the structure of a particular application database, it is also used constantly by the DBMS in response to user access commands. A system catalog accessible by the DBMS in this manner is called an **active data dictionary**. All modern relational databases provide an active data dictionary. In certain older systems, the DBMS software didn't have dynamic access to all aspects of the data descriptions. Nevertheless, these systems frequently provided an organizing facility which allowed the user to record the various entity and attribute names. This facility was called a **passive data dictionary**.

SUMMARY

Domains are specified sets of values, which form the base-level components of a relational database application. Most database products provide only the traditional domains (e.g., integer, string, float), although some systems allow user-defined domains. An attribute is an ordered pair (N, D), where N is the name of the attribute, and D is the domain supplying values for the attribute. A relation consists of a schema and a body. The schema is a named finite collection of attributes. The attributes have no pre-established order. An association, based on an attribute (N, D), is an ordered pair (N, x), where $x \in D$. A tuple under a relational schema is an unordered collection of associations based on the schema attributes. The body of a relation is a collection of tuples under the corresponding schema. The tuples are not ordered. The degree of a relation is the number of attributes in its schema, and the cardinality is the number of tuples in its body. A relational database is a finite set of relational schemas, together with the bodies of those relations. Within a given relational database, all relations bear unique names. Within a given relation, all attributes bear unique names. However, attributes from different relations may have the same name.

A superkey of a relation is a subset of schema attributes of the relation, together with the constraint that no two distinct tuples in the body can ever agree on the chosen subset. A key of a relation is a minimal superkey, that is, a superkey from which no attribute can be removed without destroying the superkey property. Defining a relation as a set ensures that each relation has at least one key.

Relations are identified with tables, attributes with columns, and tuples with rows. An important aspect of the relational model is that it provides a single mode of expression, the relation (table), for both data and relationships. A relationship is an application-determined connection among several relations. A relationship instance is a meaningful grouping of tuples from the participating relations, where "meaningful" exemplifies the connection defining the relationship.

Binary relationships involve only two tables. A one-to-many relationship is binary; each instance groups exactly one tuple of the dominant (parent) relation with zero, one, or more tuples of the non-dominant (child) entity. You express one-to-many relationships by embedding a key of the parent tuple in the child tuples. Each instance of a many-to-many relationship is a pair of tuples from the participating entities. The number of times a given tuple, from either entity, can appear in the collection of pairs is unlimited. Because the relational model can't directly represent many-to-many relationships, you must factor them through an intersection entity. Often the intersection entity corresponds to some concept in the application. A one-to-one relationship can be viewed as a limiting case of a many-to-many relationship, in which a given tuple can appear in at most one pair. Sometimes a one-to-one relationship presents a case for merging the two entities involved. The relational model stores relationships by matching values in common attributes across tables.

Higher-degree relationships involve more than two participating relations. You can tabulate these relationships as n-tuples, containing one tuple, via its key, from each relation. The resulting tabulation acts as an intersection entity that stands in a many-to-one relationship with each of the original entities. The relational model can accept this factored form. An n-degree relationship is not equivalent to a collection of pairwise binary relationships among the entities. Relationships of degree higher than three are rare.

In a recursive binary relationship, the two participating entities coincide. In this case, the entity acts in two separate roles. Many-to-many recursive relationships can be factored in the usual manner.

A database constraint limits the data appearing in the bodies of relations. Domain constraints limit attribute values to certain specified domains. A key constraint forbids a relation to contain multiple tuples that have the same values in the key attributes. A functional dependency, $X \longrightarrow Y$, is a constraint that allows two tuples to exist with the same values for the X attribute, provided they also have the same values for the Y attributes. A key constraint is a special case of a functional dependency. A foreign key is a subset of a relation's attributes that refers to a superkey in another table. Foreign keys support relationships. Entity integrity is a constraint that requires key values in tuples to be nonnull. Referential integrity is a constraint that requires foreign key values, if present, to refer to existing tuples in the referenced relation.

The most common tool used in designing a database is the entity-relationship (ER) diagram. In this notation, entities appear as rectangles, surrounded by their attributes. An alternative format lists the attributes inside the rectangle, with certain conventions for special kinds of attributes. For example, a key attribute is underlined, and a derived attribute is marked with an asterisk. ER diagrams express relationships as diamonds with connecting lines to the participating entities. The lines can be single, indicating partial participation, or double, indicating total participation of the connected entity. Annotations, such as multiplicity ratios and participation limits, capture certain constraints imposed by the application on the relationship.

The Data Definition Language (DDL) of the DBMS describes the conceptual view of the application in a schema. Ideally a schema description includes the domains, relations, attributes, and constraints. In practice, domains are usually restricted to a few generic types, and there is seldom any provision for constraints beyond entity integrity. The Data Manipulation Language (DML) of the DBMS manipulates the tuples in the relations defined by the DDL.

A set of special tables, called the system catalog, stores metadata, that is, data about the application data. The names of the relations and attributes are examples of important metadata that render the database self-describing. Typically, the system catalog serves as an active data dictionary, and the DBMS can continually refer to it when interpreting user commands.■

An informal illustration of a relational database

Without attempting a systematic approach to information retrieval, answer the following queries by manually scanning the tables of Figure 2.1.

1. Find the names of blue fish.

2. Find the names of blue fish that live in a tank named cesspool.

3. Find the names of species represented in some tank named cesspool.

4. Find the names of species represented in *all* tanks in the database.

5. Find the names of species represented in *all* red tanks in the database.

Binary relationships

Analyze the following situations to determine the appropriate relationships. Illustrate them with Bachman diagrams, and factor any many-to-many relationships.

6. The city of Megopolis maintains a library system comprising several library buildings, each of which houses a large collection of books. Of course, the more popular books can be found in several of the libraries.

7. The city of Megopolis maintains a library system consisting of several buildings, many books, and a set of patrons who periodically borrow the books. As above, a book can exist in duplicate copies in several library buildings. Moreover, patrons may borrow from any library in the system.

8. A university consists of several colleges, each containing several departments. For example, the College of Engineering contains Electrical, Civil, Mechanical, and Chemical Engineering Departments. The College of Liberal Arts contains the departments of History, Anthropology, and Foreign Languages, and so forth. Each department maintains a staff of professors. There are no joint appointments: a professor teaches within a single department. Students major in the various departments. However, unlike a professor, a student can major simultaneously in more than one department.

Higher-degree relationships

The following situations involve higher-degree relationships. Analyze them with Bachman diagrams, factoring where appropriate to permit representation within the relational model. In each case, provide sample data illustrating that the higher-degree relationship is not equivalent to the collection of pairwise binary relationships.

9. A manufacturer's outlet holds many items for sale. A customer and a sales clerk work together to complete a transaction by facilitating the customer's purchase of an item. A customer can purchase a given item in any quantity, and this information should also be recorded in the database.

10. There are fields to plow, tractors to do the plowing, and farmers to ride the tractors. When all three factors come together, some work is accomplished.

Recursive relationships

The following situations contain recursive relationships. Analyze them with Bachman diagrams as in the preceding exercises. In each case indicate whether cycles in the relationships are meaningful.

11. A computer program consists of a collection of subprocedures, which call each other for services. In general, a given subprocedure calls other routines in order to break the task into smaller components. However, a given procedure can also be invoked by many different host procedures.

12. A literary collection contains a number of books, each with a bibliographic section referencing other books.

Constraints

Below is a table of land parcels. Express the following constraints as functional dependencies.

(Parcel id) pid	(Location) loc	(Area) area	(Assessed value) aval	(Tax rate) rate	(Owner) owner
38	Chicago	5000	45000	0.01	jones
74	Minneapolis	6500	51000	0.02	jones
94	Chicago	5000	45000	0.01	smith
51	Louisville	4000	40000	0.02	baker

13. Parcel id is a key to the relation.

14. Parcels of the same area in the same location will be assessed at the same value.

15. The tax rate will be uniform for a given location.

In the aquarium database of Figure 2.1, tno, sno, and fno are keys for the tank, species, and fish relations respectively. Within the fish table, tno and sno are foreign keys that reference the tank and species tables respectively. Each of the following questions suggests a tuple for entry into the body of the fish relation. Considering the current content of the fish relation, as given in Figure 2.1, indicate if the tuple is acceptable. If it is not acceptable, indicate whether the problem is a key violation, an entity integrity violation, or a referential integrity violation. For a given question, assume that any tuples added from preceding questions have been removed so that the context is always as depicted in Figure 2.1.

16. fno = 74, fname = able, fcolor = blue, tno = 42, sno = 18

17. fno = null, fname = baker, fcolor = red, tno = 42, sno = 18

18. fno = 83, fname = charlie, fcolor = green, tno = null, sno = 22

Prove the following propositions. Each proof is only a few lines, an almost immediate consequence of the definitions. Capital letters toward the end of the alphabet (X, Y, Z) stand for arbitrary subsets of the attributes of some relation R. Capital letters toward the front of the alphabet (A, B, C) are individual attributes of R. Juxtaposition indicates union. For example, XY is the union of the subsets X and Y.

19. $X \longrightarrow X$.

20. If $X \longrightarrow Y$, then $AX \longrightarrow Y$.

Elementary entity-relationship diagrams

21. Prepare an ER diagram for the following application without introducing any new entities. A library system contains libraries, books, authors, and patrons. Key attributes are libno, bookno, authno, and patno respectively. Libraries are further described by a libname and location, books by a title and page count (pages), authors by an authname, and patrons by a patname and patweight. An author is related to many books, namely to all that he has written; each book is related to a single author. Library and book participate in a many-to-many relationship in the sense that a library can hold many copies of a book, and a book can appear in many libraries. When a book and library become related, by virtue of sharing a copy, a cost attribute is attached to this relationship instance. A patron becomes related to a library by borrowing a book from it, and he becomes related to a book in the same way. Both relationships are many-to-many. When a book is borrowed, the attribute duedate is attached to the relationship instance.

22. Sketch an ER diagram of the library application of the preceding exercise, using only one-to-many relationships. Introduce new entities as appropriate to decompose any many-to-many or higher-degree relationships.

The two next exercises concern a university application. The university consists of several colleges, each with several departments. Each department must belong to a single college. Each department maintains a staff of professors. There are no joint appointments, and there are no professors without appointment. That is, a professor teaches within exactly one department. Students major in the various departments, and a student can major simultaneously in more than one department. Indeed, a student need not have a major. The relationship between department and student carries the attribute regdate, giving the date the student established a major in the department. The entities college, department, professor, and student have key fields cno, dno, pno, and sno respectively. Each is further described with a name attribute (e.g., cname, dname).

23. Construct an ER diagram showing the relationships among colleges, departments, professors, and students, without introducing any additional entitites.

24. Sketch a revised ER diagram of the university application, using only one-to-many relationships.

Schema specification

Describe a relational database schema for each situation below, using the format of Figure 2.29, which elaborates all the features, domains, relations, attributes, keys, foreign keys, and constraints. Assume that the DBMS provides elementary domains, such as integer, string, currency, and date.

25. The city of Megopolis maintains a library system consisting of several library buildings, each housing a large book collection. Of course, the more popular books can be found in several of the libraries. Attributes of book are title and author. Attributes of a library building are name and location. None of these attributes is unique to a particular instance. An author can write two books with the same title, or the location Ward 6 can have two libraries named Wilson Library.

26. The city of Megopolis maintains a library system consisting of several buildings, many books, and a set of patrons who periodically borrow the books. As above, a book can exist in duplicate copies in several library buildings. Moreover, patrons can borrow from any library in the system. The attributes of library and book are the same as the previous exercise. The attributes of patron are p-name and address, neither of which is to be considered unique to a particular patron.

27. A university consists of several colleges, each containing several departments. Each department maintains a staff of professors. There are no joint appointments: a professor teaches within a single department. Students major in the various departments. However, unlike a professor, a student can major simultaneously in more than one department. Attributes of a college are c-name and c-location; of a department, d-name and d-location; of a professor, p-name and age; and of a student, s-name and status (e.g., freshman, sophomore). None of the attributes is unique.

28. A manufacturer's outlet holds many items for sale. A customer and a sales clerk work together to complete a sales transaction by facilitating the customer's purchase of an item. The customer can purchase more than one of a given item. Attributes of an item are i-name and i-price; of a customer, c-name and age; of a sales clerk, s-name and experience (e.g., 1 year, 2 years). An attribute of a sale is date. None of these attributes is unique.

29. There are fields to plow, tractors to do the plowing, and farmers to ride the tractors. When all three factors come together, some work is accomplished. Attributes of a field are f-name and area; of a tractor, t-name and horsepower; of a farmer, fa-name and age. None of these attributes is unique.

30. A computer program comprises a collection of sub-procedures, which call each other for services. In general, a given sub-procedure calls other routines in order to break the task into smaller components. However, a given procedure can also be invoked by many different host procedures. Attributes of a procedure are pr-name and signature (parameter list). Names of procedures are unique.

31. A literary collection has a number of books, each with a bibliographic section referencing other books. The book attributes are title and author. Neither is unique.

3 Relational Algebra

CERTAIN OPERATIONS MANIPULATE THE TABLES OF A RELATIONAL database to produce new tables. For example, suppose you want the names of all red fish in the aquarium database. The following operation extracts that information by first isolating the tuples with fcolor = red (a horizontal section) and then retaining only the fname column (a vertical section). You can envision the transformation as follows.

Fish					
fno	fname	fcolor	fweight	tno	sno
164	charlie	orange	12	42	74
347	flipper	black	25	35	17
228	killer	white	32	42	22
281	charlie	orange	27	85	22
483	albert	red	45	55	17
119	bonnie	blue	51	42	22
388	cory	purple	12	35	93
654	darron	white	84	42	93
765	elsie	white	73	42	22
438	fran	black	61	55	74
277	george	red	33	42	93
911	helen	blue	48	44	74
104	indira	black	19	42	17
302	jill	red	28	38	17
419	kilroy	red	49	55	74
650	laura	blue	55	85	17
700	maureen	white	71	44	17

$\Longrightarrow$

< ··· >
fname
albert
george
jill
kilroy

Such operations constitute a Data Manipulation Language (DML), and this chapter discusses a particular DML called relational algebra. **Relational algebra** is a collection of operations that build new relations from existing ones. Because relations are the operands for relational algebra operators, and because relations are mathematical sets, you will find the familiar set operators: union, intersection, and difference. Other operators correspond to the horizontal and vertical sectioning activities seen in the previous example.

Relational algebra is a system of operators, each of which accepts one or two relations as operands and returns another relation as a result.

Applying a relational operator to one or more operand relations always yields another relation. This relation is then available for further manipulation by additional operators. A group of objects and operators is **closed** if any operation on the objects produces a result within the group. Therefore, the collection of relations and relational operators is closed. You can exploit the closure property to write larger relational expressions, where the results of one operation become the operands for another. These sequences then become queries, which can systematically extract information from the database. The chapter's goals are to present the relational operators and to categorize database queries into categories, each corresponding to a certain pattern of relational operators that computes the solution.

In this chapter and the next, I use the symbols $\wedge$ and $\vee$ for the logical operations of "and" and "or" respectively.

Renaming and set operators

In database queries, you often need to compare two tables. For example, you might ask if one table forms a subset of another. That is, do all the rows of the first table also appear in the second? Although a straightforward examination of the table rows seems sufficient, you must remember that a table only approximates a relation. The contents of the relations are actually tuples, which are collections of associations, which in turn are attribute-value pairs. Suppose one relation contains the tuple $(A = 6, B = 8, C = 4)$ while another contains $(X = 6, Y = 8, Z = 4)$. Although both tuples appear as $(6, 8, 4)$ in table form, it's not truly meaningful to ask if the first tuple occurs in the second relation. The tuples are not directly comparable because they involve different attributes. Nevertheless, you'll need to compare such constructions, so you must have an operation for copying one of them onto a new relation in which the attribute names are compatible with those in the other.

An assignment notation allows you to rename an entire relation. In the aquarium example, $X =$ Species creates a new relation named X that has the same schema as the Species relation. The attributes remain sno, sname, and sfood, each associated with its corresponding domain. Because the attribute names are unchanged, copies of the tuples in the original relation transfer to the new relation with no difficulty. To rename one or more attributes of a relation, you use the renaming operator, ρ_n, where n gives a list of attribute names to be changed, together with their new names. For example, the expression on the left below produces a new table, illustrated on the right.

$\rho_n(\text{Species})$,

where $n = (\text{sno} \longrightarrow s, \text{sname} \longrightarrow t)$

$<\cdots>$		
s	t	sfood
17	dolphin	herring
22	shark	anything
74	guppy	worm
93	shark	peanut butter

Two attributes of the argument relation acquire new names, but the third attribute keeps its original name. Because an attribute is actually a name-domain pair, you stipulate that the domains remain unchanged in either case. Copies of the species tuples transfer to the new relation by adopting the new name in each association. For example, the tuple (sno = 17, sname = dolphin, sfood = herring) becomes (s = 17, t = dolphin, sfood = herring) in the new relation. Within each association, the attribute name changes, but the value remains fixed. In the example above, the new relation itself doesn't have a specific name, and you can assume that the DBMS assigns a unique name that isn't relevant to the discussion of the moment. If necessary, you can give the result relation a specific name by using an assignment, such as $X = \rho_n(\text{Species})$.

You often need to rename all the attributes of a relation by prefixing the table name to each attribute name. You use the notation $\breve{\rho}$ for this operation. An attribute name with one or more table prefixes is a **qualified name**. For example, the expression on the left below produces the new relation on the right, where each attribute name assumes a qualified form.

$X = \breve{\rho}(\text{Species})$

X		
Species.sno	Species.sname	Species.sfood
17	dolphin	herring
22	shark	anything
74	guppy	worm
93	shark	peanut butter

This operation is useful in combining relations with overlapping attribute names. Because the qualified names don't conflict, they can coexist in some newly constructed table. The unadorned attribute names from the original database relations are **base names**. For example, sno, sname, and sfood are base names. As the various relational algebra operators produce new relations, these base names can acquire one or more prefixes. So various tables can contain such names as $X.S$.sno or $Y.S$.sname. Just as the $\breve{\rho}$ operator extends names with prefixes, the $\hat{\rho}$ operator removes the leftmost qualifier from each attribute name of its argument relation. For example, $X = \hat{\rho}(\breve{\rho}(\text{Species}))$ produces a new relation X with the same attribute names as the Species relation. The second operator removes the qualifying prefixes introduced by the first. Successive applications of $\hat{\rho}$ eventually strip attribute names back to their base forms. Subsequent applications of $\hat{\rho}$ have no further effect.

Two relations are **union-compatible** if they have the same schema. Matching attributes from the two relations will have the same names and domains. Of course, if the names aren't the same, you can make them union-compatible with the renaming operators if the values in the relational bodies come from the same domains. Under these circumstances, the tuples from the two relations can coexist within a single new relation. If relations R_1 and R_2 are union-compatible, then the union operator, $\cup$, combines them to produce a third relation, R_3, as follows. Recall the notational convention: If R is a relation, then R also stands for the set of attributes of R, and $r(R)$ stands for the body of R.

- The schema of R_3 is a copy of the schema of R_1 (or of R_2, since both must be identical). That is, $R_3 = R_1$.

- The body of R_3 consists of all tuples that are either in R_1 or in R_2. That is $r(R_3) = r(R_1) \cup r(R_2)$.

The relational union between compatible operands is simply the familiar set union between their bodies. For relational union, you write $R_3 = R_1 \cup R_2$ and depend on the context to avoid confusion with the union of the attribute sets. Similarly, if R_1, R_2 are union-compatible, the intersection operator, $\cap$, combines the two relations to produce a third, $R_3 = R_1 \cap R_2$. R_3 inherits its schema from R_1 (or R_2), and $r(R_3)$ contains those tuples that are in both R_1 and R_2. Finally, the set difference for two union-compatible relations produces $R_3 = R_1 - R_2$. The schema of R_3 duplicates that of R_1 or R_2, and $r(R_3)$ contains those tuples that are in R_1 but not in R_2. Therefore, **union-compatible** actually means compatible for the traditional set operations of union, intersection, and difference.

The assignment (=) and renaming (ρ) operators copy an entire table, renaming the table itself or selected attributes. The set operators ($\cup, \cap, -$) combine table bodies through union, intersection, or set difference.

Select-project-join operators

Unary operators: selection and projection

You extract horizontal slices from relations with a family of operators called **selection** operators, denoted by σ_b. The subscript b gives the boolean predicate that isolates the horizontal section. For example, suppose you want to extract a horizontal section from the Tank relation, choosing tuples with tvolume greater than 150. The operation and its corresponding table transformation appear below.

$\sigma_b(\text{Tank})$,

where $b = (\text{tvolume} > 150)$

Tank			
tno	tname	tcolor	tvolume
55	puddle	green	200
42	cesspool	blue	100
35	lagoon	red	400
85	cesspool	blue	100
38	beach	blue	200
44	lagoon	green	200

$\Longrightarrow$

< · · · >			
tno	tname	tcolor	tvolume
55	puddle	green	200
35	lagoon	red	400
38	beach	blue	200
44	lagoon	green	200

The $< \cdots >$ indicates that the new relation has an arbitrary name that isn't relevant for the purpose at hand. If it's necessary to name the new relation for future reference, you can use an assignment, such as LargeTanks $= \sigma_b(\text{Tank})$.

A relation is **compatible** with a particular selection operator, σ_b, if the predicate b involves only constants and attributes from the relation. You can apply a selection operator only to a compatible relation.

The family of **projection** operators, π_q, complements the the selection operators by extracting vertical sections. The subscript specifies the attributes to retain in the vertical slice. For example, the expression on the left below produces the table transformation on the right.

$\pi_q(\text{Tank})$,

where $q = (\text{tno, tcolor})$

Tank			
tno	tname	tcolor	tvolume
55	puddle	green	200
42	cesspool	blue	100
35	lagoon	red	400
85	cesspool	blue	100
38	beach	blue	200
44	lagoon	green	200

$\Longrightarrow$

< ··· >	
tno	tcolor
55	green
42	blue
35	red
85	blue
38	blue
44	green

The new relation's schema contains only tno and tcolor attributes, and the body contains shrunken tuples from Tank. Each tuple retains only those attributes mentioned in the operator subscript. If you view the relation as a table, this operation extracts a vertical slice. The body of the new relation starts with all the shrunken tuples from Tank, but because the new relation is a *set*, any duplicates are then removed. The example has no duplicates because the new relation includes the tno attribute, which is a key in the original relation. However, the expression on the left below projects onto tcolor, and after duplicate removal, the resulting table is shorter than the argument table.

$\pi_q(\text{Tank})$,

where $q = \text{tcolor}$

Tank			
tno	tname	tcolor	tvolume
55	puddle	green	200
42	cesspool	blue	100
35	lagoon	red	400
85	cesspool	blue	100
38	beach	blue	200
44	lagoon	green	200

$\Longrightarrow$

< ··· >
tcolor
green
blue
red

A relation is compatible with a projection operator π_q if the attribute list q contains only attributes from the relation. You can apply a projection only to a compatible relation.

A selection $\sigma_b(R)$ has the same schema as R and a body containing those tuples from R for which the predicate b is true. The schema of a projection $\pi_q(R)$ is the list specified in q, and the tuples of the body are those of R, each reduced to the retained attributes. Duplicates are removed.

The selection and projection operators are sufficient to express single-table queries, which correspond to simple horizontal and vertical slices of a table. For example, the expression on the left below finds the colors of tanks named lagoon. The σ_b operator extracts a horizontal section, retaining only those tuples for which tname = lagoon. The π_q process then takes a vertical slice, keeping only the tcolor column.

$\pi_q(\sigma_b(\text{Tank}))$, $\pi_q(\sigma_b(\text{Tank}))$,

where b = (tname = "lagoon")   where b = (tname = "lagoon" $\wedge$ tvolume > 100)

       q = (tcolor) q = (tcolor, tvolume)

More complicated query conditions simply mean more complicated booleans in the selection operator; more information from the selected tuples simply means longer attribute lists in the projection operator. For example, the query on the right above requests the color and volume of each tank named lagoon that contains more than 100 gallons of water.

Cartesian product

To deal with queries involving more than one table, you need an additional relational operator, the **Cartesian product**. The Cartesian product of two or more relations produces a new relation, in which the attribute schema is the union of the operands' attributes. The symbol for the Cartesian product operator is ×, as in $R_1 \times R_2$. The following example illustrates the operation with three relations.

R_1	
A	B
1	2
3	4

×

R_2		
C	D	E
x	y	z
u	v	w

×

R_3	
F	G
α	β
γ	δ

=

			$<\cdots>$			
A	B	C	D	E	F	G
1	2	x	y	z	α	β
1	2	x	y	z	γ	δ
1	2	u	v	w	α	β
1	2	u	v	w	γ	δ
3	4	x	y	z	α	β
3	4	x	y	z	γ	δ
3	4	u	v	w	α	β
3	4	u	v	w	γ	δ

A slight problem with names occurs because the resulting relation's attributes are the union of the operands' attributes. If the same attribute name appears in two or more operands, a single copy appears in the union. However, you want *all* the operands' attributes to be in the result, even in the case where a name duplication would normally exclude an attribute from the union. You, therefore, restrict the operation to relations that have no attribute names in common, achieving this condition by renaming if necessary. Two relations are **compatible for Cartesian product** if they have no attribute names in common. For example, the following expression projects a vertical slice from Species (sno, sname) and from Fish (fno, fname, sno) and then qualifies the attributes names before taking the Cartesian product. Figure 3.1 illustrates the process.

$$Z = (X = \breve{\rho}(\pi_{\text{sno, sname}}(\text{Species}))) \times (Y = \breve{\rho}(\pi_{\text{fno, fname, sno}}(\text{Fish})))$$

Without the attribute name adjustments, the Species and Fish projections are not Cartesian product compatible because they share the attribute sno. The $\breve{\rho}$ operators qualify the attribute names, thereby rendering them unique. To reduce the accumulation of parentheses in extensive relational algebra expressions, you can adopt the convention that unary operators have precedence over binary operators. Moreover, a sequence of unary operators evaluates in right-to-left fashion: the operator nearest the argument executes first, and then the next operator to the left is applied to the result, and so forth. Because Cartesian product is a binary operation, it executes after any sequences of unary operators. Except for naming the final result, the previous construction then appears as $\breve{\rho}\pi_q(\text{Species}) \times \breve{\rho}\pi_r(\text{Fish})$, where $q = $ sno, sname and $r = $ fno, fname, sno.

The attributes ordering in the Cartesian product isn't significant. In this way, a relational Cartesian product differs from a mathematical Cartesian product. The mathematical Cartesian product of two sets, $A \times B$, generates a set of *ordered* pairs of the form (a, b) with $a \in A$ and $b \in B$. By contrast, the relational Cartesian product contains the unordered attributes from both operands, even though a tabular representation seems to indicate a left-to-right order. In general, you can take the Cartesian product of n relations by generating all the combinations formed with exactly one segment from each relation.

Two relations are compatible for Cartesian product if they have no attributes in common. If $R_3 = R_1 \times R_2$, then the schema of R_3 is the union of the attributes from R_1 and R_2. The body of R_3 consists of all tuples obtained by the union of a tuple from R_1 with a tuple from R_2. Viewed as tables, the rows of R_3 are all possible concatenations of a row from R_1 and a row from R_2.

Usually two relations that share certain common attributes can be rendered compatible for Cartesian product with the $\breve{\rho}$ operator. Certainly $\breve{\rho}$ can force Cartesian product compatibility on any two distinct tables from the original database. However, two copies of the same table present a special situation. Applying $\breve{\rho}$ to both copies leaves the qualified names identical. The proper approach is to apply $\breve{\rho}$ to only one of the copies or to use assignment to provide a different relation name for one of the copies before invoking $\breve{\rho}$. Suppose you want to form the Cartesian product from two copies of Fish. You can write either $\breve{\rho}(\text{Fish}) \times \text{Fish}$ or $\breve{\rho}(\text{Fish}) \times \breve{\rho}(X = \text{Fish})$.

The natural join

The Cartesian product typically exhibits many tuples that aren't meaningful. In Figure 3.1, each species pairs with each fish, even if the fish doesn't represent the species. A real query solution usually follows a Cartesian product with a selection operator to remove the inappropriate combinations. The following expression removes the tuples in which the fish segment disagrees with the species segment in the sno attribute.

$$\sigma_b(\breve{\rho}(\text{Species}) \times \breve{\rho}(\text{Fish})), \text{ where } b = (\text{Species.sno} = \text{Fish.sno}).$$

Y		
Fish.fno	Fish.fname	Fish.sno
164	charlie	74
347	flipper	17
228	killer	22
281	charlie	22
483	albert	17
119	bonnie	22
388	cory	93
654	darron	93
765	elsie	22
438	fran	74
277	george	93
911	helen	74
104	indira	17
302	jill	17
419	kilroy	74
650	laura	17
700	maureen	17

X	
Species.sno	Species.sname
17	dolphin
22	shark
74	guppy
93	shark

$\times$ $\implies$

Z				
Species.sno	Species.sname	Fish.fno	Fish.fname	Fish.sno
17	dolphin	164	charlie	74
17	dolphin	347	flipper	17
17	dolphin	288	killer	22
17	dolphin	281	charlie	22
17	dolphin	483	albert	17
17	dolphin	119	bonnie	22
17	dolphin	388	cory	93
17	dolphin	654	darron	93
17	dolphin	765	elsie	22
17	dolphin	438	fran	74
17	dolphin	277	george	93
17	dolphin	911	helen	74
17	dolphin	104	indira	17
17	dolphin	302	jill	17
17	dolphin	419	kilroy	74
17	dolphin	650	laura	17
17	dolphin	700	maureen	17
22	shark	164	charlie	74
22	shark	347	flipper	17
⋮	⋮	⋮	⋮	⋮

Figure 3.1   Illustrating a Cartesian product from the aquarium application

Two columns of the result, Fish.sno and Species.sno, contain identical values in any given tuple. Therefore, only one of them is necessary. The projection operator accomplishes this simplification as follows.

$\pi_q \sigma_b(\breve{\rho}(\text{Species}) \times \breve{\rho}(\text{Fish}))$,

$$\begin{aligned}\text{where } b \quad &= \quad (\text{Species.sno} = \text{Fish.sno}) \\ q \quad &= \quad (\text{Species.sno, Species.sname, Species.sfood,} \\ & \qquad \text{Fish.fno, Fish.fname, Fish.fcolor, Fish.fweight, Fish.tno})\end{aligned}$$

Now the qualified names in the result are unnecessary because the base names don't conflict. This encounter illustrates a frustration that often occurs in composing relational algebra operations. You rename certain attributes to avoid or to exploit name conflicts, and then the name extensions become redundant in later steps of the process. In that case, you use the $\hat{\rho}$ operator to simplify the attribute names of the result.

$\hat{\rho}\pi_q \sigma_b(\breve{\rho}(\text{Species}) \times \breve{\rho}(\text{Fish}))$, where b, q are as above.

Of course, this overall operation is the most frequently required combination of Species and Fish. The Cartesian product associates all species tuples with all fish tuples, capturing the appropriate connections together with many nonsensical combinations. The selection operator removes the offending tuples by forcing a match between values in columns with the same base name. The projection operator removes one column from each common-name pair, and finally, a renaming operator restores the base names. This sequence of operations is so common that it has a special operator symbol, $*$, called the **natural join**. So $\text{Species} * \text{Fish} = \hat{\rho}\pi_q \sigma_b(\breve{\rho}(\text{Species}) \times \breve{\rho}(\text{Fish}))$, where b, q are as above. The natural join produces the expected extension of each fish tuple with its species information, as shown in Figure 3.2.

The formal definition of the natural join operator is as follows. Let R_1 and R_2 be two relations, where R_1 and R_2 are distinct names. Let $\mathcal{C}_1$ and $\mathcal{C}_2$ be the attributes of $\breve{\rho}(R_1)$ and $\breve{\rho}(R_2)$ respectively. Let $\mathcal{A} = a_1, a_2, \ldots, a_m$ be attributes whose names appear in both R_1 and R_2. Then the **natural join**, $R_1 * R_2$, is:

$$\begin{aligned}R_1 * R_2 &= \hat{\rho}\pi_q \sigma_b(\breve{\rho}(R_1) \times \breve{\rho}(R_2)), \\ \text{where } b \quad &= \quad (R_1.a_1 = R_2.a_1 \wedge R_1.a_2 = R_2.a_2 \wedge \ldots R_1.a_m = R_2.a_m) \qquad (3.1) \\ q \quad &= \quad (\mathcal{C}_1 \cup \mathcal{C}_2) - \{R_2.a_1, R_2.a_2, \ldots, R_2.a_m\}.\end{aligned}$$

 The natural join, $R_1 * R_2$, is a reduction of the Cartesian product that removes those tuples that don't have the same values in matching attribute pairs. Just one column from each such pair is retained, and the remaining columns revert to their unqualified names.

With the Cartesian product and natural join operators, you can now answer multi-table queries. For example, the expression on the left below finds the colors of fish representing a species named shark. The natural join extends each fish with information about its species; then the horizontal sectioning operator isolates the tuples with sname shark.

$\pi_q \sigma_b(\text{Fish} * \text{Species})$

$$\begin{aligned}\text{where } b \quad &= \quad (\text{sname} = \text{"shark"}) \\ q \quad &= \quad (\text{fcolor})\end{aligned}$$

$\pi_q \sigma_b(\text{Species} * \text{Fish}) * \text{Tank}))$

$$\begin{aligned}\text{where } b \quad &= \quad (\text{sname} = \text{"shark"} \wedge \text{tname} = \text{"cesspool"}) \\ q \quad &= \quad (\text{fname})\end{aligned}$$

Species		
sno	sname	sfood
17	dolphin	herring
22	shark	anything
74	guppy	worm
93	shark	peanut butter

*

Fish					
fno	fname	fcolor	fweight	tno	sno
164	charlie	orange	12	42	74
347	flipper	black	25	35	17
228	killer	white	32	42	22
281	charlie	orange	27	85	22
483	albert	red	45	55	17
119	bonnie	blue	51	42	22
388	cory	purple	12	35	93
654	darron	white	84	42	93
765	elsie	white	73	42	22
438	fran	black	61	55	74
277	george	red	33	42	93
911	helen	blue	48	44	74
104	indira	black	19	42	17
302	jill	red	28	38	17
419	kilroy	red	49	55	74
650	laura	blue	55	85	17
700	maureen	white	71	44	17

$\Longrightarrow$

$<\cdots>$							
sno	sname	sfood	fno	fname	fcolor	fweight	tno
74	guppy	worm	164	charlie	orange	12	42
17	dolphin	herring	347	flipper	black	25	35
22	shark	anything	228	killer	white	32	42
22	shark	anything	281	charlie	orange	27	85
17	dolphin	herring	483	albert	red	45	55
22	shark	anything	119	bonnie	blue	51	42
93	shark	peanut butter	388	cory	purple	12	35
93	shark	peanut butter	654	darron	white	84	42
22	shark	anything	765	elsie	white	73	42
74	guppy	worm	438	fran	black	61	55
93	shark	peanut butter	277	george	red	33	42
74	guppy	worm	911	helen	blue	48	44
17	dolphin	herring	104	indira	black	19	42
17	dolphin	herring	302	jill	red	28	38
74	guppy	worm	419	kilroy	red	49	55
17	dolphin	herring	650	laura	blue	55	85
17	dolphin	herring	700	maureen	white	71	44

Figure 3.2   Illustrating a natural join from the aquarium application

As another example, what are the names of fish representing a species named shark and inhabiting a tank named cesspool? The relational algebra on the right above constructs the answer. The natural join, Species * Fish, contains tno as a common attribute with Tank. By the convention for naming intermediate relations, the natural join, Species * Fish, acquires a unique name from the system, and thus qualified names from Species * Fish don't collide with qualified names from Tank. The two natural joins result in a table, where each fish appears joined with its species and tank information. This table, however, has only one sno and one tno column. The selection and projection operators then filter the desired tuples and eliminate all but the fname column from the final answer.

By tracing through the implied operations, you can verify that (Species * Fish) * Tank = Species * (Fish * Tank). However, either of these two natural joins is also equal to (Species * Tank) * Fish. Even if the first natural join is between relations with no common attributes, the final result is still the same. When forming Species * Tank, you first qualify the attribute names and construct the Cartesian product. You next use the selection operator to remove any tuples that disagree on columns with the same base name. Because there are no such pairs of columns, no tuples are eliminated. Finally, you remove the qualifying prefixes from the attribute names. Therefore Species * Tank = Species × Tank. Now Species * Tank contains two attributes in common with Fish, namely sno and tno. So (Species * Tank) * Fish selects tuples that agree on *both* pairs of columns. In a particular tuple, if the species-tank combination doesn't have the same sno and tno values as the fish, the tuple disappears from the table. This interpretation again aligns a fish with its species and tank information, and the subsequent projection and renaming operations deliver the same result as (Species * Fish) * Tank or Species * (Fish * Tank). This argument shows that the natural join and the Cartesian product are both commutative and associative. Now because the order of the natural joins among Species, Tank, and Fish isn't significant, you can omit the parentheses that order these operations. The solution then appears as

$$\pi_q \sigma_b(\text{Species} * \text{Fish} * \text{Tank}), \text{ where } b \quad = \quad (\text{sname} = \text{``shark''} \wedge \text{tname} = \text{``cesspool''})$$
$$q \quad = \quad (\text{fname}).$$

 You can reassemble a string of Cartesian products or natural joins in any order with the same result.

As a final example, find the names of cohabiting fish. You will need to construct a table that contains pairs of fish in the same tuple. However, you can't use a direct natural join (Fish * Fish) to construct a table of fish pairs because, even after qualification, the operands are not compatible for Cartesian product. The solution below uses the Cartesian product directly on two copies of the fish relation, but only after renaming one of the copies (as X) to make them compatible. Each tuple then contains two sets of fish attributes, one with attributes qualified by Fish and the other with attributes qualified by X. It is then a simple matter to select tuples in which Fish.tno = X.tno.

$$\pi_q \sigma_b(\check{\rho}(\text{Fish}) \times \check{\rho}(X = \text{Fish})), \text{ where } b \quad = \quad (\text{Fish.tno} = X.\text{tno})$$
$$q \quad = \quad (\text{Fish.fname}, X.\text{fname})$$

Other variations on the join theme

The natural join isn't an absolute necessity but, instead, a convenience. You can always replace it with its defining sequence of Cartesian product, selection, projection, and renaming operations. Three other convenient operators are the θ-**join**, the **equijoin**, and the **semijoin** — all variations on the Cartesian product theme.

Let θ denote any one of the comparison operators, $=, <, >, \leq, \geq$, or one of their complements, such as $\neq$. Then define the θ-join analogously to the natural join, except (1) the condition of equality between values under matching columns becomes a θ-condition between them, and (2) both columns from each matching pair are kept, together with the qualifying names. The definition of a θ-join is as follows.

Let R_1 and R_2 be two relations with distinct names. Let $\mathcal{C}_1$ and $\mathcal{C}_2$ be the attributes of $\check{\rho}(R_1)$ and $\check{\rho}(R_2)$ respectively. Let $\mathcal{A} = a_1, a_2, \ldots, a_m$ be attributes whose base names appear in both R_1 and R_2. Let θ be one of the comparison operators, $=, <, >, \leq, \geq$, or one of their complements. Then the θ-**join**, $R_1 \bowtie_\theta R_2$, is

$$R_1 \bowtie_\theta R_2 = \sigma_b(\check{\rho}(R_1) \times \check{\rho}(R_2)), \quad \text{where} \quad b = ((R_1.a_1 \ \theta \ R_2.a_1) \wedge (R_1.a_2 \ \theta \ R_2.a_2) \wedge \ldots). \tag{3.2}$$

 The θ-join of two relations, R_1 and R_2, is a new relation, obtained by forming the Cartesian product and then removing those tuples whose values in matching attributes don't θ-relate to each other.

A θ-join retains certain combinations from the Cartesian product that might seem inappropriate. For example, suppose that the tno attributes in tank tuples represent an increasing sequence with a larger tno value implying a better tank. Perhaps tanks with a high tno have better environmental controls. In any case, suppose you want to associate fish with tanks that are inferior to those in which they currently swim. Rather than the normal association, where the tno value in the fish segment matches the tno value in the tank segment, you need an association of the form tno-in-tank < tno-in-fish.

To make the example specific, consider the following query. Find the names of tanks that are inferior to the home of a fish named flipper. One relational algebra translation appears on the left below using a θ-join. On the right is an equivalent solution that uses the Cartesian product and renaming operations that underlie the θ-join.

$$\pi_q \sigma_b(\text{Tank} \bowtie_\theta \text{Fish}), \qquad\qquad \pi_q \sigma_b(\check{\rho}(\text{Tank}) \times \check{\rho}(\text{Fish})),$$

where b	=	(Fish.fname = "flipper")		where b	=	(Tank.tno < Fish.tno $\wedge$
q	=	(Tank.tname)				Fish.fname = "flipper")
θ	=	<		q	=	(Tank.tname)

Figure 3.3 shows the differences among Cartesian product (assuming prior attribute name qualification), natural join, θ-join (for $\theta = $ '<'), and equijoin (defined below). The θ-join is an abbreviation for a Cartesian product followed by a selection, where the operands

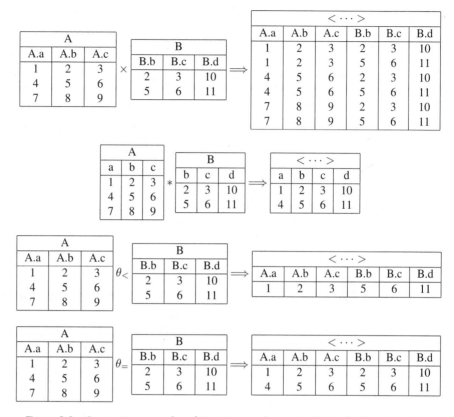

Figure 3.3 Contrasting examples of Cartesian product, natural join, θ-join, and equijoin

for the selection are the matching columns introduced by the Cartesian product. This notation allows the concatenation of tuples when the matching columns compare with an inequality. This condition is different from that normally implied by common attribute names. The natural join represents a frequent sequence of more basic operations while the θ-join is less often applicable.

A θ-join where θ is the '=' comparison operator is an **equijoin**. An equijoin is very similar to a natural join, except that it contains two columns in the result for each pair of matching columns from the initial Cartesian product. Of course, two such columns are redundant. Name qualification prefixes remain in the equijoin. See Figure 3.3.

A natural join followed by a projection on the first operand is a **semijoin**, written $R_1 \ltimes R_2$. So $R_1 \ltimes R_2 = \pi_{R_1}(R_1 * R_2)$. Because only R_1 attributes enter into the answer relation, the purpose of R_2 is simply to reduce R_1 to those tuples for which the common attribute values also appear in R_2. This operation is useful in a distributed environment, where R_1 and R_2 reside at different sites. The semijoin implementation ships only the common columns of R_2 to the site where R_1 resides and then performs a natural join at that site. That is, if q is a list of common attributes, $R_1 \ltimes R_2 = R_1 * \pi_q(R_2)$.

Existential queries

Consider the query: what are the names of species represented in a tank named cesspool? You imagine each species tuple competing for inclusion in the solution set. Some species succeed; others fail. A successful species links to some fish, and that fish in turn links to some cesspool tank. In other words, a species is successful if a path connects it to a known anchor tuple elsewhere in the database. In this case, the anchor tuple is the known cesspool tank. This pattern defines a large class of queries called existential queries.

In an **existential query**, the inclusion of a candidate tuple in the answer depends on the existence of some calculated path through the database. This condition is general; the details vary greatly. For example, the path can be shorter or longer depending on the number of intermediate tuples that occur in it. A short path suffices for the current example because a single intermediate link (a fish) connects the candidate species to the anchor cesspool tank. In all cases, however, the query will specify a set of candidate tuples and a set of known anchor tuples. Those candidate tuples that command a path to an anchor contribute to the solution set.

Figure 3.4 illustrates the process for the example query. The species tuple indicated by the question mark is under test. Matching attributes forge the links along the path, sno from species to fish and then tno from fish to tank. Many paths may connect a particular species tuple to a given cesspool tank. Indeed, there will be a path for each fish representing the species and swimming in the cesspool. The size of this path bundle isn't relevant. To add a tuple to the answer, you need only verify the existence of one such path.

 In an existential query, a candidate tuple qualifies to contribute to the solution if some path connects it to an anchor tuple in the database.

Each link in the connecting path is a tuple from some database table or from some intermediate table constructed with relational algebra. The Cartesian product of these intermediate tables includes all possible combinations. Therefore, it certainly contain tuples corresponding to the desired path, if such a path exists. You can use a selection operator to remove those nonsense connections where adjacent links don't properly match in the common attributes. The solution to the example query appears on the left below. Because the natural join also removes inappropriate combinations, the shorter version on the right is equivalent.

$$\pi_q \sigma_b (\check{\rho}(\text{Species}) \times \check{\rho}(\text{Fish}) \times \check{\rho}(\text{Tank})),$$
$$\text{where } b = (\text{Species.sno} = \text{Fish.sno} \wedge$$
$$\text{Fish.tno} = \text{Tank.tno} \wedge$$
$$\text{Tank.tname} = \text{``cesspool''})$$
$$q = (\text{Species.sname})$$

$$\pi_q \sigma_b (\text{Species} * \text{Fish} * \text{Tank}),$$
$$\text{where } b = (\text{tname} = \text{``cesspool''})$$
$$q = (\text{sname}).$$

Longer paths to the anchor tuple

The following query again searches for species connected to a known anchor tuple: find the names of species swimming with a shark. In Figure 3.5, the species tuple with the question mark attempts to contribute to the answer set. To do so, it must command a path connecting

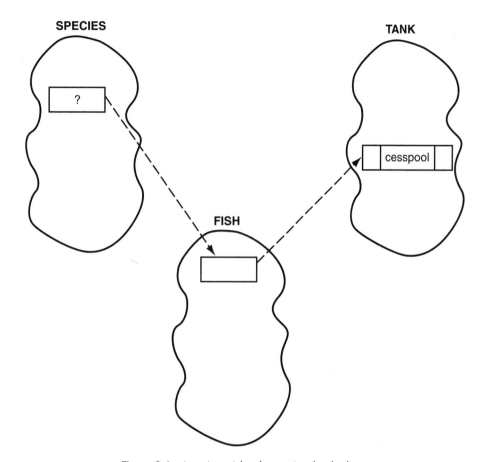

Figure 3.4 An existential path crossing the database

it to a fish, which is swimming in a tank, where another fish swims, which belongs to a species named shark. Five tuples and four links occur in the qualifying chain. These links connect a species (the one in question), a fish, a tank, another fish, and a final species, which is the anchor shark. By arranging five tables in the Cartesian product, you are sure to capture the particular tuples that properly link to form the qualifying chain, *if* the chain exists.

Because natural joins shortened the preceding example, you might first consider that approach, which constructs Species * Fish * Tank * Fish * Species. Unfortunately, this arrangement involves too many common columns. The natural join operation forces the attribute values from the two fish copies to line up, which makes the fish tuples identical. It then eliminates one of them. However, as shown in Figure 3.5, the second fish segment must represent a potentially different fish from the first fish segment. In other words, you need a fish representing the first species, swimming in a tank where *another* fish swims representing *another* species, namely a shark. You can circumvent this difficulty by stripping away attributes that force unwanted comparisons in the natural joins. The expression on the

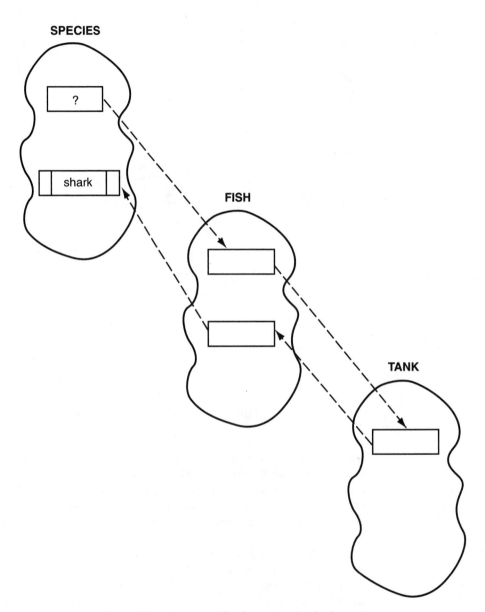

Figure 3.5   An existential path crossing the database twice

left below computes a list of species names, each associated with the key of a tank where it is represented. The expression on the right produces a table of tno keys, one for each tank containing a shark (i.e., a sharky tank).

$$\pi_q(\text{Species} * \text{Fish} * \text{Tank}),$$
$$\text{where } q = (\text{sname, tno})$$

$$\pi_r\sigma_b(\text{Tank} * \text{Fish} * \text{Species}),$$
$$\text{where } b = (\text{sname} = \text{``shark''})$$
$$r = (\text{tno}).$$

The two intermediate tables have only the tno attribute in common. Their natural join then produces a table having attributes (sname, tno) where the tno must be both the key to a sharky tank and the key of a tank where a species named sname swims. The full solution is:

$$\pi_s(\pi_q(\text{Species} * \text{Fish} * \text{Tank}) * \pi_r\sigma_b(\text{Tank} * \text{Fish} * \text{Species})), \text{ where } b = (\text{sname} = \text{``shark''})$$
$$q = (\text{sname, tno})$$
$$r = (\text{tno})$$
$$s = (\text{sname}).$$

The species name shark appears in the answer because the shark in a sharky tank certainly swims with a shark, namely itself. The solution doesn't exclude the case where the two fish links are the same fish. So the shark species links to fish X, swimming in tank T, where fish X swims again, which represents species shark. You reject the direct sequence of natural joins (Species $*$ Fish $*$ Tank $*$ Fish $*$ Species) because the self-referential case is the *only* possible connection. The correct solution must include this boundary case, plus the more general case where the fish links are distinct fish.

The final solution is correct but is slightly more complicated than necessary. The tank entity appears twice, but in each case, there is reference only to the tno attribute. However, you can obtain that attribute from Fish, where it serves as an embedded foreign key, giving the following abbreviated solution.

$$\pi_s(\pi_q(\text{Species} * \text{Fish}) * \pi_r\sigma_b(\text{Fish} * \text{Species})), \text{ where } b = (\text{sname} = \text{``shark''})$$
$$q = (\text{sname, tno})$$
$$r = (\text{tno})$$
$$s = (\text{sname})$$

A solution template for existential queries

These examples show how to construct the qualifying path in sections, where each section avoids name conflict problems with the natural join by having at most one copy of any particular operand table. The first segment uses Species $*$ Fish $*$ Tank, all distinct operands; the second uses Tank $*$ Fish $*$ Species, again all distinct within that segment. You can apply this method to longer database paths where even more table repetitions appear in the overall expression. However, you must think carefully about how to break the overall path into the proper segments. A better approach simply renames each table as it enters the Cartesian product and uses the $\breve{\rho}$ operator to qualify the attribute names. This policy guarantees that no name conflicts occur. The disadvantage is that you must specifically compose the selection boolean to remove nonsense paths. In the current example, you know that a successful path must originate with a candidate species, pass through a fish, then a tank, then another fish, and finally terminate on a shark species. You line up the five tables as follows, giving each a new table name.

$$\pi_q \sigma_b (\breve{\rho}(S = \text{Species}) \times \breve{\rho}(F = \text{Fish}) \times \breve{\rho}(T = \text{Tank}) \times \breve{\rho}(G = \text{Fish}) \times \breve{\rho}(H = \text{Species}))$$

where b = $(S.\text{sno} = F.\text{sno} \wedge F.\text{tno} = T.\text{tno} \wedge T.\text{tno} = G.\text{tno} \wedge G.\text{sno} = H.\text{sno} \wedge H.\text{sname} = \text{"shark"})$

q = $(S.\text{sname}).$

So to solve any existential query: (1) line up renamed copies of the tables needed for the path links and then (2) use a selection to remove inappropriate combinations and to force the end of the path to coincide with the specified anchor.

To illustrate this solution pattern, consider the following query: What are the names of species that are swimming with a species represented in a cesspool tank? This query requires three excursions across the database, as shown Figure 3.6. To qualify a species as swimming with some other species duplicates the chain of the previous example, with the difference that the second species need not be a shark. The final segment of the chain forces that second species to be in a cesspool tank. The qualifying chain then has seven links. The candidate species (1) links to a fish (2), which swims in a tank (3). That tank then links to another fish (4), which represents another species (5). Finally, that species connects to yet another fish (6), which swims in the anchor tank (7) named cesspool. Applying the existential pattern, you obtain the following solution.

$$\pi_q \sigma_b (\breve{\rho}(S = \text{Species}) \times \breve{\rho}(F = \text{Fish}) \times \breve{\rho}(T = \text{Tank}) \times \breve{\rho}(G = \text{Fish}) \times \breve{\rho}(R = \text{Species}) \times \breve{\rho}(H = \text{Fish}) \times \breve{\rho}(Q = \text{Tank})),$$

where b = $(S.\text{sno} = F.\text{sno} \wedge F.\text{tno} = T.\text{tno} \wedge T.\text{tno} = G.\text{tno} \wedge$
$G.\text{sno} = R.\text{sno} \wedge R.\text{sno} = H.\text{sno} \wedge H.\text{tno} = Q.\text{tno} \wedge Q.\text{tname} = \text{"cesspool"})$

q = $(S.\text{sname})$

 The pattern for a relational algebra solution to an existential query first lines up the renamed tables needed for the path links. It then removes inappropriate combinations with a selection operation.

In the examples so far, the actual data reported in the answer table has always been some attribute in the tuple at the head of the chain. In general, however, you can extract information from any of the links. For example, find the names of species swimming with a shark and also report the tank names where this cohabitation occurs. The solution lines up the five renamed tables needed for the links exactly as in the previous case, which requested no tank information. The final projection simply extracts the tname attribute along with the sname value, giving the following solution.

$$\pi_q \sigma_b (\breve{\rho}(S = \text{Species}) \times \breve{\rho}(F = \text{Fish}) \times \breve{\rho}(T = \text{Tank}) \times \breve{\rho}(G = \text{Fish}) \times \breve{\rho}(H = \text{Species})),$$

where b = $(S.\text{sno} = F.\text{sno} \wedge F.\text{tno} = T.\text{tno} \wedge T.\text{tno} = G.\text{tno} \wedge G.\text{sno} = H.\text{sno} \wedge S.\text{sname} = \text{"shark"})$

q = $(S.\text{sname}, T.\text{tname}).$

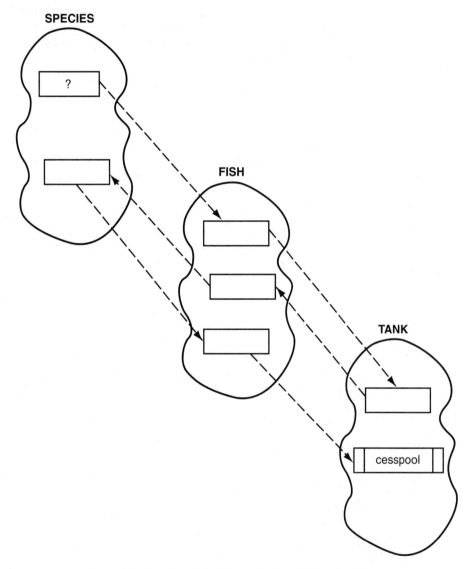

Figure 3.6   An existential path crossing the database three times

Universal queries

A nonexistential query is: find the names of species represented in all tanks. A candidate species tuple can't qualify for the solution set merely by originating a path to an anchor tuple. Instead, it must originate a bundle of paths that embrace an anchor collection, namely all tanks in the database. The distinction is important because the number of paths in the qualifying bundle depends on the current state of the database. *If* you know that there are exactly two tanks in the database, say tno = **56** and tno = **34**, you can construct two existential solutions, each giving the species connected to one of the anchor tanks. These intermediate sets, X and Y, are as follows.

$$X = \pi_q \sigma_b(\breve{\rho}(S = \text{Species}) \times \breve{\rho}(F = \text{Fish}) \times \breve{\rho}(T = \text{Tank})),$$
$$\text{where} \quad b \quad = \quad (S.\text{sno} = F.\text{sno} \wedge F.\text{tno} = T.\text{tno} \wedge$$
$$T.\text{tno} = 56$$
$$q \quad = \quad (S.\text{sname})$$

$$Y = \pi_r \sigma_c(\breve{\rho}(S = \text{Species}) \times \breve{\rho}(F = \text{Fish}) \times \breve{\rho}(T = \text{Tank})),$$
$$\text{where} \quad c \quad = \quad (S.\text{sno} = F.\text{sno} \wedge F.\text{tno} = T.\text{tno} \wedge$$
$$T.\text{tno} = 34$$
$$r \quad = \quad (S.\text{sname})$$

The intersection, $X \cap Y$, then gives the names of species that are represented in both tanks, which in this case is all the tanks. However, if the content of the tank table changes, this solution isn't valid. If there were a third tank, you could change the solution to intersect three components, each obtained with an existential construction. However, the best solution delivers the correct answer regardless of the database content. In summary, you can't qualify a candidate species by finding a path to an anchor tuple. Nor can you qualify it by finding some fixed number of paths to a collection of anchor tuples. Instead, you must consider a new approach, one that can investigate a bundle of paths simultaneously. The new method must also accommodate a variable bundle size, depending on the database conditions.

Figure 3.7 illustrates the necessary condition that characterizes a second large class of queries—universal queries. In a **universal query**, a candidate tuple qualifies to contribute to the answer by originating a complete bundle of paths embracing a specified collection of anchor tuples.

 In a universal query, a candidate tuple contributes to the answer only if a path bundle connects it with a specified collection of anchor tuples.

If you take a more circuitous approach to the problem of species represented in all tanks, you first construct a list L_1 of (sno, sname, tno) triplets. You insist that all possible combinations of sno and tno occur in the list, regardless of whether a fish connects the species sno and tank tno. However, the sname value does correspond to the species identified by sno. The expression on the left below easily accomplishes this construction.

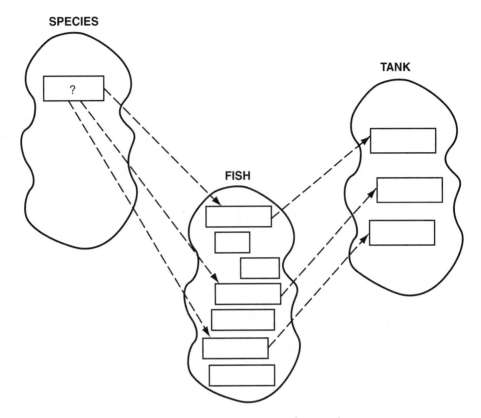

SPECIES

TANK

FISH

Figure 3.7 Path bundle characteristic of universal queries

$$L_1 = \pi_q(\text{Species} \times \text{Tank}),$$
where $q = (\text{sno, sname, tno})$

$$L_2 = \pi_r(\text{Species} * \text{Fish} * \text{Tank}),$$
where $r = (\text{sno, sname, tno})$

Now you construct a second list L_2 of (sno, sname, tno) triplets, this time requiring that a fish connect the sno and tno. The relational algebra for L_2 appears on the right above. Now consider $L_3 = L_1 - L_2$. If a particular sno appears in a triplet (sno, sname, tno) in L_3, that triplet doesn't occur in L_2. That is, sno doesn't link to tno: no fish of species sno swims in tank tno. Therefore, species sno isn't represented in at least one tank, and it can't be part of the answer to the query. Conversely, if a particular sno appears in no triplet of L_3, an L_2 triplet must have erased every L_1 triplet containing sno. But within L_1, sno appears with every tno in the database. So subtracting L_2 erased all these occurrences. That is, a triplet of the form (sno, sname, tno) must occur in L_2 for *every* tno in the database. Stated differently, sno does *not* appear in L_3 if and only if sno links to *all* tanks in the database. So, L_3 is a complement of the required answer because it contains all the sno (and corresponding sname) values that should *not* appear in the answer. You can rectify this inversion by subtracting the sno values projected from L_3 from the set of all sno values projected from Species. The resulting list contains exactly those species represented in all tanks in the database. The final relational algebra then assumes the form:

$$\pi_s\{\pi_r(\text{Species}) - \pi_r[\pi_q(\text{Species} \times \text{Tank}) - \pi_q(\text{Species} * \text{Fish} * \text{Tank})]\},$$

$$\text{where} \quad q \quad = \quad (\text{sno, sname, tno})$$
$$r \quad = \quad (\text{sno, sname})$$
$$s \quad = \quad (\text{sname}).$$

The division operator

The set-difference argument occurs often enough to merit a special operator in relational algebra, namely, relational division. I want to approach this concept from a slightly different point of view, but I will eventually show that the alternative approach coincides with the double set difference construction in the last example. If X and Y are disjoint sets such that $X \cup Y$ are the attributes of a relation R, $(x : y)$ denotes a tuple in R. The first part, x, contains the associations over X; the second part, y, contains those over Y. Viewing R as a table, you can imagine the attributes X on the left and the attributes Y on the right.

Recall the convention that the name of a relation can also stand for the set of its attributes. Two relations R_1 and R_2 are compatible for division in the form R_1/R_2 if, as sets of attributes, $R_2 \subset R_1$ and $R_2 \neq R_1$. Suppose that R_1 and R_2 are compatible for division in the form R_1/R_2. That is, $R_2 \subset R_1$ and $R_1 - R_2 \neq \varphi$ as attribute sets. Then $R_3 = R_1/R_2$ is the **quotient** of R_1 divided by R_2. The schema of R_3 is $R_1 - R_2$: the attributes of R_1 that are not also attributes of R_2. To construct $r(R_3)$, the body of the quotient, imagine each tuple in $r(R_1)$ to be a segment of the form $(a : b)$, where a holds associations over the attributes $R_1 - R_2$, and b holds the remaining associations, necessarily over R_2. Each a is a candidate for inclusion in $r(R_3)$. A particular a actually achieves inclusion in $r(R_3)$ if there is a tuple of the form $(a : b) \in R_1$, for *every* $b \in R_2$. That is, $R_3 = \{a | (\forall b)(b \in R_2 \Rightarrow (a : b) \in R_1)\}$. As a concrete example, consider the following division.

A				
a	b	c	d	e
1	2	3	10	42
1	2	3	10	14
1	2	3	32	25
4	5	6	11	65
4	5	6	32	25
7	8	9	32	25
6	5	9	32	25
6	5	9	10	14

$/$

B	
d	e
10	14
32	25

$\Longrightarrow$

< $\cdots$ >		
a	b	c
1	2	3
6	5	9

The two operands are division compatible because $(d, e) \subset (a, b, c, d, e)$, and $(a, b, c, d, e) - (d, e) = (a, b, c) \neq \varphi$. The schema of the quotient relation, therefore, is (a, b, c). The candidates for inclusion in the body of the quotient are $\pi_{(a,b,c)}(A)$, namely $(1, 2, 3)$, $(4, 5, 6)$, $(7, 8, 9)$, and $(6, 5, 9)$. $(1, 2, 3)$ transfers to the quotient because it occurs in the numerator as a prefix of *every* tuple from the denominator. That is, $(1, 2, 3 : 10, 14)$ and $(1, 2, 3, : 32, 25)$ both occur in the numerator. $(4, 5, 6)$ fails to transfer to the quotient because the combination $(4, 5, 6 : 10, 14)$ fails to occur in the numerator. Similarly, $(7, 8, 9)$ fails to transfer, but $(6, 5, 9)$ succeeds.

Let Y be the attributes of R_2, and let $X \cup Y$ be the attributes of R_1. Then the quotient relation, $R_3 = R_1/R_2$ has schema X. The body of R_3 consists of those tuples $x \in \pi_X(R_1)$ such that $(x : y) \in R_1$ for all $y \in R_2$.

This construction captures the essence of the double set difference used to solve the earlier example that found the species represented in all tanks. To see this correspondence, think of the attributes of the dividend as consisting of a prefix and a suffix, where the suffix contains the attributes of the divisor. Also, imagine each tuple as a prefix-suffix concatenation of values. The schema of the quotient then contains the prefix attributes, and the prefix of a tuple from the dividend transfers to the body of the quotient if it pairs somewhere in the dividend with *every* suffix from the divisor. Stated differently, a prefix becomes part of the quotient precisely when it is *not* among the prefixes that are *not* connected to some suffix in the divisor.

So assuming R_1 and R_2 are compatible for division in the form R_1/R_2, consider the following relational algebra constructions, where $q = R_1 - R_2$

$$X = \pi_q(R_1), Y = (X \times R_2) - R_1, Z = X - \pi_q(Y)$$

X isolates all the candidate prefixes from the dividend. X is now Cartesian product compatible with R_2 because their schemas have disjoint attributes. The Cartesian product creates all possible prefix-suffix pairs, where a prefix comes from the appropriate part of R_1 and a suffix comes from R_2. In forming Y, the set difference removes any prefix-suffix pair that is also in R_1. So a prefix vanishes completely if the process removes every prefix-suffix pair in which it occurs. This erasure happens when the prefix pairs, somewhere in R_1, with *every* possible suffix from R_2. The remaining prefixes are those that should *not* be part of the quotient. These prefixes are projected from Y and subtracted from the pool of all possible prefixes, X, to form the final answer, Z. Assembling the components, you can write the final division as follows, where $q = R_1 - R_2$.

$$R_1/R_2 = \pi_q(R_1) - \pi_q[(\pi_q(R_1) \times R_2) - R_1] \tag{3.3}$$

Because relational division corresponds to the double set difference construction, you can recast the solution to the example in the new form. Recall that the example seeks the names of species represented in all tanks. First, you compose the list, L_1, of triplets (sno, sname, tno) where the species sno links to the tank tno and sname is the sname attribute of the species. These triplets are simply the appropriate projection of the Species $*$ Fish $*$ Tank natural join. You then compose a second list, L_2, by projecting the tno attribute values from Tank. Note the meaning of L_1/L_2 in this context. The quotient contains each pair (sno, sname) that is a prefix of a triplet (sno, sname, tno) in L_1 for *every* tno in L_2. The quotient captures the species that link to *all* tanks, which is precisely the required solution. The complete relational algebra equivalent appears on the left below.

$$\pi_s[\pi_q(\text{Species} * \text{Fish} * \text{Tank})/\pi_r(\text{Tank})],$$

where q = (sno, sname, tno)

r = (tno)

s = (sname)

$$\pi_s[(\pi_q\sigma_b(\text{Species} * \text{Fish} * \text{Tank})/\pi_r\sigma_c(\text{Tank})],$$

where b = (sfood = "peanut butter")

q = (sno, sname, tno)

c = (tcolor = "red")

r = (tno)

s = (sname)

You can accommodate variations in the pattern by adjusting the divisor to represent the appropriate collection of target tuples. In particular, the divisor describes the targets that must be reachable from a particular candidate, if that candidate is to contribute to the answer. For example, the expression on the right above produces the names of species with an sfood value of **peanut butter** that have a representative in all red tanks. Recall the convention that binary operators, such as division, evaluate after unary operators. Therefore, the expressions above need no additional parentheses to isolate the numerator and denominator.

A solution template for universal queries

The solution of a universal query as a quotient of two relations is a general pattern, which you can tailor to the details of a specific query. The numerator contains prefix-suffix pairs, in which each candidate tuple appears in the prefix position. The suffixes attached to a particular prefix are all the anchor elements with a path from that prefix. The denominator contains all the anchor suffixes that must be reached to qualify a prefix to contribute to the answer. The definition of the quotient then ensures that any prefix that transfers to the quotient must reach *all* of the denominator set. Applying the pattern to the last example, you construct the numerator as all (sno, sname, tno) triplets where the (sno, sname) species likes peanut butter and links to the tno tank through some fish. The denominator contains all tno values from red tanks. The quotient then retains those (sno, sname) prefixes from the numerator that appear with all tno suffixes from the denominator. Such (sno, sname) pairs correspond to species that like peanut butter and appear in all red tanks.

Longer path bundles are possible. For example, find the names of species represented in *all* tanks containing representatives of *all* species with a worm diet (the wormy species). The solution pattern appears in Figure 3.8, where each tank on the right contains all the wormy species. Isolating this tank subset is similar to the query above, which involves, for each tank, a path bundle across the database to the wormy species. In this part of the query, the wormy species constitute the anchor tuples, and the quotient contains the tanks that link to all the anchors. These tanks then become the anchor tuples for a second division operation. A second bundle of paths connects each successful candidate species to all the tank anchors. So the quotient of the first part becomes the denominator of the second part. Proceeding in steps, you can then construct the components as follows:

$$X = \pi_q\sigma_b(\text{Species}))$$
$$Y = \pi_r(\text{Tank} * \text{Fish} * \text{Species})/X$$
$$Z = \pi_t[\pi_s(\text{Species} * \text{Fish} * \text{Tank})/Y]$$

where b = (sfood = "worms")

q = (sno)

r = (tno, sno)

s = (sno, sname, tno)

t = (sname).

X collects all the sno values such that species sno has sfood = **worms**. Y contains the tno keys of tanks that link to all the sno values in X. The quotient in Z collects the (sno,

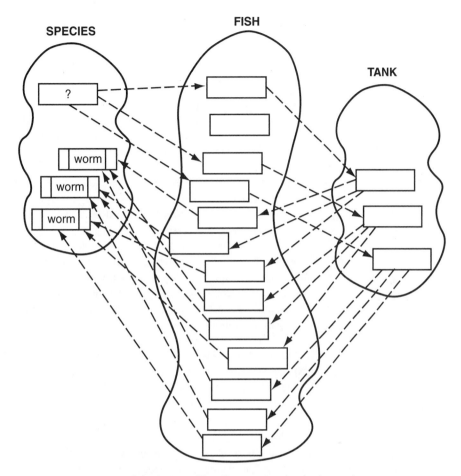

Figure 3.8 Universal bundles crossing the database twice

sname) pairs such that species (sno, sname) connects with all the tno tanks in Y. Finally, a projection extracts the required sname values. Assembling the components into a single expression, you arrive at the following solution:

$$\pi_t\{\pi_s(\text{Species} * \text{Fish} * \text{Tank})/[\pi_r(\text{Tank} * \text{Fish} * \text{Species})/\pi_q\sigma_b(\text{Species})]\}.$$

Expected size of the quotient relation

Suppose the cardinalities of the numerator, denominator, and quotient relations are $t_n, t_d,$ and t_q respectively. According to the definition, each tuple in the quotient must serve as the prefix of t_d tuples in the numerator. Therefore, t_q can be no larger than the integer part of t_n/t_d, and it can be significantly smaller. For example, some tuples in the numerator correspond to prefixes that fail to transfer to the quotient. To illustrate the point, suppose that a quotient R_1/R_2 is such that every prefix in R_1 pairs with every suffix from R_2. Then $t_q = t_n/t_d$. Now add new tuples to R_1 containing new prefixes that don't pair with *any* suffixes from R_2. The quotient doesn't change because none of the new prefixes is eligible to transfer. However, t_n becomes larger so that $t_q < t_n/t_d$.

Another condition can inflate the numerator's size without a corresponding increase in the quotient. Some tuples in R_1 can reflect prefixes that do transfer to the quotient but that associate with excessive suffixes beyond R_2. Continuing with the construction, add further tuples to R_1, but now use prefixes that do appear in the quotient and pair them with arbitrary suffixes. The quotient remains unchanged. Once the prefix qualifies to transfer to the quotient, it has all the suffixes it needs. Additional suffixes can't result in any new entries in the quotient. Therefore, you can only say that the quotient won't exceed $\lfloor t_n/t_d \rfloor$ in size.

Regardless of the eventual size of the quotient, decreasing the denominator's size tends to increase the quotient's size. Compare the following two queries.

Q_1: Find the names of species represented in all red tanks.

Q_2: Find the names of species represented in all tanks.

You expect more tuples in the solution to Q_1 than in the solution to Q_2. In general, there will be fewer red tanks than tanks of all colors, which will reduce the size of the denominator in the Q_1. Similarly, if you decrease the size of the numerator, the size of the quotient will tend to decrease as well. Fewer candidate prefixes will attempt to transfer to the quotient, and a given prefix will have less opportunity to qualify for transferal. For example, compare the following two queries.

Q_3: Find the names of species with a diet of **peanut butter** represented in all tanks.

Q_4: Find the names of species represented in all tanks.

You expect fewer tuples in the solution to Q_3. In general, there will be fewer species with an sfood value of **peanut butter** than species with any sfood value whatsoever. Therefore, a smaller numerator occurs in the Q_3 solution than in Q_4.

Generalized Division

Relational division generalizes to situations where the divisor attributes aren't necessarily a proper subset of the dividend attributes. In normal division, if $X \cup Y$ and Y are the attributes of R_1 and R_2 respectively, then the computation of $r(R_1/R_2)$ is:

$$\{x \in \pi_X(R_1) \mid R_2 \subset \{y|(x:y) \in R_1\}\}.$$

The body of the quotient contains all prefixes x such that the collection of $(x:y)$ pairs in the dividend contains all the y entries in the divisor. If a prefix x qualifies in this way, it doesn't matter if there are additional $(x:y)$ combinations in the dividend for which the y is *not* in the divisor. In other words, it's acceptable for a successful x to be paired with an excessive set of y entries as long as it pairs at least with all the divisor y entries.

Now suppose X, Y, and Z are disjoint attribute sets, such that $X \cup Y$ are the attributes of R_1 and $Y \cup Z$ are the attributes of R_2. In other words, Y is the list of common attributes between R_1 and R_2. Unless $Z = \varphi$, R_1 and R_2 aren't compatible for division in the normal sense. However, they are compatible for generalized division, defined as follows. The notation $/_G$ indicates generalized division.

$$R_1/_G R_2 = \{(x:z) \in \pi_X(R_1) \times \pi_Z(R_2) \mid \{y|(y:z) \in R_2\} \subset \{y|(x:y) \in R_1\}\}.$$
$$(3.4)$$

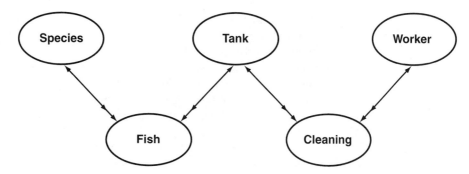

Figure 3.9   An extension of the aquarium database

A pair $(x : z)$ appears in the quotient when the prefix x appears in R_1 paired with *all* of a selected group of y suffixes. This selected group contains those y prefixes that appear in R_2 with the fixed z suffix.

As an example of generalized division, consider the extended aquarium database in Figure 3.9. Assume that the Worker entity includes the key wno and that the Cleaning entity includes the foreign keys wno and tno. Now consider the query: find the names of species-worker pairs, (sno, wno), where the species sno is represented in all tanks that the worker wno cleans. First, you compose two lists. L_1 contains (sno, tno) pairs where species sno links to tank tno; L_2 contains (tno, wno) pairs where worker wno cleans tank tno. Then $L_1 /_\mathrm{G} L_2$ gives the required (sno, wno) pairs. You might also want the names of the final species and worker tuples. The following construction carries along the sname and wname attributes and projects them as the final answer:

$$\pi_q[(\pi_r(\text{Species} * \text{Fish} * \text{Tank}))/_\mathrm{G} (\pi_s(\text{Tank} * \text{Cleaning} * \text{Worker}))],$$

where q =   (sname, wname)
         r =   (sno, sname, tno)
         s =   (tno, wno, wname).

You can express this query with ordinary division, but the construction is much more complicated. You should verify the stepwise approach below.

$W = \rho_{n_1} \sigma_{b_1} (\pi_{q_1} \check{\rho}(A = \text{Worker}) \times \pi_{q_2} \check{\rho}(B = \text{Worker}))$
$X = \rho_{n_2} \pi_{q_3} (\text{Species} * \text{Fish} * \text{Tank})$
$Y = X \times W$
$Z = Y / \rho_{n_3} \pi_{q_4} (\text{Worker} * \text{Cleaning} * \text{Tank})$

where q_1 =   (A.wno)
         q_2 =   (B.wno)
         b_1 =   (A.wno = B.wno)
         n_1 =   (A.wno $\longrightarrow w_1$, B.wno $\longrightarrow w_2$)
         q_3 =   (sno, tno)
         n_2 =   (sno $\longrightarrow s_1$, tno $\longrightarrow t$)
         q_4 =   (tno, wno)
         n_3 =   (tno $\longrightarrow t$, wno $\longrightarrow w_2$).

W is a list of tuples of the form (w_1, w_2), where both entries are wno values of the same worker. W is essentially a list of workers, but each entry has wno duplicated in two columns under different attribute names. X is a list of the form (s_1, t) where species s_1 shares a common fish with tank t. Y is then the Cartesian product of these related (s_1, t) pairs with the list of doubled workers. That is, Y is a list of the form (s_1, t, w_1, w_2), where s_1 and t are a species and tank related by some common fish and w_1 and w_2 identify a single worker. The worker need not have a connection with species s_1 or with tank t. The denominator of Z is a list of the form (t, w_2), where worker w_2 cleans tank t. The quotient is then the set of (s_1, w_1) pairs that appear in the numerator paired with every (t, w_2) suffix in the denominator.

What does this condition mean? Suppose a particular $(s_1 = a, w_1 = b)$ appears in the quotient. You can then reason as follows. If worker b cleans tank c, there is a $(t = c, w_2 = b)$ pair in the denominator. But then there must be a $(s_1 = a, t = c, w_1 = b, w_2 = b)$ tuple in the numerator, meaning that species a is represented in tank c. So a is represented in all tanks cleaned by b. Conversely, suppose that species a is represented in every tank cleaned by worker b. Then each $(t = c, w_2 = b)$ in the denominator forces a $(s_1 = a, t = c, w_1 = b, w_2 = b)$ in the numerator. Therefore, $(s_1 = a, w_1 = b)$ occurs in the quotient. In summary, the quotient is the set of (s_1, w_1) pairs such that sno is represented in every tank cleaned by worker w_1.

You can, of course, collapse the components into a single lengthy expression using only conventional division, and you can carry along the sname and wname attributes to project as the final answer. However, the direct division approach is obviously much more complicated than generalized division.

Before leaving this example, consider Figure 3.10, which shows the path bundles associated with this universal query. The required (sno, wno) pairs don't lie along a normal chain of connections across the database. Instead, they come from a collection of candidates where sno bears no special relation to wno, that is, from a Cartesian product of Species and Worker. For a fixed (species, worker) pair in the Cartesian product, the anchor collection is the set of tanks cleaned by the worker. A candidate (species, worker) pair originates a bundle of paths to the tanks where the species is represented. If these tanks contain the anchor collection, the (species, worker) pair enters the answer.

An interesting reduction occurs when one or the other denominator components is empty. Writing $R_1(X, Y)$ for the numerator emphasizes that the attributes of R_1 are $X \cup Y$. Similarly, $R_2(Y, Z)$ is the denominator with attributes $Y \cup Z$. If $Z = \varphi$, then the definition of generalized division gives:

$$R_1(X, Y)/_G R_2(Y) = \{x \in \pi_X(R_1) | R_2 \subset \{y|(x : y) \in R_1\}\} = R_1(X, Y)/R_2(Y).$$
(3.5)

So generalized division reduces to ordinary division when the numerator and denominator are compatible for division.

Now let $\mathcal{V}$ stand for the set of tuples over a void attribute set. If Y is empty, generalized division reduces to Cartesian product:

$$R_1(X)/_G R_2(Z) = \{(x : z) \in (R_1 \times R_2) | \mathcal{V} \subset \mathcal{V}\} = R_1(X) \times R_2(Z).$$
(3.6)

The first $\mathcal{V}$ arises because the suffixes of a given x are void, given that x occupies the entire tuple in R_1. The second $\mathcal{V}$ represents the prefixes of the fixed z in R_2, which are also nonexistent.

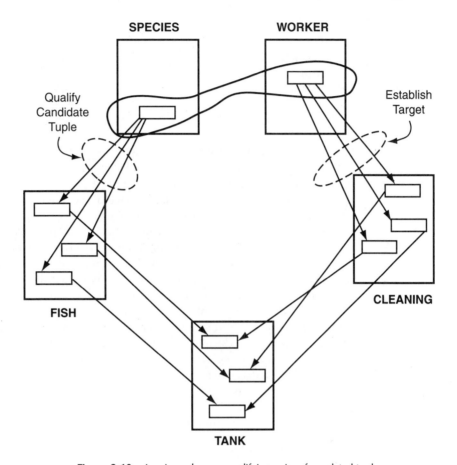

Figure 3.10 A universal query qualifying pairs of unrelated tuples

Aggregates and partitions

A **partition** of a relation classifies the tuples into disjoint groups, with the members of each group sharing some common characteristic. The tuples within each partition group serve as operands for certain **aggregate** operators, namely, sum, average, count, min, and max. Relational algebra provides a family of aggregate operators, Ψ_p^f, to perform such operations. The subscript defines a partition with a list of attributes, and the superscript specifies the aggregate functions, their arguments, and the new names for the resulting columns. For example, suppose you want to know the number of fish representing each species and also the maximum (alphabetical) fcolor value for each species. The relational algebra expression on the left below produces the answer table on the right, assuming the data in Figure 2.1.

$\pi_r \Psi_p^f \pi_q(\text{Species} * \text{Fish}),$

where q = (sno, sname, fno, fcolor)
        p = (sno)
        f = (fishCount = count(fno),
                maxColor = max(fcolor))
        r = (sno, sname, fishCount, maxColor)

< ··· >			
sno	sname	fishCount	maxColor
17	dolphin	6	white
74	guppy	4	red
22	shark	4	white
93	shark	3	white

The projection π_q of the natural join produces an intermediate table of (sno, sname, fno, fcolor) tuples, where the (fno, fcolor) fish belongs to the (sno, sname) species. The Ψ_p^f operation first stratifies this relation into non-overlapping groups, each distinguished by a common sno value. The operation then reduces each group to a single tuple, choosing a single value for each of the sno, sname, fno, fcolor attributes as follows. If the same value occurs in every tuple of the group under a particular attribute, this common value fills that attribute position in the reduced tuple. In this case, all the tuples in a group contain the same sno values because equal sno values define the group. The sno value of the reduced tuple, therefore, contains that value. Because sno is a key to the species relation, the sname values within a group must be the same across all tuples. This common sname value then appears as the sname value of the reduced tuple. If an attribute contains varying values across the tuples of the group, that position contains the null value in the reduced tuple. In this case, both fno and fcolor exhibit varying values across the tuples of a group, where many different fish belong to the same species. Both fno and fcolor, therefore, receive a null value in the reduced tuple.

Finally, the process adds a new attribute to the result table for each aggregate specified in the superscript of the Ψ_p^f operator. The value of the reduced tuple in one of these newly created positions is the result of applying the corresponding aggregate to the values in the argument columns. Here, the two aggregates are count and max with attribute names fishCount and maxColor respectively. So the schema for the resulting table contains (sno, sname, fno, fcolor, fishCount, maxColor). Under the fishCount attribute, the reduced tuple receives the number of entries in the group's fno column. Under maxColor, it receives the maximum of the group's fcolor values. Normally, you mask off the null attributes, as indicated by the final projection in the example above.

 A partition of a relation breaks the tuples into disjoint groups based on common values in specified attributes. An aggregate operator Ψ_p^f defines a partition with the attribute list p. It then applies the functions in the list f to specified columns and reduces each group to a single tuple.

Syntactical variations on the aggregate operator

Three convenient variations on the Ψ_p^f syntax are useful for formulating queries. First, the "distinct" keyword indicates that only distinct values enter into the calculation. For example, the expression on the left below determines the number of distinct fish names in each species.

$\pi_r \Psi_p^f \pi_q(\text{Species} * \text{Fish})$,

where q = (sno, sname, fno, fname)
$\qquad p$ = (sno)
$\qquad f$ = (nameCount = count(distinct fname))
$\qquad r$ = (sno, sname, nameCount)

$\pi_r \Psi_p^f \pi_q(\text{Species} * \text{Fish})$,

where q = (sno, sname, fno)
$\qquad p$ = (sno)
$\qquad f$ = (fishCount = count(*))
$\qquad r$ = (sno, sname, fishCount).

Second, the function "count(*)" in the superscript list calculates the number of tuples in each group. For example, the expression on the right above delivers the number of fish for each species. Finally, aggregate operators can take the form Ψ^f, where the partition-defining subscript isn't present. In this case, the aggregate functions in the f list operate on the entire table as a single large group. The expression on the left below counts the number of fish in the entire database.

$\pi_r \Psi^f(\text{Fish})$,

where f = (fishCount = count(*))
$\qquad r$ = (fishCount)

$\pi_r \Psi_p^f(\text{Fish})$,

where p = (sno, tno)
$\qquad f$ = (fishCount = count(*))
$\qquad r$ = (sno, tno, fishCount).

The partition-defining subscript can contain several attributes, as in the expression on the right above. It counts the fish associated with each species-tank combination. The answer is a list of (sno, tno, fishCount) tuples, where the fishCount value gives the number of fish that represent species sno *and* live in tank tno. This solution uses the embedded tno and sno foreign keys in the Fish relation. If you want the counts with the names of the species and tanks, you would use the following construction.

$\pi_r \Psi_p^f(\text{Species} * \text{Fish} * \text{Tank})$,

where p = (sno, tno)
$\qquad f$ = (fishCount = count(*))
$\qquad r$ = (sname, tname, fishCount).

Here the aggregate operator stratifies the natural join Species * Fish * Tank into groups, one for each combination of sno and tno. It then reduces each group to a single tuple, treating the columns as necessary for different circumstances. Under fno, fname, fcolor, and fweight columns, the values become nulls. As usual, a subsequent projection removes these columns.

Further examples of aggregate queries

Following are more examples of aggregate queries. The expression on the left below produces the minimum, maximum, and average volume of red tanks; the right construction computes the total tank volume associated with each species. In the second example, note that the final projection (sno, tno, tvolume) produces a table of sno species and their related tanks *before* application of the aggregate operator. The natural join returns many tuples for each species-tank pair, one for each fish that connects them. If the projection weren't used, the average (tvolume) calculation would encounter many copies of the same tvolume value, one for each fish connecting the tank with the fixed species of the group. This overcounting would lead to an erroneous average. However, the projection reduces each related species-tank pair to a single occurrence because the projection result, a relation, must suppress duplicates. The many species-fish-tank tuples from the natural join, corresponding to a particular species-tank pair, become duplicates when the fish attributes are stripped away. Only one representative tuple is retained, and the subsequent aggregate then produces the correct average values.

$\pi_r \Psi^f \sigma_b(\text{Tank}),$

where
$$
\begin{aligned}
b &= (\text{tcolor} = \text{"red"}) \\
f &= (\text{minVol} = \min(\text{tvolume}), \\
 &\quad \text{maxVol} = \max(\text{tvolume}), \\
 &\quad \text{avgVol} = \text{average}(\text{tvolume})) \\
r &= (\text{minVol}, \text{maxVol}, \text{avgVol}).
\end{aligned}
$$

$\pi_r \Psi_p^f \pi_q(\text{Species} * \text{Fish} * \text{Tank}),$

where
$$
\begin{aligned}
q &= (\text{sno}, \text{tno}, \text{tvolume}) \\
p &= (\text{sno}) \\
f &= (\text{totalVol} = \text{sum}(\text{tvolume})) \\
r &= (\text{sno}, \text{totalVol}).
\end{aligned}
$$

You can follow an aggregate operator with a selection in which the boolean tests the newly computed aggregate values. For example, consider the following query. Find the average volume of tanks associated with each species, but only for species represented in two or more tanks. The relational algebra solution appears on the left below. The aggregate operator computes the desired average volume and also the count needed to qualify certain groups for the answer.

$\pi_r \sigma_b \Psi_p^f \pi_q(\text{Species} * \text{Fish} * \text{Tank}),$

where
$$
\begin{aligned}
q &= (\text{sno}, \text{tno}, \text{tvolume}) \\
p &= (\text{sno}) \\
f &= (\text{averageVol} = \text{average}(\text{tvolume}), \\
 &\quad \text{tankCount} = \text{count}(*)) \\
b &= (\text{tankCount} >= 2) \\
r &= (\text{sno}, \text{averageVol}).
\end{aligned}
$$

$X = \pi_p \sigma_b \Psi_p^f(\text{Fish}),$

where
$$
\begin{aligned}
p &= (\text{sno}) \\
f &= (\text{fishCount} = \text{count}(*)) \\
b &= (\text{fishCount} >= 10)
\end{aligned}
$$

$\pi_s(X * \Psi_q^g \pi_r(\text{Species} * \text{Fish} * \text{Tank})),$

where
$$
\begin{aligned}
r &= (\text{sno}, \text{sname}, \text{tno}, \text{tvolume}) \\
q &= (\text{sno}) \\
g &= (\text{avgVol} = \text{average}(\text{tvolume})) \\
s &= (\text{sno}, \text{sname}, \text{avgVol}).
\end{aligned}
$$

Sometimes a query requires two or more different partitions. For example, the following query needs one partition to isolate the tuples for an aggregate calculation and a second to qualify the reduced tuples for inclusion in the answer. Find the average tank volume associated with each species, for species represented by 10 or more fish. Here you must group a species with all its associated tanks in order to apply the average aggregate. However, you must also group a species with its corresponding fish to determine if it belongs in the answer set. The excerpt on the right above shows the relational algebra solution in two steps. First it builds the context necessary to count the fish of each species. The result contains the sno values of those species represented by 10 or more fish. Because sno is an embedded foreign key in Fish, this operation needs only that one table. The result is the intermediate table denoted by X. The second step constructs the partition necessary to compute the average tank volume of each species. The natural join of this result with X eliminates species represented by fewer than 10 fish.

The natural join's ability to remove tuples produced by a separate process is useful in many circumstances. The general situation is as follows. Suppose that R_1 contains attributes K and X, where K is a key and X is the balance of the attributes. In general, R_1 is a result of certain operations on the original database tables. In the example above, R_1

is $\Psi_q^g \pi_r$(Species $*$ Fish $*$ Tank)). Now suppose that R_2 is a separately computed table of keys. That is, R_2 contains the single attribute K. Then $R_1 * R_2$ eliminates tuples from R_1 whose key value isn't present in R_2.

Arithmetic computations beyond aggregates

Aggregate functions can contain arithmetic combinations of the sum, count, average, min, and max operators. They can also contain attributes that are meaningful in a reduced group, such as attributes that are constant over the tuples of each group. Consider, for example, the following query. Find the total tank volume associated with each species. Express the tvolume attribute in quarts, although values in the database are in gallons. The relational algebra solution appears on the left below. The aggregate function that extracts the sum across a partition grouping also performs the required multiplication.

$\pi_q \Psi_p^f \pi_r$(Species $*$ Fish $*$ Tank),

where $\quad r \quad = \quad$ (sno, sname, tno, tvolume)

$\qquad\quad p \quad = \quad$ (sno)

$\qquad\quad f \quad = \quad$ (totalVol = 4 $*$ sum(tvolume))

$\qquad\quad q \quad = \quad$ (sname, totalVol)

$\pi_q \Psi_p^f$(Tank),

where $\quad p \quad = \quad$ (tno)

$\qquad\quad f \quad = \quad$ (newVol = 4 $*$ tvolume))

$\qquad\quad q \quad = \quad$ (tname, newVol).

Even if a query doesn't specify an aggregate (i.e., count, sum, average, min, max), an aggregate operator can calculate other arithmetic expressions. In this case, you must specify the operator's grouping subscript such that each group contains exactly one tuple. To achieve this, you can group on a key, or in the extreme case, on the entire collection of attributes in the table. For example, suppose you want the each tank's volume in quarts even though the tvolume values are in gallons. The solution to the right above treats each tank as a separate group.

Limits on the expressive power of relational algebra

Relational algebra also contains simple operators for inserting, deleting, and modifying tuples. However, even with these additional operators, the full relational algebra suffers a serious deficiency. Consider the one-relation employee database in Figure 2.19. The Employee table attributes are eno, ename, and sno. The key is eno, the employee's identifying number; the sno foreign key holds the eno of the employee's supervisor. A many-to-one relationship exists between the Employee table and itself. Each employee has at most one supervisor, but a supervisor can have many employees. No employee works for himself, either directly or through any number of subordinates. Now consider the following query: find the names of employees who work, either directly or indirectly, for eno 45. The relational algebra on the left below locates the employees who work directly for eno 45. As illustrated on the right, a union then computes the employees who work either directly for eno 45 or for some individual who works directly for eno 45. The latter solution obtains the employees who work for eno 45 down through two levels of supervision.

$\pi_q \sigma_b \check{\rho}(E = \text{Employee}),$

$[\pi_q \sigma_b \check{\rho}(E = \text{Employee})] \cup [\pi_q \sigma_c(\check{\rho}(E = \text{Employee}) \times \check{\rho}(F = \text{Employee}))],$

where b = $(E.\text{sno} = 45)$

q = $(E.\text{ename}).$

where b = $(E.\text{sno} = 45)$

q = $(E.\text{sname})$

c = $(E.\text{sno} = F.\text{eno} \wedge F.\text{sno} = 45).$

If you consider those employees reported by the second component of the union as once-removed workers, you can extend the pattern by requesting the names of employees who work for employee 45 directly, once-removed, or twice-removed. The solution then appears as a union of three components, as shown below.

$$[\pi_q \sigma_b \check{\rho}(E = \text{Employee})] \cup [\pi_q \sigma_c(\check{\rho}(E = \text{Employee}) \times \check{\rho}(F = \text{Employee}))] \cup$$
$$[\pi_q \sigma_d(\check{\rho}(E = \text{Employee}) \times \check{\rho}(F = \text{Employee}) \times \check{\rho}(G = \text{Employee})),$$

where b = $(E.\text{sno} = 45)$

q = $(E.\text{sname})$

c = $(E.\text{sno} = F.\text{eno} \wedge F.\text{sno} = 45)$

d = $(E.\text{sno} = F.\text{eno} \wedge F.\text{sno} = G.\text{eno} \wedge G.\text{sno} = 45).$

The point is that you must know, in advance, the maximum number of supervisory levels to construct the relational algebra. You can't compose an expression to find the those employees who work for employee 45 directly or indirectly at any level. The number of levels under employee 45 might be one, ten, or none, depending on the actual values in the database. The fundamental deficiency is that relational algebra has no facility for looping an indeterminate number of times, in the manner of a "while loop" in a traditional programming language. Looping a fixed number of times, three in the example above, presents no conceptual difficulty, although the syntax is awkward. Using the pattern above, you can find the names of employees who work for employee 45 at any level of indirection through some fixed limit, say ten. Unfortunately, the construction involves the union of ten increasingly lengthy components. If the level of indirection isn't bounded independently of the data, then relational algebra can't express the query.

Extending the relational algebra with a **recursive closure** operator eliminates this problem. Suppose that k is a key of relation R; that f is a foreign key within R referring back to R; and that $S = \sigma_c(R)$ is some initial selection of tuples from R. Consider a sequence of operations for $i = 0, 1, 2, \ldots$ as follows:

$$X_0 = S \tag{3.7}$$
$$X_i = X_{i-1} \cup \pi_R \sigma_{b_i}(\check{\rho}(X_{i-1}) \times R), \quad i > 0, \ b_i = (X_{i-1}.k = f).$$

The **recursive closure** of S in R, denoted by $\Sigma_{f=k}(R, S)$, is calculated as follows:

$$\Sigma_{f=k}(R, S) = \min\{i | X_i = X_{i+1}\}. \tag{3.8}$$

The subset $S \subset R$ is a set of tuples from R that serves as a seed. The attribute names of S are the same as for R. X_0 evaluates to this seed, and each subsequent X_{i+1} set adds R-tuples to its predecessor. Because the number of tuples in R is finite, there must be some i such that X_{i+1} adds no more tuples: $X_i = X_{i+1} = X_{i+2} = \ldots$. This stable value of X_i is the recursive closure of S in R.

Suppose, for example, that R is the Employee relation from the example above. Then the initial seed S is the single tuple with eno = 45. That is, $S = \sigma_c(R)$, where $c = $ (eno = 45). Now, letting $b_i = $ (sno = X_{i-1}.eno), the calculation proceeds as follows:

$$X_0 = S$$
$$X_1 = X_0 \cup \pi_R \sigma_{b_1}(\breve{\rho}(X_0) \times R)$$
$$X_2 = X_1 \cup \pi_R \sigma_{b_2}(\breve{\rho}(X_1) \times R)$$
$$\vdots$$

X_1 contains the seed employee (eno = 45), plus employees indicating eno 45 as a supervisor. X_2 contains X_1 plus employees reporting to any supervisor in X_1. The construction continues to build up workers who report to employee 45 at increasing levels of indirection. Because these tuples all accumulate from the Employee relation, the chain of workers reporting to employee 45 at any level must eventually terminate. Recall that there are no cycles in the chain of supervisor-worker relationships. So the recursive closure answers the unbounded query as follows:

$$\pi_q \Sigma_b(\text{Employee}, \sigma_c(\text{Employee})), \text{ where } \quad c = (\text{eno} = 45)$$
$$b = (\text{sno} = \text{eno})$$
$$q = (\text{ename}).$$

Here is the Employee relation from Figure 2.19.

Employee		
eno	ename	sno
53	albert	14
42	bernice	14
86	candice	53
45	dennis	
14	frank	45

The sequence of X_i sets computes as follows:

X_0		
eno	ename	sno
45	dennis	

X_1		
eno	ename	sno
45	dennis	
14	frank	45

X_2		
eno	ename	sno
53	albert	14
42	bernice	14
45	dennis	
14	frank	45

X_3		
eno	ename	sno
53	albert	14
42	bernice	14
86	candice	53
45	dennis	
14	frank	45

Because X_3 now contains all of the Employee relation, the progression stabilizes here, giving the recursive closure of employee 45 equal to the full Employee relation.

The recursive closure operator, $\Sigma_b(R, S)$, expands a seed relation $S \subset R$ by accumulating tuples from R that link to the tuples of S either directly or indirectly. The subscript b specifies the linkage via primary and foreign keys in the same table.

Elementary query optimization

Our examples have shown that relational algebra expressions often contain extensive Cartesian product or natural join operators. These operations are computationally time-consuming and produce large intermediate tables. To respond efficiently to queries, a relational algebra system must consider alternative expressions that deliver the same result. The process of transforming a relational algebra expression into one that's more efficient is called **query optimization**.

A simple example illustrates the dramatic difference in processing complexity that can exist between two equivalent relational algebra expressions. Consider again the aquarium example. Assume that each of the species and tank relations has 100 tuples and that there is an average of 1000 fish in each tank, giving 100,000 fish in the database. Suppose there are approximately 1000 fish of each species in the overall population. Now, consider the following query: find the names of fish swimming in cesspool tanks. The straightforward relational algebra solution appears on the left below. The natural join constructs 100,000 $\times$ 100 = 10,000,000 tuples and then scans this large collection to remove the inappropriate combinations. In total, this operation manipulates 20,000,000 tuples and produces an intermediate table of 100,000. The subsequent selection operator scans these 100,000 tuples to filter out the cesspool tuples, resulting in a few thousand tuples. From these tuples, the final projection operator extracts unique fname values. If you assume that a single tank possesses the name cesspool, this final scan processes approximately 1,000 tuples. The total number of tuples manipulated is then approximately 20,201,000.

$$\pi_q \sigma_b(\text{Fish} * \text{Tank}), \qquad\qquad \pi_q(\text{Fish} * \sigma_b(\text{Tank})),$$

where	b	=	(tname = "cesspool")	where	b	= (tname = "cesspool")
	q	=	(fname)		q	= (fname).

You can also solve the query by first isolating the cesspool tanks and then performing the natural join with this potentially much smaller set. This alternative appears on the right above. If there is a single cesspool tank, the initial selection manipulates 100 tuples to extract the cesspool tuple. The natural join then creates 100,000 extended tuples with its underlying Cartesian product and scans them to remove the inappropriate combinations. This process results in approximately 1,000 tuples, from which the final projection extracts the unique fname values. The total manipulation count is 100 + 2(100,000) + 1000 = 201,100 tuples, less than 1% of the tuples in the previous solution.

Even larger savings are possible with more complex queries. Consider again the query that finds the names of species swimming with a shark. The pattern for existential queries produces the following solution:

$\pi_q \sigma_b(\check{\rho}(S = \text{Species}) \times \check{\rho}(F = \text{Fish}) \times \check{\rho}(T = \text{Tank}) \times \check{\rho}(G = \text{Fish}) \times \check{\rho}(H = \text{Species}))$

where b = $(S.\text{sno} = F.\text{sno} \wedge F.\text{tno} = T.\text{tno} \wedge T.\text{tno} = G.\text{tno} \wedge G.\text{sno} = H.\text{sno} \wedge H.\text{sname} = \text{"shark"})$

q = $(S.\text{sname})$.

The Cartesian product creates $100 \times 100,000 \times 100 \times 100,000 \times 100 = 10^{16}$ tuples! The selection operator then scans this large intermediate table before a final pass projects the required sname values. So, the total number of operations exceeds 2.0×10^{16}. This count obviously represents an enormous amount of processing. If each tuple-handling operation consumed just 1 nanosecond, the entire operation would require about a year to complete!

The Cartesian products are the villains in the play because these operations rapidly inflate the number of tuples that must be scanned by subsequent operations. The first goal of query optimization, therefore, is to reduce the number of Cartesian product operations and the size of their operands. In this example, a first optimization omits the tank relation because it serves only to place fish F and G in the same tank. You can equate the embedded keys F.tno and G.tno directly to accomplish the same result. Because the tank relation adds a factor of 100 to the tuples of the extended Cartesian product, this modification reduces the tuple count of the overall query by that factor. Instead of a year, the query now takes about 3.6 days.

You can break the long boolean expression of σ_b into segments and apply each component to the appropriate part of the growing Cartesian product. Let $b_1 = (H.\text{sname} = \text{"shark"})$. You can use this component to reduce the size of the H operand *before* it participates in a Cartesian product. (See below.) The number of shark species is likely to be much less than the full 100 species in the database. Indeed, a credible estimate for that number is 1. By moving the selection σ_{b_1} directly adjacent to the H relation, you can reduce the size of that operand to the Cartesian product by a factor of 100. As soon as the Cartesian product has united the reduced H table with the G table, you can apply the component $\sigma_{b_2} = (G.\text{sno} = H.\text{sno})$, thereby reducing the operand of the next Cartesian product. This process continues to yield the following expression:

$\pi_q \sigma_{b_4} \{ \check{\rho}(S = \text{Species}) \times \sigma_{b_3} [\check{\rho}(F = \text{Fish}) \times \sigma_{b_2}(\check{\rho}(G = \text{Fish}) \times \sigma_{b_1} \check{\rho}(H = \text{Species}))]\},$

where b_1 = $(H.\text{sname} = \text{"shark"})$

b_2 = $(G.\text{sno} = H.\text{sno})$

b_3 = $(F.\text{tno} = G.\text{tno})$

b_4 = $(S.\text{sno} = F.\text{sno})$

q = $(S.\text{sname})$.

Approximate tuple manipulation counts appear in the table below. X_1 is formed by selecting the one shark tuple from the 100 entries of $H = \text{Species}$. The subsequent Cartesian product with $G = \text{Fish}$ then manipulates only 100,000 tuples. The next operation scans X_2 to remove the inappropriate combinations, which results in approximately 1000 tuples, each representing a fish of the shark species. The following join with $F = \text{Fish}$ produces $1000 \times 100,000 = 10^8$ tuples. Here each shark fish pairs with every other fish. The next selection, σ_{b_3}, retains only those pairs inhabiting a common tank. If you assume 1000 sharks uniformly distributed across the 100 tanks, there are about 10 sharks per tank. Each of these 10 sharks occurs with the 1000 fish of the tank, giving $100 \times 10,000 = 10^6$ tuples after the selection. The final Cartesian product with S raises the count to 10^8 again, and the σ_{b_4} selection reduces it back to 10^6. At 1 nanosecond each, the total count now requires 0.25 seconds.

This represents an improvement of roughly 10^8 over the initial expression.

100	$X_1 = \sigma_{b_1}(H)$
	– reduces operand to 1 tuple
100,000	$X_2 = G \times X_1$
100,000	$X_3 = \sigma_{b_2}(X_2)$
	– reduces operand to 1000 tuples
100,000,000	$X_4 = F \times X_3$
100,000,000	$X_5 = \sigma_{b_3}(X_4)$
	– reduces operand to 1,000,000 tuples
100,000,000	$X_6 = S \times X_5$
100,000,000	$X_7 = \sigma_{b_4}(X_6)$
	– reduces operand to 10^6 tuples
4.0×10^8	Approximate total tuple handling count

SUMMARY

Relational algebra is a system of operations on relations. It is a closed system because each operation returns a new relation, which can then serve as an operand for further operations. The basic operators of relational algebra are union ($R_1 \cup R_2$), set difference ($R_1 - R_2$), Cartesian product ($R_1 \times R_2$), selection ($\sigma_b(R)$), projection ($\pi_q(R)$), renaming ($\rho_n(R)$), and aggregation ($\Psi_p^f(R)$). Union and set difference require that the operands be union-compatible: they must have the same number of attributes, and the attributes must carry the same names. Renaming can force union-compatibility. The Cartesian product forms all possible concatenations of the form $(x : y)$, with the prefix taken from one operand and the suffix taken from the other. Operands must be Cartesian product compatible, in the sense that attribute name conflicts must not occur in the combined schema for the two operands. Again, renaming can force compatibility if needed. Two renaming operators are particularly convenient. The $\check{\rho}$ operator extends the attribute names of its argument relation by prefixing them with the name of the relation itself. The $\hat{\rho}$ operator reverses this action by removing the left-most prefix from each attribute name. Selection and projection perform horizontal and vertical sectioning operations respectively. The aggregate operator isolates groups of tuples having common values in certain chosen attributes, and it reduces each group to a single tuple. Aggregate functions and arithmetic expressions perform simple calculations on attribute values within a group. You can simulate arithmetic expressions on single tuples with the aggregate operator by forcing each partition to contain a single tuple.

Certain combinations of the basic seven operators define convenient extensions, which can simplify the expressions for certain categories of queries. The natural join, $R_1 * R_2$, consists of a Cartesian product, followed by a selection that forces equality for pairs of common attributes. The process removes one of each pair of common attributes from the final relation, and it renames the attributes to remove any qualification forced by the Cartesian product. The natural join is the typical method used to associate tuples from several relations to form a path through the database. Natural join operations are associative and commutative.

Other variations on the Cartesian product theme include θ-join, equijoin, and semijoin. The θ-join enforces a relationship, θ, between values in common columns and retains both of each pair of common columns. θ is any one of the arithmetic comparison operators:

$<, >, \leq, \geq$, and $=$, or their complements. When θ is the equality operator, the operation becomes an equijoin. A semijoin is a natural join followed by a projection on the attributes of the first operand. All join operations can be defined in terms of Cartesian products and selection operations.

Two relations are division compatible if the denominator attributes are a proper subset of the numerator attributes. In this case, the quotient attributes consist of the excess attributes in the numerator. The body of the quotient consists of those prefixes from the numerator that appear with all suffixes from the denominator. That is, $X/Y = \{z|(z:y) \in X$ for all $y \in Y\}$.

In an existential query, a candidate tuple contributes to the answer if it commands a path to an anchor tuple. You can express such queries in relational algebra by constructing the Cartesian product of the linking tables along the existential path. You use a subsequent selection operator to enforce the proper linkages through the foreign keys and to specify the defining conditions on the anchor tuple.

In a universal query, a candidate tuple contributes to the answer if it commands a bundle of paths that completely embrace a collection of anchor tuples. Universal queries use relational division in their solutions. A prefix in the numerator represents a candidate for the answer table, and the set of suffixes paired with that prefix identifies the collection of target objects reachable from the candidate. The denominator isolates the collection of anchor targets. In more complex universal queries, the anchor targets can vary with the candidate tuple under test. In this case, a variation of the division operator is useful for abbreviating the relational algebra expression. This variant is generalized division. Both conventional and generalized division can be defined in terms of the basic relational algebra operators.

Query optimization is a method for rewriting relational algebra expressions to increase efficiency while maintaining functional equivalency. Vastly superior performance results from such simple expedients as moving selection operators closer to their operands and removing intermediate tables that aren't essential for maintaining the links in database paths. Query optimization's primary goal is to reduce the number and size of operands of Cartesian product operations.∎

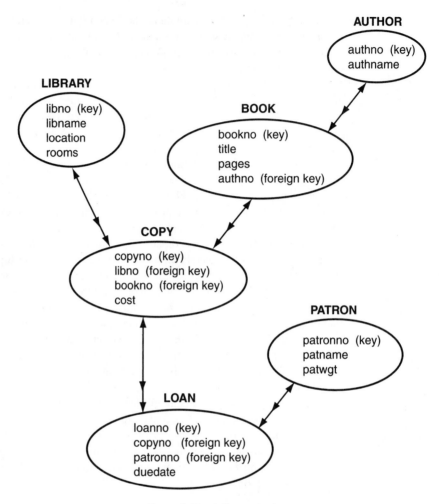

Figure 3.11 A library database

Many of these exercises deal with the library database in Figure 3.11, where the common attributes for maintaining the five binary one-to-many relationships have the same name in corresponding tables. The key attributes (e.g., libno, bookno) are unique within a table, but any of the other attributes may be duplicated. For example, two books can have the same title, but they will have distinct bookno values. Most attribute names are self-explanatory. In the library table, the rooms and pages attributes refer to the number of rooms in a library and to the number of pages in a book. The cost attribute in the copy table records how much the library paid for the copy. The patwgt attribute provides the weight of the patron.

Select-project-join operators and existential queries

Write relational algebra for the following queries.

1. Find the names of libraries located in Seattle.

2. Find the names and locations of libraries that feature books written by Salinger.

3. Find the names of libraries where the book collection overlaps with a library located in Seattle. That is, a library is part of the answer set if it contains a copy of at least one book that is also available at a Seattle library.

4. Find the book titles that are available from a library patronized by a patron named joe.

5. Find all pairs of book titles that have copies in the same library. A pair (x, y) of titles is part of the answer if there is some library which has both a copy of x and a copy of y. Phrase the query to remove pairs of the form (x, x) from the answer set and to provide just one of the pairs (x, y) or (y, x) when both qualify.

6. Find all triplets of names from distinct collocated libraries.

   Describe (in English) the intent of the following relational algebra expressions. Assume that previous relational algebra has assigned copies of Library, Copy, Book, Author, Loan, and Patron to $L, C, B, A, U,$ and P respectively. U represents Loan in order not to duplicate L, which stands for Library. Think of U as Usage.

7. $\pi_q \sigma_b (B * C * U * P)$, where $\quad q = $ (title)
   $$b = \text{(patwgt} > \text{pages)}$$

8. $\pi_q \sigma_b (\check{\rho}(Y = A * B) \times \check{\rho}(X = B * A))$, where $\quad q \;=\;$ (Y.authname, X.authname)
   $$b \;=\; (Y\text{.title} = X\text{.title} \wedge Y\text{.authno} < X\text{.authno})$$

9. $\pi_q \sigma_b (\check{\rho}(X = P * U * C * L) \times \check{\rho}(Y = (L * C * U * P) \times \check{\rho}(Z = P * U * C * L))$

   where $\quad q \;=\;$ (X.patname)
   $$b \;=\; (X\text{.libno} = Y\text{.libno} \wedge Y\text{.patronno} = Z\text{.patronno} \wedge Z\text{.location} = \text{``Minneapolis''})$$

Universal queries

Construct relational algebra expressions for the following queries.

10. Find the names of libraries holding no books.

11. Find the names of patrons who have used every library in the database.

12. Find the names of patrons who deal with all libraries located in Seattle that possess a book written by Salinger.

13. Find the names of all Minneapolis libraries that house all books with more than 300 pages that appear in all Seattle libraries.

14. Find the names of patrons weighing more than 100 pounds who deal with all libraries with more than 25 rooms that house all books written by Salinger.

15. Find the names of patrons who have checked out all books with more than 300 pages.

16. Find the titles of books that have copies in all Seattle libraries that feature copies of all books written by Mailer.

   Describe the following relational algebra expressions in English.

17. $\pi_q [\pi_r (\text{patron} * \text{loan} * \text{copy} * \text{book} * \text{author}) / \pi_s (\text{author})]$,

   where $\quad s \;=\;$ (authno)
   $$r \;=\; \text{(patronno, patname, patwgt, authno)}$$
   $$q \;=\; \text{(patname, patwgt)}$$

18. $\pi_q\{\pi_r(\text{library} * \text{copy})/[\pi_s(\text{copy})/\pi_t\sigma_b(\text{copy} * \text{library})]\}$,

$$\begin{array}{rcl}
\text{where} \quad b & = & (\text{location} = \text{``Seattle''}) \\
t & = & (\text{libno}) \\
s & = & (\text{bookno, libno}) \\
r & = & (\text{libno, libname, bookno}) \\
q & = & (\text{libname})
\end{array}$$

For the following queries, write relational algebra expressions using conventional or generalized division, whichever is more appropriate.

19. Find the names of libraries whose collections are precisely the set of books with more than 300 pages.

20. Find the names of patrons who deal with precisely those libraries located in Seattle.

21. Find the names of library-patron pairs such that the set of books containing more than 300 pages that appear in the library is the same as the set of books written by Salinger that the patron has borrowed.

Describe the following relational algebra expression in English.

22. $\pi_q[(\pi_r(L * C)/\pi_s\sigma_b(B)) - \pi_t\sigma_c(L * C * B)]$,

$$\begin{array}{rcl}
\text{where} \quad b & = & (\text{pages} > 300) \\
s & = & (\text{bookno}) \\
r & = & (\text{libno, libname, bookno}) \\
c & = & (\text{pages} <= 300) \\
t & = & (\text{libno, libname}) \\
q & = & (\text{libname})
\end{array}$$

Aggregates and partitions

Compose relational algebra expressions for the following queries.

23. Find the titles of books that have fewer than ten copies.

24. Find the location of the library with the most rooms.

25. For each book title-library name combination, find the number of copies of the book that appear in the library.

26. Compute the average size of libraries (i.e., number of rooms) used by each patron. Restrict the answer to those patrons who have borrowed books.

27. For each book with at least one copy, find the minimum, average, and maximum cost of the copies.

28. Find the names of patrons whose weight is greater than the average weight of patrons who have read a book entitled **The Name of the Rose**.

Describe the following relational algebra expressions in English.

29. $\pi_q\Psi_p^f\pi_r(\text{library} * \text{copy} * \text{book})$,

$$\begin{array}{rcl}
\text{where} \quad r & = & (\text{libno, libname, bookno, pages}) \\
p & = & (\text{libno}) \\
f & = & (\text{totalPages} = \text{sum(pages)}) \\
q & = & (\text{libname, totalPages})
\end{array}$$

30. $\pi_q \sigma_b \Psi_p^f \pi_r$(library * copy * loan * patron),

$$\begin{array}{rcl}
\text{where} \quad r & = & \text{(libno, libname, rooms, patronno, patwgt)} \\
p & = & \text{(libno)} \\
f & = & \text{(avgWgt = 2 * average(patwgt))} \\
b & = & \text{(rooms > avgWgt)} \\
q & = & \text{(libname)}
\end{array}$$

31. $\pi_q \Psi_p^f$(copy * loan),

$$\begin{array}{rcl}
\text{where} \quad p & = & \text{(libno, bookno, patronno)} \\
f & = & \text{(loanActivity = count(loanno))} \\
q & = & \text{(libno, bookno, patronno, loanActivity)}
\end{array}$$

Write relational algebra expressions to solve the following queries.

32. For each library whose collection includes more than 100 titles, find the average number of pages in the books in the collection.

33. For each author whose total number of pages written exceeds the total weight of the patrons who have read some of his work, find the average size of the libraries that carry his books. The total number of pages written is *not* increased by multiple copies of a book.

34. Find the number of libraries used by each patron, for those patrons who use a library larger than the average size of those libraries that carry a copy of a book entitled The Name of the Rose.

Limits on the expressive power of relational algebra

Consider the following relation in which k is a key and f is a foreign key referring to the same relation.

X	
k	f
1	–
2	1
3	1
4	2
5	2
6	3
7	3
8	4
9	4
10	5
11	5
12	6
13	6
14	7
15	7

35. Suppose that S is $\{(k = 15, f = 7), (k = 4, f = 2)\}$. Compute the recursive closure: $\Sigma_{k=f}(X, S)$.

36. Compute $\cap_{i=1}^{15}\{\Sigma_{k=f}(X, \sigma_i(X))\}$, where σ_i is $(k = i)$.

Elementary query optimization

Assume the library database contains 100 libraries and 10,000 books. Also assume that each library contains an average of 2 copies of each of 2,000 books, for a total of 400,000 copies in the system. Assume that 10% of the libraries are in Seattle and that there are about 40 copies of each book overall. Each question below presents two equivalent relational algebra solutions. Determine the approximate ratio of the number of tuples handled by the less efficient expression to the number handled by the more efficient expression.

37. Find the names of libraries that hold a copy of The Name of the Rose.

   (1) $\pi_q \sigma_b$(library $*$ copy $*$ book),

$$
\begin{array}{lll}
\text{where} & b & = & \text{(title = "The Name of the Rose")}\\
& q & = & \text{(libname)}
\end{array}
$$

   (2) π_q(library $*$ (copy $*$ σ_b(book))),

$$
\begin{array}{lll}
\text{where} & b & = & \text{(title = "The Name of the Rose")}\\
& q & = & \text{(libname)}
\end{array}
$$

38. Find the names of libraries that hold a copy of a book that is also available from a Seattle library.

   (1) $\pi_q \sigma_b (\breve{\rho}(L = \text{library}) \times \breve{\rho}(C = \text{copy}) \times \breve{\rho}(B = \text{book}) \times \breve{\rho}(D = \text{copy}) \times \breve{\rho}(M = \text{library}))$,

$$
\begin{array}{lll}
\text{where} & b & = & (L.\text{libno} = C.\text{libno} \wedge C.\text{bookno} = B.\text{bookno} \wedge B.\text{bookno} = D.\text{bookno}\\
& & & \wedge D.\text{libno} = M.\text{libno} \wedge M.\text{location} = \text{"Seattle"})\\
& q & = & (L.\text{libname})
\end{array}
$$

   (2) $\pi_q \{ (\pi_r(\text{library} * \text{copy})) * \pi_s(\text{copy} * \sigma_b(\text{library}) \}$,

$$
\begin{array}{lll}
\text{where} & r & = & \text{(libno, libname, bookno)}\\
& b & = & \text{(location = "Seattle")}\\
& s & = & \text{(bookno)}\\
& q & = & \text{(libname)}
\end{array}
$$

4 Relational Calculus

L IKE RELATIONAL ALGEBRA, RELATIONAL CALCULUS IS A LANGUAGE FOR
manipulating the contents of a relational database. However, relational calculus is
non-procedural. In other words, where relational algebra procedurally specifies a
sequence of operations, relational calculus merely specifies *what* information is needed but
not *how* to retrieve it. In the most general terms, a relational calculus query takes the form:
retrieve database items X such that condition Y holds. The DBMS applies condition Y
to the mass of tuples in the database, resulting in some successes and some failures. The
query syntax emphasizes the test condition itself rather than the procedures that conduct the
test. Selection of successful tuples uses a predicate, a function that returns true (success)
or false (failure) when applied to a particular candidate.

The study of predicates and their logical combinations, a field known as the predicate
calculus, has a long tradition in mathematics. Relational calculus is a natural extension of
predicate calculus to the problems of database retrieval. Indeed, relational calculus is the
well-known predicate calculus tailored to the case where the most elementary judgments
extract specific facts from a relational database.

A certain asymmetry exists between the existential and universal relational algebra
examples in Chapter 3 because the standard template for a universal query is significantly
more complicated. Relational calculus, however, expresses universal and existential queries
in a parallel manner. Unfortunately, because it is based on traditional predicate calculus,
the notation is more mathematical and therefore further removed from the language of the
application. Despite its mathematical format, relational calculus has an obvious advantage
over procedural relational algebra because the user doesn't need to specify the operational
sequence to transform existing tables into a solution table.

Review of predicate calculus

A **predicate** is a function whose value is true or false, depending on the values of its
arguments. These functions are familiar from the previous chapter, where for example,
they were used in the subscripts of selection operators. The simplest predicates are **atomic**

a	b	$\neg a$	$(a \wedge b)$	$(a \vee b)$	$(a \Rightarrow b)$
T	T	F	T	T	T
T	F	F	F	T	F
F	T	T	F	T	T
F	F	T	F	F	T

Figure 4.1 Truth tables for logical operators

predicates, and they return elementary true-false judgments about application objects. For example, if t is a tuple from the aquarium database, the atomic predicate redTank(t) renders a judgment on t. If t is a tank tuple with tcolor = red, the judgment is true. Otherwise it is false.

In this example, the domain of the atomic predicate redTank is the collection of tuples in the aquarium database. The complete definition of an atomic predicate must specify the domain of each argument. As an example from a different domain, let $P(x)$ be the predicate $x < 4$ with domain the natural numbers, $0, 1, 2, \ldots$. $P(x)$ is true for $x = 0, 1, 2, 3$, but it is false for other values in the domain. Predicates can depend on several variables. For example, suppose that $P(x, y)$ is $x + y < 6$, with the domain of each argument being the natural numbers. For certain (x, y) pairs this expression is true; for others it is false. A predicate might have *no* arguments, in which case it has a constant true or false value. For example, if P is the expression $2 + 4 = 6$, it is always true. Predicates with no arguments are **propositions**.

 An atomic predicate is a function that evaluates to true or false, reflecting an elementary judgment on the application domain. The domain of an atomic predicate is the set of elements for which the predicate returns such a judgment.

A **well-formed formula (WFF)** is an expression composed ultimately of atomic predicates. A WFF is itself a predicate, which assumes a true or false value depending on the argument values in its constituent atomic predicates. The simplest WFFs are the atomic predicates themselves. From this seed collection, you form additional WFFs by combining existing WFFs with logical operators. For example, if a, b are two WFFs, then $(a \wedge b)$ is also a WFF. $(a \wedge b)$ is true for precisely those argument values of a and b for which both a and b are true. Figure 4.1 gives the basic set of logical operators that can be used to produce new WFFs from existing WFFs; it also shows the truth values of the new WFF as a consequence of the truth values of the components. In particular, if X and Y are WFFs, then so are $\neg X$, $(X \wedge Y)$, $(X \vee Y)$, and $(X \Rightarrow Y)$. These combinations are negation, logical "and," logical "or," and logical implication respectively.

Atomic predicates constitute the first layer of WFFs. The operations of Figure 4.1 then combine the atomic predicates into a second layer. Further application of the same operations then produces yet more complicated WFFs, and so on indefinitely. The arguments of a WFF are all the arguments of the constituent atomic predicates, each with its associated domain. For example, if P_1, P_2, P_3 are atomic predicates, the following expression defines a WFF with three arguments:

$$Q(x, y, z) = ((P_1(x, y) \land P_2(x)) \lor \neg P_3(y, z)).$$

Two further operations create new WFFs from existing ones: existential and universal quantification. Each produces a result with fewer arguments than its operand. As an example of existential quantification, consider

$$Q(w, x) = (\exists y, z)(P(w, x, y, z)).$$

For a fixed (w, x) pair, if $P(w, x, y, z)$ is true for some choice of a (y, z) pair, $Q(w, x)$ is true. Otherwise it is false. The arguments of an atomic predicate, or of a WFF over such predicates using the connectives of Figure 4.1, are called **free variables**. These variables are free to assume any value in their respective domains, thereby determining the truth value of the composite WFF. In the example above, $w, x, y,$ and z are free variables in $P(w, x, y, z)$. The truth value of P varies as these variables assume different values within their domains. However, in the expression $(\exists y, z)(P(w, x, y, z))$, the variables y and z are no longer free. They are "consumed" in the process of quantifying P. Only w and x remain free to assume any value in their domains. When w and x settle on values, then $(\exists y, z)(P(w, x, y, z))$ assumes a value. That value is true *if P is true for some felicitous choice of (y, z), together with the fixed values of (w, x)*. On the other hand, $(\exists y, z)(P(w, x, y, z))$ is false if all (y, z) pairs in their respective domains leave $P(w, x, y, z)$ false. So the value of $(\exists y, z)(P(w, x, y, z))$ is determined once (w, x) is determined. In the expression $(\exists y, z)(P(w, x, y, z))$, the variables y and z are called **bound variables**.

In a WFF, each variable is either free or bound. A variable is bound if a quantifier introduces it. Bound variables are consumed in the process that determines the truth value of the WFF. A variable that isn't bound is free.

Suppose that $P(x, y)$ is the expression $y^2 = x$ and that the domains of both variables are the natural numbers, $0, 1, 2, \ldots$. Then $Q(x) = (\exists y)(P(x, y))$ depends only on x. $Q(7)$ is false because there is no choice of y in the natural numbers such that $y^2 = 7$. However, $Q(16)$ is true because the choice $y = 4$ makes $4^2 = 16$ true. The free variables of a predicate, atomic predicate or WFF, serve as ports. When certain values from the corresponding domains bind to these ports, the predicate delivers a true or false judgment on that combination of values. When existential quantification is applied to a WFF, any variables mentioned in the $(\exists \cdots)$ portion become bound, and the resulting WFF no longer reflects these variables as arguments. For a more complex example, note that the result of the following quantification contains a single free variable.

$$Q(x) = (P_1(x) \lor (\exists y)(P_2(x, y) \land (\exists z)(P_3(x) \lor P_4(x, y, z)))).$$

You can envision intermediate WFFs as follows, each with the free variables indicated.

$$
\begin{aligned}
Q_1(x, y, z) &= (P_3(x) \lor P_4(x, y, z)) \\
Q_2(x, y) &= (\exists z)(Q_1(x, y, z)) \\
Q_3(x, y) &= (P_2(x, y) \land Q_2(x, y)) \\
Q_4(x) &= (\exists y)(Q_3(x, y)) \\
Q(x) &= (P_1(x) \lor Q_4(x)).
\end{aligned}
$$

If the target of an existential quantification doesn't contain one or more of the variables specified in the $(\exists \cdots)$ portion, that portion of the quantification is redundant and can be removed. For example,

$$(\exists y)(P(x)) = P(x).$$

$(\exists y)(P(x))$ is true if some inspired choice of y permits $P(x)$ to be true. Because $P(x)$ doesn't depend on y, however, any choice for y is as good as any other. If the domain of y is the natural numbers, for example, choose $y = 1$. The truth value of $(\exists y)(P(x))$ then reduces to the truth value of $P(x)$. If $P(x)$ is true, then the chosen y suffices and $(\exists y)(P(x))$ is true. If $P(x)$ is false, then the chosen y fails, but any other choice would have failed as well. Therefore, $(\exists y)(P(x))$ is false. Because the target of the quantification below doesn't depend on x, you can reason that

$$(\exists x, y)(P(y, z)) = (\exists y)(P(y, z)).$$

Universal quantification is similar, except that the composite WFF is true when *all* choices of the quantified variable render the target true. For example,

$$Q(y) = (\forall x)(P(x, y))$$

is true, for some fixed y, when all domain values of x render $P(x, y)$ true. As with existential quantification, the variables specified with the quantifier are "consumed" in the process of determining the truth value of the result. So if x is a free variable in $P(\ldots, x, \ldots)$, it is bound in $(\forall x)(P(\ldots, x, \ldots))$.

Suppose all domains are the natural numbers and that $P(x, y)$ is $x + y > 4$. Then $Q(x) = (\forall y)(P(x, y))$ depends only on x because y is used up in the calculation. If $x = 0, 1, 2, 3$, or 4, then $Q(x)$ is false. In each of these cases, the choice $y = 0$ makes $x + y \leq 4$ and therefore $P(x, y)$ false. However, for $x > 4$, any choice of y in the natural numbers yields $x + y > 4$, and therefore $P(x, y)$ is true for all such choices of y. This observation makes $Q(x) = (\forall y)(P(x, y))$ true for $x > 4$.

You can remove from a universal quantification any variable that isn't present in the target predicate. For example,

$$(\forall x, y)(P(y, z)) = (\forall y)(P(y, z)).$$

The following formulas convert existential quantification into universal quantification and vice versa.

$$(\forall x)(P(x, y)) = \neg(\exists x)(\neg P(x, y)). \tag{4.1}$$
$$(\exists x)(P(x, y)) = \neg(\forall x)(\neg P(x, y)).$$

For a given y, $(\forall x)(P(x, y))$ is true if there are no counterexamples. That is, if there are no x values that render $P(x, y)$ false. If it's not the case that there exists a x with $\neg P(x, y)$ true. Conversely, if there are no x values that render $P(x, y)$ false for a given fixed y, then $P(x, y)$ must be true for all values of x and that fixed y. Similar reasoning establishes the second formula.

The set of well-formed formulas (WFFs) arises from the initial atomic predicates by recursive application of the logical operators $(\wedge, \vee, \neg, \Rightarrow, (\exists \cdots), (\forall \cdots))$ to existing members of the collection. Precise rules assign a truth value to the composite WFF in terms of the truth values of its atomic predicates.

At the lowest level, a WFF contains atomic predicates. The atomic predicates evaluate to true or false depending on the values of their arguments. These truth values then propagate out to determine the truth values of the intermediate expressions and, finally, the truth value of the composite WFF. Consider the WFF

$$Q(x, y) = ((\exists z)(P_1(x, z)) \wedge (\forall z)(P_2(y, z))).$$

For a fixed (x, y), suppose there is a value z_1 such that $P_1(x, z_1)$ is true and a second value z_2 such that $P(y, z_2)$ is false. Then $(\exists z)(P_1(x, z))$ is true, but $(\forall z)(P_2(y, z))$ is false. Therefore, $Q(x, y)$ is false.

A WFF is a formal string of symbols. It is "well-formed" because it's a proper assembly of the underlying atomic predicates. For example, $(P_1(x, y) \wedge P_2(y)$ isn't a WFF because it lacks the final closing parenthesis. An algorithm can check whether a candidate expression is a WFF. A valid WFF achieves meaning in some problem domain only through the truth values returned by its lowest level components, the atomic predicates. These predicates reveal interesting conditions and relationships within the application; a WFF merely reflects standard combinations of these basic informational elements. An atomic predicate is then an indecomposable function that extracts a single elementary fact from the application domain. In terms of its atomic predicates, a WFF represents a truth judgment on a more complicated statement about the application domain. So a WFF differs from an atomic predicate only because the WFF is a more complicated true-false judgment. Because of this similarity, the term predicate will, from now on, refer either to an atomic predicate or to a WFF constructed on such atomic predicates.

 A predicate is a function that evaluates to true or false depending on the values of its free variables. It can be an atomic predicate, which is an indecomposable truth judgment of some elementary fact in the application domain, or it can be a WFF, which is a logical combination of elementary judgments.

Some slight simplification of the notation will be helpful. As defined above, a WFF is a formal string of symbols, constructed through some sequence of rules from its atomic predicates. The rules are either the connectives of Figure 4.1 or the quantifiers. The composition of a WFF can accumulate numerous of parentheses, which detract from the interpretation of the result. The first simplification omits any parentheses at the outermost level. For example, write $(a \wedge b)$ as $a \wedge b$. Second, regard the unary operators, $\neg, (\exists \cdots), (\forall \cdots)$, as having higher precedence than the binary operators, $\wedge, \vee, \Rightarrow$. Apply unary operators from right to left, starting with the one closest to its argument. For example, write $(\forall x)(\exists y)\neg(\exists z)(P(x, y, z, w))$ instead of $(\forall x)((\exists y)(\neg(\exists z)(P(x, y, z, w))))$. Finally, because $\wedge$ and $\vee$ are associative, certain parentheses are redundant. For example, $a \wedge (b \wedge c)$ has the same truth table as $(a \wedge b) \wedge c$. So, define $a \wedge b \wedge c$, without any parentheses, as either one of the previous expressions. In this manner, a sequence of conjuncts (i.e., operands separated by a $\wedge$) requires no intervening parentheses. A similar statement holds for a sequence of disjuncts, which are operands separated by a ($\vee$).

Selection via a predicate

The familiar set-builder notation, $\{x \mid P(x)\}$, expresses a query by means of a predicate. Here, x ranges over the collection of candidate elements, and $P(x)$ is a predicate, which evaluates to true for those candidates that should be part of the answer. For example, if the domain of candidates is the set of natural numbers, the solution set $\{4, 5, 6, 7\}$ answers the query $\{x \mid 4 \le x \le 7\}$. If the domain of candidates is the set of tuples in a relational database, this notational system is called **tuple relational calculus**. An example of a tuple relational calculus expression is: $\{t \mid \text{tank}(t) \wedge \text{tcolor}(t) = \text{"red"}\}$. The domain of candidates is the set of all tuples from the aquarium relational database. The atomic predicate tank(t) responds true when the tuple t is an element of the tank relation. The function tcolor(t) returns the tcolor value of the tuple t, and the atomic predicate tcolor$(t) = \text{"red"}$ tests the returned value against a constant. Therefore the complete predicate (WFF) isolates the tuples corresponding to red tanks.

This example illustrates the need for two types of atomic predicates, which render elementary truth judgments on the database. The first type tests membership in some named relation. Each table in the database gives rise to an atomic predicate of the same name, which takes one argument. The predicate returns true when the argument is a tuple within the table, and it returns false in all other cases. For example, tank(t) is true when the tuple t is an element of the tank relation, and it's false otherwise. In the aquarium example, the predicates species(t), fish(t), and event(t) provide similar judgments for the other tables.

The second type of atomic predicate permits judgments about the attribute values within tuples. Every attribute in the database gives rise to a one-argument function of the same name. When the argument is a tuple that contains an association over the named attribute, then the function returns the corresponding value. If the tuple doesn't contain such an association, then the function returns the value null. For example, tcolor(t) returns the tcolor value of the tuple t, that is, red, blue, or green, if t contains a tcolor value. Otherwise, tcolor(t) returns null. The latter case occurs, for example, if t is a fish tuple, which contains no tcolor attribute. Atomic predicates arise from traditional arithmetic or string comparisons between the values returned by these attribute functions and constants, or between two such returned values. For example, tcolor$(t) = \text{"red"}$ is true if tuple t has a tcolor value and that value is red.

The domain of both kinds of atomic predicates is the collection of all tuples in the database. Therefore, each domain element is a set of associations over the attributes of a relation. Each element also carries the name of its home relation so that a table membership predicate can give a true or false judgment on it. For the aquarium database, Figure 4.2 shows several elements of this common domain for all predicates.

 For each table R, $R(t)$ is true when t is a tuple from the body of R. $A(t)$ returns the value of attribute A from tuple t, if t has such a value. Otherwise, $A(t)$ returns null. Arithmetic and string comparisons combine attribute functions to form atomic predicates.

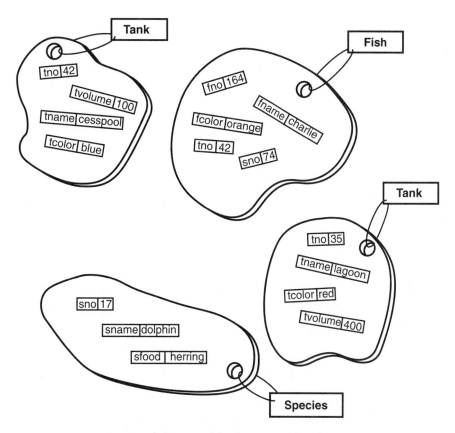

Figure 4.2   Typical elements of the domain pool for relational calculus

In summary, relational calculus is a notation for extracting information from a database by means of an extended predicate. The predicate is a WFF over a restricted set of atomic predicates:

- $R(t)$, where R is the name of a relation in the database

- $a(t) \, \theta \, v$, where a is an attribute name, v is a constant and θ is one of the comparison operators, $<, \le, >, \ge, =$, or one of their complements, such as $\ne$

- $a(t) \, \theta \, b(s)$, where a and b are attribute names and θ is as above

A query expression uses set-builder notation, with a collection of free variables to the left of a vertical bar and the predicate to the right. The predicate can introduce additional bound variables with existential and universal quantifiers.

Relational calculus is a notation for expressing queries in set-builder form $\{x \mid P(x)\}$.
The predicate $P(x)$ is a WFF over atomic predicates, which extract two types of
elementary facts: relation membership, such as $R(t)$, or attribute comparison, such as
$a(t) = b(s)$.

The following single-table query, for example, finds the red tanks with volume greater than 300. The defining predicate is a WFF in the argument t. It isolates the large red tanks from the mass of other database tuples.

$$\{t \mid \text{tank}(t) \wedge \text{tcolor}(t) = \text{``red''} \wedge \text{tvolume}(t) > 300\}.$$

Because most queries request specific attributes of the isolated tuples, the set-builder format requires further notation to report such attributes values. You simply indicate the desired attributes with the functions already available. If you want the names of red tanks of volume greater than 300, you rewrite the query above as:

$$\{\text{tname}(t) \mid \text{tank}(t) \wedge \text{tcolor}(t) = \text{``red''} \wedge \text{tvolume}(t) > 300\}.$$

For multitable queries, certain quantifications conduct implicit searches for matching tuples. For example, consider the query: find the colors of fish representing a **shark** species.

$$\{\text{fcolor}(f) \mid \text{fish}(f) \wedge (\exists s)(\text{species}(s) \wedge \text{sname}(s) = \text{``shark''} \wedge \text{sno}(f) = \text{sno}(s))\}.$$

Besides the free variable f, the predicate uses a bound variable s, which is consumed in evaluating the predicate for a particular value of f. Although s ranges over all tuples in the database, the target of the existential quantification, $(\text{species}(s) \wedge \ldots)$, immediately fails if the s value is outside of the species relation. When s assumes values in the species relation, the first part of the target returns true. The second part, $(\text{sname}(s) = \text{``shark''})$, then checks for the proper sname value. Certain s tuples fail at this point, but others continue to the final part, $(\text{sno}(f) = \text{sno}(s))$, which checks for identical sno values between that wandering s and the fixed f. If somewhere in species an s occurs that satisfies these conditions, the quantified target returns true and allows the f to contribute its fcolor value to the answer.

Unlike the natural join, the corresponding construction in relational algebra, existential quantification doesn't build a new table. It specifies only the desired result, without indicating a particular mechanism for the search. The question is simply: does there exist, somewhere in the combined mass of database tuples, some particular s that satisfies all conditions of the quantified target? If so, f currently represents a fish that should contribute to the answer. If no such s exists, f makes no contribution.

Extension to more tables is straightforward. For example, find the names of fish representing a species named shark and swimming in a pool named cesspool.

$$\{\text{fname}(f) \mid \begin{aligned}[t] &\text{fish}(f) \wedge (\exists s, t)(\text{species}(s) \wedge \text{tank}(t) \wedge \\ &\text{tno}(f) = \text{tno}(t) \wedge \text{sno}(f) = \text{sno}(s) \wedge \text{sname}(s) = \text{``shark''} \wedge \text{tname}(t) = \text{``cesspool''})\}. \end{aligned}$$

As the free variable f ranges across all tuples in the database, the fish(f) predicate immediately disqualifies those bindings where f isn't a fish. For the f that are fish, a further test requires that the s and t variables bind to a species and tank respectively, which properly connect the f to a shark and to a cesspool.

These conditions should be familiar. A candidate contributes to the answer if a path exists to an anchor tuple elsewhere in the database. This condition is the defining characteristic of an existential query. Indeed, the name "existential" comes from the use of existential quantifiers in the relational calculus solution. The pattern for constructing a relational calculus expression for an existential query is apparent. You first force a free variable to represent the type of tuple under search, and then you forge the required links with new variables introduced through an existential quantifier. Consider the longer query: find the names of species swimming in the same tank with a species named shark.

$$\{\text{sname}(s) \quad | \quad \text{species}(s) \wedge (\exists f, t, f_1, s_1)(\text{fish}(f) \wedge \text{tank}(t) \wedge \text{fish}(f_1) \wedge \text{species}(s_1) \wedge$$
$$\text{sno}(s) = \text{sno}(f) \wedge \text{tno}(f) = \text{tno}(t) \wedge \text{tno}(t) = \text{tno}(f_1) \wedge$$
$$\text{sno}(f_1) = \text{sno}(s_1) \wedge \text{sname}(s_1) = \text{``shark''})\}.$$

Recalling the relational algebra solution in Chapter 3, you will remember that the tank t served only to provide a tno value, forcing the two fish tuples f and f_1 to cohabit. You can omit the tank variable here because you can enforce the cohabitation condition by directly equating the foreign keys in the fish tuples. The expression then simplifies to

$$\{\text{sname}(s) \quad | \quad \text{species}(s) \wedge (\exists f, f_1, s_1)(\text{fish}(f) \wedge \text{fish}(f_1) \wedge \text{species}(s_1) \wedge$$
$$\text{sno}(s) = \text{sno}(f) \wedge \text{tno}(f) = \text{tno}(f_1) \wedge \text{sno}(f_1) = \text{sno}(s_1) \wedge \text{sname}(s_1) = \text{``shark''})\}.$$

Both solutions involve multiple copies of the fish and species relations. Relational algebra requires certain renaming operations to distinguish among the copies. In relational calculus, however, all variables already range over all tuples in the database. Therefore, a given variable certainly visits the relation where it is needed to form a link in the database path under construction. The predicate associated with this intended relation eliminates extraneous possibilities. In the example above, the predicate fish(f) ensures that any combinations in which f isn't a fish tuple won't contribute to the path under construction. Also, the bound variables, f_1 and s_1, are effectively constrained to particular relations, Fish and Species, by the predicates fish(f_1) and species(s_1), which occur immediately after the variables appear.

Another query from the previous chapter illustrates that you can select several attributes for the answer and that these selections can come from different free variables. Find the names of pairs of fish swimming in the same tank.

$$\{\text{fname}(f_1), \text{fname}(f_2) \mid \text{fish}(f_1) \wedge \text{fish}(f_2) \wedge \text{tno}(f_1) = \text{tno}(f_2) \wedge \text{fno}(f_1) < \text{fno}(f_2)\}.$$

The following query demonstrates a yet longer existential path: Find the names of species swimming in the same tank with a species that is represented in a red tank. The relational algebra solution lines up enough copies of the relevant tables to capture the necessary path with a Cartesian product.

$$\pi_q \sigma_b (\check{\rho}(S = \text{species}) \times \check{\rho}(F = \text{fish}) \times \check{\rho}(T = \text{tank}) \times \check{\rho}(G = \text{fish}) \times \check{\rho}(H = \text{species}) \times \check{\rho}(I = \text{fish}) \times \check{\rho}(J = \text{tank})),$$
$$\text{where } b \quad = \quad (S.\text{sno} = F.\text{sno} \wedge F.\text{tno} = T.\text{tno} \wedge T.\text{tno} = G.\text{tno} \wedge G.\text{sno} = H.\text{sno} \wedge H.\text{sno} = I.\text{sno} \wedge$$
$$I.\text{tno} = J.\text{tno} \wedge J.\text{tcolor} = \text{``red''})$$
$$q \quad = \quad (S.\text{sname}).$$

The relational calculus solution follows a similar pattern. It constrains a free variable to the species relation, where it systematically visits each candidate. For each candidate, the relational calculus expression introduces a collection of bound variables with an existential quantifier, attempting to capture the path to a red tank tuple. The expression immediately constrains each bound variable to a particular relation where it will play the proper role in extending the chain.

$$\{\text{sname}(s) \quad | \quad \text{species}(s) \wedge (\exists f, t, g, h, i, j)(\text{fish}(f) \wedge \text{tank}(t) \wedge \text{fish}(g) \wedge \text{species}(h) \wedge \text{fish}(i) \wedge \text{tank}(j) \wedge$$
$$\text{sno}(s) = \text{sno}(f) \wedge \text{tno}(f) = \text{tno}(t) \wedge \text{tno}(t) = \text{tno}(g) \wedge \text{sno}(g) = \text{sno}(h) \wedge$$
$$\text{sno}(h) = \text{sno}(i) \wedge \text{tno}(i) = \text{tno}(j) \wedge \text{tcolor}(j) = \text{``red''})\}.$$

Existential queries

In an existential query, a candidate tuple contributes to the answer if a path exists that links it to an anchor tuple elsewhere in the database. The path typically links tuples through matching values in their common attributes. The standard form of a relational algebra solution is as follows, where the selection operator enforces the linkages. Here the $b_1, b_2, \ldots$ are the linking attributes, and the $a_1, a_2, \ldots$ are the attributes requested in the query. The notation $(X_i.a_1, X_j.a_2, \ldots)$ means that the attribute values in the answer come from various tables along the path.

$$\pi_q \sigma_b (\breve{\rho}(X_1 = R_{i_1}) \times \breve{\rho}(X_2 = R_{i_2}) \times \breve{\rho}(X_3 = R_{i_3}) \times \ldots, \text{ where} \quad b \quad = \quad (X_1.b_1 = X_2.b_1 \wedge X_2.b_2 = X_3.b_2 \wedge \ldots)$$
$$q \quad = \quad (X_i.a_1, X_j.a_2, \ldots).$$

The relational calculus equivalent is easy to construct. You first draw a distinction between the links that contribute values to the answer and those that remain anonymous in the path. For example, suppose the query requests the names of species-tank pairs such that the species resides in the tank with a **shark**. Five tables must line up to provide the proper path, but only two contribute values to the answer. In the following relational algebra solution, species S and tank T contribute sname and tname values to the answer. The remaining tables serve only to construct the path and to specify the anchor species.

$$\pi_q \sigma_b (\breve{\rho}(S = \text{species}) \times \breve{\rho}(F = \text{fish}) \times \breve{\rho}(T = \text{tank}) \times \breve{\rho}(G = \text{fish}) \times \breve{\rho}(H = \text{species}))$$
$$\text{where} \quad b \quad = \quad (S.\text{sno} = F.\text{sno} \wedge F.\text{tno} = T.\text{tno} \wedge T.\text{tno} = G.\text{tno} \wedge G.\text{sno} = H.\text{sno} \wedge H.\text{sname} = \text{``shark''})$$
$$q \quad = \quad (S.\text{sname}, T.\text{tname}).$$

For the equivalent relational calculus, you specify free variables, $t_1, t_2, \ldots$, for each relation that contributes to the answer. The first part of the relational calculus solution indicates how to extract the selected attributes from these tuples and how to restrict the tuples to particular tables. The expression then begins as follows:

$$\{a_1(t_1), a_2(t_1), a_3(t_2), \ldots \quad | \quad R_1(t_1) \wedge R_2(t_2) \wedge \ldots\}.$$

The template shows two attributes extracted from table R_1 (a_1 and a_2), one from R_2, and the pattern continues as necessary. In general, any table in the path can contribute any number of attributes. The first part of the boolean condition forces t_1 to range over R_1, t_2 to range over R_2, and so forth. In the example above, the reported attributes are sname and tname, which are drawn from the species and tank relations respectively. So this query begins as follows:

$$\{\text{sname}(s), \text{tname}(t) \quad | \quad \text{species}(s) \wedge \text{tank}(t) \wedge \ldots\}.$$

Next, you assign bound variables, $v_1, v_2, \ldots$, to the remaining relations in the path. An existential quantifier introduces these variables, and the scope of the quantifier contains conditions to restrict each variable to its proper table and to match up the links in the chain. The complete general form then appears as follows.

$$\{a_1(t_1), a_2(t_1), a_3(t_2), \ldots \quad | \quad R_1(t_1) \wedge R_2(t_2) \wedge \ldots \wedge (\exists v_1, v_2, \ldots)(S_1(v_1) \wedge S_2(v_2) \wedge \ldots$$
$$\wedge b_1(v_i) = b_1(t_j) \wedge \ldots \wedge c_1(v_k) = \text{"anchor value"})\}.$$

The tables $S_1, S_2, \ldots$ serve as links in the existential chain, but they don't deliver any attributes to the answer set. You must restrict each of the existentially quantified variables to one of these tables. In truth, the variables are free to range over all tuples in the database. However, unless a variable, say v_1, assumes a value in its proper table, S_1, the predicate $S_1(v_1)$ returns false, and the entire condition fails. So "restricted to a particular table" really means that only values in a particular table have a chance of making the overall condition true.

The rest of the boolean expression forces the tuples to line up as required for the database path, and it also identifies the anchor tuple. The pattern shows $b_1(v_i) = b_1(t_j)$, meaning that attribute b_1 links the tables over which v_i and t_j range. The arrangement shown implies that one of the tables is the range of a free variable and the other of a bound variable. This is just one of several possibilities because tables corresponding to free and bound variables can occur interwoven in the path. Adjacent matches might involve two bound variables, two free variables, or one of each. In the example above, the tables corresponding to the free variables occur in positions 1 and 3 in the 5-table path. The final solution to that query takes the form:

$$\{\text{sname}(s), \text{tname}(t) \quad | \quad \text{species}(s) \wedge \text{tank}(t) \wedge (\exists f, g, h)(\text{fish}(f) \wedge \text{fish}(g) \wedge \text{species}(h) \wedge$$
$$\text{sno}(s) = \text{sno}(f) \wedge \text{tno}(f) = \text{tno}(t) \wedge \text{tno}(t) = \text{tno}(g) \wedge \text{sno}(g) = \text{sno}(h) \wedge$$
$$\text{sname}(h) = \text{"shark"})\}.$$

This format indicates a final boolean component that compares the anchor value with some attribute of a bound variable. In general, however, the anchor value could compare with one of the free variables.

Although this simple algorithm readily translates existential relational algebra queries into relational calculus, the more frequent requirement is the reverse translation. The basic information retrieval question is: find the desired information. The problem, of course, is isolating the desired information from the larger mass of irrelevant data in the same database tables. Therefore, for each fact that might be reported, a test must exist to determine if it's appropriate for the query under consideration. In other words, there must be a predicate that will return true for precisely the desired facts. It follows that the original query will likely occur in a non-procedural predicate form and require a translation into the procedural relational algebra for execution.

You can easily reverse the algebra-to-calculus translation above *if* you start with a relational calculus expression in the proper form. That format must have a sequence of free and bound variables, each restricted to a particular table, and a boolean expression forcing correct foreign key alignments. The format must also use a single existential quantifier to introduce several bound variables.

 Tuple relational calculus expresses an existential query by first assigning free variables to all relations that contribute values to the answer. It then introduces sufficient bound variables with an existential quantifier to identify the anchor tuple and to define a path to it. It restricts each variable to a single table.

Universal queries

Consider the query: find the names of tanks that contain no fish. You can construct a relational calculus solution by negating an existential quantification, as shown below.

$$Q = \{\text{tname}(t) \mid \text{tank}(t) \land \neg(\exists f)(\text{fish}(f) \land \text{tno}(t) = \text{tno}(f))\}. \qquad (4.2)$$

The corresponding relational algebra uses a set difference to subtract the inhabited tanks from the collection of all tanks.

$$\pi_q(\pi_r(\text{tank}) - \pi_r(\text{tank} * \text{fish}))), \text{ where } \quad r \;=\; (\text{tno, tname})$$
$$q \;=\; (\text{tname}).$$

A negated existential quantification means that a certain subset is empty, as emphasized in the alternative form:

$$Q \quad = \quad \{\text{tname}(t) \mid \text{tank}(t) \land Q_1(t) = \varphi\}$$
$$Q_1(t) \quad = \quad \{f \mid \text{fish}(f) \land \text{tno}(t) = \text{tno}(f)\}.$$

To see that Equation 4.2 is a disguised case of universal quantification, you can use Equations 4.1 to convert the negated existential quantification into non-negated universal quantification.

$$Q = \{\text{tname}(t) \mid \text{tank}(t) \land (\forall f)(\neg\text{fish}(f) \lor \text{tno}(t) \neq \text{tno}(f))\}.$$

A tank qualifies for the answer if, for all tuples f in the database, either f isn't a fish, in which case it's not relevant; or f is a fish, but it doesn't swim in the tank. If p and q are arbitrary predicates, $\neg p \lor q$ is equivalent to $p \Rightarrow q$. This condition, therefore, is equivalent to an implication. In other words, a tank qualifies if, for all tuples f in the database, $\text{fish}(f) \Rightarrow$ (f doesn't swim in the tank). Symbolically,

$$Q = \{\text{tname}(t) \mid \text{tank}(t) \land (\forall f)(\text{fish}(f) \Rightarrow \text{tno}(t) \neq \text{tno}(f))\}.$$

As a second example, consider again a universal query from the previous chapter: find the names of species represented in all tanks. A species qualifies if, for all tuples t in the database, either t isn't a tank; or t is a tank, and it holds a representative of the species. Either of the two equivalent forms below expresses this condition.

$$\{\text{sname}(s) \mid \text{species}(s) \wedge (\forall t)(\neg\text{tank}(t) \vee (\exists f)(\text{fish}(f) \wedge \text{tno}(t)$$
$$= \text{tno}(f) \wedge \text{sno}(f) = \text{sno}(s)))\}. \tag{4.3}$$

$$\{\text{sname}(s) \mid \text{species}(s) \wedge (\forall t)(\text{tank}(t) \Rightarrow (\exists f)(\text{fish}(f) \wedge \text{tno}(t)$$
$$= \text{tno}(f) \wedge \text{sno}(f) = \text{sno}(s)))\}. \tag{4.4}$$

To see how these solutions compare with the standard relational algebra approach, you can transform Equation 4.3 to convert the quantification to existential form.

$$Q = \{\text{sname}(s) \mid \text{species}(s) \wedge \neg(\exists t)(\text{tank}(t) \wedge \neg(\exists f)(\text{fish}(f) \wedge \text{tno}(t) = \text{tno}(f) \wedge \text{sno}(f) = \text{sno}(s)))\}.$$

As in the first example of this section, you can then replace the negated existential quantifications with set comparisons to obtain

$$\begin{aligned}
Q &= \{\text{sname}(s) \mid \text{species}(s) \wedge Q_1(s) = \varphi\} \\
Q_1(s) &= \{t \mid \text{tank}(t) \wedge Q_2(s,t) = \varphi\} \\
Q_2(s,t) &= \{f \mid \text{fish}(f) \wedge \text{tno}(t) = \text{tno}(f) \wedge \text{sno}(f) = \text{sno}(s)\}.
\end{aligned}$$

$Q_2(s,t)$ is the collection of fish associated with some (s,t) species-tank pair. You can envision $Q_2(s,t)$ as the segmented table shown on the left below. Each segment is an (s,t) pair, containing all of the related fish in the third column. A segment appears for every (s,t) pair *unless* that (s,t) pair have no fish in common. Carrying along only the key and name attributes, you can construct Q_2 with relational algebra as

$$Q_2 = \pi_q(\text{species} * \text{fish} * \text{tank}), \text{ where } q = (\text{sno, sname, tno, tname, fno, fname}).$$

$Q_1(s)$ is likewise envisioned as a segmented table, with one segment for each s value. A second column holds the tanks, t, such that the corresponding (s,t) segment of the $Q_2(s,t)$ table is empty. The Q_1 table appears in the center below.

$Q_2(s,t)$			$Q_1(s)$		Q
species	tank	fish	species	tank	species
s_1	t_1	f_{111}	s_1	t_1	s_1
s_1	t_1	f_{112}	s_1	t_2	s_2
s_1	t_1	f_{113}	s_1	t_3	s_3
$\vdots$	$\vdots$	$\vdots$	$\vdots$	$\vdots$	$\vdots$
s_1	t_2	f_{121}	s_2	t_1	
s_1	t_2	f_{122}	s_2	t_2	
$\vdots$	$\vdots$	$\vdots$	$\vdots$	$\vdots$	

You can construct the Q_1 table in relational algebra by starting with the collection of all (s,t) pairs and then subtracting the (s,t) pairs that appear in Q_2 with one or more fish:

$$Q_1 = \pi_r(\text{species} \times \text{tank}) - \pi_r(Q_2), \text{ where } r = (\text{sno, sname, tno, tname}).$$

An (s,t) pair appears in Q_1 if and only if it isn't erased by a corresponding (s,t) pair projected from Q_2. This non-erasure happens precisely when the (s,t) segment of Q_2 is empty. Finally, Q corresponds to a table of species in which s appears if the corresponding segment of Q_1 is empty. The Q table, shown on the far right above, is constructed as follows:

$$Q = \pi_t(\text{species}) - \pi_t(Q_1), \text{ where } t = (\text{sno, sname}).$$

Putting the three pieces together, with a modification to project only sname in the final answer, you obtain the double-set-negation in Chapter 3, which led directly to the definition of relational division.

$$Q = \pi_q\{\pi_r(\text{species}) - \pi_r[\pi_s(\text{species} \times \text{tank}) - \pi_s(\text{species} * \text{fish} * \text{tank})]\},$$

where s = (sno, sname, tno, tname)
       r = (sno, sname)
       q = (sname).

Recalling Equation 3.3, $R_1/R_2 = \pi_q(R_1) - \pi_q[(\pi_q(R_1) \times R_2) - R_1]$, where q lists the excess attributes of R_1 over R_2, you can identify

$R_1 = \pi_s(\text{species} * \text{fish} * \text{tank})$ where s = (sno, sname, tno, tname)
$R_2 = \pi_v(\text{tank}),$ v = (tno, tname).

If a single tank exists in which species s isn't represented, $Q_1(s) \neq \varphi$, implying that $s \notin Q$. Therefore, although the construction for Q starts with the species table (from which certain subtractions are made), it can use the set of species projected from (species * fish * tank) instead and produce the same final result. Any species that don't appear in the join can't compete to enter Q. However, such species wouldn't succeed in entering Q anyway. Also, $\pi_s(\text{species} \times \text{tank}) = \pi_r(\text{species}) \times \pi_v(\text{tank})$. So a final rewrite of Q produces:

$$Q = \pi_q\{\pi_r(R_1) - \pi_r[\pi_r(\text{species}) \times \pi_v(\text{tank}) - R_1]\} = \pi_q\{\pi_r(R_1) - \pi_r[\pi_r(R_1) \times R_2 - R_1]\} = \pi_q(R_1/R_2).$$

You should now recognize the standard format for a universal query in relational algebra. Equation 4.3 leads to two negated existential quantifiers, which in turn lead to a double-set-difference construction in relational algebra. This last construction is equivalent to a relational division, which is the standard format for a universal query.

The alternative form of Equation 4.4 provides a more natural template for directly expressing universal queries in relational calculus. Recall the defining characteristic of a universal query: a candidate tuple contributes to the answer by originating a full bundle of paths sufficient to embrace a collection of anchor tuples elsewhere in the database. Examining the format of Equation 4.4, you find the usual conditions that restrict the variables to specific tables plus a universal quantification of the form:

$$(\forall t)((t \text{ is an anchor}) \Rightarrow (t \text{ is reachable from the candidate})).$$

In Equation 4.4, the universally quantified component of the predicate states: if t is an anchor tuple (i.e., a tank), it must be reachable from s (i.e., the candidate tuple). The existence of a common fish then expresses the reachability condition.

Relational calculus expresses a universal query by assigning free variables to the relation providing the candidates. It then introduces a universally quantified component, stating $(\forall t)((t\text{ is an anchor}) \Rightarrow (t\text{ is reachable from the candidate}))$.

Consider the following, more extensive universal query, which illustrates a universal bundle of paths traversing the database twice. Find the names of species represented in all tanks that contain representatives of all species with a diet of worms. A stepwise construction proceeds as follows.

$$Q = \{\text{sname}(s) \quad | \quad \text{species}(s) \land (\forall t)(P_1(t) \Rightarrow (\exists f)(\text{fish}(f) \land$$
$$\text{sno}(f) \quad = \quad \text{sno}(s) \land \text{tno}(f) = \text{tno}(t)))\}, \tag{4.5}$$

where $P_1(t)$ is true when t is a tank that contains all the wormy species. The universally quantified component expresses the condition: if t is an anchor (i.e., one of an elite set of tanks), it is reachable from the candidate through a common fish. Therefore, $P_1(t)$ is

$$P_1(t) = \text{tank}(t) \land (\forall s_1)(P_2(s_1) \quad \Rightarrow \quad (\exists f_1)(\text{fish}(f_1) \land$$
$$\text{sno}(f_1) \quad = \quad \text{sno}(s_1) \land \text{tno}(f_1) = \text{tno}(t))), \tag{4.6}$$

where $P_2(s_1)$ is true when s_1 is a wormy species. That is,

$$P_2(s_1) = \text{species}(s_1) \land \text{sfood}(s_1) = \text{``worms''}. \tag{4.7}$$

Substituting P_2 into P_1 and then P_1 into Q gives a single WFF that effectively filters the database for the requested species names.

Equation 4.4 typifies the standard format for universal queries in relational calculus. However, the alternative format of Equation 4.3 is useful in demonstrating equivalence with the standard relational algebra format. To illustrate yet another format, consider again the query: find the names of species that are represented in all tanks. Here the anchor collection is the entire tank table, and the standard format gives the following expression.

$$\{\text{sname}(s) \mid \text{species}(s) \land (\forall t)((t\text{ is a tank}) \Rightarrow (t\text{ is connected to } s))\}.$$

An equivalent condition uses a set containment predicate:

$$\{\text{sname}(s) \mid \text{species}(s) \land (\text{set of anchor tuples}) \subset (\text{set of appropriate reachable tuples})\}. \tag{4.8}$$

In the example, the set of anchor tuples is the tank table, and the set of appropriate reachable tuples is the tanks sharing a common fish with the candidate species. Rephrasing the query emphasizes the set containment condition: find the names of species such that the set of tanks where the species is represented contains all tanks in the database. The symbolic translation is:

$$\{\text{sname}(s) \quad | \quad \text{species}(s) \land [\text{tank} \subset \{t' \mid \text{tank}(t') \land (\exists f)(\text{fish}(f) \land$$
$$\text{sno}(s) \quad = \quad \text{sno}(f) \land \text{tno}(f) = \text{tno}(t'))\}]\}.$$

Although this approach appears to avoid universal quantification, it doesn't. A set containment predicate is equivalent to a universally quantified predicate on the set members. That is, $A \subset B$ is equivalent to $(\forall x)((x \in A) \Rightarrow (x \in B))$.

Set comparison	Equivalent predicate
$\{t \mid P_1(t, \ldots)\} \subset \{t \mid P_2(t, \ldots)\}$	$(\forall t)(P_1(t, \ldots) \Rightarrow P_2(t, \ldots))$
$\{t \mid P_1(t, \ldots)\} \not\subset \{t \mid P_2(t, \ldots)\}$	$(\exists t)(P_1(t, \ldots) \wedge \neg P_2(t, \ldots))$
$\{t_0 \in \{t \mid P(t, \ldots)\}$	$P(t_0, \ldots)$
$\{t_0 \notin \{t \mid P(t, \ldots)\}$	$\neg P(t_0, \ldots)$
$\{t \mid P_1(t, \ldots)\} = \{t \mid P_2(t, \ldots)\}$	$(\forall t)(P_1(t, \ldots) \Rightarrow P_2(t, \ldots)) \wedge (\forall t)(P_2(t, \ldots) \Rightarrow P_1(t, \ldots))$
$\{t \mid P_1(t, \ldots)\} \neq \{t \mid P_2(t, \ldots)\}$	$(\exists t)(P_1(t, \ldots) \wedge \neg P_2(t, \ldots)) \vee (\exists t)(P_2(t, \ldots) \wedge \neg P_1(t, \ldots))$

Figure 4.3 Equivalence of set comparisons and quantified expressions

To use the set containment condition, you must extend the rules for WFFs to allow set comparisons. A query expression is then a set construction whose WFF can itself contain other set-comparison constructions. These interior set constructions mirror the format of the overall query because each contains another WFF to define its membership. That WFF can again contain set comparisons, involving the construction of new sets at a yet lower level. This recursion can continue to any depth, but at the lowest level the atomic predicates don't involve any further set comparisons but rather use the traditional atomic predicates of table membership (e.g., tank(t)) and attribute comparisons (e.g., tcolor(t) = "red").

You can remove all set comparisons by introducing the appropriate quantifications. The process starts with the most deeply nested sets and works outward. Any set used in a comparison appears in the standard set-builder form: $\{t \mid P(t, \ldots)\}$, where $P(t, \ldots)$ is a predicate in t and possibly other variables from the scope where the set is defined. Figure 4.3 shows how to replace various set comparisons with quantified predicates.

Aggregates and partitions

You could consider aggregates and partitions as post-processing activities, which are undertaken after retrieving the raw data from the database. This viewpoint relieves the query language of the responsibility for these features. Because Structured Query Language (SQL) includes aggregates and because the DBMS translates SQL queries into relational algebra for execution, relational algebra must also provide aggregates. However, relational calculus doesn't play an explicit role in the DBMS processing. Instead, it serves as a theoretical framework for describing data retrieval concepts, thereby providing a basis for the more user-friendly SQL. For this reason, most database texts don't include aggregates in their relational calculus discussions. Nevertheless, a brief treatment of aggregates appears here to make the relational calculus presentation parallel to the earlier relational algebra discussion and to the SQL development to come.

Minor extensions to the WFF format easily imply the necessary computations. This section adopts the relational algebra notation for sum, min, max, count, and average but introduces additional notation to apply these operations to sets arising from previous operations. In simple cases, the aggregate operator applies to the final set delivered by the retrieval portion of the query. In general, however, the aggregates can apply to intermediate sets within the overall predicate. In the aquarium database, the simple case is illustrated by the query: sum the volumes of tanks containing a shark.

$$Q = \{\text{tvolume}(t), \text{tno}(t) \mid \text{tank}(t) \wedge (\exists f, s)(\text{fish}(f) \wedge \text{species}(s) \wedge \text{tno}(t) = \text{tno}(f) \wedge$$
$$\text{sno}(f) = \text{sno}(s) \wedge \text{sname}(s) = \text{``shark"})\}$$
$$\text{Sum}(\text{tvolume}, Q).$$

The set defined by a relational calculus expression is a set of tuples. For the moment, assume that the attribute names in these tuples come from the tables where the values are extracted. So the expression Q above defines a set of (tvolume, tno) pairs. In the second expression, the Sum-function takes two arguments: an attribute name and a set of tuples. It sums the specified attribute values across the tuples in the given set. In this example, the final result is a single number. In the general case, however, it may be a set of numbers. To emphasize that the answer is a set, you should enclose the final expression in braces. The proper notation is then as follows.

$$Q_1 = \{\text{tvolume}(t), \text{tno}(t) \mid \text{tank}(t) \wedge (\exists f, s)(\text{fish}(f) \wedge \text{species}(s) \wedge \text{tno}(t) = \text{tno}(f) \wedge$$
$$\text{sno}(f) = \text{sno}(s) \wedge \text{sname}(s) = \text{``shark"})\}$$
$$Q = \{ \text{Sum}(\text{tvolume}, Q_1) \}.$$

The final answer, Q, is a set of tuples; each tuple contain one value. In this case, of course, the set is a singleton, and its only member contains a value but no corresponding attribute name. Because anonymous attribute names must be resolved before this expression can be included as part of a larger computation, the notation must be extended to allow new attribute names for computed values. So far, relational calculus expressions haven't encountered name conflicts. By contrast, relational algebra depends heavily on attribute names to define its operations, and frequent renaming is necessary to avoid conflicts. Extending relational calculus to aggregate operations on partitioned sets produces summary sets, which contain tuples that are used in other parts of the overall expression. Unambiguous names are necessary for these references.

When a relational calculus expression defines a tuple set, the predicate determines which *values* occur in the tuples. However, what attribute names associate with these values? In the simplest case, the values come directly from tuples in the database, and each such tuple has attribute names associated with its values. In this case, a tuple value in the newly created set keeps the associated attribute name. In the last example, the tuples of Q_1 were (tno, tvolume) pairs. Q then uses Q_1 to define a new set of tuples over unnamed attributes. The single component of a Q-tuple comes from an aggregate function rather than from some attribute of another table. A renaming notation solves this dilemma:

$$Q_1 = \{\text{tvolume}(t), \text{tno}(t) \mid \text{tank}(t) \wedge (\exists f, s)(\text{fish}(f) \wedge \text{species}(s) \wedge \text{tno}(t) = \text{tno}(f) \wedge$$
$$\text{sno}(f) = \text{sno}(s) \wedge \text{sname}(s) = \text{``shark"})\}$$
$$Q = \{\text{totVol} = \text{Sum}(\text{tvolume}, Q_1)\}.$$

The set Q is now a collection of (totVol) tuples. Actually, the set contains a single tuple, which reflects the total volume of all tanks containing a shark. The Sum-aggregate reduces the entire span of the intermediate set Q_1 to a single tuple by treating all of Q_1 as one large grouping. To break up the calculation across numerous groupings requires further notation.

You could, of course, combine the expressions as follows, but a stepwise process is more informative.

$$Q = \{\text{totVol} = \text{Sum}(\text{tvolume}, \{\text{tvolume}(t), \text{tno}(t) \mid \text{tank}(t) \wedge (\exists f, s)(\text{fish}(f) \wedge \text{species}(s) \wedge \text{tno}(t) = \text{tno}(f) \wedge$$
$$\text{sno}(f) = \text{sno}(s) \wedge \text{sname}(s) = \text{``shark"})\})\}.$$

Fish					
fno	fname	fcolor	fweight	tno	sno
164	charlie	orange	12	42	74
228	killer	white	32	42	22
119	bonnie	blue	51	42	22
654	darron	white	84	42	93
765	elsie	white	73	42	22
277	george	red	33	42	93
104	indira	black	19	42	17
347	flipper	black	25	35	17
388	cory	purple	12	35	93
281	charlie	orange	27	85	22
650	laura	blue	55	85	17
483	albert	red	45	55	17
438	fran	black	61	55	74
419	kilroy	red	49	55	74
302	jill	red	28	38	17
911	helen	blue	48	44	74
700	maureen	white	71	44	17

Figure 4.4   A quotient set constructed over the fish relation

Equivalence classes and quotient sets

Suppose you decompose a set into non-overlapping subsets, with all the members of a given subset sharing some common feature. Under these circumstances, each subset is an **equivalence class**. Because they share a common feature, the members of an equivalence class are equivalent to each other in some sense. This operation is actually a frequently occurring mathematical technique that can be developed in a more general form, but the details aren't necessary for this discussion. The set to be broken up will always be a set of tuples, and an equivalence class will consist of tuples that agree on some specified attributes. The notation is as follows. If R is a relation, and if $a_1, a_2, \ldots$ is some subset of its attributes, then $R/\{a_1, a_2, \ldots\}$ is a new set whose members are *subsets* of R. Within any such member, all elements agree on the attributes $a_1, a_2, \ldots$. The set $R/\{a_1, a_2, \ldots\}$ is a **quotient set**. For example, Figure 4.4 shows the quotient set fish/$\{$tno$\}$. It is important to understand that the quotient set contains 6 members, not 17, and that each member is itself a set.

 $R/\{a_1, a_2, \ldots\}$ *denotes a quotient set whose members are subsets of R. Each member is an equivalence class of tuples agreeing on the attributes $a_1, a_2, \ldots$.*

Equivalence classes provide the necessary partition groupings to answer more complicated aggregate queries. For example, find the tank count and average volume separately for each species. The solution is:

$$R_0 \;=\; \{\mathrm{sno}(s), \mathrm{sname}(s), \mathrm{tno}(t), \mathrm{tvolume}(t) \;\mid\; \mathrm{species}(s) \wedge \mathrm{tank}(t) \wedge (\exists f)(\mathrm{fish}(f) \wedge$$
$$\mathrm{sno}(s) = \mathrm{sno}(f) \wedge \mathrm{tno}(f) = \mathrm{tno}(t))\}$$

$$R_1 \;=\; R_0/\{\mathrm{sno}\}$$
$$R_2 \;=\; \{\mathrm{sno}(t), \mathrm{sname}(t), \mathrm{tcount} = \mathrm{Count}(\mathrm{tno}, t), \mathrm{avgtvol} = \mathrm{Average}(\mathrm{tvolume}, t) \;\mid\; R_1(t)\}.$$

In constructing the set R_2, you restrict the single free variable t to R_1. When t assumes a value in R_1, that value is a *subset* of tuples from the underlying set R_0. You can apply an attribute function, such as $\mathrm{sno}(t)$, to a subset of tuples. It returns the common value if all tuples in the subset agree on that attribute. If the tuples disagree, or if one or more of the tuples doesn't contain that attribute, the function returns null. In this case, $\mathrm{sno}(t)$ returns the common sno value of all tuples in the subset t. However, $\mathrm{tno}(t)$ would return null. The aggregate functions operate as described previously. In this case, the Count-function counts the number of tno entries in t; the Average-function averages the corresponding tvolume entries. So the attributes of the relation R_2 are sno, sname, tcount, and avgtvol. You could combine the various intermediate sets to give one complicated predicate, but it's more informative to leave the solution in pieces.

The pattern for applying the aggregate functions (i.e., Sum, Count, Average, Min, and Max) places the function name directly before two arguments: an attribute name and a set. The set is a collection of tuples, and the attribute name specifies which tuple values to pass to the computation. In the example above, the component $\mathrm{tcount} = \mathrm{Count}(\mathrm{tno}, t)$ appears. The Count-aggregate operates on the set of tno values extracted from the tuples in t. In this case, t happens to be an element of the quotient set, R_1, so it's a collection of (sno, sname, tno, tvolume) tuples that agree on sno.

 For $t \in R/\{a_1, a_2, \ldots\}$, the notation Sum$(b, t)$ sums the values under attribute b within an equivalence class t. Similar notation applies to the remaining aggregate functions.

You can use arithmetic combinations to return constants or simple computations in new attribute columns, as shown in the following relational algebra, its equivalent relational calculus, and the resulting table.

$\pi_q \Psi_p^f(\mathrm{tank})$,

where p = (tno)

$\quad\quad f$ = (quarts = 4 * tvolume, constantBlue = "blue")

$\quad\quad q$ = (tname, quarts, constantBlue)

$\{\mathrm{tname}(t), \mathrm{quarts} = 4 * \mathrm{tvolume}(t), \mathrm{constantBlue} = \text{"blue"} \mid \mathrm{tank}(t)\}.$

< ··· >		
tname	quarts	constantBlue
puddle	800	blue
cesspool	400	blue
lagoon	1600	blue
beach	800	blue
lagoon	800	blue

Multiple partitions

Chapter 3 presented some queries requiring several partitions or several computations on a single partition in the relational algebra solution. Similar situations occur in relational calculus. Consider the following query, which uses the result of an aggregate to remove certain groupings before the final projection. find the average volume of tanks associated with each species, but only for those species that appear in two or more tanks. The relational algebra solution is as follows:

$$\pi_q \sigma_b \Psi_p^f \pi_r (\text{species} * \text{fish} * \text{tank}), \text{ where } r = (\text{sno, sname, tno, tvolume})$$

$$\begin{aligned}
p &= (\text{sno}) \\
f &= (\text{avgtvol} = \text{average(tvolume)}, \text{tcount} = \text{count(tno)}) \\
b &= (\text{tcount} >= 2) \\
q &= (\text{sname, avgtvol}).
\end{aligned}$$

You can imitate this process in relational calculus. Q_1 constructs the table corresponding to the argument of the aggregate operator, Ψ_p^f.

$$\begin{aligned}
Q_1 &= \{\text{sno}(s), \text{sname}(s), \text{tno}(t), \text{tvolume}(t) \mid \text{species}(s) \wedge \text{tank}(t) \wedge (\exists f)(\text{fish}(f) \wedge \\
&\quad \text{sno}(s) = \text{sno}(f) \wedge \text{tno}(f) = \text{tno}(t))\} \\
Q_2 &= \{\text{sno}(t), \text{sname}(t), \text{avgtvol} = \text{Average(tvolume}, t) \mid t \in Q_1/\{\text{sno}\} \wedge \text{Count(tno}, t) >= 2\}.
\end{aligned}$$

As a second example, find the average tank volume associated with each species, provided that the species is represented by 10 or more fish. The query requires two partitions: one to group a species with its tanks in order to apply the average aggregate and a second to group a species with its fish in order to determine if it belongs in the answer set. The relational algebra for this situation is:

$$\begin{aligned}
X &= \pi_p \sigma_b \Psi_p^f (\text{Fish}), & \text{where} \quad p &= (\text{sno}) \\
Y &= \pi_s (X * \Psi_q^g \pi_r (\text{Species} * \text{Fish} * \text{Tank})), & f &= (\text{fishCount} = \text{count}(*)) \\
& & b &= (\text{fishCount} >= 10) \\
& & r &= (\text{sno, sname, tno, tvolume}) \\
& & q &= (\text{sno}) \\
& & g &= (\text{avgtvol} = \text{average(tvolume})) \\
& & s &= (\text{sno, sname, avgtvol}).
\end{aligned}$$

You can accumulate the solution in relational calculus as follows:

$$\begin{aligned}
Q_1 &= \{\text{sno}(s), \text{fno}(f) \mid \text{species}(s) \wedge \text{fish}(f) \wedge \text{sno}(s) = \text{sno}(f)\} \\
Q_2 &= \{\text{sno}(x) \mid x \in Q_1/\{\text{sno}\} \wedge \text{Count(fno}, x) >= 10\} \\
Q_3 &= \{\text{sno}(s), \text{sname}(s), \text{tno}(t), \text{tvolume}(t) \mid \text{species}(s) \wedge \text{tank}(t) \wedge (\exists s_1, f)(Q_2(s_1) \wedge \text{fish}(f) \wedge \\
&\quad\quad\quad\quad\quad\quad\quad\quad\quad \text{sno}(s) = \text{sno}(s_1)) \wedge \text{sno}(s) = \text{sno}(f) \wedge \text{tno}(t) = \text{tno}(f))\} \\
Q_4 &= \{\text{sno}(y), \text{sname}(y), \text{avgtvol} = \text{Average(tvolume}, y) \mid y \in Q_3/\{\text{sno}\}\}.
\end{aligned}$$

By adding equivalence classes, you can now write a relational calculus equivalent for any relational algebra query. However, to translate in the reverse direction, you must restrict the relational calculus to so-called "safe" expressions. This policy prevents certain nonsense expressions, such as $\{x \mid \neg\text{fish}(x)\}$, in which a variable ranges over some combination of incompatible tables.

The relational calculus notation parallels the generic query: find all items x where $P(x)$ holds. Therefore, relational calculus is a promising query language. The pattern is $\{x \mid P(x)\}$, where $P(x)$ is a WFF over the atomic predicates that directly address the database. Atomic predicates answer, for example, "Is tuple t in the body of relation R?" or "Is the tcolor value of tuple t equal to red?" Two problems arise with this syntax. First, many users don't appreciate the mathematical notation. To achieve widespread acceptance, the format should be more user-friendly. Second, although existential quantification is relatively simple, universal quantification and aggregates are much less so. Developing a more user-friendly syntax that retains all the possibilities of the predicate calculus is difficult. Structured Query Language (SQL) is a popular variation on relational calculus, but it doesn't retain the full range of WFF predicates. In particular, it avoids the heavily mathematical notation and uses only existential quantification in the predicate.

Domain relational calculus

The relational calculus described to this point is officially called the **tuple relational calculus** because the implicit range of all variables is the pool of all tuples in the database. An equivalent system uses variables that range over the attribute domains. In the aquarium database, pooling the values from all attribute domains gives 17, shark, worm, charlie, purple, 84, 42, Hatched, 05/14, green, cesspool, lagoon, 9875, jill, flipper, and many more elements. The pool is one large, heterogeneous domain. The new system is called the **domain relational calculus** because all query variables take on values from this common domain.

In contrast with the pool of tuples depicted in Figure 4.2, the domain of the free and bound variables in domain relational calculus expressions is shown in Figure 4.5. A basic difference is that the pool of domain values is typically infinite, whereas the pool of tuples in the database at any given time is finite. Because free and bound variables assume values in this common domain, a notation is necessary for assembling a collection of such values and then testing it for table membership. Accordingly, the basic atomic predicate has the form: $R(a_1 = x, a_2 = y, \ldots)$, where $a_1, a_2, \ldots$ are attribute names and R is a relation. The predicate is true for a particular set of values for $x, y, \ldots$ precisely when the assembled tuple $(a_1 = x, a_2 = y, \ldots)$ appears in relation R. Each table in the database gives rise to such a predicate. For example, the following expression requests the names of red tanks.

$$\{x \mid (\exists w, y)(\text{tank}(\text{tno} = w, \text{tname} = x, \text{tcolor} = \text{"red"}, \text{tvolume} = y))\}.$$

For a fixed candidate x, the variables w and y range over the pool of elements in the common domain and attempt to lock on to values such that the assembled tuple appears in the tank relation. If w and y can achieve such values, x is the name of a red tank.

The primary atomic predicates judge table membership, just as in tuple relational calculus. However, you need more variables to flesh out the argument. Atomic predicates of the form $(x \, \theta \, \text{constant})$ and $(x \, \theta \, y)$, where x and y are free or bound variables and θ is a comparison operator, are also allowed. For example, the following expression finds the names of red tanks with volume greater than 300.

$$\{x \mid (\exists w, y)(\text{tank}(\text{tno} = w, \text{tname} = x, \text{tcolor} = \text{"red"}, \text{tvolume} = y) \wedge y > 300)\}.$$

Existential queries

Existential queries extend to several tables, just as in the tuple relational calculus case, by using existential quantification to introduce enough variables to represent all links in the qualifying path. For example, find the names of fish that represent a species named shark.

$$\{f_2 \mid (\exists f_1, f_3, f_4, t, s_1, s_2)(\text{fish}(\text{fno} = f_1, \text{fname} = f_2, \text{fcolor} = f_3, \text{fweight} = f_4, \text{tno} = t, \text{sno} = s_1) \wedge \\ \text{species}(\text{sno} = s_1, \text{sname} = \text{"shark"}, \text{sfood} = s_2))\}.$$

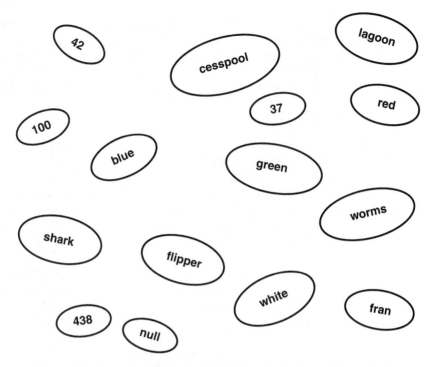

Figure 4.5   Values available for variable bindings in domain relational calculus

The existentially quantified expression returns true only if the variable s_1 binds to a value that simultaneously serves as an sno for a fish tuple and for a species tuple. This common value establishes the linkage between the two. Longer existential queries merely extend this pattern. For example, find the names of species represented in a tank with a shark.

$$\{s_2 \mid (\exists s_1, s_3, f_1, f_2, f_3, f_4, t_1, t_2, t_3, t_4, g_1, g_2, g_3, g_4, h_1, h_2)(\text{species}(\text{sno} = s_1, \text{sname} = s_2, \text{sfood} = s_3) \wedge$$
$$\text{fish}(\text{fno} = f_1, \text{fname} = f_2, \text{fcolor} = f_3, \text{fweight} = f_4, \text{tno} = t_1, \text{sno} = s_1) \wedge$$
$$\text{tank}(\text{tno} = t_1, \text{tname} = t_2, \text{tcolor} = t_3, \text{tvolume} = t_4) \wedge$$
$$\text{fish}(\text{fno} = g_1, \text{fname} = g_2, \text{fcolor} = g_3, \text{fweight} = g_4, \text{tno} = t_1, \text{sno} = h_1) \wedge$$
$$\text{species}(\text{sno} = h_1, \text{sname} = \text{``shark''}, \text{sfood} = h_2))\}.$$

Many existentially bound variables serve only as place holders in the table membership predicates. You can simplify the notation by adopting a "don't care" symbol ($*$), which means that an anonymous existentially quantified variable has been omitted. Each $*$ stands for a distinct such variable. With this convention, the previous query appears as follows. The explicit variables take on key values.

$$\{s_2 \mid (\exists s_1, f_1, t_1, g_1, h_1)(\text{species}(\text{sno} = s_1, \text{sname} = s_2, \text{sfood} = *) \wedge$$
$$\text{fish}(\text{fno} = f_1, \text{fname} = *, \text{fcolor} = *, \text{fweight} = *, \text{tno} = t_1, \text{sno} = s_1) \wedge$$
$$\text{tank}(\text{tno} = t_1, \text{tname} = *, \text{tcolor} = *, \text{tvolume} = *) \wedge$$
$$\text{fish}(\text{fno} = g_1, \text{fname} = *, \text{fcolor} = *, \text{fweight} = *, \text{tno} = t_1, \text{sno} = h_1) \wedge$$
$$\text{species}(\text{sno} = h_1, \text{sname} = \text{``shark''}, \text{sfood} = *))\}.$$

Here, species(sno $= s_1$, sname $= s_2$, sfood $= *$) stands for $(\exists s_3)$(species(sno $= s_1$, sname $= s_2$, sfood $= s_3$)). Similarly, fish(fno $= f_1$, fname $= *$, fcolor $= *$, fweight $= *$, tno $= t_1$, sno $= s_1$) means $(\exists f_2, f_3, f_4)$(fish(fno $= f_1$, fname $= f_2$, fcolor $= f_3$, fweight $= f_4$, sno $= s_1$, sno $= s_1$), and so forth. Further economy of expression results from specifying a fixed order for the predicate arguments. For example, you can assume that the species predicate always interprets the first argument as an sno, the second as an sname, and the third as an sfood. This convention runs counter to the assumption that a tuple is an unordered collection of attribute-value pairs, but you can adopt it anyway to simplify the notation. The table membership predicates then interpret argument values positionally as follows.

- species(sno, sname, sfood)
- tank(tno, tname, tcolor, tvolume)
- fish(fno, fname, fcolor, fweight, tno, sno)
- event(eno, edate, enote, fno)

With this convention, the example becomes much shorter.

$$\{s_2 \quad | \quad (\exists s_1, f_1, t_1, g_1, h_1)(\text{species}(s_1, s_2, *) \wedge \text{fish}(f_1, *, *, *, t_1, s_1) \wedge \text{tank}(t_1, *, *, *) \wedge \\ \text{fish}(g_1, *, *, *, t_1, h_1) \wedge \text{species}(h_1, \text{``shark''}, *))\}.$$

The linkage between two tuples usually requires the equality of certain attributes, which you express by using the same variable in both places. However, if you need some other comparison, such as $<, >, \leq, \geq$, you must use additional clauses. For example, find the names of cohabiting fish.

$$\{f_2, g_2 \quad | \quad (\exists f_1, t, g_1)(\text{fish}(f_1, f_2, *, *, t, *) \wedge \text{fish}(g_1, g_2, *, *, t, *) \wedge f_1 < g_1)\}.$$

The final boolean component, $f_1 < g_1$, prevents pairs of the form (a, a) in the answer, and it also removes one of each redundant pair $(a, b), (b, a)$. Because the condition isn't an equality constraint, you can't express it with a single variable playing different roles in table membership predicates.

Universal queries

Universal quantification is used to express the condition: if a tuple belongs to the anchor collection, it is reachable by some path from the candidate. Consider the query: find the names of species represented in all red tanks. The solution is:

$$\{s_2 \quad | \quad (\exists s_1)(\text{species}(s_1, s_2, *) \wedge (\forall t_1)(\text{tank}(t_1, *, \text{``red''}, *) \Rightarrow \text{fish}(*, *, *, *, t_1, s_1)))\}.$$

For more complicated queries, it is often convenient to accumulate the solution in several steps. In this case, you need to refer to the tuples in the tables assembled by previous steps. You use the same naming convention as the tuple relational calculus. In other words, each construction creates a new table of tuples with attribute names as specified. For example, to emphasize that it defines a collection of specName values, you can write the last query as follows:

$$\{\text{specName} = s_2 \quad | \quad (\exists s_1)(\text{species}(s_1, s_2, *) \wedge (\forall t_1)(\text{tank}(t_1, *, \text{``red''}, *) \Rightarrow \text{fish}(*, *, *, *, t_1, s_1)))\}.$$

Suppose you want the names of species represented in all red tanks where representatives of all species with a worm diet swim. You first isolate the species with a diet of worms as Q_1, a collection of sno values. You then construct the set of red tanks that are connected to all elements of Q_1. This collection is Q_2, a set of tno values. Finally, you define the set of species that connect to all the anchors in Q_2. The operation proceeds as follows.

$$Q_1 = \{\text{sno} = s_1 \quad | \quad \text{species}(s_1, *, \text{``worms''})\}$$
$$Q_2 = \{\text{tno} = t_1 \quad | \quad \text{tank}(t_1, *, \text{``red''}, *) \land (\forall x)(Q_1(x) \Rightarrow \text{fish}(*, *, *, *, t_1, x))\}$$
$$Q_3 = \{\text{sname} = h_2 \quad | \quad (\exists h_1)(\text{species}(h_1, h_2, *) \land (\forall y)(Q_2(y) \Rightarrow \text{fish}(*, *, *, *, y, h_1)))\}.$$

The operations of domain relational calculus are parallel to those of tuple relational calculus, but at finer level of resolution. Because the variables range over a pool of values, a tuple must be assembled before it can be checked with a table membership predicate. However, there is the benefit that the variables directly represent attribute values, and therefore attribute extraction functions are unnecessary. You can also extend the syntax to include partitions and aggregates. With those additions, you can compose a domain relational calculus equivalent for any relational algebra expression.

In domain relational calculus the variables range over a pool of values, the union of all domains in the database schema. The atomic predicates permit table membership tests on assembled tuples, and they allow direct θ-comparisons between the variables.

SUMMARY

Predicates are functions that return true or false, depending on the values of their arguments. The simplest predicates are atomic, and they deliver elementary judgments on the problem domain. A well-formed formula (WFF) is assembled from atomic predicates using logical connectives and quantifications. A WFF is also a predicate, which expresses a more complex condition through standard combinations of the elementary judgments. Tuple relational calculus is a notation that tailors the traditional predicate calculus to a given database by restricting the atomic predicates to table membership tests and θ-comparisons between extracted attribute values.

If R is a relation and a and b are attribute names, then the two types of atomic predicates are typified by $R(t)$, which is true precisely when the tuple t appears in R, and by $a(t) \; \theta \; b(s)$, which is true when the a attribute value of tuple t θ-relates to the b attribute value of tuple s. θ is one of the comparison operators, $<, >, =, \leq, \geq$, or one of their complements. An attribute value can also be compared with a constant.

In an existential query, each solution member qualifies by originating a path to some anchor tuple. Relational calculus express an existential query by assigning free variables to range over the candidate relations. It then introduces bound existentially quantified variables to identify the anchor tuple and to capture a path to that anchor.

In a universal query each solution member qualifies by originating a bundle of paths sufficient to embrace some collection of anchors. The expression for a universal query starts in the same manner, with a free variable restricted to the candidate relation. A further condition then forces

$$(\forall t)((t \in \text{anchor collection}) \Rightarrow (\exists p)(p \text{ describes a path from the candidate to } t)).$$

A relation can be stratified into groups suitable for the application of aggregate functions. If R is a relation, and $a_1, a_2, \ldots$ are a subset of its attributes, $R/\{a_1, a_2, \ldots\}$ denotes a new set, the quotient set. Each member of the quotient set is an equivalence class of tuples from R. Each member of the quotient set is a subset of R containing tuples that agree on the attributes $a_1, a_2, \ldots$. The notation $\{\text{Sum}(\{b(t') \mid t' \in t\} \mid t \in R/\{a_1, a_2, \ldots\}\}$ sums the b attribute values within each equivalence class t of the quotient set. The remaining aggregate functions have similar expressions. With these extensions, relational calculus can imitate the partition and aggregate features of relational algebra.

Domain relational calculus is similar to tuple relational calculus, but it differs in the range of its variables. Tuple relational calculus uses variables that range over the pool of tuples in the database; domain relational calculus uses variables that range over the union of all domains in the database. Therefore, the atomic predicates, while still extracting elementary facts from the database, differ in form. A table membership test is available in both versions, but in domain calculus a tuple must be assembled from a combination of variables before the test is applied. You don't need attribute functions to extract values from tuples in domain calculus because these values are already available as the variables from which the tuples were assembled. Attribute value comparisons, therefore, are replaced with direct comparisons of the variables. Tuples from different relations are linked with a common variable in the matching attributes. Development of domain relational calculus parallels that of tuple relational calculus. With the addition of syntax to handle partitions and aggregates, domain calculus can express any relational algebra query.■

The exercises below assume the context of the library database of Figure 3.11. The relations Library, Copy, Book, Author, Loan, and Patron are abbreviated as $L, C, B, A, U,$ and P respectively.

Selection via a predicate and existential queries

Write tuple relational calculus for the following queries.

1. Find the names of libraries located in Seattle.
2. Find the names and locations of libraries featuring books written by Salinger.
3. Find the names of libraries that have a book in common with a Seattle library.
4. Find the titles of books available from a library used by a patron named joe.
5. Find all pairs of book titles that have copies in the same library. Phrase the query to exclude pairs of the form (x, x) from the answer set and to provide just one of the pairs (x, y) and (y, x) when both qualify.
6. Find all triplets of library names that are collocated. Eliminate triplets of the form (x, x, x), (x, x, y), (x, y, x), and (y, x, x) from the answer. Provide just one of the six permutations of (x, y, z) when the triplet qualifies.

Describe the following relational calculus expressions in English.

7. $\{\text{pages}(b) \quad | \quad B(b) \wedge (\exists c_1, u_1, u_2, c_2, c_3, l)(C(c_1) \wedge U(u_1) \wedge U(u_2) \wedge C(c_2) \wedge C(c_3) \wedge L(l) \wedge$
$\text{bookno}(b) = \text{bookno}(c_1) \wedge \text{copyno}(c_1) = \text{copyno}(u_1) \wedge \text{patronno}(u_1) = \text{patronno}(u_2) \wedge$
$\text{copyno}(u_2) = \text{copyno}(c_2) \wedge \text{bookno}(c_2) = \text{bookno}(c_3) \wedge \text{libno}(c_3) = \text{libno}(l) \wedge$
$\text{location}(l) = \text{"Denver"})\}.$

8. $\{\text{patname}(p), \text{patwgt}(p) \quad | \quad P(p) \wedge (\exists u, c, b, l)(U(u) \wedge C(c) \wedge B(b) \wedge L(l) \wedge \text{patronno}(p) = \text{patronno}(u) \wedge$
$\text{copyno}(u) = \text{copyno}(c) \wedge \text{bookno}(c) = \text{bookno}(b) \wedge \text{libno}(c) = \text{libno}(l) \wedge$
$\text{title}(b) = \text{"Molecular Biology"} \wedge \text{location}(l) = \text{"Seattle"} \wedge \text{patwgt}(p) > 150)\}.$

9. $\{\text{authname}(a_1), \text{authname}(a_2) \quad | \quad A(a_1) \wedge A(a_2) \wedge (\exists b_1, c_1, u_1, u_2, c_2, b_2)(B(b_1) \wedge C(c_1) \wedge U(u_1) \wedge U(u_2) \wedge$
$C(c_2) \wedge B(b_2) \wedge \text{authno}(a_1) = \text{authno}(b_1) \wedge \text{bookno}(b_1) = \text{bookno}(c_1) \wedge$
$\text{copyno}(c_1) = \text{copyno}(u_1) \wedge \text{patronno}(u_1) = \text{patronno}(u_2)$
$\wedge \text{copyno}(u_2) = \text{copyno}(c_2) \wedge \text{bookno}(c_2) = \text{bookno}(b_2) \wedge$
$\text{authno}(b_2) = \text{authno}(a_2) \wedge \text{authno}(a_1) < \text{authno}(a_2))\}.$

Construct tuple relational calculus expressions equivalent to the following relational algebra.

10. $\pi_q \sigma_b (B * C * L)$, where $\quad b \quad = \quad (\text{rooms} > 25)$
$q \quad = \quad (\text{title}).$

11. $\pi_q \sigma_b (\pi_r \check{\rho}(X = P * U * C) \times \pi_s \check{\rho}(Y = C * U * P)),$

where $\quad r \quad = \quad (X.\text{patname}, X.\text{libno})$
$s \quad = \quad (Y.\text{libno}, Y.\text{patname})$
$b \quad = \quad (X.\text{libno} = Y.\text{libno} \wedge Y.\text{patname} = \text{"joe"})$
$q \quad = \quad (X.\text{patname}).$

12. $\pi_q \sigma_b (P * U * C * L)$, where $\quad b \quad = \quad (\text{location} = \text{"Seattle"})$
$q \quad = \quad (\text{patname}).$

13. $\pi_q \sigma_b (U * C * B * A * L)$, where $\quad q \quad = \quad (\text{authname}, \text{title})$
$b \quad = \quad (\text{location} = \text{"Denver"} \wedge \text{rooms} > 25).$

14. $\pi_q \sigma_b (\check{\rho}(X = P * U * C * L) \times \check{\rho}(Y = (L * C * U * P) \times \check{\rho}(Z = P * U * C * L)),$

where $\quad q \quad = \quad (X.\text{patwgt})$
$b \quad = \quad (X.\text{libno} = Y.\text{libno} \wedge Y.\text{patronno} = Z.\text{patronno} \wedge Z.\text{location} = \text{"Denver"}).$

Universal queries

Construct tuple relational calculus expressions for the following queries.

15. Find the names of libraries that have no books available.

16. Find the names of patrons who have used every library in the database.

17. Find the names of patrons who deal with all libraries located in Seattle that possess a book written by Salinger.

18. Find the names of Minneapolis libraries that house all books longer than 300 pages that are featured in all Seattle libraries.

19. Find the names of patrons weighing more than 100 pounds who deal with all libraries with more than 25 rooms that house all books written by Salinger.

20. Find the names of patrons who have checked out all books with more than 300 pages.

21. Find the titles of books that have copies in all Seattle libraries that own copies of all books written by Mailer.

Construct tuple relational calculus equivalents for the following relational algebra.

22. $\pi_q[\pi_r(L * C * B)/\pi_s\sigma_b(B)]$, where

r	=	(libname, libno, bookno)
s	=	(bookno)
b	=	(pages > 1000)
q	=	(libname).

23. $\pi_q[\pi_r\sigma_b(P * U * C)/\pi_s(B)]$, where

b	=	(patwgt > 150)
r	=	(patronno, patname, bookno)
s	=	(bookno)
q	=	(patname).

24. $\pi_q[\pi_r(P * U * C * B * A)/\pi_s(A)]$, where

s	=	(authno)
r	=	(patronno, patname, patwgt, authno)
q	=	(patname, patwgt).

25. $\pi_q\{\pi_r(L * C)/[\pi_s(C)/\pi_t\sigma_b(C * L)]\}$, where

b	=	(location = Seattle)
t	=	(libno)
s	=	(bookno, libno)
r	=	(libno, libname, bookno)
q	=	(libname).

Write tuple relational calculus expressions for the following queries.

26. Find the names of libraries whose collections are precisely the set of books with more than 300 pages.

27. Find the names of patrons who deal with precisely those libraries located in Seattle.

28. Find the names of library-patron pairs such that the set of books containing more than 300 pages that are featured by the library is the same set of books written by Salinger that have been borrowed by the patron.

Translate the following relational algebra into equivalent tuple relational calculus.

29. $\pi_q[(\pi_r(L * C)/\pi_s\sigma_b(B)) - \pi_t\sigma_c(L * C * B)]$, where

b	=	(pages > 300)
s	=	(bookno)
r	=	(libno, libname, bookno)
c	=	(pages $<= 300$)
t	=	(libno, libname)
q	=	(libname).

Aggregates and partitions

Compose tuple relational calculus expressions for the following queries.

30. Find the titles of books that have fewer than 10 copies in circulation.

31. Find the location of the library with the most rooms.

32. For each book-library combination, find the number of copies of the book owned by the library.

33. For each patron, find the average number of rooms in libraries used by him.

34. For each book with at least one copy, find the minimum, average, and maximum cost of the copies.

35. Find the names of patrons whose weight is greater than the average weight of patrons who have read a book entitled **The Name of the Rose**.

Write tuple relational calculus expressions equivalent to the following relational algebra.

36. $\pi_q \Psi_p^f \pi_r (L * C * B)$, where

$$
\begin{aligned}
r &= \text{(libno, libname, bookno, pages)} \\
p &= \text{(libno)} \\
f &= \text{(totalPages = sum(pages))} \\
q &= \text{(libname, totalPages)}.
\end{aligned}
$$

37. $\pi_q \sigma_b \Psi_p^f \pi_r (L * C * U * P)$, where

$$
\begin{aligned}
r &= \text{(libno, libname, rooms, patronno, patwgt)} \\
p &= \text{(libno)} \\
f &= \text{(avgWgt = 2 * average(patwgt))} \\
b &= \text{(rooms > avgWgt)} \\
q &= \text{(libname)}.
\end{aligned}
$$

38. $\pi_q \Psi_p^f (C * U)$, where

$$
\begin{aligned}
p &= \text{(libno, bookno, patronno)} \\
f &= \text{(loanActivity = count(loanno))} \\
q &= \text{(libno, bookno, patronno, loanActivity)}.
\end{aligned}
$$

Write relational calculus expressions to solve the following queries.

39. For each library with a collection of 100 titles or more, find the average number of pages in the books in the collection.

40. For each author whose total number of pages written exceeds the total weight of the patrons who have read some of his work, find the average size (i.e., number of rooms) of the libraries that carry his books. The page total isn't increased by the existence of multiple copies of a book.

41. Find the number of libraries used by each patron, for those patrons who use some library larger than the average size of libraries that carry a copy of a book entitled **The Name of the Rose**.

Domain relational calculus

Write domain relational calculus for the following queries. Assume that the table membership predicates take positional arguments as follows.

- library: L(libno, libname, location, rooms)
- author: A(authno, authname)
- book: B(bookno, title, pages, authno)
- copy: C(copyno, cost, libno, bookno)
- patron: P(patronno, patname, patwgt)
- loan: U(loanno, duedate, copyno, patronno)

42. Find the names of libraries located in Seattle.

43. Find the names and locations of libraries that own books written by Salinger.

44. Find the titles of books available from a library patronized by a patron named joe.

Construct domain relational calculus expressions equivalent to the following relational algebra.

45. $\pi_q \sigma_b (B * C * L)$, where $\quad b \quad = \quad$ (rooms > 25)

$\qquad\qquad\qquad\qquad\qquad\quad q \quad = \quad$ (title).

46. $\pi_q [\pi_r (P * U * C) * \pi_s \sigma_b (C * U * P)]$, where $\quad r \quad = \quad$ (patronno, patname, libno)

$\qquad\qquad\qquad\qquad\qquad\qquad\qquad\qquad\qquad\quad s \quad = \quad$ (libno)

$\qquad\qquad\qquad\qquad\qquad\qquad\qquad\qquad\qquad\quad b \quad = \quad$ (patname = "joe")

$\qquad\qquad\qquad\qquad\qquad\qquad\qquad\qquad\qquad\quad q \quad = \quad$ (patname).

47. $\pi_q \sigma_b (P * U * C * L)$, where $\quad b \quad = \quad$ (location = "Seattle")

$\qquad\qquad\qquad\qquad\qquad\qquad\quad q \quad = \quad$ (patname).

Construct domain relational calculus expressions for each of the following queries.

48. Find the names of libraries that own no books.

49. Find the names of patrons who have used every library in the database.

50. Find the names of patrons who deal with all libraries located in Seattle that own a book written by Salinger.

51. Find the names of Minneapolis libraries that house all books longer than 300 pages that are also owned by all Seattle libraries.

5 Basic SQL

BOTH RELATIONAL ALGEBRA AND RELATIONAL CALCULUS CAN EXPRESS complex queries. However, because of their mathematical notation, neither is appropriate for a non-technical user interested in a general-purpose database access language. A better language for a general-purpose audience is Structured Query Language (SQL). It retains the non-procedural feature of relational calculus but uses non-mathematical notation. SQL is the most widely used interface to relational databases, and every commercially successful relational DBMS product accepts SQL statements, even if SQL isn't the primary access language. SQL's popularity is due to its status as a query standard and its relatively simple syntax.

In the 1970s, IBM developed the first version of SQL, known then as Structured English Query Language (SEQUEL). In 1986, the American National Standards Institute (ANSI) adopted the language as the access standard for relational databases. SQL continues to evolve, and as this book goes to press, the latest release is SQL2, also called SQL-1992. Meanwhile, the ANSI design committee is studying further extensions, the basis for a future SQL3. This chapter introduces the core features of SQL2; the next chapter takes up more advanced features.

Basic SQL allows a user, either a person or a program, to manipulate the database tuples. SQL's most powerful component, the select statement, enables information retrieval under widely varying circumstances. Accordingly, this chapter treats data retrieval operations in the greatest detail and abbreviates the coverage of the remaining operations—insertion, deletion, and update. Most relational databases provide an interactive environment, which allows the user to launch SQL statements for immediate execution. Although an interactive environment is the most convenient access channel for a person, it isn't appropriate for database commands coming from a computer program. To service program clients, SQL allows certain operations to be included within standard programming languages as subprocedure calls. This feature is called **embedded SQL** because you embed database commands directly in the code of a host language, such as COBOL, Pascal, or C. The discussion of embedded SQL uses the C language as an example host.

Conceptual model for simple retrieval queries

Queries from a single table

The basic form of an SQL retrieval statement appears on the left below. To the right are an example from the aquarium database (Figure 5.1) and the resulting table. The solution table assumes the aquarium data of Figure 2.1.

select *attributes*
from *relations*
where *boolean*.

```
select tcolor
from Tank
where tname = "lagoon".
```

< ··· >
tcolor
red
green

The components of the basic SQL statement are: the select-clause, the from-clause, and the where-clause. The select-clause attributes specify the columns (i.e., attributes) to include in the answer table. The from-clause relations give the tables involved in the query. Explicit table names are necessary because the same attribute name might appear in several tables. In this case, the DBMS can't infer the relevant source tables from the select-clause attributes alone. Finally, the where-clause boolean provides a condition for deciding which tuples to include in the answer. The keywords **select**, **from**, and **where** appear in all retrieval statements, but the attributes, relations, and boolean vary with the given application and the information sought. The multiline format, of course, is a concession for the human reader. The DBMS interprets all white space equally, whether it be a space, an end-of-line character, a tab, or multiple instances of these symbols.

Single-table queries are especially simple. For example, the above query requests the colors of tanks named lagoon. Imagine the DBMS examining each tuple of the tank table, excluding those with a tname value other than lagoon. This operation produces a horizontal slice of the original table, retaining only a portion of the tuples. Figure 5.2 roughly describes the process, although the retained tuples aren't necessarily adjacent. Recall that the tuples in a relation aren't ordered, so "adjacent tuples" isn't a meaningful concept. Figure 5.2 suggests that if you think of the relation as a table, ignoring the minor misrepresentation for the moment, and if you group together the tuples satisfying the boolean, then you can envision the result as a horizontal slice from the table.

All the columns are still present in this horizontal slice, but the DBMS then reduces the slice to those attributes identified in the query. In this case, the process retains the tcolor values and shears away the other columns. In other words, the DBMS extracts a vertical slice from the previously truncated table, keeping only the requested attributes. The final result is an unnamed new table.

The query can request several attributes, and it can specify more complex boolean conditions. The underlying processing model is unchanged. The where-clause boolean isolates a horizontal section, and the select-clause attributes then define a vertical subset of that horizontal section. For example, what are the colors and volumes of tanks named lagoon having volumes greater than 100? The SQL solution is:

```
select tcolor, tvolume
from Tank
where tname = "lagoon" and tvolume > 100.
```

Again, the database starts with the specified table, extracts a horizontal slice containing those tuples satisfying the where-clause, and finally discards all columns not mentioned in

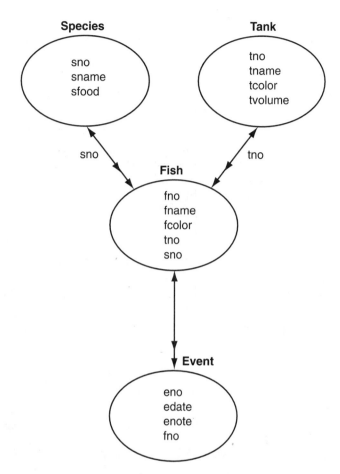

Figure 5.1 The aquarium database layout

the select-clause. This two-slice process is only a model to explain how the proper result might be constructed. Although the DBMS must deliver the same result, it may substitute more efficient operations. The non-procedural nature of the language allows this flexibility. For example, the DBMS might maintain a hidden dictionary to quickly locate tuples with a given tname value. It could use this dictionary to find all tuples with tname lagoon, examine this smaller set, and then discard tuples with tvolume less than or equal to 100. With this shortcut, the DBMS could avoid examining every tuple in the tank relation.

As an extreme example of an alternative processing strategy, suppose the DBMS stores the query result in a temporary table. Then, when the user asks the same query again, the DBMS notes that there has been no update activity since the previous query and simply returns the temporary table as the answer. In this case, the DBMS completely avoids the tank relation. Although the DBMS probably doesn't contain special code to behave in this manner, the scenario emphasizes that the user can't know which strategy the DBMS will use to process a particular query. In general, the DBMS will evaluate several alternatives in

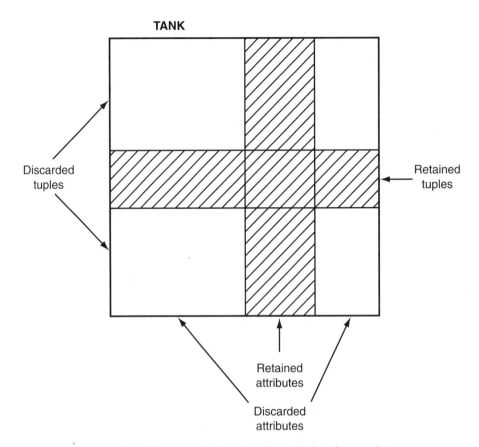

Figure 5.2 SQL extracts horizontal and vertical slices from a relation

terms of table sizes, intermediate results, hidden facilities (e.g., the dictionary speculated above), and the work necessary to perform the calculations.

Even if the DBMS doesn't evaluate a query with the two-slice process, you should still imagine that it does because the process lets you determine the exact meaning of the query. Later sections will extend the two-slice process to cover more complicated SQL features.

The width of the query result table is the number of attributes requested, which is the width of the vertical slice. However, the height of the result table isn't necessarily equal to the height of the horizontal slice. Consider again the example: what are the colors of tanks named lagoon? If several red tanks have tname lagoon, the horizontal slice includes all these tuples. But when the vertical slice removes the tno, tname, and tvolume attributes, these tuples become indistinguishable; they all contain the single value red. Because the answer is a relation, a set allowing no duplicates, only one of the red entries is kept. Therefore, the final table height can be less than the horizontal-slice height.

Despite this argument, many relational DBMS products don't remove duplicates from the vertical slice. In fact, the SQL standard states that duplicates should be retained. In the strictest sense, this deficiency prevents the answer table from qualifying as a true relation, although it does provide some additional information to the user. When working with strict ANSI SQL-compliant products, you must use the keyword "distinct" in the select-clause to force the duplicate removal. The SQL to find the colors of tanks named lagoon then appears as:

```
select distinct tcolor
from Tank
where tname = "lagoon".
```

As illustrated by its treatment of duplicates, SQL often compromises the set-theoretical relational model. SQL generally takes a table-oriented view of a relational database. The table view isn't completely accurate because it allows duplicates and suggests an ordering of tuples and attributes. Nevertheless, certain SQL operations rely on these table features. In this text, assume that an SQL query constructs a true relation without duplicates, even if the "distinct" keyword is omitted.

If you omit the where-clause, all tuples qualify for the horizontal slice. For example, to determine the names of all tanks, you use the SQL:

```
select tname
from Tank.
```

Name qualification and aliases

A **comma-list** is a list of items separated with commas. For example, a comma-list specifies the desired answer attributes in the select-clause; another comma-list provides the from-clause tables.

The where-clause boolean references certain decision attributes. In a single-table query, these attribute names aren't ambiguous. They must belong to the single from-clause table, or the SQL is erroneous. However, if the from-clause specifies several tables, two or more tables may have attributes with the same name. In writing SQL, you can qualify attribute names, if necessary, to make them distinct. A **qualified attribute name** is the basic attribute name prefixed with a table name. You can also follow this practice in single-table queries, even though the attribute names don't need qualification. Consider once again the query: what are the colors of tanks named lagoon? The solution on the left below gives the same answer table as before, but the attribute qualifications ensure that tcolor and tname come from the tank table.

```
select Tank.tcolor                    select X.tcolor chrominance
from Tank                             from Tank X
where Tank.tname = "lagoon".          where X.tname = "lagoon".
```

Besides qualifying attributes, you can specify aliases for table names, attribute names, or both. An **alias** is a synonym used elsewhere in the query. This practice allows abbreviations in the query and permits additional control over the answer table format. You give an alias to a select-clause attribute by inserting the alias name directly after the attribute, separated by white space or the word "as," but before any comma leading to another attribute. You give aliases to tables in the from-clause in the same manner. For example, you can give the alias X to Tank because it is shorter, and you might refer to it many times in composing the boolean. Also, you might want to call tcolor "chrominance" in the answer table. With these notations, you write the SQL in the center above to find the colors (chrominance) of tanks named lagoon. The answer table appears to the right. The first line of the SQL uses the Tank alias before the second line defines it. These forward references are valid because the DBMS regards the query as a unit.

As another example, consider again the query: what are the colors and volumes of tanks named lagoon having volumes greater than 100? Using aliases, you can compose the SQL on the left below. Using the data of Figure 2.1, the answer table appears to the right.

```
select X.tcolor chrominance, X.tvolume size
from Tank X
where X.tname = "lagoon" and X.tvolume > 100.
```

< ··· >	
chrominance	size
red	400
green	200

Table aliases usually provide abbreviations for later references and clarify references when several instances of the same table appear. Queries with multiple copies of the same table occur later in this chapter. Attribute aliases provide user-specified column names for the answer table.

Simple SQL queries extract a horizontal section from a single table and reduce it to the desired attribute values. Within an SQL query, an alias is a temporary synonym for an attribute or a relation, which is valid for the duration of the query.

Queries from multiple tables

Consider the following query, which requires information from two tables: what are the colors of fish representing a species named shark? In the following solution, table aliases shorten the boolean expression.

```
select fcolor
from Species S, Fish F
where S.sno = F.sno and S.sname = "shark".
```

In the user's mind, the DBMS responds to a multitable query by first forming all possible tuple combinations from the specified tables before the horizontal and vertical slicing processes. This operation is a **Cartesian product**. Figure 2.1 indicates that the species table contains four tuples and the fish table has seventeen. Pairing each species tuple with each fish tuple generates an intermediate table with $4 \times 17 = 68$ entries. Obviously, some combinations are nonsense from the query's viewpoint because they pair a fish with the wrong species. Part of this intermediate table appears in Figure 5.3.

The Cartesian product of two relations produces a third relation, whose attribute order isn't significant. In this way, a relational Cartesian product differs from a mathematical

Cartesian product. The mathematical Cartesian product of two sets, $A \times B$, generates a set of *ordered* pairs of the form (a, b) with $a \in A$ and $b \in B$. By contrast, the relational Cartesian product contains the unordered attributes from both operands, even though a table representation indicates a left-to-right order. Generalizing, you can take the Cartesian product of n relations by generating all combinations with exactly one segment from each relation. The following example illustrates the point with three relations.

R_1	
A	B
1	2
3	4

$\times$

R_2		
C	D	E
x	y	z
u	v	w

$\times$

R_3	
F	G
α	β
γ	δ

$=$

$< \cdots >$						
A	B	C	D	E	F	G
1	2	x	y	z	α	β
1	2	x	y	z	γ	δ
1	2	u	v	w	α	β
1	2	u	v	w	γ	δ
3	4	x	y	z	α	β
3	4	x	y	z	γ	δ
3	4	u	v	w	α	β
3	4	u	v	w	γ	δ

A Cartesian product of a collection of relations is a new relation whose tuples contain all possible combinations of tuples from the original relations.

The Cartesian product of Figure 5.3 has many duplicate entries and inappropriate combinations. For example, the species tuple with sno = 17, a dolphin, appears with every fish tuple, including those that represent dolphins as well as those that don't. Indeed, only six fish tuples represent dolphins: those in which sno = 17 appears in the fish tuple. Fortunately, among the redundant and nonsensical pairings, the appropriate combinations also appear. The second entry, for example, prefixes the fish tuple (fno = 347) with the species tuple (sno = 17), and it so happens that the fish tuple entry for sno is also 17. Therefore, this brute force juxtaposition of tuples from different tables does align fish tuples with the species they represent. It just happens to produce many extra tuples in the process. However, you can eliminate the nonsensical pairings by including the condition F.sno = S.sno in the where-clause boolean. The subsequent horizontal slice then eliminates the inappropriate combinations.

After you apply the boolean to the Cartesian product, the resulting horizontal slice contains only tuples with F.sno = S.sno and sname = shark, as shown in the much shorter table on the left below. At this point, each tuple corresponds to a fish with an extension that includes the appropriate species attributes. Moreover, only fish of a shark species have been retained. A final vertical slice isolates the fcolor values and produces the final answer on the right.

Cartesian product of Species and Fish								
Species.sno	sname	sfood	fno	fname	fcolor	fweight	tno	Fish.sno
17	dolphin	herring	164	charlie	orange	12	42	74
17	dolphin	herring	347	flipper	black	25	35	17
17	dolphin	herring	288	killer	white	32	42	22
17	dolphin	herring	281	charlie	orange	27	85	22
17	dolphin	herring	483	albert	red	45	55	17
17	dolphin	herring	119	bonnie	blue	51	42	22
17	dolphin	herring	388	cory	purple	12	35	93
17	dolphin	herring	654	darron	white	84	42	93
17	dolphin	herring	765	elsie	white	73	42	22
17	dolphin	herring	438	fran	black	61	55	74
17	dolphin	herring	277	george	red	33	42	93
17	dolphin	herring	911	helen	blue	48	44	74
17	dolphin	herring	104	indira	black	19	42	17
17	dolphin	herring	302	jill	red	28	38	17
17	dolphin	herring	419	kilroy	red	49	55	74
17	dolphin	herring	650	laura	blue	55	85	17
17	dolphin	herring	700	maureen	white	71	44	17
22	shark	anything	164	charlie	orange	12	42	74
22	shark	anything	347	flipper	black	25	35	17
22	shark	anything	288	killer	white	32	42	22
22	shark	anything	281	charlie	orange	27	85	22
22	shark	anything	483	albert	red	45	55	17
22	shark	anything	119	bonnie	blue	51	42	22
22	shark	anything	388	cory	purple	12	35	93
22	shark	anything	654	darron	white	84	42	93
22	shark	anything	765	elsie	white	73	42	22
22	shark	anything	438	fran	black	61	55	74
22	shark	anything	277	george	red	33	42	93
22	shark	anything	911	helen	blue	48	44	74
22	shark	anything	104	indira	black	19	42	17
22	shark	anything	302	jill	red	28	38	17
22	shark	anything	419	kilroy	red	49	55	74
22	shark	anything	650	laura	blue	55	85	17
22	shark	anything	700	maureen	white	71	44	17
74	guppy	worm	164	charlie	orange	12	42	74
74	guppy	worm	347	flipper	black	25	35	17
74	guppy	worm	288	killer	white	32	42	22
74	guppy	worm	281	charlie	orange	27	85	22
⋮	⋮	⋮	⋮	⋮	⋮	⋮	⋮	⋮

Figure 5.3 Initial Cartesian product of Species and Fish

Cartesian product of Species and Fish								
Species.sno	sname	sfood	fno	fname	fcolor	fweight	tno	Fish.sno
22	shark	anything	228	killer	white	32	42	22
22	shark	anything	281	charlie	orange	27	85	22
22	shark	anything	119	bonnie	blue	51	42	22
22	shark	anything	765	elsie	white	73	42	22
93	shark	peanut butter	388	cory	purple	12	35	93
93	shark	peanut butter	654	darron	white	84	42	93
93	shark	peanut butter	277	george	red	33	42	93

< ⋯ >
fcolor
white
orange
blue
purple
red

At this point, the processing model has three steps: (1) form an intermediate table containing all tuple combinations from the from-clause tables (2) extract a horizontal slice from this intermediate table by invoking the where-clause boolean, and finally, (3) extract a vertical slice by discarding any attributes not mentioned in the select-clause. The first step creates a large intermediate table, containing as many tuples as the product of the constituent tables' cardinalities. Moreover, most of them will involve nonsensical combinations, which will later be discarded by some portion of the where-clause boolean. Of course, the DBMS logic will try to avoid actually constructing the large intermediate table if a more efficient route is available, but the final result must remain unchanged.

You can easily extend the method to handle more than two tables. For example, what are the names of fish representing a shark species and inhabiting a cesspool tank?

```
select F.fname
from Species S, Fish F, Tank T
where S.sno = F.sno and F.tno = T.tno and S.sname = "shark" and T.tname = "cesspool".
```

Assuming the data of Figure 2.1, the intermediate Cartesian product contains $4 \times 17 \times 6 = 408$ tuples! However, the first two boolean conditions keep only those combinations where the fish segment matches both the species and tank segments. Only 17 tuples remain after this reduction. Each of the remaining tuples contains fish information extended with the details of the species represented and the tank inhabited. At this point, a simple operation augments the boolean to remove any tuples that don't correspond to a shark species or a cesspool tank. A final vertical slice isolates the fname values of the survivors.

From SQL's table-oriented viewpoint, the Cartesian product contains all concatenations of tuples from the component relations. However, considered as sets, the component tuples are sets of associations, each containing an attribute name and value. From the set-oriented viewpoint, the Cartesian product is a new relation whose schema is the union of the component schemas, with appropriate name qualifications to ensure attribute name uniqueness. To generate a tuple for the new relation, one tuple (i.e., association set) is chosen from each component of the Cartesian product. These tuples are merged (i.e., union of the association sets) to create a new larger tuple, which enters the Cartesian product. All tuples constructed in this manner appear in the new relation's body. Therefore, what appears to be a concatenation of rows in the tabular view is actually a union of tuples, where each participating tuple is an association set.

Queries that use multiple copies of tables

What are the names of species swimming in the same tank with a shark? By forming the Cartesian product of Species, Fish, and Tank and removing the nonsensical combinations, you can isolate the "sharky" tanks. Following the SQL process, you extract a horizontal slice from the Cartesian product, restrict the result to tuples with sname shark, and then take a vertical slice to isolate the tno values of the remaining tuples. These tno values represent the sharky tanks. Now the problem reduces to finding the species swimming in these sharky tanks. Working from the opposite direction, you can form the Cartesian product of the sharky tanks with a second copy of Fish and Species, again discarding nonsensical entries. The query solution is precisely the sname values from the second copy of Species.

If you compose a two-part solution in SQL, you must keep the intermediate table of sharky tanks for use in the second part. SQL provides an into-clause for this purpose. The first part of the solution isolates the sharky tanks, and because only the tno attribute is necessary to identify a tank, the proper SQL is as follows:

```
select T.tno as sharkytankno              select S.sname
from Species S, Fish F, Tank T            from SharkyTank X, Fish F, Species S
where S.sno = F.sno and F.tno = T.tno     where S.sno = F.sno and F.tno = X.sharkytankno.
    and S.sname = "shark"
into SharkyTanks.
```

Table SharkyTanks now exists with a single attribute, sharkytankno. It contains the tno values of those tanks with a shark fish. An alias gives the single SharkyTanks attribute a name and allows reference to it in a later query. The subsequent query on the right then obtains the species swimming in the sharky tanks.

You can also obtain the result with a single query. In the following solution, the aliases aren't simply convenient abbreviations; they distinguish the multiple copies of the participating relations.

```
select H.sname
from Species S, Fish F, Tank T, Fish G, Species H
where S.sno = F.sno and F.tno = T.tno and S.sname = "shark" and
    T.tno = G.tno and G.sno = H.sno.
```

S	F	T	G	H
...	...	...	...	...
...	...	...	...	...
...	...	...	...	...
...	...	...	...	...

You can reason as follows to verify that this construction delivers the correct answer. The Cartesian product constructs, in theory, a huge table, which generally looks like the one to the right above. S and H represent the full complement of species attributes; F and G represent fish attributes. T stands for the tank attributes, which appear only once. The Cartesian product body contains every possible alignment, including those arrangements where the S.sname value is shark, the T.tno value identifies a tank containing a fish F of that shark species, and the H.sname value contains the name of a species represented in that same tank by the fish G. These connections imply that the H.sname values of these particular arrangements are precisely the answer to the query. You can extract these special alignments from the large Cartesian product with the appropriate horizontal section. Consider each Cartesian product tuple as composed of five segments, as suggested by the table above. The first line of the where-clause then imposes conditions that retain only those tuples where the S segment describes the species attributes of the particular fish in the F segment, where the T segment describes the tank associated with that fish, and where the S.sname value is shark. In other words, it forces the T segment to be a sharky tank. The second line of the where-clause further reduces these remaining tuples to those where the second set of fish attributes (G) describe another (possibly the same) fish, swimming in the same tank, and where the H segment gives the species details of this second fish. A vertical section then keeps only the H.sname values. Applying this query to the data of Figure 2.1 gives the table on the right below.

In this solution, shark appears legitimately because both shark species (i.e., sno 22 and 93) appear in tank 42. Even if this weren't the case, shark would still appear in the answer table because a shark fish swims with itself according to the above construction. Because all possible combinations appear in the Cartesian product, some tuples will have the S and H segments representing the same species and the F and G segments representing the same fish. When the S segment is a shark, the boolean allows this special tuple into the horizontal section. If you want to exclude shark from the answer, you can use the following SQL:

```
select H.sname
from Species S, Fish F, Tank T, Fish G, Species H
where S.sno = F.sno and F.tno = T.tno and S.sname = "shark" and
      T.tno = G.tno and G.sno = H.sno and H.sname not = "shark".
```

However, you might want to keep shark in the answer if a shark swims in the same tank with a *different* shark fish. You must then modify the query to force the F and G segments to represent distinct fish. If the fno attribute is a key of the fish relation, this new query takes the following form. The last condition of the boolean makes the difference.

```
select H.sname
from Species S, Fish F, Tank T, Fish G, Species H
where S.sno = F.sno and F.tno = T.tno and S.sname = "shark" and
      T.tno = G.tno and G.sno = H.sno and F.fno not = G.fno.
```

As a second example, find the names of all pairs of cohabiting fish. You should be able to verify the SQL solution on the left below. Using the data of Figure 2.1, a portion of the answer appears next to the SQL code. Note that pairs of the form (a, a) appear and that there is some duplication because if (a, b) appears, so does (b, a). The first form occurs because the F and G segments of the Cartesian product can indeed be the same fish. The second form is due to the query's reflexive nature. If fish a inhabits the same tank as fish b, then obviously fish b inhabits the same tank as fish a. For every tuple that survives the horizontal sectioning with given F and G values, a mirror tuple will also survive with reversed F and G values. A simple addition to the where-condition removes these redundancies.

```
select F.fname first, G.fname second
from Fish F, Fish G
where F.tno = G.tno.
```

< ··· >	
first	second
charlie	charlie
charlie	killer
killer	charlie
george	indira
⋮	⋮

Subqueries

The DBMS tests each candidate tuple from the Cartesian product, using the where-clause condition to determine if it contributes to the answer. So far the condition has involved only comparisons among the tuple attributes. It can, however, refer to information beyond the candidate tuple. Recall the earlier solutions to the query: find the names of species swimming in the same tank with a shark. The two-part solution first computed the sharky tanks and then determined the species represented in those tanks. This solution is easier to understand than the eventual single SQL construction, which lines up five tables in a from-clause. However, a single SQL expression can still capture the flavor of the stepwise approach by using a subquery to compute the sharky tanks.

```
select S.sname
from Species S, Fish F, Tank T
where S.sno = F.sno and F.tno = T.tno and T.tno in
        (select Q.tno
        from Species H, Fish G, Tank Q
        where H.sno = G.sno and G.tno = Q.tno and H.sname = "shark").
```

The second select-statement, embedded within the where-clause, is a **subquery**. By itself, the subquery obtains the tno values of the sharky tanks. The mental execution model is unchanged. The DBMS computes the Cartesian product of Species, Fish, and Tank, using the aliases S, F, and T. It then discards the inappropriate combinations with the first two where-clause conditions. In the S, F, and T segments of the remaining tuples, S gives species information about the fish F, and T gives the corresponding tank data. At this point, the species line up with the tanks where they are represented, but some of these tanks may be non-sharky. The last boolean condition checks if the tno of the T section is among the sharky tanks. For this purpose, it constructs the set of sharky conditions on the fly, just to evaluate the one candidate tuple under test.

In this case, the set of sharky tanks is constant because it doesn't depend on the candidate tuple. In general, however, the tuple set computed by the subquery can be different for each candidate tuple, and therefore the DBMS theoretically reevaluates it for each use. In other words, the mental model of the DBMS operation in the presence of a subquery changes slightly. The initial step is as before: after forming the Cartesian product, the DBMS methodically checks each tuple for inclusion in the horizontal section. If the check involves a subquery, the DBMS reevaluates it in the context of each candidate. In our example, you can imagine the DBMS reconstructing the set of sharky tanks once for each candidate tuple. Of course, it gets the same intermediate set of sharky tank numbers each time, so the process is inefficient. Remember, however, that this process is only a mental model to let you visualize the correct solution. The DBMS can take a different route, as long as the final result remains the same. In this case, the DBMS could notice that the subquery makes no reference to the candidate tuple and must therefore compute a constant set. After the first computation, the DBMS could save the subquery set for use with subsequent candidates.

In this particular example, the subquery is unnecessary; two earlier SQL solutions used no subqueries. This example is just an introduction to the notation; it emphasizes how the boolean test can pause on a candidate tuple to perform some intermediate calculation.

When a subquery occurs within a host query, the subquery's table names are local to that subquery. This same scoping rule appears in most block-structured programming languages, such as Pascal or Ada. A host procedure can't reference local subprocedure variables. The subprocedure, however, can make free use of the host variables. In other words, a procedure can look outward to the larger scope to satisfy references to variables, but it can never look inward to the smaller scopes of its own nested procedures. Likewise, a subquery can refer to the tables of its host query, but the host can't refer to the subquery tables. If the subquery uses a table name or alias identical to one employed by the host, the subquery loses the ability to reference the outer table. The local name "hides" the host name. Using this scoping rule, you can rephrase the example above as shown on the left below, overloading the S, F, and T aliases. You should think of the S, F, and T subquery tables as *new* copies of the species, fish, and tank tables. Because the new aliases duplicate those of the host query, the subquery loses the ability to reference the attributes of the candidate tuple. In this case, it doesn't need the candidate tuple's attributes because it is computing a constant set.

```
select S.sname
from Species S, Fish F, Tank T
where S.sno = F.sno and F.tno = T.tno
    and T.tno in
        (select T.tno
        from Species S, Fish F, Tank T
        where S.sno = F.sno and
            F.tno = T.tno and
            S.sname = "shark").
```

```
select sname
from Species, Fish, Tank
where Species.sno = Fish.sno and
    Fish.tno = Tank.tno and
    Tank.tno in
        (select Tank.tno
        from Species, Fish, Tank
        where Species.sno = Fish.sno and
            Fish.tno = Tank.tno and
            sname = "shark").
```

As a matter of fact, except for convenience, the aliases aren't necessary at all, as illustrated by the version on the right. Qualification remains necessary for the sno and tno attributes.

 A subquery is an auxiliary select-statement embedded in a host query. The subquery can use table or alias names from the host query unless they are hidden by identical names in the subquery.

A modification of the example illustrates how a subquery set can vary with the candidate tuple: find the names of species that have a representative swimming in a tank with a shark of the same color. That is, the representative has the same fcolor as the shark. A one-step solution with no subqueries is possible, as illustrated on the left below. However, a subquery allows step-by-step progress toward a final expression, as illustrated on the right. Here the intermediate set is the collection of color-coordinated sharky tanks: they have a shark of the same color as the fish representing the candidate species.

```
select H.sname
from Species S, Fish F, Tank T,
    Fish G, Species H
where S.sno = F.sno and F.tno = T.tno and
    S.sname = "shark" and T.tno = G.tno and
    G.sno = H.sno and F.fcolor = G.fcolor.
```

```
select S.sname
from Species S, Fish F, Tank T
where S.sno = F.sno and F.tno = T.tno
    and T.tno in
        (select T.tno
         from Species S, Fish G, Tank T
         where S.sno = G.sno and G.tno = T.tno
            and S.sname = "shark"
            and F.fcolor = G.color).
```

The DBMS must reevaluate the subquery for each tuple from the outer Cartesian product because the subquery where-clause refers to the F.fcolor attribute from the outer host query. The expression safely uses the same convenient species and tank names in both query and subquery, but it must use a distinct fish alias in the subquery to keep access to the host's F segment.

A subquery evaluation returns a set of values. Therefore, when a subquery appears in a boolean expression, it must be part of a set comparison. Figure 5.4 lists the operations that can participate in boolean expressions with subqueries. The notation allows two interpretations of a one-member set: as a set or as the single element of the set. Under the second interpretation, you can compare a one-member set with an attribute value or with a constant using the usual θ-operations: $<, >, =, <=,$ and $>=$. The unary predicates, exists and not exists, return true if the set in question is non-empty or empty respectively. Standard SQL doesn't provide the set-containment, set-equality, or set-inequality comparisons, but they are available as extensions in some relational database systems. Set containment is interpreted to include the equality case: set A contains set B if $A = B$ or if A properly contains B.

Certain set operations allow SQL to impose its table-oriented perspective on the underlying relations. For example, suppose you want the names of fish whose color matches that of a tank with volume greater than 100. The following SQL solves the query:

```
select F.fname
from Fish F
where F.fcolor in
    (select T.tcolor
     from Tank T
     where T.tvolume > 100).
```

Technically, the F.fcolor value of a candidate tuple is an association involving the attribute fcolor. It will never be found in a set of associations involving the different attribute, T.tcolor. This question asks if an apple occurs in a box of oranges. Nevertheless, SQL allows such comparisons. It considers F.fcolor to be a one-row table containing the color (i.e., a string) of the candidate fish. The subquery constructs a table of colors (i.e., strings) from the qualifying tanks. The expression is now testing a string for membership in a table of strings. You can imagine that you are now comparing the *names* of apples with the *names* of oranges.

left operand	connective	right operand
element	in	set of elements
element	not in	set of elements
set	=	set
set	not =	set
set	contains	set
set	not contains	set
	exists	set
	not exists	set

left operand	connective	right operand
element	>	one-element set
element	<	one-element set
element	=	one-element set
element	not =	one-element set
element	>=	one-element set
element	<=	one-element set

Figure 5.4   Connectives for embedding subqueries in a where-clause

These divergences from the set-theoretical model provide additional flexibility for queries. Another variation allows SQL to use the left-to-right ordering in the query when the tuple being checked for set membership contains several components. For example, you can write

```
select X.a
from X, Y, Z
where (X.b, Y.c, Z.d) in
    (select A.e, B.f, C.g
    from A, B, C).
```

The DBMS compares the three-element row from the Cartesian product candidate, (X.b, Y.c, Z.d), in left-to-right order with the three-element rows returned by the subquery. Again, SQL is exploiting an implied ordering that isn't present in the underlying sets. It can do this because the query specifies the order.

The following queries illustrate some of the set predicates of Figure 5.4. First, find the tanks that are inhabited. The solution on the left below closely follows the intuition suggested by the query because a tank is inhabited when fish exist in it. The asterisk symbol in the subquery is a standard abbreviation, meaning all attributes of the from-clause tables. The notation is useful here because the exists-predicate isn't concerned with the tuples' attributes; it is concerned only with the their existence.

```
select T.tname                    select T.tname
from Tank T                       from Tank T, Fish F
where exists                      where T.tno = F.tno.
    (select *
    from Fish F
    where F.tno = T.tno).
```

The SQL on the right, also a solution, doesn't use a subquery. A tank with no fish won't survive the horizontal sectioning operation because it appears in Cartesian product paired only with fish from other tanks.

For another example, find the names of fish matching the color of the fish with fno = 164. Because fno is a key of the fish table, at most one fish tuple has fno = 164. You first verify that there is exactly one such fish, as shown on the left below. Then, assuming fish 164 exists, you probe further with the SQL on the right. The expression uses the convention that an element can be compared with a set if the set contains exactly one element of the same type—a string in this case.

```
select *                     select F.fname
from Fish F                  from Fish F
where F.fno = 164.           where F.fcolor =
                                 (select F.fcolor
                                 from Fish F
                                 where F.fno = 164).
```

Now find the names of species represented in all tanks. A candidate species tuple can't succeed by virtue of a connection to other database elements. Instead, it must possess a bundle of connections, sufficient to relate it to all the tanks. In other words, this is a universal query, whereas the examples to this point have all been existential queries. A universal query will always involve subqueries in its SQL solution. By contrast, the existential examples above used subqueries for a more natural step-by-step decomposition of the problem. However, they weren't necessary. An SQL solution for the species represented in all tanks is:

```
select S.sname
from Species S
where
    (select T.tno
    from Fish F, Tank T
    where S.sno = F.sno and F.tno = T.tno)
=
    (select T.tno
    from Tank T).
```

The first subquery determines all tanks holding a representative of the candidate species. The second subquery determines the set of all tanks in the database. If the two sets are equal, the candidate species appears in all tanks.

As a final example, find again the names of species represented in a tank named cesspool. Because this is an existential query, a solution without subqueries is possible. The SQL on the left below performs horizontal and vertical extractions from a Cartesian product. However, an alternative solution with nested subqueries, as shown on the right, demonstrates a chain of relationships stretching from the candidate species.

```
                                                    select S.sname
                                                    from Species S
                                                    where exists
    select S.sname                                     (select *
    from Species S, Fish F, Tank T                     from Fish F
    where S.sno = F.sno and F.tno = T.tno              where S.sno = F.sno and exists
        and T.tname = "cesspool".                         (select *
                                                           from Tank T
                                                           where F.tno = T.tno and
                                                               T.tname = "cesspool")).
```

Although commercial implementations may have some limit, SQL expressions can, in theory, nest subqueries to an arbitrary depth. In practice, however, more than two levels are rarely encountered. At each level, the scoping rules permit a subquery to reference the tables, or aliases, of the host queries above it. Of course, a reference into an outer scope is valid only if the subquery doesn't "hide" the name by redeclaring it in its own scope.

Existential queries

By definition, a candidate tuple contributes to the answer of an existential query if it can originate a path to some anchor tuple. For existential queries, previous chapters developed relational algebra and calculus formats, which used a standard form to capture the required path. This section extends those formats to SQL.

An existential query always has an SQL solution that doesn't use subqueries. The relational algebra format aligns tables for an extended Cartesian product, which captures the required database path, if it exists. It also captures many inappropriate combinations but discards them with a subsequent selection operation. Consider again the last example: find the names of species represented in a cesspool tank. The database path comprises three links: a candidate species, a connecting fish, and a cesspool tank. Accordingly, the relational algebra format aligns three tables, as shown to the left below.

$$\pi_q \sigma_b (\check{\rho}(S = \text{Species}) \times \check{\rho}(F = \text{Fish}) \times \check{\rho}(T = \text{Tank})),$$

where b = (S.sno = F.sno $\wedge$ F.tno = T.tno $\wedge$ T.tname = "cesspool")

q = (S.sname).

```
select S.sname
from Species S, Fish F, Tank T
where S.sno = F.sno and F.tno = T.tno
    and T.tname = "cesspool".
```

SQL can achieve the same effect with a from-clause alignment of the same three tables, as shown to the right. Where relational algebra avoids attribute name conflicts with a renaming operator, SQL uses aliases. Where relational algebra removes nonsensical combinations with a σ_b operator, SQL uses the same boolean conditions in a where-clause. The standard SQL format for existential queries, therefore, is a direct translation of the standard relational algebra format.

The SQL solution to an existential query aligns the path tables in a from-clause. The where-clause boolean removes the inappropriate combinations and identifies the anchor.

Although subqueries are never necessary for existential queries, they sometimes provide a more readable solution. The last section included an alternative solution to find the species in the cesspool tanks. It used a chain of subqueries to emphasize the existence of the qualifying database path. For a longer path, with multiple copies of some tables, consider again the query: find the names of species swimming with a shark. The qualifying chain involves five tuples: the candidate species, a fish, a tank, another fish, and a final species. By arranging five tables in the Cartesian product, you are sure to capture the chain, if it exists. A where-clause boolean can then remove all nonsensical entries where the foreign-to-primary key links don't match. The standard SQL solution appears on the left below, above the relational algebra that it imitates. On the right is an equivalent SQL expression, which uses subqueries to emphasize the existence of the qualifying path.

```
select S.sname
from Species S, Fish F, Tank T, Fish G, Species H
where S.sno = F.sno and F.tno = T.tno and
   T.tno = G.tno and G.sno = H.sno and
   H.sname = "shark".
```

```
select S.sname
from Species S
where exists
   (select *
   from Fish F
   where S.sno = F.sno and exists
      (select *
      from Tank T
      where F.tno = T.tno and exists
         (select *
         from Fish G
         where T.tno = G.tno and exists
            (select *
            from Species H
            where G.sno = H.sno and
               H.sname = "shark")))).
```

$$\pi_q \sigma_b (\breve{\rho}(S = \text{Species}) \times \breve{\rho}(F = \text{Fish}) \times \breve{\rho}(T = \text{Tank}) \times$$
$$\breve{\rho}(G = \text{Fish}) \times \breve{\rho}(H = \text{Species})),$$

$$\text{where} \quad b \quad = \quad (S.\text{sno} = F.\text{sno} \wedge F.\text{tno} = T.\text{tno} \wedge$$
$$T.\text{tno} = G.\text{tno} \wedge G.\text{sno} = H.\text{sno} \wedge$$
$$H.\text{sname} = \text{``shark''})$$
$$q \quad = \quad (S.\text{sname}).$$

The tank link isn't necessary in this example: it serves only to place fish F and G in the same tank. You can enforce that constraint directly by equating the tno foreign keys in the fish tuples. This simplification reduces the number of tables from five to four in the relational algebra expression, and a similar reduction is possible in the SQL equivalent. The new solutions then appear as follows.

```
select S.sname
from Species S, Fish F, Fish G, Species H
where S.sno = F.sno and F.tno = G.tno and
   G.sno = H.sno and H.sname = "shark".
```

$$\pi_q \sigma_b (\breve{\rho}(S = \text{Species}) \times \breve{\rho}(F = \text{Fish}) \times$$
$$\breve{\rho}(G = \text{Fish}) \times \breve{\rho}(H = \text{Species})),$$

$$\text{where} \quad b \quad = \quad (S.\text{sno} = F.\text{sno} \wedge F.\text{tno} = G.\text{tno} \wedge$$
$$G.\text{sno} = H.\text{sno} \wedge H.\text{sname} = \text{``shark''})$$
$$q \quad = \quad (S.\text{sname}).$$

For a still longer path, consider again the following query: find the names of species swimming with some species represented in a cesspool tank. This query requires three excursions across the database and uses seven tuples to capture the qualifying path. Below are the relational algebra and calculus solutions, which both use the standard formats. The third expression is the equivalent SQL. All three constructions use the same idea, just different notation. The relational algebra aligns the tables for a Cartesian product. The relational calculus introduces existentially quantified variables and immediately restricts them to the proper tables. The SQL aligns the tables in the from-clause. In all cases, a boolean expression removes inappropriate combinations.

(1) $\pi_q \sigma_b (\check{\rho}(S = \text{Species}) \times \check{\rho}(F = \text{Fish}) \times \check{\rho}(T = \text{Tank}) \times \check{\rho}(G = \text{Fish}) \times$
          $\check{\rho}(R = \text{Species}) \times \check{\rho}(H = \text{Fish}) \times \check{\rho}(Q = \text{Tank})),$
          where b $=$ (S.sno = F.sno $\wedge$ F.tno = T.tno $\wedge$ T.tno = G.tno $\wedge$
                      G.sno = R.sno $\wedge$ R.sno = H.sno $\wedge$ H.tno = Q.tno $\wedge$ Q.tname = "cesspool")
                q $=$ (S.sname).

(2) $\{\text{sname}(s)$ $|$ $\text{species}(s) \wedge (\exists f, t, g, r, h, q)$
                      $(\text{fish}(f) \wedge \text{tank}(t) \wedge \text{fish}(g) \wedge \text{species}(r) \wedge \text{fish}(h) \wedge \text{tank}(q) \wedge$
                      $\text{sno}(s) = \text{sno}(f) \wedge \text{tno}(f) = \text{tno}(t) \wedge \text{tno}(t) = \text{tno}(g) \wedge$
                      $\text{sno}(g) = \text{sno}(r) \wedge \text{sno}(r) = \text{sno}(h) \wedge \text{tno}(h) = \text{tno}(q) \wedge$
                      $\text{tname}(q) = \text{"cesspool"})\}.$

(3)   ```
select S.sname
from Species S, Fish F, Tank T, Fish G, Species H, Fish X, Tank Y
where S.sno = F.sno and F.tno = T.tno and T.tno = G.tno and G.sno = H.sno and
    H.sno = X.sno and X.tno = Y.tno and Y.tname = "cesspool".
```

In the examples to this point, the answer table has included only an attribute from the head of the qualifying chain. However, as with relational algebra or calculus solutions, you can extract information from any of the chain links. For example, find the names of species swimming with a shark, and report the cohabiting tanks. The SQL isolates the qualifying chain as before, but it broadens the final vertical section to include the tank name attribute from the chain.

```
select S.sname, T.tname
from Species S, Fish F, Tank T, Fish G, Species H
where S.sno = F.sno and F.tno = T.tno and T.tno = G.tno and
    G.sno = H.sno and H.sname = "shark".
```

Universal queries

In a universal query, a candidate tuple can't qualify for the answer merely by the existence of a path to an anchor tuple. Instead, the candidate must be able to reach each member of an anchor collection. Consider again the query: find the names of species represented in all tanks. A candidate species tuple can't qualify by the existence of a path to some tank. It must satisfy a more stringent condition: it must be able to reach *all* tanks. SQL can't solve this query without using subqueries. Without subqueries to bring other sets into the condition, the where-clause boolean operates independently on each tuple from the Cartesian product. These isolated comparisons can use only the attribute values for the single Cartesian product candidate tuple. The segments of this tuple represent a single path from species to anchor although the need is for information on a collection of paths. By contrast, a subquery suspends the tuple under test and constructs an additional set.
```

Comparison of the frozen candidate tuple and the new set allows a decision based on many paths.

The set containment solution

The left expression below repeats an earlier solution to the example. The SQL expression constructs two sets for each candidate species: one containing all tanks in the database and the other containing the tanks reachable from the candidate through some fish. The where-clause boolean can now reach a decision about the candidate species tuple by verifying that the set of reachable tanks contains the set of all tanks.

```
select S.sname                          select S.sname
from Species S                          from Species S
where                                   where
  (select T.tno                           (select T.tno
   from Fish F, Tank T                      from Fish F, Tank T
   where S.sno = F.sno and F.tno = T.tno)   where S.sno = F.sno and F.tno = T.tno)
=                                       contains
  (select T.tno                           (select T.tno
   from Tank T).                            from Tank
                                            where tcolor = "red").
```

A modified version appears on the right: find the species represented in all red tanks. Here, the contains-predicate is necessary because the set of reachable tanks might be larger than the set of red tanks. These examples illustrate a standard format for SQL solutions to universal queries. Subqueries generate two sets for each candidate: the anchor tuples and the reachable tuples. A set comparison then determines if the reachable set contains the anchor set. If it does, the candidate contributes to the answer.

 The SQL solution to a universal query involves two subqueries. One computes the set of anchor tuples, and the other computes the set of reachable tuples.

The doubly negated construction

An alternative approach to universal queries avoids the contains-construction but is less intuitive. Unfortunately, some database products don't support the contains-predicate, and in these cases, the alternate must be used. Consider again the query: find the names of species represented in all tanks. The following SQL is a correct solution, but you may need to study it carefully to convince yourself.

```
select S.sname
from Species S
where not exists
    (select *
    from Tank T
    where not exists
        (select *
        from Fish F
        where S.sno = F.sno and F.tno = T.tno)).
```

The query requests the sname value from certain species tuples—those where a certain calculated set is empty. That set is the set of tanks with no connection to the candidate species. The reasoning is: if the set of tanks with no connection to the candidate species is empty, the species must be connected to all tanks. The first subquery computes this set of tanks. As usual, the candidate species is frozen during the subquery evaluation, and the subquery can use its attributes. To determine the set of tanks with no connection to the frozen species tuple, the subquery selects from the tank relation those tuples for which *another* calculated set is empty. This set is calculated anew for each tank, so in the second subquery, a frozen tank and a frozen species are available. The set contains the fish tuples that act as a bridge between the frozen species tuple and the frozen tank tuple. Again, the reasoning is: if the set of fish connecting a given species and a given tank is empty, the tank has no connection with the species. If this set is empty, the tank isn't connected to the candidate species and belongs to the set under construction by the first subquery.

Using the data of Figure 2.1, you see that sno 17 appears in all six tanks of the database and that sno 22 appears only in tno 42 and 85. Therefore, the sname dolphin should appear as part of the answer table and the sname shark shouldn't. If you evaluate the first subquery for sno 17, you will get an empty set because no tank is *not* connected to sno 17. In other words, every tank is connected. The double negative is confusing and grammatically flawed, but it parallels the double negative in the SQL. Because the set is empty, the sname associated with sno 17 (dolphin) becomes part of the answer.

However, when you evaluate the first subquery for sno 22, you get a non-empty set, containing tanks tno = 55, 35, 38, and 44, because none is connected to sno 22. For example, when considering tno 55, the second subquery returns the empty set because no fish exist with tno 55 and sno 22. Therefore, the not-exists predicate is true, and tno 55 enters the accumulating set of the first subquery. The DBMS can terminate the first subquery at this point. Once tno 55 has been placed in the subquery's result table, further computation only accumulates additional tanks (35, 38, 44)—all unconnected to sno 22. These additional entries don't change the non-empty status to be tested when the construction is complete.

The doubly negated construction provides an alternative template for the SQL solution of universal queries. As with the set-containment construction, two subqueries are needed. They are now, however, nested within one another. The outer subquery computes the set of anchors that aren't reachable from the candidate. If this set is empty, the candidate can reach all the anchors, and it contributes to the answer. The inner subquery computes the links between the candidate and a fixed anchor object. No links implies an unreachable anchor.

 An alternative SQL solution to a universal query uses two nested subqueries in a doubly negated construction. The subqueries compute the set of anchor tuples that aren't reachable by a candidate.

The doubly negated construction compares directly with the relational calculus format. The relational calculus solution to the example appears below. The first line comes from the standard template; succeeding lines provide equivalent formulations, which work toward a doubly negated expression.

$$\{\text{sname}(s) \quad | \quad \text{species}(s) \wedge (\forall t)(\text{tank}(t) \Rightarrow (\exists f)(\text{fish}(f) \wedge \text{tno}(t) = \text{tno}(f) \wedge \text{sno}(f) = \text{sno}(s)))\}.$$

$$\{\text{sname}(s) \quad | \quad \text{species}(s) \wedge (\forall t)(\neg\text{tank}(t) \vee (\exists f)(\text{fish}(f) \wedge \text{tno}(t) = \text{tno}(f) \wedge \text{sno}(f) = \text{sno}(s)))\}.$$

$$\{\text{sname}(s) \quad | \quad \text{species}(s) \wedge \neg(\exists t)(\text{tank}(t) \wedge \neg(\exists f)(\text{fish}(f) \wedge \text{tno}(t) = \text{tno}(f) \wedge \text{sno}(f) = \text{sno}(s)))\}.$$

The third form corresponds to the doubly negated SQL construction. It qualifies a species if there are no tanks to which it is not connected. An earlier derivation showed how to derive the relational algebra division format from the standard relational calculus template. Therefore, the division construction from relational algebra, the universal quantification construction from relational calculus, and the doubly negated subquery construction from SQL all represent the same reasoning.

Longer universal path bundles

Suppose you want the names of species represented in all tanks containing representatives of all species whose diet is worms. The relational algebra solution is as follows. The anchor set, Y, for the overall query is itself a separate universal query. Y contains the tanks connected to all worm-eating species.

$$X = \pi_q \sigma_b(\text{Species})) \qquad \text{where} \quad b \; = \; (\text{sfood} = \text{``worms''})$$
$$Y = \pi_r(\text{Tank} * \text{Fish} * \text{Species})/X \qquad\qquad\qquad q \; = \; (\text{sno})$$
$$Z = \pi_t[\pi_s(\text{Species} * \text{Fish} * \text{Tank})/Y] \qquad\qquad r \; = \; (\text{tno}, \text{sno})$$
$$s \; = \; (\text{sno}, \text{sname}, \text{tno})$$
$$t \; = \; (\text{sname}).$$

A similar approach, using either the set-containment or doubly negated construction, works in SQL. Both solutions appear below. You can paraphrase the English to conform more closely to the leftmost SQL as follows. Find those species where the associated tanks include all members of a special tank set. The special tanks, computed as a subquery, are those whose associated species include all species with an sfood value of worm.

```
select S.sname
from Species S
where
   (select T.tno
   from Fish F, Tank T
   where S.sno = F.sno and F.tno = T.tno)
contains
   (select T.tno
   from Tank T
   where
      (select S.sno
      from Species S, Fish F
      where S.sno = F.sno and F.tno = T.tno)
   contains
      (select S.sno
      from Species S
      where S.sfood = "worm")).
```

```
select S.sname
from Species S
where not exists
   (select *
   from Tank T
   where not exists
      (select *
      from Species S
      where S.sfood = "worm" and not exists
         (select *
         from Fish F
         where F.sno = S.sno and F.tno = T.tno))
   and not exist
      (select *
      from Fish F
      where F.sno = S.sno and F.tno = T.tno)).
```

According to the SQL expression to the right above, a species qualifies if the set of wormy tanks to which it isn't connected is empty. This special tank set is computed by a subquery that questions each tank to determine (1) if it is wormy and (2) if it's not connected to the candidate species. As usual, the second part is decided by the absence of fish connecting the tank and species. However, the first part requires that the species represented in the tank contain all species with a sfood value of worm. Avoiding the contains-predicate a second time forces an embedded double negation. That is, the set of species with a worm diet that aren't connected to the tank must be nonexistent.

Besides creating difficulty with repeated negatives, this version makes substantial appeal to the scoping rules to determine which copies of Species, Tank, or Fish are under reference at a given point in the extended predicate. The set-containment predicate is clearly preferable, if it is available. Even if it's not, certain aggregate functions can sometimes be used to avoid the double negation, as you will see in the next section.

Most day-to-day SQL involves only existential queries, which don't require subqueries. Indeed, the figure is often quoted as 80% or greater. Of those that do require subqueries, few are as complicated as the examples discussed above. An understanding of these examples should leave the you very well-prepared to use SQL under normal circumstances.

Mixed existential and universal queries

The following query illustrates a mixed strategy between the pure existential and universal approaches. Find the tanks that are inhabited by *some* species present in *all* red tanks. The qualifying path for a candidate tank starts with a single extension to an associated species but then splits into a bundle of paths for the remaining connections. This is still a universal query because the candidate species can't qualify for the answer based on the existence of a single path. A subquery, therefore, must appear in the SQL solution. Figure 5.5 illustrates the solution; the SQL expression follows:

```
select T.tname
from Tank T, Fish F, Species S
where T.tno = F.tno and F.sno = S.sno and not exists
   (select *
   from Tank Q
   where Q.tcolor = "red" and not exists
      (select *
      from Fish G
      where G.tno = Q.tno and G.sno = S.sno)).
```

An identifying feature of a universal query is that a candidate tuple attempts to reach a collection of anchor tuples through a bundle of connecting paths. In this chapter's examples, the anchor collection is independent of the candidate. However, it can vary with the candidate under test. Because a subquery builds the anchor set, with the candidate frozen during the construction, the candidate's attributes are available to influence the anchor set contents. Therefore, the standard SQL templates for universal queries, set containment or double negation, remain valid.

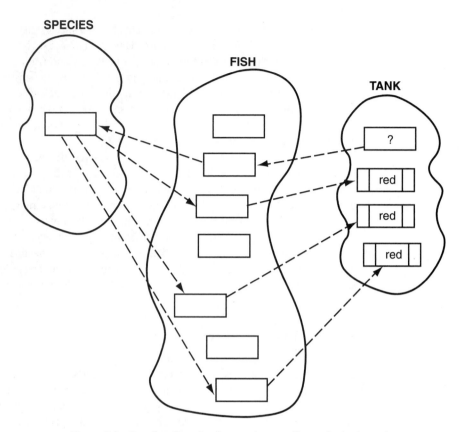

Figure 5.5   Bundles diverging from an intermediate point in the path

Aggregates and partitions

After obtaining a query solution with certain horizontal and vertical sections of a Cartesian product, you might want to organize the result table into several tuple groups. SQL provides two clauses for grouping tuples. The orderby-clause is the simpler because it merely sorts the output tuples before displaying them. The groupby-clause is more complicated because it first bundles tuples into groups according to common attribute values and then computes summary functions within each group. For example, it can separately calculate the average of an attribute value across each group. A **partition** is a segregation of tuples into disjoint groups, with the members of each group agreeing on some specified attributes. The tuples within each group serve as operands for certain **aggregate operators**, such a sum, average, and count.

 In an SQL query, a partition is a conceptual grouping of the Cartesian product tuples for the purpose of performing computations on the attribute values within each group.

The orderby-clause

To illustrate the orderby-clause, consider the query: find the names of species and their associated fish, grouped by species in the output display. Assuming the data of Figure 2.1, the uppermost SQL below produces the table on the right.

```
select S.sname species, F.fname fish
from Species S, Fish F
where F.sno = S.sno
orderby S.sname.
```

< · · · >	
species	fish
dolphin	flipper
dolphin	albert
dolphin	indira
dolphin	jill
dolphin	laura
dolphin	maureen
guppy	charlie
guppy	fran
guppy	helen
guppy	kilroy
shark	killer
shark	charlie
shark	bonnie
shark	elsie
shark	cory
shark	darron
shark	george

```
select S.sname species, F.fname fish
from Species S, Fish F
where F.sno = S.sno
orderby S.sname, F.fname.
```

The first attribute in an orderby-clause becomes the primary sort key, which determines how to group the tuples into bundles. Each bundle contains tuples that agree on the specified attribute. This example has a single sort key, sname, so the alphabetical ordering doesn't extend to the fish names within each species. For group of items with the same primary sort key value, the next orderby-attribute provides a secondary sort key, which determines the sort order within the group. You could use a third orderby-attribute to specify an order among tuples that agree on the first two sort keys, and so forth. To order the output first by sname and then by fname within each group of constant sname, you can rephrase the query as shown in the second SQL expression above. This version produces a similar table (not shown), where the fish names appear alphabetically within each species grouping. In this case, each partition grouping contains tuples that agree on both sname and fname. You expect each grouping to contain one tuple, but a grouping can contain several tuples, if several fish of the same species share a common name.

The orderby- and groupby-clauses are independent of each other. The principal use of a groupby-clause is to partition the answer set *before* computing a summary function from the tuples of each grouping. For example, you might want to know the number of tuples in each grouping or the average value of some attribute. By contrast, the orderby-clause simply makes certain groupings visible in the output display, *after* all database retrieval operations are finished.

The SQL orderby-clause specifies a sort-key sequence, which orders the final display of the answer table.

In the mental model for SQL processing, the orderby-clause imposes the partition on the Cartesian product of the from-clause tables *after* the where-clause extracts the horizontal slice but *before* the select-clause takes the vertical slice to isolate the attributes for the answer. This operational sequence allows you to order the display by some attribute that doesn't even appear in the answer—a feature of limited usefulness. For example, you can modify the previous example to select species and their associated fish and to order the display by fish color. Of course, the displayed table shows no apparent order because the fish color doesn't appear. The SQL is:

```
select S.sname species, F.fname fish
from Species S, Fish F
where F.sno = S.sno
orderby F.fcolor.
```

Because the operation appears to have no effect, some database systems don't allow the orderby-clause to contain attributes that don't appear in the answer table.

The orderby-clause has no counterpart in relational algebra or calculus. The algebra and calculus are notations for constructing new relations, which happen to conform to some query. By definition, the new relations aren't ordered. In SQL, the orderby-clause is a postprocessing feature. The table-building features construct new tables, and they have relational algebra and calculus counterparts. After the answer table has been constructed, the orderby-clause simply commands a particular order for displaying that table.

The groupby-clause

SQL provides five aggregate functions for performing computations on the tuples within a partition grouping: count, sum, average, min, and max. Each function takes an argument to indicate which attribute to summarize. Sum and average apply only to numerical attributes and to certain number-type attributes provided by some systems, such as money and time intervals.

For a first example, find the number of fish representing each species. Assuming the data of Figure 2.1, the SQL appears on the left below, and the result on the right.

```
select S.sno SpeciesNo, S.sname Species,
    count(F.fno) as fishCount
from Species S, Fish F
where F.sno = S.sno
groupby S.sno.
```

| < · · · > | | |
SpeciesNo	Species	fishCount
17	dolphin	6
74	guppy	4
22	shark	4
93	shark	3

 An aggregate is a function—count, sum, average, maximum, or minimum—which operates on some specified column. The aggregate is applied separately inside each partition grouping.

The DBMS applies select-clause aggregates independently within each partition grouping generated by the groupby-clause. The aggregate reduces each group to one line (i.e., one tuple) in the answer. In the example above, the groupby-clause generates four groups, one for each distinct sno in the species table. Four tuples, therefore, appear in the answer. Because each grouping is reduced to a single tuple, the select-clause can contain only two types of expressions: (1) an aggregate of some attribute, which reduces the multiple values within a group to a single value, or (2) an attribute value that is constant across group tuples. In the example, you can't ask for fname in the select-clause. Because each group becomes a single line in the answer, which of the many fname values in a group should appear in the output line? On the other hand, you can ask for sname. Because the tuples within a given group have the same sno value and because sno is a key to the species table, they all must also have identical sname values. Therefore, the one output line for the group has an unambiguous sname value.

By definition, any groupby-clause attribute will have a constant value across the group tuples. However, unless the database schema includes information on key or functional dependency constraints, the DBMS can't know for certain that any other attributes will be constant across a group. For this reason, some database system restrict the targets of the select-clause, in the presence of aggregates, to other aggregates and to the groupby-clause attributes. Other systems take a more liberal interpretation and allow attributes that are constant across the tuples of the group (for whatever reason) as well as aggregates. Our discussion here will assume the latter interpretation. However, if you find yourself working with a database system that takes the more restrictive view, and if you know that some attribute must be constant across groups because of a functional dependency constraint, then you can simply include the attribute in the groupby-clause. Because the attribute is already constant across the partition groups, the partition won't change. You can now use the attribute in the select-clause. Using this trick, you can rephrase the query above as shown below. Within a group of constant S.sno values, the S.sname values are also constant, so the partition groupings don't change.

```
select S.sno SpeciesNo, S.sname Species, count(F.fno) fishCount
from Species S, Fish F
where F.sno = S.sno
groupby S.sno, S.sname.
```

This query computes the number of tuples in each group by counting the entries in the fno column. However, you can count the entries under any attribute because the count simply gives the number of tuples in the group. For this reason, the notation "count(*)" is often used. The aggregate count(*) instructs the DBMS to count the tuples in each group without reference to any particular column. Using this notation, the more common SQL expression for the previous example appears on the left below. Of course, the answer table doesn't change.

```
select S.sno SpeciesNo, S.sname Species,      select S.sno SpeciesNo, S.sname Species,
   count(*) as fishCount                          count(distinct F.fname) as fishCount
from Species S, Fish F                         from Species S, Fish F
where F.sno = S.sno                            where F.sno = S.sno
groupby S.sno.                                 groupby S.sno.
```

If you want the number of distinct values of some attribute within each group, you must use the keyword "distinct" with the count function, and you must specify an attribute whose distinct entries are to be counted. For example, the expression on the right above answers the query: find the number of distinct fname values within each species.

If an aggregate appears in the select-clause but no groupby-clause is present, the entire answer table is treated as one group. For example, the left expression below counts the number of fish in the database, and the right one counts the number of fish that inhabit red tanks.

```
select count(*) fishCount
from Fish F.
```

```
select count(*) fishCount
from Fish F, Tank T
where F.tno = T.tno and T.tcolor = "red".
```

 In the presence of aggregates, an optional groupby-clause partitions the horizontal section of the Cartesian product. The aggregates reduce each group to a single tuple. An optional orderby-clause then sorts the summary tuples for display purposes. The select-clause extracts a vertical section containing the desired attributes.

Distinction between orderby and groupby

Both the orderby- and groupby-clauses can list several attributes. The tuples within each computational group agree on all groupby-clause attributes. However, the orderby-clause attributes merely determine the sort order of the display, with the leftmost attribute being the most significant sort key. Consider the query: find the names of fish, and report them by species and tank. The SQL solution appears on the left below; the answer table is to the right.

```
select S.sno speciesNo, T.tno tankNo,
    F.fname as fishName
from Species S, Fish F, Tank T
where S.sno = F.sno and F.tno = T.tno
orderby S.sno, T.tno.
```

Answer		
speciesNo	tankNo	fishName
17	35	flipper
17	38	jill
17	42	indira
17	44	maureen
17	55	albert
17	85	laura
22	42	killer
22	42	bonnie
22	42	elsie
22	85	charlie
74	42	charlie
74	44	helen
74	55	fran
74	55	kilroy
93	35	cory
93	42	darron
93	42	george

Because the query specifies no aggregates, a groupby-clause isn't appropriate. Instead, the orderby-clause forces the answer to be displayed in a clustered fashion. The answer table uses the data of Figure 2.1. The horizontal lines emphasize the groupings, but they wouldn't appear in the raw output from the DBMS.

However, if you want to cluster the data for certain calculations, then you must specify the groupby option instead. For example, suppose you want to count the fish by species and by tank, rather simply displaying them in those clusters. The following SQL performs this function and gives the answer on the right.

< ··· >		
speciesNo	tankNo	fishCount
17	35	1
17	38	1
17	42	1
17	44	1
17	55	1
17	85	1
22	42	3
22	85	1
74	42	1
74	44	1
74	55	2
93	35	1
93	42	2

```
select S.sno speciesNo, T.tno tankNo,
    count(*) as fishCount
from Species S, Fish F, Tank T
where S.sno = F.sno and F.tno = T.tno
groupby S.sno, T.tno
orderby S.sno, T.tno.
```

If you give an aggregate an alias, you can use it to sort the display by the calculated values. For example, suppose you want the average fish weight by species, and you want to present the results in descending average fish weight. By creating an alias for the computed column, the following SQL allows a reference to it in the subsequent orderby-clause. Ascending sort order is assumed for each sort key, unless descending order is explicitly specified.

```
select S.sno as speciesNo, S.sname as speciesName, average(F.fweight) as fishWeight
from Species S, Fish F
where S.sno = F.sno
groupby S.sno
orderby fishWeight descending.
```

Possible overrepresentation in partition groupings

Certain aggregate queries can introduce subtle errors if you don't carefully follow the underlying processing model. For example, suppose you want the total tank volume associated with each species. Your first attempt might produce the following expression, which contains an error.

```
select S.sno speciesNo, sum(T.tvolume) totalVol
from Species S, Fish F, Tank T
where S.sno = F.sno and F.tno = T.tno
groupby S.sno.
```

The problem is overcounting. In the grouping for a given sno, a particular tank and its volume appear many times, once for each fish connecting the tank and the fixed species. The sum aggregate then computes an inaccurate total because the tank enters into the summation too many times. You can't correct this overcounting by specifying "sum(distinct T.tvolume)" because two or more distinct tanks in the same group might have the same volume. The correct solution acquires all combinations of species and tank, without mentioning the connecting fish, and then constructs a subquery to eliminate the inappropriate combinations:

```
select S.sno speciesNo, sum(T.tvolume) totalVol
from Species S, Tank T
where exists
   (select *
   from Fish F
   where S.sno = F.sno and F.tno = T.tno)
groupby S.sno.
```

Here a species pairs with a given tank only once. That pair survives the horizontal sectioning only if there is a fish connecting them. Then the partition groups the tuples by sno. The group for a particular sno contains exactly one copy of each tank connected to that species. The sum aggregate then computes the correct value.

 Subqueries are sometimes necessary to prevent overrepresentation of tuples in partition groupings.

The max and min aggregates operate on both numerical attributes and character strings. In string operations, alphabetical order determines which string is larger. For example, the following SQL finds the minimum tank color associated with a dolphin species.

```
select min(T.tcolor) as minColor
from Tank T, Fish F, Species S
where T.tno = F.tno and F.sno = S.sno and S.sname = "dolphin".
```

Without a groupby-clause, the entire Cartesian product, after the horizontal extraction, becomes one large group. Overcounting occurs because a tank appears many times in the group, once for each fish connecting it with a dolphin species. Unlike the sum operation, the min function still gives the right answer. Duplicates in a list don't change the minimum or maximum value. A separate subquery isn't necessary to produce the proper horizontal section.

Suppressing partitions

After conceptually partitioning the Cartesian product tuples with a groupby-clause, SQL provides a final opportunity to reject certain groups before it applies the reductions specified by the select-clause aggregates. A having-clause determines which groups remain in the partition. For example, suppose you want the average tank volume associated with each species, but only for those species represented in two or more tanks. The SQL solution is:

```
select S.sno species, average(T.tvolume) avgVol
from Species S, Tank T
where exists
  (select *
  from Fish F
  where S.sno = F.sno and F.tno = T.tno)
groupby S.sno
having count(*) >= 2.
```

The subquery prevents the sum aggregate from overcounting a particular tank because of multiple connecting fish. The having-clause boolean can contain only comparisons that apply to a group as a whole. This restriction is necessary because, unlike the where-clause boolean, the having-clause boolean qualifies an entire group, rather than an individual tuple. Valid operands are aggregates, which reduce the disparate column values in a group to a single value, or attributes that have the same value across a group. This is the same reasoning that constrains the select-clause entries when an aggregate is present.

The having-clause can contain subqueries although some database system don't allow them. All features of the primary select-statement are recursively available in subqueries. For example, the following SQL finds the names of tanks whose volume is above average. Recall the convention that allows a set containing a single number to be compared directly with another number.

```
select T.tname
from Tank T
where T.tvolume >
    (select average(T.tvolume)
    from Tank T).
```

Sometimes a query needs more than one partition. In that case, you can apply aggregates to only one of them, but you can still investigate other partitions with subqueries. For example, the SQL on the left below answers the query: find the average tank volume for each species, provided that 10 or more fish represent the species. Here you must group a species with all its tanks to apply the average aggregate. However, you must also group a species with its fish to determine if it belongs in the answer.

```
select S.sno, S.sname, average(T.tvolume) avgVol
from Species S, Tank T
where exists
  (select *
  from Fish F
  where S.sno = F.sno and F.tno = T.tno)
and
  S.sno in
    (select S.sno
    from Species S, Fish F
    where S.sno = F.sno
    groupby S.sno
    having count(*) >= 10)
groupby S.sno.
```

```
select S.sno, S.sname,
    average(T.tvolume) avgVol
from Species S, Tank T
where exists
  (select *
  from Fish F
  where S.sno = F.sno and F.tno = T.tno)
and
    (select count(*)
    from Fish F
    where S.sno = F.sno) >= 10)
groupby S.sno.
```

Many database systems don't allow having-clauses in where-clause subqueries or subqueries in having-clauses booleans. If you work with such a restricted system, you could rephrase the query to avoid the having-clause in the subquery, as shown on the right.

As a final example of aggregates, consider this alternative method for solving the universal query: find the names of species represented in all tanks. Earlier sections have already developed two SQL solutions: one with a set-containment predicate and the other with a doubly negated construction. With aggregates, you can qualify a candidate species by counting the tanks connected to the candidate and comparing the result with the total number of tanks in the database. This strategy gives the SQL:

```
select S.sname
from Species S
where
   (select count(*)
   from Tank T
   where exists
      (select *
      from Fish F
      where S.sno = F.sno and F.tno = T.tno))
=
   (select count(*)
   from Tank T).
```

The full select syntax

The features discussed in the previous sections provide the full power of the SQL select-statement. Later chapters add some additional conveniences, but the new features don't increase the retrieval power of the language. The full select-statement syntax follows. The first two clauses are required; the rest are optional.

Syntax of the SQL select statement:
   select *attributes and/or aggregates and/or expressions*
   from *relations*
   where *where-boolean*
   groupby *attributes*
   having *having-boolean*
   orderby *attributes*
   into *temporary relation*.

The select-clause targets contain attributes from the from-clause tables, aggregates based on these attributes, or arithmetic expressions from either of these sources. The examples to this point have illustrated both attributes and aggregates in the select-clause. The extension to arithmetic combinations of these items is straightforward. For example, suppose you want the total volume, in quarts, of tanks for each species. If the tvolume values are in gallons, an arithmetic conversion is necessary. You can specify the conversion directly in the select-clause as follows.

```
select S.sname speciesName, 4 * sum(T.tvolume) as quartVol
from Species S, Tank T
where exists
  (select *
  from Fish F
  where S.sno = F.sno and F.tno = T.tno)
groupby S.sno
orderby S.sname.
```

A mental model for visualizing SQL activity

You can envision the DBMS responding to an SQL query with the following nine-step procedure.

1. Form the Cartesian product of the from-clause tables.

2. Use the where-clause boolean to extract a horizontal section. This step may temporarily suspend a candidate tuple to compute subqueries. In the subqueries, the table attributes from the primary query are available for reference, except where local aliases hide such access. The where-clause boolean can contain only constants and attributes of the tables in the from-clause. The exception is in subqueries, which can introduce additional tables. If the where-clause is absent, all tuples from the Cartesian product enter into the horizontal section.

3. Create a partition over the tuples of the horizontal section, generating one group for each distinct value of the groupby-clause attributes. If aggregates appear in the select-clause, but the groupby-clause is absent, the entire horizontal section becomes one large group.

4. Reject any group that doesn't satisfy the having-clause boolean. The having-clause boolean can contain only expressions that make sense for a group as a whole: aggregates that reduce a column to a single value within a group, attributes that have the same value across all tuples within a group, and constants. The having-clause boolean can contain subqueries although some database products don't allow this extension. If the having-clause is absent, all groups are retained.

5. Add columns to accommodate any aggregates or expressions in the select-clause.

6. If an aggregate appears in the select-clause, or if a groupby-clause is present, reduce the answer table to one tuple for each remaining group. Place values in the reduced tuple's columns as follows. If the column arises from an aggregate, the value comes from the specified operation on the specified column values in the group. If a column exhibits the same value in each tuple within the group, that common value is used. If the column corresponds to an arithmetic expression, the operands must be aggregates, attributes with uniform values across the group, or constants. In this case, the arithmetic expression is evaluated to obtain the required value. Any remaining columns receive the null value, but the syntax restrictions don't allow these columns to appear in the select-clause.

7. To display the answer, order the tuples as directed by the orderby-clause. Without an orderby-clause, the output display order is arbitrary. If the output order depends on an

aggregate or expression, that entry must appear in the select-clause, and it must have an alias so that the orderby-clause can mention it.

8. Isolate a vertical section by retaining only the select-clause attributes.

9. Place the answer into a temporary relation as specified by the into-clause. In this case, any effect of the orderby-clause is lost because the temporary relation, like all relations, retains no order among its constituent tuples.

Relational algebra from SQL

To execute an SQL statement, the DBMS must translate it into a procedural expression, such as relational algebra. This section develops an algorithm to transform an SQL select-statement into relational algebra. The resulting relational algebra isn't very efficient, but it provides a starting point for subsequent optimization.

The first step rewrites the SQL, if necessary, to give a distinct alias to every from-clause table and to every aggregate or arithmetic expression in the select-clause. The having-clause may contain further aggregates or arithmetic expressions that don't appear in the select-clause. These too acquire distinct aliases. For example, this initial step transforms the SQL on the left below to the format on the right.

```
select Tank.tno, tname, average(fweight)      select T.tno, T.tname,
from Tank, Fish                                  average(F.fweight) as avgWgt
where Tank.tno = Fish.tno                     from Tank T, Fish F
groupby Tank.tno                              where T.tno = F.tno
having count(*) > 10.                         groupby T.tno
                                              having (count(*) as fishCount) > 10.
```

In the simplest case, no subqueries appear in the where- or having-clauses. The translation is then a where-clause selection from the Cartesian product of the from-clause components. If aggregates are present, this intermediate result is followed with an aggregate operator and a having-clause selection. Finally, a projection isolates the elements requested in the select-clause. Following these rules, you can translate the above example as follows.

$$
\begin{array}{llll}
X_1 &=& \check{\rho}(T = \text{tank}) \times \check{\rho}(F = \text{fish}) & \text{where} & b &=& (T.\text{tno} = F.\text{tno}) \\
X_2 &=& \sigma_b(X_1) & & p &=& (T.\text{tno}) \\
X_3 &=& \Psi_p^f(X_2) & & f &=& (\text{avgWgt} = \text{average}(F.\text{fweight}), \text{fishCount} = \text{count}(*)) \\
X_4 &=& \sigma_c(X_3) & & c &=& (\text{fishCount} > 10) \\
X_5 &=& \pi_q(X_4) & & q &=& (T.\text{tno}, T.\text{tname}, \text{avgWgt}).
\end{array}
$$

Note that a single aggregate operator calculates any aggregates or arithmetic expressions in the having-clause or in the select-clause. Of course, if there are no aggregates, the process omits the steps giving X_3 and X_4. In that case, $X_5 = \pi_q(X_2)$.

The where-clause boolean extracts the horizontal section X_2 from the Cartesian product X_1. In the example above, the condition contains a single comparison, $T.\text{tno} = F.\text{tno}$. If the condition is more complicated, you can rewrite it in **disjunctive normal form**, which is a sequence of clauses separated by $\vee$ operators. Each clause is a sequence of attribute comparisons separated by $\wedge$ operators. The general format for the where-clause boolean is then:

$$b = (b_{11} \wedge b_{12} \wedge \ldots) \vee (b_{21} \wedge b_{22} \wedge \ldots) \vee (b_{31} \wedge b_{32} \wedge \ldots) \ldots .$$

The DBMS extracts the horizontal section by applying the individual components, b_{ij}, separately to the Cartesian product X_1 and then assembling X_2 through intersections and unions of the results. In other words, it calculates X_2 as follows:

$$X_2 = (\sigma_{b_{11}}(X_1) \cap \sigma_{b_{12}}(X_1)\ldots) \cup (\sigma_{b_{21}}(X_1) \cap \sigma_{b_{22}}(X_1)\ldots) \cup (\sigma_{b_{31}}(X_1) \cap \sigma_{b_{32}}(X_1)\ldots) \cup \ldots.$$

Although this format is less efficient than a single selection on X_1, it conveniently generalizes to the case where one or more of the conditions involves a subquery. Suppose that one of the $\sigma_{b_{ij}}$ is a subquery condition rather than a simple attribute comparison. Possibilities for the condition appear in the following list, where θ is one of the arithmetic comparisons: $<, >, =, \leq,$ or $\geq$. The condition could also be a negation of one of these formats. The last format presumes that the subquery returns exactly one tuple. The tuple must have a single component comparable to a_1.

- exists (select …)
- (select …) contains (select …)
- $(a_1, a_2, \ldots)$ in (select …)
- $a_1 \, \theta$ (select …)

I will illustrate the general translation idea with the first format; the others follow in a similar fashion. To be specific, suppose the SQL to be translated is:

```
select S.sno, S.sname, average(T.tvolume) as avgVol
from Species S, Tank T
where exists
    (select *
    from Fish F
    where S.sno = F.sno and F.tno = T.tno)
groupby S.sno.
```

Following the pattern above, the progression $X_1, X_2, \ldots X_5$ represents the step-by-step solution to the overall query, and $Y_1, Y_2, \ldots, Y_5$ denotes the progressive solution to the subquery. The algorithm proceeds as before, except that the host context, X_1, is included among the components of the Cartesian product, Y_1. For convenience, I extend the notation for the projection operator, so that π_{X_1} means the projection on all the attributes of X_1.

$$X_1 = \breve{\rho}(S = \text{species}) \times \breve{\rho}(T = \text{tank})$$

$$Y_1 = X_1 \times (F = \text{fish})$$
$$Y_2 = \sigma_d(Y_1)$$
$$Y_5 = \pi_r(Y_2)$$

$$X_2 = \pi_{X_1}(Y_5)$$
$$X_3 = \Psi_p^f(X_2)$$
$$X_5 = \pi_q(X_3)$$

where
$$
\begin{aligned}
d &= (S.\text{sno} = F.\text{sno} \wedge F.\text{tno} = T.\text{tno}) \\
r &= (S.\text{sno}, S.\text{sname}, S.\text{sfood}, \\
& \quad T.\text{tno}, T.\text{tname}, T.\text{tcolor}, T.\text{tvolume}, \\
& \quad F.\text{fno}, F.\text{fname}, F.\text{fcolor}, F.\text{fweight}, F.\text{tno}, F.\text{sno}) \\
p &= (S.\text{sno}) \\
f &= (\text{avgVol} = \text{average}(T.\text{tvolume})) \\
q &= (S.\text{sno}, S.\text{sname}, \text{avgVol}).
\end{aligned}
$$

Y_1 is a segmented table where each tuple of X_1 appears paired with all possible tuples from the subquery. Envision Y_1 as follows, where each species-tank combination of X_1 appears as a segment.

Y_1		
X_1		
species part	tank part	fish part
s_1	t_1	f_1
s_1	t_1	f_2
$\vdots$	$\vdots$	$\vdots$
s_1	t_2	f_a
s_1	t_2	f_b
$\vdots$	$\vdots$	$\vdots$

Because the host Cartesian product, X_1, is a component of Y_1, the host attributes are available in the boolean selection that forms Y_2. That selection removes those tuples from Y_1 where the fish part doesn't properly align with the species and tank parts. If a given species-tank prefix aligns with no fish, the entire segment disappears. Therefore, X_2 is formed by shearing off the extra attributes of Y_5 beyond X_1. Any species-tank prefix for which the subquery is empty isn't represented in the segmented table and, therefore, doesn't appear in X_2. The rest of the query then proceeds as in the earlier example.

A summary of the algorithm is:

- Form X_1 as the Cartesian product of the from-clause tables.

- Break the where-clause boolean into individual predicates. Each is either an attribute comparisons or a set comparison involving subqueries.

- Form X_2 as the union of the intersections of certain selections from X_1. Each selection applies a component of the where-clause predicate to X_1.

  - If the component is a simple attribute comparison, the selection is a simple horizontal extraction σ_b, where b is the attribute comparison.

  - If the component is a subquery predicate, each possibility is treated somewhat differently. Generally, the host Cartesian product X_1 becomes a segment in the subquery's Cartesian product. The subquery then evaluates in the typical fashion with two modifications. First, the host attributes are available for comparisons. Second, the final projection must retain all the attributes of the host query in addition to any indicated by the subquery. If further nested subqueries are encountered, this process is continued recursively. Certain operations on the subquery result produce the appropriate selection for contributing to X_2. The example above illustrated an "exists (select ...)" condition where the appropriate operation is $\pi_{X_1}(Y_5)$. Other subquery operations are similar. For example, the required operation for a "not exists (select ...)" subquery is $X_1 - \pi_{X_1}(Y_5)$.

- Form X_3 by applying an aggregate operator to X_2, if necessary.

- Form X_4 by applying a selection to X_3, if required by a having-clause. Subqueries in the having-clause are treated similarly to subqueries in the where-clause.

- Form the final result, X_5, by projecting the specified select-clause items from X_4 (or from X_2 if aggregates aren't involved).

A few syntactical loose ends

A useful feature allows the answer display to be ordered by an aggregate result, using an alias to identify it in the orderby-clause. An earlier example showed how to assign an alias to the aggregate for this purpose. The SQL on the left below uses this method for the query: find the average volume of tanks by species, and order the results by this average volume value. An alternative method specifies a position in the select-clause list as the data source for grouping or ordering, as shown in the equivalent SQL on the right.

```
select S.sno, average(T.tvolume) avgVol        select S.sno, average(T.tvolume)
from Species S, Tank T                         from Species S, Tank T
where exists                                   where exists
   (select *                                      (select *
   from Fish F                                    from Fish F
   where S.sno = F.sno and F.tno = T.tno)        where S.sno = F.sno and F.tno = T.tno)
groupby S.sno                                  groupby 1
orderby avgvol.                                 orderby 2.
```

The into-clause lets you construct an answer in stages by explicitly storing intermediate tables in the database. For example, a single query can't feed the results of one calculation into another. Suppose you want the average of the list of avgVol values returned by the query above. In other words, you want to find the average tank volume associated with each species, and then you want an average over that set of numbers. No manipulation of subqueries will deliver this result in one operation because it involves an intermediate calculation that must be actively used, not just checked, in a second computation. However, by storing the first set of values in a temporary relation, X, you can obtain the result in two steps, shown as the left and right SQL expressions below.

```
select S.sno sno, average(T.tvolume) avgVol        select average(avgvol)
from Species S, Tank T                             from X.
where exists
   (select *
   from Fish F
   where S.sno = F.sno and F.tno = T.tno)
groupby S.sno
into X.
```

Finally, SQL provides a facility to accumulate the answer table as the union of compatible SQL select-statements. The format on the left below is valid SQL syntax.

```
select attributes and/or aggregates and/or expressions        select S.sname name
from relations                                                 from Species S
where where-boolean                                       union
groupby attributes                                             select F.fname name
having having-boolean                                          from Fish F
union                                                     union
   select attributes and/or aggregates and/or expressions      select T.tname name
   from relations                                               from Tank T.
   where where-boolean
   groupby attributes
   having having-boolean
union
   ⋮
```

Set unions can usually merge only union-compatible relations. This means that the number of attributes (or aggregates or expressions) selected by each component must be equal, and these attributes must have the same names. The naming requirement presents no problem because you can use distinct aliases for the attributes, if necessary. However, taking a table-oriented viewpoint, SQL relaxes this requirement by using the first component's names and assuming that elements delivered by subsequent components (in select-clause order) must line up compatibly with these names. You can attach orderby- and into-clauses to the first component, and they will apply to the entire answer table. For example, suppose you want a list of the names in the aquarium database without distinguishing among species names, fish names, and tank names. The SQL to the right above accomplishes this task.

Data editing operations

SQL insertions

The SQL insert-statement populates a table with tuples. The left format below inserts individual tuples one at a time. For example, the expression to the right adds a new species tuple with sno = 48, sname = halibut, and sfood = herring.

```
insert                                  insert
into target-table                       into Species
values attribute-values.                values (48, "halibut", "herring").
```

The values associate with the species attributes in the order specified when the table was created. The Data Definition Language (DDL) expression on the left below repeats a portion of the schema of Figure 2.29, which creates the species table. Therefore, the data (48, halibut, herring) provide values for attributes sno, sname, and sfood respectively.

```
relation species {                      insert
   attribute sno keyvalue key           into Species (sname, sno)
   attribute sname namestring           values ("halibut", 48).
   attribute sfood namestring
   }.
```

If you don't have all the new entity's data values, or if you prefer to enter the data in an order different from the table definition, you must indicate a list of attributes to receive the insert-statement values. You place this list in the into-clause after the table name. For example, if you don't know the new tuple's sfood value and you want to enter the sname value before the sno value, you compose the insert-statement to the right above.

Because populating a large table one tuple at a time is tedious, another variation of the insert-statement allows you to generate the data from existing tables with a select-statement. The general syntax appears to the left below. For example, suppose the aquarium maintains a display of the red tanks and their fish in a 24-hour "eternal room." The SQL expression to the right retrieves the eternal-room table contents from existing tables.

```
insert                      select *
into target-table           from Tank T, Fish F
select-subquery.            where T.tno = F.tno and T.tcolor = "red".
```

However, where do you put the new tuples? You need a new table, which you can create by adding the following excerpt to the DDL that creates the database. The domain names (e.g., keyvalue, tankcolor) remain as shown in schema of Figure 2.29.

```
relation eternal {
    attribute tno keyvalue key
    attribute tname namestring
    attribute tvolume volvalue
    attribute fno keyvalue key
    attribute fname namestring
    attribute fcolor fishcolor
    attribute sno keyvalue foreign key - > species.sno
    }.
```

The new table description omits the tank color because it will always be red. It also removes the foreign key status of F.tno because tank and fish data appear together in the eternal table. With the new table available, you can use the alternative syntax for the insert-statement that loads the eternal table:

```
insert
into eternal
    select T.tno, T.tname, T.tvolume, F.fno, F.fname, F.fcolor, F.sno
    from Tank T, Fish F
    where T.tno = F.tno and T.tcolor = "red".
```

Although this variation permits the rapid loading of a large number of tuples, it has certain drawbacks, particularly in this example. First, the data must already be in the database. The new insert-statement doesn't solve the one-at-a-time loading problem; it merely shifts the problem to other tables. Second, the new table duplicates data from other tables, which conflicts with the database goal of storing data nonredundantly. Finally, if the data in the tank or fish table change, the eternal table will be out-of-date and require a reload. Even if you refresh it periodically, the tables may be inconsistent between updates.

With the exception of the first problem, these difficulties emphasize an application's need to view a tailored arrangement of the underlying conceptual database. The usual SQL solution involves a new creation, called a view, which allows a user to operate as though the entire database were materialized according to some select statement. The details of SQL views appear in the next chapter.

The remaining problem is that the insert-statement loads the new table from data that are already in the database. How do you get the data into the source tables without tedious one-at-a-time tuple insertions? Most database systems provide a utility program that reads data values from a prepared file. You can use any convenient data-entry method to prepare this file, such as word processor. For example, suppose the fish information exists on a file named "fishdata." Either of the following expressions will load the data into the fish relation. The first assumes that the file contains complete information for each fish, and the second assumes that the fish records contain only fno, sno, tno, and fname values, in that order.

```
load from "fishdata" delimiter ","      load from "fishdata" delimiter ","
insert into Fish.                       insert into Fish (fno, sno, tno, fname).
```

In either case, the data for each fish appear as a separate fishdata record. The delimiter-clause in the load-statement specifies how the attributes within a fish record are separated. In this case, the separating character is a comma. Tables are very amenable to mass loading from files because table rows correspond directly with file records.

 The SQL insert-command adds new tuples to database tables. Many databases provide a utility to load tables from text files.

SQL deletions

An SQL delete-statement is similar to a select-statement, but it restricts the from-clause to a single database table, rather than to a comma-list of tables. The general format is shown on the left below. A horizontal section determines the tuples to be deleted, using the where-clause boolean, just as with a select-statement. The boolean can contain subqueries to specify complex conditions extending beyond the attributes of the candidate tuple. For example, the SQL on the right deletes all fish from the red tanks.

```
delete                    delete
from target-table         from Fish F
where boolean.            where F.tno in
                              (select T.tno
                               from Tank T
                               where T.tcolor = "red").
```

Some database systems relax the constraint of a single from-clause table. You can then delete tuples from a Cartesian product over several tables. The effect on the database is somewhat complicated and is best understood in the context of SQL views. The details will appear in the next chapter.

Of course, if you can identify the tuples to be deleted with a boolean on the target table, you don't need to use a subquery. For example, the expression to the left below deletes all fish named "albert." However, unless you can identify the target tuples through their attributes alone, you must invoke a subquery to isolate them properly. This complication arises because only a single table can appear in the from-clause.

```
delete                              delete
from Fish F                         from Fish.
where F.fname = "albert".
```

The delete format permits massive deletion of a large number of tuples with simple syntax. For example, as with the select-statement, the absence of a where-clause qualifies every tuple in the from-clause table. The SQL on the right above deletes the entire body of the fish relation. An interactive SQL environment usually requires confirmation of mass deletion commands.

A more subtle danger associated with mass deletions is that the resulting database can be inconsistent with respect to some application constraint. For example, suppose you have taken great care to ensure referential integrity between the fish tuples and their corresponding tanks. The foreign key tno in each fish tuple refers to an existing tank tuple. Deleting a tank can leave the database in a state that violates referential integrity. Specifically, suppose you execute the following SQL, which removes tanks containing a shark.

```
delete
from Tank
where Tank.tno in
    (select T.tno
    from Species S, Fish F, Tank T
    where S.sno = F.sno and F.tno = T.tno and S.sname = "shark").
```

All shark fish now reference a nonexistent tank through the tno foreign key, thus violating referential integrity. A reference to a nonexistent tuple is a **dangling reference**. The latest SQL version allows constraint specifications in the schema to intercept this operation. However, few database products currently support this feature. Instead, referential integrity support, if present at all, only rejects attempts to add a tuple that would cause a violation. To protect referential integrity during a massive deletion of tanks, the DBMS must maintain information about all the other relations that depend on tanks. It must then scan these other tables for compliance in the new context. This activity is complex and computationally expensive. Therefore, it's not a standard feature of most DBMS products.

 The SQL delete-statement removes tuples from database relations. Delete operations can compromise referential integrity.

SQL updates

The full power of a select-subquery is available to identify tuples to be modified. For example, suppose you want to change the color of all tanks containing a dolphin to red. The SQL is on the left below. The general format is on the right, where the *comma-list of assignments* contains items of the form: *attribute name = expression.*

```
update Tank T                          update target-table
set T.tcolor = "red"                   set comma-list of assignments
where Tank.tno in                      where boolean.
  (select T.tno
  from Species S, Fish F, Tank T
  where S.sno = F.sno and F.tno = T.tno
    and S.sname = "dolphin").
```

The where-clause boolean can be a simple expression in the target table's attributes, or it can involve a subquery as in the example. You can use the simpler form to change all fish names of albert to einstein, as coded on the left below. The more complex example on the right uses old values to compute new ones. Any references to attributes on the right of the assignment operator ($=$) evaluate to the old values—the values before any changes due to the update-statement itself. This example increases the volumes of all red tanks by 10%.

```
update Fish F                          update Tank T
set F.fname = "einstein"               set T.tvolume = 1.1 * T.tvolume
where F.fname = "albert".              where T.tcolor = "red".
```

When you want to update several attributes in each target tuple, you can group the attribute names in one list and then equate it to a second list of corresponding values. The general form of the alternative syntax is:

```
update target-table
set (comma-list of attribute names) = (comma-list of expressions)
where boolean.
```

For example, if you want to increase the volume of all red tanks by 10% and recolor them blue, you can phrase the operation as follows.

```
update Tank T
set (T.tvolume, T.tcolor) = (1.1 * T.tvolume, "blue")
where T.tcolor = "red".
```

Updating the primary key of a relation might trigger extensive behind-the-scenes activity, such as relocating the record to a new hash address or updating a collection of indices. Indeed, some database systems don't allow changes to the key attributes. In these cases, you update with a deletion followed by an insertion. Just as with deletions, updates can result in referential integrity violations by modifying primary or foreign keys. Given the level of constraint enforcement available with existing database products, you can't expect the DBMS to detect such violations.

 The SQL update-statement modifies existing tuples. Updates of key values are sometimes restricted because of effects on entity or referential integrity constraints.

Embedded SQL

SQL operations are set-oriented rather than tuple-oriented. A select-statement returns a tuple set, which is, in fact, another relation. Similarly, an insertion, deletion, or update affects a set of tuples. Set operations are convenient when you converse with the DBMS across an interactive interface. However, problems can arise when the interaction is between the DBMS and another software program. Suppose a C program commands a database retrieval activity. After requesting a block of tuples, the program enters a loop to examine the tuples individually. Where does the program hold the tuples during this examination? Although the program could have a data structure for this purpose, this solution isn't robust. The database might return too many tuples for the structure to hold. A better arrangement has the program receive the tuples one at a time from the DBMS. In other words, the DBMS places a single tuple's attribute values in program variables, where the language's operations can manipulate them. A traditional program loop can repeat this process, eventually consuming the entire answer set.

The interface between set-oriented SQL and one-at-a-time, tuple-oriented programming is called an **impedance mismatch** between the two processing systems. The term comes from the telecommunications field, where similar difficulties arise when mating two transmission systems with different characteristics, such as two coaxial cables with different electrical parameters. SQL provides an alternative syntax, **embedded SQL**, to address the impedance mismatch. Embedded SQL statements are coded inline with the host language statements, allowing the program to control the database. The program requests data from the database, and the DBMS responds by doling out the answer tuples one at a time. The program can also insert, delete, and update tuples. I will use C as a host language for the following examples, but the concepts apply to any procedural language.

 Embedded SQL refers to SQL statements that are issued from within a procedural host program, such as C.

Other issues arise beyond reconciling SQL's set-oriented activity with the program's tuple-oriented processing:

- How does C transmit and receive data from the database?

- How can SQL syntax be disguised as C syntax?

- How does the DBMS inform the program of completion and error conditions?

- How can C contain SQL statements that aren't known in their entirety until the program is executed?

- How are the data types within the database made compatible with C data types?

The SQL standard now provides constructions for dealing with all of these problems. Even if a DBMS product doesn't support the latest SQL version, it usually has some mechanism for commanding database activity from within a host program.

Immediate execution
To distinguish SQL activity from the surrounding C code, each SQL statement starts with some fixed character sequence. The standard specifies the sequence "exec sql," but a given database product may use some special symbol, such as a $, at the beginning of SQL

statements. In either case, the statement terminates in the normal manner with a semi-colon. A preprocessor recognizes the SQL statements with the characteristic prefix and converts them to specialized library calls. These library calls invoke routines provided with the database, and they appear in the preprocessed C code as external, procedure-call statements. The preprocessed C code is fed into the traditional C compiler, and the resulting object code is linked with the required library routines before execution.

Suppose, for example, that you embed the statement on the left below in a C program that manipulates the aquarium database.

```
exec sql execute immediate
   "delete
   from Tank                    ⇒ dbExecImm("aquarium", "delete from Tank where tvolume < 100");
   where tvolume < 100";
```

The preprocessor recognizes the leading "exec sql" and replaces the statement with a library call in standard C syntax, as illustrated on the right. The library call invokes a routine, supplied with the DBMS product, that is prepared to parse strings and execute them against the database.

This example illustrates one method that a program can use to execute an SQL statement. In this method, it is as if the statement had been entered in an interactive session. However, this format isn't sufficient for all the program's SQL needs. Three disadvantages hinder the widespread use of this technique. First, the DBMS interprets the SQL string at runtime, converting it into executable code. This means the argument string much be reparsed each time the statement is executed. Second, the entire SQL string must be passed to the library routine as a unit. The SQL expression frequently depends on the contents of program variables, which aren't known when the program is written. For example, the threshold volume for deleting tanks, 100 in the example, may not be a constant. Of course, the program can assemble the correct string in some string variable, say sqlsource, and change the SQL statement to reflect this variable source. For example, suppose the integer variable, delThreshold, holds the threshold volume. You can use the C utility, sprintf, to "print" this value into a buffer (called suffix below), converting it to a character string. You can then concatenate this string onto the end of the fixed part of the SQL statement: "delete from Tank where tvolume >." The sequence then appears as follows.

```
sprintf(suffix, " %d", delThreshold);
strcpy(sqlsource, "delete from Tank where tvolume < ");
strcat(sqlsource, suffix);
exec sql execute immediate :sqlsource;
```

This example shows that SQL statements can use host language variables, provided they are flagged as such. The standard specifies a leading colon as the identifying marker for a host variable. The SQL source string is still inefficiently interpreted at runtime.

The third disadvantage of the immediate execution technique is that it can't retrieve data from the database because there is no place to put it. Therefore, immediate execution has limited usefulness.

Completion and error feedback

After completing each commanded database activity, the DBMS must inform the program of the outcome: an error or a successful conclusion. Before returning from an SQL activity, the library routine sets a host program variable to a completion code. The code describes the activity's outcome. A code of 0 usually means that the operation completed without incident, a code of 100 typically signals a data-not-found condition, and other codes describe specific classes of errors. The SQL standard specifies that the program should create a **diagnostics area** to hold the return code. The program can then determine an SQL statement's fate by interrogating this area. Because any SQL activity can raise several error conditions, the program must specify the size of the diagnostics area. The DBMS discards errors beyond the number specified.

To deal with error and completion feedback, the example above needs some preparatory code. A more complete excerpt appears on the left below. The "number" parameter obtained from the diagnostics area is the number of exceptions stored in that area. If none are there, the operation completed without incident. In theory, a program should follow every SQL activity with a diagnostics area check to determine the database response. If an error is detected, further information, such as a prose description of that error, is available through additional statements. The details aren't important for this discussion.

```
exec sql set transaction diagnostics size 10;

  .
  .
  .
exec sql execute immediate
  "delete
  from Tank
  where tvolume < 100";
exec sql get diagnostics :code = number;
if (code > 0)
  /* error processing activity */

  .
  .
  .
```

```
#include <sqlca.h>

  .
  .
  .
exec sql execute immediate
  "delete
  from Tank
  where tvolume < 100";
if (sqlca.sqlcode > 0)
  /* error processing activity */

  .
  .
  .
```

DBMS products that don't support the latest SQL standard must still provide feedback through some program variable. These systems usually provide a declaration file for inclusion in interfacing programs. The file declares a data structure (usually named sqlca, for SQL control area) that contains fields, such as sqlcode and errmsg. After an SQL command completes, the program can examine this structure to determine the outcome. The code on the right illustrates this alternative approach. The disadvantage of this older method is that access to the completion code is language dependent, using in this case the syntax of a "C struct." The standard proposes an access technique that uses library calls, which are independent of the host language.

For brevity, the following examples omit error checking. However, an SQL activity can fail for a bewilderingly large number of reasons, so you should always check the diagnostics areas after each call. The examples will continue to check for benign exceptions, such as a data-not-found condition.

Prepared SQL statements

You can avoid the repeated runtime parsing of an SQL string with a prepare-statement, which compiles the statement and stores the executable code in the database. You supply an identifier for the statement, which you can reference as often as desired in subsequent executions. The identifier isn't a host variable; it is database name for an executable procedure. To execute a prepared SQL statement, you use a simple "execute," rather than an "execute immediate." In this new form, the preceding example appears on the left below. The deltank identifier isn't declared in the C program. It is a database identifier, and the DBMS handles its storage.

```
exec sql prepare deltank from        sprintf(suffix, " %d", delThreshold);
   "delete                           strcpy(sqlsource, "delete from Tank where tvolume < ");
   from Tank                         strcat(sqlsource, suffix);
   where tvolume < 100";             exec sql prepare deltank from :sqlsource;
      .                                    .
      .                                    .
      .                                    .
exec sql execute deltank;            exec sql execute deltank;
      .                                    .
      .                                    .
```

Instead of coding the SQL directly in the prepare-statement, you can assemble it dynamically in a string variable and then refer to that variable in the prepare-statement. For example, if the integer variable, delThreshold, contains the deletion volume threshold, you would use the equivalent form on the right.

Why should you prepare the delete-statement? After its first execution, no tanks will remain in the database with tvolume less than 100, so there is no reason to execute it a second time. However, suppose the execute-statement appears in a loop, which inserts and deletes tanks as part of some larger process. You can place the prepare-statement outside the loop. The code is then compiled just once and executed many times.

Using the second form above, you can reexecute the SQL command many times; the deletion threshold, however, is fixed at the value originally supplied in the delThreshold variable. If the deletion threshold changes, you must recompile the SQL with another prepare-statement. This defeats the efficiency gained by the compilation. To address this difficulty, SQL provides a variation of the prepare and execute-statements. You can compile the SQL source and leave room for certain parameters to be substituted when it is executed. You write the SQL as follows, using the question mark as a placeholder in the SQL source.

```
strcpy(sqlsource, "delete from Tank where tvolume < ?");
exec sql prepare deltank from :sqlsource;
   .
   . /* code to obtain proper threshold in delthreshold */
exec sql execute deltank using :delThreshold;
   .
   .
```

The DBMS stores deltank as a parameterized procedure. You can execute it repeatedly, supplying a different parameter each time. In other words, you can change the deletion volume threshold without recompiling the SQL. The prepare-statement can have several placeholders, and a subsequent execute-statement must provide the same number of substitution values in left-to-right order in its using-clause. You need not convert the integer delThreshold into a string. Because the SQL expression uses the placeholder in a comparison with tvolume, the DBMS expects a numerical value in the execute statement.

The example above illustrates input parameters to a compiled SQL procedure. You can also use output parameters although they don't need placeholders in the SQL statement. Consider the following situation, where fno is known to be a key of the fish relation. The prepared SQL statement returns the fname, fcolor, and associated sname for a certain fish. At runtime, the fish is identified in the host variable, theFish. The construction below uses a placeholder for the fno information, which is an input parameter. The output values are the selected attributes of the fish, and the into-clause of the execute-statement specifies the host variables to receive them. You can use this technique only if the select-statement returns a single tuple. If many tuples are returned, you must use a more complex syntax, which will be discussed shortly.

```
exec sql prepare getfish from
   "select S.sname, F.fname, F.fcolor
   from Species S, Fish F
   where S.sno = F.sno and F.fno = ?";
   :
   : /* code to get proper value in theFish */
exec sql execute getfish into :specname, :fishname, :fishcolor using :theFish;
   :
```

In summary, the execute-statement allows both input and output parameters. The inputs appear in the using-clause, and they fill placeholders in the prepared SQL. The outputs appear in the into-clause, and they indicate the host variables to receive the results.

 A prepare-statement compiles an SQL string for subsequent, and perhaps repeated, execution. The SQL can include placeholders, which must be supplied with values when it is executed. If it returns a single tuple, the into-clause specifies the destination variables for the attributes.

SQL cursors

If a prepared select-statement returns a set of tuples, the output parameters of a later execute-statement can't hold the entire answer. In this case, you need to write a program loop, which successively acquires each tuple in turn. Embedded SQL provides a special feature, called a **cursor**, for doling out tuples one at a time in a program loop. You specify a cursor in several stages. First, you give the cursor a name and associate it with a prepared query. Suppose, given a tank (tno) and a species (sno), you want to loop through the fish that inhabit the tank and represent the species. You start as follows.

```
exec sql prepare getfish from
  "select F.fname, F.fcolor, F.fweight
  from Fish F
  where F.tno = ?  and F.sno = ?";
exec sql declare fishdetails cursor for getfish;
  ⋮
```

The DBMS doesn't evaluate the query at this time, so you usually insert this initialization code early in the program's preamble. Later, when the program wants to obtain the desired tuples, it issues the following statements. Assume that the C variables, tnoCurrent and snoCurrent, hold the tno and sno values for the fish to be retrieved.

```
  ⋮
exec sql open cursor fishdetails using :tnoCurrent, :snoCurrent;
exec sql fetch fishdetails into :fnameCurrent, :fcolorCurrent, :fwgtCurrent;
exec sql get diagnostics :code = number;
while (code == 0) {
    ⋮ /* C code to process the current fish */
  exec sql fetch fishdetails into :fnameCurrent, :fcolorCurrent, :fwgtCurrent;
  exec sql get diagnostics :code = number; }
exec sql close cursor fishdetails;
  ⋮
```

The first statement opens the cursor, accepting the input parameters from the using-clause. The DBMS executes the prepared SQL statement at this time. It obtains the full tuple set satisfying the query but doesn't pass them en masse to the program. Subsequent fetch operations then retrieve these tuples, one at a time, placing the attribute values in host variables. The into-clause of the fetch-statement identifies the host variables.

Note the similarity between a cursor operation and an execute-immediate command. The execute-immediate command passes input parameters in its using-clause and indicates the receiving host variables in its into-clause. The cursor passes the input parameters in the open-statement because the prepared SQL is executed when the cursor is opened. However, a using-clause passes the parameters, just as in an execute-immediate command. Subsequent fetch-statements actually retrieve the tuples, so the into-clause appears in their syntax.

When no tuples remain to return, the fetch-statement places a special return code in the diagnostics area. Because the examples don't anticipate DBMS failures, any entry in the diagnostics area must mean that the tuple supply is exhausted. Therefore, the processing loop continues as long as the diagnostics area has no entries. In practice, you should distinguish the response code for "no more tuples" from other errors. The while loop, which is standard C code, performs the desired processing on a tuple and then executes another fetch. When a fetch fails, the loop terminates, having processed all the returned tuples.

A cursor is an embedded SQL feature, which returns tuples, one at a time, from a select-statement to the calling program.

When the program opens a cursor, the DBMS executes the underlying SQL select-statement and makes the answer table available for subsequent fetch-statements. The DBMS initially positions the cursor before the first tuple of the answer set. Each fetch moves the cursor forward one tuple. After the fetch, the cursor "points" to the tuple just retrieved. When the cursor points to the last tuple, a final fetch returns an error condition to the diagnostics area. After dispatching the error condition, the DBMS positions the cursor just after the last tuple.

Suppose the program needs to delete all fish representing a certain species. It obtains the species name at runtime and places it in the variable, snameDelete. The following C excerpt achieves the desired effect.

```
exec sql prepare delSpeciesReps from
  "delete
  from Fish F
  where exists
    (select *
    from Species S
    where F.sno = S.sno and S.sname = ?)";
  ⋮
  /* code to place name of targeted species in :snameDelete */
exec sql execute delSpeciesReps using :snameDelete;
  ⋮
```

Now suppose instead that the program wants to scan through the target fish, report the fish details to the user, and let the user decide which to delete. While the cursor is pointing to a tuple, the program can direct an update or delete operation to that tuple with the phrase, "current of cursor." The left portion of Figure 5.6 implements the user's decision with a "current of cursor" phrase. The prepared delete-statement uses the "current of fishscan" reference to direct the delete activity to the tuple currently under the cursor.

The program can also impose an update on a tuple that is currently under an open cursor. If, in the example above, the program wants to update certain user-chosen fish, rather than deleting them, the delSpeciesReps prepared SQL is replaced with an updateSpeciesReps construction, as illustrated in the right portion of Figure 5.6.

For insertions, data flows from the program to the database, so a cursor isn't needed. Instead, the program loops through a prepared, parameterized insertion-statement. For example, the following excerpt inserts a collection of species tuples.

```
exec sql prepare speciesReps from                exec sql prepare speciesReps from
  "select F.fname, F.fcolor                         "select F.fname, F.fcolor
  from Fish F                                        from Fish F
  where exists                                       where exists
    (select *                                          (select *
    from Species S                                     from Species S
    where F.sno = S.sno and S.sname = ?)";             where F.sno = S.sno and S.sname = ?)";
exec sql declare fishscan                         exec sql declare fishscan
  cursor for speciesReps;                            cursor for speciesReps;
exec sql prepare delSpeciesReps from              exec sql prepare updateSpeciesReps from
  "delete                                            "update Fish
  from Fish                                          set F.fcolor = 'blue'
  where current of fishscan";                        where current of fishscan";

  : /* targeted species into snameDelete */          : /* targeted species into snameUpdate */
exec sql open fishscan using :snameDelete;        exec sql open fishscan using :snameUpdate;
exec sql fetch fishscan                           exec sql fetch fishscan
  into :fnameCurrent, :fcolorCurrent;                into :fnameCurrent, :fcolorCurrent;
exec sql get diagnostics :code = number;          exec sql get diagnostics :code = number;
while (code == 0) {                               while (code == 0) {

    : /* display fnameCurrent, etc.  */               : /* display fnameCurrent, etc.  */

    : /* get user decision */                         : /* get user decision */
  if (deleteOrder)                                  if (updateOrder)
    exec sql execute delSpeciesReps;                  exec sql execute updateSpeciesReps;
  exec sql fetch fishscan                          exec sql fetch fishscan
    into :fnameCurrent, :fcolorCurrent;              into :fnameCurrent, :fcolorCurrent;
  exec sql get diagnostics :code = number; }      exec sql get diagnostics :code = number; }
close cursor fishscan;                            close cursor fishscan;
```

Figure 5.6   Illustrating "current of cursor" for delete and update operations

```
exec sql prepare newSpecies from
  "insert into Species
  values (?, ?, ?)";

  : /* acquire first species (snoCurrent, snameCurrent, sfoodCurrent) and set eof if no more */
while (!eof) {
  exec sql execute newSpecies using :snoCurrent, :snameCurrent, :sfoodCurrent;

    : /* acquire next species information and set eof if no more */
}
```

Input and output descriptors

In the examples to this point, the programmer knows the general format of the SQL state-ments while he is writing the program. Although prepared statements accept certain input parameters at runtime, the programmer knows the number and data types of the parameters beforehand. He also knows the number and types of any output parameters. For example, in the left portion of Figure 5.6, the programmer knows to supply a single string parameter when he executes the prepared speciesReps statement or opens a cursor on it. Similarly, he knows that each fetch from the cursor returns two string parameters. This information is available when the program is written, and the programmer uses it to prepare the SQL, to declare a cursor, and to fetch tuples through the cursor.

This information, however, may not be available when the program is written. Instead, the program might learn at runtime the number and types of the parameters. For example, the programmer may know only that an SQL select-statement has been assembled in some string variable, say, sqlsource. He can prepare the statement and declare a cursor on it without knowing the number of input or output parameters, but he can't open the cursor or fetch tuples without this information.

SQL provides a facility to obtain this information dynamically in a systematic fashion. The describe-statement operates on a prepared select-statement and returns information about its input and output requirements. For example, suppose the program assembles a select-statement at runtime in the string variable sqlsource. The program can determine its input requirements by reserving space for some maximum number of input parameters, preparing the SQL, declaring the cursor, and asking the DBMS to describe the inputs. The code, which assumes a maximum of 10 input parameters, appears below.

```
exec sql allocate descriptor "sqlin" with max 10;
    ⋮

exec sql prepare sqlprep from :sqlsource;
exec sql declare sqlcursor cursor for sqlprep;
exec sql describe input sqlprep using sql descriptor "sqlin";
    ⋮
```

In this example, the describe-statement places information about the input requirements of the unknown SQL select-statement in the sqlin descriptor. With certain additional calls, the program can retrieve this information in a manner similar to that used to obtain error status information from the diagnostics area. The descriptor contains a field, count, which contains the number of input placeholders in the SQL. It also contains an array of elements, which give the data types and other information associated with each placeholder. Suppose that the prepared SQL is the following selection.

```
select T.tcolor
from Tank T
where T.tname = ?  and T.tvolume > ?.
```

Two input placeholders appear. After the describe operation, the sqlin descriptor holds information about these two parameters. The C excerpt below transfers the number of input parameters to the host variable, nparams, and loops to obtain the parameters' data types—a string and an integer.

```
exec sql get descriptor "sqlin" :nparams = count;
for (i = 1; i <= nparams; i++) {
  exec sql get descriptor "sqlin" value :i :dataType = type :dataLength = length;
    ⋮
    ⋮ /* code to set up the required input for the placeholder */
  }
    ⋮
```

The DBMS represents each supported data type with an integer code, such as 1 = integer and 2 = string. When i = 1, the get-descriptor-statement sets the host variable dataType to 2, indicating a string is required, and it sets the host variable, dataLength, to indicate the maximum length of that string. When i = 2, dataType is set to 1. The program can use this information in many ways. For example, it might ask the user for the two parameters just before opening a cursor on the prepared SQL. Now that it knows the number and data types of the parameters, it can perform error checking to ensure that the user enters proper values.

The code for opening the cursor can't specify a using-clause because the programmer doesn't know how many parameters to list there. Instead, the program loops through the descriptor and inserts values obtained at runtime to serve as actual parameters when the cursor is opened. The program then opens the cursor with the phrase "using sql descriptor ..." in place of the expected "using ..." list of input variables. The following segment illustrates these techniques. Although it set the inputs to the simple values, "lagoon" and 2000, the descriptor information can be used to calculate these values in arbitrarily complex ways.

```
          ⋮
exec sql set descriptor "sqlin" value :1 data = "lagoon";
exec sql set descriptor "sqlin" value :2 data = 2000;
exec sql open cursor sqlcursor using sql descriptor "sqlin";
          ⋮
```

Outputs are handled similarly: space is reserved for some maximum number of output descriptors, and the DBMS is asked to provide information about the output parameters. Continuing with the example, the following excerpt will appear just after the input describe-statement. Assume the select-statement has already been prepared into sqlprep, and the cursor sqlcursor has been declared over it.

```
exec sql allocate descriptor "sqlout" with max 10;
exec sql describe output sqlprep using sql descriptor "sqlout";
          ⋮
```

In the example select-statement, each returned tuple has one component: T.tcolor. The program can request the count parameter from the sqlout descriptor, and it will obtain a 1. It can then ask for the data type associated with the output and obtain the code for a character string. Using this information, the program can anticipate the number of components (1) and the data type (string) that will be returned from each fetch statement. The processing then proceeds as follows, where the normal "into ..." specifying C variables is replaced with "into sql descriptor sqlout." The tcolor value of the fetched tuple appears in the output descriptor, and the program can transfer it to a host variable with the get-descriptor statement, as shown below.

```
    ⋮
exec sql fetch sqlcursor into sql descriptor "sqlout";
exec sql get descriptor "sqlout" value :1 :currentColor = data;
    ⋮
```

 When programmers don't know the number and data types of parameters in advance, they use the describe-statement, which is a general purpose facility for processing input and output parameters of a prepared SQL select-query.

The examples here have illustrated embedded SQL with C. If you aren't familiar with C, you should still appreciate the issues that must be faced when a host program interfaces with a database. In any language, a mechanism must specify variables for shuttling information back and forth between the program and the database. A cursor must mediate between the DBMS's set-oriented SQL activities and the program's tuple-oriented activities. A preprocessor step must comb the code for database statements and transform them into ordinary subprocedure calls. After compilation, the program must be linked with a library provided by the database vendor to perform the database functions. Finally, some policy must exist to report the status of a previously commanded database activity back to the program. The programmer uses this signal to control the paths in the code that handle error and end-of-data conditions.

Because the DBMS product must provide the library of subroutines to perform the interface tasks, you can't simply match any programming language with any database. Instead, the database product must explicitly support the language. The latest SQL standard provides syntax to reduce the dependence on the peculiarities of the host language. In any case, the subprocedure calling sequences are similar across languages, so a program can often use small code segments from another language. For example, suppose the database supports a C language interface, but you need to connect with a database from Pascal. The Pascal and C subroutine calling procedures are quite similar, differing only in the order that arguments are pushed onto the runtime stack and the responsibility (caller or callee) for restoring the stack upon subroutine termination. Taking these items into account, you can call C code from Pascal, and you can then call the database from C.

SUMMARY

The most complex SQL construction is the select-statement. It is composed of two mandatory clauses followed by five optional clauses:

> select *attributes and/or aggregates and/or expressions*
> from *relations*
> where *where-boolean*
> groupby *attributes*
> having *having-boolean*
> orderby *attributes*
> into *temporary relation*.

You can envision a nine-step process to construct the answer table. The where-boolean filters the Cartesian product of the from-clause tables, and the groupby-clause attributes then partition the resulting horizontal section. The having-boolean rejects certain partition groups, and the aggregate functions reduce the remaining groups. The select-clause attributes impose a final vertical section, and the orderby-clause attributes sort the tuples for the display. Using the into-clause, you can place the final unordered tuples in a temporary table instead. This process is only a conceptual device to help you understand the meaning of the SQL statement. The DBMS will probably evaluate the query in a more efficient way. It usually considers several evaluation alternatives before choosing one based on performance expectations.

In general, nested subqueries can appear in the boolean conditions of the where- and having-clauses. A subquery suspends a candidate tuple while it computes auxiliary information from other tuples. SQL can always express an existential query without subqueries. However, universal queries always require subqueries.

Compared with data retrieval, the insert, delete, and update operations are much simpler. You can insert tuples into a table one at a time, or you can load them from an SQL select-statement. Furthermore, most DBMS products provide a utility to load a table from a file. The full power of the select-statement, including subqueries, is available to identify a set of tuples for deletion or update. Referential integrity can suffer if deletes or updates affect keys or foreign keys.

Embedded SQL enables database operations from within a host program. Our examples illustrated this feature with the C language, but the typical DBMS supports many language interfaces. The interface addresses the following issues:

- a coding policy, that allows a preprocessor to recognize embedded SQL statements and transform them into subprocedure calls

- a host language variable or a diagnostics area for the database to inform the program about the success or failure of an SQL activity

- a cursor to buffer the set-oriented results of SQL operations and to pass the tuples to the program sequentially

- a policy for dynamically passing input-output parameters to SQL statements at runtime

- a describe-statement to determine the number and data types of the parameters, if these aren't known when the program is written. ∎

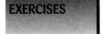

These exercises deal with the library database of Figure 3.11.

Conceptual model for simple retrieval queries

Write SQL for the following queries.

1. Find the names of libraries located in Seattle.

2. Find the names and locations of libraries that feature books written by Salinger.

3. Find the names of libraries having a book in common with a Seattle library.

4. Find the titles of books available from a library that serves a patron named joe.

5. Find all pairs of book titles that have copies in the same library. Phrase the query to exclude pairs of the form (x, x) from the answer set and to provide just one of the pairs (x, y) or (y, x) when both qualify.

6. Find all triplets of libraries that are collocated. Report the library names in the form (a, b, c). Eliminate triplets of the form (x, x, x), (x, x, y), (x, y, x), and (y, x, x) from the answer and provide just one of the six permutations of (x, y, z) when the triplet qualifies.

   Describe the following SQL queries in English.

7. ```
   select L.libname
   from library L, copy C, loan LN, patron P
   where L.libno = C.libno and C.copyno = LN.copyno and LN.patronno
       = P.patronno and P.patwgt > 150.
   ```

8. ```
   select B1.title "first title", B2.title "second title"
   from book B1, book B2
   where B1.authno = B2.authno and B1.bookno < B2.bookno.
   ```

9. ```
   select P1.patname
   from patron P1, loan LN1, copy C1, library L1, copy C2, loan LN2,
       patron P2, loan LN3, copy C3, library L2
   where P1.patronno = LN1.patronno and LN1.copyno = C1.copyno and C1.libno
       = L1.libno and L1.libno = C2.libno and C2.copyno = LN2.copyno and
       LN2.patronno = P2.patronno and P2.patronno = LN3.patronno and
       LN3.copyno = C3.copyno and C3.libno = L2.libno and L2.location
       = "Seattle".
   ```

Subqueries

Write SQL for the following queries, forcing the use of a subquery even if it isn't necessary.

10. Find the titles of books available at a Seattle library.

11. Find the names of patrons who have used a library that has also served a patron named joe.

12. Find the names of libraries that have no books available.

13. Find the names of patrons who have used all libraries.

Describe the following SQL queries in English.

14. ```
    select B.title
    from book B
    where not exists
        (select *
        from copy C, loan LN
        where B.bookno = C.bookno and C.copyno = LN.copyno).
    ```

15. ```
    select L.libname
    from library L
    where L.libno in
      (select L.libno
      from library L, copy C, book B, author A
      where L.libno = C.libno and C.bookno = B.bookno and
        B.authno = A.authno and A.authname = "Salinger").
    ```

Existential and universal queries

Translate the following relational algebra into SQL.

16. $\pi_q \sigma_b(\breve{\rho}(L = \text{library}) \times \breve{\rho}(C = \text{copy}) \times \breve{\rho}(B = \text{book}))$,

    where b = (L.libno = C.libno $\wedge$ C.bookno = B.bookno $\wedge$ B.title = "The Name of the Rose

    q = (L.location).

17. $\pi_q[\pi_r \sigma_b(\breve{\rho}(L = \text{library}) \times (C = \text{copy})) \cap \pi_r \sigma_c(\breve{\rho}(L = \text{library}) \times \breve{\rho}(C = \text{copy}))]$,

    where b = (L.libno = C.libno $\wedge$ C.bookno = 18)

    c = (L.libno = C.libno $\wedge$ C.bookno = 42)

    r = (L.libno, L.libname)

    q = (L.libname).

18. $\pi_q[\pi_r(\text{patron} * \text{loan} * \text{copy} * \text{library})/\pi_s \sigma_b(\text{library})]$,

    where b = (location = "Seattle")

    s = (libno)

    r = (patronno, patname, libno)

    q = (patname).

19. $\pi_q \sigma_b(\breve{\rho}(P = \text{patron}) \times \breve{\rho}(U = \text{loan}) \times \breve{\rho}(C = \text{copy}) \times \breve{\rho}(D = \text{copy}) \times \breve{\rho}(V = \text{loan}) \times \breve{\rho}(Q = \text{patr}$

    where b = (P.patronno = U.patronno $\wedge$ U.copyno = C.copyno $\wedge$ C.libno = D.libno and

    D.copyno = V.copyno and V.patronno = Q.patronno and

    Q.patname = "jim")

    q = (P.patname).

Write SQL for the following queries, using the specified construction.

20. Find the names of patrons who have checked out all books with more than 300 pages. Use the double-negation construction.

21. Find the names of Seattle libraries that feature all books written by Mailer. Use the set-containment predicate.

Describe the following query in English.

22. ```
    select P.patname
    from patron P
    where P.patwgt > 150 and not exists
      (select *
      from book B
      where not exists
        (select *
        from copy C, loan LN
        where B.bookno = C.bookno and C.copyno = LN.copyno and
          LN.patronno = P.patronno)).
    ```

Aggregates and partitions

Write SQL for the following queries.

23. Find the titles of books that have fewer than 10 copies.

24. Find the location of the library with the most rooms.

25. For each book-library combination, find the number of copies of the book available at the library.

26. For each patron, find the average size (i.e., number of rooms) of libraries used by him.

27. For each book, find the minimum, average, and maximum cost of its copies.

28. Find the names of patrons whose weight is greater than the average weight of patrons who have read a book entitled The Name of the Rose.

Describe the following SQL statements in English.

29.
```
select L.libno, L.libname, average(B.pages) pagecount
from library L, book B
where exists
  (select *
  from copy C
  where L.libno = C.libno and C.bookno = B.bookno)
groupby L.libno
orderby pagecount.
```

30.
```
select P.patronno, P.patname, sum(B.pages) readingload
from patron P, loan LN, copy C, book B
where P.patronno = LN.patronno and LN.copyno = C.copyno and C.bookno = B.bookno
groupby P.patronno
orderby readingload.
```

31.
```
select L.libno, B.bookno, P.patronno, count(*) "total loans"
from library L, copy C, book B, loan LN, patron P
where L.libno = C.libno and C.bookno = B.bookno and C.copyno = LN.copyno
    and LN.patronno = P.patronno
groupby L.libno, B.bookno, P.patronno
orderby L.libno, B.bookno, P.patronno.
```

Suppressing partitions

Write SQL statements to solve the following queries.

32. For each library whose collection includes more than 100 titles, find the average number of pages in its books.

33. For each author whose total number of pages written exceeds the total weight of the patrons who have read some of her work, find the average size of the libraries that carry her books. The total number of pages written isn't increased by the existence of multiple copies of a book.

34. For each patron who uses some library of size (i.e., number of rooms) greater than the average size of libraries that hold a copy of a book entitled The Name of the Rose, find the number of libraries used by that patron.

Describe the following SQL query in English.

35. ```
select P.patronno, P.patname, count(*) "copies borrowed"
from patron P, loan LN, copy C
where P.patronno = LN.patronno and LN.copyno = C.copyno
groupby P.patronno
having average(C.cost) >
  (select average(C.cost)
  from copy C, book B, author A
  where C.bookno = B.bookno and B.authno = A.authno and
    A.authname = "Salinger").
```

## The full select syntax

36. Give an example, other than the one cited in the text, of a query that can't be solved with a single SQL statement but that can be solved by producing an intermediate table with the into-clause. Write SQL to solve the query in that way.

Accumulate the relational algebra translation of the following SQL statements, following the algorithm of the text.

37. ```
select B.title
from Book B
where B.pages > 200.
```

38. ```
select L.libname
from Library L
where
    (select B.bookno
    from Book B, Copy C
    where L.libno = C.libno and C.bookno = B.bookno)
contains
    (select B.bookno
    from Book B
    where B.pages > 300).
```

39. ```
select L.libname, sum(B.pages)
from Library L, Book B
where exists
    (select *
    from Copy C
    where L.libno = C.libno and C.bookno = B.bookno)
groupby L.libno
having count(*) > 4.
```

40. ```
select L.libname
from Library L
where not exists
    (select *
    from Book B
    where not exists
        (select *
        from Copy C
        where L.libno = C.libno and C.bookno = B.bookno)).
```
```

Data editing operations

Write SQL for the following data manipulation activities.

41. Add a collection of library tuples to the database. The collection exists on a file called "newlib." Each file record (i.e., each character string terminated by a newline character) represents a library tuple. The location attribute is missing, and the remaining attributes are given in the order libno, rooms, libname, separated by commas. Assume that the DDL has created the database with the attributes in the order given by Figure 3.11.

42. Update all Seattle libraries by adding two rooms to each.

Embedded SQL

Write C code excerpts to perform the following database activities with embedded SQL.

43. Loop through the libraries located in Seattle. For each library, loop through its books. Prompt the user for the fate of each book (keep or discard). If the user chooses "discard," remove all copies of the book from the library and also remove all loan records associated with the discarded copies.

44. For each book, display the range (i.e., maximum minus minimum) of the weights of patrons who have checked out the book.

6 Advanced SQL

PREVIOUS CHAPTERS HAVE INVESTIGATED SEVERAL ASPECTS OF THE relational model: (1) component definitions—domains, attributes, schemas, associations, tuples, relations, and constraints; (2) the basic data manipulation capabilities of SQL; (3) relational algebra, which serves as a procedural implementation language for SQL; and (4) relational calculus, which is the mathematical basis of SQL. However, SQL provides many other features to help you model an application more closely. The advanced features discussed in this chapter include virtual tables, outer joins, and outer unions. The chapter also explores a systematic treatment of null values and a more comprehensive method for enforcing constraints. The chapter closes with a discussion of the relational model's inherent deficiencies, which provide some reasons for the development of the post-relational models discussed in later chapters.

Views

Table expressions in the from-clause

The general format of an SQL select-statement is:

```
select attributes and/or aggregates and/or expressions
from relations
where where-boolean
groupby attributes
having having-boolean
orderby attributes
into temporary relation.
```

Examples to this point have used only database tables in the from-clause. However, the format allows a comma-list of relations, so the first extension is generalizes table expressions in the from-clause. With the extended format, you can accumulate intermediate tables in a single SQL statement by nesting select-clauses.

For example, consider again the existential query: find the names of species swimming with a shark. You can embed an expression in the from-clause to isolate the sharky tanks, as illustrated below. The third Cartesian product component is the intermediate relation, ST, which contains the single attribute sharkytno. ST holds the tank numbers of the tanks with a shark. Of course, this feature adds no new retrieval power to the language. A previous solution to this example used multiple copies of the species and fish tables directly in the from-clause. In any case, you can, if necessary, use the into-clause to construct an intermediate table. You can then use the intermediate table in a second SQL expression. The new feature merely allows you to combine these multiple statements into one.

```
select S.sname
from Species as S, Fish as F,
    (select T.tno as sharkytno
    from Tank T, Fish G, Species H
    where T.tno = G.tno and G.sno = H.sno and H.sname = "shark") as ST
where S.sno = F.sno and F.tno = ST.sharkytno.
```

A consequence of this extended format is that the having-clause is now superfluous. You can replace a having-clause condition with a where-clause in the outer scope. For example, consider again the query: find the average tank volume associated with those species represented in two or more tanks. The left excerpt below repeats the solution from an earlier chapter. The new format on the right performs the aggregate calculations within a nested selection in the from-clause. The computational results are then available as simple attributes in the outer scope.

```
select S.sno species,                    select sno, avgVol
    average(T.tvolume) avgVol             from
from Species S, Tank T                        (select S.sno as sno,
where exists                                      average(T.tvolume) as avgVol,
    (select *                                     count(*) as tankCount
    from Fish F                               from Species S, Tank T
    where S.sno = F.sno and F.tno = T.tno)    where exists
groupby S.sno                                     (select *
having count(*) >= 2.                             from Fish F
                                                  where S.sno = F.sno and F.tno = T.tno)
                                              groupby S.sno)
                                          where tankCount >= 2.
```

The extended from-clause flexibility also solves the problem of composing aggregate functions, which to this point has required a sequence of SQL statements and temporary relations. For example, suppose you want the average of the avgVol values returned by the query above. In other words, you want to find the average tank volume associated with those species represented in two or more tanks, and then you want an average over that set of numbers. You can use the entire solution above as a from-clause entry to produce the second-level average, which gives the left construction below. For comparison, the two-part solution involving a temporary table is repeated on the right.

```
select average(avgVol)                    select S.sno as species, average(T.tvolume) as avgVol
from                                       from Species S, Tank T
   (select species, avgVol                   where exists
   from                                          (select *
      (select S.sno as species,                 from Fish F
         average(T.tvolume) as avgVol,          where S.sno = F.sno and F.tno = T.tno)
         count(*) as tankCount             groupby S.sno)
      from Species S, Tank T               having count(*) >= 2
      where exists                         into Temp.
         (select *
         from Fish F
         where S.sno = F.sno and
            F.tno = T.tno)
      groupby S.sno)                       select average(avgVol)
   where tankCount >= 2).                  from Temp.
```

 SQL allows nested select-statements in the from-clause of a host select-statement. This feature removes the need for temporary tables or having-clauses.

The view as a virtual table

The extended from-clause syntax is helpful in explaining SQL views. A **view** is a virtual relation, specified with an SQL select-statement, which you can treat as though it actually exists in the database. For example, suppose certain users (people or programs) in the aquarium environment have been long accustomed to a single-file data model. Each file record contains information on one fish, including the species and tank information. Furthermore, these users don't deal with the event entity, and they are unaware that the fish and tanks have colors. Also, some attributes have different names, such as fishname instead of fname, and the tank volume is given in quarts rather than in gallons. Their view of the aquarium is as follows. The parenthesized entries refer to the actual database names.

< ··· >							
fishno	fishname	specno	specname	specfood	tankno	tankname	tankvolume
(fno)	(fname)	(sno)	(sname)	(sfood)	(tno)	(tname)	(tvolume)

You can use an SQL statement to create this view and to make it available as though it were an actual database table.

```
create view oldaqua as
    (select F.fno as fishno, F.fname as fishname, S.sno as specno,
        S.sname as specname, S.sfood as specfood, T.tno as tankno,
        T.tname as tankname, 4 * T.tvolume as tankvolume
    from Species S, Fish F, Tank T
    where S.sno = F.fno and F.tno = T.tno).
```

The real tables are **base tables**, and the views are **virtual tables**. A base table possesses a concrete representation in the hardware disk structures, but a virtual table is only an abbreviation for an SQL select-statement. When another SQL statement refers to the virtual table, the DBMS substitutes the expanded form.

For example, suppose you are operating with the oldaqua view, and you want the names of species swimming in tanks named cesspool. The SQL on the left below uses the virtual table, oldaqua. The DBMS substitutes the definition of the oldaqua view in the from-clause, obtaining the equivalent form on the right. The DBMS then executes the second form.

```
select specname                    select specname
from oldaqua                       from
where tankname = "cesspool".          (select F.fno as fishno, F.fname as fishname,
                                          S.sno as specno, S.sname as specname,
                                          S.sfood as specfood, T.tno as tankno,
                                          T.tname as tankname, 4 * T.tvolume as tankvolume
                                       from Species S, Fish F, Tank T
                                       where S.sno = F.fno and F.tno = T.tno)
                                   where tankname = "cesspool".
```

You can join base tables with views. The following equivalent formats find the colors of fish swimming in tanks named cesspool. The DBMS substitutes the definition of oldaqua and processes the query on the right.

```
select F.fcolor                    select F.fcolor
from Fish F, oldaqua Q             from Fish F,
where F.fno = Q.fishno and            (select F.fno as fishno, F.fname as fishname,
   Q.tankname = "cesspool".              S.sno as specno, S.sname as specname,
                                          S.sfood as specfood, T.tno as tankno,
                                          T.tname as tankname, 4 * T.tvolume as tankvolume
                                       from Species S, Fish F, Tank T
                                       where S.sno = F.fno and F.tno = T.tno) as Q
                                   where F.tno = Q.tankno and Q.tankname = "cesspool".
```

You can answer many existential queries with a simple, single-table selection from oldaqua because the view presents a unified combination of species, fish, and tanks. You no longer envision a from-clause Cartesian product of the species, fish, and tank tables. The Cartesian product reappears, of course, when the DBMS substitutes the view definition, but the users need not be aware of that complication. To them, the query addresses a single table.

Existential queries requiring longer chains might need several copies of oldaqua. For example, the following SQL finds the names of species swimming with a shark.

```
select X.specname
from oldaqua X, oldaqua Y
where X.tankno = Y.tankno and Y.specname = "shark".
```

An earlier solution aligned six tuples to form the qualifying chain for a successful candidate. The new solution needs only two tuples from the oldaqua view because, in a manner of speaking, the chain comprises larger links. Each tuple in oldaqua represents a three-tuple minichain from the original tables.

A view is a virtual table specified as an SQL select-statement. The view isn't a temporary table. Instead, the DBMS merges the view definition with the rest of any SQL statement where it appears, which results in a new expression involving only the base tables.

Views are more flexible than temporary relations constructed with an into-clause. A temporary relation is valid only during a particular SQL session. The data aren't updated if the contents of the underlying tables change. A temporary table is a static snapshot of some portion of the database, taken when its defining SQL select-statement is executed. By contrast, the database stores the view definition, making it available across sessions. Moreover, the DBMS rematerializes the virtual relation anew each time it is referenced. Because the DBMS recalculates the view for each SQL statement that uses it, any changes in the underlying tables are immediately reflected in the view.

Database systems deliver services at three levels: physical, conceptual, and external. Views support the highest level, the external database description, which can vary from one user to another. A view protects its interfacing application from changes in the lower levels.

At the lowest level, the physical description serves as a foundation, which supports the intermediate level—the conceptual schema. Changes in the physical hardware or in the disk data structures need not disturb the conceptual schema, which models the application as a collection of relations, domains, attributes, and relationships. Of course, certain DBMS routines may require modification to accommodate the new physical environment, but that job rests with the database vendor. Any application software built on the conceptual schema remains valid. In the terminology of Chapter 1, isolating the conceptual schema from the underlying hardware, operating system, and data structures is called physical data independence.

Physical data independence has a counterpart at the next level. Changes in the schema (e.g., adding new tables or new attributes to existing tables) need not affect an application with a protective view. The view definition may require modification, but the application continues to function as before, provided that the new view materializes the expected relations. This characteristic of views is called logical data independence. The isolation isn't total, however. For example, if the database designer drops an attribute from the conceptual schema and your view uses that attribute, you probably won't be able to restore it in the view. Instead, you'll have to rewrite the application and use a new view.

 A view provides logical data independence and isolates application software from schema changes.

Updating tuples through a view

Information retrieval through a view involves a straightforward substitution of the view definition in the probing query. Insertions, deletions, and updates through views, however, are more complex. For example, suppose you have the following view, which materializes a single column of fish colors. As indicated on the right below, the view gives a peephole into the fish relation by revealing only the fish colors.

Fish				
fno	fname	fcolor	tno	sno
164	charlie	orange	42	74
347	flipper	black	35	17
228	killer	white	42	22
281	charlie	orange	85	22
483	albert	red	55	17
119	bonnie	blue	42	22
388	cory	purple	35	93
654	darron	white	42	93
765	elsie	white	42	22
438	fran	black	55	74
277	george	red	42	93
911	helen	blue	44	74
104	indira	black	42	17
302	jill	red	38	17
419	kilroy	red	55	74
650	laura	blue	85	17
700	maureen	white	44	17

```
create view fishColor as
    (select F.fcolor as fcolor
    from Fish F).
```

$\Rightarrow$

FishColor
fcolor
orange
black
white
red
blue
purple

Now what are the effects of the following SQL operations?

```
delete from fishColor              insert into fishColor (fcolor)
where fcolor = "red".              values ("red").
```

Because a view has no explicit counterpart in physical storage, the DBMS must apply any changes to the underlying base tables. In this case, which of the four red fish should the DBMS delete from the fish table? For the insertion, what values should the DBMS place in other attributes when it creates a new tuple with fcolor red? In particular, what value should it put in the key attribute, fno? Because these questions have no satisfactory answers, you can't update this view.

In general, a view is updatable if it has a single base table and includes a key to that table. If an update or insert produces a base-table row with nulls in nonkey positions, the consequences aren't as severe as when the key acquires null values. The entity integrity constraint isn't violated. Also, the deleting a view row affects exactly one row in the underlying table because the key value appears in the view. Therefore, deletions are also well-defined.

Some database products take the safe route and allow no data modifications through views. On these systems, views are available only for customized data retrieval, and data modification operations must refer to the base tables. Other database products allow data modifications through certain views, provided the view definition and the modifying SQL together can determine the precise effect on the underlying base tables. One criterion is that the view be based on a single table and that it include the key attributes.

The criteria in the SQL standard are more complicated. They require that the view be based on a single table, and they list several additional constraints that force a view-row change to translate to a well-defined change of the underlying base table. In particular, the view need not include the key attributes if it satisfies the rest of the rules. Although relations are mathematical sets, SQL returns multisets as query responses. In other words, duplicates aren't removed. This perspective sometimes allows the DBMS to retain a connection between the view rows and the base table rows, even in the absence of the key. In the fish color example above, the DBMS might materialize the view as follows.

Fish						FishColor
fno	fname	fcolor	tno	sno		fcolor
164	charlie	orange	42	74		orange
347	flipper	black	35	17		black
228	killer	white	42	22		white
281	charlie	orange	85	22		orange
483	albert	red	55	17		red
119	bonnie	blue	42	22		blue
388	cory	purple	35	93		purple
654	darron	white	42	93	$\Rightarrow$	white
765	elsie	white	42	22		white
438	fran	black	55	74		black
277	george	red	42	93		red
911	helen	blue	44	74		blue
104	indira	black	42	17		black
302	jill	red	38	17		red
419	kilroy	red	55	74		red
650	laura	blue	85	17		blue
700	maureen	white	44	17		white

The DBMS could maintain the connection between the duplicated view rows and the corresponding rows in the fish relation, although this connection isn't visible to the user. In this case, an update through the view is well-defined. The fishColor view, therefore, would be updatable in the SQL standard. The SQL rules allow updates for a view over a single table, without a "distinct" qualifier in the select-statement, which selects only simple attributes—no aggregates or arithmetic expressions. However, modifying data through this view is risky. You are probing in the dark as to which row of the underlying table will be affected. Therefore, even if the standard is more lenient, you should restrict data modification through views to situations where the view contains the key attributes of its single underlying base table.

A special case arises for a view over the parent and child relations of a one-to-many relationship. Some database systems allows modifications through such views, provided that they affect only the child attributes. For example, suppose you create a TankFish view as follows.

```
create view TankFish as
    (select T.tno as tno, tname, tcolor, tvolume, fno, fname, fcolor, fweight
    from Tank T, Fish F
    where T.tno = F.tno).
```

This view materializes the one-to-many relationship between Tank and Fish by extending each fish tuple with the relevant tank information. Because the T.tno value duplicates F.tno, the view retains only one copy, which it calls tno. The one-to-many relationship ensures that a given view row corresponds to exactly one row in the fish table. Therefore, any changes to the view attributes fno, fname, fcolor, or fweight translate unambiguously to corresponding changes to those attributes in the base fish table. The DBMS interprets a view-row deletion as a deletion of the fish portion only. With that interpretation, deletions are also well-defined.

This perspective stretches somewhat the typical meaning of deletion. When you delete a row from the view, that row does disappear. However, it disappears only because the fish portion is no longer available. If the tank contains other fish, those rows remain unchanged because the tank portion isn't removed from the underlying table. Similarly, the DBMS can understand a view insertion because both tank and fish portions are specified. The DBMS simply ignores the tank part of the insertion if the tank is already in the base tank table. Because the view suppresses the foreign key of the fish table, updates that might affect the relationship grouping aren't possible. The DBMS interprets the visible tno attribute as belonging to the tank relation and therefore allows no changes to it.

Although some database products take this approach, allowing modifications to the child portion of a view that materializes a one-to-many relationship, it's not standard SQL. Because they are making increasing use of database forms, these database systems permit this non-standard treatment of one-to-many relationships. A **database form** is a two-dimensional display, which is optimized for data entry and editing operations. In many ways, a form is similar to a view because both provide a customized interface to the database. Forms, however, emphasize the visual effects of the display. The forms facility of some advanced systems provides graphical features for emphasizing relationships, scroll boxes for managing lists, and command buttons for navigating among application screens. One particularly frequent form provides an appealing display of a one-to-many relationship.

Figure 6.1 illustrates how a form shows the one-to-many relationship between Fish and Tank. You use a mouse to invoke the form's features. In the language of a windows' interface, the object at the top is a retracted listbox. Clicking on the downward-pointing triangle causes a drop-down list to appear, which contains the database tanks. Clicking on one of these entries copies the chosen tank into the rectangular area that remains visible after the list retracts. The fish associated with the chosen tank then fill the object at the bottom of the form, a scrollable listbox. This listbox provides room for a few entries, usually 10 or less. You can scroll the contents forward or backward by clicking the arrows on its right edge. You can also choose a particular fish by clicking on it with the mouse. Some visual effect confirms the choice, such as a different color or reverse video. Double clicking (i.e., two rapid clicks of the mouse button without moving its position) selects the fish and also moves it to the editing area in the center of the screen, where you can modify its attributes. Clicking the save button below the edit area installs the modified fish in the list. You can insert a new fish and connect it to the current tank by entering the data in the edit area and clicking the save button. Finally, you can delete a selected fish by clicking the delete button.

The form's function corresponds to the modification scenario described earlier for a view that materializes a one-to-many relationship. When you choose a tank in the retractable listbox, the DBMS selects the appropriate rows from the TankFish view to source the lower listbox. The form's modification activities all occur through the view.

tno	tname	tcolor	tvolume	
42	cesspool	blue	100	▽

fno	fname	fcolor	sno

INSERT   SAVE   DELETE

fno	fname	fcolor	sno	
164	charlie	orange	74	▽
228	killer	white	22	
119	bonnie	blue	22	
654	darron	white	93	☐
765	elsie	white	22	
277	george	red	93	
104	indira	black	17	△

Figure 6.1   A database form displaying the fish-tank relationship

The DBMS restricts data modification through views, but the rules vary from one database system to another. However, all require that a change to the view must translate to an unambiguous change in the underlying base tables.

The check option for a view

Suppose you define the LargeTanks view as shown on the left below. Because this view is based on a single table and includes the tno key attribute, assume that you can perform insertions, updates, and deletions through the view. Now, consider the SQL activities to the right.

```
create view LargeTanks as          insert into LargeTanks (tno, tname, tcolor, tvolume)
   (select *                       values (71, "BigMuddy", "brown", 150).
   from Tank
   where tvolume > 200).           select *
                                   from LargeTanks.
```

The newly inserted tank won't appear in the answer to the subsequent query. The insert-statement adds a row to the underlying tank relation, specifying a new tank with a volume of 150. Because the definition of LargeTanks admits only those tanks whose volumes exceed 200, the DBMS excludes the new tuple from the LargeTanks relation, even though it has just successfully inserted it. A user could be confused if he couldn't recover a tuple that he had just inserted. To prevent this, you can append the phrase *with check option* to the view definition. This clause causes an insert-statement to fail if the tuple being inserted doesn't qualify for admission to the view. The left definition below illustrates a view that behaves consistently. A query will display any tuple that has been successfully inserted. The check also blocks any update through the view if the updated tuple would disappear.

```
create view LargeTanks as          create view SmallTanks as
   (select *                          (select *
   from Tank                          from LargeTanks
   where tvolume > 200)               where tvolume < 300)
   with check option.                 with check option.
```

You can construct a view over an existing view. Using the LargeTanks view of the previous example as a base, you can create a second view as shown on the right above. Can you insert a tuple with tvolume 100 into SmallTanks? The new tuple passes the check option of the SmallTanks definition, but it fails the check option of LargeTanks. Will the DBMS reject the insertion? Yes, the insert will fail because, by default, view conditions cascade to subsequent views. The SQL standard specifies further clauses to modify the default behavior.

 A check option in a view definition blocks the insertion or update of tuples that would subsequently be excluded from the view.

Null values

In any large database application, you inevitably encounter missing data. All database systems provide some internal code for a null value, which you can substitute for a missing attribute value. Unfortunately, the null value takes different meanings on different occasions. For example, null may mean that the value exists, but you don't know what it is. Suppose you are entering a worker in the employee table of a personnel database. You might specify the height attribute as null because you don't know the person's height. Certainly the new hire has a height. You can also answer some questions about the height even though the value is unknown. For example, an SQL predicate, E.height < 5 meters, is true because no person is taller than 5 meters. On other occasions, the null value may mean "not applicable." For example, suppose the attribute cruisingAltitude occurs in a vehicle table. Airplanes have cruising altitudes; automobiles don't. Although you can expect all vehicles that have a cruising altitude to have a value greater than 10 feet, you still can't assume that the predicate, V.cruisingAltitude > 10, is always true. It might not apply to the vehicle V. For a car, V.cruisingAltitude > 10 is neither true nor false.

a	b	not a	a and b	a or b
true	true	false	true	true
true	false	false	false	true
true	unknown	false	unknown	true
false	true	true	false	true
false	false	true	false	false
false	unknown	true	false	unknown
unknown	true	unknown	unknown	true
unknown	false	unknown	false	unknown
unknown	unknown	unknown	unknown	unknown

Figure 6.2   Definition of logical operators in the presence of unknown truth values

An application can avoid the use of nulls by choosing, for each attribute, some value that will never occur among the valid entries for that attribute. In other words, the null choice must lie outside that attribute's domain. For example, you might choose the string Invalid for the lastName attribute in a person table. The difficulty is that the database may be in use for many years, and eventually the attribute's domain might expand to include the null value code. Having chosen the string Invalid for the lastName attribute, you might well encounter Ms. Jane Invalid as an employee several years later. Even if you can find suitable codes for null values, they will probably differ from one attribute to another. You might choose Invalid for a string attribute and -1 for an integer attribute. This variation leads to complicated interface programs because they must handle each case separately.

To address these difficulties, SQL provides a uniform facility for handling nulls. The DBMS selects some internal representation to use as a placeholder for any null attribute value. This internal representation is the same for every attribute in every relation in every database. The precise internal representation is implementation dependent, but that detail isn't important from the user's viewpoint. The code is simply called "null" at the SQL interface, and it is used for all cases of missing data, whether the intent is an unknown value or an inapplicable circumstance.

Operations with null values

In the presence of null values, each arithmetic operation exhibits slightly modified behavior, returning null if any of its operands is null. For example, null + null produces null, as does 3 + null. Boolean operations extend to a three-valued logic: true, false, and unknown. Each comparison operation returns the truth value unknown if any of its operands is null. For example, $6 <$ null gives unknown. Even null = null returns unknown. The logical operations (i.e., and, or, not) accept arguments in the three-valued range (i.e., true, false, unknown) and return values in this same range. In some case, a logical operation can return a definitive true or false value, even if one of its operands is unknown. For example, true "or" unknown returns true; false "and" unknown returns false. Figure 6.2 shows the extended truth tables for the logical operators.

An arithmetic operation returns null if any of its operands is null. Comparisons in the presence of nulls return values in the three-state logic system: true, false, unknown. The three-state values can be combined with the standard logical connectives: and, or, not.

The exists-predicate, when applied to a table constructed with a subquery, always returns true or false—unknown. Even if the table contains only null tuples, it's still not empty, and the exists-predicate returns true. Because the not-operator returns false or true when applied to true or false operands, the not-exists predicate also returns a solid true or false value, never an unknown.

To retain a tuple in the horizontal section of the from-clause Cartesian product, the where-clause boolean must be true. If it evaluates to false or unknown, the tuple is suppressed. Likewise, to retain a partition grouping, the having-clause boolean must be true. For the most part, these extensions accord with intuition, and queries perform as expected. However, you should carefully think through the logic because surprises can occur. Suppose you want the names of fish with a null color. The SQL on the left below doesn't deliver as expected.

```
select fname          select fname
from Fish             from Fish
where fcolor = null.  where fcolor is null.
```

As a matter of fact, it delivers an empty table. Why? If a fish has an fcolor value of red, the condition takes the form, red = null, which returns unknown. Therefore, the fish is excluded from the answer. If the fish has a null fcolor value, the condition becomes null = null, which also evaluates to unknown. Again, the fish is excluded.

Because of this non-intuitive behavior, SQL disallows the word "null" in comparisons. Instead, it provides special syntax to probe an attribute for a null value. The correct predicate takes the form "attribute-name is null" or "attribute-name is not null." This predicate always returns a true or false, never an unknown. The SQL on the right above rewrites the previous example with the new predicate. This SQL does indeed recover the names of fish with a null color.

Suppose you want the names of fish that aren't red. The solution attempt on the left below delivers only those fish that have a nonnull, non-red color. The predicate, "fcolor not = red," is the same as "not (fcolor = red)," which evaluates to unknown when fcolor is null. Assuming that the query intends to deliver all fish that don't explicitly have fcolor red, it should also report the fish with null colors. The correct solution must specifically allow for the null case, as illustrated on the right.

```
select fname              select fname
from Fish                 from Fish
where fcolor not = "red". where fcolor not = "red" or fcolor is null.
```

SQL provides special comparisons to probe a predicate for any of the three truth values. For any predicate P, you can ask: P is true, P is false, P is unknown. These constructions always return a solid true or false result, never an unknown. You can also use the complements: P is not true, P is not false, P is not unknown. With these constructions, you could rewrite the above example as follows. The full predicate returns true if (fcolor = red) is either false or unknown.

```
select fname
from Fish
where fcolor = "red" is not true.
```

Because of the three-valued logic, (not P) is not the same as (P is not true). The first can return an unknown, but the second returns true or false.

For a more subtle example, suppose you want the names of tanks with volumes larger than all tanks containing a shark. A tank contributes to the answer if it dominates all the sharky tanks in volume. Now, suppose one of the sharky tanks has a null volume. You expect no tanks in the answer because the comparison with the sharky tank of null volume produces an unknown. Because this is a universal query, a successful tank must produce a true comparison for each sharky tank. Therefore, each tank will fail when it receives an "unknown" when compared with the null-volume, sharky tank. Two tentative SQL solutions appear below.

```
select T.tname                          select tname
from Tank T                             from Tank T
where                                   where not exists
   (select Q.tno                           (select *
   from Tank Q                             from Tank Q, Fish F, Species S
   where T.tvolume > Q.tvolume)            where Q.tno = F.tno and F.sno = S.sno
contains                                      and S.sname = "shark" and
   (select Q.tno                              not (T.tvolume > Q.volume).
   from Tank Q, Fish F, Species S
   where Q.tno = F.tno and F.sno = S.sno
      and S.sname = "shark").
```

Consider first the query on the left. For a given candidate, T, the first subquery isolates the tanks that T dominates in volume. The second subquery delivers the sharky tanks. If the first set contains the second, T must dominate all sharky tanks in volume, and T should contribute to the answer. Because there is a sharky tank, say T_1, which has a null volume, the volume comparison returns unknown. So T_1 doesn't appear in the first set, regardless of the candidate T. Because T_1 is a sharky tank, it appears in the second set. Therefore, the first set never contains the second, regardless of the candidate tank, and no tanks appear in the answer. This solution behaves as expected. In particular, suppose there is a tank, say T_2, that does dominate all sharky tanks in volume, in those cases where the sharky tank does indeed have a volume. T_2 still doesn't appear in the answer.

Now consider the doubly negated solution on the right. A tank contributes to the answer if the set of sharky tanks that it doesn't dominate is empty. This rewording is simply another way of saying that the tank dominates all sharky tanks. Now, consider tank T_2, which dominates all sharky tanks with a nonnull volume. When T_2 is the candidate, the predicate in the subquery returns false for all sharky tanks with a nonnull volume because the component (T_2.tvolume > Q.tvolume) is true. However, it returns unknown for the sharky tank with a null volume. In any case, it never returns a true, so the subquery constructs an empty set for the candidate T_2. This allows T_2 into the answer. So the doubly negated construction delivers a different answer than the set-containment construction. Moreover, it delivers the wrong answer. T_2 shouldn't be selected because you can't be sure that it dominates the null-volume, sharky tank.

You can obtain the expected answer from the doubly negated solution by explicitly checking for the nonexistence of tanks, Q, for which T.tvolume $>$ Q.volume isn't true. The modified doubly negated solution then appears as follows.

```
select tname
from Tank T
where not exists
  (select *
   from Tank Q, Fish F, Species S
   where Q.tno = F.tno and F.sno = S.sno and S.sname = "shark" and
     T.tvolume > Q.volume is not true.
```

These examples emphasize the potential traps associated with null values. Although most queries execute as expected, you must remain alert for possible misinterpretations when null values are present. In general computer programming, you always check boundary values as possible sources of unexpected errors. You should follow the same precaution when programming SQL queries. The rules are simple enough:

- All arithmetic involving a null value returns a null value.

- All comparisons involving a null value return the truth value unknown.

- Logical operations involving unknowns evaluate to true or false if the unknown quantity isn't relevant; otherwise they evaluate to unknown.

- Where- and having-clauses must evaluate to true (neither false nor unknown) to retain a tuple or a partition.

Therefore, you can always determine in advance just how a query will behave in the presence of null values. You must then judge if the response is suitable for the given query. You can frequently adjust a query to deliver the expected results by requesting an explicit truth value. In other words, you convert a predicate P into one of the formats: P is true, P is false, or P is unknown.

 You should carefully check the behavior of where- and having-clause predicates for boundary conditions involving null values. Unexpected behavior arises when the application interprets nulls differently from the SQL standard.

Behavior of nulls with aggregates and SQL predicates

The aggregates min, max, sum, and average ignore null values unless all values in their range of operation are null. If all are null, the aggregate returns null. Otherwise, it produces the min, max, sum, or average over the nonnull values. The count aggregate behaves differently because its purpose is to count the group tuples, regardless of their content. A count over a column that includes nulls returns the true number of entries in the column, including the nulls. A count over an empty column returns 0; the other aggregates return null when confronted with an empty column.

With the exception of count, the aggregate functions ignore null values unless the entire range of operands contains only nulls.

The full SQL standard allows predicates in where- and having-clauses beyond those investigated in Chapter 5. For the most part, these constructions are self-explanatory. The earlier chapter omitted them because they weren't important for the concepts under discussion. However, in the presence of null values, the new predicates' behavior becomes more significant.

The **between-predicate** specifies a range of possible attribute values. For example, the following SQL requests the names of tanks with volumes in a certain range.

```
select T.tname
from Tank T
where T.tvolume between 100 and 600.
```

The definition of (x between y and z) is ($x >= y$ and $x <= z$). If any operand is null, the between-predicate is never true although it can be false or unknown. Therefore, a tank with a null volume won't appear in the solution set of the example.

Besides attribute comparisons, you can compare rows by using a left-to-right lexicographic ordering. This feature marks another example of SQL's departure from the strict unordered-set definitions in the relational model. For example, you can request equality or inequality conditions between two 2-tuples as follows.

```
select T.tname                          select T.tname
from Tank T                             from Tank T
where (T.tcolor, T.tvolume) = ("blue", 500).   where (T.tcolor, T.tvolume) < ("blue", 500).
```

You can also invoke implicit comparisons with a between-predicate, such as the following.

```
select T.tname
from Tank T
where (T.tcolor, T.tvolume) between ("blue", 100) and ("green", 400).
```

Rows under comparison must have the same number of entries, and the corresponding entries must be comparable. In other words, corresponding entries must both have a character string type, or both have numeric type, or both have a special database type, such as date or currency. Suppose that the two rows are $(a_1, a_2, \ldots, a_n)$ and $(b_1, b_2, \ldots, b_n)$. Then $(a_1, a_2, \ldots, a_n) = (b_1, b_2, \ldots, b_n)$ if $a_1 = b_1$ and $a_2 = b_2$ and so forth, through $a_n = b_n$. If any one of the comparisons is false, the overall result is false. If no false comparisons appear, but a null occurs in any position, the result is unknown.

In an inequality comparison between two rows, the **pivot position** is the leftmost position, i, where $a_i = b_i$ is not true. Then, $(a_1, a_2, \ldots, a_n) < (b_1, b_2, \ldots, b_n)$ is true if $a_i < b_i$ for the pivot position i. This condition is equivalent to lexicographic order. If the two sequences are equal from the beginning out to some pivot position, where they differ, then the comparison at the pivot position determines which is smaller. In this situation, a true or false value is returned even when there are null values in some positions, provided the nulls occurs beyond the pivot position. A null can't appear before the pivot position because, by definition, that position is the first in which $a_i = b_i$ isn't true. If a null appears at the pivot position, the comparison returns the truth value unknown.

$(a_1, a_2, \ldots, a_n) > (b_1, b_2, \ldots, b_n)$ is defined in a similar manner. Denoting the rows simply as a and b, the compound condition $a <= b$ is defined as $a < b$ or $a = b$. This predicate can also return solid true or false even if nulls appear in some operand positions, provided the nulls appear beyond the pivot position for the $a < b$ portion. $a >= b$ is similarly evaluated. Because x between y and z is evaluated as $x >= y$ and $x <= z$, you can obtain a true or false value in the presence of nulls in the operands, provided the nulls are beyond the pivot.

A **like-predicate** is available for limited pattern recognition in character strings. It takes the form: "x like y." For example, to find all tanks with the substring **pool** in their names, you can use the following SQL.

```
select T.tname
from Tank T
where T.tname like "%pool%".
```

Two wildcard characters are available. An underscore matches any single character, and a percent sign matches any sequence of zero or more characters. A null value in either operand of the like-predicate results in a truth value of unknown.

The match predicate and referential integrity

The SQL **match-predicate** checks for corresponding tuple fragments in different tables. In the absence of null values, it corresponds to the set-membership test of Chapter 5. For example, the two SQL excerpts below find the names of tanks containing a species that is also represented in a cesspool tank. The SQL on the left uses constructions from previous chapters; the other illustrates the new match-predicate.

```
select T.tname
from Tank T, Fish F, Species S
where T.tno = F.tno and F.sno = S.sno
   and (S.sno, S.sname) in
      (select X.sno, X.sname
       from Species X, Fish Y, Tank Z
       where X.sno = Y.sno and Y.tno = Z.tno
          and Z.tname = "cesspool").
```

```
select T.tname
from Tank T, Fish F, Species S
where T.tno = F.tno and F.sno = S.sno
   and (S.sno, S.sname) match
      (select X.sno, X.sname
       from Species X, Fish Y, Tank Z
       where X.sno = Y.sno and Y.tno = Z.tno
          and Z.tname = "cesspool").
```

Set-membership predicates typically test a single attribute—usually a key from the candidate tuple—for inclusion in a single-column set. In truth, however, a full row is being tested for membership in a table of compatible rows. The examples above use the pair (S.sno, S.sname) to emphasize this fact. The row comparison uses lexicographic ordering.

In the absence of nulls, if r is a row and T is a table, r match T is the same as r in T. The predicate, r match T, is true if there is some row in T that matches r, that is, if there is a row r_1 in T for which $r_1 = r$ is true. Otherwise, it returns false.

The match test never returns unknown. When null values are present, therefore, the DBMS must deviate somewhat from its standard treatment of nulls to guarantee a true or false return. One possible variation is as follows. Either a row is found for which the equality predicate returns true, or it isn't. Consider the effects of different null value locations, with the binary constraint that you either find a row delivering a true comparison, or you don't. If the a null appears in a T row, an equality comparison between that row and r will return unknown. This situation presents no difficulty; there is simply one less T row available to deliver true. However, if the null value appears in r, all the equality tests against T rows deliver unknown, which forces the match to return a false.

Although this behavior is consistent with the rules for handling null values, it's not quite what is needed to describe referential integrity constraints. The set-membership predicate is already available for situations where the only concern is the consistent treatment of null values. The match-predicate is a special test, which applies to referential integrity situations. Referential integrity requires that a foreign key either match an existing key in some remote table or be null. The match-predicate, as described so far, comes close to providing the needed conditions. If r is the foreign key and T is the list of primary keys, then r match T works properly if no nulls appear in either location or if nulls appear in T. In either case, it delivers true if and only if r matches an existing entry in T. However, if r is null, the match returns false under the behavior pattern explained above. For r match T to check referential integrity, it should return true when r is null. So SQL adjusts the match-predicate behavior in the presence of null values to be exactly what is needed.

The predicate r match T returns true if either r contains a null value or there exists a row r_1 in T such that $r = r_1$ is true. Otherwise, it returns false. As an example of the match-predicate's usefulness in a referential integrity context, consider the predicate on the left below. It states that no fish tuple exists with a nonnull tno that doesn't match a tno in Tank. This condition expresses precisely the fact that no referential integrity violations arise from the Fish-Tank relationship.

```
not exists                      not exists
   (select *                       (select *
   from Fish F                     from Fish F
   where not (F.tno match          where not ((F.tno, F.sno) match
      (select T.tno                   (select T.tno, S.sno
      from Tank T))).                 from Tank T, Species S)).
```

You could write another constraint to enforce the referential integrity between Species and Fish via the sno attributes. However, suppose you attempt to express both constraints in a single statement, as shown on the right above. A problem arises here because referential integrity could be violated even though the predicate returns true. This case occurs if F.tno is null, but the F.sno value isn't among the S.sno entries of the constructed table. The match still returns a true value because any null value in the left operand forces a true result. To accommodate such situations, SQL allows a further specification in the match expression. If r is a row and T is a table, you can assemble a match predicate in any of the following three formats: (1) r match T, (2) r match partial T, or (3) r match full T.

The first format's behavior has been described above, and it delivers proper expressions for referential integrity where the matching keys each consist of a single attribute. The second format, r match partial T, returns true if *every* component of r is null, or if there is a row of T, say r_1, such that $a = b$ returns true whenever a is a nonnull component of r, and b is the corresponding element in r_1. Otherwise, it returns false. This condition is typically appropriate for independent referential integrity constraints with two or more remote relations. If you rephrase the example above to specify the partial match-predicate, the expression captures the exact meaning of the two separate referential integrity constraints: Fish-Tank and Species-Tank. The SQL expression appears below. Now part of (F.tno, F.sno) can be null, but the other part must match its counterpart in the constructed table.

```
not exists
   (select *
   from Fish F
   where not ((F.tno, F.sno) match partial (select T.tno, S.sno from Tank T, Species S)).
```

This interpretation still isn't correct, however, if the row represents a composite key to a single remote table. The third format addresses that interpretation. The final version, r match full T, returns true if *every* component of r is null, or if there is a row in T, say r_1, such that $r = r_1$ is true. Otherwise, it returns false. The full match is the expected condition when the foreign key is composite and refers to a composite primary key in a single remote table. For example, suppose that parent table P has (x, y) as a composite primary key and the child table C also has (x, y) as a composite foreign key. The appropriate referential integrity constraint is:

```
not exists
   (select *
   from C
   where not ((C.x, C.y) match full (select P.x, P.y from P)).
```

Any and all predicates

Two other predicates are available for comparing a single row with a constructed table. Both behave according to the basic rules for null values. So if the match-predicate's adjusted behavior to accommodate referential integrity constraints isn't appropriate, you can use these predicates instead. The first is the **any-predicate**, illustrated by the following alternative to the set-membership test. The query finds the names of tanks containing a species that is also represented in a cesspool tank.

```
select T.tname
from Tank T, Fish F, Species S
where T.tno = F.tno and F.sno = S.sno and (S.sno, S.sname) =any
   (select X.sno, X.sname
   from Species X, Fish Y, Tank Z
   where X.sno = Y.sno and Y.tno = Z.tno and Z.tname = "cesspool").
```

In general, if r is a row and T is a table, $r\ \theta\text{any}\ T$ returns true if there is a row, say r_1, in T such that $r\ \theta\ r_1$ returns true. If r compares false for every row of T, then false is returned. Otherwise, the truth value unknown is returned. As usual, θ is any of the comparison operators: $<, >, =, \leq,$ or $\geq$. The any-predicate, $r = \text{any}T$, is the same as r in T. In the presence of null values, the lexicographic ordering and the nature of the pivotal position determine the returned value, in accordance with the standard rules. In particular, a true value may result even if there are nulls among the components of r or the matching T row, provided the nulls appear after the pivot position.

The **all-predicate**, $r \, \theta \text{all} \, T$, returns true if $r \, \theta$-compares true with *every* row of T. It returns false if there is some row, say r_1, of T such that $r \, \theta \, r_1$ is false. Otherwise, it returns unknown.

The behavior of both the θany- and the θall-predicates is well-defined and consistent with the standard treatment of null values. Of course, you should always check null boundary situations to ensure that they behave as the application expects. For example, consider again the query: find the names of tanks that dominate all sharky tanks in volume. An earlier analysis showed that the set-containment predicate behaves as expected but the doubly negated solution needs special attention in the presence of null values. Recall that you expect an empty answer table if one or more of the sharky tanks has a null volume. The following solutions use the $>$ all and $\leq$ any predicates.

```
select T.tname                          select T.tname
from Tank T                             from Tank T
where T.tvolume >all                    where not (T.tvolume <=any
  (select Q.tvolume                       (select Q.tvolume
  from Tank Q, Fish F, Species S          from Tank Q, Fish F, Species S
  where Q.tno = F.tno and F.sno = S.sno   where Q.tno = F.tno and F.sno = S.sno
    and S.sname = "shark").                 and S.sname = "shark")).
```

Consider first the solution on the left. If there is a sharky tank with a null volume, that particular comparison will yield the truth value unknown, preventing the $>$all predicate from ever returning a true. Therefore, the construction delivers the expected empty answer table. The solution on the right arises from the rephrased query. Find the names of tanks that are *not* dominated or matched by some sharky tank in volume. If there is a sharky tank with a null volume, a comparison with that element returns the truth value unknown, precluding the $<=$any predicate from ever returning a false value. Therefore, the not $<=$any predicate can't return a true value, and no tanks will be selected for the answer. So the second construction also delivers the expected answer.

The standard treatment of null values generally provides the expected behavior. Surprises occur only with the predicates, such as exists and match, that can't return the unknown truth value. In other cases, acceptable behavior usually results because the where-clause rejects both false and unknown truth values. Of course, in the example above, you could have wanted the names of tanks that dominate the sharky tanks in volume, with the understanding that null volumes among the sharky tanks should be ignored. This alternative interpretation isn't unreasonable: it is, for example, consistent with the standard SQL treatment of aggregates. However, the SQL above doesn't deliver according to the changed expectations. Correct SQL for this new interpretation reads as follows. Here a single false comparison will reject a candidate tank, but any number of unknowns won't. As usual, the adjustment probes the predicate for a particular state of its three-valued logic.

```
select T.tname
from Tank T
where (T.tvolume >all
  (select Q.tvolume
  from Tank Q, Fish F, Species S
  where Q.tno = F.tno and F.sno = S.sno and S.sname = "shark")) is not false.
```

Finally, because SQL allows tables with duplicate entries, a **unique-predicate** is provided to detect multisets. If T is a table, the predicate "unique T" returns false if there are two distinct rows in T, say r_1 and r_2, such that $r_1 = r_2$ is true. Otherwise, it returns true. Because comparisons with nulls deliver unknown truth values, this predicate judges a table with two null rows as unique.

 SQL provides a variety of predicates for the where- and having-clauses. You should carefully check boundary conditions, but all predicates, except match and exists, behave consistently with the general rules for null values.

Outer operations

Previous examples illustrated nested select-statements in the from-clause of a main query. SQL also permits other expressions in the from-clause, provided they evaluate to tables. For example, consider again the query: find the names of species represented in cesspool tanks.

```
select R.sname
from ((Species S natural join Fish F) natural join Tank T) as R
where R.tname = "cesspool".
```

The table expression in the from-clause computes the natural join in the relational algebra sense: a horizontal section from the Cartesian product containing those combinations that agree on like-named attributes. A where-clause restriction to remove inappropriate combinations is, therefore, no longer necessary.

If you use only the word "join" rather than "natural join," you must list the match attributes in a using-clause. With this syntax, the example would appear as follows. The common attributes appear in parentheses because the general case could have a list of names.

```
select R.sname
from ((Species S join Fish F using (sno)) join Tank T using (tno)) as R
where R.tname = "cesspool".
```

A third variation is available if the match attributes have different names, as shown below.

```
select R.sname
from ((Species S join Fish F on S.sno = F.sno) as Q join Tank T on Q.tno = T.tno) as R
where R.tname = "cesspool".
```

Because the match attributes in this example have the same names in both tables, the third form isn't very illustrative. For a better example, recall the employee relation used for recursive queries in Chapter 5. The foreign key, sno (i.e., supervisor number), refers to the primary key, eno (i.e., employee number), in the same relation. Therefore, a natural join in the new notation takes the form:

```
select E.ename
from (Employee E join Employee F on E.sno = F.eno).
```

The new notation adds nothing to the language's retrieval power. It merely allows you to apply certain where-clause booleans implicitly in the from-clause construction. The entire condition can remain implicit when the match attributes from the different relations have the same names.

The from-clause join notation leads to a new concept, the outer join, which will be discussed in the next section. The joins illustrated to this point are formally called inner joins. Indeed, you can choose to use the descriptive term *inner* in the join syntax. For example, the following SQL expression finds the names of species represented in a cesspool tank. The meaning is the same as the earlier expression without the "inner." The alternatives for specifying attribute names remain available. The inner join is the default join.

```
select R.sname
from ((Species S natural inner join Fish F) natural inner join Tank T) as R
where R.tname = "cesspool".
```

 SQL permits expressions in the from-clause that evaluate to tables. In addition to embedded subqueries, such expressions include:

- *A natural [inner] join B*

- *A [inner] join B on conditions*

- *A [inner] join B using attribute-list*

The outer join

With an inner join, if a row from the left operand doesn't match any row from the right operand, it doesn't appear in the result. Suppose that Tank 42 (cesspool) contains no fish, and consider the query: list the fish associated with each tank. Neither of the SQL solutions below contains an entry for Tank 42.

```
select R.tno, R.tname, R.fno, R.fname
from (Tank T natural inner join Fish F) as R.
```

```
select T.tno, T.tname, F.fno, F.fname
from Tank T, Fish F
where T.tno = F.tno.
```

This omission isn't due to a new format in the from-clause. Instead, it results because tuples are dropped from the Cartesian product if they don't agree on matching attributes. This same omission occurs with the old format, as shown on the right above. Sometimes this interpretation satisfies the application's needs, and sometimes it doesn't. Because you asked for a list of the fish associated with each tank, you might accept the omission of tank 42. You understand that the SQL won't report a tank without any fish.

However, if you want a count of the fish in each tank, the omission is less satisfactory. Instead of the solution on the left below, which contains no row for tank 42, you would probably prefer a solution that included tank 42 with a count of zero. You could laboriously include the special case as illustrated on the right. However, this extension is awkward because it doubles the query length just to handle the boundary case.

```
select R.tno, R.tname, count(*) as fishCount
from (Tank T natural inner join Fish F) as R
groupby R.tno.
```

```
select R.tno, R.tname, count(*) as fishCount
from (Tank T natural inner join Fish F) as R
groupby R.tno

union

select T.tno, T.tname, 0 as fishCount
from Tank T
where not exists
  (select *
  from Fish F
  where T.tno = F.fno).
```

A new construction, an outer join provides a more satisfactory solution. The DBMS constructs a **left outer join** like an inner join, except that it retains non-matching rows from the left operand in the result. It places null values in the attributes that would usually come from the right operand. Variations include the **right outer join**, which retains non-matching attributes from the right operand, and the **full outer join**, which retains non-matching attributes from both operands. The syntax is as follows.

$$
X \quad [\text{natural}] \quad
\begin{Bmatrix} \text{left} \\ \text{right} \\ \text{full} \end{Bmatrix}
\quad \text{outer join} \quad Y \dots.
$$

 An outer join retains non-matching entries for one or both operands, using null values where you expect the missing attributes to appear.

In the example, you can use a left outer join to retain tanks without fish. Assuming the data of Figure 2.1, with all fish removed from tank 42, the SQL expression on the left below produces the table on the right.

```
select R.tno, R.tname, R.fno, R.fname
from (Tank T natural left outer join Fish F) as R.
```

< ··· >			
tno	tname	fno	fname
35	lagoon	347	flipper
35	lagoon	388	cory
38	beach	302	jill
44	lagoon	911	helen
44	lagoon	700	maureen
55	puddle	483	albert
55	puddle	438	fran
55	puddle	419	kilroy
85	cesspool	650	laura
85	cesspool	281	charlie
42	cesspool	--	--

Even though it has no matching fish, tank 42 still appears in the answer. The outer join fills the fish portion of the Cartesian product with null values, two of which appear in the final selection. You can use a right outer join to retain fish that have no matching tank or a full outer join to retain fish without tanks and tanks without fish. Suppose you want to count the fish in each tank. Unfortunately for this example, the count aggregate includes nulls. Therefore, it returns the value 1 over the partition associated with tank 42. This result is shown below and again assumes the data of Figure 2.1, with all fish removed from tank 42.

```
select R.tno, R.tname, count(*) as fishCount
from (Tank T natural left outer join Fish F) as R
groupby R.tno.
```

< ··· >		
tno	tname	fishCount
35	lagoon	2
38	beach	1
44	lagoon	2
55	puddle	3
85	cesspool	2
42	cesspool	1

You can obtain tank 42's proper count of zero as follows. This illustrates SQL's limited ability to pull a value from one of several sources, depending on the circumstance. The construction is similar to the case statement of many procedural programming languages (or the switch statement in C).

```
select X.tno, X.tname, sum(X.trueFish) as fishCount
from
   (select Y.tno as tno, Y.tname as tname,
     (case when Y.fno is null then 0 else 1) as trueFish
   from (Tank T natural left outer join Fish F) as Y) as X
groupby X.tno.
```

< ··· >		
tno	tname	fishCount
35	lagoon	2
38	beach	1
44	lagoon	2
55	puddle	3
85	cesspool	2
42	cesspool	0

The outermost from-clause expression constructs table X, which contains certain selections from an outer join Y. The attributes tno and tname are selected, and a third attribute, trueFish, is computed as a 0 for those tuples where the fno is null (indicating an unmatched tank) and as a 1 otherwise. So trueFish is 1 if the tuple is a true fish attached to its home tank. The DBMS then partitions these selections on X.tno and sums the trueFish values. Each true fish contributes a 1 to the sum within its partition, and each single tuple partition corresponding to a tank with no matching fish produces a sum of 0. The final answer table appears on the right.

The natural left, right, or full outer join uses like-named attributes in the two tables to retain tuples from the Cartesian product. As with the inner join, alternative formats are available if you want to use a subset of the common attributes or if you need to match attributes with different names. The more complete format is as follows. The word "outer" is optional; only the left, right, or full designation is necessary to command the corresponding outer join.

$$X \quad [\text{natural}] \quad \left\{ \begin{array}{l} \text{left} \\ \text{right} \\ \text{full} \end{array} \right\} \quad [\text{outer}] \quad \text{join} \quad Y \quad \left\{ \begin{array}{l} \text{on } attribute\text{-}list \\ \text{using } conditions \end{array} \right\} \cdots$$

From-clause expressions in an SQL select-statement can include various forms of the outer join:

- *A natural left outer join B*

- *A natural right outer join B*

- *A natural full outer join B*

The usual alternatives to a natural join—attribute lists or join conditions—are also available.

At this time, many commercial database products don't support all features of the latest SQL standard. For example, the case statement for conditional selection is a recent addition, as are general table expressions in the from-clause. Even though these features aren't present, many database products still support some form of outer join. In these products, the syntax usually attaches the "outer" specification directly to the affected table. On such a system, the following SQL is a typical formulation of the query: find the fish associated with each tank and retain an entry for tanks that have no fish.

```
select T.tno, T.tname, F.fno, F.fname
from Tank T, outer Fish F
where T.tno = F.tno.
```

The join condition is still specified in the where-clause, even though the attributes share a common name. The keyword "outer" appears with the table where null values can appear, so the example corresponds to a left outer join in the language of the current standard. It retains unmatched tanks and extends null values across the associated fish attributes. This arrangement is somewhat counterintuitive because a left outer join attaches the keyword "outer" to the right table. However, until recently outer joins were a frequently occurring, but non-standard feature, and these variations aren't unexpected.

The outer union

Strictly speaking, the union of two relations requires that they have the same schema. Under this condition, the DBMS forms the union by retaining the common schema and constructing a new body from the set-theoretical union of the operand bodies. A well-defined relation results because the tuples in both operands are associations over the same attribute set.

However, you might need to merge two relations with similar but not identical schemas. Chapter 5 demonstrated a relaxed syntax for this case. It allows the operand's corresponding attributes to have different names, provided the tuple values are compatible. In other words, the tuple values must come from the same domain. The DBMS then uses the first operand's attribute names for the result relation. Of course, each operand must have the same number of attributes, and in the absence of common names, some convention must determine which attributes correspond. Taking a table-oriented viewpoint, the DBMS determines the attribute correspondence from the left-to-right ordering in the SQL expression. The following operation illustrates this point. Attribute names for the result come from the first operand, and the body comprises rows from both operands. This process, for example, places the 11 value of attribute "d" under attribute "a" in the result.

```
select a, b, c
from A

union

select d, e, f
from B.
```

A		
a	b	c
1	2	3
4	5	6
7	8	9

∪

B		
d	e	f
11	12	13
14	15	16

⇒

< ··· >		
a	b	c
1	2	3
4	5	6
7	8	9
11	12	13
14	15	16

Because the new syntax allows you to construct a union directly in the from-clause, the left expression below is a simpler version of the example above. Because no attribute lists are present, the DBMS uses the attribute order from the definitions that create A and B.

```
select *                    select a, b, c         select *
from A union B.             from A                 from A union all B.
                           union all
                           select d, e, f
                           from B.
```

Contrary to standard SQL practice, which retains duplicates by default, the union operation removes duplicate rows from the result unless the keyword "all" is specified. To retain duplicates, you must use one of the variations to the right above. In these cases, the number of duplicates of a given row in the answer is $n_A + n_B$, where n_A and n_B are the number of duplicates of the row in tables A and B respectively.

Using the same left-to-right method of aligning incompatible column names, the DBMS can also perform set intersection or set difference, as illustrated on the left below. Note that set difference employs the keyword "except." As with the union operation, you can include the keyword "all" to command special treatment of duplicates. If you omit the "all," the intersect- and except-statements remove duplicates from the answer table. The variations that retain duplicates appear to the right. The intersect operation retains a given row in the answer n times, where $n = \min(n_A, n_B)$, n_A is the number of times the row appears in A, and n_B is the number of times that it appears in B. Similarly, the set difference retains a given row in the answer n times, where $n = \max(0, n_A - n_B)$.

```
select *                    select *
from A intersect B.        from A intersect all B.


select *                    select *
from A except B.           from A except all B.
```

For each of the set operations—union, intersect, and except—SQL provides alternative formats for the more rigorous case where common attribute names are to govern. In such a case, the desired behavior is that like-named attributes should line up, even if they occupy different places in the left-to-right definitions of the operand tables. The following union, for example, drops any columns from A or B that aren't common to both tables. It then performs an ordinary set union, retaining the common attributes for the result schema and filling the new body with the tuples from the modified operands. The left-to-right attribute order in the table definitions doesn't affect the result.

A union corresponding B.

A		
a	b	c
1	2	3
4	5	6
7	8	9

∪

B		
a	b	d
11	12	13
14	15	16

⇒

< ··· >	
a	b
1	2
4	5
7	8
11	12
14	15

As usual, the DBMS removes duplicates unless the word "union all" is specified. Similar formats are available for intersection and set-difference operations.

 You can specify the following set-theoretical operations as expressions in the from-clause of an SQL select statement:

- *A union [all] [corresponding] B*

- *A intersect [all] [corresponding] B*

- *A except [all] [corresponding] B*

The optional "all" commands special treatment of duplicates, and the optional "corresponding" lines up common attributes, overriding the normal left-to-right alignment and dropping attributes appearing in only one of the operands.

Finally, suppose you want to produce the following operations on the relations A and B of the preceding example. You want to force tuples from both operands into compatible forms, not with left-to-right attribute matching, but rather with an extension that guarantees all operand tuples will possess all attributes. This requires adding to operand A those attributes of operand B that aren't already present. Similarly, operand B is augmented with the excess attributes from operand A. When new attributes are added to a relation, existing tuples receive null values under the new columns.

A		
a	b	c
1	2	3
4	5	6
7	8	9

∪

B		
a	b	d
11	12	13
14	15	16

⇒

< ··· >			
a	b	c	d
1	2	3	null
4	5	6	null
7	8	9	null
11	12	null	13
14	15	null	14

This operation is called the **outer union** of A and B. Because the resulting attribute configuration is the same as for a Cartesian product or for any joins based on the Cartesian product, the SQL standard calls this construction a **union join**. Using the new terminology, the SQL on the left below constructs the table shown above. The equivalent expression on the right embeds the union join in a from-clause.

A union join B.

```
select *
from A union join B.
```

An outer union, or union join, forces a set-theoretic union between incompatible tables by constructing a new schema that contains all attributes from both operands. Each operand tuple is extended with null values to fit the new schema.

Like the outer join, the outer-union operation occurs frequently in database products, even though the product might not conform to the latest SQL standard. These products usually generate the outer union as follows.

```
select *
from A
outer union
select *
from B.
```

Constraints

Chapter 2 introduced some common database constraints: domain constraints, key constraints, entity and referential integrity constraints, and functional dependencies. In each case, the constraint disallows certain database states by judging them invalid in the application context. For example, a key constraint might state that tno is a key of the tank relation. This constraint captures the designer's intent that a tno value uniquely identify a tank. Two distinct tuples with the same tno values, therefore, could never appear in the tank relation. Constraints arise from an analysis of the database application. The designer can include some of them in the database schema, which allows the DBMS to enforce them.

Chapter 2 showed a hypothetical schema definition that permitted specification of the domain, key, and entity and referential integrity constraints. It also allowed functional dependencies in the schema. Because most database products don't provide such flexible schemas, Chapter 2 also illustrated a scaled-down schema, representative of the more common case.

The SQL standard provides extensive facilities for DDL capture of many constraints, including all those mentioned above. With the new facilities, you can create customized application domains, which you can then use in the attribute definitions. You can hold the domains, tables, and attributes accountable to local constraints, and you can globally constrain the database as a whole. This section investigates the details of these constraint mechanisms.

Purpose and format of SQL constraint

The designer uses constraints to tailor the database to a particular application. A DBMS is a general-purpose and flexible tool, which you can customize to many specific tasks. It offers detailed syntax for defining and manipulating the application data, but, by necessity, it can't contain specialized features for some particular application. For example, you can't expect the DBMS to restrict tcolor values to red, blue, or green as a general practice. You might, however, want to enforce that condition for the aquarium application. When you adapt a general-purpose DBMS to a particular application, you are using it to construct a semantic model of the application. In other words, you are attempting to represent as much of the application meaning as possible in the database.

The purpose of SQL constraints is to adapt a general-purpose relational DBMS to the given application. Without constraints, the table bodies can contain any data whatsoever. Each constraint forces them to align more closely with the meaning of the application. Newer database models are challenging the relational model's ability to capture application semantics; the latest SQL standard's increased emphasis on constraints is an attempt to strengthen the relational model in this area.

Although constraints appear in the DDL, rather than in the DML, they assume the predicate form of the where-clause or having-clause conditions of SQL select-statements with one important difference. In a select-statement, a where-clause condition must evaluate to true to pass a tuple into the horizontal section. Similarly, a having-clause condition must be true to retain a partition grouping. By contrast, the constraint conditions must evaluate to false to abort a database operation. The difference lies in the treatment of unknown truth values. In a where- or having-clause, unknown is treated as false: the candidate tuple or partition grouping doesn't participate in future processing. In a constraint condition, however, unknown is treated as true: the constraint is satisfied and processing continues.

Constraints tailor the database model to respond more closely to the given application's meaning. Constraints are introduced in the schema definition as SQL predicates.

Figures 6.3, 6.5, and 6.6 describe more completely the aquarium database using the SQL constraint specification facilities. The new definitions customize the situation of Figure 2.29 to respond more closely to the aquarium application. The discussion that follows explains the constraint features in detail.

Domain constraints

First consider the specialized domain constraints of Figure 6.3. You create application-specific domains by restricting the native database types (e.g., integer, char(n), bit(n), smallint) with constraint conditions. You then use these domains to specify allowable values for columns in the table definitions, as shown in Figure 6.5.

You can give a specific default value for each domain, such as the noColor string associated with the tankcolor and fishcolor entries in the schema. With this feature, you can circumvent the complex rules for treating null values. For example, whenever the DBMS inserts a tuple with a missing attribute value over the tankcolor domain, it substitutes noColor, rather than null, for that omission. This flexibility allows the application to deal with missing colors in a specialized manner.

When the schema associates an attribute with a domain, the DBMS assumes responsibility for maintaining attribute values compatible with the declared domain. It rejects an insertion or update that attempts to install a value outside the chosen domain. A legal value must not only conform to the specified native data type (e.g., integer, char(n)—see Figure 6.4), but it must also satisfy any domain-check conditions. You specify domain-check conditions as an SQL predicate, using the dummy keyword "value" to represent any value under test. Several examples appear in Figure 6.3, such as check (value in ("noColor", "blue", "red", "green")), which restricts the tankColor domain to these particular strings.

```
create domain keyvalue as integer
     check (value > 0)
     check (value is not null)
create domain refvalue as integer
     check (value > 0)
create domain tankcolor as char(10)
     default "noColor"
     check (value in ("noColor", "blue", "red", "green"))
create domain fishcolor as char (10)
     default "noColor"
     check (value in ("noColor", "blue" "red", "orange", "black", "white", "purple"))
create domain namestring as char(25)
     default "noName"
     check (upper(value) between A% and Z%)
create domain wgtvalue as integer
     check (value > 0)
create domain volvalue as integer
     default 0
     check (value >= 0 and value <= 5000)
     check (value - 100 * (value / 100) = 0)
     .
     .
     .
```

schema continued in Figure 6.5

Figure 6.3 Domain portion of the aquarium schema featuring SQL constraints

Data type designation	Interpretation
character(n)	fixed length character string
character varying (n)	variable length character string of maximum length n
integer	integer
numeric(p, q)	numeric value, p digits with decimal point q places from the right
date	calendar dates
time	times, hours through fractions of a second

Figure 6.4 Some of the native data types available in SQL

The aquarium schema creates the keyvalue domain to supply primary keys for all tables. The definition includes a check condition that disallows null values in any attribute over this domain. In this way, entity integrity is ensured. Similarly, the refvalue domain supplies values for the foreign-key attributes. Null values aren't disallowed here because the aquarium application chooses to allow a null value in the fish relation's tno foreign key. This is a conscious choice, taken by the database designer to respond more closely to the aquarium context. The aquarium can register a fish in the database without a tno value, which indicates that it hasn't yet been assigned to a tank. So the constraint must allow nulls in that foreign key. On the other hand, suppose the aquarium doesn't want to include any fish representing an anonymous species. In this case, you want the fish foreign key, sno, to always match the primary key, sno, of an existing species tuple. Since both foreign keys use the same domain (i.e., refvalue), you allow nulls in the refvalue domain definition and specify an additional constraint on the sno foreign key in the fish-table definition. Table constraints will be discussed shortly.

The schema restricts each of the fishcolor and tankcolor domains to a finite set of strings, and it constrains namestring values to begin with a letter. The "upper" function converts a value to upper case, simplifying the test for an initial letter. A "lower" function and other common string processing operations, such as trimming blanks, counting characters, and extracting a substring, are also available. The wildcard characters, % and underscore, have the same meanings here as in the like-predicate. Note the calculation used to restrict the volvalue domain to integral multiples of 100.

Domain constraints restrict values to a native data type, such as integer or character, and impose further checks with SQL predicates. You can specify default values to circumvent the standard treatment of nulls.

Now consider the table definitions of Figure 6.5, which use the previously defined domains to indicate the column data types. You can also use the native data types here. The schema declares the event table's edate column to be of type date, which is a native data type for storing calendar dates. The column enote of the same table is specified as type varchar(500). This is also a native data type, corresponding to strings of varying length up to 500 characters. The notation is an abbreviation of the full form: enote character varying (500).

Each column definition can specify a default value. The column default overrides the corresponding domain default if a conflict arises. For example, the species table uses the string unnamedSpecies for a missing sname value. Providing defaults at the table level allows differentiated treatment of missing values across attributes with the same domain. Functions are available to return the current date, time, and user. These values can be specified as defaults in certain places, such as the edate column of the event table.

Table constraints: primary-key, foreign-key, and check constraints

Each table definition includes not only the columns and their domains, or native data types, but also any table constraints. The constraint primary key $(a_1, a_2, \ldots)$ evaluates to false if two distinct rows in the table agree on the attributes $a_1, a_2, \ldots$. It is implemented with the predicate: not unique (select $a_1, a_2, \ldots$).

The constraint foreign key $(a_1, a_2, \ldots)$ references $T(b_1, b_2, \ldots)$ evaluates as $(a_1, a_2, \ldots)$ match (select $b_1, b_2, \ldots$ from T). The match-predicate always evaluates to true or false, never unknown. It is true if the left operand contains a null value or if there is a row, say r, in the right operand with $a_1 = r.b_1$ and $a_2 = r.b_2$ and ....

For a single-attribute foreign key, this behavior is appropriate. However, for a composite foreign key that references a corresponding composite primary key in another table, the required condition is: every component of left operand is null or there exists a matching row in right operand. In other words, the foreign-key constraint must evaluate as $(a_1, a_2, \ldots)$ match full (select $b_1, b_2, \ldots$ from T). To obtain the necessary evaluation, you must specify the constraint as follows: foreign key $(a_1, a_2, \ldots)$ references $T(b_1, b_2, \ldots)$ match full.

```
create table tank (
   tno keyvalue,
   tname namestring
      default "unnamedTank",
   tcolor tankcolor,
   tvolume volvalue,
   primary key (tno)
   )
create table species (
   sno keyvalue,
   sname namestring
      default "unnamedSpecies",
   sfood namestring
      default "unspecifiedDiet",
   primary key (sno)
   )
create table fish (
   fno keyvalue,
   fname namestring
      default "unnamedFish",
   fcolor fishcolor,
   fweight wgtvalue,
   tno refvalue,
   sno refvalue,
   primary key (fno),
   check (sno is not null),
   foreign key (tno) references tank (tno),
   foreign key (sno) references species (sno)
   )
create table event (
   eno keyvalue,
   edate date,
      default current_date,
   enote varchar(500),
   fno refvalue,
   primary key (eno),
   foreign key (fno) references fish (fno)
   ).
```

schema continued in Figure 6.6

Figure 6.5   Base table schemas for the aquarium database using SQL constraints

You can replace the "match full" specification with "match partial" if you want a partially null row to match when its nonnull elements align with a row in the referenced table. This intermediate level of matching corresponds to the match-partial predicate. Because the aquarium application uses single-attribute foreign keys, you can suppress the match-option of the foreign-key constraint. Match, match-full, and match-partial all evaluate to the same result when the left operand is a single attribute.

If you omit the attribute list of the referenced relation from a foreign-key constraint, the DBMS automatically uses the primary keys of that relation. For example, you can abbreviate the foreign-key constraint of the fish table as: `foreign key tno references tank`.

You can also include check constraints in the table definitions. For example, you can use a check to force the sno attribute of the fish table to a nonnull value. This will capture the application constraint that no fish can enter the fish table unless it is linked to an existing species. Although the check condition appears within a table definition, it can refer to other tables. For example, if you want to enforce the condition that a white fish must always be a shark, you can place the following constraint in the fish table:

```
check (fcolor not = "white" or exists
    (select *
    from Species S
    where S.sno = fish.sno and S.sname = "shark")).
```

Table constraints specify primary and foreign keys and apply additional checks through SQL predicates.

Column constraints: primary-key, reference, and check constraints

You can also attach constraints directly to the column definitions. Keep in mind, however, that you can also express any column constraint as a table constraint through one of the three types already discussed: primary-key, foreign-key, and check. An alternative definition of the fish table, using column constraints rather than table constraints, appears below. It shows that you can designate a column as a primary or foreign key. Although they aren't applicable in this example, the match-full and match-partial options are available if needed for composite foreign keys. You can also specify check conditions, but they refer only to the column under definition. A column definition usually starts with the column's name, followed by its domain or native data type, followed by an optional default specification, followed by any number of constraints. The allowed constraint types are primary-key, references, and check. All are illustrated in the new definition of the fish table below.

Column constraints are primary-key, references, and check. They can be used in place of the corresponding table constraints, but they add no further capability.

```
create assertion volColorFD check (not exists
    (select *
    from tank T, tank U
    where T.tvolume = U.tvolume and T.tcolor <> U.tcolor))
create assertion comfyShark check (not exists
    (select *
    from Species S, Fish F, Tank T
    where S.sno = F.sno and F.tno = T.tno and
        S.sname = "shark" and T.tvolume < 3000))
create assertion populationDensity check (not exists
    (select *
    from
        (select T.tno as t, T.tvolume as v, count(*) as fCount
        from Tank T, Fish F
        where T.tno = F.tno
        groupby T.tno)
    where v / fCount < 100)).
```

Figure 6.6 Global constraints on the aquarium database

```
create table fish (
    fno keyvalue
        primary key,
    fname namestring
        default "unnamedFish",
    fcolor fishcolor,
    fweight wgtvalue,
    tno refvalue
        references tank (tno)
    sno refvalue
        check (sno is not null),
        references species (sno)
    ).
```

Global constraints

Figure 6.6 concludes the schema specification with certain global constraints on the database state. The first assertion implements the functional dependency: tvolume⟶tcolor. Recall that a functional dependency, $a \longrightarrow b$, means that two tuples agreeing on attributes a must also agree on attributes b. You formulate functional dependency constraints with a check condition, using the not-exists SQL construction. Specifically, if T is the table in question, the condition is as follows:

```
not exists
    (select *
    from T as X, T as Y
    where X.a = Y.a and not (X.b = Y.b)).
```

The constraint tvolume —→tcolor takes this form in Figure 6.6. Two further constraints also appear there. The volume of a tank containing a shark must not be less than 3000, and no tank volume may decrease below 100 gallons per fish. The schema calls these constraints comfyShark and populationDensity respectively.

 The schema specifies global constraints with create-assertion statements. They typically use a not-exists subquery.

The schema names the global constraints, and it could have named the domain and table constraints. For example, you could redefine the fish table as follows, specifying names for the primary-key, foreign-key, and check constraints.

```
create table fish (
    fno keyvalue,
    fname namestring
        default "unnamedFish",
    fcolor fishcolor,
    fweight wgtvalue,
    tno refvalue,
    sno refvalue,
    constraint fishEntity primary key (fno),
    constraint identifiedFish check (sno is not null),
    constraint fishTank foreign key (tno) references tank (tno),
    constraint fishSpecies foreign key (sno) references species (sno)
    ).
```

Named constraints are useful in cases where they might be temporarily violated during a sequence of data manipulation activities. A sequence of activities that the DBMS treats as an indivisible unit is a **transaction**. When it processes a transaction, the DBMS may need to suspend certain constraints until the full transaction has been completed. All constraints are then reasserted, and if a violation exists, the transaction is rolled back. In other words, the DBMS restores the database to the state that existed before the transaction started. Suppose, for example, that a global constraint requires the aquarium database always to contain at least three tanks. You specify the constraint in the schema as follows.

```
create assertion minTanks check ((select count(*) from tank) >= 3).
```

An attempt to enter the first tank into the database fails because it violates the minTanks assertion. Inserting the three tanks with an indivisible transaction will solve the problem. The precise SQL for a transaction is beyond this chapter's scope, but the solution runs along these lines:

1. Defer constraint minTanks.

2. Start a transaction sequence.

3. Insert the first tank, insert the second tank, insert the third tank.

4. Apply constraint minTanks.

5. Commit the transaction sequence.

You can defer named constraints across a sequence of data manipulation activities that might result in temporary violations.

Triggers

The DBMS generally responds in two ways to data modification that causes a constraint violation. It can reject the modification and restore the database state as it existed before the transaction, or it can undertake further adjustments to make the database back comply with the constraints. So far, we have assumed the first solution. The second possibility allows the DBMS to execute a compensatory procedure to regain a consistent state. These compensatory procedures are called **triggered** routines. In the most general case, they involve arbitrary application code. Although general triggers aren't available in SQL-1992, they are under consideration for future releases. Meanwhile, the current SQL standard does provide specialized triggers for maintaining referential integrity in the face of primary- or foreign-key modifications. This sections discusses those features.

The full format for a foreign-key constraint in a schema table definition is:

```
foreign key (a₁, a₂, ...)
    references T(b₁, b₂, ...) [match {full | partial }]
    [on delete {no action | cascade | set default | set null}]
    [on update {no action | cascade | set default | set null}].
```

The match-full and match-partial options have already been discussed. The emphasis here is on the on delete ... and on update ... phrases. When the DBMS deletes or updates a parent row in a one-to-many relationship grouping, these clauses specify the clean-up activity to maintain referential integrity. The alternatives are: no action, cascade, set default, and set null. If the foreign-key definition clause omits the trigger clauses, the DBMS assumes "no action" by default.

Assume initially that Figures 6.3 through 6.6 are the defining schema for the aquarium application. If you delete a species tuple, any fish representing that species become orphans. The sno value of an abandoned fish references a nonexistent species tuple—a clear violation of referential integrity. However, instead of rejecting the deletion, the application might require that the orphan fish also be deleted. This decision rests entirely with the application. You could follow a different strategy when a tank tuple is deleted: you could leave the homeless fish in the database but set their tno values to null. Again, this is the database designer's decision, and it reflects the nature of the aquarium application. Either solution, however, maintains referential integrity.

You can tailor the fish-tank relationship to respond differently to a referential integrity challenge than the fish-species relationship. This flexibility further illustrates how you can customize a database to a given application. In other words, you capture more of the application semantics in the database, which relieves the interfacing programs of much special purpose code. You can use on delete ... and on update ... options to ensure referential integrity in the aquarium database. The revised schemas for the fish and event relations appear in Figure 6.7. The other tables aren't affected because they contain no foreign keys.

```
create table fish (
  fno keyvalue,
  fname namestring
    default "unnamedFish",
  fcolor fishcolor,
  tno refvalue,
  sno refvalue,
  primary key (fno),
  check (sno is not null),
  foreign key (tno) references tank (tno)
    on delete set null
    on update cascade,
  foreign key (sno) references species (sno)
    on delete cascade
    on update cascade
).
 create table event (
   eno keyvalue,
   edate date,
     default current_date,
   enote varchar(500),
   fno refvalue,
   primary key (eno),
   foreign key (fno) references fish (fno)
     on delete cascade
     on update cascade
   ).
```

Figure 6.7: Revised base table schemas for the aquarium database, using delete and update triggers

When a foreign key maintains a one-to-many relationship, the on-delete clause of the foreign-key constraint allows four choices when a parent tuple is deleted. One possibility, indicated with the phrase "on delete cascade," deletes all the children. The second possibility frees the children in the database, breaking the connection with the parent tuple. You invoke this option with the phrase "on delete set null." These are the two possibilities that preserve referential integrity. Two further options are also available. In the aquarium database, the schema specifies "set null" for the tno foreign key in the fish relation, but it chooses "cascade" for the rest.

When cascade is specified, the child tuples of a deleted parent are also deleted. If a doomed child tuple is parent to further children in yet another relation, the DBMS consults the foreign-key constraint of the grandchild relation. If cascade is specified there, the grandchildren are also deleted. This necessitates an investigation of their children, and so on, recursively as needed. However, if the DBMS encounters an action other than cascade at some point in the tree of descendants, the investigation stops at that point. If the investigation stops because a "set null" action is encountered, the DBMS detaches the tuples at the arresting level by setting their foreign keys to null. It deletes tuples at the higher levels.

The entire deletion scenario can fail at this point. For example, suppose a constraint disallows null values where they must be inserted. If the triggered procedure can't complete successfully, the DBMS falls back to the other method for maintaining the constraints: it rejects the transaction.

The two remaining possibilities, no action or set defaults, can also cause the entire deletion order to fail. Suppose, for example, the schema specifies no action or omits the on-delete clause in the foreign-key constraint of the event relation. Deleting a species requires the deletion of all its associated fish because the cascade option appears in the fish table. However, each fish might own many events. Because no action is specified for the events, a referential integrity violation occurs if the DBMS deletes the species and its corresponding fish. Certain events would contain fno foreign keys that refer to nonexistent fish tuples. Therefore, the DBMS must reject the original species deletion order.

Suppose you revise the foreign-key constraint for tno in the fish relation to specify "on delete set default." In this case, the DBMS must be able to derive a default value, either from the tno column definition in the fish table or from the domain for that column. Because neither source provides a default in this example, the effect is the same as "on delete set null."

To illustrate the "on delete set default" option, you can establish a virtual tank, inTransit, to hold fish that don't belong to a specific tank. You must give the tank a distinct tno value, such as 500, and specify that value as a default in the tno column definition in the fish relation. Incidentally, you must also give the tank a large volume to comply with the comfySharks global constraint of Figure 6.6. Finally, you must be careful not to have too many fish in transit at the same time, or you will violate the global constraint, populationDensity. In any case, you use the action "on delete set default" to set a fish's tno value to 500, pointing to the inTransit tank, when its home tank is deleted.

SQL intends that you use the triggering rules to support two kinds of one-to-many relationships. You use the first kind when the existence of a child makes no sense in the absence of the parent. Consider, for example, grades associated with a student or rooms associated with a building. You use the second kind for more transient attachments, such as fish in a tank, persons assigned to a department, or paintings displayed in a museum. The first type of relationship should specify "on delete cascade," and the second "on delete set null." Specifying no action, or allowing this intention to stand by default, will likely cause constraint violations.

 The on-delete clause of a foreign-key constraint enables the DBMS to launch compensatory activity to repair referential integrity threats posed by a parent deletion in a one-to-many relationship. The cascade option deletes the children if possible, consulting additional on-delete clauses that may appear in the grandchildren. The set null option detaches the children, if possible.

The on-update clause, also shown in Figure 6.7 for the aquarium example, operates in a parallel manner. If an SQL expression updates a parent's primary key, the cascade option forces a foreign-key update in all its children. This retains the group integrity of the parent with its children. The set-null option detaches the children if possible. The set-default option attempts to set the foreign keys to a specified default value. If the final results lead to a constraint violation, the DBMS rolls back the entire update sequence. Otherwise, it accepts the update along with any modifications imposed by the triggered procedures.

The cascading changes brought into play by a deletion or update are part of that deletion or update activity. The entire process either plays through to a consistent conclusion, or no part of it is executed. You can imagine that the database clones a copy of itself and then modifies the clone to reflect the data modification and any triggered effects. When it has finished, it checks the clone for constraint violations. If there are none, the DBMS discards the real database and replaces it with the clone. If there is a violation, the clone is discarded, and the real database remains unaffected. The violation is, of course, reported back to the user. This scenario is inefficient, the DBMS actually uses some equivalent process that is less computationally expensive. As a mental model, however, the scenario emphasizes the all-or-nothing nature of deletions and updates in the presence of triggered procedures.

Extended definition of a relational database

Chapter 2 defined a relational database as a finite collection of relations and a relation in terms of domains, attributes, associations, and tuples. According to the definitions, table structures are the sole building blocks for application modeling. Subsequent chapters investigated access issues, such as SQL queries, and semantic extensions, such as views and constraints. Building on this material, this section revisits the definitions and provides a more complete list of features and philosophies that constitute the relational model.

E. F. Codd, widely regarded as a founder of relational databases, places the model's characteristics in three broad categories. First, structural features are support the relational view of the data. They include relations and their underlying components and views and queries, both mechanisms for creating virtual tables. Second, integrity features support entity and referential integrity and also application-specific constraints. Finally, data manipulation features include the methods for tuple retrieval, insertion, deletion, and update. These features must be able to emulate any operation from relational algebra. Certain conveniences such as outer joins and unions are also expected.

Codd provides a set of 12 rules, which in his view qualify a database product as relational. In other words, to merit the name *fully relational*, a database product should provide the three categories of features—structure, integrity, and data manipulation—and it should abide by the following rules:

1. Tabular structures represent all information.

2. You can address each information item by specifying the relation name, the key value of the containing tuple, and the attribute name of the storage cell.

3. A systematic mechanism exists for treating null values.

4. An active catalog stores information about the names and dispositions of the tables and their components.

5. A language is available, both interactively and through host programs, to perform data definitions (DDL) and data manipulations (DML).

6. The problem of updating information through views is systematically addressed.

7. The interface language supports set-oriented operations. It contains primitives that accept complete relations as operands and return complete relations as results.

8. The conceptual schema buffers applications from changes to the physical hardware.

9. The view mechanism buffers applications from changes in the conceptual schema.

10. The database management system is capable of storing and enforcing integrity constraints.

11. Distributing the database across several sites doesn't diminish the system's functional.

12. The system has a security mechanism that can't be defeated by accumulating small transactions.

This list paraphrases the rules somewhat. See Codd's writings for the originals. The relational philosophy is that the tabular structure alone is a sufficient basis for a powerful modeling technique. Codd's rules, except for the last two on multisite distribution and security, then insists that a relational DBMS have the features discussed in the last several chapters. These features provide flexible data-manipulation capabilities and permit a database designer to capture much of the application semantics in the database schema.

Shortcomings of the relational model

The relational model has evolved through many stages since its appearance in the early 1970s. Performance was an early concern. However, you can measure performance in two arenas: performance at execution time, when the data is actually being manipulated, and performance during design and implementation, when the database is under construction. In the second arena, the relational model was a clear winner from the start. Moreover, the relational model has overcome its initial performance deficiencies, and it's now comparable or superior to its hierarchical and network predecessors. Although the slow processing speeds of early relational implementation were often attacked by its critics, the relational model no longer suffers from this shortcoming.

The access language SQL, together with its earlier progenitors and competitors, also received a great deal of criticism. Early SQL versions weren't uniform in the treatment of certain constructs. For example, subqueries defining embedded tables could occur in the where-clause but not in the from-clause. Also, although the overall query and any subqueries are isomorphic in format, subqueries didn't have the same structural freedom reserved for the overall query. A subquery, for example, couldn't contain a having-clause. The problems with null values and with data updates through views were handled in an ad hoc fashion, and domain and integrity constraints weren't supported. The most recent version of the SQL standard has addressed these concerns. So, just like the performance issue, the SQL interface has silenced its early critics.

However, philosophical questions remain concerning the relational model's ability to adapt to the application semantics. The new extended support for constraints certainly enhances its viability in this respect, but some researchers feel that the table structure is inherently flawed. To retrieve an application object, you must be aware of the various tables that contain its components. You must then invoke a join operation to assemble them. For example, to retrieve a fish, complete with its species, tank, and event information, you must construct a new table as follows.

```
select *
from Species S, Fish F, Tank T, Event E
where S.sno = F.sno and F.tno = T.tno and F.fno = E.fno.
```

Because an event is at the bottom of the tree of one-to-many relationships, each row of this large intermediate table corresponds to one event, extended with its related fish, species, and tank information. Why should this construction be necessary to retrieve a complete picture of a fish? Doesn't this mechanism bring unnecessary storage details up to the application level? Should a user in the application environment really be concerned that the fish information is spread across several tables for economy of storage? In other words, you want to retrieve a fish, and the multiple-table representation is a distraction. It mixes application objects with their database representation details. This mixing is fine for the database designer because his charge is to model the application with the available resources. However, a users might consider the multiple-table representation irrelevant for their purposes.

This is a serious charge against a modeling language. The model's basic intent is to allow interactions that are meaningful in the application, while suppressing any hint that an entity under manipulation is anything other than an application object itself. Therefore, a model affords a closer match with the application if it permits the direct manipulation of application objects. Unfortunately, this isn't the only shortcoming of the relational representation scheme.

The idea that an object's attribute should be a single value doesn't always coincide with reality. When you examine a fish object, you see certain single-valued attributes, such as the fname attribute, which is a single string. Other fish characteristics, however, are inherently multivalued, such as its set of events. Arranging the events in single-valued cells in a disjoint table is unnatural. The event set is a fish attribute on par with its name. Other fish attributes, such as the species or tank, are single-valued, but their values aren't taken from the native data types or from domains constructed over these types. Instead, their values are other application objects.

 Critics of the relational model claim that it unnecessarily exposes the user to a dispersed tuple collection that should more naturally appear as a single application object. You can reassemble the object with SQL joins, but that implementation detail is irrelevant at the application level.

A second deficiency of the relational model is that it stores only data, not procedures. The relational model sees SQL queries and other data manipulation activities as external to the DBMS. Some relational database products do store compiled versions of SQL queries for reuse, but the model provides no general mechanism for organizing the storage and retrieval of active routines. The trigger procedures that clean up after deletions and updates offer some progress in this direction. Future versions of SQL may well offer general trigger procedures so that a database transition can launch arbitrary application code.

However, a major rearrangement of the model would be necessary to allow tables to possess procedures that would function naturally in conjunction with the table's application role. For example, the fish table might have a function to automatically retrieve the species information for a targeted tuple, which would relieve the application of the need to join the separated pieces. Considering data objects as static attribute collections, as opposed to dynamic agents, is an extension of the previous shortcoming. The data objects don't faithfully model their real-world counterparts. They fail to provide sufficiently representative attributes, and they fail to capture behavior. Object-oriented databases, which will be discussed in the next chapters, evolves to address these shortcomings of the relational model.

Another shortcoming is that the relational model can't easily handle non-textual data. Many modern applications include graphical data, such as engineering drawings. Some involve soundtracks or even multimedia combinations of these elements. How can you store these data elements in table structures? How can you retrieve them as functions of their attributes? For example, how can you formulate the following query in SQL? Find the dominant polygons in all the images that contain a triangle in the lower left-hand quadrant. Beyond the obvious questions concerning the storage and retrieval of non-textual information, equally difficult problems arise with the retrieval language itself. For example, you might want to highlight a bracket on a drawing and ask for a list of assemblies where a component of that general shape appears. Current database products can't respond to these challenges. Specialized systems are found in experimental situations, but a systematic treatment of graphics, image, and sound information hasn't been developed.

Multimedia information can't be arranged easily in tables. Nevertheless, some existing relational database products do permit the use of image files. The simple solution stores the image on a separate file in some standard format, such as a bitmap, and records the *name* of the file a table cell. For example, you can augment the fish relation to include a photo attribute with data type bitmap. You can then include bitmap photos, generated with separate software packages, in the fish tuples. This will result in a table such as the following.

Fish					
fno	fname	fcolor	tno	sno	photo
164	charlie	orange	42	74	char164.bmp
347	flipper	black	35	17	flip347.bmp
228	killer	white	42	22	kill228.bmp
:	:	:	:	:	:

The data-type bitmap is nothing more than a string, and the photos are only minimally accessible. You can answer the query: find the photos of fish that represent a shark. But the system must now be prepared to display bitmap image files. You can't, however, solve a query that refers to any aspect of the photos themselves. For example, you can't find the names of fish with a fin area greater than 30% of the body area. Of course, you could add normal attributes for fin area and body area, but you can't hope to capture all aspects of the photos in a reasonable number of such traditional attributes. Moreover, an unhealthy dependency would exist between the extracted attributes and the photos. Suppose you update the photo of a given fish. How would you make sure that the fin and body area attributes are changed?

Although some relational products handle images and soundtracks in a primitive fashion, access to these attributes is usually shallow. Earlier criticism of the relational model's semantic conformance capability noted that object-oriented techniques hold the promise of enhanced semantic modeling. For the difficulties associated with non-textual data types, the object-oriented model is may be somewhat better, but it doesn't settle all the problems. Its advantage lies in its philosophical position on the nature of an attribute. The object-oriented model already accepts complex objects for attribute values, so accepting an image, a drawing, or a soundtrack presents no conceptual problem. Also, when probed for a feature, an object can undertake any amount of hidden processing, including the dispatching of help messages to other objects. Therefore, a role already exists, for example, for a pattern recognition routine to filter images for a desired ratio of fin area to body area. This pattern recognition routine functions in the same manner as a routine that acquires the species name of the fish. In the relational model, by contrast, a pattern recognition routine constitutes a clear exception to the normal routines that align tuples from various relations and extract answers from the certain cells.

 Another criticism of the relational model is its limited ability to handle non-textual data types, such as graphics, images, and soundtracks.

A final criticism is that SQL isn't a computationally complete language. Earlier examples showed that relational algebra can't compute recursive closures. Because SQL and relational algebra are equivalent, SQL can't either. Recall the employee relation, where each tuple represents a worker and an sno attribute identifies the worker's supervisor in the same table. To determine the workers reporting to X, either directly or indirectly at any level, you must invoke a sequence of join operations. You can't know in advance, moreover, how many such joins are needed. Iterative loops of indeterminate length, as provided by the familiar while-loops of many programming languages, are essential for this type of processing. Recursive procedure calls would also work, but SQL has neither of these features. Certain computations, therefore, can be undertaken only with embedded SQL, where the host language provides the missing capabilities.

SQL has accumulated certain programming features as it has evolved. One of these forms appeared briefly in the discussion of outer joins. The case statement computes a value according to one of several expressions. The example computed a 0 or 1, depending on the nullity of the fno attribute: (`case when Y.fno is null then 0 else 1`). The general syntax is as follows.

```
case
      when condition-1 then expression-1
      when condition-2 then expression-2
             ⋮
      else expression-n.
```

The DBMS evaluates the when-clauses in the order given until one of them returns a true value. It then chooses the corresponding expression as the value of the case statement. However, this branching capability is limited to a scalar expression. It can't be used, for example, to make a choice of tables in a from-clause.

As more programming features appear in the language, SQL might evolve to include a while-loop, which would render it computationally complete.

SUMMARY

Besides explicit table references, SQL allows expressions in the from-clause that evaluate to tables. In particular, it allows embedded subqueries. This extension allows you to collapse sequences of SQL queries that communicate through temporary tables into a single statement. As consequences of this facility, you no longer need temporary tables or having-clauses, and you can nest aggregate functions.

A view is a virtual table defined with an SQL query. In contrast with a base table, a view has no independent existence in the database. Instead, the DBMS materializes it as needed by substituting the view definition for its reference in a from-clause. A view differs from a temporary table. A temporary table, created with an into-clause in an SQL query, is a static snapshot, taken when the DBMS executes the query. Subsequent references to the temporary table won't see any updates since its creation. A view, however, is materialized anew with each reference; it immediately reflects any updates in the underlying tables. Views implement the logical independence that buffers applications programs from changes to the conceptual schema. If such a change occurs, you can often rewrite the view definition to materialize the old context for existing application programs.

Updating through views presents difficulties. Generally, you can update a view based on a single relation if it includes the relation's primary key. Some database products permit updates through a view that materializes a one-to-many relationship, provided the updates are restricted to the child attributes. The check option instructs the DBMS to reject a view insertion or update if the new tuple would immediately disappear from the view because it fails the defining criteria. If you construct a view over other views, this check can be complicated because conditions on a lower view can cause a modified tuple to disappear. View conditions typically cascade to subsequently defined views, so the DBMS rejects a tuple if it fails the criteria of any view in the hierarchy.

SQL includes a systematic treatment of null values. Any arithmetic involving a null value returns a null value. Any comparison involving a null value returns the truth value unknown. The three truth values—true, false, and unknown—form a three-valued logic system. The rules for the logical connectives are adjusted to accommodate these values. To qualify a tuple or a partition for inclusion in a query answer, the where-clause predicate must evaluate to true. The DBMS rejects both false and unknown returns. You should carefully examine predicates for their behavior in the presence of null values. Some predicates, such as exists and match, avoid the unknown truth value and are most likely to produce unexpected results. Because the match-predicate is tailored to be useful in checking referential integrity, it produces results slightly different from those reached through the standard treatment of nulls.

SQL also includes convenience predicates, which aren't strictly necessary but are useful in some queries: "like" for limited string pattern matching, "between" for checking ranges, "any" and "all" for comparisons between a constructed row and a generated table, and "unique" for checking for duplicate rows. When using any of these predicates, you should carefully investigate the boundary cases involving null operands.

Other from-clause expressions include inner and outer joins and unions. The join referenced in other chapters, the inner join, consists of a selection from a Cartesian product for tuples that agree on certain named attributes. SQL provides a concise syntax for inner joins, particularly when the matching attributes have the same names. A left outer join retains tuples from the left operand, even when they match no entries from the right. Null values fill the positions that would be occupied by the matching right-operand tuple. A right outer join retains tuples from the right operand, even though there are no matches. A full outer join retains non-matching entries from both operands.

Various union operators are available. Some permit the union of tables with dissimilar attribute names by aligning columns in a left-to-right order. An outer union, called a union join in the latest SQL standard, creates a new relation with the same schema as a Cartesian product. However, instead of populating it with operand concatenations, the DBMS extends each operand tuple with nulls to accommodate the missing attribute values. The set operations of intersect and difference are also available. Unlike other SQL operations, they remove duplicates unless commanded otherwise.

The database schema can provide constraints at the global, table, column, or domain level. Domain constraints restrict values to native data types and then apply further restrictions with check predicates. Table constraints consist of three types: primary-key, foreign-key, and check. The first two enforce non-duplication of primary key values and referential integrity in one-to-many relationships. You can attach some table constraints directly to the affected column, such as primary-key, references (used for a foreign-key column), and check. You specify global constraints with create-assertion statements. Each provides a predicate that must not evaluate false in any database state. A constraint predicate returning the truth value unknown doesn't trigger a violation. Because the DBMS rejects data manipulation commands that would lead to a constraint violation, constraints tailor the database model more closely to the application semantics. You can defer named constraints across a sequence of activities to accommodate temporary violations.

A trigger is a database event that launches a compensatory process to recover a consistent state. Although the most general triggers, which execute application-specific routines, aren't supported by the current SQL standard, specialized triggers are available to repair damage to one-to-many relationships that may occur when parent tuples are modified. You can tailor the response to detach the children of an affected parent or to cascade the modification recursively to them. If you specify a cascade action, a parent deletion will force the deletion of all its children. The deletion can propagate to the children's children, and so forth. If a child is detached, the DBMS sets its foreign-key values to null, which continues referential integrity after the parent has been deleted. The DBMS executes a deletion or update, together with any repair of the foreign keys, as an indivisible unit. If the final result violates a constraint, the DBMS rolls back the entire operation.

The relational model emphasizes the use of a single data structure, the relation, for all application modeling. SQL, however, heavily exploits the table representation. Codd elaborates three categories of modeling features for a relational product: structural (e.g., tables, attributes, domain, views, and queries), integrity (entity, referential, and application-specific), and data-manipulation (the relational algebra operations). He also presents twelve rules to distinguish a true relational database product from those that are deficient in some important area.

The relational model does have its critics. One of its shortcomings is its limited ability to conform to application semantics. This deficiency manifests itself both in the dispersion of application objects across several tables and in the artificial separation of data and procedures. A second problem is its incompatibility with non-textual data types, such as images and soundtracks. Finally, SQL isn't a computationally complete language, although it is evolving toward one.■

EXERCISES

These exercises use the library database of Figure 3.11.

Views

Using embedded subqueries in the from-clause, solve the following queries with a single SQL statement without a having-clause.

1. For each library holding 100 book copies or more, find the average cost of the copies.

2. For each patron, find the average cost of the copies that he has borrowed, provided the average number of pages in the corresponding books is greater than 300.

Given the primary- and foreign-key designations of Figure 3.11, comment on the following views' ability to process updates.

3. create view dearBooks as
```
   (select title, pages
   from book B
   where exists
     (select *
     from copy C
     where C.bookno = B.bookno and C.cost > 300)).
```

4. create view libCollection as
```
    (select L.libno, L.libname, B.title, B.pages, C.cost
    from library L, copy C, book B
    where L.libno = C.libno and C.bookno = B.bookno).
```

5. create view abbrLib as
```
    (select distinct libname, location
    from library).
```

Null values

Suppose the library database tables can contain null values. Comment on the following queries and their proposed SQL solutions. If the SQL doesn't behave as expected, explain how to modify it to obtain the desired results. Assume that the primary keys aren't null.

6. Find the names of libraries that aren't located in Seattle.
```
   select libname
   from library
   where location <> "Seattle".
```

7. Find the names of libraries that have more rooms than all libraries that hold a book written by Salinger.

```
select L.libname
from library L
where not exists
  (select *
  from library M, copy C, book B, author A
  where M.libno = C.libno and C.bookno = B.bookno and B.authno = A.authno and
    A.authname = "Salinger" and M.rooms >= L.rooms).
```

If T is the table to the right, determine the truth value of the following predicates.

8. (21, 18, null, null) $<$ (21, 20, null, 36).

9. (21, 18, null, null) = (21, 18, null, null).

10. (9, 40, 83, 15) $<$any T.

11. (null, 12, 10, 3) $<$any T.

12. (10, null, null, 14) match T.

13. (10, null, null, 14) match full T.

T			
a	b	c	d
10	null	null	14
20	32	null	null
17	41	84	null
32	54	96	64

Outer operations

Rewrite the following SQL statements using only the simple constructs of Chapter 5. In other words, restrict the from-clause to existing relations. You will need to compute a constant column of null values in the select-clause of some of your solutions.

14.
```
select libname
from (library natural inner join copy) natural inner join book
where title = "The Name of the Rose".
```

15.
```
select libname, title
from library union join book.
```

16.
```
select libname, average(cost) as avgCost
from library natural left outer join copy
groupby libno.
```

Constraints

Figure 6.8 contains an initial schema for the library database of Figure 3.11. The following exercises request schema modifications to include constraints appropriate to the library situation.

17. Add a table constraint to maintain referential integrity between author and book.

18. Add a table constraint to maintain referential integrity between book and copy.

19. Add a table constraint to ensure that the foreign key linking a copy to its parent book will never be null.

20. Add a table constraint to maintain referential integrity between library and copy.

21. Add a column constraint to maintain referential integrity between copy and loan.

22. Add column constraints to ensure that neither of the two foreign keys linking loan to its parents will ever have a null value.

23. Add a column constraint to maintain referential integrity between patron and loan.

24. Add the global constraint: the set of patrons using all Seattle libraries always includes a patron named joe.

```
create domain keyvalue as integer
   check (value > 0)
   check (value is not null)
create domain refvalue as integer
   check (value > 0)
create domain namestring as char(25)
   default "nullString"
   check (upper(value) between A% and Z%)
create domain countvalue as integer
   default 0
   check (value >= 0)
create domain decimalvalue as numeric(7, 2)
   default 0.0
   check (value >= 0.0)
create table library (
   libno keyvalue primary key,
   libname namestring,
   location namestring,
   rooms countvalue
   )
create table author (
   authno keyvalue primary key,
   authname namestring,
   )
```

```
create table book (
   bookno keyvalue primary key,
   title namestring,
   pages countvalue,
   authno refvalue
   )

create table copy (
   copyno keyvalue primary key,
   libno refvalue,
   bookno refvalue,
   cost decimalvalue
   )

create table patron (
   patronno keyvalue primary key,
   patname namestring,
   patwgt decimalvalue
   )

create table loan (
   loanno keyvalue primary key,
   copyno refvalue,
   patronno refvalue,
   duedate date
      default current_date
   ).
```

Figure 6.8 A partial schema for the library database

Triggers
Continuing with the schema development in Figure 6.8, add the additional constraints directed below.

25. If a book is deleted, all its copies should also be deleted. If the book's primary key is updated, then its copies should remain attached to the book.

26. If a copy is deleted, then all loans dependent on that copy should also be deleted. If the copy's primary key is updated, the corresponding loans should remain attached.

7 Object-Oriented Databases

O NE CRITICISM OF THE RELATIONAL MODEL IS THAT IT DISPERSES an application entity across several relations. In the aquarium database, for example, your mental image of a tank includes the fish that inhabit it. The join operation that aligns fish with their home tanks is an implementation detail. Suppose you want to know the number of fish in a tank. If you were physically present in the aquarium, you would walk over to the tank and simply count the fish. A preprocessing step to first populate the tank with its fish seems unnatural because the fish are already present. The nature of the application is that the tanks contain their fish on a continuing basis. The preliminary join in the relational database model is an accidental consequence of a storage detail of relational model; it doesn't arise from any conceptual separation between the application entities.

Of course, the dispersed representation serves the goals of storage economy and data consistency, and I am not arguing that it should be abandoned. Instead, the user should *perceive* the abstract model objects as faithful representatives of the corresponding application objects. If a real aquarium tank contains fish, then an abstract tank in the database should contain abstract fish. If the DBMS must use join operations to construct this illusion from dispersed relations, it should keep these operations hidden. Out of sight, these operations won't distract the user who is thinking in terms of the application objects.

The object-oriented database model adopts this viewpoint, building on similar concepts in object-oriented programming languages. These languages supplement the simple data types—integers, reals, and strings—with complex types, which have properties that more closely approximate their real-world counterparts. Other useful concepts flow naturally from this viewpoint. For example, application objects evolve through time as they interact with each other. In the model, an object's evolution is reflected through attribute changes. For example, a tank that was blue can become red. The events that trigger such changes are messages passed among objects. For example, a fish can dispatch a paintTank message to its home tank. When it receives the message, the tank modifies its color attribute. This chapter investigates these object-oriented programming concepts and extends the ideas to define a new database model.

Informal illustration of an object-oriented database

Figure 7.1 shows the principle entity of the aquarium, the fish. The aquarium's purpose is to support, nurture, display, and process fish. Alternative views are, of course, possible. For example, a tank salesman thinks of the aquarium as a consumer of tanks. You will see that the object-oriented model can also accommodate this viewpoint, but for the moment, suppose that the fish is the main entity.

Like the relational model, the object-oriented model defines a fish with a set of attributes, which distinguish it from other fish. Here the fish has three simple attributes: name, color, and weight. The relational fish contained an fno attribute, which served as a key. An fno value represented its corresponding fish tuple in various database relationships. The object-oriented model departs from that important convention: it doesn't assign a key attribute to an entity. Instead, it represents each fish as a distinct object, which retains its identity even if all its attributes change. The DBMS gives each object a unique object identifier (OID). This OID serves many of the same purposes as a key attribute. An object's OID, however, is stronger than a key because it is unique across the entire database, not just within a particular table. Another advantage the OID enjoys over a key attribute is that the DBMS maintains it. The designer, therefore, is relieved of concerns about its nullity and its uniqueness.

Attribute values can be other objects

The name, color, weight, and fno complete the descriptive fish attributes from the relational perspective. Although a fish is connected to its home tank, its representative species, and its set of events, the relational model doesn't consider these items as descriptive attributes. Why not? Because the relational model uses tables as the basic building blocks, and it restricts table cells to traditional data types, such as numbers and character strings. The relational model can't put tanks, species, or event sets in table cells because they have internal structure. Therefore, it elevates these entities to the status of separate relations and maintains the relationships to fish with foreign keys.

The object-oriented model, however, doesn't make a distinction between a complex attribute, such as home (i.e., a tank), and a simple attribute, such as name (i.e., a character string). Referring again to Figure 7.1, you see the aquarium as a collection of fish objects. The diagram magnifies one fish object for a closer inspection, which reveals three simple attributes (name, color, and weight) and two complex objects (home and breed). Although name contains a string, home contains a tank. Of course, an implementation represents the tank by its OID, which allows the DBMS to recover it in its entirety, if necessary. However, for purposes of the mental model, you should think of the entire tank as contained inside the fish. Although home is a tank, which possesses internal structure and involves potentially unwieldy representation problems, this isn't a relevant distinction from the application standpoint. Like its name, color, and weight strings, the fish's home is a meaningful attribute of its existence. The important point is that each object maintains a set of attributes and that an attribute can contain a complex object value at any given time.

Without further restrictions, you can freely assign any objects to any attribute. For example, you can replace the string killer in the fish name attribute with a tank. Of course, a fish with a tank for a name instead of a string is unusual, but conceivable. Objects' attributes are usually restricted with domain constraints, just as in the relational model. The point

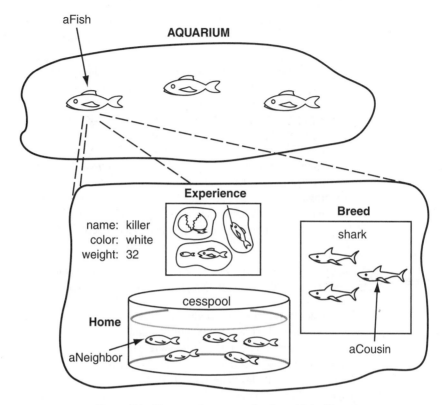

Figure 7.1   The aquarium as a collection of fish objects

here, however, is that an object's attribute value can theoretically be any type: a simple string or another complex object. It can even be the hosting object itself.

You can assign the same object to different attributes. Because several fish inhabit a given tank, the home attributes of these fish all contain the same tank. Because the implementation uses an OID to represent the tank, it can easily accommodate this multiple assignment. An object isn't "used up" when it serves as an attribute value. To present an extreme example, give each fish another attribute, called "self." The value of self at any time is a fish object, namely the fish object that contains the attribute currently under definition. In other words, each fish contains itself as an attribute value. Of course, that fish, when inspected more closely, also contains a self attribute whose value is the same fish. Moreover, that fish contains itself yet again, and so forth. The implementation simply uses the OID of the fish object under definition to fill the self attribute slot, which truncates the endless recursion. Conceptually, however, the infinite regression remains available. You can examine a fish and retrieve the value of the self attribute (i.e., the same fish). You can then examine that fish, retrieving the value of its self attribute, which is again the same fish. You can continue in this manner until you realize that you aren't deriving much new information from the experiment.

Referring again to Figure 7.1, you see that each fish contains a breed attribute, whose value is the representative species. As with the home attribute, this value is a complex object, whose internal details you can examine, if necessary. You see that the magnified breed value of the fish (i.e., a species object) contains, in its reps attribute, other fish of the same species. These are cousins of the fish under discussion. The home value (i.e., a tank) contains, in its population attribute, fish swimming in the same tank with the fish in question. These are neighboring fish. A final attribute, labeled experience, contains a more complex object, namely a collection of event objects. The event objects are the fish's experiences. The experience attribute value is yet more complex than the home or breed attributes. First, the object that fills the experience slot is a *collection*. Therefore, in allowing attribute values beyond traditional strings and numbers, the object-oriented model departs further from the relational model where attribute values must be single-valued atomic entries. Second, the members of the collection object are themselves complex objects. In other words, a fish's experience attribute is an object, which is a collection of event objects.

 Attribute values in an object are less constrained than those in a relational tuple. An object attribute value can be another object or even a collection of objects.

The object-oriented model also organizes species, tanks, and events as objects. A tank contains three attributes whose values are traditional strings: its name, volume, and color features. It contains one attribute, population, whose value is a fish object collection, containing those fish inhabiting the tank. A species object contains name and food strings and a reps attribute. The reps attribute value is the collection of fish that represent the species. Finally, an event object contains date and note attributes, which assume character string values, and a subject attribute, whose value is the fish that owns the event.

Figure 7.1 exhibits the aquarium as a collection of fish, each with internal detail that you can pursue to recover other objects of interest. Figure 7.2 takes a different viewpoint by representing the aquarium as a tank collection. Within a tank, the population attribute delivers the fish collection that inhabits the tank. You can recursively examine a fish to reveal its species and its collection of events.

Extracting query solutions from objects

You can maintain several aquarium views at the same time, using the most appropriate as the launching point for a particular query. For example, what are the colors of tanks named lagoon? Starting with the aquarium as a tank collection, you sequentially examine each tank. If the name attribute is the string lagoon, you add the color attribute string to the accumulating answer set.

For a more complicated example, how many fish live in a tank named cesspool and represent a species named shark? The most appropriate starting point is the aquarium as a fish collection. You examine each fish in turn, contributing one or zero to an accumulating count, depending on whether the fish satisfies the query conditions. To make this determination for a fish, you first examine its home attribute, a tank. You probe the name attribute of the tank. If it contains the string cesspool, the test continues. Otherwise you discard the fish without incrementing the count. If the test does continue, you next probe the breed attribute for its name attribute. If the value is the string shark, you increment the

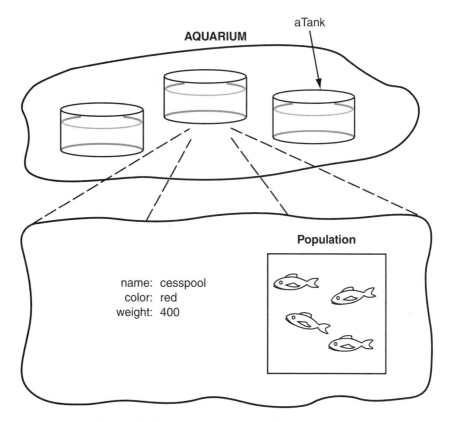

AQUARIUM

aTank

Population

name: cesspool
color: red
weight: 400

Figure 7.2   The aquarium as a collection of tank objects

accumulating count. In any case, you continue the task with the next fish object. When you have processed all fish in the aquarium, the count is complete.

Although the fish object collection may be the most natural starting point for the last query, you can initiate the process from another collection. For example, you can start with the aquarium as a tank collection, as shown in Figure 7.2. You examine each tank in turn, immediately rejecting tanks where the name attribute isn't the string cesspool. You further interrogate each cesspool tank for its population attribute, which is a fish collection. You examine the collection, one by one, to see if the breed attribute contains the name value shark. If so, you increment the count by one. When you finish the collection, you repeat the process for the next cesspool tank. When you have exhausted the cesspool tanks, the count is complete.

These examples illustrate the general approach for probing interrelated objects. The exact syntax will come later. From some starting collection, you examine the attributes of the first-level objects. Because these values are themselves objects, you can subject them to the same treatment, providing a second-level examination. The process continues until you can make a decision about the path under study. In many ways the procedure is similar to the mental model in Chapter 5 for constructing solutions to existential queries. There, tentative paths start from a candidate tuple and stretch across the database through matching attributes to some anchor tuple. In the query above, you attempt to connect a fish object to a cesspool tank. However, instead of exploring connections through a common tno value, you look within the fish itself for the tank. If it is there, you find the qualifying path by searching within a candidate object, where you continue recursively as necessary into the internal details of other objects discovered along the way.

Occasionally you must construct intermediate objects, just as you perform intermediate calculations with SQL subqueries. For example, suppose you want the names of species represented in all tanks. This is a universal query, and its SQL solution requires subqueries. In the object-oriented model, you start with the aquarium as a species collection, as shown in Figure 7.3. You test each species object to determine if it appears, via some fish, in all tanks. If so, you include the corresponding name string in the answer. The test proceeds by constructing a new collection, which is initially empty. You probe the reps attribute of the candidate species to obtain the collection of associated fish, and you then ask each fish for its home tank. As you receive each new tank, you add it to the new collection. Because the DBMS maintains the new collection as a set, it suppresses duplicates. When all fish have contributed, the new collection contains the unduplicated home tanks of all fish representing the candidate species. Finally, you compare it with the aquarium as a collection of tank objects. If the two collections are equal, the species in question appears in all tanks. Otherwise, it doesn't.

The DBMS identifies each object with a unique OID, as shown in Figures 7.4 and 7.5. The aquarium is then redundantly represented by the collections of Figure 7.6. These interface collections have names, such as TheTanks and TheFish, which you can access as the starting point of a query. In the above example, the query solution started with the collection of all species, then probed the associated fish, and finally requested the home tanks of these fish. A query solution can, in general, start with any of the interface collections.

In terms of the OIDs in Figures 7.4 and 7.6, the universal query example proceeds as follows. Recall that you want the names of species represented in all tanks. From TheSpecies of Figure 7.6, the candidate species are OID-5001, 5002, 5003, and 5004. The first, OID-5001, contains a reps attribute of OID-4001, a set yielding OID-5041, 5044, 5052, 5053, 5055, and 5056 and representing a collection of fish. These fish deliver home attributes of OID-5022, 5020, 5021, 5024, 5023, and 5025 respectively. Because this collection is equal to TheTanks from Figure 7.6, the name attribute of OID-5001, dolphin, becomes the first entry in the answer set.

The second species, OID-5002, contains a reps attribute of OID-4002, a set (OID-5042, 5043, 5045, 5048), and these fish deliver home attributes OID-5021, 5023, 5021, and 5021 respectively. After removing duplicates, the tanks containing species OID-5002 are OID-5021 and 5023, which don't encompass the list of OIDs in TheTanks. This species, therefore, doesn't contribute to the developing answer list. When the DBMS recovered the fish for species OID-5002, it found only four, hardly sufficient to cover the six tanks of the database even if they were as widely dispersed as possible. The same is true for the remaining two species, OID-5003 and OID-5004, which have four and three fish respectively. Therefore, the answer set is the single string dolphin.

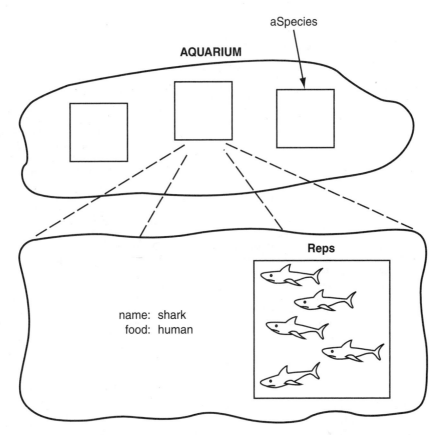

Figure 7.3   The aquarium as a collection of species objects

Relationship representation through logical inclusion

The object-oriented model represents relationships with logical inclusion. The objects related to a candidate are present within the candidate at some level of recursion. Therefore, besides allowing more complex attribute values, the object-oriented model differs from the relational model in relationship representation. The term *logical inclusion* describes the relationship mechanism because the inclusion of a guest object within a host isn't implemented by nesting the corresponding data structures. Instead, it is accomplished by using an OID to represent the included object. You can think of the OID as a pointer to the related object.

 Where the relational model uses common attributes to maintain relationships, the object-oriented model uses logical inclusion.

The results of the example queries to this point have been collections of strings that have an obvious printable form. However, if you phrase the queries differently, a difficulty arises

OID	attributes
5001	name ("dolphin"), food ("herring"), reps (OID-4001)
5002	name ("shark"), food ("anything"), reps (OID-4002)
5003	name ("guppy"), food ("worm"), reps (OID-4003)
5004	name ("shark"), food ("peanut butter"), reps (OID-4004)
5020	name ("puddle"), color ("green"), volume (200), population (OID-4005)
5021	name ("cesspool"), color ("blue"), volume (100), population (OID-4006)
5022	name ("lagoon"), color ("red"), volume (400), population (OID-4007)
5023	name ("cesspool"), color ("blue"), volume (100), population (OID-4008)
5024	name ("beach"), color ("blue"), volume (200), population (OID-4009)
5025	name ("lagoon"), color ("green"), volume (200), population (OID-4010)
5040	name ("charlie"), color ("orange"), breed (OID-5003), home (OID-5021), experience (OID-4011)
5041	name ("flipper"), color ("black"), breed (OID-5001), home (OID-5022), experience (OID-4012)
5042	name ("killer"), color ("white"), breed (OID-5002), home (OID-5021), experience (OID-4013)
5043	name ("charlie"), color ("orange"), breed (OID-5002), home (OID-5023), experience (OID-4014)
5044	name ("albert"), color ("red"), breed (OID-5001), home (OID-5020), experience (OID-4015)
5045	name ("bonnie"), color ("blue"), breed (OID-5002), home (OID-5021), experience (OID-4016)
5046	name ("cory"), color ("purple"), breed (OID-5004), home (OID-5022), experience (OID-4017)
5047	name ("darron"), color ("white"), breed (OID-5004), home (OID-5021), experience (OID-4018)
5048	name ("elsie"), color ("white"), breed (OID-5002), home (OID-5021), experience (OID-4019)
5049	name ("fran"), color ("black"), breed (OID-5003), home (OID-5020), experience (OID-4020)
5050	name ("george"), color ("red"), breed (OID-5004), home (OID-5021), experience (OID-4021)
5051	name ("helen"), color ("blue"), breed (OID-5003), home (OID-5025), experience (OID-4022)
5052	name ("indira"), color ("black"), breed (OID-5001), home (OID-5021), experience (OID-4023)
5053	name ("jill"), color ("red"), breed (OID-5001), home (OID-5024), experience (OID-4024)
5054	name ("kilroy"), color ("red"), breed (OID-5003), home (OID-5020), experience (OID-4025)
5055	name ("laura"), color ("blue"), breed (OID-5001), home (OID-5023), experience (OID-4026)
5056	name ("maureen"), color ("white"), breed (OID-5001), home (OID-5025), experience (OID-4027)
5080	subject (OID-5040), date ("01/26"), note ("Hatched")
5081	subject (OID-5041), date ("05/14"), note ("Born")
5082	subject (OID-5041), date ("05/15"), note ("Swimming")
5083	subject (OID-5041), date ("05/30"), note ("Takes fish from trainer")
5084	subject (OID-5042), date ("04/30"), note ("Hatched")
5085	subject (OID-5043), date ("05/23"), note ("Hatched")
5086	subject (OID-5044), date ("06/25"), note ("Born")
5087	subject (OID-5044), date ("06/30"), note ("Doubled in length")
5088	subject (OID-5045), date ("07/22"), note ("Hatched")
5089	subject (OID-5045), date ("08/05"), note ("Monopolized food")
5090	subject (OID-5046), date ("02/04"), note ("Hatched")
5091	subject (OID-5047), date ("02/08"), note ("Hatched")
5092	subject (OID-5048), date ("04/19"), note ("Hatched")
5093	subject (OID-5049), date ("09/25"), note ("Hatched")
5094	subject (OID-5050), date ("10/02"), note ("Hatched")
5095	subject (OID-5051), date ("11/12"), note ("Hatched")
5096	subject (OID-5052), date ("12/25"), note ("Born")
5097	subject (OID-5053), date ("06/04"), note ("Born")
5098	subject (OID-5054), date ("01/11"), note ("Hatched")
5099	subject (OID-5055), date ("04/23"), note ("Born")
5100	subject (OID-5056), date ("05/09"), note ("Born")

Figure 7.4   An implementation view of aquarium objects

Set Usage	OID	Contents
Fish Set	4001	OID-5041, 5044, 5052, 5053, 5055, 5056
in reps	4002	OID-5042, 5043, 5045, 5048
attribute	4004	OID-5040, 5049, 5051, 5054
Fish Set	4005	OID-5044, 5049, 5054
in population	4006	OID-5040, 5042, 5045, 5047, 5048, 5050, 5052
attribute	4007	OID-5041, 5046
	4008	OID-5043, 5055
	4009	OID-5053
	4010	OID-5051, 5056
Event Set	4011	OID-5080
in experience	4012	OID-5081, 5082, 5083
attribute	4013	OID-5084
	4014	OID-5085
	4015	OID-5086, 5087
	4016	OID-5088, 5089
	4017	OID-5090
	4018	OID-5091
	4019	OID-5092
	4020	OID-5093
	4021	OID-5094
	4022	OID-5095
	4023	OID-5096
	4024	OID-5097
	4025	OID-5098
	4026	OID-5099
	4027	OID-5100

Figure 7.5   An implementation view of aquarium set objects

OID	Name	Contents
6001	TheSpecies	(OID-5001, 5002, 5003, 5004)
6002	TheTanks	(OID-5020, 5021, 5022, 5023, 5024, 5025)
6003	TheFish	(OID-5040, 5041, 5042, 5043, 5044, 5045, 5046, 5047, 5048, 5049, 5050, 5051, 5052, 5053, 5054, 5055, 5056)
6004	TheEvents	(OID-5080, 5081, 5082, 5083, 5084, 5085, 5086, 5087, 5088, 5089, 5090, 5091, 5092, 5093, 5094, 5095, 5096, 5097, 5098, 5099, 5100)

Figure 7.6   Alternative representations of the aquarium database as collections of objects

in displaying the answer set. For example, suppose you ask for the species represented in all tanks, rather than the names of those species. Then, instead of constructing a collection of strings, such as dolphin, the DBMS constructs a collection of species objects. How does it display the collection? The OIDs are meaningless to the user because the DBMS generates and maintains them. You might expect the DBMS to display an object by displaying all its attributes. However, some of the attribute values might be complex objects, requiring a recursive display of all their attributes. Suppose the DBMS tries to display a species object in this manner. First, it displays the name and food strings, then the reps attribute. Because reps is a fish collection, it must display the entire collection. Proceeding to display the first fish, it outputs the name, color, and weight strings and then attempts to display the breed attribute. However, that value is a species. Worse yet, it is the same species that the DBMS is attempting to display at the top level. The situation, therefore, degenerates into an infinite loop.

Because a systematic listing of all the attributes of an object is impossible in some cases, the DBMS simply displays the simple attributes (e.g., numbers and strings) and provides only a generic class value for more complex attributes. For example, the printable form of a species object is (name = dolphin, food = herring, reps = aFishCollection). A typical fish is reported as (name = charlie, color = orange, weight = 12, home = aTank, breed = aSpecies). The rest of the chapter assumes that each object has a printable form of this nature.

For display purposes, each object has a printable form. This form displays simple attributes but gives only a generic class indication for complex-valued attributes.

Object-oriented terminology

The previous section discussed four object-oriented features that contrast sharply with the relational approach:

- Attribute values can be complex objects, as opposed to simple strings and numbers.

- An attribute value can be a collection of objects.

- Relationships among objects are represented by logical inclusion, a technique that embeds OIDs within an object's attributes to link it to related objects.

- Unless otherwise specified, object attributes aren't typed. Because an attribute isn't necessarily associated with a particular domain, it can contain an arbitrary object.

This section explores additional features that are useful in object-oriented database design.

Object-oriented features can appear in a programming language, with or without provisions for database manipulation. Indeed, the difference is slight. In a pure programming language, such as Smalltalk or C++, you can use object-oriented ideas to organize the program's data structures and to control access to these structures. If database operations are available, the same concepts extend to database objects. A database object differs from a conventional data object, as declared in a programming language, only in its **persistence** and its **shareability**. A database object persists after the process that created it terminates, and it is available to multiple users simultaneously. Consequently, for the rest of this section, the term *system* refers either to the object-oriented environment where a program is designed and executed or to an object-oriented DBMS, which provides similar services with database extensions. Likewise, objects refer either to transient, memory-based objects in a program or to database objects, which represent the persistent stored model of an application.

Object communication with signals

Objects interact with one another and with the user interface by means of signals. A **signal** is a message transmitted from an object or from the user interface to a target object. The target object is expected to respond in a predictable manner. Possible responses include attribute modification, calculations, secondary signal transmissions to other objects, database manipulation activity, and feedback to the user interface. Signals are also called messages, and this discussion will use the two terms interchangeably.

Although objects respond differently to signals, all responses have two aspects in common. First, the target object always responds to the signal. You can think of the acknowledgment as the return of the control flow to the object that transmitted the signal, just as a called procedure eventually returns control to its caller. Second, the target object always returns a completion object to the sender. The returned object can be a simple string, such as **success** or **failure**, which informs the sender of outcome, or it can be a complex object with internal structure available for further interrogation. The returned value can even be a collection of objects.

 A signal, a message dispatched from a sending object or the user interface to a target object, requests some service. The target object complies with the signal instructions and returns a completion object to the sender.

Of course, the intent is that the model objects faithfully represent the corresponding real-world application objects. Messages elicit responses from the model objects, just as similar requests would address their real-world counterparts. For example, when you send a fish object a message requesting its name value, the object responds with a string, say, **flipper**. In the real-world application, this procedure corresponds to obtaining the fish name, say, by walking over to the tank, fetching the fish with a net, and reading the tag attached to its tail. You can also ask a fish object for its home attribute value, and it replies with a tank object. You can then direct further messages to the tank to continue your investigation.

All objects respond to signals that request an attribute value; they also accept signals that force an attribute value change. The latter signals must carry a parameter to identify the new value. The actual syntax for initiating and responding to signals varies with the support system. Writing the signal after the target object indicates a signal transmission. (The Smalltalk language uses the same convention.) As in most languages, the target object appears as a program variable, but it is actually an OID. For example, if the variable aFish holds OID-5040, the code excerpt on the left below requests the value of the object's home attribute. Assuming that the variable aTank holds the OID of a tank, the code on the right changes the aFish's home attribute to the new value, aTank. The new value, aTank, is a parameter, which the signal home: carries to the object, aFish.

```
aFish home.                      aFish home:  aTank.
```

Each message has a unique **signature**, which is its name and a specified number of parameters. The examples above illustrate two distinct messages. The first has a signature consisting of the name home without any parameters. The second signature is the name home:, together with one parameter. The trailing colon is part of the signature; it indicates that the signal will carry one parameter. Signatures for messages with one or more parameters use alternating keywords and colons to introduce the parameters. For example, the following code dispatches a message with three parameters to the object, targetObject. The signature is takeAction:using:andAlso:. When you transmit the message to an object, you must insert a parameter object after each colon.

```
targetObject takeAction:  param1 using:  param2 andAlso:  param3.
```

 A message signature is a sequence of keywords, alternating with colons, which specifies the generic format for invoking the signal. An invocation must insert a parameter after each colon. If a signal involves no parameters, its signature is a single keyword with no colon.

This chapter and the next will use this syntax for signal transmission. However, other object-oriented systems use different syntax. For example, some systems use traditional C procedure calls, specifying the target object as the first parameter. In these systems, you change the home attribute of aFish to aTank with the call: home(aFish, aTank);. C++ uses a mixture of the two notations. It selects the message signature from the receiving object with the same format used to select a field from a record structure. It then passes the parameters like a traditional procedure call. In C++, you change the home attribute of aFish to aTank with the code: aFish.home(aTank);.

Attribute signals

The four kinds of aquarium objects respond to the signals of Figure 7.7. An unparameterized signature corresponds to a request for an attribute value, and the parameterized counterpart is a command to change the attribute value. The signals that read and write attribute values are called **attribute signals**. For signatures, they use the attribute names, without a colon for reading and with a colon for writing.

The message recipient always returns a completion object to the sender. The sender can assign the returned object to a variable, such as bTank, and it can then send more messages to bTank. The operations to the left below illustrate the use of object variables by assigning the collection of fish swimming in the same tank with aFish to the variable, aFishCollection. The code to the right obtains the same result in one line. The parenthesized expression returns the home tank, which is then probed with the population message.

```
bTank := aFish home.                    aFishCollection := (aFish home) population.
aFishCollection := bTank population.
```

To avoid unnecessary parentheses in signal expressions, this text adopts the convention that dispatches unparameterized signals in left-to-right order as they follow the target object.

Object Class	Read signal	Write signal	Object Class	Read signal	Write signal
Fish	name	name:	Tank	name	name:
	color	color:		color	color:
	weight	weight:		volume	volume:
	home	home:		population	population:
	breed	breed:	Event	note	note:
	experience	experience:		date	date:
Species	name	name:		subject	subject:
	food	food:			
	reps	reps:			

Figure 7.7   Attribute signals accepted by aquarium objects

You can then write the above expression as follows. The target, aFish, receives the `home` signal and responds with a tank object. That tank then receives the `population` signal and returns a fish collection.

```
aFishCollection := aFish home population.
```

When unparameterized and parameterized signals appear in the same expression, the unparameterized signals receive the precedence. For example, you can modify the population of aFish's home with the following statement. You don't need parentheses because the unparameterized home signal takes precedence. The object aFish returns its home (i.e., a tank), which then receives the `population:` signal carrying the new value.

```
aFish home population: aFishCollection.
```

Another convention is that write-attribute signals return the target object itself. This convenience allows you to cascade attribute-write commands. For example, the following code sets the name and color attributes of aFish.

```
(aFish name: "marley") color: "blue".
```

The `name:` signal sets the name attribute of aFish to marley and returns the target object, aFish, which then receives the `color:` signal. The parentheses are necessary to avoid confusion with a signal having the `name:color:` signature.

Signals are operations on objects that return other objects. As such, the system of objects and signals is closed in the same sense as relational algebra. Indeed, you can consider an object and signal system as an algebra. You apply signals to objects, resulting in further objects, which you can then probe with additional signals. This viewpoint will be useful in formulating queries against an object-oriented database, and you will find the process very similar to relational algebra and SQL. The details are in the next chapter.

Many objects can meaningfully reply to the same signal. For example, Figure 7.7 indicates that all fish objects respond to the `name`, `color`, `weight`, `breed`, `home`, and `experience` signals. An object responds to a message by executing a procedure. Where should the procedure code reside? All fish objects, for example, exhibit similar behavior in response to a given signal. One fish returns the string charlie in response to a name signal; another returns flipper. However, the algorithm for processing the signal is the same in both cases: it fetches the string in the object's name attribute. For efficiency, all fish objects use the same procedure to process the name message. Similarly, another procedure is shared among all fish objects for the name: message, which changes the name attribute. In general, all the signal implementation code for behavior-similar objects can be shared. All fish objects share procedures for name, color, weight, breed, and experience messages. All species objects share procedures for name, food, and reps messages.

Classes and methods

Procedure sharing leads to the principal idea of the object-oriented model, the concept of class. The model groups objects with similar behavior into a class, a sort of meta-object. The class holds the code for processing messages received by objects of the group. A procedure that responds to a message is called a **method**.

In truth, class is a more fundamental concept than object, and many textbooks define it first. A **class** is a template that specifies the skeletal aspects of a group of similar objects. These common features include the attribute names and the methods for processing signals. When you need a new object from a particular class, you mint it from the class template. Immediately upon creation, the new object can process signals associated with the class.

In keeping with the model's philosophy, you use a message to create an object from a class template. The class, say Fish, is a sort of second-level object, but an object nevertheless. It responds to the new signal by returning a freshly minted fish object, with null values in all the attributes but with full awareness of the need to deal with such signals as home, breed, and name. The left excerpt below illustrates the operation. The notation uses a period to separate adjacent statements. You send the new signal to the fish class and store the returned fish object in the variable, aFish. You then use the name: signal to set the name attribute to the string flipper. Because unparameterized signals take precedence, you can abbreviate the code, as shown on the right.

```
aFish := Fish new.
aFish name: "flipper".        aFish := Fish new name: "flipper".
```

How does the fish class come to be available for this operation? If fish *objects* are stamped out by sending new signals to the fish *class*, how is the fish class itself created? As you will see later, specifying the application classes amounts to a schema definition, with appropriate adjustments for the object-oriented context. For the rest of this section, assume that classes are available for the aquarium entities: Fish, Species, Tank, and Event.

A class is roughly equivalent to a relation's schema. A relation's schema determines the structure (i.e., attribute names) of tuples that appear in the body. A class determines the structure (i.e., both attribute names and message responses) of objects created from that class. You can compare a class with a set of table headings and an object created from the class with a table row. This comparison isn't perfect because the class also includes a dynamic aspect—defining the objects' reactions to signals. Although the most recent SQL versions provide some triggered processes, most features of relational tables are passive. External agents act on table rows, for example, by SQL directives. In contrast, objects incorporate behavior as part of their definitions.

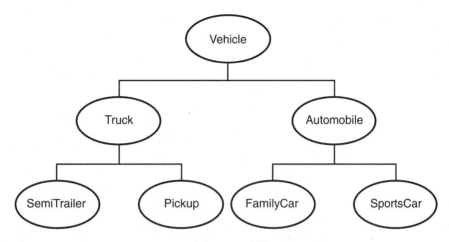

Figure 7.8   A hierarchy of vehicle classes

 You create objects from a generic template, called a class, which specifies the attribute names and the behavioral methods. A method is a procedure that an object invokes when it receives a message.

Class hierarchies and inheritance

Classes are organized in a hierarchy, so that each class represents a specialization of its immediate parent. For example, consider the arrangement of Figure 7.8. An entry toward the bottom of the diagram represents a specialization of the class immediately above it. A sports car is a special kind of automobile. In turn, an automobile is a special kind of vehicle. If you obtain a new sports car object by dispatching a new signal to the class SportsCar, you expect it to contain all the attributes of that class. The new object does contain the expected attributes, but it also contains automobile and vehicle attributes. The parents' attributes appear in a child object through **inheritance**. All attributes, those directly specified in the class SportsCar and those inherited from parent classes, are initially null.

Suppose the vehicle class specifies attributes serialNumber and weight, expecting a number and a string value respectively. The vehicle class also specifies the methods for the corresponding attribute signals. The messages to the left below create a vehicle object and establish its initial attributes.

```
aVehicle := Vehicle new.              anAutomobile := Automobile new.
aVehicle weight:  4200.               anAutomobile audioPackage:  "Quadraphonic Sound".
aVehicle serialNumber:  "Z409-71-80942".   anAutomobile seats:  4.
```

Now suppose the automobile class specifies attributes audioPackage and seats, expecting a string and a number respectively, and the methods for the corresponding attribute signals. You can create an automobile object and establish its initial attributes as shown to the right above. Because an automobile is a special kind of vehicle, it contains, in addition to the attributes explicitly declared in its class, the attributes of a vehicle. Moreover, it responds to the attribute signals intended for a vehicle. For example, the following code is valid.

```
anAutomobile := Automobile new.
anAutomobile audioPackage:  "Quadraphonic Sound".
anAutomobile seats:  4.
anAutomobile weight:  4200.
anAutomobile serialNumber:  "Z409-71-80942".
```

Now suppose the subclass SportsCar specializes Automobile even further by adding the attributes tachometerLimit and turningRadius, together with the attribute methods. An object created through SportsCar has the structure shown in the rightmost part of Figure 7.9. Attributes from its ancestor classes are available as a sort of superstructure. The object responds to attribute signals associated with these inherited parameters.

You use classes to represent the generic application entities, just as you use tables in a relational database. By positioning the application classes in an existing hierarchy, you can exploit inherited resources. When you create an object from an application class, it automatically receives the attributes from all higher ancestors, and it also shares the ancestors' methods for responding to messages. In the vehicle example, you need to write less support code for the automobile class because it uses existing methods from the vehicle class. Of course, this convenience depends on the prior existence of a class that can be specialized to the given application entity.

The class hierarchy imposes a partial order on its classes. When a new class specializes an existing class by providing additional attributes and methods, it is a **subclass** of the existing class. The original class is then called the parent class or **superclass**. In this terminology, a subclass object inherits attributes and methods from its superclasses.

 Classes are arranged in a hierarchy. You can create subclasses by specialization, which specifies additional attributes and methods for an existing class. Objects created through a subclass inherit all attributes and methods of the parent class. Some of these inherited features may themselves have been inherited from higher classes in the hierarchy.

The native hierarchy of frequently used classes

The object-oriented modeling environment provides an initial hierarchy of frequently-used classes, such as numbers, strings, collections of various sorts, and input/output streams. In designing an object-oriented database, you insert the application classes at appropriate points in the hierarchy, exploiting the signal processing methods from the parent classes. Figure 7.10 shows an abbreviated set of native classes. This hierarchy is based on two commercial products: the GemStone object-oriented database and the Smalltalk/V object-oriented programming language. You can compare the built-in classes with the native data types available in a programming language or in a relational database system. The full collection of object-oriented classes is typically much larger than the excerpt of Figure 7.10.

Each of the built-in classes provides a repertoire of methods for manipulating its objects. For example, a collection object has methods to test its empty status, to add objects, to remove objects, to iterate over its member, and to calculate its size. These methods are self-explanatory and will be used as needed to illustrate object-oriented queries.

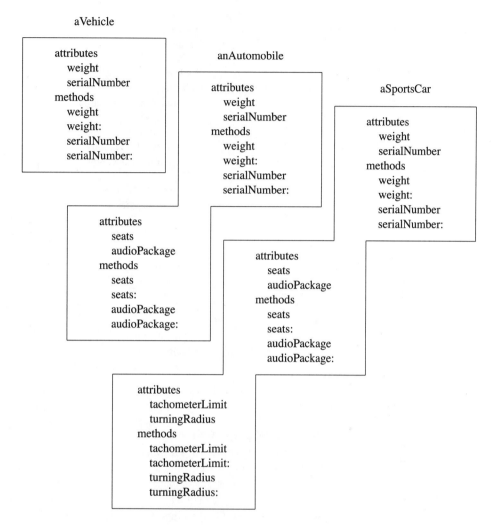

Figure 7.9 Inheritance of attributes and methods from superclasses

You can position new classes anywhere in the hierarchy. Usually, application designers place the application classes, such as Fish, Species, Tank, and Event, directly under the root class Object. Some designers interpose a single superclass directly over the application classes to provide attributes common to all database objects, such as creator and creation timestamp. A typical arrangement for the aquarium example appears to the right. To insert a subclass, you send the appropriate signal to the superclass object, requesting that it admit a specialization. The actual syntax will be studied in a later section.

```
Object
  AquariumClass
    Fish
    Tank
    Species
    Event
      ⋮
```

```
                          Object
                             Association
                             Behavior
                                Class
                             Boolean
                             Collection
                                SequenceableCollection
                                   Array
                                   String
                                   OrderedCollection
                                      SortedCollection
                                Bag
                                   Set
                                      Dictionary
                             Magnitude
                                Character
                                DateTime
                                Number
                                   Float
                                   Fraction
                                   Integer
                             Stream
                                ReadStream
                                WriteStream
                                   ReadWriteStream
```

Figure 7.10   Hierarchy of built-in classes

Method installation and polymorphism

The model insists that an object always respond to a signal, and the class hierarchy provides a convenient mechanism for guaranteeing a universal response. Besides installing specific methods in the application classes, you place default methods for all application signals in a common ancestor class. Then, if an object receives an inappropriate signal, it responds with the inherited default method. On the other hand, a legitimate signal invokes the legitimate method of the class, which prevents a search up the hierarchy for an inherited method of the same name. In the aquarium example, you simply place methods in the superclass, AquariumClass, to handle all the application messages. You install a method installation, as expected, by sending a message carrying the procedure code as a parameter. The following code installs the food method in the AquariumClass class.

```
AquariumClass method:  "food" code:  [^self signalError:  "food"].
```

This one line introduces several new ideas. First, the intention is to intercept signals that might be sent to objects not prepared to process them. For example, suppose a fish object receives the food signal. Because food isn't a fish attribute, the fish object might appear at a loss to interpret it. However, the fish object inherits attributes and methods from its superclasses. So it invokes the food method from its parent class, AquariumClass. The code segment above then processes the signal.

If a species object receives the food signal, it responds with its own food method, which returns the attribute value. The more immediate method takes precedence over any inherited method with the same signature. This scoping convention is the same as in conventional programming languages. When a local identifier is declared in a subprocedure, it hides access to a like-named identifier in the host procedure. Similarly, when an attribute or method is declared in a subclass, it hides access to any like-named attribute or method in its superclasses.

 A class definition can override attributes or methods inherited from a parent class. An inherited method processes a message only if the class definition doesn't provide the required method.

In summary, species objects behave properly when probed with a food signal. Fish objects, however, use the inherited method from AquariumClass. That method executes the code: ^self signalError: "food".

The opening caret (^) is the return operator. It returns to the message sender the object constructed by the expression to its right. The return operator has the lowest precedence, so the rest of the line is evaluated before it is invoked. In this case, the return value is the object obtained by sending the signalError: signal to the object "self." Self is a system variable, which you can reference from any procedure. However, it stands for different objects in different contexts. For example, when self occurs in a method that is executing on behalf of a fish object, say aFish, then it stands for aFish. When that same code is executing on behalf of a different object, say bFish, then it stands for bFish. In other words, self stands for the object that received the signal that invoked the method. In the example, you have a fish object, which has inadvertently received the food signal. Therefore, the food method in the parent class, AquariumClass, is executing on behalf of that fish object. So the code sends the signal signalError:, carrying the string parameter food, to the fish.

The next step is to place the signalError: method in AquariumClass, where it is available by inheritance to all the application objects. Below is the installation code, which uses the method:code: message illustrated earlier. As usual, the second parameter is a procedure that describes how an object should respond to a signalError: message. This time, however, the procedure is a one-parameter code block. This means that you must supply one parameter when you invoke the method. The dummy variable param represents the parameter in the method description.

```
AquariumClass method:   "signalError" code:   [param |
   "Signal " display.  param display.
   " not understood by object (" display.  self display.  ")" display.
   ^self].
```

Recall that each object is assumed to have a printable form. Complex objects are reported by printing simple attributes (e.g., strings and numbers) and by providing a generic indication for complex attributes. The display signal activates this process through a method inherited from a superclass in the system hierarchy. A string, such as Signal, responds by echoing itself on the screen. So a fish object responds to an inadvertent food signal by displaying the following message:

```
Signal food not understood by object ("charlie" "orange" 12 aSpecies aTank anEvent).
```

The misbehaving fish object itself is then returned to the sender. The sending code segment expects, of course, a food string at this point, so subsequent signals can also misfire. Nevertheless, the application has responded by serving notice of the unexpected situation.

The final feature introduced here is **polymorphism**, a property that allows methods in different classes to respond to the same message signature. Previous examples have already introduced this idea. The `signalError:` method dispatched the `display` signal several times to accumulate the error message string on the output screen. It is sent to several strings, the constant string object Signal and the string parameter `param`, for example. It is also sent to the fish object, using the pseudo-variable "self." The actual method selected to process a message isn't known, therefore, until an object receives the message. At that point, the methods available to the object's class are investigated for a matching signature. The method that displays a string is different from that which displays a fish object. The latter must iterate over the attribute fields, displaying the simple ones and providing a generic indication of the complex ones.

Polymorphism is also called "late binding" because the code associated with a message is selected at run-time rather than at compile-time. When the `signalError:` code is being compiled, the system doesn't know what class of object will be passed as the dummy `param`. Only when the display message is dispatched will that information be available.

 Polymorphism refers to the use of the same message signature to address different methods in different classes. When you send a signal to an object, the method from the object's class, possibly inherited, processes the signal.

In the example, all application objects—fish, species, tanks, and events—process the message `signalError:`. However, this variety of signal recipients isn't an example of polymorphism. A single signalError method handles all the messages. It is contained in AquariumClass where it is accessible through inheritance by all application objects. On the other hand, the `name` signal is an example of polymorphism. Different code segments are invoked when the `name` signal is sent to a tank, a fish, or a species object. As another example, suppose the species class contains the method `numberOfFish`, specified as follows:

```
Species method:  "numberOfFish" code:  [^reps size].
```

Assume that reps, as a fish collection, responds to the `size` signal by returning the size of the collection. In this case, it is the number of fish representing the species that is processing the message. Now, suppose that the tank class contains the following method with the same signature:

```
Tank method:  "numberOfFish" code:  [^population size].
```

When sent to a tank object, the `numberOfFish` signal returns the size of its population collection. When sent to a species object, it returns the size of its reps collection. The same signal signature invokes different code segments, depending on the target object's class. This binding of the signal to different code segments under different circumstances is polymorphism.

The distinguishing features of object-oriented data modeling are:

- *Complex, multi-valued, and untyped attribute values.*

- *Encapsulation. Attributes are protected; they can be accessed only through attribute signals. The corresponding methods are private within each class.*

- *Classification. Objects are categorized into classes, which are arranged in a hierarchy.*

- *Inheritance. Attributes and methods of ancestor classes are available to objects created through a subclass.*

- *Polymorphism. The same message signature invokes different methods, depending on the class of the receiving object.*

The encapsulation feature is subtle. It's true that objects protect their attributes, allowing access only through predefined messages. However, when an attribute signal returns a complex value (i.e., an object), subsequent operations can change that value. If the object serves as an attribute value inside another unrelated object, the modification compromises the strict spirit of encapsulation. For example, suppose fish objects aFish and bFish both contain the same home value: they are swimming in the same tank. The operation, aFish home color: "red", changes the state of the home tank of both aFish and bFish, even though bFish doesn't appear in the expression. The home attribute of aFish is actually an OID pointing to a particular tank. Object bFish contains the same OID in its home attribute. So the color change appears in both places, as illustrated in Figure 7.11. This vulnerability is similar to passing pointer variables by value in a program. The data referenced by the pointer is subject to change by the called procedure even though the data address in the calling routine is protected.

This example concerns a single tank. When aFish exposes it to a color: message, its color changes to red, and both aFish and bFish must live with the consequences. They are sharing a tank in the real application; bFish therefore shouldn't be overly protective about changes to that tank. The behavior is appropriate for the application. However, note that bFish does protect its home tank against a change that substitutes a new tank. Such a substitution requires a home: signal directed at bFish, which gives bFish an opportunity to control the access.

A parallel situation will help you appreciate the subtleties of the encapsulation. Suppose you control access to your car in the following sense. No agent can substitute another car without your approval. However, other agents can change every component of the car, down to the radiator cap, without your approval. The agent just asks you for a pointer to the front bumper, for example. Although you deliver a copy of the pointer, you feel secure because your original pointer still addresses your front bumper. Because the external agent can now address messages to the front bumper, he can shorten it, paint it, and adorn it with dents. Without further involvement on your part, your pointer now addresses the mutilated front bumper.

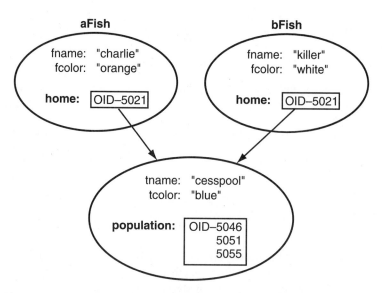

Figure 7.11 Circumventing object encapsulation with complex-valued attributes

You can enforce stronger access control of the encapsulated attributes. For a given application, it's a matter of determining the need. A later section, dealing with constraints, will present a situation where the population of a tank, aTank, must be limited to 50 fish. How can you prevent the following operation, where you assume that aFish is a newly available fish?

```
aTank population add:  aFish.
```

The object aTank delivers its population value (a set of fish), which then receives an `add:` signal. The `population:` signal, typically used to change the value of the population attribute, hasn't been invoked. Therefore, any safeguards within that method aren't applicable. The solution is actually relatively simple and will be discussed later. The point here is that the level of protection afforded by object encapsulation must be well understood.

Signal precedence: unary, binary, keyword

In the absence of parentheses, a default precedence order governs the application of signals. You can always use parentheses to clarify the situation if there is any doubt. Signals fall into three groups: unary, binary, and keyword. Unary signals contain a single keyword and no parameters. Consequently, no colons appear in the signature of a unary signal. Earlier discussion referred to unary signals as unparameterized signals. For example, all the read-attribute signals are unary signals. Unary signals have the highest priority. Assuming that the variable anEvent contains an event object, the code segment `anEvent subject home name:  "cesspool"` involves two unary signals. The expression dispatches them in left-to-right order, and they return first the fish object in the target's subject attribute and then the home tank of that fish object. Finally, the keyword signal `name:` changes the tank name to cesspool.

Unary signals are so named because they involve only one object—the signal receiver. Keyword signals, by contrast, involve two or more objects, depending on the number of parameters. Keyword signals are distinguished by a sequence of keywords separated by colons. An invocation places actual parameters after the colons. A keyword signal with one colon involves two objects—the signal target and a parameter object. The write-attribute signals are all keyword signals, each with one parameter. Keyword signals have lowest priority. They are dispatched in left-to-right order after the results of any unary and binary signals have been received.

Binary signals involve exactly two objects—the signal target and one parameter. You could write these signals as keyword signals because the definition above allows for the case of exactly two objects. The syntax, however, permits a special case for certain binary operations because a more intuitive form results. For example, a number object responds to the `plus:` signal by returning a new number object, equal to the sum of the target and the parameter. Although the left excerpt below correctly sets the variable aNumber to 6, you are likely to prefer the alternative form on the right.

```
aNumber := 4 plus:  2.                          aNumber := 4 + 2.
```

The + symbol is the signature of a binary signal. You write it between two objects with the understanding that the leftmost object is the signal target and the rightmost object is the parameter. Other arithmetic operators are similarly defined, allowing you to use the traditional forms. Comparison operators also have binary forms. For example, `aBoolean := aNumber < bNumber` means that the less-than signal is sent to the aNumber object, carrying the parameter bNumber. A boolean is returned, either the true object or the false object, depending on the relative sizes of the operands. Booleans themselves participate in binary operations with other booleans. For example, `newBoolean := aBoolean & bBoolean` means that the logical-and signal is sent to aBoolean, carrying the parameter bBoolean. The result is a new boolean value, true or false, depending on the values of the operands. A vertical bar is the binary signal for a logical-or operation, as in `newBoolean := aBoolean | bBoolean`.

Binary signals have intermediate priority. Unary signals are first dispatched in left-to-right order, and the returned objects are incorporated into the expression under evaluation. The binary signals are then sent, again in left-to-right order, and the completion objects are substituted into the expression. Finally, the keyword signals are sent, also in left-to-right order.

 Unary signals have a single keyword signature. You write binary signals in infix notation, with the left operand as the target. A keyword signal passes parameters, and its signature is a sequence of keywords separated by colons. An invocation places actual parameters after the colons. Signal priority is: unary, binary, keyword.

The binary equal-signal has two variations. $A == B$ returns the boolean object true if A and B are indeed the same object. In other words, they hold the same OID. Having the same OID is called **strong equality**. **Weak equality**, denoted by $A = B$, returns true if A and B belong to the same class and their corresponding attributes are equal in the same weak sense. Therefore, $A = B$ if two tests are passed. First A and B must belong to the same class. If the testing gets this far, then the attribute names for A and B must correspond (e.g., $a_1, a_2, \ldots$). Then, for each a_i, you must have $(A\ a_i) = (B\ a_i)$. Note that the values returned by the attribute signals, a_i, can themselves be complex objects with internal structure. In this case, the weak equality tests are repeated recursively on those objects. If A and B are sets, then $A = B$ if there exists a one-to-one correspondence between the sets, such that corresponding elements are equal in the weak sense.

If $A == B$, then clearly $A = B$ because there is actually a single OID involved. However, $A = B$ does not imply $A == B$. Suppose you have a class Gadget, involving two attributes, width and height. The excerpt below creates aGadget and bGadget from the Gadget template and sets their attributes to identical values.

```
aGadget := Gadget new.
bGadget := Gadget new.
aGadget width:  6.
bGadget width:  6.
aGadget height:  4.
bGadget height:  4.
cGadget := aGadget
```

The comparison aGadget = bGadget returns true because both are instances of Gadget and their corresponding attribute values are equal. However, aGadget == bGadget returns false because two different OIDs are involved. Nevertheless, the last comparison, cGadget == aGadget returns true because assigning an object to an identifier merely copies the OID. An OID behaves much like a pointer in C.

Weak equality can be tricky because of possible cycles in the recursive checks. Suppose you have two tank objects, aTank and bTank, and you want to check aTank = bTank. Both are instances of the tank class, so you proceed to check weak equality of their attributes. Checking the name, color, and volume attributes presents no difficulty because these values are simple numbers and strings. However, checking equality of the population attributes is more difficult. You must find a one-to-one correspondence between aTank population and bTank population that allows corresponding fish to be weakly equal. If the populations are different sizes, the condition obviously fails. But if they are the same size, say n, you need to check $n!$ possible one-to-one correspondences. In addition to the large number of possibilities, you encounter another complication. The check for weakly equal fish must test the weak equality of their home tanks. But these home tanks are aTank and bTank, so you return to the original question: is aTank = bTank? Therefore, a weak equality check may end up checking that same equality further down in the recursive nest, which leads to an infinite loop in the computation.

Because of these difficulties, you should try to use strong equality, if possible, and restrict weak equality to situations that compare only simple strings and numbers beyond the first level of the recursive descent. You can implement this compromise by redefining the weak equality operator for certain application classes. For example, for tanks you could insist that the string and number attributes be weakly equal and that the complex attributes be strongly equal. Then aTank = bTank if they weakly agree on name, color, and volume and strongly agree on population.

Strong equality of objects means they have the same OID. Weak equality means that corresponding components have the same values, recursively determined in a weak sense. Weak equality checks can involve excessive computation and infinite loops.

Definition of an object-oriented database

Chapter 1 defined a database as a self-describing collection of data elements and relationships that presents a uniform user interface. Chapter 2 then defined a relational database as a collection of relations, each consisting of a schema and a body. The schema and body were described in terms of domains, attributes, associations, and tuples. The relational model satisfies the spirit of the introductory definition. A relational database is self-describing through its system tables. It contains data elements (tuples) and relationships among them (through common attributes). SQL provides the uniform interface.

An **object-oriented database** (OODB) is a database, in the sense of the introductory definition, where the data elements are objects and relationships are maintained through logical inclusion. The application entities are represented as classes. Self-description is achieved because the classes are meta-objects, which contain the attributes names and signal methods. An OODB provides a systematic approach to relationship representation, and the uniform user interface is a system of messages, which can probe the objects and their interconnections.

 In an object-oriented database (OODB), the application entities are classes, entity instances are objects created from the classes, and relationships are maintained through logical inclusion. A system of signals and methods for processing them provide a uniform interface to the database.

The support system that provides the design and execution environments for an OODB is called an object-oriented database management system (OODBMS). You expect the OODBMS to provide an initial hierarchy of classes and methods for handling generic operations on these classes. For example, the OODBMS should provide a method for iteration over a collection's members. You specify an OODB with a schema. Where a relational schema describes the application tables, an object-oriented schema describes the application classes and the methods. To illustrate the underlying concepts more completely, consider a more complicated aquarium example.

First, refer to the name and color attributes of species, tanks, and fish with the simple identifiers name and color instead of sname, tname, tcolor, fname, and fcolor. When you probe these attributes with attribute signals, the OODBMS chooses the appropriate method according to the polymorphism property. Second, assume the aquarium now contains two varieties of tanks: those used for carefully controlled scientific experiments and those used to display fish to the public. All tanks have name, color, volume, and population attributes, but scientific tanks have the additional attributes temperature and salinity, each expecting a numerical value. The display tanks have additional attributes lightingEffect and soundTrack, which hold strings describing the display atmosphere, such as blue subdued background and Theme from Seahunt. The aquarium also categorizes fish into two classes: experimental fish and display fish. All fish have attributes name, color, weight, home, breed, and experience. However, experimental fish also have the attribute examinations, a collection of events describing physical examinations of the fish. Display fish have no additional attributes. Experimental fish inhabit scientific tanks, and display fish inhabit display tanks.

Placing application classes in the native hierarchy

The following hierarchy organizes the database classes for the expanded aquarium application. The attributes appear in parentheses.

```
Object
    AquariumClass (creator, creationDate, modificationDate)
        Tank (name, color, volume, population)
            ScientificTank (temperature, salinity)
            DisplayTank (lightingEffect, soundTrack)
        Species (name, food, reps)
        Fish (name, color, weight, home, breed, experience)
            ExperimentalFish (examinations)
            DisplayFish
        Event (date, note, subject).
```

Objects created through a subclass inherit attributes from their ancestor classes and respond to the corresponding attribute signals. For example, assuming that you have created the aScientificTank object from the ScientificTank class, the code aScientificTank population delivers a collection of fish objects corresponding to the fish that inhabit the tank. The population attribute is inherited from the tank superclass.

A detailed schema for the aquarium database appears in Figures 7.12 and 7.13. In composing the schema, you first create subclasses to represent the application entities. You send the subclass:instanceVariables:constraint: signal to the root class, Object, to create the overall application class, AquariumClass. Attributes of AquariumClass are then inherited by all application objects: tanks, species, fish, events, and their subclass objects. You constrain these application-wide attributes to String, one of the OODBMS's built-in classes. You next define the applications classes as subclasses of AquariumClass. Each subclass provides the required attributes and constrains them to the proper values. The specification of ExperimentalFish not only adds an attribute, examinations, but also places a tighter constraint on the home attribute. An experimental fish's home must be a scientific tank, not just a general tank. Similar reasoning applies to the specialized classes DisplayFish, DisplayTank, and ScientificTank.

After specifying the application classes, you establish certain sets as subclasses of the built-in class Set. These classes accommodate the various collections that appear in the application objects' attributes. By placing them under Set in the hierarchy, you let them inherit all the convenient system methods for dealing with sets—a procedure for iterating over the members, for example. All application sets are placed under a superclass called AquariumSet, where you can conveniently concentrate methods that are applicable to all the various application collections. Figure 7.12 concludes by creating the global names (e.g. TheSpecies, TheTanks), each conceptually holding the entire database.

```
Object subclass:  "AquariumClass"
  instanceVariables:  ("creator", "creationDate", "modificationDate")
  constraints:  (("creator", String), ("creationDate", String),
       ("modificationDate", String)).
AquariumClass subclass:  "Species"
  instanceVariables:  ("name", "food", "reps")
  constraints:  (("name", String), ("food", String), ("reps", FishSet)).
AquariumClass subclass:  "Tank"
  instanceVariables:  ("name", "color", "volume", "population")
  constraints:  (("name", String), ("color", String), ("volume", Number),
    ("population", FishSet)).
Tank subclass:  "ScientificTank"
  instanceVariables:  ("temperature", "salinity")
  constraints:  (("temperature", Number), ("salinity", Number),
    (population, ExperimentalFishSet)).
Tank subclass:  "DisplayTank"
  instanceVariables:  ("lightingEffect", "soundTrack")
  constraints:  (("lightingEffect", String), ("soundTrack", String),
    ("population", DisplayFishSet)).
AquariumClass subclass:  "Fish"
  instanceVariables:  ("name", "color", "weight", "home", "breed", "experience")
  constraints:  (("name", String), ("color", String), ("weight", String),
    ("home", Tank), ("breed", Species), ("experience", EventSet).
Fish subclass:  "ExperimentalFish"
  instanceVariables:  ("examinations")
  constraints:  (("examinations", EventSet), ("home", ScientificTank)).
Fish subclass:  "DisplayFish"
  instanceVariables:  ()
  constraints:  (("home", DisplayTank)).
AquariumClass subclass:  "Event"
  instanceVariables:  ("date", "note", "subject")
  constraints:  (("date", DateTime), ("note", String), ("subject", Fish)).

Set subclass: "AquariumSet".  AquariumSet subclass:  "SpeciesSet" constraint:  Species.
AquariumSet subclass:  "TankSet" constraint:  Tank.
AquariumSet subclass:  "FishSet" constraint:  Fish.
AquariumSet subclass:  "EventSet" constraint:  Event.
FishSet subclass:  "ExperimentalFishSet" constraint:  ExperimentalFish.
FishSet subclass:  "DisplayFishSet" constraint:  DisplayFish.

TheSpecies := SpeciesSet new.
TheTanks := TankSet new.
TheFish := FishSet new.
TheEvents := EventSet new.
```

Figure 7.12   Object-oriented schema for the aquarium database

The collection of all objects belonging to a particular class is called the **extent** of the class. For example, TheSpecies, which contains all application species objects, is the extent of the species class. By iterating over this set, queries can systematically probe for related information. Each of these base collections is initially empty; you must add the member objects by sending the proper signals. A discussion of these topics follows shortly.

Attribute methods and error traps

Figure 7.13 provides a partial listing of the methods needed to handle the attribute signals. To establish a method, you send the method:code: signal to the class. The first parameter names the method and, consequently, its triggering signal. The second passes the code block that processes the signal. Each attribute requires two such methods: one to read the attribute and a second to write it from an external parameter. A method always executes on behalf of the target object that receives the triggering signal. During execution, the method code can directly access, by name, the target object's attributes. Therefore, each attribute method simply operates on its corresponding attribute. Methods can't access the attribute values of other objects by name. Instead, they must launch secondary attribute signals if they need such information.

 A method can directly access the target object's attributes by name, including any attributes inherited from ancestor classes. However, it must access other objects' attributes with secondary signals.

The AquariumClass provides an initialize method that is available to all application subclasses. It sets the creator attribute to the current user, a string solicited from the System object, and it sets the creationDate and modificationDate in a similar fashion. AquariumClass also includes the signalError: method for intercepting signals that are sent to inappropriate applications objects. Although this schema specifies the error handling mechanism, the OODBMS usually has built-in methods already available for this purpose.

You don't use the AquariumClass template directly to create objects. Instead, you generate objects through the subclasses (i.e., Species, Fish, Tank, and Event) and allow them to function as specialized AquariumClass objects through inheritance. A class that doesn't directly give rise to objects is called an **abstract** class. Most code in an abstract class deals with generalities common to all its subclasses. In the aquarium schema, for example, the error response method appropriately appears in the abstract superclass.

Instead of writing your own signalError: method, you can use the built-in method, subClassResponsibility. You need to revise those portions of Figure 7.13 that invoke signalError:, as suggested below. Of course, when an inappropriate signal is intercepted, some pre-established system message now appears rather than the user-specific choice associated with signalError.

```
AquariumClass method:  "name" code:  [^self subClassResponsibility].
AquariumClass method:  "color" code:  [^self subClassResponsibility].
AquariumClass method:  "weight" code:  [^self subClassResponsibility].
    ⋮
```

```
AquariumClass method:  "creator" code:  [^creator].
AquariumClass method:  "creator:" code:  [param | creator := param.  ^self].
AquariumClass method:  "creationDate" code:  [^creationDate].
AquariumClass method:  "creationDate:" code:  [param | creationDate := param.  ^self].
AquariumClass method:  "modificationDate" code:  [^modificationDate].
AquariumClass method:  "modificationDate:" code:  [param | modificationDate := param.  ^self].
AquariumClass method:  "initialize" code:  [
  creator:  (System user); creationDate:  (System today); modificationDate:  (System today).
  ^self].
AquariumClass method:  "signalError" code:  [param |
  "Signal " display.  param display.
  " not understood by object (" display.  self display.  ")" display.
  ^self].
AquariumClass method:  "name" code:  [^self signalError:  "name"].
AquariumClass method:  "color" code:  [^self signalError:  "color"].
    ⋮

Species method:  "name" code:  [^name].
Species method:  "name:" code:  [param | name := param.  ^self].
Species method:  "food" code:  [^food].
Species method:  "food:" code:  [param | food := param.  ^self].
Species method:  "reps" code:  [^reps].
Species method:  "reps:" code:  [param | reps := param.  ^self].

Tank method:  "name" code:  [^name].
Tank method:  "name:" code:  [param | name := param.  ^self].
Tank method:  "color" code:  [^color].
Tank method:  "color:" code:  [param | color := param.  ^self].
Tank method:  "volume" code:  [^volume].
Tank method:  "volume:" code:  [param | volume := param.  ^self].
Tank method:  "population" code:  [^population].
Tank method:  "population:" code:  [param | population := param.  ^self].
    ⋮
```

Figure 7.13   Partial listing of the standard attribute methods for the aquarium database

Creating the application objects

With the object-oriented schema in place, you now need to create application objects, place them in the appropriate collections, and ensure the proper cross-connections within the attributes. Because sets respond to the add: signal, you can populate the database as follows. You create a tank, cesspool, and establish its attributes; then you create a species, shark, and its attributes. Next, you repeatedly create fish, establish their attributes, and connect them to the cesspool tank and the shark species.

```
aTank := ScientificTank new.
aTank initialize; name:  "cesspool"; color:  "blue"; volume:  400; temperature:  30;
   salinity:  1.6; population:  (ExperimentalFishSet new).
TheTanks add:  aTank.
aSpecies := Species new.
aSpecies initialize; name:  "shark"; food:  "anything"; reps:  (FishSet new).
TheSpecies add:  aSpecies.
anExperimentalFish := ExperimentalFish new.
aTank population add:  anExperimentalFish.
aSpecies reps add:  anExperimentalFish.
anExperimentalFish initialize; name:  "charlie"; color:  "orange"; weight:  34; home:  aTank;
   breed:  aSpecies; experience:  (EventSet new); examinations:  (EventSet new).
TheFish add:  anExperimentalFish.
anExperimentalFish := ExperimentalFish new.
aTank population add:  anExperimentalFish.
aSpecies reps add:  anExperimentalFish.
anExperimentalFish initialize; name:  "killer"; color:  "white"; weight:  150; home:  aTank;
   breed:  aSpecies; experience:  (EventSet new); examinations:  (EventSet new).
TheFish add:  anExperimentalFish.
   ⋮
```

The syntax provides a convenient notation for sending a sequence of signals to the same object. Of course, if each signal returns the target object, you can accomplish the sequential transmission by accumulating the signatures to the right of the object, perhaps with parentheses if there is a conflict with the default precedence. However, if the signals don't return the target object, you can use a semicolon to separate a sequence of messages addressed to the same object. The code above uses this syntax. In general, the sequence $\{T\ s_1; s_2; s_3.\}$ is equivalent to $\{T\ s_1.\ T\ s_2.\ T\ s_3.\}$.

The code adds a each new fish to the population and reps attributes of the proper tank and species objects. It also sets the home and breed attributes of the fish. This constructs the logical inclusion links in both directions. A fish can look inside its home attribute to find its tank, and a tank can look inside its population attribute to find its fish.

Relationships

Binary relationships

Binary relationships appeared repeatedly in the previous section's examples. Species and their associated fish were one such relationship. In all cases, the relationship instances involved a mutual embedding. A species object contained its collection of representative fish; a fish object contained its classifying species. In general, if objects A and B are related, some attribute of A contains B and some attribute of B contains A. Because attribute values can be complex objects, the embedded object isn't represented with a key, as in the relational model. Instead, the object itself appears within its host. Moreover, the inclusion can be a collection because an attribute value can be any object. In particular, it can be a set. In the aquarium example, a fish contains its tank in its home attribute. Similarly, the tank contains its collection of fish in its population attribute. When you insert data into the database, you must be careful to establish the proper inclusions in both directions.

Because collections can serve as attribute values, you can directly represent many-to-many relationships in the object-oriented model. Factoring through a third entity, as required in the relational model, isn't necessary. However, in many cases the third entity should still be present, not because it is needed to model the relationship, but because it is an important application entity. For example, you can directly represent the many-to-many relationship between tanks and species without fish objects. You simply place the attribute speciesPresent in the tank class. For a given tank object, the attribute value is the collection of species represented in the tank. Similarly, you can place the attribute tanksUsed in the species class. The concept of fish, therefore, isn't necessary for a many-to-many relationship between tanks and species. However, the fish entity should be present in any case because it is an essential part of the aquarium application.

Chapter 2 explained a many-to-many relationship between boats and sailors. The investigation led to the discovery of a third entity, race, which mediated the relationship. This third entity isn't necessary to represent the many-to-many relationship in an object-oriented context. You can introduce a sailors attribute into the boat class and a boats attribute into the sailor class, each designed to hold the collection of related objects from the other class. Figure 7.14 illustrates this mutual containment. However, as in the aquarium application, you probably want to retain the race class because of its relevance in the yacht club application.

The need to distinguish among one-to-many, many-to-many, and one-to-one binary relationships is less pressing in the object-oriented model. You represent all in the same manner—with logical inclusion. They differ only in the nature of included attribute: sometimes it's a single object, and sometimes it's a set.

Higher-degree relationships

Consider again the higher-degree relationship, Ship-Cargo-Port, from Chapter 2. In that example, a triple, such as (Enterprise, Beans, Boston), constituted a meaningful grouping for the relationship. The earlier discussion used an auxiliary relation, called mission, to tabulate the triples. This new relation factored the ternary relationship into three one-to-many binary relationships. The analysis also showed that a collection of pairwise decompositions wasn't equivalent in meaning. Now, how is this relationship represented in the object-oriented model?

As a first approach, you can imitate the relational decomposition of Chapter 2 and introduce the mission entity. You then establish all four entities as classes. A mission contains three attributes, holding its ship, cargo, and port. Each of the other classes contains a collection of missions. This arrangement gives the standard mutual embedding associated with one-to-many relationships, and it is exactly parallel to the aquarium situation. A fish contains its tank and its species, and tank and species each contain a fish collection. Figure 7.15 shows the embeddings used in this representation of the ship-cargo-port relationship.

This approach is fine. It has the advantage of introducing the mission entity, which can then serve as a repository for additional information generated by a ship-cargo-port encounter. For example, you can record the mission date as an attribute. However, in the object-oriented model, you can avoid the extra entity altogether.

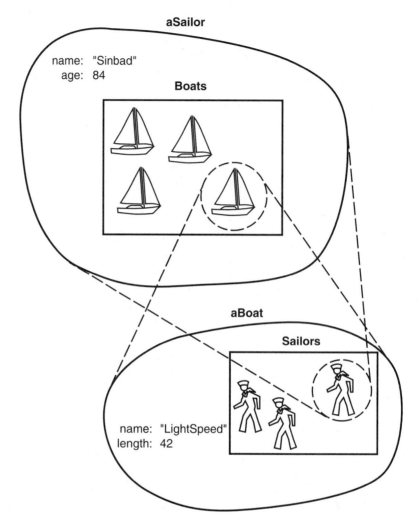

Figure 7.14   Direct many-to-many relationship between sailor and boat classes

Before giving the new solution, I'll dispense with one misleading possibility, which results in the same ambiguity as the attempted pairwise decomposition in Chapter 2. Suppose you include attributes cargo and ports in the ship class, each intended to hold the related collections of cargo and ports. Similarly, attributes ships and ports are included in the cargo class, and ships and cargo are included in the port class. Figure 7.16 shows these embeddings.

Recall the discussion of Chapter 2 where two different situations led to the same database structure, proving that the pairwise decomposition couldn't faithfully model the application. You can adapt this scenario to the object-oriented case. In particular, suppose the ship Enterprise has never carried beans to Boston. However, the Enterprise has carried

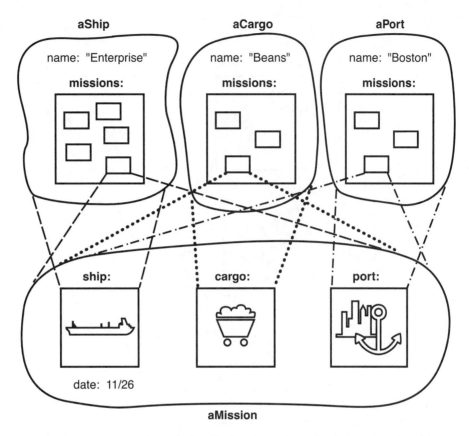

Figure 7.15 Representing a higher-degree relationship in the object-oriented model

beans somewhere, just not to Boston. So Enterprise appears in the ships collection of beans, and beans appears in the cargo collection of Enterprise. Also, some ship has carried beans to Boston, just not the Enterprise. So beans appears in the cargo collection of Boston, and Boston appears in the ports collection of beans. Finally, the Enterprise has delivered some cargo to Boston, just not beans. Therefore, Boston appears in the ports collection of Enterprise, and Enterprise appears in the ships collection of Boston. In other words, each of the objects—Enterprise, beans, and Boston—is related to the other two, just not through a single mission. As such, each already contains the other two in its appropriate attribute collections, and no additional entries appear if the mission (Enterprise, beans, Boston) is now undertaken. The database remains in exactly the same state. It can't distinguish between the situation where the (Enterprise, beans, Boston) grouping exists and the more circuitous situation where three groupings exist: (Enterprise, beans, · · ·), (Enterprise, · · ·, Boston), and (· · ·, beans, Boston). As in Chapter 2, the conclusion is that a collection of pairwise groupings can't accurately represent the ternary relationship.

However, you can embed ship-cargo *pairs* in a port object, and you can construct similar arrangements for the inclusions in ship and cargo. Then, in the example above, Boston

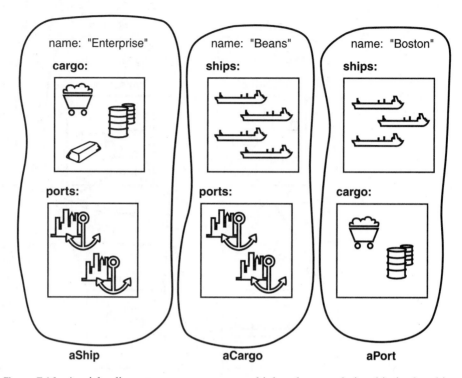

Figure 7.16: A misleading attempt to represent a higher-degree relationship in the object-oriented model

contains Enterprise-X and Y-beans pairs for the first scenario, but the pair Enterprise-beans appears only when the mission (Enterprise, beans, Boston) actually occurs. Therefore, the two situations can be distinguished. Ship-port pairs within a cargo object record the roundabout situation as Enterprise-X and Y-Boston pairs and the straightforward mission as Enterprise-Boston. Similarly, cargo-port pairs within ship distinguish between the two sets of circumstances.

But, to maintain a collection of pairs as an attribute value, you must first define the class from which the pairs are created. At this point, you encounter again the same pairwise decomposition. Ship-cargo pairs constitute precisely the shipment entity of Chapter 2, which mediates the many-to-many relationship between ship and cargo. Similarly, ship-port pairs correspond to the docking tuples of Chapter 2, and cargo-port pairs are arrivals. The object-oriented model, however, contains additional structure. A collection of ship-cargo pairs is embedded in a port object, which provides an additional many-to-many relationship between port and ship-cargo pairs (shipments). If you tabulate this last relationship, the (Enterprise, beans, Boston) mission appears as ((Enterprise, beans), Boston). By contrast, the circuitous situation appears as three tuples: ((X, beans), Boston), ((Enterprise, Y), Boston), and (Enterprise, beans), Z). The two scenarios are distinguishable. The Enterprise has indeed carried beans to Boston if and only if the pair ((Enterprise, beans), Boston) appears in the tabulation.

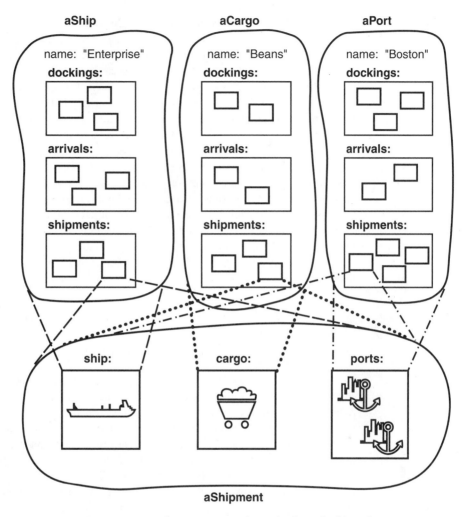

Figure 7.17 Accommodating a ternary relationship by embedding object pairs

A tabulation of pairs, one of whose components is already a pair, is the same as a tabulation of triples. So this solution doesn't actually avoid the triples; it simply disguises them as pairs by grouping the first two elements. In this form, you have another many-to-many binary relationship, which you already know how to represent. Therefore, the embedding of a collection of ship-cargo pairs (shipments) within a port object (and similar embeddings for the ship and cargo objects) amounts to the standard technique for avoiding an intersection entity when representing a many-to-many relationship. It just so happens that one of the entities is already a tabulation of pairs, which represents another many-to-many relationship. Figure 7.17 illustrates the inclusions, although only a shipment is selected for expansion.

In Figure 7.17, you see a shipment (a ship-cargo pair) extended to include a ports attribute as well. That extension occurs when you implement the relationship between port and shipment, which forces inclusions in both directions. Also, all the primary classes contain a collection of shipments. Ship and cargo certainly contain such collections to record the pairs in which they participate. Port must also contain a collection of shipments to represent the final many-to-many relationship derived above. Similar reasoning shows that ship, cargo, and port must each contain collections of the other pairings, arrivals and dockings. Therefore, to represent the ternary relationship in this approach properly, the solution introduces *three* new classes (shipment, arrival, and docking), corresponding to the three pairwise decompositions of Chapter 2. It then embeds three collections within each of the primary classes to preserve the illusion of triples masquerading as pairs. This approach is much more complex than the first considered, where the single mission class corresponded to the triplet tabulation of the relational solution.

Because the more complicated solution provides no advantages, the simpler approach is recommended. You should factor higher-degree relationships in the object-oriented model, which introduces a new entity (class). A number of one-to-many relationships result from the process, and you can implement them with standard attribute inclusions.

 You represent higher-degree relationships in the object-oriented model—just as in the relational model—by factoring them through an intersection class. The resulting collection of one-to-many relationships lends itself to standard attribute embeddings.

If you carefully examine the more complex solution of Figure 7.17, you find that the shipment objects are somewhat duplicated by the arrival and docking objects. Each is a roundabout representation of the auxiliary table of triples, which was needed in the relational model. Therefore, you can eliminate two of the three pairings although this reduction destroys the relationships' symmetry. Suppose you retain shipments and delete arrivals and dockings. All primary classes now contain collections of shipments. You determine all the missions related to port Boston as follows. You ask Boston to deliver its shipments. Each shipment contains a unique ship and cargo. When paired with Boston itself, this ship-cargo pair constitutes one triple to the answer. You can pursue a similar strategy to recover the missions associated with a cargo or a ship. This solution is biased toward the ship-cargo pairing, giving the impression that the shipment entity is more essential to the application than the arrival or docking entities. In terms of a relational decomposition, this last approach appears as Figure 7.18.

In summary, the object-oriented model offers several techniques for representing higher-degree relationships. Although the prose descriptions are somewhat complicated, the diagrams quickly reveal that all share the common goal of recording *triples* of objects that participate in the relationship. The least complicated and most symmetric solution creates a new class, which then enters into many-to-one relationships with each of the original classes. You can easily handle these many-to-one relationships with the standard logical inclusion technique.

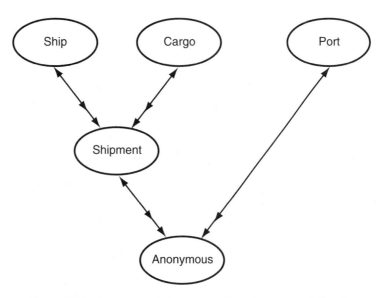

Figure 7.18 An asymmetrical decomposition of a ternary relationship

Recursive relationships

Recursive relationships present no difficulty in the object-oriented model because you can embed an object in itself by using its OID. The employee example in Chapter 2 provided an example of a recursive one-to-many relationship. Each employee had at most one supervisor. A supervisor, also an employee, could manage many workers. The tree of employees under a given supervisor had no cycles. You can transfer the example to the object-oriented context by organizing the Employee class as shown in Figure 7.19. Each employee object contains a set of subordinate employees.

Chapter 2 also examined a many-to-many recursive relationship, which involved assemblies and their subcomponents. The basic entity was a part, a manufactured item. In the role of an assembly, a given part contained many other parts. In the role of a component, a given part contributed to many assemblies. The relational solution offered the traditional factoring of the many-to-many relationship through a third entity, quantity. Translating to the object-oriented model, you find that the quantity entity isn't necessary, although it could still be useful for storing the number of times a given subpart appears in an assembly. A part now simply contains two collections of parts as attributes. One collection holds those parts (assemblies) to which it contributes; the other holds those parts (components) that it comprises. Therefore, the structure of Figure 7.20 is sufficient to maintain the relationship.

 You represent recursive binary relationships in the object-oriented model in the standard manner through mutual inclusions.

The earlier discussion of recursive relationships led to certain queries that neither SQL nor its mathematical counterparts (relational algebra and calculus) could express. These

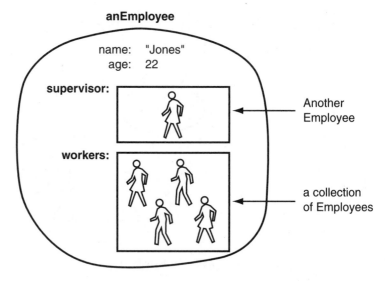

Figure 7.19   A one-to-many recursive relationship in the object-oriented model

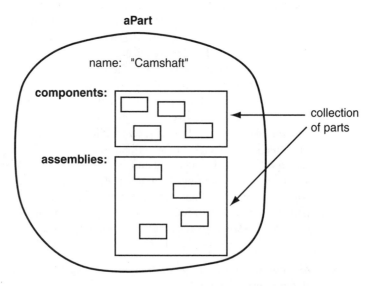

Figure 7.20   A many-to-many recursive relationship in the object-oriented model

queries involve iterations where the number of cycles is a function of the data. For example, find all the employees that report to employee Jones at any level of indirection. Or find the hierarchy of parts needed to construct a Camshaft. Because SQL lacks the equivalent of a while-loop, it isn't computationally complete. You can use embedded SQL for these queries because you can use the looping capabilities of the host language. But as you will see in the next chapter, the query syntax for the object-oriented model is procedural, and it is complete. Therefore, you can solve these troublesome queries with the signaling mechanisms of object-oriented database systems.

Constraints

General constraints: domain, key, entity integrity, and referential integrity

The object-oriented schema definition has already introduced certain constraints. As the schema defined each class, it restricted the instance variables to values from specified classes. If the constraint class was a collection, an additional clause constrained the membership. Therefore, an object-oriented schema directly incorporates the equivalent of relational domain constraints.

The structure of the object-oriented model automatically enforces key constraints, entity integrity constraints, and referential integrity constraints. In the relational model, a key constraint forces a table's tuples to have unique values under an attribute or a group of attributes. Such a constraint is necessary so that the attribute value can represent a unique tuple in relationships with other tables. In the object-oriented model, each object has a unique OID, which is generated and maintained by the system. It is guaranteed to be unique across the entire database. Therefore, this OID can serve on any occasion where unique representation of an object is needed.

In the relational model, the entity integrity constraint insists that key attributes not have null values. Given the representative role of the key attribute, a null key prevents a tuple from participating in relationships. In a manner of speaking, the real-world instance corresponding to that tuple is lost in the database. There is always the chance that all other attribute values might be duplicated in other tuples, which would make it impossible to identify the tuple in question. The reason for insisting on nonnull keys in the relational context is that the key value is a "handle" for a tuple. Without a handle, you can't address the tuple as a single unit. In the object-oriented model, with the OID assuming the handle function, the concept of a null key doesn't arise. An OID is never null. Entity integrity, therefore, is always preserved.

Finally, referential integrity enforces a constraint on a foreign key in the relational model. Either the value is null, or it refers to an existing primary key value in the referenced table. In the object-oriented model, a related object is conceptually embedded in its host. If it's there, it's an existing object. In truth, its OID appears in a host attribute, but the same argument holds. If an OID is there, it refers to an existing object. The system doesn't permit dangling OIDs. It carefully tracks all references to an object and prevents deletion while any references exist.

The object-oriented structure automatically enforces the more generally applicable relational constraints: domain, key, entity integrity, and referential integrity.

Functional dependency constraints

Although the properties of the OID handle the structural constraints (i.e., key, entity integrity, referential integrity), they don't automatically enforce functional dependencies. For example, the aquarium application has the functional dependency (FD) constraint: volume $\longrightarrow$ color. Recall that the FD, $X \longrightarrow Y$, restricts any relation containing X and Y, such that two tuples with identical X values must also have identical Y values. In this case, volume $\longrightarrow$ color means that two tank tuples with the same volume must have the same color. To enforce this FD in the object-oriented model, you must incorporate the appropriate checks into the attribute methods that modify the volume and color values.

Suppose a tank object receives the signal volume: 300. The attribute method specified in the schema (Figure 7.13) simply assigns the value 300 to the volume attribute and returns the tank object. If there is a second tank object with a volume of 300 and a different color, the FD is violated. To prevent this violation, you must modify the method that handles the volume attribute signal. You first launch a query to determine if conflicting objects exist. If they do, you abort the volume attribute assignment and initiate error feedback. The revised method takes the following form:

```
Tank method: "volume:" code: [newVolume |
  |tmp|
  tmp := TheTanks select: [aTank |
    (aTank == self) not & (aTank volume = newVolume) & (aTank color = color) not].
  tmp isEmpty
    ifTrue:  [volume := newVolume]
    ifFalse: [self FDviolation: "volume determines color"].
  ^self].
```

A one-parameter block specifies the code for processing the volume: signal, just as in the simple attribute method of Figure 7.13. However, instead of assigning the parameter to the volume attribute, the new method first queries for the existence of other tanks. The vertical bars at the beginning of the code introduce a temporary variable. The code sends a select: signal to TheTanks, which holds all tanks in the database. The parameter passed with the signal is a one-parameter code block that executes once for each element of the target set. In other words, each tank in the database is sequentially bound to the dummy parameter, aTank. As aTank ranges over the tanks in TheTanks, a boolean is constructed for each one. All the tanks with a true boolean are collected into a new set, which is returned value of the select: signal. Therefore, tmp contains a tank collection. Each tank in tmp (1) is not equal to the target tank (the one whose volume is under tentative modification), (2) has a volume value equal to newValue, and (3) differs from the target tank in the color attribute. So tmp contains the collection of tanks that would conflict with the target tank after assignment of the newVolume value. The collection tmp is sent the isEmpty signal, to which it responds with a boolean: true if empty, false if not. If tmp is indeed empty, the newVolume assignment can be made without fear of a violation. However, if tmp isn't empty, the assignment isn't made, and a signal FDviolation: is sent to the target tank. This signal is handled by the superclass, AquariumClass, in the same spirit as the signalError: method discussed earlier.

Besides using the binary signals for strong and weak equality, this example uses the signals not and ifTrue:ifFalse:. A boolean responds to the not signal by returning its complement. A boolean responds to the ifTrue:ifFalse signal by executing one of the parameters (both are code blocks), depending on the true or false nature of the target boolean.

To completely enforce the functional dependency, you must also provide a new color: method. The corresponding code segment is similar to the new volume: method. The point is that you can instrument the objects to launch arbitrary information-gathering expeditions before modifying their attributes. In this way, you can check any application constraints for possible violations before committing the database change.

Triggers for more general constraints

Suppose the aquarium application limits the number of tanks to 50. An earlier discussion illustrated how to insert objects into the database. The example created a tank named cesspool and placed it in TheTanks, the global set containing all database tanks. The add: signal was then used to put the new tank into TheTanks. Since TheTanks is an instance of the class TankSet, it is automatically an instance of the system superclass Set, where the add: signal is available. You can intercept the add: signal at the TankSet level by redefining it there. As the signal travels up the hierarchy looking for a matching method, it passes through the application class TankSet before reaching the system class Set. Therefore, if an add: method is available there, it will be used. You can then implement the desired constraint as follows. The solution contains certain deficiencies, which I'll discuss later, but for the moment, it introduces the concept with a minimum of complications.

```
TankSet method:  "add:" code:  [newTank |
   (self includes:  newTank) | (self size < 50)
     ifTrue: [super add:  newTank]
     ifFalse: [self constraintViolation:  "Tank collection is of maximum size"].
   ^self].
```

Now consider an add: signal dispatched to TheTanks. If the new tank is already a member of TheTanks, as ascertained by the includes: signal directed to self (TheTanks), or if the collection's current size is less than 50, no violation will occur upon adding the new tank. In this case, the OODBMS adds the newTank by redirecting the add: signal up the hierarchy with the "super" variable.

The super variable is similar to the self variable. Both stand for the object that received the signal that invoked the method. However, a signal sent to self begins the search for a matching method in the target object's class; a signal sent to super begins in the next higher superclass. In the example, the target object is a TankSet. When it receives an add: aTank signal, it invokes the method above, binding the dummy parameter, newTank, to the actual parameter, aTank. Assuming the current size of TheTanks is less than 50, add: aTank is dispatched to super, that is, to the original TankSet on behalf of which the method is executing. The OODBMS suspends the current method until a completion object returns from the super add: aTank operation. Because super stands for the original TankSet, that object receives the signal, but it doesn't search for the matching method among the methods of its immediate class, TankSet. If it did, it would invoke the suspended method anew, which would lead to an infinite loop. Instead, it starts the search among the methods of the immediate superclass of TankSet, namely AquariumSet. Not finding a matching signature there, the search continues in the system superclasses, Set, Bag, Collection, ..., until the default method is found.

Therefore, you can bypass an interception by the current method if you send a signal to super. The application-specific method, add:, is first intercepted in the TankSet class, where a constraint check is evaluated. If no violation is detected, you'll wish you hadn't intercepted the signal because the default behavior would have been satisfactory. Dispatching a new add: signal to super invokes the required default behavior.

In a manner of speaking, you can say that the add: signal triggers a constraint check, which results in some variation in the default behavior. This mechanism is similar to relational database triggers, discussed in Chapter 6. The following excerpt, for example, appeared in the schema description of the fish table. It uses the enhanced SQL facilities of Chapter 6.

```
create table fish (
        ⋮
    foreign key (tno) references tank (tno)
        on delete set null
        on update cascade,
    foreign key (sno) references species (sno)
        on delete cascade
        on update cascade
        ⋮
```

The on-delete and on-update clauses act as triggers that launch compensatory activity when referential integrity is challenged. In this case, the DBMS sets the tno foreign key to null if the referenced tank is deleted. It also deletes any fish associated with a deleted species. You can implement these triggers in the object-oriented model by intercepting certain signals. The following discussion illustrates this process by showing how to enforce the equivalent of the "on delete set null" constraint between tanks and their fish.

You delete a tank from the database by removing it from the global set TheTanks. For example, suppose you want to delete all tanks named cesspool. You first gather the collection of cesspool tanks into a new set with the select: signal. You then use the removeAllPresent: signal to remove these selected tanks from the global collection. The code appears as follows.

```
| tanksToDelete |
tanksToDelete := TheTanks select:  [aTank | aTank name = "cesspool"].
tanksToDelete do:  [aTank | aTank population do:  [aFish | aFish home:  null] ].
TheTanks removeAllPresent:  tanksToDelete.
```

The temporary variable tanksToDelete holds the collection of cesspool tanks. However, before removing them from the global collection, TheTanks, you probe each tank with a code segment that adjusts the home attribute of the affected fish to null. You perform this iteration by sending the do: signal to the tanksToDelete set. The signal carries a one-parameter code block, which the OODBMS executes once for each member of the target set. During that execution the selected member is represented by the dummy variable, aTank. You retrieve aTank's population collection with the population signal and then probe the returned fish set with another do: signal, which writes null into each home attribute.

Variables, such as TheTanks, are called global variables because they aren't instance variables in any class. The global variables provide the ultimate external handles for the database. The global identifier, TheTanks, contains a collection of tanks. The tanks, in turn, contain references to fish objects. The fish objects contain references to species objects, which, in turn, reference additional fish objects, more tank and species objects, and so forth. Any OID that can't be reached by a path from a global variable is considered inessential and is automatically scavenged from the system by a background "garbage collector."

You can modify the code above to remove the selected cesspool tanks from TheTanks without first adjusting the home attributes of the affected fish. However, you can still reach the deleted tanks indirectly. Starting with TheFish, you can reach the various fish associated with the cesspool tanks, and you can then reach the tanks themselves by using the home attributes of these fish. Therefore, although the OODBMS would remove the cesspool tanks from TheTanks, it would leave them in the database because of their indirect links to the global object, TheFish.

However, if you first nullify the home attributes of the affected fish, removing the tanks from TheTanks is fatal. No attributes of any objects contain the targeted tanks. Therefore, shortly after their removal from TheTanks, the OODBMS permanently disposes of the tanks and reclaims their storage for other uses.

Sharpening a constraint's focus

Certain problems arise with the some of the constraint solutions developed so far. Because the FD volume $\longrightarrow$ color is enforced directly within the attribute methods for volume and color, it is invoked only when the FD is threatened. The other solutions, however, are more remote from the attribute methods, and they may interfere in situations where the constraint isn't an issue.

A previous example implemented a constraint in the TankSet class to limit the number of tanks to 50. The intent was to prevent a specific object, TheTanks, from exceeding size 50. However, the implementation applied to all TankSet objects, not just TheTanks. Other collections of tanks exist in the model, including, for example, the tanksToDelete in the deletion code above. In this case, the constraint check doesn't interfere because tanksToDelete is a subset of TheTanks. It can't, therefore, be larger than the full set of tanks in the database. In general, however, the OODBMS shouldn't invoke a constraint check where it isn't applicable because it could lead to interference with the legitimate activities of unrelated objects.

The problem is that the constraint implementation is too broad. It's meant to apply to one object, but because methods must be installed in a class, it actually affects all objects of that class. One solution is to create a separate class for the TheTanks object, the only object in the class, and put the constraint code there. You modify the hierarchy related to sets as follows. The new or modified entries are marked with an asterisk. The new subclass, TankHandle, is a subclass of TankSet, and consequently its members are already constrained to be tank objects. You then initialize the global identifier, TheTanks, as a TankHandle object, which again serves as an external handle to the database. You relocate the constraint code to the TankHandle class, as shown after the modified classes. Other TankSet collections now respond to the add: signal by searching for the matching method above the TankHandle class, thereby avoiding this code segment. Only an add: directed to TheTanks invokes the constraint code.

```
  Set subclass:  "AquariumSet".                    TheSpecies := SpeciesSet new.
  AquariumSet subclass:  "SpeciesSet"           *  TheTanks := TankHandle new.
    constraints:  Species.                         TheFish := FishSet new.
  AquariumSet subclass:  "TankSet"                 TheEvents := EventSet new.
    constraint:  Tank.
* TankSet subclass:  "TankHandle".
  AquariumSet subclass:  "FishSet"
    constraint:  Fish.
  AquariumSet subclass:  "EventSet"
    constraint:  Event.
  FishSet subclass:  "ExperimentalFishSet"
    constraint:  ExperimentalFish.
  FishSet subclass:  "DisplayFishSet"
    constraint:  DisplayFish.

TankHandle method:  "add:" code:  [newTank |
   (self includes:  newTank) | (self size < 50)
     ifTrue:  [super add:  newTank]
     ifFalse:  [self constraintViolation:  "Tank collection is of maximum size"].
   ^self].
```

A second solution doesn't create a separate class for TheTanks and leaves the constraint code in the TankSet class. However, it checks the identity of the target collection before interfering with the add: signal. The revised constraint code for this solution is as follows:

```
TankSet method:  "add:" code:  [newTank |
   (self == TheTanks) not | (self includes:  newTank) | (self size < 50)
     ifTrue:  [super add:  newTank]
     ifFalse:  [self constraintViolation:  "Tank collection is of maximum size"].
   ^self].
```

This second solution isn't very attractive because it burdens a general method with a special case. One of the arguments for concentrating methods in the class definition is that all class objects should exhibit generically similar behavior in response to a given signal. So the second solution violates the spirit of the class. Therefore, the first solution is preferable.

Assuming you have adopted the first solution, you now have a special subclass, TankHandle, holding the single object, TheTanks. This special subclass turns out to have other uses, beyond constraints on the database tanks. In particular, reconsider the constraint that emulated the on-delete clause from the relational schema. The idea is to adjust the home attribute of a fish object to null when its home tank is deleted. The previous solution involved a check within the deletion operation to perform this operation, but the code didn't exist within a class. Although it should be, such external code isn't part of the database proper. The responsibility for maintaining integrity across a delete operation should rest with the stored methods of the database, not with external code that probes the database. Methods are indeed part of the database, but user code segments are external agents commanding certain database activities. To remain faithful to the spirit of the on-delete clause, the mechanism should be part of the database itself.

You can integrate the special referential integrity checks into the database by controlling access to TheTanks in a special manner. Because this handle now resides in a special subclass, you can easily intercept all methods that modify TheTanks. The earlier analysis showed how to intercept the add: signal to maintain a constraint on the number of tanks in the database. To protect a referential-integrity constraint, you can also intercept other signals, such as the removeAllPresent: used to delete tanks.

Assume that all signals that change the contents of TheTanks have been redefined in the special subclass TankHandle to simply return an error indication. Assume also that the add: signal functions to ensure that the tank collection doesn't exceed 50 tanks. Now you can redefine the removeAllPresent: method as follows, where the parameter carries the tank set to be deleted from TheTanks.

```
TankHandle method:  "removeAllPresent:" code:  [aTankSet |
   aTankSet do:  [aTank | aTank population do:  [aFish | aFish home:  null] ].
   ^super removeAllPresent:  aTankSet
   ].
```

Now any user can remove tanks with the removeAllPresent signal as follows. The detachment of the affected fish occurs automatically. Because signals that don't change the content of TheTanks aren't intercepted, the select: signal behaves as previously described.

```
TheTanks removeAllPresent:  (TheTanks select:  [aTank | aTank name = "cesspool"]).
```

Possible breach of object encapsulation with the read attribute signal

As a final example of object manipulation subtleties, recall the earlier discussion about attribute returns that can breach encapsulation. Remember your car with the vulnerable front bumper. In the aquarium example, the analysis noted that you can change the population of a tank without invoking the population: attribute signal. For example, you can add aFish to the population collection of aTank with the following code:

```
aTank population add:  aFish.
```

The read attribute signal population returns the collection of fish objects associated with aTank. The add: signal places aFish in that collection without any mention of the write attribute signal population:. Therefore, you encounter difficulties enforcing constraints such as "blue tanks must not contain more than 10 fish." You don't want to monitor the add: signal in the FishSet class because that would constrain all FishSet objects. Instead you would like to prevent an overly large FishSet object from occupying the population attribute of a blue tank.

The problem lies in the default behavior of the read attribute signal `population`. That signal submits the collection to an external agent. This removes control from the tank object, which could respond to constraint threats, and delivers control to the FishSet object, where a constraint would apply too broadly. You can, however, redefine the `population` method to deliver a *copy* of the fish collection. The external agent can change that copy in an uncontrolled manner, but to reestablish the altered copy as the tank's population value, it must use the `population:` signal. At that point, the constraint can be checked. The attribute methods then appear as follows:

```
Tank method:  "population" code:  [
  |populationCopy|
  populationCopy := FishSet new.
  population do:  [aFish | populationCopy add:  aFish].
  ^populationCopy].
Tank method:  "population:" code:  [newPopulation |
  (color = "blue") & (newPopulation size > 10)
    ifTrue:  [self constraintViolation:  "blue tanks limited to 10 fish"]
    ifFalse:  [population := newPopulation].
  ^self].
```

The general technique of exporting a copy of an attribute allows a subsequent check on any attempt to reinstall the attribute in an altered state. The decision to export attribute values in this protected manner rests with the application. Any constraints that require close monitoring of modifications may require close control of attribute values. In this case, you should consider exporting copies. This approach does, however, involve an added burden because you must now remember to reinstall modified attribute values.

One final path remains that can circumvent the constraint enforcement coded above. You can change the tank color to red and then continually add fish to its population collection until you exceed the 10 fish limit. You can do this because the prevention mechanism isn't invoked on red tanks. After you have established the large fish collection, you return the tank color to blue. This is a general problem that arises when the values of two attributes must be coordinated. Another example was the volume $\longrightarrow$ color functional dependency, where you had to adjust both the `volume:` and the `color:` methods to properly enforce the constraint. The solution in the present case follows the same pattern. You modify the `color:` method to prevent a color change to blue if the population size is too large:

```
Tank method:  "color:" code:  [newColor |
  (newColor = "blue") & (population size > 10)
    ifTrue:  [self constraintViolation:  "blue tanks limited to 10 fish"]
    ifFalse:  [color := newColor].
  ^self].
```

The examples in this section have occasionally set an attribute value to null. As more complicated methods are developed, continually checking an attribute's nullity before sending it a signal becomes inconvenient. In this chapter and the next, assume that null responds appropriately to signals so that continued processing isn't affected. For example, if the null object receives the `select:` signal, it returns an empty set. If it receives a `do:` signal, it performs no processing and returns null. If it receives an arithmetic signal, it returns null. Finally, if the null object receives a comparison signal, it returns false. This default behavior simplifies certain methods in the exercises for this section and in the next chapter.

Comparison of object-oriented and relational databases

The relational model represents application entities as tables and entity instances as rows (tuples). In the aquarium example, the application fish entity corresponds to a fish table in the database. Instances of the fish entity are the actual fish, each represented by a row in the fish table. In the object-oriented model, the application entities become classes in the database, and entity instances are objects in the appropriate class. In the aquarium example, fish objects are created from the fish class.

The relational table specifies the structure of its constituent tuples with its column headings. The values under a given attribute are restricted to some predefined domain, usually one of the traditional types: number, string, currency, date, or time. Recent relational implementations have broadened this selection somewhat, allowing bitmap images and formatted documents, for example, to be stored in a table cell. However, even with these extensions, the DBMS treats a cell's data element as an atomic unit. For instance, a relational database might store bitmap images, but it can't use their internal structure for building relationships. Instead, the bitmap must be used as a complete unit, for example, by displaying it on the output screen. You can't compose a query requesting all tuples where the bitmap contains a triangle.

Consider a simple composite structure: an address with a street number and name, a city, a state, and a zip code. The relational models flattens this structure so that each components appears separately among the table attributes. Strict adherence to the relational model requires that the table cells contain only atomic attributes, devoid of internal structure from the application viewpoint. By contrast, most programming languages provide composite structures (e.g., the C struct) as a strong feature for organizing data representations within a program. Therefore, even at its inception, the relational model was at odds with the prevailing trend in programming languages. However, the highly decomposed nature of relational tables, which contributing to the simplicity of the model and to the consequent easy construction of database applications, was proclaimed a desirable feature.

Beyond disassembling natural application structures, such as the address noted above, the relational model further decomposes entities by distributing their components across several tables. This process, termed *normalization*, will be discussed in detail later. Normalization addresses legitimate design goals, which arise from an analysis of the given application. For example, in a complex application the boundaries between entities may not be intuitively obvious. If you have only fish, tanks, and species, you can trust your intuition to distinguish them. But suppose that you are dealing with hundreds of attributes, attempting to group them into robust tables. Suppose the application is a factory, and you confront the question of the light fixtures in each room. Are these fixtures attributes of the room? Perhaps they belong to the building because the lighting remains fixed while moveable walls can be readjusted? Perhaps they belong to the electrical system? Or perhaps they constitute an independent entity with relationships to these other items? The normalization process helps the designer cope with these questions, but the result is a dispersal of application components across many tables. Any reassembly is performed as needed through join operations on common attributes.

The normalization process also addresses general concerns about storage economy and reduced risk of inconsistent representation. The general rule is: store a value in a single location and refer to it as needed through the system of foreign keys. Unfortunately, the application then sees the dispersed representation. In the aquarium example, the real tank contains its fish on a continuing basis while the model must reacquire its fish through a join process each time they are referenced.

The object-oriented model takes the opposing view that such dispersal of application objects isn't helpful, particularly in complex situations. With a dispersed view, both the designer and the eventual user must remain aware of the dispersed state and command proper reassembly when needed. The argument isn't that a dispersed storage scheme should be abandoned. Instead, it is that the user shouldn't have to deal with its inconveniences.

Breaking with the relational tradition, the object-oriented model allows objects to contain complex attributes. In other words, the attribute value can have arbitrarily complicated internal structure. An attribute value can be a collection, for example, which is in sharp contrast with the relational restriction to a single atomic value. Moreover, an attribute value can be another complex object or even a collection of objects. Thus, an object contains within itself, at some level of recursion, all the other database objects to which it is related. The mechanism for maintaining relationships is logical inclusion rather than matching common attributes. An actual implementation embeds objects by reference, using the OIDs. A search for a related object, therefore, follows the chain of OIDs, just as it follows foreign key links in the relational model. However, the user doesn't need to know this implementation detail. The concept of logical inclusion is sufficient to proceed from an object to related objects without dealing with the actual links.

 In contrast with the relational model, the object-oriented approach allows complex attributes, leading to a more natural representation of the application. The mechanism for maintaining relationships then becomes logical inclusion, which locates related objects within the host object at some level of recursion.

Beyond the representation issue, the object-oriented model takes a more active view of its objects. Apart from certain minor extensions with database triggers, a relational database is a passive collection of organized data elements and relationships. External agents probe the database with SQL queries. By contrast, an object-oriented database captures the data elements, their relationships, and their behavior. The behavior of each object is specified through methods, which respond to signals from other objects and from the user interface. The simplest use of such signals is to retrieve and modify attribute values, but you can also use them for more complex purposes, such as constraint enforcement. The system of objects and signals is closed in the sense that an object receiving a signal provides another object as a return value. Therefore, you can compose objects and signals into lengthy expressions, which control complex data manipulation tasks. Proponents of the object-oriented methodology argue that people are accustomed to viewing their world as a collection of cooperating agents (i.e., objects) exchanging communications (i.e., signals). It is natural and intuitive to model an application in this manner.

Whereas a relational database is a passive collection of data elements, an object-oriented database contains the data elements, their relationships, and their behavior. Behavior is described with methods, which are code segments that enable objects to respond to signals.

Unlike the tables of the relational model, classes in an OODB exist in a hierarchy. Designers can insert their application classes in an existing system hierarchy. An object created through a class contains not only the attributes and methods defined in that class but also the attributes and methods of its superclasses. This mechanism allows you to define new classes incrementally. The new class specifies only how it extends its immediate parent class. The aquarium example exploited this feature to specialize the classes of ScientificTank and DisplayTank as subclasses of the existing tank class. Only the new attributes and methods particular to the subclasses needed definition. The inherited properties of the tank class provided most of the behavior of the subclass objects.

The relational model can accommodate such specializations, but many of the advantages are lost. Suppose you want to represent the extended aquarium schema of Figure 7.12 in the relational model. As a first approach, you can maintain separate tables for the two kinds of tanks, and likewise for the two kinds of fish. Such an arrangement appears in Figure 7.21. Many of the attribute names in ScientificTank are duplicated in DisplayTank, but there is no duplication of actual tuples because a tank is either in one category or the other. However, simple queries become complicated by the unnatural breakup of tanks and fish. Suppose you want the names of tanks with volume greater than 400. You must query two tables, and the SQL becomes a union of two simpler queries. Moreover, a more complex aquarium might contain ten different kinds of tanks.

A second approach retains some of the flavor of the hierarchical arrangement by adding category tables above the specialized variants of Tank and Fish, as shown in Figure 7.22. The table TankCategory contains only two tuples, "scientific" and "display." The actual tanks contain a foreign key that refers to the appropriate category. The foreign key serves as a flag field, marking a tank as belonging to one of the two categories. The fish categories use a similar arrangement. The queries that troubled the previous solution now revert to their simpler form. However, the constraint that an experimental fish must inhabit a scientific tank is more difficult to enforce. It is no longer sufficient to indicate a foreign key constraint, forcing the tank reference in fish to point to an existing tank tuple. Instead, it must point to an existing tank tuple with a particular category flag.

Although both solutions recover some of the characteristics of the aquarium of Figure 7.12, they don't provide the richness of the complete hierarchy. In the object-oriented model, for example, every application object can obtain a printable version of itself, suitable for output display, because application objects are specializations, at some level, of the root system class Object. The ability to respond to a display message is inherited from the system Object.

Beyond a fundamentally different view of data elements and relationships, the object-oriented model is enriched by a variety of concepts adopted from object-oriented programming languages. These features include encapsulation of behavior through signals and methods and the incorporation of application classes into an existing system hierarchy. The relational model has no equivalent features.

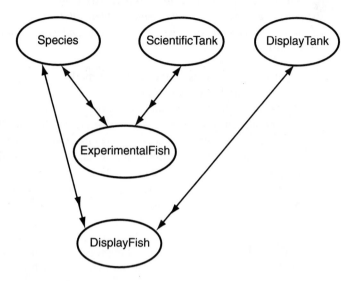

Figure 7.21 A relational organization to handle specialized tanks and fish

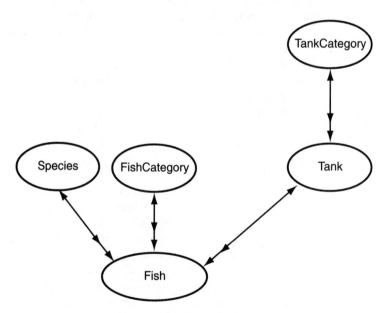

Figure 7.22 An alternative relational approach to specialized classes

The relational model has no equivalents of the object-oriented concepts: inheritance, encapsulation, polymorphism, and complex attributes.

SUMMARY

Object-oriented modeling refers to a particular software design methodology, which views an application as a collection of interacting objects. The general philosophy is applicable to many areas, such as databases, operating systems, and programming languages. The primary features of the object-oriented approach are:

- Data elements are encapsulated into objects that interact with each other and with the user through the exchange of messages. Each object has a unique identity, implemented as a system-generated object identifier (OID), which remains constant regardless of changes to the object attribute values.

- Objects are created from class templates. All objects created from a given class contain the same set of attributes and respond to the same signals. Of course, objects of the same class can have different attribute values, so the specific responses to signals can vary. Attribute values are themselves complex objects or collections of objects.

- A method is a code segment, resident in a class, that processes matching signals directed to objects of the class.

- The classes are arranged in a hierarchy such that objects of a given class are also indirectly members of its superclasses. An object is endowed with the attributes of its class, and it inherits the attributes of all its superclasses. A name conflict, however, can hide an inherited property.

- An object also inherits additional methods from its superclasses. Therefore, an object can respond to certain signals even though its class doesn't possess a matching method. When an object receives a signal, it searches for the matching method, starting with the methods of the object's class. If this search fails, it considers methods of its parent superclass. This pattern continues up the hierarchy into the various system classes, finally terminating at the predefined Object class.

- The same signal can elicit different behavior from different objects. In a particular expression, an identifier is bound to an object as a result of some preceding code execution. At compile-time, some identifiers can be associated with a class, but others can't. In the latter case, only at run-time, when the object receives a signal, is the identifier's class known. The method actually invoked depends on the class, and perhaps the superclasses, of the target object, and it can involve different processing when directed to objects of different classes. This flexible treatment of signals is called polymorphism.

Applied to databases, these features allow you to model the application entities as classes and entity instances as objects belonging to the classes. The ability to use complex-valued attributes allows objects to contain related objects, which in turn contain more distantly related objects. The concept of logical inclusion describes this technique of maintaining relationships. Although an actual implementation uses OIDs to maintain the illusion of endless recursion, the user doesn't need to be concerned with that level of detail. From a user perspective, an object contains, at some level of recursion, all other objects that are related to it.

An object-oriented database is simply a database that uses object-oriented concepts to provide additional structure. It provides a uniform interface with a system of signals and their corresponding methods. The object-oriented model easily accommodates binary relationships with logical inclusion and without the need for intersection entities, as required by the relational model in the case of many-to-many relationships. The object-oriented model expresses higher-degree relationships by creating the intersection entity as described in Chapter 2 and then providing mutual inclusions between the intersection and the original relationship participants. Recursive relationships introduce no particular difficulty.

Certain generic constraints that are crucial in all relational applications are the domain, key, entity integrity, and referential integrity constraints. The object-oriented model handles domain constraints in a similar manner: the schema specifies the kind of object that can fill an attribute slot. The other generic constraints are automatically enforced by the model's structure. Key attributes are unnecessary because a system-generated OID serves in that capacity. Consequently, no questions arise as to a key's nullity or to its possible reference to a nonexistent object.

Constraints that arise from the application, however, must be handled by modifying the methods that access attributes. Usually the modification involves a query to determine if a constraint will be violated before changing an attribute value. These checks bear some resemblance to the database triggers of Chapter 6, and they can be used, for example, to imitate an on-delete clause in a relational schema.

When compared with the relational model, the object-oriented model proves to be the stronger modeling tool. Where the relational model restricts attributes to atomic values, frequently of the traditional data types (string, number, and the like), the object-oriented model allows complex object values and even collections of such objects. Where a relational database is a passive collection of organized data, an object-oriented database stores behavior patterns with the data. The relational model disperses the components of an application object across several tables and depends on join operations to reconstruct the pieces when necessary. By contrast, the object-oriented model collects all the components necessary to faithfully represent an application object into a single software object and uses logical inclusion to handle potentially complex components.■

Informal illustration of an object-oriented database

Refer to the aquarium database of Figures 7.4 and 7.6. Without attempting a systematic approach to information retrieval, obtain answers to the following queries by manually coordinating the objects in the figures.

1. Find the names of blue fish.

2. Find the names of species represented by a blue fish.

3. Find the names of species represented by a blue fish in a tank named cesspool.

4. Find the names of species represented in all red tanks.

Definition of an object-oriented database

Prepare object-oriented schemas for the following situations in the spirit of Figure 7.12. You don't need to append the attribute signal definitions (Figure 7.13). Besides the complex-valued attributes that maintain relationships among objects, assume that each object also contains a simple string attribute, name.

5. A university consists of several colleges, each containing several departments. For example, the College of Engineering contains the departments of Electrical, Civil, Mechanical, and Chemical Engineering. The College of Liberal Arts contains the departments of History, Anthropology, and Foreign Languages. Each department has a staff of professors. There are no joint appointments: a professor teaches in a single department. Students major in the various departments. However, unlike a professor, a student can major simultaneously in more than one department. Students and faculty are both specializations of the more general classification, person.

6. An amusement park features a wide variety of rides, some duplicated in different locations in the park. In other words, there may be three ferris wheel rides. Of course, the park accommodates a horde of visitors, and each visitor can enjoy any ride, any number of times.

7. An art gallery holds many original paintings. It has produced a limited number of prints of each painting. The prints are sold to patrons, and the original paintings are loaned to patrons.

Relationships

The following situations involve higher-degree or recursive relationships. Draw diagrams in the spirit of Figure 7.15 to illustrate how the object-oriented model maintains these relationships.

8. There are fields to plow, tractors to do the plowing, and farmers to ride the tractors. When all three factors come together, some work is accomplished.

9. A computer program comprises a collection of subprocedures, which call each other for services. In general, a given subprocedure calls other routines in order to break the task into smaller components. However, a given procedure can be invoked by many different host procedures.

10. A computer graphics image consists of a collection of two-dimensional curves. A given curve is related to other curves with which it shares an intersection.

Constraints

Implementing most constraints requires a familiarity with the query format of the next chapter. However, the exercises here are based on the constraint examples of this chapter. In all the exercises, assume that a special class has been designated for each of the external handle objects (e.g., TheTanks, TheSpecies). The portion of the application class hierarchy dealing with sets then takes the form shown in Figure 7.23.

```
Set subclass:  "AquariumSet".          AquariumSet subclass:  "EventSet"
AquariumSet subclass:  "SpeciesSet"       constraint:  Event.
  constraints:  Species.                EventSet subclass:  "EventHandle".
SpeciesSet subclass:  "SpecHandle".     FishSet subclass:  "ExperimentalFishSet"
AquariumSet subclass:  "TankSet"          constraint:  ExperimentalFish.
  constraint:  Tank.                    FishSet subclass:  "DisplayFishSet"
TankSet subclass:  "TankHandle"           constraint:  DisplayFish.
AquariumSet subclass:  "FishSet"
  constraint:  Fish.                    TheSpecies := SpecHandle new.
FishSet subclass:  "FishHandle".        TheTanks := TankHandle new.
                                        TheFish := FishHandle new.
                                        TheEventSet := EventHandle new.
```

Figure 7.23   Revised set definitions for the aquarium database

11. The text modified the volume-attribute method to enforce the FD volume⟶color. The constraint could still be violated, however, by changing the color attribute. Provide a modification for the `color:` method to protect against such violations.

12. Suppose that each species in the database is associated with fish of a particular weight range and that the weight ranges for different species don't overlap. For example, aSpecies may have representative fish in the range 10–50, bSpecies in the range 51–100, cSpecies in the range 101–150, and so forth. Compose a functional dependency for this constraint and provide the appropriate attribute method adjustments to enforce it.

13. Suppose that the number of events associated with fish in red tanks is not to exceed 50. Adjust the attribute methods to enforce this constraint.

   Figure 7.24 gives an object-oriented schema for the library database used in previous exercises. External collections (e.g., TheLibraries, TheBooks) provide the starting points for signals. Assume that the read and write attribute methods are available.

14. Write a code segment to accomplish the following.

   • Insert a new author with name Hemingway.

   • Insert a new book with title The Sun Also Rises and with a page count of 350. Properly connect the book with the author Hemingway.

   • Insert a new library with name Wilson Memorial, location Seattle, and a room count of 25. Place three copies of The Sun Also Rises, each at a cost of four dollars, in the new library.

   • Insert a new patron named Jones with weight 170. Check out one of the copies of "The Sun Also Rises" from the previously established Seattle library to Mr. Jones. Date the loan with today's date as obtained from the System object.

15. Modify the appropriate methods to enforce the constraint that loans can't have null values in either the patron or copy attributes.

16. Modify the attribute methods of the library database to enforce the constraint that patrons weighing more than 150 pounds can't check out books written by Mailer.

```
Object subclass:  "ApplicationClass"
  instanceVariables:  ("creator", "creationDate", "modificationDate")
  constraints:  (("creator", String), ("creationDate", String),
      ("modificationDate", String)).
ApplicationClass subclass:  "Library"
  instanceVariables:  ("name", "location", "rooms", "copies")
  constraints:  (("name", String), ("location", String),
      ("rooms", Number), ("copies", CopySet)).
ApplicationClass subclass:  "Author"
  instanceVariables:  ("name", "books")
  constraints:  (("name", String), ("books", BookSet)).
ApplicationClass subclass:  "Book"
  instanceVariables:  ("title", "author", "pages", "copies")
  constraints:  (("title", String), ("author", Author),
      ("pages", Number), ("copies", CopySet)).
ApplicationsClass subclass:  "Copy"
  instanceVariables:  ("cost", "library", "book", "loans")
  constraints:  (("cost", Number), ("library", Library),
    ("book", Book), ("loans", LoanSet)).
ApplicationClass subclass:  "Patron"
  instanceVariables:  ("name", "weight", "loans")
  constraints:  (("name", String), ("weight", Number), ("loans", LoanSet)).
ApplicationClass subclass:  "Loan"
  instanceVariables:  ("date", "patron", "copy")
  constraints:  (("date", String), ("patron", Patron), ("copy", Copy)).

Set subclass:  "ApplicationSet".
ApplicationSet subclass:  "BookSet" constraint:  Book.
ApplicationSet subclass:  "CopySet" constraint:  Copy.
ApplicationSet subclass:  "LoanSet" constraint:  Loan.
ApplicationSet subclass:  "AuthorSet" constraint:  Author.
ApplicationSet subclass:  "LibrarySet" constraint:  Library.
ApplicationSet subclass:  "PatronSet" constraint:  Patron.
AuthorSet subclass:  "DatabaseAuthors".
BookSet subclass:  "DatabaseBooks".
LibrarySet subclass:  "DatabaseLibraries".
PatronSet subclass:  "DatabasePatrons".

TheAuthors := DatabaseAuthors new.
TheBooks := DatabaseBooks new.
TheLibraries := DatabaseLibraries new.
ThePatrons := DatabasePatrons new.
```

Figure 7.24   Object-oriented schema for the library database

8 Object-Oriented Queries

THIS CHAPTER REVISITS THE SQL QUERY CATEGORIES—existential, universal, and aggregate—and develops standard approaches for object-oriented solutions. An object-oriented query is a signal expression, similar to the relational algebra expressions of Chapter 3. That chapter investigated an algebra of operations and relations, including such operators as $\pi, \sigma, \bowtie$, and $*$ for implementing queries. Relational algebra forms a closed system. In other words, the operations accept relations as arguments and return new relations as results. Consequently, you can compose relational algebra operations into lengthy expressions, which are capable of expressing complex queries. Objects and messages exhibit this same property. An object accepts a message and returns another object. Therefore, you can also compose expressions involving many objects and messages. The returned object from one signal acts as the recipient of the next and so forth as long as necessary. This chapter's goal is to develop signal composition patterns that correspond to the various query categories.

Besides resembling relational algebra as a closed system of objects and operators, signal expressions also parallel relational algebra's procedural approach to query solution. Just like relational algebra, signal expressions constitute a procedural language because they provide a detailed plan for computing the desired results. By contrast, SQL is a non-procedural language that specifies only the desired result, not the computational path. Nevertheless, the translation of SQL into signal expressions is a mechanical task, which can be easily automated. Moreover, the object-oriented database community has developed the Object Query Language (OQL), which exhibits a non-procedural syntax, which is very similar to SQL.

Conceptual model for simple data retrieval

The previous chapter defined several object-oriented schemas for the aquarium database. Figure 8.1 summarizes the final structure. A view emphasizing the tank collection appears in Figure 8.2. Four base objects serve as external handles to the database: TheTanks, TheFish, TheSpecies, and TheEvents. Each of these objects is the single instance of its class. For example, TheTanks is the sole object of the TankHandle class. Special methods in the handle classes control access to the global collections, enforcing application constraints. These classes, and all other application collections, are defined as direct or indirect subclasses of the system-provided class, Set, which provides the default methods for adding and removing set members.

With the notable exception of global objects (e.g., TheTanks and TheSpecies), a typographical convention uses names beginning with a capital letter for classes and names with lower-case initial letters for object, signal, and method identifiers.

You can approach the database from any of the global base objects. Figure 8.2 shows the structure as it unfolds from the TheTanks handle. In particular, the TheTanks object, as a collection, contains several tanks. Figure 8.2 expands one of the tanks to reveal its structure: simple descriptive attributes and a collection of fish objects. You can probe the fish to obtain yet more related objects. Alternatively, you can start with TheSpecies, where you find several species objects, as shown in Figure 8.3. Again, recursive examination of the attribute values leads to related objects. A view with TheFish as the starting point appears in Figure 8.4, and a similar pattern uses the TheEvents handle as an entry object. These approaches all illustrate logical inclusion as the linking mechanism in the mental model for information recovery.

Queries directed to a single class

Consider first a query involving a single class: find the colors of tanks named lagoon. Recall the do: signal from the previous chapter. You send it, carrying a single-parameter code block, to a target collection. The OODBMS executes the code once for each member of the collection and binds the dummy parameter to a different member for each iteration.

```
TheTanks do:  [aTank | aTank name = "lagoon" ifTrue:
                       [aTank color display.  Newline display] ].
```

Here, you interrogate each tank in the global collection under the guise of the dummy parameter, aTank, using an attribute signal to retrieve the name value. You compare the name with the string lagoon and send a nested code block to the resulting boolean. If the boolean is true, the block displays the tank color. To construct organized screen output displays, assume that each output continues on the screen from where the previous output operation left off. The system object, Newline, responds to the display signal by starting a new line.

Some signals, such as the read attribute signals, retrieve information directly from database objects. These signals return a completion object containing the desired information. However, other signals command some activity for which a returned value isn't important. The write attribute signals, for example, behave this way. The convention is that these signals return the target object by default, which facilitates a signal cascade to the same target. Suppose you want to display the colors of tanks named lagoon and the names of red tanks. As in the previous example, you dispatch the do: signal to iterate over TheTanks. Because it isn't intended to return specific information, it returns its target, TheTanks. You can then send a second do: message to TheTanks without repeating the target identifier. The first code excerpt below illustrates this technique. The parentheses are necessary to avoid confusion with a signal having the do:do: signature. You can also

```
Object subclass: "AquariumClass"
   instanceVariables: ("creator", "creationDate", "modificationDate")
   constraints: (("creator", String), ("creationDate", String),
       ("modificationDate", String)).
AquariumClass subclass: "Species" instanceVariables: ("name", "food", "reps")
   constraints: (("name", String), ("food", String), ("reps", FishSet)).
AquariumClass subclass: "Tank" instanceVariables: ("name", "color", "volume", "population")
   constraints: (("name", String), ("color", String), ("volume", Number),
       ("population", FishSet)).
Tank subclass: "ScientificTank" instanceVariables: ("temperature", "salinity")
   constraints: (("temperature", Number), ("salinity", Number),
      (population, ExperimentalFishSet)).
Tank subclass: "DisplayTank" instanceVariables: ("lightingEffect", "soundTrack")
   constraints: (("lightingEffect", String), ("soundTrack", String))
       ("population", DisplayFishSet)).
AquariumClass subclass: "Fish"
   instanceVariables: ("name", "color", "weight", "home", "breed", "experience")
   constraints: (("name", String), ("color", String), ("weight", String),
       ("home", Tank), ("breed", Species), ("experience", EventSet)).
Fish subclass: "ExperimentalFish" instanceVariables: ("examinations")
   constraints: (("examinations", EventSet), ("home", ScientificTank)).
Fish subclass: "DisplayFish"
   instanceVariables: () constraints: (("home", DisplayTank)).
AquariumClass subclass: "Event" instanceVariables: ("date", "note", "subject")
   constraints: (("date", DateTime), ("note", String), ("subject", Fish)).

Set subclass: "AquariumSet".
AquariumSet subclass: "SpeciesSet" constraints: Species.
SpeciesSet subclass: "SpecHandle".
AquariumSet subclass: "TankSet" constraint: Tank.
TankSet subclass: "TankHandle".
AquariumSet subclass: "FishSet" constraint: Fish.
FishSet subclass: "FishHandle".
AquariumSet subclass: "EventSet" constraint: Event.
EventSet subclass: "EventHandle".
FishSet subclass: "ExperimentalFishSet" constraint: ExperimentalFish.
FishSet subclass: "DisplayFishSet" constraint: DisplayFish.

TheSpecies := SpecHandle new.
TheTanks := TankHandle new.
TheFish := FishHandle new.
TheEvents := EventHandle new.
```

Figure 8.1 Object-oriented schema for the aquarium database

TheTankCollection

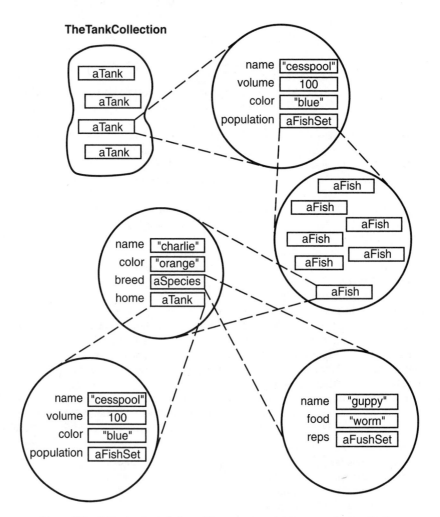

Figure 8.2 Object-oriented view of the aquarium database as a tank collection

use a separating semicolon between signals, giving the second version below, where the parentheses are no longer needed.

```
(TheTanks do:  [aTank | aTank name = "lagoon" ifTrue:  [aTank color display.  Newline display] ])
    do:  [aTank | aTank color = "red" ifTrue:  [aTank name display.  Newline display] ].
TheTanks do:  [aTank | aTank name = "lagoon" ifTrue:  [aTank color display.  Newline display];
    do:  [aTank | aTank color = "red" ifTrue:  [aTank name display.  Newline display] ].
```

You can use more complicated booleans and request more than one attribute value. For example, find the colors and volumes of tanks named lagoon with volume greater than 100. To format the output, you use the Tab object. Tab is another convenient system object, similar to Newline, which responds to the display signal by tabbing the screen cursor.

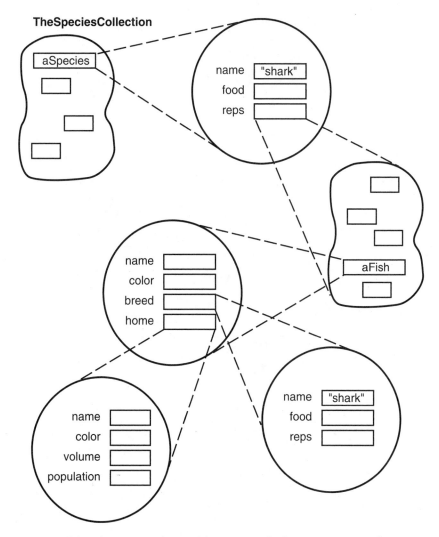

Figure 8.3   Object-oriented view of the aquarium database as a species collection

```
TheTanks do:   [aTank | (aTank name = "lagoon") & (aTank volume > 100) ifTrue:   [
    aTank color display.   Tab display.   aTank volume display.   Newline display] ].
```

The scoping rules for nested code blocks are the same as in block-structured programming languages, such as Pascal or C. The rules are also the same as for nested subqueries in SQL. A nested block retains access to the variables of its host, and, by extension, to any other block that contains the host. The reverse isn't true. Moreover, a nested block loses access to a host variable when it hides the name with a local declaration. In the example above, the code argument for the ifTrue: signal retains access to the aTank variable in its host. The host in this case is the code block for the do: signal.

TheFishCollection

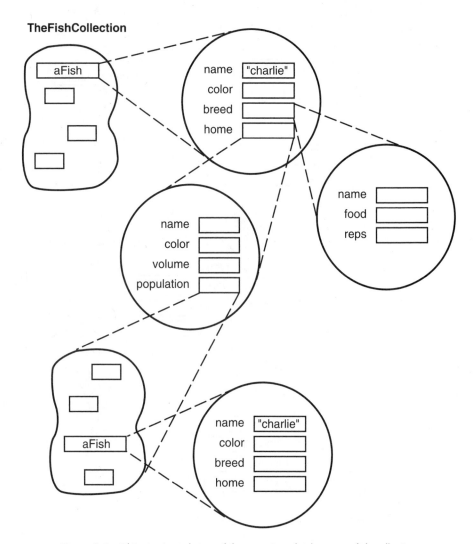

Figure 8.4 Object-oriented view of the aquarium database as a fish collection

A final concern is that the solutions to this point don't remove duplicates values from the answer. Instead they display each component of the answer as soon as it is discovered. With a slightly more complicated expression, you can accumulate the answer strings, remove the duplicates, and then display them as a unit after finishing the database probes. This technique will appear in later queries.

Queries directed to multiple classes

Consider an example that requires information from objects across several classes: what are the colors of fish that represent a species named shark? You can start by interrogating TheSpecies for its sharks or by selectively choosing fish from TheFish, using the breed attribute to find the sharks. Both approaches appear below. The second solution is shorter because it doesn't probe any multivalued attributes. The breed signal returns a single species object, and the name signal then acquires a single string. In contrast, the first solution probes the reps attribute, receiving a collection, which requires a second iteration.

```
TheSpecies do:  [aSpecies |
    aSpecies name = "shark" ifTrue:  [
      aSpecies reps do:  [aFish |
        aFish color display.  Newline display] ] ].
```

```
TheFish do:  [aFish |
    aFish breed name = "shark" ifTrue:  [
      aFish color display.  Newline display] ].
```

The query expression probes within objects to find related objects. This is in contrast with the relational model where the probes cross multiple tables through common attributes. The object-oriented approach is as simple as the relational one, and it provides a distinct advantage because it allows more complex structures. From the user's standpoint, information retrieval is a matter of recursively examining the contents of some base object in a very intuitive manner. The same process would be used if the objects could be physically manipulated.

Consider the last query again. You want the colors of the sharks. Imagine the box of fish on your desk. The box is TheFish. Upon opening the box, you find a collection of smaller boxes, each containing a fish. You examine these objects sequentially. Opening a fish box, you find several string attributes and also a box labeled breed. Opening the breed box, you find the species attributes, including the name string. If that name value is **shark**, you write out the color string from the opened fish box. If not, you close the breed box, close the fish box, and move to another fish. This tangible metaphor guides the construction of signal expressions for arbitrarily complicated queries. When faced with a complicated query, it helps to adopt this viewpoint. Imagine that the database, in the form of one of the global collections, is on your desk. You can unpack the internal structure as you methodically search for the desired information. When you have figured out how to proceed, you simply translate your unpacking activities into the corresponding signals.

Try out the box-unpacking scenario on the following query: what are the names of fish representing a shark species and inhabiting a cesspool tank? You should be able to understand each of the following three solutions, which differ only in the choice of the starting object. The first solution is shortest because it probes no multivalued attributes.

```
TheFish do:  [aFish | (aFish breed name = "shark") & (aFish home name = "cesspool") ifTrue:  [
  aFish name display.  Newline display] ].
```

```
TheSpecies do:  [aSpecies |
    aSpecies name = "shark" ifTrue:  [
      aSpecies reps do:  [aFish |
        aFish home name = "cesspool"
          ifTrue:  [
            aFish name display.
            Newline display] ] ] ].
```

```
TheTanks do:  [aTank |
    aTank name = "cesspool" ifTrue:  [
      aTank population do:  [aFish |
        aFish breed name = "shark"
          ifTrue:  [
            aFish name display.
            Newline display] ] ] ].
```

As another example, find the names of species swimming in the same tank with a shark species. Following the containment model (i.e., boxes within boxes within boxes), you filter the sharks from TheSpecies and examine each to obtain its representative fish and then the tanks where they swim. These tanks' populations are fish collections, and the breed attributes from these fish contain the required species. You construct the query exactly along these lines, as shown on the left below.

```
TheSpecies do: [aSpecies |
  aSpecies name = "shark" ifTrue:  [
    aSpecies reps do:  [aFish |
      aFish home population do:  [bFish |
        bFish breed name display.
        Newline display] ] ] ].
```

```
TheSpecies do:  [aSpecies |
  aSpecies name = "shark" ifTrue:  [
    aSpecies reps do:  [aFish |
      aFish home population do:  [bFish |
        bFish breed name = "shark"
        ifFalse:  [
          bFish breed name display.
          Newline display] ] ] ] ].
```

The SQL solution of this query places the string shark in the answer because it considers a shark to be swimming with itself. In the object-oriented solution, the aFish home structure provides the tank housing a shark. Then aFish home population returns the tank's fish collection, which surely includes the shark, aFish. In the subsequent iteration, bFish takes on the value aFish at some point, and then bFish breed name returns the string shark to be displayed. So the behavior is the same as the SQL equivalent. In the SQL case, you suppressed the shark string by rewriting the boolean to reject shark strings. You can follow the same logic in the signal expression, as shown in the parallel code on the right above.

Because the solution is actually a procedural program, you can explicitly code any variation you want. You might, for example, want to include shark in the answer if two distinct shark fish swim in the same tank. The SQL for this case included a clause to force the two fish representing the two species to be distinct, as shown below. Because the fno attribute was a key of the fish table, the last boolean of the where-clause ensured that two distinct fish appeared in the database path. The equivalent signal expression follows the same idea, as demonstrated in the second solution below. Because the objects contain no keys, the object-oriented solution uses the strong equality check to test if two variables are bound to the same object.

```
select H.sname
from Species S, Fish F, Tank T, Fish G, Species H
where S.sno = F.sno and F.tno = T.tno and S.sname = "shark" and T.tno = G.tno and
   G.sno = H.sno and F.fno not = G.fno.

TheSpecies do:  [aSpecies |
  aSpecies name = "shark" ifTrue:  [
    aSpecies reps do:  [aFish |
      aFish home population do:  [bFish |
        bFish == aFish ifFalse:  [display bFish breed name.  Newline display] ] ] ] ].
```

Now consider the query: find all pairs of cohabiting fish. In SQL, you join two copies of the fish relation. In the object-oriented case, a fish already contains, at some level of inspection, all the fish that are swimming with it. If you want to pursue the recursion further, this fish contains all the fish swimming with those neighbors, and all the fish swimming with those twice-distant neighbors, and so forth. Therefore, you can solve the query by asking each fish to deliver its home, a tank, which you then ask to deliver its population, the cohabiting fish. The solution appears on the left below.

```
TheFish do: [aFish |
   aFish home population do: [bFish |
      bFish name display. Tab display.
      aFish name display. Newline display] ].
```

```
TheFish do: [aFish |
   aFish home population do: [bFish |
      aFish name < bFish name ifTrue: [
         bFish name display. Tab display.
         aFish name display. Newline display] ] ].
```

You can adopt the strategy from the corresponding SQL to prevent the display of the form (a a) and to suppress one the redundant pairs (a b) or (b a). You just display qualifying pairs where the names appear in alphabetical order. This adjustment appears on the right.

Signal expressions equivalent to SQL subqueries

Although subqueries in SQL can often provide more intuitive solutions for existential queries, they are necessary only for universal queries. Subqueries introduce subsidiary computations and set comparisons into the where- and having-clause booleans. The set comparisons include set equality, set containment, and element membership checks. These operations are also available in signal expressions. Although they don't materially simplify the signal expressions for existential queries, they are necessary for universal queries.

In a signal expression, a subquery takes the form of an auxiliary computation, which results in an intermediate object that you can use in the hosting activity. Consider again the query: find the names of species swimming in the same tank with a shark species.

```
|sharkytanks answer|
answer := Set new.
sharkytanks := TankSet new.
TheTanks do: [aTank |
   aTank population do: [aFish |
      aFish breed name = "shark" ifTrue: [sharkytanks add: aTank] ] ].
TheSpecies do: [aSpecies |
   aSpecies reps do: [aFish |
      (sharkytanks includes: aFish home) ifTrue: [answer add: aSpecies name] ] ].
answer do: [aString | aString display. Newline display].
```

The query uses two temporary variables: sharkytanks and answer, which are declared within the vertical bars at the beginning of the code. The sharkytanks variable will hold a collection of specially selected tanks, namely those holding a shark. The answer variable will hold a set of strings, which, at the conclusion of the operation, will correspond to the names of species that swim with sharks.

Duplicate members aren't permitted in sets. All sets respond to the add: signal, which carries a parameter object to be added to the set. If the parameter object is already in the set, the operation doesn't add the second copy. The OODBMS typically uses strong equality for the duplication test; for strings and numbers, however, it substitutes weak equality. Two strings are equal, therefore, if they contain the same sequence of characters, even if they are two separate objects when considered as character arrays. The add: method compares the arriving objects with existing members using the equality method associated with their class. Two objects from different classes are obviously not equal, while two of the same class are judged according the class method. For strings and numbers, equality is weak equality. By accumulating the successful name strings in the answer set before displaying those strings, you can suppress duplicates.

In the example, you ask each tank, aTank, to report its population. You then ask each of the population's fish to deliver its breed name. You compare the breed name string with shark. If a match occurs, you add the tank to the sharkytanks collection. You will add a given tank to sharkytanks several times, once for each shark that it contains. However, the collection suppresses this duplication because TankSet is a subclass of Set.

Next you send a second do: signal to TheSpecies, asking each species if it has a representative fish in one of the sharky tanks. All sets respond to the includes: signal with a boolean, true if the parameter is in the set, false otherwise. On each iteration, aFish represents the species, aSpecies. If aFish home is a member of sharkytanks, you add aSpecies name to the answer set, provided it isn't already there. Finally, you send a do: signal to the answer set. It iterates over the member strings, displaying each on the screen.

This signal expression is more complicated than the earlier solution, which didn't use subsidiary computations. Indeed, it is more complicated than the SQL version below, which uses a subquery. Despite its length, the signal expression has the advantage that it computes the set of sharkytanks only once. The SQL, on the other hand, implies a recomputation for each candidate tuple. Of course, the DBMS can optimize the final computation to avoid the redundancy.

```
select S.sname
from Species S, Fish F, Tank T
where S.sno = F.sno and F.tno = T.tno and T.tno in
    (select T.tno
    from Species S, Fish F, Tank T
    where S.sno = F.sno and F.tno = T.tno and S.sname = "shark").
```

Some further examples illustrating the calculation of intermediate objects

You can always solve existential queries without calculating intermediate objects. Because universal queries require intermediate objects, below are a few more examples to illustrate the technique. The first is a variation of the above query: find the names of species that have a representative swimming in a tank with a shark of the same color. In other words, the color of the fish representing the candidate species is the same as the shark's color. You must recompute the intermediate object because it varies across the candidate objects.

```
|answer|
answer := Set new.
TheSpecies do:  [aSpecies |
   aSpecies reps do:  [aFish |
      |sharkytanks|
      sharkytanks := TankSet new.
      TheTanks do:  [aTank |
         aTank population do:  [bFish |
            (bFish breed name = "shark") & (bFish color = aFish color) ifTrue:  [
               sharkytanks add:  aTank] ] ].
      (sharkytanks includes:  aFish home) ifTrue:  [answer add:  aSpecies name] ] ].
answer do:  [aString | aString display.  Newline display].
```

For each fish in the candidate species' reps collection, you recompute the sharkytank collection as those tanks that contain a shark of the same color as the fish. The example illustrates how temporary variables are declared in the code block that uses them. As shown below, this query has a more straightforward solution, although it leaves some duplication among the answer strings.

```
TheSpecies do:  [aSpecies |
   aSpecies reps do:  [aFish |
      aFish home population do:  [bFish |
         (bFish breed name = "shark") & (bFish color = aFish color) ifTrue:  [
            aSpecies name display.  Newline display] ] ] ].
```

For a second example, find the uninhabited tanks. Although this query involves an empty status check of a set, it doesn't require an intermediate computation. The set to be checked already exists in the database structure. This advantage over the equivalent SQL occurs because attributes can hold collections directly, so the OODBMS doesn't have to recompute them. All collections respond to the isEmpty signal, returning true if the set is empty. The signal expression is then as follows.

```
TheTanks do:  [aTank |
   aTank population isEmpty ifTrue:  [aTank name display.  Newline display] ].
```

Finally, consider a query that does require the computation of an intermediate object, a computation that corresponds to the mandatory use of a subquery in SQL. Find the names of species represented in all red tanks.

```
|redtanks|
redtanks := TankSet new.
TheTanks do:  [aTank | aTank color = "red" ifTrue:  [redtanks add:  aTank] ].
TheSpecies do:  [aSpecies |
   |mytanks|
   mytanks := TankSet new.
   aSpecies reps do:  [aFish | mytanks add:  aFish home].
   (mytanks contains:  redtanks) ifTrue:  [aSpecies name display.  Newline display] ].
```

The query computes the collection of red tanks and stores the result in the temporary variable redtanks. Then, for each species, aSpecies, it calculates the collection of tanks where the species is represented. It assigns the second collection to the temporary variable mytanks. If mytanks contains redtanks, it reports the name value of the species.

Sets respond to the `contains:` signal in the expected manner, returning true if the parameter object is a subset of the signal target. An earlier example used the `includes:` signal, which returns true if its parameter is a member of the target set. So `contains:` and `includes:` serve slightly different purposes: `includes` takes a single-object parameter, and `contains` takes a set.

Existential queries

In an existential query, a candidate contributes to the answer if a path connects it to certain anchor elements. In a relational database, the qualifying path stretches across tuples linked with common attributes. In an object-oriented database, the qualifying path stretches from the candidate object into its internal structures.

Explicit probes into attribute objects

Reconsider the query: find the names of species swimming with a shark. Figure 8.5 shows the qualifying path as a series of magnifications that recursively expand the candidate species' internal details. The species object with a question mark is attempting to enter the answer set. Actually, its name string attribute will enter the answer if the species qualifies. Expanding its reps attribute details allows a closer inspection of the fish representing the species. Enlarging one of these fish, say Fish X, shows further internal structure, including its home tank. The tank expansion reveals its population attribute, which contains the fish cohabiting the tank with the Fish X. Expanding one of these neighboring fish shows its breed, which on closer examination, contains a species object with name string shark. The desired path has been found.

You encounter fish collections at two points in the exploration. Each time, you choose one fish to continue the investigation. The actual query must sequence through the fish collection in its search for the qualifying path. This exhaustive exploration is wasteful because the species qualifies as soon as one complete path has been discovered. Therefore, the object-oriented solution needs an optimization step. The concern here, however, is with systematic programming for the general existential query solution, so program optimization is left to the OODBMS. The signal expression below corresponds to the expansions of Figure 8.5. It uses `do:` signals to iterate over the fish collections.

```
|answer|
answer := Set new.
TheSpecies do:  [aSpecies |
   aSpecies reps do:  [aFish |
      aFish home population do:   [bFish |
         bFish breed name = "shark" ifTrue:   [answer add:  aSpecies name] ] ] ].
answer do:  [aString | aString display.  Newline display].
```

TheSpeciesCollection

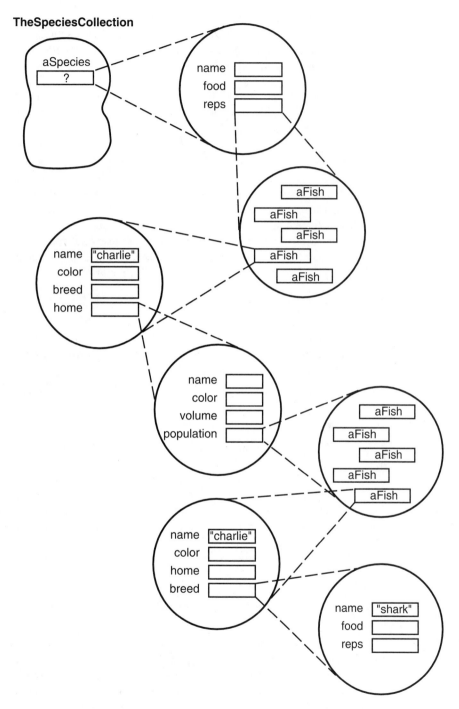

Figure 8.5   Consecutive expansions reveal an existential path

A shortcut syntax using database paths

The complexity of the above query solution is due to iterations over collections returned by multivalued attribute signals. A shortcut syntax allows a collection to respond to an attribute signal and to return a collection of values, one solicited from each member through the same attribute signal.

The `collect:` signal behaves much like the `select:` signal of the previous chapter. When a target collection receives a `select:` signal, the `select:` method builds a new collection, a subset of the target, which it returns to the sender. The target collection remains unchanged. The method decides which of the target's members to place in the new collection by executing the parameter code block for each member. If the last calculation of the block produces a true boolean, the member enters the accumulating subset. The `collect:` signal operates in an analogous manner, except that the result of the calculation on each member, rather than the member itself, enters the new collection. In this case, the final computation of the block need not produce a boolean: it can produce any object whatsoever. The accumulated collection of these final computation objects, one for each member of the target, is returned to the sender. For example, the following excerpt collects all the tank names, which results in a collection of strings.

```
tmp := TheTanks collect:  [aTank | aTank name].
```

Using the built-in `collect:` signal, you can make the TankSet collection respond directly to an attribute signal, such as `name`, by programming it to collect the name attributes from each member. Using the following methods, you also program TankSet collections to assemble their volume numbers and color strings.

```
TankSet method:  "name" code:  [^self collect:  [aTank | aTank name] ].
TankSet method:  "volume" code:  [^self collect:  [aTank | aTank volume] ].
TankSet method:  "color" code:  [^self collect:  [aTank | aTank color] ].
```

`TheTanks` volume now returns a Set object, containing the unduplicated volumes of all tanks in the database. In this case, the returned collection is a set of numbers. A different attribute collection, however, might contain application objects, such as a set of fish. You would want it to be a FishSet object, rather than a generic Set object. For example, if you collect the population values from a tank collection, you obtain a set of fish, which you would like to be a FishSet. So you install the `population` method as follows:

```
TankSet method:  "population" code:  [
  |aFishSet|
  aFishSet := FishSet new.
  (self collect:  [aTank | aTank population]) do:  [bFishSet | aFishSet addAll:  bFishSet].
  ^aFishSet].
```

Collecting the population values across the tanks gives a collection of lumps, each a FishSet object as specified in the schema. The `addAll:` signal behaves like the `add:` signal, except that it adds many elements at the same time. Its parameter, therefore, is a set of elements rather than a single element. Each population lump is added to the accumulating aFishSet object. The returned value is then a set of fish, and it is a proper instance of the FishSet class.

Assume now that the application set classes—TankSet, FishSet, SpeciesSet, EventSet—have attribute retrieval methods. A TankSet object responds to `name`, `color`, `volume`, and `population` signals. The first two signals assemble string collections, the third a number collection, and the last a fish collection. A SpeciesSet object responds to `name`, `food` and `reps` signals, and so forth. Finally, you instrument the Set class to respond to the `display` signal by passing it to each member of the set. The member responds by displaying itself on a separate line.

```
Set method:  "display" code:  [^self do:  [anObject | anObject display.  Newline display] ].
```

With these signals available, consider again the last query: find the names of species swimming with a shark. The new solution below is much simpler:

```
(TheSpecies collect:  [aSpecies |
   (aSpecies reps home population breed name includes:  "shark")
      ifTrue:  [aSpecies name] ifFalse:  [null]
   ]) display.
```

The concatenation of attribute signals, `reps home population breed name`, accumulates the names of species cohabiting with the target object. You proceed one signal at a time for a given aSpecies. First, `reps` returns its collection of fish. Then `home` returns the unduplicated collection of home tanks from these fish. Next `population` returns a FishSet, containing the fish from these home tanks, which are fish swimming with a representative of aSpecies. Finally, `breed` collects the species of the co-swimmers, and `name` gathers the names of the species. If the string shark appears in this final set, you ask aSpecies for its name string as the last computation of the `collect:` block. That name string becomes part of the return collection of the hosting `collect:` signal. However, if the shark string doesn't occur in the set returned by `reps home population breed name`, then null is the last object handled by the block, adding nothing to the accumulating `collect:` return object. When the `collect:` signal returns its names, you display them by dispatching the modified `display` signal to the set.

Besides being shorter, this form more clearly illustrates the existential nature of the query. The `reps home population breed name` expression constitutes a **database path**, which stretches from a candidate species object to the names of other species objects. This path is a direct parallel with the corresponding SQL mechanism.

 A database path is a sequence of attribute signals, each probing the set of objects returned by its predecessor.

For another example, which illustrates a longer path, find the names of species swimming with a species represented in a cesspool tank. Instead of stopping at a shark species as in the previous query, you must continue the chain back to a cesspool tank. Figure 8.6 shows the required expansions, and the following signal expressions examine the interconnecting attributes in the same sequence. The first solution uses explicit iterations over the intermediate sets; the second uses database paths.

```
|answer|
answer := Set new.
TheSpecies do: [aSpecies |
   aSpecies reps do: [aFish |
      aFish home population do:  [bFish |
         bFish breed reps do:  [cFish |
            cFish home name = "cesspool" ifTrue:  [answer add:  aSpecies name] ] ] ] ].
answer do:  [aString | aString display.  Newline display].
```

```
(TheSpecies collect:  [aSpecies |
   (aSpecies reps home population breed reps home name includes:  "cesspool")
      ifTrue:  [aSpecies name] ifFalse:  [null].
   ]) display.
```

As in SQL existential solutions, the answer can include information collected along the qualifying path, not merely attributes of the candidate object at the head of the chain. For example, find the names of species swimming with a shark and also the names of the common tanks. The brute force solution, without duplication suppression in the answer, is:

```
TheSpecies do: [aSpecies |
   aSpecies reps home do:  [aTank |
      (aTank population breed name includes:  "shark") ifTrue:  [
         aSpecies name display.  Tab display.  aTank name display.  Newline display] ] ].
```

You must break the database path, reps home population breed reps home name, after the home message to retain access to the common tank. This tank is available for display in the aTank variable if a shark is located in its population. You can remove duplicates from the answer by storing (species name : tank name) concatenations as single strings in a set. The concatenation operator is a comma, and it is a binary operator. The construction string1, string2 sends the concatenate signal to string1 carrying string2 as a parameter. The returned object is a new string with prefix string1 and suffix string2. Using this device, you can rephrase the query as:

```
|answer|
answer := Set new.
TheSpecies do:  [aSpecies |
   aSpecies reps home do :[aTank |
      (aTank population breed name includes:  "shark") ifTrue:  [
         answer add:  aSpecies name, Tab, aTank name] ] ].
answer do:  [aString | aString display.  Newline display].
```

You can envision the database path notation as constructing all possible leaf elements in a tree that starts with the target object. Assuming aSpecies is a species object, the expression below constructs the set of strings in the leaf nodes of Figure 8.7.

```
aSpecies reps home population breed name.
```

TheSpeciesCollection

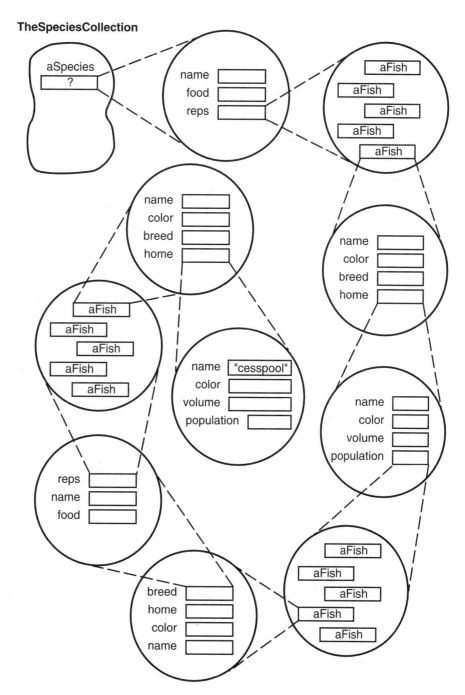

Figure 8.6   Consecutive expansions along a lengthy existential path

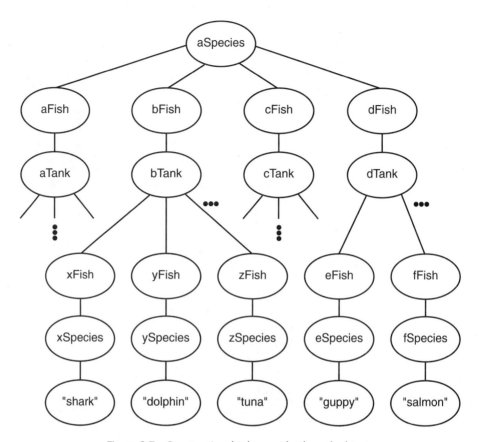

Figure 8.7   Constructing database paths through objects

If shark occurs among these strings, you conclude that the originating object is a species that swims with a shark. However, an interior node of the tree represents the tank in which the cohabitation occurs, and that object isn't available with the database path notation.

Figure 8.7 also emphasizes the rapidly growing set of leaf objects at the frontier of an expanding path. The retrieval mechanism constructs and examines all paths from the root object to the leaves. The resulting combinatorial explosion of leaf nodes becomes cause for performance concerns. SQL constructions present a similar problem when many tables appear in a from-clause. Consequently, an optimization step is needed in either language before executing a query.

Universal queries

Signal expressions for universal queries must calculate intermediate objects, just as the equivalent SQL must involve subqueries. In a universal query, a candidate doesn't quality to contribute to the answer merely by the existence of a path connecting it to an anchor. Instead, the candidate must originate a path bundle sufficient to embrace a collection of anchor objects. In a signal expression, this situation requires the computation of intermediate sets.

Imitating the set containment solution in SQL

As a first example, consider again the query: find the names of species represented in all red tanks. Although it can be shortened slightly, the following solution uses explicit variables to emphasize the intermediate sets:

```
|redTanks|
redTanks := TheTanks select:  [aTank | aTank color = "red"].
TheSpecies do:  [aSpecies |
  |myTanks|
  myTanks := aSpecies reps home.
  (myTanks contains:  redTanks) ifTrue:  [aSpecies name display.  Newline display] ].
```

Figure 8.8 shows a candidate species examined in ever-increasing detail through a sequence of attribute expansions. You examine the reps attribute to reveal a collection of fish. You then examine each fish to retrieve its home attribute. These home attributes constitute the collection of tanks where the candidate species is represented. As tank objects, they form a subset of TheTanks, which is the collection of all tanks. The question then is whether the constructed tank set encompasses all the red tanks. Figure 8.8 implies an affirmative answer. It shows the collection of tanks holding the candidate species as containing both red tanks and also a blue one.

You can always test the general condition for a universal query with a containment predicate. The set of anchor objects is one collection; the set of reachable objects is a second collection. If the second collection contains the first, the criterion is met. In the solution above, redtanks holds the anchor objects, and mytanks, recalculated as appropriate for the candidate species, holds the reachable objects.

Imitating the SQL solution with double negation

SQL also allows a doubly negated construction to express universal queries. Some database products require the doubly negated solution because the contains-predicate isn't available. You can mimic the doubly negated SQL solution in a signal expression, as illustrated by the next example. Consider again the query solved immediately above: find the names of species represented in all red tanks. The doubly negated SQL solution is as follows:

```
select S.sname
from Species S
where not exists
  (select *
  from Tank T
  where T.tcolor = "red" and not exists
    (select *
    from Fish F
    where S.sno = F.sno and F.tno = T.tno)).
```

You can reword the English to parallel the SQL: find the names of species for which the set of red tanks to which they are not connected is empty. SQL constructs the required sets with two nested subqueries. In the signal expression below, the untouchedRedTanks set holds,

TheSpeciesCollection

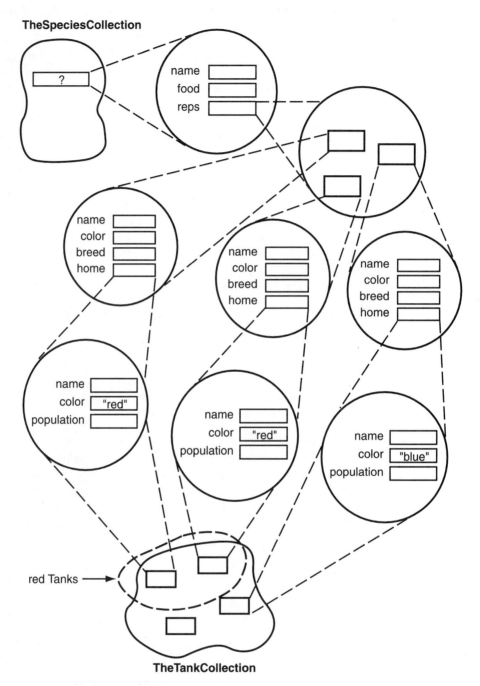

TheTankCollection

Figure 8.8   The bundle of extensions associated with a universal query

for each candidate species, the collection of red tanks to which the species isn't connected. The species qualifies if this calculated set is empty. You can test the empty status of a set with the isEmpty signal.

```
TheSpecies do:  [aSpecies |
  |untouchedRedTanks|
  untouchedRedTanks := TheTanks select:  [aTank |
    (aTank color = "red") & (aTank population intersect:  aSpecies reps) isEmpty].
  untouchedRedTanks isEmpty ifTrue:  [aSpecies name display. Newline display] ].
```

Initially, all tanks are candidates for inclusion in the untouchedRedTanks. After you discard the non-red tanks, however, a remaining red tank qualifies only if its fish population is disjoint from the representatives of the candidate species. In other words, it's "untouched" by that species. The two fish sets are readily available. You obtain the tank's fish population from its population attribute, and you get the candidate species' representatives from its reps attribute. You test the two fish sets for disjointness with the intersect: message. A set responds to the intersect: signal by returning a new set, which contains the intersection of the receiver and the signal parameter.

The reason for the doubly negated SQL construction, or for its equivalent set-containment operation, is that all quantification in SQL is implicitly existential. If you could directly express universal quantification in SQL, you could avoid the double negation. Because relational calculus allows direct universal quantifications, it can solve the query above as follows. Here, S is the species relation, T is Tank, and F is Fish.

$$\{s.\text{sname} \mid S(s) \wedge (\forall t)(\neg(T(t) \wedge t.\text{tcolor} = \text{"red"}) \vee (\exists f)(F(f) \wedge s.\text{sno} = f.\text{sno} \wedge f.\text{tno} = t.\text{tno}))\}.$$

You can directly test universal quantification in a signal expression by iterating the predicate over the collection's elements and accumulating the result through a logical-and operation with a temporary variable that was initialized to true. If the variable is still true at the conclusion of the iterations, the predicate is true for all members of the collection. For example, the expression below checks if every member of a collection is odd. Suppose the collection is called OddFellows and that its members (i.e., numbers) respond to the odd signal by returning the appropriate boolean.

```
|allOdd|
allOdd := true.
OddFellows do:  [aNumber | allOdd := allOdd & aNumber odd].
```

When the do: signal returns, the variable allOdd is true if and only if $(\forall n)(\neg(n \in \text{OddFellows}) \vee n$ is odd). Using this pattern, you can mimic the relational calculus solution to the above query in a signal expression. The result appears below.

```
TheSpecies do:  [aSpecies |
  |qualified|
  qualified := true.
  TheTanks do:  [aTank |
    qualified := qualified &
      ((aTank color = "red") not | (aTank population intersect:  aSpecies reps) isEmpty not)].
  qualified ifTrue:  [aSpecies name display.  Newline display] ].
```

Some further examples

The SQL examples in Chapter 5 investigated a variation of the query above. The modified query required that the path bundle extend three times across the database. Although this query was more complicated than any that might typically be encountered, it showed that you can construct universal queries in an algorithmic manner. The query was: find the names of species represented in all tanks containing all species with a worm diet. The SQL and its equivalent signal expression follow.

```
select S.sname
from Species S
where
   (select T.tno
   from Fish F, Tank T
   where S.sno = F.sno and
      F.tno = T.tno)
contains
   (select T.tno
   from Tank T
   where
      (select S.sno
      from Species S, Fish F
      where S.sno = F.sno and
         F.tno = T.tno)
   contains
      (select S.sno
      from Species S
      where S.sfood = "worm")).
```

```
|wormySpecies wormyTanks|
wormySpecies := TheSpecies select:  [aSpecies |
   aSpecies food = "worm"].
wormyTanks := TheTanks select:  [aTank |
   aTank population breed contains:  wormySpecies].
TheSpecies do:  [aSpecies |
   aSpecies reps home contains:  wormyTanks ifTrue:  [
      aSpecies name display.  Newline display] ].
```

The wormySpecies form the first group of comparison objects. You then compute the wormyTanks—those tanks connected to all wormySpecies—by constructing a bundle of attribute extensions to encompass the wormySpecies. A candidate species qualifies if it embraces all the wormyTanks.

As a final example, consider the earlier SQL query that illustrated a mixed strategy between the existential and universal approaches: find the tanks inhabited by some species that is represented in all red tanks. A candidate tank need only exhibit the existence of a single attribute-extension sequence to an anchor species, but that species must command a bundle of extensions to encompass all the red tanks. The attribute extension from a candidate tank to an anchor species in the likesRedTanks subset is characterized by a non-empty intersection between the tank's species and likesRedTanks. The code appears as follows:

```
|redTanks likesRedTanks|
redTanks := TheTanks select:  [aTank | aTank color = "red"].
likesRedTanks := TheSpecies select:  [aSpecies | aSpecies reps home contains:  redTanks].
TheTanks do:  [aTank |
   (aTank population breed intersect:  likesRedTanks) isEmpty not
      ifTrue:  [aTank name display.  Newline display] ].
```

Object class	Signal	Action	Returned object or class
Boolean	ifTrue: aBlock	conditional execution	receiver
	ifFalse: aBlock	conditional execution	receiver
	ifTrue: tBlock ifFalse: fBlock	conditional execution	receiver
	not	logical complement	Boolean
	& aBoolean	logical "and" with parameter	Boolean
	| aBoolean	logical "or" with parameter	Boolean
Set	includes: anElement	membership test	Boolean
	contains: aSet	containment test	Boolean
	do: aBlock	iterate code for each element	receiver
	add: anObject	insertion	receiver
	isEmpty	empty test	Boolean
	select: aBlock	select a subset or receiver	selected subset
	collect: aBlock	accumulate contributions of members	Set

Figure 8.9 Summary of simple signals needed to simulate SQL queries

Figure 8.9 summarizes the surprisingly small number of signals needed to express the examples. You must supplement these operations with the common arithmetic operations, a few string manipulation functions, and the attribute signals.

Aggregates and partitions

Imitating the SQL orderby-clause

In SQL, you can group tuples that agree on the groupby-clause attributes, and you can compute simple statistics over the attributes within each such group. These aggregate computations include count, min, max, average, and sum. You can use an independent orderby-clause to display the answer in a specified order. Because signal expressions are a general-purpose programming language, these capabilities are also available with an object-oriented database. As a first example, find the names of species with their corresponding fish and order the answer by species name. The SQL and its equivalent signal expression are:

```
select S.sname species, F.fname fish
from Species S, Fish F
where F.sno = S.sno
orderby S.sname.
```

```
(TheSpecies asSortedCollection:
 [a b| a name < b name]) do:
   [aSpecies | aSpecies reps do: [aFish |
      (aSpecies name, Tab, aFish name) display.
      Newline display] ].
```

All instances of the Set class respond to the signal asSortedCollection: by returning a new set, which contains the same members arranged in a sorted order. The new set responds to subsequent iteration signals by supplying its members in sorted order. The code block parameter of the asSortedCollection signal specifies a predicate that determines when two elements are deemed to be in sorted order. In this case, you want the species objects ordered alphabetically by their name strings. Therefore, two species objects, a and b, are in order if the predicate a name $<$ b name is true. The output display uses the concatenation operator to join the name strings with an intervening tab. If you want to arrange the fish names in order within each species, you can cast the reps set as a sorted collection, as shown below.

```
(TheSpecies asSortedCollection:  [a b| a name < b name]) do:  [aSpecies |
    (aSpecies reps asSortedCollection:  [a b| a name < b name]) do:  [aFish |
        (aSpecies name, Tab, aFish name) display.  Newline display] ].
```

An alternative approach accumulates the output strings in an answer set, which you convert to a sorted collection before displaying it. The following segment illustrates the point.

```
|answer|
TheSpecies do:  [aSpecies |
    aSpecies reps do:  [aFish |
        answer add:  (aSpecies name leftJustify:  20), Tab, aFish name] ].
answer asSortedCollection do:  [aString | aString display.  Newline display].
```

The asSortedCollection method requires a code block parameter only when the objects to be sorted have a complex structure and don't respond to the ordinary "<" binary signal. Because strings respond to this default ordering signal, the code block isn't required in the example above. The default code block is [a b| a < b]. The example uses the leftJustify: signal to left justify a string in a blank-filled field of a given size. This produces a more coherent display because it does a better job than a single tab in keeping the species portion of the string separate from the fish portion.

Imitating the SQL groupby-clause

Reconsider the following query: find the number of fish representing each species. Below are the SQL, recovered from Chapter 5, and the equivalent signal expression.

```
select S.sno, S.sname, count(*)          TheSpecies do:  [aSpecies |
from Species S, Fish F                       (aSpecies name, Tab, aSpecies reps size) display.
where F.sno = S.sno                          Newline display].
groupby S.sno.
```

In a signal expression, you must isolate the objects to be grouped for the counting operation. In this case, the fish of a given species are already isolated in the reps attribute of that species. The very structure of the database provides the required partition. To perform the actual counting, you use the size signal. All collections respond to the this signal by returning the number of elements they contain. The example assumes that the concatenation operator (i.e., the comma) is overloaded to accommodate a parameter of class Number. Of course, the key field, sno, is an unnecessary component in the object-oriented representation, so it isn't part of the answer.

Sometimes, as in the example above, the partition already exists as part of the database definition. However, some queries require a calculated partition. Consider a slight variation of the query: count the fish by species and tank. In other words, for each species-tank combination, how many fish represent the species and inhabit the tank? The SQL solution adds the tno attribute to the groupby argument. The resulting SQL and its signal expression equivalent appear below. The signal expression subdivides the reps attribute in each species into fish groups associated with each tank.

```
select S.sno, S.sname, T.tno,          TheSpecies do:  [aSpecies |
   T.tname, count(*)                      aSpecies reps home do:  [aTank |
from Species S, Fish F, Tank T              (aSpecies name, Tab, aTank name, Tab,
where F.sno = S.sno and F.tno = T.tno         (aSpecies reps select:  [aFish |
groupby S.sno, T.tno.                           aFish home = aTank
                                              ]) size) display.
                                          Newline display] ].
```

The other SQL aggregate queries of Chapter 5 have signal expression equivalents. First, find the total number of fish in the database. The SQL omitted the groupby-clause, which forced all the selected tuples into one default group. The signal expression simply exploits the fact that the collection of fish already exists as the global variable TheFish:

```
TheFish size display.
```

Next, find the number of fish that inhabit red tanks. You extract the subset of TheFish where the home attribute is red. You then request its size.

```
(TheFish select:  [aFish | aFish home color = "red"]) size display.
```

Now, find the average volume of all red tanks.

```
|sumVolume redTanks|
sumVolume := 0.
redTanks := TheTanks select:  [aTank | aTank color = "red" ].
redTanks do:  [aTank | sumVolume := sumVolume + aTank volume].
redTanks size = 0 ifTrue:  [(sumVolume / redTanks size) display].
```

Next, find the total volume of tanks by species.

```
TheSpecies do:  [aSpecies |
   |sumVol|
   sumVol := 0.
   aSpecies reps home do:  [aTank | sumVol := sumVol + aTank volume].
   (aSpecies name, Tab, sumVol) display.  Newline display].
```

Recall that SQL exhibits a subtlety in this matter. You must be careful to avoid overcounting in a group that contains multiple copies of a tank due to multiple interconnecting fish. This problem doesn't arise in the signal expression because the database path reps home returns a TankSet. Because it is a set, TankSet suppresses any duplicates that might be introduced by two fish in the reps collection belonging to the same tank.

Now, find the volume of the largest tank containing all species. The max: signal, directed at a number or a string, compares the target with the parameter and returns the larger.

```
|maxVol|
maxVol := 0.
(TheTanks select:  [aTank | population breed contains:  TheSpecies])
   do:  [aTank | maxVol := maxVol max:  aTank volume].
maxVol display.
```

Like an SQL having-clause, a signal expression can also reject certain groupings from a partition. The following example lists the average volume of tanks associated with each species, but only for those species represented in two or more tanks.

```
TheSpecies do:  [aSpecies |
   aSpecies reps home size >= 2 ifTrue:  [
      |avgVol|
      avgVol := 0.
      aSpecies reps home do:  [aTank | avgVol := avgVol + aTank volume].
      aSpecies reps home size > 0 ifTrue:  [avgVol := avgVol / aSpecies reps home size].
      (aSpecies name, Tab, avgVol) display.  Newline display] ].
```

Now, find the total tank volume associated with each species, provided that the species is represented by 10 or more fish. This query involves two partitions: one partition isolates the fish of the candidate species, and the other isolates the tanks where the candidate is represented. The first serves to qualify the candidate for inclusion in the answer; the second provides a group for calculating the total volume. The required signal expression is:

```
TheSpecies do:  [aSpecies |
   aSpecies reps size >= 10 ifTrue:  [
      |sumVol|
      sumVol := 0.
      aSpecies reps home do:  [aTank | sumVol := sumVol + aTank volume].
      (aSpecies name, Tab, sumVol) display.  Newline display] ].
```

Finally, consider a query where the result of an aggregate must be passed to another aggregate. The SQL solution creates an intermediate table with the into-clause, or it uses embedded SQL to access a general-purpose programming language. A signal expression is already a program in a general-purpose language, so the latter route is readily available. The query is: compose a list of the average tank volumes associated with each species and then report the average of those numbers. The signal expression below adapts an earlier solution, which reported the average volume by species.

```
|listOfAverages finalAvg|
listOfAverages := Set new.
TheSpecies do:  [aSpecies |
   |avgVol|
   avgVol := 0.
   aSpecies reps home do:  [aTank | avgVol := avgVol + aTank volume].
   aSpecies reps home size > 0 ifTrue:  [avgVol := avgVol / aSpecies reps home size].
   listOfAverages add:  avgVol.]
finalAvg := 0.
listOfAverages do:  [aNumber | finalAvg := finalAvg + aNumber].
listOfAverages size > 0 ifTrue:  [finalAvg := finalAvg / listOfAverages size].
finalAvg display.
```

SQL can't express certain recursive queries where the depth of the recursion depends on the data. Instead, you must use embedded SQL to access a more general programming language. However, signal expressions already have access to the necessary features of a general-purpose language. Therefore, recursive queries present no difficulty, as you will see in the next section.

Recursive queries

One-to-many recursive relationships

Consider the employee database from Chapter 2. In the equivalent object-oriented database, the single entity is the employee class, and each instance contains strings to identify an employee: name, address, and phone. Each instance also contains a supervisor attribute (i.e., another employee) and a set of workers. Figure 8.10 summarizes the situation, showing two layers of the recursion.

Chapter 3 discussed the query: find the workers who report to a specified employee through any number of levels in the chain of command. The query is beyond the capabilities of relational algebra because the number of recursive layers can't be bounded independently of the data. Neither SQL, nor its underlying mathematical equivalents, relational algebra or calculus, provides an iteration mechanism to handle the case where the number of iterations isn't a constant. In other words, these access languages have no equivalent of the traditional while-loop, which is available in all procedural languages. They have only the equivalent of a restricted for-loop in which the bounds are constants.

Of course, embedded SQL can handle the query because it provides access to a general-purpose host language. For the same reason, signal expressions can also process the query. The following segment reports the names of all employees who are named joe or who report to joe at any level below him. Assume all the employees are available in the global collection TheEmployees. Also assume that employee objects respond to the usual attribute signals. The database schema in Figure 8.11 sketches the situation. Also assume, as in Chapter 2, that the relationship between an employee and his workers is one-to-many and that no cycles appear in the chain of command. In the absence of cycles, the inchain collection in the solution below can never process the same employee more than once. Therefore, it must eventually become empty, and the algorithm will terminate.

```
|inchain|
inchain := TheEmployees select:  [aEmployee | anEmployee name = "joe"].
[inchain isEmpty] whileFalse:  [
   |anEmployee|
   anEmployee := inchain choose.
   inchain remove:  anEmployee.
   inchain addAll:  anEmployee workers.
   anEmployee name display.  Newline display].
```

The idea is to start the inchain collection with all workers named joe and then to remove these workers, one at a time, report their names, and place all their subordinate workers back in the inchain collection. As long as inchain isn't empty, workers who haven't been reported remain in the chain of command under joe.

The whileFalse: signal, addressed to a code block, provides the traditional while loop. Of course, the whileTrue: method is also available. When a code block receives the whileFalse: signal, it evaluates itself to obtain a boolean. If the boolean is false, the

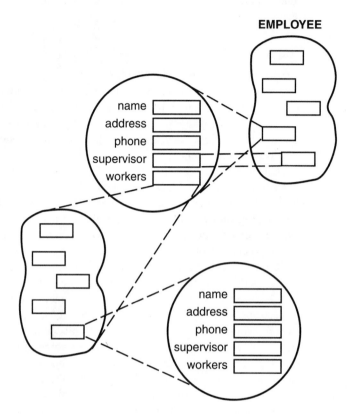

Figure 8.10   A one-to-many recursive relationship in an object-oriented context

```
Object subclass:  "Employee"
  instanceVariables:  ("name", "address", "phone", "supervisor", "workers")
  constraints:  (("name", String), ("address", String), ("phone", String),
    ("supervisor", Employee), ("workers", EmployeeSet)).
Set subclass:  "EmployeeSet" constraint:  Employee.
EmployeeSet subclass:  "EmployeeDatabase".

TheEmployees := EmployeeDatabase new.
```

Figure 8.11   Schema for the object-oriented recursive Employees database

parameter block is evaluated, and control loops back to evaluate the receiver again. If the boolean is true, the parameter code isn't executed, and control leaves the statement. The solution above also uses the choose signal to select an arbitrary element from a set. The target set returns null if it's empty.

Many-to-many recursive relationships

Consider the parts explosion example, which was also introduced in Chapter 2. In this case, the relationship between the parts class and itself is many-to-many. A part comprises many subparts, and it is also a component in many superparts. Figure 8.12 summarizes the situation. Each part has a string attribute, name, and two set attributes: subparts, which contains all its component parts, and superparts, which contains all the assemblies in which it participates. The object-oriented schema appears in Figure 8.13. You need to assume the usual attribute methods.

A signal expression easily handles the traditional parts explosion query, as shown in the code segment below. The code implements a generic explode: method for the part class. The output to the right illustrates an explosion of front suspension, assuming the data of Figure 2.21. Although you could solve this query with an iterative technique, this solution illustrates direct recursion in a method definition.

```
Part method: "explode:" code: [anIndentation |           front suspension
  |temp|                                                    axle bracket
  temp := anIndentation.                                    wheel
  [temp > 0] whileTrue: [                                     tire
    Tab display. temp := temp - 1].                           hub
  self name display. Newline display.                         bearing race
  self subparts do: [aPart |                                  ball bearing
    aPart explode: anIndentation + 1] ].                    bolt
                                                           axle
Parts do: [aPart |                                         cotter pin
  aPart name = "front suspension" ifTrue: [
    aPart explode: 0] ].
```

Data editing operations

You can insert, update, and delete database information through the appropriate signals, most of which have already appeared in the examples to this point.

Insertion of new objects

Inserting new objects is straightforward: you create them from the appropriate class template, establish their attribute values, and connect them with related objects. Suppose you want to add a new green fish named calvin. Calvin is a shark and will live in the cesspool tank. For this example, suppose the names of the species and tank are sufficient to locate the objects. Because there are no keys and because OIDs aren't accessible, you must take care to ensure that you can identify each application object. If the names, color, and volumes of the tanks are all subject to duplication, you'll probably want to include a tankNumber attribute as a unique identifier from the application viewpoint. For the moment, however, assume that a tank or a species can be uniquely identified by its name. The following excerpt adds the new fish and connects it properly with other database objects.

TheParts

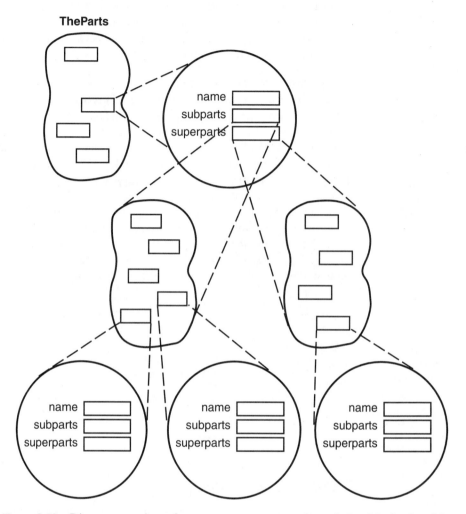

Figure 8.12: Direct expression of a many-to-many recursive relationship in the object-oriented model

```
Object subclass:  "Part"
   instanceVariables:  ("name", "subparts", "superparts")
   constraints:  (("name", String), ("subparts", PartSet), ("superparts", PartSet))
Set subclass:  "PartsSet" constraint:  Part.
PartsSet subclass:  "PartsDatabase".

TheParts := PartsDatabase new.
```

Figure 8.13   Partial object-oriented schema for the Parts database

```
|aSpecies aTank aFish|
aSpecies := (TheSpecies select:  [bSpecies | bSpecies name = "shark"]) choose.
aTank := (TheTanks select:  [bTank | bTank name = "cesspool"]) choose.
aFish := Fish new; initialize; breed:  aSpecies; home:  aTank;
   name:  "calvin"; color:  "green"; experience:  (EventSet new).
TheFish add:  aFish.
aSpecies reps:  (aSpecies reps add:  aFish).
aTank population:  (aTank population add:  aFish).
```

You add the new fish not only to the overall collection, TheFish, but also to the aSpecies reps and aTank population sets. These adjustments maintain the referential links between the fish and its species and between the fish and its tank. Because the reps signal might deliver a copy of its fish collection, the modified collection is reinstated with the reps: signal. Exporting attribute values by copy was discussed in Chapter 7 in connection with constraints. Whether these precautions are necessary is determined by the application. The insertion code installs the new fish in the reps attribute collection and then writes that collection back into the attribute. The update, therefore, is registered in the species object, regardless of the method used to export the reps attribute. A similar procedure is followed to adjust the population attribute of the tank containing the new fish.

Of course, adding fish one at a time is tedious, as was the case with the SQL insert statement. Recall that most relational DBMS products automate the process with a load utility, a feature outside of SQL proper. Because you compose signal expressions in the context of a general programming language, you can easily accommodate loading from an external file. For example, suppose you want to load a large number of fish from a file named "fishfile." The file format presents each fish on a single line, which gives the name and color strings followed by the species and tank names. The general form of the file manipulation activity follows.

```
|aFile|
aFile := File open:  "fishfile".
[aFile endOfFile] whileFalse:  [
  |aFish aSpecies aTank aString|
  aFish := Fish new; initialize; experience:  (EventSet new).
  aFish name:  (aFile readString); color:  (aFile readString).
  aString := aFile readString.
  aSpecies := (TheSpecies select:  [bSpecies | bSpecies name = aString]) choose.
  aString := aFile readString.
  aTank := (TheTanks select:  [bTank | bTank name = aString]) choose.
  fish breed:  aSpecies; home:  aTank.
  TheFish add:  aFish.
  aSpecies reps:  (aSpecies reps add:  aFish).
  aTank population:  (aTank population add:  aFish)].
aFile close.
```

The system class File responds to the open: signal by delivering an open file with the specified name, positioned at the beginning of its information stream. Of course, there are variations that specify how to proceed if the file doesn't exist, but you won't need those details. The file object then responds to a variety of file manipulation signals, such as `readString` and `endOfFile`. The first returns the next string from the file—the next sequence of characters delimited by "white space" (i.e., spaces, tabs, and newline markers); the second returns true when no characters remain to be read.

Deletion of objects

Just as in SQL, you can also undertake mass deletions. All the apparatus developed earlier to locate objects before displaying them is also available to identify a collection of objects to purge from the database. For example, the following excerpt deletes the fish in red tanks:

```
|markedFish|
markedFish := (TheTanks select:  [aTank | aTank color = "red"]) population.
markedFish do:  [aFish |
   aFish home population:  (aFish home population remove:  aFish).
   aFish breed reps:  (aFish breed reps remove:  aFish).
   aFish experience do:  [anEvent | anEvent subject:  null].
   TheEvents removeAll:  aFish experience.
   aFish experience:  null.  aFish home:  null.  aFish breed:  null.
   TheFish remove:  aFish].
```

Using a database path construction to accumulate the contributions from the red tanks, you assemble the fish to be deleted in a collection called markedFish. You then delete them, not only from TheFish but also from the specialized collections associated with their tanks and species. Note that the solution also removes the event objects belonging to a doomed fish. The solution accommodates the possibility that the reps and population attributes are exported by copy.

Chapter 7 discussed constraints that behave the same as the on-delete trigger in SQL. If such a constraint has been established, the code doesn't need to deal with removing the event objects in the experience attribute of a fish. That compensatory activity will be launched when the fish is removed from the global collection. The above solution still works, however, because the cascading deletion simply finds no event objects. They have already been deleted before the command to remove the fish. Moreover, the experience, home, and breed attributes of the doomed fish have all been set to null to reflect the severed connections. This precaution isn't strictly necessary because these attributes won't be available after the fish are deleted.

A deletion operation through signal expressions suffers somewhat in comparison with SQL because you must clean up the relationships that might be damaged. In the example above, you must remove the targeted fish object from the population collection of its home tank and from the reps collection of its breed species. In SQL, these references to tank and species are contained within the target fish tuple, and therefore you don't need to give them special consideration. The reverse connection, from tank to fish, for example, isn't represented in SQL. Because connections exist in both directions in the object-oriented model, you must be careful not to leave any dangling references to a deleted object.

Consider again the following query from Chapter 5: delete the tanks containing a species named shark. The deletion challenges referential integrity because fish swimming in the deleted tanks will contain a dangling reference. From the system standpoint, the reference isn't dangling because the garbage collector won't remove a tank while it is reachable from a global collection. As long as a tank is reachable through a fish in TheFish, it will remain in the system. But the reference is dangling from an application viewpoint. When you remove a tank from TheTanks, you intend to remove it completely from the database. The deletion code should accomplish this goal, or all remove: signals should be intercepted to coordinate the activity in one place. The first solution appears below. You maintain referential integrity by setting the home attribute to null for each fish inhabiting a doomed tank.

```
|markedTanks|
markedTanks := TheTanks select:  [aTank |
    aTank population breed name includes:  "shark"].
markedTanks do:  [aTank |
    aTank population do:  [aFish | aFish home:  null].
    TheTanks remove:  aTank].
```

The second approach adheres to the spirit of similar constraints from Chapter 7. It allows the OODBMS to enforce referential integrity by intercepting the remove: signal in the TankHandle class, where TheTanks is the only object. The method code appears below. You can imitate it to establish similar referential integrity constraints between species and fish and between fish and events.

```
TankHandle method:  "remove:" code:  [aTank |
    aTank population do:  [aFish | aFish home:  null].
    ^super remove:  aTank].
```

Updating objects

Updates in SQL can challenge referential integrity when a key attribute is changed. Because keys aren't necessary in an object-oriented representation, this problem doesn't occur in signal expressions for updates. For example, you can change any attribute of a tank object, and it still remains the home of its collection of fish. The home attribute of a fish refers to a tank through a system-guaranteed identity that is independent of any of its attributes.

   Suppose you want to change the tank color of those tanks containing a dolphin. The new color is to be red. The solution appears on the left below.

```
|markedTanks|                                          TheTanks do:  [aTank |
markedTanks := TheTanks select:  [aTank |                   aTank color = "red" ifTrue:  [
   aTank population breed name includes:  "dolphin"].          aTank volume:  1.1 * aTank volume] ].
markedTanks do:  [aTank | aTank color:  "red"].
```

Of course, you can calculate the replacement value in an update from the old entry. For example, the code on the right above increases the volume of all red tanks by 10%.

Signal expressions from SQL

The examples so far have demonstrated that signal expressions can imitate all the features of SQL. Moreover, several examples have illustrated cases where signal expressions are better than SQL. For example, to solve recursive queries where the depth of the recursion is data-dependent, you must use embedded SQL to gain access to a while-loop. By contrast, you can construct recursive methods directly with signal expressions.

Despite the simplicity of the object-oriented model, the signal expressions in this chapter seem no more intuitive than non-procedural SQL. Although you have the benefit of a simple and powerful mental model, you must still assemble the various signal alternatives into a plan to retrieve the desired data. In short, you must still write a program to access an object-oriented database. With a relational DBMS, on the other hand, you need only describe the desired information. Besides its equivalent or greater simplicity, SQL enjoys another advantage: many people are familiar with SQL as a database access language. For both these reasons, an SQL interface to object-oriented databases is needed. The interface allows you to use object-oriented methodology during the database design and implementation phases, and it permits the users of the final product to continue with the familiar SQL. Most commercial object-oriented databases have an SQL interface, usually called OOSQL. Within certain broad restrictions, this interface isn't difficult to construct, as you will see in this section. It must simply accept an SQL statement and generate a corresponding signal expression.

Restricting translation to a particular SQL format

At the outset, you should realize that certain far-fetched SQL queries can never be automatically translated into signal expressions because they involve keys and foreign keys from the relational tables in unexpected ways. In the aquarium database, for example, find the tanks where the tno value is equal to the volume. You can easily formulate this ad hoc query in SQL as follows:

```
select T.tname
from Tank T
where T.tno = T.tvolume.
```

Although it's conceivable that you might pose such a query, the response isn't very meaningful in terms of the application. The tno values serve to identify the tanks through a concise attribute and to maintain relationships between tanks and their fish. A different assignment of tno values can accomplish this same purpose but yield a different answer to the query. When you ask for a tank whose tno value is equal to its volume, you are asking for a tank that accidentally satisfies some criterion. These queries appear from time to time, mostly in academic textbooks, but they aren't common.

Although signal expressions can imitate key-matching activity that corresponds to the intended usage of the keys, they can't use the key values as part of an arbitrary condition. The reason, of course, is that the object-oriented model doesn't store any keys. Entity integrity is already guaranteed because an object-oriented database maintains objects in a record-oriented, as opposed to value-oriented, fashion. Once you create an object, its existence is independent of its attribute values. A relational tuple, on the other hand, maintains its identity only across changes to its nonkey attributes. When the key is changed, it becomes a different tuple. For all practical purposes, the key is the tuple's identity. When you model an application object as a database object, you don't need a key attribute with its associated metaphysical connotations and constraints. In effect, the object's machine address (i.e., OID) plays the role of a key, and that address isn't subject to user manipulation. In particular, it can't be null. Similarly, because it uses logical inclusion to maintain relationships, the object-oriented model has no need for foreign keys. However, referential integrity isn't automatically guaranteed. Previous examples have illustrated cases where it might be violated through updates or deletions.

Therefore, the algorithmic translation of SQL into signal expressions will deal only with SQL statements that use keys and foreign keys to reference the intended relationships. They can appear in equality comparisons in the where-clause boolean to remove inappropriate combinations from the Cartesian product of the from-clause. They can also appear in the groupby-clause, but they can't occur in the select-, orderby-, or having-clauses. Nor can they be arguments of aggregate functions.

Converting relational tables to classes

Translating SQL automatically into signal expressions depends on a fundamental alignment between the relational tables and the object classes. Assume the following context. Each relational table, R, corresponds to an application entity. A corresponding class, R, appears as follows in the system hierarchy. The intervening ApplicationClass holds attributes common to all the application classes, such as creator and creationDate.

```
Object                              Set
    ApplicationClass                    ApplicationSetClass
        R₁                                  R₁-Set
        R₂                                  R₂-Set
          ⋮                                   ⋮
```

Objects belonging to class R correspond to the tuples in relation R. Moreover, each R is associated with a corresponding R-Set, positioned under the system Set class as shown above. The objects corresponding to the R-tuples are contained in an instance of R-Set, called The-Rs. This setup is consistent with the notation used with the aquarium database. That is, you have a fish class, matching the fish table schema, and a FishSet class, from which you can clone sets of fish, including TheFish that corresponds to the body of the fish table. Of course, the attributes of the relation R correspond to the instance variables of the class R.

Because of this correspondence and because the classes parallel the relational tables, object-oriented translation will have only one-to-many relationships. Relational tables can't directly represent many-to-many relationships. You could translate SQL, with references to factored many-to-many relationships, into a signal expression for a database that doesn't contain the intersection objects. However, you would have to accommodate signals to phantom classes. Such an interface is possible, but it is more complicated than what is needed here. The discussion here will retain the simpler one-to-one correspondence between relational tables and user-defined classes and its consequent constraint of one-to-many relationships in the object-oriented translation.

When table R_1 contains foreign key a_1, referencing a tuple in table R_2, assume that the instance variable a_1, defined in class R_1, is constrained to an object of class R_2. An object of class R_1 then contains the referenced object of class R_2 in attribute a_1. For example, the tno attribute (a_1) of the fish table (R_1) refers to a tuple in the tank table. Then attribute tno (a_1) of a fish object contains the tank object corresponding to the referenced tank tuple. This attribute has been called "home" in the examples so far. However, because the correlated object-oriented schema must now be constructed algorithmically from a relational schema, the available foreign-key attribute name, tno, is used instead.

The relational model provides for a reference from the "many" relation to the "one" relation, but not for a reference in the reverse direction. For example, the fish table contains a reference, tno, to the tank table, but the tank table contains no reference to the fish table. However, the object-oriented model contains mutual references. So if a_1 is a foreign key in table R_1, referencing a tuple in table R_2, then each object in class R_2 contains an attribute r_1, which contain the *set* of objects in R_1 that reference it. For example, the fish table (R_1) contains the foreign key tno (a_1) referencing the tank table (R_2). Therefore, each tank object contains an attribute "fish," which contains the set of fish objects referring to the tank. Earlier sections called this attribute "population." In the automatic translation, it is generated from the name of the table containing the foreign key reference. Therefore, it has the derived name "fish."

Summarizing the last two paragraphs in terms of the fish and tank tables of the aquarium database, you have each fish object with an attribute, tno, containing its home tank, and each tank object with an attribute, fish, containing its set of fish. In general, each foreign key that links two tables gives rise to two reciprocal attributes in the corresponding classes.

The notation can become awkward in unusual circumstances. For example, assume there are two one-to-many relationships between the species and fish tables. The first associates a fish with the species it represents, and the second associates a fish with the species that it imitates at the annual Halloween party. In this case, the translated fish class needs two sno attributes to refer to its two species. However, the relational schema already deals with that problem. So you can expect sno-real and sno-pretend attributes in the fish table, and you can use these names in the translation to a fish class. However, the translated species class needs two "fish" attributes, one for each of its populations. The relational schema doesn't take care of this direction, so the translation must install two fish populations, say, fish$_1$ and fish$_2$. In general, the translation algorithm must install a pair of attributes for each one-to-many relationship in the relational schema. If name conflicts occur, additional notation is necessary to maintain the distinctions. Because multiple relations between the same pair of tables don't occur in the aquarium database, this issue doesn't arise.

Using these conventions, the aquarium relation schema of Chapter 2 then translates to the object-oriented schema of Figure 8.14.

The general form of a select-project-join query to be translated

Designing an SQL interface is a lengthy undertaking because it must consider all SQL features. The more modest intent here is to argue that an automatic translation from SQL to signal expressions is possible within the framework discussed above. Therefore, the following discussion will develop the algorithm to show how to translate select-project-join queries in some detail. You will then learn how to incorporate further SQL features into the procedure.

The starting point is an SQL expression of the general form on the left below and a list of the one-to-many relationships of the form $R_1.a = R_2.b$, interpreted as follows. The foreign key, a, in relation R_1 refers to the primary key, b, in relation R_2. For the aquarium database these relationships appears on the right below.

```
Object subclass:  "AquariumClass"
  instanceVariables:  ("creator", "creationDate", "modificationDate")
  constraints:  (("creator", String), ("creationDate", String),
      ("modificationDate", String)).
AquariumClass subclass:  "Species"
  instanceVariables:  ("sname", "sfood", "fish")
  constraints:  (("sname", String), ("sfood", String), ("fish", FishSet)).
AquariumClass subclass:  "Tank"
  instanceVariables:  ("tname", "tcolor", "tvolume", "fish")
  constraints:  (("tname", String), ("tcolor", String), ("tvolume", Number),
      ("fish", FishSet)).
AquariumClass subclass:  "Fish"
  instanceVariables:  ("fname", "fcolor", "fweight", "tno", "sno", "event")
  constraints:  (("fname", String), ("fcolor", String), ("fweight", Number),
     ("tno", Tank), ("sno", Species), ("event", EventSet)).
AquariumClass subclass:  "Event"
  instanceVariables:  ("edate", "enote", "fno")
  constraints:  (("edate", DateTime), ("enote", String), ("fno", Fish)).

Set subclass:  "AquariumSet".
AquariumSet subclass:  "SpeciesSet"
  constraint:  Species.
AquariumSet subclass:  "TankSet"
  constraint:  Tank.
AquariumSet subclass:  "FishSet"
  constraint:  Fish.
AquariumSet subclass:  "EventSet"
  constraint:  Event.

TheSpecies := SpeciesSet new.
TheTanks := TankSet new.
TheFish := FishSet new.
TheEvents := EventSet new.
```

Figure 8.14   Object-oriented aquarium schema translated from the relational format

```
select output list          Fish.tno = Tank.tno
from table list             Fish.sno = Species.sno
where where boolean         Event.fno = Fish.fno.
orderby orderby list
```

Each reference to a relational table, R, either directly or through an alias, translates into a signal directed to the corresponding global set, The$R$s. For example, the appearance of the fish table in the from-clause results in a do: signal being sent to TheFish. Although an example is used here to develop the algorithm, the translation actually proceeds mechanically. To demonstrate the translation, consider the query: find the names of species swimming with a shark and order the results by species name. The initial SQL is:

```
select S.name
from Species S, Fish F, Tank T, Fish G, Species H
where S.sno = F.sno and F.tno = T.tno and T.tno = G.tno and G.sno = H.sno and H.name = "shark"
orderby S.name.
```

The overall format of the translation algorithm

Step one is to lay out a series of nested do: signals, one for each table mentioned in the SQL from-clause. If the SQL gives a unique alias to a table, use the alias as the dummy variable in the do: parameter code block. Otherwise, give each table a unique alias for this purpose and qualify all references to attributes with these aliases. You send the do: signals to the global collections that correspond to the from-clause tables.

The final layer in the innermost nest is controlled by the object-oriented equivalent of the where-boolean, to which you send an ifTrue: signal. Any code placed in the innermost segment of the nest can simultaneously deal with an instance from each of the application classes. A dummy variable represent each instance, and the dummy variables are all visible in the innermost segment. Of course, some of the signals indicated in the boolean aren't meaningful because they involve key attributes that aren't maintained in the object-oriented version. These elements will be removed in subsequent steps. In constructing the where-boolean, replace qualified attribute names (e.g., F.color) with the corresponding attribute signals (e.g., F color). In the example, the method plan then starts as follows:

```
TheSpecies do:  [S |
   TheFish do:  [F |
      TheTanks do:  [T |
         TheFish do:  [G |
            TheSpecies do:  [H |
               (S sno = F sno) & (F tno = T tno) & (T tno = G tno) &
               (G sno = H sno) & (H sname = "shark") ifTrue:  [······] ] ] ] ] ].
```

Next, examine the where-clause boolean for any entries that correspond to equality conditions in the list of relationship mappings. For each of these items, remove the loop associated with the table on the right side of the equality (i.e., the "one" side of the relationship), and replace its dummy variable with a temporary variable of the same name. Place the temporary variable inside the loop corresponding to the table on the left side of the equality (i.e., the "many" side of the relationship). Next, assign the temporary variable a value, which you obtain calling the attribute signal of the foreign key in the mapping rule. Finally, remove the offending item from the boolean. This explanation is much more complicated than the actual operation. In the example, you find F.sno = S.sno in the boolean, which corresponds to one of the entries in the relationship mapping list. This relationship rule mentions Species and Fish, but you operate in the context of the aliases to identify S with Species and F with Fish. So you remove the loop associated with the S variable, establish a temporary variable of the same name, S, within the F loop, and assign to S the object returned by the call F sno. Finally, you shorten the boolean by removing the F.sno = S.sno component. The code segment appears below:

```
TheFish do:  [F |
  |S|
  S := F sno.
  TheTanks do:  [T |
    TheFish do:  [G |
      TheSpecies do:  [H |
        (F tno = T tno) & (T tno = G tno) &
        (G sno = H sno) & (H sname = "shark") ifTrue:  [·····] ] ] ] ].
```

Note that the innermost nested segment still has access to all the objects from the various components that make up the query. However, the S variable is now always bound to the species that the F fish object represents. In other words, the S species and the F fish are aligned so that F represents S. This alignment is exactly the intent of the first part of the where-clause.

Next, you find the F.tno = T.tno entry in the boolean and the corresponding relationship list entry. Following the rule, you discard the T loop and replace its dummy variable with the reference F.tno, which results in the following reduced code:

```
TheFish do:  [F |
  |S T|
  S := F sno.  T := F tno.
  TheFish do:  [G |
    TheSpecies do:  [H |
      (T tno = G tno) & (G sno = H sno) & (H sname = "shark") ifTrue:  [·····] ] ] ].
```

You now encounter G.tno = T.tno in the boolean, which corresponds again to the relationship entry Fish.tno = Tank.tno. This discovery provokes an attempt to discard the T loop. However, you have already discarded that loop. In this case, you dispense with the loop elimination and new variable declaration parts of the process. You simply replace the boolean condition with T = G tno, which gives the following expression:

```
TheFish do:  [F |
  |S T|
  S := F sno.  T := F tno.
  TheFish do:  [G |
    TheSpecies do:  [H |
      (T = G tno) & (G sno = H sno) & (H sname = "shark") ifTrue:  [·····] ] ] ].
```

A final application of a mapping rule processes G sno = H sno to remove the H loop and gives the following shell:

```
TheFish do:  [F |
  |S T|
  S := F sno.  T := F tno.
  TheFish do:  [G |
    |H|
    H := G sno.
    (T = G tno) & (H sname = "shark") ifTrue:  [·····] ] ].
```

Finally, you concatenate the strings to be displayed and place them in an answer collection, which you must declare as a temporary variable at the outermost level. This final step gives the following solution to the translation problem:

```
|answer|
answer := Set new.
TheFish do:  [F |
  |S T|
  S := F sno.  T := F tno.
  TheFish do:  [G |
    |H|
    H := G sno.
    (T = G tno) & (H sname = "shark") ifTrue:  [answer add:  S sname] ] ].
answer asSortedCollection do:  [aString | aString display.  Newline display].
```

An alternative transformation of the initial translation shell

An alternative algorithm is useful for handling aggregates. Consider again the algorithm above. When you process a foreign-key matchup in the where-clause, you retain the loop on the "many" side of the relationship and introduce a dummy variable on the "one" side. Another possibility is to keep both loops but replace the do: target of the "many" side with an intersection of the current target and the inverse attribute of the foreign key. Again, this description sounds complicated, but the operation is actually quite simple. For example, the initial shell of the solution is the same as before:

```
TheSpecies do:  [S |
  TheFish do:  [F |
    TheTanks do:  [T |
      TheFish do:  [G |
        TheSpecies do:  [H |
          (S sno = F sno) & (F tno = T tno) & (T tno = G tno) &
          (G sno = H sno) & (H sname = "shark") ifTrue:  [······] ] ] ] ] ].
```

You want to remove the component S sno = F sno from the boolean construction in the innermost loop. Taking the alternative route, you keep both the S and F loops but replace TheFish with the intersection of TheFish and S fish because fish (in a species object) is the inverse attribute associated with sno (in a fish object). You also take care that the S loop lies outside of the F loop. (The algorithm calls for one loop for each table of the from-clause, but it doesn't specify a particular order.) Because TheFish contains all fish, the intersection is simply S fish, which gives the expression:

```
TheSpecies do:  [S |
  S fish do:  [F |
    TheTanks do:  [T |
      TheFish do:  [G |
        TheSpecies do:  [H |
          (F tno = T tno) & (T tno = G tno) &
          (G sno = H sno) & (H sname = "shark") ifTrue:  [······] ] ] ] ] ].
```

Continuing this process with the remaining foreign keys, you arrive at the following expression. You need to complete the ellipsis in the innermost construction as before to accumulate S sname strings in an answer set.

```
TheSpecies do:  [S |
   TheTanks do:  [T |
      (S fish intersect:  T fish) do:  [F |
         TheSpecies do:  [H |
            (T fish intersect:  H fish) do:  [G |
               (H sname = "shark") ifTrue:  [······] ] ] ] ] ].
```

Both algorithms yield inefficient signal expressions, but they are functionally correct. Optimization can start at this point. In the second expression, just above, the boolean depends only on the H binding. Therefore, you can move the H loop and its immediate test for H sname = "shark" to the outermost level. Because no more components remain in the boolean, the mere existence of non-empty target objects in the innermost loop places a string in the answer set. So you can rearrange the solution as follows:

```
TheSpecies do:  [H |
   H sname = "shark" ifTrue:  [
      TheSpecies do:  [S |
         (S fish intersect:  T fish) isEmpty not &
         (T fish intersect:  H fish) isEmpty not) ifTrue:  [······] ] ].
```

Suppose that the query requests, in addition to the species name, the names of the cohabiting tanks. Suppose that it also asks for a presentation order by species name and by tank name within species. Below is the SQL starting point.

```
select S.sname, T.tname
from Species S, Fish F, Tank T, Fish G, Species H
where S.sno = F.sno and F.tno = T.tno and T.tno = G.tno and G.sno = H.sno and H.sname = "shark"
orderby S.sname, T.tname.
```

The translation differs only in the detail of the concatenated strings added to the answer set in the innermost loop. Using the first approach, you eliminate loops associated with the "one" side of any many-to-one relationship. This gives the following solution:

```
|answer|
answer := Set new.
TheFish do:  [F |
   |S T|
   S := F sno.  T := F tno.
   TheFish do:  [G |
      |H|
      H := G sno.
      (T = G tno) & (H sname = "shark") ifTrue:  [
         answer add:  (S sname leftJustify:  20), Tab, T tname] ] ].
answer asSortedCollection do:  [aString | aString display.  Newline display].
```

You can algorithmically translate SQL into signal expressions by providing a nest of do: *signals, one for each from-clause table. You place the where-clause boolean in the innermost scope and remove conditions corresponding to foreign-key alignments. Appropriate changes in the looping structure are also required.*

Extending the algorithm to subqueries

The algorithm extends to subqueries because you can use it recursively to build the subquery sets. Consider the query: find the names of worm-eating species that inhabit all red tanks by means of a fish weighing more than 30 pounds. The starting point is the SQL solution on the left below. You build the shell of the translation as in the previous example, leaving the subquery for a subsequent pass through the algorithm. The initial shell appears on the right.

```
select S.sname                              |answer|
from Species S                              answer := Set new.
where S.sfood = "worm" and not exists       TheSpecies do:  [S |
   (select *                                  |subQuery|
   from Tank T                                   :
   where T.tcolor = "red" and not exists         : {construct subquery set here}
      (select *                                   :
      from Fish F                              (S sfood = "worm") & (subQuery isEmpty)
      where F.tno = T.tno and F.sno = S.sno       ifTrue:  [answer add:  S sname] ].
        and F.weight > 30)).                 answer do:  [aString |
                                                aString display.  Newline display].
```

You construct the subquery by selecting tank objects as directed by the SQL. A loop simply acquires the red tanks where a further subquery is empty.

```
subQuery := Set new.
TheTanks do:  [T |
   |subSubQuery|
      :
      : {construct innermost subquery set here }
      :
   (T tcolor = "red") & (subSubQuery isEmpty) ifTrue:  [subQuery add:  T] ].
```

The innermost subquery commands a similar construction. Note that the S and T variables from the hosting loops are available for the boolean.

```
subSubQuery := Set new.
TheFish do:  [F |
   (F tno = T) & (F sno = S) & (F fweight > 30) ifTrue:  [subSubQuery add:  F] ].
```

When you substitute the subquery components into the original shell, you obtain a final translation of the query.

Extending the algorithm to partitions and aggregates

The translation of SQL with aggregates presents complications in the general case. The discussion here covers the special situation where an application class defines the partition. The example involves grouping by sno. Because sno is a key, this is the same as grouping by species. The translation places the loops corresponding to the grouping variables at the outermost levels and adopts a foreign-key resolution policy that retains these loops. For example, consider the query: find the species cohabiting with a shark, count the number of cohabiting tanks for each such species, compute the smallest, largest, and average volumes of these tanks, and report in order of species name. The SQL solution appears as follows:

```
select S.sname, count(*) tankCount, min(T.tvolume) minVol,
   avg(T.tvolume) avgVol, max(T.tvolume) maxVol
from Species S, Tank T
where exists
   (select *
   from Fish F, Fish G, Species H
   where S.sno = F.sno and F.tno = T.tno and T.tno = G.tno and
      G.sno = H.sno and H.name = "shark"
groupby S.sno
orderby S.name.
```

You start with two nested loops for the S and T variables, keeping the S loop outermost because the groupby-clause specifies species as the grouping criterion. The algorithm recognizes the attribute sno as a key because of its position in the relationship rule: F.sno = S.sno. Just inside the loops for the groupby classes, you establish temporary variables as needed for the aggregates. By adopting aliases for each of the selected aggregates (if not already given in the SQL), you have a ready source for these variable names.

```
|answer|
answer := Set new.
TheSpecies do:  [S |
   |tankCount minVol, avgVol, maxVol|
   tankCount := 0.  minVol := null.  avgVol := 0.  maxVol := null.
   TheTanks do:  [T |
      |subquery|
      subquery := Set new.

         ⋮

      subquery isEmpty not ifTrue:  [
         tankCount := tankCount + 1.
         maxVol = null
            ifTrue:  [maxVol := T tvolume] ifFalse:  [maxVol := maxVol max:  T tvolume].
         minVol = null
            ifTrue:  [minVol := T tvolume] ifFalse:  [minVol := minVol min:  T tvolume].
         avgVol := avgVol + T tvolume] ].
   tankCount > 0 ifTrue:  [
      answer add:  (S sname leftJustify:  20), " ", tankCount, " ", minVol, " ",
         (avgVol / tankCount), " ", maxVol] ]
answer asSortedCollection do:  [aString | aString display.  Newline display].
```

The nested computation for the subquery starts as follows. It establishes a shell with loops for F, G, and H.

```
TheFish do:  [F |
   TheFish do:  [G |
      TheSpecies do:  [H |
         (S sno = F sno) & (F tno = T tno) & (T tno = G tno) &
         (G sno = H sno) & (H name = "shark") ifTrue:  [subquery add:  F] ] ] ].
```

Noting an opportunity to replace the S loop because of the S.sno = F.sno in the boolean, you realize that the S loop is outside the scope of the subquery because it refers to a variable from the hosting loop. Therefore, you replace the condition with S = F sno. Similarly, F.tno = T.tno and T.tno = G.tno become F tno = T and T = G tno respectively. However, the term G.sno = H.sno does allow you to remove the H loop. The patch then becomes:

```
TheFish do:  [F |
   TheFish do:  [G |
      |H|
      H := G sno.
      (S = F sno) & (F tno = T) & (T = G tno) &
      (H sname = "shark") ifTrue:  [subquery add:  F] ] ].
```

 The translation extends to subqueries. It uses the previous version to accumulate the sets commanded by the subquery computations. The translation also extends to aggregates by placing the groupby loops at the outermost level.

Object Query Language (OQL)

The goal of the Object Database Management Group (ODMG) is to standardize the features of object-oriented database products. One of the ODMG proposals is a standard access language called Object Query Language (OQL). OQL retains as much of the SQL format as possible while adapting it to an object-oriented context. This section briefly revisits some of the earlier queries of this chapter and shows you how to translate them into OQL. In the following discussion, Smalltalk notation refers to the way signal expressions have been written so far in the chapter; OQL refers to the new notation.

OQL notation

The OQL notation for attribute signals is slightly different. Instead of following the target object with the signal, such as f name, you use the format f.name. The new syntax is consistent with a field specification in a C/C++ structure. Database paths are allowed, provided that each step in the path delivers precisely one object. For example, if e is an event object, you can compose the path: e.subject.home.name, which recovers the name of the tank containing the fish that experienced the event e. Each reference delivers a single object: e.subject delivers a fish, and then e.subject.home delivers a tank, and so forth.

Paths that spread out into collections of objects can't be composed with the simple dot-notation. Instead, you must accumulate them with a format that constructs a set, namely a select-statement. For example, if t is a tank object, Smalltalk notation uses the database path t population breed name to obtain the names of species represented in t. However, t.population isn't a single object; it is the collection of fish swimming in tank t. Therefore, in OQL the format t.population.breed isn't defined.

The expression below uses Smalltalk notation for the query: find the names of tanks containing a shark.

```
TheTanks do:  [aTank |
    (aTank population breed name includes:  "shark")
        ifTrue:  [aTank name display.  Newline display] ].
```

To compose the equivalent OQL expression, you can follow the same database path. But as soon as you reach a component that delivers a set, you must compose a select-statement to provide a container for the set. This approach appears on the left below. The OQL subquery creates a set of strings, and the predicate then checks to see if shark is among them.

```
select t.name
from t in TheTanks
where "shark" in                    select f.home.name
   (select f.breed.name            from f in TheFish
   from f in t.population).         where f.breed.name = "shark".
```

Because database paths don't need to be interrupted as long as they are single-valued, you can use the simpler variation on the right. You iterate over TheFish set, probing in one direction with a single-valued database path to obtain its species name and in the other direction to obtain its home tank name.

OQL examples

Consider the following existential query: find the names of species swimming with a shark. A database path in a signal expression extends from a candidate species s as follows: s reps home population breed name. The result is a set of strings, the names of all species cohabiting with s. The signal expression merely tests to see if this set contains the string shark.

However, the equivalent OQL path, s.reps ..., stalls after the first link because a set appears rather than a single object. Therefore, imitating the simpler construction above, you start the OQL as shown on the left below. The select-statement gathers all the sharky tanks, and it corresponds to the final part of the database path: ... home population breed name. The expression extends single-valued database paths in both directions from a fish. You can now complete the query by requesting the species name from those fish whose home tank appears in the first construction. The final form then appears on the right.

```
select f.home                    select g.breed.name
from f in TheFish                from g in TheFish
where f.breed.name = "shark".    where g.home in
                                     (select f.home
                                     from f in TheFish
                                     where f.breed.name = "shark").
```

Now, suppose that the aquarium database directly represents the many-to-many relationship between species and tanks. Each species object contains a tanks attribute, which holds the tanks where it is represented. Similarly, each tank object contains a species attribute, which holds the associated species. The excerpt on the left below is the OQL solution to: find the names of species represented in a cesspool tank. The center OQL excerpt obtains the name of species swimming with a shark.

```
select s.name              select s.name              select s.name
from s in TheSpecies       from s in TheSpecies       from s in TheSpecies
where "cesspool" in        where exists               where for all t in
   (select t.name             (select t                   (select t
    from t in s.tanks).         from t in s.tanks            from t in TheTanks
                                where "shark" in             where t.color = "red") :
                                  (select g.name               (exists f in TheFish :
                                   from g in t.species)).          f.breed = s and f.home = t).
```

The SQL interface to an object-oriented DBMS in the last section restricted the object-oriented schema to one-to-many relationships. From the last two examples, you can see that OQL suffers no such restriction.

For a final example, consider the universal query: find the names of species represented in all red tanks. The OQL solution appears on the far right above. It again assumes the original arrangement where the many-to-many relationship between species and tanks appears as two one-to-many relationships: fish-species and fish-tank. The format illustrates that you can express universal quantification directly in OQL. This provides a distinct advantage over SQL. Therefore, the solution structure follows a universally quantified relational calculus expression more closely than an SQL expression. The OQL format for a universally quantified predicate is for all x in C : B(x). Here, C is a collection, which can be an existing set, such as TheFish, or a computation generated with an embedded select-statement. B(x) is a boolean, with x ranging over the collection. The format for explicit existential quantification is similar, and both are illustrated in the example.

 OQL retains much of the SQL syntax while accommodating new object-oriented features, such as universal quantification and queries that directly traverse many-to-many relationships.

Signal expressions are an access language for manipulating information in an object-oriented database. Each of the SQL query categories from Chapter 5 (i.e., existential, universal, aggregate) has an equivalent object-oriented solution. You solve an existential query by probing into the internal structure of a candidate to seek a path to an anchor object. You solve a universal query by constructing two sets: the objects reachable from a candidate and the anchor objects for the candidate. The first set must contain the second for the candidate to contribute to the answer. Because the query language for an object-oriented database is a computationally complete programming language, you can solve aggregate

Object class	Signal	Action	Returned object or class
Boolean	ifTrue: aBlock	conditional execution	receiver
	ifFalse: aBlock	conditional execution	receiver
	ifTrue: tBlock ifFalse: fBlock	conditional execution	receiver
	not	complementation	Boolean
	and: aBlock	logical and with result of code	Boolean
	or: aBlock	logical or with result of code	Boolean
	&	logical and	Boolean
	|	logical or	Boolean
Collection	includes: anElement	membership test	Boolean
	contains: aCollection	containment test	Boolean
	intersect: aCollection	intersection operation	Collection
	do: aBlock	iterate code for each element	receiver
	add: anObject	insertion	receiver
	addAll: aCollection	mass insertion	receiver
	asSortedCollection	sorting operation	SortedCollection
	collect: aBlock	assemble contributions	Collection
	select: aBlock	subset via a predicate	Collection
	inject: anObject into: aBlock	accumulating computation	anObject
	remove: anObject	removal	receiver
	isEmpty	empty test	Boolean
Class	subclass: aString instanceVariables: anArray constraints: an Array	subclass definition	receiver
	method: aString code: aBlock	method definition	receiver
Block	whileTrue: aBlock	data-dependent iteration	receiver
	whileFalse: aBlock	data-dependent iteration	receiver

Figure 8.15   Methods associated with object-oriented query formulation

queries by performing the required manipulations—partitioning, rejecting certain groups, and calculating summary statistics over the remaining groups—in that language.

The schema definitions establish application classes and also Set subclasses for holding various collections. Objects from these classes respond to attribute signals and to a wide variety of system signals. You express queries as programs of such signals. Figure 8.15 summarizes the signals illustrated in this chapter's examples. With these signals, you can compose signal expressions equivalent to any SQL query. Moreover, they go beyond SQL in solving recursive queries.

You can instrument the Set class to respond to attribute signals by collecting the results contributed by each member when probed with the same signal. This generalization leads to the notion of a database path, a sequence of attribute signals that constructs the tree of objects reachable through attribute probes. For example, if aSpecies is a species object, `aSpecies reps home` accumulates the unduplicated tank objects where aSpecies is represented. `aSpecies reps home population` accumulates the fish objects swimming in tanks where aSpecies is represented. `aSpecies reps home population breed` collects all the species objects that are represented in tanks where aSpecies is represented, and so forth. Because this notation removes the do: signals that iterate over collections, it leads to a simplified format for queries.

An algorithm can automatically translate SQL statements into signal expressions. Each from-clause table has a corresponding database handle. The fish table, for example, corresponds to TheFish, which is a global collection of all fish objects. The translation starts by nesting do: signals: one level for each from-clause table. The do: signals target the corresponding database handles. In the innermost level of the nest, you insert a boolean expression that corresponds to the where-clause. The boolean controls a code segment that inserts the select-clause strings into an accumulating answer set. Because the boolean contains references to the table keys and because the corresponding classes don't have keys, you must use a sequence of transformations to remove those references. The result is a correct, but inefficient, signal expression, which delivers the same answer as the original SQL. The algorithm extends to subqueries, partitions, and aggregates.

Object Query Language (OQL) provides an alternative to SQL translation. The syntax retains the general format of SQL but incorporates useful features from the object-oriented model. For example, OQL can directly exploit unfactored many-to-many relationships, and it can directly express universal quantification. OQL uses database paths but restricts them to single-object returns at each stage of the path.∎

EXERCISES

These exercises refer to the object-oriented library database schema of Figure 7.24. Assume that all attribute methods are defined.

Conceptual model for simple data retrieval

Write signal expressions for the following queries. Don't be concerned with duplicate suppression. For this section, don't use attribute signals directed to collections.

1. Find the names of libraries located in Seattle.

2. Find the names and locations of libraries that feature books written by Salinger.

3. Find the names of libraries whose collection of books overlaps a library located in Seattle.

4. Find the titles of books available from a library that is patronized by a patron named joe.

5. Find all pairs of book titles that have copies in the same library.

6. Find the names of library triplets that are collocated. Eliminate triplets of the form (x, x, x), (x, x, y), (x, y, x), and (y, x, x) from the answer.

Convert the following SQL statements into equivalent signal expressions. Each assumes the existence of the keys and foreign keys from the relational database of Figure 3.11. Therefore, you will need to translate the SQL intention into the corresponding logical signals. Don't follow the mechanical translation at the end of the chapter. Instead, interpret the SQL to determine the query's intent and then write a signal expression.

7.
```
select L.libname
  from library L, copy C, loan LN, patron P
  where L.libno = C.libno and C.copyno = LN.copyno and LN.patronno = P.patronno
    and P.patwgt > 150.
```

8.
```
select B1.title "first title", B2.title "second title"
  from book B1, book B2
  where B1.authno = B2.authno and B1.bookno not = B2.bookno.
```

9. ```
   select P1.patname
   from patron P1, loan LN1, copy C1, library L1, copy C2, loan LN2, patron P2,
      loan LN3, copy C3, library L2
   where P1.patronno = LN1.patronno and LN1.copyno = C1.copyno and C1.libno = L1.libno and
      L1.libno = C2.libno and C2.copyno = LN2.copyno and LN2.patronno = P2.patronno and
      P2.patronno = LN3.patronno and LN3.copyno = C3.copyno and C3.libno = L2.libno and
      L2.location = "Seattle".
   ```

Write signal expressions for the following queries. Construct an auxiliary collection for the subquery even if it isn't strictly necessary. As before, you must reconcile any references to keys or foreign keys, such as libno and bookno, with the object-oriented format.

10. ```
    select B.title
    from book B
    where not exists
       (select *
       from copy C, loan LN
       where B.bookno = C.bookno and C.copyno = LN.copyno).
    ```

11. ```
    select L.libname
    from library L
    where L.libno in
       (select L.libno
       from library L, copy C, book B, author A
       where L.libno = C.libno and C.bookno = B.bookno and
          B.authno = A.authno and A.authname = "Salinger").
    ```

Existential and universal queries

Write signal expressions for the following queries. Database paths have now been introduced, and you can use them to abbreviate the syntax.

12. Find the titles of books that have copies in all Seattle libraries.

13. Find the names of Seattle libraries that feature all books written by Mailer.

14. ```
    select L.libname
    from library L
    where L.rooms > 25 and
       (select B.bookno
       from copy C, book B
       where L.libno = C.libno and C.bookno = B.bookno)
    contains
       (select B.bookno
       from book B, author A
       where B.authno = A.authno and A.authname not = "Salinger").
    ```

```
15. select B.title
    from book B, author A
    where B.authno = A.authno and A.authname = "Mailer" and not exists
      (select *
      from library L
      where L.location = "Seattle" and not exists
        (select *
        from copy C
        where B.bookno = C.bookno and C.libno = L.libno)
      and
        (select P.patronno
        from patron P, loan LN, copy C
        where P.patronno = LN.patronno and LN.copyno = C.copyno and C.libno = L.1
      contains
        (select P.patronno
        from patron P
        where P.patwgt > 150)).
```

Aggregates and partitions

Write signal expressions for the following queries.

16. Find the location of the library with the most rooms.

17. For each library-book combination, find the number of related copies. Report in sorted order on library name and book title.

18. For each patron, find the average size (i.e., number of rooms) of libraries used by that patron.

19. For each book, find the minimum, average, and maximum cost of its copies.

20. Find the names of libraries that have fewer than 10 book copies.

```
21. select L.libname, B.title, count(*) copies
    from library L, copy C, book B
    where L.libno = C.libno and C.bookno = B.bookno and L.location = "Seattle"
    groupby L.libno, B.bookno.
```

```
22. select sum(P.patwgt)
    from patron P
    where exists
      (select *
      from loan LN, copy C, book B, author A
      where P.patronno = LN.patronno and LN.copyno = C.copyno and C.bookno = B.bo
        and B.authno = A.authno and A.authname = "Mailer").
```

```
23. select L.libname
    from library L
    where L.rooms >
      (select average(P.patwgt)
      from patron P
      where exists
        (select *
        from loan LN, copy C
        where L.libno = C.libno and C.copyno = LN.copyno and LN.patronno = P.patr
```

24. ```
    select L.libname, max(C.cost) "largest expense"
    from library L, copy C
    where L.libno = C.libno and L.location = "Seattle"
    groupby L.libno.
    ```

25. For each patron who weighs 150 pounds or more, find the average size (i.e., number of rooms) of the libraries that he patronizes.

26. For each library for which the average weight of its patrons exceeds 150 pounds, find the number of patrons named joe.

27. ```
    select L.libname, sum(B.pages) totalpages
    from library L, book B
    where exists
      (select *
      from copy C
      where L.libno = C.libno and C.bookno = B.bookno)
    groupby L.libno
    having average(B.pages) >
      (select average(B.pages)
      book B).
    ```

28. ```
    select A.authname, max(L.rooms) maxspace
    from author A, library L
    where exists
      (select *
      from book B, copy C
      where A.authno = B.authno and B.bookno = C.bookno and C.libno = L.libno)
    groupby A.authname
    having count(*) > 10
    orderby maxspace.
    ```

Recursive queries

For the exercises in this section, change the Book subclass definition to include the cites and citedIn attributes, each holding BookSet object. For a Book object B cites contains all books cited by B; citedIn contains all books that reference B. The Book part of the schema now reads as follows. Also assume that sets have been instrumented as described in the text to respond to the choose signal by supplying an arbitrary member of the set.

```
ApplicationClass subclass: "Book"
  instanceVariables: ("title", "author", "pages", "copies", "cites", "citedIn")
  constraints: (("title", String), ("author", Author), ("pages", Number),
    ("copies", CopySet), ("cites", BookSet), ("citedIn", BookSet)).
```

29. Find the titles of all citations, either direct or indirect, in books written by Umberto Eco. In other words, find the titles of books cited by Eco, cited by a book that is cited by Eco, and so forth.

30. Find the titles of books that directly cite a work written by Umberto Eco.

Data editing operations

Write signal expressions for the following data manipulation activities.
```

31. Add library objects to the database. The library descriptions are available on the newlib file. Each line of the file represents either a new library or a book copy belonging to the previous library. If the record represents a library, it starts with the string, library, followed by the number of rooms and the library name. The location attribute is missing. A set of book copy records follows each library. A book copy starts with the string, bookcopy, followed by the cost of the copy, the book title, and the author's name. Assume that both the book title and the author's name are unique across the database. The corresponding books and authors already exist in the collections TheBooks and TheAuthors. You can repeatedly send the readString signal to the file to sequentially read the character strings of the records. The skip signal abandons the remaining strings in a record by moving past the next newline marker.

32. Delete all books that have been read by a patron named joe. Include the activity that should be taken to maintain referential integrity: remove copies and loans associated with the doomed books.

33. Update all Seattle libraries by adding two rooms to each.

34. Delete patrons weighing more than 150 pounds who have dealt with all libraries in Seattle. Remove any loans associated with these patrons.

Signal expressions from SQL

Using the algorithm in the text, convert the following SQL to signal expressions. The foreign key mappings that maintain the five one-to-many relationships of the library database are:

Book.authno = Author.authno   Copy.libno = Library.libno
Copy.bookno = Book.bookno   Loan.copyno = Copy.copyno
Loan.patronno = Patron.patronno

You have been able to deal with queries to this point without explicit handles, TheCopies and TheLoans, because the copies and loans attributes of the remaining classes contain the appropriate subsets. So you have had no need to address the set of all database copies or loans as a starting point in a query. However, in dealing with the algorithmic translation from the SQL, you must establish a loop for each table in the where-clause; you must have the global collections of copies and loans. Therefore, assume for this section of exercises that these handles are available.

Assume also that the attributes of the application classes have been patterned after the corresponding relational tables in the manner discussed in the text. In particular, a foreign-key attribute contains its reference, and an inverse reference is established in the referenced object. For example, a copy object contains a library object in its libno attribute, and each library object contains a copies attribute, which holds the set of copies that reference the library. Similar arrangements exist between copy and book, between book and author, between copy and loan, and between loan and patron.

35.
```
select P.patname, L.location
from Library L, Copy C, Loan U, Patron P
where L.libno = C.libno and C.copyno = U.copyno and U.patronno = P.patronno
    and P.patwgt > 150.
```

36.
```
select L.libname, count(*) K
from Library L, Book B
where exists
    (select *
    from Copy C
    where L.libno = C.libno and C.bookno = B.bookno)
groupby L.libno
orderby L.libname.
```

Object Query Language (OQL)

Compose OQL solutions for the following queries. Assume the library schema of Figure 7.24, with the addition of two handles, TheCopies and TheLoans, which hold the extents of the Copy and Loan classes respectively.

37. Find the names of libraries located in Seattle.

38. Find the titles of books with more than 300 pages that have been written by Salinger.

39. Find the titles of books that are available from a library that is patronized by a patron named jim.

40. Find the names of Seattle libraries that hold all books written by Mailer.

9 Deductive Databases

As defined in Chapter 1, a database offers a systematic interface for extracting the facts and relationships that it contains. As illustrated by the query solutions in the relational and object-oriented models, you can obtain new information about the application by combining the existing facts in various combinations. Query solutions in the relational and object-oriented models illustrated this activity. In the relational model, a query forges database paths through common attribute links; in the object-oriented model, it uses recursive probes into the attribute values. Although a query assembles the consequences of the existing data and relationships into a answer table or answer object, these answers are considered external to the database.

A deductive database emphasizes inference rules, which construct new facts from the basic data or from previously constructed facts. However, the DBMS considers the inferred information to be a permanent part of the database. The inferred data form a sort of shadow of logical implications, which greatly enlarges the actual stored data. In this setting, a query takes the form of a logic program, which invokes inference rules as it proceeds from known data toward the required information. These Inference rules become part of the application database and give the appearance that certain facts are available when they actually must be derived upon demand. Somewhat similar to SQL's view facility, this feature is ultimately more powerful.

Logic programming in a database context

Logic programs resemble the relational calculus expressions of Chapter 4. Where relational calculus expressions combine atomic predicates with logical operations (e.g., $\wedge$, $\vee$, $\neg$, $\forall$, and $\exists$), logic programs incorporate the predicates into inference rules. The following discussion of logic programming uses a framework similar to the Prolog programming language, but it adapts the language to a database context.

Database and arithmetic predicates

A **database predicate** is a boolean function of its arguments. The truth value associated with particular argument values is chosen to reflect the given application. To a database designer, who is trying to model an application, the database predicates assert elementary truths about the application. In the aquarium example, you can create a database predicate fish (X, Y, Z, W, A, B), which means that a fish exists in the database with fno = X, fname = Y, fcolor = Z, fweight = W, tno = A, and sno = B. You assign true to the predicate fish (164, "charlie", "orange", 12, 42, 74) because a fish of that description exists in the application. On the other hand, you assign false to the predicate fish (164, "flipper", "white", 12, 42, 22) because the arguments don't identify an application fish. Here you are thinking of a fish as a table row, with attributes fno, fname, fcolor, fweight, tno, and sno. As you'll see in the next section, it isn't necessary to envision the data as table rows. What is important is that you have a notation for asserting elementary facts about the application objects.

A **binding** is a substitution of constant values for the variables in a predicate or sequence of predicates. Part of the application definition is the list of database predicate bindings that should be regarded as true. (The other part is the list of valid inference rules, which will be discussed later.) For example, you would assert the following bindings to be true for the aquarium application.

```
fish (164, "charlie", "orange", 12, 42, 74)
fish (347, "flipper", "black", 25, 35, 17)
fish (228, "killer", "white", 32, 42, 22)
                  ⋮
```

Next, you would make similar assertions for database predicates describing the other objects in the aquarium. You would have species, tank, and event predicates. In this notation, a positional correspondence exists between each database predicate argument and an attribute of the corresponding application entity. In the fish (X, Y, Z, W, A, B) example, the predicate will be true for a binding where X is the fno of some fish, Y is the name of that fish, and so forth. However, the variables can assume other bindings, even bindings with a nonsensical entry such as one with green in the fno slot. In these cases, the predicate is false. For example, fish ("green", "charlie", "purple", 12, 42, 74) is false because no application fish has this set of attributes. The predicate returns false, therefore, for nonsensical bindings and also for reasonable bindings that don't correspond to an application object.

You specify the database **content** as a list of database predicates, with specific bindings substituted for all the arguments. You explicitly assert all expressions in the content to be true. The database predicates with any other bindings are implicitly false. The collection of constants appearing in the database content is the **universe of discourse**, or simply the universe, and it is denoted by U. For the aquarium database, the universe is the heterogeneous set containing all attribute values from any fish, species, tank, or event predicate in the content list. Using the data from the aquarium relational database of Figure 2.1, you tabulate U as follows. The tabulation omits quotes from the string constants for legibility. Note that the universe is a finite set. The universe, augmented with constants appearing in user commands, supplies all variable bindings for predicates.

U =   (164, 347, 228, 281, 483, 119, 388, 654, 765, 438, 277, 911, 104, 302, 419, 650, 700, charlie, flipper, killer, albert,
       bonnie, cory, darron, elsie, fran, george, helen, indira, jill, kilroy, laura, maureen, orange, black, white, red, blue,
       purple, 55, 42, 35, 85, 38, 44, puddle, cesspool, lagoon, beach, green, 200, 100, 400, 17, 22, 74, 93, dolphin,
       shark, guppy, 3456, 6653, 5644, 5645, 6789, 5211, 6719, 6720, 9874, 9875, 2176, 2285, 2874, 3116, 3651, 3884,
       2992, 4004, 5118, 6233, 7555, 01/26, 05/14, 05/15, 05/30, 04/30, 05/23, 06/25, 06/30, 07/22, 08/05, 02/04, 02/08,
       04/19, 09/25, 10/02, 11/12, 12/25, 06/04, 01/11, 04/23, 05/09, Hatched, Born, Swimming, Takes fish from trainer,
       Doubled in length, Monopolized food).

 A binding specifies values for a function's variables. A database predicate is a boolean function whose true bindings give elementary facts about the application. The database content is a list of the database predicates with their true bindings. The universe of discourse is the set of all constants mentioned in the database content list.

An **arithmetic predicate** is a boolean function of the form $X \theta Y$, where θ is one of the operators $<, >, =, \leq, \geq$, or one of their complements, such as $\neq$. Bindings for arithmetic predicates are limited to the universe of discourse, so the set of true bindings for an arithmetic predicate is finite. A **literal** is a database predicate, an arithmetic predicate, a derived predicate, or the negation of one of these forms. Derived predicates will be defined shortly, but for now, just think of them as boolean functions that return true or false when their arguments are bound to values from the universe.

A literal can contain a mixture of constants and variables in its arguments. For example, `fish (X, "charlie", "orange", W, A, B)` is a literal. A **ground literal** is a literal that contains only constants in its argument list. So `fish (164, "charlie", "orange", 12, 42, 74)` is a ground literal. Arithmetic predicates are included in this specialization. So $42 < 74$ is a ground literal; $X < 74$ isn't. A ground literal has an absolute true or false value. If the ground literal is a database predicate, it is true if it occurs in the database content list and false if it doesn't. If the ground literal is an arithmetic predicate, it is true if the arithmetic comparison between the constants is meaningful and correct, and it is false otherwise. If the ground literal is a derived predicate, its truth value follows from certain inference rules, which will be discussed shortly.

A **negated literal** is a literal preceded with the negation symbol ($\neg$). A negated ground literal is true precisely when its counterpart without the negation symbol is false, and vice versa. Of the examples below, the first two are non-negated literals, and the last two are negated.

`fish (X, Y, Z, A, B);`   `X < Y;`   `¬fish (X, Y, Z, A, B);` $\neg(X < Y)$

Because these examples aren't ground literals, their truth values are indeterminate without additional information. The truth values depend on the variable bindings.

 A literal is a database, arithmetic, or derived predicate. A negated literal contains a leading negation symbol ($\neg$). A ground literal is a literal with constant arguments. The database content is the collection of non-negated ground literals arising from the database predicates.

Inference rules and derived predicates

In terms of literals, the database content is the collection of non-negated ground literals arising from the database predicates. These ground literals are chosen to represent elementary facts about the application; more complex facts correspond to other ground literals, associated with derived predicates. You can easily determine the truth value of a ground literal arising from a database predicate: you just look it up in the database content list. If it appears, it's true. However, for ground literals arising from other predicates, a different process, governed by a set of inference rules, determines if they are true. An **inference rule** is an expression of the form $P(X, Y, \ldots) \vdash Q_1, Q_2, Q_3, \ldots$. Here, P is a predicate that is *not* a database predicate. The predicate P is the **head** of the rule. The set of literals $Q_1, Q_2, \ldots$ is the **body**. Note that the head is a predicate and therefore a non-negated literal. However, the body components are literals; therefore, they can be negated. Each of the body literals is a **subgoal**. A **derived predicate** is one that appears as the head of one or more inference rules. An inference rule must follow a specific format:

- The head must not be a database predicate or an arithmetic predicate.

- The head must not be negated.

- Each of the head arguments must be a distinct variable. In the head, the same variable must not appear in more than one position. No constants may appear.

- The arguments of the body literals can include variables from the head, other variables, and constants.

 An inference rule contains a head and a body, the latter consisting of one or more subgoals. A derived predicate is a predicate that appears as the head of one or more inference rules.

If inference rules mention constants that aren't currently in the universe of discourse, the universe expands to include them. Because the inference rules are finite in number, and because each of them involves a finite number of symbols, this expansion retains a finite universe. Therefore, the set of true bindings for any given predicate is a finite tabulation.

Each derived predicate gives rise to a large collection of ground literals, which correspond to the many possible bindings for its argument variables. Which do you consider true? This question is complicated and will be addressed shortly. Assume for the moment that you have somehow assigned a truth value to all the ground literals. You can now determine when the rule body, under some binding that reduces all its subgoals to ground literals, is true. To make this judgment, you treat the body as the logical conjunction of its subgoals. You also rearrange the order of the subgoals, if necessary, to collect all the negated subgoals together. For example, you transform the following body as indicated.

$$G_1(X, Y, A, B), G_2(Z, A, C), \neg G_3(X, Z, A, D), \neg G_4(Y, B, D, E).$$
$$G_1(X, Y, A, B) \wedge G_2(Z, A, C) \wedge \neg G_3(X, Z, A, D) \wedge \neg G_4(Y, B, D, E).$$
$$[G_1(X, Y, A, B) \wedge G_2(Z, A, C)] \wedge \neg [G_3(X, Z, A, D) \vee G_4(Y, B, D, E)].$$

You always interpret an inference rule in the context where the head variables are bound. So suppose the body above is part of the rule

$$H(X, Y, Z) \vdash G_1(X, Y, A, B), G_2(Z, A, C), \neg G_3(X, Z, A, D), \neg G_4(Y, B, D, E).$$

For a specific binding of the head variables, say $(X = x, Y = y, Z = z)$, the body takes the following form:

$$[G_1(x, y, A, B) \wedge G_2(z, A, C)] \wedge \neg[G_3(x, z, A, D) \vee G_4(y, B, D, E)],$$

which you can write as a positive part and a negative part:

$$\mathcal{P}(x, y, z, A, B, C) \wedge \neg\mathcal{N}(x, y, z, A, B, D, E).$$

As the example illustrates, a binding of the head variables can leave additional unbound variables in the rule body. These unbound variables are the **free variables**. You can categorize free variables into two groups: positive free variables appear in a non-negated subgoal; all the others are negative free variables. In the example, A, B, and C are positive free variables. D and E are negative free variables. Note that a positive free variable can appear in a negated subgoal, but it must also appear in a non-negated subgoal. By contrast, a negative free variable appears only in negated subgoals.

To obtain a rule body's truth value for a specific binding of the head variables, you separate the rule body into its positive ($\mathcal{P}$) and negative ($\mathcal{N}$) parts. The body is true if (1) there exists a binding for the positive free variables that makes $\mathcal{P}$ true, and (2) after substituting that successful binding for the positive free variables in all negated subgoals, no binding for the negative free variables can make $\mathcal{N}$ true. Otherwise, the body is false. Therefore, for the head binding $(X = x, Y = y, Z = z)$, the body above is true if there exists a binding $(A = a, B = b, C = c)$ such that $[G_1(x, y, a, b) \wedge G_2(x, a, c)]$ is true, and $[G_3(x, z, a, D) \vee G_4(y, b, D, E)]$ is false for *all* bindings of D and E. Otherwise, it is false.

A rule is **satisfied** if every binding of the head variables that makes the body true also makes the head true. A binding of the head variables reduces the head to a ground literal, and the truth values of all ground literals are known (by assumption at this point). In the example rule, you can check as follows to see if it is satisfied. Start with the rule:

$$H(X, Y, Z) \vdash G_1(X, Y, A, B), G_2(Z, A, C), \neg G_3(X, Z, A, D), \neg G_4(Y, B, D, E).$$

Next test each binding of the head variables. For example, test the following expression, where $x, y,$ and z are constants from the universe of discourse:

$$H(x, y, z) \vdash G_1(x, y, A, B), G_2(z, A, C), \neg G_3(x, z, A, D), \neg G_4(y, B, D, E).$$

If $H(x, y, z)$ is true, this binding succeeds, regardless of the truth values of the subgoals, and you go on to consider another binding. However, if $H(x, y, z)$ is false, you must investigate the body. If the body is false, this binding succeeds, and again you proceed with another binding. However, if the body is true while the head is false, the rule isn't satisfied, and you don't need to consider any other bindings.

The rule satisfaction problem reduces to determining the body's truth value after binding the head variables to constants. In this example, the non-negated free variables are A, B, and C; the negative free variables are D and E. For the head binding $(X = x, Y = y, Z = z)$, the body is true if there is a binding $(A = a, B = b, C = c)$ with these properties: (1) $G_1(x, y, a, b)$ is true, (2) $G_2(z, a, c)$ is true, and (3) for all bindings $(D = d, E = e)$, both $G_3(x, z, a, d)$ and $G_4(y, b, d, e)$ are false. Otherwise the body is false.

The procedure is much simpler and more intuitive if negated subgoals aren't present. In that case, all the free variables are positive free variables, and the body is true if there is a binding of the free variables that simultaneously converts all the subgoals into true ground literals. The next best case is to have negated subgoals but no negative free variables. In other words, any variables appearing in the negated subgoals also appear in non-negated subgoals. Then the body is true if there is a binding of the free variables that converts all the non-negated subgoals into true ground literals, and the ground literals obtained by removing the negation symbol from the negated subgoals are all false. Consider, for example, the modified rule:

$$H(X, Y, Z) \vdash G_1(X, Y, A, B), G_2(Z, A, C), \neg G_3(X, Z, A, B), \neg G_4(Y, B, C).$$

For the head binding $(X = x, Y = y, Z = z)$, the body $G_1(x, y, A, B)$, $G_2(z, A, C)$, $\neg G_3(x, z, A, B)$, $\neg G_4(y, B, C)$ is true if there is a binding $(A = a, B = b, C = c)$ such that $G_1(x, y, a, b)$ and $G_2(z, a, c)$ are true while $G_3(x, z, a, b)$ and $G_4(y, b, c)$ are false.

 A free variable is a variable that appears in the rule body but not in the head. A negated free variable appears only in negated subgoals. All the other free variables are positive free variables.

Possible worlds and inference rule models

Assuming that you have classified all ground literals as true or false, you now know how to test a rule for satisfaction. But how is this classification done? When you substitute constant bindings from the universe of discourse for a derived predicate's variables, you obtain a ground literal. Unlike the ground literals arising from the database predicates, however, you can't look up this literal in a list to determine its truth value. So how do you make that determination?

Intuitively, the ground literal arising from a derived predicate should be true when it appears as the head of an inference rule with a true body. For example, consider the following rule, which expresses the condition that X is the fno value of a red fish.

```
redFish (X) ⊢ fish (X, Y, "red", W, A, B).
```

You want a particular ground literal, say redFish (483), to be true if there exists binding for Y, W, A, and B such that the subgoal fish (483, Y, "red", W, A, B) is true. This process seems simple enough. A ground literal arising from a derived predicate is true if it is forced true by some inference rule. This forcing is caused by some substitution for the remaining variables that renders all the subgoals true. However, some of the subgoals might also involve derived predicates. In that case, you must recursively pursue the same strategy until all the subgoals are reduced to database predicates, whose truth values are available in the database content list.

The problem with this approach is that there may be cycles in the inference rules. Somewhere in the chain of inferences associated with the subgoals, you may encounter the head predicate again. Because you haven't yet determined the head predicate's truth value, you can't determine the truth value of the subgoal that depends on it. The example with the `redFish` predicate doesn't have this problem, but other predicates may involve more complicated definitions. So consider the situation from a larger perspective. Suppose you just assign an arbitrary value (true or false) to every ground literal arising from every derived predicate. Can you distinguish one set of assignments as most appropriate for the application?

In other words, you can assign either truth value, true or false, to a ground literal arising from a derived predicate. But the consequences will render certain assignments more meaningful than others. Remember, the aquarium application lurks in the background, and you want the true ground literals arising from *all* of the predicates—database predicates and derived predicates—to represent true facts about that application. Recall also that you determined the true bindings for the database predicates by simply listing them as the database content. In a manner of speaking, you were free to choose which were true and which were false. If the collection (fno = 483, fname = albert, fcolor = red, fweight = 28, tno = 55, sno = 17) happened to identify a fish (and its species and tank connections), then you chose to include the fact `fish (483, "albert", "red", 28, 55, 17)` in the database content list. Otherwise you didn't. Actually, you weren't assigning arbitrary truth values. Instead, you allowed a binding to be true only when it reflected the application reality.

In a similar manner, you can arbitrarily assign truth values to the ground literals arising from the derived predicates. If the derived predicates are numerous or if they contain many variables, the number of bindings quickly becomes intractably large. So you should think of this assignment as a mental experiment. Conceptually you proceed as follows. You gather all the derived predicates together in preparation for arbitrarily assigning true or false to each ground literal that can arise from them through substitution from the universe of discourse. Although a given derived predicate can appear as the head of several rules, you include only one copy in the working collection.

Consider the first derived predicate on the worktable. If it has p variables and if the universe of discourse has n entries, there are n^p possible bindings. Although the task is large, you can nevertheless imagine assigning true or false to the ground literal arising from each binding. You then operate on the next derived predicate in the same way, and so on until you have finished with all of them. You now have a huge pile of ground literals that represent "truth." Of course, the database content list is there, but it is dwarfed by the other "facts" that you have arbitrarily created. You simply discard the collection of ground literals that were assigned false. The true pile is your concern; it captures the application's intent.

But does it? Although you exercised some discipline in discerning the true cases for the database predicates, you were rather cavalier about assigning truth values to the derived predicates. As you might expect, this assignment probably doesn't accord with the application. Suppose, for example, that `redFish (X)` is one of the derived predicates, and you intend it to be true when X binds to the fno value of a red fish. However, in your haste you assigned false to `redFish (483)` although the fish with fno = 483 is red.

The arbitrary assignment of truth values to the ground literals arising from the derived predicates is a **possible world**. More specifically, a possible world consists of the true ground literals from the derived predicates plus the true ground literals in the database content list. If you're unhappy with your possible world, you can create a different one by repeating the assignment process with different choices. Suppose there are m derived predicates, $P_1, P_2, \ldots, P_m$, and that the ith predicate involves p_i variables. Continue to assume that the universe of discourse contains n elements. Then the creation of one possible world requires $N = n^{p_1} + n^{p_2} + \ldots + n^{p_m}$ truth value assignments. Because there are 2^N ways of assigning true or false to the N ground literals, there are 2^N possible worlds.

A **deductive system** is a database content list and a collection of inference rules. A possible world is a **model** of a deductive system if all the rules are satisfied. Recall that a rule is satisfied if every head binding that makes the body true also makes the head true. For a given possible world, establishing the truth value of either a rule head or its body isn't difficult. For a particular head binding, the head becomes a ground literal, whose truth value was fixed when the possible world was created. Moreover, you have a process for determining the truth value of a body in the context of a head binding. This process searches for a binding for the positive free variables such that the positive part of the body is true and all further bindings for the negative free variables fail to make the negative part true. In evaluating candidates in the search process, you continually assess the truth value of boolean expressions of ground literals. This isn't a problem because the truth value of all these ground literals was decided when the world was created. So in any possible world, you can mechanically check to see if the rules are satisfied.

As you consider all head bindings, remember that the only case where the rule is endangered is when the body is true. In this case, the head must also be true or else the rule fails. Therefore, to check a rule, you only have to check those bindings where the body is true. If the head is also true in these cases, the rule is satisfied. If all rules check out, the possible world is a model of the system.

For brevity of notation, equate a possible world with the collection of ground literals that are true in that world. This collection includes the true ground literals arising from the database predicates, the database content list, and also all true ground literals arising from derived predicates. In this sense, a possible world is just a subset of the collection of all possible ground literals. All possible worlds have a common subset of ground literals arising from the database predicates (i.e., the database content), but they differ in which ground literals arising from the derived predicates are present.

 You create a possible world by assigning truth values to all ground literals arising from derived predicates. The ground literals that are assigned the value true, together with the database content list, form the possible world. A possible world where all the inference rules are satisfied is a model.

This discussion uses the term *model* differently than the term *database models*. A database model is an organizational structure for managing data elements and their relationships. At this point you have studied the relational and object-oriented database models, and you are now investigating the deductive database model. In the logical sense, however, a model is a collection of ground literals, in the presence of a set of inference rules, with the following property: if all the ground literals in the model are considered true, and all ground literals not in the model are considered false, then all inference rules are satisfied.

An earlier example considered a possible world that assigned false to `redFish (483)` although `fish (483, "albert", "red", 28, 55, 17)` appeared in the database content. When checking the rule

$$\text{redFish (X)} \vdash \text{fish (X, Y, "red", W, A, B)}$$

with the bindings

$$\text{redFish (483)} \vdash \text{fish (483, "albert", "red", 28, 55, 17)},$$

you confront the situation where the single subgoal is true, but the head is false. Therefore, the rule isn't satisfied. So the possible world that makes a false assignment to `redFish (483)` isn't a model of the system.

Minimal models

Do the truth assignments of a model align more closely with the application than the truth assignments of an arbitrary possible world? The truth assignments of a model have the following advantage: under a model assignment, all the database predicates are true, and the derived predicates are true in those cases demanded by the rules. However, a model may still diverge from the application's desired interpretation. Suppose that the `redFish` derived predicate occurs in just the one rule above. Now suppose that the model world assigns true to `redFish (164)` although one of the database content entries, `fish (164, "charlie", "orange", 12, 42, 74)`, strongly suggests that the corresponding fish is actually orange. It so happens that the model remains consistent with all of the rules. As long as `redFish (X)` is assigned true for all the truly red fish, it doesn't matter if it is assigned true for other fish. The only way to invalidate a rule is to make the body true and the head false. However, `redFish (X)` occurs as the head of a single rule. So asserting that `redFish (164)` is true can't invalidate any rule. The rule stands, and because `redFish` doesn't enter into any other rules, the model stands.

The problem is that rules never force a derived predicate to be false. A rule either forces a derived predicate to be true, or it's silent on the matter. In the example above, you can even have an `orangeFish (X)` derived predicate with the expected derivation, `orangeFish (X) ⊢ fish (X, Y, "orange", W, A, B)`. The model can assign true to both `orangeFish (164)` and to `redFish (164)` without internal contradiction. The rules simply say that *if* a fish is orange, the `orangeFish` predicate must be true for that fish. However, if the fish is red, the `orangeFish` predicate can still be true because the rule exerts no coercive force. In other words, the rule isn't invalidated because the body is false. The truth value of the head, therefore, isn't relevant.

Consequently, if you equate a model with the collection of true ground literals, you prefer a model with as few entries as possible. You need enough to satisfy the rules, but you should avoid gratuitous true entries if you want to conform closely to the application. If all models, considered as collections of true ground literals, were comparable through set inclusion, you could determine the smallest by intersecting them. However, all models aren't comparable. You will soon encounter a situation where the intersection of two models isn't a model.

To summarize to this point, you start with a list of ground literals arising from the database predicates. In keeping with the application intent, you assert these literals to be true by definition. This collection forms the core of any possible world, to which you add other true facts arising from the derived predicates. You want this extended collection of facts to represent the extended database content. It should be a faithful rendition of the application and register not only the initial data elements but also other facts that are logically consistent deductions from the inference rules and the initial elements. Therefore, you certainly want to choose a possible world where the inference rules are all satisfied. This observation justifies the preoccupation with models, as opposed to possible worlds where some rules might remain unsatisfied. However, even a model that is consistent with the rules can diverge from the application intent by containing more facts than are necessary to satisfy the rules. So you want the extended database to correspond to a minimal model, one that satisfies all the rules but contains no extraneous facts.

Considering models as sets of true ground literals, you can partially order them by set inclusion. A **minimal model** is a model $\mathcal{M}_0$, such that if $\mathcal{M}$ is a model and $\mathcal{M} \subset \mathcal{M}_0$, then $\mathcal{M} = \mathcal{M}_0$. Once you have a model, you can easily obtain a minimal model by removing any ground literals that aren't needed to satisfy the rules. You repeatedly select a ground literal, remove it from the model, and verify that the smaller possible world remains a model. If it doesn't, you reinstate the ground literal and choose another. If it does, you leave the literal out and continue. Because the model is a finite set, you must eventually reach a point where no ground literal can be thrown out with jeopardizing the model status of the possible world. At this point, you have a minimal model.

 A minimal model is a collection of true ground literals arising from the database and derived predicates, with the property that if any member is removed, the collection is no longer a model.

A minimal model represents the extended database as intended by the application through its initial data elements and inference rules. There are no superfluous facts, such as an assertion that an orange fish is red simply because no rule violations occur. However, two disconcerting issues remain. First, could there be several minimal models? If so, which constitutes the application's real meaning? All models contain the core database content, and all satisfy the rules. They differ only in the derived facts that are asserted to be true. In the application, you usually have an understanding about the facts that should be derivable. For example, if you employ a rule to define the predicate redFish (X), you want it to be true precisely when X is the fno value of a red fish. If the minimal models can vary in the truth values of the derived predicates, the true application facts aren't well defined.

The second problem is operational. Creating a minimal model with the process above is tedious. You must first elaborate the possible worlds, each involving a very large number of assignments to the ground literals arising from the derived predicates, and you must then choose one that satisfies all the inference rules (i.e., you must choose a model). Finally, you must minimize the model by removing ground literals as long as the remaining collection still satisfies all the rules. These problems with minimal models will be addressed later in the chapter. Until then, assume that a satisfactory minimal model is available.

Logic programs

A **logic program** is a collection of inference rules that allows the deduction of new facts from an initial set. The initial set of facts is the database content, a list of true ground literals arising from the database predicates. This set of initial facts constitutes the **axioms** of the system. Inference rules build on the axioms, and on each other, to express more complicated facts. Although the database stores certain generic inference rules as part of the application, you can assert more specialized inference rules as a logic program to elicit new information from the database. In other words, you use logic programs to answer queries. To solve a query, you augment the general collection of inference rules in the database with specialized rules for the query situation. The merged collection of rules is a logic program. The system follows this program to report the true ground literals associated with some minimal model of these rules. The next section provides a few intuitive examples from the deductive version of the aquarium database.

The axioms of a system are the set of true ground literals arising from the database predicates; they constitute the initial database content. A logic program is a collection of inference rules that allows new facts to be deduced from the axioms. In other words, a logic program answers a query.

Informal illustration of a deductive database

Assume the aquarium data in Figure 2.1. Each table gives rise to a database predicate of the same name. The species table, for example, corresponds to the `species()` predicate. The predicate is true or false depending on the values of its arguments, which appear in domain relational calculus format. In other words, a positional correspondence exists between the arguments and the attributes of the corresponding table. The following ground literals arise from the `fish` database predicate:

```
fish (164, "charlie", "orange", 12, 42, 74)
fish (167, "anonymous", "blue", 33, 80, 26).
```

The first is true because the bindings correspond to a row in the fish table. The second is false. The general form of the `fish` database predicate is `fish (X, Y, Z, W, A, B)`.

Query syntax

Following the pattern above, you can tabulate the true ground literals (i.e., the axioms) arising from the database predicates: tank, species, fish, and event. A query is either a database or a derived predicate with free variables in some of its arguments. For example, suppose you want the names of all blue fish. Mindful of the correspondence between the argument positions and the fish attributes, you compose the following statement. The system responds with the table on the right, which lists all the bindings that make the predicate true.

`fish (W, X, "blue", C, Y, Z).`

W	X	C	Y	Z
119	bonnie	51	42	22
911	helen	48	44	74
650	laura	55	85	17

The search space is the universe of discourse—the union of all attribute values from all database tables. Although you get the desired fish names under the X column, you must tolerate the other attributes reported in the rest of the table. The solution below removes the unwanted information. It also illustrates a specialized inference rule for a query. You first define a new derived predicate, `bluefishName (X)`, which extends the database to certain synthesized facts. Besides the four predicates from the original database tables, you can now use the new predicate `blueFishName`. The new solution table appears to the right.

	Q
`blueFishName (X) ⊢ fish (W, X, "blue", C, Y, Z).`	bonnie
`bluefishName (Q).`	helen
	laura

The system deduces this solution as follows. It searches for a Q binding that will make `blueFishName (Q)` true. This information forms part of all minimal models for the system, where the system now comprises the axioms, all inference rules asserted before this time, and the new rule for `blueFishName`. Assume for the moment that a unique minimal model exists and that it is a faithful reflection of the aquarium situation. However, the minimal model hasn't been laboriously computed with the process discussed in the previous section. Storing all the facts derivable from the database content would be very inefficient. Instead, the system pursues a search strategy that discovers the values of Q such that `blueFishname (Q)` would be in the minimal model, if it had been fully constructed. A rough outline of the search strategy follows.

Because the `blueFishName` predicate doesn't correspond to a database predicate, the system looks for inference rules with `blueFishName` in the head. Finding the rule above, it reasons that `blueFishName (Q)` must be true if `fish (fno = W, fname = Q, fcolor = "blue", tno = Y, sno = Z)` is true. The rule variables aren't taken literally; they are merely placeholders (i.e., dummy variables) that coordinate substitutions in the rule. The rule thus directs the DBMS to find a binding that makes the subgoal true. Because the rule must be satisfied, the value bound to fname then makes the head predicate true. Whether you call this value X or Q doesn't matter; it becomes part of the query solution.

Derived predicates are useful for extracting attributes from tuples. Some examples are:

```
fname (X) ⊢ fish (A, X, B, C, D, E).     tname (X) ⊢ tank (A, X, B, C).
fcolor (X) ⊢ fish (A, B, X, C, D, E).    tcolor (X) ⊢ tank (A, B, X, C).
```

You must remember, of course, the positional correspondences for the arguments. For example, the third rule above states that X is the tname value of a tank if there is an axiom `tank (A, X, B, C)`. The axiom must match the head binding for the tname position, but the bindings for the remaining positions are unconstrained. An axiom such as `tank (42, "cesspool", "blue", 100)` suffices to render `tname ("cesspool")` true.

A more useful predicate associates an attribute value with a key of the same table. The predicate `fishHasName (X, Y) ⊢ fish (X, Y, A, B, C, D)` is true precisely when X and Y are bound to the fno and fname values, respectively, of some fish tuple. To illustrate these predicates, you need additional rules to access the relationships implied by the foreign keys. For example, the following rules allow you to test when a fish inhabits a tank, when a fish represents a species, and when an event belongs to a fish.

```
fishInhabitsTank (X, Y) ⊢ fish (X, A, B, C, Y, D).
fishRepresentsSpecies (X, Y) ⊢ fish (X, A, B, C, D, Y).
eventConcernsFish (X, Y) ⊢ event (X, Y, A, B).
```

These predicates represent relationships between tuples because their arguments use only the keys fno, tno, sno, and eno. fishInhabitsTank (X, Y) is true if a fish exists with fno value X and tno value Y. For this purpose, you could always use the single subgoal on the rule's right side, but it involves extra variables that may not be relevant to the given query. For example, you can now solve the query for the names of fish in cesspool tanks as follows. First, you assert the rule query (X) to provide the system with a route for deducing the names of the desired fish.

```
query (X) ⊢ fishHasName (Y, X), tankHasName (Z, "cesspool"), fishInhabitsTank (Y, Z).
```

You then launch the query proper with the statement: query (X). To return true for a particular value of X, the rule must find additional values from the universe of discourse to make all three subgoals true. In other words, it must find a Y (fno) and a Z (tno), with Y inhabiting Z and Z named cesspool.

Permanent inference rules and logic programs arising from queries

Of the inference rules discussed to this point, all except blueFishName and query are useful beyond the queries where they originated. They express the condition that an application object has a certain attribute value, for example, fishHasName (X, Y), or that a certain relationship holds between two application objects, such as fishInhabitsTank (X, Y). These rules belong in the database because they are a natural extension of the application model. They express application facts that will remain universally true, regardless of the current query. The other rules (e.g., blueFishName (X)) are less generally useful, but you still expect them to remain universally true in the aquarium application. So you might consider them part of the database, or you might consider them as part of a query from the user interface. This ambiguous boundary between the database and its access language is one of the characteristics of deductive database systems.

Several problems arise if the database accumulates all the rules asserted in preparation for queries. First, a new rule can have a head predicate that already exists in the database. In that case, the new rule provides additional circumstances that can render the old predicate true. This interpretation may not be satisfactory because you may have forgotten the old rules when you composed the new query rule. In this case, the reported true bindings will be larger than expected.

Second, a new rule may contradict an existing one. Suppose the existing rule structure allows you to deduce that a certain tank is red. You don't want to add a new rule that concludes the tank is blue. In particular, suppose you have previously asserted the following rules.

```
redTank (X) ⊢ tank (X, Y, "red", Z).
blueTank (X) ⊢ tank (X, Y, "blue", Z).
redTank (X) ⊢ tank (X, Y, Q, Z), ¬blueTank (X).
```

The first two rules let you deduce that a tank, represented by its tno attribute X, is red or blue directly from the database predicate. The database predicate, in turn, directly reflects the tank-table content. The third rule states that a tank is red if it isn't blue. Now suppose the database contains no red tanks and no blue tanks, but it does contain a single green tank. The database content list, in other words, is the single axiom: `tank (10, "emerald", "green", 2000)`. Because no rule forces `blueTank (10)` to be true, you conclude that `blueTank (10)` is false, and therefore that `redTank (10)` is true. Although you have contradicted reality, you haven't yet contradicted the rules. You have simply located a tank that isn't blue, and according to the last rule, a non-blue tank is red. The rule says that the term *red tank* means either a true red color or a color other than blue. However, suppose you now assert another rule, which claims that non-red tanks must be blue.

$$\text{blueTank (X)} \vdash \text{tank (X, Y, Q, Z), } \neg\text{redTank (X).}$$

Because the last rule of the first set and the new rule reference each other, problems arise in evaluating either the blueTank or redTank predicate. In particular, both the following two contradictory solutions satisfy all the rules. Remember that the tank table has no tanks with a tcolor attribute of red or blue and that it contains a single tank with a tcolor attribute of green.

> Solution 1: `redTank (10)` is true, and `blueTank (10)` is false.
> Solution 2: `redTank (10)` is false, and `blueTank (10)` is true.

Recall that the four inference rules are:

redTank (X) $\vdash$ tank (X, Y, "red", Z).		redTank (X) $\vdash$ tank (X, Y, Q, Z), ¬blueTank (X).
blueTank (Y) $\vdash$ tank (X, Y, "blue", Z).		blueTank (X) $\vdash$ tank (X, Y, Q, Z), ¬redTank (X).

For either solution, the first two rules are satisfied because the actual color of tank tno = 10 is green. Therefore, the bodies are false, and the rules are satisfied regardless of the truth values of the head predicates. Both solutions also satisfy the last two rules. If `redTank (10)` is true and `blueTank (10)` is false, the third rule has a true body (both subgoals) and a true head while the fourth rule has a false body (the second subgoal). On the other hand, if `redTank (10)` is false and `blueTank (10)` is true, the third rule has a false body (second subgoal) while the fourth rule has a true body (both subgoals) and a true head.

If you assume the database contains a single green tank and no species, fish, or events, you have found two minimal models for the system: $\mathcal{M}_1$ and $\mathcal{M}_2$.

$\mathcal{M}_1$: tank (10, "emerald", "green", 2000)
          redTank (10).

$\mathcal{M}_2$: tank (10, "emerald", "green", 2000)
          blueTank (10).

Both assignments (possible worlds) are models because both satisfy all the rules. Both are minimal. You can't remove `redTank (10)` from $\mathcal{M}_1$ without violating the third rule, and you can't remove `blueTank (10)` from $\mathcal{M}_2$ without violating the fourth rule.

This situation is disconcerting because no matter how you redefine the meaning of a red tank, you can't reconcile the fact that both `redTank (10)` true and `redTank (10)` false are consistent with all the rules. However, the example unrealistically insists that tanks be either red or blue, despite an axiom revealing a green tank. If conflicting minimal models can be restricted to such unlikely situations, you might hope to avoid them in practice. This situation will be discussed more fully later; for the moment, note that negated predicates and cyclic rules are tricky.

The last section stated that models weren't necessarily comparable via set inclusion and that the intersection of two models wasn't necessarily a model. This example provides the counterexample that proves both statements. You have neither $\mathcal{M}_1 \subset \mathcal{M}_2$ nor $\mathcal{M}_2 \subset \mathcal{M}_1$. Moreover, $\mathcal{M}_1 \cap \mathcal{M}_2$ contains the single axiom tank (10, "emerald", "green", 2000), which isn't a model because it violates both the third and fourth rules.

In the presence of negated subgoals and cyclical rules, you can have several competing minimal models. These models introduce ambiguity in the true facts that can be derived about the application.

Provided you avoid the problems of the last example, you can continue to add rules to the database. Each rule adds to the repertoire of facts that can be derived from the underlying database predicates. However, some of the rules may be very specialized and used very infrequently. In these cases, you must decide whether to retain the rules as part of the permanent database or to assert them temporarily as part of a query. Assume the rules of Figure 9.1 have been permanently installed as part of the aquarium database. With these rules, you can extract descriptive attributes associated with a key, and you can match tuples participating in a relationship. Queries will require additional rules, but the DBMS will remove them after reporting the query solution.

Consider a final query, which illustrates the need for temporary, customized rules. Find the names of species swimming with a shark. Assume the rules of Figure 9.1 are in effect, and assert two further inference rules specifically for this query:

```
sharkyTank (X) ⊢ fishInhabitsTank (Y, X),
                 fishRepresentsSpecies (Y, Z),
                 speciesHasName (Z, "shark").
```

```
query (X) ⊢ speciesHasName (Y, X),
            fishRepresentsSpecies (Z, Y),
            fishInhabitsTank (Z, W),
            sharkyTank (W).
```

The statement query (X) launches the query. A successful X value must be the sname value of a species tuple with sno value Y, represented by a fish with fno value Z that inhabits a tank with tno value W. Moreover, sharkytank (W) must be true. To check out this condition, rename the dummy variables in the sharkytank rule to avoid confusion with the variables already in use.

```
sharkyTank (W) ⊢ fishInhabitsTank (A, W),
                 fishRepresentsSpecies (A, B),
                 speciesHasName (B, "shark").
```

W must be the tno value of a tank tuple inhabited by a fish with fno value A, and that fish must represent a species with sno value B. Finally, the sno B must appear in a species tuple with an sname value **shark**.

This process should seem familiar. It traces an existential path from a candidate species tuple across the database to a tank where it is represented and then back to a second species tuple containing a **shark** sname. In its search to find appropriate bindings to satisfy the rules, the system follows the same abstract approach as an SQL query. Although the query appears as a logic program instead of a relational calculus expression, the search strategy remains the same.

Database predicates	
Predicate	argument order
`species (X, Y, Z)`	sno, sname, sfood
`tank (W, X, Y, Z)`	tno, tname, tcolor, tvolume
`fish (U, V, W, X, Y, Z)`	fno, fname, fcolor, fweight, tno, sno
`event (W, X, Y, Z)`	eno, fno, edate, enote

To assert an attribute value
`speciesHasName (X, Y) ⊢ species (X, Y, Z)`
`speciesHasFood (X, Y) ⊢ species (X, Z, Y)`
`tankHasName (X, Y) ⊢ tank (X, Y, W, Z)`
`tankHasColor (X, Y) ⊢ tank (X, W, Y, Z)`
`tankHasVolume (X, Y) ⊢ tank (X, W, Z, Y)`
`fishHasName (X, Y) ⊢ fish (X, Y, U, V, W, Z)`
`fishHasColor (X, Y) ⊢ fish (X, U, Y, V, W, Z)`
`fishHasWeight (X, Y) ⊢ fish (X, U, V, Y, W, Z)`
`eventHasDate (X, Y) ⊢ event (X, W, Y, Z)`
`eventHasNote (X, Y) ⊢ event (X, W, Z, Y)`

To assert a relationship between two application instances
`fishRepresentsSpecies (X, Y) ⊢ fish (X, U, V, W, Z, Y)`
`fishInhabitsTank (X, Y) ⊢ fish (X, U, V, W, Y, Z)`
`eventConcernsFish (X, Y) ⊢ event (X, Y, W, Z)`

Figure 9.1   Built-in inference rules and axiom shells for the aquarium database

Definition of a deductive database

Representation of axioms

The informal illustration in the previous section formed the database predicates from the equivalent relational tables. However, the axioms' supporting structure doesn't have to be relational. For example, by inserting the appropriate class methods, you could build the same predicates (Figure 9.1) over the object-oriented schema of Figure 7.12. The important building blocks for queries, in the upper right and lower center of Figure 9.1, assert that objects have attribute values and participate in relationships. You can implement the predicate `speciesHasName (X, Y)` with the following method. A species object receives the corresponding signal, which carries a string parameter (Y).

X speciesHasName: Y.

The target object X returns true if X is a species object with a name attribute equal to the parameter Y. You install the code in the Object class to make it available to all application objects and to the strings, numbers, and other objects that might appear as variable bindings. Those objects that don't belong to the species class immediately reply false. Species objects respond by comparing the parameter with their name attribute. The following method code implements this strategy.

```
Object method:  "speciesHasName" code:  [aString |
    self class == Species
        ifTrue:  [^self name = aString]
        ifFalse:  [^false] ].
```

You can also implement the relationship rules of Figure 9.1 with signals. The signal on the left below computes the predicate fishInhabitsTank (X, Y); the corresponding method appears on the right.

X fishInhabitsTank: Y.

```
Object method:  "fishInhabitsTank" code:  [aTank |
    self class == Fish
        ifTrue:  [^self home == aTank]
        ifFalse:  [^false] ].
```

So you can use relational tables, object classes, or even some less familiar data representation scheme to implement the database predicates. The important point is that a deductive database rests on an initial collection of predicates, called the **axioms**. How the DBMS evaluates the axioms for particular bindings is an implementation detail, which doesn't appear in the definition of a deductive database.

Figures 9.2 and 9.3 show the axioms for the aquarium database. The symbols, such as s_1, s_2, t_1, and t_2, denote application instances. In a particular implementation, they might be OIDs (object-oriented) or keys (relational). In the deductive model, however, these symbols literally stand for themselves. For example, s_1 is an element of the universe of discourse, which is available for binding to variables in inference rules and queries. These symbols are no different than the other constants that appear in the axioms, such as lagoon, red, 200, cesspool, herring, and flipper. For legibility, Figure 9.3 omits quotes from the constant strings.

Inference rules for relationships, constraints, and implied facts

An inference rule defines a new predicate, which ultimately depends on the axioms for its truth value. With the following rule, you can ascertain that X is a red fish that represents a shark species and swims in a cesspool tank.

```
redSharkInCesspool (X) ⊢ fishInhabitsTank (X, Y), fishRepresentsSpecies (X, Z),
                        tankHasName (Y, "cesspool"), speciesHasName (Z, "shark")
                        fishHasColor (X, "red").
```

Besides building rules over the axioms, you can construct rules over other rules. For example, given the previous rule, the following expression states that X is the name of a fish having a red shark cousin (same species) living in a cesspool.

```
cousinOfRedSharkInCesspool (X) ⊢ fishHasName (Y, X), fishRepresentsSpecies (Y, Z),
                        fishRepresentsSpecies (W, Z), redSharkInCesspool (W), W ≠ Y.
```

Recall that a database is a self-describing collection of data elements and relationships with a systematic user interface. A **deductive database** is a database where the data elements and elementary relationships are given by **axioms**. **Inference rules** extend the axioms to more

speciesHasName (s_1, dolphin)	speciesHasFood (s_1, herring)
speciesHasName (s_2, shark)	speciesHasFood (s_2, anything)
speciesHasName (s_3, guppy)	speciesHasFood (s_3, worm)
speciesHasName (s_4, shark)	speciesHasFood (s_4, peanut butter)

tankHasName (t_1, puddle)	tankHasColor (t_1, green)	tankHasVolume (t_1, 200)
tankHasName (t_2, cesspool)	tankHasColor (t_2, blue)	tankHasVolume (t_2, 100)
tankHasName (t_3, lagoon)	tankHasColor (t_3, red)	tankHasVolume (t_3, 400)
tankHasName (t_4, cesspool)	tankHasColor (t_4, blue)	tankHasVolume (t_4, 100)
tankHasName (t_5, beach)	tankHasColor (t_5, blue)	tankHasVolume (t_5, 200)
tankHasName (t_6, lagoon)	tankHasColor (t_6, green)	tankHasVolume (t_6, 200)

fishHasName (f_1, charlie)	fishHasColor (f_1, orange)	fishHasWeight (f_1, 12)
fishHasName (f_2, flipper)	fishHasColor (f_2, black)	fishHasWeight (f_2, 25)
fishHasName (f_3, killer)	fishHasColor (f_3, white)	fishHasWeight (f_3, 32)
fishHasName (f_4, charlie)	fishHasColor (f_4, orange)	fishHasWeight (f_4, 27)
fishHasName (f_5, albert)	fishHasColor (f_5, red)	fishHasWeight (f_5, 45)
fishHasName (f_6, bonnie)	fishHasColor (f_6, blue)	fishHasWeight (f_6, 51)
fishHasName (f_7, cory)	fishHasColor (f_7, purple)	fishHasWeight (f_7, 12)
fishHasName (f_8, darron)	fishHasColor (f_8, white)	fishHasWeight (f_8, 84)
fishHasName (f_9, elsie)	fishHasColor (f_9, white)	fishHasWeight (f_9, 73)
fishHasName (f_{10}, fran)	fishHasColor (f_{10}, black)	fishHasWeight (f_{10}, 61)
fishHasName (f_{11}, george)	fishHasColor (f_{11}, red)	fishHasWeight (f_{11}, 33)
fishHasName (f_{12}, helen)	fishHasColor (f_{12}, blue)	fishHasWeight (f_{12}, 48)
fishHasName (f_{13}, indira)	fishHasColor (f_{13}, black)	fishHasWeight (f_{13}, 19)
fishHasName (f_{14}, jill)	fishHasColor (f_{14}, red)	fishHasWeight (f_{14}, 28)
fishHasName (f_{15}, kilroy)	fishHasColor (f_{15}, red)	fishHasWeight (f_{15}, 49)
fishHasName (f_{16}, laura)	fishHasColor (f_{16}, blue)	fishHasWeight (f_{16}, 55)
fishHasName (f_{17}, maureen)	fishHasColor (f_{17}, white)	fishHasWeight (f_{17}, 71)

Figure 9.2   Axioms of the aquarium database

complex relationships. **Logic programs** provide the uniform user interface. An axiom is a predicate with constant arguments whose truth value represents an elementary judgment about the application. The precise mechanism for determining the axioms' truth values isn't important for the definition. Beyond the simple relationships given by the axioms, a deductive database contains inference rules, which you can combine into logic programs to derive more complex facts.

A deductive database's **schema** contains the shells of the axioms and an initial collection of inference rules. The schema's rules derive facts of general utility and express constraints particular to the application. The **initial content**, or simply the **content**, of the database is the collection of axioms. The **extended content** of the database is a minimal collection of all true ground literals. In other words, the database's extended contents constitute a minimal model of the axioms and inference rules. Figure 9.4 shows the deductive schema for the aquarium database. The axioms serve two purposes: to pass judgment on attribute values and to assert elementary relationships.

eventHasDate $(e_1,\ 01/26)$	eventHasNote $(e_1,\ \text{Hatched})$
eventHasDate $(e_2,\ 05/14)$	eventHasNote $(e_2,\ \text{Born})$
eventHasDate $(e_3,\ 05/15)$	eventHasNote $(e_3,\ \text{Swimming})$
eventHasDate $(e_4,\ 05/30)$	eventHasNote $(e_4,\ \text{Takes fish from trainer})$
eventHasDate $(e_5,\ 04/30)$	eventHasNote $(e_5,\ \text{Hatched})$
eventHasDate $(e_6,\ 05/23)$	eventHasNote $(e_6,\ \text{Hatched})$
eventHasDate $(e_7,\ 06/25)$	eventHasNote $(e_7,\ \text{Born})$
eventHasDate $(e_8,\ 06/30)$	eventHasNote $(e_8,\ \text{Doubled in length})$
eventHasDate $(e_9,\ 07/22)$	eventHasNote $(e_9,\ \text{Hatched})$
eventHasDate $(e_{10},\ 08/05)$	eventHasNote $(e_{10},\ \text{Monopolized food})$
eventHasDate $(e_{11},\ 02/04)$	eventHasNote $(e_{11},\ \text{Hatched})$
eventHasDate $(e_{12},\ 02/08)$	eventHasNote $(e_{12},\ \text{Hatched})$
eventHasDate $(e_{13},\ 04/19)$	eventHasNote $(e_{13},\ \text{Hatched})$
eventHasDate $(e_{14},\ 09/25)$	eventHasNote $(e_{14},\ \text{Hatched})$
eventHasDate $(e_{15},\ 10/02)$	eventHasNote $(e_{15},\ \text{Hatched})$
eventHasDate $(e_{16},\ 11/12)$	eventHasNote $(e_{16},\ \text{Hatched})$
eventHasDate $(e_{17},\ 12/25)$	eventHasNote $(e_{17},\ \text{Born})$
eventHasDate $(e_{18},\ 06/04)$	eventHasNote $(e_{18},\ \text{Born})$
eventHasDate $(e_{19},\ 01/11)$	eventHasNote $(e_{19},\ \text{Hatched})$
eventHasDate $(e_{20},\ 04/23)$	eventHasNote $(e_{20},\ \text{Born})$
eventHasDate $(e_{21},\ 05/09)$	eventHasNote $(e_{21},\ \text{Born})$

fishInhabitsTank (f_1, t_2)	fishRepresentsSpecies (f_1, s_3)
fishInhabitsTank (f_2, t_3)	fishRepresentsSpecies (f_2, s_1)
fishInhabitsTank (f_3, t_2)	fishRepresentsSpecies (f_3, s_2)
fishInhabitsTank (f_4, t_4)	fishRepresentsSpecies (f_4, s_2)
fishInhabitsTank (f_5, t_1)	fishRepresentsSpecies (f_5, s_1)
fishInhabitsTank (f_6, t_2)	fishRepresentsSpecies (f_6, s_2)
fishInhabitsTank (f_7, t_3)	fishRepresentsSpecies (f_7, s_4)
fishInhabitsTank (f_8, t_2)	fishRepresentsSpecies (f_8, s_4)
fishInhabitsTank (f_9, t_2)	fishRepresentsSpecies (f_9, s_2)
fishInhabitsTank (f_{10}, t_1)	fishRepresentsSpecies (f_{10}, s_3)
fishInhabitsTank (f_{11}, t_2)	fishRepresentsSpecies (f_{11}, s_4)
fishInhabitsTank (f_{12}, t_6)	fishRepresentsSpecies (f_{12}, s_3)
fishInhabitsTank (f_{13}, t_2)	fishRepresentsSpecies (f_{13}, s_1)
fishInhabitsTank (f_{14}, t_5)	fishRepresentsSpecies (f_{14}, s_1)
fishInhabitsTank (f_{15}, t_1)	fishRepresentsSpecies (f_{15}, s_3)
fishInhabitsTank (f_{16}, t_4)	fishRepresentsSpecies (f_{16}, s_1)
fishInhabitsTank (f_{17}, t_6)	fishRepresentsSpecies (f_{17}, s_1)

eventConcernsFish (e_1, f_1)	eventConcernsFish (e_2, f_2)	eventConcernsFish (e_3, f_2)
eventConcernsFish (e_4, f_2)	eventConcernsFish (e_5, f_3)	eventConcernsFish (e_6, f_4)
eventConcernsFish (e_7, f_5)	eventConcernsFish (e_8, f_5)	eventConcernsFish (e_9, f_6)
eventConcernsFish (e_{10}, f_6)	eventConcernsFish (e_{11}, f_7)	eventConcernsFish (e_{12}, f_8)
eventConcernsFish (e_{13}, f_9)	eventConcernsFish (e_{14}, f_{10})	eventConcernsFish (e_{15}, f_{11})
eventConcernsFish (e_{16}, f_{12})	eventConcernsFish (e_{17}, f_{13})	eventConcernsFish (e_{18}, f_{14})
eventConcernsFish (e_{19}, f_{15})	eventConcernsFish (e_{20}, f_{16})	eventConcernsFish (e_{21}, f_{17})

Figure 9.3   Axioms of the aquarium database (continued)

Attribute assertion axioms	
Predicate	Intended meaning
`speciesHasName (X, Y)`	string Y is the name of species X
`speciesHasFood (X, Y)`	string Y is the food of species X
`tankHasName (X, Y)`	string Y is the name of tank X
`tankHasColor (X, Y)`	string Y is the color of tank X
`tankHasVolume (X, Y)`	number Y is the volume of tank X
`fishHasName (X, Y)`	string Y is the name of fish X
`fishHasColor (X, Y)`	string Y is the color of fish X
`fishHasWeight (X, Y)`	number Y is the weight of fish X
`eventHasDate (X, Y)`	string Y is the date of event X
`eventHasNote (X, Y)`	string Y is the note of event Y
Relationship assertion axioms	
Predicate	Intended meaning
`fishRepresentsSpecies (X, Y)`	fish X belongs to species Y
`fishInhabitsTank (X, Y)`	fish X inhabits tank Y
`eventConcernsFish (X, Y)`	event X happened to fish Y
Relationship assertion rules	
Inference rule	Intended meaning
`neighbor (X, Y) ⊢   fishInhabitsTank (X, Z),` `                    fishInhabitsTank (Y, Z).`	fish X and fish Y swim in the same tank
`cousin (X, Y) ⊢   fishRepresentsSpecies (X, Z),` `                  fishRepresentsSpecies (Y, Z).`	fish X and fish Y belong to the same species

`cohorts (X, Y) ⊢   eventConcernsFish (E, X),`
`                   eventConcernsFish (F, Y),`
`                   eventHasNote (E, "Hatched"),`
`                   eventHasNote (F, "Hatched"),`
`                   eventHasDate (E, Z),`
`                   eventHasDate (F, Z).`
	fish X and fish Y are the same age

Constraints	
Constraint rule	Intended meaning

`false ⊢   tankHasVolume (X, Y),`
`          tankHasVolume (Z, Y),`
`          tankHasColor (X, A),`
`          tankHasColor (Z, B),`
`          A ≠ B.`
	tanks of the same volume must have the same color

Figure 9.4   Deductive schema for the aquarium database

 A deductive database maintains the data elements and elementary relationships as axioms. Inference rules construct more complex relationships. The deductive schema asserts the axioms' format and an initial collection of general inference rules.

In addition to the axioms, the aquarium schema provides three derived relationships. You can use the predicates `neighbor`, `cousin`, and `cohort` to test if two fish belong to the same species, swim in the same tank, or possess **Hatched** events with the same datestamp. The database's extended content contains the axioms of Figure 9.2 plus such ground literals as `neighbor` (f_1, f_3) and `cousin` (f_{12}, f_{15}). The first is true because fish f_1 and f_3 inhabit the common tank t_2; the second is true because fish f_{12} and f_{15} belong to the common species s_3.

The last entry in the schema expresses the constraint that tanks with the same volume must have the same color. In other words, the functional dependency volume $\longrightarrow$ color must hold. Because a rule must be satisfied under all circumstances, a constant `false` head means that the body must always evaluate to false. No matter what you substitute for the variables, one of the subgoals must fail. Suppose two tanks have the same volume. So the first two subgoals are true when X is the first tank, Z the second, and Y their common volume. A and B can now successfully bind to their colors, making the third and fourth subgoals true. Therefore, if the rule is satisfied, the last subgoal must fail, which forces the colors to be equal.

An earlier discussion addressed the possibility of two contradictory rules. If two rules are such that any possible world satisfying one doesn't satisfy the other, no model can exist, much less a minimal model. For example, if the database content contains ground literals asserting two tanks with the same volume but different colors, then no assignment of truth values to the derived predicates will satisfy all the rules. In particular, bindings among the initial content will always violate the constraint rule of Figure 9.4. Therefore, no model can exist among the possible worlds. A set of axioms and rules that possesses no model is **inconsistent**. A deductive database representing a real-world application must remain consistent at all times. For this reason, a consistency test must follow each database update. If the test fails, the system must roll back the update. In the example above, the system wouldn't allow the installation of a second tank agreeing with an existing tank in volume but not in color.

Acyclic deductive database and a unique minimal model

A deductive database with no cyclical references among its inference rules is an acyclic deductive database. A precise definition will come later. Acyclic deductive databases present a more manageable situation when several minimal models compete to define the extended database content. Recall the previous discussion that defined red tanks in terms of blue tanks and blue tanks in terms of red tanks. Two different minimal models existed in that case, and each was consistent with all the rules. In one model, `redTank (10)` was true; in the other it was false. This situation is confusing because the minimal model defines the extended database, which in turn asserts the true facts about the application. However, this example isn't an acyclic deductive database because the inference rules depend on each other. Although you can't completely avoid the existence of several minimal models, you can, in the absence of cyclical rules, choose the most natural minimal model to represent the extended database content.

Acyclic deductive databases are exactly equivalent to relational databases under relational algebra or SQL. In an acyclic deductive database, therefore, logic programs exist for all the queries from the previous chapters.

A **dependency graph** is a directed graph whose nodes represent the database and derived predicates. An arc runs from node p to node q precisely when some inference rule has head q and a body containing either p or $\neg p$ as a subgoal. No arcs enter the database predicate nodes because these predicates can't appear as the head of an inference rule. An **acyclic dependency graph** is a dependency graph that contains no cycles. An **acyclic deductive database** is a deductive database with an acyclic dependency graph.

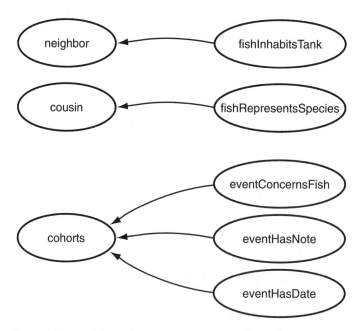

Figure 9.5 Initial dependency graph for the aquarium deductive schema

Although the deductive schema specifies initial inference rules, you must add other rules for query solutions. In this sense, the database schema is never complete. As you add and remove inference rules, the set of derivable facts varies to reflect the changed meaning. In an acyclic deductive database, the full collection of inference rules never produces cycles in the dependency graph. Figure 9.5 illustrates the initial dependency graph for the aquarium database. It omits database predicates that don't serve as subgoals for any rules. The arcs come from the relationship assertion rules of Figure 9.4. Of course, this graph evolves as you add rules either to refine the extended content of the database or to assist in query formulations.

 The dependency graph of a deductive database links each derived predicate with the predicates of its subgoals. In an acyclic deductive database, the dependency graph has no cycles.

Given these definitions, the previous troublesome example isn't an acyclic deductive database. The dependency graph for the example appears in Figure 9.6. It shows a single database predicate, `tank`, and two derived predicates, `redTank` and `blueTank`. The rule for `redTank` produces an arc from `blueTank` to `redTank`, while the rule for `blueTank` produces an arc in the opposite direction, completing a cycle.

You can order the database and derived predicates in an acyclic deductive database such that any given predicate receives dependency arcs only from predicates earlier in the list. Moreover, you can put the database predicates at the beginning of the list because

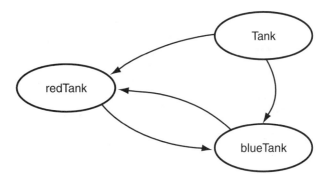

Figure 9.6 Dependency graph for the example yielding multiple minimal models

these predicates have no incoming arcs. A list with these properties is a **topological sort**. A simple algorithm constructs a topological sort from an acyclic graph.

Start with an empty list, and choose any node from the graph. Move with the flow of the arcs until you reach a node with no outgoing arcs. Because no cycles occur in the graph and because the graph contains a finite number of nodes, this condition must eventually hold. At this point, add the blocked node to the beginning of the list and remove it from the graph. Also remove any arcs that lead into it. Repeat this procedure until you have transferred all the nodes to the list. When you place a node in the list, no arcs remain leading out of the node. This means that any derived predicates depending on the node are already in the list. Because the process constructs the list from tail to head, when you reinstall the dependency arcs, they all point toward the tail. If the database predicates don't appear in a contiguous segment at the beginning of the list, simply move them there. That movement can't upset the list's order because these predicates have no incoming arcs. Once you have linearized the dependency graph in this manner, you can redraw the arcs. They will all run in the same direction: from front to back.

Acyclic deductive databases can still exhibit a multitude of minimal models. Consider again the example where the aquarium database has a single green tank, but no fish, species, or events. The database content is the single ground literal, tank (10, "emerald", "green", 2000). Now add the following inference rules.

```
redTank (X) ⊢ tank (X, Y, "red", Z).
antiRedTank (X) ⊢ tankHasColor (X, Y), ¬redTank (X).
```

The situation is acyclic, and a topological sort gives tank, redTank, antiRedTank. Each inference rule uses subgoal predicates that come earlier in the list than its head predicate, and all the database predicates are first. You can't reverse the two derived predicates violating this property. You can obtain the database's extended content (i.e., a minimal model) by traversing the list from front to back and tabulating all the true ground literals introduced at each stage. Below is the resulting model.

$$\mathcal{M}_1: \quad \begin{array}{l} \text{tank (10, "emerald", "green", 2000).} \\ \text{antiRedTank (10).} \end{array}$$

The first literal is the single entry in the database content list. Because the body of the redTank rule can't be true for any bindings, you don't include redTank (10) in the model. You could include it without violating the rule because a false body places no demands on the head's truth value. However, reasoning directly from the database content (i.e., the axioms), you find no reason to include redTank (10). Moreover, even if you were to include it, you might have to remove it later to produce a minimal model. Moving to the last predicate of the sorted list, you find you must add antiRedTank (10) to the model because ¬redTank (10) is now true. Thus you arrive at model $\mathcal{M}_1$. You can easily verify that $\mathcal{M}_1$ is minimal because discarding antiRedTank (10) violates the antiRedTank rule. Now consider a second model, $\mathcal{M}_2$.

$$\mathcal{M}_2: \quad \begin{array}{l} \text{tank (10, "emerald", "green", 2000).} \\ \text{redTank (10).} \end{array}$$

Here you include redTank (10) although the corresponding rule didn't force you. Because the antiRedTank rule now has a false body, which places no demands on the head predicate, you omit antiRedTank literals from the model. You now discover that this model is minimal even though you exercised an unnecessary generosity by including redTank (10). If you try to remove redTank (10), you discover that the antiRedTank rule would be violated. So you have a competing minimal model.

However, $\mathcal{M}_2$ is a less intuitive solution because it isn't forced directly by the database content. Instead, it depends on the addition of an unnecessary fact, which is later solidified by a rule more distant from the axioms. Building out from the axioms, the rules state (1) redTank (X) if X is the number of a red tank and (2) antiRedTank (X) if X is the number of a tank but not a red one. Because the database contains a single green tank, the first model captures an intuitively plausible set of facts: antiRedTank (10) is true. Model $\mathcal{M}_2$ takes the less intuitive view that the single tank is red because there is no axiom says otherwise. Then antiRedTank (10) becomes false and cements that decision.

So although several competing minimal models may exist, you can arrive at a preferred model by adding ground literals only when forced by an inference rule and by working forward in the predicates' topological sort. In summary, you proceed as follows to construct the preferred minimal model associated with an acyclic deductive database:

- Produce a topological sort of the predicates, placing the database predicates at the beginning. Maintain the property that any rule's subgoals appear before the head of that rule.

- Initialize the model with the axioms, which are the ground literals arising from the database predicates.

- Add literals arising from the derived predicates by considering them in the topological sort order. When working with a given derived predicate, include a literal only if forced by some inference rule and the collection of literals already in the model. Don't add literals just because they don't violate any rules.

This process clearly produces a minimal model because a literal is added only when forced by a rule. The predicates involved in the subgoals have already been processed by the time the literal is forced into the model, and they are never reconsidered by the algorithm.

Therefore, if the literal were removed later, the forcing rule would be violated because the subgoal bindings that forced the literal into the model would still be available.

The topological sort isn't a unique ordering. Several orderings might exist with the property that a given predicate depends only on predicates earlier in the list. Suppose a rule for p_1 refers to p_2, a rule for p_2 refers to p_3, and similar dependencies exist among q_1, q_2, and q_3. Assuming the leading ellipsis stands for the database predicates, the following two sequences are both valid topological sorts.

$$\ldots, p_3, p_2, p_1, q_3, q_2, q_1.$$
$$\ldots, p_3, q_3, p_2, q_2, p_1, q_1.$$

A disturbing question is then: does the procedure construct different minimal models from the two sort sequences? The answer is no. Because there are no dependencies between the p and q predicates, the ground literals contributed to the model by a p aren't influenced by any literals already contributed by a q, and vice versa. The procedure constructs the same minimal model for both orderings. The general argument is as follows. Let $\mathcal{L}_1$ and $\mathcal{L}_2$ be two topological sorts of the predicates, each with the following properties:

- The database predicates occur first in the list.

- Any rules for a derived predicate reference only predicates earlier in the list.

Suppose $\mathcal{M}_1$ and $\mathcal{M}_2$ are minimal models constructed from the two lists. If $\mathcal{M}_1 \neq \mathcal{M}_2$, let p be the first predicate in $\mathcal{L}_1$ where the models disagree. In other words, for some specific binding, p is true in $\mathcal{M}_1$ and false in $\mathcal{M}_2$, or vice versa. Now, all predicates that appear as subgoals for p appear earlier than p in *both* lists. So if p is the first disagreement, both models must agree on all possible bindings for all subgoals contributing to p. But they must then also agree on p because the process adds a literal only if leaving it out would violate a rule. If some subgoal bindings force p to be true, p must be part of both models. On the other hand, if no subgoal bindings force p to be true, the process leaves p out of both models. So, p is either in both models or in neither, which contradicts the assumption that the models differ on p. Therefore, the two models must be the same.

 An acyclic deductive database allows the construction of a unique preferred minimal model by working outward from the axioms, adding literals only when forced by a rule.

Unless otherwise noted, assumes an acyclic deductive database with a minimal model constructed according to the above procedure. The DBMS doesn't tabulate the minimal model as explicit data. It stores only the axioms and inference rules and derives any ground literals in the extended database content as needed for a query response. However, the preferred minimal model exists conceptually to provide a unique solution for each query. A database or derived predicate with a specific variable binding is true precisely when the resulting ground literal is in the preferred minimal model.

Query solution as goal satisfaction

A **query** is a predicate with one or more variable arguments. A **query solution** is a binding for the query's variable arguments such that the resulting ground literal is in the extended

```
void queryProcessor() {
    void createLiteralList(), addToLiteralList(), reportBinding();
    bindTable *binding;
    literalList *query;
    char inputString[100];

    while (scanf("%s", inputString) > 0) {
        createLiteralList (&query);
        addToLiteralList (&query, inputString);
        binding = null;
        while satisfy (query, &binding)
            reportBinding (binding); } }
```

Figure 9.7   A query processing routine for calculating true bindings

database content. Because the database is acyclic, the extended content is the unique
minimal model constructed with the algorithm above. When presented with a query, the
DBMS displays all the solutions. The DBMS takes the query as a **goal**, which is satisfied
by certain variable bindings. It solves the query by finding those bindings.

A query solution algorithm in the absence of negative free variables

This section presents a mental model, by which the DBMS could systematically investigate
all possible bindings for the query variables. Although inefficient, the process illustrates how
to systematically discover all query solutions. Another deficiency of this initial algorithm
is that it works only when the inference rules contain no negative free variables. In other
words, no variables appear in a negated subgoal unless they also appear in the head or in a
non-negated subgoal. A later variation will remove this restriction.

The candidate bindings come from the universe of discourse. If the query has n variables
and the universe has p constants, the algorithm must consider p^n possible bindings. It first
orders these candidate bindings and then steps through them sequentially. The presentation
below represents literals, ground or non-ground, negated or non-negated, as simple character
strings. To manipulate the literals, it uses the data structures literalList and bindTable.
As you might expect, a literalList holds a list of literals; the algorithm uses it to
manipulate inference rule bodies. The algorithm assumes the necessary support routines
to create these lists and to add elements to them. A bindTable structure holds a list of
variables and their current bindings from the universe of discourse. Again, the algorithm
assumes support routines, such as one to display the current table bindings.

The outermost structure of the algorithm appears in Figure 9.7 although it defers detailed
activity to other routines. The user enters a query as a character string, which becomes
the first literal in a newly created literalList called query. The initial binding table,
bindings, is null. The satisfy routine then sequences through the possible bindings,
reporting those that satisfy the query. The code for satisfy follows.

```
boolean satisfy (literalList *Q, bindTable **B) {
    literalList *groundQ, *bind();

    groundQ = bind (Q, B); /* acquire next binding (or first if B refers to a null table) */
    while ((*B != null) && !truthValue (groundQ))
        groundQ = bind (Q, B);
    return (*B != null); }
```

The satisfy routine returns true if it finds a true binding for the literalList argument. The actual binding appears in the bindTable argument at that time. Because this same routine must probe for additional bindings, it always proceeds forward from the bindTable value upon entry. This policy implies that the possible bindings are ordered, a simple enough matter since the universe of discourse is finite. The subprocedure bind acquires the next binding for consideration. If the entry bindTable is null, the next binding is the first. If the entry bindTable contains the last binding, the next binding is null. If the next binding is well-defined, the bind procedure installs it in the bindTable and also performs the substitutions from the new bindTable on the literalList to produce a ground literalList, which it returns to its caller.

Upon receiving a list of ground literals from the bind routine, the satisfy routine checks the list's truth value. It's true if all the ground literals in the list are true. The auxiliary procedure truthValue determines the truth value with the algorithm of Figure 9.8. It makes a direct determination for a database or arithmetic predicate; for a derived predicate, it resorts to a recursive investigation of the subgoals.

The routine marches through the sequence of ground literals, testing each in the appropriate manner. The code assumes routines to determine if a literal arises from a database predicate (databasePredicate) or if it is an arithmetic predicate (arithmeticPredicate). In these cases, the routine axiom checks the database content, or the arithEval procedure computes the arithmetic comparison. The only complication occurs when the ground literal involves a derived predicate. The procedure unifyRule then identifies the first rule with the appropriate head, makes the corresponding substitutions in the body, and returns a new literalList containing the substituted body. A recursive call to satisfy determines if some binding of the newly introduced variables can render all the body true. If not, the unifyRule routine obtains the next applicable rule. Eventually, a rule will succeed, or the unifyRule routine will adjust the rule pointer to null, indicating that the last applicable rule has failed.

Elimination of negative free variables

Because the bind operation in satisfy provides substitutions for all variables in a literalList, it reduces a rule body to a sequence of ground literals before passing it to the truthValue routine. What happens if a rule introduces negative free variables? Suppose you have the rule

$$H(X) \vdash \neg G_1(X, Y), G_2(X)$$

where G_1 and G_2 are database predicates. Now launch the query $H(X)$. The query processor calls satisfy with the literalList $H(X)$ and an empty bindTable. Satisfy acquires the first binding for X, say x, and calls truthValue with the ground literal $H(x)$. TruthValue detects the derived predicate and unifies it with the rule, passing the body

```
boolean truthValue (literalList *Q) {
    boolean success, inverted, databasePredicate(), axiom();
    boolean arithmeticPredicate(), arithEval(), negated();
    bindTable *binding;
    literalList *R, *T, *copyLiteralList(), *unifyRule();
    char *subgoal, *removeLiteralList(), *removeNegation();
    int lengthLiteralList();
    rule *r;

    success = true;
    R = copyLiteralList (Q);
    while (success && (lengthLiteralList (R) > 0)) {
        subgoal = removeLiteralList (&R);
        if (negated (subgoal)) {
            subgoal = removeNegation (subgoal));
            inverted = true; }
        else
            inverted = false;
        if (databasePredicate (subgoal))
            success = axiom (subgoal);
        else if (arithmeticPredicate (subgoal))
            success = arithEval (subgoal);
        else { /* derived predicate */
            success = false;
            r = null;
            T = unifyRule (subgoal, &r);
            while (!success && (r != null)) {
                binding = null;
                success = satisfy (T, &binding);
                T = unifyRule (subgoal, &r); } }
        if (inverted)
            success = !success; }
    return success; }
```

Figure 9.8   Determining the truth value of a collection of subgoals

$\neg G_1(x, Y), G_2(x)$ to satisfy with an empty bindTable. If satisfy can find a binding for Y that makes the body true, then x will be reported as part of the answer. However, $G_1(x, Y)$ must fail for every Y substitution for the subgoal to succeed.

Satisfy produces the first binding for Y, namely x again, and passes the resulting ground literal $\neg G_1(x, x), G_2(x)$ to truthValue. TruthValue considers each subgoal in turn. Assuming that $G_1(x, x)$ isn't in the database content list, it successfully negotiates the first subgoal. Then, assuming that $G_2(x)$ is in the database content list, the second goal also succeeds. Therefore, truthValue returns true for $\neg G_1(x, x), G_2(x)$, and satisfy returns true for $\neg G_1(x, Y), G_2(x)$. Unwinding further, truthValue then returns true for $H(x)$, and queryProcessor reports x as a query solution. Unfortunately, this scenario remains valid even if there is another binding y such that $G_1(x, y)$ is in the database content. In this case, x shouldn't be part of the answer set.

The negative free variable causes this problem. If these variables aren't present, any meaningful test of a negated subgoal involves only the ground case. Because all the variables occur in the head or in non-negated subgoals, you only need to test the negated subgoal in circumstances where the variables are already compatibly bound. For example, suppose you change the rule to

$$H(X) \vdash \neg G_1(X, X), G_2(X).$$

Under the assumptions of the previous trace, the solution x appears through the same series of calls. However, this time x does belong in the answer because a true rule body doesn't require that $G_1(x, Y)$ fail for all Y. It requires only that $G_1(x, x)$ fail.

You can eliminate negative free variables by introducing additional rules. Consider the rule:

$$H(X, Y, Z) \vdash G_1(X, Y, A, B), G_2(Z, A, C), \neg G_3(X, Z, A, D), \neg G_4(Y, B, D, E).$$

For a particular binding $(X = x, Y = y, Z = z)$, the algorithm attempts to determine the body's truth value with these substitutions. In other words, it attempts to find a true binding for

$$G_1(x, y, A, B), G_2(z, A, C), \neg G_3(x, z, A, D), \neg G_4(y, B, D, E).$$

This body is true if there exists a binding $(A = a, B = b, C = c)$, such that $G_1(x, y, a, b)$ and $G_2(z, a, c)$ are both true, and both $G_3(x, z, a, D)$ and $G_4(y, b, D, E)$ fail for every substitution for the negative free variables D and E. That is, the following ground literals must all be true:

$$G_1(x, y, a, b), \quad G_2(z, a, c), \quad \neg G'(x, y, z, a, b).$$

Here $G'(X, Y, Z, A, B)$ is defined by the two rules:

$$G'(X, Y, Z, A, B) \vdash G_3(X, Z, A, D).$$
$$G'(X, Y, Z, A, B) \vdash G_4(Y, B, D, E).$$

Indeed, the single ground instance $\neg G'(x, y, z, a, b)$ succeeds precisely when there are no bindings for D and E that make either G_3 or G_4 true. Stated differently, both G_3 and G_4 fail for every substitution for D and E.

So you can modify the procedure as follows. Suppose you encounter a rule containing negated subgoals with negative free variables. Suppose these subgoals are $\neg G_1, \neg G_2, \ldots$, involving positive free variables $X_1, X_2, \ldots$ and negative free variables $Y_1, Y_2, \ldots$. You replace all these subgoals with the single subgoal $\neg G'(X_1, X_2, \ldots)$, which involves only positive free variables, and you add new rules for G' as follows.

$$G'(X_1, X_2, \ldots) \vdash G_1.$$
$$G'(X_1, X_2, \ldots) \vdash G_2.$$
$$\vdots$$

You can, of course, instrument the queryProcessor routine to take this action automatically.

The algorithm delivers solutions from the preferred minimal model

If the inference rules admit a unique minimal model, the algorithm above will deliver query solutions from that model. Moreover, if the inference rules admit several competing models, the algorithm will deliver query solutions form the preferred model.

An earlier example had a preferred minimal model although at least two competing minimal models existed. The database, a stripped-down version of the aquarium application, contained a single axiom, tank (10, "emerald", "green", 2000), and the following two inference rules:

```
redTank (X) ⊢ tank (X, Y, "red", Z).
antiRedTank (X) ⊢ tank (X, Y, W, Z), ¬redTank (X).
```

The rule with a negated subgoal contains no negative free variables. The more natural minimal model is the one where antiRedTank (10) is true and redTank (10) is false. You obtain this minimal model by expanding outward from the database predicates, adding all ground instances arising from a particular predicate before moving on to consider predicates that are further along in the topological sort. Now suppose you enter the query antiRedTank (A) in the input loop of the queryProcessor routine. The universe of discourse contains the values 10, "emerald", "green", 2000, and the satisfy routine must return A-bindings from this universe that render the query true. So you expect the solution A = 10.

The algorithm composes a literalList with the one goal, antiRedTank (A), and its first call to satisfy passes this goal list and a null binding table. Satisfy forms a ground literal by binding A to the first value from the universe of discourse and then calls truthValue to determine the truth value of that ground literal. So the ground literal at this point is antiRedTank (10), or antiRedTank ("green"), or some other substitution. But continue to think of it as antiRedTank (A), with the understanding that A is actually some constant. TruthValue makes a copy, R, of the argument list, and noting that the list's only subgoal is a derived predicate, it constructs a new literalList from the first rule applicable to antiRedTank. It modifies the rule body to use the substitution already present in the head. The new list of subgoals, T, takes the form tank (A, Y, W, Z), ¬redTank (A), where A is some constant at this point but Y, W, and Z are still variables. It now calls satisfy recursively to obtain bindings, if possible, for Y, W, and Z that make this list of subgoals true. The new invocation of satisfy produces the first binding for Y, W, and Z from the universe of discourse, and it proceeds to call truthValue again with the resulting ground literal. This ground literal list now has the form tank (A, Y, W, Z), ¬redTank (A), where all of A, Y, W, and Z have specific substitutions. TruthValue notes that the first subgoal arises from a database predicate and checks it against the existence of an axiom. This test fails, and the entire process back to the first satisfy call in queryProcessor fails unless the bindings happen to be A = 10, Y = "emerald", W = "green", Z = 2000. For this particular binding, the subgoal succeeds, and it pursues the second subgoal, ¬redTank (10).

The truthValue loop notes the negated subgoal and substitutes its non-negated counterpart, redTank (10). It sets the inverted flag to remember this variation. It then locates the appropriate rule and seeks bindings for Y and Z in the new subgoal list: tank (10, Y, "red", Z). Satisfy fails to find bindings in this case because the fixed component, "red," precludes any match with the single axiom. TruthValue prepares to return false, but because the inverted flag has been set, it reports true instead. Therefore, the algorithm reports the ground literal tank (10, "emerald", "green", 2000), ¬redTank (10) true, which leads it to report antiRedTank (10) true also, as expected.

This example emphasizes two aspects of the algorithm. First, it delivers the solution from the preferred minimal model. It suspends judgment on the truth value of any ground literal arising from a derived predicate while it evaluates evidence from the subgoals of the supporting inference rules. If this evidence involves additional derived predicates, the truth judgment of these components is also deferred until their subgoal predicates are considered. The algorithm takes direct action only on a database or arithmetic predicate, and these predicates don't depend on inference rules. Therefore, the algorithm discovers the truth values of derived ground literals in the same order as a topological sort of the derived predicates. This policy delivers the preferred minimal model.

A second observation is that you avoided tracing the behavior on a specific binding by keeping the variable notation and making a mental note that a substitution had occurred. You can pursue this policy more formally to remove some of the algorithm's inefficiency. Instead of investigating all possible bindings in a sequential fashion, the algorithm can use the variables as generic placeholders for the substitutions until it arrives at the database or arithmetic predicates. At that point, it can identify the successful bindings.

As a preview of Chapter 10's deductive query solutions, find the names of species represented in a cesspool tank where some other distinct species with the same food preference is also represented. Assume the axioms of Figures 9.2 and 9.3 and the schema of Figure 9.4. You start by asserting a temporary inference rule that identifies the desired species names.

```
desiredSpeciesName (X) ⊢ speciesHasName (Y, X), fishRepresentsSpecies (U, Y),
                         fishInhabitsTank (U, Z), tankHasName (Z, "cesspool"),
                         fishInhabitsTank (W, Z), ¬cousin (W, U),
                         fishRepresentsSpecies (W, V), speciesHasFood (V, F),
                         speciesHasFood (Y, F).
```

You then launch the query by entering the goal, desiredSpeciesName (X), in the input loop of the queryProcessor routine. The backtracking mechanism searches for bindings X, Y, Z, W, V, and F, such that Y is a species with name X and food preference F, for which there exists a representative fish U swimming in tank Z with name cesspool, in which swims an unrelated (i.e., different species) fish W, representing species V, with V also having food preference F.

Relationships

A deductive database represents elementary relationships by ground instances of the database predicates. The axioms of Figure 9.3 list fishInhabitsTank (f_1, t_2) and fishRepresentsSpecies (f_1, s_3) as instances of elementary relationships. The abstract relationship is fish-inhabits-tank, expressed with the predicate fishInhabitsTank (X, Y). A specific binding that makes the predicate true is an instance of the relationship. The schema also constructs more complex relationships with inference rules. For example, you can derive cousin (f_1, f_{10}) from the inference rule for cousin in the schema of Figure 9.4. The derived predicate, cousin (X, Y), expresses the abstract relationship that allows two fish to become cousins: they must represent the same species. When the backtracking algorithm of the previous section returns a true variable binding for cousins (X, Y), the resulting ground literal expresses a fact about the aquarium application. In this case, the fact is that the binding constants are fish and that they are cousins.

The schema's inference rules take no precedence over those asserted in the query solution process. When you assert new inference rules, new relationships come into existence. Because the new rules simply enrich the model's semantic content, rendering it a more faithful reflection of the application, you could have included them in the schema. This illustrates again the blurred boundary between the access language and the database definition. For example, suppose you want a predicate speciesInTank (X, Y) to be true when tank Y holds a representative of species X. You can assert this relationship with the inference rule:

speciesInTank (X, Y) ⊢ fishRepresentsSpecies (Z, X), fishInhabitsTank (Z, Y).

This predicate simplifies certain queries. For example, you can find the names of species represented in cesspool tanks by asserting the following new rule and launching the query cesspoolSpecies (A).

cesspoolSpecies (A) ⊢ speciesHasName (X, A), tankHasName (Y, "cesspool"), speciesInTank (X, Y).

The list of possible relationships, however, has no end. You could define camouflaged-Shark (X) to be true when X is the name of a fish representing a shark species and swimming in a tank of the same color as the fish. Although you expect the rule to remain valid in the aquarium application, it would have limited usefulness.

In practice, inference rules in the schema establish the basic relationships: the one-to-many or many-to-many connections between the application entities. You then create more complex relationships as needed by asserting new inference rules, typically as part of a query process. New rules allow you to derive new facts. Stated differently, they allow new ground literals to enter the preferred minimal model. However, new rules can also cause previously established facts to be removed from the minimal model. Certain facts that were true before the assertion of a new rule may no longer be true. How can this happen?

Because the database is acyclic, no cycles appear in the predicates' dependency graph, even when you add new rules. However, a new rule can still force new true ground literals to arise from an existing predicate. That development, in turn, can cause a negated subgoal based on that predicate to become false where it was previously true. This can force the head ground literal out of the minimal model. Consider again the simplified aquarium with a single green tank, tank (10, "emerald", "green", 2000), and the following two inference rules:

redTank (X) ⊢ tank (X, Y, "red", Z).
antiRedTank (X) ⊢ tank (X, Y, W, Z), ¬redTank (X).

The rules assert that redTank (X) is true when X is a tank with color attribute red and that antiRedTank (X) is true when X is a tank but redTank (X) is false. Although this system has two competing minimal models, the preferred minimal model is the one where `antiRedTank (10)` is true. In other words, the aquarium contains a single tank, and it isn't red. But suppose you now assert the rule:

$$redTank~(X)~\vdash~tank~(X,~Y,~"green",~Z).$$

In doing so, you have changed the application semantics. The term *red tank* means either a red tank or a green tank. This interpretation of red is unusual, but you're in charge of this application. If you want red to mean "red or green," you are free to use the term in this specialized sense. (If this argument is confusing, pretend you have redefined red to mean reflecting light in the wavelength ranges 500–550 and 650–700 millimicrons.) Now `redTank (10)` is true, and `antiRedTank (10)` becomes false. The fact `antiRedTank (10)`, previously in the preferred minimal model, has been dropped.

When you assert new rules that define *new* derived predicates, any facts existing to that point remain true. This is because the new predicate isn't used in any of their derivations. When a new rule provides additional avenues to derive ground instances of *existing* predicates, however, some old facts may disappear. When you add a new rule to facilitate a query solution, you usually introduce new derived predicates that are useful for that query. This operation leaves all old facts intact, and it extends the minimal model to other facts that are relevant for the query. If these new predicates remain in the database, however, they might accidentally confound subsequent queries when overlapping predicate names occur. Because of this danger, you should remove query inference rules after the system delivers the solution. For the remainder of this chapter and the next, assume that the DBMS removes the rules of a logic program after running it.

 The deductive model represents relationships with ground instances of database predicates. Inference rules augment this base of relationship instances. Although the database schema specifies some inference rules, most arise from query solutions.

Binary relationships

Ground instances of database predicates are sufficient to represent both one-to-many and many-to-many relationships. For example, a collection of `fishInhabitsTank (X, Y)` ground instances captures the one-to-many relationship between tank and fish. The collection is actually just a tabulation of the corresponding fish-tank pairs, as shown on the left below. A given fish appears at most once in the tabulation because it associates with at most one tank. On the other hand, a given tank can occur many times, which implies that it associates with many fish.

fishInhabitsTank (f_1, t_2)		f_1	t_2
fishInhabitsTank (f_2, t_3)		f_2	t_3
fishInhabitsTank (f_3, t_2)		f_3	t_2
fishInhabitsTank (f_4, t_4)		f_4	t_4
fishInhabitsTank (f_5, t_1)		f_5	t_1
fishInhabitsTank (f_6, t_2)		f_6	t_2
fishInhabitsTank (f_7, t_3)		f_7	t_3
fishInhabitsTank (f_8, t_2)		f_8	t_2
fishInhabitsTank (f_9, t_2)	$\Rightarrow$	f_9	t_2
fishInhabitsTank (f_{10}, t_1)		f_{10}	t_1
fishInhabitsTank (f_{11}, t_2)		f_{11}	t_2
fishInhabitsTank (f_{12}, t_6)		f_{12}	t_6
fishInhabitsTank (f_{13}, t_2)		f_{13}	t_2
fishInhabitsTank (f_{14}, t_5)		f_{14}	t_5
fishInhabitsTank (f_{15}, t_1)		f_{15}	t_1
fishInhabitsTank (f_{16}, t_4)		f_{16}	t_4
fishInhabitsTank (f_{17}, t_6)		f_{17}	t_6

speciesInTank (s_1, t_1)		s_1	t_1
speciesInTank (s_1, t_2)		s_1	t_2
speciesInTank (s_1, t_3)		s_1	t_3
speciesInTank (s_1, t_4)		s_1	t_4
speciesInTank (s_1, t_5)		s_1	t_5
speciesInTank (s_1, t_6)		s_1	t_6
speciesInTank (s_2, t_2)	$\Rightarrow$	s_2	t_2
speciesInTank (s_2, t_4)		s_2	t_4
speciesInTank (s_3, t_1)		s_3	t_1
speciesInTank (s_3, t_2)		s_3	t_2
speciesInTank (s_3, t_6)		s_3	t_6
speciesInTank (s_4, t_2)		s_4	t_2
speciesInTank (s_4, t_3)		s_4	t_3

A many-to-many relationship takes the same form, except that a given instance from either entity can occur many times in the tabulation. For example, the speciesInTank (X, Y) derived predicate illustrated earlier can instead appear as a database predicate. Then certain ground instances of the predicate appear in the database content list, corresponding to tabulation on the right above. A given species, say s_1, occurs in several pairs, each associating s_1 with a different tank. A given species, therefore, is related to many tanks. Likewise a given tank, say t_1, occurs in many pairs, corresponding to different species. So a given tank is related to many species. The tabulation is very similar to the intersection entity, which appears when you decompose a many-to-many relationship in the relational model. Indeed, if you add a column for the quantity of fish that connect a given species and a given tank, you almost have the fish table from the relational aquarium database. Only the distinction among the connecting fish is missing.

Higher-degree relationships

As shown by the above examples, the deductive model represents binary relationships with two-argument database predicates. Similarly, it represents higher-degree relationships through database predicates with longer argument lists. Consider again the ternary relationship among ships, cargoes, and ports. The deductive analog of the mission table of Chapter 2 or the mission class of Chapter 7 is a predicate mission (S, P, C). This predicate is true precisely when ship S has called at port P carrying cargo C. Corresponding to the degree of the relationship, the predicate has three arguments.

In both the relational and object-oriented settings, the ternary relationship wasn't equivalent to three binary relationships among the participants. The same conclusion holds in the deductive model. Suppose you have three binary predicates: (1) docking (S, P), true when ship S calls at port P; (2) shipment (S, C), true when ship S carries cargo C; and (3) arrival (P, C), true when port P receives cargo C. You might attempt to derive the mission predicate as follows.

```
mission (S, P, C) ⊢ docking (S, P), shipment (S, C), arrival (P, C).
```

But as before, this arrangement can't distinguish between the two situations: (1) the ship Enterprise has carried beans to Boston; and (2) the ship Enterprise has not carried beans to Boston, but the Enterprise has carried some cargo to Boston, the Enterprise has carried beans somewhere, and some ship has brought beans to Boston. In either case, the derived predicate mission ("Enterprise", "Boston", "beans") is true. Therefore, you conclude, for the third time, that a piecewise decomposition of a ternary relationship into three binary relationships isn't equivalent to the original relationship.

However, introducing a single database predicate mission (S, P, C) is valid, and if you examine the ground instances, you find that it is essentially a tabulation of the mission triples from the relational situation. Moreover, you can then derive the docking, shipment, and arrival predicates from the mission predicate.

```
docking (S, P) ⊢ mission (S, P, C).
shipment (S, C) ⊢ mission (S, P, C).
arrival (P, C) ⊢ mission (S, P, C).
```

The situation generalizes to higher-degree relationships. A relationship of degree n requires n one-to-many relationships in the relational model, each linking one of the participating entities to a newly created intersection entity. In a deductive database, you express an n-degree relationship with an n-ary database predicate whose true instances are part of the database content.

 The deductive model expresses higher-degree relationships with database predicates. The number of arguments in the predicate matches the degree of the relationship.

Recursive relationships

Recursive relationships present no special problems in the deductive model. Consider again the employee table from Chapter 2 where each employee tuple contains an sno to identify her supervisor's employee number. A typical table appears on the left below; the corresponding ground instances are to the right. The database predicate is supervises (S, E), true when employee (eno) E reports to supervisor (eno) S.

Employee		
eno	ename	sno
53	albert	14
42	bernice	14
86	candice	53
45	dennis	
14	frank	45

```
supervises (14, 53).
supervises (14, 42).
supervises (53, 86).
supervises (45, 14).
```

You can query for the employees reporting to employee number 14 with supervises (14, X). You can also consider two levels of management and query for the employees reporting directly to employee 14 or reporting to someone who reports to employee 14.

```
under14TwoLevels (X) ⊢ supervises (14, X).
under14TwoLevels (X) ⊢ supervises (14, Y), supervises (Y, X).
```

The first rule finds Employees 53 and 42, and the second rule recovers employee 86 through the binding Y = 53. Continuing the pattern, you obtain the employees reporting to employee 14 through three levels as follows.

```
under14ThreeLevels (X) ⊢ supervises (14, X).
under14ThreeLevels (X) ⊢ supervises (14, Y), supervises (Y, X).
under14ThreeLevels (X) ⊢ supervises (14, Z), supervises (Z, Y), supervises (Y, X).
```

Although you can extend this pattern to recover the employees reporting to a given supervisor through any known number of levels, you can't obtain the employees down through an unknown number of levels. That query requires cyclical inference rules. The system can tolerate these cycles under certain controlled conditions. A later discussion will lift the acyclic dependency graph requirement, and this query can then be analyzed in greater detail. For the moment, consider the following solution.

```
over (X, Y) ⊢ supervises (X, Y).
over (X, Y) ⊢ over (X, Z), supervises (Z, Y).
```

To determine all the employees reporting to employee 14 through any number of levels, you launch the query with the command over (14, Y). Assume that the search algorithm considers the rules in the order given. The first attempt tries to satisfy over (14, Y) by recursively attempting to satisfy supervises (14, Y). The procedure succeeds for the bindings Y = 53 and Y = 42. The attempt to satisfy over (14, 86) fails with the first rule, but the second rule then tries to satisfy the list over (14, Z), supervises (Z, 86), for some Z binding. The binding Z = 53 expands the first subgoal to supervises (14, 53), which succeeds; the second subgoal then becomes supervises (53, 86), which also succeeds. Although no further solutions exist for this particular example, the pattern should be clear. The second rule allows workers at any distance from Employee 14 to be reached eventually, which properly accumulates the query solution.

However, this solution is a fortuitous result of the order that the algorithm invokes the rules. Suppose it tries the recursive rule first. Then an attempt to satisfy over (14, 53) expands in the following sequence, which introduces an endless sequence of new variables.

```
over (14, A), supervises (A, 53)
over (14, B), supervises (B, A), supervises (A, 53)
over (14, C), supervises (C, B), supervises (B, A), supervises (A, 53)
    ⋮
```

The first subgoal continues to expand indefinitely, and the algorithm enters an infinite loop. So recursive rules can prove useful, but their invocations must be carefully planned. In this case, the difficulty arises from the order that the algorithm invokes the rules. As you will see in the Chapter 10, other difficulties can arise when negated predicates appear in the dependency graph cycles.

Therefore, the discussion here will continue to assume an acyclic deductive database even though certain queries will remain unsolvable. This problem also appeared with relational algebra and with SQL, neither of which are computationally complete. Neither of these languages can express the query to find the employees reporting to a given supervisor through an arbitrary number of levels. A later section will show that an acyclic inference rule system is exactly equivalent to SQL and relational algebra in expressive power. Therefore, both should fail on the same queries. However, the careful introduction of cyclic rules gives a system that can solve queries beyond the range of relational algebra or SQL.

The employee example illustrates a one-to-many recursive relationship. A many-to-many recursive relationship appears in the bill of materials database considered in Chapter 2. (See Figure 2.20.) The primary entity is a part. A given part has many components, and it also contributes to many assemblies. The relational solution relied on an intersection table, which listed all pairs of parts, (p_1, p_2), where p_1 contains p_2. You can imitate that solution in the deductive model with the database predicate uses (X, Y), which is true when part X uses part Y as a component. You can easily formulate queries requesting information from a known segment of the hierarchy. For example, the left excerpt below finds the immediate components of part carburetor, and the right finds the subparts of a carburetor to two levels. You launch the query with the command contains ("carburetor", Y) or inCarbtoTwoLevels (Y).

```
                              inCarbtoTwoLevels (Y) ⊢ uses ("carburetor", Y).
uses ("carburetor", Y).       inCarbtoTwoLevels (Y) ⊢ uses ("carburetor", Z), uses (Z, Y).
```

However, a parts explosion through an arbitrary number of levels requires cyclic inference rules. You can successfully write this query as follows if you assume that the processing algorithm considers the rules in the order given. You launch the explosion query with the expression: contains ("carburetor", Y).

```
            contains (X, Y) ⊢ uses (X, Y).
            contains (X, Y) ⊢ uses (X, Z), contains (Z, Y).
```

A parts implosion, a listing of all the parts directly or indirectly containing a carburetor, uses the same recursive rules. You launch the implosion query with the expression: contains (X, "carburetor").

The deductive model represents recursive relationships in the usual way—through database predicates that associate related instances. Careful use of self-referential rules allows the expression of queries where the recursion depth isn't bounded in advance.

Constraints

The relational model enforces constraint through SQL assertions in the database schema. The object-oriented model employs special checks in the methods that modify object attributes. The deductive model uses special inference rules to enforce constraints.

An inference rule takes the form $q \vdash p_1, p_2, \ldots, p_n$, and all rules must be satisfied for all variable bindings. The satisfaction process interprets the rule as a logical implication, equivalent to a disjunctive clause. The two forms are as follows.

$$p_1 \wedge p_2 \wedge \ldots \wedge p_n \Rightarrow q. \qquad\qquad \neg p_1 \vee \neg p_2 \vee \ldots \vee \neg p_n \vee q.$$

A **disjunctive clause** is a sequence of literals connected with logical-or operators. A **Horn clause** is a disjunctive clause that contains at most one non-negated literal. As you can see in the form above, an inference rule with no negated subgoals corresponds to a Horn clause with exactly one non-negated literal, the head. Restricting inference rules to Horn clauses gives rise to a well-behaved form of logic programming. In particular, a Horn clause system always has a unique minimal model, and the question of a preferred minimal model doesn't arise. With only one model, there is no competition. However, a Horn clause system can't express universal queries, and it is, therefore, inferior to relational algebra.

In acyclic systems, certain inference rules don't correspond to Horn clauses. A negated predicate in the body produces a non-negated literal when you transform the rule into a disjunctive clause. Because the head also produces a non-negated literal, the number then exceeds one, which violates the Horn clause definition. This form is still useful to demonstrate how to express constraints with inference rules.

Consider a rule without a head literal. The expression is hardly an inference rule because there is nothing to derive. However, you can formally manipulate it into a disjunctive clause and obtain

$$\neg p_1 \vee \neg p_2 \vee \ldots \vee \neg p_n.$$

A disjunctive clause retains the same truth value, regardless of bindings, if you append the constant literal false to it. In particular, the clause is true precisely when there exists a true literal among the original entries. So the following expression is equivalent.

$$\neg p_1 \vee \neg p_2 \vee \ldots \vee \neg p_n \vee \text{false}.$$

Translating back to an inference rule, you obtain:

$$\text{false} \vdash p_1, p_2, \ldots, p_n.$$

For this rule to be satisfied for all possible bindings, at least one of the subgoals must fail for each binding. These rules with a false head open the possibility that a system may have no minimal model. For example, suppose you have a simple system with the four axioms on the left below and the single inference rule on the right.

```
tankHasVolume (t₁, 2000).
tankHasVolume (t₂, 2000).
tankHasColor (t₁, "red").
tankHasColor (t₂, "green").
```

$$\text{false} \vdash \text{tankHasVolume } (X, Y),$$
$$\text{tankHasVolume } (Z, Y),$$
$$\text{tankHasColor } (X, A),$$
$$\text{tankHasColor } (Z, B),$$
$$A \neq B.$$

This constraint is the volume $\longrightarrow$ color functional dependency that was included in the sample schema of Figure 9.4. The ground instances of the database predicates, which form the core of any minimal model, already violate the rule. In particular, the binding $X = t_1$, $Y = 2000$, $Z = t_2$, $A =$ "red", $B =$ "green" makes all the subgoals true simultaneously. Therefore, no minimal model exists because a model must contain all the ground literals arising from the database predicates.

When such a situation develops, the inference rules take precedence. In other words, the rules stand, and the database content becomes invalid. This same situation arose in the relational model. There, a constraint specified that certain relational bodies were invalid in terms of the application. The DBMS then controlled modifications to the relational bodies so that they never entered an invalid state. A deductive DBMS also checks a proposed modification of the database content list against the inference rules. If the modification causes a rule violation, the DBMS doesn't permit it.

In a deductive database content modification, only a constraint rule (i.e., a rule with a false head) can cause a violation. But the modification may affect a derived predicate. For a given derived predicate, some new ground instance might become true, or some previously true ground instances might become false. However, these changes reflect the intended ramifications of the new database content. They correspond to changes in the preferred minimal model to accommodate the new situation. They never force the minimal model to vanish. On the other hand, a rule with a false head can derive a flat contradiction, which does cause all minimal models to vanish. At that point the system is overdetermined and can't simultaneously accommodate the proposed database content and the rule system.

 A constraint in the deductive model is an inference rule without a head or with a constant false head. In the presence of constraints, a given database content list and associated inference rules may admit no models. In that case, the conflicting database content is an invalid database state.

You can check for constraint violations with the same algorithm that solves queries. The query-processing algorithm accepts a predicate and searches for variable bindings that render the predicate true. Although such queries typically involve a single predicate, the mechanism can handle a predicate list because its recursive expansion soon encounters such lists anyway. Therefore, you can check a constraint rule simply by passing its body to the query-processing algorithm. If it finds any true bindings, the constraint is violated.

Enforcing structural constraints with inference rules

What kind of constraints appear in a deductive database? First, you generally want to guarantee that an application object's descriptive attributes are unambiguous. For example, the database content list may contain tankHasColor (t₁, "red"), which you interpret to mean that the application tank t_1 is red. However, no contradiction arises if you add `tankHasColor` $(t_1,$ `"green"`) to the database content list. The preferred minimal model adjusts itself to the new circumstances, some query solutions change, but no rules are violated. Although this situation opens opportunities for multivalued attributes, you usually want an application object's descriptive attributes to be unambiguously specified. You can use a constraint rule to enforce this expectation as follows.

$$\text{false} \vdash \text{tankHasColor (X, A), tankHasColor (X, B), A} \neq \text{B}.$$

In the presence of this rule, the attempt to enter the second ground instance, `tankHasColor` $(t_1,$ `"green"`), into the database content forces a violation, and the DBMS doesn't permit the insertion. In this spirit, you expect the deductive schema to contain constraints enforcing the attribute uniqueness. A partial listing of the attribute uniqueness constraints for the aquarium application appears in top portion of Figure 9.9. These constraint rules follow an obvious mechanical pattern, and the DBMS can generate them automatically on behalf of the designer. In that case, the schema need only indicate which predicates judge the application objects' descriptive attributes.

You can also use constraint rules to enforce the one-to-many nature of elementary relationships. For example,

$$\text{false} \vdash \text{fishInhabitsTank (X, Y), fishInhabitsTank (X, Z), Y} \neq \text{Z}$$

forces a given fish to associate with at most one tank. Figure 9.9 contains additional examples.

The entity and referential integrity concerns from the relational model present no difficulties in the deductive model. This fortunate situation also applies to the object-oriented model because a system-generated OID, if present, always refers to an existing object. Suppose that the axiom `fishInhabitsTank` (f_1, t_2) or `fishHasName` $(f_1,$ `"charlie"`) occurs in the database content list. You can interpret the axioms as evidence of the existence of a fish f_1 and a tank t_2. Suppose `fishInhabitsTank` (f_1, t_2) occurs, but no descriptive predicates for fish f_1 appear. You interpret this situation as confirming the existence of a fish f_1, which currently has no assigned name, color, or weight. Likewise the presence of `fishInhabitsTank` (f_1, t_2) implies the existence of a tank t_2 even if that tank has no further descriptive predicates. With such an interpretation, it's impossible to violate referential integrity. Simply referring to a tank causes it to exist, so a fish can't associate with a nonexistent tank.

Although this argument suggests that entity and referential integrity concerns aren't a problem in the deductive model, the situation still isn't ideal. You might want to explicitly assert the existence of an application object so that you can more carefully control references to it. A few additional database predicates achieve this goal. In the aquarium example, they are `fish (X)`, `species (X)`, `tank (X)`, and `event (X)`, which are intended to be true when the argument is a fish, species, tank, or event respectively. You must augment the database content list of Figures 9.2 and 9.3 to include the following ground instances.

species (s_1)	tank (t_1)	fish (f_1)	event (e_1)
species (s_2)	tank (t_2)	fish (f_2)	event (e_2)
species (s_3)	tank (t_3)	fish (f_3)	event (e_3)
$\vdots$	$\vdots$	$\vdots$	$\vdots$

Enforcing unique descriptive attributes
false ⊢ speciesHasName (X, Y), speciesHasName (X, Z), Y ≠ Z.
false ⊢ speciesHasFood (X, Y), speciesHasFood (X, Z), Y ≠ Z.
false ⊢ tankHasName (X, Y), tankHasName (X, Z), Y ≠ Z.
false ⊢ tankHasColor (X, Y), tankHasColor (X, Z), Y ≠ Z.
false ⊢ fishHasColor (X, Y), fishHasColor (X, Z), Y ≠ Z.
⋮

Enforcing one-to-many relationships
false ⊢ fishInhabitsTank (X, Y), fishInhabitsTank (X, Z), Y ≠ Z.
false ⊢ fishRepresentsSpecies (X, Y), fishRepresentsSpecies (X, Z), Y ≠ Z.
false ⊢ eventConcernsFish (X, Y), eventConcernsFish (X, Z), Y ≠ Z.
⋮

Enforcing entity integrity
false ⊢ speciesHasName (X, Y), ¬species (X).
false ⊢ speciesHasFood (X, Y), ¬species (X).
false ⊢ tankHasName (X, Y), ¬tank (X).
false ⊢ tankHasColor (X, Y), ¬tank (X).
false ⊢ tankHasVolume (X, Y), ¬tank (X).
⋮

Enforcing nonnull descriptive values
false ⊢ species (X), ¬speciesHasName (X, Y).
false ⊢ fish (X), ¬fishHasColor (X, Y).
⋮

Enforcing referential integrity
false ⊢ fishInhabitsTank (X, Y), ¬tank (Y).
false ⊢ fishRepresentsSpecies (X, Y), ¬species (Y).
false ⊢ eventConcernsFish (X, Y), ¬fish (Y).

Figure 9.9 Inference rules expressing constraints in the aquarium database

With these predicates available, you can formulate the following equivalent of an entity integrity constraint.

$$\text{false} \vdash \text{fishHasName (X, Y), } \neg\text{fish (X)}$$
$$\text{false} \vdash \text{fishHasColor (X, Y), } \neg\text{fish (X)}$$
$$\text{false} \vdash \text{fishHasWeight (X, Y), } \neg\text{fish(X)}.$$

The rules prevent the association of a descriptive attribute value with a symbol that doesn't represent a fish. In the relational model, such an assignment corresponds to entering a tuple into a table with a null key, a clear entity integrity violation. You can construct similar rules to control the descriptive predicates for tanks, species, and events.

The following constraint shows how to prevent a descriptive attribute from assuming a null value.

$$\text{false} \vdash \text{fish (X), } \neg\text{fishHasName (X, Y)}.$$

The deductive model represents a null attribute value by the absence of a ground instance of the corresponding descriptive predicate. The rule above, therefore, asserts that a violation occurs if X binds to a symbol declared to represent a fish but no binding for Y satisfies the descriptive predicate fishHasName.

This example marks the first natural encounter with a negated subgoal that introduces negative free variables. You could depend on the query-processing algorithm to remedy the situation, but the following alternative rule set accomplishes the same purpose and is perhaps more intuitive.

```
false ⊢ fish (X), ¬namedFish (X).
namedFish (X) ⊢ fishHasName (X, Y).
```

An explicit referential integrity constraint, say that a fish must inhabit an existing tank, takes the form

```
false ⊢ fishInhabitsTank (X, Y), ¬tank (Y).
```

Figure 9.9 concludes with several referential integrity constraints from the aquarium database.

When studying the advanced SQL syntax of Chapter 6, you encountered situations where constraints had to be lifted while a sequence of database modifications was undertaken. Although the end result was a valid database state, certain intermediate states might have caused constraint violations. Suppose the following axioms, which describe the characteristics of a certain fish, are in the database content list.

```
fish (f₁).
fishHasName (f₁, "charlie").
fishHasColor (f₁, "orange").
```

Suppose you have asserted the following constraint rules. The first two deal with the entity integrity of a fish symbol, such as f_1; the rest enforce nonnull name and color attribute values.

```
false ⊢ fishHasName (X, Y), ¬fish (X).
false ⊢ fishHasColor (X, Y), ¬fish (X).
false ⊢ fish (X), ¬namedFish (X).
namedFish (X) ⊢ fishHasName (X, Y).
false ⊢ fish (X), ¬coloredFish (X).
coloredFish (X) ⊢ fishHasColor (X, Y).
```

Now, suppose you want to remove the fish from the database. Removing the axiom fish (f_1) causes immediate violations of the first two rules, and removing either of the descriptive axioms causes a violation of the corresponding nullity constraint. However, removing all three axioms returns the database to a consistent state. You encounter a similar difficulty when you insert a new fish. So, as with relational databases, you must use a transaction—an indivisible sequence of modifications that succeeds or fails as a unit.

Functional dependency constraints

A simple functional dependency constraint, volume ⟶ color, appeared in the schema of Figure 9.4. You can extend that pattern to enforce an arbitrary functional dependency whose components are all descriptive attributes of the same application object. For example, the functional dependency on the left below translates into the rules on the right.

$$\begin{aligned}
\text{false} \vdash\ & a_1\ (\text{X, A}_1),\ a_2\ (\text{X, A}_2),\ \ldots,\ a_n\ (\text{X, A}_n),\\
& a_1\ (\text{Y, A}_1),\ a_2\ (\text{Y, A}_2),\ \ldots,\ a_n\ (\text{Y, A}_n),\\
& b_1\ (\text{X, B}),\ b_1\ (\text{Y, C}),\ \text{B} \neq \text{C}.\\
\text{false} \vdash\ & a_1\ (\text{X, A}_1),\ a_2\ (\text{X, A}_2),\ \ldots,\ a_n\ (\text{X, A}_n),\\
& a_1\ (\text{Y, A}_1),\ a_2\ (\text{Y, A}_2),\ \ldots,\ a_n\ (\text{Y, A}_n),\\
& b_2\ (\text{X, B}),\ b_2\ (\text{Y, C}),\ \text{B} \neq \text{C}.\\
& \vdots\\
\text{false} \vdash\ & a_1\ (\text{X, A}_1),\ a_2\ (\text{X, A}_2),\ \ldots,\ a_n\ (\text{X, A}_n),\\
& a_1\ (\text{Y, A}_1),\ a_2\ (\text{Y, A}_2),\ \ldots,\ a_n\ (\text{Y, A}_n),\\
& b_m\ (\text{X, B}),\ b_m\ (\text{Y, C}),\ \text{B} \neq \text{C}.
\end{aligned}$$

$$a_1, a_2, \ldots, a_n \longrightarrow b_1, b_2, \ldots, b_m.$$

Here, a_i (V, W) is a descriptive database predicate, which asserts that object V has value W for attribute a_i. The first rule then states that two objects, X and Y, with the same bindings for the attributes $a_1, a_2, \ldots, a_n$ but with different bindings for the attribute b_1 constitute a violation. The other rules enforce similar constraints on the remaining members of the functional dependency's right side.

You can also formulate functional dependencies when the components lie in separate entities. Suppose the aquarium insists that fish of the same color swim in tanks of the same color. If a green fish inhabits a blue tank, all other green fish must inhabit blue tanks. You can express this constraint as follows.

```
false ⊢ fishHasColor (X, Y), fishHasColor (Z, Y),
        fishInhabitsTank (X, A), fishInhabitsTank (Z, B),
        tankHasColor (A, C), tankHasColor (B, D), C ≠ D.
```

The relationship predicates derive the proper tanks before the descriptive predicates compare their colors. An alternative approach asserts a rule to attach the home tank color to a fish, making it an indirect fish attribute. The constraint rule then falls under the previous category, and you can write it as follows.

```
fishHasTankColor (X, Y) ⊢ fishInhabitsTank (X, Z), tankHasColor (Z, Y).
false ⊢ fishHasColor (X, Y), fishHasColor (Z, Y),
        fishHasTankColor (X, A), fishHasTankColor (Z, B), A ≠ B.
```

Aggregate predicates and associated constraints

Certain quantitative constraints remain awkward in the notation developed to this point. Suppose, for example, that you want the database to contain less than three fish. This constraint appears below.

```
thirdFish (X) ⊢ fish (X), fish (Y), fish (Z), X ≠ Y, X ≠ Z, Y ≠ Z.
false ⊢ thirdFish (X).
```

Similarly, the following constraint asserts that the database contains at least three fish.

$$\text{false} \vdash \text{fish (X)}, \neg\text{thirdFish (X)}.$$

But you would have to write a very long and awkward rule to constrain the database to have at least a thousand fish. The point is that the current notation can't perform arithmetic operations; in fact, it can't compute functions of any kind. Therefore, besides having difficulty with quantitative constraints, you can't express aggregate queries.

The logic programming process could be augmented with functions so that the predicate arguments could include computations on their variables. These functions, in turn, could have their arguments computed by other functions, leading to a much richer set of logic expressions. However, instead of developing the complex machinery to consider these more complicated logic programs, there is a simple expedient for extracting the traditional aggregates (i.e., sum, average, count, min, and max) from the bindings delivered by a deductive query. The process creates new predicates, where the true bindings reflect various aggregates and arithmetic combinations computed from an existing predicate's table of true bindings.

This approach compromises, to a certain degree, the non-procedural specification of derived predicates to this point. Until now, inference rules defined each derived predicate. However, when a query solution requires the true binding values, a recursive procedure follows these inference rules back to the database predicates, where the true ground instances are available as axioms. The DBMS stores these axioms as tables. Therefore, although you can view a derived predicate as a non-procedural specification, an operational algorithm determines its table of true bindings. In a similar manner, the new aggregate predicates ultimately derive their true bindings from tables. Instead of storing these tables in the database, however, the DBMS computes them as needed.

Suppose $P(X_1, X_2, \ldots X_n)$ is a predicate of arity n. P may be a database predicate or a derived predicate. This predicate gives rise to a family of new predicates: $P_i^f(X_1, X_2, \ldots, X_i, Y)$, for $0 \leq i \leq n$. If $i < n$, then f can be any of the standard aggregates: count, sum, average, min, or max. If $i = n$, then f can be any arithmetic expression in the variables $X_1, X_2, \ldots, X_n$.

Before formally defining these predicates, consider the following operation on the aquarium database. Suppose you have the derived binary predicate tankHousesFish $(X_1; X_2)$, which is true when tank X_1 contains fish X_2. The reverse of the fishInhabitsTank database predicate, its definition is:

$$\text{tankHousesFish } (X_1, X_2) \vdash \text{fishInhabitsTank } (X_2, X_1).$$

The predicate $\text{tankHousesFish}_1^{\text{count}}(X_1; Y)$ is true when X_1 is bound to a tank and Y is bound to the number of fish in that tank. Operationally, the DBMS obtains these true bindings as follows. First, it tabulates the true bindings for the unsubscripted base predicate. It then partitions the table using the first argument. Next, it counts the number of entries in each group and produces a new table with one row for each group. A group's row contains the constant value of X_1 for that group and the count. The DBMS interprets the final table as the true ground instances of $\text{tankHousesFish}_1^{\text{count}}(X_1; Y)$. The transformation on the left below illustrates the process.

X_1	X_2
t_1	f_5
t_1	f_{10}
t_1	f_{15}
t_2	f_1
t_2	f_3
t_2	f_6
t_2	f_8
t_2	f_9
t_2	f_{11}
t_2	f_{13}
t_3	f_2
t_3	f_7
t_4	f_4
t_4	f_{16}
t_5	f_{14}
t_6	f_{12}
t_6	f_{17}

$\Longrightarrow$

X_1	Y
t_1	3
t_2	7
t_3	2
t_4	2
t_5	1
t_6	2

X_1	X_2	X_3
s_1	200	t_1
s_1	100	t_2
s_1	400	t_3
s_1	100	t_4
s_1	200	t_5
s_1	200	t_6
s_2	100	t_2
s_2	100	t_4
s_3	200	t_1
s_3	100	t_2
s_3	200	t_6
s_4	100	t_2
s_4	400	t_3

$\Longrightarrow$

X_1	Y
s_1	1200
s_2	200
s_3	500
s_4	500

The count aggregate computes the number of entries in each group, and therefore it isn't concerned with the values in the second column of the true binding table for `tankHousesFish`. However, the other aggregates use a column's values for their computations. You might, for example, have the predicate `speciesVolTank` that associates each species with the tanks where it is represented and with their volumes. Therefore, the `speciesVolTank` table below gives rise to a table of true bindings for $\text{speciesVolTank}_1^{\text{sum}}(X_1; Y)$, as shown on the right above.

```
speciesVolTank (X₁, X₂, X₃) ⊢ fishRepresentSpecies (F, X₁), fishInhabitsTank (F, X₃),
                    tankHasVolume (X₃, X₂).
```

These examples illustrate why a predicate $P(X_1, X_2, \ldots, X_n)$ of arity n gives rise to aggregate predicates P_i^f only for subscripts $i < n$. The first i columns of the true binding table for P define the partition, and column $i + 1$ supplies values for the aggregate computation. If the subscript is n, the partition definition uses all the columns, which results in one group for each tuple. In this case f can be any arithmetic combination of the preceding columns. For example, suppose that the table of true bindings for $P(X_1, X_2, X_3)$ is as shown on the left below. Then the transformed table on the right defines the true ground instances of $P_3^{2*X_1+X_2-X_3}(X_1, X_2, X_3, Y)$.

X_1	X_2	X_3
2	3	5
4	6	1
8	3	2
6	6	7

$\Longrightarrow$

X_1	X_2	X_3	Y
2	3	5	2
4	6	1	13
8	3	2	17
6	6	7	11

For a formal definition, if $P(X_1, X_2, \ldots, X_n)$ is a predicate of arity n, the DBMS determines as follows the true ground instances of the **aggregate predicate** $P_i^f(X_1, X_2, \ldots, X_i, Y)$, where $0 \le i < n$ and f is one of the standard aggregates. It tabulates the true ground instances for P with a call to the query-processor algorithm. It then puts the table columns in the order: $X_1, X_2, \ldots, X_n$. It next partitions the table on the first i columns so that all rows in a given group have the same values under X_1 through X_i. Within each group, it applies the f aggregate to the values in column $i + 1$, producing a new table with a single row for each group. The new table has column headings $X_1, X_2, \ldots, X_i, Y$. Under each X_i is the constant value from column X_i in the group. Under Y is the result of the aggregate on column $i + 1$. The DBMS uses the transformed table to determine the true ground literals for $P_i^f(X_1, X_2, \ldots, X_i, Y)$.

Note that i can be zero. In this case, the DBMS aggregates the first column of P over one large group, which runs the full table length. This produces $P_0^f(Y)$. If $i = n$ and f is an arithmetic expression in $X_1, X_2, \ldots, X_n$, the new table contains a row for each tuple in the true binding table for P. Within each row, a final column for Y contains the specified arithmetic results on the values in the previous columns.

An immediate concern is that the bindings required for Y don't necessarily occur in the universe of discourse. To this point, all argument bindings have been restricted to that domain. The DBMS can easily circumvent this by simply adding all constants produced by the process to the universe of discourse. This expansion of the universe is temporary, lasting only for the duration of the query-processing or constraint-checking activity that uses the constructions.

 The DBMS defines an aggregate predicate with a computed tabulation of its true ground instances. It obtains the table by partitioning and aggregating the true ground instances of an existing predicate.

Evaluating such an aggregate predicate, say P_i^f, involves computing the true bindings for the predicate P and then partitioning and aggregating the resulting table. Therefore, when an aggregate predicate occurs in an inference rule body, the rule head depends implicitly on the predicate P. This requires an arc in the dependency graph from P to the head. Even with the addition of such arcs, an acyclic database must continue to avoid cycles in the dependency graph. Consequently, a topological sort of the predicates is still possible, and the earlier query-processing algorithm still draws solutions from the preferred minimal model.

When the algorithm reaches an aggregate subgoal, say $P_i^f(X_1, X_2, \ldots, X_i, Y)$, it constructs the table of true ground instances as described above. Because no cycles exist in the dependency graph, the intermediate table for the true bindings of $P(X_1, X_2, \ldots, X_n)$ is fixed. In other words, the set of true ground instances arising from P can't change as a result of the rule where the aggregate occurs. For this reason, the system can treat aggregate predicates in the same manner as database predicates; each has an underlying table of true instances. The difference is that the DBMS must calculate the table for an aggregate at a particular point in the goal satisfaction process. By contrast, the table for a database predicate is always available in the database content list.

With aggregate predicates, you can express certain quantitative constraints, such as the restriction that the number of fish in the database be at least 1000. You build an aggregate predicate over the database predicate fish (X), which asserts the existence of fish X.

$$\text{false} \vdash \text{fish}_0^{\text{count}}(Y), \ Y < 1000.$$

The only true instance of $\text{fish}_0^{\text{count}}(Y)$ occurs when Y is bound to the number of fish in the tabulation of the true ground instances of fish (X). If this binding for Y is less than 1000, the second subgoal is satisfied, which produces a violation.

 You can use headless inference rules to express a variety of constraints, including the uniqueness of descriptive attributes, the one-to-many nature of relationships, entity and referential integrity, nonnull attributes, and certain quantitative restrictions derived from the standard aggregates.

Chapter 10 will discuss aggregate predicates in greater detail as part of a systematic analysis of deductive queries. As a preview, however, consider the following quantitative constraint: if at least one tank contains a shark, the average volume of tanks containing sharks must be at least 3000. You can express this constraint as follows.

$$\text{sharkyTank}\ (X_1, X_2) \vdash \text{tank}\ (X_2), \text{fishInhabitsTank}\ (F,\ X_2), \text{tankHasVolume}\ (X_2, X_1),$$
$$\text{fishRepresentsSpecies}\ (F, S), \text{speciesHasName}\ (S, \text{"shark"}).$$
$$\text{false} \vdash \text{sharkyTank}_0^{\text{average}}(Y), \ Y < 3000.$$

The sharkyTank predicate constructs a table of tanks with sharks. It includes the tank volume in each case and places it first. To keep the table from suppressing duplicates, which would reduce tanks with the same volume to a single row, the table retains the tank itself as the second argument. If at least one sharky tank exists, the first rule pair produces true instances of sharkyTank. Considering the table as one large group, the DBMS transforms it by averaging the elements of its first column, the tank volumes. Therefore, the first subgoal is true when Y is that average. Finally, if the average is less than 3000, the second subgoal becomes true, which forces a violation.

A change in the database content can force a violation in many ways. Adding a new fish can transform a non-sharky tank into a sharky one, which can change the average volume. Removing a fish can convert a sharky tank into a non-sharky one, again changing the average volume. Modifying the volume attribute of a sharky tank will also change the average volume. The constraint rule monitors all these possibilities.

SUMMARY Incorporating concepts from logic programming, deductive databases represent an application as a core of explicit facts supplemented with inference rules. The inference rules allow the DBMS to compute a consistent extended collection of derived facts on demand. The basic information unit is the predicate, which occurs in three varieties: database, arithmetic, and derived. Database predicates assert elementary application facts, and arithmetic predicates allow comparisons between constants. Derived predicates obtain their truth values through the inference rules.

A predicate is a boolean function, whose arguments are restricted to a finite set of values called the universe of discourse. A literal is a predicate where the arguments can be variables or constants. A literal with all constant arguments is a ground literal. A binding is an assignment of constants from the universe to the variables of some list.

Database predicates are elementary judgments about the application. The true ground literals arising from the database predicates are simply tabulated in a database content list. For example, a database predicate fishHasColor (X, Y) is true when fish X has color value Y. fishHasColor (f_1, "red") is an example of a true ground literal arising from this database predicate. The database content establishes the application objects' attributes and their elementary relationships. All the constants mentioned in the database content make up the universe of discourse, which is augmented with any constants appearing in the inference rules. After the universe of discourse has been defined, arithmetic predicates express comparisons between the values.

Inference rules allow the definition of derived predicates in terms of subgoals. An inference rule contains a head and a body. The head is a derived predicate, and each subgoal is a literal, possibly negated. The DBMS interprets an inference rule as a logical inference. The inference rule is satisfied in all cases except when all the subgoals are true but the head is false. An arbitrary assignment of truth values to all the ground literals arising from the derived predicates creates a possible world. Formally defined, a possible world contains the database content in addition to all the true ground literals arising from the derived predicates. A possible world where all inference rules are satisfied is a model. A minimal model is a model where no ground literal can be returned to false without destroying the model with a rule violation.

Ideally, the database content and the inference rules cooperate to produce a unique minimal model. The ground literals in this unique minimal model become application facts that are derivable from the initial database content. However, in general, several contradictory minimal models compete for the application "meaning." In this case, a preferred minimal model may be discernible.

The dependency graph of a collection of predicates and inference rules contains a node for each predicate. A directed arc runs from node q to node p if either q or $\neg q$ appears in the body of an inference rule having p as the head. A dependency graph with no cycles is acyclic; a deductive database with an acyclic dependency graph is an acyclic deductive database. The predicates in an acyclic deductive database admit a topological sort, a linearized list where a given predicate depends only on predicates that occur earlier in the list. When the dependency graph is linearized in this fashion, all arcs point forward from earlier nodes toward later nodes in the list. You can generate a preferred minimal model by starting with the database content and adding ground literals from derived predicates, taken in the order of the topological sort. At any given point, the process adds a ground literal only if some rule forces it to be true. An algorithm can mechanically compute a predicate's true bindings in the preferred minimal model. The preferred minimal model contains true ground literals that correspond to the facts computable with relational algebra from an equivalent relational database.

A query is a predicate assertion with variables for one or more of its arguments. The query-processing algorithm solves the query by searching for those bindings that render the predicate true in the preferred minimal model.

By definition, a deductive database is a database where the elementary data elements and relationships are represented by ground instances of database predicates. These initial facts are axioms. A deductive database is further characterized by inference rules, which permit the calculation of other true ground literals, all drawn from the preferred minimal model. Logic programs, consisting of additional inference rules, constitute a systematic user interface to the database.

Inference rules can also enforce constraints because a headless inference rule must always have a false body, regardless of the variable bindings. The deductive schema specifies the axiom shells and an initial collection of inference rules, which represent both derived relationships of general utility and database constraints. You can use inference rules to express the traditional constraints of entity and referential integrity. You can also force the uniqueness of attribute values, the one-to-many status of relationships, and nonnull entries.

The DBMS interprets aggregate predicates with a procedure that transforms the true binding table for an auxiliary predicate. It partitions the table and applies one of the aggregate operators (i.e., sum, average, count, min, or max) to the resulting groups. For example, if $P(X_1, X_2)$ is a predicate, $P_1^{sum}(X_1, Y)$ is true for those bindings of X_1 and Y that appear in the transformed table. The DBMS computes that table by launching the query $P(X_1, X_2)$ and accumulating the true bindings in an intermediate table. It partitions that table on constant values of X_1 and places one row in the transformed table for each group. The row contains the constant X_1 value and the sum of the X_2 values across the group. These aggregate predicates allow you to express certain quantitative constraints with inference rules.■

EXERCISES

Logic programming in a database context

1. Suppose you are dealing with a database of trees where the attributes are height, diameter, and age. The database predicate tree (W, X, Y, Z) means that the tree with tree-number W has height X, diameter Y, and age Z. Suppose the database contains the following axioms and inference rules. Find the unique minimal model.

```
tree (10, 56, 0.8, 27).        largeTree (W) ⊢ tree (W, X, Y, Z), Y > 1.5.
tree (20, 74, 1.2, 45).        smallTree (W) ⊢ tree (W, X, Y, Z), Y < 1.0.
tree (30, 84, 1.6, 58).
```

2. Expand the previous problem to include the following rules. Find all the distinct minimal models for the new collection of axioms and rules. Do you have an intuitive preference for one of the models?

```
largeTree (W) ⊢ tree (W, X, Y, Z), Y > 1.5.
smallTree (W) ⊢ tree (W, X, Y, Z), Y < 1.0.
smallTree (W) ⊢ tree (W, X, Y, Z), ¬largeTree (W).
```

3. Expand the first problem to include the following rules. Find all the distinct minimal models for the new collection of axioms and rules. Do you have an intuitive preference for one of the models?

```
largeTree (W) ⊢ tree (W, X, Y, Z), Y > 1.5.
smallTree (W) ⊢ tree (W, X, Y, Z), Y < 1.0.
smallTree (W) ⊢ tree (W, X, Y, Z), ¬largeTree (W).
largeTree (W) ⊢ tree (W, X, Y, Z), ¬smallTree (W).
```

For the next group of questions, assume database predicates are available to return descriptive information about the library database entities. The ground instances of the following predicates appear in the database content list.

Database predicate	Order of arguments	Database predicate	Order of arguments
library (W, X, Y, Z)	libno, libname, location, rooms	book (X, Y, Z)	bookno, title, pages
author (X, Y)	authno, authname	copy (X, Y)	copyno, cost
patron (X, Y, Z)	patno, patname, patwgt	loan (X, Y)	loanno, duedate

4. What additional database predicates are needed to express the one-to-many relationships between the following entities: author and book? library and copy? book and copy? copy and loan? patron and loan?

Use the database predicates developed for the previous question as needed in the inference rules that follow.

5. Compose an inference rule for sisterLibraries (X, Y), which is true when X and Y are libno values and the corresponding libraries share the same location.

6. Compose an inference rule for sibling (X, Y), which is true when X and Y are bookno values and the corresponding books have the same author.

7. Compose inference rules for thinNearBook (X) and thickOrFarBook (X). ThinNearBook (X) is true when X is a bookno corresponding to a book with less than 100 pages that is available from a Seattle library. ThickOrFarBook (X) is true when X isn't a thinNearBook.

8. Compose an inference rule for sameLiteraryTaste (X, Y), which is true when X and Y are patno values, referring to patrons who have read a common book.

Definition of a deductive database

Prepare deductive schemas for the following situations in the spirit of Figure 9.4. You don't need to invent any constraint rules for the applications. Each schema should give the shells of the database predicates needed to represent application entity instances and to express the one-to-many relationships. Include at least one additional relationship derived through an inference rule.

9. An engineering firm has several projects in progress. Each project occupies the full attention of several engineers. Each engineer has a crew of laboratory assistants who report only to him. Each laboratory assistant owns a collection of instruments. There is no joint ownership of instruments.

10. A molecule contains many atoms, and it is important to record the number of each kind of atom in the molecule. For example, methane, CH_4, contains one carbon and four hydrogen atoms. Atoms appear in many different molecules.

11. Draw a dependency graph for the following situation.

Axioms	Inference Rules
tree (10, 56, 0.8, 27).	largeTree (W) ⊢ tree (W, X, Y, Z), Y > 1.5.
tree (20, 74, 1.2, 45).	smallTree (W) ⊢ tree (W, X, Y, Z), Y < 1.0.
tree (30, 84, 1.6, 58).	smallTree (W) ⊢ tree (W, X, Y, Z), ¬largeTree (W).
	largeTree (W) ⊢ tree (W, X, Y, Z), ¬smallTree (W).

Query solution as goal satisfaction

12. Consider the following rule set, where E and F are database predicates. Using variables to indicate generic substitutions from the universe of discourse, show the hierarchy of arguments passed to the recursive satisfy routines while searching for solutions to the query: A (P, Q).

$$A (X, Y) \vdash B (X, Z), C (Z, Y).$$
$$B (X, Y) \vdash E (X, Z), F (Z, Y).$$
$$C (X, Y) \vdash E (Y, Z), E (Z, X).$$

13. Using the aquarium schema predicates of Figure 9.4, compose inference rules to solve the query: find the names of tanks having volume greater than 3000 and containing a shark species.

Relationships

The following situations involve higher-degree or recursive relationships. In each case, compose a deductive schema, which features database predicates for the descriptive entity attributes and for the relationships.

14. There are fields to plow, tractors to do the plowing, and farmers to ride the tractors. When all three factors come together, some work is accomplished.

15. A computer program consists of a collection of subprocedures, which call each other for services. In general, a given subprocedure calls other routines to break its task into smaller components. However, a given procedure can also be invoked by many different host procedures.

16. A literary collection consists of books. Each contains a bibliographic section referencing other books.

17. A computer graphics image consists of a collection of two-dimensional curves. A given curve is related to other curves that it intersects.

Constraints

A deductive schema for the library database appears in Figure 9.10. Using these primitives, construct inference rules to express the following constraints.

18. Patrons weighing more than 100 pounds may not check out books with less than 300 pages.

19. (Entity integrity.) A descriptive attribute may not be associated with a nonexistent entity.

20. (One-to-many relationship enforcement.) The following relationships must be one-to-many: author-book, library-copy, book-copy, copy-loan, and patron-loan.

21. (Nonnull descriptive values.) All the descriptive predicates for a given entity instance must be present. Use auxiliary rules as necessary to avoid negative free variables.

22. Compose an inference rule for `patReadsAuth (X, Y)`, true when patron X has checked out a book written by author Y. Then use an aggregate predicate to express the constraint that a patron may not read books written by more than 10 different authors.

Entity existence assertion axioms	
Predicate	Intended meaning
`library (X)`	X is a library
`author (X)`	X is an author
`patron (X)`	X is a patron
`book (X)`	X is a book
`copy (X)`	X is a copy of a book
`loan (X)`	X is the record of the loan of a copy to a patron

Attribute assertion axioms	
Predicate	Intended meaning
`libHasName (X, Y)`	string Y is the name of library X
`libHasLocation (X, Y)`	string Y is the location of library X
`libHasRooms (X, Y)`	string Y is the number of rooms in library X
`authHasName (X, Y)`	string Y is the name of author X
`bookHasTitle (X, Y)`	string Y is the title of book X
`bookHasPages (X, Y)`	number Y is the page count of book X
`copyHasCost (X, Y)`	string Y is the dollar cost of copy X
`patHasName (X, Y)`	string Y is the name of patron X
`patHasWeight (X, Y)`	string Y is the weight of patron X
`loanHasDate (X, Y)`	string Y is the due date of loan Y

Relationship assertion axioms	
Predicate	Intended meaning
`authWritesBook (X, Y)`	author X has written book Y
`libHoldsCopy (X, Y)`	library X holds copy Y
`bookHasCopy (X, Y)`	book X has copy Y
`copyHasLoan (X, Y)`	copy X has loan record Y
`patHasLoan (X, Y)`	patron X has loan record Y

Figure 9.10   Deductive schema for the library database

10 Deductive Queries

T HIS CHAPTER'S FOCUS IS THE DEDUCTIVE QUERY. It will develop a standard approach for each of the query categories: existential, universal, and aggregate. For each type of query, the deductive solution strategy is similar to the relational and object-oriented cases already studied—only the notation is new.

Consider first the existential query. In a relational database, you solve an existential query by constructing a database path through the relations. You link adjacent tables with common attribute values and eventually connect a candidate tuple with a specified anchor. In an object-oriented database, you pursue the same strategy, except the database path is a recursive search into the candidate object's attributes. Existential queries in a deductive database are just a variation on this theme: common bindings in subgoals serve as links in the database path.

Universal queries in a relational database are solved by demonstrating a bundle of paths sufficient to connect a candidate to all members of an anchor collection. This strategy requires a subquery in SQL, a division operator in relational algebra, and a universal quantifier in relational calculus. Because quantification is implicit and existential in SQL, you must use complex expressions for universal queries, such as set-containment and doubly negated subqueries. In an object-oriented database, you imitate the set-containment solution. For a given candidate object, if the set of reachable objects contains the set of anchors, the candidate contributes to the answer. In the deductive model, you follow the doubly negated SQL solution because existential quantification is implied for subgoal variables in inference rules. The resulting pattern uses two cascading rules with negated subgoals.

The relational model handles aggregate queries with special operators that let you partition a table and summarize the resulting groups. The object-oriented model can imitate these operations because it uses a general purpose programming language as an interface. The last chapter introduced aggregate predicates, which extend the capabilities of inference rules to imply similar constructions. With aggregate predicates, you can solve aggregate queries in a deductive database.

Although this chapter's primary goal is to show you how to express the various query categories with logic programs, it also develops some theoretical results. It demonstrates that acyclic inference rule systems are equivalent to relational algebra and then investigates variations on the inference rule format. If you weaken the acyclic inference system by disallowing negated predicates, you avoid the problem of competing minimal models, but the system becomes less expressive than relational algebra. On the other hand, if you strengthen the system by allowing dependency graph cycles, you can express queries beyond the range of relational algebra, but a preferred minimal model may not be distinguishable.

This chapter's examples use the aquarium application, specifically the schema of Figure 9.4 plus the entity existence axioms: `species (X)`, `tank (X)`, `fish (X)`, and `event (X)`. The returned query bindings use the database content of Figures 9.2 and 9.3.

Existential queries

Queries involving a single application object

In the simplest existential queries, a candidate qualifies directly on the basis of its immediate attributes; no probes into related objects are necessary. For example, find the colors of tanks named lagoon. On the left below is the SQL solution, which involves a selection from a single relation. The adjacent code shows the corresponding logic program. In the deductive solution, the database predicates constrain the answers to lagoon tanks and associate the chosen tanks with their colors. The query processor response appears on the right.

```
select tcolor          query (X) ⊢ tankHasName (Y, "lagoon"),        X
from Tank                         tankHasColor (Y, X).              ─────
where tname = "lagoon".  query (X).                                  red
                                                                     green
```

Unless otherwise specified, assume that after it has reported the solution, the DBMS removes any inference rules asserted during a query process. So you can reuse the `query` predicate as needed for different queries without fear of interference from previous activities.

Because a rule's subgoal list represents a conjunction of conditions, you can translate logical-and operations in an SQL where-clause to a sequence of subgoals. For example, to find the colors of tanks named lagoon with volume greater than 100, you translate the SQL as follows.

```
select tcolor, tvolume                    query (X) ⊢ tankHasName (Y, "lagoon"),
from Tank                                            tankHasVolume (Y, Z),
where tname = "lagoon" and tvolume > 100.            Z > 100, tankHasColor (Y, X).
                                          query (X).
```

Logical-or conditions in the where-clause, however, translate to additional rules. The following SQL and its translation find the colors of tanks that are either named lagoon or have a volume greater than 100.

```
select tcolor, tvolume                query (X) ⊢ tankHasName (Y, "lagoon"),
from Tank                                        tankHasColor (Y, X).
where tname = "lagoon" or tvolume > 100.   query (X) ⊢ tankHasVolume (Y, Z), Z > 100,
                                                 tankHasColor (Y, X).
                                      query (X).
```

Following the query-processing algorithm, bindings for X and Y that fail the `tankHasName` subgoal get a chance to satisfy the second rule. So a tank Y can deliver its color X if it's named lagoon or if it has a volume greater than 100.

An alternative approach first isolates the contributing tanks and then binds the color. The first part requires two rules because of the disjunction in the SQL where-clause. This variation appears on the left below.

```
targetTank (Y) ⊢ tankHasName (Y, "lagoon").    targetTank (Y) ⊢ tank (Y),
targetTank (Y) ⊢ tankHasVolume (Y, Z),                           tankHasName (Y, "lagoon").
                 Z > 100.                      targetTank (Y) ⊢ tank (Y),
query (X) ⊢ targetTank (Y),                                      tankHasVolume (Y, Z),
            tankHasColor (Y, X).                                 Z > 100.
query (X).                                     query (X) ⊢ targetTank (Y),
                                                               tankHasColor (Y, X).
                                               query (X).
```

Here Y must bind to a tank because the `tankHasName` database predicate produces only axioms for tank objects. However, you can explicitly force Y to bind to a tank with the `tank (Y)` existence axiom. The parallel code on the right above shows this alternative. In this example, it isn't necessary to use the existence axiom because the attribute assertion predicate `tankHasName (X, Y)` forces Y to be a tank. But this precaution is necessary under other circumstances. Suppose you want all tanks except lagoon. Imitating the pattern to this point, you might attempt the following solution.

```
query (X) ⊢ ¬tankHasName (X, "lagoon").
query (X).
```

As expected, the single subgoal succeeds for those symbols X from the universe of discourse, such as t_1, t_2, t_4, which are tanks but for which `tankHasName (X, "lagoon")` is false. However, it also succeeds for nonsensical bindings, such as X = "green" because `tankHasName ("green", "lagoon")` doesn't appear among the axioms, and therefore it is false. The problem is that a negated subgoal can succeed in unexpected ways by binding to some value outside the intended range. Therefore, when negated subgoals are present, you need other subgoals to eliminate nonsensical bindings. The simplest solution is to add a subgoal that restricts a variable to the intended range. In this example, you intend X to range over the tanks and to bind successfully to those with a name other than lagoon. So you can rephrase the query as shown on the left below.

```
query (X) ⊢ tank (X),                  query (X) ⊢ tankHasColor (Y, X),
            ¬tankHasName (X, "lagoon").              ¬tankHasName (Y, "lagoon").
query (X).                             query (X).
```

Now X must indeed be a tank, and furthermore, its name must not be lagoon. If X binds in a nonsensical manner, such as X = "green", then tank (X) fails, and the truth value of ¬tankHasName (X, "lagoon") isn't relevant. This precaution isn't necessary if some other subgoal already constrains the variable to a proper range. The parallel code on the right above, for example, finds the colors of tanks that aren't named lagoon. Here the non-negated subgoal, tankHasColor, can succeed only if Y is bound to a tank. This eliminates any extraneous bindings that satisfy the negated subgoal.

Queries involving multiple application objects

When a candidate enters the solution set by virtue of its relationships with other objects, the logic program must investigate database paths to these related objects. It does this with common bindings in the relationship predicates. The expressions below find the colors of fish swimming with a shark. The SQL lines up the relevant tables to capture all species-fish combinations, and it then removes the inappropriate combinations with the where-clause. The deductive equivalent uses the fishRepresentsSpecies relationship predicate to achieve the same purpose.

```
select fcolor                          query (X) ⊢ fishHasColor (Y, X),
from Species, Fish                                 fishRepresentsSpecies (Y, Z),
where Species.sno = Fish.sno and                   speciesHasName (Z, "shark").
      sname = "shark".             query (X).
```

You can envision the fishRepresentsSpecies predicate as a tabulation of the fish-species pairs where the fish is a representative of the species. In other words, the predicate's true ground instances give the natural join of the species and fish relations. When you use fishRepresentsSpecies as one of the subgoals, you restrict the successful bindings to fish-species pairs that satisfy the foreign-key matchup in the SQL where-clause. A further subgoal then forces the species to be a shark.

This pattern extends to longer database paths. For example, find the names of fish that represent a shark species and inhabit a cesspool tank. The SQL aligns a sequence of database tables and then filters the resulting combinations. The corresponding logic program connects species to fish to tank with the relationship predicates and accomplishes the same goal. The two approaches are shown below.

```
                                       query (X) ⊢ fishRepresentsSpecies (Y, Z),
select F.fname                                     fishInhabitsTank (Y, W),
from Species S, Fish F, Tank T                     speciesHasName (Z, "shark"),
where S.sno = F.sno and F.tno = T.tno and          tankHasName (W, "cesspool"),
      S.sname = "shark" and T.tname = "cesspool".  fishHasName (Y, X).
                                       query (X).
```

The direction along the database path is less intuitive in the deductive solution than in the SQL. The deductive path starts with the fish and extends in both directions to the species and to the tank. You can imitate the SQL more directly by asserting two additional rules that allow you to view the relationships from either end.

```
speciesClassifiesFish (X, Y) ⊢ fishRepresentsSpecies (Y, X).
tankHousesFish (X, Y) ⊢ fishInhabitsTank (Y, X).
```

Because these rules are generally useful, assume they remain in the database. Later queries will use them without further assertions. You can now express the previous query with a path that closely parallels the SQL.

```
query (N) ⊢ speciesClassifiesFish (S, F), fishInhabitsTank (F, T), speciesHasName (S, "shark"),
          tankHasName (T, "cesspool"), fishHasName (F, N).
query (N).
```

The pattern extends to longer database paths. For example, find the names of species swimming with a shark. Imitating the SQL on the left below, you obtain the deductive solution on the right. The deductive expression aligns the relationship predicates in the same order as the table linkages in the SQL where-clause.

```
select H.sname
from Species S, Fish F, Tank T,
    Fish G, Species H
where S.sno = F.sno and F.tno = T.tno and
    S.sname = "shark" and T.tno = G.tno and
    G.sno = H.sno.
```

```
query (N) ⊢ speciesClassifiesFish (S, F),
          fishInhabitsTank (F, T),
          tankHousesFish (T, G),
          fishRepresentsSpecies (G, H),
          speciesHasName (H, "shark"),
          speciesHasName (S, N).
query (N).
```

An SQL variation of this query eliminates the string shark from the answer when it occurs only because a fish swims with itself. The logic program for this variation appears below. With the subgoal G ≠ F, it forces the candidate fish and the shark fish to be distinct.

```
query (N) ⊢ speciesClassifiesFish (S, F), fishInhabitsTank (F, T),
          tankHousesFish (T, G), fishRepresentsSpecies (G, H), G ≠ F
          speciesHasName (H, "shark"), speciesHasName (S, N).
query (N).
```

Because a different variable represents each path link, the link attributes are available for reporting or for further restriction. For example, find the names of species swimming with a blue shark and also report the names of the common tanks. As seen on the left below, the SQL shows that all the database chain links are available. The same accessibility is present in the corresponding logic program, as shown on the right.

```
select H.sname, T.tname
from Species S, Fish F, Tank T,
    Fish G, Species H
where S.sno = F.sno and F.tno = T.tno and
    S.sname = "shark" and T.tno = G.tno and
    G.sno = H.sno and G.fcolor = "blue".
```

```
query (N, M) ⊢ speciesClassifiesFish (S, F),
             fishInhabitsTank (F, T),
             tankHousesFish (T, G),
             fishRepresentsSpecies (G, H),
             speciesHasName (H, "shark"),
             fishHasColor (G, "blue"),
             speciesHasName (S, N),
             tankHasName (T, M).
query (N, M).
```

This flexibility contrasts with the object-oriented solution, where you must interrupt the database path with iteration signals to access intermediate components. For example, you can write a concise object-oriented expression for the earlier query, which imposed conditions only on the database path endpoints. That query found the names of species swimming with a shark.

```
(TheSpecies select:  [aSpecies |
    aSpecies reps home population breed name includes:  "shark"]) name display.
```

When the query must access intermediate elements, you must interrupt the path. For example, find the names of species swimming with a blue shark and report the names of the common tanks. The object-oriented solution appears below. Clearly, SQL and logic programs have the advantage here.

```
|answer|
answer := Set new.
TheSpecies do:  [aSpecies |
    aSpecies reps home do:  [aTank |
        aTank population do:  [aFish |
            aFish color = "blue" & (aFish breed name = "shark") ifTrue:  [
                answer add:  aSpecies name, " ", aTank name] ] ] ].
answer display.
```

Finally, reconsider the following query, which requires an existential path crossing the database three times. Find the names of species swimming with a species represented in a tank named cesspool. The pattern uses successive subgoals to forge the path links. The SQL aligns the relations while the corresponding logic program aligns relationship predicates.

```
select S.sname
from Species S, Fish F, Tank T, Fish G, Species H, Fish X, Tank Y
where S.sno = F.sno and F.tno = T.tno and T.tno = G.tno and G.sno = H.sno and
    H.sno = X.sno and X.tno = Y.tno and Y.tname = "cesspool".
```

```
    query (N) ⊢ speciesClassifiesFish (S, F), fishInhabitsTank (F, T),
                tankHousesFish (T, G), fishRepresentsSpecies (G, H),
                speciesClassifiesFish (H, X), fishInhabitsTank (X, Y),
                tankHasName (Y, "cesspool"), speciesHasName (S, N).
    query (N).
```

 Existential queries in deductive databases use common bindings in relationship predicates to forge a path from a candidate object to a specified anchor. The common bindings in relationship predicates correspond to common attributes in SQL.

Universal queries

Consider the universal query: find the names of species represented in all tanks. Earlier chapters developed three SQL solutions. The first and most intuitive method used a set-containment condition between two subqueries. The second used a doubly negated exists-construction, which transformed the universal quantification into existential quantification.

The third solution used the count aggregate although it was a thinly disguised version of double negation. The three solutions appear below.

```
select S.sname              select S.sname              select S.sname
from Species S              from Species S              from Species S
where                       where not exists            where 0 =
   (select T.tno               (select *                   (select count (*)
   from Fish F, Tank T         from Tank T                 from Tank T
   where S.sno = F.sno and     where not exists            where 0 =
      F.tno = T.tno)              (select *                   (select count (*)
contains                          from Fish F                 from Fish F
   (select T.tno                  where S.sno = F.sno and     where S.sno = F.sno and
   from Tank).                       F.tno = T.tno)).             F.tno = T.tno)).
```

A logic program can imitate only the doubly negated expression. For a given candidate species, you require that it not miss a tank. The query then starts as follows.

query (N) ⊢ speciesHasName (S, N), ¬speciesMissesTank (S).

For a species S to succeed, it must not miss a single tank. So speciesMissesTank (S) must be true when there exists a tank where species S isn't represented. You state this rule as follows.

speciesMissesTank (S) ⊢ tank (T), ¬connected (S, T).

For a particular species S, speciesMissesTank (S) must now fail for every binding of the free variable T if the species is to contribute to the answer. All nonsensical bindings for T fail immediately because of the subgoal tank (T). For a binding T that does represent a tank, speciesMissesTank (S) fails only if connected (S, T) succeeds. Stated differently, for every tank T, you must have a connection between species S and tank T. This rewording corresponds exactly to the intent of the query, so only the rule for connected (S, T) remains to complete. This predicate should be true when the species and the tank share a fish. The complete query then appears as follows. Note the double negation that characterizes universal queries. In a logic program, this feature appears as two negated subgoals.

```
query (N) ⊢ speciesHasName (S, N), ¬speciesMissesTank (S).
speciesMissesTank (S) ⊢ tank (T), ¬connected (S, T).
connected (S, T) ⊢ speciesClassifiesFish (S, F), fishInhabitsTank (F, T).
query (N).
```

This pattern is the basic template for universal queries, but you must tailor it to accommodate query variations. Suppose you want the names of species with a worm diet represented in all red tanks via a blue fish. You proceed as follows.

```
query (N) ⊢ speciesHasName (S, N), speciesHasFood (S, "worms"), ¬speciesMissesRedTank (S).
speciesMissesRedTank (S) ⊢ tankHasColor (T, "red"), ¬connectedWithBlue (S, T).
connectedWithBlue (S, T) ⊢ speciesClassifiesFish (S, F), fishInhabitsTank (F, T),
                           fishHasColor (F, "blue").
query (N).
```

Here a successful species S must have a worm diet, and the predicate `speciesMisses-RedTank` (S) must fail. Such a failure occurs if no T has `tankHasColor` (T, "red") true but `connectedWithBlue` (S, T) false. If you compose `connectedWithBlue` (S, T) to mean that S and T share a blue fish, this condition is precisely the query's intent.

As with existential queries, longer universal paths are possible. For example, find the names of species represented in all tanks that contain all species with a worm diet. From an SQL standpoint, a successful species tuple must originate a path bundle to embrace all of a target tank group. Moreover, each tank in the target group must originate a path bundle to embrace all the species with sfood worms. Stated differently, a successful species tuple must not miss any of the target tanks. Therefore, the first part of the query follows the established pattern.

```
query (N) ⊢ speciesHasName (S, N), ¬speciesMissesTarget (S).
```

Now speciesMissesTarget (S) must be true when there exists a target T that isn't connected to S. The following rule expresses the intent.

```
speciesMissesTarget (S) ⊢ target (T), ¬speciesConnected (S, T).
speciesConnected (S, T) ⊢ speciesClassifiesFish (S, F), fishInhabitsTank (F, T).
```

Now, `target` (T) must be true when T is a tank that doesn't miss any of the worm-eating species. In other words, a target tank is itself given by a universal query. The following rules complete the query.

```
target (T) ⊢ tank (T), ¬tankMissesWormySpecies (T).
tankMissesWormySpecies (T) ⊢ speciesHasFood (S, "worms"), ¬tankConnected (T, S).
tankConnected (T, S) ⊢ tankHousesFish (T, F), fishRepresentsSpecies (F, S).
```

 A universal query in a deductive database uses negated predicates to imitate the doubly negated SQL construction. You usually develop the query with several rules, which correspond to the nested subqueries in the SQL equivalent.

Some queries use a mixed existential and universal strategy. For example, find the names of tanks inhabited by some species that is present in all red tanks. A successful tank must originate a single database path to a target species, but that target species must command a path bundle to embrace all the red tanks. In SQL, you align relations to capture an existential path to a target species. You then use the doubly negated construction to qualify that target. The SQL solution appears below; its equivalent logic program follows.

```
select T.tname
from Tank T, Fish F, Species S
where T.tno = F.tno and F.sno = S.sno and not exists
    (select *
    from Tank K
    where K.tcolor = "red" and not exists
        (select *
        from Fish G
        where G.tno = K.tno and G.sno = S.sno)).
```

```
query (N) ⊢ TankHasName (T, N), tankHousesFish (T, F),
         fishRepresentSpecies (F, S), ¬speciesMissesTarget (S).
speciesMissesTarget (S) ⊢ tankHasColor (K, "red"), ¬connected (S, K).
connected (S, K) ⊢ speciesClassifiesFish (S, G), fishInhabitsTank (G, K).
query (N).
```

Aggregates and partitions

Chapter 9 showed how to use an existing predicate to construct aggregate predicates. You launch an intermediate query to tabulate the true bindings for the existing predicate. Then you partition that table to obtain groups that agree on an initial column set and apply the aggregate to the next column. The transformed table contains the true ground instances of the aggregate predicate.

As a first example, find the number of fish representing each species. The inference rules already contain a derived predicate that tabulates related fish-species pairs: speciesClassifiesFish (S, F). So you can build the count aggregate directly over this predicate and obtain the following simple expression.

$$\text{speciesClassifiesFish}_1^{\text{count}} \text{ (S, C)}.$$

To determine the true bindings for S and C, the DBMS evaluates the query speciesClassifiesFish (S, F) and aggregates the resulting table by groups to obtain a reduced table. The table transformation on the left below illustrates the process. The reduced table defines the true bindings for S and C in the $\text{speciesClassifiesFish}_1^{\text{count}}$ (S, C) predicate, which constitutes the query solution. For example, $\text{speciesClassifiesFish}_1^{\text{count}}$ (s_1, 6) is true, and $\text{speciesClassifiesFish}_1^{\text{count}}$ (s_1, 5) is false.

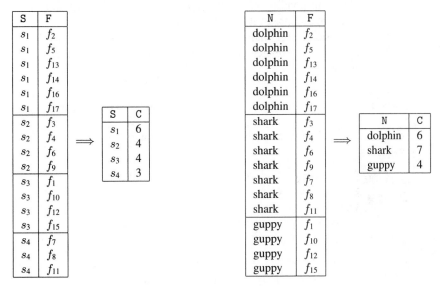

Suppose you construct a table of species names with their corresponding fish and then count the fish in each group. Because species names aren't unique, you get fewer groups than the four in the previous example. The logic program and its intermediate process appear as follows, and the table transformation to the right above illustrates the process.

```
speciesNameAndFish (N, F) ⊢ speciesHasName (S, N),
                            speciesClassifiesFish (S, F).
speciesNameAndFish₁ᶜᵒᵘⁿᵗ (N, C).
```

Because two species are named shark, the partitioning process combines them into a single group. So when you construct an aggregate predicate, you should build it over a predicate where the partitioning arguments are object identifiers. Then the process won't combine the groups for several application objects.

Some constructions in SQL can overrepresent a group element. For example, calculate the average tank volume by species. The SQL on the left below produces an erroneous average because a tank volume repeats in a group—once for each fish connecting the tank to the candidate species. The proper solution aligns the species and tanks and then uses a subquery to eliminate the inappropriate combinations. In the correct solution, each related species-tank pair appears just once, and the average function computes the right answer. The correct approach appears on the right.

```
select S.sno S.sname, average (T.tvolume)      select S.sno S.sname, average (T.tvolume)
from Species S, Fish F, Tank T                 from Species S, Tank T
where S.sno = F.sno and F.tno = T.tno          where exists
groupby S.sno.                                     (select *
                                                   from Fish F
                                                   where S.sno = F.sno and F.tno = T.tno)
                                               groupby S.sno.
```

The corresponding logic program doesn't encounter this difficulty because the species-VolumeTank predicate tabulates species-tank pairs. A pair succeeds when the DBMS can find a successful binding for F in the connecting subgoals, as shown below. The tabulation contains each related species-tank pair just once, and the DBMS computes the correct average.

```
speciesVolumeTank (S, V, T) ⊢ speciesClassifiesFish (S, F), fishInhabitsTank (F, T),
                              tankHasVolume (T, V).
query (S, N, A) ⊢ speciesHasName (S, N), speciesVolumeTank₁ᵃᵛᵉʳᵃᵍᵉ (S, A).
query (S, N, A).
```

When a zero subscript appears in an aggregate predicate, the DBMS operates on a single group, which contains the entire table of true bindings for the underlying predicate. It applies the aggregate to the first column. For example, find the number of red fish. Below are the logic program and its associated table transformation.

```
redGroup (F) ⊢ fishHasColor (F, "red").
query (C) ⊢ redGroup₀ᶜᵒᵘⁿᵗ (C).
query (C).
```

You can combine aggregates with the existential and universal patterns of the previous sections. For example, find the name of the largest tank that contains all species with sfood worms. You acquire the candidate tanks with the universal query pattern and then construct the appropriate aggregate to find the tank with maximum volume in this set. Of course, the answer may contain several names if several target tanks all have the same maximum volume. The solution follows.

```
target (T) ⊢ tank (T), ¬missesWormySpecies (T).
missesWormySpecies (T) ⊢ speciesHasFood (S, "worms"), ¬connected (T, S).
connected (T, S) ⊢ tankHousesFish (T, F), fishRepresentsSpecies (F, S).
wormyTank (V, T) ⊢ target (T), tankHasVolume (T, V).
query (N) ⊢ target (T), tankHasVolume (T, M), wormyTank$_0^{max}$ (M), tankHasName (T, N).
query (N).
```

SQL can reject certain partition groupings with a having-clause. You can imitate a having-clause filter with a subgoal because all aggregates are available as variable bindings. For example, list the average volume of tanks associated with each species, but only for species involved with two or more tanks. You can count the tanks and average their volumes, per species, with aggregate predicates. You can then use the resulting variables in an arithmetic predicate to remove the unwanted groups. The logic program is:

```
speciesTank (S, T) ⊢ speciesClassifiesFish (S, F), fishInhabitsTank (F, T).
speciesVolTank (S, V, T) ⊢ speciesTank (S, T), tankHasVolume (T, V).
speciesTankCount (S, C) ⊢ speciesTank$_1^{count}$ (S, C).
speciesTankAvgVol (S, V) ⊢ speciesVolTank$_1^{average}$ (S, V).
query (S, N, V) ⊢ speciesHasName (S, N), speciesTankCount (S, C),
                 C >= 2, speciesTankAvgVol (S, V).
query (S, N, V).
```

This example illustrates how to access aggregate values in supplementary subgoals. As another example, find the names of tanks whose volume is larger than average. The query below uses an aggregate predicate to bind the A variable to the average tank volume. An arithmetic predicate then compares A with the volume of a candidate tank.

```
volTank (V, T) ⊢ tankHasVolume (T, V).
query (N) ⊢ tankHasName (T, N), tankHasVolume (T, V), volTank$_0^{average}$ (A), V > A.
query (N).
```

Some query solutions use more than one partition. For example, find the average tank volume for each species, provided the species is represented by 10 or more fish. The SQL solution, on the left below, groups a species with its tanks to apply the average aggregate. It uses a subquery to verify that the species is represented by 10 or more fish. In SQL, you must compute all aggregates with a single partition. If you must apply conditions to those aggregates, you use a having-clause. However, if you must apply conditions to a different partition, as in this example, you must employ a subquery. In a logic program, separate subgoals develop all necessary aggregate information, either for reporting or for rejecting certain groups. So the logic expression is more symmetric. An equivalent logic program appears on the right below.

```
select S.sno, S.sname,
    average(T.tvolume) avgVol
from Species S, Tank T
where exists
    (select *
    from Fish F
    where S.sno = F.sno and
        F.tno = T.tno)
and
    S.sno in
        (select S.sno
        from Species S, Fish F
        where S.sno = F.sno
        groupby S.sno
        having count(*) >= 10)
groupby S.sno.
```

```
speciesVolTank (S, V, T) ⊢ speciesClassifiesFish (S, F),
                            fishInhabitsTank (F, T),
                            tankHasVolume (T, V).
speciesAvgVol (S, A) ⊢ speciesVolTank₁^average (S, A).
speciesCountFish (S, C) ⊢ speciesClassifiesFish₁^count (S, C).
query (S, N, A) ⊢ speciesHasName (S, N),
                  speciesCountFish (S, C),
                  C >= 10, speciesAvgVol (S, A).
query (S, N, A).
```

You can construct an aggregate predicate over another such predicate provided you introduce no cycles into the dependency graph. Suppose you want to sum the tank volumes by species and then average that set of numbers. The following logic program accomplishes this goal.

```
speciesVolTank (S, V, T) ⊢ speciesClassifiesFish (S, F), fishInhabitsTank (F, T),
                            tankHasVolume (T, V).
speciesTotalVolume (Q, S) ⊢ speciesVolTank₁^sum (S, Q).
query (A) ⊢ speciesTotalVolumes₀^average (A).
query (A).
```

 With inference rules, you can operationally define aggregate predicates to capture the corresponding SQL computations. The aggregate results are available for use in other subgoals, which allows you to imitate the SQL having-clause.

Logic programs and relational algebra

The queries that you can solve with logic programs over an acyclic deductive database are the same as those that you can solve with relational algebra over the corresponding relational database. This section proves the equivalence. Chapter 5 showed how to translate SQL into relational algebra. The reverse translation is also possible, and therefore SQL and relational algebra are capable of exactly the same query solutions. So the proof that logic programs over acyclic deductive databases are equivalent to relational algebra also shows the equivalence of SQL and acyclic logic programs.

Correspondence between relations and database predicates

To prepare for a comparison, align the relational database with its deductive counterpart as follows. Suppose you have a relational system with relations $R_1, R_2, \ldots$, where relation R_i has attributes $a_1, a_2, \ldots$. Adopt a fixed ordering of the R_i attributes, say $a_{i1}, a_{i2}, \ldots$, and declare a database predicate $R_i(a_{i1}, a_{i2}, \ldots)$. For a given binding $a_{i1} = v_1, a_{i2} = v_2, \ldots$, the ground instance $R_i(v_1, v_2, \ldots)$ is true precisely when the tuple $(a_{i1} = v_1, a_{i2} = v_2, \ldots)$ occurs in relation R_i. Therefore, you obtain the axioms of an equivalent deductive system from the relations. You can reverse the process to obtain a relational system from a deductive system. Each database predicate gives rise to a relation, where the attribute names are the argument variables. Each relation's body, which comes from the database content list, contains the true bindings for its corresponding predicate. You can start, for example, with the relational version of the aquarium database, comprising the relations and attributes on the left below, and derive the database predicates on the right.

Relations
species (sno, sname, sfood)
tank (tno, tname, tcolor, tvolume)
fish (fno, fname, fcolor, fweight, tno, sno)
event (eno, fno, edate, enote)

$\Longrightarrow$

Database predicates
species (sno, sname, sfood)
tank (tno, tname, tcolor, tvolume)
fish (fno, fname, fcolor, fweight, tno, sno)
event (eno, fno, edate, enote)

The predicate arguments appear strange but only because you have been accustomed to single uppercase letters for variables. However, by using the relation's attributes, you have a mnemonic for each argument position in the predicate. You obtain the true ground instances of the newly established database predicates from the bodies of the corresponding relations. For example, the species relation on the left below gives rise to the axioms on the right.

Species		
sno	sname	sfood
17	dolphin	herring
22	shark	anything
74	guppy	worm
93	shark	peanut butter

$\Longrightarrow$

Axioms
species (17, "dolphin", "herring")
species (22, "shark", "anything")
species (74, "guppy", "worm")
species (93, "shark", "peanut butter")

Now suppose you want to translate in the reverse direction—from a deductive system into a relational system. You can't expect to start with database predicates that are exactly parallel to the relational tables. Instead, you usually have axioms in the categories of Figure 9.4. Certain database predicates assert the existence of application objects, such as fish (X); others assert descriptive attributes of those objects, such as fishHasName (X, Y). A final group asserts relationships between objects, such as fishInhabitsTank (X, Y). You can start with those database predicates and create corresponding tables as illustrated below.

Database predicates
species (X)
fish (X)
tank (X)
event (X)
speciesHasName (X, Y)
speciesHasFood (X, Y)
tankHasName (X, Y)
tankHasColor (X, Y)
tankHasVolume (X, Y)
fishHasName (X, Y)
fishHasColor (X, Y)
fishHasWeight (X, Y)
eventHasDate (X, Y)
eventHasNote (X, Y)
fishRepresentsSpecies (X, Y)
fishInhabitsTank (X, Y)
eventConcernsFish (X, Y)

$\implies$

Database relations
species (X)
fish (X)
tank (X)
event (X)
speciesHasName (X, Y)
speciesHasFood (X, Y)
tankHasName (X, Y)
tankHasColor (X, Y)
tankHasVolume (X, Y)
fishHasName (X, Y)
fishHasColor (X, Y)
fishHasWeight (X, Y)
eventHasDate (X, Y)
eventHasNote (X, Y)
fishRepresentsSpecies (X, Y)
fishInhabitsTank (X, Y)
eventConcernsFish (X, Y)

Using the argument variables as attribute names leads to some confusion about attribute meanings. Moreover, the predicates use X and Y repeatedly, so the common column names don't carry the same interpretation as in a normal relational schema. Nevertheless, you will see that the relational algebra equivalents of logic programs can use these artificially induced relations to obtain the proper query solutions. So, for the moment, you should tolerate the strange attribute names that occur when you convert a deductive system to a relational one.

Because you understand the meanings associated with the variable positions, you can easily reconstruct the more familiar aquarium relations from the list above. For example, you obtain the original species relation as follows.

$$\rho_n(\text{species}) * \rho_m(\text{speciesHasName}) * \rho_p(\text{speciesHasFood}), \text{ where}$$
$$n \;=\; (\text{X} \rightarrow \text{sno})$$
$$m \;=\; (\text{X} \rightarrow \text{sno}, \text{Y} \rightarrow \text{sname})$$
$$p \;=\; (\text{X} \rightarrow \text{sno}, \text{Y} \rightarrow \text{sfood}).$$

The renaming operator changes the artificial names to the more familiar ones (e.g., sno, sname, sfood). Natural joins then reassemble the full species table. Unfortunately, null values can cause a problem at this point. If a species instance has a null value for a descriptive attribute, it doesn't appear in the natural join. If sno = 17 has a null value for sname, no ground instance of the form speciesHasName (17, $\cdots$) appears in the database content list, and the corresponding relational table has no entry for sno = 17. Then the natural join construction above also omits sno = 17 even if it has other attributes.

One solution allows the value <null> in the universe of discourse. You can then represent missing attribute values with ground literals of the form speciesHasName (17, <null>). In a deductive-to-relational mapping, these ground literals produce tuples with a null value under the appropriate column. In the reverse mapping to a deductive system, a tuple with null values in its components produces an axiom with <null> in its bindings. This solution amounts to substituting an outer join for the natural join in the translation process. To avoid unnecessary complications, assume for this section that null values don't appear in the database.

In the species reconstruction above, the table arising from the existence predicate doesn't contribute materially to the join. If an entity exists, and if it has nonnull attribute entries, then it will be present in all the tables arising from the descriptive predicates. So you can omit the first operand of the join.

Now assume you start with a relational database and construct the corresponding database predicates and axioms. The resulting deductive database is acyclic because it has no inference rules at all. However, you now equate each relational algebra operation with an inference rule because the operation produces a new table, which corresponds to the true ground instances of a derived predicate.

Relational algebra operations can never introduce cycles. Relational algebra operators accept existing relations and produce new ones. These new relations can then serve as operands for further algebraic expressions, which result in additional relations. But this process can't produce a table that has already appeared earlier in the chain of constructions. The relational algebra syntax specifies sequential operations, where existing tables produce new ones. Even an expression such as $X = X * Y$ means that the *old* version of X enters into a natural join operation with Y. The process then renames the result as X, which destroys the old X. The result X and the operand X are different tables. You can replace any sequence of relational algebra operations that reuses a table name with an equivalent sequence that uses new names for each new relation. Assume this convention is in force for all relational algebra expressions in this section. As you'll see, the new tables give rise to derived predicates. Because the operations continually introduce new names, no cycles ever arise in the dependency graph.

To summarize, each relational database corresponds to a canonical acyclic deductive database, constructed as illustrated above. Each table produces a database predicate and a collection of true ground instances. Each relational algebra expression also produces one or more inference rules, which never cause cycles in the dependency graph.

A relational database has a natural acyclic deductive equivalent, and vice versa. You take the axioms from the bodies of the relations, and in the reverse direction, you obtain relations from the database predicates.

From relational algebra to inference rules

Chapter 3 defined seven crucial relational algebra operators: Cartesian product, projection, selection, union, difference, aggregate, and renaming. You can achieve the results of the other operators by combining these basic seven. This section shows that any of the basic relational algebra operators, except the renaming operator, produces a result table whose content is precisely the true bindings of a derived predicate.

The renaming operator produces an unchanged table body with new attribute names. Because you can choose arbitrary variable names when you use a predicate, you don't need an inference rule to derive a table with the new names. Suppose you have the correspondence

Relations
species (sno, sname, sfood)
tank (tno, tname, tcolor, tvolume)
fish (fno, fname, fcolor, fweight, tno, sno)
event (eno, fno, edate, enote)

$\Longrightarrow$

Database predicates
`species (sno, sname, sfood)`
`tank (tno, tname, tcolor, tvolume)`
`fish (fno, fname, fcolor, fweight, tno, sno)`
`event (eno, fno, edate, enote)`

and the relational algebra expression

$$\text{temp} = \rho_n(\text{species}) \times \rho_m(\text{species}), \text{ where } \begin{aligned} n &= (\text{sno} \rightarrow s_1, \text{sname} \rightarrow n_1, \text{sfood} \rightarrow q_1) \\ m &= (\text{sno} \rightarrow s_2, \text{sname} \rightarrow n_2, \text{sfood} \rightarrow q_2). \end{aligned}$$

The new relation, temp, has attributes $s_1, n_1, q_1, s_2, n_2,$ and q_2 and contains the Cartesian product of species with itself. You can construct a derived predicate, `temp`, whose arguments correspond to these attributes:

$$\text{temp } (s_1, n_1, q_1, s_2, n_2, q_2) \vdash \text{species } (s_1, n_1, q_1), \text{ species } (s_2, n_2, q_2).$$

You associate each predicate with a table where the column headings are the variables and the table body is the set of true bindings for these variables. The inference rule variables are simply placeholders; therefore any names will do. Because you're free to choose variable names, you can accomplish the effect of a renaming operation by simply choosing the new variable names as needed.

From the schema conversion, predicates are already available for the database tables. Proceeding by induction, assume you have a predicate for any new table created with relational algebra operators to this point. If you create another new table with one of the basic relational algebra operators, you can construct inference rules for a corresponding derived predicate as follows. The new table's rows will be the new predicate's true bindings.

The first possibility is the Cartesian product. Suppose you create the new table, carProd, as the Cartesian product of tables R_1, with attributes $a_{11}, a_{12}, \ldots,$ and R_2, with attributes $a_{21}, a_{22}, \ldots$. Two tables are compatible for Cartesian product when they have no attribute names in common. You can rename the operands, if necessary, to achieve this compatibility. So assume the attribute lists for R_1 and R_2 have no names in common. Consider the following derived predicate, where the tables of true bindings for the predicates R_1 and R_2 are the relations R_1 and R_2.

$$\text{carProd } (a_{11}, a_{12}, \ldots, a_{21}, a_{22}, \ldots) \vdash R_1(a_{11}, a_{12}, \ldots), R_2(a_{21}, a_{22}, \ldots).$$

If $a_{11} = v_1, a_{12} = v_2, \ldots, a_{21} = w_1, a_{22} = w_2, \ldots$ is a ground instance of `carProd` that is forced true by this rule, then $a_{11} = v_1, a_{12} = v_2, \ldots$ must be a true ground instance arising from R_1, and $a_{21} = w_1, a_{22} = w_2, \ldots$ must be a true ground instance arising from R_2. Therefore, the tuple $(a_{11} = v_1, a_{12} = v_2, \ldots)$ must be in the relation R_1, and the tuple $(a_{21} = w_1, a_{22} = w_2, \ldots)$ must be in the relation R_2. Then the tuple $(a_{11} = v_1, a_{12} = v_2, \ldots, a_{21} = w_1, a_{22} = w_2, \ldots)$ is in the Cartesian product $R_1 \times R_2$. The argument is reversible. If the double-size tuple is in the Cartesian product, it also represents a true binding for the `carProd` predicate.

A rule with two subgoals, which each contain disjoint argument lists, derives a new predicate whose true instances correspond to the Cartesian product of the subgoal tables.

Next consider the union operator. If R_1 and R_2 are union compatible, they have the same attribute names. Then unionRel = $R_1 \cup R_2$ also has these same attributes, and its body contains tuples that are in R_1, R_2, or both. Let $a_1, a_2, \ldots$ be the common attributes of R_1 and R_2. Because the two tables are union compatible, this list encompasses all attributes. The following two rules introduce a derived predicate unionRel, whose table of true bindings is exactly the union of the tables R_1 and R_2.

$$\text{unionRel } (a_1, a_2, \ldots) \vdash R_1(a_1, a_2, \ldots).$$
$$\text{unionRel } (a_1, a_2, \ldots) \vdash R_2(a_1, a_2, \ldots).$$

A binding $a_1 = v_1, a_2 = v_2, \ldots$ is true for unionRel if and only if it is forced true by one of the rules. It is forced true by one of the rules if and only if it is a true binding for R_1 or for R_2. It is a true binding for one of the predicates if and only if the tuple $a_1 = v_1, a_2 = v_2, \ldots$ is in R_1 or R_2. Finally, that tuple is in R_1 or in R_2 if and only if it is in $R_1 \cup R_2$.

No proofs are given for the remaining cases because they are similar to the two just presented.

You obtain the logical equivalent of a union operation with a pair of inference rules, which each contribute ground instances from an operand of the union.

Next consider a selection operation, selRel = $\sigma_b(R)$, where b is a boolean involving arithmetic comparisons between attributes of R or between an attribute of R and a constant. First, place b in disjunctive normal form: $b = c_1 \vee c_2 \vee \ldots \vee c_n$, where each c_i is a sequence of comparisons connected by logical-and operations. Then,

$$\text{selRel} = \sigma_{c_1}(R) \cup \sigma_{c_2}(R) \cup \ldots \cup \sigma_{c_n}(R),$$

and the previous case showed how to construct a predicate to imitate a union. So jumping ahead for a moment, if you assume you have predicates selRel$_1$, selRel$_2$, ... corresponding to the operations $\sigma_{c_1}(R), \sigma_{c_2}(R), \ldots$, then the following rules properly define the selRel predicate, where $a_1, a_2, \ldots$ are the attributes of R.

$$\text{selRel } (a_1, a_2, \ldots) \vdash \text{selRel}_1 (a_1, a_2, \ldots).$$
$$\text{selRel } (a_1, a_2, \ldots) \vdash \text{selRel}_2 (a_1, a_2, \ldots).$$
$$\vdots$$

Therefore, you only have to produce the predicates selRel$_i$. Because these are all identical, assume you are working with the expression selRel = $\sigma_b(R)$, where b is a conjunction of arithmetic comparisons. Accordingly, let $b = d_1 \wedge d_2 \wedge \ldots$, where each d_i assumes one of the following forms: $a_j \, \theta \, a_k$ or $a_j \, \theta$ constant. As usual, θ is one of the comparisons $=, <, >, \geq \leq$, or one of their complements. The predicate selRel is then

$$\text{selRel } (a_1, a_2, \ldots) \vdash R (a_1, a_2, \ldots), \ d_1, d_2, \ldots.$$

Each d_i, as an arithmetic predicate, is directly suitable for a subgoal. The rule forces the true bindings of selRel to be the subset of the true bindings of R where all the arithmetic predicates are true. That operation filters the true bindings of R for those that satisfy the boolean b. Suppose the table $R(A, B, C)$ is the relational equivalent of the predicate R (A, B, C). Below are a selection operator and its equivalent inference rules.

$S = \sigma_b(R),$

where $b = ((A = B) \wedge (A = 2 * C)) \vee (B > C))$

```
S (A, B, C) ⊢ R (A, B, C), A = B, A = 2 * C.
S (A, B, C) ⊢ R (A, B, C), B > C.
```

You can imitate a selection by placing the boolean in disjunctive normal form and composing a rule for each of the clauses. The rule for a conjunctive clause contains the predicate for the operand table as a first subgoal, followed by arithmetic subgoals commanding the comparisons of the clause.

You handle projection by restricting the arguments of the derived predicate to the operator's attribute list. In other words, if projRel $= \pi_q(R)$, where q is a subset of the R-attributes, you define the predicate projRel as:

$$\text{projRel } (a_{i_1}, a_{i_2}, \ldots) \vdash R(a_1, a_2, \ldots),$$

where the $q = (a_{i_1}, a_{i_2}, \ldots)$ is the specified subset of $a_1, a_2, \ldots$.

You can imitate a projection by deriving a head predicate containing only the projection list arguments. The rule's body contains the entire predicate, which leaves the rest of the arguments for existential binding.

If R_1 and R_2 are compatible for the difference operator, you can construct a new relation, diffRel $= R_1 - R_2$, containing those tuples that are in R_1 but not in R_2. Again assuming that the attributes of R_1 (and R_2) are $a_1, a_2, \ldots$, consider the following derived predicate.

$$\text{diffRel } (a_1, a_2, \ldots) \vdash R_1(a_1, a_2, \ldots), \neg R_2(a_1, a_2, \ldots).$$

A true binding of diffRel must correspond to a true binding for R_1 that doesn't succeed for R_2. That interpretation, however, is exactly the meaning of $R_1 - R_2$. Note that the rule contains no negative free variables, so there is no question about R_2 failing for a universally quantified set of bindings. A true binding for R_1 is removed from the result precisely when that ground literal appears in the set of bindings for R_2.

You can imitate a difference operation with a rule containing two subgoals: the first is the predicate of the first operand, and the second negates the predicate of the second operand.

In relational algebra, you specify an aggregate operation with the form aggRel $= \Psi_p^f(R)$. The subscript, p, is an attribute list defining a partition; the superscript, f, is a list of aggregate functions or arithmetic expressions. The latter includes the new names for columns produced by the aggregates. The body of aggRel then contains one tuple for each group, and each such tuple contains entries under the attributes of R plus entries under the new names. For each attribute of R that is constant over the group, the common value occurs in the result tuple. For each attribute of R that varies over the group, null occurs in the result tuple. For each new name, the DBMS performs the specified computation and uses the answer in the result tuple. The left table transformation below illustrates the computation of $\Psi_p^f(R)$, where $p = (a, b)$, and $f = (e \leftarrow \text{sum}(c), f \leftarrow \text{max}(d))$.

$\Psi_p^f \Bigl($

a	b	c	d
1	2	4	6
1	2	5	8
3	4	7	3
3	4	7	1
5	6	8	2

$\Bigr) =$

a	b	c	d	e	f
1	2	–	–	9	8
3	4	7	–	14	3
5	6	8	2	8	2

$\pi_q \Psi_p^f \Bigl($

a	b	c	d
1	2	4	6
1	2	5	8
3	4	7	3
3	4	7	1
5	6	8	2

$\Bigr) =$

a	b	e	f
1	2	9	8
3	4	14	3
5	6	8	2

Because null attributes aren't considered in this section, you can restrict your attention to the operation $\pi_q \Psi_p^f(R)$, where q includes the attributes of the partition p plus any new names introduced in the aggregate list f. The projection removes any attributes of R that might produce null values. Therefore, in the above example, $q = (a, b, e, f)$. The operation appears on the right above.

To translate the aggregate expression into an equivalent set of inference rules, you can restrict it further. If f contains an arithmetic expression, the partition p must contain all the attributes of R. In general, an arithmetic expression can unambiguously manipulate the attributes of R that define the partition, and it can combine these attribute values with an aggregate. For example, relational algebra allows the expression on the left below.

$$\pi_q \Psi_p^f(R), \text{ where } \begin{aligned} p &= (a, b) \\ f &= (d \leftarrow a * \text{sum}(c)) \\ q &= (a, b, d) \end{aligned} \qquad \pi_q \Psi_v^g \Psi_p^f(R), \text{ where } \begin{aligned} p &= (a, b) \\ f &= (e \leftarrow \text{sum}(c)) \\ v &= (a, b, c, d, e) \\ g &= (d \leftarrow a * e) \\ q &= (a, b, d). \end{aligned}$$

You can achieve the same result, however, by first performing the sum aggregate across the commanded partition, which gives a temporary column. You then append the column associated with the arithmetic onto that result by using a partition of individual tuples. Finally, you remove the extraneous column. This alternative appears on the right above. Therefore, no loss of generality results from assuming that arithmetic expressions always operate with a fine partition of individual tuples.

In this restricted context, you can easily achieve the effect of a relational algebra aggregate or arithmetic expression by using an aggregate predicate from Chapter 9. Suppose you are constructing inference rules to achieve the effect of $\text{aggRel} = \pi_q \Psi_p^f(R)$, where the attributes of R are $a_1, a_2, \ldots, a_m$. Suppose $p = (a_{i_1}, a_{i_2}, \ldots, a_{i_n})$, a subset of the attributes of R, and $f = (b_1 \leftarrow f_1, b_2 \leftarrow f_2, \ldots, b_k \leftarrow f_k)$. You prepare a separate rule for each of the f entries. For each b_j, there are two possibilities: f_j is an arithmetic combination of the attributes of p, or f_j is one of the standard aggregates. You rearrange the R attributes to place the attributes in p first. If f_j is one of the standard aggregates, you place its argument attribute, say a_{c_j}, next. Let the predicate with the reordered arguments be $_jQ$. You construct an aggregate predicate over $_jQ$ to compute a table containing the partition attributes plus b_j. The operation proceeds as follows.

$$_1Q(a_{i_1}, a_{i_2}, \ldots, a_{i_n}, a_{c_1}) \vdash R(a_1, a_2, \ldots, a_m).$$
$$\texttt{aggRel}_1(a_{i_1}, a_{i_2}, \ldots, a_{i_n}, b_1) \vdash_1 Q_n^{f_1}(a_{i_1}, a_{i_2}, \ldots, a_{i_n}, b_1),$$
$$_2Q(a_{i_1}, a_{i_2}, \ldots, a_{i_n}, a_{c_2}) \vdash R(a_1, a_2, \ldots, a_m).$$
$$\texttt{aggRel}_2(a_{i_1}, a_{i_2}, \ldots, a_{i_n}, b_2) \vdash_2 Q_n^{f_2}(a_{i_1}, a_{i_2}, \ldots, a_{i_n}, b_2),$$
$$\vdots$$
$$_kQ(a_{i_1}, a_{i_2}, \ldots, a_{i_n}, a_{c_k}) \vdash R(a_1, a_2, \ldots, a_m).$$
$$\texttt{aggRel}_k(a_{i_1}, a_{i_2}, \ldots, a_{i_n}, b_k) \vdash_k Q_n^{f_k}(a_{i_1}, a_{i_2}, \ldots, a_{i_n}, b_k),$$

Of course, you omit the argument a_{c_j} from $_jQ$ if f_j is an arithmetic expression rather than a standard aggregate. With the components $\texttt{aggRel}_j$ available, you assemble the final table:

$$\texttt{aggRel}\ (a_{i_1}, a_{i_2}, \ldots, a_{i_n}, b_1, b_2, \ldots, b_k) \vdash \texttt{aggRel}_1(a_{i_1}, a_{i_2}, \ldots, b_1),$$
$$\texttt{aggRel}_2(a_{i_1}, a_{i_2}, \ldots, b_2),$$
$$\vdots$$
$$\texttt{aggRel}_k(a_{i_1}, a_{i_2}, \ldots, b_k).$$

You can extend an aggregate predicate to imitate a relational algebra aggregate or arithmetic expression if the relational algebra expression includes a projection to remove columns that might introduce null values.

A comprehensive translation example

At this point, you can transform any relational system into an equivalent acyclic deductive system, and you can recast any relational algebra expression as a set of inference rules. Consider the following situation in the aquarium application. The relational algebra, shown below, computes the average volume of the red tanks containing each species. You want an equivalent deductive expression.

$$\text{query} = \pi_q \Psi_p^f \pi_r \sigma_b (\text{species} * \text{fish} * \text{tank}), \text{ where}$$

b	=	(tcolor = "red")
r	=	(sno, sname, tno, tvolume)
p	=	(sno, sname)
f	=	(avgVol $\leftarrow$ average (tvolume))
q	=	(sno, sname, avgVol).

You first remove the natural joins, expressing them as Cartesian products followed by selection and projection operators. Using the renaming operators to achieve Cartesian product compatibility, you then have the following equivalent query:

$$\text{query} = \pi_q \Psi_p^f \pi_r \sigma_b \hat{\rho} \pi_s \sigma_c (\check{\rho}(\text{species}) \times \check{\rho}(\text{fish}) \times \check{\rho}(\text{tank})),$$

where
b	=	(tcolor = "red")	c	=	(species.sno = fish.sno $\wedge$ fish.tno = tank.tno)
r	=	(sno, sname, tno, tvolume)	s	=	(species.sno, species.sname, species.sfood,
p	=	(sno, sname)			fish.fno, fish.fname, fish.fcolor, fish.fweight,
f	=	(avgVol $\leftarrow$ average (tvolume))			tank.tno, tank.tname, tank.tcolor, tank.tvolume).
q	=	(sno, sname, avgVol)			

Operating in parallel on the equivalent deductive database, you can assume the existence of the database predicates:

```
species (sno, sname, sfood)
fish (fno, fname, fcolor, fweight, tno, sno)
tank (tno, tname, tcolor, tvolume).
```

You now build up the required inference rules by considering the intermediate tables generated by the query. The renaming activities are no problem because you can choose the database predicate variable names as you wish and so avoid the collisions that require renaming operations in relational algebra.

$$\text{cartProd } (s_1, s_2, s_3, f_1, f_2, f_3, f_4, f_5, f_6, t_1, t_2, t_3, t_4) \vdash \text{species } (s_1, s_2, s_3), \text{ fish } (f_1, f_2, f_3, f_4, f_5, f_6),$$
$$\text{tank } (t_1, t_2, t_3, t_4).$$
$$\text{cSel } (s_1, s_2, s_3, f_1, f_2, f_3, f_4, f_5, f_6, t_1, t_2, t_3, t_4) \vdash \text{carProd } (s_1, s_2, s_3, f_1, f_2, f_3, f_4, f_5, f_6, t_1, t_2, t_3, t_4),$$
$$f_5 = t_1, \quad f_6 = s_1.$$
$$\text{sProj } (s_1, s_2, s_3, f_1, f_2, f_3, f_4, t_1, t_2, t_3, t_4) \vdash \text{cSel } (s_1, s_2, s_3, f_1, f_2, f_3, f_4, f_5, f_6, t_1, t_2, t_3, t_4).$$
$$\text{bSel } (s_1, s_2, s_3, f_1, f_2, f_3, f_4, t_1, t_2, t_3, t_4) \vdash \text{sProj } (s_1, s_2, s_3, f_1, f_2, f_3, f_4, t_1, t_2, t_3, t_4), \quad t_3 = \text{"red"}.$$
$$\text{rProj } (s_1, s_2, t_4, t_1) \vdash \text{bSel } (s_1, s_2, s_3, f_1, f_2, f_3, f_4, t_1, t_2, t_3, t_4).$$
$$\text{query } (s_1, s_2, a) \vdash \text{rProj}_2^{\text{average}}(s_1, s_2, a).$$

The reverse process: from derived predicates to relational algebra

The algorithm above translates a relational algebra expression into its equivalent logic program. For the reverse direction, you need to provide a relational algebra expression to compute the table of true bindings for a derived predicate. This section presents a brief treatment of the process because most of the ideas simply reverse the operations in the relational-to-deductive translation.

For the database predicates, the corresponding tables of true bindings are available as the database axioms. For a derived predicate, you examine the subgoals of the defining inference rules. If a derived predicate occurs at the head of n inference rules, the corresponding table of true bindings is the union of the tables delivered by the individual rules. Because the union operator is available in relational algebra to accumulate these results, it's enough to understand how to generate the true binding table for a single inference rule.

The process operates inductively along a topological sort of the rule heads. When working with a given rule, therefore, you can assume that all its subgoal already have tables of true bindings available. For the rule in question, you consider each subgoal in turn. If you encounter an aggregate predicate as a subgoal, you compute its corresponding true binding table as detailed in Chapter 9. By induction, you can assume that the underlying predicate for the aggregate already has a properly computed true binding table. Because the database is acyclic, the underlying predicate occurs earlier in the topological sort and has already been processed. The partitioning and aggregation activities, therefore, proceed without difficulty. So at this point, assuming that relations are available for all the subgoal predicates, it is sufficient to show how to translate a single rule.

If a body predicate variable repeats in several places, you replace the second and subsequent occurrences with new variables and append new subgoals, which contain arithmetic predicates that force the new variables to equal the replaced variable. The first instance of the replaced variable remains untouched. If a constant appears in a body predicate, you replace it with a new variable and then add a subgoal forcing the new variable to equal the replaced constant. For example, you transform the rule on the left below to the form on the right.

P (X, Y, Z) ⊢ Q (X, Y, X), R (Y, Z, Z),   P (X, Y, Z) ⊢ Q (X, Y, A), R (B, Z, C),
          S (X, Y, "red").   S (D, E, F), X = A, Y = B,
                                                          Z = C, X = D, Y = E,
                                                          F = "red".

These substitutions don't change the true binding table following from the rule. All the
subgoals now have different variable lists. Using the new attribute headings, you can combine their underlying tables in a Cartesian product. A subsequent selection operation, with
a boolean given by the conjunction of the arithmetic predicates, produces an intermediate
table, which contains all the true bindings of the head. The table also contains superfluous
columns corresponding to the free variables in the body. A final projection shears away the
extraneous columns. Therefore, the above example gives rise to the following relational
algebra expression. For Q, it assumes that the attributes of the true binding table are q_1, q_2,
and q_3. For R, they are r_1, r_2, and r_3. For S, they are s_1, s_2, and s_3.

$$P = \pi_a \sigma_b (\rho_q(Q) \times \rho_r(R) \times \rho_s(S)), \text{ where } \begin{aligned} q &= (X \leftarrow q_1, Y \leftarrow q_2, A \leftarrow q_3) \\ r &= (B \leftarrow r_1, Z \leftarrow r_2, C \leftarrow r_3) \\ s &= (D \leftarrow s_1, E \leftarrow s_2, F \leftarrow s_3) \\ b &= (X = A \wedge Y = B \wedge Z = C \wedge X = D \wedge Y = E \wedge F = \text{``red''}) \\ a &= (X, Y, Z). \end{aligned}$$

Consider again the aquarium example. Suppose you have relations for the database predicates of Figure 9.4, and you want to find equivalent relational algebra for the following
query.

```
specVolTank (S, N, V, T) ⊢ speciesHasName (S, N), fishRepresentsSpecies (F, S),
                           fishInhabitsTank (F, T), tankHasVolume (T, V),
                           tankHasColor (T, "red").
query (S, N, A) ⊢ specVolTank₂^average (S, N, A).
query (S, N, A).
```

The query requests the average volume of the red tanks for each species. The query is the
same one considered in the earlier relational-to-deductive translation. However, you now
start with a deductive database and with axioms different from those that arose from the
relational translation. When you produce the equivalent relational database, you find tables
such as speciesHasName and fishHasColor instead of the simple species, tank, fish, and
event tables. So you must manage the relational translation in terms of the new tables.
    The first rule's right side contains only database predicates, and the corresponding
tables are available. Because certain variables are repeated, and because a constant appears
in the body, you rewrite it in the following form.

```
specVolTank (S, N, V, T) ⊢ speciesHasName (S, N), fishRepresentsSpecies (F, B),
                           fishInhabitsTank (C, T), tankHasVolume (D, V), tankHasColor (E, F),
                           S = B, F = C, T = D, T = E, F = "red".
```

The initial tables obtained from the deductive axioms are:

Database relations				
species (X) fish (X) tank (X) event (X)	speciesHasName (X, Y) speciesHasFood (X, Y)	tankHasName (X, Y) tankHasColor (X, Y) tankHasVolume (X, Y)	fishHasName (X, Y) fishHasColor (X, Y) fishHasWeight (X, Y)	eventHasDate (X, Y) eventHasNote (X, Y)
	fishRepresentsSpecies (X, Y) fishInhabitsTank (X, Y) eventConcernsFish (X, Y)			

Employing renaming operators to assemble the table corresponding to `specVolTank`, you obtain:

$$R_1 = \text{speciesHasName}$$
$$R_2 = \text{fishRepresentsSpecies}$$
$$R_3 = \text{fishInhabitsTank}$$
$$R_4 = \text{tankHasVolume}$$
$$R_5 = \text{tankHasColor}$$
$$\text{specVolTank} = \pi_q \sigma_b (\rho_{n_1}(R_1) \times \rho_{n_2}(R_2) \times \rho_{n_3}(R_3) \times \rho_{n_4}(R_4) \times \rho_{n_5}(R_5)),$$

$$
\begin{aligned}
\text{where} \quad n_1 &= (S \leftarrow X, N \leftarrow Y) \\
n_2 &= (F \leftarrow X, B \leftarrow Y) \\
n_3 &= (C \leftarrow X, T \leftarrow Y) \\
n_4 &= (D \leftarrow X, V \leftarrow Y) \\
n_5 &= (E \leftarrow X, F \leftarrow Y) \\
b &= (S = B \wedge F = C \wedge T = D \wedge T = E \wedge F = \text{``red''}) \\
q &= (S, N, V, T).
\end{aligned}
$$

Finally, the query is given by $\pi_q \Psi_p^f(\text{specVolTank})$, where

$$
\begin{aligned}
p &= (S, N) \\
f &= (A \leftarrow \text{average}(V)) \\
q &= (S, N, A)
\end{aligned}
$$

You can mechanically transform relational algebra queries into logic programs over the equivalent deductive database, and vice versa.

Beyond acyclic deductive databases

Horn clause systems

The previous section proved the equivalence of relational databases with relational algebra and acyclic deductive databases with logic programs. This section considers certain format changes in the inference rules. To simplify the discussion, aggregate predicates are excluded from the initial discussion.

The first variation bans negated predicates from the bodies of inference rules. Deductive systems that allow no negated subgoals are called **Horn clause systems**. The lack of negated subgoals, however, reduces the subsequent logic programs below the expressive power of relational algebra. The advantage gained is that all the rules become equivalent to Horn clauses, and any such system has a unique minimal model.

Suppose $\mathcal{M}_1$ and $\mathcal{M}_2$ are two models under a Horn clause system. Let $\mathcal{M}_3 = \mathcal{M}_1 \cap \mathcal{M}_2$. Then $\mathcal{M}_3$ is also a model under these restricted circumstances. To prove this, you need to verify that all the rules are satisfied under $\mathcal{M}_3$.

Consider the rule $h \vdash g_1, g_2, \ldots, g_k$. Only head variables and positive free variables occur; there are no negative free variables. Let B be a binding of the variables, such that all the $g_i(B)$ are true in $\mathcal{M}_3$. Here $g_i(B)$ is the bound version of subgoal i. Because no negated subgoals appear, each $g_i(B)$ is one of two forms. It is a positive ground instance of a database or a derived predicate, or it is an arithmetic predicate. In the first case, $g_i(B)$ true in $\mathcal{M}_3$ implies $g_i(B) \in \mathcal{M}_3 \subset \mathcal{M}_1 \cap \mathcal{M}_2$. So $g_i(B)$ is true in both $\mathcal{M}_1$ and $\mathcal{M}_2$. In the second case, ground instances of arithmetic predicates retain the same truth value regardless of the model under consideration. The truth value of an arithmetic ground literal depends only on the indicated comparison of the constants. Therefore, if these $g_i(B)$ are true in $\mathcal{M}_3$, they must also be true in $\mathcal{M}_1$ and $\mathcal{M}_2$.

So all the $g_i(B)$ are true in both $\mathcal{M}_1$ and $\mathcal{M}_2$. Because no rules are violated in these models, $h(B)$ must also lie within both models, which proves that $h(B) \in \mathcal{M}_3$. So $h \vdash g_1, g_2, \ldots, g_k$ is satisfied under $\mathcal{M}_3$. Because the rule was arbitrarily chosen, you can conclude that all the rules are satisfied under $\mathcal{M}_3$, which implies that it is a model. In Horn clause systems, therefore, the intersection of two models is also a model.

In a deductive system composed only of Horn clauses, the intersection of two models is also a model.

At this point, you can easily argue that a minimal model must be unique. Suppose that $\mathcal{M}_1$ and $\mathcal{M}_2$ are minimal models. Then $\mathcal{M}_1 \cap \mathcal{M}_2$ is also a model, and it is contained in both $\mathcal{M}_1$ and $\mathcal{M}_2$. Therefore, by the definition of a minimal model, $\mathcal{M}_1 \cap \mathcal{M}_2 = \mathcal{M}_1$ and $\mathcal{M}_1 \cap \mathcal{M}_2 = \mathcal{M}_2$, which forces $\mathcal{M}_1 = \mathcal{M}_2$.

Note that this argument doesn't depend on the acyclic nature of the database system. Even if cycles appear in the dependency graph, a unique minimal model exists, provided no negated predicates are allowed. A unique minimal model is an attractive feature because the "true" facts to be inferred from a set of rules is a single unambiguous collection. You don't encounter the uncertainties associated with competing minimal models, and you aren't forced to use a preferred minimal model to establish a clear meaning for the extended database content.

A deductive system composed only of Horn clauses has a unique minimal model. This is true even if cycles appear in the dependency graph.

Unfortunately, a system with no negated predicates can't express solutions to universal queries and is, therefore, inferior to relational algebra. To prove this, first consider the effect of adding a new axiom—a true ground instance of a database predicate—to a Horn clause system. The new axiom can never force some other true ground literal from the minimal model. Why? A new axiom can force the minimal model to expand to include previously false ground literals, but it can never force the model to contract. Each ground literal is present in the minimal model because some rule forces it true. In the absence of negated predicates, adding another true ground literal can't falsify any ground rule body that isn't false already. Because no rule body can be made false, the conditions that force a ground literal to be true remain effective after adding a new axiom. This shows that the minimal model of a Horn clause system grows monotonically with the database content. As you add axioms to the database content list, the minimal model grows to accommodate the consequences of the new facts. It never shrinks. In other words, if $\mathcal{M}(D)$ is the minimal model associated with axiom set D, then if $D_1 \subset D_2$, $\mathcal{M}(D_1) \subset \mathcal{M}(D_2)$.

In the aquarium application of Figure 9.4, consider the query: find the names of tanks that don't contain fish. Negated predicates easily solve this query, as shown below.

```
query (N) ⊢ tankHasName (T, N), ¬fishyTank (T).
fishyTank (T) ⊢ fishInhabitsTank (F, T).
```

In fact, it can't possibly be expressed without negated predicates. To prove this point, suppose the query has been expressed with rules that don't involve negated predicates: the Horn clause feature is preserved. Suppose some tank, say t_1, with name cesspool, contains no fish under the current database content. Then query ("cesspool") is true. In other words, query ("cesspool") is part of the minimal model. Further suppose that t_1 is the only tank named cesspool, so the presence of query ("cesspool") in the minimal model is due only to the fact that t_1 contains no fish.

Next add a new axiom, fishInhabitsTank (f_1, t_1), to the database content. The ground literal query ("cesspool") should disappear from the minimal model because the tank t_1 now contains a fish. However, the minimal model grows monotonically with the database content axiom list, so the previously established true ground literal query ("cesspool") can't be removed. Therefore, the supposed query solution without negated predicates can't deliver the correct answer. The assumption that such a query solution exists must be wrong. You can conclude, therefore, that a deductive system with no negated predicates in its rules can't express some queries that are accessible with relational algebra. In this sense, Horn clause systems are weaker than relational algebra.

Actually, it's more accurate to say that Horn clause systems aren't equivalent to relational algebra. Although Horn clause systems can't express certain relational algebra queries, they can still express other queries that relational algebra can't. Recall the employee database in Chapter 9. The discussion there demonstrated that Horn clause rules could express the query to recover all employees reporting to a given supervisor at any level of indirection. No negated predicates were involved, but the inference rules did introduce cycles in the dependency graph. Therefore, forbidding negated predicates but allowing cyclical rules permits query solutions that can't be expressed in relational algebra.

 A deductive system composed entirely of Horn clauses can't express universal queries and is, therefore, weaker than relational algebra. However, it can express certain recursive queries, so in this sense, it is stronger than relational algebra.

Systems with restricted cycles in the dependency graph

The last example showed how a system with cyclical rules could express queries beyond the reach of relational algebra. The difficulty, of course, is that a deductive system with cyclical rules might have no preferred minimal model. Without a preferred minimal model, the true application facts implied by the rules are ambiguous. This section investigates how to introduce restricted cyclical rules without destroying the preferred minimal model.

You expand an initial Horn clause system as follows. First, reinstate rules with aggregate predicates, together with both negated subgoals and cyclical rules. But impose a restriction that the predicates in a cycle not depend on either negated or aggregate predicates from the same cycle. You allow negated and aggregate-based subgoals in the rules that define predicates of the cycle, but only when they are based on other predicates outside the cycle. A deductive system satisfying this test appears to offer the best of both worlds. Note that the template for universal queries uses negated predicates, but it doesn't introduce any cycles. Similarly, cyclical rules appear in the solution of unbounded recursive queries against the employee database, but they aren't mixed with negated predicates. The hopes for this approach are that it will allow the expression of universal queries, that it will permit the tracing of recursive relationships through an indeterminate number of levels, and that it will retain a preferred minimal model.

From the universal template and from the recursive solution format for the employee situation, you discover that the first two promises hold. However, the algorithm for computing the true binding table for a derived predicate may enter an infinite loop because of the cycles in the dependency graph. As you'll see, you can modify the algorithm so that it still computes a preferred minimal model.

For the remainder of this chapter, assume that a deductive database may contain cycles in its dependency graph. However, the derivation of a predicate from the cycle involves negated subgoals or aggregates only when they depend on predicates outside the cycle. This condition characterizes a **restricted deductive database**.

 A restricted deductive database allows cycles in its dependency graph and negated subgoals in its inference rules. For predicates in a cycle, however, the defining rules may contain neither negated subgoals nor aggregates based on predicates in the same cycle.

The dependency graph in Figure 10.1 shows a cyclical situation. The asterisks represent the database predicates. No arcs, of course, lead into them. The solid circles represent derived predicates. Several overlapping cycles appear: $(P_3, P_4, P_6, P_8, P_7, P_5, P_3)$ and $(P_4, P_6, P_8, P_7, P_5, P_4)$. There is also a simple cycle: $(P_{11}, P_{13}, P_{12}, P_{11})$.

Even with the cycles, you can conduct a "lumpy" topological sort of the predicates. Start with the database predicates, which have no predecessors, and then add predicates such that a newly added predicate depends only on elements already in the list. When you come to a cycle, or overlapping cycles, add the entire set of nodes associated with the cycle(s) as a lump. Below is the salvaged topological sort of the predicates of Figure 10.1:

$$D_1, D_2, D_3, D_4, P_{14}, P_{16}, P_{15}, \; (P_{13}, P_{12}, P_{11}), \; P_{10}, P_9, \; (P_3, P_4, P_6, P_8, P_7, P_5, P_3), \; P_2, P_1.$$

Consider a cluster of nodes in parentheses as a single unit. Although arcs can run backward within a unit, any arcs that leave the unit will always point forward. Any arcs that enter the unit come from earlier elements in the list.

To construct the preferred minimal model in this situation, start with the axioms—the true ground literals arising from the database predicates. Then progress along the lumpy

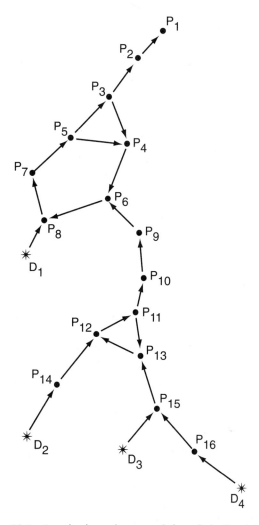

Figure 10.1 A cyclic dependency graph for a deductive database

topological sort, adding all ground literals that arise from a given predicate or lump before moving on in the list. In the example, the axioms comprise the true ground literals arising from D_1, D_2, D_3, and D_4. You then add all true ground literals arising from P_{14}. At this stage, a new ground literal enters the model only if it is forced true by a rule with P_{14} in the head. Any subgoals in such a rule involve only predicates that have already been completely defined. You then treat P_{16} and P_{15} in the same manner.

Next you encounter the lump (P_{13}, P_{12}, P_{11}). A predicate in this group depends only on predicates in the group and predicates earlier in the list. No predicate in the group appears in negated form. If you can develop a process for expanding the minimal model in one large step to include the smallest collection of true ground instances associated with the

```
accept L(E_i), 0 ≤ i ≤ m;
for (i = 0; i < n; i + +)
        L(P_i) = φ;
change = false;
do {
        for (i = 0; i < n; i + +) {
                L'(P_i) =   ground instances forced by rules with P_i in head,
                                using L(P_j) and L(E_k) to resolve references in bodies;
                change = (L'(P_i) ≠ L(P_i));
                }
        for (i = 0; i < n; i + +)
                L(P_i) = L'(P_i);
        } while (change);
return L(P_i), 0 ≤ i ≤ n;
```

Figure 10.2 Algorithm for completing tables of true ground literals for a cycle

group, then you can continue along the topological sort to completion. You will then have a deterministic preferred minimal model.

Until you encounter a lump in the topological sort, you obtain a predicate's true ground literals by working your way through the rules with the predicate in the head. For each rule, consider the set of all possible bindings. Some produce a true body, which is easy to detect because the true instances of all the subgoal predicates have already been established. For each binding that produces a true body, add the predicate, now a ground literal, to the growing model.

When you encounter a lump, you modify this procedure. First establish an empty table for each predicate in the group. You fill these tables with true ground literals arising from the predicates, but you do so in parallel, rather than sequentially as you have been doing with other predicates in the list. Next, repeatedly sequence through the predicates of the group, at each stage adding true ground literals that are forced by the rules and the current content of the growing model. Eventually you reach a point where a complete pass adds no new ground literals to the model. This stable condition completes the definition of all the predicates in the group.

The algorithm of Figure 10.2 describes the process, where the E_i represent predicates outside the group, and the P_i are the predicates in the group. E_i also contains auxiliary predicates that are defined with aggregates from other external predicates. $L(P_i)$ is the list of true ground instances arising from P_i. Each $L(P_i)$ starts empty and grows monotonically to include all instances that must be true to satisfy all the rules. $L(E_i)$ is the list of true ground literals corresponding to predicates external to the group. The list $L(E_i)$ is complete before the algorithm starts.

At any given time during the algorithm execution, the true ground literals in the model are given by the lists $L(E_i)$ and $L(P_i)$. The former don't change during execution, but the latter start empty and grow. When you add a true ground literal to one of the $L(P_i)$, the new true fact can't reverse the effect of a rule that previously installed a true ground literal in the model. This follows because the P_i never occur as negated subgoals in the rules under consideration. A new ground instance of a P_i, therefore, can only make a previously false body true. It can never make a previously true body false.

The lists $L(P_i)$ grow monotonically, and because there are only a finite number of possible ground literals, they must reach a point where further iterations make no changes in their contents. So the algorithm must terminate. The combined contents of the $L(E_i)$ and $L(P_i)$ lists then constitute a model of the rules considered to this point. These rules include the predicate group just processed and any earlier portions of the topological sort.

Moreover, the model is minimal with respect to the rules processed to this point. The process above adds true ground instances monotonically in a particular order. If some instance is superfluous, there is a first instance, say H, that is superfluous. The true body that forced H into the model comprises ground literals that entered the model before H. These rule bindings, therefore, aren't superfluous and can't be removed. So the true rule body that forced H into the model remains true after H is removed. But the rule is violated in this situation, so H can't be removed. Consequently, there is no first superfluous entry, and the model must be minimal.

Although the proof details aren't given here, the preferred minimal model generated by the revised algorithm doesn't depend on the particular topological sort of the predicates, and it doesn't depend on the order that the predicates are considered in the auxiliary process for handling the cyclic groups.

The algorithm isn't efficient, but that isn't significant here. By allowing cycles in the inference rules, you can express queries that are beyond relational algebra. You must simply make sure never to involve negated or aggregate predicates in the cycles. This precaution is easy to observe, as you'll see in the next section on recursive queries.

 A restricted deductive database possesses a well-defined preferred minimal model. There is an algorithm for populating that model.

This algorithm isn't appropriate for computing query solutions. It computes all the true ground instances in the preferred minimal model by filling tables as directed by a lumpy topological sort of the predicates. This computation can be enormously costly, both in storage space and time. Consequently, a practical query processor must be able to search the preferred minimal model without generating its large bulk. A backtracking mechanism, similar to the one for acyclic inference systems, can be constructed for this purpose.

Recursive queries

Besides retaining a preferred minimal model, restricted deductive database system allow query solutions that are beyond relational algebra. Consider the simple database of machine parts with the schema of Figure 10.3. The system has only two inference rules, and neither contains a negated or aggregate predicate. The rules do introduce a cycle into the dependency graph, an arc from contains to contains. The cycle, however, is very tight, and its two inference rules contain no negated subgoals. Because the DBMS withdraws query rules after reporting the solution, this system remains within the definition of a restricted deductive database, provided you don't introduce new rules with the contains predicate in the head.

Consider the existential query: find the names of component parts at any level in a part named turbine. You can easily express the solution without negated subgoals.

```
Entity existence axioms:
    part (X)              /* X is a species instance */
Attribute assertion axioms:
    partHasName (X, Y)              /* string Y is the name of part X */
    partHasColor (X, Y)             /* string Y is the color of part X */
Relationship assertion axioms:
    uses (X, Y, Z)           /* part X uses part Y in quantity Z */
Relationship assertion rules:
    contains (X, Y) ⊢ uses (X, Y, W).
    contains (X, Y) ⊢ uses (X, Z, W), contains (Z, Y, V).
```

Figure 10.3 Deductive schema for database of machine parts

```
query (N) ⊢ partHasName (X, "turbine"), partHasName (Y, N), contains (X, Y).
query (N).
```

Next consider a universal query: find the names of component parts used at any level in the assembly of *all* blue parts. Using the universal template, you proceed as follows:

```
query (N) ⊢ partHasName (X, N), ¬missesBlueAssembly (X).
missesBlueAssembly (X) ⊢ partHasColor (B, "blue"), ¬contains (B, X).
query (N).
```

The query introduces no additional cycles, and it doesn't modify the rule base for an existing cycle. Note that you can use the ¬contains subgoal; you just can't use it in a cycle where contains is one of the nodes. Therefore, the system remains a restricted deductive database, and there is a preferred minimal model giving unambiguous definition to the query. In general, the template for universal queries operates as expected because there is no need to tamper with the definition of the contains predicate, and that is the only place where you could violate the conditions of a restricted deductive database.

Suppose you want to tabulate the components of a part, p_1, but only the components that don't themselves comprise further subparts. In other words, you want a listing of the ultimate components of part p_1. You first establish a rule to check if a part is composite (i.e., composed of other parts):

$$\text{composite (X)} \vdash \text{uses (X, Y, Z).}$$

You then proceed as shown on the left below. The parallel entry on the right illustrates a simple aggregate in this application, retrieving the number of distinct ultimate components of part p_1.

```
query (X, N) ⊢ contains (p₁, X), ¬composite (X),       ultimate (X) ⊢ contains (p₁, X),
               partHasName (X, N).                                    ¬composite (X).
query (X, N).                                           query (C) ⊢ ultimate₀ᶜᵒᵘⁿᵗ (C).
                                                        query (C).
```

The aggregate above poses no problem because it isn't involved in a cycle. But suppose you want a predicate containsQty (X, Y, Q) to be true when part X uses a total of Q copies of part Y. In other words, Q reflects the number of Y parts that are used directly in X plus the number of Y parts that contribute at any level to the construction of other subassemblies used in X. Although it contains an aggregate in a forbidden location, the following solution does provide the correct solution. This demonstrates that you can use aggregates in cycles, but only with care.

$$G\ (X, Y, Z, A, B) \vdash uses\ (X, Y, B), Z = "*", A = 1.$$
$$G\ (X, Y, Z, A, B) \vdash uses\ (X, Z, A), containsQty\ (Z, Y, B), Z \neq Y.$$
$$H\ (X, Y, N, Z, A, B) \vdash G_{5}^{A\ *\ B}\ (X, Y, Z, A, B, N).$$
$$containsQty\ (X, Y, Q) \vdash H_{2}^{sum}\ (X, Y, Q).$$

Here you have created another cycle involving the predicates containsQty, G and H. This cycle's predicates have no negated subgoals in their defining rules, but they do depend on aggregates constructed over predicates of the same cycle. The intent of containsQty (X, Y, Q) is that part X uses Q copies of part Y at some level in its construction. G (X, Y, "*", 1, B) states that X directly contains B copies of Y; G (X, Y, Z, A, B) states that X directly contains A copies of some other assembly Z and that Z in turn contains B copies of Y at some level in its construction.

For a particular X and Y, a typical table of true bindings for G appears on the left below. The first row means that 5 copies of y directly contribute to the assembly of x. The other rows correspond to components of x other than y. These other components contribute indirect copies of y. The three direct copies of part q, for example, contribute 18 copies of y. Once you have constructed the table for G, you can obtain the total copies of y by summing the products of the last two columns. The rule for H produces a sixth column, which contains the products of columns four and five, and then reshuffles that column to the third position, directly following the X and Y columns that will define a partition. The rule for containsQty then sums that column.

X	Y	Z	A	B
x	y	"*"	1	5
x	y	q	3	6
x	y	r	2	4
x	y	s	5	7
⋮	⋮	⋮	⋮	⋮

X	Y	Q
x	y	57
x	a	2
x	b	14
x	c	28
a	y	21
a	b	5
a	c	10
b	y	3
b	c	2

You can trace the activity of the algorithm of Figure 10.2 on the components of part x, as illustrated in Figure 10.4. Part x directly contains 3 copies of y, and it indirectly contains an additional 42 copies via its a subassembly and an additional 12 copies via its b subassembly. Performing a similar summation on the other components, you see that the query containsQty (X, Y, Q) should return the table on the right above. This solution table is correctly computed by the algorithm of Figure 10.2.

You can trace through this algorithm's operation as follows. As part of the database content list, you have the relevant portion of uses (X, Y, T) shown below. Because G,

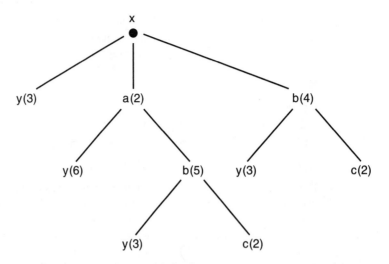

Figure 10.4 A typical part assembly for illustrating a recursive query with aggregates

H, and containsQty are all initially empty, the first pass through the algorithm's iterative loop produces the initial versions of these tables, which are also shown below. The order that you compute containsQty, G, and H isn't relevant because the computations use the tables from the previous iteration. At the beginning of the first iteration, only the uses table has entries; the rest are empty. The first rule for G (X, Y, Z, A, B) establishes the direct use of Y by X while the second rule contributes nothing because the previous version of containsQty is empty. Neither containsQty nor H acquires entries because at least one of their dependent tables from the previous iteration is empty.

uses (X, Y, T)		
X	Y	T
x	y	3
x	a	2
x	b	4
a	y	6
a	b	5
b	y	3
b	c	2

G (X, Y, Z, A, B)				
X	Y	Z	A	B
x	y	*	1	3
x	a	*	1	2
x	b	*	1	4
a	y	*	1	6
a	b	*	1	5
b	y	*	1	3
b	c	*	1	2

H (X, Y, N, Z, A, B)					
X	Y	N	Z	A	B

containsQty (X, Y, Q)		
X	Y	Q

Because the first pass changed the binding tables' contents, you start a second pass. You compute new tables for containsQty, G, and H using the old versions for references in the rule bodies. The tables then take the following form. G remains unchanged, but H now delivers the commanded arithmetic over the old G.

uses (X, Y, T)		
X	Y	T
x	y	3
x	a	2
x	b	4
a	y	6
a	b	5
b	y	3
b	c	2

G (X, Y, Z, A, B)				
X	Y	Z	A	B
x	y	*	1	3
x	a	*	1	2
x	b	*	1	4
a	y	*	1	6
a	b	*	1	5
b	y	*	1	3
b	c	*	1	2

H (X, Y, N, Z, A, B)					
X	Y	N	Z	A	B
x	y	3	*	1	3
x	a	2	*	1	2
x	b	4	*	1	4
a	y	6	*	1	6
a	b	5	*	1	5
b	y	3	*	1	3
b	c	2	*	1	2

containsQty (X, Y, Q)		
X	Y	Q

On the next pass, G and H retain their old values, but containsQty acquires non-empty content.

uses (X, Y, T)		
X	Y	T
x	y	3
x	a	2
x	b	4
a	y	6
a	b	5
b	y	3
b	c	2

G (X, Y, Z, A, B)				
X	Y	Z	A	B
x	y	*	1	3
x	a	*	1	2
x	b	*	1	4
a	y	*	1	6
a	b	*	1	5
b	y	*	1	3
b	c	*	1	2

H (X, Y, N, Z, A, B)					
X	Y	N	Z	A	B
x	y	3	*	1	3
x	a	2	*	1	2
x	b	4	*	1	4
a	y	6	*	1	6
a	b	5	*	1	5
b	y	3	*	1	3
b	c	2	*	1	2

containsQty (X, Y, Q)		
X	Y	Q
x	y	3
x	a	2
x	b	4
a	y	6
a	b	5
b	y	3
b	c	2

On the next pass, the second rule for G finally becomes active and expands the G table. Neither H nor containsQty changes because they compute from the previous values of G and H respectively. However, over the next two iterations the H table updates, reflecting the new G, and the containsQty table then updates, reflecting the new H. The following tables illustrate the situation after these three iterations.

uses (X, Y, T)		
X	Y	T
x	y	3
x	a	2
x	b	4
a	y	6
a	b	5
b	y	3
b	c	2

G (X, Y, Z, A, B)				
X	Y	Z	A	B
x	y	*	1	3
x	a	*	1	2
x	b	*	1	4
a	y	*	1	6
a	b	*	1	5
b	y	*	1	3
b	c	*	1	2
x	y	a	2	6
x	b	a	2	5
x	y	b	4	3
x	c	b	4	2
a	y	b	5	3
a	c	b	5	2

H (X, Y, N, Z, A, B)					
X	Y	N	Z	A	B
x	y	3	*	1	3
x	a	2	*	1	2
x	b	4	*	1	4
a	y	6	*	1	6
a	b	5	*	1	5
b	y	3	*	1	3
b	c	2	*	1	2
x	y	12	a	2	6
x	b	10	a	2	5
x	y	12	b	4	3
x	c	8	b	4	2
a	y	15	b	5	3
a	c	10	b	5	2

containsQty (X, Y, Q)		
X	Y	Q
x	y	27
x	a	2
x	b	14
a	y	21
a	b	5
b	y	3
b	c	2
x	c	8
a	c	10

At this point, certain bindings from the old version of containsQty, such as X = x, Y = y, Q = 3, disappear from the new version. The next three iterations produce changes in the G, H, and containsQty tables respectively and result in the tables below.

uses (X, Y, T)		
X	Y	T
x	y	3
x	a	2
x	b	4
a	y	6
a	b	5
b	y	3
b	c	2

G (X, Y, Z, A, B)				
X	Y	Z	A	B
x	y	*	1	3
x	a	*	1	2
x	b	*	1	4
a	y	*	1	6
a	b	*	1	5
b	y	*	1	3
b	c	*	1	2
x	y	a	2	21
x	b	a	2	5
x	y	b	4	3
x	c	b	4	2
a	y	b	5	3
a	c	b	5	2
x	c	a	2	10

H (X, Y, N, Z, A, B)					
X	Y	N	Z	A	B
x	y	3	*	1	3
x	a	2	*	1	2
x	b	4	*	1	4
a	y	6	*	1	6
a	b	5	*	1	5
b	y	3	*	1	3
b	c	2	*	1	2
x	y	42	a	2	21
x	b	10	a	2	5
x	y	12	b	4	3
x	c	8	b	4	2
a	y	15	b	5	3
a	c	10	b	5	2
x	c	20	a	2	10

containsQty (X, Y, Q)		
X	Y	Q
x	y	57
x	a	2
x	b	14
a	y	21
a	b	5
b	y	3
b	c	2
x	c	28
a	c	10

Subsequent iterations produce no changes in these tables, so the algorithm terminates. The final table for containsQty is exactly as anticipated. But will the algorithm always compute the correct result?

Although the tables for G, H, and containsQty don't grow monotonically with successive iterations, they do exhibit a pattern. You can exploit this pattern to show that the algorithm does indeed always compute the correct result. Once you introduce a tuple (x, y, z, a, b) into G, there will always be a tuple there of the form (x, y, z, a, $\cdots$). Moreover, after $3i$ iterations of the algorithm, the last element represents the number of copies of y that have been located through level i under x. Every three iterations, the algorithm updates the final entry of the tuple to reflect copies of y found at the next lower level under x. When it has probed all levels under x, the tuple remains constant for the rest of the process. Every three iterations, the algorithm updates H to follow the development in G. ContainsQty then follows the changes in H.

The algorithm terminates because each table grows monotonically in its entries in a selected subset of columns. Meanwhile, the entries in the remaining columns grow to represent the number of instances of a particular part found through lower and lower levels in the tree of Figure 10.4. Because that tree is finite, the changes must eventually stabilize, and the algorithm terminates. All rules are satisfied, and you have no freedom to remove an entry from any table. Because containsQty is a computed table over H, you can't remove a tuple. Similarly, H is computed over G. Finally, the only tuples in G are those that are forced there by the last iteration, which uses the current contents of uses and containsQty. Consequently, you can't remove a tuple from G without violating one of the rules.

The trace shows that the algorithm correctly computes the bindings for the containsQty predicate even though the system violates one of the requirements for a restricted deductive database. However, you can't, in general, define a predicate within a cycle using aggregates built over elements of the same cycle. Suppose, for example, that you have the following program, where E is a predicate from outside the cycle that has the constant bindings on the left below. The algorithm in Figure 10.2 generates the tables extending to the right. The tables for R and S never stabilize. So you can see that a special argument must be made for each logic program that introduces aggregates in a cycle.

```
R (X, Y) ⊢ E (X, Y).
S (X, Y) ⊢ R₁ˢᵘᵐ (X, Y).
R (X, Y) ⊢ S (X, Y).
```

E (X, Y)	
X	Y
1	2
1	3

R (X, Y)	
X	Y
1	2
1	3

S (X, Y)	
X	Y
1	5

R (X, Y)	
X	Y
1	2
1	3
1	5

S (X, Y)	
X	Y
1	10

R (X, Y)	
X	Y
1	2
1	3
1	10

S (X, Y)	
X	Y
1	15

R (X, Y)	
X	Y
1	2
1	3
1	15

S (X, Y)	
X	Y
1	2
1	3
1	20

R (X, Y)	
X	Y
1	2
1	3
1	20

......

Recursive versions of existential, universal, and aggregate queries operate within the requirements of a restricted deductive database. You can sometimes justify self-referential aggregates in cycles, but you must give a special argument to show that the algorithm terminates with a minimal model.

This section deals with recursion, as evidenced by cycles in the dependency graph, not in the application objects. The parts database is not recursive in the latter sense: a part doesn't contain itself at any level. If the parts aren't machine parts but instead abstract objects that can contain themselves, then some of the example queries are undefined. For example, suppose the parts are program procedures, which contain calls to other procedures. If you consider a procedure as containing those procedures that it calls, a procedure can contain itself, either directly or indirectly.

If a part can contain itself, the predicate containsQty isn't well-defined. Suppose that part p_1 contains one copy of part p_2 directly and that it also contains one copy of itself. Then any binding for Z in containsQty $(p_1, p_2,$ Z$)$ will satisfy Z = 1 + Z, which isn't possible. However, other queries, such as the ultimate (X) developed earlier, are still meaningful.

Because the recursive queries in this section are beyond the expressive power of relational algebra, this latest version of a deductive database can outperform its relational counterpart.

This chapter developed patterns for existential, universal, and aggregate queries in an acyclic deductive database. For an existential query, you align the relationship predicates needed to construct a path from a candidate object to the specified anchors. You use common argument bindings to link the predicates, just as you use common attributes in SQL.

For universal queries, you use negated predicates to imitate the doubly negated SQL construction. Suppose entities A and B participate in a many-to-many relationship, which

Algebra operator	Inference rule
$Q = R_1 \times R_2$	$Q \vdash R_1, R_2.$
$Q = R_1 \cup R_2$	$Q \vdash R_1.$ $Q \vdash R_2.$
$Q = \sigma_b(R)$	$Q \vdash R, d_{11}, d_{12}, \ldots.$ $Q \vdash R, d_{21}, d_{22}, \ldots.$ $\vdots$ where $b = c_1 \vee c_2 \vee \ldots$ and $c_i = d_{i1} \wedge d_{i2} \wedge \ldots.$
$Q = \pi_q(R)$	$Q(a_{i_1}, a_{i_2}, \ldots) \vdash R(a_1, a_2, \ldots).$ where $(a_{i_1}, a_{i_2}, \ldots) \subset (a_1, a_2, \ldots)$
$Q = \pi_q \Psi_p^f(R)$	$Q(a_{i_1}, a_{i_2}, \ldots, b) \vdash T_{|p|}^f(a_{i_1}, a_{i_2}, \ldots, b).$ $T(a_{i_1}, a_{i_2}, \ldots, c) \vdash R(a_1, a_2, \ldots).$ where $q = (a_{i_1}, a_{i_2}, \ldots, b).$ $\quad f = (b \leftarrow g(c))$

Figure 10.5　Equivalence of relational algebra operators and inference rules

is tabulated as entity C. So you have two relationship predicates: ac (A, C) and cb (C, B). Assuming the predicates a and b test the existence of A and B objects respectively, you obtain the set of A objects that are related to all B objects as follows:

```
query (A) ⊢ a(A), ¬missesB (A).
missesB (A) ⊢ b(B), ¬connected (A, B).
connected (A, B) ⊢ ac (A, C), cb (C, B).
query (A).
```

The aggregate predicate notation developed in Chapter 9 extends to include arithmetic predicates, which operate on partition groups with a single tuple. This operation extends each tuple to contain a new attribute, which holds the result of the arithmetic. Aggregate predicates allow you to compose inference rules that imitate the SQL aggregate functions.

Acyclic deductive databases with logic program queries are equivalent to relational databases with relational algebra queries. You can align the schemas from either direction. A relational database gives rise to its acyclic deductive equivalent by associating a database predicate with each relation. An acyclic deductive database gives rise to its relational equivalent by creating a relation from each database predicate and its corresponding axioms. After aligning the two databases in this manner, you have a one-to-one correspondence between each table and a database predicate. Relational algebra operations produce new tables that are associated with derived predicates. In particular, an inference rule can imitate each of the basic relational algebra operations. Figure 10.5 gives an abbreviated summary of these mappings.

Two variations on the acyclic theme were discussed. The first forbids negated subgoals, which restricts the rules to Horn clauses. This reduced version has the advantage of a unique minimal model, but it can't express universal queries. The advantage of a unique minimal model remains even if you allow cyclical rules. The cyclical rules let you solve certain recursive queries that lie beyond relational algebra.

A second variation allows both cycles in the dependency graph and negated subgoals, but it forbids using negated subgoals over the predicates of a cycle to derive a head predicate from the same cycle. A deductive system that respects this relaxed condition is a restricted deductive database. It still possesses a well-defined preferred minimal model. An algorithm can systematically accumulate all the true ground instances of that preferred minimal model.

Recursive queries in a restricted deductive database present no particular difficulties. Indeed, sometimes you can relax the restriction that forbids, in a given cycle, aggregates constructed over predicate in the same cycle. But you must analyze each such case to ensure that the algorithm terminates properly.■

EXERCISES

Most of the following exercises deal with the library database and use the schema of Figure 10.6.

Existential queries

Write logic programs for the following queries.

1. Find the names of libraries located in Seattle.

2. Find the names and locations of libraries that feature books written by Salinger.

3. Find the names of libraries whose book collection overlaps a Seattle library.

4. Find the titles of books that are available from a library that is patronized by a patron named joe.

5. Find all pairs of book titles that have copies in the same library. Phrase the query to exclude pairs of the form (x, x) from the answer set.

6. Find the names of all library triplets that are collocated. Eliminate triplets of the form (x, x, x), (x, x, y), (x, y, x), and (y, x, x) from the answer.

Describe the following logic programs in English.

7. query (N) ⊢ libHasName (L, N), libHoldsCopy (L, C), copyHasLoan (C, U),
            patHasLoan (P, U), patHasWeight (P, W), W > 150.
   query (N).

8. query (N, M) ⊢ bookHasTitle (B, N), bookHasTitle (X, M),
            authWritesBook (A, B), authWritesBook (A, X), B ≠ X.
   query (N, M).

9. patLib (P, L) ⊢ patHasLoan (P, U), copyHasLoan (C, U), libHoldsCopy (L, C).
   query (N) ⊢ patHasName (P, N), patLib (P, L), patLib (P2, L), patLib (P2, L2),
            libHasLocation (L2, "Denver").
   query (N).

Write logic programs for the following queries.

10. Find the titles of books that have more than one copy in a Seattle library.

11. Find the names of patrons who have used a library that has also been used by a patron named jill to borrow a book written by an author named Doyle.

Universal queries

Write logic programs for the following queries.

12. Find the names of libraries that have no books available.

13. Find the names of patrons who have used every library.

Entity existence assertion axioms	
Predicate	Intended meaning
`library (X)`	X is a library
`author (X)`	X is an author
`patron (X)`	X is a patron
`book (X)`	X is a book
`copy (X)`	X is a copy of a book
`loan (X)`	X is the record of the loan of a copy to a patron

Attribute assertion axioms	
Predicate	Intended meaning
`libHasName (X, Y)`	string Y is the name of library X
`libHasLocation (X, Y)`	string Y is the location of library X
`libHasRooms (X, Y)`	string Y is the number of rooms in library X
`authHasName (X, Y)`	string Y is the name of author X
`bookHasTitle (X, Y)`	string Y is the title of book X
`bookHasPages (X, Y)`	number Y is the page count of book X
`copyHasCost (X, Y)`	string Y is the dollar cost of copy X
`patHasName (X, Y)`	string Y is the name of patron X
`patHasWeight (X, Y)`	string Y is the weight of patron X
`loanHasDate (X, Y)`	string Y is the due date of loan Y

Relationship assertion axioms	
Predicate	Intended meaning
`authWritesBook (X, Y)`	author X has written book Y
`libHoldsCopy (X, Y)`	library X holds copy Y
`bookHasCopy (X, Y)`	book X has copy Y
`copyHasLoan (X, Y)`	copy X has loan record Y
`patHasLoan (X, Y)`	patron X has loan record Y

Figure 10.6 Library schema for the exercises

Describe the following logic programs in English.

14. query (T) ⊢ bookHasTitle (B, T), ¬inUse (B).
    inUse (B) ⊢ bookHasCopy (B, C), copyHasLoan (C, U).
    query (T).

15. query (N) ⊢ libHasName (L, N), libCarriesSalinger (L).
    libCarriesSalinger (L) ⊢ authWritesBook (A, B), authHasName (A, "Salinger"),
                            bookHasCopy (B, C), libHoldsCopy (L, C).
    query (N).

For each of the following queries, state whether it requires negated subgoals in its logic program solution.

16. Find the locations of libraries that possess a copy of a book entitled The Name of the Rose.

17. Find the names of patrons who use a library located in Seattle.

18. Find the names of patrons who use all libraries located in Seattle that hold a book written by Salinger.

Write logic programs for the following queries.

19. Find the names of patrons who have checked out all books with more than 300 pages.

20. Find the titles of books that have copies in all Seattle libraries that feature copies of all books written by Mailer.

21.
```
select P.patname
from patron P
where P.patwgt > 150 and not exists
    (select *
    from book B
    where not exists
        (select *
        from copy C, loan LN
        where B.bookno = C.bookno and C.copyno = LN.copyno and
            LN.patronno = P.patronno)).
```

Aggregates and partitions

Write logic programs for the following queries.

22. Find the titles of books that have fewer than 10 copies in circulation.

23. Find the location of the library with the most rooms.

24. For each library-book combination, find the number of copies of the book held by the library.

25. For each patron, find the average size (i.e., number of rooms) of the libraries used by the patron.

26. For each book, find the minimum, average, and maximum cost of its copies.

27. Find the names of patrons whose weight is greater than the average weight of patrons who have read a book entitled **The Name of the Rose**.

28.
```
select L.libno, L.libname, average(B.pages) pagecount
from library L, book B
where exists
    (select *
    from copy C
    where L.libno = C.libno and C.bookno = B.bookno)
groupby L.libno.
```

29.
```
select P.patronno, P.patname, sum(B.pages) readingload
from patron P, loan LN, copy C, book B
where P.patronno = LN.patronno and LN.copyno = C.copyno and C.bookno = B.bookno
groupby P.patronno.
```

30.
```
select L.libno, B.bookno, P.patronno, count(*) "total loans"
from library L, copy C, book B, loan LN, patron P
where L.libno = C.libno and C.bookno = B.bookno and C.copyno = LN.copyno
    and LN.patronno = P.patronno
groupby L.libno, B.bookno, P.patronno.
```

31. For each library whose collection includes more than 100 titles, find the average number of pages in the books in the collection.

32. For each author whose total number of pages written exceeds the total weight of the patrons who have read some of his work, find the average size of the libraries that carry his books.

33. For each patron, find the number of libraries that he uses, but only for those patrons that use some library of size greater than the average size of libraries that carry a copy of a book entitled The Name of the Rose.

34.
```
select P.patronno, P.patname, count(*) "copies borrowed"
from patron P, loan LN, copy C
where P.patronno = LN.patronno and LN.copyno = C.copyno
groupby P.patronno
having average(C.cost) >
    (select average(C.cost)
     from copy C, book B, author A
     where C.bookno = B.bookno and B.authno = A.authno and
           A.authname = "Salinger").
```

35. For each patron, p, display the average, μ_p, and variance, σ_p^2, of the number of rooms in the libraries that he patronizes. The variance of a list is the average of the squares minus the square of the average.

Logic programs and relational algebra

36. Construct a deductive system equivalent to the relational database shown below. The table keys are underlined.

L (<u>libno</u>, libname, location, rooms)
A (<u>authno</u>, authname)
P (<u>patronno</u>, patname, patwgt)
B (<u>bookno</u>, title, pages, authno)
C (<u>copyno</u>, cost, libno, bookno)
U (<u>loanno</u>, duedate, copyno, patronno)

Using the deductive schema of the previous exercise, compose logic programs to translate the following relational algebra expressions.

37. $\pi_q \sigma_b (B * C * U * P)$, where q = (title)
$\phantom{\pi_q \sigma_b (B * C * U * P), \text{where}}\ b$ = (patwgt > pages).

38. $\pi_q \sigma_b (\check{\rho}(Y = A*B) \times \check{\rho}(X = B*A))$, where q = (Y.authname, X.authname)
$\phantom{\pi_q \sigma_b (\check{\rho}(Y = A*B) \times \check{\rho}(X = B*A)), \text{where}}\ b$ = (Y.title = X.title $\wedge$ Y.authno < X.authno).

39. $\pi_q \sigma_b (\check{\rho}(X = P * U * C * L) \times \check{\rho}(Y = (L * C * U * P) \times \check{\rho}(Z = P * U * C * L))$

where q = (X.patname)
$\phantom{\text{where}}\ b$ = (X.libno = Y.libno $\wedge$ Y.patronno = Z.patronno $\wedge$ Z.location = "Minneapolis").

40. $\pi_q [\pi_r (P * U * C * B * A) / \pi_s (A)]$, where s = (authno)
$\phantom{\pi_q [\pi_r (P * U * C * B * A) / \pi_s (A)], \text{where}}\ r$ = (patronno, patname, patwgt, authno)
$\phantom{\pi_q [\pi_r (P * U * C * B * A) / \pi_s (A)], \text{where}}\ q$ = (patname, patwgt).

41. $\pi_q \{ [\pi_r (L * C * B) / \pi_s (A)] * C * U * [\pi_t \sigma_b (P * U * C * B) / \pi_s (A)] \}$,

where s = (authno)
$\phantom{\text{where}}\ r$ = (libno, libname, authno)
$\phantom{\text{where}}\ b$ = (patwgt > 150)
$\phantom{\text{where}}\ t$ = (patronno, authno)
$\phantom{\text{where}}\ q$ = (libname).

Entity existence axioms:

```
Entity existence axioms:
    routine (X)              /* X is computer subroutine */
Attribute assertion axioms:
    routineHasName (X, Y)                /* string Y is the name of routine X */
    routineHasLength (X, Y)              /* number Y is the length of routine X */
Relationship assertion axioms:
    calls (X, Y)             /* routine X calls routine Y */
Relationship assertion rules:
    uses (X, Y) ⊢ calls (X, Y).
    uses (X, Y) ⊢ calls (X, Z), uses (Z, Y).
```

Figure 10.7 Deductive schema for database of computer routines

42. $\pi_q \Psi_p^f \sigma_b (L * C * B)$, where
$$b = (\text{rooms} > 25)$$
$$f = (\text{copyCount} = \text{count(copyno)})$$
$$p = (\text{libno, bookno})$$
$$q = (\text{libno, libname, bookno, title, copyCount}).$$

43. $\pi_q \Psi_p^f (P * U * C * B)$, where
$$p = (\text{patronno})$$
$$f = (\text{pageTotal} = \text{sum(pages)})$$
$$q = (\text{patname, pageTotal}).$$

44. $\pi_q \Psi^f \pi_r \sigma_b (P * U * C * B * A)$, where
$$b = (\text{authname} = \text{"Mailer"})$$
$$r = (\text{patronno, patwgt})$$
$$f = (\text{massAdmirers} = \text{sum(patwgt)})$$
$$q = (\text{massAdmirers}).$$

45. $\pi_q \Psi_p^f (P * U * C)$, where
$$p = (\text{patronno})$$
$$f = (\text{maxCost} = \text{max(cost)})$$
$$q = (\text{patname, maxCost}).$$

Recursive queries
Figure 10.7 defines a deductive database of computer procedures. Write logic programs for the following queries in terms of this application.

46. Find the names of routines that are used by routine r_1, either directly or indirectly at any level.

47. Find the names of routines that use routine r_1, either directly or indirectly at any level.

48. Find the names of the most basic routines in the database. A basic routine is one that doesn't call other routines.

11 Network Databases

A NETWORK DATABASE STORES DATA ELEMENTS IN RECORDS, WHICH correspond very closely to relational tuples. Moreover, it organizes the records into tables, which look very much like relational tables. However, the similarity ends here because the network model embeds pointers in the records to link them into circular chains. Although these prewired relationship groupings are fast and efficient, they suffer several disadvantages in comparison with the relational model's foreign key technique.

The first problem is that the predefined links group only those relationships that the schema preselects for representation. In the aquarium example, the network DBMS can link together the fish swimming in a given tank, and it can also include the tank in the grouping. This relationship is an obvious one in the application, and the designer can assume that users will frequently access it. However, suppose a user conjures up a more ad hoc relationship that groups fish with their *compatible* tanks rather than with their home tanks. For this purpose, a compatible tank is a tank with the same color as the fish. If the database designer didn't preestablish this particular tank-fish relationship in the schema, the DBMS can't efficiently process a query based on it.

A second and more serious problem is that the network representation exposes implementation details, such as linked lists, that aren't relevant from the application viewpoint. The later database models (i.e., relational, object-oriented, and deductive) relieve the database designers of these implementation details, allowing them to think in terms of application objects. A related deficiency is that database designers must be more familiar with data structures and storage schemes when working with a network database. As you'll see, manipulating of a network database requires considerable programming skill. Finally, users must interact with a network database from a host programming language and make database calls as necessary to transfer information between the database and the program variables. Thus, the interface language is procedural, which is considered less productive than the non-procedural approaches of SQL, relational calculus, or logic programs.

Commercial network products are still available today, and many data processing systems currently operate with a network database core. In fact, the large investment in this so-called legacy code is one reason that the network model continues to be viable. Neverthe-less, I consider the model to be of historical importance only. But the network model does merit study because it illustrates another approach to the standard database challenge: how to represent data elements and their relationships. This chapter explains the components of the network model, and it shows how to construct existential, universal, and aggregate network queries.

The network model was created by the Data Base Task Group (DBTG) of the Confer-ence on Data Systems Languages (CODASYL) committee. The original definition dates from the early 1970s, with updates appearing in the late 1970s and early 1980s. In the mid-1980s, the American National Standards Institute (ANSI) released a standard syntax to define and manipulate network databases. The treatment here varies slightly from the standard because my goal is to present network database concepts, not the precise details of the standard.

Informal illustration of a network database

The entities in the aquarium application are fish, species, tank, and event. The relevant relationships are Inhabits, which groups tanks with their fish; Represents, which groups species with their fish; and Experiences, which groups fish with their events. Named relationships in the network model are called **sets** although they have nothing to do with mathematical sets. To avoid confusion in this area, this discussion will always refer to named relationships as network sets.

A **network set** is a collection of disjoint chains, as illustrated in Figure 11.1. In the figure, the tanks and fish appear as disconnected rectangles, but the DBMS actually tabulates them like records in a file. In fact, the application entities are called **record types**. A pointer connects a tank to its first fish, and another pointer connects the first fish to the second. Additional pointers continue the chain through the final fish, which points back to the tank.

The chains must be disjoint because this representation corresponds to a one-to-many relationship between the tank and its fish. Each chain contains exactly one tank, and the fish on the chain all inhabit that single tank. A chain may contain no fish, one fish, or many fish. If two chains intersected in a common fish, that common fish would belong to two different tanks, a violation of the one-to-many relationship. You might protest that the two chains could intersect in a common tank, but that would be equivalent to a single chain that happens to return to the tank before looping out to include additional fish. The model gains no advantage by allowing such rethreading through the common tank, so it disallows such chains. For any one-to-many relationship, a single chain emerges from each dominant instance (i.e., the one side of the relationship) and passes in succession through all the dependent instances (i.e., the many side of the relationship) before returning to the dominant instance. Each disjoint chain of Figure 11.1 is an instance of the Inhabits relationship.

From Figure 11.1, you see that primary and foreign keys aren't needed to maintain the Inhabits relationship. To find the fish for a given tank, you simply follow the link from the tank to its first fish, then from that fish to the next, and so forth until you return to the tank. Similarly, to obtain the home tank of a given fish, you follow the links until you

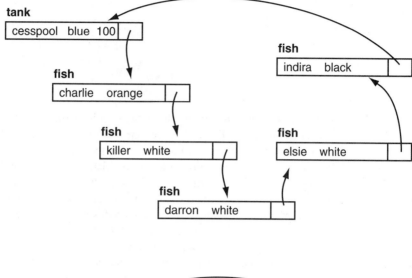

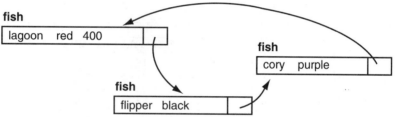

Figure 11.1   A one-to-many relationship with network chains

arrive at a tank record. Although keys aren't necessary to maintain relationships, they are frequently included for integrity or efficiency reasons.

Besides containing the application object's descriptive attributes, each record also holds pointers to link it into one or more chains. Envision the tank record tabulation as shown on the left below. The arrows indicate address pointers to the first fish of the tank's Inhabits chain. The model isn't concerned with the mechanism for implementing the links. A fish link may be the permanent disk address of the fish record, or it may be a memory address where that fish has been temporarily loaded. It may even be an fno key, which uses an auxiliary index to associate the key with the address of the actual fish record. So although the model officially suppresses keys in the representation of relationships, they can reappear at a lower level. In any case, the database designer or user views the link as a direct access route to its referenced record.

Tank			
tname	tcolor	tvolume	firstFish
puddle	green	200	●⟶
cesspool	blue	100	●⟶
lagoon	red	400	●⟶
cesspool	blue	100	●⟶
beach	blue	200	●⟶
lagoon	green	200	●⟶

Tank				
tname	tcolor	tvolume	firstFish	lastFish
puddle	green	200	●⟶	●⟶
cesspool	blue	100	●⟶	●⟶
lagoon	red	400	●⟶	●⟶
cesspool	blue	100	●⟶	●⟶
beach	blue	200	●⟶	●⟶
lagoon	green	200	●⟶	●⟶

For efficiency considerations, the network model frequently uses additional pointers to enable chain traversal in both directions and to permit a dependent instance to access its dominant partner directly, without traversing the list. In this case, each tank record contains two pointer fields: one pointing to the first fish on the chain and the other pointing to the last fish, as shown on the right above. Each fish record contains three pointer fields, which reference the previous fish, the next fish, and the dominant tank. A partial tabulation of the fish records appears below. Equipped with this more elaborate set of pointers, an instance of the Inhabits chain appears as in Figure 11.2. If you envision each of the ●⟶ symbols as an arrow pointing to another record, you see that the records are densely interconnected in a web of pointers. Another name for such a web is a network, which gives the network database model its name.

Fish					
fname	fcolor	fweight	nextFish	prevFish	tankHome
charlie	orange	12	●⟶	●⟶	●⟶
flipper	black	25	●⟶	●⟶	●⟶
killer	white	32	●⟶	●⟶	●⟶
charlie	orange	27	●⟶	●⟶	●⟶
⋮	⋮	⋮	⋮	⋮	⋮

 A network set expresses a one-to-many relationship between a dominant entity and a dependent entity. Each dominant record originates a chain that passes through zero, one, or more dependent records.

Although each instance of a network set can be a complicated set of forward and reverse pointers, together with direct pointers from dependent to dominant records, they will appear here as single lines. The diagrams will still become cluttered with cross-connections because an application entity can participate in more than one network set. Consider the situation in Figure 11.3, which suppresses the record's descriptive attributes and draws instances of different network sets with different line styles. The solid lines are instances of the Inhabits network set. As you can see, one of the tank records has no fish on its Inhabits chain. This boundary condition is valid. A tank groups with zero, one, or more fish in a one-to-many relationship. The dashed lines are instances of the Represents network set. A species record associates with zero, one, or more fish records.

Note that instances of different network sets can intersect. An intersection occurs when two chains have a record in common, not when the lines just happen to cross outside a record.

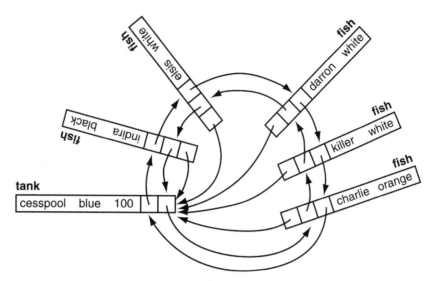

Figure 11.2   Network chain with auxiliary pointers

An earlier analysis established that chains corresponding to distinct instances of the same network set can't intersect because an intersection would violate the one-to-many nature of the relationship. This argument, however, doesn't prevent two chains from different network sets from intersecting. As you'll see, this latter type of intersection provides the crucial connection for extending database search paths to solve a query.

 Distinct chains from the same network set have no records in common. However, chains from different network sets can intersect, which provides an opportunity for network navigation from a record to related records.

Suppose you want the names of species swimming in a cesspool tank. You start by scanning the table of tank records. For each tank with tname cesspool, you follow the pointers of the Inhabits chain. On the chain, you encounter a sequence of fish records, each representing a fish that swims in the tank. For each fish record, you pause in your traversal of the Inhabits chain and take a detour on the Represents chain through the fish. On that detour, you eventually encounter a species record. That species classifies the fish where you initiated the detour, so the species must represent a fish swimming in the tank. You note the sname attribute as part of the answer and return from the detour to continue traversing the Inhabits chain. Each fish provides a detour in this manner and eventually provides an sname for the accumulating answer. Some of the sname strings may be duplicates because you may visit two fish of the same species on the tank's Inhabits chain. In the case of duplicates, you keep only a single copy in the accumulating answer list. Eventually, you finish your traversal of the tank's Inhabits chain and resume your scan of the tank table for another cesspool tank. You repeat the tour along the Inhabits chain of each cesspool tank. When you complete the tank table scan and any subsidiary

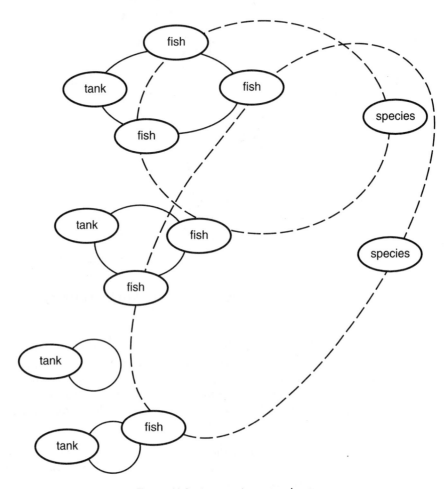

Figure 11.3 Intersecting network sets

expeditions required upon finding a cesspool record, you display the sname values of the answer list.

The process just illustrated is **network navigation**, and all query solutions in the network database model all take this form. The example consists of three nested loops. A first loop iterates through the tank table records. When it discovers a cesspool tank, a nested loop sequentially considers each fish on the tank's Inhabits chain. Within this second loop, a third iteration moves along the fish of the intersecting Represents chain to recover the species record and a possible addition to the answer list. Therefore, the processing corresponds to the usual control concepts of a programming language.

A network DBMS leaves the burden of navigation control to a **host language**. It provides the host routine with information from the database through subprocedure calls. This approach is the same as the embedded SQL of Chapter 5. The difference is that SQL does have a non-embedded counterpart, which allows direct interactive access to the database. A user of a network database must employ a host language program for all database interaction. In turn, the program controls the user interface with the input and output operations of the language. The original CODASYL proposal envisioned COBOL as the interface language. Commercial network database products, however, provide access through several languages, and this text will assume a C interface.

 In the network model, you control network navigation through a host language program, which makes calls to the network DBMS for information needed to guide the movement along the network set chains.

Consider again the example query from above: find the names of species swimming in a cesspool tank. The code segment below implements the nested loops needed to navigate from the anchor cesspool tank records to candidate species records. A later section will give more details on the database calls; for the moment, focus on the solution's format. Assume that declarative items are available as needed for this code segment, such as structures for tank and species records, which the DBMS can fill in response to a $get *<record type>* call. A feedback area, dbStatus, is also available for the DBMS to register the success or failure of the most recent call. A returned value of 0 represents unconditional success; a non-zero value provides an exception code. A particular non-zero dbStatus code, for example, signals the end of a record sequence in process. Many other dbStatus returns are possible, ranging from a benign end-of-data condition to a hardware malfunction.

```
$find first tank;
while (dbStatus == 0) {
    $get tank;
    if (strcmp(tank.tname, "cesspool") == 0) {
        $find first fish within Inhabits;
        while (dbStatus == 0) {
            $find species owner within Represents;
            $get species;
            printf("%s\n", species.sname);
            $find next fish within Inhabits; } }
    $find next tank; }
```

The outermost loop iterates through the tank records in an unspecified order. The find command brings a particular tank record into focus. A subsequent get command loads it into the corresponding memory data structure. Once resident in the memory structure, the record's attributes are available for probing with the usual C operations. In this case, the tname attribute (a character string) is compared with the constant cesspool. A true comparison activates the nested loop based on a different variant of the find command. This variation follows the links of the named network set to locate related records. For each related fish record, a third nested activity acquires the dominant species record. This last activity doesn't appear as a loop in the program because the DBMS responds to the find-owner command. The DBMS can sequence across the intervening fish on the Represents chain until it find the species record, or it can directly follow an owner pointer in the fish if such a pointer is available. The chosen method depends on how elaborately the DBMS implements the Represents network set.

Query solution in a network database is procedural: a host language program expresses the specific navigational algorithm to qualify a candidate record.

Definition of a network database

A database is an organized collection of data elements and their relationships, which presents a systematic user interface. A **network database** stores the elementary data items as records. It classifies these records under a number of **record types**, which represent the application entities. It supports only binary one-to-many relationships, which it expresses with **network sets**. For a given application, you define the network database with a **network schema**, which gives the record type and network set definitions. Although record types are similar to SQL table shells, the network sets have no counterpart in a relational database.

Network record types

The record is a familiar data structure in many programming languages. A record type is a composite structure, containing a heterogeneous collection of fields. In C, for example, you can declare a `tankType` record type as shown on the left below. Although all the fields in this example are character strings, a field can specify any available data type—a native C data type or a previously declared record type. Using a record type, you can declare variables of this type. For example, the `tank` variable on the right below is an instance of the `tankType` record structure. As shown in the code line below the declaration, you can manipulate the variable in the executable part of the program. Here the code copies a character string into one of the record components.

```
typedef struct {                    tankType tank;
    char tname[20];                          ⋮
    char tcolor[10];
    char tvolume[5];                strcpy(tank.tcolor, "blue");
    } tankType;
```

A record type definition serves as a pattern for instances that you declare and manipulate later in the program. A similar arrangement exists in a network database. A **network record type** is a data structure that represents an application entity as a heterogeneous collection of data values, also called fields. In contrast with program records, the fields of a network record type are limited to a small collection of predefined types: character strings, integers, and floats, with special forms for currency and timestamps. The database stores application entity instances as dictated by the record type format. Each instance is a **record**. Upon command, the DBMS will transfer a record from the database to a corresponding record structure in a host program, or vice versa. The aquarium network schema, for example, contains a tank record type definition. The DBMS will expect any interfacing program to contain a corresponding record data structure to act as a loading and unloading dock for database transfers.

```
schema aquarium.

record tank.                          typedef struct {              typedef struct {
    field tname is character 20.          char tname[20];               char edate[10];
    field tcolor is character 10.         char tcolor[10];              char enote[100];
    field tvolume is character 5.         char tvolume[5];              } eventType;
record species.                           } tankType;
    field sname is character 20.                                    tankType tank;
    field sfood is character 20.      typedef struct {              speciesType species;
                                          char sname[20];           fishType fish;
record fish.                              char sfood[20];           eventType event;
    field fname is character 20.          } speciesType;
    field fcolor is character 10.                                  int dbStatus;
    field fweight is character 5.     typedef struct {
                                          char fname[20];
record event.                             char fcolor[10];
    field edate is character 10.          char fweight[5];
    field enote is character 100.         } fishType;
```

Figure 11.4: Record type descriptions and corresponding header file for the aquarium network example

A network database schema contains record type and network set definitions. Each interfacing program mirrors the record types with memory data structures, which buffer records coming from or going to the database.

The left portion of Figure 11.4 shows the record type definition for the aquarium schema. When the DBMS processes the schema, it prepares a header file, which you can include in programs that reference the aquarium database. The right two columns of Figure 11.4 show the header file. You can see that it is a mechanical translation of the schema, which is tailored for the C language. Of course, the DBMS provides similar services for other interface languages.

The last entry of the header file defines the dbStatus integer variable, which informs the program of the success or failure of a database activity. The header specifies one record variable for each record type of the schema. For example, it declares a tank variable over the tankType structure, providing a compatible buffer for tank records coming from or going to the database. The remaining record types receive similar variables. In each case, the variable has the same name as the record type, so any code that references it will be somewhat self-documenting.

You can now better appreciate the query solution of the previous section. You can resolve the external references in that solution by including the header file, called aquarium.h, of Figure 11.4 in the program. The excerpt then appears as follows.

```
#include aquarium.h
$open database aquarium;
$find first tank;
while (dbStatus == 0) {
    $get tank;
    if (strcmp(tank.tname, "cesspool") == 0) {
        $find first fish within Inhabits;
        while (dbStatus == 0) {
            $find species owner within Represents;
            $get species;
            printf("%s\n", species.sname);
            $find next fish within Inhabits; } }
    $find next tank; }
$close database aquarium;
```

You identify each database call with a leading dollar symbol, which allows a preprocessor to recognize it and convert it into valid C syntax before compilation. The conversion references a library routine provided with the DBMS, which passes the text of the requested database activity and the program's buffer address. Sample conversions are:

```
$find first tank;   ⟹   dbStatus = executeNetwork ("find first tank", null);
$get tank;          ⟹   dbStatus = executeNetwork ("get tank", &tank);
```

The two-phase operation is necessary to bring a database record into the program's memory structure. The find command doesn't transfer information into the program template; it simply brings the DBMS focus to a particular database record. A subsequent get command transfers the data into the memory template. When the program brings the attention of the DBMS to a particular record, that record is the **current record**. You must use a similar two-phase operation to store information from the template into the database. The details of the data manipulation syntax appear later.

Network sets

Record types model the application entities, but they don't express relationships among the entities. Instead, network sets define the relationships. A **network set** is a named construction of the schema that references a dominant record type and a dependent record type. A network set instance is a chain of records containing exactly one record from the dominant entity and zero, one, or more records from the dependent entity. The network model supports only the network set as a means for maintaining relationships. All relationships, therefore, must be binary and one-to-many. Of course, this category includes one-to-one relationships as a special case. The constraint presents no practical difficulty because you can use the standard technique to factor a many-to-many relationship into two one-to-many relationships with an intersection entity. You can decompose higher-degree relationships in a similar manner.

Network sets appear in the schema after the record types that model the application entities. Each description specifies the dominant record type (i.e., the owner) and the dependent record type (i.e., the member). You should envision each network set instance as a linked chain containing a dominant record and any number of dependent records. You

```
network set  <network set name>.
      owner is  ⎰  < dominant record type name >  ⎱.
                ⎱  system                          ⎰
         [duplicates are not allowed.]
                      ⎧  sorted by defined keys  ⎫
                      ⎪  first                    ⎪
         [order is  ⎨  last                       ⎬.]
                      ⎪  next                      ⎪
                      ⎪  prior                     ⎪
                      ⎩  by system default         ⎭
      member is  <dependent record type name>.
         insertion is  ⎰  automatic  ⎱.
                        ⎱  manual     ⎰
                       ⎧  optional   ⎫
         retention is  ⎨  mandatory  ⎬.
                       ⎩  fixed      ⎭
         [key is  <list of fields from dependent record type>.]
                              ⎧  by application
         [set selection is  ⎨  by value of  <field name>  in  <dominant record type name>        ⎫
                              ⎪  structural  <field name>  in  <dependent record type name>  =    ⎬.]
                              ⎩              <field name>  in  <dominant record type name>        ⎭
         [check is  <field name>  in  <dependent record type name>  =
                    <field name>  in  <dominant record type name>.]
```

Figure 11.5   General format of a network set description

may want to customize the behavior of a chain for the given application. For example, you may want to impose an order among the dependent members. You may want to provide integrity checks that guard against a member being placed on the wrong chain. You may want to specify conditions that must be satisfied before the DBMS can transfer a dependent record on or off the chain. You can specify clauses in the schema to achieve these goals.

The format for a network set definition appears in Figure 11.5. The notation uses [...] to indicate an optional entry and {...} to specify a choice of several constructions. It uses < ... > to indicate a user-specified identifier. When constructing a network set, you should replace the < ... > entries with names that are meaningful for the application. Following this pattern, Figure 11.6 shows the network set definitions for the aquarium database.

A schema can specify two kinds of network sets: owner-coupled and system. In an **owner-coupled network set**, the dominant entity is a previously defined record type in the schema. Each owner-coupled network set comprises many chains, one for each dominant record instance. In the aquarium schema, Inhabits is an owner-coupled network set. Each tank record owns a chain of fish records. In a **system network set**, the dominant entity isn't a previously defined record type. Instead, the DBMS, or the "system," is the dominant partner. Each system network set comprises exactly one chain that originates with the DBMS and passes through all the member record instances before returning to the DBMS. Figure 11.7 illustrates the distinction, showing the Inhabits network set at

```
network set Inhabits.                      network set tankAlpha.
   owner is tank.                             owner is system.
      order is sorted by defined keys.           order is sorted by defined keys.
   member is fish.                            member is tank.
      insertion is manual.                       insertion is automatic.
      retention is optional.                     retention is fixed.
      key is ascending fname.                    key is ascending tname.

network set Represents.                    network set speciesAlpha.
   owner is species.                          owner is system.
      order is sorted by defined keys.           order is sorted by defined keys.
   member is fish.                            member is species.
      insertion is automatic.                    insertion is automatic.
      retention is fixed.                        retention is fixed.
      key is ascending fname.                    key is ascending sname.

network set Experiences.                   network set fishAlpha.
   owner is fish.                             owner is system.
      order is sorted by defined keys.           order is sorted by defined keys.
   member is event.                           member is fish.
      insertion is automatic.                    insertion is automatic.
      retention is mandatory.                    retention is fixed.
      key is ascending edate.                    key is ascending fname.
```

Figure 11.6   Network set description portion of the network aquarium schema

the top and the `tankAlpha` network set toward the bottom. The solid lines show several chains in the `Inhabits` owner-coupled set, but the dashed line shows a single chain in the `tankAlpha` system network set. Because it involves a single chain, a system network set is sometimes called a **singular set**.

Owner-coupled network sets use an application record type as the dominant entity. System network sets use the DBMS itself in that role. An owner-coupled network set consists of many chains, one for each dominant record. A system network set has a single chain.

With either kind of network set, the pattern allows an optional ordering-clause, which defines the order of the dependent records on the chains. The ordering-clause allows several choices. One is "sorted by defined keys." If you specify that choice, you must include a key-clause further down under the member definition. To define the sorted order, the key-clause identifies a member field (or list of fields) from the member record type. Although you use owner-coupled network sets to maintain one-to-many relationships, you use system sets primarily as indices into the record tables. Therefore, the system set description usually specifies "order is sorted by defined keys" and includes fields in the key-clause to maintain a useful order for the application. In the aquarium example of Figure 11.6, the tank, species, and fish records are ordered by tname, sname, and fname respectively through the system sets `tankAlpha`, `speciesAlpha`, and `fishAlpha`. You can use a variation of the `find` command to force the DBMS to process records as they appear on a network set chain. For

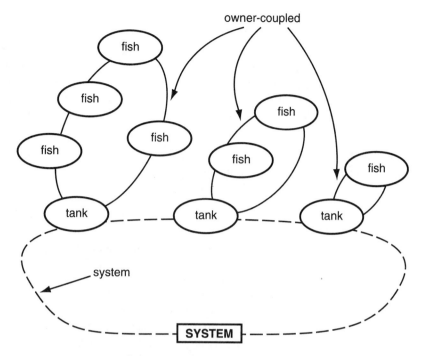

Figure 11.7 A system network set versus an owner-coupled network set

example, you can process tank records in order of increasing tname by using the `tankAlpha` network set. Data manipulation details follow later.

You can define several system network sets over the same dependent record type. For example, you can add another schema entry to Figure 11.6 by including the excerpt below. Then, if you need to process tanks in order of increasing or decreasing volume, you can use the `tankByVolume` system set.

```
network set tankByVolume.
    owner is system.
        order is sorted by defined keys.
    member is tank.
        insertion is automatic.
        retention is fixed.
        key is ascending tvolume.
```

The remaining choices of the ordering-clause are self-explanatory. The "by system default" allows the system to maintain the dependent records in any convenient order on the chain. The DBMS chooses this unordered arrangement by default if the schema doesn't provide an ordering-clause. The "first" or "last" option means that the DBMS should add a new dependent record as the first or last member of the chain as it exists when the record is added. Subsequent modifications to the chain may move the record from the end position. The "next" and "prior" options imply that a member of the chain is current due to some earlier operation and that the DBMS should add a new record either before or after the current member.

If you specify the "duplicates are not allowed" option, you must include a key-clause under the member definition. In this case, the DBMS won't add a new member to a chain if it duplicates the key value of an existing member on the chain. This facility extends the function of the clause *order is by defined keys*, which establishes an index on the chain members. When duplicates are forbidden, the index is unique.

 An ordering-clause controls the position of dependent records on a chain. In conjunction with a key-clause and a no-duplicates clause, the ordering-clause establishes an index or a unique index.

Insertion and retention clauses

The first two clauses under the member definition are the insertion and retention clauses, which specify conditions for adding or removing members from a chain. The available choices for the insertion clause are automatic and manual. If you choose automatic, the DBMS won't create a new member record without automatically attaching it to one of the chains. The Represents network set, for example, specifies automatic insertion. When you add a new fish record to the fish table, the DBMS automatically places it on one of the Represents chains. By default, the DBMS chooses the "current" chain, the one that has been most recently involved in some database activity. You can, however, force the DBMS to select a different chain with the set-selection clause. The aquarium schema doesn't specify set-selection clauses, so the current chain acquires the new member. Because system network sets have only one chain, the choice is simple. The DBMS enters the new fish on the single fishAlpha chain.

The alternative insertion choice is manual. In the aquarium example, the Inhabits network set specifies manual insertion. When you create a new fish record, the DBMS doesn't place it on any Inhabits chain. Instead, you later issue a connect command to place the fish on one of the Inhabits chains. The chain to receive the new member is the chain that is current at the time of the connect command. You can move the currency pointer between the time when you create the fish and the time when you explicitly connect it to an Inhabits chain.

The choice of automatic or manual insertion depends on the application. Therefore, this flexibility is an opportunity to tailor the network database model more closely to the application semantics. The aquarium schema uses the automatic option for the Represents network set. This means that the species of a new fish can never be in doubt. Presumably, the user has the fish in hand, and if he can't determine its species, the database designer doesn't want it in the database. By specifying automatic insertion, you guard against fish of unknown species. On the other hand, the Inhabits network set specifies manual insertion. This choice suggests that a user should enter a fish in the database even if he hasn't assigned it a home tank. The database designer wants to accommodate the possibility that a fish may arrive in a temporary container and wait for a tank assignment. In this case, the fish can continue to exist in the database, without joining any of the Inhabits chains. Arising from the application analysis, these choices are constraints that prevent certain database states. Just like constraints in the other models, they provide a mechanism for the database to adhere to the application's meaning.

 The insertion clause assigns responsibility for connecting newly created dependent records onto a network set chain. Automatic insertion gives the responsibility to the DBMS; manual insertion leaves it with the host program.

The retention clause governs how you remove dependent records from a chain. The available choices are: fixed, mandatory, and optional. If retention is fixed, once you place a dependent record on a chain, you can't disconnect it from that chain. You must distinguish between removing a record from a chain and deleting it from the database. You can delete a dependent record even if its retention is fixed. However, you can't disconnect it from its chain and leave it in the database, either free-floating away from any chain of the set or on a different chain of the set.

If retention is mandatory, you can move a dependent record from one chain of the network set to another, but you can't free-float it away from all chains of the set. The data manipulation language (DML) provides a special command, `reconnect`, to perform this operation in one indivisible action. A `reconnect` command disconnects a dependent record from one chain of a specified network set and reconnects it to another in the same network set, without returning control to the host program between the two actions.

The final choice is the least restrictive. If retention is optional, you can disconnect a dependent record from a chain and allow it to free-float in the database.

Some interesting combinations of insertion and retention are possible. If insertion is manual and retention is either fixed or mandatory, a dependent record can start out in a free-floating state with respect to the network set. It belongs to none of the network set's chains. But once you connect it to a chain, you can never recover its free-floating status.

Depending on the specific application, the insertion and retention choices represent an opportunity to tune the model to the application intent. The aquarium example chooses the manual-optional combination for the `Inhabits` network set. This selection allows a fish to arrive in a temporary container and still be recorded in the database. Moreover, the fish can go back into the temporary container at any time and still remain in the database. The automatic-fixed combination reflects a more rigid view of the `Represents` network set. You don't want unclassified fish in the database, and you don't want a fish to change its classification. A fish can't change its species as simply as it can change its home tank. The distinction is in the nature of the application reality, and you can reflect the difference in the network set descriptions. Finally, the `Experiences` network set specifies automatic-mandatory. Each event happens to a single fish, and it isn't possible to have an event without a subject fish. Therefore, the automatic insertion clause is appropriate. Fixed retention would be equally appropriate because an event that happens to one fish should never be transferred to the chain of a different fish. However, mandatory retention facilitates error correction. If you mistakenly attribute an event to the wrong fish, you can reconnect it to the correct fish. If the retention is fixed, you have to delete the event and recreate it. Because the enote field is 100 characters long, event creation is tedious.

The retention clause controls the disconnection of a dependent record from a chain. The fixed alternative forbids disconnection, but the mandatory choice allows disconnection if followed by an immediate reconnection to another chain. Optional retention allows disconnection without further conditions.

Integrity considerations: the set-selection and check-clauses

The set-selection clause specifies how the DBMS should identify the correct chain when it must connect a newly created record. The simplest alternative is "set selection is by application," which is the default route if the schema doesn't specify a set-selection clause. "Set selection is by application" implies that previous processing activity has left a current chain, and the DBMS chooses that chain to receive the new member. The current chain is the one that was most recently involved in a database activity. A later section will detail how to make a particular chain the current one.

A second alternative is "set selection is by value of *<field name>* in *<dominant record type name>*," which requires that a value in the named field must uniquely identify a dominant record. Suppose you change the species record type and the Represents network set definitions to the following.

```
record species.                          network set Represents.
   duplicates are not allowed for sname.     owner is species.
      field sname is character 20.              order is sorted by defined keys.
      field sfood is character 20.           member is fish.
                                                insertion is automatic.
                                                retention is fixed.
                                                key is ascending fname.
                                                set selection is by value of sname in species.
```

The DBMS can now locate the proper chain by finding the species record with an sname field matching the one currently installed in the species memory structure. Because each species record owns exactly one Represents chain, locating the species owner identifies the corresponding network set instance. Because species has no key, this example assumes that the sname attribute is unique across species records. If this assumption isn't justified, you have encountered one of the cases where you need a key in the record type even though it isn't strictly necessary to maintain the relationships. To illustrate the set-selection concept here, assume that sname is a unique attribute across species records.

Suppose the program must connect a newly created fish to the chain originating from the shark species. Because the Represents network set specifies an automatic insertion clause, the DBMS will perform the chain connection when it stores the new fish. The code then appears as follows.

```
        ⋮
    strcpy (species.sname, "shark"); /* get proper value into template */

        ⋮ /* intervening activity that loses currency of Represents */
    strcpy (fish.fname, "newboy");
    strcpy (fish.fcolor, "green");
    $store fish;

        ⋮
```

After you copy the string **shark** into the species memory template, subsequent processing may move the currency pointer away from the chain associated with that species. However, when the `store` command creates a new fish, the DBMS uses the set-selection clause of the `Represents` network set to reacquire the shark chain before connecting the new fish to it.

The analysis above argues that you may want to reinstate the sno attribute in the species record type if sname isn't unique, and if you want to use the set-selection alternative just described. The final set-selection possibility, illustrated below, not only argues for reinstating the sno attribute in the species record type but also for including it in the fish record type. Suppose you change the `tank`, `fish`, and `Represents` portions of the schema to the following.

```
record species.                          network set Represents.
    duplicates are not allowed for sno.       owner is species.
        field sno is character 5.                 order is sorted by defined keys.
        field sname is character 20.          member is fish.
        field sfood is character 20.              insertion is automatic.
record fish.                                      retention is fixed.
    field fname is character 20.                  key is ascending fname.
    field fcolor is character 10.                 set selection is structural
    field sno is character 5.                         sno in fish = sno in species.
```

Note the clause: "set selection is structural—sno in fish = sno in species." Now you must include an sno attribute in each fish to identify its classifying species because the DBMS matches sno values in the species and fish records to identify the proper `Represents` chain. This method, however, doesn't require you to place a search value in the species memory template to locate the proper chain. The code for storing a new fish and automatically connecting it to the proper chain now shortens to the excerpt below.

```
                ⋮
        strcpy (fish.fname, "newboy");
        strcpy (fish.fcolor, "green");
        strcpy (fish.sno, "22");
        $store fish;

                ⋮
```

When the store command creates the new fish instance, the DBMS initiates a search for the unique species record with a sno value equal to that of the new fish. The Represents chain of that species gets the new fish.

Any of these set-selection mechanisms can fail to locate a chain. If the set selection is by application, but no previous activity has established a current chain, the operation fails. If the set selection specifies a search for an owner record with certain field values, and no such record exists, the operation fails. If the set selection launches a search for an owner record that matches some field in the dependent record but finds no such match, the operation fails. In these cases, the DBMS can't connect the new dependent record to a chain. Consequently, it refuses to store the record at all. The DBMS reports the failure back to the program as a non-zero dbStatus return code.

The set-selection clause determines how the DBMS identifies a particular chain when it must connect a new dependent record. By default, the current chain receives the new member; other methods launch a search through the available chains, seeking to satisfy some matching fields.

The final clause under the member portion of a network set definition is an optional constraint check. It takes the form: check is <field name> in <dependent record type name> = <field name> in <dominant record type name>. The format of this clause is the same as the last set-selection option. It requires that primary and foreign keys appear in the dominant and dependent record types. Then, regardless of the method of set selection, an attempt to connect a dependent record to a chain will fail if the corresponding values don't match. Of course, if the schema specifies a structural set selection with the same condition, the operation will certainly succeed if the appropriate chain exists. But if the schema uses a different set-selection method, by application for example, the DBMS may find the chain, but the connection can still fail. Failure occurs if the chain's owner doesn't contain a matching value in the specified field. So the check-clause is a constraint that keeps the program from placing dependent records on the wrong chain.

The check-clause prevents the connection of inappropriate dependent records to the wrong chain. A successful connection must match certain fields in the dominant and dependent records.

Cycles in the owner-coupled network sets aren't allowed. In other words, a network set can't specify the same record type for both member and owner. Nor can the member record type serve as the owner of another network set whose member cycles back to the owner of the original set, and so forth. Stated differently, suppose you construct a graph with the record types as nodes. You draw an arc from node A to node B if there is a set with owner A and member B. This is the owner-member graph, and it can contain no cycles.

Network Data Manipulation Language (DML)

Currency pointers

The previous section discussed the network Data Definition Language (DDL), which you use to write a network schema. This section describes the Data Manipulation Language (DML), which you use to manipulate the data in a network database. You must understand the DML commands in the context of currency pointers. The DBMS maintains a collection of currency pointers on behalf of each interfacing program. At any given time, each pointer is either null, or it points to a particular *record*. Even though certain currency pointers are associated with network sets, remember that the pointer actually references some record of the network set.

The DBMS maintains a currency pointer for each record type of the schema. The aquarium example has a current of tank, a current of species, a current of fish, and a current of event. These pointers are all null when an interfacing program begins operation. As processing continues, the current of <record type> usually points to the last record of the given type that has been accessed. However, the DBMS may reset a currency pointer to null, for example, after a record deletion. The explanation of each manipulation command will indicate when it changes the current of some record type. For example, the excerpt below first establishes a current of tank record and then establishes a current of fish record. The currency pointers for different record types are independent. When the current of fish changes to the new record accessed by the second command, the previously established current of tank remains pointing to the tank that was located earlier.

```
$find first tank;
$find first fish;
      .
      .
      .
```

The DBMS also maintains a currency pointer for each network set, which points to the last record accessed on a chain of the set. It may point to the owner record, or it may point to one of the member records. In any case, it unambiguously identifies a particular chain in the network set. The aquarium example has a current of Inhabits, a current of Represents, and a current of Experiences. It also has a currency pointer for each of the system network sets—a current of speciesAlpha, tankAlpha, and fishAlpha.

A command doesn't have to refer to a network set to affect its currency pointer. The command, $find first tank, not only establishes a particular tank as the current of tank, it also establishes that same record as the current of Inhabits and the current of tankAlpha. A subsequent command, $find first fish, then changes the current of Inhabits to point to the fish that was accessed. This may or may not involve a new chain. If the fish is a member of the same chain as the previously accessed tank, the current chain remains the same. If the fish is a member of a different chain, that new chain becomes current. In either case, the current of Inhabits now points to a fish record. The current of tank and the current of tankAlpha remain unchanged.

Finally, the DBMS maintains a current of run-unit, which points to the last record of any type that has been accessed by the program. The phrase "current of program" could be used, but several versions of the same program might be running simultaneously. In that case, the DBMS maintains a separate collection of currency pointers for each copy.

Current of run-unit is thus more descriptive. The current of run-unit is an important concept because many processing activities don't specify a target record. Instead, the DBMS acts on the current of run-unit.

 The network DBMS maintains a collection of currency pointers for each interfacing program. It has a currency indicator for each record type, for each network set, and for the program as a whole.

Navigating among records

The find command has three forms:

1. find *<record type name>* owner within *<network set name>*;

2. find $\left\{ \begin{array}{l} \text{first} \\ \text{last} \\ \text{next} \\ \text{prior} \end{array} \right\}$ *<record type name>* [within *<network set name>*] [using *<field list>*];

3. find current of *<record type name>*;

The first form locates the dominant record entry on the chain identified by the currency pointer of the specified network set. Consider, for example, the following command.

$find species owner within Represents;

The command fails if the current of Represents is null. Otherwise, the DBMS identifies a particular Represents chain (i.e., the target chain) with the currency pointer. The pointer itself may refer to one of the many fish records or to the single species record. The command changes the following currency pointers, if necessary, to point to the species record of the target chain: current of species, current of Represents, current of speciesAlpha, and current of run-unit. All other currency pointers remain unchanged.

The second find-command format describes a variety of alternatives. The two optional phrases are the within-clause and the using-clause. If both are omitted, the remaining syntax provides the method for sequencing through the records of some specified record type, but in no predictable order. The code excerpt on the left below locates some tank record with the priming command $find first tank; it then locates other tank records with the $find next tank command. The DBMS guarantees that the records located with successive $find next calls will be distinct from those returned by earlier calls.

```
$find first tank;
while (dbStatus == 0) {
    .
    .       /* process tank */
    $find next tank; }
```

```
$find last tank;
while (dbStatus == 0) {
    .
    .       /* process tank */
    $find prior tank; }
```

When you locate a tank in this way, the DBMS updates the current of tank to the new tank. It also adjusts the current of `Inhabits`, `tankAlpha`, and run-unit to point to the new tank. When a `find` command fails, all currency pointers remain unchanged. When the loop above receives the last tank, a subsequent `find next tank` returns a non-zero `dbStatus` value.

The alternative processing order, shown in the parallel code on the right, achieves the same result. The `$find last` command locates some record in an unpredictable way, and subsequent `$find prior` commands return the rest of the records. Therefore, the `first-last` modifiers aren't really meaningful in the absence of a within-clause. The syntax allows a first-to-last or last-to-first choice to remain compatible with the `find ... within ...` formats, which do exploit ordering in the database. When an order is meaningful, the program can choose to process from first to last or from last to first, as defined by that order.

In the absence of a within-clause, either the `find first-next` or the `find last-prior` command returns the records as ordered in an internal table. That order isn't predictable from a programming standpoint because you can control record placement only on the chains and not in the tables. You must be careful not to move the currency pointer between `find next-prior` commands because the DBMS uses the currency pointer to give meaning to the term *next* or *prior*.

If you include a within-clause, the DBMS limits processing to the member records on some chain of the specified network set. Which chain? The DBMS uses the target chain identified by the network set currency pointer. An error occurs if the specified <*record type name*> isn't the dependent record type of the <*network set name*>. An error also occurs if no target chain is current. The modifiers—first, next, last, or prior—refer to positions along the target chain. For "next" or "prior," the current of the network set must point to one of the member records. The DBMS interprets "next" or "prior" with respect to that current member record. If the schema specifies "order is sorted by defined keys," this find-command format returns the records in that order. If the network set is a system set, this method returns the records according to a global index. If the network set is owner-coupled, the returned sequence includes only the member records of the specific target chain.

If you specify the using-clause, either with or without the within-clause, the DBMS limits the processing to records that match search values previously installed in the memory template of the specified record type. For example, the following code traverses a subset of the species member records on the single `speciesAlpha` chain. It considers only those species that have an sfood worms. The mechanism behaves as if the species having other sfood values weren't on the chain. In particular, the `$find first ...` command stops, not on the first species record of the chain, but on the first one that has an sfood value of worms. The `$find next ...` behaves similarly.

```
strcpy (species.sfood, "worms");
$find first species within speciesAlpha using sfood;
while (dbStatus == 0) {
  :
        /* get species into memory and process as desired */
  $find next species within speciesAlpha using sfood; }
```

When you locate a record with any of the find commands, the DBMS adjusts several currency pointers. After the operation, the current of the specified record type points to the new record. The current of any network set where the new record participates also points to the new record. The current of run-unit points to the newly accessed record. If the record is a candidate for inclusion on some network set chain but isn't currently on any such chain, then the current of that network set becomes null. For example, the schema requires that a fish be on some Represents chain, but not necessarily on an Inhabits chain. Therefore, a successful find ... fish ... always updates the current of fish, Represents, and run-unit. But if the accessed fish isn't currently on an Inhabits chain, the current of Inhabits becomes null.

Most of the time, the new currencies are exactly what the interfacing program requires to carry out subsequent actions. Occasionally you must suppress some of the currency pointer updates. For this purpose, you can add another clause to any of the find-command formats—the retain currency clause. The retain currency clause specifies a list of network sets whose currency pointers are to remain unchanged as a result of the find operation. However, the DBMS always updates the current of run-unit to reflect the new record, and it also unconditionally updates the current of the affected record type.

Suppose you are traversing a Represents chain, and you want to make a detour along an intersecting Inhabits chain. Figure 11.8 illustrates this situation. The solid lines are Represents chains; the dashed line is an Inhabits chain. You have stepped out to the first fish on the upper Represents chain to the fish marked X. You intend to systematically visit each fish on the chain. However, while you are paused at Fish X, you decide to investigate another fish on the same Inhabits chain as Fish X. You advance to Fish Y in Figure 11.8. After processing that fish, you now want to resume your journey along the original Represents chain. But in the process of locating Fish Y, the DBMS shifted the current of Represents to the lower chain, in particular to Fish Y on the lower chain. Therefore, a find next fish within Represents will locate Fish Y', instead of Fish X' as desired. When you moved off the upper Represents chain, you should have suppressed the update of the Represents currency pointer.

This situation occurs in solving the query: find the names of fish swimming with a shark. The correct code appears below. A retain-currency clause suppresses an inappropriate update of the current of Represents.

```
strcpy (species.sname, "shark");
$find first species within speciesAlpha using sname;
while (dbStatus == 0) {
    $find first fish within Represents;
    while (dbStatus == 0) {
        $find first fish within Inhabits retain currency for Represents;
        while (dbStatus == 0) {
            $get fish;
            printf("%s\n", fish.fname);
            $find next fish within Inhabits retain currency for Represents; }
        $find next fish within Represents; }
    $find next species within speciesAlpha using sname; }
```

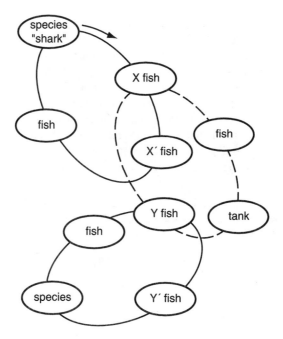

Figure 11.8 Currency hazards associated with intersecting chains

The outermost loop sequences species with an sname value of **shark**. You don't need to worry about accessing a different species record inside the outermost loop. Because the nested activity acquires only fish records, it doesn't affect the current of `speciesAlpha`. For each species of the outermost loop, the nested loop sequences across the fish on its `Represents` chain. For each such fish, the innermost loop sequences across the fish of the intersecting `Inhabits` chain. However, the `find` commands for this last activity specifically request that the `Represents` currency pointer not be updated. Consequently, the proper fish of the outermost shark species remains current when the innermost loop terminates. This allows a subsequent `find next` ... to continue traversing the `Represents` chain.

An earlier query also navigated across intersecting chains to find the names of species swimming in cesspool tanks. Why didn't it encounter currency problems? The code was:

```
$find first tank;
while (dbStatus == 0) {
    $get tank;
    if (strcmp(tank.tname, "cesspool") == 0) {
        $find first fish within Inhabits;
        while (dbStatus == 0) {
            $find species owner within Represents;
            $get species;
            printf("%s\n", species.sname);
            $find next fish within Inhabits; } }
    $find next tank; }
```

The innermost activity finds the owner of the intersecting chain directly, without first accessing any of the intervening fish records. The currency pointer of the Inhabits network set, being traversed in the next outer loop, isn't changed. When the DBMS locates the owning species, it updates the current of species, the current of Represents (same chain, different record), and the current of run-unit. However, it doesn't touch the current of Inhabits because species records don't participate in the Inhabits network set.

You use the third find-command format to update the current of run-unit to the record that is current through some record type. Suppose you located a certain tank, but subsequent processing moved the current of run-unit to another record. The following code illustrates how to reestablish the tank as the current of run-unit.

```
strcpy (tank.tname, "cesspool");
$find first tank using tname;
    :              /* processing moves current of run-unit, but not current of tank */
$find current of tank;
```

With the find command, you can sequence through the records of a specified record type in an unordered manner or in the order given by a network set. Unless the find command specifically suppresses an update, the DBMS adjusts the currency pointers automatically as it locates the records.

Although you can access records in many ways with the find command, the information remains in the database unless you issue a get command to retrieve it into the memory buffer. The get command always retrieves the current of run-unit, so it isn't strictly necessary to specify the record type. If the record type is specified, and the current of run-unit is a record of a different type, the DBMS reports an error. Therefore, you should specify the record type, both to trap the potential error and to make the program more readable. The simple format is: $get [<*record type name*>]. The examples to this point have illustrated its use.

Record insertions, updates, and deletions

When you want to store a record, you first establish its attribute values in its memory template. You then invoke the store command. For example, you can create a new tank with the code excerpt on the left below. When the DBMS successfully stores a record, it updates the current of run-unit and the current of the record type to point to the new record. If the DBMS automatically inserts the new record into one or more network sets, it also updates the currency pointers of those network sets. If the record type of the new record serves as the member of a network set with manual insertion, the current of that network set becomes null because the record isn't placed on any chain of the set.

```
strcpy (tank.tname, "fatVat");        strcpy (tank.tname, "cesspool");
strcpy (tank.tcolor, "blue");         $find first tank using tname;
strcpy (tank.tvolume, "99999");       while (dbStatus == 0) {
$store tank;                              $get tank;
if (dbStatus != 0) {                      strcpy (tank.tcolor, "blue");
   /* error processing activity */        $modify tank;
   }                                      $find next tank using tname; }
```

You can modify an existing record in a similar fashion, except that the record type specifier is optional with the modify command. The command always acts on the current of run-unit. As with the get command, you should specify the record type to trap errors and to document the program. The code segment on the right above changes the color of all cesspool tanks to blue.

Deleting records is more complicated because the erase command customizes its behavior to the retention clauses in the network sets affected by the deletion. The erase command always operates on the current of run-unit, so it isn't strictly necessary to specify the record type. But, as before, the practice is recommended. The format follows.

$erase [all] [<*record type name*>];

The alternative with the optional "all" modifier is easiest to explain. The current of run-unit is the target record. If it participates as a member in any network sets, the DBMS disconnects it from the chains. If it participates as an owner in a network set, the DBMS recursively deletes all the dependent records on its chain. Finally, the DBMS removes the record itself from its record type table. Because the owner-member graph contains no cycles, the recursive deletion operation can't again encounter the same record type that was originally under deletion.

In the aquarium example, the command $erase all tank proceeds as follows. The DBMS checks that the current of run-unit is a tank record. If it isn't, the DBMS reports an error and terminates the operation. Otherwise, the DBMS probes the target tank's dependent records on any network set chains. Because the tank owns a chain in the Inhabits network set, the DBMS recursively executes a delete operation on each fish of that chain. In other words, it performs an erase all fish command against each fish on the chain, but without requiring them to sequence through the current of run-unit. The current of run-unit remains pointing to the original target tank. When deleting a fish, the DBMS discovers that it owns an Experiences chain. So before it deletes the fish, the DBMS directs an erase all event to each event on the fish's Experiences chain. Because the events are leaf nodes in the owner-member graph, the DBMS can delete them without further complications. The owning fish is then deleted, and after all such fish are gone, the owning tank is deleted.

The current of run-unit, the current of tank, and the current of Inhabits all become null because their referenced record has vanished. If the current of fish was pointing to one of the deleted fish, the current of fish becomes null. If the current of Represents was pointing to one of the deleted fish, it also becomes null. If the current of Experiences was pointing to one of the deleted fish, it becomes null. Finally, if the current of event was pointing to one of the deleted events, it becomes null. In short, an erase command has recursive consequences: records other than the target can also be deleted. When a record is directly or indirectly deleted, the DBMS adjusts any currency pointers referencing it to null.

 An erase all *command deletes the current of run-unit, and it recursively executes an* erase all *against all members of any chains owned by the target record. Any currency pointers referencing deleted records become null.*

The deletion process draws a careful distinction between two cases: (1) the target record is a dependent record on some chain, and (2) it is the dominant record of a chain. In the former case, the DBMS disconnects the target record before its deletion, but other records on the chain remain unaffected. However, if the target record is the dominant record of a chain, the DBMS recursively deletes all other records on the chain before deleting the target itself.

If the "all" modifier isn't present, the process is slightly different. Again a recursive situation exists when the target record participates as the dominant record on one or more chains. However, instead of recursively deleting the dependent records, the erase operation may fail, either directly with the target record or with one of the dependent records encountered in the recursive activity. Therefore, the DBMS first conducts a rehearsal, marking certain records for deletion. But the marked records aren't actually deleted, pending the completion of recursive attempts to delete related records. If the rehearsal encounters a failure at any point in the exercise, the DBMS removes all the deletion marks, leaves the database unchanged, and reports the failure to the controlling program with a non-zero dbStatus return code. If the rehearsal completes successfully, the DBMS disconnects all the marked records from their chains and removes them from the database.

The rehearsal examines each chain owned by the target record—one for each owner-coupled network set that specifies the target's record type as the owner. Each chain has the potential to abort the deletion operation. Therefore, the DBMS terminates the rehearsal as soon as it encounters a failing chain. This procedure is the "owner chain test" for the target record. A loop iterates through the chains until it finds a failing chain or until it has investigated all the chains owned by the target. Within the loop, the DBMS tests the chain as follows. If the chain contains no dependent records, it passes the test. Otherwise, the DBMS looks at the retention clause of the network set. If the retention is optional, the DBMS marks all the dependent records for free-floating, and the chain passes the test. If the rehearsal completes successfully, these records will be removed from the chain and free-floated in the database, not connected to any chain of the network set. If the retention is mandatory, the chain fails the test, and the DBMS terminates the rehearsal. If the retention is fixed, the DBMS marks each dependent record on the chain for deletion, and it recursively applies the owner chain test to each dependent record. If the test succeeds for all the dependent records, the chain passes the test.

Because the owner-member graph contains no cycles, this process must eventually terminate successfully with records that own no chains, successfully with records owning only chains with optional retention clauses, or unsuccessfully with a record owning a chain with a mandatory retention clause. A failure removes all marks and reports an exception to the program. A termination at the leaf nodes of the owner-member graph succeeds by deleting or free-floating all records so marked. The idea is that the demise of a record must be accompanied by the demise of all its fixed dependents at all levels beneath it and the free-floating of all its optional dependents. If it has mandatory dependents at any level beneath it, the operation fails. It fails because a mandatory dependent must be shifted to another chain when its dominant record (and therefore its current chain) is removed. The DBMS requires that the interfacing program specifically address the reconnection before issuing the erase command.

In the aquarium example, the command erase tank can't fail because Inhabits is the only network set that specifies the tank record type as the owner, and the retention clause of Inhabits is optional. Therefore, if the target tank holds any fish, the DBMS free-floats them in the database, unconnected to any tank chain, and then deletes the tank. The command erase species, however, can fail. In the recursive rehearsal, the DBMS marks for deletion each fish on the Represents chain of the target species. It then subjects each fish to a chain probe. Each fish owns an Experiences chain, possibly containing event records. Because the retention clause of the Experiences network set is mandatory, a non-empty chain causes a failure.

The command erase fish can fail for the same reason because the target fish may possess a populated Experiences chain. But if its Experiences chain is empty, the DBMS deletes the fish without consulting the Inhabits or Represents network sets. The fish participates in these latter sets as a member, rather than as an owner. The DBMS simply disconnects the fish from the chains before deleting it. An erase event command always succeeds because event records are in the leaf nodes of the owner-member graph. They own no chains because they don't participate as owner in any network sets.

Connecting of records to network sets

The last category of commands manipulates the network sets. It includes the connect, disconnect, and reconnect commands. With these commands, the target record must be the current of run-unit. You use connect to place a dependent record on a chain of a specified network set. It's applicable only if the target record isn't currently on some chain. So you use this command for a newly created record whose record type is the member of a network set with a manual insertion clause. You also use it for a record that was previously on a chain but has been taken off with the disconnect command. This is possible only if the retention clause of the network set is optional.

In the aquarium example, the Inhabits network set specifies manual insertion and optional retention, so you can use the connect and disconnect commands to move fish records on and off tank chains. The following code excerpt creates a fish and connects it to the Inhabits chain identified by the current of Inhabits. Later, the code relocates the fish. For simplicity, assume that fname and tname are unique identifiers, which you can use to bring the fish and its new Inhabits chain into currency at the time of the relocation. You make another Inhabits chain current by locating the tank record with tname cesspool. The subsequent connect command now places the fish on the cesspool chain.

```
strcpy (fish.fname, "salty");
strcpy (fish.fcolor, "gray");
$store fish;            /* salty fish is now current of run-unit */
$connect fish to Inhabits;

       :              /* intervening processing */
strcpy (fish.fname, "salty");
$find first fish using fname;
$disconnect fish from Inhabits;
strcpy (tank.tname, "cesspool");
$find first tank using tname;
$find current of fish;            /* make salty fish the current of run-unit */
$connect fish to Inhabits;
```

You can also use a connect to place a dependent record on a chain with fixed retention, but you can't subsequently remove the record. Typically, you use fixed retention with automatic insertion, so that neither the connect nor the disconnect command is applicable. When they do apply, the connect operation updates the current of the affected network set to the dependent record just inserted. The disconnect command sets the currency pointer to null.

The reconnect command exists specifically to deal with dependent records on chains with mandatory retention. In this case, you can remove a dependent record from a chain, but you must immediately place it on another chain of the same network set. Moreover, these two operations must proceed as one indivisible transaction: the controlling program must not be allowed to exploit the interval between them. The program issues the reconnect command, and when control returns to the program, the chain transfer is complete. You can also use the reconnect command to transfer a dependent record between two chains in a network set with optional retention. In this case, however, the indivisibility of the transaction is simply a convenience because the program could be exposed to the interval between the disconnection and the reconnection without viewing an invalid database state.

A reconnection operation, however, has some subtle difficulties. First, the DBMS must now identify *two* chains. The chain where the target record now exists is simple enough to find, but how does the DBMS locate the new chain? When it makes the target record the current of run-unit, the DBMS also adjusts the current of the network set to the target record, which identifies the *old* chain—the one from which the target will be disconnected. In order to force the current of the network set to point to a different chain, you first establish the currency of the new chain and then use a retain-currency clause to hold it when the DBMS acquires the target record as the current of run-unit. The following code illustrates the technique used to move a fish from one tank chain to another. The object here is to move all the fish from the lagoon tank to the cesspool tank. Assume that the database contains only one lagoon and one cesspool tank.

```
strcpy (tank.tname, "lagoon");
$find first tank using tname;
$find first fish within Inhabits;
while (dbStatus == 0) {
    strcpy (tank.tname, "cesspool");
    $find first tank using tname;        /* new chain is current */
    $find current of fish retain currency of Inhabits;       /* fish to CRU */
    $get fish;      /* establish new check fields if needed */
    $reconnect fish within Inhabits;
    strcpy (tank.tname, "lagoon");
    $find first tank using tname;
    $find first fish within Inhabits; }
```

You continually reestablish the lagoon chain to locate subsequent fish for transfer, and you always issue a find first to get the next fish. The DBMS has already transferred the previous fish to the new chain, so a find next or find prior will discover no context for judging the next or prior member of the chain. When the loop has transferred all the lagoon fish, the find first will return a non-zero dbStatus. The reconnect operation places null in the currency pointer of the source chain, and it updates the currency pointer of the destination chain to the record just inserted.

A second subtlety associated with a reconnection is that a check-clause in the schema may require that certain fields in the dependent record match values in the dominant record. If the dependent record is now compatible with its present chain, it's likely to be incompatible with its destination chain. Moreover, you can't change the fields of the dependent record to match the intended destination because that would violate the check-clause of the present chain. Therefore, assume that a reconnect simultaneously stores the template for the dependent record, which can contain the proper context for the destination chain. Because the aquarium schema doesn't specify check-clauses, this dilemma doesn't arise. Nevertheless, the code above retrieves the fish record into the program template because the subsequent reconnect will store that template in the process of transferring the record from one chain to another.

The get, modify, erase, connect, disconnect, *and* reconnect *commands all operate on the current of run-unit. When a network set is involved in the operation, the currency pointers usually provide the proper context. Sometimes, however, you must use the retain-currency clause.*

Relationships

A relationship is a meaningful association among application entities. The degree of the relationship is the number of application entities involved, and an instance of the relationship is a grouping of application objects drawn from the participating entities. Restated in network terminology, a relationship is a meaningful association among record types. The degree is the number of record types involved, and an instance of the relationship is a grouping of records drawn from the participating record types.

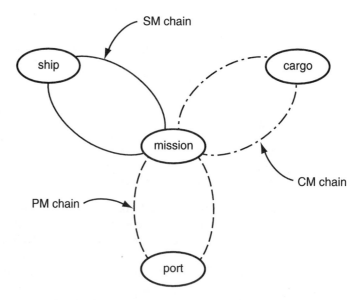

Figure 11.9 The ship-cargo-port ternary relationship in a network database

Network databases express relationships with owner-coupled network sets. Each set represents a binary one-to-many relationship between the owner record type and the member record type. You construct an owner-member graph with directed arcs from owner record types to member record types. The owner-member graph may contain no cycles. Working within these constraints, this section will show how the network model handles many-to-many, higher-degree, and recursive relationships.

The network model accommodates many-to-many binary relationships in much the same manner as the relational model—with an intersection entity and two one-to-many relationships. For example, the relationship between species and tank is many-to-many; the standard decomposition introduces the intersection entity, fish, and two one-to-many relationships: tank-to-fish and species-to-fish. The network schema uses the owner-coupled network sets Inhabits and Represents to express the derived relationships.

Higher-degree relationships

The network model handles higher-degree relationships with similar decompositions. Consider again the ternary relationship between ship, cargo, and port. In each of the relational, object-oriented, and deductive models, the optimal solution involved a new entity and three new one-to-many relationships. Using "mission" to refer to the new entity, Figure 11.9 shows this solution in the network model.

The solution introduces three network sets, with owner record types ship, cargo, and port respectively. The member record type in all cases is mission. A particular mission record is on one chain of each network set, and that intersection carries precisely the information that a given ship called at a given port carrying a given cargo. Recall the troublesome example where the ship Enterprise has not carried beans to Boston, but three

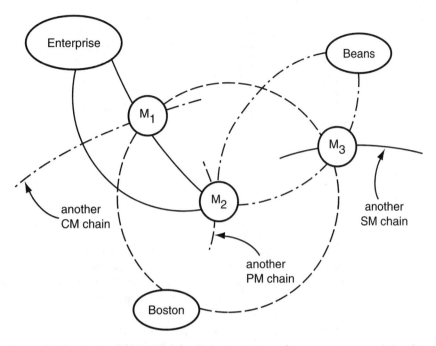

Figure 11.10 Distinguishing a set of pairwise associations from a true ternary relationship

somewhat related activities have occurred: the Enterprise has carried beans to some port, the Enterprise has called at Boston with some cargo, and some ship has carried beans to Boston. The misleading scenario circuitously suggests that the Enterprise has carried beans to Boston when, in fact, it hasn't. In this case, a mission record exists simultaneously on the Enterprise and beans chains, but that record isn't on the Boston chain. Instead, it's on the chain originating from some other port. A similar argument holds for the other two missions. Each is missing one of the specific trio: Enterprise, beans, or Boston. Figure 11.10 illustrates the misleading scenario.

The code excerpt on the left below tabulates the triples (ship, cargo, port) corresponding to the true ternary relationship. The three network sets are SM, CM, and PM, with owners ship, cargo, and port respectively. The member in all cases is mission. In the misleading scenario, the triple (Enterprise, beans, Boston) doesn't appear because no mission record is simultaneously on the three chains emanating from the Enterprise, beans, and Boston records. Therefore, the solution of Figure 11.9 correctly distinguishes between the misleading scenario and a true mission in which the Enterprise carries beans to Boston.

```
$find first mission;                    $find first shipment;
while (dbStatus == 0) {                 while (dbStatus == 0) {
   $find ship owner within SM;             $find ship owner within carries;
   $get ship;                              $get ship;
   $find cargo owner within CM;            $find cargo owner within isCarried;
   $get cargo;                             $get cargo;
   $find port owner within PM;             $find first docking within callsOn;
   $get port;                              while (dbStatus == 0) {
   print("%s,%s,%s\n", ship.sname,            $find port owner within hosts;
      cargo.cname, port.pname);               $get port;
   $find next mission; }                      printf("%s,%s,%s\n", ship.sname,
                                                 cargo.cname, port.pname);
                                              $find next docking within callsOn; }
                                           $find next shipment; }
```

If you attempt a pairwise decomposition, you encounter three new record types and six new network sets, as shown in Figure 11.11. Because the number of record types and network sets has become much larger, the figure uses the entity-relationship notation. Suppose you now look for triples (ship, cargo, port), where the ship has carried the cargo, the ship has called at the port, and the port has received the cargo. Although you can retrieve these triples from the diagram of Figure 11.11, they have an ambiguous interpretation. (Enterprise, beans, Boston) appears if the Enterprise has carried beans to Boston, or if the Enterprise hasn't carried beans to Boston but the three related activities have occurred, or both. A code excerpt for assembling the triples is on the right above. Consequently, you can conclude yet again that this pairwise decomposition isn't equivalent to the original ternary relationship.

So you represent higher-degree relationships in the network model with multiple owner-coupled sets. A relationship of degree n among the record types $R_1, R_2, \ldots, R_n$ gives rise to new record type S and n network sets. Each R_i is the owner of one of the network sets; the new record type S is the member element in all of them. An instance of the n-ary relationship is an n-tuple, $(r_1, r_2, \ldots, r_n)$, where each r_i is a record of type R_i. The tabulation of all these instances is a tabulation of the records of the newly created S record type. Of course, the network model doesn't allow other records to be stored in the fields of S, but you can remove them after you have placed the records on the correct chains. None of these fields is a descriptive attribute of an S record. Instead, each field merely identifies a chain where the record should reside. The S record doesn't need to have any descriptive fields whatsoever. However, after you create the new record type, you usually discover that it serves a meaningful purpose in the application. You then add descriptive fields to flesh out that purpose. In the ship-cargo-port example, the new record type is mission. In addition to containing pointers that place it on particular SM, CM, and PM chains, a mission record can also contain descriptive information about the mission, such as a mission date or a bill-of-lading number.

The chain from a particular $r \in R_i$ passes through all records in the tabulation having the value r under the R_i column in the S tabulation. After populating all the chains in this manner, you can remove the records indicating the chain sources from the S tabulation. This leaves empty records, whose only purpose is to link the dominant records of the network sets. In the ship-cargo-port example, each record of the newly created mission record type

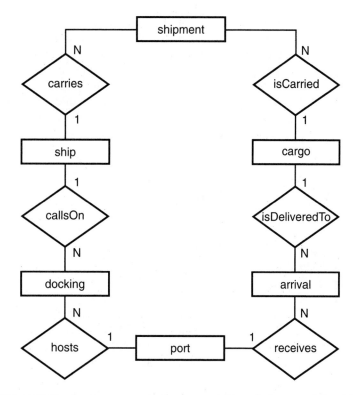

Figure 11.11   An erroneous pairwise decomposition of a ternary relationship

initially contains ship, cargo, and port fields. The field values guide the record onto the corresponding ship, cargo, and port chains, and then they are redundant.

The network model expresses a relationship of degree n with n owner-coupled network sets. Each set involves one of the participating relationship record types as the owner and the newly created intersection record type as the member.

One-to-many recursive relationships

Recursive relationships require some ingenuity because the owner-member graph doesn't allow cycles. Therefore, you express recursive relationships by creating multiple copies of certain record types, although the clones need not contain all the fields of the original. Consider again the employee database of Chapter 5. As a relational database, this example consists of a single table, as shown on the left below. The sno attribute identifies the supervisor (eno) of a given employee. Because the supervisor is also an employee, she appears in the same table with the supervised workers. Even though the relationship is one-to-many, a network schema can't express it directly. That would require a network set with identical owner and member record types, which would produce an immediate cycle in the owner-member graph. Instead you create a new record type, supervisor, whose records are mirror images of the employee records. In truth, the supervisor records can be empty because each supervisor record will be tightly paired with exactly one employee record. The network set clones accomplishes this pairing. It has supervisor as the owner and employee as the member. Each supervisor originates a clones chain, which loops through a single dependent employee record—the employee that cloned the supervisor. This network set has nothing to do with the supervisory relationship. Each employee appears on a unique clones chain and serves to flesh out the details of those few employees who are actually supervisors.

Employee		
eno	ename	sno
53	albert	14
42	bernice	14
86	candice	53
45	dennis	
14	frank	45

```
schema personnel.

record employee.
    field ename is character 20.

record supervisor.

network set clones.
    owner is supervisor.
    member is employee.
        insertion is automatic.
        retention is fixed.
```

```
network set supervises.
    owner is supervisor.
        order is sorted by defined keys.
    member is employee.
        insertion is manual.
        retention is optional.
        key is ascending ename.
```

You now express the actual supervisory relationship with a second owner-coupled network set, supervises, again with owner supervisor and member employee. Because both network sets have owner supervisor and member employee, no cycle appears in the owner-member graph. Figure 11.12 illustrates this situation, using dashed lines for clones chains and solid lines for supervises chains. The network schema appears on the right above.

Suppose you want the names of employees reporting to frank, either directly or indirectly through a sequence of intermediary supervisors. You locate Employee frank and then navigate along the clones chain to the mirror-image supervisor record. You then switch to the supervises chain and follow it to the bernice record. You dutifully report bernice as part of the answer. However, you now want to recursively pursue the employees that report to bernice (a depth-first search) before continuing on the supervises chain to albert. So you need to invoke some recursive activity on each member of the supervises chain. But you must do this without losing currency on the chain because you must be able to continue with the next member when the recursive activity completes. Will the currency pointers cooperate?

Arriving at bernice, you are on supervises chain X in Figure 11.12. To pursue the workers under bernice, you follow the clones chain through bernice to the mirror supervisor record. The current of supervises switches to chain Y in the figure. You quickly traverse this chain, discovering that bernice has no employees under her. The recursive activity on bernice is now complete, and you are ready to continue with the next record on the original supervises chain X. However, a find next ... command will return an error condition because the current chain is Y, not X. Moreover, the Y chain is empty, presenting no context for determining a "next" record. You can't suppress the currency update for supervises because you really must switch to the new supervises chain to probe the employees reporting to bernice.

You can solve this problem in several ways. When you have finished probing the workers under bernice, you can locate the supervisor owner of the supervises chain

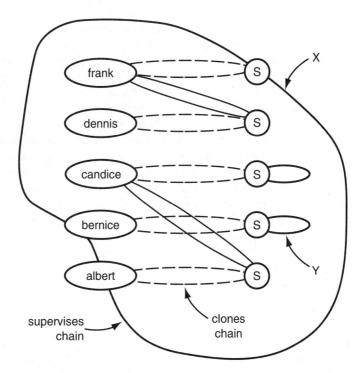

Figure 11.12   Managing recursive relationships with auxiliary network sets

associated with bernice. You can then find the first (and only) employee on its `clones` chain, which establishes bernice again as the current of `supervises` and identifies the chain X. This solution appears as the recursive routine on the left below. You launch the actual query with the excerpt on the right.

```
void worksUnder () {
     /* assumes employee is current */
$find supervisor owner within clones;
$find first employee within supervises;
while (dbStatus == 0) {
  $get employee;
  printf("%s\n", employee.ename);
  worksUnder();
  $find next employee within supervises; }
$find owner within supervises;
$find first employee within clones; }
```

```
      :
strcpy (employee.ename, "frank");
$find first employee using ename;
worksUnder ();
      :
```

Although this solution is correct, it isn't very satisfying. The operation of the recursive routine isn't clear from reading it because it depends on the hidden movement of currency pointers to maintain the proper context. This example exposes a more general deficiency of the network model: the same database manipulation command can behave differently from one occasion to the next because the currency pointers can establish varying contexts. The currency pointers' status constitutes a "side effect" of the main programming theme, and relying on side effects is now considered poor software development practice. A routine that depends on global conditions for its proper operation may well encounter situations where the global arrangement hasn't been appropriately prepared. Therefore, this programming format isn't recommended. A later section will investigate a second method that is somewhat more intuitive, but the general criticism of the network model remains. Querying a network database not only requires the ability to write computer programs in a host language, but it also demands careful attention to global currency pointers, a feature that invites mistakes.

The employee database isn't recursive in the most basic sense. No employee reports to himself, either directly or indirectly. Instead, the database is recursive because the employee entity enters into a binary relationship with itself. You can express the latter condition with owner-coupled sets and a second copy of the employee record type. You tightly link the second copy to the first through a new network set that maintains a one-to-one relationship. If the database is recursive in the first sense, with an employee who reports to herself either directly or indirectly, the above algorithm enters an infinite loop. The query itself is still meaningful, but the correct solution must avoid the recursive pursuit of an employee who has already been reported. The C code for this variation appears later as an exercise.

Many-to-many recursive relationships

Many-to-many recursive relationships are actually less complicated because the relationship already requires a new record type to decompose it into two one-to-many relationships. This decomposition produces no cycle in the owner-member graph because the new record type serves the member role in both cases. Consider again the parts database of Chapter 2. The earlier decomposition is repeated below, and the new record type is called use. In use, you can include a quantity field, which reflects the number of occurrences of part pno_2 in part pno_1. The table below includes pno_1 and pno_2 entries so you can place the quantity value in context. When you establish the network database, you can remove these identifiers from the use records and depend on the network set chains to link use records to their dominant parts.

Part			Use		
pno	pname		pno_1	pno_2	quantity
35	wagon		35	16	1
51	tire		35	10	1
52	hub		35	11	1
⋮	⋮		⋮	⋮	⋮

You can easily construct two owner-coupled network sets, component and assembly, as illustrated in Figure 11.13. The dashed lines represent component chains. A given component chain links many use records, which deliver the quantities of the components used in the dominant record. You can identify these components through the intersecting assembly chain. To find the direct components of a wagon, for example, you navigate along the component chain emanating from the wagon part and encounter five use records. Through each use record threads an assembly chain, whose owner gives the component's identity. So you pick up steering tongue, bolt, front suspension, rear suspension, and

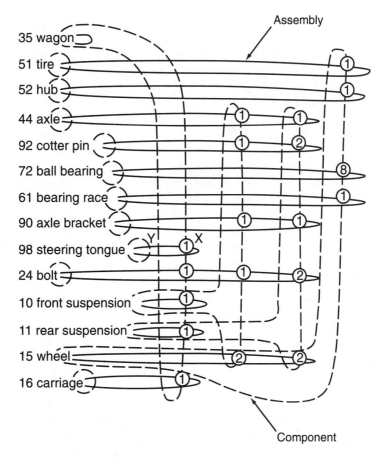

Figure 11.13 Network rendition of the many-to-many parts database

carriage as the direct components of wagon. Furthermore, you note that a wagon uses each component in quantity one.

The reverse navigation is also possible. Suppose you want to know the assemblies that use the component bolt. You follow the solid line, an `assembly` chain, from bolt and encounter three use records. Through each use record threads a `component` chain, whose owner identifies the assembly that uses the bolt. So you pick up wagon, front suspension, and rear suspension. Furthermore, you note that one bolt is used directly in a wagon, one bolt in a front suspension, and two bolts in a rear suspension.

With either of these navigations, you can pause at each use to recursively investigate the contributions of its owner on the intersecting chain. A parts explosion lists the components of a given part at any level of assembly. So to find the parts explosion list for a wagon, you traverse the `component` chain, where you note the direct contribution of steering tongue, bolt, front suspension, rear suspension, and carriage as before. However, you also pursue the components of each of these direct constituents. Suppose that you have arrived at use record X in Figure 11.13 by means of a find first use within component command. You then find the owner of the intersecting assembly chain and display steering tongue as part of the answer. Unfortunately, the current of component has now switched to chain Y in the figure. You do want to recursively investigate chain Y to determine its components (none in this case), but then you want to continue along the original component chain from point X.

You could attempt to reestablish point X by retracing your path out the assembly chain. In the general case, however, many use records might be on that chain. Which one was used on the way in? In the case of the steering tongue, you can indeed find the one and only use along the current assembly to regain point X. But what if you were investigating a wheel, which has several use records on its assembly chain? Clearly, you must remember point X in a more general manner. One solution to the dilemma is to pass the identity of the use record into the recursive routine and to expect the routine to restore that point before terminating. The identification of a particular use record is somewhat difficult because it contains a single quantity field. So you now need another feature of the network database model: the database key.

A network **database key** is a unique identifier that the DBMS assigns to each record when storing it in the database. Because the DBMS generates the database key, it is guaranteed to be unique to the record being stored. Typically, the database key is the absolute disk storage address of the record. When a get command transfers a record into its memory buffer, the DBMS also transfers the database key, using a template expansion to accommodate the additional item. The DBMS also provides an appropriate data type in the interfacing program to hold database keys. The templates for the part and use record types then appear as shown to the left below.

Using database keys, you can write a recursive routine that returns to a predetermined record after investigating the direct components of a given part. That routine appears in the center below. It accepts the name of the part to be probed, the database key of the record to be established upon conclusion, and a final parameter that indicates the depth of the recursion. You can use the last parameter to control an indentation scheme to offset the components of a given assembly, which produces the output display on the right below. The auxiliary routine displaySpaces (n) displays n spaces.

```
typedef struct {
    :
    :
} databaseKey;
typedef struct {
    int pno;
    char pname[20];
    databaseKey partKey;
} partType;
typedef struct {
    int quantity;
    databaseKey useKey;
} useType;

partType part;
useType use;
int dbStatus;
```

```
void reportComponents (char *partName,
    databaseKey returnContext, int depth) {
    char *partNameCopy;

    strcpy (part.pname, partName);
    $find first part using partName;
    $find first use within component;
    while (dbStatus == 0) {
        $get use;
        $find part owner within assembly;
        $get part;
        displaySpaces (3 * depth);
        printf("%s (%d)\n", part.pname,
            use.quantity);
        partNameCopy = strdup(part.pname);
        reportComponents (partNameCopy,
            use.useKey, depth + 1);
        $find next use within component; }
    use.partKey = returnContext;
    $find first use using partKey; }
```

```
steering tongue (1)
bolt (1)
front suspension (1)
  axle (1)
  cotter pin (1)
  axle bracket (1)
  bolt (1)
  wheel (2)
    tire (1)
    hub (1)
    ball bearing (8)
    bearing race (1)
rear suspension (1)
  axle (1)
  cotter pin (2)
  axle bracket (1)
  bolt (2)
  wheel (2)
    tire (1)
    hub (1)
    ball bearing (8)
    bearing race (1)
carriage (1)
```

To find the parts explosion for the wagon part, you launch the following query. The code finds the initial use record to give the recursive algorithm a context for returning at the outermost level. The particular use record isn't relevant because it doesn't enter into the calculation.

```
$find first use;
$get use;
reportComponents ("wagon", use.useKey, 0);
```

The use of database keys is controversial. The DBMS must ensure that the program doesn't change the database key component of the memory template and then issue a modify command. Also, database keys share a vulnerability similar to pointers in programming languages. A program can release the resource (memory released or database record deleted) while it retains a variable containing a now-invalid reference. A final problem is that frequently the unique database key is the absolute disk address of the record. If programs retain references to the address, the DBMS isn't free to relocate records in its storage management activities. Because of these problems, not all network database products include this feature.

If database keys aren't available, or if their use is forbidden in the interest of less error-prone code, you must introduce a user-defined key into record types to reestablish lost currency pointers. In the example above, you can include a uno field and take care to store each use record with a unique value in this attribute. The recursive routine then concludes as before, except that the uno, passed as the returnContext argument, is stored in the memory template, and the find command reads: find first use using uno.

As before, the term *recursive* in this situation doesn't mean that a part contains itself, either directly or indirectly. Instead, the record type part participates in a many-to-many relationship with itself. The standard decomposition produces two one-to-many relationships, which you represent with owner-coupled network sets. If the parts were abstractions of some sort, say computer programs, a part might contain itself. In that case, the algorithm developed here will enter an infinite loop. Certain queries against such a doubly recursive database are still meaningful, but you must code them more carefully.

 The network model can express recursive relationships, but it sometimes requires clones of the record types. Queries against such databases must carefully consider the currency pointers' behavior.

Constraints

Although the network database model is relatively old, it provides rather strong support for certain kinds of constraints. For example, referential integrity requires that a foreign key in a dependent table either be null or refer to an existing primary key in the dominant table. The network model maintains many-to-one relationships with network sets, and you can't place a dependent record on a nonexistent chain. With respect to a particular many-to-one relationship, a dependent record is either free-floating in the database, not connected to any dominant record, or it is on precisely one chain emanating from an existing dominant record. Therefore, because of the model's structure, referential integrity is never in question in a network database.

A key constraint requires that values in specified fields not be duplicated in more than one record. You can express this constraint in the network model in two ways. The record type in the schema can include the clause *duplicates are not allowed for* . . .. For example, to enforce the condition that sname is a key for the species record type, you can rewrite the schema entry as shown on the left below. You can also enforce the constraint by constructing a system network set where the member structure features the appropriate fields in a key-clause. You can then specify "duplicates are not allowed" in the network set definition. You can also enforce the key status of sname, for example, by rewriting the `speciesAlpha` definition as shown on the right.

```
record species.
   duplicates are not allowed for sname.
      field sname is character 20.
      field sfood is character 20.
         :
         :
```

```
network set is speciesAlpha.
   owner is system.
      order is sorted by defined keys.
      duplicates are not allowed.
   member is species.
      insertion is automatic.
      retention is fixed.
      key is ascending sname.
```

The second method generalizes to a sort of fragmented key constraint. You can require that certain fields contain unique values, but only over the records associated with a dominant record from a related entity. Suppose you want fname to be unique across the fish associated with each species, while allowing duplicate fname values for fish of different species. You can code this intent in the schema by adjusting the `Represents` network set as shown below.

```
network set Represents.
   owner is species.
      order is sorted by defined keys.
      duplicates are not allowed.
   member is fish.
      insertion is automatic.
      retention is fixed.
      key is ascending fname.
```

Entity integrity in the relational sense requires that a relation's primary key contain no null values. The reasoning behind this requirement is that the key is the only mechanism for identifying a tuple in an unordered relation. Relationships use the key as a surrogate for the tuple. Although you can define a record type so that certain fields function as keys, a particular record's integrity isn't as heavily dependent on that key as it is in the relational model. You have seen that keys aren't necessary to maintain relationships or even to distinguish between records in the network model. You can have two identical records in a table, distinguished only by their disparate connections to related records on network chains. In terms of the categorization of Chapter 1, the network database model is object-based, and the relational model is value-based. The value of the key attribute is essential to a tuple's identity in the relational model. But the mere existence of a record is sufficient for identification in the network model. Consequently, the question of entity integrity doesn't arise in the network context.

 The network model's structure is such that entity and referential integrity are never in question. You can enforce key constraints with a "duplicates are not allowed" annotation in the schema.

The network model contains no provisions for enforcing functional dependencies. However, you can enforce constraints of this sort by imposing a discipline on the interfacing programs. Suppose you want to enforce the tvolume $\longrightarrow$ tcolor functional dependency in the aquarium application. You can write the following auxiliary routine to create or update tank records. The single argument is an integer flag: 1 to update an existing tank and 2 to create a new tank. Assume that the field values for the new or modified tank are in the corresponding memory template.

```
boolean modifyTank (int flag) {              /* 1 = update, 2 = create */
    boolean violation;
    tankType newTank;

    newTank = tank; violation = false; $find first tank;
    while (!violation && (dbStatus == 0)) {
        $get tank;
        if ((flag == 2) || (tank.tankKey != newTank.tankKey))
            if ((tank.tvolume == newTank.tvolume) && (tank.tcolor != newTank.tcolor))
                violation = true;
        $find next tank; }
    tank = newTank;
    if (flag == 1)
        $find first tank using tankKey;          /* old tank to CRU if update */
    if (!violation)
        if (flag == 1)
            modify tank;
        else
            store tank;
    return violation; }
```

The code uses the database key facility in the case where it is modifying an existing record. It checks the database key to ensure that the record isn't compared with itself, and it uses the database key again to return the current of run-unit to the old record before issuing the `modify` command. Recall that the `modify` command always operates on the current of run-unit.

Writing this code solves only the smaller part of the problem. The difficulty is that there is no way to ensure that all users will create and modify records through this routine. To enforce this constraint, all users must agree to establish tank fields in the template and then to call `modifyTank (1)` to update an existing tank, or `modifyTank (2)` to create a new tank. All interfacing programs must forego the direct use of `store` and `modify` commands. Enforcing the constraint is thus beyond the control of the DBMS.

 The network model contains no provision to enforce functional dependency constraints.

The network model does enforce constraints of a different nature with the insertion and retention clauses of the network sets. For example, the specification "retention is fixed" prevents dependent records from being removed from a chain. Moreover, an `erase` operation directed at the dominant record of the chain will also erase all the dependent records. This behavior is identical to the "on delete cascade" trigger in SQL. There, the schema entry for the fish relation contained the following clauses:

```
        foreign key (tno) references tank (tno)
            on delete set null
            on update cascade,
        foreign key (sno) references species (sno)
            on delete cascade
            on update cascade.
```

When the DBMS deletes a species tuple, the "on delete cascade" triggers the recursive deletion of any fish whose foreign key points to the deleted species. You achieve the same effect in the network model with the "retention is fixed" clause. Similarly, the effect of "on delete set null" is to free-float the fish associated with a deleted species. You achieve this same result in the network model with the phrase *retention is optional*. In the relational schema, the clause *on update* ... triggers the appropriate changes in the fish tuples if the corresponding species tuple or tank tuple changes its sno or tno value. In the example above, a change of species sno propagates the new sno value into the dependent fish. A change of tank tno propagates in a similar fashion. Selecting "on update set null" free-floats the dependent records when the foreign-key referent changes. The network model, however, has no equivalents of these constraints.

 A fixed-retention clause in a network set's schema description enforces the same deletion conditions as the on-delete-cascade clause in a relational schema. Similarly, the optional-retention clause corresponds to on-delete-set-null. The network model has no equivalent of the relational update-trigger.

Network queries

This section provides a brief survey of existential, universal, and aggregate queries in a network database. Even though the solutions are coded in a programming language, they still illustrate a pattern for each type. Once you understand the format, you can solve a particular query by customizing the parameters of the appropriate pattern.

Existential queries

Examples throughout this chapter have illustrated existential queries. The format involves nested loops that navigate across intersecting chains. The navigation establishes a database path between a candidate record and a specified anchor record. The only difficulty in the process lies with the currency pointers, and you can treat this problem mechanically by systematically stacking the old context when you depart along an intersecting chain. For example, find the names of species swimming with a shark. The SQL reads as follows.

```
select S.sname
from Species S, Fish F, Tank T, Fish G, Species H
where S.sno = F.sno and F.tno = T.tno and T.tno = G.tno and
   G.sno = H.sno and H.sname = "shark".
```

You can follow the SQL in a network solution by navigating from a candidate species to a fish, then to a tank, then to another fish, and finally to the anchor shark species. You scan the species records in an outermost control loop. This processing thread appears as the vertical connection across species on the left of Figure 11.14. You implement it with find first-next commands. For each species record in the outer loop, you use a nested loop to probe the fish on its Represents chain. Referring again to Figure 11.14, you first encounter Fish X. Here, you transfer to the intersecting Inhabits chain to extend the database path toward the tank where the fish swims. You want to continue with the fish marked Y when you finish this detour. Proceeding with the detour, you find the owner record

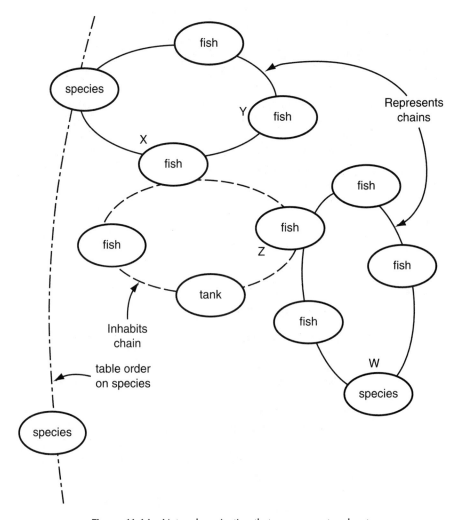

Figure 11.14   Network navigation that reuses a network set

on the intersecting Inhabits chain. At this point you have achieved the network equivalent of aligning the first three tables of the SQL from-clause. The fourth table is another copy of the fish relation. Therefore, you iterate across the fish owned by the previously located tank. Referring to Figure 11.14, you see that the planned circuit involves the current Inhabits chain, the same chain that you used to find the tank. The first such fish is at point Z. However, as soon as you locate the fish at point Z, the current of Represents shifts to that record, which loses the earlier context of the first Represents chain.

Unless you take some measure to restore the currency of the previous Represents instance, you won't be able to continue with the step to fish Y when you complete the detour. Worse yet, noting that the final table in the SQL is another copy of species, you proceed to find the owner of the newly acquired Represents chain, arriving at the species record marked W. The current of species now shifts to the W record, which disrupts the main sequential flow along the left of the diagram. In other words, the find next ... of the outermost control loop now operates in a changed currency context.

You must restore the proper currencies that are needed for the outer loops. You can't use the retain-currency clause to prevent the current of Represents from shifting to the second instance because you must transfer to this second instance to locate the final species record. Before addressing this problem, note that the database path is probing for the correct linkages. If the species record located at point W has sname shark, the original species qualifies for the answer. If it doesn't, the detour hasn't been fruitful, and you must continue with the next fish of the first Inhabits chain. Returning to the currency problem, you can restore the appropriate pointers with the general control loop structure shown below.

```
$find first <record type name> [within <network set name>];
while (dbStatus == 0) {
    /* store identifier of <record type name> record on the network set chain */
        :       /* nested activity */
    /* reacquire <record type name> record that was current at beginning of loop */
    $find next <record type name> [within <network set name>]; }
```

The format assumes that the nested activity within each loop causes the currency of the controlling network set to drift. So the loop stores an identifier for the current record, which uniquely identifies the current network set, at the top and restores it at the bottom. If the currency doesn't drift, the context restoration does no harm. Therefore, the final find next command behaves as though there were no intervening computation and therefore no opportunity for currency drift. To restore the currency pointer in this manner, you must retain a key to the initiating record at the top of the loop. For this purpose, assume that all record types of the aquarium example contain unique key fields (e.g., sno for species, fno for fish). The currency restoration process demonstrates that even though record keys aren't necessary for maintaining relationships in the network model, they are nevertheless useful. If unique record keys aren't available from the application schema, you can use the DBMS-generated database keys. The currency restoration technique remains the same.

Because the loop performs the currency restoration before it terminates, you can use a stack to hold the keys. Assume that the appropriate routines are available to manipulate a generic stack (e.g., createStack, pushStack, popStack). You can now formulate a correct network solution to the example query as shown in the left part of Figure 11.15. At the top of each loop, you push the control record's identifying key onto the stack. At the bottom of the loop, you remove it and use it to restore the record. When you reacquire the record, you simultaneously reacquire any chains that were current at the top. Therefore, the subsequent find next ... operates in the context of the previous record as desired. Any nested loops push and pop in the same manner. So when execution reaches the bottom of a loop, regardless of intervening activity, its controlling record key is at the top of the stack.

An obvious shortcoming of the previous solution is that the intermediate loops continue processing to the end, even if the candidate's sname has already been added to the answer list. In truth, when you encounter a shark at the end of the path, you can terminate both intermediate loops and continue with the main processing flow to the next candidate

```
char *candidate;                                boolean found;
list *answer;                                   char *candidate;
stack *keyStack;                                list *answer;
                                                stack *keyStack;
list = createList();
keyStack = createStack();                       list = createList();
$find first species;                            keyStack = createStack();
while (dbStatus == 0) {                          $find first species;
  $get species;                                 while (dbStatus == 0) {
  pushStack(keyStack, species.sno);               $get species;
  candidate = strdup(species.sname);              pushStack(keyStack, species.sno);
  $find first fish within Represents;             found = false;
  while (dbStatus == 0) {                          candidate = strdup(species.sname);
    $get fish;                                    $find first fish within Represents;
    pushStack(keyStack, fish.fno);                while (!found && (dbStatus == 0)) {
    $find tank owner within Inhabits;               $get fish;
    $find first fish within Inhabits;               pushStack(keyStack, fish.fno);
    while (dbStatus == 0) {                          $find tank owner within Inhabits;
      $find fish;                                    $find first fish within Inhabits;
      pushStack(keyStack, fish.fno);                 while (!found && (dbStatus == 0)) {
      $find species owner within Represents;           $find species owner within Represents;
      $get species;                                    $get species;
      if (strcmp(species.sname, "shark")               if (strcmp(species.sname, "shark") {
        addToList(answer, candidate);                    addToList(answer, candidate);
      fish.fno = popStack(keyStack);                     found = true;
      $find first fish using fno;                        }
      $find next fish within Inhabits;                 $find next fish within Inhabits;
      }                                                }
    fish.fno = popStack(keyStack);                   fish.fno = popStack(keyStack);
    $find first fish using fno;                      $find first fish using fno;
    $find next fish within Represents;               $find next fish within Represents;
    }                                                }
  species.sno = popStack(keyStack);               species.sno = popStack(keyStack);
  $find first species using sno;                  $find first species using sno;
  $find next species;                             $find next species;
  }                                               }
displayList(list);                              displayList(list);
```

Figure 11.15 Two navigational solutions to find the species swimming with a shark

species. You can achieve this enhancement with a boolean that signals when the shark has been located, which gives the parallel solution shown in the continuation of Figure 11.15. This improvement also dispenses with the stack activity in the innermost loop because the controlling Inhabits currency pointer doesn't drift.

In developing the solution to an existential query, you use the intersecting chains of the network sets to navigate among records. Sometimes you enter the chain at the dominant record and use a loop to probe all the dependent records. Sometimes you enter the chain at a dependent record and use a find ... owner ... command to locate the dominant record. In the first case, you must take precautions to restore the currency of the controlling record (and its corresponding chain) prior to the find next ... command. In the latter case, the precaution isn't necessary because no loop is involved.

 You solve an existential query in a network database by writing nested control loops to navigate across related records. You must carefully restore currency pointers at the bottoms of the loops.

Universal queries

You can compose a network solution to a universal query by imitating the set-containment SQL expression. For example, find the names of species represented in all red tanks. The SQL solution follows.

```
select  S.sname
from species S
where   (select T.tno                                      (select T.tno
         from fish F, tank T              contains          from tank T
         where S.sno = F.fno and F.tno = T.tno)             where T.tcolor = "red").
```

You can imitate this solution in the network case by constructing two lists for each candidate species: a list of tno values of red tanks and a list of tno values associated with the species. If the second list contains the first, the candidate contributes to the answer. You have to construct the first list only once because it's independent of the species under consideration. Furthermore, you can terminate the second list as soon as it grows to encompass the first list. The code appears below. The boolean variable covers becomes true as soon as the list reachable from the candidate record grows to contain the list of targets. Of course, that condition is true immediately if the list of targets is empty, which justifies the variable's initialization as shown.

```
boolean covers;
list *mytanks, *redtanks, *answer;

answer = createList(); redtanks = createList();
$find first tank;
while (dbStatus == 0) {        /* acquire list of red tanks */
    $get tank;
    if (strcmp(tank.tcolor, "red") == 0)
        addToList(answer, tank.tno);
    $find next tank; }
$find first species;
while (dbStatus == 0) {
    $get species;
    mytanks = createList();
    covers = emptyList(redtanks);        /* covers goes true when mytanks covers redTanks */
    $find first fish within Represents;
    while (!covers && (dbStatus == 0)) {        /* get list of tanks for this species */
        $find tank owner within Inhabits;
        $get tank;
        addToList(mytanks, tank.tno);
        covers = contains(mytanks, redtanks);        /* compare lists */
        $find next fish within Represents; }
    if (covers)
        addToList(answer, species.sname);
    destroyList(mytanks);
    $find next species; }
displayList(answer);
```

 The generic solution to a universal query against a network database involves the assembly and comparison of two lists: the anchor records and the records reachable from the candidate record.

Aggregate queries

Aggregate query solutions introduce no additional concepts because you perform the calculations in the host programming language. For example, find the number of fish representing each species. The SQL and its equivalent navigational solution appear below. The network version simply performs the count in the host code as it visits the target records.

 In the network model, you compute aggregates in the host programming language. You use the usual facilities for looping across a range of values to extract the desired computation.

```
select S.sno, S.sname, count(*)
from Species S, Fish F
where F.sno = S.sno
groupby S.sno.
```

```
int count;

$find first species;
while (dbStatus == 0) {
    $get species;
    count = 0;
    $find first fish within Represents;
    while (dbStatus == 0) {
        count++;
        $find next fish within Represents; }
    printf("%d, %s, %d\n", species.sno,
        species.sname, count);
    $find next species; }
```

Comparison of network databases with previous models

The examples of this chapter highlight the major disadvantage of the network database model: you must manipulate the data from a host programming language. This constraint forces the user to describe the navigation process as an explicit procedure. However, many database users aren't sufficiently familiar with computer programming to compose network queries. Although the object-oriented model also requires the user to compose query solution procedures, its proponents argue that the object-oriented programming context is less difficult to master. Viewing the application as a collection of interacting objects is strongly intuitive. Moreover, non-procedural access languages, such as OQL, exist for object-oriented databases.

A second deficiency of the network model is the complicated nature of the relationship maintenance structures. Navigating among the network sets requires continual attention to the chain transfers. For example, if you enter a chain on an owner record, you must construct a loop to investigate the dependent records. If you arrive instead on a dependent record, you use a find ... owner within ... command in place of a loop. Moreover, you must carefully monitor the currency pointers because the default updating strategy might not accord with the needs of the given query.

An advantage of the network model is its speed and efficiency when traversing relationships that have been implemented through the network sets. The chain links provide direct disk or memory addresses of related records, which allows immediate retrieval without the overhead of relational joins, recursive object-oriented attribute searches, or deductive inferences.

Because its access language is an extension of a host programming language, the network query language is computationally complete. You can easily write network queries involving recursive relationships through an unbounded number of levels. In this sense, the network query capability is more powerful than either SQL or relational algebra. However, you have seen both embedded SQL and object-oriented processes that achieve the same results because both have access to a computationally complete language. You have also seen that a deductive database can handle recursive queries through an indeterminate number of levels. The problem in the deductive case isn't with queries but rather with the theoretical implications of recursive inference rules.

The network database model evolved in response to deficiencies in the hierarchical model, which is historically the oldest model. The relational model has now supplanted the network model because the former offers simpler modeling concepts and a less complicated, non-procedural query language. Moreover, with the development of query optimization techniques and behind-the-scenes rapid indexing mechanisms, the relational model has achieved levels of speed and efficiency that make it competitive with networks.

SUMMARY

The network model uses a record type, which contains a heterogeneous collection of fields, to represent an application entity. The network schema elaborates each record type by naming and giving a data type to each field. For each interfacing language, the DBMS generates a template to be included in interfacing programs. For each record type, the template defines a buffer area, which serves as a loading or unloading dock for records in transit to or from the database. The template also declares a feedback area, where the DBMS places a code describing the outcome (i.e., success or failure) of the database activity commanded by the program.

The network model represents elementary data elements as record fields. These fields are categorized by record type and tabulated in the database. Network sets express relationships among the data elements. An owner-coupled network set links one dominant record from a specified owner record type with zero, one, or more dependent records from a distinct member record type. You can envision an owner-coupled network set as a collection of chains. From each owner record, a chain grows to pass through its dependent records before returning to the owner. A dependent record is on at most one such chain. In other words, two chains of the same network set don't intersect. Chains from different network sets, however, can intersect. These latter intersections provide the basis for network navigation in the pursuit of query solutions. A system network set, or singular set, uses the DBMS as the owning entity. You should envision it as a single chain emanating from the system and passing through selected dependent member records. You use system sets primarily as indices that return the dependent records in some sorted order.

The schema description of a network set specifies the owner (dominant) and member (dependent) record types. An order-clause governs the position of a new entry on the chain. Ordering options are: first, last, prior, next, sorted by defined keys, and by system default. You can add an annotation to prevent duplicates, as determined by the fields of a key-clause. An insertion clause assigns responsibility for connecting new records to their network set chains. Automatic insertion makes the DBMS responsible for the proper connections. Manual insertion leaves the connection to an interfacing program. A retention clause controls the removal of a dependent record from a chain. Fixed retention prevents removal; mandatory retention allows removal only when immediately followed by reconnection to a different chain; and optional retention allows removal without further conditions. You can specify a set-selection clause to determine a particular method for identifying the chain to receive a newly created member record.

The DML (Data Manipulation Language) contains several variations of the find command. These allow you to locate records absolutely from their tables or through their occurrences on chains. The get, store, modify, and erase commands control the creation, modification, and deletion of database records and the loading of their contents into memory templates. The `connect`, `disconnect`, and `reconnect` commands move dependent records among chains.

The DML commands operate in the context of currency pointers that identify the operands. For each interfacing process, the DBMS maintains a currency pointer for each record type, for each network set, and for the process as a whole (current of run-unit). The DBMS continually updates these pointers to reference the last accessed record that is associated with the record type, network set, or database in general. All database processing occurs from within some host language, with certain subprocedure calls serving to command database activity. The calls implement the DML commands, and their exact function depends on the state of the currency pointers.

The network model restricts all relationships to be binary and one-to-many. The standard decomposition mechanism reduces many-to-many relationships to this required form, and the extension to higher-degree relationships follows in the same way. You express a relationship of degree n as n owner-coupled sets, each with one of the relationship entities as the owner, and all with a newly created intersection entity as the member. Recursive relationships present a special problem because no cycles are allowed in the owner-member graph. A many-to-many recursive relationship must be decomposed through an intersection entity anyway, and that solution also works in the recursive case. The many-to-many relationship between an entity and itself becomes two one-to-many relationships between the entity and a newly-created intersection entity. This transformation removes the cycle in the owner-member graph. A one-to-many recursive relationship, however, requires a clone of the record type, which is linked to the original record type with a special network set. In the special network set, each chain has exactly one member—a clone of its owner. You must carefully monitor the currency pointers in a recursive query because they usually don't respond as needed.

Entity and referential integrity considerations aren't a problem with the network database model. You can accommodate a key constraint with a duplicates-are-not-allowed clause in the schema description. The network model provides no facility to enforce functional dependency constraints although you can substitute the disciplined use of external access routines. You can use the retention clause to achieve the same result as the on-delete-cascade or the on-delete-set-null triggers of the relational model. The network model has no equivalent of the relational update-trigger.

You can handle existential, universal, and aggregate queries by directly navigating among database records with the network sets. For existential queries, you build a database path through the intersecting network set chains. You must take care to maintain the currency pointers. For universal queries, you construct the appropriate lists to imitate the set-containment solution of SQL. You handle aggregate queries by performing the required calculations in the host language.

An older database model, the network model has been largely superseded by the relational model. The network model's primary deficiencies are the exposure of the implementation details, such as the network set chains, the difficult access through a procedural programming language, the error-prone mechanism of currency pointers, and the generally accepted attitude that proper use of a network database requires a higher and more costly level of technical expertise.■

Definition of a network database

Compose network schemas for the following applications. Defend your choices of insertion and retention clauses.

1. An engineering firm has several projects in progress. Each project occupies the full attention of several engineers. Each engineer has a crew of laboratory assistants who report only to that engineer. Each laboratory assistant owns a collection of instruments (e.g., oscilloscopes, meters). There is no joint ownership of instruments.

2. A molecule contains many atoms, and it is important to record the number of each kind of atom in the molecule. For example, methane, CH_4, contains one carbon and four hydrogen atoms. Atoms clearly appear in many different molecules.

The following exercises establish the context for later questions on the network data manipulation language.

3. The library database contains libraries, authors, books, patrons, copies, and loans. Assuming one-to-many relationships between library and copy, author and book, book and copy, copy and loan, and patron and loan, construct a network schema. Include key and foreign-key fields in the record types even though these entries aren't strictly necessary for expressing the relationships. Use check-clauses in the network set descriptions to ensure that dependent records are placed on the proper chain. Include system network sets to globally order the libraries, authors, and patrons by name. The fields associated with each record type follow. The primary keys are underlined, and foreign keys have the same names as their referents.

   - library (<u>libno</u>, libname, location, rooms)
   - author (<u>authno</u>, authname)
   - patron (<u>patno</u>, patname, patwgt)
   - book (<u>bookno</u>, title, pages, authno)
   - copy (<u>copyno</u>, cost, bookno, libno)
   - loan (<u>loanno</u>, duedate, copyno, patno)

4. Show the inclusion file that the DBMS generates while processing the schema of the previous exercise.

Network Data Manipulation Language (DML)

The following exercises assume the library schema and inclusion file generated in the last two problems.

5. Assume you have information for libraries, authors, and patrons on three files: library.txt, author.txt, and patron.txt respectively. Each file record represents one instance of the corresponding application entity. The fields are in fixed positions in the records, as shown in the upper row of tables below. The primary keys of the entities are underlined. Write C code to load these files into the database. The C code can call the DML commands as necessary. You need not include error processing contingencies; simply assume that the input files contain no errors.

library.txt	
field	position
<u>libno</u>	1 - 5
libname	11 - 30
location	41 - 60
rooms	71 - 75

author.txt	
field	position
<u>authno</u>	1 - 5
authname	11 - 30

patron.txt	
field	position
<u>patno</u>	1 - 5
patname	11 - 30
patwgt	41 - 45

book.txt	
field	position
bookno	1 - 5
title	11 - 30
pages	41 - 45
authno	51 - 55

copy.txt	
field	position
copyno	1 - 5
cost	11 - 30
bookno	41 - 45
libno	51 - 55

loan.txt	
field	position
loanno	1 - 5
duedate	11 - 30
copyno	41 - 45
patno	51 - 55

6. Assume that libraries, patrons, and authors have been loaded by the previous exercise. Write C code to load the books from the book.txt file described in the table above. The process should properly connect each book to the correct author chain.

7. Assume that libraries, authors, books, and patrons have been loaded as directed by the previous exercises. Write C code to load the copies and loans, each described by fixed field files shown in the tables above.

8. Assuming the database of the previous exercise, write C code to delete all books written by Salinger.

9. Suppose all Seattle libraries are merging into a single library. The buildings have all been stacked on top of each other. The result is a single building whose rooms total the sum of the rooms from its components. All copies of books from the constituent libraries have been consolidated into the new library. The new library is called **MegaLib**. Write C code to update the database.

Relationships

Compose network schemas to describe the following situations.

10. A manufacturer's outlet holds many items for sale. A customer and a sales clerk work together to complete a transaction by facilitating the customer's purchase of an item. A customer can purchase a given item in any quantity, and this information should also be recorded in the database.

11. A library collection consists of books, each with a bibliographic section referencing other books.

12. A botanical garden contains a variety of plants, representing many species. Plants can be propagated by taking a cutting from an existing plant, the parent, and rooting it to start a new plant, the child. A new plant is of the same species as its parent.

Consider an extension of the employee record type discussed in the text. The eno field is a key for the record type. The ename field gives the employee name, and the sno field gives the eno of the supervisor. The hours field indicates the number of hours per week that the employee is expected to work.

Employee			
eno	ename	sno	hours
⋮	⋮	⋮	⋮

13. Construct a network schema that captures the recursive supervises relationship.

14. Assume no employee can supervise himself, either directly or indirectly. For an employee who supervises no workers, define the hourCredit as the number of hours per week that the employee works. For an employee who does supervise other workers, define the hourCredit as the hours worked plus the hourCredit of each person supervised. Write C code to find the hourCredit value of all workers named joe.

Constraints

15. Write a C routine to enforce the constraint that patrons weighing more than 100 pounds may not check out a book written by Salinger.

Network queries

16. Find the names of patrons who have borrowed a book written by Salinger for which the holding library paid more than $25.

17. Find the titles of books that are available from a library that is patronized by a patron named joe.

18.
```
select L.libname, B.title
from library L, copy C, book B, author A
where L.libno = C.libno and C.bookno = B.bookno and
    B.authno = A.authno and A.authname = "Mailer".
```

19. Find the names of patrons who have used all libraries.

20. Find the titles of books that have been read by all patrons and that are available from every library.

21.
```
select L.libname
from library L
where
    (select B.bookno
    from copy C, book B
    where L.libno = C.libno and C.bookno = B.bookno)
contains
    (select B.bookno
    from book B
    where B.pages > 300).
```

22. Find the average number of pages in a book.

23. For each library, find the average weight of patrons who use it.

24. Find the names of patrons whose weight is greater than the average weight of patrons who have read a book entitled The Name of the Rose.

12 Hierarchical Databases

T HE HIERARCHICAL DATABASE MODEL PREDATES THE NETWORK MODEL, which itself has been largely supplanted by the relational model. So the hierarchical model is undeniably obsolete. However, as with network databases, many data processing systems with a hierarchical database core are still functioning. Much of this legacy software uses IBM's Information Management System (IMS) product. This highly successful product, developed in the 1960s, dominated the mainframe world of commercial database applications for many years. It left a large investment in expensively developed software to be amortized over the ensuing decades, long after the appearance of more powerful data modeling tools.

The hierarchical method of representing relationships is awkward unless the application presents a natural hierarchy. Hierarchies exhibit only one-to-many relationships, where each entity serves in at most one dependent role. For example, a business management structure is typically hierarchical. A president presides over many vice presidents; each vice president controls many divisions; each division contains many departments; and so forth. The hierarchical structure is rigid and fails to accommodate cases where an entity stands in a many-to-one relationship with two or more dominant entities. Even the simple aquarium example fails to conform to the hierarchical format because the fish entity assumes two dependent roles—under species and under tank. The hierarchical model can address this problem, but the solution isn't easy.

In earlier chapters, the discussions of the other database models used a neutral access language, which captured the essential concepts without attempting to adhere to the precise syntax of any particular database product. When you encounter a specific commercial database system of the relational, object-oriented, deductive, or network variety, you should expect minor changes in syntax and function. However, with your knowledge of the basic concepts, you should be able to adapt quickly to the local variations. The discussion here continues this approach with the hierarchical database model but diverges even farther from the native constructions of existing hierarchical products. Because of the model's age, the schema syntax and data manipulation commands reflects a bygone era of programming style. The precise hierarchical description offers no pedagogical advantage, and there is no reason for you to struggle with an unfriendly format. Consequently, the discussion here adopts a loose variant that serves the same purpose.

Informal illustration of a hierarchical database

Much of the hierarchical model's vocabulary comes from the subject of mathematical trees. You have already encountered directed acyclic graphs (DAGs), for example, in the dependency graph of an acyclic deductive database or in the owner-member graph of a network database. A node with no incoming arcs is a **source**, and a DAG must contain at least one source. A tree is a DAG with a single source, called the **root**, and with the additional property that a unique path connects the root to any other node. The root branches into several child nodes; each child branches into grandchild nodes. The branching process continues until it reaches the leaf nodes. A leaf node, also called a **sink**, is a node that has no outgoing arcs. Because of the unique path requirement, subtrees emanating from distinct nodes don't intersect. This chapter assumes some familiarity with trees, both as mathematical entities and as data structures.

Tree structures for entities and for their instances

A **database hierarchy** is a tree where the nodes are application entities. A one-to-many relationship connects each parent and child. Because the root has no incoming arcs, it doesn't participate on the many side of any relationships. However, each entity, except the root, participates on the many side of exactly one relationship. The aquarium database consists of two hierarchies, as shown in Figure 12.1. The collection (species, fish, event) forms one hierarchy because of the one-to-many relationships between species and fish and between fish and event. The fish and event entities each participate on the many side of one relationship; the species entity, the root, doesn't participate on the many side of any relationship. In the lower left portion of Figure 12.1, cascading one-to-many relationships link the three entities of the hierarchy. The collection (tank, fish, event) forms a second hierarchy, with tank serving as the root. Shorter hierarchies, (species, fish), (tank, fish), and (fish, event), also exist in the diagram.

In the terminology of mathematical trees, the entity on the one side of a one-to-many relationship is the **parent**; the entity on the many side is the **child**. The one-to-many relationship itself is a **parent-child relationship**. In a database hierarchy, the root entity serves, by definition, only in parent roles, and each non-root entity plays the child role in exactly one parent-child relationship. However, a given entity can assume any number of parent roles. In the hierarchies from aquarium example, a given entity also participates in at most one parent role. However, this example doesn't represent the most general case.

A modified aquarium application appears in Figure 12.2. It has no species entity, but it does have other application entities that illustrate a more generic hierarchy. The root is tank, which has two children, cleaning and fish. The cleaning entity has a single child, solvent, and the fish entity has two children, event and award. Both tank and fish serve in two parent roles. Every entity except tank serves in precisely one child role.

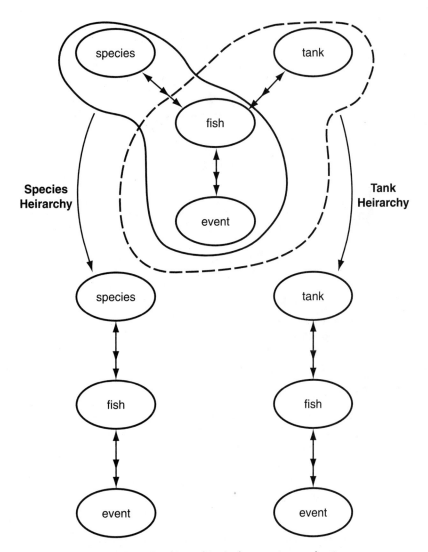

Figure 12.1   Two hierarchies in the aquarium application

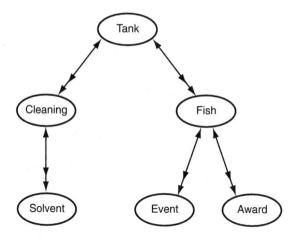

Figure 12.2　A hierarchy with nodes in multiple parent roles

 A database hierarchy is a tree of application entities with a one-to-many relationship connecting each parent and child.

You draw a database hierarchy with the root at the top and with the children of each node arranged in an arbitrary but fixed left-to-right order. In other words, when you first represent the hierarchy, you can choose any order for the children of each node. However, once you have established that order, it remains constant for any further analysis of the situation. In the tree in Figure 12.2, the ordered children of tank are (cleaning, fish), and the ordered children of fish are (event, award). In any analysis, you are free to call on the familiar properties of trees, such as subtrees and traversals, because a database hierarchy is a tree.

The **preorder traversal** of a tree is a sequential listing of its nodes according to the following recursive process. If the tree has a single node, the preorder traversal is a list containing that single node. If the tree contains more than one node, its root serves in the parent role of one or more parent-child relationships, and each child serves as the root of a subtree. Let the order of the children be $C_1, C_2, \ldots, C_n$. The preorder traversal is the list composed of the root node, followed by the preorder traversal of the C_1 subtree, followed by the preorder traversal of the C_2 subtree, and so forth. For the example of Figure 12.2, the preorder traversal follows:

$$(\text{tank, (cleaning, (solvent)), (fish, (event), (award))}).$$

The parentheses indicate the sublists constructed by the recursion. These parentheses are present only to clarify the process: they aren't part of the final preorder traversal. Unfortunately, the process isn't reversible. Given a preorder traversal, you can't reconstruct the tree. You can reparenthesize the traversal above, for example, as follows:

$$(\text{tank, (cleaning), (solvent, (fish), (event), (award))}).$$

This new grouping corresponds to the tree of Figure 12.3, which is different from the original tree of Figure 12.2. The alternative tree misrepresents the modified aquarium situation in

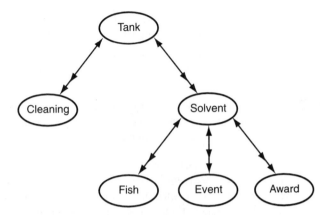

Figure 12.3 An alternative tree for a given preorder traversal

several ways. It raises the solvent node from level 3 to level 2, and it depresses the fish node from level 2 to level 3.

A later section shows how to describe a hierarchical database with a hierarchical schema. The schema describes the hierarchical tree, and the DBMS uses it to construct the preorder traversal needed for data manipulation activities. Because the DBMS is aware of the relative node positions directly from the schema, it doesn't depend on the preorder scan to reconstruct the tree.

Although the preorder traversal process isn't reversible, you can reconstruct the tree if you have some additional information. If you know which list elements are leaf nodes, and at which level, you can reverse the preorder traversal and reconstruct the tree. All you really need to do is reinsert the deleted parentheses. When the reinsertion is complete, the list assumes the form $(X, (\ldots), (\ldots), \ldots)$. This format reveals the root, X, and its subtrees. Each of the parenthesized lists following X comprises a subtree of X, which you can recover recursively in left-to-right order. Consider, for example, the parenthesized list derived from Figure 12.2: (tank, (cleaning, (solvent)), (fish, (event), (award))). You can deduce that tank is the root and that it has two subtrees: (cleaning, (solvent)) and (fish, (event), (award)). Each subtree is also of the proper form $(Y, (\ldots), (\ldots), \ldots)$, which reveals a root Y and further subtrees. Therefore, you can recover the tree of Figure 12.2.

Reinserting parentheses is simple, provided the leaf nodes are marked with their level numbers. Think in terms of different level parentheses when you perform the insertions. After you have placed all parentheses, you can remove the level markers. In a recursive process, the base step puts level-specific parentheses around the leaf nodes. For the list above, the initial step produces the following:

$$\text{tank, cleaning, } _3(\text{solvent})_3, \text{ fish, } _3(\text{event})_3, \, _3(\text{award})_3.$$

Subsequent passes insert parentheses of sequentially lower levels until a last set of parentheses at level 1 encloses the entire list. If $i > 1$ marks the highest level parentheses in the list, the next pass places level $i - 1$ parentheses around any contiguous run of level i groupings and includes the node directly in front of the run. In the example, the next pass places level 2 parentheses as shown on the first line below. A final pass produces the next line. If you now remove the subscripts, you have the original parenthesized list, and you can reconstruct the tree from there.

$$\text{tank, }_2(\text{cleaning, }_3(\text{solvent})_3)_2,\ _2(\text{fish, }_3(\text{event})_3,\ _3(\text{award})_3)_2$$
$$_1(\text{tank, }_2(\text{cleaning, }_3(\text{solvent})_3)_2,\ _2(\text{fish, }_3(\text{event})_3,\ _3(\text{award})_3)_2)_1$$

You draw a database hierarchy as a tree with a fixed left-to-right ordering of the child nodes under each parent. You can convert the tree into a linear list with a preorder traversal. You can reverse the process if you know the levels of the leaf nodes.

Subsequent discussion will use the term **type hierarchy** for a database hierarchy because its nodes are record *types*. A type hierarchy gives rise to many **instance hierarchies**, where the nodes are specific records. An instance of the hierarchy of Figure 12.2, for example, appears in Figure 12.4. Now a single tank record heads the tree. The first field of a record gives its record type, a T in the case of the root tank record. Subsequent fields are the tank attributes—tname, tcolor, and tvolume. The tank's children are cleaning and fish records in left-to-right order.

Because the cleaning entity is the leftmost child in the type hierarchy of Figure 12.2, the instance hierarchy displays all cleaning records in an arbitrary but fixed left-to-right order before taking up the fish records. According to the type hierarchy of Figure 12.2, each cleaning record possesses zero, one, or more solvent records. So the instance hierarchy shows the related solvent records in an arbitrary but fixed left-to-right order as children under the proper cleaning record. Each fish record has zero, one, or more events records and zero, one, or more award records. Because the type hierarchy displays event as the first child, the instance hierarchy shows all the event records for a given fish before starting on its award records.

You can apply a preorder traversal to linearize an instance hierarchy, just as you did for the type hierarchy. The instance hierarchy mirrors the structure of the type hierarchy. However, the traversal produces a list of records rather than record types (application entities). A preorder traversal of the instance hierarchy of Figure 12.4 gives the list below, now displayed vertically with an indentation scheme showing the location of the record types. The indentation isn't a part of the preorder traversal: it just emphasizes the list structure.

```
T cesspool blue 100
    C 7/24
        S alcohol
        S benzene
    C 8/30
        S water
    F charlie orange
        E 1/26 hatched
        A 3/17 gold star
        A 4/12 iron cross
    F bonnie blue
        E 3/5 monopolized food
    F elsie white.
```

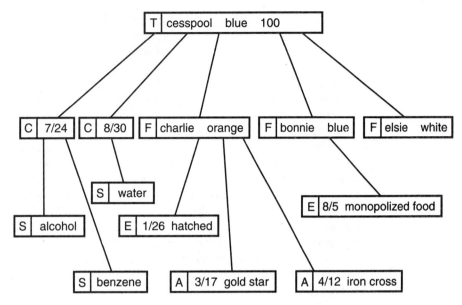

Figure 12.4   An instance tree following from the tank hierarchy

Relationships through logical adjacency

The preorder traversal preserves all the one-to-many relationships of the instance hierarchy. For example, which cleaning record is associated with the solvent benzene? The first cleaning record encountered by moving backward in the list from the benzene solvent. Which fish received the gold star award on March 17? The first fish record encountered by moving backward from the gold star award record. Where does the bonnie fish swim? In the first tank record encountered by proceeding backward from the bonnie fish record. In general, you can navigate from a child to its parent by scanning toward the front of the list from the given child record. The first record encountered of the proper type is the desired parent.

You can also move in the opposite direction, from parent to children. To find the awards associated with fish charlie, you proceed forward from the charlie fish record. Each award record encountered belongs to charlie until another fish record terminates the sequence. In truth, the sequence ends when the forward scan encounters any record type at the fish level or higher in the type hierarchy. If it encounters a tank record, for example, then any subsequent award records must belong to fish of this new tank, rather than to charlie. In any case, the linearized placement allows you to identify the group of award records that belong to charlie.

So, as with the network model, key fields aren't necessary to maintain relationships in the hierarchy. You don't even need the linked lists of the network model. Instead, the hierarchical model maintains relationships with the record positions in the linearized traversal. You find the children of a given record as the next block of records of the correct type after the given parent. Similarly, you find the parent of a given child as the closest previous record of the correct type. This identification technique requires that each record contain a type field. In the example, the symbols T, C, S, F, E, and A denote tank, cleaning, solvent, fish, event, and award records respectively.

The concept of maintaining relationships through relative positions in a linearized list is **logical adjacency**. Related records are essentially adjacent in the list because they are separated only by records of lower hierarchical types. Such intervening records are simply filler material, which you disregard when navigating across a relationship. The linearized traversal is a mental construct for visualizing the relationship mechanism. If an actual sequential list of records were used as the physical implementation, the system would suffer from the usual inefficiencies of sequential access. A search would typically have to scan through large, irrelevant segments of the list to reach a desired record. Therefore, the actual implementation of a hierarchy stores the records in more efficient ways, interlaced with pointers and indices to allow rapid access. That is why the relationship maintenance technique is called "logical adjacency," rather than simply "adjacency." Related records are logically adjacent, as implied by the preorder traversal. Whether they are physically adjacent in any sense shouldn't concern the database user. The DBMS maintains the illusion that the records exists in a linear list, and you can exploit this order to move among related records. The order established by the preorder traversal of a hierarchy is a **hierarchical order**.

 Hierarchical order is the order established by a preorder traversal of a hierarchy instance's records. You infer relationships from logical adjacencies within the hierarchical order.

Each instance of the tank hierarchy is a tree, or a preorder traversal of a tree, with a particular tank record in the root position. Each tank is then a child of a single system record representing the generic tank hierarchy itself. Figure 12.5 shows this extension. You obtain a preorder traversal of the extended tree by concatenating the preorder traversal lists of the instance trees, one for each tank. You then have a single list, which contains all tanks in the database. Following each tank record A, and preceding the next tank record, are all the records related to tank record A at whatever level in the hierarchy. All the cleaning records owned by tank A fall in this segment, as do all its fish records. Individual cleaning records are followed by their solvent records, and individual fish records are followed by their event and award records. The single list, containing all the preorder traversals of the instance hierarchies, is the **linearized record hierarchy**.

Navigating among related records

Just as with a network database, you express queries against a hierarchical database in a host language, using procedure calls to move information to and from the database. However, instead of navigating along network chains, the program moves forward and backward within the linearized record hierarchy. For example, to find the names of fish swimming in a cesspool tank, the controlling C program proceeds as follows:

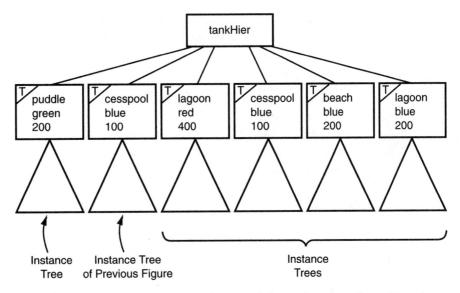

Figure 12.5   The full linearized record hierarchy following from the tank type hierarchy

```
$get first tank;
while (dbStatus == 0) {
    if (strcmp(tank.tname, "cesspool") == 0) {
        $get first child fish within parent tank;
        while (dbStatus == 0) {
            printf("%s\n", fish.fname);
            $get next child fish within parent tank; } }
    $get next tank; }
```

Although the discussion here again uses the C language to host the database activity, a hierarchical database can also support other languages. You indicate database activity in the host program with some special symbol, such as a leading dollar sign. A preprocessor replaces each marked statement with a library call in the proper host language syntax. After all such replacements, the host program is acceptable to the C compiler. A sample preprocessor translation appears as follows.

```
$get first tank;   ⟹   dbCommand("get first tank", &tank, &dbStatus);
```

As with a network database, the hierarchical DBMS provides a template, tailored to a specified language, for interfacing programs. The template defines a memory structure for each record type and declares a variable of the same name as the record type. For the example, assume that the template includes a memory structure for tank, such as the excerpt to the left below. The DBMS uses the dbStatus variable of the template to return a success or failure indication to the program. A library call always passes the address of the dbStatus variable as an argument. You should, of course, always check the status of this variable after each database activity. A returned value of zero means that the activity completed as expected; a non-zero value is an error code. If the database activity passes information to or from the database, the library call also passes the address of the appropriate template, as illustrated in the preprocessor translation above.

```
typedef struct {
    char tname[20];
    char tcolor[20];
    int tvolume;
    } tankType;

tankType tank;

int dbStatus;
```

```
T puddle green 200
    :
    :
T cesspool blue 100

    F charlie orange
        E 01/26 Hatched
    F killer white
        E 04/30 Hatched
    F bonnie blue
        E 07/22 Hatched
        E 08/05 Monopolized food
    F darron white
        E 02/08 Hatched
    F elsie white
        E 04/19 Hatched
T lagoon red 200
    F flipper black
    :
    :
```

$\rightarrow$

Unlike its network counterpart, the retrieval syntax of the hierarchical model doesn't distinguish between finding a record and importing it into memory. The hierarchical get command performs both tasks, returning a non-zero dbStatus value if it can't find the record. Each get command works in the context of a single currency pointer in a specified linearized hierarchy. The currency pointer is null before the program has accessed any record of the hierarchy. Otherwise, it lies between the last record accessed, of any type, and the next record in the linearized list. In the list on the right above, the arrow indicates a possible position for the currency pointer.

A get first <record type name> command resets the currency pointer to the beginning of the hierarchy and then moves it forward to access the first record of the indicated type. A get next <record type name> command accepts the existing status of the currency pointer and scans forward to locate the next record of the indicated type. In either case, if the scan reaches the end of the linearized list before the desired record type, the DBMS returns a non-zero dbStatus and leaves the currency pointer position unchanged.

Another variation lets you retrieve the child records for a given parent. The get first child <record type name> within parent <record type name> command moves the currency pointer backward until it encounters a record of the parent type. The pointer then scans forward to access the first record of the desired child type. The complementary form, the get next child <record type name> within parent <record type name> command, behaves similarly, except the scan proceeds forward from the current pointer position. In either case, the forward search terminates if a record of the parent type (or higher) occurs before the desired child record. This technique allows the program to loop through the child records for a particular parent and to receive a non-zero dbStatus when the child records are exhausted. Of course, additional child records might still exist farther along in the linearized list, but those records belong to a different parent record.

Suppose the tank hierarchy appears as the list to the right above. The arrow marks the location of the currency pointer. Successive get next child fish within parent tank commands successfully recover the fish records for charlie, killer, bonnie, darron, and elsie. The next attempt, however, produces a non-zero dbStatus code. Although more fish records exist farther in the list—flipper for example—the command won't process through the intervening lagoon tank record.

Although the examples above navigate from parent to child records, you can also move from child to parent by using a different form of the get command. The details will come later. For now, note that the commands all move the currency pointer in a linearized traversal of the record hierarchy. Remember, however, the linearized traversal exists only as a conceptual tool for tracking the activity of a sequence of get commands. The actual implementation will use a more complicated arrangement of pointers and indices to lace the records together in a more efficient manner. But the implementation will always support the illusion that you can move back and forth along the linearized traversal.

The complicated tank hierarchy with cleaning, solvent, and award record types illustrates how a type hierarchy can take on a tree-like appearance. The only restriction is that a non-root node serve as the child of precisely one relationship. There is no limit on the number of parent roles. However, if each non-leaf node serves in a single parent role, the special case of cascading one-to-many relationships occurs. In this case, a one-to-many relationship connects the root record type to its one and only child record type. This discussion concerns the *type* hierarchy of application entities, as depicted, for example, in the upper portion of Figure 12.6. The cascading one-to-many relationships seem to reduce the tree to a linear structure. However, an *instance* of this hierarchy still has a tree-like appearance, with the amount of branching dependent on the number of child records under each parent. Figure 12.6 illustrates the contrast between a type hierarchy and a type hierarchy instance: the lower portion shows a typical instance of the type hierarchy in the upper part.

The tank hierarchy in the original aquarium database exhibits the cascading one-to-many relationships shown in the top part of Figure 12.6. The hierarchy omits the species record type because it would be a second parent to fish, which is a forbidden condition. A later section will develop a mechanism, called a virtual relationship, which can reattach the species portion. For now, pretend that the aquarium contains only the tank hierarchy fragment. The preorder traversal is (tank, fish, event).

Assuming the data of Figure 2.1, the corresponding linearized record hierarchy appears as Figure 12.7. Key fields appear in each record even though they aren't necessary to maintain the relationships. As in the network case, the keys will be necessary to reestablish currency pointer positions and to enforce integrity constraints. The DBMS infers relationships from logical adjacency in the list. It finds related records in close proximity to a given target record. However, the get commands that navigate among related records rely on the previous positioning of a currency pointer, and nested activity can cause that pointer to drift from its desired location. Therefore, query solutions need the key fields to adjust the currency pointer.

The tank record fields are tno, tname, tcolor, and tvolume, which are all preceded by a type field that identifies the record as a tank. Tank records contain a T symbol in the first

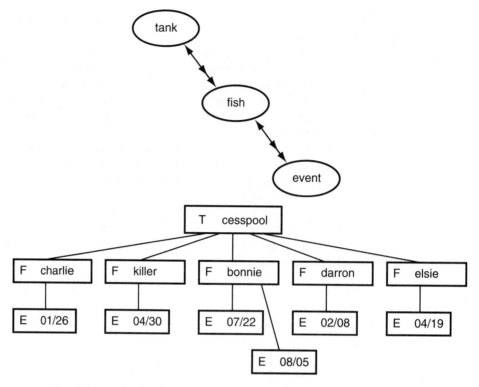

Figure 12.6 The distinction between the type hierarchy and one of its instances

field. Each fish record contains an F in the first field, followed by the fno, fname, fcolor, and fweight attributes. Each event record contains an E in the first field, followed by the eno, edate, and enote values.

An overview of the query format against a hierarchical database

This section shows how to use the linearized record hierarchy of Figure 12.7 to answer queries. It provides a prose description of the process. The precise algorithms will come later. As a first example, find the dates of events associated with a blue fish. You scan forward in the list, pausing at each fish. If the fish is blue, you scan forward within that parent to recover all its child event records. From these records, you extract the dates.

For a second example, suppose you want the names of tanks that contain a blue fish. Again you scan forward in the list, pausing at each blue fish. From a blue fish, you scan backward until you find a tank record. From the tank record, you extract the tank name as part of the accumulating answer. You then skip forward to the next tank because any further blue fish in the current tank can only add the same tank name again to the accumulating answer set. From the new position at the next tank, you continue to scan forward for more blue fish.

```
T 55 puddle green 200                      T 35 lagoon red 400
    F 483 albert red 45                        F 347 flipper black 25
        E 6719 06/25 Born                          E 6653 05/14 Born
        E 6720 06/30 Doubled in length             E 5644 05/15 Swimming
    F 438 fran black 61                            E 5645 05/30 Takes fish from trainer
        E 3116 09/25 Hatched                   F 388 cory purple 12
    F 419 kilroy red 49                            E 2176 02/04 Hatched
        E 5118 01/11 Hatched               T 85 cesspool blue 100
T 42 cesspool blue 100                         F 281 charlie orange 27
    F 164 charlie orange 12                        E 5211 05/23 Hatched
        E 3456 01/26 Hatched                   F 650 laura blue 55
    F 228 killer white 32                          E 6233 04/23 Born
        E 6789 04/30 Hatched               T 38 beach blue 200
    F 119 bonnie blue 51                        F 302 jill red 28
        E 9874 07/22 Hatched                       E 4004 06/04 Born
        E 9875 08/05 Monopolized food       T 44 lagoon green 200
    F 654 darron white 84                       F 911 helen blue 48
        E 2285 02/08 Hatched                       E 3884 11/12 Hatched
    F 765 elsie white 73                        F 700 maureen white 71
        E 2874 04/19 Hatched                       E 7555 05/09 Born.
    F 277 george red 32
        E 3651 10/02 Hatched
    F 104 indira black 19
        E 3992 12/25 Born
```

Figure 12.7 Linearized record hierarchy for the aquarium tank hierarchy

Finally, suppose you want the names of tanks that contain a fish that has an event posted on the same date as some fish in a cesspool tank. Because this query is somewhat more complicated, consider a solution in pseudo-C code. Assume you have list processing routines to maintain unduplicated lists of strings or numbers in the host language. You can reference such procedures as createList, addToList, removeFromList, and destroyList, and the data type list.

The algorithm appears below. The initial approach is simple enough. An outer loop examines each tank record in turn. If the tank has tname cesspool, you examine each of its event records. Note that event isn't a direct child of tank, rather it is a child of fish, which in turn is a child of tank. So event is a grandchild of tank. However, the get first-next child event within parent tank commands still work properly. They scan forward, searching for the next event record, until they encounter a tank record or a higher-level record. Because the fish records are lower in the type hierarchy than tank, they don't interrupt the scan. Therefore, you can use these commands to sequence through the grandchild records of a given parent. Indeed, you can also retrieve great-grandchild records because the DBMS searches the linearized record hierarchy between the target parent and the next record of that parent type or a higher type.

```
        list *answer;
        char *matchDate;

        answer = createList();
        $get first tank;
        while (dbStatus == 0) {
            if (strcmp(tank.tname, "cesspool") == 0) {
                $get first child event within parent tank;
                if (dbStatus == 0) {
                    matchDate = strdup(event.edate);
                        :
                        :   /* find tanks with matchDate events */
                    $get next child event within parent tank; } }
            $get next tank; }
        displayList(answer);
```

For each event located in the target segment, you extract the edate field and store it in the matchDate variable. You must now search the linearized hierarchy from the beginning to locate other event records with that same edate value. When you locate such a record, you move the pointer backwards to the closest tank. This accesses the tank that contains the fish that owns the event. Finally, you add the tank's tname to the answer list. This activity occurs in the ellipsis in the middle of the code excerpt.

The problem with this approach is that it loses the currency pointer for the original event (i.e., the one that contributed the matchDate). The program must restore that pointer so that the subsequent get next child event within parent tank command will function properly. You can reestablish the proper currency by retaining the key eno value from the event where the nested activity departs and restoring it before the get next ... command. Assume you have a stack for pushing key values. You can then proceed as shown in Figure 12.8. A nested activity finds other events (and their parent tanks) that match the date of the target event. This disturbs both the event and tank contexts. So you stack both the tno and eno key values. You also use a form of the get command that skips over records where certain fields don't match search arguments. The search string cesspool constrains the outermost loop to return only tanks with that tname value. Later on, a similar scan searches for event records with a particular matching edate value.

When the innermost loop locates an event with an edate value matching the target string, it moves the pointer backward until it encounters a tank. This accesses a tank that contributes to the answer. Notice that this operation actually acquires the grandparent of the child event record. The find parent ... command can successfully acquire parents of any level because it simply scans backwards in the linearized hierarchy until it encounters a record of the correct type. After adding the grandparent's tname value to the accumulating answer set, the program can't make any progress by finding additional matching event records within this tank segment of the linearized hierarchy. They would simply add the same tname to the answer list. Instead, it advances the pointer to the next tank before resuming the search.

 Queries against a hierarchical database are programs in a host language, which interfaces with the database through procedure calls. The program controls movement back and forth along the linearized record hierarchy and uses a single currency pointer to coordinate related records.

```
list *answer;
int tankid, eventid;
char *matchDate;
stack *keyStack;

answer = createList(); keyStack = createStack();
$get first tank where tname = "cesspool";
while (dbStatus == 0) {
    pushStack(keyStack, tank.tno);
    $get first child event within parent tank;
    while (dbStatus == 0) {
        pushStack(keyStack, event.eno);
        matchDate = strdup(event.edate);
        $get first event where edate = currentDate;
        while (dbStatus == 0) {
            $get parent tank of child event;
            addToList(answer, tank.tname);
            $get next tank;
            if (dbStatus == 0)
                $get next event where edate = currentDate; }
        eventid = popStack(keyStack); $get first event where eno = eventid;
        $get next child event within parent tank; }
    tankid = popStack(keyStack); $get first tank where tno = tankid;
    $get next tank where tname = "cesspool"; }
displayList(answer);
```

Figure 12.8   Illustrating motion along the linearized hierarchy in query solution

The linearized record hierarchy list is a sequence of segments, one for each record of the root type. Each segment contains a single root record, which is followed by a sequence of subsegments, one for each child record (by whatever relationship) of the root. Continuing the pattern, each subsegment is a sequence of subsubsegments, one for each grandchild record by way of the particular child. The process finally terminates with the leaves of the hierarchy. The scheme is a clever one because it preserves the relationship among records with a simple proximity arrangement, which avoids the overhead of network chains or foreign keys. However, as you'll see in the next section, the scheme has a serious flaw.

Relationships

You can easily represent one-to-many binary relationships in the hierarchical database model, provided no record type participates on the many side of more than one relationship. This constraint is serious because the forbidden condition frequently arises. In the complete aquarium example, the fish record type participates simultaneously in relationships with species and with tank. Moreover, it appears on the many side of both relationships. You can't represent these situations in a hierarchy. Worse yet, an application can contain many-to-many relationships. The standard factorization technique will decompose a many-to-many relationship into two one-to-many relationships. Unfortunately, the new intersection entity

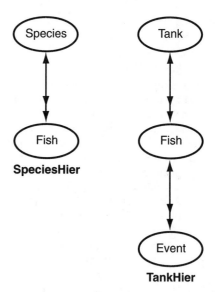

Figure 12.9   The aquarium database as two hierarchies

appears on the many side of both of the new relationships. So the problem reappears: a type hierarchy can't accommodate nodes with multiple parents.

If you think of the hierarchy after linearizing it with a preorder traversal, you can see why multiple parents aren't possible. The segment following a given parent record contains all the child records related to that parent. If such a child record has another parent, it must also appear in another segment headed by the second parent. However, the child record can't appear in two distinct places in the linearized list.

Or can it? You could duplicate the child records in a separate hierarchy. The aquarium example then appears as shown in Figure 12.9. In solving queries, you will simply switch between the hierarchies as needed. For example, to find the names of tanks containing a shark species, you proceed as shown below, keeping track of the currency pointers in both hierarchies.

```
list *answer;

answer = createList();
$get first species where sname = "shark";
while (dbStatus == 0) {
    $get first child fish within parent species;
    while (dbStatus == 0) {
        $sync tankHier to speciesHier;
        $get parent tank of child fish;
        addToList(answer, tank.tname);
        $get next child fish within parent species; }
    $get next species where sname = "shark"; }
displayList(answer);
```

The outer loop scans the species hierarchy for species records with sname shark. Pausing at each such record, it initiates a nested loop to probe for the fish records within the species hierarchy segment following the shark. When the nested loop finds a fish record, it issues a synchronization command to move the currency pointer in the tank hierarchy to access the matching fish record there. It then moves the currency pointer in the tank hierarchy to access the owning tank, which contributes to the answer. Meanwhile, the currency pointer in the species hierarchy has been patiently waiting, positioned just after the fish record that triggered the activity in the tank hierarchy. You can, therefore, properly access the next fish within the parent species record.

Although this solution does allow multiple parents, it's somewhat unsatisfactory because it duplicates the fish records in two hierarchies. The redundant scheme wastes storage space. It also invites inconsistencies in the database because you must install a change to a fish record in two places. Moreover, in the general case, a record type may require more than two copies because it must be replicated once for each relationship where it plays the child role.

You could pass over these difficulties by deferring them to the implementation. For the database systems studied so far, the discussions emphasized that the relationship maintenance techniques were mental models. They allow you to visualize the DBMS response to interface commands. However, the DBMS can implement the physical storage and the manipulation algorithms in a more efficient manner, provided it projects the proper illusion for the user. Faced with the duplication problems in the hierarchical model, therefore, you could say that the implementation must deal with the matter. It must deal with efficiency issues while still projecting the illusion that a record type can exist in more than one hierarchy. The interface language then needs a command to move the currency pointer in a remote hierarchy to the same record that is currently in focus in an active hierarchy. The example above postulates a sync command for this purpose.

However, when you study the hierarchical model, you are stepping back about 30 years in time. In the 1960s, the distinction between database implementation and application logic wasn't as clear as it appears now. The hierarchical database model was an attempt to provide the first integrated data processing environment, and it naturally responded to deficiencies in the prevailing practice of the time. That practice involved a host of disconnected programs, each with its own customized data files. Because the existing environment required meticulous attention to data structures and algorithms for manipulating information, the hierarchical model's designers didn't consider it unreasonable that this new database model should also involve these details. They desired progress on a different front. Instead of a large collection of repetitive, and possibly inconsistent, data files that were legible only in the context of their particular programs, the new database would provide a self-documenting central data repository, accessible by all agents. The hierarchical model did make considerable progress toward this goal by organizing a chaotic data collection into a systematic structure. Only then did the underlying problem of confounding database implementation detail and application logic become apparent. Subsequent database models then began to emphasize the advantages of separating the database implementation aspects from the application abstractions.

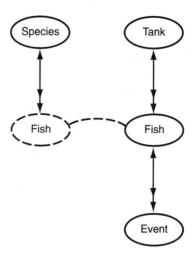

Figure 12.10   Using a virtual relationship to represent the aquarium hierarchical database

Virtual children outside of the linearized hierarchy

So how does the hierarchical model accommodate multiple parentage? It uses a technique similar to the duplication discussed above. However, it exposes the method of suppressing the undesirable repetition of records in various hierarchies, and it reveals the chaining process for linking record clones across hierarchies. Although it retains the possibility of several hierarchies, it allows two types of child nodes: physical and virtual. If a record type participates in the child role of two or more one-to-many relationships, the designer chooses one occurrence as the physical child. As a physical child, the record type appears in a hierarchy under its parent via the chosen relationship. In all other occurrences, the record type is a **virtual child**. When a virtual child occurs in a hierarchy, the actual record instances reside elsewhere, perhaps in a different hierarchy, where the record type plays the physical child role. Using a dashed line to indicate a virtual child, Figure 12.10 shows the aquarium database as the two hierarchies. A dashed link also connects the virtual child to its physical counterpart in another hierarchy.

You don't use a linearized traversal to pack virtual child records after their parent. Instead, you use a collection of pointers, called **child-sibling** pointers. The parent of a virtual child is called, as might be expected, the **virtual parent**, to distinguish it from the physical parent in the remote hierarchy where the physical child resides. So in the aquarium example of Figure 12.10, fish is the physical child of tank, and fish is a virtual child of species. Tank is the physical parent of fish, and species is a virtual parent of fish. The DBMS packs the instance records of a particular record type after the physical parent record in the usual linearized traversal. However, virtual child records don't follow a virtual parent in its linearized hierarchy. Instead, a virtual parent contains an address pointer to the first of its virtual children. Each virtual child record contains a pointer to its next sibling under the same virtual parent.

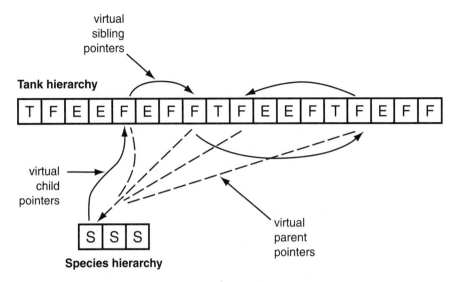

Figure 12.11   Child-sibling pointers maintain a virtual relationship

 A virtual child is the child of a one-to-many relationship whose records aren't packed after the parent in the linearized record hierarchy. Instead, the DBMS uses a chain of pointers to locate these records, which can reside in another hierarchy.

A typical arrangement for the aquarium database is shown in Figure 12.11. The species linearized hierarchy contains only species records because the only other entry in the hierarchy is the virtual child, fish. Because it is a virtual child, its records aren't packed with the species owners. From each species emanates a virtual child pointer that locates the first fish of that species. That fish then contains a virtual sibling pointer that locates the next fish of the species, and so forth along the chain until the final fish contains a null virtual sibling pointer. These pointers provide a path for recovering the fish records associated with a given species even though they are located in a different hierarchy. Because you will also need to navigate from a fish record to its species parent, each fish contains a virtual parent pointer back to the owning species record.

In general, a record type that participates in n relationships in the child role must provide $n - 1$ pairs of pointers to facilitate navigation across the $n - 1$ virtual relationships. The application designer promotes one of the relationships to physical status, and the DBMS holds the child records of this relationship in proximity to the physical parent. The pointer pair for a given virtual relationship contains one virtual sibling pointer, used to locate the next child record in the virtual relationship, and one virtual parent pointer, used to refer back to the virtual parent in a different hierarchy. Moreover, each virtual parent must contain a virtual child pointer to locate the first virtual child. A program can then retrieve subsequent child records along the chain of virtual sibling pointers.

Consider the example in the top part of Figure 12.12, where record type D appears in the child role of three one-to-many relationships. The central part of the figure shows a decomposition into three hierarchies. B is the physical parent of D. In addition to its attribute fields, each D record contains two pairs of pointers: the first pair for the CD relationship and the second for the AD relationship. The first pointer of each pair is the virtual sibling pointer that extends the chain of child records; the second is the virtual parent pointer.

Because of the relationships' one-to-many nature, a D record will be on at most one chain originating from a C record, and it will be on at most one chain originating from an A record. C-chains and A-chains don't intersect. However, a given D record can exist simultaneously on a C-chain and on an A-chain. These constraints and possibilities are similar to those encountered with network chains. However, the BD relationship constitutes a hidden chain. Each D record associates with precisely one B record—the B that is closest to it toward the beginning of the linearized hierarchy.

When you choose to treat some relationships as virtual and others as physical, you express the choice in the hierarchical schema, which will be covered in the next section. Each variant of the get command can include the qualifier "virtual" before the word "child" or "parent" to clarify how to move the currency pointers. The syntax of the data manipulation commands will also be covered in the next section.

Using virtual relationships, you can now express multiple parentage in the hierarchical database model. Consequently, you can represent many-to-many relationships. You use the standard technique to decompose a many-to-many relationship into two one-to-many relationships between the original entities and a newly created intersection entity. For example, the relationship between tank and species in the aquarium database is many-to-many, and it decomposes into two one-to-many relationships: tank-fish and species-fish. The intersection entity, fish, is already part of the database in this case. However, the intersection entity could be a newly discovered application object.

Higher-degree relationships

Virtual relationships also accommodate the decomposition of higher-degree relationships. Consider again the ship-cargo-port ternary relationship. This example first appeared in a relational setting in Chapter 2 (see Figures 2.14 through 2.18), and subsequent chapters revisited it in the contexts of other database models. The solution creates an intersection entity, called mission, with one-to-many relationships: ship-mission, cargo-mission, and port-mission. The resulting diagram, Figure 12.13, is similar to Figure 12.12, which you have already solved. Proceeding in parallel with that solution, you choose one of the relationships for a physical parent-child expression, and you relegate the other two to virtual status. The lower portion of Figure 12.13 shows the three linearized hierarchies, interlaced with child-sibling pointers that link virtually related records. Each mission record contains, in addition to its attribute fields, two pairs of pointers. The first pair maintains the relationship between port and mission; the second pair deals with the ship-mission relationship. Placing the records in the center linearized hierarchy implicitly represents the cargo-mission relationship.

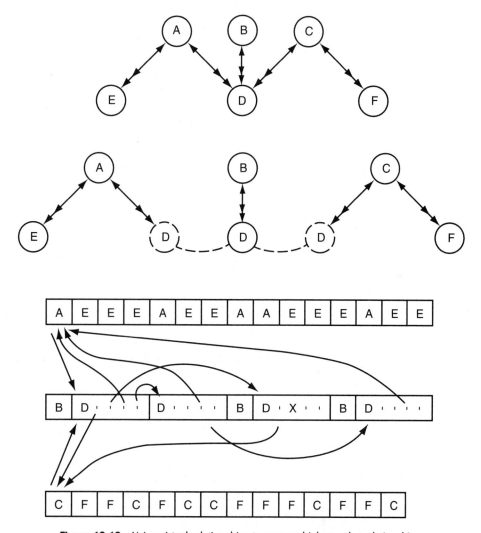

Figure 12.12   Using virtual relationships to express higher-order relationships

 You use virtual relationships to express higher-order relationships, including many-to-many binary relationships. You decompose them into a number of one-to-many relationships. The intersection entity then participates in multiple child roles, and it appears as a virtual child in all except one of them.

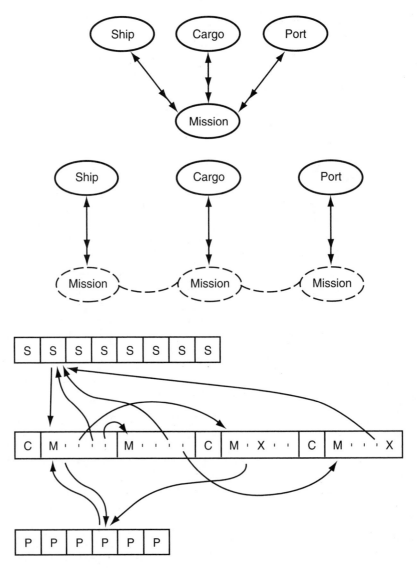

Figure 12.13 Decomposing the ship-cargo-port ternary relationship into hierarchies

Hierarchical definition and data manipulation

The hierarchical schema

You describe a hierarchical database with a **hierarchical schema**, which lists the record types, their fields, and their parents in the hierarchies. Typical of 1960s programming specifications, the details appear as a dense collection of abbreviations and physical requirements. In the language of IMS, for example, part of the aquarium hierarchical description appears below.

```
DBD     NAME=AQUARIUM
SEGM    NAME=TANK,BYTES=60
FIELD   NAME=(TNAME,SEQ),BYTES=20,START=1
FIELD   NAME=TCOLOR,BYTES=20,START=21
FIELD   NAME=TVOLUME,BYTES=20,START=41
SEGM    NAME=FISH,BYTES=40,PARENT=TANK
FIELD   NAME=(FNAME,SEQ),BYTES=20,START=1
FIELD   NAME=FCOLOR,BYTES=20,START=21
  ⋮         ⋮
```

See the IMS manuals—they should still be available—for more details. Instead of IMS syntax, the discussion here will use a hypothetical language that expresses the data definition and manipulation concepts but in a format more representative of how they might be presented today. In this spirit, Figure 12.14 shows the hierarchical schema for the aquarium application. Each record type is a **segment**. The schema locates each segment in a hierarchy by specifying its physical parent. The root segment is an exception, of course, because it has no parent. The schema simply identifies it as the root.

If a segment serves as a virtual child, you instrument it with virtual parent and sibling pointers—a pair of pointers for each virtual relationship that involves the segment. You have to note only the names of the virtual parent and sibling segments, without a data type, because the field contents will always be address pointers. Similarly, a segment that serves as a virtual parent contains a pointer to its first virtual child. The no-duplicates clause elevates a field to the status of a unique key. The aquarium schema includes segment keys even though they aren't necessary to maintain relationships. As you'll see shortly, keys are essential for adjusting the currency pointer so that retrieval commands operate properly.

Although the format of Figure 12.14 shows the essential features of a hierarchical database, the schema layout for a typical hierarchical product usually contains additional restrictions. For example, a virtual child may not be allowed to have children, or a second level schema may specify which segments are **sensitive**. Non-sensitive segments aren't accessible in an application that attaches to the second level schema. The interfacing program, however, must be aware of their presence to navigate the hierarchies.

Certain rare circumstances can't be handled by this simplified schema description. For example, suppose you physically include the fish entity in the species hierarchy. (This is a different arrangement from Figure 12.14.) You then want to express *two* virtual relationships between tank and fish. The first associates a fish with the tank where it swims; the second connects a fish with its preferred tank, say, by virtue of temperature and salinity. The tank segment description then contains two virtual child pointers, one for the chain of fish that inhabit the tank and the other for the chain of fish that would like to inhabit the tank. The

```
segment tank;                          segment event;
   root of tankHier;                      parent fish;
      field tno integer no duplicates;       field eno integer no duplicates;
      field tname char(20);                  field edate char(20);
      field tcolor char(20);                 field enote char(100);
      field tvolume integer;
                                       segment species;
segment fish;                             root of speciesHier;
   parent tank;                              field sno integer no duplicates;
      field fno integer no duplicates;       field sname char(20);
      field fname char(20);                  field sfood char(20);
      field fcolor char(20);                 virtual child fish;
      virtual parent/sibling species/fish;
```

Figure 12.14   Hierarchical schema for the aquarium database

syntax of Figure 12.14 doesn't allow you to distinguish between these two virtual child pointers. Similarly, the fish segment has two pairs of pointers, each giving a virtual parent tank and a virtual sibling fish. But it contains no information to distinguish the chains. A more complicated schema description could accommodate this situation, but the simpler syntax is sufficient to illustrate the essential concepts.

 A hierarchical schema describes the application segments (i.e., record types) and places them in hierarchies. It expresses virtual relationships by indicating the target segments of the virtual pointers.

Locating records with the `get` command

The data manipulation commands of a commercial hierarchical database system are usually dense and cryptic, which reflects the practice of the age. For example, IMS uses the command GU (get unique) to locate the first record of a particular type in a hierarchy. It uses subsequent GN (get next) commands to sequence through the collection. The GNP (get next within parent) command sequences through a segment of the linearized hierarchy governed by a given parent record. The variations, GHU, GHN, and GHNP, announce the program's intention to modify the retrieved record. The H stand for "hold."

A more user-friendly syntax achieves the same goals with the `get` command. This retrieval command has two basic forms: one to navigate from a child to its parent, and the other to navigate from a parent to its children. The brackets [...] denote an optional entry, the braces {...} indicate a choice, and the < ... > specify a user-supplied identifier. The first get form is:

get [virtual] parent <*segment name*> of child <*segment name*>.

For this command to operate properly, previous database activity must have positioned the currency pointer appropriately in the linearized hierarchy where the child segment physically resides. The pointer must be just after a child record. In that case, that particular child record is **current**. If a child record isn't current, an error occurs, and the DBMS returns a non-zero `dbStatus`. If a child record is current, and if the command doesn't specify the virtual qualifier, the DBMS moves the currency pointer toward the beginning of the linearized hierarchy until it encounters a record of the required parent type. The parent record becomes current, and the DBMS imports its contents into the controlling program's memory. If a child record is current and the virtual qualifier is specified, the child record must contain a virtual parent pointer. The virtual parent pointer locates a record of the parent type, possibly in a different hierarchy. The DBMS adjusts the currency pointer of the hierarchy that physically contains the parent record type to make the parent record current. If the DBMS can't locate the parent record, it returns a non-zero `dbStatus` and leaves all currency pointers unchanged.

A certain asymmetry exists between the processes for locating a physical and a virtual parent. The `find parent` ... command can locate a parent, grandparent, great-grandparent, and so forth because it merely scans backward in the linearized hierarchy until it finds a record of the proper type. That record must be the desired ancestor. However, a `find virtual parent` ... command follows the virtual parent pointer of the child to a specific parent record. You must use additional commands to access grandparents and other more remote ancestors.

The second format of the `get` command is:

$$\texttt{get} \left\{ \begin{array}{l} \textit{first} \\ \textit{next} \end{array} \right\} \texttt{ [[virtual] child] } \textit{} \texttt{ [within parent } \textit{}\texttt{] [where } \textit{<search argument>}\texttt{] .}$$

You use the `get first` ... option to initiate a search through a linearized hierarchy or across a chain of virtual children. You then use the `get next` ... format to continue the sequence. The `get next` ... form accepts the current position of the currency pointer, which must reference an instance of the target record type. The `get first` ... form reestablishes currency at the beginning of the linearized hierarchy, or just past the parent record as required by other clauses. If the `child` qualifier appears before the desired record type, the `within parent` clause must also appear. In this case, the DBMS restricts the search to the segment of the linearized hierarchy owned by a particular parent record (physical scan) or to the chain of child records emanating from the parent record (virtual scan). In either case, the optional search argument provides a boolean expression involving the fields of the target record type and constants. If a search option is present, the DBMS further restricts the scan to those target records that satisfy the search argument.

For example, assuming the schema of Figure 12.14, the aquarium database contains two hierarchies, tankHier and speciesHier. The former physically contains the tank, fish, and event segments; the latter contains species segments. The schema instruments species as a virtual parent of the virtual child fish. In this context, find the names of species that are represented by a blue fish in a tank of volume 4000 gallons or more.

The code is shown below. The outermost loop sequences along the linearized species hierarchy. It pauses at each species record to undertake the nested activity. Just after it has imported a species record into the program's memory structure, a typical iteration through the outermost loop leaves the currency pointer in the species hierarchy as shown by arrow 1 in Figure 12.15. That species record, marked with an S in the figure, is the virtual parent of a chain of fish records. Two appear in the diagram. The program locates the first blue fish with the `get first virtual child fish` ... command. Assuming that the first fish of the chain qualifies, the DBMS moves the currency pointer of the tank hierarchy to arrow 2 in the figure, just after that fish. The get parent tank ... command then moves the tank hierarchy's currency pointer back to the parent tank at position 3 in the figure. If this tank is large enough, the program records the sname value from the species S in the accumulating answer list. It also sets the boolean found to note that investigating more fish from this species isn't necessary. However, if the tank isn't large enough, the program must continue along to the next blue fish at position 4.

Here a problem arises with the currency pointer in the tank hierarchy. Because the currency pointer is now at position 3, no current fish record provides the context needed for the subsequent find next virtual child fish ... command. Therefore, the program must restore the currency pointer to point 2 before attempting to retrieve the next virtual fish. The code does this by retaining the fno key value of the fish at location 2 before moving the currency pointer to access its tank. A fresh scan of the tank hierarchy recovers the required position by using the key value as a search argument.

```
list *answer;
boolean found;

answer = createList();
$get first species;
while (dbStatus == 0) {
   $get first virtual child fish within parent species where fcolor = "blue";
   found = false;
   while (!found && (dbStatus == 0)) {
      currentFish = fish.fno;              /* retain identity of fish */
      $get parent tank of child fish;
      if (tank.tvolume >= 4000) {
         found = true;
         addToList(answer, species.sname); }
      else {
         $get first fish where fno = currentFish;            /* restore current fish */
         $get next virtual child fish within parent species where fcolor = "blue"; } }
   $get next species; }
displayList(answer);
```

Although this example is simple, it still requires a currency pointer adjustment. Unlike the network model, the hierarchical model maintains only one currency pointer for all record types in a given hierarchy. Even a small amount of nested processing can overload this pointer, and the program must then reestablish it properly.

 The hierarchical get command has variations that navigate from parent to child, and from child to parent. Default movement is along the linearized hierarchy, but you can use the "virtual" qualifier to move across the virtual pointers instead.

Record insertions

To insert records, you position the currency pointer and then issue an insert command. The DBMS stores the data in the memory template as a new record, inserting it physically

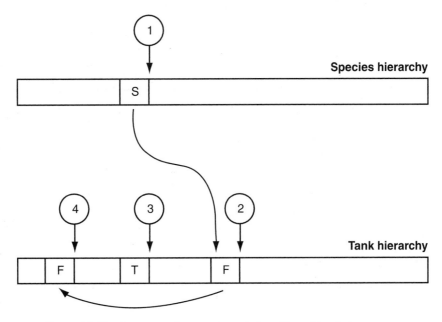

Figure 12.15 Currency pointer movement along hierarchies during a query

as close as possible after the currency pointer. The new record becomes the current record. The record enters as a physical child in the appropriate relationship, as governed by its position in the linearized list. If no previous activity has established the currency pointer, the insertion occurs at the beginning of the hierarchy.

If the inserted entry's record type is a virtual child in other relationships, the virtual parent must be current in a remote hierarchy so that the DBMS can insert the new record on the proper chains. The format of the insert command is:

insert .

As shown below, you can use this form to insert a new fish in the tank hierarchy. The code forces the new fish to belong to the first cesspool tank from the beginning of the hierarchy. The code also inserts the new fish as the sixth fish in hierarchical order under that tank, provided that five fish already swim there. Otherwise, it inserts the new fish last. Besides becoming a physical child of the appropriate tank record, the new fish becomes a virtual child of the species record with sno 22.

```
$get first tank where tname = "cesspool";
if (dbStatus == 0) {
   for (i = 0; (dbStatus == 0) && (i < 5); i++)
      $get next child fish within parent tank;
   $get first species where sno = 22;
   :
   :            /* place data for new fish fields in template */
   $insert fish; }
```

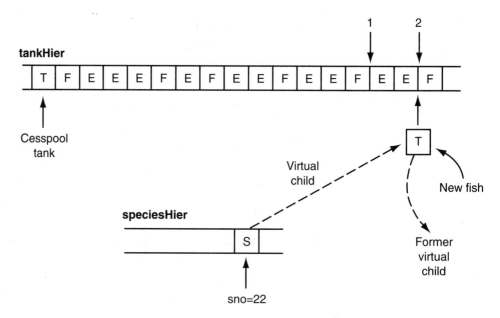

Figure 12.16   Determining the hierarchical sequence of a new record

Figure 12.16 shows the positioning of the currency pointer, assuming that the tank record on the left of the linearized hierarchy is the first cesspool. The positioning activity leaves the currency pointer at arrow 1 in the figure. The `insert` command places the new fish record just after the location marked by arrow 2. Because each fish is followed by its event records, the DBMS can't insert the new fish directly at that point. If the DBMS put the fish there, the subsequent event records would belong to the new fish because they would follow it in hierarchical sequence. The next logical place that can accommodate a new fish is position 2. The DBMS also places the new fish record at the beginning of the chain of virtual child records emanating from the chosen species. In particular, it sets the new fish's sibling pointer to reference the species' former virtual child, and the species' virtual child pointer to reference the new fish. Finally, it sets the new fish's virtual parent pointer to refer back to the chosen species.

Deleting and updating records

Deletion is a simple operation although it involves a significant side effect. To delete a record, you move the currency pointer to the target record and issue a `delete` command. That command takes the form:

$$\text{delete } <segment\ name>.$$

When the DBMS deletes a record from the linearized hierarchy, it also deletes all its children. That, in turn, deletes all the children's children, and so forth. If the DBMS didn't remove the physical child records, they would implicitly change parents. The new parent would be the closest parent record of the proper type earlier in the list. The DBMS must also removes the virtual children because the source of the parent-sibling pointer chain no longer exists.

When the DBMS removes the target (and its physical and virtual children), it disrupts other virtual pointer chains, namely those that pass through the deleted records. Because these one-way chains are difficult to repair, the DBMS may leave the deleted records in the database. In this case, it marks the records as deleted, and it must check that status whenever they are accessed. However, their links are then available to complete any virtual chains that pass through them. The DBMS handles these details without user intervention.

As an example, the following code excerpt deletes all cesspool tanks and, by necessity, all fish swimming in those tanks and all events associated with those fish. This default behavior is the same as that commanded by the on-delete-cascade clause in SQL or the fixed-retention clause in the network model. The deleted fish may serve as links in virtual chains, which note that the fish represent certain species. The DBMS is responsible for preserving the integrity of those chains. The currency pointer becomes undefined when the DBMS deletes the target record. Therefore, the code uses a get first ... command to acquire the next tank rather than a get next ... command.

```
$get first tank where tname = "cesspool";
while (dbStatus == 0) {
   $delete tank;
   $get first tank where tname = "cesspool"; }
```

 When the DBMS deletes a record from a hierarchical database, it also deletes its physical and virtual children at all levels.

You can always handle updates with a deletion followed by an insertion. Most products, however, provide a more efficient update command. The general procedure acquires the target record, modifies the field values in the memory template, and issues an update command.

Constraints

In the language of Chapter 1, the hierarchical database model is object-based rather than value-based. The identity of an application instance depends on the existence of a record object and is independent of any field values. You don't need a key to distinguish an instance from its fellows. Two records with identical fields can represent distinct application instances of the same type. You may be able to distinguish them because they have different children or simply because they occupy different locations in the hierarchical sequence.

Therefore, entity integrity isn't an issue in a hierarchical database. In the relational model, entity integrity specifies that the primary key of an instance can't be null. Entity integrity is important in the relational model because the instance's primary key represents that instance in remote parts of the database. It forms the basis for relationships. However, the hierarchical model maintains relationships with logical adjacency, complicated with chains of virtual children if necessary. It needs no keys to maintain the relationships although keys are sometimes convenient for other purposes. The hierarchical model's structure always enforces entity integrity.

The hierarchical model's structure also enforces referential integrity. You can't insert a record in the hierarchical sequence without implicitly associating it with a physical parent. Whatever parent record lies closest in the backward direction in the linearized hierarchy becomes the parent of the newly inserted record. If no such parent record exists, the insertion operation fails. Similarly, if the DBMS can't locate the parent of a virtual relationship— through the currency pointer of a remote hierarchy or through some other means—the insertion operation fails. In any case, a successful insertion automatically establishes parent records for all relationships where the new record participates as a child. In a like manner, the `delete` command removes all physical and virtual children of a targeted record. A child then can't reference a nonexistent parent.

In relational terms, referential integrity means that a foreign key must either be null or point to an existing tuple in the parent relation. In the hierarchical case, the model's structure enforces a stronger condition: a child record must always reference an existing parent. The reference can't even be null. Referential integrity, therefore, is always enforced in the hierarchical model.

A key constraint on a relation specifies that an attribute, or sequence of attributes, must contain unique values across the tuples of the relation's body. You can specify a key constraint in the hierarchical model, as illustrated by the no-duplicates clause attached to certain fields in the examples. In an actual hierarchical product, the syntax is usually more cryptic. For example, the following entry appeared in an earlier IMS schema: FIELD NAME=(TNAME,SEQ),BYTES=20,START=1. The entry establishes TNAME as a sequence field, meaning that no duplicates are allowed.

The hierarchical model has no provisions for enforcing functional dependencies. Just as in the network case, you must develop update routines that check for functional dependency violations. For example, suppose you want to enforce the tvolume $\longrightarrow$ tcolor functional dependency in the aquarium application. You can adapt the `modifyTank` routine from Chapter 11 to the this situation as follows. The procedure assumes that you have already installed the new tank values in the memory template and that you have positioned the currency pointers of the various hierarchies for the modification. For a new tank, you position the currency pointer of the tank hierarchy just after an existing tank. If you are updating an old tank, you position it just after that tank. The solution is only slightly changed from the network case.

```
boolean modifyTank (int flag) {          /* 1 = update, 2 = create */
    boolean violation, tanksPresent;
    tankType newTank;

    newTank = tank;        /* save new tank information */
    violation = false;
    $get first tank; tanksPresent = false;
    while (!violation && (dbStatus == 0)) {
        if ((flag == 2) || (tank.tno != newTank.tno))
            if ((tank.tvolume == newTank.tvolume) && (tank.tcolor != newTank.tcolor))
                violation = true;
        tanksPresent = true;
        $get next tank; }
    if (tanksPresent)
        $get first tank where tno = newTank.tno;          /* currency to old tank */
    tank = newTank;
    if (!violation)
        if (flag == 1)
            update tank;
        else
            insert tank;
    return violation; }
```

Generally, you can enforce any constraint, if you are willing to write a special program to check for violations before changing the database. However, the challenge is to ensure that all database modifications use the procedure. In the relational and later models, a strong reason for including constraint enforcement in the DBMS itself is to prevent users from circumventing special check procedures.

 The hierarchical model's structure automatically enforces entity and referential constraints. You can specify key constraints with a no-duplicates clause in the schema, but no provisions are available for functional dependency constraints.

Hierarchical queries

Existential queries

You have already seen examples of hierarchical solutions to existential queries. As with network databases, you solve an existential query against a hierarchical database by constructing a program in a host programming language. Instead of navigating across intersecting chains, however, you move back and forth in the linearized record hierarchy. In either case, the goal is the same: construct a database path from a candidate record to an anchor record. In a hierarchical database, two complicating factors arise: traversing virtual relationships and carefully monitoring the currency pointer in the hierarchy.

Consider the request: find the names of species that swim with a shark. Figure 12.17 shows the path commanded by a successful species. The question mark is the candidate record. A virtual child (VC) pointer leads to the first of a chain of fish, and virtual sibling (VS) pointers continue the chain. Each fish on the chain resides in a tank hierarchy segment,

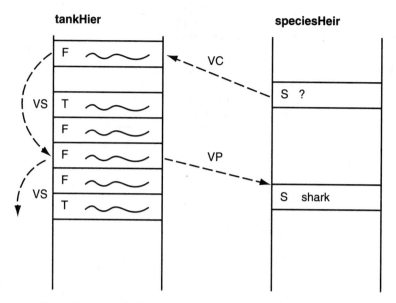

Figure 12.17   A database path extending twice between hierarchies

which is dominated by a particular tank. Therefore, each fish on the chain appears in a cluster of neighboring fish, in the sense that they all swim in the same dominating tank. The diagram indicates that one of the neighboring fish contains a virtual parent (VP) pointer to a shark species. This qualifies the original candidate species to contribute to the answer.

You can approach the solution from either end of the database path. You can navigate from target to anchor or from anchor to target. One possible algorithm appears below. The outermost loop scans the anchor species, each named shark. However, nested activity locates other species that share a common tank, so the currency pointer isn't reliable at the bottom of the loop. Accordingly, you save the sno key and use it to restore the active anchor before moving to the next one. Within the outermost loop, a second loop moves along the chain of virtual fish belonging to the anchor species. However, within that loop further nested activity moves off to investigate other fish in the same tank. Therefore, you save the fno of the chained fish. You use it later to restore the fish to currency before following a virtual sibling pointer to the next fish on the anchor chain. The nest activity disturbs the memory templates, so you use program variables to retain the key values for restoring the currency pointers. You can also use a stack, as you did in the network case.

```
            int fishKey, speciesKey;
            list *answer;

            answer = createList();
            $get first species where sname = "shark";
            while (dbStatus == 0) {
                speciesKey = species.sno;
                $get first virtual child fish
                    within parent species;
                while (dbStatus == 0) {
                    fishKey = fish.fno;
                    $get parent tank of child fish;
                    $get first child fish within parent tank;
                    while (dbStatus == 0) {
                        $get virtual parent species of child fish;
                        addToList(answer, species.sname);
                        $get next child fish within parent tank; }
                    $get first fish where fno = fishKey;
                    $get next virtual child fish
                        within parent species; }
                $get first species where sno = speciesKey;
                $get next species where sname = "shark"; }
            displayList(answer);
```

You solve an existential query in a hierarchical database by writing nested control loops to navigate through related records. Sometimes the navigation proceeds along virtual chains; other times it investigates a segment of a linearized record hierarchy.

Universal queries

You also solve universal queries in the host language. You can use the same logic developed in Chapter 11 for the network model. An example will illustrate the point: find the names of species represented in all red tanks. The control program constructs two lists: a list of tno values from the red tanks and a list of tno values associated with a candidate species. If the second list contains the first, the candidate contributes to the answer. The program's structure resembles the network case; the difference lies in the database activity needed to construct the lists. The hierarchical solution appears below, following the equivalent SQL set-containment solution. The hierarchical solution reconstructs the activity envisioned for the SQL. However, it explicitly terminates the construction of the candidate species' tanks as soon as that list grows large enough to cover the list of red tanks. The covers boolean keeps track of this fact.

```
select S.sname
from species S
where   (select T.tno                                      (select T.tno
            from fish F, tank T              contains       from tank T
            where S.sno = F.fno and F.tno = T.tno)          where T.tcolor = "red").
```

```
boolean covers;
list *mytanks, *redtanks, *answer;

answer = createList();
redtanks = createList();
$get first tank where tcolor = "red";
while (dbStatus == 0) {              /* acquire list of red tanks */
    addToList(answer, tank.tno);
    $get next tank where tcolor = "red"; }
$get first species;
while (dbStatus == 0) {
    mytanks = createList();
    covers = emptyList(redtanks);           /* covers goes true when mytanks covers redTanks */
    $get first virtual child fish within parent species;
    while (!covers && (dbStatus == 0)) {         /* get list of tanks for this species */
        $get parent tank of child fish;
        addToList(mytanks, tank.tno);
        covers = contains(mytanks, redtanks);       /* compare lists */
        $get first fish where fno = fish.fno;    /* restore currency */
        $get next virtual child fish within parent species; }
    if (covers)
        addToList(answer, species.sname);
    destroyList(mytanks);
    $get next species; }
displayList(answer);
```

 You solve universal queries in a hierarchical database by constructing two sets in the host language program: the set of anchors and the set reachable from the candidate. If the second list contains the first, the candidate is part of the answer.

Aggregate queries

Aggregate queries against a hierarchical database present little difficulty because you can perform the appropriate computations in the host language. The equivalent SQL can serve as a guide for that computation. For example, find the number of fish representing each species. The SQL solution and the hierarchical equivalent appear below.

```
select S.sno, S.sname, count(*)
from Species S, Fish F
where F.sno = S.sno
groupby S.sno.
```

```
int count;
$get first species;
while (dbStatus == 0) {
    count = 0;
    $get first virtual child fish within parent species;
    while (dbStatus == 0) {
        count++;
        $get next virtual child fish within parent species; }
    printf("%d, %s, %d\n", species.sno, species.sname, count);
    $get next species; }
```

You compute aggregates in the host programming language by using database calls to navigate through related records. The usual precautions concerning currency pointers apply.

SUMMARY

The hierarchical database model is the oldest of the five organizational methods studied in this text. Chronologically, the hierarchical and network models represent the past. The relational model represents the present, and the object-oriented and deductive models represent probable trends for the future.

In its simplest incarnation, the hierarchical model uses logical adjacency to represent relationships. Related records are kept close to each other in a hierarchical sequence. This mechanism can't accommodate multiple parentage, so the model adds virtual relationships, which it maintains with chains. With its dependence on visible chains, the hierarchical model reveals a major asymmetry and provides one of the motivating reasons for its successor, the network model.

A type hierarchy is a collection of application entity types, which are connected with one-to-many relationships. The entity types form the nodes of a tree. The relationships are also called parent-child relationships. The parent entity is on the one side of the relationship, and the child is on the many side. The tree structure imposes two further constraints on a hierarchy. First, a distinguished entity, the root, doesn't assume the child role in any relationship. Second, all non-root nodes serve in exactly one child role. The number of parent roles isn't limited for any node.

The type hierarchy appears as a tree when you extend arcs from parent to child. You can derive an instance hierarchy from a type hierarchy by replacing the root entity with one of its records and displaying its child records. If the type hierarchy root has several children, you arrange them in an arbitrary but fixed left-to-right order. An instance hierarchy cloned from the type hierarchy then exhibits the children of the root record in a similar fashion.

Both the type hierarchy and its instances permit linearization with a preorder traversal. You obtain a linearized record hierarchy by concatenating the preorder traversals of all instances of a given type hierarchy. From a particular record in the linearized hierarchy, you can locate related records by moving forward or backward in the list. You navigate from a child to its parent by moving backward from the child until you encounter a record of the proper parent type. You find the children of a given parent in the segment delimited by the parent and the next record of the parent type. This arrangement is called logical adjacency, and you can exploit it to solve queries. The DBMS doesn't actually maintain the records in this linearized fashion. But it projects the illusion that it does, which allows you to construct a program that moves back and forth along the list as the query requires.

Because the model constrains type hierarchies to one-to-many relationships and single parentage, it can't directly represent many-to-many or higher-degree relationships. However, you can establish several type hierarchies in the same database by duplicating certain record types in several places. The duplication is virtual: the records actually exist in a single hierarchy, and the clones are pointer references. When an entity appears as the child of two or more relationships, you choose one relationship for physical representation in a hierarchy. In that hierarchy, the child is a physical child. In the other relationships, the child is virtual, and you access it with a system of pointers. A virtual parent contains a virtual child pointer to locate its first virtual child record. You locate subsequent children by following virtual sibling pointers in the child records. Each child also contains a virtual parent pointer. With this enhancement, the hierarchical model can accommodate multiple parentage. You can then use the standard decomposition technique to replace higher degree and many-to-many relationships with a collection of one-to-many relationships involving multiple parentage.

A hierarchical schema declares the record types, called segments, their fields, their locations in a physical hierarchy, and any pointers necessary to maintain virtual relationships. The get command has variations to move from parent to child and from child to parent within the physical hierarchy or along the virtual chains. A query solution then takes the form of a program in a host language, similar to those developed for the network model. Control loops allow you to investigate the records systematically by accessing them in the hierarchical order. A single currency pointer provides context in each hierarchy. The get commands depend on this pointer to move among related records. Because nested activity can move the currency pointer, you must often restore its proper position at the bottom of a control loop before accessing the next record in the sequence. You can handle this adjustment with a stack of key values, just as in the network case, provided you have included key fields in the schema.

Entity integrity constraints aren't applicable to a hierarchical database because records don't depend on keys for identity or for relationships. The model's structure enforces referential integrity because a record can't exist in a hierarchy without a parent. Positioning a new record in a physical hierarchy identifies a physical parent, namely the one immediately to the left in the linearized hierarchy. The DBMS won't insert a record if a parent record doesn't exist to the left. Nor will it insert a record if it can't find the proper virtual parent. The delete command always removes all children of the target record, which provides the final cleanup necessary to ensure referential integrity. You can specify key constraints with a no-duplicates clause, but the hierarchical model has no provision for enforcing more general constraints, including functional dependencies. ∎

EXERCISES

Informal illustration of a hierarchical database

1. Construct a preorder traversal of the tree in Figure 12.18.

2. Extract all the hierarchies from the library system database, as illustrated in Figure 12.19. Construct a preorder traversal of each.

The level-specific parentheses below indicate the leaf nodes of preorder traversals. Insert lower level parentheses to recapture the tree structure.

3. A, B, $_3(G)_3$, C, E, $_4(J)_4$, $_4(K)_4$, $_3(F)_3$, H, $_4(L)_4$, $_4(M)_4$, $_3(I)_3$, $_2(D)_2$

4. A, B, C, $_4(D)_4$, E, $_5(F)_5$, $_5(G)_5$

Using the linearized record hierarchy of Figure 12.7, find the information requested by the following queries. Don't write code. Instead, derive the information from the linearized hierarchy by observation.

5. Find the names of fish swimming in blue tanks.

6. Find the names of tanks that contain a fish of the same color as the tank.

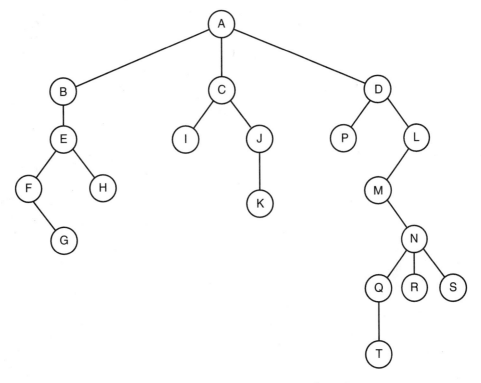

Figure 12.18   Tree for preorder traversal exercise

Write C code to solve the following queries. Take care to track the currency pointer in the linearized hierarchy of Figure 12.7. Assume the availability of list and stack routines as used in the text.

7. Find the names of fish swimming in blue tanks.

8. Find the names of tanks that contain a fish of the same color as the tank.

Relationships, hierarchical definition, and data manipulation

Compose a hierarchical schema for the following situations. Use virtual relationships as necessary.

9. An engineering firm has several projects in progress. Each project occupies the full attention of several engineers. Each engineer has a crew of laboratory assistants who report only to that engineer. Each laboratory assistant owns a collection of instruments (e.g., oscilloscopes, meters). Instruments aren't jointly owned.

10. A molecule contains many atoms. It is important to record the number of each kind of atom in the molecule. For example, methane, CH_4, contains one carbon and four hydrogen atoms. Atoms clearly appear in many different molecules.

The following exercise constructs a hierarchical schema for the library application.

11. The library database consists of libraries, authors, books, patrons, copies, and loans. Assuming one-to-many relationships between library and copy, author and book, book and copy, copy and loan, and patron and loan, construct a hierarchical schema reflecting this arrangement. You will need to break the schema into several hierarchies. You should include primary key fields in the

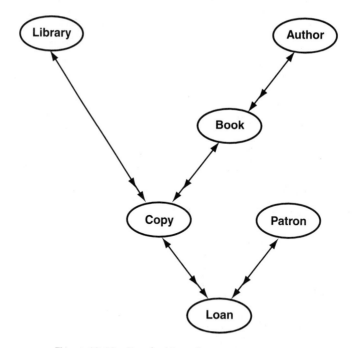

Figure 12.19   Tree for hierarchy extraction exercise

record types even though these entries aren't necessary for expressing relationships. The key fields will be useful for reestablishing the currency pointer in a control loop when it has drifted because of nested activity. The fields associated with each record type are as follows. The primary key is underlined. It isn't necessary to include the foreign keys in the schema.

- library (<u>libno</u>, libname, location, rooms)
- author (<u>authno</u>, authname)
- patron (<u>patno</u>, patname, patwgt)
- book (<u>bookno</u>, title, pages, authno)
- copy (<u>copyno</u>, cost, bookno, libno)
- loan (<u>loanno</u>, duedate, copyno, patno)

12. Assume you have information for libraries, authors, and patrons on three files: library.txt, author.txt, and patron.txt respectively. Each file record represents one instance of the corresponding application entity, and the fields are in fixed record positions in the record according to the following format. The primary keys of the entities are underlined. Write C code to load the files into the hierarchical database described above. You don't need to include error-processing contingencies.

library.txt	
field	position
<u>libno</u>	1 – 5
libname	11 – 30
location	41 – 60
rooms	71 – 75

author.txt	
field	position
<u>authno</u>	1 – 5
authname	11 – 30

patron.txt	
field	position
<u>patno</u>	1 – 5
patname	11 – 30
patwgt	41 – 45

13. Write C code to delete all books written by Salinger.

14. All Seattle libraries are merging into a single library. The buildings have all been stacked on top of each other, and the new building contains all the rooms of its components. All copies of books

from the constituent libraries have been consolidated into the new library. The new library is called MegaLib. Write C code to update the database.

Constraints

15. Write a C routine to enforce the constraint: libraries outside Seattle must not have books with more than 300 pages. How must the routine be used to ensure that the constraint isn't violated?

16. Write a C routine to enforce the constraint that patrons weighing more than 100 pounds may not check out a book written by Salinger.

Hierarchical queries

17. Find the titles of books written by Salinger that contain 300 pages or more.

18. Find the titles of books that are available from a library that is patronized by a patron named joe.

19.
```
select L.libname
from library L, copy C, loan LN, patron P
where L.libno = C.libno and C.copyno = LN.copyno and LN.patronno = P.patronno
    and P.patwgt > 150.
```

20. Find the titles of books that have been read by all patrons and are available from every library.

21.
```
select L.libname
from library L
where
    (select B.bookno
    from copy C, book B
    where L.libno = C.libno and C.bookno = B.bookno)
contains
    (select B.bookno
    from book B
    where B.pages > 300).
```

22. Find the average number of pages in a book.

23. Find the names of patrons whose weight is greater than the average weight of patrons who have read a book entitled **The Name of the Rose**.

24.
```
select L.libno, L.libname, sum(B.pages) totalpages
from library L, book B
where exists
    (select *
    from copy C
    where L.libno = C.libno and C.bookno = B.bookno)
groupby L.libno
having average(B.pages) >
    (select average(B.pages)
    from book B).
```

13 Comparing the Database Models

Model similarities

So far this text has surveyed five database models: hierarchical, network, relational, object-oriented, and deductive. Although preceding chapters have emphasized their differences, it's important to remember that the five models exhibit some fundamental similarities. Figure 13.1 provides an overview of the models' similarities and differences.

The most obvious similarity is that all five models possess features for storing both application entity descriptions and instances of these entities. Regardless of the database model, an application entity description is an attribute collection; an entity instance is a collection of values under these attributes. Different application entities have different attribute collections. In the aquarium example, a tank is a (tno, tname, tcolor, tvolume) collection; a species is a (sno, sname, sfood) collection. These differences allow you to distinguish among the entities in the real-world application. You don't confuse a tank with a species because the former exhibits tno, tname, tcolor, and tvolume values that you associate with a tank. You perceive a species as belonging to a different entity, which comprises sno, sname, and sfood values. Within an application entity, all instances use the same attributes. You can, however, distinguish among the instances because they have different attribute values. One tank is the value set (tno = 42, tname = cesspool, tcolor = blue, tvolume = 100); another is (tno = 35, tname = lagoon, tcolor = red, tvolume = 400).

To maintain application entities and their instances, all five database models also use some form of table format. Each application entity becomes a separate table. The instances of a given entity become rows in its table. All five database models use some generalization of the table format in this fashion. The relational model, of course, explicitly specifies tables as the storage mechanism. In a relational schema, you describe a table shell for each application entity. In subsequent processing, you manipulate the table rows as instances of the corresponding application entity. In a network schema, you specify a record type for each application entity. A file of records then represents the instances. A file is a

Model	Data element organization	Relationship organization	Identity	Access language
Relational	Tables	Identifiers for rows of one table are embedded as attribute values in another table.	value-based	non-procedural
Object-Oriented	Objects, which logically encapsulate both attributes and behavior	Logical containment. Related objects are found within a given object by recursively examining its attributes. The attributes are themselves objects.	record-based	procedural
Deductive	Base facts that can be arranged in tables	Inference rules that permit related facts to be generated on demand	value-based	non-procedural
Hierarchical	Files, records	Logical proximity in a linearized tree	record-based	procedural
Network	Files, records	Intersecting chains	record-based	procedural

Figure 13.1   Comparison of the five database models

generalized table, where the repeating elements are records rather than rows. Each record, however, corresponds exactly to a row because it is a sequence of field values, just as a row is a sequence of attribute values. In a hierarchical schema, you specify a segment for each application entity. Except for the notation, however, a segment description is the same as a network record type description. Both contain a list of named fields and imply a file of records that are compatible with the fields. If you broaden the definition of a table to include a file of records, you can conclude that the relational, network, and hierarchical database models all use tables to store the application entities and their instances.

The object-oriented and deductive database models can also use tables. However, these models' philosophies de-emphasize storage structure and leave the choice to a given implementation. In the object-oriented model, an application entity becomes a class; the instances become objects created from the corresponding class. A class encapsulates an attribute collection, and each object from the class provides specific values for the attributes. Although the model provides no further storage details, you can still envision the objects as rows in a table. Each row provides the values for the class attributes, which appear across the top of the table. In this representation, the object identifier (OID) is just another attribute. Similarly, the deductive model can store the axioms in a tabular form. The deductive schema specifies the axiom shells, such as `tankHasName (X, Y)`, and you can envision the appropriate ground instances arrayed as rows in a corresponding table. In this case, the `tankHasName` table could appear as follows:

tankHasName	
t_1	puddle
t_2	cesspool
t_3	lagoon
t_4	cesspool
t_5	beach
t_6	lagoon

A deductive database also contains inference rules. Each inference rule comprises two strings: a head and a body. You can, therefore, store the inference rules in a table where each row corresponds to a different rule. The table has two columns: one for the head strings and another for the body strings.

In addition to using tables to store the application entities and their instances, all five database models also provide some arrangement for navigating through relationships to extract query solutions. The representative structures have evolved from primitive linking schemes that expose the implementation structures to more abstract relationship concepts that suppress implementation detail. In all cases, however, query solutions still exploit the available relationship mechanism to assemble related data elements.

Specific patterns characterize the query categories: existential, universal, and aggregate. In an abstract sense, a query solution in a given category is the same across all the models. You always solve an existential query by searching for database paths between a candidate and an anchor. Only the details for expressing the path vary from one model to the next. In the relational model, the path proceeds across one-to-many relationships by linking tuples where the foreign-key value in the dependent entity matches the primary-key value in the dominant entity. In the network model, you construct the path by traversing the record chains of the network sets. This navigation again proceeds across one-to-many relationships because each chain corresponds to a relationship instance, which links a dominant record with its dependent partners. The path can enter on a dominant record and depart from a dependent record, or it can enter on a dependent record and depart from the dominant one. In a hierarchical database, you encounter both physical and virtual one-to-many relationships as you construct the existential path. The process for a virtual relationship is the same as in the network case: you move along linked chains from the dominant to a dependent record or vice versa. For a physical relationship, you move within a linearized hierarchy of records. You move backward to the first record of the proper type to link a dependent record with its dominant partner. You scan forward to obtain the dependents associated with a given dominant record.

In an object-oriented database, an existential path burrows into the candidate's attributes. Because attribute values can be complex objects, this process continually discovers related objects, and it can continue the probe by investigating their attributes. Although the model provides no further implementation detail, you can imagine an existential path passing through table rows, just as in the relational case. Where a relational path jumps from a foreign-key value to a matching primary-key value in a row of a remote table, an object-oriented path jumps from an attribute OID to a matching object in a remote table. This viewpoint, of course, assumes that objects are arrayed in tabular rows as discussed above. In the aquarium example, suppose a fish object contains OID-5021 in its home attribute. In the table of tank objects, one of the rows will have an OID attribute equal to 5021. In a sense, the home attribute in the fish is a foreign key, which points to a particular row in the tank-object table. The situation is only slightly different from the corresponding relational representation. In the relational model, the primary-key values for each tank come from the application. Users must provide tno values, just as they must supply tname, tcolor, and tvolume values. In the object-oriented model, the DBMS provides the OIDs, which ultimately serve the same purpose.

A deductive schema specifies axioms for the basic relationships, such as `fishInhabitsTank (X, Y)`. By using common variable names in adjacent subgoals, you can construct an existential path with these relationship predicates. Suppose you want the names of species represented in red tanks. The following inference rule expresses this existential query:

```
query (X) ⊢ speciesHasName (A, X), fishRepresentsSpecies (B, A),
               fishInhabitsTank (B, C), tankHasColor (C, "red").
```

In a successful binding, the variable A points to a particular species. You can think of the A value as a primary key in each of the attribute tables. Assuming the tabular representation discussed above, the ground instances of `speciesHasName (P, Q)` appear as table rows. Each row contains the primary key of a species and its corresponding sname string. In the `fishRepresentsSpecies (B, A)` subgoal, the same A value occurs. Here, it acts as a foreign key, which points to the corresponding primary keys in the attribute tables `speciesHasName` and `speciesHasfood`. In the successful binding, the B value must now be the primary key of a fish that represents species A. Similar interpretations apply to the remaining links in the query. So an existential database path in a deductive database proceeds along common variable names in subgoals, and the successful bindings act much like the links between foreign and primary keys in relational tuples.

Solving universal queries is also similar for all five models. You construct two sets: the anchors and the elements reachable from a candidate. If the second set includes the first, the candidate contributes to the answer. Only the details of the set constructions vary across the models. Two approaches are available in the relational model: the set-containment approach and the doubly negated approach. In the former, you explicitly construct the two sets with subqueries and then test for containment. In the doubly negated solution, the set containment is tested one element at a time, without explicitly building the sets. Set A is contained in set B if and only if $(\forall x)(x \in A \implies x \in B)$. Equivalently, set A is contained in set B if and only if $\neg(\exists x)(x \in A \land \neg(x \in B))$. The two negations produce two not-exists subqueries in the Structured Query Language (SQL) expression. In both the hierarchical, network, and object-oriented models, you must accumulate the two sets in a host language program, which makes appropriate calls to the database. You also test the set containment with the host language features. The deductive model follows the doubly negated SQL solution, and you can, therefore, interpret the solution as following the same pattern as in the other models. If the set of reachable objects includes the set of anchor objects, the candidate contributes to the answer. The two negations appear in linked subgoals, as in the following example: find the names of tanks that contain all species.

```
           query (N) ⊢   tankHasName (T, N), ¬tankMissesSpecies (T).
tankMissesSpecies (T) ⊢   species (S), ¬connected (T, S).
      connected (T, S) ⊢   fishInhabitsTank (F, T), fishRepresentsSpecies (F, S).
```

The final category, aggregate queries, involves a summarizing computation over a partitioned table. In the hierarchical, network, and object-oriented models, you explicitly program the calculations in a host language program, which calls the database as needed. The process is implicit in the relational and deductive models although the DBMS must set up the same partitioning and summarizing activities that you program in the other models.

The deductive model, in particular, must use an operational definition of its aggregate predicates, which brings the underlying computation into the user's view even though he doesn't have to program it.

The models' strengths and weaknesses

Although the five database models do share significant similarities, they have varying strengths and weaknesses. As expected, the older hierarchical and network models are deficient in many respects, and in today's database environments, it's difficult to find any compensating strengths. The relational model, by contrast, remains a strong contender in the face of its newer competitors, the object-oriented and deductive models. Starting with the older models and working forward, this section discusses the five models' relative strengths and weaknesses. For the older models, you should expect mostly weaknesses. Indeed, the earlier models' shortcomings provided the impetus for their replacements. For the newer models, you should expect mostly strengths.

The hierarchical and network models

As illustrated in the query solutions of Chapters 11 and 12, the hierarchical and network models share many features. Both represent data as records, and both include navigation commands for moving among related records. Both also express queries and update activities in a host program that makes library procedure calls to transfer information back and forth with the database. These common features lead to common weaknesses.

The hierarchical model has overly complicated structures for maintaining relationships. Although logical adjacency is a straightforward organizational principle, it isn't sufficient for multiple parentage situations. In these cases, the hierarchical model introduces a second scheme for maintaining relationships—virtual chains. This solution forces an asymmetry into the model: some relationships use logical adjacency, and some use virtual chains. You must remain constantly aware of the distinction when writing navigational queries. Moreover, the hierarchical model involves database designers in yet more programming details because they must direct the DBMS in constructing the type hierarchies. Should the records contain one-way or two-way links? Should dependent records contain parent pointers? Should the root records enjoy a fast access path, such as a hash table? These questions are far from the application domain where the designers should be working.

The hierarchical model actually employs the network set concept, disguised as virtual chains, but doesn't elevate it to full status with appropriate commands for using it. Instead, it mixes database commands with programming language control methods, such as threaded trees. Because the hierarchical model is so tightly bound with a host control language, you must be a capable programmer to use it. Under these conditions, writing database manipulation programs is a difficult and specialized task. The syntax of commercial hierarchical products makes the problem worse because it is typically dense and cryptic, with many references to physical storage details.

Offsetting the cumbersome representation of relationships is the relative speed and efficiency of the network and hierarchical models. To maintain network sets or virtual relationships, they use pointer chains, which provide direct disk addresses of related records. The application designer can also specify rapid retrieval structures for the logical adjacency implementation, such as pointer arrays, indices, or hash tables. These devices circumvent the sequential search implied by the physical parent-child relationship in the linearized hierarchy. For relationships that are built into the applications, these methods locate the disk addresses of related records with less overhead than in the relational or post-relational models.

For ad hoc relationships that appear after the database is in use, however, the pre-wired disk address links provide no assistance, and the performance degenerates to sequential searches. For example, a designer of the aquarium database could easily foresee that the relationship between a fish and its home tank should be pre-established. A user could, however, imagine a new relationship, where the fish is associated with a tank of compatible color. In the relational model, this relationship would automatically be supported through matching values in the fcolor and tcolor attributes of the two entities. In the hierarchical and network models, it wouldn't be supported at all. Any queries that used the new relationship would have to search the files sequentially for matching records. Therefore, although the lower-level linkage mechanisms increase the older models' efficiency, they don't make up for the less flexible relationship representation methods.

Because they manipulate data in a host programming language, the access languages of the hierarchical and network models are more powerful than SQL. In particular, you can express recursive queries with unbounded depths. Of course, the price of this flexibility is long and potentially expensive programming. Moreover, the ability to probe recursive relationships is usually wasted in the hierarchical case because a hierarchical DBMS typically doesn't allow recursive relationships. Although you can stretch the virtual pointer chains to accommodate recursive relationships, commercial hierarchical products usually don't allow the extension. This deficiency simply reflects the products' age. At the time they were developed, many problems were more pressing than recursive relationships, and now there would little profit in rewriting these old systems.

The hierarchical model was an early attempt to bring some organization to data processing systems of the 1950s and 1960s. At that time, an application was distributed across a suite of programs and their tailored files. Considered against this background, the model does make some progress by providing a common description of the data hierarchies and a central data repository to serve many programs. Judging it against the generic database definition of Chapter 1, however, you can conclude that the hierarchical model is hardly self-describing. It contains no provisions for metadata, and therefore a program can't query the database about its organization. In comparison with more modern models, the user interface isn't systematic. A large programming effort is necessary to extract information from a hierarchical database, and the asymmetry between physical and virtual relationships complicates that programming.

The network model corrects the hierarchical model's most troublesome oversight—the awkward representation of multiple parentage. It also raises relationships to the status of named database elements, network sets, and it introduces commands for manipulating them. These extensions enable more realistic modeling of real-world situations. They also conform directly with the features of entity-relationship diagrams, which are currently the most popular database design methods. For a user interface, however, the network model still uses database calls from a host language control program. This approach is certainly very flexible because, in theory, you can program any user interface. However, these programs are expensive and involve a lot of duplicated effort. Furthermore, they discourage nontechnical users, who aren't proficient in the host language. The network model also retains a relationship maintenance mechanism (i.e., network sets) that exposes the underlying data structures (i.e., linked chains). Because it requires a familiarity with computer science constructs, this feature further limits the number of potential users.

In short, both the hierarchical and network models suffer from complicated relationship schemes, which require both database designers and users to possess considerable technical expertise. Furthermore, the user must be familiar with a host programming language to access a hierarchical or network database. The network model is slightly more acceptable because it has a consistent method for representing relationships in the face of multiple-parentage or higher-degree relationships. The only compensating advantage is that both models offer efficient access to related records through pointers to disk addresses.

The relational model

The relational model was designed to remove the host-language access requirement and to suppress the subsidiary structures for maintaining relationships. From the user's viewpoint, matching values in common attributes implicitly lace together related tuples in disjoint tables. The DBMS can use indices, linked lists, and other structures to enhance performance, but it hides these technical details from the user. SQL provides a systematic, nonprocedural interface, which removes the need for the user to understand a host programming language. Although SQL itself is a programming language, it is simple compared to the procedural hosts of the hierarchical and network models. Because it is patterned after structured English, SQL is accessible to a wide range of nontechnical users. After writing query solutions for the hierarchical and network models, you can surely appreciate why the relational model received such a warm welcome.

Relational DBMS products also derived significant benefits from years of database research. The relational model has a rigorous mathematical base. The concept of a relation itself is a mathematical one. Each attribute has an associated domain, and the relation's body at any time is, except for the attribute order, a subset of the Cartesian product of these domains. The mathematical definition of a relation over a finite collection of domains is essentially the same: a subset of the Cartesian product. The only difference is that the relational definition removes the attribute order that is inherent in the mathematical Cartesian product. The model's name, therefore, comes from its mathematical counterpart. The definitions of the relational database components also proceed from mathematical concepts. A domain is a set of values. An attribute is a name-domain pair. An association over an attribute is a name-value pair, where the name comes from the attribute and the value comes from the corresponding domain. A relational schema is a set of attributes. A tuple over a relational schema is a set of associations over the corresponding attributes. A relational body is a set of tuples over the corresponding relational schema. Finally, a relational database is a set of relations, each comprising a schema and a body.

Other strengths of a relational DBMS also arose from relational research, which culminated in Codd's twelve rules. The rules for a relational DBMS include the following important criteria:

- Only table structures are visible to the user.

- An active catalog stores metadata, which makes the database self-describing.

- The user interface employs a set-oriented language.

- A conceptual schema buffers applications from changes to the underlying physical storage. A view mechanism buffers applications from changes in the conceptual schema.

Relational databases maintain relationships with common attributes in related tables. This method disposes with, or at least hides, the complicated chains or linearized trees of the earlier models. A nontechnical audience can easily visualize one-to-many relationships laced together with foreign-key references.

In summary, the relational model's advantages over its predecessors are its simple tabular schema, its uncomplicated relationship representation scheme, its comparatively simple access language, SQL, and its strong mathematical foundation for the underlying concepts.

Of course, the relational model isn't without its shortcomings. In a way, the model has generated its own deficiencies by enabling the exploration of more difficult problem domains, such as databases with pictures and soundtracks. Some difficulties touch on philosophical data modeling issues, such as dispersing an application entity across several tables. Others are simple inconveniences, which seldom provoke practical problems. For example, SQL isn't computationally complete, but this deficiency is barely noticed outside of academic textbooks. The post-relational models do, however, address these issues.

The object-oriented model

In the object-oriented model, the application entities become database classes, and entity instances become objects under the appropriate class. A class corresponds roughly to a table shell in the relational model, and an object corresponds to a row in the table. A class is actually a more expressive modeling feature than a table because it captures the behavior of its objects in addition to their static attributes. Moreover, an object's attribute values aren't limited to the simple strings and numbers of the earlier models: they can be other objects. The DBMS can, therefore, represent an object as a compact structure that contains its related objects. By contrast, the relational model visibly maintains related tuples in separate tables. Relationship representation through logical inclusion is at least as straightforward as through common attribute links. Many would argue that logical inclusion is simpler because it frequently corresponds more naturally with the real-world relationship. In the aquarium example, the relationship between a tank and its fish exhibits physical inclusion. The corresponding relationship in the object-oriented database exhibits logical inclusion. The tank contains a home attribute, whose value is the appropriate fish collection.

Because an application object contains related objects within itself, at some level of recursion, you can construct query solutions by probing the candidate object's attributes. This approach is procedural, so you might suspect it is inferior to the non-procedural SQL. But the required procedures are, in fact, simple in comparison with the host language programming of the hierarchical and network models. Furthermore, non-procedural extensions, such as OQL, salvage much of SQL's convenience while still exploiting the model's object-oriented features.

As a data modeling tool, the object-oriented model offers another advantage over the relational model: the class hierarchy. You can insert application classes at appropriate points in an existing system structure. An object instantiated through an application class then contains not only the attributes and methods defined in that class, but also the attributes and methods of its superclasses. So you can define a new class incrementally by specifying only how it extends its immediate parent. In general, all the strengths of object-oriented modeling are available in an object-oriented database: inheritance, encapsulation, polymorphism, and message-passing among objects.

In summary, the object-oriented models possesses the following advantages over its relational predecessor: a class structure, which encapsulates behavior as well as the traditional static attributes; a simple relationship mechanism, logical inclusion, which often corresponds with its real-world equivalent; and application-modeling features adopted from object-oriented software development, such as inheritance and polymorphism. One regression appears to be the reappearance of a host programming language for user access to the database. The object-oriented language syntax is, however, less difficult than the host languages of the earlier models. In any case, a non-procedural query language, Object Query Language (OQL), is available. OQL retains the flavor of SQL but provides access to the database's object-oriented features.

The deductive model

The deductive database represents another post-relational line of research. Although it retains tables for the core information (i.e., the axioms), most of the database exists only as an implicit collection of facts that are consistent with the axioms and the inference rules. Like the relational model, a deductive system is strongly based on mathematical reasoning. By restricting the format of the inference rules, you can prove the existence of a minimal model, which is a large collection of facts that extends the axioms and conforms closely to the application. Inference rules define derived predicates, which in turn correspond to virtual tables. However, the DBMS doesn't store these virtual tables. Instead, it materializes them as needed in the query solution process.

The operational meaning of inference rules is closely related to relational algebra because the inference rules guide the reassembly of a virtual table. Because a deductive database uses an implicit reassembly process, it doesn't encapsulate application objects as compactly as its object-oriented equivalent. Instead, the deductive viewpoint is closer to the relational one: it just uses different methods to assemble dispersed information.

The deductive model handles relationships with relationship predicates, which you can envision as tabulations of relationship instances, much like the intersection tables in relational databases. This method then shares the advantages of the relational method: no technical constructions, such as linked lists, appear at the user interface. In comparison with the object-oriented model, however, the deductive model doesn't make as much progress in bringing the model closer to the reality of the application. Application objects in a deductive database still contain only attributes, not behavior, and they are still dispersed across many tables. In the aquarium example, a fish object has ground instances tabulated under the `fish`, `fishHasName`, `fishHasColor`, and `fishHasWeight` axioms. Moreover, the attributes are still limited to numbers and strings, which provide only shallow modeling capabilities when compared with complex-valued attributes.

In truth, the deductive model is actually just another viewpoint on the relational representation. Inference rules replace queries as instruments for combining stored information in new ways. The difference is that the deductive model considers the set of initial inference rules, plus subsequent query rules, as defining the application on a continuous basis. As the inference rules change, the minimal model adjusts to encompass exactly the facts that should be true about the real-world application. Except for name conflicts, you should never have to withdraw any inference rules that you used in a query solution. The inferred facts remain true as additional rules continue to refine the meaning of the database. This viewpoint is prevalent in artificial intelligence studies, where much research concentrates on automated reasoning techniques. Against this background, an advantage of deductive databases is that research results and techniques from artificial intelligence studies can be applied to database modeling situations.

The deductive model thus shares the strengths of the relational model and invites further features from the realms of artificial intelligence and automated reasoning. Its access language of inference rules is more powerful than SQL because, under proper conditions, it can handle recursive queries. Because of its similarity to the relational model, the deductive model also exhibits the shortcomings of the relational model: a dispersed representation of application objects, no complex-valued attributes, and no encapsulated behavior.

DISK STORAGE MANAGEMENT

PART I EMPHASIZED THE STRUCTURES DATABASE MODELS USE TO STORE data elements and maintain relationships among them. Because the database content can be large and because it must survive machine shutdowns and failures, the DBMS retains the database structures on secondary storage, typically magnetic disk packs. The DBMS transfers small sections from the database to computer memory for processing, and it writes any changes back onto the disk. Unfortunately, a data packet exchange between disk and memory is three to five orders of magnitude slower than the same operation between two memory structures.

To appreciate this speed difference, suppose you are working steadily on an assembly line at the rate of one operation per second. You might, for example, be stapling the pages of a report. It takes about one second to pick up the report pages, square them off, place the corner under the stapler head, and strike it. If a source supplies you with a continual stream of unstapled reports, you can continue to work at this pace. Now, suppose the source interrupts the supply stream while it fetches a new batch from a remote printing location. To make the situation comparable to a disk access delay, suppose it takes 10^5 times as long as a basic stapling operation. The delay is then 10^5 seconds or about 30 hours! You must obviously integrate a delay of this size carefully into the work schedule.

Similarly, the disk organization that responds to database commands must minimize the required disk accesses. Compared with the time needed to recall data from disk into memory, the time needed to actually process the data is negligible. So Part II will emphasize techniques for organizing data storage on disks and for rapidly finding particular data elements in that storage.

The first chapter surveys physical organization schemes for disk storage units and then discusses the particular storage needs of database management systems. Traditional data files use a repeating record structure; the operating system intervenes to allow a controlling program to sequence through these homogeneous records. Unfortunately, a DBMS deals with many different data types, and for efficiency reasons, it must pack different record types into adjacent file records. A DBMS, therefore, views disk storage as individually addressable pages and takes over the management of these pages from the operating system.

Of course, the pages store application data, but they also contain links to related records and pointers for rapid retrievals.

Chapter 14 analyzes the advantages and disadvantages of two file organization techniques: indexed sequential and hashed. Both enable the rapid retrieval of target records based on key field values. By themselves, these organizations improve performance by dividing the search space into a collection of smaller segments. Further improvement comes from auxiliary files, called indexes, that accelerate access to the main data file. Chapter 15 presents two kinds of indexes: hierarchical indexes and B^+-trees. Finally, Chapter 16 revisits the five database models and considers file organization schemes that are appropriate for their operations.

14 File Structures

ARLIER CHAPTERS EMPHASIZED THE ORGANIZATIONAL METHODS FOR storing data elements, maintaining relationships among them, and responding to user commands. However, these discussions gave little attention to the physical storage details necessary to implement the organizations. For example, the relational model expresses relationships with common attributes across disparate tables. When you need to assemble related tuples, you invoke join operations, either directly through relational algebra or indirectly through SQL. In your mind's eye, the DBMS forms a Cartesian product of the relevant tables and filters out the entries that don't agree on the common attributes. But the DBMS will typically avoid the wasteful Cartesian product construction because the subsequent filtering operation normally rejects most of it anyway.

You can envision a more efficient process that retrieves the tables' tuples in sorted order on the common attributes. Suppose two tables, A and B, have the common attribute x. A has n tuples; B has m. To form the Cartesian product, the DBMS must cycle the entire B table past each A tuple, which requires mn operations. The time consumed depends on the tuples' storage format, but a rough estimate of the operation count is proportional to the time. If you can retrieve the tuples from A and B in sorted order on attribute x, you can complete the join with one sequential pass through each table. Assume that the computer memory is large enough to hold, at the same time, all the A tuples and B tuples with a particular x value, say, $x = v_1$. You start simultaneous position markers at the heads of tables A and B. As long as the x values don't match, you advance the marker with the smaller x value. When a match occurs, say $x = v_1$, you import into memory buffers all the tuples from A and B with $x = v_1$, advancing the A and B markers as you transfer the tuples. In memory, you form all combinations with a prefix from A and a suffix from B and emit the resulting tuples to the accumulating join table. You then continue advancing the marker with the smaller x value until you discover another match. This process requires only $m + n$ tuple accesses, which is much smaller than the mn needed for the Cartesian product. Of course, this more efficient process needs the tuples in sorted order. This chapter and Chapter 15 discuss techniques for achieving the required order.

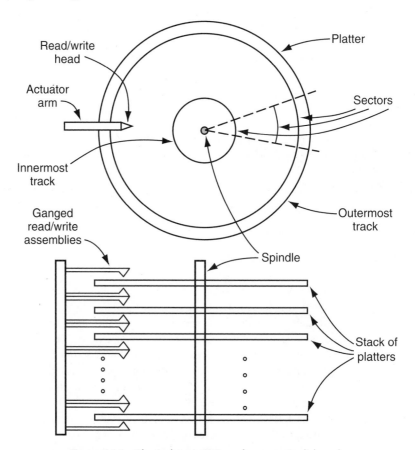

Figure 14.1   Physical organization of a magnetic disk pack

Physical organization of a disk storage unit

This section examines the physical parameters of disk storage units—those that determine its storage capacity and its data transfer rate to and from main memory. As shown in Figure 14.1, a disk contains a stack of platters on a common spindle. A thin, uniform film of magnetic material covers each platter's surface. The platters spin close to a recording head, which can electrically coerce a small patch of the film into one of two possible polarities without affecting adjacent patches. These two polarities are the ubiquitous 0 and 1 of the binary alphabet. Groups of adjacent patches form bytes for data storage.

When you store data as patterns of magnetized states on the disk surface, the storage is **persistent**. Even if you remove power from the disk unit, the patterns remain until the recording head stimulates them to change. Persistent storage is fundamentally different from computer memory, where stored patterns vanish when the power is removed. **Volatile** storage describes a memory device that loses its stored patterns when power is removed.

Each disk surface contains subdivisions, called regions, where you can reliably store and retrieve data bytes. **Formatting** is the process that establishes the regions, which you address hierarchically through cylinders, tracks, and sectors. The disk's physical construction directly determines the address parameters, as discussed below.

The platters are rigidly attached to the central spindle, which rotates them at a uniform speed—typically 3600 revolutions per minute. On the periphery of the spinning platters is the recording head, which contains a single read-write sensor for each platter surface. (See Figure 14.1.) Although the sensor mechanism's arms are stationary—they don't rotate with the platters—they can still extend back and forth in the space between the platters to position the read-write head at some varying radial distance from the spindle. A precise stepper motor controls the in-and-out motion, allowing the head to stop only at certain radial positions called **tracks**. The radial position closest to the platter edge is the outermost track, or track 0; the position corresponding to the maximal extension of the read-write arms is the innermost track, or track $N - 1$. The number of tracks, N, is a parameter that determines the disk's storage capacity. N is about 100 for small floppy diskettes and about 1000 for larger sealed units. Each track position defines a circular path on each platter surface, which repeatedly circulates beneath the read-write head for that surface as long as the actuator arms hold their radial position.

Each track contains further subdivisions, called **sectors**. A sector is an angular extent along a track. As illustrated in Figure 14.1, the track sectors form pie-shaped wedges that fan out from the spindle and cross all the tracks on a platter. You can store the same number of bytes in any sector, regardless of its track. Because the outermost track is farther from the spindle, the linear extent of a sector is greater than for the innermost track. This disparity means that the small magnetized areas that define the bytes must be packed more closely on the innermost track than on the outermost. It also means that the innermost track can't be too close to the spindle because that would require extremely tight packing of the magnetized areas. Consequently, the innermost track is typically about half-way from the spindle to the edge of the disk, resulting in a packing density ratio of about 2:1 from the innermost to the outermost track. Because the platter rotates at a uniform angular velocity, the time required for a sector to pass beneath the read-write head is the same, regardless of its track. The formatting process establishes a fixed angular position as the beginning of sector 0 (across all tracks), and the other sectors then assume consecutively higher numbers up to some limit, $M - 1$. M is a second manufacturing parameter that determines the disk's storage capacity. Typically, M ranges from 20 to 50. The number of bytes, B, that you can store in each sector also varies with the disk unit, but it is usually a power of 2 in the range of 512 to 4096.

The last parameter needed to determine the disk's storage capacity is the number of platter surfaces, P. P can vary from 1 for single-sided floppy disks to as many as 50 for larger units. The total byte capacity is then the product $PNMB$. If you take the upper end of the parameter ranges, you calculate a storage capacity of $50 \cdot 1000 \cdot 50 \cdot 4096 \approx 10^{10}$, or 10 gigabytes. This figure is on the high end for current commercial products. However, disks of a few gigabytes do exist, and rapid progress in disk storage technology continues to provide larger and larger storage capacities.

Because the read-write heads for the platters are grouped together, the same track number circulates under the head for each platter surface. A **cylinder** is the collection of tracks with the same number from the various platter surfaces. Cylinder 0 contains all the outermost tracks from the surfaces; cylinder $N - 1$ contains all the innermost tracks. The concept of a cylinder is important because you can access data from the tracks in a cylinder without moving the radial position of the read-write head. Each sector on the disk has a unique disk address consisting of the cylinder number, the platter surface number, and the angular sector number. A sector is also known as a page.

 A disk unit contains a stack of platters, each providing two surfaces for storage. Each surface holds a sequence of concentric tracks, each track holds a fixed number of sectors, and each sector holds a fixed number of bytes. You can individually address each sector (page) on the disk.

The hardware conducts all data transfers between the disk unit and computer memory in complete sectors. Moreover, transfers occur without continuous attention from the computer's central processor. The central processor gives the disk controller a command, which specifies the sector address, the location of a memory buffer, and the direction of the intended transfer (to disk or from disk). The central processor then continues with its program while the disk controller undertakes the transfer and provides an interrupt when it is complete. This independent operation is **direct memory access (DMA)**.

The time required to complete a transfer is the sum of three delays. First, the read/write heads must move to the proper cylinder, which usually takes 10 milliseconds. This is the **seek time**. The head must then wait for the required sector to rotate beneath its sensors, which generally takes about 8 milliseconds. This is the **rotational latency**. Finally, the head must read or write the data as the sector passes by. This is the **transmission time**, perhaps 0.5 millisecond. The given values are averages. The read-write heads may already be on the required track, and the proper sector may be just ready to rotate past the sensor. In this case, the time would be 0.5 millisecond for the transfer. However, such luck is rare, and this chapter will use 15 milliseconds as a rough estimate of the time needed to access a disk sector. Newer disk units are pushing this value lower, but it will always be in the millisecond range because it involves physically moving parts. This is roughly a million times slower than the nanosecond range for computer memory operations.

Because a disk storage unit is a common resource across all computer processes, the operating system manages access to it. A user, including a sophisticated user such as a DBMS, regards the disk as a collection of files, each holding records of a particular format. The most common structure, for example, is a stream of characters. The operating system typically interposes two levels of abstraction between the user and the actual storage medium: the file manager and the disk manager. Figure 14.2 illustrates the chain of command.

Suppose you request record 26 of the "myfile.txt" file. The file manager maintains tables for each named file, which identify the pages devoted to that file. These tables must also reside on the disk because they must be persistent, but the operating system handles those details. In response to your request, the file manager supplies sector addresses to the disk manager and asks the disk manager to return the corresponding file pages. The disk manager, in turn, asks the disk controller to transfer the sectors and supplies the address of a memory buffer to hold the returned information. The disk manager deals with pages and isn't concerned with the pages' content. The file manager is aware of the page arrangement

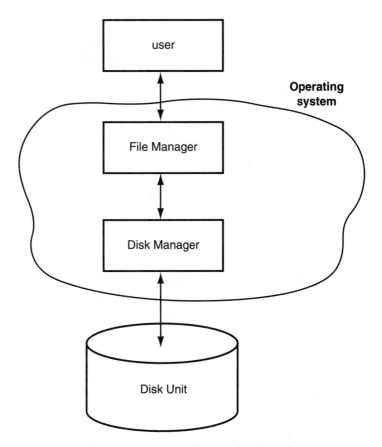

Figure 14.2   Layers of management between the disk and a user program

that constitutes a particular file, and it knows the record format within the pages. So even though it isn't concerned with the record's contents, the file manager can deliver the records to the user. In the end, your program receives a memory image of the requested record. It may then copy elements into local variables, or it may manipulate the data directly in the buffer.

Hoping to receive additional requests for the previously accessed pages, the disk manager can hoard pages in its internal buffers. In that case, it can deliver the required data without a disk access. So that all updates are persistent, however, it must always ensure that the actual disk pages are faithful reflections of the memory images. The disk manager also maintains a list of empty pages that it can assign to a file upon request by the file manager. This policy allows files to grow and shrink dynamically.

This division of labor works fairly well for ordinary programs that regard files as uniformly organized structures (i.e., some persistent repeating pattern). However, a DBMS often mixes different structures on the same file. In the aquarium application, for example, the DBMS may mix the tank records with the fish records. Because it anticipates a frequent need for both kinds of records in a given relationship group, the DBMS wants to store fish records on the same page as their home tanks. Such variations complicate the conventional file manager's job, so the DBMS subsumes the file manager function. The DBMS regards each file as a collection of pages, and depending on the file organization, it retains certain information about the pages' disk addresses. The DBMS can then interact directly with the disk manager to obtain new pages or to reacquire existing pages. The DBMS also handles any schemes for integrating the pages into higher-level structures.

The computer operating system usually controls disk access through a disk manager, which reads and writes pages at the file manager's request. The file manager keeps track of which pages belong to which files and allows an application program to view a file as a named collection of records. Because it needs to store different kinds of records in the same file, a DBMS usually interacts directly with the disk manager.

Block layout schemes

The established literature refers to the DBMS' elementary storage unit as a **block**. The smallest unit of disk transfer, the block contains 512 to 4096 bytes depending on the particular disk unit. A block is usually a page. However, to make the DBMS more independent of the hardware platform, the DBMS map between blocks and disk sectors might not be one-to-one. If the block is larger than a page, the disk manager must combine several pages to form the block. If the block is smaller than the page, the disk manager can pack several blocks per page. In either case, the disk manager handles the mismatch and supplies DBMS blocks upon request. The disk manager supplies a unique block address when it delivers a new block to the DBMS, and the DBMS retains the address to regain access to the block at a later time. The block address is generally a cylinder-platter-sector designation.

The DBMS must organize record storage within blocks, and it must handle references to remote records from within a given record. The latter concern arises because of relationships among records. If all records stored on a block contain fixed-length fields, you can simply pack them into the block. If the block size isn't evenly divisible by the record length, you would waste some space at the block end rather than split a record across two blocks. The address of a record is then the concatenation $(b : r)$, where b is the block address and r is the record number within the block. The count, r, starts with $r = 0$ in each block. If each record contains n fields, with lengths $l_0, l_1, \ldots, l_{n-1}$, the beginning of field i of record $(b : r)$ is at byte $rL + \sum_{j<i} l_j$ of block b, where $L = \sum l_j$ is the record length.

Although some database files take this simple form, most don't. Variable-length records are a more common occurrence for several reasons. First, many fields are character strings, and specifying a fixed length is wasteful if many strings are considerably shorter. A fixed length also introduces an uncomfortable exception when a string exceeds the maximum length. Second, some data types, even more so than character strings, exhibit extreme variations in length. For example, pictures and audio samplings are long byte sequences of widely varying lengths. Finally, for access efficiency, the DBMS may pack several record types into the same block. The different record types will have different record lengths, even if they are uniform for a given type.

For variable-length records, you can't calculate a record's starting point from the record number in the block. You could use the combination $(b : o)$ as the record address, where b is the block address and o is a byte offset from the beginning of the block. However, records refer to each other with these record addresses, so a record's address shouldn't change once it has been established. A record whose address is used in other records is said to be **pinned** because you can't move it from that address without modifying all its references. Because you usually don't know the extent of these references, you must assume a record is pinned in the absence of evidence to the contrary. When you update a field in a variable-length record, you may change its size. This would displace adjacent records to new offset values and require an undesirable change in the $(b : o)$ address.

Figure 14.3 illustrates a better addressing scheme: it maintains constant record addresses even when the records relocate. You place a small directory of record locators at the block end. The directory terminates with a null entry—an X in the figure. Each locator contains the byte offset from the beginning of the block to the first byte of a given record. This offset appears as an arrow in the figure. Each locator also contains a delete flag (D in the figure), which the DBMS sets when it deletes the record.

Now the record address is the combination $(b : l)$, where b is the block address and l is the relative position of the locator from the block end, starting with $l = 0$. For example, you locate record $(b : 2)$ by consulting the third locator from the block end. Because the locators are all the same size, you can easily find any particular locator. If the block size is 4096, for example, you need 12 bits for the offset pointer plus one bit for the delete flag. Allocating 2 bytes per locator accommodates these needs. Therefore, the locator for record $(b : 2)$ occupies bytes 4090 and 4091 of block b.

If a record moves within a block, you must change the offset in its locator, but all external references will still find the record. Because the locator update occurs on the same block as the record itself, the process involves no additional block retrieval penalty. Of course, if a record expands to push itself or one of its neighbors off the block, the scheme breaks down. But you can salvage the idea by replacing a record that has moved off the block by a reference to its new location. The reference will be the combination $(b' : l')$, where b' is the new block and l' is the offset of the new locator in that block. All references to the record still use $(b : l)$, targeting the old block. However, the system can chase down the current record location by noting that it isn't at the prescribed location but has left a forwarding address. If the record moves a second time, you update the reference at $(b : l)$ to the final destination. In this scheme, the record itself must carry the original address as a prefix field, so that you can find the old location for the update. In summary, you need at most one extra block retrieval to find a record that has been pushed off its initial block.

When you find a record through its locator, you must be able to determine if the record is physically there or if it has moved to a forwarding address. This information is only one example of a variety of subsidiary items that accompany each record. In the case of varying field lengths, you also need information about the beginning offset and length of each field. A field doesn't necessarily extend from its beginning offset to the beginning of the next field. Padding bytes may exist between the fields to force data types to line up on particular byte boundaries. For example, some systems constrain integers to begin at byte

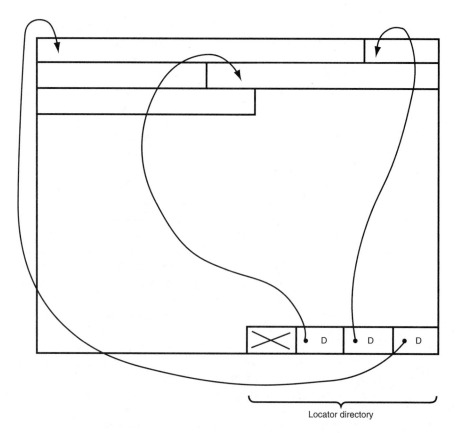

Figure 14.3 Finding records within a block with locators

addresses that are evenly divisible by four. Therefore, you need both the field offset and its length in the general case. If you pack records of several types in a single block, each record must contain a type identification field.

A record header can accommodate all these needs. A more complete block organization appears in Figure 14.4. A record address is again the combination $(b : l)$, where l gives the position of the record's locator from the end of block b. The offset of the locator points to the beginning of the record, where header information precedes the actual record fields. A particular F (flag) value, say 0, implies that the record is present in its original location after the header. A different F value, say 1, implies that the record has moved to a forwarding address and that the forwarding address itself begins directly after the T flag. A third F value, say 2, implies that the record is present after the header but that it has been relocated from its initial block. In this case, the old address appears after the F marker and before the rest of the header. The T flag denotes the record type, a DBMS code. In the aquarium example, suppose that tank records use code 1, fish records use code 2, and so forth. The DBMS assigns these codes when it creates the entities. Following these two flags is a field directory that gives each field's offset and length. The directory terminates

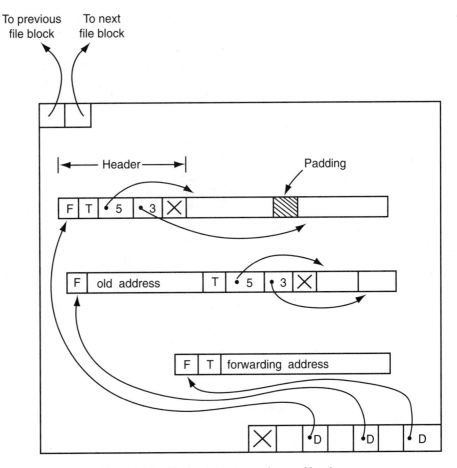

Figure 14.4 Block organization with record headers

with a null entry, denoted by an X. This organization has the flexibility to locate fields in variable-length records and to move the records without changing their external addresses.

Usually the record fields hold the data, but sometimes this arrangement isn't practical. You can always hold the traditional data types (e.g., integers, floats, and reasonably short character strings) directly in the field. You just note the starting byte and length in the record header. However, splitting records across blocks isn't convenient, so there is a practical limit to the size of character strings that can fit in a single block. That limit may be quite large, perhaps 4000 or so for large blocks holding records with few other fields, but it is nevertheless bounded independently of the amount of disk storage available. More difficulties arise if a field contains a bitmapped image or an audio sampling because either can greatly exceed the capacity a single block's capacity. For such data, the field stores the beginning block address of a remote block chain that contains the full data. For each record type, the database stores the data type of its fields. Consequently, the correct interpretation is available for each field.

When you delete a record, you can't reuse its $(b : l)$ address for another record because references elsewhere in the database may point to the address. If you store another record at the address, it may be mistaken for the deleted record by some process following the references. Therefore, you can't recycle the locator addresses although you can reclaim the storage actually occupied by the record. When you delete a record, the system sets the D flag in its locator. The DBMS interprets the D flag properly when following references from other records. If you happen to know that a record isn't pinned, you can recycle its locator.

Because the DBMS assumes responsibility for the file blocks, it usurps the first entries in each block to store the addresses of the next and previous file blocks. If the DBMS imposes no further organization on the file, it must retain only the file name and its first block address. It can locate subsequent blocks by following the next block pointers; it can locate records within a block by sequencing through the locator directory. If the DBMS enters the file at some intermediate point—by following a $(b : l)$ reference from another record, for example—it can still navigate to adjacent records. In either case, however, the DBMS has only sequential access to the file blocks. Sequential access is efficient only in those rare cases where all the records are relevant to a given data processing activity. More often, only a small subset of records is relevant. To avoid unnecessary block retrievals for irrelevant records, the DBMS needs further organization to allow efficient access to the desired records.

 DBMS files are collections of fixed-size blocks. A locator directory allows record relocation within a block while leaving the record's external address unchanged. For pinned records, the external address should never change.

The primitive file organization of this section is a **sequential file**, also called a **heap**. The system places the records in no particular order in the file blocks, and it can only access them sequentially.

Indexed sequential files

This section retains the block organization of Figure 14.4 but adds features to locate particular records. Suppose a sequential file is spread over B blocks. You must dispatch $B/2$ block retrievals, on the average, to find a particular record. You need the full B block retrievals to discover that the target record isn't in the database. Using the estimate of 15 milliseconds per access for a file of 100,000 blocks, the average retrieval figure of $B/2$ accesses translates to $(50,000)(0.015) = 750$ seconds $= 12.5$ minutes. In the worst case, you must scan the entire file, which requires 25 minutes.

Frequently, you know a key value of the desired record. If most search activity against the file is of this key-search type, you can achieve some efficiency by maintaining the file in sorted order on the key field. Suppose you arrange the records as shown in Figure 14.5. You subdivide the file into a collection of miniheaps, each indicated by a horizontal string of blocks. The records in a given miniheap aren't necessarily in sorted order, but the collection does exhibit an overall order. All the records in the first miniheap have key values less than the smallest key of the second miniheap. Similarly, all records of the second miniheap have key values less than the smallest key of the third miniheap, and so forth. So the organization exhibits sorted clusters, with the elements of cluster i having smaller key values than the elements of cluster $i + 1$. Ideally, each miniheap comprises a single block, and you initially create the file that way. However, as the file grows, you must insert records into particular blocks to maintain the sorted order, so eventually the original blocks will overflow. To delay the overflow, it's common practice to leave about 20% empty space in each block in a newly created file.

Assuming that each block conforms to the variable-length record format described in the previous section, a directory of record locators appears at the end and next-previous block pointers appear at the beginning. Under the clustered scheme, these block pointers lace together blocks of the same miniheap. The locators function in the usual fashion to point to records and to note deletions. The locator offset forms part of a record address, $(b : l)$, and because external references may use the address, it must remain stable. Therefore, you can't keep the locators in sorted order, and you must assume that the individual miniheaps aren't ordered. The organization of Figure 14.5 is a variation on a general theme called **indexed sequential** file format. As the name suggests, an auxiliary file (i.e., an index) usually accompanies these files to guide the system in selecting the correct miniheap to search for a target record. Your concern now is organizing the data file itself; Chapter 15 will provide details on auxiliary indexes.

Instead of retaining a single block pointer to the first block of a sequential file, the DBMS now stores an ordered array of block addresses to the first blocks of the various miniheaps. A block address is typically 4 bytes long, so the block pointer array for the example file of 100,000 blocks requires 400,000 bytes of memory. For comparison purposes, suppose the file is organized as an indexed sequential file and it hasn't yet grown sufficiently to require overflow blocks on any of the 100,000 initial miniheaps. In other words, each miniheap is a single block. You can conduct a binary search for a target record. You first access the middle block and determine which half of the file contains the desired record. Since the middle miniheap contains a single block, you can search it in memory for the largest and smallest keys. Even if the miniheap contains more than one block, assume that the system maintains the largest and smallest key in a special location in the first block. Comparing these values with the target key, you determine the target's location, if it is present at all. It is in the middle block, an earlier block, or a later block. If it's in the middle block, you can return it without further disk accesses. Otherwise, you have divided the search space in half, and you repeat the process on the appropriate half.

Let B be the total number of blocks. Because each access divides the search space in half, the size will be less than one block after $n = \log_2 B$ probes. In the example, at most $\log_2 100000 \approx 17$ accesses reduces the search segment to one block, where the target record must exist if it's in the file. Using the estimate of 15 milliseconds per access, you find that the worst case performance of this search is 0.26 seconds, compared with a worst case scenario of 25 minutes for the sequential organization.

Of course, this performance deteriorates as blocks overflow, producing larger heaps at each point in the subdivision. However, even if every block overflows into a full second block, the 17 accesses become only 18, giving a retrieval time of 0.27 seconds. For each probe, except the last, the largest and smallest keys are available in the first block of the miniheap, so you can make the decision on which half to search next without reading the second block. On the final probe, the target record may be in the second block, which

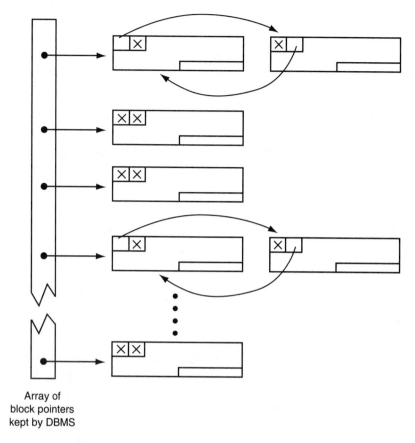

Figure 14.5 An indexed sequential file organization

adds one to the count from the previous analysis. In the corresponding sequential case, the original file would grow to 200,000 blocks and require 50 minutes to scan.

In a non-database situation, when the performance of an indexed sequential file deteriorates to an unacceptable level, you can read out the records sequentially and build another indexed sequential file with no overflow blocks. However, this reorganization option isn't usually available for a database file because the records are pinned. Each combination of a block address and a locator offset, $(b : l)$, is a potential reference target of other database records, so the reorganization must retain the old blocks to hold forwarding addresses. This constraint so compromises the reorganization's retrieval efficiency that the operation isn't considered feasible for database files of pinned records.

 Provided the DBMS can retain the array of block addresses in memory and no miniheap overflows onto a second block, you can locate a target record in an indexed sequential file with at most $\log_2 B$ accesses, where B is the number of blocks in the file.

If the array of block addresses is too large to retain in memory and you don't want to resort to an auxiliary file structure (i.e., an index) to facilitate address access, you can decrease the number of miniheaps by allowing some of them to overflow immediately on file creation. In the example, if the 400,000 bytes of storage dedicated to the array is too large, you can reduce it in half by using two blocks in each miniheap. Then, 50,000 addresses, using 200,000 bytes of memory, appear in the array, and the maximum access time remains the same. Locating a target record now requires at most $1 + \log_2 50000 \approx 17$ probes, again about 0.26 seconds.

If the file needs B blocks and each miniheap contains h blocks, the file needs B/h miniheaps, and the DBMS array of block addresses is of size B/h. The maximum number of probes to locate a target record is then $(h - 1) + \log_2 B/h$. For the example of 100,000 blocks, the following tabulation shows how the access time increases with the miniheaps' size. As you can see, you can considerably reduce the size of the DBMS address array with only modest penalties in retrieval time.

h	DBMS array size	maximum number of probes	access time (seconds, at 0.015 per probe)
1	100,000	17	0.255
2	50,000	17	0.255
4	25,000	18	0.270
8	12,500	21	0.318
16	6,250	28	0.420
32	3,125	43	0.645

Although the performance improvement over sequential files is impressive, three problems arise with indexed sequential organization. First, the performance deteriorates as the file ages and the miniheaps overflow into chains of blocks. Second, the block pointer array can become so large that the DBMS can't hold it in memory. In that case, the DBMS must expend additional accesses to page back and forth among the disk blocks that hold the array. Although you can use larger miniheaps to reduce the address array size, the array can still be very large for a large data file. When the address array grows to an unwieldy size, it becomes a sort of secondary file structure, used to facilitate access to the main data file. Such an auxiliary file is an **index**, and you must then consider methods for rapid access to the index records. Finally, you can construct an indexed sequential organization over a single field or a concatenation of fields, but you can't simultaneously order the file on two or more different fields. If you maintain the aquarium's tank file as an indexed sequential file on tno, you can't simultaneously order it by tcolor. This simple fact follows because the indexed sequential organization physically places a record in the proper miniheap based on the ordering field value. If the tno value places it in miniheap x and the tcolor value places it in miniheap y, the system obviously can't satisfy both conditions. It can maintain the file on the combination (tno, tcolor), where the major ordering is tno and records with the same tno value appear in tcolor order. However, that arrangement isn't in tcolor order in a global sense. Because the indexed sequential organization can support only one ordering field, the response deteriorates to sequential access if the search criterion involves a different field.

If the indexed sequential file is sorted by a nonkey field, you must modify the search method. The **ordering field** refers to the field(s) on which records are sorted. If the ordering field isn't a key, duplicate records can appear with the same ordering field value.

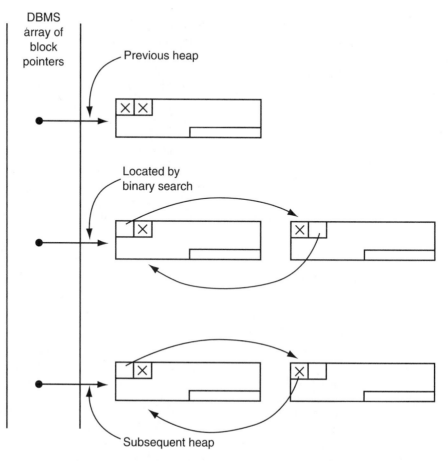

Figure 14.6   Multiple occurrences of the ordering field value are contained in adjacent miniheaps

You can conduct a binary search to find a block with the nonkey target value. In general, this process locates a miniheap corresponding to a particular block address in the DBMS array. If the target value is the lowest or highest value in the miniheap, you must also read earlier or later miniheaps from the DBMS array. These subsequent block accesses aren't inefficient because you must read them anyway to obtain all the target records. As shown in Figure 14.6, if the target records spill onto other blocks, they are in adjacent miniheaps and require no further search. Therefore, the number of accesses is $\log_2 B$ plus one for each adjacent block that contains additional target records. By contrast, a sequential search requires you to search all B blocks to ensure that you have found all the targets. For the example of 100,000 blocks, a search for records with a non-unique key requires at most 17 accesses to locate a miniheap with one of the targets, plus additional accesses to acquire the remaining targets from adjacent blocks. If the 100,000 blocks were organized sequentially, you would have to expend 100,000 accesses to ensure that you had found all the targets.

If a is a record field in a particular file f, $I_f(a)$ is the **image of a in f**. It is the number of distinct values that occur in field a in the file. In the aquarium example, two of the fish attributes are fcolor and fweight. If I_f(fcolor) is 5, five different fish colors appear in the file. Similarly, I_f(fweight) might be 100. The image of a field provides a rough estimate of the number of records (or blocks) associated with a particular field value. For example, if the fish file contains $B = 100,000$ blocks, you can use B/I_f(fcolor) $= 100,000/5 = 20,000$ as an estimate of the number of blocks containing records with a particular fcolor, say blue. If you maintain the file as an indexed sequential file on fcolor, you expect to retrieve about 20,000 blocks in recovering records with fcolor blue. Of course, these disk accesses are beyond those necessary to locate the miniheaps where blue records reside.

The image of an attribute in a file serves a useful purpose in estimating the expense, usually, the number of disk accesses, associated with a retrieval strategy. The DBMS can easily maintain an accurate value for $I_f(a)$, provided it has a rapid access mechanism for locating records with a given a-value. For example, if the DBMS maintains the file as an indexed sequential file on a, a binary search can quickly determine if the file contains a record with a given a-value. When the DBMS adds a new record, it searches the file for a record with the same a-value. If it finds none, it increments $I_f(a)$. When it deletes a record, it again searches the file. If it finds no other record with the same a-value, it decrements $I_f(a)$.

If the DBMS packs records of various types into one file, it can apply the indexed sequential organization only to the outermost record of the repeating group. Suppose the file organization in the aquarium application follows each tank record with its fish records and each fish record with its events. The repeating group is (tank, fish, event). Because fish records appear fragmented after their owning tanks, the file can't maintain order on any fish field. Similarly, it can't use event fields to order the records. However, you can consider the fish and event records as a sort of padding that follows each tank record, and you can organize these extended tank records as an indexed sequential file on a tank attribute. In this case, tank is the outermost member of the repeating group.

Hash files

Indexed sequential organization exploits the advantages of dividing the file into a collection of miniheaps. A record falls in a particular miniheap as a function of its ordering field value. A second approach also divides the file into miniheaps based on the records' ordering field values, and it achieves even faster access. This alternative organization is a **hash file**. In a hash file, the individual miniheaps are traditionally called **buckets**. In a hash file, you determine the bucket for a target record from a calculation on the ordering field value. In this case, the ordering field is the **hash field**. As with an indexed sequential organization, the general case allows multiple records with the same hash field value. However, in most practical cases, the hash field is a unique key, and this discussion will assume that the hash key is unique. The search mechanism immediately locates the correct miniheap (i.e., bucket) by performing a calculation that requires no disk accesses. By contrast, an indexed sequential search must sample the various miniheaps in some systematic fashion, typically with a binary search, to determine the correct miniheap.

From the standpoint of the DBMS, a hash file appears much the same as an indexed sequential file. (See Figure 14.7.) The DBMS maintains an array of bucket addresses, indexed from 0 through $N - 1$, where N is a predetermined maximum number of buckets. It places a record in the file by **hashing** the hash field value to obtain an index in the range 0 to $N - 1$. A **hash function**, $f(k)$, specifies the calculation. You should choose the hash function to spread the key values uniformly across the range 0 to $N - 1$. The DBMS retrieves the bucket at the array address returned by the hash function, and places the new record there. Assuming you know the hash field value, record retrieval proceeds in the same manner. The DBMS hashes the field to produce an offset into the DBMS array of bucket addresses. It retrieves the identified bucket and probes it for the target record.

 The DBMS stores a record in the hash file bucket identified by hashing the hash field value. A popular hash function is $f(k) = k \bmod N$, where k is the hash key value and N is the number of available buckets.

Choosing a hash function

Ideally, each bucket is one block, as was the ideal case for indexed sequential files. But because of non-uniformities in the hash function and subsequent file growth, some buckets usually overflow onto additional blocks. In any case, the DBMS maintains the buckets as miniheaps, laced together with pointers, that it must search sequentially. Therefore, the overall organization is much the same as an indexed sequential file, except that the number of probes to locate the proper miniheap is reduced to 1, as compared with $\log_2 N$ in the indexed sequential case. Assuming each bucket is one block, the recovery time is then a uniform 0.015 seconds for any file record.

Even if the buckets comprise several blocks, the DBMS must still search only $1/N$ of the blocks, which provides an N-fold speed-up over the sequential organization. With the example of a 100,000 block file, you achieve a speedup of 10^5 if you maintain 100,000 buckets. If the address array for 100,000 buckets is too large to fit in memory, you can use fewer buckets, but each bucket will be spread over several blocks. For example, you can use 10,000 buckets for the example file of 100,000 blocks, but the performance advantage over the sequential organization falls from 10^5 to 10^4, resulting in a worst case access time of 0.15 seconds. In this case, you can still locate the correct bucket with a hashing calculation, but each bucket contains about ten blocks. In the worst case, you must retrieve them all, which requires $(10)(0.015) = 0.15$ seconds.

For the simple hashing scheme described here, you specify the total number of buckets, N, in advance. You then develop a hash function that spreads the range of key values over the interval 0 to $N - 1$. Several factors influence the choice of N. If you choose a large N for a given file size, each bucket will spread over few blocks, resulting in fast access time. In the limit, with an N sufficiently large that the buckets are single blocks, the access time for any record will be equal to one block retrieval time, about 0.015 seconds. However, if N is large, the DBMS must maintain a large array of bucket addresses in memory. Using small values of N reduces the memory array size, but it increases the access time as the buckets spill across several blocks.

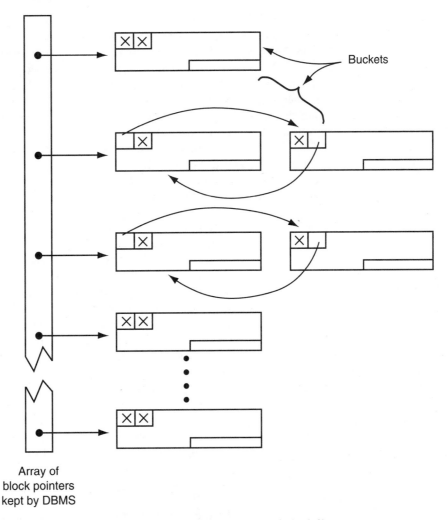

Figure 14.7   The bucket structure of a hash file

A second problem is that hash functions seldom achieve uniformity in mapping the range of key values into the interval $[0, N - 1]$. Suppose that you decide to distribute the example file of 100,000 blocks across 100,000 buckets. You anticipate one block per bucket and a fast access time of 0.015 seconds. Suppose you choose the hash function to be $f(k) = k \bmod 100000$, which produces values in the required range of $[0, 99999]$. Now suppose the record keys are all numeric but the last three digits are always 000. It follows that each k is divisible by 1000, and therefore $f(k)$ is divisible by 1000. (Write $k = 100000a + f(k) = 1000b$ for some a, b, which implies that $f(k) = 1000(b - 100a)$, which is divisible by 1000.) The only $f(k)$ values delivered by the hash function, therefore, are 0, 1000, 2000, ..., 99000, so all the records will crowd into 100 buckets. The remaining 99,900 buckets will be empty! Even if you assume that the 100 buckets are hit uniformly, each bucket will contain $1/100$ of the file, or 1000 blocks. This will raise the worst case retrieval time from 0.015 seconds to 15 seconds!

The choice of a hash function, therefore, must take some account of the record key values. It isn't realistic to assume that you have the entire set of keys when you design the file structure because some of the keys will appear later as the file grows. But you should have a representative sample in advance to avoid the bad luck of the previous example. If you use the popular form $f(k) = k \bmod N$, you should choose N to avoid the extremely lumpy distribution shown above.

Choosing N to be a prime number reduces the chances of a lumpy distribution, but it doesn't entirely eliminate the possibility. Indeed, given *any* N and *any* hash function, you can concoct a set of keys that hash in a lumpy fashion. Simply hash a very large number of keys and observe the resulting bucket contents. Because all the keys are disappearing into the finite collection of N buckets, you can make at least one of the buckets receive an arbitrarily large number of keys by hashing enough of them. Now choose the most heavily populated bucket's contents for the misbehaving set of keys and discard all the other keys. The chosen set now hashes to a single bucket, and the remaining buckets are all empty, which is a very lumpy distribution.

So a bit of a game is involved. For a known hashing scheme, a malicious adversary can contrive a set of key values that will defeat the rapid access mechanism of the hash file. However, if you know all the keys in advance, you can construct a hash function to spread them uniformly across the desired range. A representative sample of the keys is usually sufficient to construct a hashing scheme that will reasonably approximate a uniform distribution. An adversary won't be able to degrade the performance and still leave the sample representative of the total key set. Moreover, the application context—not a malicious mechanism—determines the key values.

Even if it avoids the above catastrophic failure, the hashing function probably won't achieve a uniform distribution. Therefore, it is traditional to choose N, the number of buckets, to be about 25% larger than the time-space tradeoff demands. For example, if you decide to use 50,000 buckets for the 100,000 block file, you anticipate each bucket to be spread over 2 blocks, which will require 2 probes for half of the retrievals. This is about $(0.015 + 0.030)/2 = 0.022$ seconds on the average. Because the distribution may be non-uniform, you should use 62,500 buckets. The extra room allows the lumps to disperse somewhat, and it also provides space for future growth.

Calculating the distribution of records across the buckets

With some probability arguments, you can estimate how much unevenness to expect in the distribution of records across a hash file's buckets. As an initial goal, assume you want a hash file where each bucket comprises a single block. If the DBMS can hold the address array in memory, it will need one disk access, about 0.015 seconds, to retrieve a random record with a known key value. Let q be the record capacity of a block, an average value if the blocks contain variable-length records. An array of N buckets can then accommodate Nq records without any block overflows. If you store Nq records in the file, it is fully loaded. In other words, it has a load factor of 1. In general, if you store r records in N buckets and the block capacity is q, then the file's **load factor** is r/Nq. The load factor is the fraction of the non-overflowing capacity in use. Denoting the load factor by α, you have:

$$\alpha = \frac{r}{Nq}. \tag{14.1}$$

For any $\alpha \leq 1.0$, no file block has to overflow. However, some will probably overflow anyway because the hash function won't achieve a perfectly uniform distribution of records to buckets. How severe will the overflow problem become as the file grows to capacity? The question doesn't have a general answer because each hash function distributes the keys differently. However, you can analyze a probabilistic situation where the hash function places each record by randomly choosing a bucket from a uniform distribution. If the file contains N buckets, the probability that a particular record hashes to a particular bucket is then $1/N$. This doesn't mean that the hash function is random. If you present the same hash field value again, it will hash to the same bucket. Instead, you suppose the first placement of a hash field value operates randomly. Thereafter, the function remembers if it has already chosen a bucket for a particular value. This behavior is obviously difficult for a real calculation. But it's a convenient model for the expected behavior of a real calculation that does manage to spread the hash field values uniformly.

As a first step in the analysis, you need $D(x)$, the fraction of buckets that receive exactly x records. To calculate this value, suppose you have distributed r records across N buckets according to the uniform hashing function. Each bucket has one or more blocks of capacity q. Choose a particular bucket, say b_0, and ask the following question. What is the probability that bucket b_0 received exactly x records, for some $0 \leq x \leq r$? Because there are N^r possible distributions of r records into N buckets, the question becomes: what fraction of the N^r distributions assign exactly x records to bucket b_0?

You can simplify the matter by choosing a specific set of x records. Then how many distributions assign the chosen record set to b_0? A successful distribution can assign each of the x fixed records in only one way, namely to b_0. However, it can assign each of the remaining $r - x$ records in $N - 1$ ways, namely to any one of the other $N - 1$ buckets. So the number of distributions that assign the specific set of x records to b_0 is $1 \cdot 1 \cdot \ldots \cdot 1 \cdot (N - 1) \cdot (N - 1) \cdot \ldots \cdot (N - 1)$, a product of x factors of the form (1) and $r - x$ factors of the form $(N - 1)$. In other words, the function can achieve the required assignment in $(N - 1)^{r-x}$ ways.

Because each possible choice of x specific records delivers $(N - 1)^{r-x}$ configurations with exactly the chosen x records in b_0, you can infer the following expression for the probability, $P(b_0, x)$, that bucket b_0 receives exactly x records.

$$P(b_0, x) = \frac{\binom{r}{x} (N - 1)^{r-x}}{N^r}. \tag{14.2}$$

$\binom{r}{x} = \frac{r!}{x!(r-x)!}$ is the total number of ways you can choose x records from the r available. Because the uniform hashing scheme isn't biased, it treats all buckets equally. Therefore, the probability of *any* bucket receiving exactly x records is the same as for b_0. So $P(b, x) = P(b_0, x)$ for any bucket b. Because the value doesn't depend on b, call it simply $P(x)$, the probability that a given bucket receives x records.

You can now reason that the expected number of buckets that receive exactly x records is the total number of buckets, N, times the probability that any one of them will receive exactly x records.

A more familiar example may clarify the point. Suppose you know the chances are 3 out of 4 that a person attending a basketball game will wear a red cap. If you know that N persons will attend a particular game, how many red caps would you predict? By analogy, you expect the number of buckets receiving exactly x records to be $NP(x)$. So $D(x)$, the fraction of buckets with exactly x records, is $NP(x)/N = P(x) = P(b_0, x)$. Substituting $P(b_0, x)$ from Equation 14.2, you obtain:

$$D(x) = \frac{\binom{r}{x}(N-1)^{r-x}}{N^r}. \tag{14.3}$$

From Equation 14.1, $r = \alpha N q$, so

$$D(x) = \frac{\binom{\alpha N q}{x}(N-1)^{\alpha N q - x}}{N^{\alpha N q}}. \tag{14.4}$$

For large N and $\alpha N q$, in comparison with x, you can approximate Equation 14.4 by

$$D(x) = \frac{(\alpha q)^x e^{-\alpha q}}{x!}. \tag{14.5}$$

The approximation doesn't depend on N. The $D(x)$ values for the following tables and graphs, based on $N = 100000$, were calculated from both formulas, and the results were identical to four decimal places. Figure 14.8 tabulates $D(x)$ for various load factors; Figure 14.9 shows the same results graphically. In both cases, the total number of buckets, N, is 100,000, and the bucket capacity is 10. For a load factor, α, less than one, the file is partially full, and you might expect the buckets to be proportionally full. If $\alpha = 0.2$, the file is 20% full. Because the buckets are all the same size (10) and the uniform hash function treats them equally, you might expect each bucket to be about 20% full. Each bucket would then contain about two records. In general, if the load factor is $\alpha < 1$, you might expect each bucket to contain about αq records.

However, this expectation isn't borne out by Figures 14.8 and 14.9. They do show that the fraction of buckets having the expected population, αq, is the highest. For example, with a load factor of 0.7, the fraction of buckets having population $(0.7)(10) = 7$ is larger (or as large) than for any other population. But a significant fraction of the buckets have populations above or below the expected value. As the load factor increases, the distribution of bucket populations spreads out in both directions from its expected value. For a load factor of 1.0, a significant number of buckets have populations larger than 10. These buckets overflow into a second block. Some buckets even have populations greater than 20, which produces overflows into a third block.

	load factor, α									
x	0.1	0.2	0.3	0.4	0.5	0.6	0.7	0.8	0.9	1.0
0	0.3679	0.1353	0.0498	0.0183	0.0067	0.0025	0.0009	0.0003	0.0001	0.0000
1	0.3679	0.2707	0.1494	0.0733	0.0337	0.0149	0.0064	0.0027	0.0011	0.0005
2	0.1839	0.2707	0.2240	0.1465	0.0842	0.0446	0.0223	0.0107	0.0050	0.0023
3	0.0613	0.1804	0.2240	0.1954	0.1404	0.0892	0.0521	0.0286	0.0150	0.0076
4	0.0153	0.0902	0.1680	0.1954	0.1755	0.1339	0.0912	0.0573	0.0337	0.0189
5	0.0031	0.0361	0.1008	0.1563	0.1755	0.1606	0.1277	0.0916	0.0607	0.0378
6	0.0005	0.0120	0.0504	0.1042	0.1462	0.1606	0.1490	0.1221	0.0911	0.0631
7	0.0001	0.0034	0.0216	0.0595	0.1044	0.1377	0.1490	0.1396	0.1171	0.0901
8	0.0000	0.0009	0.0081	0.0298	0.0653	0.1033	0.1304	0.1396	0.1318	0.1126
9	0.0000	0.0002	0.0027	0.0132	0.0363	0.0688	0.1014	0.1241	0.1318	0.1251
10	0.0000	0.0000	0.0008	0.0053	0.0181	0.0413	0.0710	0.0993	0.1186	0.1251
11	0.0000	0.0000	0.0002	0.0019	0.0082	0.0225	0.0452	0.0722	0.0970	0.1137
12	0.0000	0.0000	0.0001	0.0006	0.0034	0.0113	0.0263	0.0481	0.0728	0.0948
13	0.0000	0.0000	0.0000	0.0002	0.0013	0.0052	0.0142	0.0296	0.0504	0.0729
14	0.0000	0.0000	0.0000	0.0001	0.0005	0.0022	0.0071	0.0169	0.0324	0.0521
15	0.0000	0.0000	0.0000	0.0000	0.0002	0.0009	0.0033	0.0090	0.0194	0.0347
16	0.0000	0.0000	0.0000	0.0000	0.0000	0.0003	0.0014	0.0045	0.0109	0.0217
17	0.0000	0.0000	0.0000	0.0000	0.0000	0.0001	0.0006	0.0021	0.0058	0.0128
18	0.0000	0.0000	0.0000	0.0000	0.0000	0.0000	0.0002	0.0009	0.0029	0.0071
19	0.0000	0.0000	0.0000	0.0000	0.0000	0.0000	0.0001	0.0004	0.0014	0.0037
20	0.0000	0.0000	0.0000	0.0000	0.0000	0.0000	0.0000	0.0002	0.0006	0.0019
21	0.0000	0.0000	0.0000	0.0000	0.0000	0.0000	0.0000	0.0001	0.0003	0.0009

Figure 14.8: Fraction of buckets with population x, as a function of load factor α (block capacity = 10)

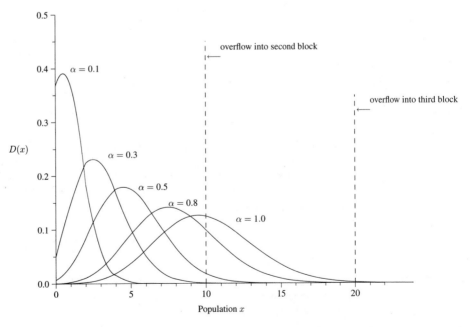

Figure 14.9 Fraction of buckets, $D(x)$, having population x, for $\alpha \leq 1.0$ (block capacity = 10)

A hashing function will introduce unavoidable variations from a uniform distribution of records across the available buckets. Some blocks become overpopulated, perhaps to the point of overflowing into additional blocks.

The average number of disk probes per random retrieval

You can use the distribution profile, $D(x)$, to determine the average number of block retrievals to obtain a randomly chosen record. Suppose you retrieve all $\alpha N q$ records in some random order. For each record, assume you know the hash field value. You apply the hash function to determine the record's bucket. Depending on its location in the bucket, you have to retrieve one, two, or more blocks to obtain the record. Consider a particular bucket, say b_0, containing x records. Over the course of the experiment, you eventually retrieve all x records. The q records in the base block, which corresponds to the bucket address in the DBMS memory array, each require one block retrieval. If $x \leq q$, this count covers all the records. But, if $q < x$, the next q records each require two block retrievals—one to acquire the base block and one to follow the linking pointer to the next block of the bucket. Therefore, if $q < x \leq 2q$, you have to expend $q + 2(x - q)$ block retrievals.

Let $T(x)$ be the number of block retrievals necessary to recover, in a random order, all the records in a bucket with x records. Note the random order of the record retrievals. To determine the average number of probes to retrieve a target record, you must sum the probes associated with each independent target and divide by the number of targets. So you can't read all the records from a block once you retrieve it. Instead you must search independently for each record. The general pattern for $T(x)$ is then:

$$
T(x) = \begin{cases}
x, & x \leq q \\
q + 2(x - q) = 2x - q, & q < x \leq 2q \\
q + 2q + 3(x - 2q) = 3x - 3q, & 2q < x \leq 3q \\
\quad \vdots & \\
jx - j(j-1)q/2, & (j-1)q < x \leq jq \\
\quad \vdots &
\end{cases}
\tag{14.6}
$$

Because there are $ND(x)$ buckets that contain x records, you obtain the average number of probes by summing the $T(x)$ probes required by each such bucket and then dividing by the number of records. Q, the average number of block accesses to retrieve a target record, is given by the following formula. The summation starts at $x = 1$ because no records lie in buckets with population zero.

$$
Q = \frac{1}{\alpha N q} \sum_{x=1} ND(x)T(x) = \frac{1}{\alpha q} \sum_{x=1} D(x)T(x).
\tag{14.7}
$$

For large N, you can use Equation 14.5 to approximate $D(x)$. Therefore, for large N, the average number of probes depends only on the load factor, α, and the block capacity, q.

Figures 14.10 and 14.11 show the average number of disk accesses needed to retrieve a random record from the hash file. Results are best, of course, for large block capacities and small load factors. Block size has a greater influence on performance. For example, a

q	load factor, α									
	0.1	0.2	0.3	0.4	0.5	0.6	0.7	0.8	0.9	1.0
1	1.0500	1.1000	1.1499	1.1998	1.2494	1.2986	1.3472	1.3950	1.4416	1.4868
2	1.0060	1.0221	1.0456	1.0747	1.1081	1.1447	1.1838	1.2249	1.2675	1.3112
4	1.0002	1.0020	1.0080	1.0196	1.0377	1.0620	1.0916	1.1258	1.1635	1.2039
6	1.0000	1.0002	1.0018	1.0067	1.0169	1.0338	1.0577	1.0879	1.1235	1.1631
8	1.0000	1.0000	1.0005	1.0025	1.0084	1.0203	1.0397	1.0669	1.1010	1.1404
10	1.0000	1.0000	1.0001	1.0010	1.0044	1.0129	1.0288	1.0533	1.0860	1.1254
20	1.0000	1.0000	1.0000	1.0000	1.0003	1.0020	1.0081	1.0230	1.0499	1.0888
30	1.0000	1.0000	1.0000	1.0000	1.0000	1.0004	1.0029	1.0123	1.0347	1.0726

Figure 14.10   Average disk accesses for a random retrieval for load factor α and block capacity q

block capacity $q = 10$ and a load factor $\alpha = 0.8$ produces an average of 1.05 disk accesses per record retrieval, which translates to an average retrieval time of $(1.05)(0.015) = 0.0158$ seconds. Occasionally, a record will require $(2)(0.015) = 0.03$ seconds or even $(3)(0.015) = 0.045$ seconds, but the statistics guarantee that most records will require just one disk access. Therefore, the average is just slightly more than one access time.

Figure 14.11 illustrates the validity of the rule-of-thumb: provide 25% surplus space, which corresponds to $\alpha = 0.8$. For block capacities of 10 or more, $\alpha = 0.8$ marks the load factor where the curve starts to rise significantly from the nominal value of one disk access per retrieval.

 The average number of probes to retrieve a randomly selected record from a hash file increases with the load factor and decreases with the block capacity. With a load factor of 0.8, you can keep the average below 1.5, even for small block capacities.

Extending the analysis for $\alpha > 1.0$

A load factor of 1.0 corresponds to a full file in the sense that the base blocks of the buckets could accommodate all the records. Because of chance variations, however, certain buckets will overflow, and others will contain less than their full capacities. For a certain load factor, α, and a certain block capacity, q, the last section developed expressions for the fraction of buckets with given populations, $D(x)$, and for the average number of disk accesses needed to retrieve a randomly selected record, Q. A review of these arguments shows that they don't depend on $\alpha \le 1.0$, so they are also valid for overloaded hash files. The approximation for $D(x)$, Equation 14.5, remains valid for $\alpha > 1.0$ if x is still small in comparison with N and $\alpha N q$. The average retrieval time gets worse with overloaded files because most buckets then comprise several blocks. Figures 14.12 and 14.13 show the increases in bucket population densities and average disk accesses associated with higher load factors.

In Figure 14.13, the average number of disk probes for a random retrieval grows with the load factor in an approximately linear fashion, for the portion of the curve corresponding to overloaded files (i.e., $\alpha > 1$). The figure also shows that larger block capacities, beyond 10 or so, bring little performance improvement. When $q = 1$, you can see the linear

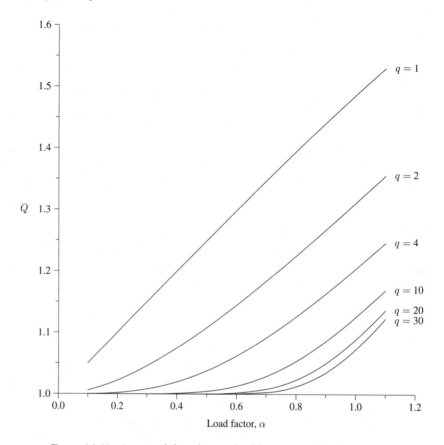

Figure 14.11   Average disk probes vs. load factor α and block capacity q

relationship between average retrieval probes and load factor even in the unsaturated region where $\alpha < 1$. You can also see this linearity in Figure 14.11.

You can manipulate Equation 14.7 to show that the average number of disk accesses does reduce to a linear form for larger values of α. That reduction appears below. To follow the mathematics, you should remember the power series expansion for the exponential function: $e^t = \sum t^n/n!$. The development starts with $T(x)$, the number of probes needed to retrieve each record randomly from a bucket containing x records. The general expression developed earlier reduces to a simpler form when x is a multiple of the block capacity q:

$$T(x) = q(1)+q(2)+\ldots+q(x/q) = q\sum_{i=1}^{x/q} i = q(x/q)(x/q+1)/2 = x(x+q)/2q. \quad (14.8)$$

When x isn't a multiple of q, Equation 14.8 still gives an approximation for $T(x)$. It is exact for x values that are multiples of q, and it is monotonically increasing between these values. The approximation is more accurate for higher values of α because most buckets in an overloaded file exhibit a chain of full blocks, which terminates in a partially filled block.

Equation 14.8 accurately includes the full blocks' contributions, but it approximates the last block's contribution. For large α, the last block's contribution is a small component when compared with the full blocks. Therefore, you can take Equation 14.8 as an approximation of the number of probes required to retrieve the records from a bucket with population x.

To compute the average number of probes to access a target record, you sum the number of probes for each record and divide by the number of records. You can simplify Equation 14.7 by using the above approximation for $T(x)$.

$$
\begin{aligned}
Q &= \frac{1}{\alpha q}\sum_{x=1} D(x)T(x) = \frac{1}{\alpha q}\sum_{x=1}\frac{1}{x!}(\alpha q)^x e^{-\alpha q}\frac{x(x+q)}{2q} = \frac{e^{-\alpha q}}{2\alpha q^2}\sum_{x=1}\frac{1}{x!}(\alpha q)^x x(x+q) \\[2mm]
&= \frac{e^{-\alpha q}}{2\alpha q^2}\sum_{x=1}\frac{1}{(x-1)!}(\alpha q)^x(x+q) = \frac{e^{-\alpha q}}{2\alpha q^2}\sum_{x=0}\frac{1}{x!}(\alpha q)^{x+1}(x+1+q) \\[2mm]
&= \frac{(\alpha q)e^{-\alpha q}}{2\alpha q^2}\sum_{x=0}\frac{1}{x!}(\alpha q)^x(x+1+q) = \frac{e^{-\alpha q}}{2q}(q+1)\sum_{x=0}\frac{1}{x!}(\alpha q)^x + \frac{e^{-\alpha q}}{2q}\sum_{x=1}\frac{x}{x!}(\alpha q)^x \\[2mm]
&= \frac{e^{-\alpha q}}{2q}(q+1)e^{\alpha q} + \frac{e^{-\alpha q}}{2q}\sum_{x=1}\frac{1}{(x-1)!}(\alpha q)^x = \frac{q+1}{2q} + \frac{e^{-\alpha q}}{2q}\sum_{x=0}\frac{1}{x!}(\alpha q)^{x+1} \\[2mm]
&= \frac{q+1}{2q} + \frac{e^{-\alpha q}}{2q}(\alpha q)\sum_{x=0}\frac{1}{x!}(\alpha q)^x = \frac{q+1}{2q} + \frac{\alpha}{2} = \frac{1}{2q} + \frac{1+\alpha}{2} \\[2mm]
&\approx \frac{1+\alpha}{2}, \quad \text{for large } q
\end{aligned}
$$

The last expression shows the linear growth with α. It also shows the decreasing influence of q, once q has grown past 10 or so. This approximation accounts for the Q values of Figure 14.13 for $\alpha > 1$.

Hashing non-numeric values

The hashing discussion so far has assumed that the hash field values are numeric so that the hash function can process them. However, many record types have ordering fields that aren't numeric. The hash field may be a part number, which is a sequence of alphanumeric characters, or it may be a unique name of some sort. You can always consider a character string hash field as a number by using the binary number from its encoding. The string abcdefg, for example, has the ASCII encoding 095 096 097 098 099 100 101, and you can consider it to be the number 095096097098099100101. The representation uses three digits for each character because each character is a one-byte code in the range 000 to 255. The problem is that character strings can be long, in fact so long that the resulting number may be too large for the computer registers. Many computers restrict integers to 16, 32, or 64 bits. One solution breaks the number into groups of a small fixed size, say, m digits. The process starts on the right and adds the groups, retaining only the least significant m digits on each addition. For the example, suppose $m = 4$. This breaks 095096097098099100101 into 0 9509 6097 0980 9910 0101. You then add the groups as follows, keeping only the rightmost four digits after each operation.

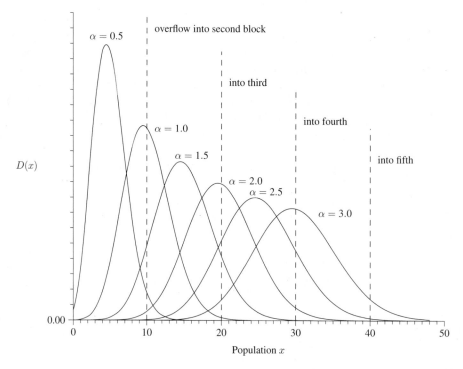

Figure 14.12: Fraction of buckets, $D(x)$, having population x, for overloaded hash files (block capacity is 10)

$$0000 + 9509 = 09509 \rightarrow 9509$$
$$9509 + 6097 = 15606 \rightarrow 5606$$
$$5606 + 0980 = 06586 \rightarrow 6586$$
$$6586 + 9910 = 16496 \rightarrow 6496$$
$$6496 + 0101 = 06597 \rightarrow 6597$$

This technique, called **folding**, produces a numeric value in the range appropriate for computer arithmetic. The hash function then operates on the numeric value to determine the bucket. In the example above, the hash field **abcdefg** translates to the number 6597, which is appropriate for the hash function.

Dynamic file structures

Both indexed sequential and hashed file organizations exploit a segmentation of the data file. Each uses a characteristic mechanism to determine which segment to search for a target record. Hash files use a calculation; indexed sequential files use a sequence of test probes patterned after a binary search. In either case, the DBMS must retain the segments' base block addresses in memory. This requirement can be excessive if the files are long enough. The memory array of block addresses can be extensive, even if the file is relatively short, because the DBMS must allocate a large number of base blocks to allow room for the file

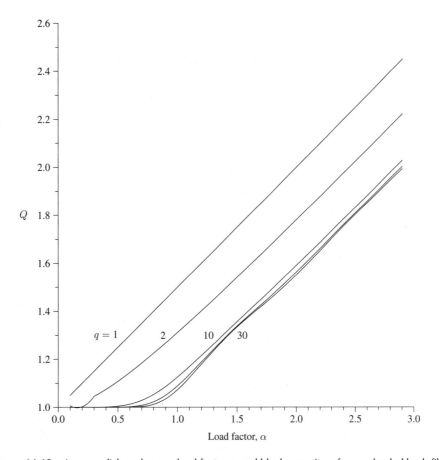

Figure 14.13 Average disk probes vs. load factor α and block capacity q for overloaded hash files

to grow. For an indexed sequential file, the DBMS apportions the extra space across the base blocks by filling them only partially when it creates the initial file. For a hash file, the DBMS uses a small initial load factor, which results in underfilled buckets.

For example, suppose the initial file contains sufficient records to fill 100 blocks, but you expect it to grow to 1000 blocks. For an indexed sequential file, the DBMS allocates 1000 blocks, which results in a memory array of 1000 block addresses. It loads the initial (sorted) records into the first 10% of each block and leaves 90% free to accept future file additions. If the key values of the initial 100 blocks of records are spread in a representative fashion across the full range of possible key values, future additions should fill the empty space with few overflows. However, a pathological case can defeat the plan. Suppose the records of the initial 100 blocks contain key values all beginning with the letter 'a.' If later additions contain only keys beginning with the letter 'b' or higher, the DBMS directs all of them toward the last miniheap, which quickly overflows onto a 900 block chain. However, if the distribution of key values in the initial 100 blocks is representative of the final distribution, this problem shouldn't arise.

If the DBMS uses a hash file, it again allocates 1000 blocks, giving a load factor of 0.1 after it loads the initial 100 blocks. Subsequent records then spread across the 1000 buckets. Assuming a reasonably uniform hashing function, you expect only small overflow chains early in the process.

In both these scenarios, the DBMS must retain the full memory array of block addresses even though a much smaller array is sufficient for the initial, small file. This section investigates methods that allow the DBMS to start with a small array of block addresses, commensurate with the initial file size, which can then grow as the file size increases. These methods involve massive record relocations, so certain inefficiencies result if the records are pinned. The techniques discussed below are generally applicable only to files of unpinned records.

Dynamic indexed sequential files

First consider an indexed sequential organization that can dynamically alter its size. Suppose you have a small initial file, requiring N blocks. You deploy the records in the usual fashion by distributing the sorted records across the N blocks but filling each block to capacity. The DBMS then maintains a small memory array to address the N blocks. N can be small because the DBMS allocated only a small number of blocks in comparison with the number that it will eventually allocate as the file grows.

When the DBMS adds a new record, it attempts to insert it in its proper order in the file. A binary search locates the target block, and if the block has a vacancy, it accepts the new record. If the block is full, the DBMS allocates a new block and relocates half the records from the target block into the new block, say the half with the largest key values. If the records are pinned, it must install appropriate forwarding addresses. The DBMS enlarges its memory array to include the new block address at a location just after the address of the original target block. The new record belongs in one of the two blocks, and there is now room for it because both blocks are only half full. Figure 14.14 summarizes the situation.

In this scheme, when a block overflows, the DBMS integrates an overflow block into the array of base blocks, which avoids an overflow chain on the original base block. The DBMS memory array increases each time an overflow occurs, and it eventually reaches some maximum size. When the memory array can no longer grow, the DBMS must chain new blocks onto the overflowing miniheaps, just as in the original indexed sequential organization. The new algorithm can easily handle this regression to the indexed sequential behavior. When the DBMS obtains a new block from the disk manager, it places the address in the memory array—if the array hasn't reached its maximal size. Otherwise, it chains the block to the overflowing miniheap. The advantages of the dynamic allocation method are that disk blocks aren't allocated until needed and the DBMS doesn't need to accommodate an array of block addresses any larger than required by the current file size.

Moreover, the method doesn't suffer if the original key values aren't representative of the range of key values encountered as the file grows. For example, if the original records have key values all beginning with the letter 'a,' the DBMS packs them all in the original few blocks. Subsequent entries with key values beginning with 'b' or higher force the splitting of the last block, which adds new block addresses at the end of the memory array. So this troublesome case presents no problem when the allocation is dynamic.

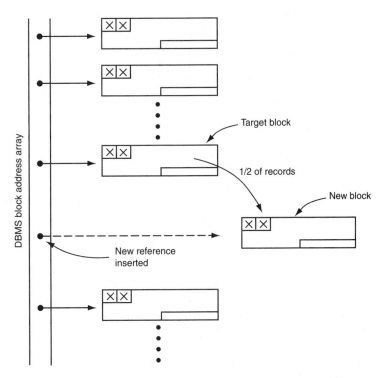

Figure 14.14   Splitting a block in a dynamic indexed sequential file

 A dynamic indexed sequential file allocates new blocks as needed and integrates them into the array of block addresses, which avoids overflow chains on the base blocks. The DBMS doesn't need to preallocate disk blocks to accommodate the final file size.

Dynamic hashing by modulus doubling

Hash files can grow dynamically in several ways. One method systematically changes the hash function to produce a larger range of bucket addresses. This is potentially expensive because, in general, if the hash function changes, all the records will relocate. However, by carefully choosing the hash functions' form, you can leave most records in their original buckets and relocate only those in an overflowing block.

To analyze this method, suppose the current hash function is $f(k) = k \bmod N$, where N is the number of currently available buckets and k is the key value. Suppose you now double the number of buckets to $2N$ and introduce a new hash function, $g(k) = k \bmod 2N$. The bucket addresses produced by $f(k)$ are correlated with those produced by $g(k)$. Suppose $f(k) = t$, for some $0 \le t < N$. Then $k = aN + t$ for some integer a, and a is either even or odd. If a is even, $k = 2bN + t$ for some integer b, which means that $g(k) = t = f(k)$. If a is odd, $k = (2b+1)N + t = 2bN + (N+t)$, which means that $g(k) = (N+t) = f(k) + N$. So when you change the hashing function from f to g, every record in bucket 0 either remains in bucket 0 or relocates to bucket N. Similarly, each record in bucket 1 either remains in bucket 1 or relocates to bucket $N + 1$. The pattern continues through bucket $N - 1$, where records either remain in place or relocate to bucket $2N - 1$.

Now suppose you allocate N blocks for an initial hash file, just sufficient for the size of the original file and with a little extra space to prevent excessive overflow—say $\alpha = 0.8$. You don't expect too many overflows in loading the initial file although you do expect significant overflows as the file grows. By cleverly switching hash functions, you can manipulate the structure so that the DBMS memory array will eventually incorporate all the overflow blocks. Therefore, buckets won't grow into lengthy chains of blocks even when you later add many records.

Initially, the DBMS memory array contains the N bucket addresses, and the hash function is $f_1(k) = k \bmod N$. The function $f_1(k)$ delivers a value in the range $0 \le f_1(k) < N$, which the DBMS uses to choose a bucket address from the memory array. The DBMS also maintains a single parameter, r, which indicates the next bucket to be split because of an overflow. Initially $r = 0$.

You now load the records into the hash file. The DBMS hashes each record with $f_1(k)$ to locate the target bucket. If the target bucket can accommodate the record, it does so without further adjustment. But if the target bucket overflows, the DBMS adjusts the hashing scheme. It does *not* split the overflowing target bucket; the target overflows onto a second chained block in the normal manner. Instead, it splits bucket r. The DBMS obtains a new block from the disk manager and places its address at position $N + r$ in the memory array. It applies the hash function $f_2(k) = k \bmod 2N$ to each record of block r, and these records either remain in block r or relocate to the new block, $N + r$. The DBMS then increments r by 1. Figure 14.15 illustrates the situation to this point, showing the first overflow in block i. This forces a split of block 0.

It appears the DBMS has split the wrong block. Block i overflowed onto a second block, but the DBMS split block 0 and relocated about half its contents into block N. The reason for this apparently illogical choice is that the DBMS wants to split the blocks in order. It will first split block 0, then block 1, then block 2, and so forth. The DBMS doesn't want to change completely to the new hashing function $f_2(k)$ because that would require relocating records from all the blocks. That massive relocation would demand the allocation of all N new blocks at the same time. The systematic process of splitting the blocks in order, regardless of the source of the overflow, allows the DBMS to allocate new blocks one at a time. Each record in the single block being split will either remain in place or relocate to the newly acquired block. When block $r = 0$ splits, those records that must relocate in accordance with the new hash function go to block $0 + N$, the newly allocated block just after $N - 1$. Later, when block 1 splits, any relocations will go to block $1 + N$, the next allocated block. Therefore, the adjustment involves only two blocks, the splitting block (not necessarily the overflowing block) and the new block obtained from the disk manager.

After the adjustment, you can still locate any record. You apply the hashing function $f_1(k)$ to its hash key value and note the result. If it is less than r (the new r, after incrementing), you know that the original destination bucket has split, so you apply $f_2(k)$ to determine whether the record has moved to bucket $f_1(k) + N$. If the result of $f_1(k) \ge r$, the destination bucket hasn't yet split, and the record must be in that bucket, although it might be on an overflow block chained to the base block.

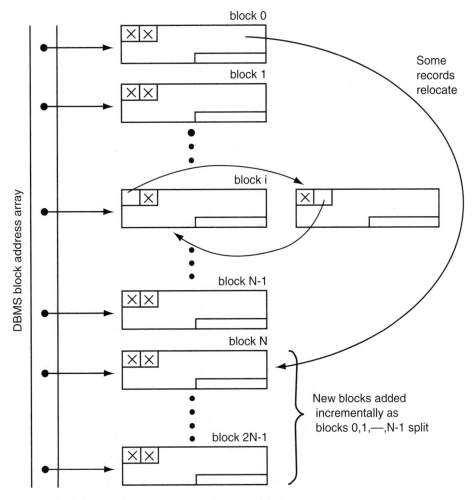

Figure 14.15 Splitting block 0 when the first overflow occurs

When the next overflow occurs, the DBMS splits bucket $r = 1$ and advances r to 2. It again obtains a new block from the disk manager and places the new block's address at position $N + 1$ of the memory array. Block 1 may have an overflow chain attached to it; the overflow that forced block 0 to split may have occurred in block 1. If an overflow chain exists, the DBMS uses one of the overflow blocks as the new block instead of requesting a new block from the disk manager. In any case, all the records of bucket 1—base block plus any overflow—redistribute themselves between block 1 and block $N + 1$. Typically, any chained blocks disappear during this relocation. However, it may happen that all the records remain in block 1, and the DBMS must retain the overflow chain. Equally unlikely but possible, all the records may transfer to block $N + 1$, which would force the overflow chain to that block.

Each time an overflow occurs, the value of r advances as the DBMS splits the next element of the base block array. As r increases, you expect fewer overflows because records originally hashing via $f_1(k)$ to buckets 0 through $r - 1$ now have twice as much room via $f_2(k)$ in buckets 0 through $r - 1$ and N through $N + r - 1$. Therefore, if the records hash uniformly via $f_1(k)$, overflows will decrease once r has increased somewhat. If r manages to increase to $N - 1$, the next overflow forces the last of the original blocks to split. At this point, the entire file conforms to the second hashing function, $f_2(k)$. The algorithm resets r to 0, and $f_2(k)$ becomes the hashing function for the entire file. You no longer need to test $f_1(k)$ to determine if $f_2(k)$ should be applied: $f_1(k)$ is superfluous at this point. The splitting can resume in the same manner as after the original allocation, except that $2N$ buckets are now available and the new $f_1(k) = k \bmod 2N$. The next overflow after this changeover starts the allocation of blocks $2N$ through $4N - 1$ from the disk manager and the use of a new $f_2(k) = k \bmod 4N$ on records that hash to buckets 0 through $r - 1$.

It's unlikely that r will run the full gamut up to $N - 1$ during the initial load. Indeed, if the original N blocks correspond to $\alpha = 0.8$ in terms of the initial file size, and if r manages to increase to $N - 1$, then twice as many blocks will be in use. This corresponds to $\alpha = 0.4$. For reasonable block capacities, 10 for example, essentially no overflow will occur at $\alpha = 0.4$. (See Figure 14.11.) However, as the file grows beyond its original size, r will eventually increase to $N - 1$, forcing a new cycle to climb toward $4N$ allocated blocks. Further growth may eventually produce yet another cycle, which will push the block allocation toward $8N$, and so forth.

To determine when a block will split, an overflow is deemed to occur when the DBMS must obtain a new block from the disk manager to accommodate the next record in a bucket. Therefore, if a bucket has an overflow chain, subsequent entries into the last block of the chain won't trigger a block split as long as the last block can accommodate new records. But if the last chain block is full, the next record hashing to the bucket will trigger a block split, even though that same bucket may have triggered an earlier block split in the same cycle. Of course, if the hash functions distribute the records uniformly across the buckets, it's unlikely that a bucket will grow a lengthy overflow chain before it splits into two buckets.

The DBMS array of block addresses increases one block at a time, just as in the case of dynamic indexed sequential files. Moreover, if the hash functions spread the records uniformly, the new blocks eliminate overflow chains that may have developed earlier in the cycle. This keeps the number of retrieval probes close to one. As in the case of dynamic indexed sequential files, this process can continue only as long as the DBMS can accommodate the increasing size of its array of block addresses. When that limit is reached, block splitting ceases, and overflow chains start to accumulate. This algorithm can easily handle the switchover because it permits overflow chains throughout the process. After the process reaches the maximum size of the DBMS memory array, it just doesn't reabsorb the overflows with further block splitting.

Because the file structure can evolve in so many ways, analyzing the performance of a dynamic hash file is difficult. However, a straightforward simulation can distribute records to randomly selected buckets and split the buckets as required by the dynamic process. At each point, the simulation tracks the buckets' populations, so it can determine the average number of probes needed to retrieve a randomly selected record. Suppose, at a given time, that the process has allocated N buckets and that the simulation has retained their populations as $p_0, p_1, \ldots, p_{N-1}$. Then Q', the average number of disk accesses to retrieve a randomly selected record, is:

$$Q' = \frac{\sum_{i=0}^{N-1} T(p_i)}{\sum_{i=0}^{N-1} p_i}. \tag{14.9}$$

$T(x)$ comes from Equation 14.7. Figure 14.16 illustrates a typical situation, obtained from a simulation with the following parameters: block capacity = 10, initial allocation = 100 blocks, initial record count = 800. Because this arrangement can hold 1000 records, the initial load would correspond to a load factor of 0.8, if it weren't for the dynamic splitting algorithm requesting more blocks when it detects overflows. The upper portion of Figure 14.16 shows the load factor rising toward the 0.8 mark as the initial records are loaded. It achieves only about 0.7 because some splitting increases the number of allocated blocks. As the simulation adds more records, the load factor continues upward to about 0.9, where the splitting process holds it in check. As records pile up in the blocks, tending to increase the load factor, more frequent overflows occur, forcing new block allocations and tending to decrease the load factor. These two processes balance each other at a load factor of about 0.9.

The lower portion of Figure 14.16 displays the average number of probes required to retrieve a randomly selected record from the file, as a function of the number of records currently in the file. The average number of accesses for a random retrieval rises as buckets that aren't in line to split acquire overflow chains. As splitting progresses across the buckets, a bucket with an overflow chain has the opportunity to split, which reduces, or even eliminates, the overflow chain. Therefore, you observe periodic decreases in the average number of disk accesses per retrieval. As the process allocates new blocks, it integrates them into the memory array of hash addresses. The simulation allows this array to grow to a maximum of 1000 buckets, which is ten times the size of the original allocation. At that point, noted in the graphs where approximately 9500 records have been inserted, the simulation suppresses further splitting. Both the load factor and the average disk accesses per retrieval then resume their upward climb. When 16,000 records have been inserted, α has risen to 1.6 because the limiting allocation of 1000 buckets can accommodate only 10,000 records without overflow. At that point, Q', the average number of disk accesses per retrieval, is about 1.44, which is the value expected from a traditional hashing scheme with these parameters.

You can conclude that the block-splitting process of the dynamic hashing algorithm keeps the file load factor from migrating into an overloaded state. In other words, it keeps $\alpha < 1$. It does eventually reach a point where the block address array is too large to allow further growth. When you add more records, the load factor then continues its upward climb, eventually assuming the behavior of an overloaded hash file.

The dynamic hashing scheme just described can be called **modulus doubling**, although other names exist in the literature. The hash functions must be of the form $f(k) = k \bmod M$, for some modulus M, and, at any given time, two such functions are operational: one for blocks that have already split and the other for blocks that haven't yet split. The modulus of the former is always double the modulus of the latter. This scheme can effectively allocate blocks as a file grows, while maintaining a reasonable average retrieval time of slightly more than one disk access. Moreover, you can easily incorporate the

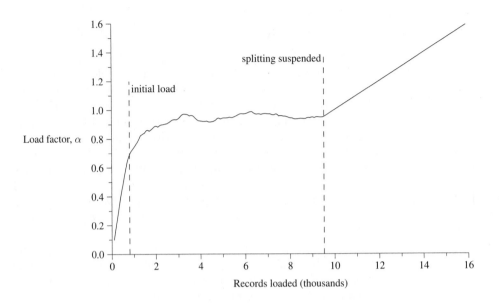

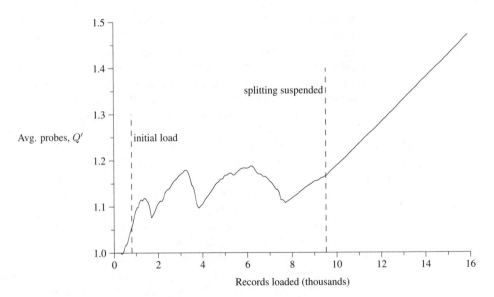

Figure 14.16   Performance of a modulus-doubling dynamic hash file (block capacity = 10)

dynamic algorithm into a standard hashing scheme: you simply suppress the block splitting upon reaching some maximum number of buckets.

 Dynamic hashing by modulus doubling systematically splits blocks in order of their occurrence in the memory array, regardless of the source of the triggering overflow.

Dynamic hashing by directory doubling

The modulus doubling method isn't applicable if the hash function isn't of the proper form. This section investigates an alternative dynamic hashing technique called **directory doubling**. Placing no restrictions on the hash function, the new method expands the memory array of block addresses in a lumpy fashion (by doubling it at strategic times) in contrast with the incremental growth associated with modulus doubling. However, it still allocates the actual data storage blocks in an incremental fashion, one at a time as needed.

You start by establishing the largest memory array of bucket addresses that the DBMS can comfortably handle and then rounding that value down to the closest power of 2. Denote this value by $N = 2^n$. Eventually, the DBMS memory array will expand to N cells, each pointing to a bucket. During the dynamic phase of file growth, each bucket comprises exactly one block, so performance is exactly one disk access for any record. At some point, however, the dynamic allocation of buckets must cease in order not to exceed the predetermined limit of N. At that point, the existing buckets start to accumulate overflow chains, and the performance deteriorates just as with the modulus-doubling scheme.

You next choose a hashing function, $f(k)$, so that $0 \leq f(k) < N$ for all hash field values that will ever appear in file records. The hash function doesn't need to involve modular division, but it should spread the expected hash field values uniformly across the range 0 to $N - 1$. Because $N = 2^n$, you consider the values returned by $f(k)$ as n bit quantities, and you precede the smaller values with leading 0s if necessary. The subscripted function, $f_i(k)$, extracts the ith bit of $f(k)$. In other words, $f_{n-1}(k)$ is the most significant bit; $f_{n-2}(k)$ the next most significant bit; and so forth. $f_0(k)$ is the least significant bit. Each $f_i(k)$ is either 0 or 1.

With this hashing method, the DBMS memory array of block addresses is called a directory. The file starts with one bucket, which contains one block. The DBMS directory contains a single entry, which hold the address of the one data block and a flag that keeps track of the block's splitting history. At the outset, no splitting has occurred, so the directory appears as in the upper portion of Figure 14.17. The DBMS maintains a parameter, r, that indirectly indicates the directory's current size. You initialize r to 0 because the directory starts with $2^r = 2^0 = 1$ bucket address. As the process unfolds, the number of directory entries is always a power of 2. Therefore, r climbs from 0 toward its maximal value of n.

As the file starts to receive records, the DBMS places them all in the single data block, regardless of the value of $f(k)$. When that block is full, the next new record triggers a splitting of the initial block into two blocks, as shown in the lower portion of Figure 14.17. The DBMS obtains a new block from the disk manager and doubles the directory to two entries. The first entry keeps the original block's address; the second stores the new block's address. The DBMS sets the flag in each directory cell to 1 because the cells point to "first

r=0

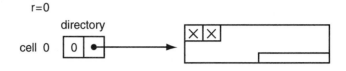

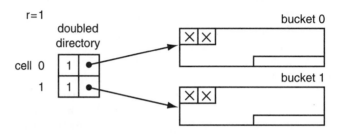

Figure 14.17   Early evolution of a directory-doubling dynamic hash file

generation daughter blocks" of the original single data block. It also updates r to 1 to reflect the new directory size of 2^1. The DBMS then applies $f_{n-1}(k)$ to each record in the original block, which examines the first bit of its hash value. If the value is 0, the record remains in the first bucket, now called bucket 0. If the value is 1, the record relocates to the new block, now called bucket 1. Typically about one-half of the records relocate to the new block, so each block is approximately one-half full. The DBMS now places the new record in bucket 0 or 1 according to its $f_{n-1}(k)$ value.

Although most unlikely, all the records could remain in block 0 or relocate to block 1. In that case, one of the blocks fills up. This extreme case isn't likely if the hash function distributes the keys uniformly across the range 0 to $N-1$ because about one-half of the bit expressions for 0 to $N-1$ have the first bit equal to zero and the rest have the first bit equal to 1. So in the typical case, either block can accommodate the new record. The extreme case, where the new record tries to enter a full block, triggers further splitting, which is discussed below.

Before adding more records and tracing further splits, note that the hashing scheme can still recover the records after the first split. To locate a record, you hash the key value and use the first r bits of the result as an index into the directory. If $r = 0$, no bits are needed because the directory contains only one cell. If $r = 1$, as in the example after the first split, the first bit of the hash value selects directory cell 0 or cell 1. These cells contain the proper block addresses for the records with the same first bits in their hash values. As r grows larger, this technique continues to locate the bucket that holds the target record.

Now you can continue to add records by using the first $r = 1$ bits of the hash value to place them in bucket 0 or in bucket 1. Eventually, one of the buckets, say bucket 1, overflows, and the directory doubles again. Each cell gives rise to two cells as shown in the upper portion of Figure 14.18. The DBMS increases r to 2, reflecting the new directory

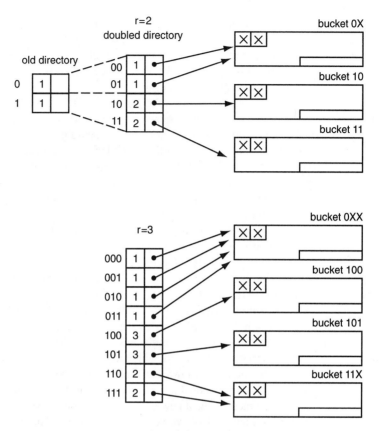

Figure 14.18 Continuing evolution of a directory-doubling dynamic hash file

size of $2^2 = 4$ cells. The two cells arising from cell 0 point to the same block because that one didn't overflow. Call this one bucket 0x because it contains records with a 0 in the first bit of their hashed keys and an irrelevant value in the second bit. The flags in these two cells still contain the value 1, indicating that the data block is a first generation split from the original data block.

The two cells arising from cell 1, however, point to different blocks. The upper cell, now called cell 10, continues to point to the block that cell 1 referenced—the overflowing cell, previously called bucket 1. You now call it bucket 10. The lower cell, now called cell 11, points to a new block obtained from the disk manager. You relocate the records in bucket 10 according to the second bit of their hash values. The first bit of their hash values is 1, of course, because all the relocating records used to be bucket 1. If $f_{n-2}(k)$ is 0, the record remains in bucket 10; if $f_{n-2}(k)$ is 1, it relocates to bucket 11. In the typical case, about one-half of the records relocate. The new record can fit in either block, depending on the first two bits of its hash value—10 or 11. The first bit of the hash value can't be 0 because the record was trying to enter bucket 1 when the overflow was detected. Only records with the first bit equal to 1 would attempt to enter bucket 1.

Retrieval operations continue to function appropriately. You apply the hash function to the key field and use the first $r = 2$ bits as an index into the memory array. A hash value with a 0 in the first bit selects either cell 00 or 01. Both cells point to bucket 0x (the old bucket 0). A hash value of 10 or 11 selects the corresponding cell and obtains a reference to bucket 10 or 11 as required.

You have now arrived at the general case where the history flags in the directory cells contain values less than or equal to r. Recall that r reflects the number of times the directory has doubled, but a cell flag tracks the number of generations its data block is removed from the original single data block that started the file. After the first split, the directory flags can contain any value from 1 through r, depending on the blocks' overflow order. For example, the lower portion of Figure 14.18 shows the configuration after a new record attempts to enter a full bucket 10. Bucket 10 becomes bucket 100, and the disk manager supplies a new block to form bucket 101. The directory doubles, so the single cell pointing to bucket 10 becomes two cells: the upper pointing to bucket 100 and the lower pointing to bucket 101. The records in bucket 100 (previously bucket 10) redistribute between buckets 100 and 101 according to $f_{n-3}(k)$, the third bit of their hash values. The unaffected directory cells also double, but they continue to point to their old data blocks, and their history flags remain unchanged. The old buckets acquire new names, 0xx and 11x, that indicate which records are stored in the blocks. An 'x' in this context means "either 0 or 1." So, for example, bucket 0xx holds records with a hash value beginning with a 0. The retrieval mechanism still locates records with a single disk access. The first $r = 3$ bits of the hash value select the appropriate directory cell, which in turn provides the correct block address.

When a block overflows, the directory must double if the history flag of the corresponding directory cell is equal to r. Otherwise, the directory doesn't double but rearranges the pointers to incorporate a new block. Suppose, for example, that the situation in the lower portion of Figure 14.18 evolves to the point where bucket 0xx overflows. Bucket 0xx becomes bucket 00x, and a new block becomes bucket 01x. The history flags in the associated directory cells increase to 2, and Figure 14.19 shows the rearranged pointers. The records in bucket 00x (the old 0xx) relocate depending on $f_{n-2}(k)$, the second bit of their hash values.

Thus, the scheme allocates data blocks incrementally to offload about half the contents of a full block that is about to overflow. If the bursting block corresponds to a directory cell with a maximal history flag (i.e., a history flag equal to r), the directory doubles. If the bursting block corresponds to a directory cell with a less than maximal history flag, the DBMS incorporates the new block into the existing directory structure. Eventually the process reaches the directory size limit. Although further directory doubling isn't possible at that point, cells that haven't yet reached the maximal history flag value can continue to readjust to accommodate new blocks. Unlike the modulus-doubling scheme, the dynamic adjustment's demise phases in gradually. The dynamic adjustment starts to be suppressed when the first block with a history flag of n can't split. Some adjustment remains possible as the other directory cells' history flags increase toward their maximal value of n. The process ceases completely when all directory cells have a history flag of n. When a block can't split because of the size limit, it starts accumulating overflow blocks on a chain, and the performance starts deteriorating.

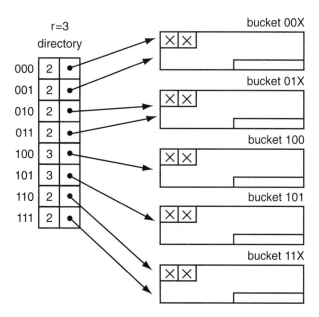

Figure 14.19   Alternative evolution of a directory-doubling dynamic hash file

Because the directory structure can evolve in so many ways, the performance of a directory-doubling hash file is difficult to analyze mathematically. However, you can easily simulate the algorithm. Using a block capacity of 10, Figure 14.20 illustrates a typical performance profile. Until it must deny a splitting request for the first time, the dynamic algorithm keeps the average accesses per retrieval at an absolute minimal value of 1.0. From that point on, the value rises uniformly and merges into the expected values for normal hashing when the algorithm stops all splitting attempts. The algorithm suppresses all splitting when all directory cells have history flags equal to the maximal directory doubling count, n. All buckets must then grow overflow chains. Freely available splits keep the load factor in the 0.75 range. When splitting opportunities start to decline, the load factor begins a gradual rise, and it also merges smoothly into the expected values associated with normal hashing.

 Dynamic hashing by directory-doubling maintains an absolute minimal value of 1.0 for the average number of accesses per retrieval, as long as free splitting is available. When splitting is restricted, the performance gradually merges with that of with normal hashing.

Other hashing schemes

Hashing techniques have been an extensive computer science research topic for many years, so many variations are available. This chapter presents the general methods, but it certainly doesn't claim exhaustive coverage. Another popular method is **open address hashing**, which places overflow records in the first available bucket beyond the target.

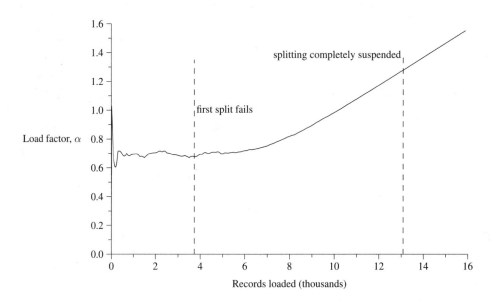

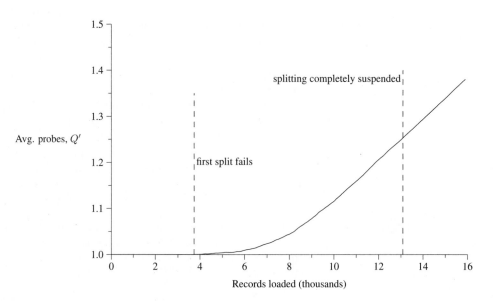

Figure 14.20   Performance of a directory-doubling dynamic hash file (block capacity = 10)

It uses a cyclical counter, such that bucket 0 follows bucket $N - 1$. Hash tables that reside in memory (e.g., program identifiers in a source language compilation) frequently use open addressing, and the method can also be extended to disk buckets. Its advantage is that it allocates no new disk blocks as long as space exists anywhere in the existing bucket collection. The disadvantage is that overflows from one bucket reduce the following buckets' effective capacity, which forces them to overflow sooner. The average number of probes for a random retrieval also suffers as the file fills and many records reside away from their home bucket.

Another interesting variation involves an **order-preserving** hash function. In other words, if $k_1 \leq k_2$, then $f(k_1) \leq f(k_2)$. This hash function allows you to retrieve the records in key order by accessing the buckets in numerical order. All records in bucket i have keys that are less than or equal to the smallest key of bucket $i + 1$, which produces an organization similar to an indexed sequential file. Suppose the record keys are m-bit quantities, and you are hashing to 2^n buckets, where $n < m$. A simple order-preserving hash function extracts the n most significant bits of the key by right-shifting the least significant $m - n$ bits off the register: $f(k) = k >> (m - n)$. However, this function is usually not effective in spreading the keys uniformly over the buckets. In the worst case, all the keys may have the same leading n bits. In general, effective order-preserving hash functions are difficult to invent, particularly if the full set of keys isn't known when the file is created.

Partitioned hashing functions concatenate bit strings obtained by separately hashing the values from different record fields. You can use the scheme to reduce the search space size if the key values are only partially available. For example, suppose you have a database of sites, each characterized by a latitude and longitude and holding additional data on the facility located at that point. Suppose you hash the records into 1024 buckets. You obtain the first five bits of the ten-bit bucket address by hashing the latitude. You similarly hash the longitude to obtain the second five bits. For a random retrieval, if you have both the latitude and longitude, you can obtain the correct bucket immediately by hashing the two values and concatenating the bit strings. If you have only the latitude, however, you can still hash that part, obtaining, say, 10110. Now you know that the record must be in one of the 32 buckets with addresses of the form 10110xxxxx, so you have reduced the search space by a factor of 32. A similar argument holds if only the longitude is given.

SUMMARY

A disk storage unit is a stack of magnetic platters that rotate around a common spindle. You can envision the surface of each platter as a collection of concentric rings, called tracks, where the mechanism can linearly store data bytes. The set of tracks directly above and below each other on the various platters is a cylinder. Each track's circumference comprises a number of sectors. Each track contains the same number of sectors, and each sector contains the same number of data bytes, regardless of its track. The sector is the unit of data transfer between the disk and the computer memory. Each sector has a unique address of the form (cylinder, platter, angular position). Typical sector sizes are 512 to 4096 bytes. The nominal time required to transfer a sector between disk and computer memory is about 15 milliseconds.

The DBMS deals with disk pages, also called blocks. Ideally, a page is a sector. However, to accommodate varying disk sizes, a mapping may associate many pages with a sector or many sectors with a page. For performance reasons, the DBMS needs to pack records of various types onto a page, which results in varying record lengths. To implement relationships, records must be able to refer to other records, and these references frequently take the form of disk addresses. When other records reference a record, it is said to be pinned; pinned records shouldn't change their addresses. Therefore, you express the record address as a block address, combined with the offset to a locator at the bottom of the block. This locator points to the actual location of the record in the block, with suitable arrangements for a forwarding address if the record moves off the block. Each record usually possesses a header that identifies the record type, flags forwarding addresses, and provides pointers and length specifications for the fields. Each block also contains forward and backward pointers to other blocks, so the DBMS can link the file into one long chain or into a collection of short chains.

If the file records aren't in any particular order, the file is a sequential file, or a heap. The sequential organization links all the blocks into one long chain, and the DBMS retains only the first block's address. The average number of disk accesses required to acquire a target record from a sequential file is excessive because, on the average, the DBMS must search half the file.

An appealing alternative divides the file into many segments, called miniheaps or buckets, and provides a mechanism for rapidly determining which miniheap to search for a target record. This chapter discussed two such division techniques: indexed sequential and hashed. An indexed sequential organization orders the records by a key field, not necessarily unique, and disburses the records across the miniheaps. The records in the first miniheap have key values less than or equal to the keys of the second miniheap, and so forth. The DBMS keeps the block addresses of the first block of each miniheap in a memory array. It can then conduct a rapid binary search by first accessing the middle block and noting the relationship between the block's key values and the target record's key value. This information places the target in one half of the file, and the DBMS repeats the subdivision process until it reduces the search segment to a single block. The maximum number of accesses is $\log_2 N$ plus the accesses needed to search the block in the final miniheap. N is the number of elements in the DBMS memory array.

Although an indexed sequential organization reduces the search time to a logarithmic function of the file length, a hash file can approach the absolute minimum of one disk access per retrieval. For a hash file, the DBMS also maintains an array of bucket addresses, but it calculates the array cell to be probed from the target record's key field. The calculation uses a hash function, which, in the ideal case, spreads the records uniformly across the buckets. Because of probabilistic variations, some buckets will overflow into a second block, and others will receive fewer records than they can accommodate. On average, however, the process holds the number of disk accesses per random retrieval to just slightly above 1. The ratio of the number of records stored to the number that can be accommodated in the allocated buckets, assuming one block per bucket, is the file's load factor. Judicious combinations of low load factors and large block sizes can keep the average number of disk accesses per retrieval very close to the minimal value of 1.

A disadvantage of both the indexed sequential and hashed organizations is that the DBMS must allocate a full sized memory array and the associated initial data blocks when it creates the file. Subsequent file growth fills in the empty space in the structure. An uneven distribution of keys can result in overflow chains on the miniheaps and decreased performance. In many instances, a file's final size is unknown, and you would prefer to start the file with a small number of data blocks and a small DBMS memory array.

A dynamic indexed sequential file places new records in newly allocated blocks and integrates the new block addresses into the DBMS memory array. The process involves block-balancing operations when a new block relieves an overflowing existing block so that problems associated with a non-representative set of initial key values don't arise. Of course, moving pinned records requires additional processing to update forwarding addresses. Therefore, a dynamic indexed sequential file is most appropriate for unpinned records.

Several dynamic techniques achieve a similar efficiency by allowing hash files to grow as needed from a small initial allocation. The modulus-doubling scheme applies if the hashing function is of the form $f(k) = k \bmod M$. It spreads records over an increasing range of buckets by systematically doubling the modulus M. Because the process doesn't immediately split overflowing buckets, the average disk accesses per retrieval climbs slightly above 1.0, but eventual relief decreases the value again. By contrast, the directory-doubling technique applies to any hashing function. It uses an ever larger sequence of initial bits from the hash value. When the file is small, a few such bits are sufficient to distinguish among the allocated buckets. When the file grows to the envisioned capacity, all the bits are necessary to distinguish among the allocated buckets. When a bucket becomes full, it splits in such a way to integrate the new bucket into the directory scheme, possibly increasing the number of bits used from the hash value. Because the process splits the overflowing buckets, the number of accesses per random retrieval remains at the absolute minimal value of 1.0. Eventually a predetermined maximal size of the DBMS memory array forces certain splits to be denied, and the performance starts to deteriorate. Both dynamic hashing schemes revert to the performance of normal hashing when splitting opportunities are foreclosed.

Physical organization of a disk storage unit and block layout schemes

1. The time required to position the read-write sensors over a disk track varies with the sensors' current position. Suppose that the time required to move from track x to track y is given by the following expression, where t_0 and t_1 are positive constants. If the disk platters contain N tracks, derive an expression for the average **seek time**, that is, the average time necessary to move the read-write sensors to a target track.

$$T(x, y) = \begin{cases} 0, & \text{if } x = y \\ t_0 + t_1 |x - y|, & \text{if } x \neq y. \end{cases}$$

Indexed sequential files

2. Suppose a sequential file contains B blocks, each holding q records. The DBMS maintains only the block address of the file's first block. Each block contains forward and backward pointers chaining it into the complete file. The text uses the figure $B/2$ as the average number of disk accesses needed to find a target record. Show that this average is actually $(B + 1)/2$.

3. Suppose one block of a sequential file is in memory from a previous operation when a request arrives to acquire a target record. Using the parameters of the preceding exercise, show that the average number of disk accesses to retrieve the target is $(B^2 - 1)/3B \approx B/3$ for large B.

4. Suppose the miniheaps of an indexed sequential file contain records with keys from the table below. The block capacity is 2 records. The first data column is the base block, the middle column is the first chained block, and the last column is the second chained block. Directly calculate the average number of data probes per retrieval by tracing the retrieval of each key and summing the required disk accesses. Comment on your answer in light of the fact that $\log_2(7) \approx 3$.

Miniheap	Contents					
0	18	55	79	87	116	135
1	177					
2	179	193	242			
3	254	277	291	311	324	370
4	398	403	419			
5	428					
6	460	500	526	528	540	575

5. Suppose you add a record with key value 412 to the indexed sequential file of the preceding exercise. Which miniheap receives the new record? How does it affect the average number of disk accesses per random retrieval?

6. Consider a portion of the library database, consisting of libraries, books, and copies. Each entity appears on a separate file with structures as shown below. The parentheses indicate primary keys. Copy has foreign keys bookno and libno, which implement the many-to-one relationships between copy and book and between copy and library.

Entity	File	Attributes
Library	L	(libno), libname, location, . . .
Book	B	(bookno), title, pages, . . .
Copy	C	(copyno), cost, bookno, libno

Suppose all three files are organized as sequential files. So each file is one long chain of blocks requiring sequential search methods. There are $N_L = 2000$ libraries, stored 20 per block. There are $N_B = 20,000$ books, stored 20 per block. There are $N_C = 1,000,000$ copies, stored 100 per block. Estimate the number of disk accesses, and therefore the processing time, needed to perform the natural join, $L * C * B$, disregarding any buffering of disk blocks.

7. Suppose the library file, L, and the book file, B, of the preceding exercise are now organized as indexed sequential files on libno and bookno respectively. Assume L has 100 miniheaps of one block each, and B has 1000 miniheaps of one block each. As before, each block in the L miniheap contains 20 library records, and each block in the B miniheap contains 20 book records. The copy file, C, remains a sequential file. Under these new circumstances, estimate again the number of disk accesses and the processing time required to construct the natural join $L * C * B$.

8. Suppose, in addition to the indexed sequential organization of the library and book files, that the copy file, C, is also so organized, but on the foreign key bookno. Assume that the image of bookno in file C is 20,000. In other words, all books are represented. Estimate again the number of disk accesses and the processing time required to construct the natural join $L * C * B$.

Hash files

9. Suppose the library and book files of the last exercise are now organized as hash files, with the load factor adjusted such that the average retrieval time is 1.1 disk accesses from either file. Continue to assume that the copy file is organized in an indexed sequential manner on the foreign key bookno. Estimate again the number of disk accesses and the processing time required to construct the natural join $L * C * B$.

10. Can you gain substantial savings over the preceding exercise by changing the copy file to an indexed sequential file on the foreign key libno, rather than on bookno? Estimate the processing cost with this new organization and comment on the savings achieved.

11. Show that for large N, $\alpha N q$ Equation 14.4,

$$D(x) = \frac{\binom{\alpha N q}{x} (N-1)^{\alpha N q - x}}{N^{\alpha N q}},$$

reduces to Equation 14.5,

$$D(x) = \frac{(\alpha q)^x e^{-\alpha q}}{x!}.$$

Dynamic file structures

12. Load the records with the following keys into an initially empty modulus-doubling hash file. The initial modulus is 10, and the initial bucket allocation is 10. The block capacity is 2. Each time a you acquire new data block, give a snapshot of the organization: the bucket contents, the two hash functions in use, and the value r used to determine if the second hash function is applicable.

1246	1290	1326	1359	1380	1405	1442	1477	1492	1522
1555	1602	1633	1676	1688	1711	1712	1758	1775	1780
1816	1839	1879	1892	1933	1957	1970	2002	2038	2048
2066	2112	2145	2159	2195	2225	2251	2275	2319	2333

13. What is the load factor and average number of disk accesses per random retrieval for the final configuration of the preceding exercise?

14. Load records with the following keys into an initially empty directory-doubling hash file. The block capacity is 2, and directory doubling is allowed to proceed through 3 levels. In other words, the maximum directory size is 8 cells. The hash function is $f(k) = k \bmod 8$, a 3 bit quantity. The hashed value appears as the parenthesized entry following each key in the table. Each time you acquire a new data block, give a snapshot of the directory contents and the data blocks.

1095 (111)	1104 (000)	1155 (011)	1181 (101)	1231 (111)
1283 (011)	1334 (110)	1383 (111)	1402 (010)	1444 (100)

15. What is the load factor and average disk accesses per random retrieval for the final configuration of the preceding exercise?

15 Indexes

CHAPTER 14 DISCUSSED TWO ORGANIZATIONS THAT SUBDIVIDE A LARGE file into a collection of miniheaps: indexed sequential and hashed. Compared with a sequential organization, a decomposition into N miniheaps reduces the disk access cost for a given search by $1/N$. The tradeoff is that the DBMS must maintain a memory array of N block addresses, which can't grow indefinitely because of memory limitations. Consequently, the individual miniheaps eventually become large chains of blocks in themselves, which compromises the performance within each miniheap.

An obvious solution stores the array of block addresses on disk along with the data blocks. The DBMS then pages it partially into memory as needed. An auxiliary file of this nature is an **index**, and its records contain key values and correlated block addresses. In some cases, the block addresses refer to the main data file indicate where you can find a target record. In other cases, the block addresses refer to other portions of the index, and you must probe further to find the data reference. When determining the retrieval cost of a record, you must, of course, count the overhead disk accesses that read the index. Consequently, you want to organize the index file to minimize this expense.

You can generally organize an index around any field, or field group, of the data file records. Several indexes can serve the same data file to accelerate record recovery based on different field values. In the aquarium example, the fish file can have two indexes: one on fcolor and another on fweight. If you know the target record's fcolor, you can use the first index to retrieve the record. You use the second index if you know the fweight value. In either case, the index overhead should be only a few disk accesses beyond those needed to retrieve the target data blocks. This chapter investigates several techniques that permit indexes to achieve these goals.

Sparse hierarchical indexes

A sparse index of unduplicated keys

A **sparse hierarchical index** accelerates access to an indexed sequential file. It uses the same field, or field group, as the indexed sequential organization: the **ordering field** of the

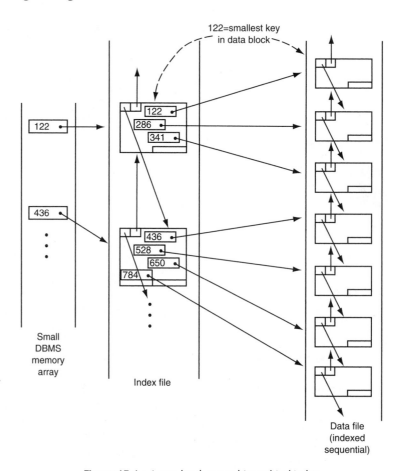

Figure 15.1   A one-level sparse hierarchical index

file. A sparse hierarchical index is so named because it exhibits a hierarchical structure and can catalog the entire data file by tracking only a subset of the ordering field values. A sparse hierarchical index is sometimes called an ISAM index, an acronym standing for Indexed Sequential Access Method.

Figure 15.1 illustrates the simplest form of a sparse hierarchical index. It distributes the data across many blocks and typically fills each block only partially to allow room for growth. It then chains the data blocks together to reflect the records' ordering field values. In other words, the ordering field values in block i are less than or equal to the smallest ordering field value in block $i + 1$. So the data file organization is indexed sequential.

However, an additional structure now appears, the index file, which delivers the following advantages. First, the file can grow, adding new blocks as necessary, without producing overflow chains and without enlarging the DBMS memory array of block addresses. Second, the maximum number of disk accesses needed to retrieve a target record will be two or three, even for a file with a very large number of blocks. If N is the number of data blocks, recall that the bare indexed sequential method required $\log_2 N$ to find the proper miniheap, plus overflow accesses as needed to recover the data. The disadvantage of the index file is that you must continually update the index as you modify the data file.

Just like the data file, the index file of Figure 15.1 contains blocks, but the block records contain key values and block addresses pointing to the data file. For the moment, assume that the data file's ordering field values are unique. In other words, the ordering field is a key. The index file contains one *record* for each data file *block*. Although the content of an index record varies slightly across implementations, the situation in Figure 15.1 is typical. Each index record contains the address of a data file block, together with the smallest key value in the data block.

You pack the index records tightly into blocks, but a block of index records represents many data blocks, which in turn represent many data records. Within an index block, you maintain the records in order by increasing key value. You then chain the index blocks, just as in the data file. In other words, the largest key of index block i is smaller than the smallest key of index block $i + 1$. Because memory operations don't count in the cost equation, no advantage accrues from insisting on ordered records within the index blocks. You can find any record by scanning the block after transferring it to memory. Nevertheless, the discussion is simpler if the index records are in sorted order in the blocks, and the examples and illustrations will reflect this convention. Moreover, index records usually aren't pinned, and you can easily move them to maintain the desired order.

An index that doesn't contain an entry for each data file record is a **sparse index**. By contrast, an index with an entry for each data file record is a **dense index**. Therefore, the index of Figure 15.1 is sparse, justifying its classification as a sparse hierarchical index.

An index can be much smaller than its data file for two reasons. First, the index can be sparse, so it directly represents only a fraction of the data records. Second, the index contains only the key field and a block address; therefore, more index records fit in a block. For example, suppose you have 4096 byte blocks, with data records packed 10 to the block. Using a typical size of 4 bytes for a block address and 20 bytes for a key value, you can pack about 170 index records in each block. Suppose the data file has 1,000,000 records, which require 100,000 fully packed blocks. A sparse index file then needs only 100,000 records—one for each data block. You can pack these records in $100,000/170 = 589$ blocks. Although the block address array for the data file may be too large to retain in memory, the smaller block address array for its index file stands a much better chance. In this example, the DBMS must retain only 589 block addresses to acquire any index block.

Figure 15.1 shows an index block with the same general form as any other block. Forward and backward pointers chain it in the complete file, and a locator array appears at the block end. Although you can envision arrangements where index records are pinned, such conditions are rare. Remote references exist to the index *blocks*, for example, from the DBMS memory array, but not to the individual index records. Nevertheless, the locator arrays are necessary because the keys in the index records vary in length. As shown in Figure 15.2, an index block then looks a bit like a porcupine, bristling with references to its data file.

The DBMS memory array, which is now much smaller than the number of data blocks, contains an entry for each index block. Each cell holds not only an index block pointer, but also the lowest key in that index block. The DBMS keeps the memory array sorted on these

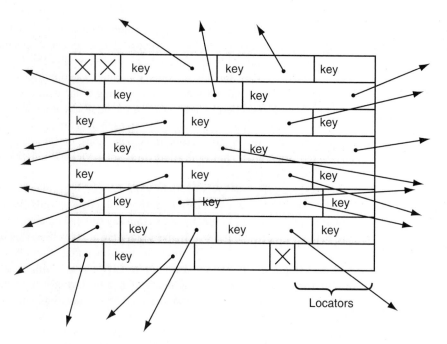

Figure 15.2 An index block bristling with references to data blocks

key entries. To locate a target record with key value x, you first find the array entry with the largest key not exceeding x. You can do this most easily by scanning the memory array backwards until you encounter an entry i with key value $v_i \leq x$. This process takes place in memory and therefore contributes nothing to the cost of the search. You then expend a disk access to retrieve index block i, which must contain a reference to the target's data block, if it exists in the file. All higher index blocks, $i + 1$ and up, have keys that are strictly larger than x; the lowest key in index block i is less than or equal to x. You next search index block i for the record, say j, with the largest key $u_j \leq x$. Similar reasoning guarantees that the target record lies in the data block referenced by record j. A second disk access now retrieves the data block. Therefore, two disk accesses, or 0.03 seconds, are sufficient to obtain any record in the file.

You can compare the sparse hierarchical index with the unadorned indexed sequential organization. Assume a file of 1,000,000 records. Data records are packed 10 to the block; index records average 24 bytes in length, which allow 170 index records to the block. The score then appears as follows.

	straight indexed sequential	with sparse hierarchical index
Data records	1,000,000	1,000,000
Data blocks	100,000	100,000
DBMS memory array (entries)	100,000	589
Memory array size (bytes)	400,000	14,136
Accesses per retrieval	17	2

The DBMS memory array size falls from 100,000 entries, one for each miniheap of the data file, to 589, one for each block of the index file. However, the entries' size increases to include a key, growing from 4 bytes for a block address to a typical value of 24 bytes for a block address and a key value. Nevertheless, the memory array still shrinks from 400,000 to 14,136 bytes, a reduction factor of about 30. Even more important, the disk accesses needed for a random retrieval decreases. In the straight indexed sequential organization, you need 17 probes to conduct a binary search of the 100,000 miniheaps represented in the memory array. With the assistance of the sparse hierarchical index, you need only two probes: one to obtain the appropriate index block and a second to obtain the data block.

If the memory array is still too large, you can generalize the process to more levels. The memory array entries of Figure 15.1 are identical in format to the index records. Therefore, you can consider the memory array as a higher-level index, which provides addresses for the index blocks of the next lower level. So the structure of Figure 15.1 is actually a two-level index, but the first level resides in memory. If the memory level structure is too large, you can pack the records into blocks and store them on disk. A third, smaller level is then necessary to coordinate access to the new index blocks.

For example, Figure 15.3 shows a three-level sparse hierarchical index. First-level entries, in the DBMS memory array, point to second-level index blocks. The key value in a first-level entry is the smallest key among the records of the second-level index block under reference. A second-level record points to a third-level index block and contains the smallest key among the records there. Finally, a third-level record points to a data block and contains the smallest key there.

Continuing with the 1,000,000 record data file from above, you can pack references to the 589 index blocks into $589/170 \approx 4$ first-level blocks, which requires a memory array of only four entries. You must now expend three disk accesses to retrieve a record. The search strategy remains the same, and you simply repeat it at each level until you reach a data block. Suppose x is the target record key. You search the first-level index in memory for the entry i with the largest key $v_i \leq x$. This entry supplies a block address, which you use to retrieve a second-level index block. You search there for record j with the largest key $u_j \leq x$ and use the corresponding block address pointer to retrieve a third-level index block. One more repetition locates the pointer to the data block containing record x. The third and final disk access transfers the data block into memory. Three disk accesses, or 0.045 seconds, is still considerably better than the 17 accesses needed by the binary search without the index. Moreover, the DBMS memory array is now insignificantly small.

An appropriate maximum size for the memory-resident level is one block. Using the figures from the examples, this is about 170 entries. Assuming two additional levels on disk, plus the data file, you can catalog 4.9 million data blocks, calculated as follows. The 170 entries in the first-level memory-resident index constitute a sparse set of pointers to 170 blocks of second-level entries, which contain $(170)^2 = 28,900$ more index records. These records point to 28,900 blocks of third-level entries, which contain $(170)^3 = 4,913,000$ final index records. Each points to a data block. Therefore, you can retrieve any one of 4.9 million data blocks with three disk accesses (about 0.045 seconds).

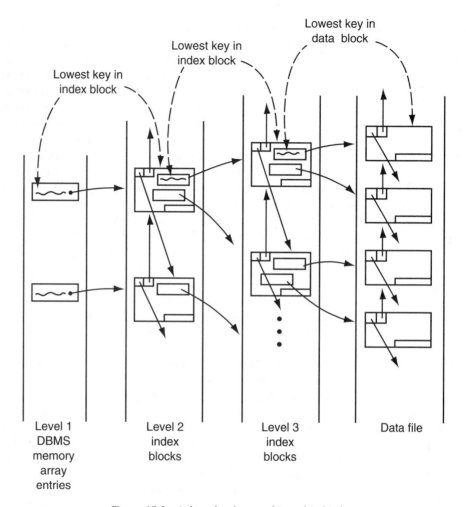

Figure 15.3 A three-level sparse hierarchical index

 If you can pack K index entries per block, an n-level sparse hierarchical index can catalog K^n data blocks and keep the first level (one block) in memory. You can then reach any data record in n disk probes.

A sparse index with duplicated keys

What happens if you relax the condition that the ordering field must be a key? Multiple records can then appear with the same ordering field value. Let's call them duplicate records, even though only the keys are the same. The indexed sequential organization forces duplicate records into adjacent positions in the data file although they might occupy more than one block. However, the blocks will be adjacent in the file chain, and nothing is lost if you omit index references to the intermediate blocks. The index entries for the chain segment's endpoints are sufficient to locate all the duplicate the records. Because you can't distinguish among them with the ordering field, you must read all the data blocks anyway. So you first follow the index to one end of the data chain for the target value and then follow the forward or backward pointers to recover the rest of the target records.

To be specific, assume an index reference always points to the last data block where target records reside. This choice works well with the file update activities you'll consider shortly. You then retrieve duplicate records through index references to the terminal data block, where you find some of the target records. From there, you follow the backward data block pointers to retrieve the rest of them. You terminate the backward scan when you reach a block containing a record with a lower ordering field value than the target. No earlier blocks can contain target records.

Figure 15.4 illustrates the point with index field values $x_0 < x_1 < x_2$. The entry x_0 appears in the bottom-level index with a pointer to the first block. Note that x_1 records also appear in the block, but only in the upper part. The smallest ordering field value in the block is x_0. The next index entry is x_1, with a pointer to the last block in which x_1 records appear. The intermediate blocks, all completely filled with x_1 records, don't have index entries.

The retrieval mechanism locates all x_1 records as follows. Upon reaching the bottom-level index block, you scan it for the largest key not exceeding x_1 and obtain a vector to the last block where x_1 records appear. You acquire earlier blocks by following the backward links. These subsequent block accesses don't count in the cost equation because you would have to read them anyway to obtain the target records. For an n-level index, the number of disk accesses is still n to place the search at the final block of target records.

If the targets occupy several blocks, they are immediately available—without further searching—through the chain pointers. This policy keeps the index from filling up with useless pointers to intermediate data blocks of duplicate records. For example, if you organize a file of 1,000,000 persons into an indexed sequential format on gender, about 500,000 entries appear for each of the two ordering field values. However, instead of the three-level index illustrated earlier for 1,000,000 records, a one-level index suffices. The one level contains two entries: one pointing to the highest block containing females and the other to the highest block containing males. The ordering field becomes unique in the index, even if it isn't a key in the data file. In the index, each ordering field value occurs at most once and points to the last block containing target records with the given value.

 A sparse hierarchical index can accommodate non-unique values in the ordering field. The ordering field becomes a key in the index file.

Maintaining a sparse hierarchical index during deletions

As a data file undergoes modifications, its index must be updated. After learning how to update the index for a data file change, you can handle the case where you create an index simultaneously with the data file. Both start empty, and if you keep the index current with the data file, you will have a fully functional index when you finish loading the data file.

The retrieval process functions properly if the index record key is *less than or equal* to the smallest key in the referenced block. However, it shouldn't be so low as to drop

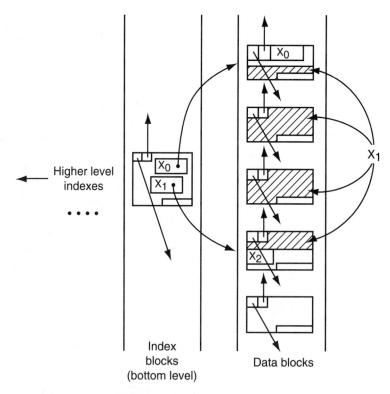

Figure 15.4   A sparse hierarchical index with a non-unique ordering field

below the largest key in the preceding data block. So far, the index record has contained the smallest key in the referenced block. The retrieval method works, however, even if the index key doesn't exist in the referenced block—as long as it is less than any key that does exist there.

Suppose you want to retrieve record 70 from the arrangement of Figure 15.5. The largest first-level entry not exceeding 70 is 2, which points to the first block of the next level. There, the largest entry not exceeding 70 is 45, which points to the data block containing record 70. To take advantage of this flexibility, you can change the key entries of the first record of the first block of all index levels to $-\infty$, a value less than any legal ordering field value. The $-\infty$ value may be the empty string for character string ordering fields, or it may be -1 for non-negative integer ordering fields. The index then appears as in Figure 15.6.

This policy leads to an especially simple method for updating an index when a data record is deleted: leave the index unchanged because it's still valid. Suppose you delete record 60 from the scheme of Figure 15.6. Because 60 isn't the smallest key in the block, it doesn't appear in the sparse index. You can reclaim the data space for record 60 but not its locator because the record may be pinned. Instead, you set the D flag in the locator. The retrieval process still functions to recover any existing file record.

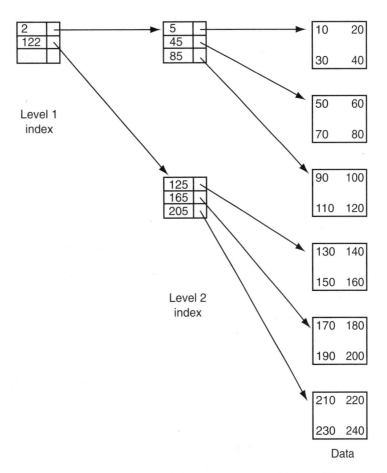

Figure 15.5 Keys in a sparse index need only be less than the smallest key of the referenced block

Upon deleting record 130, you note that 130 does appear in an index entry, but you simply leave it there. The key 130 isn't so small that it overlaps records in the preceding block (they extend only to 120), and 130 serves just as well to guide the retrieval process as the actual smallest key of the data block. The index also remains valid when the ordering field isn't unique. For example, multiple 130-records appear in Figure 15.7, and you can verify that removing any 130-record leaves the search algorithm intact.

If a data block suffers enough deletions, it can become empty. If the data records are pinned, the block must continue to exist because its locators appear in external references. In this case, the block remains in the chain and may cause some inefficiency. For example, you may have to traverse it to recover other records with the same target value. In any case, even if the data records aren't pinned, you may want to leave the data block in the chain to accommodate future growth.

If the data records aren't pinned and you decide to return empty blocks to the disk manager, you must adjust the structure accordingly. You must repair the chain of data

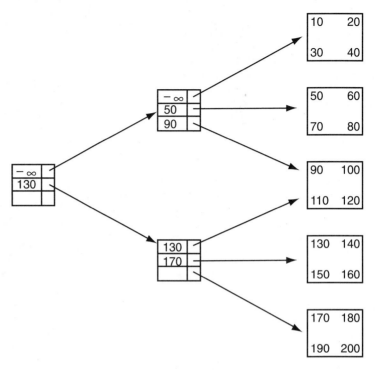

Figure 15.6 A sparse hierarchical index with $-\infty$ adjustments on the first blocks of each level

blocks to thread across the missing block, and you must consider the effect on the index. If no index entry points to the data block, the index isn't affected. If the data block has an index entry but the preceding block doesn't, you adjust the index entry to point to the preceding block. This case occurs when the block is the last of a chain associated with a fixed key value. Finally, if the data block and its preceding neighbor both have index entries, you remove the entry for the vanishing data block. The remaining index continues to function properly although you now have an index block that is only partially filled. You can reclaim this space when new data blocks appear.

Because index blocks aren't pinned, you can return an empty index block to the disk manager after removing its reference in the next higher level. The release of index blocks then propagates up the structure into the DBMS memory array, which is actually the highest-level index. The DBMS array shrinks as blocks on the next lower level vanish.

In summary, the index structure is amazingly robust when confronted with deletion operations on the data file. Indeed, you don't have to touch the index at all, and it will continue to function properly to retrieve the remaining data file records. If you want to release unused blocks back to the disk manager, you must make slight readjustments up through the index levels.

Unfortunately, these adjustments can lead to an unbalanced structure. Consider the situation of Figure 15.8, where four levels of index blocks reference data blocks (not shown) at the right of the diagram. Assume the blocks shown represent only a part of the structure

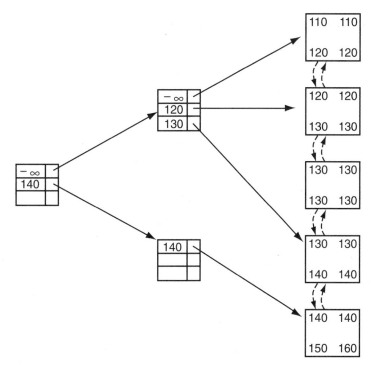

Figure 15.7: A sparse hierarchical index cataloging multiple records with the same ordering field value

and additional blocks extend in both directions off the top and bottom edges of the diagram. In other words, assume the index blocks are fully packed with references at all levels, so a vector from the first-level index leads to n^3 data blocks. In Figure 15.8, n is 3 to make the diagram manageable, but in practice this fanout figure is much larger—often on the order of several hundred.

Now suppose you delete all the data records in the blocks referenced by index keys 20 through 270. Many index blocks become empty. Returning the empty blocks to the disk manager results in the situation of Figure 15.9. Note the superfluous levels leading to the data block associated with key 10. A vector from key 10 in the highest level fans out to just 1 data block, while the rest of the keys in the highest level fan out to n^3 data blocks. You can prevent this unbalanced deterioration by judiciously relocating adjacent index records when blocks become nearly empty. Indeed, this balancing is the distinguishing characteristic of B-tree indexes, a topic for a later section.

 A sparse hierarchical index remains valid when you delete data records. However, some index adjustment is necessary if you return empty blocks to the disk manager. These adjustments can eventually lead to an unbalanced structure.

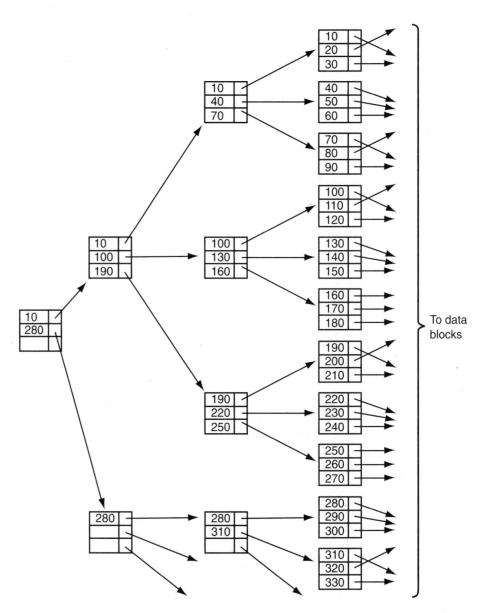

Figure 15.8   A heavily populated sparse hierarchical index before massive data record deletions

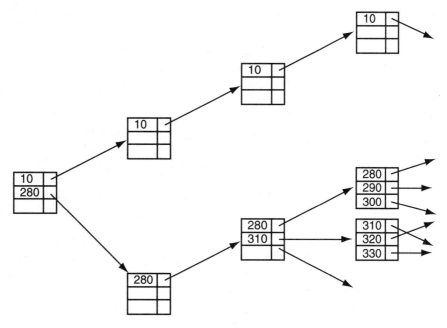

Figure 15.9 An unbalanced sparse hierarchical index resulting from massive data deletions

Maintaining a sparse hierarchical index during insertions

Now consider new data record insertions. Suppose you want to insert a record with ordering field value x. Other x-records may exist in the file, or other x-records may have existed in the file at an earlier time. A variety of increasingly complicated scenarios are possible. You make an attempt to locate a record in the existing file with ordering field value x. If none exists, the process directs you to the data block through an index entry less than or equal to x. You will always be directed to some data block because the entry $-\infty$ doesn't exceed x for any x. The target block may be empty due to previous deletions, or it may have records with key values greater than x. However, because the index brought you to this particular data block, you know that the subsequent block contains records with keys strictly greater than x. You also know that if the preceding block contains any x-records, then x-records spread over several blocks or did so in the past. In that case, the index entry for the target block must be exactly x. In any case, if it will fit, you can add the record to the target block without changing the index.

If another record with ordering field value x does exist in the file, you arrive at the last block where records with that value now reside or resided at some time in the past. Again, the subsequent block contains records with keys strictly greater than x, and the preceding block can contain x-records only if the index entry to the target block is exactly x. In the latter case, the x-records in the preceding block represent the highest keys in that block. So again you can add the record to the data block without changing the index. Therefore, the index structure is robust when confronted with data file insertions, provided the data block targeted by the index isn't full.

If the target data block is full, you must consider the index entry leading to the block, as well as those leading to adjacent blocks. Suppose v is the index value that directs the process to the data block i. Therefore, $v = \max\{u | u \leq x\}$, where u varies over the bottom-level index key values. Let v^- and v^+ be the key values of the preceding and subsequent index records respectively. These index records point to the preceding and subsequent data blocks, and of course $v^- < v < v^+$.

You first check to see if you can place the new record in the preceding block. If $v = x$, the preceding block can contain x-records, but they all must represent the highest key. In this case, you retrieve the preceding block, and if the new record will fit, you install it there. Otherwise, you obtain a new block from the disk manager and chain it into the structure just after the overflowing block. You then relocate some records from the overflowing block into the new block to make room for the new record in the appropriate order. Because you chain the new block *after* the overflowing block, the relocation moves the records with the largest ordering field values.

Record relocation isn't a pleasant task because the data records may be pinned, and you must tend to the forwarding addresses. If you must relocate records, you can achieve greater balance by moving half the records from the overflowing block into the new block. The index may remain valid. Let y be the smallest key relocated to the new block. If $y = v^+$, all the relocated records must contain y values, so the new arrangement represents the case where y-records extend across several blocks. In this case, the new block needs no index entry, and the index is correct as it stands. The old block now receives the new record. This particular scenario appears in Figure 15.10, where a record with ordering field 55 attempts to enter a full data block.

If $y \neq v^+$, you must alter the index. The next best situation is that $y = v$. In this case, all the remaining records in the old block must be y-records, so these records now extend across two or more blocks. A minimal index adjustment is necessary to advance the index pointer associated with v to point to the new block. The old block now needs no index entry. Figure 15.11 shows this arrangement, where a new record with ordering field 60 attempts to enter a full block.

The final possibility is that $v < y < v^+$, and you must create a new index record for the new block. The new index entry contains key y and the new block's address. You insert it into the lowest-level index block, just after the record with key v. Suppose for the moment that the new index record will fit there. You now place the new x-record in either the old data block or the new one, as appropriate. This final case appears in Figure 15.12, where a record with key 65 attempts to enter a full block.

In summary, you must consider four possibilities if a data block overflows: (1) a position in the preceding block, (2) a new block that happens to require no index entry, (3) a new block referenced by the old index entry, and (4) a new block and a new index entry. The first three cases are necessary only because the ordering field may not be unique. If the ordering field is a key in the data file, only the last possibility applies.

Of course, when you create a new index record, it may not fit in the proper index block. Figure 15.12 illustrates this case. You must allocate a new index block and chain it into position just after the overflowing one. You move half of the index records to the new block and place the new record in whichever block is now appropriate. You then compose a new index record, reflecting the new index block, and place it in the next higher index. Because

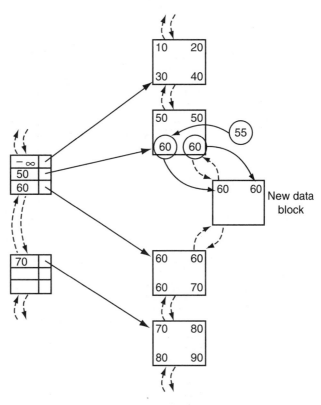

Figure 15.10   A data block splitting that doesn't affect the sparse hierarchical index

the ordering field is a key in the index blocks, each block split forwards a new index record to the next higher level. When the propagation reaches the highest level, the single-block, memory-resident DBMS array must accommodate the arriving entry. If that isn't possible, the level of the index system increases by one. The DBMS array becomes two half-filled blocks in the new level, and the DBMS array itself shrinks to two entries pointing to these two new blocks.

 Insertions in a sparse hierarchical data file periodically require the allocation of new data blocks, which forces index record adjustments. Lower index levels can absorb the adjustments, or they can propagate to higher levels. In the extreme case, the DBMS memory array enlarges, or a new index level appears.

Considering both insertions and deletions, you can conclude that the sparse hierarchical scheme can expand with a data file, although the algorithm gets complicated. Because of the massive relocation of data file records, the method quickly incurs excessive overhead costs in maintaining the forwarding addresses of pinned records. Consequently, this indexing method is most appropriate for files with unpinned data records. Moreover, deletions can

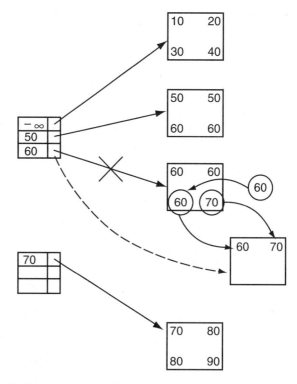

Figure 15.11   A data block splitting that requires an index pointer adjustment

introduce inefficiencies in the structure unless you take steps to consolidate partially filled blocks.

Sparse hierarchical indexes aren't as popular as they were in the past. They do have some advantages. You can process the file in sorted order on the ordering field, and you can use a sparse index. Unfortunately, the disadvantages are frustrating. The organization doesn't adjust gracefully to data block modifications, and it can become significantly unbalanced in the sense that the fanout from adjacent index entries can vary greatly. The variant discussed here is somewhat more flexible than the average ISAM structure. A typical commercial ISAM file exhibits a fixed number of levels and suffers overflow chains rather than attempting to adjust the index. In these systems, you must regenerate the file to reorganize the index, an operation that often isn't available for database files of pinned records. Finally, the need to maintain ordered data blocks adds to the overhead expense of update operations.

Dense Indexes

Hierarchical indexes aren't limited to indexed sequential files. You can adapt them to any data file, provided you sacrifice the sparse property of the lowest level. The lowest level of a sparse hierarchical index can function with a single record per data block because you can

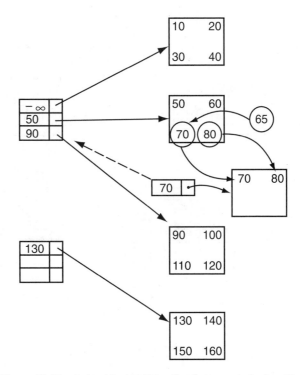

Figure 15.12   A data block splitting that forces an index insertion

infer all the data block's ordering field values from that one index entry and its neighbors. In particular, if the ith index entry contains the key value x_i, its data block contains records with ordering field values y in the range, $x_i \leq y < x_{i+1}$, and these records can appear in no other file location. An exception occurs with a non-unique ordering field, where x_i-records can spill into prior blocks.

If the data blocks aren't organized in an indexed sequential fashion, the lowest-level index must contain an entry for each data *record*. In other words, it must be dense. However, the upper levels build on this lowest level in the same sparse manner as before. If you can pack K index records on a block, an n-level sparse index can catalog K^n data *blocks* and still keep the highest level in a single memory-resident block. If you switch to a dense representation at the lowest level, the same scheme can now catalog only K^n data *records*. The new figure is a reduction by a factor equal to the data blocks' capacity. For example, if you pack the data records 10 to the block, a dense index catalogs only one-tenth as many records as does a sparse index of the same depth.

Figure 15.13 illustrates a dense hierarchical index. The upper levels remain sparse because index records appear in sorted order. The order allows you to infer a block of keys from a single higher-level entry and its neighbors. An index record in the lowest level, with key value x, points to the data record with that ordering field value. Therefore, the reference at the lowest level is a record address—the block address and locator offset combination, $(b:l)$, that uniquely locates the record. So the data records are pinned by the index, even if

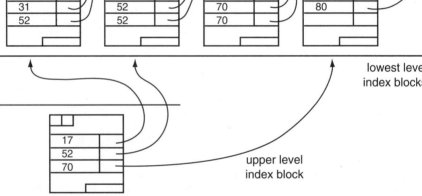

Figure 15.13   A dense hierarchical index

they aren't pinned by other references in the system. Although the index records appear in order on the ordering field, the corresponding data records can appear anywhere in the file.

As before, the pointers in the upper levels of the index are block pointers. If the ordering field isn't a unique key, multiple data records can appear with the same ordering field value. Because the lowest-level index records point to individual records, several index records can now occur with the same ordering field value. Because the multiple data records may be dispersed, you can't elevate the ordering field to key status in the lowest index level. However, ordering field values are unique at the next higher index level. The treatment of the key 70 in Figure 15.13 illustrates the point.

The search strategy remains unchanged. To locate the records with ordering key x, you search the highest-level index for the entry with the largest key not exceeding x and use the corresponding block pointer to retrieve a block from the next lower index level. You repeat the search process at that level to obtain a vector to the next lower level, and so forth. The lowest-level index block contains references to the desired targets. Other references can exist in preceding index blocks at the lowest level, so the search must follow the backward pointers until it finds an index record with a value strictly less than x. In any case, you must still issue individual block retrievals for each data record.

If the ordering field is a unique key, the search pattern takes n probes to recover the target, assuming that the highest-level index is memory-resident. However, if many targets exist with the given ordering field value, then $n - 1$ search probes brings you to the group of adjacent index records pointing to the targets. You must then expend an additional probe for each target. Because you must retrieve an entire block to find a single target, the recovery is much less efficient. Recall that for an indexed sequential file, a data block retrieval recovers many targets because they are packed together according to the ordering field.

You can process the data records in index order by scanning the lowest level of the index file and moving across the forward block pointers to adjacent index blocks. While in each index block, you must dispatch separate probes to retrieve each data record. To illustrate this inefficiency, suppose you have 1,000,000 records organized as an indexed sequential file. If you pack the records 10 to the block, you need 100,000 block accesses to process the file in index order. You can achieve this processing order without reference to an index by following the forward pointers in the data blocks themselves. So the process incurs no index overhead. The 100,000 block accesses consume about 100,000 (0.015) = 1500 seconds, or about 25 minutes.

By contrast, suppose the data is dispersed across the file in an unordered fashion. You can still construct a dense hierarchical index. Using the estimate of 170 index records per block, the lowest level of that index contains about $1,000,000/170 \approx 5883$ blocks. To process all the data in index order, you don't need the upper index levels. Instead you read through the lowest-level index blocks in order and follow the individual record pointers to the data. Therefore, you must make 1,000,000 separate disk accesses to recover the data records in the desired order, and you must also read 5883 index blocks, for a total of 1,005,883 accesses. This translates to 1.51×10^4 seconds or about 4.2 hours.

 Using a dense hierarchical index of n levels, you can arrive at a packed group of data references in $n - 1$ disk probes, assuming the highest-level index is memory-resident. However, you must then expend a separate disk access for each data target.

You can use a dense hierarchical index to impose a new order on an existing indexed sequential file. Suppose the aquarium's fish file is organized as an indexed sequential file on tank number (tno) and has a sparse hierarchical index, also on tno. This organization accelerates natural joins with tank records, which is a frequent operation. Independently of the sparse index on tno, you can construct a dense hierarchical index on fish number (fno). Processing the records in fish number order can be useful in other contexts. For example, a one-to-many relationship exists between fish and event: each fish experiences many events. So you also expect frequent navigation from an event to its owning fish. This operation is much faster if you can quickly retrieve a fish record with a given fno value.

The fact that the data file may possess some independent organization isn't relevant in constructing a dense index because the record addresses in the lowest-level index blocks can point anywhere. In the extreme case, you can create a dense index on every data field. Although this involves a great deal of extra disk storage for the index blocks, you can then recover a target from any field's value. A file with an index on every field is a **fully inverted file**. You usually process a file by proceeding from the record to its fields. In other words, given a record, you interrogate it for field values. The alternative direction is from field to record. Given a field value, you ask for the corresponding records. So an inverted file is reversed in the sense that it lets you proceed in the less obvious direction from field to record. If the file contains indexes on some, but not all, of its fields, it is a **partially inverted file**.

As a data file undergoes modifications, the adjustments to a dense index structure are similar to those for a sparse index. If you delete a data record, the index remains valid. The deletion sets the D flag in the record's locator and reclaims the actual data space. You usually can't remove the locator anyway because the record may be pinned. You can remove the lowest-level index entry without disturbing the search path to other records. In this way, a bottom-level index block can eventually become empty, and you can return it to the disk manager. If this happens, you must remove the corresponding entry at the next higher index level. So, just as with a sparse hierarchical index, contractions propagate up the index levels, causing minor adjustments to the index blocks. Also in parallel with the sparse case, the structure can evolve to unbalanced fanout or superfluous levels.

When you insert a new data record, you must create a bottom-level entry in the dense index. Because the bottom-level index blocks have an indexed sequential structure, you must insert the new index record in proper order. You invoke the search process to arrive at the proper bottom-level block. You then place the new index record there according to the earlier scenarios for a sparse hierarchical index:

- The index block may have room for the new record. You just insert it there.

- A boundary case may allow the new record to occupy the preceding index block. This occurs if records with the same ordering field value spill into the preceding block, and that block isn't full. You just insert the new record in the preceding block.

- You must chain a new index block into position, but it doesn't require a higher-level entry. This occurs if the records shifted to the new block continue a sequence of keys from the old block, which retains the higher-level entry. You insert the new record into one of the two blocks.

- You must chain a new index block into position, but you can shift the index entry at the next higher level to this new block. This also occurs because the relocated records continue a sequence across the two blocks. In this case, however, the old block holds the continuation, and the higher-level index entry must target the new block. You insert the new record into one of the two blocks.

- You must chain a new index block into position and propagate a new index entry to the next higher level. You again relocate records between the overflowing block and the new one, and you place the entering record in one of the two blocks. The process then repeats as the next higher level tries to absorb its new entry.

You can also construct a dense hierarchical index over a hash file. The hash file has its own problems associated with the movement of pinned data records. Recall from Chapter 14 the problems you can encounter with dynamic hashing schemes. These difficulties, however, don't extend to the dense index system. Once you surmount the difficulties and place a new record, its ordering field value and its $(b : l)$ address form a new index record. You insert the record into the dense index structure, where no pinned records complicate the operation.

 A dense hierarchical index is decoupled from the record relocation difficulties of its underlying data file. Therefore, you can adjust the index to remain current with its data file. However, the structure can exhibit unbalanced fanout and extra levels as a result of data block modifications.

An interesting arrangement allows data records to be pinned *only* by a dense index on a key field. In other words, any references from other data files must specify the record key rather than its disk address. You then use the dense index to locate the actual disk address. Of course, instead of one disk access to retrieve the record (or two if you encounter a forwarding address), you must tolerate the n accesses of an n-level index. This penalty isn't extreme because $n = 3$ suffices for a very large file. The advantage is that the records are essentially unpinned. Because a *single* reference to the record address exists in the lowest level of a specific index, you can update that reference when a record relocates, instead of maintaining a forwarding address in the original position. Therefore, you can reclaim the original data space and its locator when you delete a record.

If dense indexes exist on other fields, their lowest level contains not record addresses but record keys. When using one of these secondary indexes, you arrive at the lowest level in the usual manner, where you find a record key instead of the expected record disk address. You then use this record key to search the primary key index, and you find the target record's disk address at the bottom level. If the ordering field for the secondary index isn't unique, the bottom level yields a collection of records, and each provides the key of one of the desired target data records. If there are m such targets, you must conduct m separate searches on the primary index. Again, this penalty isn't too onerous because you must dispatch separate data probes for each target in any case. Each probe now requires $n \approx 3$ disk accesses, instead of the one or two that would be needed if the record disk addresses were present at the bottom level of the secondary index.

B-trees

A B-tree index is a generalization of the dense hierarchical index but with the ability to reorganize itself dynamically to avoid unbalanced structures. With its several variations, the B-tree family of structures is currently the most popular method for implementing indexes in database management systems. This section explores one variation in detail, the B^+-tree, and briefly reviews some of the other variants. For now, assume that the ordering field for the index is a key in the data file.

In the upper levels of a dense hierarchical index, you don't really need the first key entry in an index block. Therefore, you can omit it, as long as you retain its reference pointer. In the first block of a given level, that key is $-\infty$, which is simply a default category that directs the search if no other key qualifies. In searching for the largest key that doesn't exceed a target value x, you take the $-\infty$ route if all other keys in the block are greater than x. In subsequent blocks of a given level, the first key usually duplicates the key of the next higher-level block in the descent. Actually, as long as the upper-level, directing key is less than or equal to the smallest key of the referenced block, the search makes a correct descent through the various levels. However, nothing is lost by assuming that the first key of a lower block duplicates the directing key in its parent. The search method continues to function properly under this assumption. A glance back at Figure 15.8 confirms these observations.

Omitting the first key in each index block leaves more reference pointers than keys and suggests a rearrangement, at least conceptually, where the keys appear *between* the pointers. For example, consider Figure 15.14. Each key in an upper-level block associates with the pointer to its right. The unattached pointer at the extreme left of a block corresponds to the suppressed first key. Therefore, at the top level, a search for a target key $x \geq 3000$ proceeds via the rightmost pointer. A search for a key in the range $2000 \leq x < 3000$ takes the pointer between 2000 and 3000, the pointer associated with 2000. So the search criterion is the same as in the hierarchical index blocks. The largest key not exceeding the target provides a pointer to the next level block. If all keys in the block exceed the target, you follow the default pointer at the extreme left.

Figure 15.14 provides a four-level index into the data file (not shown), and the bottom level provides a dense reference to each data record. The use of the pointers in the bottom level is somewhat different. Again, each key associates with the pointer to its right, but the pointer is now a record address, a $(b : l)$ combination, that references some data record. The extra pointer on the extreme left now points to the next index block at that level. Therefore, the lowest level constitutes a dense index into the data records, and you can use this layer to recover the data in sorted order. For this reason, the collection of bottom-level blocks is called the **sequence set** of the index. Retaining only the address of the first block of the sequence set, the DBMS can follow the leftmost pointers across the chain to recover all data records in key order. The other index blocks are collectively called the **index set**.

For practice, locate record 1260. Searching the single block at the top level, you discover $1000 \leq 1260 < 2000$, so you follow the pointer associated with 1000, the one to its right, to the next level. There you note $1200 \leq 1260 < 1500$ and follow the pointer associated with 1200, which leads to a third-level block. You find $1250 \leq 1260 < 1350$ there, which directs you to the bottom-level block. At this lowest level, you find the disk address of record 1260.

Search spans

In general, blocks contain a varying number of keys, but the pointers always outnumber the keys by exactly one. If a block in level q has t keys, refer to them with the notation $k_i^{(q)}$, for $1 \leq i \leq t$ and $k_1^{(q)} < k_2^{(q)} < \ldots < k_t^{(q)}$. In a similar manner, $p_i^{(q)}$ refers to the ith pointer in the level q block, for $0 \leq i \leq t$. So the actual arrangement of the block elements is:

$$p_0^{(q)}, k_1^{(q)}, p_1^{(q)}, k_2^{(q)}, p_2^{(q)}, \ldots, k_t^{(q)}, p_t^{(q)}$$

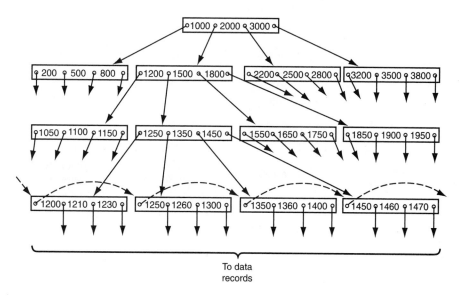

Figure 15.14 Evolving a hierarchical index toward a B^+-tree

Each block also contains two shadow keys: the left shadow, $k_0^{(q)}$, and the right shadow, $k_{t+1}^{(q)}$. These keys don't actually exist in the block, but you can infer their values, and they are useful in describing the operations on the structure. Because the pointer $p_i^{(q)}$ associates with the key $k_i^{(q)}$, for $1 \leq i \leq t$, you continue the tradition and associate $p_0^{(q)}$ with the shadow key $k_0^{(q)}$. At the top level, you set $k_0^{(1)} = -\infty$ and $k_{t+1}^{(1)} = +\infty$.

After adding the two shadow keys to the top-level block, you can distinguish a sequence of non-overlapping adjacent intervals of the form: $[k_0^{(1)}, k_1^{(1)}), [k_1^{(1)}, k_2^{(1)}), \ldots, [k_t^{(1)}, k_{t+1}^{(1)})$, where each interval $[k_i^{(q)}, k_{i+1}^{(q)})$ denotes the key range $k_i^{(q)} \leq x < k_{i+1}^{(q)}$. The bracket on the left end means that the search span includes the left endpoint; the parenthesis on the right means that it doesn't include the right endpoint. An interval $[k_i^{(q)}, k_{i+1}^{(q)})$ is a **level q search span**. For example, the single top-level block of Figure 15.14 contains the shadow keys $-\infty$ and $+\infty$ and the level-one search spans $[-\infty, 1000), [1000, 2000), [2000, 3000)$, and $[3000, +\infty)$.

With the shadow keys and the search spans well-defined at the top level, $q = 1$, you can proceed recursively to establish these elements at the lower levels. If you count the shadow keys, each pointer in the top-level block lies between two keys. In other words, $p_i^{(1)}$ lies between $k_i^{(1)}$ and $k_{i+1}^{(1)}$. In the child block reached via $p_i^{(1)}$, these two keys become the left and right shadow keys respectively. That is, $k_0^{(2)} = k_i^{(1)}$ and $k_{s+1}^{(2)} = k_{i+1}^{(1)}$ in the child block at level two, assuming that the child block has s actual keys. This procedure establishes the shadow keys and the search spans in the level-two blocks. You can repeat the method to define shadow keys and search spans in the lower levels. Continuing with the example of Figure 15.14, the blocks at the various levels have search spans that fan out as follows:

$$
[-\infty, 1000) \quad \rightarrow \quad
\begin{cases}
[-\infty, 200) & \rightarrow \quad \cdots \\
[200, 500) & \rightarrow \quad \cdots \\
[500, 800) & \rightarrow \quad \cdots \\
[800, 1000) & \rightarrow \quad \cdots
\end{cases}
$$

$$
[1000, 2000) \quad \rightarrow \quad
\begin{cases}
[1000, 1200) & \rightarrow \quad \cdots \\
[1200, 1500) & \rightarrow \quad
\begin{cases}
[1200, 1250) & \rightarrow & \text{address of records} & 1200, 1210, 1230 \\
[1250, 1350) & \rightarrow & \text{address of records} & 1250, 1260, 1300 \\
[1350, 1450) & \rightarrow & \text{address of records} & 1350, 1360, 1400 \\
[1450, 1500) & \rightarrow & \text{address of records} & 1450, 1460, 1470
\end{cases} \\
[1500, 1800) & \rightarrow \quad \cdots \\
[1800, 2000) & \rightarrow \quad \cdots
\end{cases}
$$

$\vdots$

The leftmost search span of a child block inherits its lower limit from the previous level; the rightmost search span inherits its upper limit. Each search span associates with exactly one pointer, the one that falls between its limiting keys in the alternating sequence of pointers and keys. In other words, the level q search span $[k_i^{(q)}, k_{i+1}^{(q)})$ gives rise to the child block at level $q + 1$ reached by following $p_i^{(q)}$. For example, suppose you are locating record 1210 in the layout of Figure 15.14. You have $1000 = k_1^{(1)} \leq 1210 < k_2^{(1)} = 2000$ from the first level. Following the pointer associated with 1000, you arrive at the second-level block, where $1200 = k_1^{(2)} \leq 1210 < k_2^{(2)} = 1500$. Following the pointer associated with 1200, you arrive at the third level, where $1200 = k_1^{(2)} = k_0^{(3)} \leq 1210 < k_1^{(3)} = 1250$. Finally, following the pointer associated with 1200, the default pointer, you arrive at the bottom level, where the reference to record 1210 resides.

Therefore, at each layer in the index except the bottom, you find $k_i^{(q)} \leq x < k_{i+1}^{(q)}$, where one of the limits may be inherited from the preceding level. The top level, which can't inherit from a preceding layer, uses the values $\pm\infty$ on the ends. The leaf nodes don't inherit shadow keys. Instead, the pointer p_i gives the address of the record with key k_i, and the extra pointer p_0 links the block to its successor. See Figure 15.14.

Although the B^+-tree organization provides some storage efficiency by suppressing an unnecessary key reference in each index block, this isn't its most impressive feature. Most significant is that insertion and deletion operations on the B^+-tree leave it balanced: all blocks are always at least half-full and all bottom-level blocks are always at the same distance from the single top-level block. A dense hierarchical index also possesses the latter property, but in some examples, intermediate levels are sparsely populated, which results in uneven fanout in subsequent levels. B^+-trees don't exhibit such degenerate forms.

The defining properties of a B^+ tree
The index blocks of a B^+-tree are the **nodes**, and the single top-level block is the **root**. The nodes at a given level are the child nodes of a parent on the immediately preceding level. The bottom level consists of **leaf nodes**, which contain the data's record addresses.

A B^+-tree index is then a tree with the following constraints:

1. Each node contains an ordered collection of keys and pointers of the form: $(p_0^{(q)}, k_1^{(q)},$ $p_1^{(q)}, k_2^{(q)}, p_2^{(q)}, \ldots, k_t^{(q)}, p_t^{(q)})$, where $k_1^{(q)} < k_2^{(q)} < \ldots < k_t^{(q)}$. The superscript gives the node's depth in the tree, with the root having depth one. For each non-leaf node, the keys define a sequence of non-overlapping search spans: $[k_j^{(q)}, k_{j+1}^{(q)})$, for $0 \le j \le t$, where $k_0^{(q)}$ and $k_{t+1}^{(q)}$ are inherited from the parent or are equal to $-\infty$ or $+\infty$ in the case of the root. Pointer $p_j^{(q)}$ leads to a child node, where the keys $\hat{k}_1^{(q+1)}, \hat{k}_2^{(q+1)}, \ldots \hat{k}_s^{(q+1)}$ all lie within the jth search span, *excluding* the left end unless the child is a leaf node. When search span $[k_j^{(q)}, k_{j+1}^{(q)})$ gives rise to a child node with keys $\hat{k}_1^{(q+1)} < \hat{k}_2^{(q+1)} < \ldots < \hat{k}_s^{(q+1)}$, then:

$$k_j^{(q)} < \hat{k}_i^{(q+1)} < k_{j+1}^{(q)}, 1 \le i \le s, \quad \text{if the child isn't a leaf}$$
$$k_j^{(q)} \le \hat{k}_i^{(q+1)} < k_{j+1}^{(q)}, 1 \le i \le s, \quad \text{if the child is a leaf}$$

Finally, if the node is a leaf node, say L, pointer p_j is the address of the data record with key k_j, for $1 \le j \le t$, and p_0 points to another leaf node that contains the smallest key exceeding all keys in L. If L contains the largest set of keys, p_0 is null.

2. The number of keys in a node can't exceed a maximum value, n, the **order** of the B^+-tree. The smallest order for a B^+-tree is two, but usually n is much larger.

3. Let t be the number of keys in an arbitrary node, other than the root. Then $\lfloor n/2 \rfloor \le t \le n$. For the root, $1 \le t \le n$, unless the tree is empty.

4. All paths from the root to a leaf node are of equal lengths.

The first constraint is a formal restatement of the earlier discussion concerning the suppression of the first key in an index block and the fact that the keys in a child node lie within the originating search span of the parent. Starting with some $[k_{i_1}^{(1)}, k_{i_1+1}^{(1)})$ in the root, proceeding to some $[k_{i_2}^{(2)}, k_{i_2+1}^{(2)})$ in the child that arises from it, and so forth, you generate a sequence of nested search spans until you reach the lowest level, v, where you pick a key, say $k_{i_v}^{(v)}$. The following relationship then holds:

$$k_{i_1}^{(1)} < k_{i_2}^{(2)} < \ldots < k_{i_{v-1}}^{(v-1)} \le k_{i_v}^{(v)} < k_{i_{v-1}+1}^{(v-1)} < k_{i_{v-2}+1}^{(v-2)} < \ldots < k_{i_1+1}^{(1)}. \quad (15.1)$$

The terms listed form a non-decreasing sequence. $-\infty$ can occur on the far left, and then several of the leading $k_{i_j}^{(j)}$ values can be $-\infty$ through the inheritance of shadow keys. Obviously, the relation between adjacent $-\infty$ symbols should be $=$, rather than $<$. However, as you pass across expression 15.1 from left to right, once a $k_{i_j}^{(j)}$ becomes some finite value, the relationship remains $<$ until you reach the key value at the lowest level. The relationship between the left end of the search span immediately above the leaf $k_{i_{v-1}}^{(v-1)}$ and the key in the leaf node is $\le$, as indicated. As you encounter the right endpoints $k_{i_j+1}^{(j+1)}$ beyond the central key, the relationship remains $<$, unless one of the entries is $+\infty$. From that point on, all remaining terms to the right must also be $+\infty$, and the relationship changes to $=$. This nesting of search spans along any path from the root to a leaf guarantees that the search method properly locates a record address. Therefore, algorithms for modifying the structure must leave Equation 15.1 intact.

The remaining conditions guarantee that the tree won't become significantly unbalanced. Except for the root, you can't have some nodes reduced to a single key, while other parts of the tree are fully packed. All nodes, except the root, must contain at least half their capacity. Moreover, the tree must achieve this balance while keeping the path lengths to the leaf nodes at some uniform value. Therefore, the number of disk accesses needed to retrieve a randomly selected record is the same for every record in the file.

 A B^+-tree structure maintains all its nodes, except the root, at least half-full. It also maintains all leaf nodes at a uniform distance from the root. The search spans in a path from root to leaf form a nested sequence of intervals of decreasing size.

Scenarios for maintaining balance during insertions

The algorithm that maintains a balanced structure is somewhat difficult to program but easily illustrated with an example. Assume $n = 4$, which allows reasonably compact diagrams. In practice, however, the typical case has n on the order of several hundred. You start with an empty tree, containing no nodes. The B^+-tree insertion algorithm isn't concerned with placing records in the underlying data file. That file may have any organization whatsoever, and it may have its own problems with record locations. However, after you have placed the record in the data file, by whatever means, you have its key and address available for insertion into the B^+-tree. The insertion algorithm takes over at this point.

As you add the first several keys, the root comes into existence. Until the number of keys exceeds four, the root remains the single leaf node. Suppose the first four keys are 1000, 2000, 3000, and 4000, as shown in the top portion of Figure 15.15. As you add the keys, the organization remains legal at all times because the root can contain any number of keys less than or equal to the maximum. However, when other nodes come into existence, they will be restricted to contain at least $\lfloor 4/2 \rfloor = 2$ keys. In this particular example ($n = 4$), the non-root nodes are constrained only slightly more than the root. With an unrealistically low B^+-tree order of four, however, this case is unusual. The lower limit on the non-root node populations is typically on the order of 100.

The order of the first four key insertions doesn't matter. The block contents adjust to maintain the order. Suppose you now add the key 1500. You must undertake a major adjustment because the single node can't hold more than four keys. An overflowing block usually has several alternatives available, such as looking at underpopulated sibling nodes for relief. In this case, however, no other nodes exist. So you obtain a new block from the disk manager and chain it to the right of the current block, using the leftmost pointer of the existing block. You then relocate a minimal group of $\lfloor 4/2 \rfloor = 2$ of the largest keys to the new block, leaving three keys in the original block. The old block temporarily has $n + 1$ keys while you resolve the overflow. Note also that $n + 1 - \lfloor n/2 \rfloor = \lceil n/2 \rceil + 1 \geq \lfloor n/2 \rfloor + 1 > \lfloor n/2 \rfloor$, so the old block retains at least the minimum number of keys.

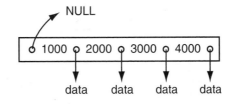

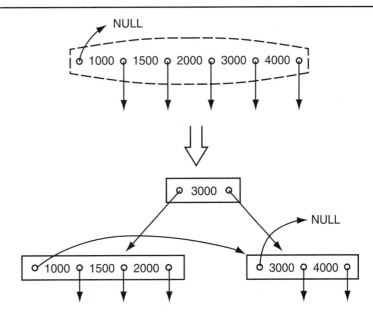

Figure 15.15 Growth of a B^+-tree of order four

The two blocks now become the lowest level of the index, and the disk manager supplies another new block for the new root. You install the smallest key from the new block in the new root and establish pointers to the two leaf nodes on either side of it. The original root didn't have search spans because it was also a leaf. However, the new root now contains the two search spans $[-\infty, k)$ and $[k, +\infty)$ with k being the smallest key in the new block. So you establish the nesting property of the search spans when you create the first non-leaf node. The lower part of Figure 15.15 shows the situation.

Once the tree has grown reasonably large, a root split is rare because a wide variety of other relief measures are available to accommodate a splitting lower-level node. These other measures are always invoked first, and if all else fails, the root splits. Splitting the root raises the tree's depth by one and adds one disk access to the retrieval path of every data record. A root split is also the only time when you need two new blocks from the data manager. In all other cases, a single new block is sufficient.

Now add the key 3500. Applying the search criterion, you arrive at the rightmost bottom-level index node, where you would find an address for key 3500 if it were in the tree. You add 3500 to that node, and because the node isn't at capacity, it simply absorbs the

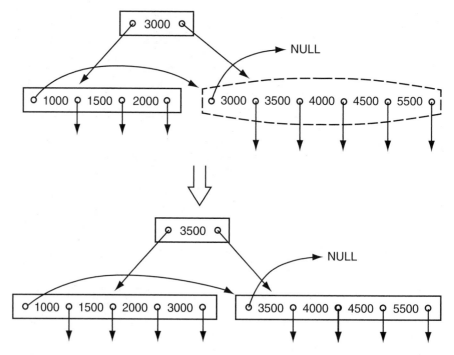

Figure 15.16 An overloaded leaf node being relieved by an underpopulated sibling

key. The procedure affects no index nodes above the bottom-level node. The search spans followed in the path to the leaf node constitute a nested sequence of intervals of decreasing size, and 3500 is in all of them. So you can place the key 3500 in the bottom-level node without violating the relationships among the search spans in the index.

Now add keys 4500 and 5500, both targeted toward the right child. This leads to the bloated node shown in the top part of Figure 15.16. The overflowing node looks to its parent, attempting to find an underpopulated sibling. In the parent, the overflowing node arises from a search span $[k_{i_1}^{(q)}, k_{i_1+1}^{(q)})$ via pointer p_{i_1}. A left sibling arises from search span $[k_{i_1-1}^{(q)}, k_{i_1}^{(q)})$ via pointer $p_{i_1-1}^{(q)}$ in the parent; a right sibling arises from $[k_{i_1+1}^{(q)}, k_{i_1+2}^{(q)})$ via pointer p_{i_1+1}. In this case, the troubled node has no right sibling, but its left sibling is in a position to help because it contains fewer than the maximum number of keys. You shift the smallest key-pointer combination to the left sibling and change the key in the parent between the two siblings to 3500, which is the new lowest key in the right child.

The nesting property, Equation 15.1, remains valid. You adjusted the boundary between two adjacent search spans in the parent to place the relocated key inside the search span that gives rise to the sibling. The lower part of Figure 15.16, shows the new configuration, just after you adjusted the original search spans in the parent: $[-\infty, 3000)$ and $[3000, +\infty)$ became $[-\infty, 3500)$ and $[3500, +\infty)$. The last span includes the shifted key, 3000, of the left sibling.

Load sharing between siblings can take several forms. The specific form depends on whether the nodes are interior nodes or leaf nodes and whether the underpopulated sibling is to the left or to the right of the overflowing node. The details vary slightly in each case, and handling these minutiae makes the algorithm difficult to program. In leaf node exchanges, the idea is to move the smallest key and its associated record pointer to the left sibling or to move the largest key and its data pointer to the right sibling. Of course, such siblings must exist, and they must be underpopulated. You then adjust the key in the parent between the two siblings to change the two adjacent search spans. The new search spans must cover the spread of keys in the two altered nodes. The case of key sharing between interior nodes will arise in a later example.

Next, add key 1700 to the latest configuration in the lower portion of Figure 15.16. The search for an existing 1700 leads to the left child node, where the new key overloads the node. No left sibling exists, and the right sibling is already fully populated. Therefore, the node must split. You start with the technique established earlier. You chain a new block into position after the overflowing one and relocate a minimal collection of keys. However, because the splitting node isn't the root, a new variation occurs at this point. You dispatch the smallest key in the new node and a pointer to the new block, in the order (k, p), toward the parent. There you insert the package just to the right of the pointer connecting parent and child, as summarized in Figure 15.17. A pair of the form (k, p), inserted just after an existing pointer, maintains the alternation of pointers and keys in the parent. Moreover, the search span in the parent $[x, y)$ divides into two adjacent search spans, $[x, k)$ and $[k, y)$. Because all the keys in the overflowing block must lie in the original span $[x, y)$, the keys as distributed in the two blocks lie in the two new search spans. The smallest key of the new block is the proper limiting value.

A complication arises if the parent node can't accept another key to split the search span that gives rise to the overflowing child. The parent will either be the root, or it will be an interior node of the tree. First, consider the root. You can evolve the last configuration of the example to force an overflowing root. Toward this end, add keys 1800, 2200, and 2400, which fill the leaf nodes in the bottom portion of Figure 15.17 to capacity. Then add 3200. This forces a split of the center leaf node and the creation of a new node, which you promptly fill with 2600, 3300, and 3400. The configuration now appears as the top portion of Figure 15.18. The figure suppresses the data pointers and the chaining of the lowest-level nodes. Adding 6000 causes another split and fills the root to capacity. Adding 4600, 6200, and 6400 fills the leaf nodes to capacity and sets the stage for a root split on the next insertion. This intermediate configuration appears in the center portion of Figure 15.18. Now add key 4800. This leads to the overloaded root shown at the bottom of Figure 15.18.

The root has no siblings, so the only recourse is to split, which increases the depth of the entire tree. You obtain a new node and relocate the largest $\lfloor n/2 \rfloor$ keys, together with their pointers on *both* sides, to the new block. This process leaves the alternating pointer-key sequence in the old block ending with a key, rather than with a pointer, which violates a constraint on the structure. You now lift that dangling key to yet another new node, which becomes the new root. After you have relocated the $\lfloor n/2 \rfloor$ keys to the new node, $n + 1 - \lfloor n/2 \rfloor = \lceil n/2 \rceil + 1 \geq \lfloor n/2 \rfloor + 1$ keys remain in the old node. So you can remove the dangling key to the new root and still leave the minimum number of keys in the

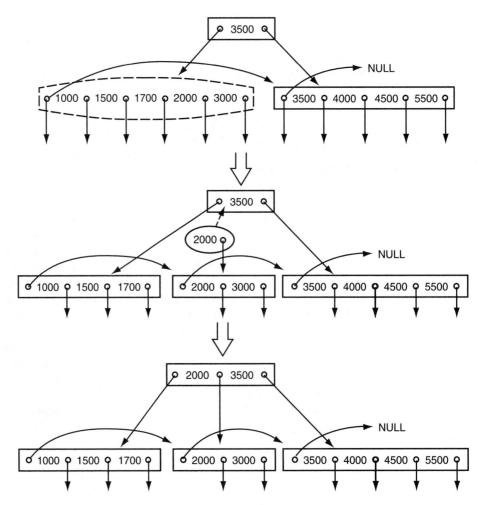

Figure 15.17 A splitting leaf node divides the search span of its parent

old node. You then install pointers in the new root: one on the left of the key leading to the old node and one on the right side to the new one.

In the example of Figure 15.18, you place the key 3500 in the new root and deploy the remaining keys as shown in Figure 15.19. The key elevated to the root becomes the inherited upper limit of the old block and the inherited lower limit of the new block. So all the subtree pointers associate with the same search spans as before the split. Moreover, the two search spans in the new root, $[-\infty, k)$ and $[k, +\infty)$, where k is the elevated key, properly encompass the search spans of the two child nodes.

The discussion so far has illustrated the following cases: (1) splitting the root when it is also a leaf, (2) relieving an overloaded leaf node via an underpopulated sibling, (3) splitting a leaf node that isn't the root, and (4) splitting the root when it isn't a leaf. The remaining possibilities deal with an overloaded interior node, which is neither root nor leaf. Suppose

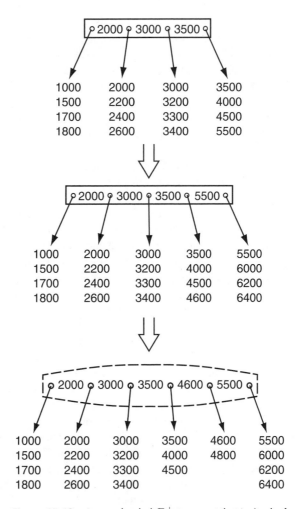

Figure 15.18   An overloaded B^+-tree root that isn't a leaf

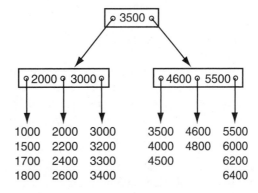

Figure 15.19   Splitting an overloaded B^+-tree root that isn't a leaf

that you create an overflowing interior node that isn't the root, as suggested by top portion of Figure 15.20. The uniform height of the triangles descending from the nodes means that all the subtrees at those points are the same height. All operations so far have preserved the property that all paths from the root to a leaf are the same length. This more complicated case must also maintain that property.

In the figure, the overflowing node has an underpopulated left sibling, so you can attempt a redistribution. The situation is slightly more complex than the balancing achieved earlier with leaf nodes. In this case, subtrees complicate the flow of keys between adjacent nodes. As shown in the center of Figure 15.20, you bundle the smallest key and the subtree to its left into a package, which you dispatch toward the parent. There, you temporarily install the package just to the left of the pointer connecting parent and child. A packet of the form (p, k) properly integrates into the alternating sequence of pointers and keys when installed in the parent in this fashion. The resulting configuration, shown at the bottom of Figure 15.20, violates the B^+-tree constraints because the subtree that was lifted to the parent is now one level shorter than the subtrees that were left behind. However, you aren't finished with the maneuver because your intent is to transfer material to the sibling, not to the parent. Consequently, you continue as shown in Figure 15.21, where the package consisting of 3500 and its stunted right subtree descend to occupy the last position in the left sibling. A packet of the form (k, p) integrates properly into the alternating sequence of keys and pointers when it is placed in the final position. The wandering subtree also returns to a position where it is the proper height. So no path from root to leaf has changed length as a result of the full operation.

You can show that this load sharing operation between siblings preserves the relationships among the search spans in the nodes. Let $[x, y)$ be the search span in the parent giving rise to the overflowing node. Let $[w, x)$ be the search span of its left sibling. Because you are moving the leftmost key and subtree from the overflowing node, the lower limit of the search span for that subtree must be inherited from the parent and must therefore be x. So if k is the key to be moved, $[x, k)$ is the search span of the subtree to be moved with it. You have $w < x < k < y$, and you replace the two search spans of the rearranged parent with $[w, k)$ and $[k, y)$ respectively. Now that the subtree has moved to the left sibling, its search span, $[x, k)$, nests in the span $[w, k)$ as required. The remaining subtrees in the left sibling continue to nest properly because their search spans haven't changed and the search span in the parent has widened from $[w, x)$ to $[w, k)$. The remaining subtrees in the relieved node have search spans with lower limits greater than or equal to k because they all lie to the right of the removed key, k. Therefore, they continue to nest in the altered search span, $[k, y)$, of the parent.

Again, several cases arise that vary slightly in the details. But the general idea is to exploit an underpopulated sibling to relieve an overflowing interior node. If a left sibling is used, the smallest key and its left subtree, in the form (p, k), are raised to the parent, where they take up a position just *before* the pointer connecting parent to child. The new configuration isn't a proper B^+-tree, but you can correct that by composing another package in the form (k, p), consisting of the parent key between the two siblings and the subtree just raised. You lower that package into the left sibling, where it occupies the rightmost position. If a right sibling is used, the largest key and its right subtree, in the form (k, p), are raised to the parent, where they take up a position just *after* the pointer connecting parent

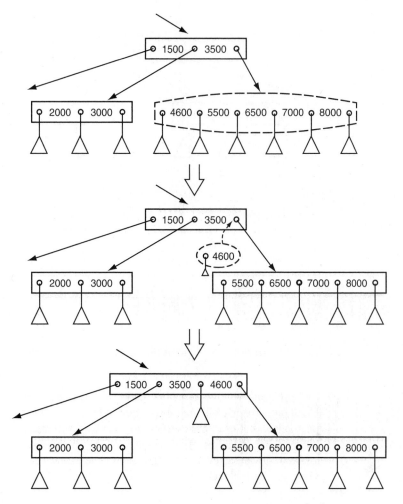

Figure 15.20   Load sharing between interior nodes in a B^+-tree

and child. You compose a new packet in the form (p, k), containing the wandering subtree and the parent key between the two siblings, and lower it into the right sibling, where it occupies the leftmost position. In either case, if an underpopulated sibling is available, no split occurs, and no new nodes appear. Because the parent node holds the extra key only temporarily, it can serve in this role even if it already has a full complement of keys.

The last case deals with an overflowing interior node that has no underpopulated sibling. The situation appears in the upper portion of Figure 15.22. The mechanism is similar to a root split because you populate a new node with the $\lfloor n/2 \rfloor$ largest keys, moving their subtrees *on both sides* with them. The alternating sequence in the old node then ends improperly with a key, instead of with a pointer. You elevate this key, together with a pointer to the new node, in the form (k, p) to the parent. There you insert them just after

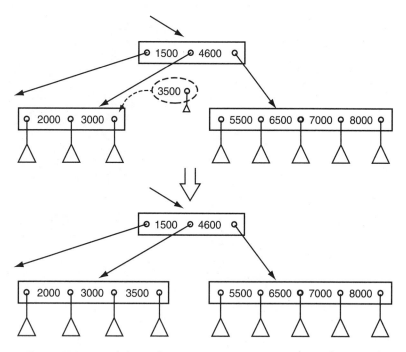

Figure 15.21   Load sharing between interior nodes in a B^+-tree (continued)

the pointer connecting parent and child. The new entry splits the original search span in the parent, properly dividing it as required for the two child nodes. If the parent becomes overloaded as a result of absorbing the new key, you make a second adjustment to relieve that overload. A sibling of the parent may be available to share the load, or the parent may split and forward a key to the grandparent. The base case for this recursion is the root split, which you have already studied.

The B^+-tree insertion algorithm chooses among several options to maintain a population balance in the nodes. Underpopulated nodes can accept new keys directly or as part of a strategy to share the load of their siblings. Splitting occurs as a last resort and propagates up the tree as necessary.

Scenarios for maintaining balance during deletions

Removing a key from the B^+-tree index uses similar methods to maintain the balance. If the removal causes a node to fall below the minimum of $\lfloor n/2 \rfloor$, you can transfer a key from an overpopulated sibling. You carry out the transfer as described for insertions. The details will differ depending on the leaf or non-leaf status of the node.

    If no overpopulated sibling is available, the node coalesces with one of its siblings. First, suppose the node in crisis is a leaf node, but not the root. (Because the root has no minimum population, it never enters an underpopulated state.) To merge with its left

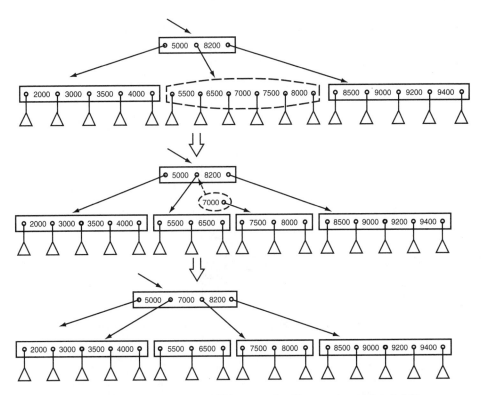

Figure 15.22 Splitting an interior B^+-tree node with no underpopulated siblings

sibling, all its remaining keys, together with their data pointers, move to the left sibling. Because the node has just become undersized, the relocation involves exactly $\lfloor n/2 \rfloor - 1$ keys. Moreover, because the left sibling isn't overpopulated, it must contain exactly $\lfloor n/2 \rfloor$ keys. When you merge the populations, the total doesn't exceed n. You then return the node to the disk manager and remove its pointer in the parent. You also remove the parent key between the two siblings. This scenario appears in Figure 15.23. The operation for merging with a right sibling is similar. Of course, when the parent suffers the deletion of a key-pointer pair, it may fall below the minimal population. This doesn't occur in Figure 15.23, but it does in Figure 15.24, which produces an example of an interior node in an underpopulated state.

A key disappears from an interior node because it was removed in the process of merging the contents of its right and left subtrees. This observation is certainly valid for the level just above the leaves, as demonstrated in the preceding paragraph, and you'll see that it holds recursively for higher levels in the tree. Therefore, the general case is as shown in Figure 15.24, where a key and one of its adjacent subtrees are deleted. The node maintains its proper alternating sequence of keys and pointers, but it drops below the minimal number of keys. If the node in crisis isn't a leaf node, it must have a sibling because it can't be the root. Because that sibling isn't overpopulated, it must contain exactly $\lfloor n/2 \rfloor$ keys. Moreover, because the affected node has just dropped below the minimum, it must contain

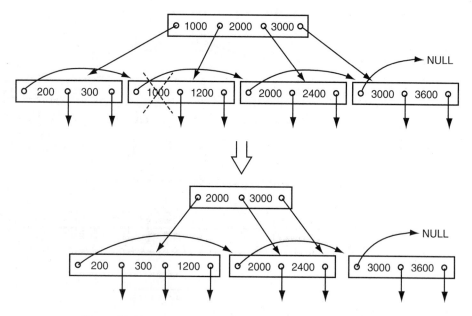

Figure 15.23   Merging an underpopulated leaf node in a B^+-tree

exactly $\lfloor n/2 \rfloor - 1$ keys. If you add the key in the parent between the two siblings to these two collections, the total is $2\lfloor n/2 \rfloor \leq n$. So all of them will fit into a single node.

However, you must give proper attention to the subtrees, so that the search spans continue to nest properly. Figure 15.24 shows the case where the key 1700 and its left subtree disappear from an interior node, presumably as the result of previous coalescence deeper in the tree. With the loss of 1700 and its left subtree, the node still contains a proper alternating sequence of keys and pointers, but the sequence is too short. If the node is combined with its left sibling, the resulting alternating sequence will have two adjacent pointers where they join, which is also undesirable. Worse yet, when the vacated node returns to the disk manager, the parent will lose a pointer, which will leave it with two adjacent keys. However, you can insert the key from the parent between the adjacent pointers in the child to rectify both situations. The case associated with a left sibling merge is shown in the lower portion of Figure 15.24. A merge with a right sibling is an analogous operation. In either case, it is the key between the two coalescing siblings that descends to separate the two adjacent pointers in the child.

The parent now falls below the minimum population in the example of Figure 15.24, so you must perform a second adjustment on that node. In general, the coalescence of two siblings at level i removes a key from the common parent at level $i - 1$. If the parent can't tolerate the loss or compensate for it by shifting a key from a sibling, the parent must coalesce with one of its siblings, which forces a key removal from the grandparent at level $i - 2$. The recursion terminates when the parent is the root or when a parent can indeed tolerate the loss, with or without the help of an overpopulated sibling. The root can decrease to one key without violating the rules. A further decrease means that its only two child

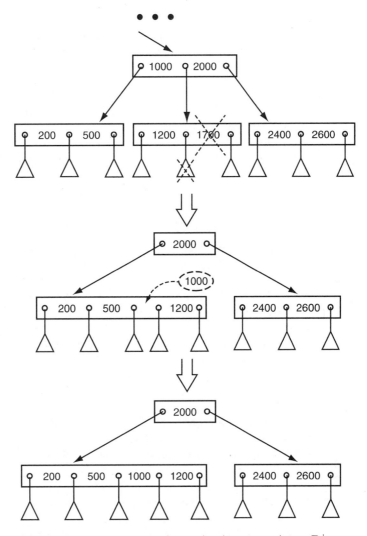

Figure 15.24 Merging an underpopulated interior node in a B^+-tree

nodes have merged into a single node. That single node then becomes the new root, and the old root node returns to storage. A vanishing root node reduces the depth of the tree by one, shortening all the paths to the data records by a uniform amount.

When two leaf siblings merge, they arise from adjacent search spans in the parent, say $[x, y)$ and $[y, z)$. So all the keys in the two siblings are in the span $[x, z)$, which becomes the new search span in the parent when you remove the key between the siblings. The merge thus preserves the nesting property. When two non-leaf siblings merge, all the search spans in the left sibling nest in a search span in the parent, say $[x, y)$; all the spans in the right sibling nest in an adjacent span in the parent, say $[y, z)$. y is the inherited upper limit of the rightmost span in the left sibling, and it is the inherited lower limit of the leftmost span in the right sibling. Therefore, when the siblings merge, with the key y inserted between them, the search spans in the coalesced node are exactly those of the sibling nodes. They all nest in $[x, z)$, the span created in the parent when you remove y and a pointer to the vanishing node. Consequently, Equation 15.1 remains intact for this final operation.

Deletions from a B^+-tree structure share keys among siblings to forestall a reduction below the minimal population. When an overpopulated sibling isn't available, a node must coalesce with a sibling by extracting a key from their common parent. The contraction can propagate up the tree, and in the extreme case, the root can vanish, which lowers the depth of the entire tree by one.

Performance statistics for B^+ trees

Illustrations to this point have shown B^+-tree nodes holding only keys and pointers. Actually, they use the general block structure, where some reserved space holds forward-backward block pointers and a locator array. Because the forward-backward block pointers are available, the extra leftmost pointers in the leaf nodes aren't necessary. The block pointers can maintain the chain across the bottom of the tree. Moreover, you can follow the chain backwards, which is useful when duplicate records are present. In this case, you can follow the pointers to the left or to the right of the target key as you descend the tree. The resulting path terminates in the midst of the target entries at the leaf level. The forward-backward block pointers then enable access to adjacent leaf nodes, which contain the target entries.

The locator array is also useful because the keys, and therefore the index entries, are of varying lengths. A locator entry gives the offset of the corresponding data entry in the block. Therefore, you can array the fixed-length pointers in the upper portion of the block and pack the corresponding keys in the lower portion. An interpreting program then overlays the block with two array structures: one covering the pointers and one covering the locators. The latter gives indirect access to the keys.

B^+-tree indexes are the structures of choice for existing database management systems. The self-balancing property amortizes the reorganization of the index over many records, so a large reorganization is never necessary. Many insertions drop directly into the accommodating leaf node, which requires no adjustment beyond writing the new leaf node to disk. When additional adjustment is necessary, it is limited to the path extending from the root to the leaf where the modification is made. The DBMS can keep these node blocks in memory as the search descends to the node. From a parent node in the path, you can infer the existence of siblings, so you need three extra disk accesses to read a sibling, execute the transfers if possible, adjust the search spans in the parent, and write the modified sibling and parent. If the sibling is full, the read operation on that sibling is wasted, and you need three additional accesses to execute the maneuver on the other sibling. If both are full, you have wasted two read accesses, and you need three more to acquire a new block, split the overflowing block, adjust the parent (already in memory), and write all modified blocks to disk. So, depending on the scenario followed, the insertion requires 1, 4, 5, or 6 disk accesses to update the index. If a parent overflows as a result of a block split, you need an additional 3, 4, or 5 accesses to update the next level. This pattern continues up the tree as necessary. The algorithm is biased: insertions that affect a large number of nodes occur much less frequently that those that are limited to the lower levels of the tree. So the average number of accesses per index update remains in the 2–3 range for B^+-trees of reasonably high order.

Figure 15.25 shows simulation results for B^+-trees of varying orders. It gives the average number of disk accesses required to update the index when you insert records in the underlying data file. The keys inserted in the simulation were chosen randomly from a large range. A B^+-tree can unfold in many different configurations, depending on the key insertion order and the opportunities for adjacent nodes to share entries. Therefore, the trends of Figure 15.25 should be considered typical, but not exact in any given case. Although the algorithm forces all nodes, except the root, to remain at least one-half full, the simulation reveals that nodes run, on the average, about 80

You expect splitting at the lowest level to occur about once every q insertions, if q is the order of the B^+-tree. For example, if you insert keys in increasing sequence, the balancing mechanism ensures that the nodes fill in a left-to-right order. A new node is then needed every q entries. However, in a less than ideal situation, a sparse leaf can become isolated from an overflowing leaf by an intervening full sibling. Because the algorithm looks no further than one sibling away to relieve an overflowing node, a split occurs even though a more extensive adjustment could accommodate the new key without a split. Therefore, splitting at the lowest level occurs somewhat more frequently than once per q entries. This isolation effect is more noticeable for small values of q. The simulation reports the following frequency of splitting at various levels.

Order	Splitting frequency						Total
	Leaf		$\Longrightarrow$			Root	
4	0.292	0.068	0.016	0.003	0.000	0.000	0.381
8	0.149	0.019	0.002	0.000	0.000		0.171
16	0.075	0.004	0.000	0.000			0.080
32	0.037	0.001	0.000				0.038
64	0.018	0.000	0.000				0.018
128	0.009	0.000					0.009

For order $q = 4$, for example, about 29% of the insertions produce a split at the leaf level. This is about 4% higher than the $1/q = 0.25 = 25\%$ expected for an ideal insertion sequence. Similarly, the level just above the leaf nodes experiences a split, on the average, on 6.8% of the insertions. An ideal insertion sequence, splitting only when no possible rearrangement can accommodate the new entry, would give $1/q^2 = 0.0625 = 6.25\%$. Higher-order B^+-trees exhibit even less difference between the simulated frequency of splits and that expected for an ideal insertion sequence.

For a B^+-tree of order q, simulations show that the splitting frequency at the leaf level is somewhat greater than $1/q$ because the insertion algorithm can't fully exploit underpopulated siblings remote from an overflowing node.

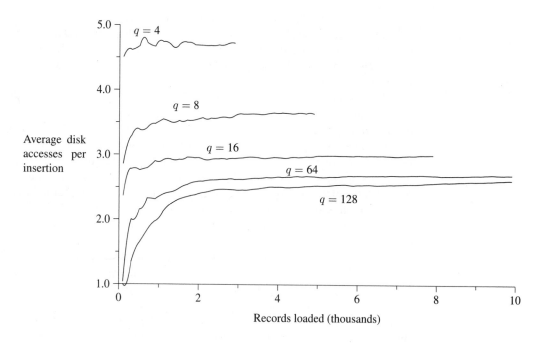

Figure 15.25   Average disk accesses per insertion for a B-tree index of order q

You obtain great leverage by making the nodes as large as possible. In other words, you should choose a large value for the order q of the B^+-tree. A high-order B^+-tree incurs less overhead in node splitting and therefore exhibits a lower update expense, as shown in Figure 15.25. Moreover, a high-order tree remains relatively flat, which keeps the number of accesses per retrieval correspondingly low. Recall that the number of index accesses needed to locate a target record is the same for all records in the underlying file and that this value is equal to the depth of the B^+-tree.

The most densely packed B^+-tree of order q has q keys and $q+1$ pointers in the root, $q(q+1)$ keys and $(q+1)^2$ pointers in the next lower level, $q(q+1)^2$ keys and $(q+1)^3$ pointers in the third level down, and so forth. At the leaf level, it has $q(q+1)^{d-1}$, if you designate the root as level one and proceed through the leaf nodes at level d. An ideal insertion sequence grows this most densely packed tree, which keeps the depth to a minimum. No q-order B^+-tree can contain $q(q+1)^{d-1}$ keys with a depth less than d. On the other hand, the most degenerate B^+-tree contains one key and two pointers in the root, $2\lfloor q/2 \rfloor$ keys and $2(\lfloor q/2 + 1 \rfloor)$ pointers in the next level, and so forth, for a total of $2\lfloor q/2 \rfloor (\lfloor q/2 \rfloor + 1)^{d-2}$ keys in the leaf nodes. Therefore, if R_{min} and R_{max} are the minimum and maximum number of leaf keys in a B^+-tree of depth d and order q, you have the relationships:

$$
\begin{aligned}
R_{min} &= 2\lfloor q/2 \rfloor (\lfloor q/2 \rfloor + 1)^{d-2} \\
R_{max} &= q(q+1)^{d-1}.
\end{aligned} \tag{15.2}
$$

R	$q = 4$	$q = 8$	$q = 16$	$q = 32$	$q = 64$	$q = 128$
10^1	$(2, 2)$	$(2, 2)$	$(1, 1)$	$(1, 1)$	$(1, 1)$	$(1, 1)$
10^2	$(4, 4)$	$(3, 3)$	$(2, 2)$	$(2, 2)$	$(2, 2)$	$(1, 1)$
10^3	$(5, 5)$	$(4, 4)$	$(3, 3)$	$(2, 3)$	$(2, 2)$	$(2, 2)$
10^4	$(6, 7)$	$(5, 5)$	$(4, 4)$	$(3, 3)$	$(3, 3)$	$(2, 3)$
10^5	$(8, 9)$	$(6, 7)$	$(5, 5)$	$(4, 4)$	$(3, 4)$	$(3, 3)$
10^6	$(9, 10)$	$(7, 8)$	$(5, 6)$	$(4, 5)$	$(4, 4)$	$(3, 4)$
10^7	$(11, 12)$	$(8, 9)$	$(6, 7)$	$(5, 6)$	$(4, 5)$	$(4, 4)$
10^8	$(12, 14)$	$(9, 11)$	$(7, 8)$	$(6, 7)$	$(5, 6)$	$(4, 5)$
10^9	$(14, 15)$	$(10, 12)$	$(8, 9)$	$(6, 7)$	$(5, 6)$	$(5, 5)$
10^{10}	$(15, 17)$	$(11, 13)$	$(9, 10)$	$(7, 8)$	$(6, 7)$	$(5, 6)$

Figure 15.26   Minimal and Maximal B^+-tree depths for a given number of entries

You can solve for the minimal and maximal B^+-tree depths associated with R-leaf level index entries as follows:

$$d_{\min} \quad = \quad 1 + \left\lceil \log_{q+1} \frac{R}{q} \right\rceil \tag{15.3}$$

$$d_{\max} \quad = \quad 2 + \left\lfloor \log_{\lfloor q/2 \rfloor + 1} \frac{R}{2\lfloor q/2 \rfloor} \right\rfloor.$$

Because of the logarithmic variation in depth, the difference between the shortest and the tallest B^+-trees for a fixed number of index entries is quite small, especially for higher-order B^+-trees. Figure 15.26 exhibits this small difference over a wide range of index sizes, R. An entry, (x, y), in the table means that the shortest B^+-tree capable of holding the given number of entries is x, and the tallest tree that could evolve for that number of entries is y. Clearly, the balancing mechanism works rather well, even though it is somewhat shortsighted in checking only the closest siblings in an attempt to avoid a node split.

According to an earlier argument, an estimate of the splitting frequency at the lowest level should be somewhat higher than $1/q$, where q is the order of the B^+-tree. You can use Equations 15.2 and 15.3 to calculate an upper and lower bound on the *total* splitting frequency, which is the ratio of the number of splits, at whatever level, to the number of leaf-level keys. Assume that q is even to avoid the rounding notation for $\lfloor q/2 \rfloor$. So $\lfloor q/2 \rfloor = q/2$. The number of splits, s, is equal to $n - d$, where n is the total number of nodes in the tree and d is the depth. This observation holds because each root split produces two new nodes, and each non-root split produces one new node. So if k is the number of leaf-level keys, the splitting frequency is: $\gamma = (n - d)/k$. The configuration corresponding to the most splits is the tallest possible tree. In that case, you have $k = R_{\min} = q(q/2+1)^{d-2}$ leaf-level keys in a tall tree of depth d. The root has one node with one key. The next level has two nodes with $2(q/2 + 1)$ pointers. The third level has $2(q/2 + 1)$ nodes with $2(q/2 + 1)^2$ pointers, and so forth. Therefore n, q, and d are related as follows:

$$
\begin{aligned}
n \quad &= \quad 1 + 2 + 2(q/2 + 1) + 2(q/2 + 1)^2 + \ldots + 2(q/2 + 1)^{d-2} = 1 + 2\sum_{i=0}^{d-2}(q/2 + 1)^i \\
&= \quad 1 + 2\frac{(q/2 + 1)^{d-1} - 1}{(q/2 + 1) - 1} = 1 + \frac{4}{q}[(q/2 + 1)^{d-1} - 1].
\end{aligned}
$$

The splitting frequency calculated from this tallest tree is the worst scenario. The actual splitting frequency is somewhat better. In other words, for large q:

$$\gamma = (n-d)/k \leq \frac{\frac{4}{q}[(q/2+1)^{d-1}-1]-(d-1)}{q(q/2+1)^{d-2}} < \frac{\frac{4}{q}(q/2+1)^{d-1}}{q(q/2+1)^{d-2}} = \frac{4}{q^2}(q/2+1) < 2/q + 4/q^2 \approx 2/q.$$

You already know that $\gamma \geq 1/q$ because the leaf level alone needs a new node every q insertions. Actually, the tree must fill the first few levels before the inequality holds because the first split acquires two nodes, and it takes some time to amortize this surplus over the subsequent insertions. So for trees of large order q with depth greater than three or so, you have:

$$1/q \leq \gamma \leq 2/q. \tag{15.4}$$

You can instrument the earlier simulation to count the number of splits at regular points during the insertion process. This gives the data below, which confirm Equation 15.4. An observed γ competes for the lower end of the observed range only when the tree has depth three or more, a situation that wasn't simulated in the case of $q = 128$.

q	$1/q$	Observed γ range	$2/q$
4	0.2500	0.3550 - 0.3900	0.5000
8	0.1250	0.1550 - 0.1755	0.2500
16	0.0625	0.0760 - 0.0824	0.1250
32	0.0313	0.0364 - 0.0400	0.0625
64	0.0156	0.0183 - 0.0200	0.0313
128	0.0080	– - 0.0098	0.0156

Other members of the B-tree family

Many variations exist on the B^+-tree theme. So great are the advantages of a high-order B^+-tree that you might consider using several disk blocks for each node. The insertion and deletion algorithms incur additional overhead because you then need several disk accesses to view a node completely. However, you often need only a part of the node. This is the case, for example, in descending a search path. If the first block of the node contains the desired search span, you don't need to access the remaining blocks.

A second variation takes a different view of the constraint that the non-root nodes must be half-full. Instead of interpreting half-full to mean one half of some maximum number of keys, you judge the population of a node in terms of the space available. For example, if a node can hold 4096 bytes, a population of 2048 bytes or less is considered sparse, even if that 2048 bytes includes a large number of keys. This situation can occur in the case of varying length keys, where the content of the node happens to involve only small keys. In this case, you can use the node to offload an overflowing sibling, regardless of the number of keys that it contains. This variation allows nodes to contain a varying number of keys, as long as the fraction of free space in the node isn't more than half. Although you must change the details of the insertion and deletion algorithms, the procedures carry over to the new situation.

Traditionally, a B-tree node (not a B^+-tree) contains keys and two kinds of pointers: data pointers and index pointers. The index pointers are interwoven with the keys in an alternating sequence. However, each key also possesses a data pointer that gives the disk address of the record with that key. Therefore, the upper levels of the B-tree can direct the search to the target record, if the target happens to coincide with an endpoint of a search span. With this scheme, the search doesn't always need to continue to the leaf nodes because it occasionally encounters the target key in the upper levels of the tree. However, most of the nodes of a tree are in the bottom level, so you enjoy this advantage only infrequently.

For a fully developed B-tree of order q, about $q/(q + 1)$ nodes are at the leaf level. Because the order of the B-tree is usually 100 or more, less than one percent of the nodes appear in the upper levels. Any advantage gained from data pointers in the upper levels is confined, therefore, to this small subset of entries. Moreover, because a node is typically a fixed-size disk block, the presence of additional data pointers in the upper-level nodes reduces the order of the B-tree. Another disadvantage of having data pointers in the tree's interior is that deletion can then start in non-leaf nodes, which complicates the deletion algorithm. For these reasons, the preferred structure is the B^+-tree, where data pointers appear only in the leaf nodes.

Yet another variation is the B^*-tree. Here the minimum population of a non-root node must be at least two-thirds of the maximum value. The maximum value is the order of the B^*-tree, and is again denoted by q. A splitting node, other than the root, must have at least one fully populated sibling. The split then combines the $q + 1$ keys in the overflowing node, the q keys of the full sibling, and the key in the parent between them, which gives a total of $2q + 1$ keys. Because $2q + 1 \geq 3\lfloor 2q/3 \rfloor$, this collection of keys is sufficient for *three* nodes, which replace the original overflowing node and its sibling. You distribute the keys across a new node, the overflowing node, and the chosen sibling. You then dispatch a packet of the form $(p_l, k_m, p_m, k_r, p_r)$ toward the parent. The l, m, and r tags denote left, middle, and right. The pointers then reference the left, middle, and right nodes of the redistributed trio; the keys are the smallest values in the middle and right nodes. This packet replaces the segment (p, k, p') in the parent, where the pointers reference the overflowing child and its sibling.

The number of keys in the parent increases by one, which may cause further overflow that can propagate up the tree. Thus, the general case splits two nodes into three, rather than one into two, as is the case with B^+-trees. You must give special consideration to the root because a root split involves no sibling. In particular, you must allow the root to be oversized so that it can contain up to $2\lfloor 2q/3 \rfloor$ keys. When the root must split, because of the insertion of one key beyond this limit, it can then supply enough keys for two minimal sized daughters and still retain a key for the new root.

A similar operation coalesces nodes when a node enters a crisis state by falling below $\lfloor 2q/3 \rfloor$ in population. The general case combines three nodes into two, so you must give special consideration to the case of an overflowing leftmost or rightmost child. Except for these extremes, if a node falls below $\lfloor 2q/3 \rfloor$ keys and has no opportunity for load sharing with a sibling, then it must have two siblings of minimal size. The $\lfloor 2q/3 \rfloor - 1$ keys remaining in the underflowing node, plus the $2\lfloor 2q/3 \rfloor$ keys from its two thin siblings, plus the two keys in the common parent separating the pointers to the child nodes, total $3\lfloor 2q/3 \rfloor + 1 \leq 2q + 1$ keys. So you discard one of the three siblings back to the disk manager and distribute its keys into the remaining two, possibly filling both of them with one key left over. The center key and pointers to the two remaining nodes constitute a packet of the form (p, k, p') that you dispatch to the parent. There, it replaces the segment $(p_l, k_m, p_m, k_r, p_r)$ associated with the three merging children. Because you dispatch one key upward, the boundary case, where the keys total $2q + 1$, results in two completely full child nodes but no overflow. The parent has now suffered the replacement of a two-key segment with a one-key segment, so a further contraction can propagate up the tree.

If the underflowing node is the rightmost or leftmost child of a parent, you must transfer a key from the adjacent sibling, even if it is already at the minimal population. The underflowing node is then legal, but its neighbor may now be in an underflowing state. This operation has effectively transferred the crisis to one of the interior nodes, where it now has two siblings and falls under the general coalescence scheme above. You can ensure that a parent always has some node with both right and left siblings by limiting $q \geq 3$. Under this constraint, the parent will always contain at least two keys and must therefore have at least three children. The final exception is the root, which may have just one key and two children. In this case, the root and the two children, one of which is underflowing, total $1 + \lfloor 2q/3 \rfloor + \lfloor 2q/3 \rfloor - 1 = 2\lfloor 2q/3 \rfloor$, which is the capacity of the oversized root. All three nodes can combine into a single root, and the tree depth decreases by one.

 Some variations on the B-tree scheme involve the storage of data pointers in the interior nodes, a constraint that non-root nodes be at least two-thirds full, and an interpretation of the node load in terms of total bytes available, rather than by the number of keys.

SUMMARY

An index is an auxiliary file that provides rapid access to a data file's records. The index uses a target value of the ordering field to obtain the disk addresses of the desired records. You can construct an index over unique or non-unique ordering fields. A hierarchical index exploits the fact that the ordering field values are typically much smaller than their records. Therefore, you can pack them tightly into disk blocks, together with references to the full records. Because you maintain the index references in order, a higher-level reference needs to note only the smallest ordering field value in a lower-level block. You can infer the remaining values from that single entry's relationship to its neighboring entries at the upper level.

If the bottom level of a hierarchical index contains 1,000,000 entries, packed 100 to the block, the next higher level can track all these entries with just 10,000 pointers, one for each block of the lower level. In turn, you can pack these 10,000 pointers perhaps 100 to the block, which necessitates 100 entries or just one block at the highest level. In general, if K is the number of index references that you can pack in a block, you achieve a fanout of $K : 1$ at each level of the index. With a single-block top level, an n-level index can then reference K^n data records.

If an indexed sequential file organizes the data on the same ordering field, the index doesn't need to contain an entry for each data record: one entry per data block is sufficient. An index with n levels can then catalog K^n data blocks. An index that contains an entry for each data record is a dense index. An index that isn't dense is a sparse index. Either scheme is robust in the face of data file modifications. However, certain changes do propagate up the index levels, and a sequence of changes can result in an unbalanced structure.

The B-tree family provides indexing structures that remain balanced as the underlying data file evolves. The most popular member of this family is the B^+-tree. Disk blocks form the nodes of a tree, with the leaf nodes providing addresses of the cataloged records. Interior nodes contain key values that divide the range of possible ordering field values into search spans. As the search process descends the tree, it passes through a nested sequence of search spans that represent ever more closely the records that agree with the ordering field's target value.

The algorithms for inserting and deleting maintain balance by requiring that all non-leaf nodes be at least half-full. An overloaded node attempts to share with a sibling before initiating a split to introduce a new node. This negotiation with siblings occurs both at the leaf level and in the interior of the tree, which allows entire subtrees to shift in an attempt to forestall a node split. The algorithm accommodates this shifting by adjusting the search spans in a common parent so that the nested search span condition remains valid on any path from root to leaf. Similarly, a deletion also seeks to avoid node coalescence by requesting a spare key from an overpopulated sibling. If this route isn't available, an underflowing node vanishes by merging with one of its minimally populated siblings. This removes the intervening key in their common parent. Thus, deletions can also propagate up the tree.

The tree depth changes only when the root splits or coalesces with its two minimally populated children. Therefore, the tree always maintains all leaf nodes at the same distance from the root. You then need an equal number of disk probes to retrieve any record of the file. All nodes are restricted to some maximum number of keys, called the order of the B^+-tree. In a typical situation, the B^+-tree order is in the 100 to 200 range, which provides a very large fanout.

The B-tree family has other members. A plain B-tree stores record addresses in interior nodes as well as in the leaf nodes. This allows the search to strike the target occasionally without descending to the leaf level. The advantage is small because $q/(q+1)$ of the nodes of a fully populated B-tree are leaf nodes. The insertion and deletion algorithms are also more complicated than their B^+-tree counterparts. A B^*-tree tightens the constraint on minimal node population to two-thirds full; other variations interpret the minimal density in terms of the available bytes in the node, rather than by the number of keys. Because of the significant advantage afforded by a high-order B^+-tree, another variation explores the possibility of spreading a node over several disk blocks.

Hierarchical and dense indexes

1. Suppose you organize a data file in an indexed sequential fashion and pack the records 20 to the block. The key value occupies 2% of the record length. Suppose further that there are 20,000,000 data records and that they are tightly packed into 1,000,000 blocks. Assume that block addresses alone could be packed 1000 to the block if they weren't accompanied by key values. How many levels are required for a sparse hierarchical index if the uppermost level must be contained in one block?

2. Suppose you organize the data file of the preceding exercise as a sequential heap with no regard for the ordering field. Assume that a record address is 20% longer than a block address, with the extra bits used for the locator-offset portion of the address. How many levels are required for a dense hierarchical index so that the uppermost level is a single block?

3. For purposes of drawing compact diagrams, assume a block can hold four index records or two data records. With these parameters, suppose you have an indexed sequential file configured as shown in Figure 15.27. The figure shows a portion of the two lowest levels. The ordering field is a key, and the data blocks show only the keys. The index is a sparse hierarchical index. You want to enter a record with key 3500 into the file. Show the resulting structure after following the text's method for index adjustment.

B-trees

4. Starting with an empty B^+-tree of order $q = 3$, draw a picture of the tree after each of the following five operations. Each operation assumes that the preceding operations have been successfully completed. In all cases, insert key entries in the order listed and always consult the left sibling first, if it's present, in an attempt to offload an overflowing node.

    - Add records with keys 100, 600, 1000, 900.
    - Add records with keys 400, 800, 1200.
    - Add records with keys 1300, 1400, 1500, 1600, 1700, 1100.
    - Add records with keys 1120, 1130, 1140, 1150, 1160, 1050.
    - Add a record with key 2000.

5. What is the average occupancy of the non-root nodes in the final configuration of the preceding exercise? Is this average within the expected bounds?

6. What is the splitting frequency per record inserted in the final configuration of the exercise above? In other words, what is the ratio of the number of splits to the number of leaf keys inserted? How does this value compare with the upper and lower bounds developed in the text?

7. Draw a picture of the B^+-tree after each of the following operations on the final configuration of the exercise above. Execute the deletions in the order listed and always consult the left sibling first, if it's present, in an attempt to borrow a key for an underflowing node. Coalescence, if necessary, merges with the left sibling, if present.

    - Delete the records with keys 1140, 1150, 1160.
    - Delete the records with keys 1300, 1400.
    - Delete the records with keys 1600, 1700, 2000.
    - Delete the record with key 1200.

8. Compose a sequence of insertion and deletion keys that will result in a B^+-tree of order four and depth three with the fewest number of nodes.

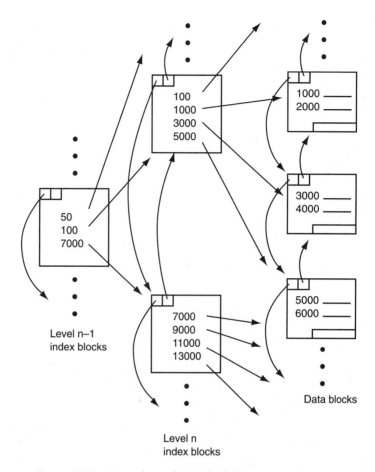

Figure 15.27   Sparse hierarchical index before entering key 3500

9. Is it possible to grow the tallest B^+-tree of order four and depth three through insertions alone? If so, give a sequence of insertions that will result in such a tree. If not, explain why.

10. Let t be the ratio of the maximum number of leaf keys that can be contained in a B^+-tree of order q and depth d to the minimum number of leaf keys that can be held in a tree with the same parameters. Show that $t < 2^{d-2}(q+1)$, for even q.

11. Consider a B^+-tree of order q, where q is even and $q > 3$. Let t be the height difference between the tallest such tree that can hold R leaf node keys and the shortest tree that can hold R leaf node keys. Show that $t < 1 + \log_{q+1}(R/q)$.

12. Prove that a B^+-tree of order q and depth $d \geq 2$ with the maximal number of nodes has at least $q/(q+1)$ of the nodes at the leaf level.

13. Show that the splitting frequency of a B^*-tree, γ, satisfies the following, for trees of depth $d \geq 3$ and order q divisible by three.

$$\frac{1}{q} \leq \gamma \leq \frac{3}{2q}\left(1 + \frac{3}{2q}\right)$$

16 File Structures for the Database Models

A
T THE IMPLEMENTATION LEVEL, ALL APPLICATION OBJECTS APPEAR AS records. The records contain fields, which hold data values. The relational model is the simplest in this regard because the entire structure consists of relations, which are named collections of tuples. Each relation translates directly into a similarly named collection of records. The hierarchical and network models both rely on the concept of a record type, a collection of application-specific fields, which is augmented with system fields to facilitate references to other records. The basic data element in the object-oriented model is the object, which is a collection of attributes patterned after a class template. These attributes can be data fields of the usual variety (e.g., strings, numbers, or booleans), or they can be other objects. In the latter case, the field value is an object identifier (OID), which can be the key or disk address of another record. The deductive model exhibits the greatest variation because it uses two types of basic data elements: axioms and inference rules. An axiom is simply an assertion that a certain application object possesses a particular attribute, such as fishHasWeight (X, Y). You can obviously tabulate these facts as records. For example, you can have a fishhasWeight file of records with fields X and Y. A given record then contains a fish's OID, X, and the fish's weight, Y. You can view the inference rules as one-to-many relationships between heads and bodies, which are character strings with placeholder variables. Therefore, you can tabulate the heads and give them internal unique identifiers. You tabulate the bodies separately and give each an embedded foreign key to identify its head. So you can also store the inference rules as records.

Therefore, with some imagination, you can envision each model's basic data elements as records within files. However, the resulting file system must be strengthened with structures to accelerate query and update operations, particularly for the efficient use of relationships. Recall that each of the five database models uses a distinct conceptual mechanism for handling relationships. This chapter discusses how to adapt the file and index structures of the preceding chapters to implement those mechanisms. Although each database model has a conceptual standard, their implementations don't. Indeed, database products compete by promoting clever implementation structures for enhanced performance. The only rule is that the resulting product must deliver the illusion associated with the corresponding model.

The relational model, for example, must perform frequent joins. You can greatly accelerate these joins with indexes on the common attributes. However, a relational database product isn't required to support indexes. In fact, it could perform joins in a brute-force manner by cycling every tuple of one operand past every tuple of the other. But the performance would be poor, and the database product would have little commercial appeal. By contrast, a viable implementation might opt to maintain hash tables on the primary keys, or it might internally string together the records of a relationship instance. The variations are too voluminous to survey exhaustively, and many implementation methods are proprietary secrets of the database vendors. So you should consider this chapter's techniques as typical practice, but you should also expect a great deal of variation across commercial products.

The relational model

The relational schema provides the field names and data types for each table. The data type either implies or explicitly states the storage requirements for its field (e.g., char(10)). Most relational products also allow variable length character strings (e.g., varchar(50)), and some of the newer products allow extremely long and varying data fields to store images and sound tracks. The block layout scheme of the preceding chapters accommodates these variations with locator arrays, record headers, and indirect references to lengthy data objects. Using these devices, you could assign each relation to a separate file. This is a popular choice although other arrangements provide better performance by grouping related records from different tables in the same file.

A well-designed relational database adheres to the entity integrity constraint, which doesn't allow null values in the primary key field. Using the most recent SQL specifications, you can identify the key field in the schema, and the DBMS will assume responsibility for entity integrity. Even if the application doesn't specify a key, the DBMS usually assigns each tuple a unique identifier. Sometimes the user can access this field under a name such as "rowid" or "TID" (tuple identifier).

References between relations use embedded foreign keys. It follows that the underlying records are never directly pinned by other application objects. A remote tuple can refer to a given tuple's key value but not to its disk address. Consequently, if no system structures, such as index files, pin the tuple records, the DBMS can relocate them without the overhead of forwarding addresses. For example, if you implement two relations as hash files on their common field, you can efficiently process joins, and all data records remain unpinned. In this case, insertions and deletions can rearrange records in a bucket to reclaim both unused data space and unused locators.

Hash files, however, aren't as popular as B^+-tree indexes for accelerating joins. You don't want to ask the application designer to specify a hash function because this implies that the designer knows about hash functions. In an effort to bring database design to an ever larger audience, the current trend is to minimize implementation details. A second problem is that the designer must know the hash file's eventual size. Even with the dynamic hashing schemes, the number of bits in the hash result or the maximum modulus is an input to the algorithm. By contrast, a B^+-tree index grows gracefully without a preestablished upper limit and requires no technical input from the designer. If the primary keys are available in the schema, the DBMS can automatically establish a B^+-tree index. Indeed, the DBMS can assume full responsibility for trading off the advantages and disadvantages of the index. It can abandon the index when confronted with massive updates to avoid the overhead of keeping it current. Depending on the computational expense, the DBMS may even create the index specifically for a given join operation.

Unfortunately, B^+-trees do pin the data records with references from the leaf nodes. To escape the undesirable consequences of pinned records, the DBMS can insist that a B^+-tree index on the primary key contain the *only* external references to record addresses of the associated relation. In this case, adjusting the leaf reference when a record relocates may be comparable (in terms of disk accesses) to setting up a forwarding address. This would likely be the case if the index comes and goes as needed for query assistance; sometimes the records wouldn't be pinned at all.

You can construct a B^+-tree over any underlying file organization. For example, you can place a B^+-tree over a hash file. Although a large fanout B^+-tree provides access to a target in 2 to 3 disk probes, a good hashing scheme reduces this figure, on the average, to the 1.0 to 1.5 range. Therefore, if you need the extra performance edge, you can still implement hashed access even though the B^+-tree is present on some other ordering field.

You can implement the aquarium application as shown in Figure 16.1. To execute a join operation, you recover the selected records from the many side of a one-to-many relationship and use the index to obtain the matching parent records. For example, you can join a collection of fish records with their tank and species components by using the foreign keys in the fish records (i.e., tno and sno) as search targets for the B^+-tree indexes on the tank and species files. Similarly, a collection of event records refers to the owning fish, and you can obtain the parent fish records through the fno index on the fish file. Figure 16.1 thus provides an index to accelerate the joins for each one-to-many relationship. The index organizes the dominant side of the relationship according to its primary key.

Because the event entity doesn't appear on the dominant side of a relationship, you can omit the index over that file. However, if you include it, you can keep the event records minimally pinned by directing other references through the single index. These other references can arise in connection with the select operator of relational algebra. Most queries deal with only a small subset of the tuples in the targeted relations, and an effective method for isolating the desired subset can greatly accelerate the query solution. For example, you can speed up the following query by joining only the fish subset with fcolor red and the tank subset with tname lagoon.

```
select fname, tvolume
from Fish F, Tank T
where tname = "lagoon" and fcolor = "red".
```

Indexes on fcolor and tname can achieve this efficiency. To maintain the data records' minimally pinned status, you can establish B^+-trees that terminate in fno and tno values, respectively, rather than in record addresses. Of course, when you obtain keys from the index's leaf nodes, you must present them to the primary index to acquire the selected records. Figure 16.1 suggests this arrangement with the cascading B^+-tree symbols.

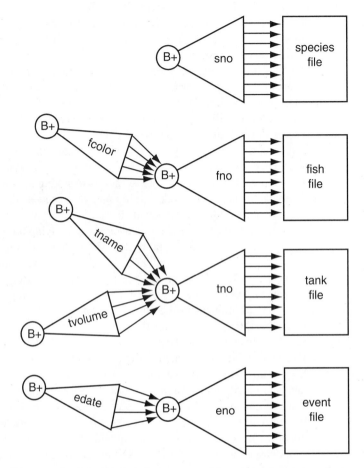

Figure 16.1   An indexed implementation of the relational aquarium database

Although the most symmetric approach assigns a separate file to each relation, this separation isn't necessary. In fact, some relational databases store all the relations in a single file. At the other extreme, a dispersed solution can be more convenient, for example, in a distributed situation where certain parts of the relation are primarily active at certain sites. Intermediate arrangements are possible as well, and Figure 16.2 illustrates one of them. Here, tank and fish tuples share a single tank-fish file. To facilitate the join of tank and fish records, you physically follow each tank record with the fish records that it owns, as shown in the upper portion of the figure. Because the records are only minimally pinned by the primary index, you can relocate them when the number of fish associated with a given tank expands or contracts. Although you can address the fish segments individually through the fno index, you can also consider them as a trailer on the tank record. This provides a permanent join that you don't need to construct on demand.

With this arrangement, the above query can now proceed as follows, without an explicit join. You first use the index on tname to obtain the keys of tank records with tname lagoon.

You then introduce each key into the primary index on tno to obtain the actual tank record. On the same block, or perhaps on succeeding blocks, are all the related fish records. You extract the fname from each red fish, pair it with the tvolume from the fixed tank, and add the result to the accumulating output list.

In this way, you can pack any natural hierarchy in the application schema. In the aquarium example, the cascade tank-fish-event comprises such a hierarchy, and you can interweave all three record types in a single file. The arrangement then exhibits a preexisting join of tank records with their fish and with the events owned by their fish. But the species record type remains outside of this cozy nesting, so you still need another index to facilitate species-fish joins. You could choose to nest the cascade species-fish-event, but then the tank record type would lie outside the packing scheme. You can't pack the fish records simultaneously in close proximity to the owning tank and to the owning species. Such is the nature of intersecting one-to-many relationships.

Strictly speaking, any index structures in the relational model are implementation details that shouldn't appear in the interface language. The user simply commands table operations (e.g., create table, drop table) and tuple operations (e.g., insert, select, update, delete) as SQL expressions, without regard to any efficiencies afforded by indexes. Most relational database products, however, provide SQL-like commands to create and drop indexes. For example, the following typical SQL creates an explicit index, which uses the tno attribute as an ordering field. The SQL doesn't specify the particular form of the index, but it is usually a B^+-tree.

```
create unique index tankIndex on tank(tno).
```

You use the "unique" qualifier to inform the index that there will be no duplicate tno values. For many relational products, specifying a unique index is the only approach for enforcing a key constraint, although you will recall from Chapter 6 that the most recent SQL version allows constraint specification in the table schema. For example, the definition of the tank table, excerpted from Figure 6.5, appears below. The primary key (tno) clause enforces the constraint that tno values must be distinct across tank tuples. But many relational products don't support this enhanced level of SQL. Instead, they usually rely on an index creation command to enforce a key constraint.

```
                ⋮
create table tank (
    tno keyvalue,
    tname namestring
        default "unnamedTank",
    tcolor tankcolor,
    tvolume volvalue,
    primary key (tno).
    )
                ⋮
```

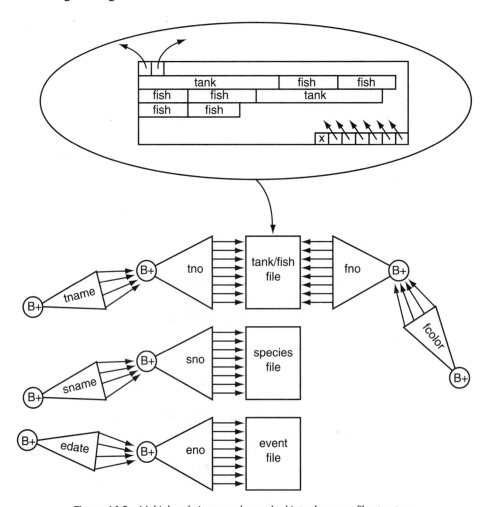

Figure 16.2 Multiple relations can be packed into the same file structure

SQL commands for creating and dropping indexes allow you to remove indexes during massive updating activities. This avoids the overhead expense of updating them. You can regenerate the indexes when you need them later for retrieval operations. The pure relational model allows the DBMS to make those decisions based on the mix of update and query operations directed against the database. Although index creation incurs disk accesses, it can still be the most efficient approach to a given query.

You can assign relations to separate files, or you can require several relations to coexist on a single file. You may even split a single relation across several files. The relational model needs indexes for join efficiency, and many relational products provide explicit commands for creating and dropping indexes.

The network model

The network database model stores record types and network sets. A network set is a named schema element, which implements a one-to-many relationship between a dominant (owner) record type and a dependent (member) record type. For example, you can implement the one-to-many relationships between species and fish and between tank and fish in the aquarium application with the owner-coupled sets Represents and Inhabits. The following excerpt from Figure 11.6 illustrates the definition of network sets.

```
network set Inhabits.                          network set Experiences.
   owner is tank.                                 owner is fish.
      order is sorted by defined keys.               order is sorted by defined keys.
   member is fish.                                member is event.
      insertion is manual.                           insertion is automatic.
      retention is optional.                         retention is mandatory.
      key is ascending fname.                        key is ascending edate.

network set Represents.
   owner is species.
      order is sorted by defined keys.
   member is fish.
      insertion is automatic.
      retention is fixed.
      key is ascending fname.
```

You can store network sets in several ways. The simplest storage scheme imitates the conceptual chains of Chapter 11. In other words, an instance of Inhabits is a chain containing one tank record and zero, one, or more fish records. The block layout scheme already provides header fields for each stored record. These fields hold organizational items needed to access the record: field offsets, field lengths, and flags noting a forwarding address or an indirect reference to a more voluminous storage location. In the network database model, you also encode network set information in the record headers.

Consider, for example, the fish record type in the aquarium application. For each network set with fish as the owner, a chain extends from each fish record and passes through the member records. So you must reserve a field in the fish record header for a pointer to the first member record of the chain. In this case, fish plays the owner role in the network set Experiences, and event is the member. Each fish record then contains a pointer to the first event on its chain. The pointer may be null if the fish owns no events, or it may be the disk address of a particular event record. Figure 16.3 illustrates this situation. The pointer to the first event appears in the fish record header, just after the F flag (forwarding address status) and the T flag (record type).

The situation is more complicated when the record type appears as the member of a network set. In a complete implementation, the record header contains three pointers for each such set: a pointer to the owning parent record, a pointer to the next member of the chain, and a pointer to the previous member of the chain. Some network products, however, use less than the full complement of three pointers. Indeed, you can obtain full functionality with just the pointer to the next member record. This pointer lets you follow the chain from

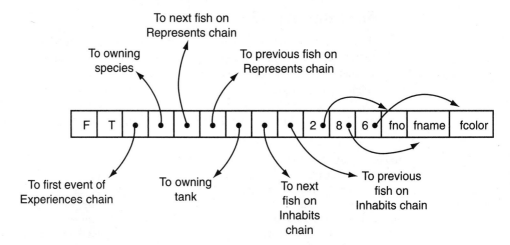

Figure 16.3   Record header fields required for network set implementations

the owner through all the members and back to the owner. But you'll see better performance if you can access the owner directly from each member.

In the aquarium application, the fish record type plays member roles in both the Inhabits and Represents network sets. Each affiliation gives rise to three pointers, as shown in Figure 16.3. Because network set pointers are record addresses (i.e., block address and locator offset $(b : l)$ combinations), they are all the same size. The DBMS knows the number of network pointers in the header from the schema's set specifications. So by coding these pointers immediately after the F and T flags, the DBMS will always find them in fixed header locations. It can then calculate where the rest of the header begins.

With this scheme, the pointer overhead varies from one record type to the next, depending on the roles that the record type plays in the network sets. Assuming the three sets above are the only network sets in the aquarium schema, the tank record type occurs as the owner of Inhabits, but it doesn't occur as a member of any set. Therefore, each tank record header needs a single pointer to the first fish of its Inhabits chain. Similarly, the species record type occurs only as the owner of Represents, and each species header contains a single pointer to the first fish of its Represents chain. The fish record type is the most complicated because it is the owner of Experiences and a member of Inhabits and Represents. Each fish record header can then hold as many as seven pointers, as illustrated in Figure 16.3. Finally, the event record type appears only as a member of the Experiences network set. The header of an event record thus contains three pointers: one to the owning fish record, one to the next event on a given chain, and one to the preceding event. The nature of a one-to-many relationship prevents a member record from residing simultaneously on more than one chain of a given network set. So an event record can appear on at most one Experiences chain, and a single pair of next-prior pointers is sufficient to link it into that chain.

Maintaining chains of linked records is time-consuming because adjacent links can be on different disk blocks. Moreover, note that the schema excerpts above specify that the

Inhabits and Represents chains must be ordered on the fish's fname attribute. Each Experiences chain must be ordered on the event's edate attribute. So when you connect a new member record, you must traverse the chain to the proper location before rewiring the links.

Figure 16.4 shows an alternative approach: an owner record points not to the first member of its chain, but to the root node of a private index over all the members belonging to that owner. For example, a tank record contains the block address of the root of a private B^+-tree that catalogs, on the basis of fname value, just the fish belonging to that tank. For a given tank, the indexed fish records are typically a small subset of the total fish file. In that case, the root node of the private index may very well be the only node. With this arrangement, the expensive linked chains are no longer necessary, and the number of pointers in the record headers is significantly reduced. Figure 16.4 shows that you now need only three pointers in the fish header and one pointer in each of the other three record types. The sequence set of the index now maintains the order commanded by the schema. Most insertions require only an update of the single index node.

This approach generalizes to handle system network sets. A system network set contains a single chain, in contrast with owner-coupled network sets, which have a disjoint chain for each owner record. The single chain globally links all the records of the specified member type. A system set usually specifies an ordering on the chain and therefore corresponds to a global index of the member record type. So you can implement a system network set with a global B^+-tree. The following excerpt from the aquarium network schema specifies a global index on the tank records with ordering field tname.

```
network set tankAlpha.
    owner is system.
        order is sorted by defined keys.
    member is tank.
        insertion is automatic.
        retention is fixed.
        key is ascending tname.
```

Although you envision this structure as a system-owned chain linking all the tank records in tname order, the actual implementation uses a B^+-tree on tname. B^+-tree indexes— global for system network sets or local for owner-coupled network sets—facilitate the find command, which takes the following form.

$$\text{find} \left\{ \begin{array}{l} \text{first} \\ \text{last} \\ \text{next} \\ \text{prior} \end{array} \right\} \textit{<record type name>} \text{ [within } \textit{<network set name>}\text{] [using } \textit{<field list>}\text{]}.$$

When you specify the optional [using <field list>] clause, you assume that the program's record template contains target values for the listed fields. If no within-clause appears, the find command requests target records that have certain values in the specified fields. If the using-clause mentions just one field, a global index on that ordering field will quickly return the required record set without searching the entire file. If the clause mentions several fields, the DBMS will use a global index, if available, on the field with the largest image, for reasons

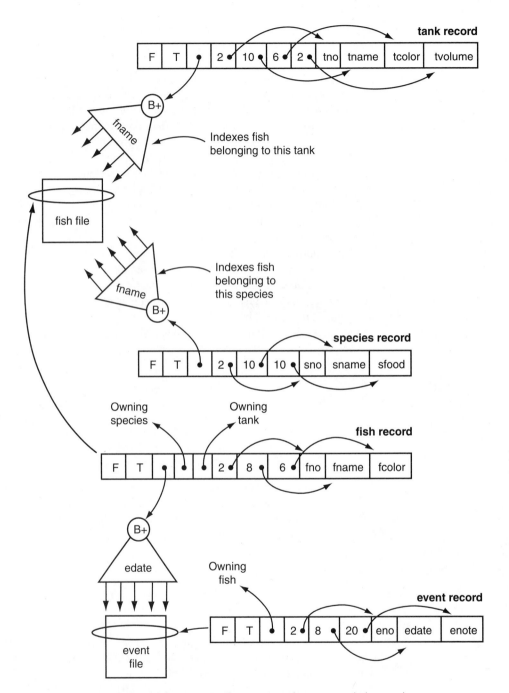

Figure 16.4 An alternative implementation of owner-coupled network sets

explained below. This index will return the smallest record subset, and the DBMS must process these records to filter out those that don't match the remaining field specifications. If the command specifies a within-clause, the request is restricted to the member records of a particular owner-coupled chain. The DBMS search strategy is the same except that it uses a local index, if available, over the member records of the owner-coupled chain.

An index is most valuable when it significantly reduces the candidates in a search effort. For example, an index on gender in a personnel file isn't very effective because it typically reduces the search space only by half. Suppose you have a file of 1,000,000 people and want to process only the females. A B^+-tree index on gender allows you to quickly arrive at the sequence set, which contiguously stores references to the females. Because these references constitute a dense index, you need a separate disk probe for each. This means you must dispatch 500,000 disk probes to retrieve the females, regardless of how they are packed on the data file. If the data records are packed 10 to the block, you can process the entire file in only 100,000 probes by simply ignoring the male records when they occur. So an index on a binary-valued attribute, such as gender, isn't effective. On the other hand, an index on social security number is very effective in reducing the search space because a particular social security number refers to a single personnel record.

The above discussion of the find command noted that, given a choice, the DBMS will use an index over a field with a large image. The image of a file attribute, $I_f(x)$, is the number of distinct values occurring in the x-attribute across the file records. If $I_f(x)$ is large, the number of records having a particular x-value is small. In the absence of more detailed information, you can use the estimate $N/I_f(x)$ for the expected number of records having a particular value for attribute x, where N is the number of records in the file. An index constructed over an attribute with a large image is called a **discriminating index**. If you specify a particular target value for the ordering field x, you expect a discriminating index to return relatively few records. In other words, the index is capable of fine discrimination among records. An index on social security number is a discriminating index; an index on gender isn't.

When designing a network application, you can choose the implementation method for the network sets, either as private indexes or as linked chains. In making the decision, you should consider both the expected chain populations and the discriminating nature of the ordering field. If you expect the typical chain to have few members, an indexed representation wastes an entire block for the root node of an essentially empty index. The linked chain representation is then less expensive. Another condition that argues for the linked chain is a non-discriminating sort field. If you use a B^+-tree, you will get a non-discriminating index, which appears as chained block segment at the lower level for each target value. So the chains reappear anyway, and you may just as well use them directly in the network set representation.

How should you assign record types to files in the network model? Unlike the relational model, the network model allows the database designer to specify many of the physical storage details, including the method for implementing network sets. Another such detail influences the assignment of record types to files. The record type portion of the schema provides for an optional clause, called the **location mode**. The option takes one of three forms:

$$\text{location mode is} \left\{ \begin{array}{l} \texttt{direct} \\ \texttt{calc} <\textit{procedure name}> \texttt{using} <\textit{field list}> \\ \texttt{via} <\textit{set name}> \end{array} \right.$$

The `direct` mode provides rapid access to a record only if you know its database key. The database key is the record address, the block address and locator offset combination where the record is stored. This storage mode assigns the record type to a file with sequential organization. However, it doesn't imply that the record type is the file's sole occupant, as you'll see shortly. If you don't know the target's database key, the only available search mechanism is sequential access to the file blocks through the forward-backward pointers. Chapter 11 used database keys in connection with queries that backtracked across network sets already in use. The query program used database keys to restore a context that had been lost when the currency pointers migrated in the second use of the network set. Database keys are available, even if the schema indicates a location mode other than direct. The `direct` location mode relieves the DBMS of any responsibility for providing a rapid access path to records with particular application field values. Only if you have accessed the record before and have retained its database key, can you expect the DBMS to rapidly retrieve the record a second time.

The `calc` mode specifies a hash file organization and allows the designer to provide the hash function. The schema also specifies the hash field, and the user must ensure that hash field values are acceptable by the specified hash function. This storage mode assigns the record type to a hash file and determines the number of buckets as the largest value returned by the hash procedure. The schema doesn't specify the maximal bucket number in advance. When the hash function returns a value larger than any previously seen, the DBMS acquires new blocks from the disk manager to extend the file through that bucket. As with `direct` location, `calc` location doesn't imply that the record type is the file's sole occupant.

The `via set` location mode requires the DBMS to store records of the type under description in close proximity to the owning record in the named network set. The record type under description must be the specified member record type of the named set. "Close proximity" means on the same block or on adjacent blocks in the event of overflow. The `via set` location specification places no restriction on the storage mode of the network set's owner record type. You can use a location-mode clause in the owner's record type description to store the owner in any manner: `direct`, `calc`, or `via set` based on some other network set.

In the aquarium example, you can specify a location mode of `calc` for tank records and `via set Inhabits` for fish records. In this case, the DBMS groups the fish records for a particular tank after that tank as a sort of trailer. It then assigns the entire collection a bucket in the tank file according to the specified hashing scheme. If the schema locates event records `via set Experiences`, the DBMS packs all event records for a fish after that fish. It then packs the lot after the owning tank. The entire collection then represents a preestablished join of a tank with its fish and with their events. The DBMS assigns the collection to a bucket with the hash function from the `calc` location mode of the tank record type.

In summary, the `direct` and `calc` modes assign a new file to the record type under description. Later `via set` modes, however, can force other record types into those files.

SpeciesHier   TankHier

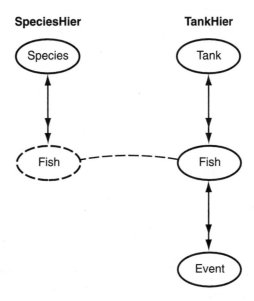

Figure 16.5   Hierarchical decomposition of the aquarium database

The `direct` and `calc` modes do provide additional access paths to their base record types, which supplement any system sets that may appear in the schema.

 The network model stores records in hashed files, sequential files, or interwoven in close proximity to their owners via some network set. It implements the network sets with pointers in the record headers or with local indexes.

The hierarchical model

Although the relational and network models allow implementations to store different record types in the same file, the storage scheme isn't really visible as part of the conceptual model. By contrast, the hierarchical model groups disparate record types in each hierarchy, and these groupings are visible at the conceptual level in the schema. Related records occupy adjacent positions in a preorder traversal.

Recall that the schema presents a system of hierarchies. Within a hierarchy, a given record type plays the dependent role in at most one, one-to-many relationship. Some record types are virtual: the DBMS materializes them as needed through references to the existing records in another hierarchy. For example, you decomposed the aquarium database into two hierarchies, TankHier and SpeciesHier, as illustrated in Figure 16.5. Because the fish entity plays the dependent role in two one-to-many relationships, it appears in both hierarchies. Fish records are physically present in TankHier, but you can reference them from SpeciesHier through a system of pointers.

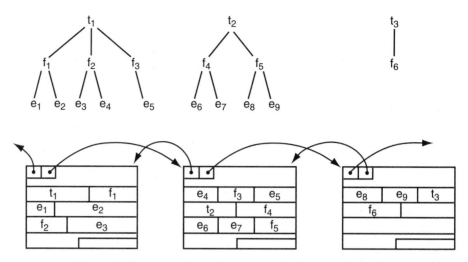

Figure 16.6   Instance hierarchies from the TankHier type hierarchy

How do you store a hierarchy in a file system? First, consider a hierarchy of physical (i.e., non-virtual) record types, such as the TankHier in Figure 16.5. The database contains multiple instances of this hierarchy, as shown in the upper portion of Figure 16.6. Each instance mirrors the type hierarchy, TankHier. A tank record appears at the root and branches into multiple fish subtrees. Each subtree has a fish at the root, followed by multiple event records. The hierarchical sequence of the leftmost instance of Figure 16.6 is $(t_1, f_1, e_1, e_2, f_2, e_3, e_4, f_3, e_5)$. Within a given instance, you can order the fish records by some fish attribute. Within a fish subtree, you can order the events by some event attribute. The tank, its fish, and their events exhaust the record types of the example hierarchy. However, in the general case, you can order the children within a given subtree first by record type and then by an attribute within each record type. The full hierarchical sequence for the entire TankHier forest is the concatenation of the instance sequences. You can use some tank attribute to determine the concatenation order.

The simplest file organization for a type hierarchy is a sequential file, where the records appear in hierarchical sequence. The linearized record sequence is then exactly parallel to the logical adjacency pattern that you use to envision query solutions. Because no records are pinned, you can easily relocate them when you chain new blocks into the structure to relieve overflows. The block structure of this sequential file appears in the lower portion of Figure 16.6. In a sense, the format preestablishes the relationship joins because related records are now physically adjacent.

Recall that the get command takes the form:

$$\text{get} \left\{ \begin{array}{c} first \\ next \end{array} \right\} \text{[[virtual] child] } <segment\ name> \text{ [within parent } <segment\ name>] \text{ [where } <search\ argument>].$$

The where-clause specifies boolean search conditions that restrict the retrieval to records with certain field values. Because the target records may constitute a small subset of the linearized hierarchy, you need further index structures to accelerate the search. A sequential search of the linearized hierarchy would be very inefficient. You can apply the B^+-tree index method of Chapter 15 to this problem because the index doesn't rely on the data file's underlying structure. For historical accuracy, however, the following describes the approaches used by Information Management System (IMS), the well-established hierarchical product from IBM.

The unadorned physical adjacency solution of Figure 16.6 is the **Hierarchical Sequential Access Method** (HSAM). The next step toward improved performance provides indexed access to the instance hierarchy roots but retains the physical adjacency of subsegments under each root. If you construct this index with the same ordering field that you used to concatenate the instance hierarchies in the sequential arrangement, you maintain the overall order. In essence, the index points you quickly to a tank record, and you find a sequential trailer leading from it. The trailer contains the related fish and event records. This alternative is the **Hierarchical Indexed Sequential Access Method** (HISAM).

Figure 16.7 demonstrates the HISAM organization. The H symbol in the index triangle means that the index is hierarchical. A B^+-tree index would function equally well, but IMS predates the B^+-trees. The ordering field is tname. If the underlying data file maintains the extended tank records in tname order, a sparse hierarchical index is sufficient. This condition will be satisfied if the data file is a sequential run of instance hierarchies. In that case, the index specifies only block addresses at the lowest level, and the data records remain unpinned. You can then relocate data records to adjacent blocks as the structure grows, and the index requires minimal maintenance.

Using the HISAM organization, a search can use a given tname value to receive rapid access to the target tank, but it then degenerates into a sequential search through the related fish and event records. Although the sequential part is slow, the full hierarchical sequence is still available, with the forward-backward threads linking the data blocks. Therefore, you still have preestablished relationship joins, and the index quickly isolates the segment of the linearized hierarchy where they reside.

At the conceptual level, relationships in the hierarchical model depend on logical adjacency, not physical adjacency. So the preorder traversal of a hierarchy instance can involve non-adjacent records, provided a pointer scheme connects them properly. In the aquarium example, you can have separate files for the tank, fish, and event records, but the records are then heavily pinned with references from other records. In particular, each record needs two pointers in its header to reference the next and preceding records in the hierarchical sequence. Child-sibling pointers can provide further processing shortcuts.

For example, you can lace the tank hierarchies with hierarchical sequence pointers as illustrated in the top portion of Figure 16.8. The figure shows only the forward pointers, but each has a parallel reference in the opposite direction. With these pointers, you can follow the hierarchical sequence. Unfortunately, each link may involve a separate disk access because the subsequent or preceding record may reside in a different block, perhaps even in a different file. So you need to skip portions of the hierarchy that aren't relevant to a particular processing activity. If you are processing the fish in a given tank, for example, you don't want to visit their intervening event records, particularly when each visit may involve a separate disk access. The child-sibling pointers, shown in the center portion of Figure 16.8, enable this skip navigation. Each record contains two additional pointers: one to its leftmost child at the next hierarchical level and another to its right sibling under

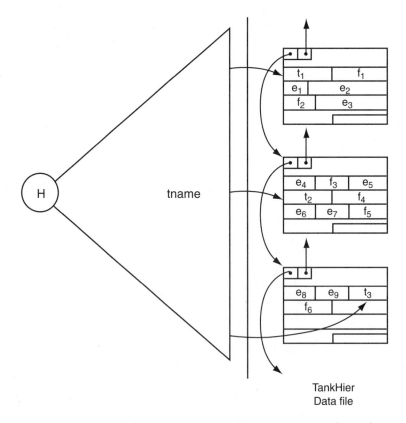

Figure 16.7 Indexed access to the roots of hierarchy instances (HISAM)

their common parent. You could add more pointers to allow two-way navigation among siblings, to provide direct access to the parent record from a child, and to access the right-most child directly from the parent. Even without these elaborations, the record headers now bristle with references to other records in a manner reminiscent of the network model. The lower portion of Figure 16.8 shows a sketch of a fish record header. It exhibits hierarchical next-prior pointers (HN and HP), a leftmost child pointer (LC), and a right sibling pointer (RS).

IMS provides two other organizations that use hierarchical and child-sibling pointers to lace together the records of the hierarchy instances while still providing more immediate access to the root records. The first is the **Hierarchical Indexed Direct Access Method** (HIDAM). It constructs a hierarchical index over the root record type, using the highest-level ordering field of the hierarchical sequence. Upon reaching a root record through the index, you use child-sibling pointers to continue the search into related records. In Figure 16.8, the HIDAM method can provide an index into the tank records. Each tank record then maintains the appropriate pointers to navigate to the rest of the hierarchy. The final method is the **Hierarchical Direct Access Method** (HDAM). HDAM provides hashed access to the root records and child-sibling pointers for traversing related records.

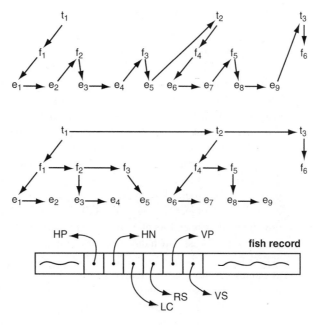

Figure 16.8 Hierarchical and child-sibling pointers allow direct access to a hierarchy

When virtual record types appear in a hierarchy, the corresponding actual record types must provide additional pointers to maintain the virtual chain. These pointers play roughly the same roles as the child-sibling pointers in the physical implementations described above. The difference is that the pointers provide references across hierarchies. From an implementation standpoint, the difference isn't significant because you already assume that all pointers reference remote blocks, and possibly even remote files.

In the aquarium example, the fish entity reappears in the SpeciesHier hierarchy as a virtual child of the species entity. Each species record then contains a pointer to its first virtual child, and each fish provides a virtual sibling pointer to continue the chain. This arrangement is almost the same as the child-sibling pointers that allow skip processing of the fish within a tank. A major difference is the ability to navigate from child to parent. In the TankHier, a child can eventually find its parent by back-navigating along the hierarchical pointers. The first record of the proper type is the desired parent. However, a fish record can't find its virtual species parent in this manner because it resides in a separate type hierarchy. Therefore, yet another pointer burdens each fish record to refer to its virtual parent. These items appear in the fish header of Figure 16.8 as the VP and VC pointers.

 A hierarchical database file structure imitates the linearized record sequence used to maintain the one-to-many relationships in the type hierarchies. You can organize the records linearly in this sequence (HSAM, HISAM), or you can disperse them and provide pointers for the reassembly process (HIDAM, HDAM).

The object-oriented model

The notion of class replaces the concept of relation in the object-oriented database model. This represents a philosophical retreat from a mathematical abstraction to a behavioral description. In the relational model, an application entity is an attribute collection, and each instance is an element of the Cartesian product of the corresponding domains. In the object-oriented model, an entity is an attribute collection plus a set of behavior patterns. An entity instance, an object, is still an element of the Cartesian product of the attribute domains, but that characterizes only its static nature. Because it can respond to messages by invoking a behavior pattern, it also has a dynamic nature.

You represent an object of class A as a record with the usual header information, which gives class identification and a forwarding address if necessary. Class identification now plays the role associated with the record type flag of the preceding models. When the DBMS creates a new object, it assigns an OID. The OID is the object record's storage address: the block address and locator offset combination. Relocation off the home block uses the forwarding address mechanism discussed earlier. If you know an object's OID, you can access it with one disk probe (two, if it has relocated off its home block). The object's attributes can hold basic elements (e.g., character strings or numbers) or more complex objects. The record fields then frequently contain OIDs of other objects, and you need additional disk probes to retrieve the details of these related objects.

In comparison with the relational case, further complications arise here because a class can inherit attributes from its ancestors. Each relation, on the other hand, has an independent definition. Consider the class hierarchy of Figure 16.9. Class A has attributes a_1 and a_2. Class B is a subclass of class A with additional attributes b_1, b_2 and b_3. Finally, class C is a subclass of class B with the additional attribute c_1. A sample A record appears in the lower part of the figure. The F flag carries forwarding address information; the T flag denotes the class, A in this case. Assume that attribute a_1 is a character string and that a_2 is another object. So you find the a_1 value directly in the record, but you must expend another retrieval to recover a_2. Although the figure shows the familiar field lengths and offset information in the header, this arrangement wastes some space in storing the OID field lengths. All OIDs have the same known length. However, this arrangement does allow you to mix OIDs, strings, and numbers in an arbitrary order.

In the figure, a typical B record layout appears beneath the A record. Because class B objects inherit the attributes of the ancestor class A, you include space in the B record to store the attributes, a_1 and a_2, in addition to the newly introduced attributes b_1, b_2, and b_3. Similarly, a C record is an extension of a B record, as shown in the last layout of the figure. When a class inherits from a single hierarchy of ancestors, the DBMS can infer an attribute position in the offset and data-length array by assuming that each subclass adds its attributes to the end of those inherited from its ancestors. If a class inherits from multiple parents, however, you must use a more complicated scheme to associate an entry in the offset and data-length header array with a particular attribute.

Certain classes, such as Collection and Array, contain a variable number of anonymous attributes. The corresponding object records must then encode the number of fields in the record header. Subject to these considerations, objects become variable-length records, similar to tuples, at the implementation level. Because the object-oriented model expresses relationships with logical containment, you can achieve some efficiency by packing related

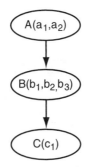

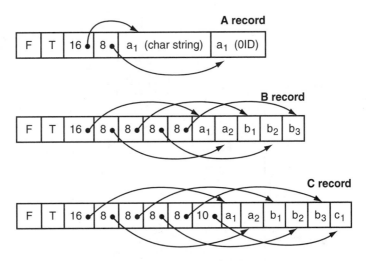

Figure 16.9   Record layouts for objects of nested subclasses

records on the same block. For example, in the object-oriented aquarium application, a tank object has three traditional attributes: name, color, and volume. You can encode these field values directly in the corresponding record. However, the tank object also has a population attribute, whose value is an object of class Set. So the tank record contains an OID in its population attribute slot, and you would prefer that the population OID reference an object on the same disk page. Moreover, the population object contains many OIDs, all anonymous attributes that refer to the fish that populate the tank. You would also prefer that these fish objects reside on the same disk block with the tank or on adjacent disk blocks if an overflow situation develops. Figure 16.10 summarizes this preferred arrangement. Because of the nature of the application, an operation on the tank will probably consult the fish that swim in that tank. This approach to packing related records is then similar to the one used in the relational model to avoid extensive join operations.

For an ordering field that is a traditional data type (e.g., character string or number), index construction is no different than in the other models. You erect a B^+-tree to guide

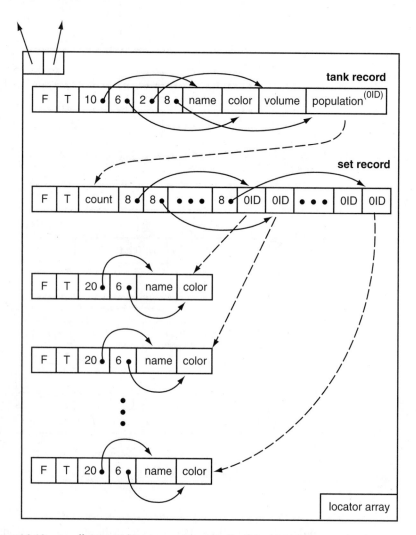

Figure 16.10 An efficient packing arrangement for the fish objects associated with a given tank

the search to the leaf nodes. There you find record addresses leading to the target objects. Following is a typical operation, which filters the tanks for a given name. Here you can use an index on the tank objects, with ordering field "name," to accelerate the `select:` operation.

```
TanksToDelete := TheTankCollection select: [aTank | aTank name = "cesspool"].
```

However, you may want to index objects on an ordering field within a complex-valued attribute. Suppose you are selecting fish that inhabit red tanks as follows:

```
FishToDelete := TheFishCollection select:  [aFish | aFish home color = "red"].
```

The concatenation aFish home color is an example of a database path that extends recursively within an object to probe its attribute values. These paths can become quite lengthy, as you saw in Chapter 8's query solutions. To accelerate the operation above, an index must catalog fish records according to a remote attribute in their home tanks. Conceptually, you can envision the index as follows. A B^+-tree guides you to the leaf level by providing a pointer at each level. At each level, you choose the proper pointer by comparing the given tank color with those stored in the index nodes. At the leaf level, you find record addresses, which direct you to the target records. The targets are fish objects although the B^+-tree guides the search by comparing tank colors. This mixing of tank and fish attributes doesn't affect your use of the index. You descend the index by comparing character strings, and you find record addresses at the bottom. You didn't have to access any tank objects to obtain the comparison strings. However, maintaining the index is burdensome. If a tank changes color, many index entries become invalid even though the fish file hasn't changed.

An index that catalogs objects on the basis of returns from database path signals is a **path index**. In general, a database path in a selection operation is a signal concatenation of the form $Xa_1a_2\ldots a_n = v$, where X ranges over the objects under selection. The final comparand, v, is the target value (i.e. a string or number). Suppose X is a collection of class X_1 objects. Then a_1 is an attribute signal, appropriate for class X_1, which returns an object of class X_2. Similarly, a_2 is an attribute signal appropriate for class X_2, which returns an object of class X_3, and so on. Each signal, a_i, elicits an object of class X_{i+1}, which is appropriate for the following signal. An object of class X_n receives the final signal, a_n, and returns a string or number for comparison with the target v.

An index to accelerate these selections must catalog objects of class X_1 in terms of the ordering field a_n of class X_n. You can construct this index without difficulty. To each object of class X_1, you send the database path signal sequence. You insert the returned ordering field value and the X_1 object OID into the B^+-tree. However, maintaining the index is difficult. Data modifications in objects quite remote from the indexed objects can invalidate large portions of the index.

A more direct solution replaces the single index with n indexes as follows. You create an index over class X_n objects with the traditional (i.e., string or numeric) ordering field a_n. The leaf nodes of this index contain the OIDs (i.e., record addresses) of the X_n objects corresponding to particular values of the ordering field. An OID is a bit string, and although it isn't generally meaningful as a number, you can still use it as a number to guide a search through a second B^+-tree. With the OIDs recovered from the first B^+-tree as target values, you enter the second B^+-tree. The leaf nodes of the second index contain OIDs of the X_{n-1} objects that contain a target OID in attribute a_{n-1}. Continuing this process back along the database path, you construct a final B^+-tree that catalogs objects of class X_1 that have a_1 attributes equal to the OIDs from the previous stage. A set of indexes that work together in this manner to simulate a path index is called a **multi-index**.

To apply this philosophy to the short database path aFish home name, you need two indexes. The first catalogs tank objects according to the ordering field "name" and delivers OIDs in the leaf nodes. For example, entering this index with a target value of red locates the OIDs of all red tanks. A second index then catalogs fish objects according to the ordering field "home," which contains only OIDs. However, if you enter the second index with an OID obtained from the first index search, you are requesting fish objects that contain a red tank in their home attribute. The targets recovered from this second index search satisfy the requirement: aFish home name = "red".

The advantage of this approach is that a change in tank objects affects only the first index, which is indeed an index on tank objects. In the general case, a change in class X_i objects affects only the index that catalogs X_i objects. Localizing update consequences makes the index scheme more manageable, but unfortunately it is also less efficient in terms of disk probes. Instead of the two to three probes associated with a single index, you now have $2n$ to $3n$ probes involving n indexes. For long database paths that find frequent use, this penalty is unacceptable. Developing more powerful methods for indexing object-oriented databases continues to be an active area of research.

Object-oriented databases represent objects as records with the usual relocation information and a class identifier. Besides traditional data elements (i.e., strings and numbers), fields can contain OIDs of other objects. You can index objects over attributes that are embedded via other attributes. This results in multi-indexes and path indexes.

The deductive model

Chapter 10 compared logic programs with relational algebra and described how to translate between database predicates and relations. In a deductive database, the axioms declare elementary facts about the application entities, and these facts can be represented in tables. To store the axiom portion of a deductive database, you can therefore use the familiar techniques already described for storing relational tuples. You first pack the records into blocks. You can then construct indexes over the resulting files to accelerate inference-rule processing that involves the ordering field. Suppose a query involves the subgoal fishHasName (X, "flipper"), and assume that you have consolidated the fish entity axioms into a table. You can then use an index on that table's file to quickly locate records pertaining to the fish flipper.

The heads of inference rules define derived database predicates, and according to the correspondence of Chapter 10, you can represent the predicates as tables. So when you use a derived predicate, you are actually generating a temporary relation, at least conceptually. Chapter 9 showed how the inference rules for the derived predicate correspond to the relational algebra operations that construct the temporary relation. The following inference rule, for example, corresponds to a natural join between the relations associated with the predicates A and B.

$$A \ (X, \ Y, \ Z) \ \vdash \ B \ (X, \ Z), \ C \ (Z, \ Y).$$

Because you have already studied indexes that facilitate relational algebra operations, you can apply the same techniques to accelerate inference-rule processing. In this example, you need indexes on the B and C relations, both with ordering field Z. You can use the indexes to scan B and C in sorted order, which allows you to generate the A table in one pass through the operands.

Deductive database operations typically involve the recursive expansion of inference rules to bind query variables to acceptable values. Chapter 9 described a backtracking engine for this purpose and offered suggestions for improved performance. An important requirement is that the deductive query processor have rapid access to the inference rule collection. Usually, the backtracking algorithm is working on a ground instance arising from a subgoal and needs a rule body to expand it. Therefore, you should index the rule collection by the head predicates.

You can implement a deductive database as a collection of tables. Relational algebra operations on the tables generate new tables corresponding to derived predicates. You need indexes to accelerate access to records with particular known fields and to acquire rule bodies for known head predicates.

SUMMARY

You can combine the file organization and rapid access methods of Chapters 14 and 15 to support efficient database operations. For all five database models, the block layout format of Chapter 14 packs records of varying types and lengths into blocks, which allows efficient placement of related records. All the models require joins among the underlying records although the operation is implicit in some models. In all cases, B^+-tree indexes can accelerate join operations.

The relational model offers the cleanest implementation because tables and files, and also table rows and file records, are directly comparable. Moreover, the file representation can achieve unpinned, or minimally pinned, data records. You can implement the deductive model with relations to hold the axioms and with relational algebra to construct new tables equivalent to derived predicates. So you can also achieve minimally pinned data records in the deductive case. The remaining models require data records with headers that bristle with references to related records. Consequently, these records are heavily pinned. The references provide rapid access to related records, but for performance reasons, you must still consider storing related records on the same disk block with their owner. If overflow develops, the related records should appear on adjacent blocks.

In the network database model, you can use the location-mode clause in the schema to command record storage in close proximity to the owner of a relationship chain. By default, the hierarchical model stores records in a physical sequence corresponding to the conceptual hierarchical sequence that defines relationships. However, you can also employ pointer schemes to store records disjointly under indexed or hashed organizations. IMS provides four variations on this theme: Hierarchical Sequential Access Method (HSAM), Hierarchical Indexed Sequential Access Method (HISAM), Hierarchical Indexed Direct Access Method (HIDAM), and Hierarchical Direct Access Method (HDAM). These methods expedite access to the root record of a hierarchy instance but degenerate into slower sequential traversal, or pointer chasing, within each such instance.

The object-oriented model can store objects as file records, but the attribute fields frequently contain OIDs that reference related objects. These OIDs offer the same advantages and disadvantages as the record headers in the network and hierarchical cases. They provide direct disk references for related records, but they pin their host record and therefore complicate record relocations. You need indexes to accelerate query operations, but you may want to index objects according to attribute values in some related objects. For example, you may want to index fish objects according to the color of their home tanks. A direct implementation of this kind of index is a path index. Unfortunately, changes to objects from remote classes can invalidate path index entries. One solution uses a multi-index, a collection of several indexes that separately account for the contributions from each link in the database path.

The relational model

1. The relational version of the library system database has six relations; three of them appear in the following table. Parentheses indicate the primary keys. The last entry for each relation states how many records you could pack into a block if the block were devoted to the single relation type. The packing densities include accommodations for record headers containing flags and an array of field offsets and lengths.

Relation	Attributes	Record count	Maximum records per block
book	(bookno), title, pages, authno	20,000	20
copy	(copyno), cost, bookno, libno	1,000,000	100
library	(libno), libname, location, rooms	2,000	20

Suppose $I_{copy}(\text{libno}) = 2,000$ and $I_{copy}(\text{bookno}) = 20,000$. In other words, the copy records represent all libraries and books. Suggest a file arrangement to accelerate the natural join library $*$ copy $*$ book.

The network model

2. Assume the data volume and distribution of the preceding exercise: 2,000 library records, each 1/20 of a block long, and so forth. Now suppose you store the data in a network database with location modes as specified in the schema excerpt below. You represent network sets with links in the record headers, and you instrument them with the full complement of record pointers. An owner record contains a pointer to the first member record of its chain, and each member record contains forward and backward pointers to other chain members and a pointer to the owner. Assume these pointers are record addresses, each occupying 0.001 block. The record lengths in the table above don't include linkage pointers in the header. Analyze the effort needed to construct the join library $*$ copy $*$ book, and compare the result with the preceding exercise.

```
record library.
   duplicates are not allowed for libno.
   location mode is direct.
      field libno is integer.
      field libname is character 20.
      field location is character 20.
      field rooms is integer.
record book.
   duplicates are not allowed for bookno.
   location mode is calc hashfunc using bookno.
      field bookno is integer.
      field title is character 20.
      field pages is integer.
      field authno is integer.
record copy.
   duplicates are not allowed for copyno.
   location mode is via libHoldsCopy.
      field copyno is integer.
      field cost is integer.
      field bookno is integer.
      field libno is integer.
```

```
network set libHoldsCopy.
   owner is library.
      order is by system default.
   member is copy.
      insertion is automatic.
      retention is mandatory.
      set selection is by application.
      check is libno in copy = libno in library.
network set bookHasCopy.
   owner is book.
      order is by system default.
   member is copy.
      insertion is automatic.
      retention is fixed.
      set selection is by application.
      check is bookno in copy = bookno in book.
```

The hierarchical model

3. Suppose you store the libraries, books, and copies of the preceding exercise in a hierarchical database. Put libraries and copies in one physical hierarchy and put books and virtual copies in a second. Assume virtual parent and child pointers are the same size as the network set linkages of the preceding exercise: 0.001 block. Analyze the join library ∗ copy ∗ book, and compare the result with the network organization above. Assume a HSAM organization of the library-copy hierarchy, and assume that virtual relationships use a virtual child pointer in the parent and virtual parent-sibling pointers in the children.

4. In the hierarchical organization above, assume the book title field occupies 10% of its record length. Suppose further that the image of location across the library records is 200. You want to use the join from the preceding exercise to determine the titles of books available in Seattle libraries. In other words, you want to evaluate the relational algebra expression below. Suggest a processing strategy.

$$\pi_q \sigma_b (\text{library} * \text{copy} * \text{book}), \text{ where } \begin{array}{rcl} b &=& \text{location} = \text{``Seattle''} \\ q &=& \text{title.} \end{array}$$

5. Can you reduce the processing time of the preceding exercise by using a HISAM organization for the library-copy hierarchy? Assume HISAM uses a sparse hierarchical index with a fanout of 100 at each level.

DATABASE DESIGN

PARTS I AND II INVESTIGATED FIVE DATABASE MODELS FROM A CONCEPTUAL viewpoint and presented file organizations that support these conceptual abstractions. Part III takes up design issues. When you design a database application, you must address certain issues that are independent of the particular database model or product that you will use. What are the fundamental application entities, and what are the relationships among them? What constraints restrict the legal database states? Will the database be used primarily as a static reference, or will it continually undergo modifications? What kind of queries will occur? How much technical training will the users have? The design techniques in Part III provide a systematic approach to some of these problems. In particular, you will see that the application constraints and relationships influence how the entities should be dispersed across relational tables.

Database design is a process that discovers the application entities, relationships, and constraints and maps them onto the structures of a given commercial database product. Secondary issues accompany this primary goal, including indexes for performance acceleration, translations from existing application practices, and user interface design. However, the design techniques of Part III deal only with efficiently capturing the application entities, relationships, and constraints.

Chapter 17 presents entity-relationship notation, which allows you to document an evolving database design in a concise manner. The entity-relationship (ER) diagrams don't constitute a database schema because no existing product adheres directly to the notation. Instead, the diagrams serve as a tool for designers while they are working on the database definition. They also serve as documentation for the completed design. The chapter will show how to use ER diagrams to capture the application semantics and how to map the final configuration into a schema for any of the five database models.

To the extent possible in the chosen database model, the DBMS should automatically enforce the application constraints, so users don't have to check continually for database consistency. In many cases, you can ensure constraint enforcement by choosing a particular dispersion of related entities across tables. For example, if the design stores each data element in one place, an update can't change one copy of the element and leave an obsolete second copy at another location. You can express many constraints of this nature as functional dependencies. Chapters 18 and 19 discuss normalization processes, which automatically enforce functional dependencies and similar constraints.

17 Application Design Capture

C REATING A LARGE DATABASE APPLICATION IS A DEMANDING SOFTWARE development task, even without considering the various interfacing programs that will use the database. Moreover, the database component is often just one aspect of a larger project, whose overall goal is to automate the information flow of an enterprise. The previous chapters discussed conceptual mechanisms for organizing application entities and their relationships, but always in the context of a particular database model. This chapter investigates design capture techniques that are independent of the eventual database setting and are therefore suitable for describing the abstract database component of a larger project.

The chapter discusses two database design methodologies: the entity-relationship (ER) model and the object modeling portion of the Object Modeling Technique (OMT). The ER approach is the most widely used database design method, but it is nevertheless only one example of a **semantic** modeling tool. A semantic modeling tool purports to capture subtle aspects of the application meaning. OMT is a more recent approach, which is used primarily in conjunction with object-oriented software design. In either case, you must further transform the outputs of these tools to map a general database design into a specific database schema. This chapter also discusses these mappings.

Software development usually commences with a requirements specification phase, which documents the proposed system behavior. This activity analyzes the application world, the objects that reside in that world, and their interactions. The tools discussed in this chapter represent approaches to organizing the information in the requirement specifications, particularly with regard to the project's database component.

The entity-relationship model

A popular tool for capturing and communicating an application database design, the entity-relationship (ER) data model was developed by P. Chen in the 1970s. The ER model has evolved into several variations, all aspiring to the same goal: the concise capture of the application semantics in terms appropriate for subsequent mapping to a specific database model. As its name implies, the ER model provides a systematic representation

693

of the application entities and their relationships. Although the original ER model gives a philosophical view of how entities, relationships, and constraints can capture the inherent meaning of an application, its most significant contribution is the technique for diagramming the application in a concise, descriptive manner. This discussion deals only with ER diagrams, which are communication devices for designers working to define the database. No commercial database product implements the ER model directly. After defining the application, through the ER diagrams and other documentation, you must translate it to a specific database schema.

 ER diagrams provide a notation for documenting a tentative database design. You capture the important application features with ER diagrams, which you then translate into a specific database schema.

Chapter 2 discussed elementary ER diagrams, and you may want to review that section to refresh your memory on the notation for entities, attributes, and relationships. ER notation represents application entities (classes) as rectangles with the attributes listed inside. Certain typographical conventions indicate key, multivalued, composite, or derived attributes. Because you expect an object to respond to signals appropriate for its class, the lower portion of the entity rectangle lists any special signals beyond the usual read-write actions on the attributes. Relationships are named diamonds with lines connecting the vertices to the participating entities. You can directly represent many-to-many, higher-degree, and recursive relationships, and you can use notations (e.g., multiplicity ratios or participation limits) to document relationship parameters.

ER notation provides the **weak entity** concept for a situation where the entity's objects aren't meaningful as isolated objects in the database. Instead, the objects are meaningful only in the presence of related objects, their dominant partners. In other words, the weak object provides further description of the dominant object, somewhat similar to an attribute but with more complex structure. You make this judgment in the application context. In the aquarium application, you can consider *event* as weak entity. You envision the events for a fish as further descriptive elements of the fish, which help distinguish it from its colleagues. Indeed, in the object-oriented model, the fish's events are the contents of the experience attribute. Therefore, as you'll see later, when you translate an ER diagram into an object-oriented schema, you simply incorporate a weak entity into its dominant entity as an attribute. However, most database models don't support attributes whose values are sets of complex objects. So the weak entity concept is most useful in the ER diagram design phase.

A weak entity is always the dependent participant in a one-to-many or a one-to-one relationship with its dominant partner. ER diagrams use doubled borders to indicate a weak entity and its vital relationship. The weak entity's participation must be total because a weak object can't exist outside the context of its dominant partner. In the aquarium application, for example, an isolated event object isn't meaningful. An event must belong to some fish. In terms of database modification operations, if you delete a fish, you must also delete all its events. The related events aren't meaningful in the absence of the fish, nor can you meaningfully transfer them to some other fish. Figure 17.1 shows the weak entity event with the doubled-border notation.

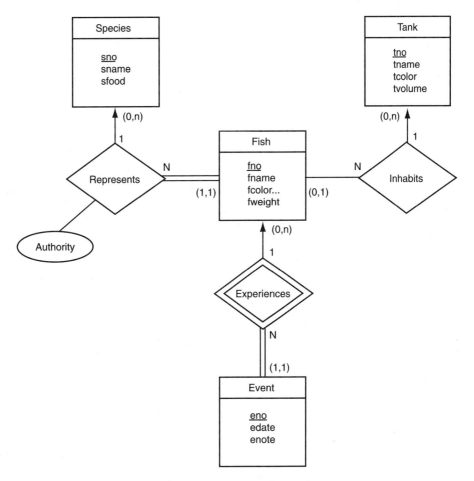

Figure 17.1   Weak entities in an ER diagram

Class hierarchies and inheritance

Although the original entity-relationship model didn't include class hierarchies and lattices, later enhancements added these facilities. These features are most useful if the eventual database deployment will occur in an object-oriented setting. However, even if a different database model is the ultimate target, a superclass-subclass arrangement among the application entities captures more of the application's meaning, and you can map class hierarchy information to non-object-oriented database schemas.

To illustrate subclass hierarchies, consider again the more complex aquarium example of Chapter 7, whose schema appears in Figure 7.12. All aquarium objects are instances of the superclass AquariumClass, which stores general attributes such as creator, creationDate, and modificationDate. Because all objects contain these information items, you have a more efficient representation when the objects inherit the attributes from a common superclass. Subclasses of AquariumClass then define the more specific application entities:

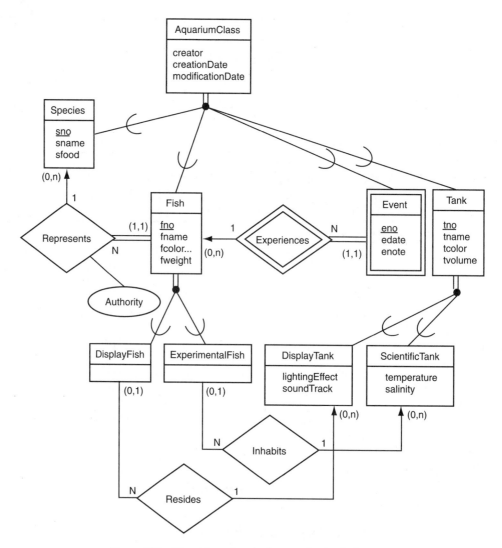

Figure 17.2 Class hierarchies in the aquarium's ER diagram

Species, Tank, Fish, and Event. However, the application needs two specializations of Tank, ScientificTank and DisplayTank; it also needs two kinds of Fish, ExperimentalFish and DisplayFish. The ER diagram in Figure 17.2 summarizes the class structure. Note the mathematical subset symbol, $\subset$, superimposed on a connecting line between a superclass and a subclass. The symbol's closed end appears on the subclass side, in the sense that ScientificTank $\subset$ Tank, because if x is a ScientificTank, it is necessarily a Tank.

As illustrated in Figure 17.2, entities at all levels of the class hierarchy can participate in relationships. The fish entity is a direct participant in the Represents and Experiences relationships. The subclasses, DisplayFish and ExperimentalFish, engage in relationships with subclasses of Tank. When you create a fish object, it is prepared to store fno, fname, fcolor, and fweight values, and also creator, creationDate, and modificationDate values. It inherits the latter attributes from the superclass, AquariumClass. The fish object is also prepared to enter into a Represents relationship with a species object. Indeed, because the diagram specifies total participation of the fish entity in the Represents relationship, the fish object must belong to a Represents relationship grouping. The fish object is also prepared to enter into an Experiences relationship grouping with event objects.

However, you haven't further classified the fish as experimental or display, and therefore it can't enter into either the Inhabits or the Resides relationship. This is unfortunate because the fish object needs to swim in some kind of tank. In this case, you need a notation to specify that a fish object must be further classified as a display fish or an experimental fish. This requirement is a variation on the total participation theme of relationships, and it uses a similar notation. If you double the line leaving the superclass, you imply that all superclass objects must belong to at least one of the subclasses. Stated differently, the superclass objects are the union of the subclass objects. In the aquarium of Figure 17.2, all superclasses are the union of their subclasses.

Class specialization and generalization

The process that derives subclasses from a superclass is **specialization**. A subclass object is a special instance of the superclass. In the aquarium application, a scientific tank is a special kind of tank. Typically, the subclass contains additional attributes that are appropriate for the special instance. For example, the temperature and salinity attributes of a scientific tank are relevant for these special tank objects, but they aren't important for a more generic tank. Note, however, the interaction with the total status of the specialization. According to Figure 17.2, you can never have a generic tank. The notation classifies each tank as display or scientific. Also note that the subclass need not exhibit additional attributes. For example, the DisplayFish and ExperimentalFish specializations of Fish in Figure 17.2 contain no additional attributes. However, these subclasses do provide a basis for insisting that display fish associate with display tanks and that experimental fish associate with scientific tanks.

The process that abstracts from a collection of specialized subclasses to a superclass is **generalization**. So the Tank class is a generalization of the subclasses DisplayTank and ScientificTank. In an application, you may need to view the same object at different levels of abstraction. At times, you may be concerned only with the tank object's more generic attributes: its name, color, and volume. Under other circumstances, you may want to deal with attributes such as temperature and salinity. In this case, you perceive the object in a more concrete manner—as a scientific tank.

You can say that a relationship exists between Tank and ScientificTank, in the sense that the former generalizes the latter. However, you shouldn't confuse this relationship with a traditional database relationship. A database relationship is a pattern, say species-fish, that gives rise to groupings of related objects, say $(s_1, f_1, f_2, f_3, f_4)$. The relationship between superclass and subclass emphasizes different perspectives of the *same* object. You can view a scientific tank as a tank if you aren't concerned with the fine detail that further distinguishes a scientific tank. But you must remember that you aren't dealing with a grouping of related objects. To avoid confusion, this discussion will use the term *relationship* only in the database sense—as a grouping of distinct related objects.

Passing from a superclass to a subclass is a specialization to a more detailed description. Rising from a subclass to a superclass is a generalization to a more generic description.

Consider the fish objects arising from the class structure of Figure 17.2. You don't classify them into display or experimental fish on the basis of some attribute or predicate. Instead, you explicitly create each fish as an instance of the proper subclasses. You may, however, want to use an attribute of the generic fish class to determine the proper subclass. Such an attribute is a **discriminator**. When an object has a discriminator attribute, it can start its existence as an instance of the superclass. Later, you can set the discriminator value and signal the object to change its class to a subclass, as determined by the discriminator.

In the upper part of Figure 17.3, the attribute ftype serves as a discriminator of the fish class. If you place the string display in the ftype attribute of a given object, you intend the object to be a display fish. Likewise, the string experimental indicates the experimental fish specialization. When a discriminator is present, the collection of subclasses is an **attribute-defined specialization**. The discriminator values for the various subclasses appear on the connecting lines, as shown in Figure 17.3.

An alternative to a discriminator is a procedure that the DBMS can invoke to determine the subclass specialization. A procedure can distinguish the subclasses in more complex ways than a discriminator attribute. For example, a procedure may classify a fish object as a display fish if the fname attribute begins with a letter beyond M, if the fcolor attribute is bright orange, if the fweight is less than 10 pounds, and if the object owns more than 25 events. Otherwise, the fish is experimental. In this case, the subclasses are a **procedurally-defined specialization**. The procedure name appears on the connecting line to a subclass, together with the return value for the subclass. The lower portion of Figure 17.3 illustrates a procedurally-defined specialization.

Overlapping subclasses and multiple inheritance

In certain cases, the subclasses don't constitute a disjoint specialization of the superclass. The examples so far classify each generic superclass object into exactly one of the specialized subclasses. This reflects the nature of the aquarium application. Other applications will present more complicated specializations. For example, suppose you upgrade the aquarium to a larger biological park with a more diverse animal population. You classify animals as land-based, water-based, or air-based, as shown in the class hierarchy of Figure 17.4. A particular animal object, say an amphibian (e.g., a frog or a turtle), can then belong to *two* specializations.

In general, you can have an object that resides simultaneously in several subclasses. When the specializations of a superclass aren't disjoint, you need additional notation to emphasize the overlapping subclasses. Various conventions, such as a small "d" or "o" near the branch point leading to the subclasses, denote disjoint or overlapping respectively. This discussion uses the device shown in Figure 17.4, where an arc extends through lines leading to overlapping subclasses. This notation is compatible with the Object Modeling Technique, a competing documentation style that will be discussed later.

The amphibian class occurs as a specialization of both the land-based and water-based classes. An amphibian object then inherits the attributes and operations of both superclasses—an example of **multiple inheritance**. Multiple inheritance changes the

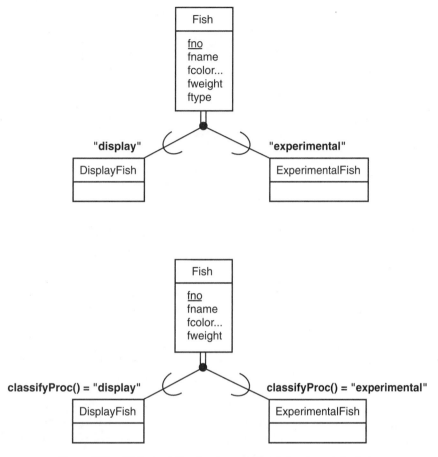

Figure 17.3 Attribute-defined and procedure-defined specializations

topology of the superclass-subclass diagram from a hierarchy to a lattice. The connections between classes are still directed, in the sense that they always proceed from a superclass to a subclass, but they no longer fan out in a strict tree-like fashion.

The application class diagram is a directed acyclic graph (DAG). The DAG can have more than one source. (Recall that a source is a node with no incoming arcs. A tree is a DAG with a single source—the root—and a unique path from the root to any node.) In the absence of multiple inheritance, each node is connected to a single source through a unique path. If you gather all the source nodes as subclasses of an overall application superclass, such as the overriding AquariumClass in the aquarium example, the diagram becomes a tree, provided no multiple inheritance situations occur. After this operation, the original sources nodes are no longer sources because they are now subclasses of the overall application superclass. This overall superclass is the only source in the revised diagram.

On the other hand, a lattice is a DAG without the property that a unique path connects each node to exactly one source. In a lattice, multiple paths can connect a node to the

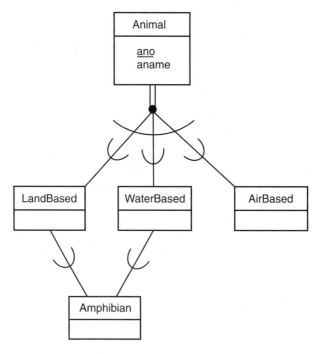

Figure 17.4   Overlapping specialization subclasses

same source or to several sources. If multiple inheritance is present, the application class diagram remains a lattice, even if you gather all the source nodes as subclasses of an overall application superclass.

In Figure 17.4, the amphibian subclass arises when the initial specialization into land-based and water-based subclasses merges to account for objects that fall into both categories. The figure implies that all objects are instances of an ancestor root superclass, Animal. This observation is generally true if the application structure contains a generic application class above all the specific application entities. However, an ER diagram doesn't necessarily represent an object-oriented system where an Object class rules as the ultimate ancestor of all other classes. So multiple inheritance may create a class from two superclasses that don't share a common ancestor. You can simulate this situation in Figure 17.4 by removing the animal superclass. The land-based, water-based, and air-based classes remain, and two of them conspire to produce the amphibian subclass. Note that if a common ancestor exists upstream on two or more paths leading to a subclass created through multiple inheritance, the fanout from that common ancestor must involve overlapping specialization.

The subclasses' disjoint or overlapping nature is independent of the total or partial specialization discussed earlier. A specialization is total if you must classify every superclass object into one or more of the subclasses. The specialization is partial if superclass objects can exist without belonging to any of the subclasses. In either case, you can constrain those superclass objects that are further classified to fall into exactly one subclass (disjoint specialization), or you can allow them to fall simultaneously into several subclasses (overlapping specialization).

 Specialization can be (1) total and disjoint, (2) partial and disjoint, (3) total and overlapping, or (4) partial and overlapping.

When a superclass specializes into subclasses, some aspect of the application usually provides the basis for classifying a superclass object into a particular subclass. For attribute-defined and procedurally-defined specializations, the discriminating criteria appear in the objects as attributes or functions of the attributes. In other cases, the designer envisions a specialization across subclasses but lets the user assign particular objects to particular subclasses. In any case, the classification must use some feature of the application objects. In the example of Figure 17.4, the feature is habitat. You classify an animal according to its habitat: land-based, water-based, or air-based.

You can specialize a superclass on the basis of two or more features. For example, as suggested by Figure 17.5, you can classify a species object as either plant or animal, the traditional first-level breakout of the biological taxonomy. With respect to a different criterion, you can also classify the object as land-based, water-based, or air-based. Multiple inheritance then establishes six additional subclasses: land-based animals (LBA), land-based plants (LBP), water-based animals (WBA), water-based plants (WBP), air-based animals (ABA), and air-based plants (ABP). Subclass objects inherit the appropriate habitat features and also the proper attributes for a plant or an animal.

Subclasses created through multiple inheritance present implementation problems, as you'll see later. The problems aren't insurmountable, and if the final environment is an object-oriented database that supports multiple inheritance, you can easily resolve them. In any case, you should determine that the application truly needs multiple inheritance before including it in your design. If superclasses giving rise to a common subclass have a common ancestor, the specialized subclasses immediately below the common ancestor must overlap. Therefore, you should reconsider the discriminating criterion for that specialization. Can you redefine the specialization so that the subclasses are disjoint? Because multiple inheritance occurs when two of the specialized subclasses merge lower in the lattice, it disappears if the subclasses above become disjoint.

In the aquarium application, the subclasses immediately below the generic Aquarium-Class are Tank, Species, Fish, and Event. Can an object simultaneously be a tank and a species? No. Such overlap isn't in the nature of the application, and similar reasoning holds for the other subclasses. Therefore, this first specialization is disjoint, and the fanout of subclasses under Tank can't have a subclass in common with the fanout under Species. The same is true for any other pair in the first-level specialization. A multiple inheritance situation can still occur *within* the sublattice under Tank, Species, Fish, or Event. But, if this occurs, it is because a common ancestor lower in the hierarchy gives rise to an overlapping specialization. For example, when Tank subdivides into DisplayTank and ScientificTank, that specialization could be overlapping and lead to a multiple inheritance situation within the Tank sublattice. (However, as shown in Figure 17.2, that specialization isn't overlapping, and no multiple inheritance situations occur in the aquarium application.)

702   Database Design

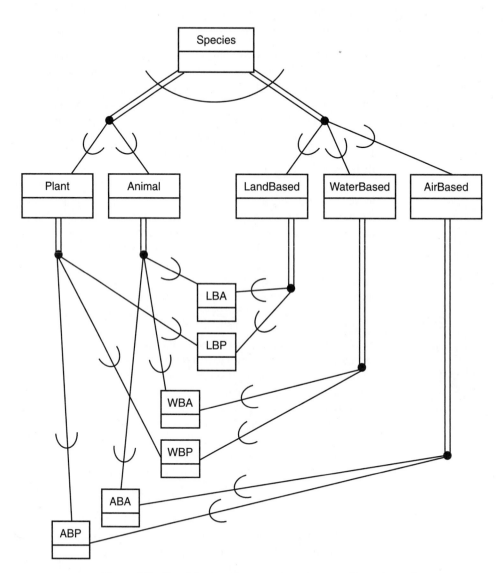

Figure 17.5 Specialization of a superclass along two dimensions

You should always challenge an overlapping specialization with the intent of rendering it disjoint. But keep in mind that overlapping subclasses are sometimes the proper application description. Suppose the application is a university database, where the person entity figures prominently. You need to classify a person object into the subclasses Faculty, Student, Staff, and Administrator because the different person categories have different attribute sets. Inevitably, a faculty member will register for a course and require the additional attributes of a student. Likewise, an administrator will occasionally teach a course, acting like faculty, and a student will monitor a laboratory, acting like faculty. Worse yet, some enterprising person will become involved as faculty, staff, student, and administrator at the same time. Although you might challenge the overlapping specialization in Figure 17.6, you can't reduce it to a disjoint one.

Deeper in the lattice, you can encounter $\begin{pmatrix} 4 \\ 2 \end{pmatrix} = 6$ subclasses that represent persons in two roles, $\begin{pmatrix} 4 \\ 3 \end{pmatrix} = 4$ subclasses that represent persons in three roles, and $\begin{pmatrix} 4 \\ 4 \end{pmatrix} = 1$ subclass for persons in all four roles. Moreover, the subclass for persons in three roles should inherit from the appropriate two-role subclasses, rather than from the original faculty, student, staff, and administrator classes. With this more indirect inheritance, you can generalize the three-role person to any of his two-role possibilities. Similarly, the four-role subclass should inherit from all the three-role subclasses, so you can treat a four-role person as any of the three-role personalities if the need arises.

All eleven multiple inheritance subclasses appear in Figure 17.6. The figure shows how a subclass can inherit the same attributes from different parents because the parents obtained those attributes from a common ancestor. For example, FacStuStaff inherits faculty attributes from FacStaff and also FacStu. In this case, just one set of faculty attributes exists in the FacStuStaff. The application can now view a FacStuStaff object as a FacStaff object, a Staff object, or a Person object. Although Figure 17.6 doesn't illustrate additional attributes, each subclass in the intertwined lattice could contain attributes other than those inherited from ancestors, which would allow the application to discriminate among persons involved in various combinations of roles.

 Overlapping specializations afford opportunities for subsequent merging of the descendants of the specialized subclasses. These merged subclasses represent multiple inheritance situations, which can raise problems in mapping to a database model.

ER diagrams have their limitations. The diagram's intent is to capture the application meaning in a concise visual format. However, the notation supports only certain features, such as entities, various kinds of attributes, relationships, multiplicities, participation limits, subclasses, and inheritance. It has no provision for specifying nonkey functional dependencies. For example, in the original description of the aquarium database in Chapter 2, a constraint specified that tank volume determines tank color. That is, $tvolume \longrightarrow tcolor$. You can't convey this constraint in ER notation.

Other constraints are also beyond ER diagrams' expressive ability. For example, a diagram can't express a constraint that limits the number of sharks in a tank to four. You

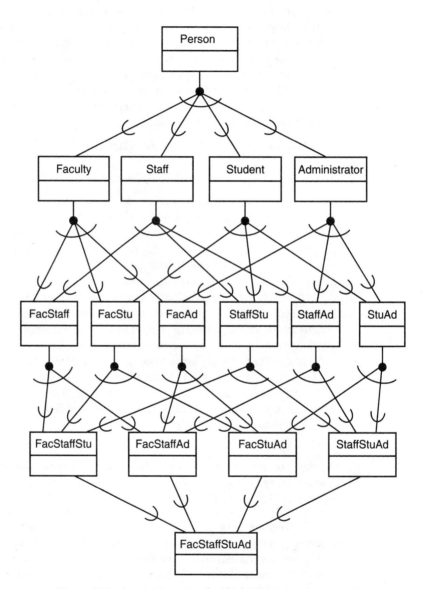

Figure 17.6   An extreme case of multiple inheritance opportunities

can annotate the diagram with additional constraints, but even with such enhancements, you should consider the ER diagram as a partial documentation of the design. You also need a prose commentary to elaborate on the reasoning behind the subclass arrangement, the relationships' meaning, and the attributes' expected domains. The documentation supplements the ER diagram and provides a complete design that you can then map to a particular database schema.

Mapping from ER diagrams to database schemas

This section's first goal is to map an ER design into a relational database schema. As this process unfolds, the discussion addresses the more general problem of expressing the ER diagram's semantic intent through the available features of a particular database model. These same problems arise later in the section, where you learn how to translate an ER design into network, hierarchical, object-oriented, and deductive database schemas. Sometimes you can exactly capture an ER constraint in a database schema. Sometimes you can only approximate it. The supported features and the degree of compromise needed for approximately supported features vary with the database model.

Mapping to a relational schema

In the absence of subclass lattices, you can easily convert an ER diagram into a relational schema. You first examine each entity's attributes. If a composite attribute appears, you flatten the structure and represent each of the leaf attributes separately. For example, you can transform an elaborate version of the fish entity as shown below. You abandon the upper levels of a composite attribute and represent the bottom levels directly in the listing with the other attributes. If the application must refer to the collection of title, first, and last with a single identifier, the interfacing software must reassemble the composite structure from the basic elements. With this transformation, the relational database representation loses a semantic nuance that was present in the ER diagram: the attributes title, first, and last form a meaningful group. This loss is one cost of using the less expressive relational model. It is only the first of many compromises that you must take in the mapping process.

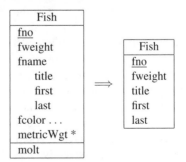

Note also that the mapping above removes the fcolor. . . and metricWgt attributes. Because it is a derived attribute, you can compute metricWgt from more basic sources. You then leave that computation to the interface. For example, you can define a view that materializes metricWgt using a computation over other values. You must remove the multivalued attribute fcolor. . . because a relation can contain only atomic values in each cell. You create instead a new entity, FishColor, and a one-to-many relationship between Fish and FishColor. Each fish can now own many FishColor objects, and each contributes one color to the fish's color scheme. FishColor is then a weak entity that depends on Fish via the IsColored relationship. It contains the single attribute, fcolor, that you transferred from the fish entity. You specify a participation limit of $(1, n)$ for Fish, which documents a constraint that the fcolor... can't be null.

In the absence of subclass complications, the aquarium ER diagram is as shown in Figure 17.1. Only the multivalued attribute fcolor... proved troublesome. Therefore, after resolving this problem by introducing the FishColor entity, you have the transformed diagram in Figure 17.7.

You must factor each many-to-many or higher-degree relationship in the ER diagram by introducing one-to-many relationships and an intersection entity. If necessary, you give key attributes to the original participants of the decomposed relationship. These keys become the foreign keys in the intersection entity. After such decompositions, all relationships are binary and one-to-many. All dominant entities have key attributes. This precaution sets the stage for implementing each one-to-many relationship with a foreign key. You insert the foreign-key attribute in the dependent entry, where it matches the key attribute in the dominant partner. You then shift any attributes associated with a many-to-many or higher-degree relationship to the intersection entity and remove the original relationship.

Checking Figure 17.7, you see that the aquarium example involves no many-to-many or higher-level relationships, so this decomposition step isn't necessary. However, the decomposition of the ship-cargo-port example of Figure 2.27 illustrates how to shift an attribute of a decomposed relationship to the intersection entity. Recall that a relationship attribute is a descriptive feature of a relationship grouping as a whole. When you decompose the relationship into a collection of one-to-many relationships with a new intersection entity, intersection objects are precisely the old relationship groupings. Therefore, you can properly install any relationship attribute as an entity attribute in the intersection.

The decomposition procedure provides a new entity to hold attributes of the decomposed relationship. But what should you do with attributes associated with one-to-many binary relationships that you don't decompose? For example, the Represents relationship in Figure 17.7 is a one-to-many relationship with the attribute *authority*. In these cases, you can fold the attribute into the many side of the relationship. The attribute properly describes a species-fish pair because it contains the person or agency that classified the fish into the species category. However, if you associate that person or agency with the fish, you lose no information. Because the fish-species relationship is many-to-one, you can unambiguously recover the species component if you need it.

Folding the authority attribute into the fish entity constitutes a slight semantic change from the diagram's intent. This compromise is necessary to map the diagram to a relational schema. As when you flattened composite attributes, you must pay a price to force the application into the less expressive relational model. In general, as you pursue mappings to the schemas of the various database models, you will have to compromise some of the ER diagram's semantic intent. The database models simply don't provide the features necessary to preserve all the nuances of the original design. So far you have encountered two such compromises in mapping to a relational schema: flattening composite attributes and shifting relationship attributes to the dependent entity in a one-to-many relationship.

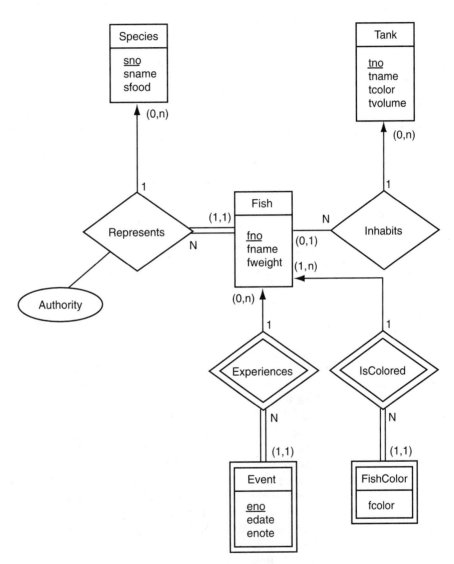

Figure 17.7   The aquarium's ER diagram after adjusting for multivalued attributes

```
create table Tank (
    tno integer,
    tname char(20),
    tcolor char(10),
    tvolume integer,
    primary key (tno) )

create table Species (
    sno integer,
    sname char(20),
    sfood char(20),
    primary key (sno) )

create table Fish (
    fno integer,
    fname char(20),
    tno integer,
    sno integer,
    primary key (fno),
    check (sno is not null),
    foreign key (tno) references tank (tno)
        on delete set null
        on update cascade,
    foreign key (sno) references species (sno)
        on delete cascade
        on update cascade )
```

```
create table FishColor (
    fno integer,
    color char(10),
    check (fno is not null),
    foreign key (fno) references fish (fno)
        on delete cascade
        on update cascade )

create table Event (
    eno integer,
    edate date,
    enote varchar(500),
    fno integer,
    check (fno is not null),
    primary key (eno),
    foreign key (fno) references fish (fno)
        on delete cascade
        on update cascade ).
```

Figure 17.8   Schema resulting from the ER diagram translation

The general rule is to remain as faithful as possible to the diagram's meaning while working within the limitations of the target database model.

The final operation on the ER diagram establishes a foreign key for each one-to-many relationship. You place the foreign key in the non-dominant entity and use the same name as the key of the corresponding dominant entity. For example, you add the attributes sno and tno to the fish entity of Figure 17.7, fno to the event entity, and fno to the FishColor entity. Finally, you define a relation for each of the entities, and the transformation is complete. You can use the primary and foreign-key clauses in SQL to document the relationships. The ER diagram of Figure 17.7 then transforms into the schema of Figure 17.8.

As shown in the figure, you can use relational schema clauses to translate some of the constraints appearing in the ER notation. The fish entity participates totally in the Represents relationship. This constraint means that a fish object must associate with a species object, and you specify that intent with the check constraint in the fish table. The check disallows a null foreign key sno. Because the foreign-key clause establishes sno as a reference to the species table, referential integrity guarantees that the sno attribute will either be null or reference an existing species tuple. The check-clause then tightens the constraint to ensure that sno always references an existing species tuple. You employ the same method to reflect the weak entity status of the event and FishColor tables. You constrain the foreign keys to be nonnull, and an event or FishColor object can then exist only as an extension of a fish tuple.

The on-delete and on-update triggers also reflect the total participation of Fish in the Represents relationship, the total participation of Event in the Experiences relationship, and the total participation of FishColor in the IsColored relationship. In particular, deleting a dominant tuple triggers the deletion of all its related tuples on the dependent side of these relationships. Updating the primary key of a dominant tuple cascades so that the dependent tuples remain linked to the modified dominant tuple.

The weak entity and total participation constraints are similar because both allow a dependent tuple to exist only when linked to a dominant partner. So you can express both in the relational schema with checks that disallow null foreign keys and cascading triggers on delete and update operations. Actually, a slight semantic difference exists between a weak entity and a totally participating entity. An object arising from a weak entity depends completely on its dominant partner for its meaning. In the aquarium case, event is a weak entity, linked to fish. An event object is a record of some experience that happened to a particular fish. If the fish weren't in the database, the event record wouldn't be meaningful. Moreover, it isn't meaningful to transfer an event to a different fish. Total participation, on the other hand, means that every dependent object must enter into a relationship grouping with a dominant object. In the aquarium case, a fish object must be associated with a species object. However, the fish would still be a meaningful application object even if its species were unknown. The constraint merely says that you don't want a fish in the database with an unknown species. The on-delete and on-update triggers aren't capable of distinguishing this difference, so you use the cascade option in both of them. Therefore, you suffer yet another compromise in the ER diagram's semantic intent as you cope with the available features of the relational schema.

In summary, transforming an ER diagram into a relational database schema proceeds as follows.

- You examine each attribute, x, of each entity, E, for the following special cases.

  - If x is a composite attribute, you flatten it. You retain only the leaf entries of the hierarchical structure.

  - If x is a derived attribute, you remove it. You can make it available through a view after you have established the database schema.

  - If x is a multivalued attribute, you create a new weak entity, E_x, and a one-to-many relationship between E and E_x. You move the multivalued attribute to E_x.

- You decompose many-to-many and higher-degree relationships into collections of one-to-many relationships. You transfer any relationship attributes to the intersection entity.

- You fold any relationship attributes attached to one-to-many relationships into the dependent entity.

- You give key attributes to all dominant entities if they aren't already present.

- You give a foreign key to the dependent entity of each one-to-many relationship; you use the same name as the key in its dominant partner.

- You prepare a create-table SQL statement for each entity of the transformed diagram and use the appropriate clauses to enforce key constraints, referential integrity, total participation, and weak entities.

- Anticipating frequent joins across the established relationships, you index all primary and foreign keys—if the database product allows explicit index creation.

 You translate an ER diagram into a relational schema by: (1) transforming multivalued and composite attributes, (2) decomposing many-to-many and higher-degree relationships, and (3) introducing keys and foreign keys. Each entity then becomes a relation.

If the ER diagram includes superclass-subclass lattices, the procedure is somewhat more complicated. Chapter 7 discussed several options for representing class hierarchies as relations, and you should review that material now. The important concept is that various ancestor classes provide more general views of a *single* object. Suppose you create an object, x, according to the class template, C. Then x inherits attributes and operations from all the ancestor superclasses of C, but these alternative views don't constitute other objects. They simply provide different descriptions of the single object, x.

You have three choices for removing a given specialization in the lattice. First, you can transfer all the attributes of the subclasses into the superclass and remove the subclasses. A given superclass object uses the attribute slots for the subclasses to which it belongs and wastes the remaining attribute slots. You place flag attributes in the superclass to mark an object as belonging to one or more of the subclasses. The second alternative transfers the superclass attributes into each subclass and removes the superclass. Because no superclass exists over the subclasses, you must now represent an object that specializes into two or more of the subclasses as two or more distinct objects. This method suffers from redundancy because the superclass attributes repeat in each of the separate objects. This alternative isn't available if the specialization is partial because it leaves no structure to store superclass objects that don't specialize. The final option retains the superclass and the subclasses as distinct entities but connects them with ordinary relationships rather than with a superclass-subclass structure. The circumstances of the particular specialization dictate which route is most appropriate. Figure 17.9 summarizes the details.

Consider the aquarium ER diagram of Figure 17.2. A generic application class, AquariumClass, specializes into the primary application entities: Species, Fish, Event, and Tank. In this case, the best approach transfers the superclass attributes (i.e., creator, creationDate, and modificationDate) to the subclasses. The collapsed ER diagram then appears as Figure 17.10. The figure also shows a different approach to specializations lower in the hierarchy, and those details will be discussed shortly. Because the specialization of AquariumClass into the four application entities is total and disjoint, every AquariumClass object must belong to exactly one of the subclasses. No isolated AquariumClass objects exist that aren't further classified, and therefore you don't need a separate table for such objects. This viewpoint is also appropriate because AquariumClass doesn't directly participate in any relationships. Instead, an AquariumClass object becomes involved with related objects only in its role as a species, fish, event, or tank object.

Even though you don't create a separate AquariumClass entity in this example, consider the configuration that would arise if you were to choose that route. Figure 17.11 shows the relevant portion of the ER diagram, where the AquariumClass remains as a separate entity. When you generate the final tables, AquariumClass becomes a distinct table, as do

Approach	When available	Disadvantages
Replace the superclass and its subclasses with a single class containing the union of all attributes from the superclass and all subclasses.	Always	An object uses only the attributes of the subclasses into which it specializes. The remaining attributes represent wasted storage space. In the extreme case, if the specialization is partial, superclass objects that don't specialize waste the storage slots of all the subclass attributes. If an individual subclass enters into a relationship, you must shift the relationship to the single new class, which raises questions about an object's eligibility for participation in the relationship.
Repeat the superclass attributes in each of the subclasses and retain only the subclasses.	Total specialization only	If the superclass enters into a relationship, you must duplicate the relationship for each subclass, which leads to a greatly expanded diagram. If an object specializes into two or more subclasses, you must represent it as two or more distinct objects, which introduces redundant storage of the superclass attributes.
Replace the superclass-subclass connecting lines with ordinary relationships. Render the subclasses as weak entities with participation limits of $(1, 1)$ and constrain the superclass side of each relationship with a participation limit of $(0, 1)$.	Always	The transformation introduces extra relationships, and inconsistencies can arise even within the constraints commanded by the participation limits.

Figure 17.9 Options for removing a subclass specialization from an ER diagram

Species, Fish, Event, and Tank. The subclasses become weak entities because an object can exist in one of these classes only if it is a specialization of an AquariumClass object. Each AquariumClass tuple relates to a tuple from exactly one of the subclass tables.

Note the participation ratios on the relationships. On the AquariumClass side, the lower participation limit must be 0 because a given AquariumClass tuple must be able to avoid the three relationships that aren't appropriate for it. For example, if a particular AquariumClass tuple is actually a tank, it will partake of an IsTank grouping, which associates it with exactly one tank tuple. The related tank tuple supplies attributes appropriate for a tank. The AquariumClass tuple doesn't partake of the IsSpecies, IsFish, or IsEvent relationships. On the other hand, the participation of the subclass entities must be total. A given fish object, for example, must partake of exactly one IsFish grouping, which associates the fish with its corresponding AquariumClass tuple.

This arrangement doesn't change the storage requirements because each application object still possesses the three AquariumClass attributes plus its subclass attributes. The difference is that Figure 17.11 splits the attribute package of an application object into two parts, keeping the creator, creationDate, and modificationDate attributes in a separate table. The adopted solution of Figure 17.10 keeps all attributes of a given application object together in a single table. Both solutions store the same number of attributes, so neither can claim a space savings over the other. A disadvantage of the separate AquariumClass solution is that it introduces an additional entity and four new relationships into the diagram. When you finally generate the relational tables, you must lace these tables together with keys. Therefore, the following discussion will assume the solution in Figure 17.10, which

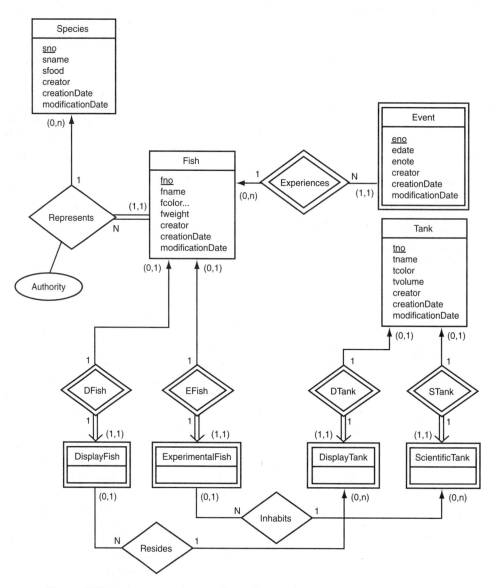

Figure 17.10   Aquarium ER diagram after collapsing the AquariumClass specialization

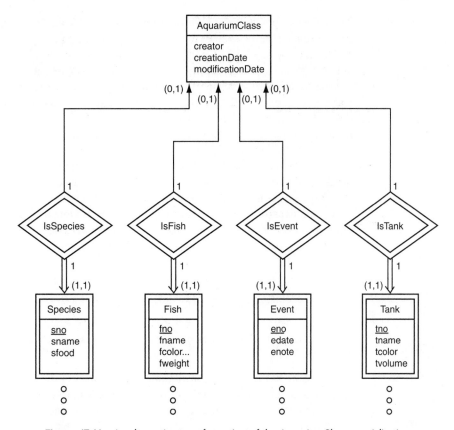

Figure 17.11 An alternative transformation of the AquariumClass specialization

abandons the AquariumClass entity and repeats its attributes in each of the specialized
subclasses.

Although the approach of Figure 17.10 simplifies the eventual relational schema, it
does have a certain disadvantage. Queries specifically concerning a general Aquarium-
Class object now become more complicated. For example, a query to find all creators of
application objects could be phrased as the left excerpt below, if the AquariumClass table
were present. But the adopted solution disperses the AquariumClass attributes across the
subclasses, so you must now express the same query as the lengthier union on the right.

```
select creator              select creator
from AquariumClass.         from Species
                            union select creator
                                    from Fish
                            union select creator
                                    from Event
                            union select creator
                                    from Tank.
```

The solutions above ignore the option in Figure 17.9 that removes the subclasses after transferring all their attributes to the superclass. In the aquarium application, this approach results in a single application class that encompasses Species, Fish, Event, and Tank. An application object is now simply an AquariumClass object, and it uses whatever attributes it needs to reflect its more specialized identity. This alternative not only wastes the storage space associated with the unused attributes, but it also destroys too much of the essential detail of the ER design. The design introduced the various subclasses because the application needs to distinguish among the different kinds of entities. The species entity, for example, partakes of different relationships than the tank entity. If you adopted this approach, the Represents relationship would exist between AquariumClass and itself, and only certain kinds of AquariumClass objects would qualify for participation in the relationship. You can't seriously consider this alternative in the aquarium application because it represents a significant departure from the ER diagram's semantic intent. This is generally the case in other applications as well. Therefore, unless otherwise directed, you should assume that only two approaches are available for removing a specialization from an ER diagram:

- Repeat the superclass attributes in the subclasses and remove the superclass.

- Insert regular relationships between the superclass and each of its subclasses.

You must study the application carefully before making a decision to retain a superclass as a separate table or to copy its attributes into the subclasses. Removing the superclass is appropriate only if the specialization is total and disjoint. If the participation isn't total, you have no choice but to retain the superclass as a separate entity; you need it to house those objects that don't further specialize. If the specialization is overlapping, you have a strong incentive to retain the superclass entity, particularly if the superclass contains a large number of attributes. Finally, if the superclass enters into a relationship and you remove it, you must duplicate the relationship to impinge on each of the subclasses. This produces a more complicated diagram, and the better approach probably retains the superclass. The case with the AquariumClass specialization of Figure 17.2 provides the most compelling scenario for removing the superclass: a total disjoint specialization of a superclass that participates in no relationships. However, removing the superclass does represent one more small deviation from the strict semantics of the ER diagram.

Returning to the solution of Figure 17.10, you decide to treat the remaining specializations by retaining the superclass. The fish superclass enters directly into the Experiences relationship, and you expect queries directed to both the generic tank and fish entities. When you retain the superclass as a separate entity, you can view the various subclasses as trailers that supply attributes appropriate for a particular specialization. For example, a tank object maintains the attributes of a generic tank (i.e., tno, tname, tcolor, tvolume), and it is related to exactly one DTank object or to one STank object, depending on its specialization. That related object acts as a trailer to supply additional attributes as circumstances dictate. In any case, the ER diagram of Figure 17.10 now contains no superclass structures, so you can convert it into a relational schema as discussed earlier.

Two methods are available to reduce superclass-subclass specializations from an ER diagram before mapping to a relational schema. You can duplicate the superclass attributes in the subclasses, or you can introduce restricted relationships between the superclass and each subclass.

Although multiple inheritance didn't occur in the aquarium example, you can handle it with the techniques discussed above. Consider the situation in the upper portion of Figure 17.12, which transforms to the lower part of the same figure. Suppose a particular A object specializes to both B and C subclasses. In the given solution, it will then participate in exactly one isB grouping with a B object and exactly one isC grouping with a C object. From a relational viewpoint, you can think of the A object as an A tuple, which associates with two extensions: one providing B attributes and the other providing C attributes. If these B and C extension objects connect with the same E object, via isE and isE' respectively, the E object serves as an additional extension, which contains the E attributes.

When you convert the entities to tables, you embed the key attribute of the superclass in the subclass extension. You can then reassemble a complete object as needed. As illustrated in Figure 17.13, an E tuple contains foreign keys b_1 and c_1, enabling recovery of the appropriate segments from the B and C tables. Each of these tuples contains a foreign key into the A table to obtain the most ancestral attributes. You must remember that the attributes $(a_1, a_2, b_1, b_2, c_1, c_2, c_3, e_1, e_2)$ describe a *single* application object. The representation with multiple tables is a convenience for mapping into a relational database system, which doesn't support subclass lattices.

The multiple table representation offers opportunities for inconsistencies to creep into the database. Suppose an E tuple references B and C extensions, as shown in Figure 17.13, but these extensions refer to different A tuples. This error shouldn't occur because it implies that two A objects are involved in the generalization of the E object. If the most recent SQL version is available, you can include a constraint assertion in the schema to prevent this error. The schema for the situation of Figures 17.12 and 17.13 would then appear as shown in Figure 17.14. Note the lattice integrity check at the bottom of the schema.

Of course, you must compose other guard assertions to prevent other inconsistencies, such as an A tuple branching to two distinct E tuples. In any case, you can stretch the relational model to accommodate class hierarchies and lattices. The extension does require some care to guard against inappropriate liaisons among the new relating entities that replace a superclass-subclass specialization. If you take proper precautions to ensure that the relational linkages don't lead to inappropriate connections, the question of attribute inheritance along two or more paths isn't troublesome. For example, in Figure 17.13, an E tuple inherits attributes a_1 and a_2 along two paths: one through the B ancestor and one through the C ancestor. However, if you properly constrain the associations with SQL assertions, either path terminates at the same A tuple, so either delivers unambiguous values for a_1 and a_2.

You can map all the features of an ER diagram, including subclass lattices, to a relational schema. Some ER constraints, particularly consistency restrictions arising from multiple inheritance, require create-assertion SQL statements.

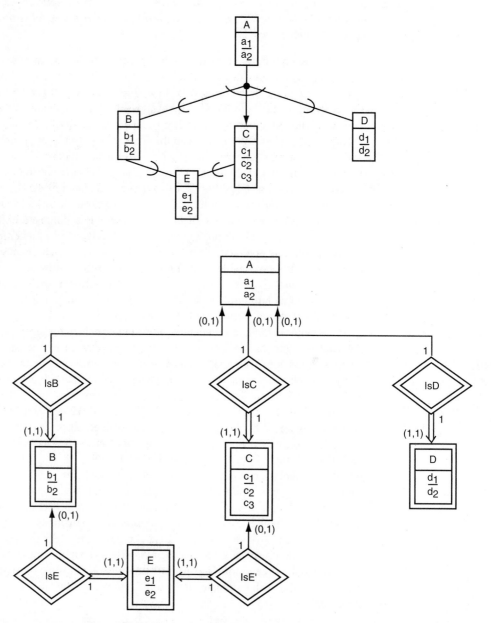

Figure 17.12 Elevating multiple inheritance classes to new entities

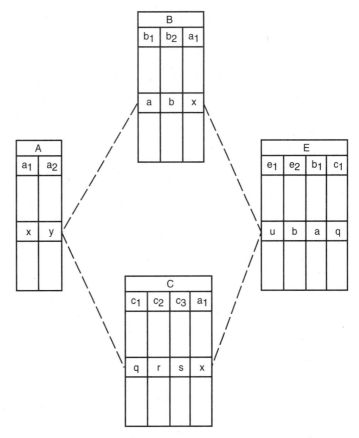

Figure 17.13   Relational tables from the multiple inheritance lattice of the preceding figure

Mapping to a network schema

Mapping from an ER diagram to a network database schema proceeds in a similar fashion. In particular, you can remove subclass hierarchies and lattices in the same way. Some network database products support composite and multivalued attributes, so in that case, you don't need to transform those specialized attributes. The original CODASYL proposal includes composite attributes, modeled after the hierarchical data structures of the COBOL Data Division. It also supports multivalued attributes, again patterned after a similar COBOL construction. If these features aren't available in the network database product at hand, you must perform the transformations discussed earlier to flatten composite attributes and to export multivalued attributes to a new weak entity. You must again remove derived attributes, under the assumption that the interfacing software can recompute them as necessary. Next, you decompose many-to-many and higher-degree relationships in the standard fashion, creating an intersection entity that can absorb any relationship attributes. If relationship attributes remain, necessarily attached to one-to-many relationships, you fold them into their associated dependent entities. Because the relationships will eventually become owner-

```
create table A (
    a₁ integer,
    a₂ integer,
    primary key (a₁) )
create table B (
    b₁ integer,
    b₂ integer,
    a₁ integer,
    primary key (b₁),
    foreign key (a₁) references A (a₁) on delete cascade on update cascade,
    check (a₁ is not null) )
create table C (
    c₁ integer,
    c₂ integer,
    c₃ integer,
    a₁ integer,
    primary key (c₁),
    foreign key (a₁) references A (a₁) on delete cascade on update cascade,
    check (a₁ is not null) )
create table D (
    d₁ integer,
    d₂ integer,
    a₁ integer,
    primary key (d₁),
    foreign key (a₁) references A (a₁) on delete cascade on update cascade,
    check (a₁ is not null) )
create table E (
    e₁ integer,
    e₂ integer,
    b₁ integer,
    c₁ integer,
    foreign key (b₁) references B (b₁) on delete cascade on update cascade,
    check (b₁ is not null),
    foreign key (c₁) references C (c₁) on delete cascade on update cascade,
    check (c₁ is not null) )
create assertion latticeIntegrity check (not exists
    (select *
    from E
    where 1 ≠
        (select count(*)
        from A
        where exists
            (select * from B where A.a₁ = B.a₁ and B.b₁ = E.b₁)
        or exists
            (select * from C where A.a₁ = C.a₁ and C.c₁ = E.c₁))).
```

Figure 17.14 An SQL assertion for consistency among classes of a subclass specialization

coupled network sets, you don't need to place primary keys in the dominant entities or foreign keys in the dependent entities. Nevertheless, a network schema can include clauses that require foreign-key references (e.g., set-selection or check), so you may want to include these keys in the dependent entities anyway. The decision depends on the given application.

If you perform these operations on the aquarium ER diagram of Figure 17.1, you obtain Figure 17.15. Assuming that the target database can't handle repeating data items, the solution exports the multivalued attribute fcolor to a new weak entity. Anticipating the need for set-selection and integrity checks in the network schema, it also includes foreign keys in the dependent entities. To generate the network schema from the revised ER diagram, you create a record type for each entity and an owner-coupled network set for each relationship.

Unlike the relational schema, the network schema can distinguish between a weak entity and a totally participating entity. You specify the total participation of a regular entity with an automatic-insertion clause and a mandatory-retention clause, as illustrated with the Represents network set of Figure 17.16. Under this arrangement, you can remove a fish record from a species chain if you immediately connect it to another species chain. By contrast, you use a fixed-retention clause with the weak entities, event and FishColor, which forces event and FishColor records to remain forever on the fish chain where they were first attached.

If subclass lattices appear in the ER diagram, you can restructure them before generating the network database schema. For example, the more elaborate aquarium diagram of Figure 17.2 transforms into Figure 17.10, just as in the relational translation. However, you must express the new relationships, such as DFish, EFish, DTank, and STank, as owner-coupled network sets. This requirement presents no technical difficulty, but unlike the relational schema, a network schema has no provision for specifying constraints to ensure that attribute packages broken across several record types recombine to form a single object. The specialization of fish into display and experimental fish is total and disjoint. Therefore, you must prevent a given fish from having records on both its DFish and EFish chains. Likewise, you must prevent a given fish from having more than one record on its DFish or EFish chain. The interfacing software must shoulder this burden because the network schema can't express the constraints.

You also handle multiple inheritance with the techniques already discussed. For example, the situation at the top of Figure 17.12 transforms to the configuration at the bottom. It represents superclasses as distinct entities that relate to their subclasses through relationships with restricted multiplicities. The only difference from the relational case is that you must express the relationships with owner-coupled network sets. The relational example of Figure 17.13 then appears as Figure 17.17 in the network case. An A record that specializes to both B and C subclasses picks up the corresponding attributes with isA and isB chains. An A record that doesn't further specialize has empty chains; an A record that specializes only as a B subclass object has an empty isC chain. In any case, at most one member record can appear on either chain. The E record inherits from both the B and C records with the isE and isE' chains. Again, you must take precautions to ensure that any such arrangement corresponds to a single application object when you reassemble the attribute packets. The network schema can't express this constraint, so you must write routines to manipulate the A, B, C, D, and E records as a group.

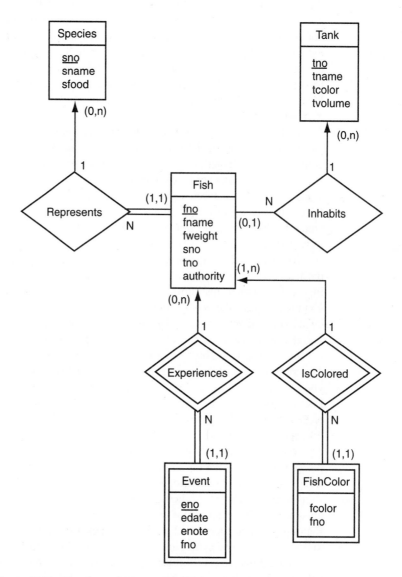

Figure 17.15 Transformed aquarium ER diagram just before generating a network schema

```
record Species.
   field sno is integer.
   field sname is character 20.
   field sfood is character 20.
record Fish.
   ⋮
network set Represents.
   owner is Species.
      order is sorted by defined keys.
   member is Fish.
      insertion is automatic.
      retention is mandatory.
      key is ascending fname.
   set selection is structural
      sno in Fish = sno in Species.
   check is sno in Fish = sno in Species.
network set Inhabits.
   owner is Tank.
      order is sorted by defined keys.
   member is Fish.
      insertion is manual.
      retention is optional.
      key is ascending fname.
   set selection is structural
      tno in Fish = tno in Species.
   check is tno in Fish = tno in Tank.
```

```
network set Experiences.
   owner is Fish.
      order is sorted by defined keys.
   member is Event.
      insertion is automatic.
      retention is fixed.
      key is ascending edate.
   set selection is structural
      fno in Event = fno in Fish.
   check is fno in Event = fno in Fish.
network set IsColored.
   owner is Fish.
   member is FishColor.
      insertion is automatic.
      retention is fixed.
   set selection is structural
      fno in FishColor = fno in Fish.
   check is fno in FishColor = fno in Fish.
```

Figure 17.16   Skeletal network schema from the ER diagram of the preceding figure

Because of this difficulty in maintaining a consistent representation, you should carefully evaluate the decision to break the lattice into separate entities linked with highly constrained relationships. An alternative route keeps all the attributes together but wastes space for those records that don't require the specialized fields. You also need flag fields to maintain the record's subclass designations, which allow you to control which records participate in which relationships. The interfacing software must then monitor the flags to make sure that inappropriate records don't enter certain relationships. An earlier discussion criticized this approach because it collapses the specializations and masks the distinctions captured in the ER diagram. Moreover, other problems arise if the individual subclasses partake of separate relationships. You must weigh these disadvantages against the added nuisance of one-record chains in each of several new network sets.

 You can map ER diagrams to a network database schema with the same transformations used for a relational target. The difference is that you use owner-coupled network sets to translate the final one-to-many relationships rather than foreign-key associations.

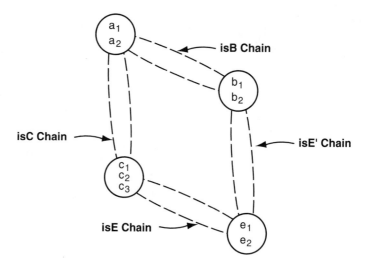

Figure 17.17 Network realization of the attribute packet links from a multiple inheritance lattice

Mapping to a hierarchical schema

If the target database environment is hierarchical, you must subdivide the ER diagram into hierarchies before you can write the schema. The preliminary operations proceed as before. You flatten composite attributes, remove derived attributes, export multivalued attributes to a new weak entity, decompose many-to-many and higher-degree relationships into one-to-many relationships with an intersection entity, and transfer relationship attributes to the intersection entities or fold them into the dependent side of a one-to-many relationship. As in the network mapping, you don't need to instrument the dependent entities with foreign keys because logical adjacency in the hierarchical schema will maintain the relationships. The network mapping for the aquarium application retained the foreign keys because they were useful for integrity checks and set-selection clauses. The hierarchical model provides neither of these features, so you should suppress the foreign keys.

These preparatory operations on the aquarium ER diagram of Figure 17.1 yield the transformed diagram of Figure 17.18, which shows two hierarchies. All entities, except species, appear in a maximal hierarchy rooted in the tank entity. The species and fish entities then constitute an auxiliary hierarchy, where fish enters as a virtual child. This choice is displayed in Figure 17.18. The alternative is a maximal hierarchy rooted in species, which contains all entities except tank. Tank and fish then constitute the auxiliary hierarchy. Without information on the nature of query and update activity, the choices are symmetrical. However, if most database activity involves the tank-fish relationship, Figure 17.18, together with a HSAM or HISAM physical organization, is the preferred choice. It packs tanks together with their fish, which facilitates processing across the more frequent relationship groupings.

Because of the hierarchical structure, all dependent entities are totally participating weak entities. A dependent record necessarily relates to the closest preceding dominant parent record in hierarchical sequence. A dependent record can't exist in the structure

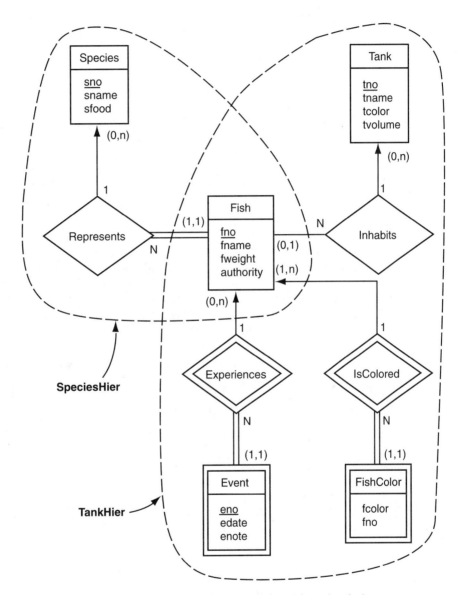

Figure 17.18   An ER diagram with hierarchies identified

```
segment Tank;                              segment Event;
    root of TankHier;                          parent Fish;
        field tno integer no duplicates;           field eno integer no duplicates;
        field tname char(20);                      field edate char(20);
        field tcolor char(20);                     field enote char(100);
        field tvolume integer;                 segment FishColor;
segment Fish;                                      parent Fish;
    parent Tank;                                   field fcolor char(20);
        field fno integer no duplicates;       segment Species;
        field fname char(20);                      root of SpeciesHier;
        field fweight integer;                     field sno integer no duplicates;
        field authority char(20);                  field sname char(20);
        virtual parent/sibling Species/Fish;       field sfood char(20);
                                                   virtual child Fish;
```

Figure 17.19 Hierarchical schema corresponding to the ER diagram of the preceding figure

without a dominant record. Therefore, you can't express the partial participation of the fish entity in the Inhabits relationship. This inaccuracy is limited to the Inhabits relationship because the remaining relationships are all total, The distinction between a weak entity and a totally participating entity, such as the fish component of the Represents relationship, is also lost. Furthermore, the participation limit, $(1, n)$, which describes the role of Fish in the IsColored relationship is beyond the syntax of a hierarchical schema. The constraint requires a fish to have at least one color, and it can have many colors. However, you can't control the number of fishColor records inserted in hierarchical sequence after a given fish. The implied participation of any dependent entity is always $(0, n)$.

If you can't capture a constraint in the schema, you must enforce it through the application software, sometimes through unnatural contortions. For example, to support the partial participation of Fish in the Inhabits relationship, you can create an artificial tank, where you place fish that aren't related to any real tank. With these warnings, the hierarchical translation of Figure 17.18 appears in Figure 17.19. It differs very little from the schema of Figure 12.14.

  An ER diagram without subclass structure translates reasonably well into a hierarchical database schema although the transformation treats all dependent entities as weak entities. You solve the multiple parentage problem in the usual manner by identifying separate hierarchies and joining them with virtual relationships.

If subclass structures appear in the ER diagram, you again look to the two principal reduction methods discussed earlier: you can repeat the superclass attributes in the subclasses or convert the superclasses into distinct entities connected to their subclasses with constrained relationships. In the latter case, the objects in the subclasses provide trailers to add the attributes associated with a particular specialization.

Consider again the more elaborate aquarium application of Figure 17.2. The first approach is appealing for the initial AquariumClass specialization. The specialization is total and disjoint, and the superclass contains only a few attributes. The first step, therefore, progresses toward the transformed diagram of Figure 17.10. But if you use the approach in Figure 17.10 for the remaining specializations, you encounter multiple parentage in the entities associated with tank and fish. You can conveniently interpret a one-to-one relationship to place the dependent entity on either side. So, reading from Figure 17.10, consider the tank entity as the parent of both DisplayTank and ScientificTank, which in turn serve as parents for DisplayFish and ExperimentalFish respectively. Because you are pursuing a hierarchy, ExperimentalFish can't have another parent, so you must interpret the one-to-one EFish relationship as connecting to the child Fish. Similarly, the DFish relationship must extend to the child Fish. However, Fish then has two parents, ExperimentalFish and DisplayFish.

You can salvage the situation by regarding Fish, with its DisplayFish or Experimental-Fish trailer, as the single child of Tank, with its appropriate trailer. However, this viewpoint actually retreats to the reduction method from Figure 17.9 that was rejected earlier as usually inappropriate. You have copied the subclass attributes into the superclass and eliminated the subclasses. In the aquarium example, the specialized subclasses of Tank and Fish add no attributes. They are present only to participate preferentially in separate relationships. To track this distinction, you can introduce flags in the enlarged superclass. The aquarium example then regresses to the simpler representation of Figure 17.20, and you can generate the hierarchical database schema as in the discussion without subclass structures. However, you can no longer associate experimental fish with scientific tanks through a relationship separate from that which connects display fish with display tanks. Instead, you must use the DispFlag, ExpFlag, and SciFlag attributes to mark the suppressed specializations and burden the application software with the task of constraining the proper subclasses of fish to the appropriate subclasses of tanks.

When you introduce new relationships to separate a superclass from its subclasses, you will probably encounter multiple parentage problems, which will make a hierarchical translation more difficult. The preceding example didn't pursue the usual route for resolving multiple parentage problems in a hierarchical database. That route identifies a distinct hierarchy that intersects the original in a virtual child. Although this approach is standard for application entities, it can multiply the number of hierarchies excessively if you use it to deal with the multitude of new relationships introduced in a superclass-subclass transformation. Therefore, the technique illustrated in the last example is preferable if you can execute it with minimal disruption to the design. This was the case in the example.

However, in general, many subclasses may specialize a given superclass, and each subclass may have a long list of attributes and participate in a separate collection of relationships. In this case, collapsing all the subclasses into the superclass destroys much of the ER diagram's semantics. So, depending on the situation, you may prefer to introduce new hierarchies and virtual relationships to keep the subclasses as distinct entities.

Multiple inheritance situations also give rise to multiple parentage problems that complicate a translation into a hierarchical database schema. Figure 17.12 illustrates this point. You can retain the transformation in the lower part of the figure if you implement it as two hierarchies. One hierarchy is rooted in A and contains C, D, and E; the other is rooted in B and contains E as a virtual child. Moreover, A contains B as a virtual child. Although this arrangement preserves the identity of all subclasses, it constructs a complicated structure

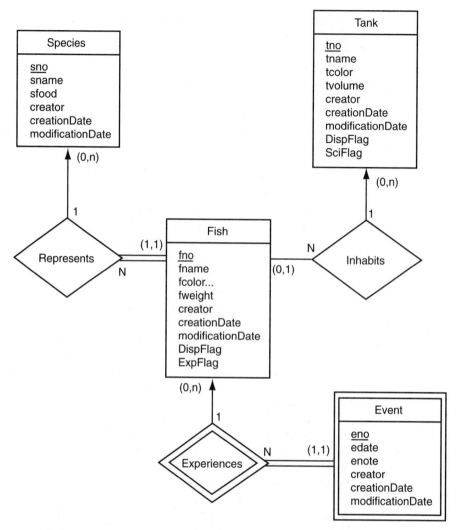

Figure 17.20   Eliminating subclasses before translating to a hierarchical schema

that may not be consistent with the rules of the hierarchical database product. Some hierarchical products, IMS, for example, don't allow a virtual child to possess a further virtual child. The solution here stipulates B as the virtual child of A and E as the virtual child of B. This solution, therefore, isn't available for an IMS database.

If the individual subclasses don't partake of separate relationships with the rest of the design, an effective approach collapses all of A, B, C, D, and E into a single entity and provides slots for all possible attributes. The single entity must contain flags to distinguish among the suppressed subclasses. Although this compression hides certain semantic features of the ER diagram, it may provide the only viable solution when the final database target is hierarchical. Recall that the hierarchical model predates by decades the more re-

```
Object subclass:  "NameStruct"
   instanceVariables:  ("title", "first", "last")
   constraints:  (("title", String), ("first", String), ("last", String)).
Set subclass:  "StringSet" constraint:  String.
Object subclass:  "AquariumClass"
   instanceVariables:  ("creator", "creationDate", "modificationDate")
   constraints:  (("creator", String), ("creationDate", String), ("modificationDate", String)).
AquariumClass subclass:  "Fish"
   instanceVariables:  ("fname", "fcolor", "fweight", "home", "breed", "experience", authority)
   constraints:  (("fname", NameStruct), ("fcolor", StringSet), ("fweight", Number),
      ("breed", Species), ("experience", EventSet), (authority, String)).
      .
      .
      .
```

Figure 17.21   Partial object-oriented translation of the aquarium ER diagram

cent development of subclass lattices. Therefore, it's not surprising that multiple inheritance situations are difficult to accommodate.

 Subclass structures, especially overlapping specialization and multiple inheritance, are difficult to incorporate into a hierarchical schema. Sometimes the only solution collapses a subclass lattice into a single entity with flags denoting the suppressed subclasses. The interfacing software assumes the burden of preferential treatment for subclass objects.

Mapping to an object-oriented schema

From the above discussion, you can conclude that ER diagrams, even those that involve subclass lattices, map rather comfortably into relational database schemas. They map less comfortably, however, into network database schemas. The greatest difficulty occurs when the database target is hierarchical: multiple parentage complications can force significant compromise of the ER diagram's semantic features. Consider now a mapping to an object-oriented schema, which directly supports subclass hierarchies. A problem arises only in the case of multiple inheritance because some object-oriented systems allow only subclass hierarchies, not the more general subclass lattice. For the moment, therefore, assume that the ER diagram contains no multiple inheritance specializations. This condition holds in the aquarium example of Figure 17.2.

Each entity in the ER diagram becomes an application class structure. You start by considering the various kinds of attributes that can appear in a class. Because the object-oriented model allows attribute values to be complex objects, you can directly accommodate multivalued and composite attributes from the diagram. You express a multivalued attribute as a collection, where you constrain the members as appropriate. For example, you can map the multivalued fcolor of the fish entity to a collection of character strings.

Using Chapter 7's notation, Figure 17.21 shows a portion of the object-oriented schema corresponding to the ER diagram in Figure 17.2. The fish class definition includes a constraint on the fcolor attribute, which restricts its value to objects of the StringSet class. The schema defines StringSet, in turn, as a collection of character strings. A fish object, therefore, contains a string collection in its fcolor attribute, which allows it to hold any number of colors. This capability means that you don't have to export multivalued attributes to weak entities, as was the case with the other models so far.

Furthermore, you don't have to flatten composite attributes before mapping to an object-oriented schema. Figure 17.2 shows fname as a composite attribute, constructed from a title, a first name, and a last name. The schema of Figure 17.21 creates a class called NameStruct by declaring three attributes—title, first, and last—each constrained to contain a string. It then requires the fname attribute to contain a NameStruct object. You can mirror any composite attribute as a nested arrangement of other objects, so you can always create a special class of objects appropriate for a composite attribute domain. In the fish class, the composite fname is a structure composed of three strings. In general, the composite can be a structure comprising many objects, and each object can itself be composite.

Finally, you can express derived attributes with class methods that perform the appropriate computations. For example, in Chapter 7's format, the following class method delivers the derived attribute, metricWeight.

```
Fish method:  "metricWeight" code:  [^(fweight / 2.2)].
```

As shown in Figure 17.21, you position the AquariumClass class directly under the generic Object class of the database environment. You then establish other application entities as subclasses of AquariumClass. The specializations DisplayFish and ExperimentalFish become subclasses of Fish; the specializations ScientificTank and DisplayTank become subclasses of Tank. Therefore, the subclass hierarchy maps directly to the object-oriented database schema, where all the various attribute types appear as objects of the appropriate class.

You then express the relationships by embedding related objects within each other. The Represents relationship of Figure 17.2 is one-to-many from Species to Fish, and the Fish participation is total. As shown in Figure 17.21, each fish object associates with exactly one species object, which occurs as the breed attribute value in the fish. A constraint restricts the breed attribute to a species object. However, you must enforce the total participation with special methods that create and modify fish objects. These methods ensure that the breed attribute isn't null. The Experiences relationship is one-to-many from Fish to Event, and you handle it in the same manner. A fish object contains its collection of events in the experience attribute, which you constrain to collections of event objects.

Both relationships involve symmetrical representations in the mating entities. A species contains a fish collection in its reps attribute; a fish contains its owning species in its breed attribute. These attributes are inverses of each other in the sense that the breed attribute of a fish, x, contains the species object that classifies the fish. In the path notation of Chapter 8, if f is a fish, $f \in f$ breed reps; and if s is a species, $s == s$ reps breed. Similarly, an event object contains a subject attribute, which holds the fish that experienced the event. These mutual inclusions are the conceptual mechanism for expressing object-oriented relationships. Because the ER notation is similar, translation into an object-oriented database schema isn't complicated with the preparatory transformations that occur in the other database models.

In summary, to translate a one-to-many relationship, you include the dominant object in the dependent entity and a collection of dependent objects in the dominant entity. You can also directly express many-to-many relationships. If the fish entity isn't present, you can still express a many-to-many relationship between Tank and Species. Each tank object will contain an attribute holding a collection of related species objects; each species object will contain an attribute holding a collection of related tank objects. The representation differs from a one-to-many relationship only because collections appear on both sides.

Although the mechanism handles many-to-many relationships without difficulty, you should still consider the possibility of factoring the relationship into two one-to-many relationships with an intersection entity. The new entity often plays a meaningful role in the application, and in any case, you may need it if relationship attributes appear in the ER diagram. You can fold relationship attributes attached to a one-to-many relationship into the dependent entity, as discussed earlier. However, you can't transfer a relationship attribute of a many-to-many relationship to either entity because the attribute describes a pair of objects, one from each participating entity. Relationship attributes, therefore, properly belong in the intersection entity.

You can also handle higher-degree relationships with direct mutual embeddings although the embedded objects become complicated structures. Suppose an n-degree relationship exists among entities $X_1, X_2, \ldots, X_n$. You can endow X_1 with an attribute containing a collection of lists. Each list takes the form $(x_2, x_3, \ldots, x_n)$, where x_i is a class X_i object. An X_1 object can then recover all its relationship groupings by adding itself to each list in the attribute. Of course, you need similar arrangements in the remaining entities. However, as discussed in Chapter 7, a simpler solution decomposes the n-degree relationship into n one-to-many relationships between the original participants and an intersection entity. Even if the intersection entity doesn't serve a meaningful application role, you need it to house relationship attributes.

 An ER diagram maps directly into an object-oriented database schema because subclass hierarchies transform directly into a class structure. You can place composite and multivalued attributes directly in the classes because they allow complex objects as attribute values. You then represent relationships with mutual embeddings.

Overlapping specialization and multiple inheritance may not be supported by the target object-oriented database environment. In this case, you perform the transformation shown in Figure 17.12, where each specialization becomes an ordinary relationship with restricted participation limits. The subclasses provide trailer objects to complete their superclass counterparts. When you translate the relationships to mutual embeddings, a related collection of objects appears, as shown in Figure 17.22. You must remember that all these objects actually correspond to a *single* application object. At the highest level of generalization, the object exhibits only a_1 and a_2 attributes. If you examine it in greater detail, the object specializes into one or more of the subclasses—B, C, and D—and you can find these extensions as embedded objects in the B-ext, C-ext, and D-ext attributes. The extensions do invoke distinct objects, but that is an unfortunate consequence of the representation arrangement, which attempts to make up for the absence of overlapping specialization.

The extension attributes provide a close-up look of the application object, which is more detailed than the class-A view. To view a further specialization as an E object, you examine the E-ext attribute of either the B or C extension. These extensions must refer to

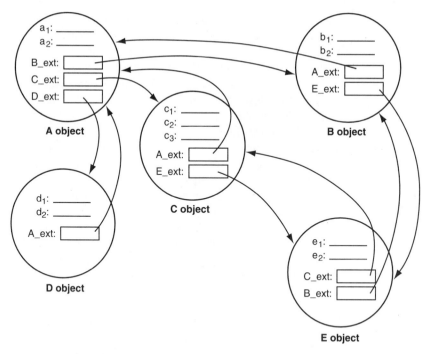

Figure 17.22: Object embeddings that arise from overlapping specialization and multiple inheritance

the same object, so an opportunity for inconsistency arises here. The methods that create and update the subclass objects must ensure that the embedded E objects arising from B and C embeddings in a single A object are identical. In the strong identity notation of Chapter 7, you must have x B-ext E-ext == x C-ext E-ext, for every A object, x. Similarly, the A objects reached through the B-ext and C-ext attributes of a given E object must be strongly identical. In general, the constraints must ensure that a reassembled package of attributes corresponds to a single application object.

Consider the example in Figure 17.12. If the subclasses don't enter into separate relationships, you can collapse all the attributes into the superclass, A, and add flags to mark the suppressed subclasses. This is the first alternative listed in Figure 17.9. However, this route has a considerable disadvantage because it collapses semantic distinctions that the ER diagram has taken pains to distinguish.

Mapping to a deductive schema

The final mapping translates the ER diagram into a deductive database schema, which is a collection of attribute and relationship predicates (i.e., the axioms) and inference rules that extend the axioms. To assert that an application object possesses some attribute value, you use predicates such as fishHasName (X, Y), which is true when fish X has fname Y. You also use existence predicates, such as fish (X), to assert that X is a fish object. Therefore, binding values, X, must exist that make the predicate true.

Existence predicates	
aqObj (X)	species (X)
fish (X)	event (X)
tank (X)	displayFish (X)
experimentalFish (X)	displayTank (X)
scientificTank (X)	

Attribute assertion predicates	
aqObjHasCreator (X, Y)	aqObjHasCreationDate (X, Y)
aqObjHasModificationDate (X, Y)	
speciesHasSno (X, Y)	speciesHasSname (X, Y)
speciesHasSfood (X, Y)	
fishHasFno (X, Y)	fishHasFname (X, Y)
fishHasFcolor (X, Y)	fishHasWeight (X, Y)
eventHasEno (X, Y)	eventHasEdate (X, Y)
eventHasEnote (X, Y)	
tankHasTno (X, Y)	tankHasTname (X, Y)
tankHasTcolor (X, Y)	tankHasTvolume (X, Y)
displayTankHasLightingEffect (X, Y)	displayTankHasSoundTrack (X, Y)
scientificTankHasTemperature (X, Y)	scientificTankHasSalinity (X, Y)

Figure 17.23 Attribute and existence predicates from the translation of the aquarium ER diagram

These binding values are tantamount to application object identifiers. To facilitate the ER diagram translation, you need an object identifier attribute in each source entity. A source entity for this purpose is an entity that doesn't have a superclass within the application. In Figure 17.2, all aquarium objects are some specialization of the root class, AquariumClass, and therefore you can place the identifying attribute in that class. If the application has several root classes, you must place separate identification attributes in each of them. You could develop the aquarium example without the unifying AquariumClass entity. In that case, you would supply identifying attributes for Species, Fish, Event, and Tank. The identifying attribute serves as a unique key for each object. Subclasses don't need such identifiers because they represent more detailed descriptions of their superclasses, and they inherit the identifier. From this point on, assume you have modified Figure 17.2 by adding the aqObj attribute to the AquariumClass entity.

You then establish the attribute predicates as illustrated in Figure 17.23. The true instances of the existence predicates occur when X binds to the aqObj attribute of an application object that specializes as indicated by the predicate. For example, fish (X) is true when X binds to the aqObj attribute of a fish object. The true instances of the attribute assertion predicates occur when the X variable binds to the aqObj attribute of an application object and the Y variable binds to the appropriate descriptive attribute of the same object. For example, the true instances of fishHasColor (X, Y) occur when X binds to the aqObj attribute of a fish object, and Y binds to a string describing one of the fish's colors.

Multivalued attributes present no problem in this context. If the aqObj value of a fish is 42, you assert that the fish has colors red, white, and blue by including the following ground literals among the axioms:

```
fishHasFcolor (42, "red")
fishHasFcolor (42, "white")
fishHasFcolor (42, "blue").
```

This representation actually differs very little from an earlier solution, where you exported the fcolor attribute into a weak entity. Here, the set of `fishHasColor (X, Y)` axioms constitutes a tabulation of that weak entity, and it relates back to the proper fish through the aqObj common attribute. You don't need to dwell on this equivalence: just note that multivalued attributes give rise to multiple entries in the axiom tabulations.

You can flatten composite attributes so that only the leaf components appear in the axiom tabulations, or you can introduce a new entity to hold structures of the appropriate type. In the ER diagram of Figure 17.2, fname is a composite attribute, consisting of three strings—title, first, and last. You can create a new entity, NameStruct, containing the three attributes: title, first, and last. If you place the new entity under AquariumClass, it inherits the object identifier, aqObj. If you make it a separate root class, you must include an object identifier attribute in it. Then, for example, you document the fact that Dr. Fried Flipper is a NameStruct object as follows.

```
nameStructHasTitle (72, "Dr.")
nameStructHasFirst (72, "Fried")
nameStructHasLast (72, "Flipper").
```

Here, 72 is the identifier of the NameStruct object. The attribute assertion `fishHasFname (X, Y)` now has the entry `fishHasfName (42, 72)` in the axiom tabulations, which reflects the fact that fish 42 has the fname attribute given by NameStruct 72.

You can express derived attributes with aggregate predicates as described in Chapters 9 and 10. For example, to obtain the metric weight of a fish, you add the following inference rule to the database:

$$\text{fishHasMetricWeight (X, Y)} \vdash \text{fishHasFweight}_2^{Z/2.2} \text{ (X, Z, Y).}$$

Recall that the DBMS evaluates aggregate predicates operationally. If $P_n^f(X_1, X_2, \ldots, X_n, Y)$ is an aggregate predicate, the DBMS first computes the table of true bindings for the underlying predicate P. It then partitions that table on the first n attributes and applies the function f to each partition grouping. Finally, it forms a new table with one row for each group. For each group, it copies the first n attributes from the old table because they must be constant over the rows of that group. For the last cell, Y, it installs the result of the computation f on the group. Chapters 9 and 10 describe the details of this operation.

The translation converts relationships in the ER diagram into relationship predicates in the deductive axiom schema. A relationship of degree n, without attached attributes, gives rise to a relationship predicate with n arguments. If relationship attributes occur, each such attribute adds another argument to the resulting predicate. For example, you can tabulate the relationships of the aquarium application (Figure 17.2) as Figure 17.24. The true instances occur when X and Y bind to aqObj values of related objects.

Predicate	Interpretation
represents (X, Y, Z)	fish X represents species Y according to authority Z
experiences (X, Y)	fish X experiences event Y
inhabits (X, Y)	experimentalFish X lives in scientificTank Y
resides (X, Y)	displayFish X lives in displayTank Y

Figure 17.24   Relationship predicates from the aquarium ER diagram

You formulate constraints as inference rules with false heads. These rules help you capture multiplicity and participation limit constraints of the ER diagram. For example, to assert the total participation of the fish entity in the Represents relationship, you add the following inference rules to the database:

$$\text{false} \vdash \text{fish (X)}, \neg\text{classifiedFish (X)}$$
$$\text{classifiedFish (X)} \vdash \text{represents (X, Y, Z)}.$$

Using an aggregate predicate, you constrain the Represents relationship to be one-to-many from Species to Fish as follows:

$$\text{fishSpecies (F, S)} \vdash \text{represents (F, S, A)}$$
$$\text{false} \vdash \text{fishSpecies}_{\text{i}}^{\text{count}} \text{(F, C)}, \text{C} > 1.$$

The following inference rules ensure that experimental fish are associated with scientific tanks:

$$\text{false} \vdash \text{inhabits (F, T)}, \text{scientificTank(T)}, \neg\text{experimentalFish (F)}$$
$$\text{false} \vdash \text{inhabits (F, T)}, \text{experimentalFish(F)}, \neg\text{scientificTank (T)}.$$

Finally, you can enforce the total specialization of Fish into its two subclasses as follows:

$$\text{false} \vdash \text{fish (X)}, \neg\text{displayFish (X)}, \neg\text{experimentalFish (X)}.$$

 An ER diagram maps to a deductive database schema with attribute and relationship predicates. You use inference rules to materialize derived attributes and to enforce the diagram's constraints.

Overlapping specialization and multiple inheritance difficulties don't occur in mapping to a deductive schema. The existence axioms catalog the application objects into their various subclasses. You then represent overlapping specialization by two or more ground instances in the axiom tabulations, which correspond to simultaneous subclassification into two or more subclasses. If the fish object with aqObj value 42 were simultaneously a display fish and an experimental fish, the following ground literals would appear among the axioms:

$$\text{fish (42)}$$
$$\text{displayFish (42)}$$
$$\text{experimentalFish (42)}.$$

You can handle multiple inheritance in a similar fashion. Consider the case of Figure 17.12, which has plagued the mappings to other database models. An axiom E (X) is available to restrict X bindings to E objects, and if the axiom tabulation is consistent, B (X), C (X), and A (X) will all deliver true ground literals for this same binding. The attributes contributed by the different subclasses are then available from the attribute predicates. Because all the bindings refer to a single application object through the unique object identifier bound to X, no question can arise about inheriting A attributes across conflicting paths.

Multiple inheritance and overlapping specialization, therefore, present no special problems in recovering information from the structure—if the axioms are consistent. You can assert further inference rules to control that consistency. Consider again the example of Figure 17.12. The following rules force an interlaced collection of A, B, C, D, and E objects to correspond to a single application object:

$$
\begin{aligned}
&\text{false} \vdash \text{E (X), } \neg\text{B (X)} \\
&\text{false} \vdash \text{E (X), } \neg\text{C (X)} \\
&\text{false} \vdash \text{B (X), } \neg\text{A (X)} \\
&\text{false} \vdash \text{C (X), } \neg\text{A (X)} \\
&\text{false} \vdash \text{D (X), } \neg\text{A (X).}
\end{aligned}
$$

You can apply similar constraints to every specialization in the diagram. Each rule simply asserts that a subclass member, as distinguished by the identifying attributes of the source classes, is also a member of its superclasses.

Object Modeling Technique (OMT)

ER diagrams contain many object-oriented concepts. However, several competing notations are used in the world of object-oriented software design and development. This section briefly presents the Object Modeling Technique (OMT) of Rumbaugh and his colleagues as an alternative to ER diagrams. OMT consists of several phases; this discussion deals only with the part that describes the static structure of the data—the attributes, the subclass lattice, and the relationships among the classes.

OMT represents entities as rectangles, just as in ER diagrams, but it immediately calls them classes. Much of the OMT notation is then devoted to describing the various subclass specializations that can occur. The apex of a small triangle points to a superclass; the base of the triangle extends to a line segment for attaching subclasses. Disjoint specialization is an open triangle; overlapping specialization is a darkened triangle.

Figure 17.25 uses OMT notation to describe the multiple inheritance configuration of Figure 17.12. You list attributes inside the class rectangles, a convenient option that was adopted for ER diagrams earlier. You indicate class methods in a lower window in the rectangle. For database design, you assume that the attribute read-write methods are always available, so you don't include them in the OMT diagram. Instead, you list specialized methods. These methods can compute a derived attribute or perform some action expected of an object in the application context. You may, for example, want a fish to respond to a molt signal by rotating its color scheme. Special annotations mark attributes as key, multivalued, or composite. This discussion continues with the underline, ellipsis, and indentation conventions from ER diagrams.

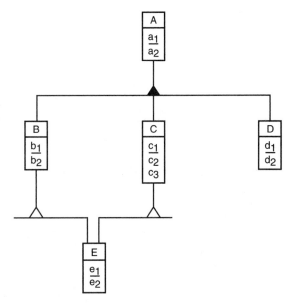

Figure 17.25   OMT notation for overlapping subclasses and multiple inheritance

Because most application relationships are binary, an OMT diagram uses the ER diamond only for the occasional higher-degree relationship. OMT notation usually doesn't name relationships: it represents a binary relationship between two classes simply as a line segment connecting the classes. However, it denotes the multiplicities of the participating classes with special terminators where the line segments impinge on the class rectangles. Suppose a line connects classes X and Y, as shown in the variations of Figure 17.26. No terminator on the Y end implies that a given X object associates with exactly one Y object. This default condition is equivalent to a participation limit of $(1, 1)$ on the X end of the relationship. An open circle on the Y end indicates that a given X object associates with zero or one Y objects, which corresponds to a participation limit of $(0, 1)$ on the X end. Finally, a closed circle on the Y end specifies that a given X object associates with zero, one, or more Y objects. In other words, the participation limit of X is $(0, n)$. Various combinations of these markings, used on both sides of the relationship, quickly convey the most common constraints. You can use numerical annotations in less frequently occurring cases. For example, a participation limit of $(2, n)$ becomes a 2^+ where the relationship line joins the constrained class. Figure 17.27 illustrates these conventions. It is the OMT equivalent of the aquarium ER diagram in Figure 17.2.

Figure 17.27 also illustrates a rectangle hanging off the relationship link to display relationship attributes. The rectangle appears as a class, except that it has no name. This convention strongly suggests the intersection class that results when you decompose a many-to-many relationship. Indeed, an earlier discussion emphasized the intersection class as the proper repository for relationship attributes. The relationship between Species and Fish in the figure is one-to-many rather than many-to-many. A one-to-many relationship presents a less persuasive argument for a separate intersection class although you could still

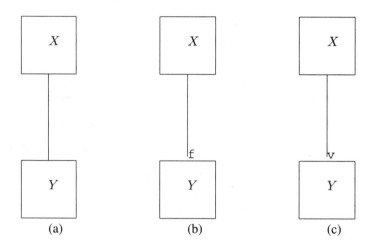

X   X   X

f   v

Y   Y   Y

(a)   (b)   (c)

Figure 17.26 Expressing relationship multiplicities with OMT diagrams

create one. As with ER diagrams, no ambiguity results if you transfer the authority attribute to the fish class, but some loss of application semantics will occur because the classifying authority actually describes a species-fish grouping.

 OMT is an alternative notation to ER diagrams. OMT emphasizes the object-oriented aspects of a database design, but it also provides graphical features to represent relationship constraints usually seen on ER diagrams.

Using a slightly more compact notation, an OMT diagram conveys the same information as an ER diagram. Therefore, you can use the same techniques to translate an OMT diagram into any one of the five database schemas. The emphasis on the class structure and the suppression of relationship names reflect the OMT's origins in object-oriented analysis, but OMT and similar tools are becoming more popular in a wider context.

OMT gives special emphasis to a particular situation where a single dominant class enters into several one-to-X relationships with its dependent classes. The relationships all share a common grouping theme: the dependent objects are components in the associated dominant object. Generally, when a dominant class associates with several dependent classes, the sense of each relationship can be different. For example, the upper part of Figure 17.28 shows a tank class entering into separate one-to-many relationships with each of Fish, Worker, and Cleaning. The sense of each relationship is unique to the participating partners. A fish object swims in the tank, a worker maintains the tank, and a cleaning record documents an activity on the tank. By contrast, the diagram at the bottom of the figure illustrates a situation where all relationships share the sense. The dependent objects are the constituents of the dominant object. Such an arrangement is an **aggregation** because

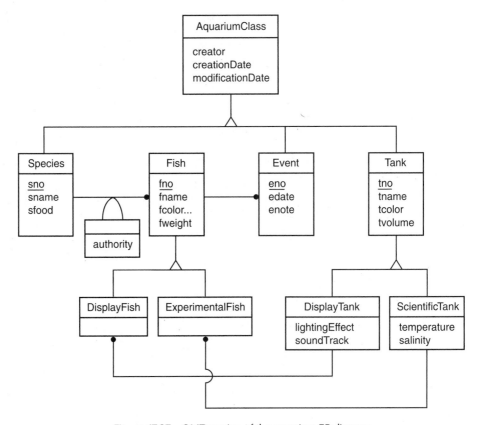

Figure 17.27   OMT version of the aquarium ER diagram

the dominant object is an aggregate of the dependent objects. This use of the term bears no relation to SQL aggregates or aggregate predicates.

OMT emphasizes this specific use of a collection of one-to-X relationships with a special notation. When the relationship sense is aggregation, OMT specifies small diamonds at the dominant ends of the connecting line segments. An aggregate class is usually the target of many such diamond-tipped relationship lines, which indicates that a dominant object is constructed from components in the dependent classes. Figure 17.29 shows the correct notation for the situation in the lower part of Figure 17.28.

You can also use this notation in the recursive case, where all the components of the dominant objects are of the same class and each serves as a dominant assembly for yet additional components. This arrangement is simply the parts database, which has appeared repeatedly in earlier chapters to illustrate recursive many-to-many relationships. The OMT diagram in the upper portion of Figure 17.30 illustrates the situation. There, an assembly is a more specialized view of a component. The more specialized view shows how to construct the assembly from its components. If desired, you can also interpret each of the components as an assembly and continue the recursion.

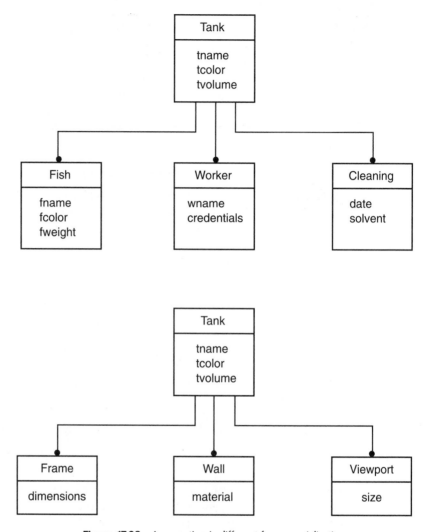

Figure 17.28 Aggregation is different from specialization

For a given root component, this reasoning generates a parts explosion. The alternative parts implosion is also available. You note that a given component contributes to many assemblies, and you then generalize each of the assemblies to a component, which is recursively housed in further assemblies.

You can factor the many-to-many relationship in the usual manner, which produces the diagram in the lower portion of the figure. In the upper diagram, the relationship attribute, quantity, stores a count of the number of times a given component appears in a given assembly. Following the standard practice, you transfer this attribute to the intersection class, Use. You can then envision an assembly as an aggregation of many Use objects, each representing a particular component. Similarly, you can interpret a component, somewhat

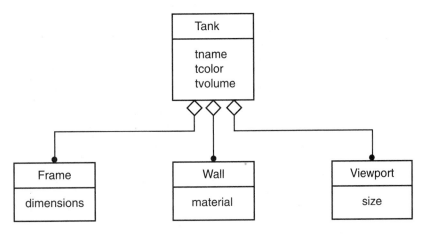

Figure 17.29 Using aggregate symbols to display relationships

broadly, as an aggregation of many Use objects, each identified with an assembly to which the component contributes.

An explosion of a particular component takes a specialized view of the component as an assembly and tabulates its related Use objects. Each Use object uniquely identifies another component, and you can recursively apply the process to that component. An implosion of a particular component tabulates its Use objects, each identifying a unique assembly. A general view of each such assembly reveals that it is a component, and you can recursively apply the process to it.

SUMMARY

In contrast with the database schemas of the previous chapters, the notational models introduced here don't provide machine-readable definitions of database designs. Instead, designers use the new models to discuss and document a database definition before they map it to a particular database schema. Entity-relationship (ER) diagrams are currently the most popular tool. However, competing notations, such as the Object Modeling Technique (OMT), are gaining acceptance because of the increasing importance of object-oriented software development methods. Both methods are semantic modeling tools: they attempt to capture subtle nuances in the application's meaning.

ER diagrams represent application entities as named rectangles, which are surrounded by ovals containing their attributes. You can also record the attributes inside the entity rectangle and use conventions for marking the various attribute types (e.g., multivalued, derived, composite, or key). You show relationships as named diamonds with connecting lines to the participating entities; you indicate relationship constraints with multiplicity ratios, participation limits, arrowheads, and total-partial participation lines.

A weak entity object is meaningful only when related to a dominant object. A weak entity always associates with its dominant partner through a many-to-one or one-to-one relationship. Graphically, you depict both the weak entity rectangle and its crucial connecting relationship with doubled borders. The participation of a weak entity must be total.

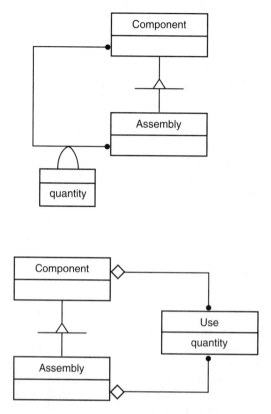

Figure 17.30 Recursive aggregation in OMT diagrams

ER diagrams use class hierarchies and lattices to show specialization of a superclass entity into subclasses. The notation is a connecting line with a superimposed subset symbol, ⊂. Subclasses inherit the attributes and operations of their superclasses. A subclass specialization can be total, meaning that you always view a superclass object as a generalized view of one or more subclasses. Or it can be partial, meaning that a superclass object can exist without further specialization. To indicate total specialization, you double the connecting line impinging on the superclass.

Independent of its total-partial status, a specialization can be disjoint or overlapping. In a disjoint specialization, an object that is further classified must belong to exactly one of the subclasses. Overlapping specialization occurs when an object belongs simultaneously to two or more subclasses. A thorny issue, which causes difficulties when mapping an ER diagram to a database schema, is multiple inheritance. In multiple inheritance, a class inherits attributes from several superclasses. Multiple inheritance and overlapping specialization frequently occur together because the subclasses of the overlapping specialization can rejoin deeper in the lattice in a multiple inheritance situation.

You can map an ER diagram to any of the five database schemas. However, the mappings frequently compromise semantic distinctions documented in the diagram. ER-to-relational mapping occurs most frequently. If there is no subclass structure, the mapping proceeds by flattening composite attributes, removing derived attributes, exporting multivalued attributes to weak entities, and factoring all many-to-many and higher-degree relationships through an intersection entity. You then transfer relationship attributes to the intersection entity, or you fold them into the dependent side of a one-to-X relationship. All dominant entities receive primary keys, and all dependent entities receive foreign keys of the same name. Each entity then becomes a relation.

If subclass specializations are present, you must remove them before the transformation. The most semantically damaging approach collapses a specialization into the superclass, providing slots for all possible attributes and flags to mark the suppressed subclasses. A less drastic alternative repeats the superclass attributes in the subclasses, but this approach is available only when the specialization is total. A final possibility converts subclasses to full-fledged entities and connects them to the superclass with restricted relationships. All three techniques share the disadvantage of masking semantic nuances in the ER diagram.

You can map the ER diagram into a network schema in much the same way, except you express the relationships with owner-coupled network sets. To translate to a hierarchical schema, you must first deal with the subclass structure and then separate the diagram into several hierarchies to avoid multiple parentage. Removing a subclass specialization frequently introduces many multiple parentage situations, which make the translation awkward. Consequently, the least appreciated approach, collapsing the specialization lattice into a single class, may often be the only reasonable solution, even though it significantly compromises the ER diagram.

An object-oriented mapping easily accommodates a class hierarchy, and you can also handle the various types of attributes without regard to their special status. Furthermore, you can directly express relationships, even many-to-many and higher-degree relationships, through mutual embeddings. Nevertheless, you will often want to factor these relationships because you must house relationship attributes in the intersection entity.

You begin a mapping to a deductive schema by establishing unique key attributes in all the application source objects. You then compose attribute assertion predicates and relationship predicates to reflect elementary facts about the objects identified by these keys. You remove subclass lattices as in the other models and use inference rules to enforce a consistent representation of an application object that has been dispersed across several subclass objects.

OMT diagrams provide an alternative to ER diagrams. They use similar graphical devices to capture analogous features of entities and relationships. Entities, now called classes, are rectangles that contain attributes and interfacing operations. Binary relationships are simple line segments connecting the participating classes, with special terminators for the most common participation limits. Subclass specialization appears as a triangle with the apex connected to the superclass and the base extended to attach the subclasses. A darkened triangle implies overlapping specialization; an open triangle means disjoint specialization. OMT has no notation for total versus partial specialization. However, it does use a distinctive notation for aggregation, a collection of one-to-X relationships that describes a dominant object constructed from dependent components.

The entity-relationship model, class hierarchies and inheritance, mappings from ER diagrams to database schemas, and Object Modeling Technique

1. Prepare an ER diagram for the following application without introducing any new entities. A library system contains libraries, books, authors, and patrons with key attributes libno, bookno, authno, and patno respectively. Libraries are further described by a libname and location, books by a title and page count (pages), authors by an authname, and patrons by a patname and patweight. Author-book is a one-to-many relationship; library-book is a many-to-many relationship. A library can hold many copies of a book, and a book can appear in many libraries. A book and a library enter into a relationship grouping by sharing a copy. This relationship instance has a cost attribute, which states how much the library paid for the book. Patron-library and patron-book are many-to-many relationships. When a patron borrows a book, the transaction creates an instance of the patron-book relationship and attaches a duedate attribute to it.

2. Sketch an ER diagram of the library application in the preceding exercise. Use only one-to-many relationships.

An engineering company has several projects in progress. Each occupies the full attention of several engineers. Moreover, each engineer is working on at least one project, and each project has at least one engineer. Each engineer has a crew of laboratory assistants who report only to that engineer. No assistant is without an engineering supervisor. Furthermore, each engineer supervises at least two assistants. Each laboratory assistant has exclusive ownership of a collection of instruments. Each instrument is owned by an engineering assistant. However, a particular assistant may own no instruments. The key attributes of project, engineer, assistant, and instrument are pno, eno, ano, and ino respectively. Each entity is further described with a name: pname, ename, aname, or iname.

3. Construct an ER diagram for the engineering application.

4. Construct a relational schema from the ER diagram of the engineering application.

5. Construct a network schema from the ER diagram of the engineering application.

6. Construct a deductive schema from the ER diagram of the engineering application.

7. Construct an object-oriented schema from the ER diagram of the engineering application.

8. Construct an OMT diagram equivalent to the ER diagram of the engineering application.

A farm has fields to plow, tractors to do the plowing, and farmers to ride the tractors. When all three factors come together, some work is accomplished. A field is a (fno, fname) pair, and fno is the key. Tractors are (tno, tname) pairs, and farmers are (fmrno, fmrname) pairs in the same tradition. When a field, a farmer, and a tractor perform work, the hours attribute in the corresponding relationship instance measures the amount of work. The relationship instance also contains a second attribute, expense, which is the hours attribute times $15.00.

9. Devise an ER diagram that can handle multiple occurrences of the same field-tractor-farmer relationship with potentially different hours and expense attachments. You must achieve this goal without decomposing the ternary relationship between fields, tractors, and farmers.

10. Revise the ER diagram of the preceding exercise to decompose the ternary relationship and absorb the relationship data into the intersection entity.

11. Create a relational schema from the revised ER diagram.

12. Create a network schema from the revised ER diagram.

13. Create a deductive schema from the revised ER diagram.

14. Create an object-oriented schema from the revised ER diagram.

15. Draw an OMT diagram equivalent to the revised ER diagram.

A literary collection contains books, each with a bibliographic section referencing other books. Suppose a book is a (bno, btitle) pair, and bno is the key. You are interested in the number of times that book Y cites book X, and therefore you attach the descriptive attribute, ncite, to the recursive relationship.

16. Construct an ER diagram showing the recursive relationship between the book entity and itself but without further decomposition.

17. Revise the ER diagram of the preceding exercise to decompose the recursive many-to-many relationship and absorb the relationship attribute.

18. Create a relational schema from the revised ER diagram.

19. Create a network schema from the revised ER diagram.

20. Create a deductive schema from the revised ER diagram.

21. Create an object-oriented schema from the revised ER diagram.

22. Draw an OMT diagram equivalent to the revised ER diagram.

18 Functional Dependency Analysis

APPLICATION CONSTRAINTS CUSTOMIZE A DATABASE SO THAT IT CLOSELY represents the corresponding application miniworld. Chapter 17 discussed notational tools for capturing an application's entities and relationships. With these tools, you can constrain the application objects in general terms. For example, you can specify multiplicity ratios and participation limits on relationships, distinguish total from partial entity participation in a relationship, establish class hierarchies and lattices, and distinguish disjoint and overlapping specializations. The database designer uses these constraints to rule out certain database states as invalid or inconsistent.

Consider the aquarium application. The ER diagram of Figure 17.1 specifies that every fish object must pair with a species. If the database state includes an unpaired fish, it is inconsistent or invalid. The database should never enter such a state because the aquarium miniworld will never exhibit the corresponding real-world state. If the database arrives in an inconsistent state, it is no longer an accurate mirror of the aquarium reality.

You can map a database design, as given by an ER or OMT diagram, onto a database schema, but the database models vary greatly in their ability to express constraints from the diagram. Sometimes you can't specify a design constraint in the schema because the target database model doesn't possess the necessary features. Sometimes you can partially express the constraint in the schema, but you must leave full enforcement to the interfacing access programs. In any case, the intent is always the same: you strive to include design constraints in the schema, if possible, so the DBMS can assume the burden of ensuring a continually consistent database state. Omitting these constraints has many disadvantages: inconsistent constraint enforcement across the suite of access programs, duplicated effort in many programs to enforce the same constraint, and the necessity to discipline the users to access the database only through controlled procedures.

In addition to the structural constraints noted on ER diagrams, functional dependencies form another broad class of constraints that frequently appear in applications. Generally speaking, a functional dependency requires that matching values appear in certain related attributes. This chapter analyzes methods that you can use to enforce functional dependency constraints. Functional dependency analysis usually assumes a relational database context, so this chapter and the next will follow that tradition.

Sources of functional dependency constraints

Recall that a relation consists of two parts: the relational schema and the relational body. The schema provides the attributes, and the body contains the tuples defined over these attributes. For this discussion, R, or some variation such as R' or R_i, will denote a relational schema and $r(R)$ will denote the corresponding body. Therefore, R is a set of attributes, and $r(R)$ is a set of tuples.

The universal relation and its projections

Chapter 2 defined a functional dependency constraint as follows. Suppose R is a relation. If X and Y are subsets of R, then $X \longrightarrow Y$ is a constraint on all relational bodies, $r(R)$, such that any two tuples from $r(R)$ that agree on the X attributes must also agree on the Y attributes. You read as $X \longrightarrow Y$ as X **determines** Y. Functional dependency is abbreviated as FD.

A simpler discussion of FDs results if all application attributes are in a single relation. In this case, any subset of the application attributes can appear on either side of an FD, and the FD will still make sense in terms of the definition above. This single relation, which contains all application attributes, is the **universal relation**. It is denoted by the unadorned symbol, R. Any other relations that appear in the discussion will use variations on the symbol (e.g., R' or R_i).

A goal of functional dependency analysis is to subdivide the universal relation into components such that the component bodies can never become inconsistent with respect to the FD constraints. Any such component, $r(R')$, must be the projection of the universal relation onto R'. That is, $r(R') = \pi_{R'}(r(R))$. With this requirement, the database state is simply the content of the universal relation. Once you specify $r(R)$, the projection determines the content of any component R'. For example, in the aquarium application, R = (sno, sname, sfood, tno, tname, tvolume, tcolor, fno, fname, fcolor, fweight, eno, edate, enote).

Next, suppose you impose constraints on the universal relation's content so that the alignment of values in a tuple reflects some meaningful fact about the application. For example, if the fno value is 347, the fname value should be the name of the fish whose fno is 347 and not the name of some other fish. Similarly, the tname value should be the name of the tank in which fno 347 is swimming. You can use functional dependencies to express these constraints. For example, if two tuples have the same tno value, say x, they should also have the same tname value. In other words, tno $\longrightarrow$ tname.

Tuple components should relate to each other as the application requires. For the aquarium application, the universal relation should correspond to the natural join of the species, tank, fish, and event relations. This construction assembles only properly related values within a given tuple. Each tuple corresponds to an event, extended with the attributes of the owning fish, its home tank, and its representative species. In this chapter, however, assume that the universal relation comes first, along with the FDs that render the tuples meaningful in application terms. Subsequent decomposition will isolate the actual application entities.

Functional dependency analysis eventually leads to a systematic decomposition of the universal relation into the application entities. You may well wonder about the necessity of this process because, with the ER and OMT modeling tools, you can directly express a design as related application entities. These methods, however, are limited. Although the ER and OMT approaches present a notation for capturing a design, they don't specify how to identify the application entities in a formal manner. By contrast, the analysis approach of this chapter is a formal process for obtaining the appropriate entities. In particular, you form the entities by packaging attribute subsets from the universal relation, but you ensure that all FD constraints are automatically enforced by the relationships among the entities. As the process continues, certain expected entities emerge as suggestive collections of attributes. In the aquarium application, for example, you expect species, fish, tank, and event to emerge as you decompose the universal relation. So functional dependency analysis is a complementary process. You can use it to discover or confirm entities in an ER or OMT diagram. Moreover, FDs can express constraints that have no graphical equivalent in the ER or OMT notation. As you will see, these hidden constraints can lead to the further decomposition of an entity that may appear to be an indivisible unit in the ER diagram.

Returning to the aquarium universal relation, you find a great deal of repetition in the tuples. Each event tuple extends to include all the attributes of its owning fish, and the fish then extends to encompass all the attributes of its tank and species. If a given fish has 100 events, they give rise to 100 almost identical tuples, which differ only in the event attributes. All fish, species, and tank attributes are identical across the 100 tuples. The universal relation, therefore, is an inefficient container for the aquarium data. It wastes space with repeating values and affords opportunities for inconsistency in the repeated values. For these reasons, you should envision the universal relation only as a mental construct. It is a starting point for a decomposition process, which culminates in a collection of more manageable relations.

 The universal relation, R, contains all application attributes. The database state is the content of R. The content of any component relation $R' \subset R$ is a projection of the content of R. You can use FD constraints to ensure that values within the same R tuple are meaningfully related in application terms.

This chapter uses the following notational conventions. Capital letters toward the beginning of the alphabet (e.g., A, B, C) denote single attributes. Capital letters toward the end of the alphabet (e.g., X, Y, Z) denote sets of attributes. Lowercase Greek letters (e.g., μ, ν, ϕ, ψ) signify tuples. $\mu(X)$ is the shorter tuple obtained from μ by retaining only the values under the attributes X. Juxtaposition indicates the union of attribute sets. For example, $XY = X \cup Y$. Calligraphic letters (e.g., $\mathcal{F}, \mathcal{G}, \mathcal{H}$) denote sets of functional dependencies.

Using this notation, the definition of an FD is as follows. Let R' be a subset of the universal relation R. Let X and Y be two subsets of R'. The functional dependency $X \longrightarrow Y$ is the constraint on $r(R')$: if $\mu, \nu \in r(R')$ with $\mu(X) = \nu(X)$, then $\mu(Y) = \nu(Y)$.

The left side of a functional dependency is a **determinant**. When the constraint $X \longrightarrow Y$ holds in R', you say that X **determines** Y in R'.

In the universal aquarium relation, for example, you expect fno$\longrightarrow$tno. If two extended tuples have the same fno value, they must also have the same tno value. After all, the two tuples correspond to two events, extended with their related fish, species, and tank attributes. If the two events relate to the same fish, clearly only one tank is involved—the one where the fish swims. Therefore, fno is a determinant, and one of the attributes that fno determines is tno.

Let $R_1 \subset R_2$, and suppose that $X \longrightarrow Y$ is a constraint on R_2. An FD, $X \longrightarrow Y$, **applies** to R_1 if $X \subset R_1$. Because $r(R_1)$ and $r(R_2)$ are both projections of $r(R)$, any FD that constrains $r(R_2)$ will also constrain $r(R_1)$, if it is applicable. The table below illustrates this situation. Because the tuples involved must be projections of tuples from the universal relation, the table shows them in that context. Because $X \longrightarrow Y$ constrains $r(R_2)$, you must have $y_1 = y_2$ and $y_1' = y_2'$ in the table. However, $X \longrightarrow (Y \cap R_1)$ then constrains $r(R_1)$. So any FD that constrains $r(R_2)$ gives rise to a similar FD that constrains $r(R_1)$, if $R_1 \subset R_2$ and the FD is applicable to R_1. The table also shows that the same argument applies to a superset. If $R_1 \subset R_2$ and $X \longrightarrow Y$ constrains $r(R_1)$, then $X \longrightarrow Y$ also constrains $r(R_2)$.

R					
R_2					$R - R_2$
R_1			$R_2 - R_1$		
X	$R_1 - XY$	Y			
x	z_1	y_1	y_1'	w_1	v_1
x	z_2	y_2	y_2'	w_2	v_2

In short, if $X \longrightarrow Y$ constrains the universal relation, $r(R)$, and $X \subset R'$, then $X \longrightarrow (Y \cap R')$ constrains $r(R')$. Conversely, any FD constraining $r(R')$ must constrain $r(R)$. This result allows you to assert an FD constraint for the application without specifying which relation must observe the constraint. If the FD applies to a relation, then the FD constrains the relation.

You can use an FD to express the notion of a superkey in a relation $R' \subset R$. A superkey of R' is a set of attributes, $K \subset R'$, with the constraint that no two distinct tuples, $\mu, \nu \in r(R')$, agree on K. In other words, if $\mu \neq \nu$, then $\mu(K) \neq \nu(K)$. In terms of FDs, the constraint $K \longrightarrow A$, for every A in R', is equivalent to K being a superkey of R'. Indeed, if K is a superkey and $\mu(K) = \nu(K)$, then μ and ν must be the same tuple. It follows that $\mu(A) = \nu(A)$ for any A, so $K \longrightarrow A$ for any A. Conversely, suppose that $K \longrightarrow A$, for any A in R'. Now, suppose two tuples, μ and ν, agree on K. Because of the FD, they must then agree on all attributes of R'. However, two tuples that agree on all attributes must be the same tuple because a relation tolerates no duplicates. Therefore, no two distinct tuples can agree on K, which means that K is a superkey. This argument proves that K is a superkey of R' if and only if $K \longrightarrow R'$.

An FD can also express the constraint that the values under a set of attributes, X, are constants. The constraint is $\varphi \longrightarrow X$. In other words, any two tuples that agree on the empty set of attributes, which is any two tuples whatsoever, must agree on X. All tuples, therefore, must agree on X, which means that the $\mu(X) = \nu(X)$ for any tuples μ and ν in the relation.

The functional dependency constraint $X \longrightarrow Y$ constrains the database state, $r(R)$, such that $\mu(X) = \nu(X)$ implies $\mu(Y) = \nu(Y)$. For a component R', if $X \subset R'$, then $X \longrightarrow Y \cap R'$ holds. A superkey K of R' means $K \longrightarrow R'$.

If possible, you should express application constraints in the database schema because the DBMS can then refuse database updates that would result in an inconsistent state. In the case of a superkey constraint, you can use the primary-key clause in an SQL create-table statement to convey the message. You can express other functional dependency constraints with SQL create-assertion statements. In the aquarium universal relation, tno is no longer a superkey because many tuples can share the same tno. The tno value identifies a tank, but each tuple of the universal relation is an event that happened to a fish in a tank. A given tank then appears in many tuples. However, tno is still a determinant. For example, tno $\longrightarrow$ tname. If two tuples agree on tno, they represent events experienced by fish with the same home tank. So the tname values should be the same. If you define the aquarium application as a single universal table R, you can express the tno $\longrightarrow$ tname constraint as follows. The expression partitions the table on tno and reports the groups with multiple tname values.

```
create assertion tnameConsistency check (not exists
    (select tno
    from R
    groupby tno
    having max(tname) ≠ min(tname))).
```

The same reasoning allows you to assert tno $\longrightarrow$ tcolor and tno $\longrightarrow$ tvolume. You may also know from the application analysis that tanks are color-coded by volume. Tanks with volumes 0–400 are blue, those in the range 401–600 are red, and so forth. So if two tuples agree on tvolume, they must agree on tcolor. Symbolically, tvolume $\longrightarrow$ tcolor. Note that the reverse isn't true. You could have two red tanks, one with volume 500 and one with volume 550.

Functional dependency constraints can arise for many reasons, but they all reflect the application semantics. In the examples above, several FDs arose because tno uniquely identifies a tank; another FD expressed a constraint on the tank color scheme. Other constraints arise from the one-to-many nature of the relationships: species-fish, tank-fish, and fish-event. For example, you assert eno $\longrightarrow$ fno to constrain an event to its owning fish. The reverse isn't true because a fish can experience many events.

Analyzing the application constraints, you can construct a set of FDs, $\mathcal{F}_{aq}$, to control the content of the universal aquarium relation. Figure 18.1 lists this set. Except for tvolume $\longrightarrow$ tcolor, the constraints $\mathcal{F}_{aq}$ are precisely those necessary to ensure that the universal relation contains only tuples from the join of individual relations in the dispersed version of this database. In other words, the constraints force $r(R) = r(\text{Species}) * r(\text{Fish}) * r(\text{Tank}) * r(\text{Event})$. The first row of Figure 18.1 constrains the (sno, sname, sfood) segments to behave as though they come from a species table. When a given sno value appears in a tuple, the sname and sfood values must tag along. This maintains consistency with the (sno,

sno ⟶ sname	sno ⟶ sfood	
tno ⟶ tname	tno ⟶ tcolor	tno ⟶ tvolume
fno ⟶ fname	fno ⟶ fcolor	fno ⟶ fweight
eno ⟶ edate	eno ⟶ enote	
tvolume ⟶ tcolor		
eno ⟶ fno	fno ⟶ tno	fno ⟶ sno

Figure 18.1   Initial set of functional dependencies, $\mathcal{F}_{aq}$, for the universal aquarium relation

sname, sfood) segments in other tuples. The next three rows in the figure enforce similar constraints on the (tno, tname, tcolor, tvolume), (fno, fname, fcolor, fweight), and (eno, edate, enote) segments. The last row expresses the many-to-one relationships that must hold between the segments.

The closure of a collection of functional dependencies

At any time, the database state is simply the content of the universal relation, $r(R)$, which determines, by projection, the content of any subset relation. Because of insertions, updates, and deletions, the database state changes over time. A database state **violates** an FD, $U \longrightarrow V$, if there exist two distinct tuples, $\mu, \nu \in R$ with $\mu(U) = \nu(U)$ and $\mu(V) \neq \nu(V)$. A database state **satisfies** an FD it doesn't violate the FD. By extension, a database state violates $\mathcal{F}$ if it violates some FD in $\mathcal{F}$, and it satisfies $\mathcal{F}$ if it satisfies all FDs in $\mathcal{F}$. A database state is **consistent** or **valid**, with respect to a collection of constraints $\mathcal{F}$, if it satisfies $\mathcal{F}$.

Although the initial FDs come from analyzing the application, you can add new FDs through a process of logical implication. Suppose you assemble a collection, $\mathcal{F}$, of FDs that reflects application constraints. Any database state that satisfies $\mathcal{F}$ will also satisfy additional FDs. Consider the collection $\mathcal{F}_{aq}$ of Figure 18.1 for the universal aquarium relation. Note that eno ⟶ tname isn't in $\mathcal{F}_{aq}$. You could have placed it there because eno is a superkey, but you didn't. Although eno ⟶ tname is an application constraint, you don't have to include it among the constraining FDs for the universal relation. Why? It is superfluous: all database states that satisfy $\mathcal{F}_{aq}$ automatically satisfy eno ⟶ tname.

To see how the constraints already in $\mathcal{F}_{aq}$ subsume eno ⟶ tname, you reason as follows. Suppose R satisfies $\mathcal{F}_{aq}$ but violates eno ⟶ tname. You must then have two distinct tuples, μ and ν, such that $\mu(\text{eno}) = \nu(\text{eno})$ and $\mu(\text{tname}) \neq \nu(\text{tname})$. Because tno ⟶ tname is in $\mathcal{F}_{aq}$, you must have $\mu(\text{tno}) \neq \nu(\text{tno})$. Because fno ⟶ tno is in $\mathcal{F}_{aq}$, $\mu(\text{fno}) \neq \nu(\text{fno})$ then follows. Finally, eno ⟶ fno in $\mathcal{F}_{aq}$ forces $\mu(\text{eno}) \neq \nu(\text{eno})$, a contradiction. Two violating tuples, therefore, can't exist, and R must satisfy eno ⟶ tname.

Generalizing from this example, if R never enters a database state that violates an FD in $\mathcal{F}$, then it always satisfies certain other FDs "for free." You don't need extra precautions to ensure that the additional FDs aren't violated because that isn't possible without violating some FD in $\mathcal{F}$. The **closure** of $\mathcal{F}$, $\mathcal{F}^+$, is the enlarged collection, $\mathcal{F}$ plus all the FDs that you enforce automatically as a by-product of enforcing $\mathcal{F}$.

The formal definition of $\mathcal{F}^+$ is as follows. You say $\mathcal{F}$ **implies** an FD, $X \longrightarrow Y$, if every database state that satisfies $\mathcal{F}$ also satisfies $X \longrightarrow Y$. You can abbreviate $\mathcal{F}$ implies $X \longrightarrow Y$ as $\mathcal{F} \models (X \longrightarrow Y)$. The alternative wording "$\mathcal{F}$ **models** $X \longrightarrow Y$" means "$\mathcal{F}$ implies $X \longrightarrow Y$." When the context $\mathcal{F}$ is clear, the phrases "$X \longrightarrow Y$ must hold" and "you have $X \longrightarrow Y$" also mean that $\mathcal{F} \models (X \longrightarrow Y)$. In symbols, the closure of $\mathcal{F}$ is:

$$\mathcal{F}^+ = \{X \longrightarrow Y \mid \mathcal{F} \models (X \longrightarrow Y)\}. \tag{18.1}$$

If $X \longrightarrow Y \in \mathcal{F}$, then $X \longrightarrow Y$ obviously holds for every database state that satisfies $\mathcal{F}$. Therefore, $\mathcal{F}$ models every FD in $\mathcal{F}$, and $\mathcal{F} \subset \mathcal{F}^+$. The FDs in $\mathcal{F}^+ - \mathcal{F}$ are the "free" constraints, which you enforce automatically as a by-product of enforcing $\mathcal{F}$.

$\mathcal{F} \models (X \longrightarrow Y)$ *means that every database state satisfying $\mathcal{F}$ also satisfies $X \longrightarrow Y$.*
$\mathcal{F}^+ = \{X \longrightarrow Y \mid \mathcal{F} \models (X \longrightarrow Y)\}.$

Some FDs in $\mathcal{F}^+$ are trivial: they express conditions that are trivial extensions of the existing constraints. Besides the FDs in $\mathcal{F}$ itself, the simplest example of a trivial extension is an FD of the form $X \longrightarrow Y$, where $Y \subset X$. *Any* database state satisfies this FD. If two tuples agree on X, then because $Y \subset X$, they must agree on Y. The trivial FDs also include situations where the right side is empty ($X \longrightarrow \varphi$) and where both sides are empty ($\varphi \longrightarrow \varphi$). Although such FDs don't customize the database states to the application at hand, they nevertheless appear in $\mathcal{F}^+$. Straight from the definition, every database state that satisfies $\mathcal{F}$ will satisfy the trivial FDs.

Therefore, $\mathcal{F}^+$ is very large. Indeed, it is exponentially large in terms of the number of attributes in the universal relation. An FD where the right side is a subset of the left side is a **reflexive FD** or a **trivial FD**. You can count the number of reflexive FDs over n attributes. If the left side of a reflexive FD has i attributes, the right side can have $0, 1, 2, \ldots, i$ attributes. There are $\binom{i}{j}$ ways of choosing a j-attribute right side from the i attributes on the left. So the number of reflexive FDs with a fixed set of i attributes on the left is

$$\sum_{j=0}^{i} \binom{i}{j} = \sum_{j=0}^{i} \binom{i}{j} 1^j 1^{i-j} = (1+1)^i = 2^i.$$

Because there are $\binom{n}{i}$ ways of choosing the particular set of i attributes for the left side, there are $\binom{n}{i} 2^i$ reflexive FDs with i attributes on the left. Because i can range over $0, 1, 2, \ldots, n$, you compute the following grand total of reflexive FDs over n attributes.

$$\sum_{i=0}^{n} \binom{n}{i} 2^i = 3^n.$$

Just with trivial reflexive FDs, therefore, $\mathcal{F}^+$ is already exponentially large. You obtain another sort of trivial extension by adding the same attributes to both sides of an existing

FD. Suppose $X \longrightarrow Y \in \mathcal{F}^+$. Then $XZ \longrightarrow YZ \in \mathcal{F}^+$, for any subset Z. To prove this, suppose you have a valid database state where two tuples agree on XZ. Then they certainly agree on X. The existing FD, $X \longrightarrow Y$, which must hold because the database state is valid, then forces them to agree on Y. Because they already agree on Z, you now have them agreeing on YZ, and the database state satisfies $XZ \longrightarrow YZ$. So in addition to the reflexive FDs, you obtain many more elements of $\mathcal{F}^+$ by strengthening both sides of $\mathcal{F}$ members with all possible subsets. This process is **augmentation**. Note that augmentation of a trivial FD produces another trivial FD.

A third way that an FD can enter $\mathcal{F}^+$ is through **transitivity**. If $X \longrightarrow Y$ and $Y \longrightarrow Z$ are in $\mathcal{F}^+$, then $X \longrightarrow Z$ is in $\mathcal{F}^+$. In a disguised form, an earlier argument used this mechanism to show $\mathcal{F}_{aq} \models$ eno $\longrightarrow$ tname. Using transitivity, you can reason directly from eno $\longrightarrow$ fno and fno $\longrightarrow$ tno to eno $\longrightarrow$ tno. You then combine that result with tno $\longrightarrow$ tname to yield eno $\longrightarrow$ tname.

The proof that transitivity creates an element of $\mathcal{F}^+$ proceeds as follows. Suppose $X \longrightarrow Y, Y \longrightarrow Z \in \mathcal{F}^+$, and $r(R)$ is a valid database state. In this situation, $\mu(X) = \nu(X)$ forces $\mu(Y) = \nu(Y)$. However, the second FD then implies that $\mu(Z) = \nu(Z)$. This proves the database state must satisfy $X \longrightarrow Z$. Stated differently, $X \longrightarrow Z \in \mathcal{F}^+$.

Armstrong's axioms

The last section discussed three processes that expand $\mathcal{F}$ to include new FDs in $\mathcal{F}^+$: reflexivity, augmentation, and transitivity. It turns out that these operations, repeated as long as they are applicable, generate all of $\mathcal{F}^+$. The proof will come shortly, but first consider three additional operations that also generate elements of $\mathcal{F}^+$. The six operations are collectively known as **Armstrong's axioms**:

1. **Reflexivity.** If $Y \subset X \subset R$, then $X \longrightarrow Y \in \mathcal{F}^+$ (regardless of $\mathcal{F}$).

2. **Augmentation.** If $X \longrightarrow Y \in \mathcal{F}^+$ and $Z \subset R$, then $XZ \longrightarrow YZ \in \mathcal{F}^+$.

3. **Transitivity.** If $X \longrightarrow Y \in \mathcal{F}^+$ and $Y \longrightarrow Z \in \mathcal{F}^+$, then $X \longrightarrow Z \in \mathcal{F}^+$.

4. **Composition.** If $X \longrightarrow Y \in \mathcal{F}^+$ and $X \longrightarrow Z \in \mathcal{F}^+$, then $X \longrightarrow YZ \in \mathcal{F}^+$.

5. **Decomposition.** If $X \dashrightarrow YZ \in \mathcal{F}^+$, then $X \longrightarrow Y \in \mathcal{F}^+$ and $X \longrightarrow Z \in \mathcal{F}^+$.

6. **Pseudotransitivity.** If $X \longrightarrow Y \in \mathcal{F}^+$ and $WY \longrightarrow Z \in \mathcal{F}^+$, then $WX \longrightarrow Z \in \mathcal{F}^+$.

From the last section, you know that the first three axioms are correct. The proofs for the others are equally straightforward. Suppose you have a valid database state with respect to $\mathcal{F}$. For the composition axiom, $\mu(X) = \nu(X)$ implies $\mu(Y) = \nu(Y)$ and $\mu(Z) = \nu(Z)$ by the hypothesis. However, you then have $\mu(YZ) = \nu(YZ)$, which shows $X \longrightarrow YZ$ holds. For decomposition, if $\mu(X) = \nu(X)$, then $\mu(YZ) = \nu(YZ)$ by the hypothesis, so $\mu(Y) = \nu(Y)$ and $\mu(Z) = \nu(Z)$. Therefore, $X \longrightarrow Y$ and $X \longrightarrow Z$. Finally, for pseudotransitivity, if $\mu(WX) = \nu(WX)$, then certainly $\mu(X) = \nu(X)$, so $\mu(Y) = \nu(Y)$ by the first part of the hypothesis. You now have $\mu(WY) = \nu(WY)$, which implies $\mu(Z) = \nu(Z)$ by the second part of the hypothesis and shows that $WX \longrightarrow Z$ must hold. At this point, you have proved that Armstrong's axioms are **sound**, meaning that applying the axioms to elements in $\mathcal{F}^+$ always yields an element of $\mathcal{F}^+$.

When you apply Armstrong's axioms to FDs in $\mathcal{F}^+$, the resulting FDs are also in $\mathcal{F}^+$.

The last three of Armstrong's axioms are conveniences: you can achieve their effects by using combinations of the first three. The equivalent sequences follow:

Composition			Decomposition	
(1) $X \longrightarrow Y$	given		(1) $X \longrightarrow YZ$	given
(2) $X \longrightarrow XY$	augmentation		(2) $YZ \longrightarrow Y$	reflexivity
(3) $X \longrightarrow Z$	given		(3) $YZ \longrightarrow Z$	reflexivity
(4) $XY \longrightarrow YZ$	augmentation		(4) $X \longrightarrow Y$	transitivity of (1) and (2)
(5) $X \longrightarrow YZ$	transitivity of (2) and (4)		(5) $X \longrightarrow Z$	transitivity of (1) and (3)

Pseudotransitivity	
(1) $X \longrightarrow Y$	given
(2) $WX \longrightarrow WY$	augmentation
(3) $WY \longrightarrow Z$	given
(4) $WX \longrightarrow Z$	transitivity of (2) and (3)

So when you derive an FD in $\mathcal{F}^+$ by repeated application of Armstrong's axioms from some initial starting point, you could, if necessary, derive the same FD by repeated application of the first three axioms alone.

Working with an initial collection of FDs, $\mathcal{F}$, consider a fixed attribute subset, X. You know that $X \longrightarrow X \in \mathcal{F}^+$ by reflexivity. From this starting point, consider all the FDs with left side X that you can generate from $\mathcal{F}$ by repeated applications of Armstrong's axioms. Now define $(X; \mathcal{F})$ as the largest right side that appears in this group. In other words,

$$(X; \mathcal{F}) = \bigcup \{A \mid X \longrightarrow A \text{ follows from } \mathcal{F} \text{ via Armstrong's axioms}\}. \qquad (18.2)$$

$(X; \mathcal{F})$ has many useful properties. From the definition of $(X; \mathcal{F})$, you have that $X \longrightarrow A$ follows by Armstrong's axioms for every $A \in (X; \mathcal{F})$. By the soundness of the axioms, $X \longrightarrow A \in \mathcal{F}^+$ for every $A \in (X; \mathcal{F})$. Because you can obtain $X \longrightarrow (X; \mathcal{F})$ from these components by repeated application of the composition axiom, you can derive $X \longrightarrow (X; \mathcal{F})$ from $\mathcal{F}$ by Armstrong's axioms, so it is in $\mathcal{F}^+$. Furthermore, from $X \longrightarrow X$, you can use decomposition to reach $X \longrightarrow A$ for every $A \in X$. Therefore, $X \subset (X; \mathcal{F})$. Finally, if $Y \subset (X; \mathcal{F})$, you can derive $X \longrightarrow Y$ with Armstrong's axioms because you can derive $X \longrightarrow A$ for every $A \in Y$. By repeated use of the composition axiom, you can then reach $X \longrightarrow Y$. Conversely, if you can derive $X \longrightarrow Y$ with Armstrong's axioms, you can also derive $X \longrightarrow A$, for every $A \in Y$. You simply use decomposition after arriving at $X \longrightarrow Y$. So $A \in (X; \mathcal{F})$, for every $A \in Y$, which implies that $Y \subset (X; \mathcal{F})$.

These results are all immediate consequences of the definition of $(X; \mathcal{F})$. They will be used frequently in the arguments to come without further comment. So keep in mind the following points:

- You obtain $(X; \mathcal{F})$ from X by using Armstrong's axioms on a specific starting set of FDs, $\mathcal{F}$. If you use a different set of FDs, $\mathcal{G}$, you get a different set of attributes in $(X; \mathcal{G})$.

- $X \longrightarrow (X; \mathcal{F}) \in \mathcal{F}^+$.

- $(X; \mathcal{F})$ has the largest right side of any FD with left side X that you can derive from $\mathcal{F}$ using Armstrong's axioms.

- $X \subset (X; \mathcal{F})$.

- $Y \subset (X; \mathcal{F})$ if and only if you can derive $X \longrightarrow Y$ from $\mathcal{F}$ with Armstrong's axioms.

Armstrong's axioms are not only sound, they are also **complete**. In other words, the axioms generate all of $\mathcal{F}^+$. The proof runs as follows. Suppose $X \longrightarrow Y \in \mathcal{F}^+$, and consider r, the two-tuple relational body below. All the attributes in $(X; \mathcal{F})$ contain 0s in both tuples, but the tuples differ in all the remaining attributes. The top tuple contains all 0s in the remaining attributes; the other contains all 1s.

$(X; \mathcal{F})$	$R - (X; \mathcal{F})$
$\ldots 000 \ldots$	$\ldots 000 \ldots$
$\ldots 000 \ldots$	$\ldots 111 \ldots$

This relation satisfies every FD in $\mathcal{F}$. This may seem outrageous because $\mathcal{F}$ is an arbitrary collection of FD constraints. However, it is true, and you can prove it as follows. Let $U \longrightarrow W$ be an FD in $\mathcal{F}$. The only way r can violate $U \longrightarrow W$ is if $U \subset (X; \mathcal{F})$. Otherwise, you can't find two distinct tuples that agree on U. So if U isn't contained in $(X; \mathcal{F})$, no violation occurs. On the other hand, if $U \subset (X; \mathcal{F})$, you can generate $X \longrightarrow U$ from $\mathcal{F}$ by repeated application of Armstrong's axioms. From $X \longrightarrow U$ and $U \longrightarrow W \in \mathcal{F}$, you can now derive $X \longrightarrow W$ by transitivity. Therefore, you have generated $X \longrightarrow W$ by repeated application of the axioms, which proves $W \subset (X; \mathcal{F})$. The two tuples then agree on W, so no violation of $U \longrightarrow W$ occurs.

Because r satisfies an arbitrarily chosen FD in $\mathcal{F}$, it follows that r satisfies all FDs in $\mathcal{F}$. By the definition of $\mathcal{F}^+$, r must then satisfy all FDs in $\mathcal{F}^+$. In particular, r must satisfy $X \longrightarrow Y$. Because $X \subset (X; \mathcal{F})$, you must have $Y \subset (X; \mathcal{F})$, or else r would violate $X \longrightarrow Y$. However, that means you can obtain $X \longrightarrow Y$ by repeated application of the axioms. This proves the axioms are complete. In other words,

$$
\begin{aligned}
\mathcal{F}^+ &= \{X \longrightarrow Y \mid F \models (X \longrightarrow Y)\} \\
&= \{X \longrightarrow Y \mid X \longrightarrow Y \text{ follows from } \mathcal{F} \text{ by repeated application of the axioms}\}.
\end{aligned}
$$

(18.3)

Starting with the FDs in $\mathcal{F}$, you can generate $\mathcal{F}^+ = \{X \longrightarrow Y \mid \mathcal{F} \models (X \longrightarrow Y)\}$ by repeated application of Armstrong's axioms.

This result provides a systematic, if inefficient, algorithm for generating $\mathcal{F}^+$ from $\mathcal{F}$. You methodically generate all the 3^n reflexive FDs from the n attributes mentioned in $\mathcal{F}$ and add them to $\mathcal{F}$ to produce a first approximation of $\mathcal{F}^+$. You then repeatedly cycle through the FDs of the approximation, adding new FDs when an opportunity arises to use one of the axioms. Because the number of attribute subsets is finite, you eventually reach a point where you can't generate an FD that isn't already in the set. At that point, you have

$\mathcal{F}^+$. Because $\mathcal{F}^+$ is exponentially large and because this algorithm is inefficient, you don't really want to generate all of $\mathcal{F}^+$. The next section shows how to use the concept of $\mathcal{F}^+$ without explicitly constructing it.

Because you know that Armstrong's axioms eventually generate all the FDs that logically follow from an initial collection, $\mathcal{F}$, you can revise the earlier definition of $(X; \mathcal{F})$.

$$(X; \mathcal{F}) = \bigcup \{ A \mid X \longrightarrow A \text{ is generated from } \mathcal{F} \text{ by Armstrong's axioms} \}$$
$$= \bigcup \{ A \mid \mathcal{F} \models (X \longrightarrow A) \}. \tag{18.4}$$

In summary, the initial collection of functional dependency constraints, $\mathcal{F}$, arises from an analysis of the application. If the DBMS takes precautions to guarantee that the database state always satisfies $\mathcal{F}$, then the database state will automatically satisfy a much larger collection of FDs, $\mathcal{F}^+$. In this sense, $\mathcal{F}^+$ represents all the FDs that are logical consequents of the FDs in $\mathcal{F}$. The following statements are then equivalent:

- $\mathcal{F} \models (X \longrightarrow Y)$.
- $X \longrightarrow Y \in \mathcal{F}^+$.
- You can derive $X \longrightarrow Y$ from $\mathcal{F}$ using Armstrong's axioms.
- $Y \subset (X; \mathcal{F})$.

Minimal covers

An algorithm to check membership in the closure

Although you don't want to generate all of $\mathcal{F}^+$ because of its exponential size, you might want to check if a given FD is a member of $\mathcal{F}^+$. This test is much easier. Indeed, $X \longrightarrow Y \in \mathcal{F}^+$ if and only if $Y \subset (X; \mathcal{F})$. Therefore, you can check if $X \longrightarrow Y \in \mathcal{F}^+$ by generating $(X; \mathcal{F})$ and checking if Y is in it. The skeletal code for the algorithm appears below. Assume that you have data types to handle attributes, sets of attributes, and sets of FDs. The procedure maxRight grows $(X; \mathcal{F})$ in an interesting manner: it uses only the FDs in $\mathcal{F}$. FDinClosure simply uses the returned value of maxRight to conduct a test for $Y \subset (X; \mathcal{F})$.

```
attributeSet maxRight(attributeSet X,
                      FDset F) {
   attributeSet Z;
   boolean changed;

   changed = true; Z = X;
   while (changed)
      if (∃U ⟶ V ∈ F with U ⊂ Z and V ⊄ Z)
         Z = Z ∪ V;
      else
         changed = false;
   return Z; }
```

```
boolean FDinClosure(attributeSet X,
                    attributeSet Y,
                    FDset F) {
/* returns true if X ⟶ Y ∈ F⁺ */
   return Y ⊂ maxRight(X, F); }
```

How do you know that maxRight correctly generates $(X; \mathcal{F})$? An invariant for the while loop of the maxRight procedure is $Z \subset (X; \mathcal{F})$. This observation is certainly true when you enter the loop because $Z = X$ at that point. Assuming that it's true at the beginning of an arbitrary pass through the loop, you reason that any change to Z adds the attributes V from an FD, $U \longrightarrow V \in \mathcal{F}$, and $U \subset Z$. But $U \subset Z \subset (X; \mathcal{F})$ means $X \longrightarrow U \in \mathcal{F}^+$. Then $U \longrightarrow V \in \mathcal{F}$ gives $X \longrightarrow V \in \mathcal{F}^+$ by transitivity. So $V \subset (X; \mathcal{F})$. When the algorithm changes Z to $Z \cup V$, the new Z remains in $(X; \mathcal{F})$. Therefore, $Z \subset (X; \mathcal{F})$ is a loop invariant, which remains true when the loop terminates. Because $\mathcal{F}$ provides only finitely many right sides to add to the growing Z, the loop must eventually terminate. At that point, $Z \subset (X; \mathcal{F})$, and Z didn't change during the last iteration.

To prove equality, look at the relational body r below, where the Z attributes are those of the final pass through the loop—the pass where you couldn't find a $U \longrightarrow V \in \mathcal{F}$ with $U \subset Z$ and $V \not\subset Z$.

Z	$R - Z$
$\ldots 000 \ldots$	$\ldots 000 \ldots$
$\ldots 000 \ldots$	$\ldots 111 \ldots$

It turns out that r satisfies all the FDs in $\mathcal{F}$. To prove this, suppose $U \longrightarrow V \in \mathcal{F}$. If $U \not\subset Z$, no violation occurs because no two tuples in r agree on U. So you must check only the case where $U \subset Z$. Because the algorithm was unable to find an FD in $\mathcal{F}$ with $U \subset Z$ and $V \not\subset Z$, you must have that $V \subset Z$. However, both tuples then agree on V, and again no violation occurs. Therefore, r satisfies all FDs in $\mathcal{F}$, and it must satisfy all FDs of $\mathcal{F}^+$, including $X \longrightarrow (X; \mathcal{F})$. Because $X \subset Z$, the two tuples agree on X, so they must agree on $(X; \mathcal{F})$. This agreement is possible only if $(X; \mathcal{F}) \subset Z$. Because the loop invariant asserts that $Z \subset (X; \mathcal{F})$ always, you then have $Z = (X; \mathcal{F})$ upon loop termination.

Determination of keys and superkeys

You can use $\mathcal{F}^+$ to determine if a particular subset of attributes is a superkey. Recall that K is a superkey of R if and only if $K \longrightarrow A$ holds for every $A \in R$. Therefore, K is a superkey if and only if $K \longrightarrow R \in \mathcal{F}^+$. Moreover, K is a key if it is a minimal superkey. The defining condition is then: $K \longrightarrow R \in \mathcal{F}^+$, but $(K - A) \longrightarrow R \notin \mathcal{F}^+$ for any $A \in K$. You can check all these conditions with the FDinClosure algorithm. Unfortunately, if R has n attributes, you must check 2^n attribute subsets for key or superkey status.

An extreme case occurs when the empty set is a key, but that restricts the relation to at most one tuple. In this case, all attribute sets are superkeys because they all contain φ. Algorithm maxRight correctly computes $(\varphi; \mathcal{F})$ to detect this unusual case, but because a relation of one tuple or less isn't an interesting database component, subsequent discussion will ignore this boundary case and assume that φ isn't a key.

If you check the non-empty subsets in order of increasing size, you can distinguish between superkey and key without checking the minimality condition. First, you check all subsets of size one. If an attribute is a superkey, it must be a key because a superkey with one attribute is minimal. You then remove from the candidate list all supersets of the one-attribute keys because all of them will be superkeys—just not minimal superkeys. You then check the remaining two-attribute candidates. If a two-attribute pair checks out as a superkey, it must be a key. It wouldn't be in contention if it were a superset of a one-attribute key. You add any two-attribute keys found this way to the list of keys, and you remove all their supersets from the candidate list. You continue in this manner through

Z	applicable FD
eno	eno $\longrightarrow$ edate
eno, edate	eno $\longrightarrow$ enote
eno, edate, enote	eno $\longrightarrow$ fno
eno, edate, enote, fno	fno $\longrightarrow$ fname
eno, edate, enote, fno, fname	fno $\longrightarrow$ fcolor
eno, edate, enote, fno, fname, fcolor	fno $\longrightarrow$ fweight
eno, edate, enote, fno, fname, fcolor, fweight	fno $\longrightarrow$ tno
eno, edate, enote, fno, fname, fcolor, fweight, tno	tno $\longrightarrow$ tname
eno, edate, enote, fno, fname, fcolor, fweight, tno, tname	tno $\longrightarrow$ tcolor
eno, edate, enote, fno, fname, fcolor, fweight, tno, tname, tcolor	tno $\longrightarrow$ tvolume
eno, edate, enote, fno, fname, fcolor, fweight, tno, tname, tcolor, tvolume	fno $\longrightarrow$ sno
eno, edate, enote, fno, fname, fcolor, fweight, tno, tname, tcolor, tvolume, sno	sno $\longrightarrow$ sname
eno, edate, enote, fno, fname, fcolor, fweight, tno, tname, tcolor, tvolume, sno, sname	sno $\longrightarrow$ sfood
eno, edate, enote, fno, fname, fcolor, fweight, tno, tname, tcolor, tvolume, sno, sname, sfood	none applicable

Figure 18.2   Deducing a key of the aquarium universal relation

subsets of size n. Of course, only one subset of size n is in the candidate list unless you have already removed it as a superset of a previously determined key. When you finish, you have a complete list of the relation's keys, and you know that the superkeys are all the supersets of these keys. Unfortunately, you must consider exponentially many subsets; a more efficient method for finding the keys of a relation isn't known.

Consider the FDs, $\mathcal{F}_{aq}$, from the aquarium universal relation, as given in Figure 18.1. Suppose you are checking various subsets of R = (sno, sname, sfood, tno, tname, tcolor, tvolume, fno, fname, fcolor, fweight, eno, edate, enote) for superkey or key status. According to the algorithm, you first check the one-attribute subsets. Figure 18.2 shows how the algorithm maxRight enlarges its Z approximation for (eno; $\mathcal{F}_{aq}$) on subsequent iterations. Because the algorithm eventually includes all of R in Z, it reports eno $\longrightarrow R$ in the closure of $\mathcal{F}_{aq}$. Therefore, eno is a key, and all supersets of eno are superkeys. You then remove all supersets of eno from the candidate list. In other words, the search for further keys must consider only subsets that don't contain eno.

Note that no FD in $\mathcal{F}_{aq}$ has eno on its right side. Because the algorithm maxRight proceeds by adding right sides of FDs in $\mathcal{F}_{aq}$ to a growing Z, it can't include eno in Z if it isn't there at the beginning. Therefore, all remaining candidates on the list will fail the superkey test because none of them contains eno and the algorithm can't add it. The growing Z can never encompass all of R. You can conclude that the only key forced by the constraints of Figure 18.1 on the aquarium universal relation is eno. The only superkeys are supersets of eno. This result is compatible with the earlier discussion of the aquarium universal relation: each row corresponds to an event, extended with the attributes of the owning fish, its home tank, and its representative species.

 You can use $\mathcal{F}^+$ to determine a relation's keys and superkeys. You don't need to generate all of $\mathcal{F}^+$ to do so.

Definition of a minimal cover

Although it avoids constructing $\mathcal{F}^+$, the process for determining keys and superkeys makes repeated scans of $\mathcal{F}$. Other activities also use $\mathcal{F}$ extensively, so the set should be as small as possible. In general, you can't simply remove an FD from $\mathcal{F}$ without changing the boundary between valid and invalid database states. However, some redundancy may exist in $\mathcal{F}$, and you may be able to work with a smaller equivalent set. For example, if $\mathcal{F}$ contains $A \longrightarrow B, B \longrightarrow C$, and $A \longrightarrow C$, you can remove the last FD because it follows from the other two by transitivity. In other words, $A \longrightarrow C$ will be in $\mathcal{F}^+$ even if you remove it from $\mathcal{F}$. It will be one of the constraints that you can enforce "for free" as a consequence of enforcing the remaining two. The discussion below investigates relationships between different sets of FDs with the eventual goal of replacing a given set of FDs with a smaller one. You will then find the replacement set more efficient when you scan it during certain checks, such as key determination.

Two sets of FDs, $\mathcal{F}$ and $\mathcal{G}$, are **equivalent** if $\mathcal{F}^+ = \mathcal{G}^+$. You write this equivalence as $\mathcal{F} \equiv \mathcal{G}$. If you have two equivalent sets of FDs, you can choose to enforce either one, and the valid database states will be the same. A consistent database state with respect to $\mathcal{F}$, say s_1, satisfies all the FDs in $\mathcal{F}^+ = \mathcal{G}^+ \supset \mathcal{G}$. Therefore, it certainly satisfies all the FDs in $\mathcal{G}$, which makes s_1 consistent with respect to $\mathcal{G}$. Similarly, if a database state is consistent with respect to $\mathcal{G}$, it is also consistent with respect to $\mathcal{F}$. Extending the previous notation, you write $\mathcal{F} \models \mathcal{G}$ to mean that $\mathcal{F} \models (X \longrightarrow Y)$, for every $X \longrightarrow Y \in \mathcal{G}$. That is, $\mathcal{G} \subset \mathcal{F}^+$. You read $\mathcal{F} \models \mathcal{G}$ as "$\mathcal{F}$ models $\mathcal{G}$" or "$\mathcal{F}$ determines $\mathcal{G}$." In this notation, you have: if $\mathcal{F} \equiv \mathcal{G}$, then $\mathcal{F} \models \mathcal{G}$ and $\mathcal{G} \models \mathcal{F}$.

The reverse is also true. If $\mathcal{F} \models \mathcal{G}$ and $\mathcal{G} \models \mathcal{F}$, then $\mathcal{F} \equiv \mathcal{G}$. To prove this, note that $\mathcal{F}^{++} = \mathcal{F}^+$. To generate $\mathcal{F}^+$, you start with $\mathcal{F}$ and repeatedly add to the collection by applying Armstrong's axioms until none of them can generate a new FD. The accumulated FDs constitute $\mathcal{F}^+$. To generate $\mathcal{F}^{++}$, you start with $\mathcal{F}^+$ and immediately find that no axiom can add a new FD. Otherwise, you wouldn't have stopped the process that was generating $\mathcal{F}^+$. Because the process adds no new FDs, $\mathcal{F}^{++} = \mathcal{F}^+$.

If $\mathcal{F} \models \mathcal{G}$, then $\mathcal{G} \subset \mathcal{F}^+ = \{X \longrightarrow Y \mid \mathcal{F} \models (X \longrightarrow Y)\}$. So $\mathcal{G}^+ \subset \mathcal{F}^{++} = \mathcal{F}^+$. Because $\mathcal{G} \models \mathcal{F}$ also, you can interchange $\mathcal{F}$ and $\mathcal{G}$ in the argument to give $\mathcal{F}^+ \subset \mathcal{G}^+$. You then have

$$\mathcal{F} \models \mathcal{G} \text{ and } \mathcal{G} \models \mathcal{F} \text{ if and only if } \mathcal{F} \equiv \mathcal{G}. \qquad (18.5)$$

You can check the equivalence of two sets of FDs with the algorithm `FDinClosure`. For each $X \longrightarrow Y \in \mathcal{G}$, you check to see if $X \longrightarrow Y \in \mathcal{F}^+$. This test proceeds by checking $Y \subset (X; \mathcal{F})$, using `maxRight` to grow $(X; \mathcal{F})$. If an FD fails, the two sets aren't equivalent. If all FDs pass, you check the other direction. For each $X \longrightarrow Y \in \mathcal{F}$, you check to see if $X \longrightarrow Y \in \mathcal{G}^+$. In other words, is $Y \subset (X; \mathcal{G})$? If an FD fails, the two sets aren't equivalent. If all FDs pass, they are.

 Two sets of FDs are equivalent if and only if each is a subset of the other's closure.

Let $\mathcal{F}$ and $\mathcal{G}$ be two sets of FDs. $\mathcal{G}$ is a **minimal cover** for $\mathcal{F}$ if $\mathcal{G} \equiv \mathcal{F}$ and $\mathcal{G}$ conforms to the following restrictions:

- The right side of every FD in $\mathcal{G}$ contains a single attribute.

- If $X \longrightarrow A \in \mathcal{G}$, then $\mathcal{G} \not\equiv \mathcal{G} - \{X \longrightarrow A\}$. That is, no FD in $\mathcal{G}$ is redundant.

- If $XA \longrightarrow B \in \mathcal{G}$, then $\mathcal{G} \not\equiv (\mathcal{G} - \{XA \longrightarrow B\}) \cup \{X \longrightarrow B\}$. In other words, no FD in $\mathcal{G}$ has a redundant attribute on its left side.

$\mathcal{F}$ is **minimal** if it is a minimal cover of itself. Obviously, $\mathcal{F} \equiv \mathcal{F}$, so a minimal set of FDs is one that satisfies the above three conditions. You prefer to work with a minimal cover for $\mathcal{F}$, rather than with the original $\mathcal{F}$, because it is "smaller" in a certain sense. The first restriction insists that the right sides of the FDs be as simple as possible. The second condition requires that no extra FDs appear in the set. In particular, you can omit any FD that ends up in the closure of the remaining FDs because it will be enforced without any effort on your part. The third condition says that the left sides of the FDs are as simple as possible.

An algorithm to calculate a minimal cover

Every set of FDs possesses a minimal cover. A constructive proof shows how to obtain such a cover. The process starts with $\mathcal{F}$ and proceeds through three steps, each transforming the previous step's result to satisfy yet another restriction for a minimal cover. Each step also preserves equivalency with the original $\mathcal{F}$. With some subtleties and improvements to come later, consider the following tentative algorithm.

```
FDset tentativeMinCover(FDset F) {
  FDset G;

  G = φ;
  for each X ⟶ A₁A₂...Aₚ ∈ F
    for (i = 1; i ≤ p; i++)
      G = G ∪ {X ⟶ Aᵢ};
  while (there exists X ⟶ A ∈ G with  G ≡ G − {X ⟶ A})
    G = G − {X ⟶ A}
  while (there exists XB ⟶ A ∈ G with  G ≡ (G − {XB ⟶ A}) ∪ {X ⟶ A})
    G = (G − {XB ⟶ A}) ∪ {X ⟶ A};
  return G; }
```

After the first step, $\mathcal{G}$ contains the FDs obtained by splitting the right sides of the FDs in $\mathcal{F}$ into separate FDs. For example, an FD of the form $X \longrightarrow ABC \in \mathcal{F}$ gives rise to the three FDs: $X \longrightarrow A$, $X \longrightarrow B$, and $X \longrightarrow C \in \mathcal{G}$. Generally, if $X \longrightarrow A_1 A_2 \ldots A_p \in \mathcal{F}$, then each of $X \longrightarrow A_i \in \mathcal{G}$, for $1 \le i \le p$. Repeated application of the composition axiom then gives $X \longrightarrow A_1 A_2 \ldots A_p \in \mathcal{G}^+$. So $\mathcal{G} \models \mathcal{F}$. Similarly, if $X \longrightarrow A$ appears in $\mathcal{G}$, it does so because there is an $X \longrightarrow AY \in \mathcal{F}$. Because $X \longrightarrow A$ follows from $X \longrightarrow AY$ by the decomposition rule, you have $X \longrightarrow A \in \mathcal{F}^+$. So $\mathcal{F} \models \mathcal{G}$, and $\mathcal{F} \equiv \mathcal{G}$. Therefore, after the first step you have a new set of FDs, $\mathcal{G}$, that is equivalent to $\mathcal{F}$ and satisfies the first condition for a minimal cover. Note that the first step fails to transfer any FDs of the form $X \longrightarrow \varphi$ that may be in $\mathcal{F}$. An FD with an empty right side places no constraint on the relational body and is therefore always redundant.

The second step ejects an FD from $\mathcal{G}$ if the remaining FDs constitute an equivalent set. When this step starts, you have $\mathcal{G}^+ = \mathcal{F}^+$ because the $\mathcal{G}$ constructed by the preceding step is equivalent to the original $\mathcal{F}$. Each time you remove an FD from $\mathcal{G}$, the remaining FDs must still be equivalent to $\mathcal{F}$. Because there are a finite number of FDs in $\mathcal{G}$ at the beginning of this step, you must reach a point where no further ejections are possible. Note that this step can't confound the preceding step's results because any FDs remaining in $\mathcal{G}$ will still have a single attribute on the right side. Therefore, after the second step, $\mathcal{G} \equiv \mathcal{F}$, and $\mathcal{G}$ satisfies the first two conditions of a minimal cover.

Finally, the last step removes attributes from the left sides of FDs in $\mathcal{G}$, as long as the set remains equivalent to the original $\mathcal{F}$. Because the left sides of the FDs in $\mathcal{G}$ have finitely many attributes to remove, this process must reach a point where no further reductions are possible. Then, $\mathcal{G} \equiv \mathcal{F}$, and the third condition of a minimal cover holds for $\mathcal{G}$. Clearly, the first restriction continues to hold because the third step doesn't disturb any right sides. Can the third step confound the second condition for a minimal cover? Even if no redundant FDs are present at the beginning of the third step, can the third step reintroduce a redundant FD?

Yes, this complication can occur. Suppose you start with $\mathcal{G}$ as given by the left table of the transformation below. If you form $\mathcal{H} = \mathcal{G} - \{AB \longrightarrow C\}$, you can verify that `maxRight` computes $(AB; \mathcal{H}) = ABD$. Because this result doesn't include C, the FD, $AB \longrightarrow C$, isn't redundant. Similar calculations reveal that none of the FDs is redundant. However, $(A; \mathcal{G}) = ADBC$, which implies that B is a redundant attribute on the left side of $AB \longrightarrow C$. So you replace the FD with $A \longrightarrow C$, which gives the equivalent collection $\mathcal{G}'$ on the right.

$\mathcal{G}$
$AB \longrightarrow C$
$A \longrightarrow D$
$D \longrightarrow B$
$C \longrightarrow D$

$\implies$

$\mathcal{G}'$
$A \longrightarrow C$
$A \longrightarrow D$
$D \longrightarrow B$
$C \longrightarrow D$

However, $A \longrightarrow D$ is now redundant. Indeed, if you let $\mathcal{G}'' = \mathcal{G}' - \{A \longrightarrow D\}$, you can compute $(A; \mathcal{G}'') = ACDB$. Because the result contains D, you can remove $A \longrightarrow D$. This example shows that an FD can be made newly redundant when the third step reduces the left side of a different FD.

You can salvage the algorithm: simply repeat steps two and three until no change occurs in either step. This stable condition must eventually appear because both steps reduce the size of $\mathcal{G}$ by removing entire FDs or by removing attributes from the left sides of FDs. In either case, because only a finite number of potential removals is available, the algorithm must eventually reach a point where no further reduction is possible. At that point, $\mathcal{G} \equiv \mathcal{F}$, and $\mathcal{G}$ satisfies all three conditions for a minimal cover. The revised algorithm, `minCover1`, then appears as follows.

```
FDset minCover1(FDset F) {
  FDset G;
  boolean change2, change3;
  G = φ; change2 = change3 = true;
  for each X ⟶ A₁A₂ ... Aₚ ∈ F
    for (i = 1; i ≤ p; i++)
      G = G ∪ {X ⟶ Aᵢ};
  while (change2 || change3) {
    if (there does not exist X ⟶ A ∈ G with  G ≡ G − {X ⟶ A})
      change2 = false;
    else {
      change2 = true;
      while (there exists X ⟶ A ∈ G with  G ≡ G − {X ⟶ A})
        G = G − {X ⟶ A} }
    if (there does not exist XB ⟶ A ∈ G with  G ≡ (G − {XB ⟶ A}) ∪ {X ⟶ A})
      change3 = false;
    else {
      change3 = true;
      while (there exists XB ⟶ A ∈ G with  G ≡ (G − {XB ⟶ A}) ∪ {X ⟶ A})
        G = (G − {XB ⟶ A}) ∪ {X ⟶ A}; } }
  return G; }
```

Consider the second step, where you try to remove an FD, $X \longrightarrow Y$, from $\mathcal{G}$. Let $\mathcal{H} = \mathcal{G} - \{X \longrightarrow Y\}$. You can remove the FD if $\mathcal{H}^+ = \mathcal{G}^+$. Equivalently, you can remove the FD if you don't change the closure. So you must check that $\mathcal{G} \models \mathcal{H}$ and $\mathcal{H} \models \mathcal{G}$. However, the first part is trivial. Because $\mathcal{H} \subset \mathcal{G}$, you have $\mathcal{H} \subset \mathcal{G} \subset \mathcal{G}^+$, which implies that $\mathcal{G} \models \mathcal{H}$. For the second part, you must show that $\mathcal{H} \models (U \longrightarrow V)$, for every $U \longrightarrow V \in \mathcal{G}$. For every $U \longrightarrow V \in \mathcal{G}$, except $X \longrightarrow Y$, you have $U \longrightarrow V \in \mathcal{H} \subset \mathcal{H}^+$, which implies that $\mathcal{H} \models (U \longrightarrow V)$. So the only significant check is whether $\mathcal{H} \models (X \longrightarrow Y)$. In other words, is $Y \subset (X; \mathcal{H})$? To check this, you grow $(X; \mathcal{H})$ without using $X \longrightarrow Y$. If it contains Y, you can remove $X \longrightarrow Y$ from $\mathcal{G}$. Otherwise, you can't.

Suppose, after the first step of minCover1, you have the table of FDs to the left below. The second column gives the maxRight return for the left side of the FD in the first column. The procedure operates in the context of the remaining dependencies: it omits the FD under consideration and also any removed in an earlier line (marked with an asterisk). If the maxRight return includes the right side of the FD under consideration, you remove the

	FD	maxRight return	Remove FD?
	$AB \longrightarrow C$	ABD	No
	$AB \longrightarrow D$	ABC	No
*	$EF \longrightarrow A$	$EFBCAD$	Yes
	$F \longrightarrow B$	F	No
	$EF \longrightarrow C$	EFB	No
	$G \longrightarrow C$	G	No
	$C \longrightarrow A$	C	No

	FD	maxRight return	Remove FD?
*	$EF \longrightarrow C$	$EFABCD$	Yes
	$AB \longrightarrow C$	ABD	No
	$AB \longrightarrow D$	ABC	No
	$EF \longrightarrow A$	EFB	No
	$F \longrightarrow B$	F	No
	$G \longrightarrow C$	G	No
	$C \longrightarrow A$	C	No

Consider the first entry, $AB \longrightarrow C$. You temporarily cross that FD off the list; the remaining FDs constitute $\mathcal{H}$ from the discussion above. Using the remaining FDs, you next compute $(AB; \mathcal{H})$. You start with $Z = AB$ and observe that the second FD has left side $AB \subset Z$. This allows you to add its right side to Z, giving $Z = ABD$. However, no more FDs in $\mathcal{H}$ have their left side in Z and their right side not in Z. Therefore, $(AB; \mathcal{H}) = ABD$, as shown in the top row of the second column. Because $C \notin ABD$, $\mathcal{H} \not\models (AB \longrightarrow C)$, so you can't remove the FD.

A similar argument shows that you must also retain the second FD. However, the third entry provides some variety. You temporarily cross out $EF \longrightarrow A$, leaving the set $\mathcal{H}$, and compute $(EF; \mathcal{H})$. Starting with EF, you extend to EFB using $F \longrightarrow B$, extend to $EFBC$ using $EF \longrightarrow C$, extend to $EFBCA$ using $C \longrightarrow A$, and finally extend to $EFBCAD$ using $AB \longrightarrow D$. Because $A \subset EFBCAD$, you can remove $EF \longrightarrow A$ from the list. You erase it permanently, and `maxRight` computations for later FDs don't use it. The next entry, $F \longrightarrow B$, gets no further than the initial F in computing $(F; \mathcal{H})$. So you can't remove it. The next entry, $EF \longrightarrow C$, starts with EF, extends to EFB using $F \longrightarrow B$, but stops there. The process could use the FD removed earlier, but it's no longer available. So you can't remove $EF \longrightarrow C$. Similarly, you must also retain the final two entries.

If you consider the FDs in a different order, you might reject a different collection of redundant FDs. In the example, you can rework the second step of the algorithm in the order shown to the right above. This time, you reject $EF \longrightarrow C$ and keep $EF \longrightarrow A$. So a minimal cover isn't a unique computation: several minimal covers can exist for a given $\mathcal{F}$.

When you remove an FD, $X \longrightarrow Y$, from $\mathcal{G}$ to form $\mathcal{H}$, then $\mathcal{H}$ is **weaker** than $\mathcal{G}$ in the sense that $\mathcal{H}$ may allow more valid database states. If a database state satisfies $\mathcal{G}$, it certainly satisfies $\mathcal{H}$ because $\mathcal{H}$ has one less FD to worry about. Therefore, $\mathcal{G} \models \mathcal{H}$ trivially. The deciding criterion for removing $X \longrightarrow Y$ in the minimal cover algorithm then becomes: Does $\mathcal{H} \models \mathcal{G}$? In other words, does removing $X \longrightarrow Y$ not actually weaken $\mathcal{G}$? You can then phrase this question as: Is $Y \subset (X; \mathcal{H})$? You could restate the conditions in algorithm `minCover1` in this less complicated form, but a similar optimization is available for the third step. So let's consider that first.

In the third step, you try to replace an FD of the form $XB \longrightarrow A$ in $\mathcal{G}$ with a reduced FD of the form $X \longrightarrow A$. Let $\mathcal{H}$ be the new set of FDs: $\mathcal{H} = (\mathcal{G} - \{XB \longrightarrow A\}) \cup \{X \longrightarrow A\}$. $\mathcal{H}$ is **stronger** than $\mathcal{G}$ in the sense that it may permit fewer valid database states. If a database state satisfies $\mathcal{H}$, it certainly satisfies $\mathcal{G}$. All the FDs in $\mathcal{G}$ are in $\mathcal{H}$, except $XB \longrightarrow A$. However, a database state that satisfies $\mathcal{H}$ must satisfy the stronger condition $X \longrightarrow A$, so it certainly satisfies $XB \longrightarrow A$. Therefore, $\mathcal{H} \models \mathcal{G}$ trivially. The question is then: does $\mathcal{G} \models \mathcal{H}$? Because $X \longrightarrow A$ is the only FD in $\mathcal{H}$ that isn't in $\mathcal{G}$, the question then becomes: does $\mathcal{G} \models (X \longrightarrow A)$? Equivalently, is $A \subset (X; \mathcal{G})$? When you tentatively strengthen $\mathcal{G}$ to $\mathcal{H}$ by replacing $XB \longrightarrow A$ with $X \longrightarrow A$, you need only check if the `maxRight` algorithm can grow $(X; \mathcal{G})$ to encompass A using the *old* set of FDs, $\mathcal{G}$.

After removing the redundant $EF \longrightarrow A$ in the example above, you arrive at the left column in the tabulation below. The second column lists an attribute that you are trying to remove from the left side of the FD in the first column. In the first line, you are trying to remove A from $AB \longrightarrow C$. You compute `maxRight` with the rest of the left side: $(B; \mathcal{G})$ $= \mathtt{maxRight}(B, \mathcal{G})$, where $\mathcal{G}$ is the entire list in the left column.

FD	Attribute	maxRight return	Remove attribute?
$AB \longrightarrow C$	A	B	No
	B	A	No
$AB \longrightarrow D$	A	B	No
	B	A	No
$F \longrightarrow B$	φ	φ	No
$EF \longrightarrow C$	E	F	No
	F	E	No
$G \longrightarrow C$	φ	φ	No
$C \longrightarrow A$	φ	φ	No

Starting with $Z = B$, you find no FD, $U \longrightarrow V \in \mathcal{G}$ with $U \subset Z$ and $V \not\subset Z$. Indeed, no FD in the left column has its left side contained in B. So maxRight returns B, which doesn't contain C. Therefore, you can't delete A from the left side of the first FD. You then try to remove B from AB but encounter the same difficulty. Actually, you can't reduce the left side of any FD in the list. So the list of the leftmost column is the final solution—a minimal cover.

An FD with a single attribute on the left side provokes a call to maxRight$(\varphi, \mathcal{G})$. The returned set is usually φ. The only circumstance where it could be larger is when an FD of the form $\varphi \longrightarrow A$ appears in $\mathcal{G}$. This extreme FD restricts the right side to be constant across all the relation's tuples. The discussion here assumes that this boundary case doesn't apply, so you don't need to apply the third step of the algorithm to an FD with a singleton left-hand side.

Steps two and three both employ a test for equivalence, after weakening the existing set of FDs by ejecting an FD or strengthening it by reducing a left side. The argument above simplifies both tests to a condition on a maxRight computation. Therefore, the final algorithm for a minimal cover is:

```
FDset minCover2(FDset F) {
  FDset G;
  boolean change2, change3;

  G = φ; change2 = change3 = true;
  for each X ⟶ A₁A₂...Aₚ ∈ F
    for (i = 1; i ≤ p; i++)
      G = G ∪ X ⟶ Aᵢ;
  while (change2 || change3) {
    if (there does not exist X ⟶ A ∈ G with  A ∈ maxRight(X, G − {X ⟶ A}))
      change2 = false;
    else {
      change2 = true;
      while (there exists X ⟶ A ∈ G with  A ∈ maxRight(X, G − {X ⟶ A}))
        G = G − {X ⟶ A} }
    if (there does not exist XB ⟶ A ∈ G with  A ∈ maxRight(X, G))
      change3 = false;
    else {
      change3 = true;
      while (there exists XB ⟶ A ∈ G with  A ∈ maxRight(X, G))
        G = (G − {XB ⟶ A}) ∪ {X ⟶ A}; } }
  return G; }
```

A comprehensive example

The third step of the minimal cover algorithm produced no changes in the last example. For a more eventful example, consider a new set of FDs, $\mathcal{F}$, as shown in the left column of the first table below. The first step of `minCover` splits the right sides to obtain the second column, $\mathcal{G}$. For each $X \longrightarrow A$ in the second column, the third column gives $(X; \mathcal{H})$, where $\mathcal{H}$ is $\mathcal{G}$ minus the FD under consideration and any FDs removed in prior lines (marked with an asterisk). If $A \in (X; \mathcal{H})$, you remove the FD (mark it with an asterisk), and it isn't available for the computation on subsequent FDs. The first column in the second table summarizes the situation when the algorithm has ejected all redundant FDs.

$\mathcal{F}$		$\mathcal{G}$	maxRight return	Remove FD?
$A \longrightarrow BD$	*	$A \longrightarrow B$	$ADCB$	Yes
$C \longrightarrow B$		$A \longrightarrow D$	A	No
$DA \longrightarrow C$		$C \longrightarrow B$	C	No
$EFG \longrightarrow HJK$		$DA \longrightarrow C$	DA	No
$EF \longrightarrow L$		$EFG \longrightarrow H$	$EFGJKLG$	No
$FL \longrightarrow G$		$EFG \longrightarrow J$	$EFGHKLG$	No
$HJ \longrightarrow K$	*	$EFG \longrightarrow K$	$EFGHJLGK$	Yes
		$EF \longrightarrow L$	EF	No
		$FL \longrightarrow G$	FL	No
		$HJ \longrightarrow K$	HJ	No

$\mathcal{G}$ from step 2	Attribute	maxRight return	Remove attribute?
$A \longrightarrow D$		omit test	
$C \longrightarrow B$		omit test	
$DA \longrightarrow C$	D	$ADCB$	Yes
$EFG \longrightarrow H$			
$EFG \longrightarrow J$			
$EF \longrightarrow L$			
$FL \longrightarrow G$			
$HJ \longrightarrow K$			

The third step then begins to reduce the left sides of the FDs. Because no FDs of the form $\varphi \longrightarrow A$ appear, you omit the test when the left side contains a single FD. The first successful encounter occurs when you try to remove D from the left side of $DA \longrightarrow C$. Using the entire left column, you start growing $(A; \mathcal{G})$, and you succeed in reaching C. Therefore, you can replace $DA \longrightarrow C$ with $A \longrightarrow C$. Because the contents of $\mathcal{G}$ change permanently at this point, you redraw the table. The development then continues as shown in the first table below, until you are able to remove G from the left side of $EFG \longrightarrow H$. At that point, you redraw the table again, which gives the situation on the right.

$\mathcal{G}$ from step 2	Attribute	maxRight return	Remove attribute?
$A \longrightarrow D$		omit test	
$C \longrightarrow B$		omit test	
$A \longrightarrow C$		omit test	
$EFG \longrightarrow H$	E	FG	No
	F	EG	No
	G	$EFLGHJK$	Yes
$EFG \longrightarrow J$			
$EF \longrightarrow L$			
$FL \longrightarrow G$			
$HJ \longrightarrow K$			

$\mathcal{G}$ from step 2	Attribute	maxRight return	Remove attribute?
$A \longrightarrow D$		omit test	
$C \longrightarrow B$		omit test	
$A \longrightarrow C$		omit test	
$EF \longrightarrow H$	E	F	No
	F	E	No
$EFG \longrightarrow J$	E	FG	No
	F	EG	No
	G	$EFLGHJK$	Yes
$EF \longrightarrow L$			
$FL \longrightarrow G$			
$HJ \longrightarrow K$			

Working with the table on the right above, you discover that you can remove G from $EFG \longrightarrow J$. The final table then appears as shown below; the algorithm's third step can make no further reductions. However, you must now scan the final left column for any newly redundant FDs that may have been introduced during the reduction of left-hand sides in the third step. Following the algorithm, you could repeat the second step, but note that all the final FDs have a different right side. Therefore, if you remove an FD, maxRight can't regrow its right side because maxRight starts from the left side and uses only the remaining FDs. Therefore, if all the FDs have distinct right sides, they must be nonredundant. The list below then constitutes a minimal cover.

$\mathcal{G}$ from step 2	Attribute	maxRight return	Remove attribute?
$A \longrightarrow D$		omit test	
$C \longrightarrow B$		omit test	
$A \longrightarrow C$		omit test	
$EF \longrightarrow H$	E	F	No
	F	E	No
$EF \longrightarrow J$	E	F	No
	F	E	No
$EF \longrightarrow L$	E	F	No
	F	E	No
$FL \longrightarrow G$	F	L	No
	L	F	No
$HJ \longrightarrow K$	H	J	No
	J	H	No

 $\mathcal{G}$ *is a minimal cover of* $\mathcal{F}$ *if (1)* $\mathcal{G} \equiv \mathcal{F}$ *and (2)* $\mathcal{G}$ *has no redundant FDs, no extraneous attributes on any left side, and single attributes for all right sides. You can construct a minimal cover for any* $\mathcal{F}$.

A minimal cover for the aquarium database constraints

As a final example, consider the set $\mathcal{F}_{aq}$ for the aquarium universal relation as shown in Figure 18.1. All FDs have single-attribute right sides, so the first step of the minimal cover algorithm produces no change. Moreover, all FDs, except tno $\longrightarrow$ tcolor and tvolume $\longrightarrow$ tcolor, have distinct right sides, so they must be nonredundant.

If you remove tno $\longrightarrow$ tcolor, you can grow (tno; $\mathcal{H}$) with the remaining FDs ($\mathcal{H}$) to include tno, tname, tvolume, and tcolor. Therefore the removal is justified. With this adjustment, the remaining FDs have unique right sides, so all are nonredundant. Finally, all left sides contain a single attribute, and in the absence of FDs of the form $\varphi \longrightarrow A$, you can't reduce these left sides. Therefore, the third step of the algorithm produces no further change. $\mathcal{F}_{aq} - \{$tno $\longrightarrow$ tcolor$\}$ is a minimal cover for $\mathcal{F}_{aq}$. For future reference, Figure 18.3 documents this minimal cover, which is called $\mathcal{F}'_{aq}$.

In this case, the original set of FDs is nearly its own minimal cover. This occurs because the aquarium application is a small example, and the constraining FDs are just those necessary to force valid database states to conform to the join, Species $*$ Fish $*$ Event $*$ Tank. However, if you collect the FDs without special attention to providing only the minimal constraints, you may easily include eno $\longrightarrow$ tname or fno $\longrightarrow$ sname. Both are consistent with the understanding that a row in the universal relation represents an event, extended with its owning fish, home tank, and representative species. However, such entries are redundant, and the minimal cover construction will force them out.

sno $\longrightarrow$ sname	sno $\longrightarrow$ sfood	
tno $\longrightarrow$ tname	tno $\longrightarrow$ tvolume	
fno $\longrightarrow$ fname	fno $\longrightarrow$ fcolor	fno $\longrightarrow$ fweight
eno $\longrightarrow$ edate	eno $\longrightarrow$ enote	
tvolume $\longrightarrow$ tcolor		
eno $\longrightarrow$ fno	fno $\longrightarrow$ tno	fno $\longrightarrow$ sno

Figure 18.3 $\mathcal{F}'_{aq}$, a minimal cover for $\mathcal{F}_{aq}$, the governing FDs for the universal aquarium relation

Lossless-join decompositions

The aquarium universal relation is a poor choice for representing the data. A great deal of repetition occurs for certain data values, and ample opportunity arises for inconsistencies. The redundancy is directly connected with the governing set of functional dependencies. An FD insists that two tuples agree on certain attributes, which results in redundant storage and possible inconsistency. Later sections study this matter more closely and present a solution by decomposing the universal relation into several smaller relations. When you disperse the data across several relations, query activities will inevitably use join operations to reassemble the components. This section discusses precautions to ensure that join operations faithfully restore the a relation's contents from its component projections.

$(R_1, R_2, \ldots, R_n)$ is a **decomposition** of a relation R' if $R' = R_1 \cup R_2 \cup \ldots \cup R_n$. A decomposition $(R_1, R_2, \ldots, R_n)$ is a **lossless-join decomposition** of $R' \subset R$ in the context of a set of FDs, $\mathcal{F}$, if $\pi_{R'}(r) = \pi_{R_1}(r) * \pi_{R_2}(r) * \ldots * \pi_{R_n}(r)$, for every *valid* database state $r(R)$ with respect to $\mathcal{F}$. Of course, $\pi_{R_i}(r) = \pi_{R_i}\pi_{R'}(r)$ because $R_i \subset R'$. So if you let $r' = \pi_{R'}(r)$, the condition reads: $r' = \pi_{R_1}(r') * \pi_{R_2}(r') * \ldots * \pi_{R_n}(r')$. In other words, a decomposition of R' is lossless if you can exactly recover the R' projection of any valid state as the join of the decomposition's components. For brevity, this discussion will use "lossless join" or "lossless decomposition" for a lossless-join decomposition.

Suppose you have the situation below, which splits R' into R_1 and R_2. Assume that the governing functional dependencies are such that the database state is valid. Let r' denote the content of R'; r' is a projection of the valid universal state, $r(R)$. You see that $r' \subset \pi_{R_1}(r') * \pi_{R_2}(r')$, but $r' \neq \pi_{R_1}(r') * \pi_{R_2}(r')$. Therefore, this decomposition isn't lossless.

R'

a	b	c	d	e
7	8	1	2	3
6	3	1	2	4

R_1

a	b	c
7	8	1
6	3	1

R_2

c	d	e
1	2	3
1	2	4

Join of components

a	b	c	d	e
7	8	1	2	3
7	8	1	2	4
6	3	1	2	3
6	3	1	2	4

You will always have r' contained in $\pi_{R_1}(r') * \pi_{R_2}(r')$. To prove this, suppose $\mu \in r'$. Then $\mu(R_1)$ and $\mu(R_2)$ must agree on the overlapping attributes of R_1 and R_2. Moreover, $\mu(R_1) \in \pi_{R_1}(r')$ and $\mu(R_2) \in \pi_{R_2}(r')$. Consequently, when you form $\pi_{R_1}(r') * \pi_{R_2}(r')$, you combine $\mu(R_1)$ and $\mu(R_2)$ in the preliminary Cartesian product, and the combination survives the subsequent test for equality in common attributes. However, that combination is precisely μ. So $r \subset \pi_{R_1}(r) * \pi_{R_2}(r)$ always.

As illustrated in the above example, the reverse inclusion doesn't always hold. Therefore, when you test a decomposition to determine if it's lossless, you need only check that the join doesn't introduce too many tuples. This result generalizes to decompositions with more than two components.

Suppose $(R_1, R_2, \ldots, R_n)$ is a decomposition of R' and r' is the body of R'. Then $r' \subset \pi_{R_1}(r') * \pi_{R_2}(r') * \ldots * \pi_{R_n}(r')$. The decomposition is lossless if $r' = \pi_{R_1}(r') * \pi_{R_2}(r') * \ldots * \pi_{R_n}(r')$, where r' is a projection of any valid database state.

A join that doesn't always restore the original relation from the projected components is a **lossy join**. A lossy join includes the original tuples, but it also includes some extraneous tuples. In this sense, it represents a loss of precision. You don't want to store the relation R in the above example as the projections R_1 and R_2 because a query join operation generates false tuples that aren't in the original relation. For example, the query on the left below operates on the original table and returns the value 1; the query on the right operates on the components and returns 2. Therefore, you must ensure that any decomposition of a relation is a lossless join decomposition.

```
select count(*)            select count(*)
from R                     from R_1, R_2
where a = 7 and b = 8.     where R_1.c = R_2.c and R_1.a = 7 and R_1.b = 8.
```

If the decomposition involves only two components, a simple test determines if it is lossless. Let $\mathcal{F}$ be the governing set of FDs. A decomposition (R_1, R_2) is lossless if and only if either $R_1 \cap R_2 \longrightarrow R_1 \in \mathcal{F}^+$ or $R_1 \cap R_2 \longrightarrow R_2 \in \mathcal{F}^+$. The proof below considers a decomposition of the universal relation. However, the result holds for the binary decomposition of any projection of the universal relation.

Suppose $R_1 \cap R_2 \longrightarrow R_1 \in \mathcal{F}^+$. Because $r \subset \pi_{R_1}(r) * \pi_{R_2}(r)$ for any database state $r(R)$, you need only show the reverse inclusion for valid database states. So suppose r is a valid database state of R, with respect to $\mathcal{F}$, and let $\mu \in \pi_{R_1}(r) * \pi_{R_2}(r)$. The preliminary Cartesian product formed μ when it combined a tuple $\mu_1 \in \pi_{R_1}(r)$ with a tuple $\mu_2 \in \pi_{R_2}(r)$. The subsequent selection then found the same values under the common attributes in both halves: $\mu_1(R_1 \cap R_2) = \mu_2(R_1 \cap R_2) = x$. Because r is a valid database state and $R_1 \cap R_2 \longrightarrow R_1 \in \mathcal{F}^+$, any tuples in R with the values x under the attributes $R_1 \cap R_2$ must agree on all attributes R_1. Therefore, the projection $\pi_{R_1}(r)$ will contain exactly one tuple with values x under attributes $R_1 \cap R_2$. Therefore, μ_1 is that one tuple, and μ_1 agrees on attributes R_1 with *all* the tuples in r that have $R_1 \cap R_2$ values x. Because $\mu_2(R_1 \cap R_2) = x$, μ_2 must be the projection of one of these tuples, say ρ. Therefore, $\mu_1 = \pi_{R_1}(\rho)$ and $\mu_2 = \pi_{R_2}(\rho)$. When you then form μ by combining μ_1 and μ_2, you produce the tuple ρ. Therefore, $\mu = \rho \in r$, and the decomposition has the lossless-join property. The argument just given is symmetric in R_1 and R_2, and therefore if $R_1 \cap R_2 \longrightarrow R_2 \in \mathcal{F}^+$, a lossless-join decomposition also results.

For a proof in the reverse direction, suppose the decomposition is lossless. Let $X = R_1 \cap R_2$. The proof assumes that neither $X \longrightarrow R_1$ nor $X \longrightarrow R_2$ is in $\mathcal{F}^+$ and derives a contradiction. If $R_1 - (X; \mathcal{F})$ were empty, then $R_1 \subset (X; \mathcal{F})$, which implies $X \longrightarrow R_1$. Therefore, $R_1 - (X; \mathcal{F}) \neq \varphi$. By a similar argument, $R_2 - (X; \mathcal{F}) \neq \varphi$. Because $X \subset (X; \mathcal{F})$, the difference $R_1 - (X; \mathcal{F})$ removes any elements of R_1 that are also in R_2. So $R_1 - (X; \mathcal{F})$ and $R_2 - (X; \mathcal{F})$ are disjoint sets, neither of which is empty. The following table breaks the attributes of R into segments, and the last two must each contain at least one attribute. Let r be the contents of the table. It turns out that r is a valid database state, which you can prove by showing that it satisfies all the FDs in $\mathcal{F}$.

R		
$(X; \mathcal{F})$	$R_1 - (X; \mathcal{F})$	$R_2 - (X; \mathcal{F})$
...000...	...111...	...222...
...000...	...333...	...444...

To violate $U \longrightarrow V \in \mathcal{F}$, you must have $U \subset (X; \mathcal{F})$. Then $X \longrightarrow U$, and $X \longrightarrow V$ follows by transitivity. So $V \subset (X; \mathcal{F})$. However, no violation then occurs because the two tuples agree on $(X; \mathcal{F})$. This table, therefore, represents a valid database state, and the lossless-join hypothesis asserts that $r = \pi_{R_1}(R) * \pi_{R_2}(R)$. You can directly compute the join of the projections to see if this statement is true. You first need to rearrange the table to show the projection components explicitly.

R				
		$(X; \mathcal{F})$		
$R_1 - X$		X	$R_2 - X$	
...111...	...000...	...000...	...000...	...222...
...333...	...000...	...000...	...000...	...444...

R_1		
		$(X; \mathcal{F}) \cap R_1$
$R_1 - X$		X
...111...	...000...	...000...
...333...	...000...	...000...

R_2		
$(X; \mathcal{F}) \cap R_2$		
X	$R_2 - X$	
...000...	...000...	...222...
...000...	...000...	...444...

Join of components				
		$(X; \mathcal{F})$		
$R_1 - X$		X	$R_2 - X$	
...111...	...000...	...000...	...000...	...222...
...111...	...000...	...000...	...000...	...444...
...333...	...000...	...000...	...000...	...222...
...333...	...000...	...000...	...000...	...444...

The computation shows that $r \neq \pi_{R_1}(R) * \pi_{R_2}(R)$ and establishes the expected contradiction.

 A decomposition (R_1, R_2) of R, in the context of a set of FDs, $\mathcal{F}$, is a lossless-join decomposition if and only if $R_1 \cap R_2$ is a superkey of at least one of the components.

You need a more elaborate test for a lossless-join decomposition into more than two components. However, you won't need that test if you achieve each multicomponent decomposition with a sequence of two-way splits. Suppose you want the decomposition $(R_1, R_2, R_3, R_4, R_5)$. You can start with the two-way decomposition $((R_1 \cup R_2 \cup R_3), (R_4 \cup R_5))$, and using the theorem above, you can show that it is lossless. You then decompose the components into $((R_1 \cup R_2), R_3)$ and (R_4, R_5) and show that each binary decomposition is lossless. A final decomposition of $(R_1 \cup R_2)$ finishes the task. If r is a valid database state for R, in the context of some set of FDs, $\mathcal{F}$, you can show that $r = \pi_{R_1}(r) * \ldots * \pi_{R_5}(r)$ by working up from the individual decompositions. In particular, the following conditions must hold because the piecewise decompositions are lossless. The expressions use an abbreviated notation, where $\pi_{R_1 \cup R_2 \cup R_3} = \pi_{123}$, and so forth.

$$
\begin{aligned}
r &= \pi_{123}(r) * \pi_{45}(r) \\
\pi_{123}(r) &= \pi_{12}(\pi_{123}(r)) * \pi_3(\pi_{123}(r)) = \pi_{12}(r) * \pi_3(r) \\
\pi_{45}(r) &= \pi_4(\pi_{45}(r)) * \pi_5(\pi_{45}(r)) = \pi_4(r) * \pi_5(r) \\
\pi_{12}(r) &= \pi_1(\pi_{12}(r)) * \pi_2(\pi_{12}(r)) = \pi_1(r) * \pi_2(r).
\end{aligned}
$$

Back-substituting, you obtain

$$
r = ((\pi_1(r) * \pi_2(r)) * \pi_3(r)) * (\pi_4(r) * \pi_5(r)).
$$

Chapter 3 showed that the natural join is associative. You can, therefore, remove the parentheses to obtain the final result.

The next section shows how to decompose the universal relation to achieve storage efficiencies and consistency enhancements. Each decomposition will be a lossless, two-way split. The final decomposition, therefore, will always be a lossless-join decomposition.

 A multicomponent decomposition will have the lossless-join property if you achieve the decomposition with a sequence of two-way, lossless-join decompositions.

Boyce-Codd normal form (BCNF)

Redundancies induced by functional dependency constraints

If you can predict a cell's content in a relation, the relation suffers two disadvantages when compared with storage schemes where such prediction isn't possible. First, if a cell's content is predictable, why should the DBMS store it? Is this not just wasted storage space? Second, if you can predict a cell's content, a user may insert a different value in the cell and make the database state inconsistent. For example, consider the following excerpt from the aquarium universal relation.

Aquarium universal relation													
eno	edate	enote	fno	fname	fcolor	fweight	tno	tname	tcolor	tvolume	sno	sname	sfood
⋮	⋮	⋮	⋮	⋮	⋮	⋮	⋮	⋮	⋮	⋮	⋮	⋮	⋮
6653	05/14	Born	347	flipper	black	150	35	lagoon	red	400	17	dolphin	herring
5644	05/15	Dies	347	—	—	—	—	—	—	—	—	—	—
⋮	⋮	⋮	⋮	⋮	⋮	⋮	⋮	⋮	⋮	⋮	⋮	⋮	⋮

You can predict each blank in the second tuple from the governing FDs, which constrain the valid database states. Noting the fno value (347) in the second tuple, you know that the second tuple represents another event in the life of fish 347. So you can copy the descriptive information about fish 347, its home tank, and its related species from the preceding tuple. A prediction like this ultimately derives from the FDs of $\mathcal{F}_{aq}$, as shown in Figure 18.1. For example, fno $\longrightarrow$ sname must hold by transitivity from fno $\longrightarrow$ sno and sno $\longrightarrow$ sname. Because the two tuples agree on fno, they must also agree on sname, and you can copy dolphin into the appropriate cell in the second tuple.

If you imagine the entire aquarium universal relation, you find that most of the cells are subject to this sort of prediction. So the universal relation not only wastes space in storing redundant information, it also invites inconsistency. The interfacing programs and interactive activities must somehow prevent users from entering information different from the predictions.

Suppose you have a collection of attributes, R, and a set of governing FDs, $\mathcal{F}$. Let $R' \subset R$. Recall that the FD, $X \longrightarrow Y$, **applies** to R' if $X \subset R'$. In this case, if $X \longrightarrow Y$ constrains $r(R)$, then $X \longrightarrow (Y \cap R')$ constrains $r(R') = \pi_{R'}(r(R))$. If an FD has an empty right side, it always holds, regardless of the database state. Therefore, it doesn't actually constrain the relation's body, and you can remove it from the constraint collection. Then, if the right side is a single attribute, the intersection with R' is the entire right side or the empty set. In the latter case, the FD doesn't actually constrain R'. The following definition deals with FDs where the right side is a single attribute. The applicable circumstance, therefore, is when R' contains both the right and left sides.

R' is in **Boyce-Codd normal form** (BCNF) with respect to $\mathcal{F}$ if the following condition holds. Whenever $X \longrightarrow A \in \mathcal{F}^+$, $XA \subseteq R'$, and $A \notin X$, then $X \longrightarrow R' \in \mathcal{F}^+$. Certain FDs are trivial because the left side contains the right side. The conditions for BCNF aren't concerned with these trivial FDs. If $A \in X$, you don't care whether $X \longrightarrow R'$ is in $\mathcal{F}^+$. Moreover, if the FD doesn't meaningfully apply to R' (i.e., if $XA \not\subseteq R'$), again you aren't concerned about whether $X \longrightarrow R' \in \mathcal{F}^+$. But if a non-trivial FD applies meaningfully to R', you insist that the left side be a superkey of R' for the relation to merit the BCNF award.

You don't require the left side to be a superkey of the universal relation R. You only require that the left side determine all the attributes of R'. An FD $X \longrightarrow A \in \mathcal{F}^+$, which meets the preconditions (e.g., $A \notin X$ and $XA \subset R'$), but fails the postcondition (e.g., X is a superkey of R'), prevents R' from achieving BCNF. This FD is a BCNF **violator**. In the context of a set of FDs, $\mathcal{F}$, an alternative statement of BCNF is then as follows:

 R' satisfies Boyce-Codd normal form if X is a superkey of R' for every non-trivial FD, $X \longrightarrow A$, that applies meaningfully to R'.

Suppose you have a table, R', in BCNF with respect to $\mathcal{F}$, and suppose you try to use an FD, $X \longrightarrow A \in \mathcal{F}^+$, to predict some cell's value. You find two tuples that agree on X, and you then know that they must also agree on A. You can, therefore, predict that the A value in the second tuple is the same as the A value in the first. However, because the relation is in BCNF, $X \longrightarrow R' \in \mathcal{F}^+$, which means that X is a superkey in R'. So only one tuple in the relation can have the given value of X. This frustrates your attempt to predict the A value of a tuple, based on the A value of a different tuple with the same X value.

Although BCNF removes redundancy problems that arise from FDs, it doesn't remove all redundancies. Other redundancies may arise from constraints other than functional dependencies; a later section will discuss these possibilities.

Removing a BCNF violator through decomposition

When you find an FD, $X \longrightarrow A \in \mathcal{F}^+$, that is a BCNF violator for R', you can decompose R' into two components such that the FD isn't a BCNF violator for either component. Moreover, the decomposition will satisfy the lossless-join property. Of course, other BCNF violators may still exist for one or both components. But the offending list will be one FD shorter, and subsequent decompositions can then deal with the other violators. The decomposition proceeds as shown below, where $X \longrightarrow A \in \mathcal{F}^+$ is a BCNF violator for R'.

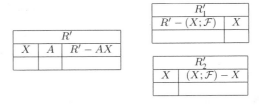

Note that $R_1' \cap R_2' = X$ and $R_2' = (X; \mathcal{F})$. Because $X \longrightarrow (X; \mathcal{F}) \in \mathcal{F}^+$, X is a superkey of R_2'. The decomposition is, therefore, lossless. Also, the superkey status of X in R_2' ensures that $X \longrightarrow A$ is no longer a BCNF violator with respect to R_2'. Because $X \longrightarrow A$ is a BCNF violator for R', you must have $A \notin X$. Also, $X \longrightarrow A$ implies that $A \in (X; \mathcal{F})$, so $A \notin R' - (X; \mathcal{F})$. Therefore, $A \notin R_1'$, and $X \longrightarrow A$ doesn't meaningfully apply to R_1'. By repeating this two-way splitting process, you can eventually reduce R' to a series of BCNF components, and the final decomposition will be lossless.

Although the decomposition technique is simple enough, it does require that you continually scan $\mathcal{F}^+$ for BCNF violators. The earlier analysis of the closure noted that $\mathcal{F}^+$ is exponentially large, so these searches are difficult. You might hope that you could always find the BCNF violators in $\mathcal{F}$ itself, but that simplification isn't valid. For example, suppose $R = (A, B, C, D, E)$ and $\mathcal{F} = (A \longrightarrow B, B \longrightarrow C, C \longrightarrow D)$. If you are dealing with a component table $R' = (A, D, E)$, you notice that none of the FDs is meaningfully applicable to the table. To qualify as a BCNF violator, the table must contain both sides of the FD. However, $A \longrightarrow D \in \mathcal{F}^+$, by repeated transitivity, and $(A; \mathcal{F}) = ABCD \not\supseteq R'$. So A isn't a superkey of R'. You then have a BCNF violator in the closure, $\mathcal{F}^+$, although no FDs in $\mathcal{F}$ is a violator. The conclusion is that you must systematically scan the closure, $\mathcal{F}^+$, for violations. A later section will develop a more efficient algorithm for locating and removing BCNF violators.

An earlier example obtained the following FDs as a minimal cover for a given set of FDs. Consider a universal relation, R, that contains all these attributes, and look for BCNF violators in $\mathcal{F}$ itself, rather than in $\mathcal{F}^+$.

$\mathcal{F}$	
$A \longrightarrow D$	$C \longrightarrow B$
$A \longrightarrow C$	$EF \longrightarrow H$
$EF \longrightarrow J$	$EF \longrightarrow L$
$FL \longrightarrow G$	$HJ \longrightarrow K$

Computing $(A; \mathcal{F}) = ADCB$, you see that A isn't a superkey of R, and $A \longrightarrow D$, $A \longrightarrow C$, and $A \longrightarrow B$ are all BCNF violators. To resolve the situation, you isolate $(A; \mathcal{F})$ in one component of a decomposition and place $A \cup (R - (A; \mathcal{F}))$ in a second component. The decomposition then appears as the second tier below.

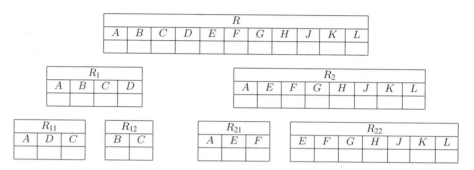

The first component, R_1, has a further BCNF violator, $C \longrightarrow B$, because $(C; \mathcal{F}) = CB \not\supseteq R_1$. So you export BC to R_{12} and leave the remaining attributes, plus the common attribute, C, in R_{11}. R_2 also needs further decomposition because $(EF; \mathcal{F}) = EFHJLGK$, which isn't all of R_2. So you break R_2 into R_{21}, containing AEF, and R_{22}, containing $EFGHJKL$. These elements establish the third tier above. R_{22} still has the BCNF violators $FL \longrightarrow G$ and $HJ \longrightarrow K$. You decompose it losslessly as follows.

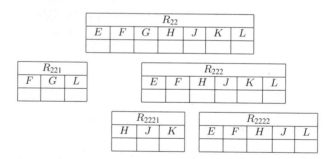

Although you searched only $\mathcal{F}$, rather than $\mathcal{F}^+$, you can still argue that all the relations in the final decomposition are in BCNF. Starting with R_{11}, recall that A is a superkey and compute $(D; \mathcal{F}) = D$ and $(C; \mathcal{F}) = CB$. These results imply that D doesn't determine any attribute outside of itself and C determines only itself and an attribute outside of R_{11}. Therefore, neither D nor C can serve as the left side of a BCNF violator for R_{11}. A similar exemption applies to the combination DC.

R_{12} contains only two attributes, and you need at least three for a BCNF violation. (If you have only two attributes, say A_1 and A_2, and $A_1 \longrightarrow A_2$, then $A_1 \longrightarrow A_1 A_2$, which implies that A_1 is a superkey.) You can make similar arguments for R_{221}, R_{2221}, and R_{2222}. Only R_{2222} has enough attributes to make this informal check burdensome.

Reducing the aquarium database to BCNF

As a second example, decompose the aquarium universal relation in the context of the governing FDs, $\mathcal{F}'_{aq}$, of Figure 18.3. You already know that supersets of eno are the only superkeys, so sno $\longrightarrow$ sname is a BCNF violator. You calculate $(\text{sno}; \mathcal{F}'_{aq}) = (\text{sno, sname, sfood})$ and break these attributes out into a separate relation, called Species. You can argue as before that sname and sfood, either individually or collectively, determine only themselves, so no further BCNF violators trouble the species relation. The other component contains the common attribute sno to link it to Species; it also contains the remaining attributes not transferred to Species.

The indentation format below indicates this first-level decomposition. Supersets of eno remain the only keys of the second component, so tno $\longrightarrow$ tname is a BCNF violator, leading to a tank table for $(\text{tno}; \mathcal{F}'_{aq}) = (\text{tno, tname, tcolor, tvolume})$. The two components from this decomposition appear at a second indentation level below. However, both components require further decomposition, the first because tvolume $\longrightarrow$ tcolor, and the second because fno $\longrightarrow$ fname. The corresponding components appear at a third indentation level.

```
eno edate enote fno fname fcolor fweight tno tname tcolor tvolume sno sname sfood
   sno sname sfood
   sno eno edate enote fno fname fcolor fweight tno tname tcolor tvolume
      tno tname tcolor tvolume
         tvolume tcolor
         tno tname tvolume
      sno tno eno edate enote fno fname fcolor fweight
         fno fname fcolor fweight tno sno
         eno fno edate enote.
```

You can argue that no further BCNF violators lurk in $(\mathcal{F}'_{aq})^+$. The final relations then appear as follows. Except for the tank relation, which decomposes into two components, the final BCNF schema is very similar to the aquarium relational database from previous chapters.

Relation	Attributes
Species	sno, sname, sfood
Tank	tno, tname, tvolume
VolColor	tvolume, tcolor
Fish	fno, fname, fcolor, fweight, sno, tno
Event	eno, edate, enote, fno

Intuitively, redundancy occurs when two or more application entities occur in the same relation. A one-to-many or many-to-many relationship between any two of the entities, say A and B, produces duplication because all the attributes from an A instance will repeat for every related B instance. Because the original aquarium database represented the application entities as separate relations, opportunities for such redundancy were rare. However, when all application entities reside in a single universal relation, much more redundant representation appears. The functional dependency decomposition process removes the redundancy and produces components that correspond to individual application entities.

From this perspective, functional dependency analysis is useful in identifying the application entity types. If the application is small, such as the aquarium example, you can expect certain entities to appear because of your comprehensive understanding of the application. You can use this knowledge to force the first several decompositions and reduce the tables to a size where you can argue, without systematically investigating the closure set, that no further BCNF violations exist in $\mathcal{F}^+$. In decomposing the aquarium universal relation, for example, you expect Species, Tank, Fish, and Event to appear because mixing these entities in a single table accounts for much of the duplication. The fact that the expected tank relation undergoes a further decomposition may come as a surprise, but by that time, the decomposing relation (Tank) has very few attributes.

An algorithm for BCNF decomposition

Suppose you are considering a component for further decomposition. A combination of nonkey attributes, X, can't be the left side of a BCNF violator if X determines only itself and attributes outside the component. You can identify such an X because $(X; \mathcal{F})$ will include only X and attributes outside the component. Most attributes simply assert some descriptive property about an application entity, so they never determine any attributes beyond themselves. In other words, they never appear on the left side of a nontrivial FD. If you can identify attributes of this nature in a component, you don't need to consider their combinations as sources of BCNF violators. In short, understanding the nature of the application frequently makes it unnecessary to scan $\mathcal{F}^+$ exhaustively for BCNF violators.

However, you can systematically scan $\mathcal{F}^+$, if necessary, with the following procedure. A decomposition is a set of attribute sets, so assume you have such a data structure, decomposition. Suppose a relation, R', has n attributes, and you are probing it for possible BCNF violations. Because a BCNF violator must have $X \longrightarrow A, A \notin X$, and X not a superkey, you can't have more than $n-2$ attributes in X. This means you must consider the n one-attribute subsets, the $\binom{n}{2}$ two-attribute subsets, and so forth, up through the $\binom{n}{n-2}$ subsets of size $n-2$ as left sides of possible BCNF violators. You probe each candidate, say X, by computing $Y = (X; \mathcal{F})$. If Y contains more than X but less than R', then X is the left side of a BCNF violator. Assume a subroutine to calculate the ith candidate subset of R', calcSubset(R', i), and one to return the number of such candidate subsets, candSubsets(R').

```
decomposition BCNFdecomp(attributeSet R, FDset F) {
  int i, m, n;
  boolean change, found;
  attributeSet X, Y, R₁, R₂;
  decomposition D₁, D₂;

  D₁ = R;  D₂ = φ;  change = true;
  while (change) {
    change = false;
    for each R′ ∈ D₁ do {
      n = |R′|;  found = false;
      m = candSubsets(R′);  /* get number of candidate subsets */
      for (i = 1; !found && (i ≤ m); i++) {
        X = calcSubset(R′, i);  /* get iᵗʰ subset */
        Y = maxRight(X, F) ∩ R′;
        if (Y − X ≠ φ && R′ − Y ≠ φ) {
          found = true;  change = true;
          R₁ = Y;  R₂ = (R′ − Y) ∪ X;
          D₂ = D₂ ∪ {R₁, R₂};  } }
    if (!found)
      D₂ = D₂ ∪ {R′};  }
    D₁ = D₂;  D₂ = φ;  }
  return D₁;  }
```

Algorithm BCNFdecomp systematically probes each relation by investigating all possible attribute subsets that could form the left side of a BCNF violator in $\mathcal{F}^+$. Starting with an application's universal relation, it delivers a decomposition where all components satisfy BCNF. However, the number of subsets of n attributes is exponential in n, so this algorithm isn't optimal. Indeed, it continually rechecks those parts of the decomposition that remain constant in the outer loop. More efficient algorithms use a computation that is polynomial in n.

In the pursuit of a BCNF decomposition, a particular algorithm may unnecessarily decompose a component. Note that if $X \longrightarrow A \in \mathcal{F}^+$, $XA \subset R'$, and $A \notin X$, you can still make a lossless-join decomposition of R' into $R_1 = XA$ and $R_2 = R' - A$, even if X is a superkey of R'. In the aquarium example, this step may decompose the species table as shown below. Although the decomposition obviously goes too far in terms of optimal representation, it doesn't violate BCNF.

Species		
sno	sname	sfood

R₁	
sno	sname

R₂	
sno	sfood

In the context of a set of FDs, $\mathcal{F}$, a decomposition of the universal relation R into $(R_1, R_2, \ldots, R_n)$ satisfies BCNF if each component satisfies BCNF. You can then summarize the results of this section as follows.

Every relation admits a lossless-join decomposition that satisfies Boyce-Codd normal form.

Dependency preservation

Suppose $\mathcal{F}$ is a set of FDs, and $(R_1, R_2, \ldots, R_n)$ is a decomposition of R. Define $\pi_{R_i}(\mathcal{F})$ as all FDs from the closure of $\mathcal{F}$ such that R_i contains their left and right sides.

$$\pi_{R_i}(\mathcal{F}) = \{X \longrightarrow Y \mid X \longrightarrow Y \in \mathcal{F}^+ \text{ and } XY \subset R_i\}. \qquad (18.6)$$

You read $\pi_{R_i}(\mathcal{F})$ as the projection of $\mathcal{F}$ on R_i, but the definition actually includes all FDs from the *closure* of $\mathcal{F}$ that are contained in R_i.

A decomposition of R into $(R_1, R_2, \ldots, R_n)$ is a **dependency-preserving decomposition** with respect to $\mathcal{F}$ if $\mathcal{F} \equiv \pi_{R_1}(\mathcal{F}) \cup \pi_{R_2}(\mathcal{F}) \cup \ldots \cup \pi_{R_n}(\mathcal{F})$. Because each $\pi_{R_i}(\mathcal{F}) \subset \mathcal{F}^+$ from the definition, you have $\mathcal{F} \models \pi_{R_i}(\mathcal{F})$, for each i. Therefore, $\mathcal{F} \models \cup_{i=1}^{n} \pi_{R_i}(\mathcal{F})$. This means that $\mathcal{F}$ is potentially stronger than the union of its projections. The essence of a dependency-preserving decomposition is that $\mathcal{F}$ isn't actually stronger; it is equivalent to the union of its projections.

A dependency-preserving decomposition is attractive because you can enforce all of $\mathcal{F}^+$ by ensuring that no violators appear in the projections, $\pi_{R_i}(\mathcal{F})$. Moreover, the FDs of a given projection involve the attributes of a single component of the decomposition. In other words, the only checks involve FDs of the form $X \longrightarrow Y$, where XY appear in a single component. Such a check, of course, needs to verify that two tuples agreeing on X also agree on Y. Because XY appear in a single table, however, you don't need expensive join operations to perform the check.

A simple example shows that not all decompositions are dependency-preserving. Consider the universal relation $R = (A, B, C)$ in the presence of $\mathcal{F} = (AB \longrightarrow C, C \longrightarrow A)$. Decompose R as shown below, and let $\mathcal{G} = \pi_{R_1}(\mathcal{F}) \cup \pi_{R_2}(\mathcal{F})$. The only possible nontrivial FDs that could project from $\mathcal{F}^+$ onto $\pi_{R_1}(\mathcal{F})$ are $B \longrightarrow C$ and $C \longrightarrow B$. However, you can apply the maxRight$(B, \mathcal{F})$ algorithm to compute $(B; \mathcal{F}) = B$, which shows that $B \longrightarrow C \notin \mathcal{F}^+$. A similar computation shows that $C \longrightarrow B \notin \mathcal{F}^+$. Therefore, $\pi_{R_1}(\mathcal{F})$ contains only trivial FDs.

R_1	
B	C

R		
A	B	C

R_2	
C	A

The only possible nontrivial FDs that could project from $\mathcal{F}^+$ onto $\pi_{R_2}(\mathcal{F})$ are $A \longrightarrow C$ and $C \longrightarrow A$. Obviously, $C \longrightarrow A \in \mathcal{F}^+$ because it is in $\mathcal{F}$. However, computing $(A; \mathcal{F}) = A$ from maxRight$(A, \mathcal{F})$, you see that $A \longrightarrow C \notin \mathcal{F}^+$. Therefore, $\pi_{R_2}(\mathcal{F})$ consists of $C \longrightarrow A$ plus trivial FDs.

So $\mathcal{G}$ contains only $C \longrightarrow A$ and trivial FDs. You can trace the computation of maxRight$(AB, \mathcal{G})$ as follows. The algorithm first initializes the approximation Z of

$(AB; \mathcal{G})$ to AB and then looks for an FD, $U \longrightarrow V \in \mathcal{G}$, such that $U \subset AB$ and $V \not\subset AB$. A trivial FD can never satisfy these criteria because if AB contains U, it also contains V. (Remember, a trivial $U \longrightarrow V$ has $V \subset U$.) The only chance then is the one substantive FD in $\mathcal{G}$: $C \longrightarrow A$. However, $C \not\subset AB$, so that FD isn't applicable. Therefore, maxRight$(AB, \mathcal{G})$ returns only AB, which doesn't contain C. This shows that $AB \longrightarrow C \notin \mathcal{G}^+$. Because $AB \longrightarrow C \in \mathcal{F}$, $\mathcal{F} \not\equiv \mathcal{G}$ and the decomposition isn't dependency-preserving.

Note that $C \longrightarrow A$ is a BCNF violator for the original R because $(C; \mathcal{F}) = CA$, which isn't all of R. However, the decomposition (R_1, R_2) does satisfy BCNF. The only nontrivial FD from $\mathcal{F}^+$ that applies to either table is $C \longrightarrow A$, and it isn't a BCNF violator because C is a superkey of R_2. The decomposition also satisfies the lossless-join property because the common attribute C is a superkey of the second component. The example, therefore, demonstrates a lossless-join decomposition of R into (R_1, R_2) that satisfies BCNF but isn't dependency-preserving.

Moreover, no other decomposition of R enjoys the lossless-join property. Suppose you decompose so that A is the common attribute. Recall from above that $(A; \mathcal{F}) = A$, which implies that A isn't a superkey of either component. A similar observation holds if you decompose using B as the common attribute. If you decompose R into disjoint components, the common attributes are the empty set, φ, which is certainly not a superkey of either component. This example, therefore, admits only one BCNF lossless-join decomposition, and that decomposition isn't dependency-preserving. This counterexample proves that you can't always obtain a BCNF, lossless-join, dependency-preserving decomposition.

 You can't always decompose a relation such that the decomposition (1) satisfies BCNF, (2) has the lossless-join property, and (3) has the dependency-preserving property.

This development is unfortunate. You want to decompose the universal relation into components that satisfy BCNF because that decomposition removes all redundancy forced by FD constraints. You must also insist on a lossless-join decomposition so that queries don't generate false results with join operations. Finally, you want the decomposition to preserve dependencies so that the DBMS can easily enforce all the FDs without resorting to joins.

In the example, you can use an SQL assertion to enforce the $AB \longrightarrow C$ constraint, but it is an expensive operation that joins the two components before checking the FD condition. You can express this constraint as follows.

```
create assertion splitFD check (not exists
    (select S.A, S.B
     from R₁ natural join R₂ as S
     groupby S.A, S.B
     having max(C) ≠ min(C))).
```

The ideal BCNF, lossless-join, dependency-preserving decomposition isn't always possible. But depending on the governing FDs, it may still be available in a particular application. When you decompose a relation, the problem occurs when you encounter a BCNF violator, $X \longrightarrow A \in \mathcal{F}^+$, where the right side A is part of a key for the relation. In the example above, the violator for R is $C \longrightarrow A$, and AB is a key for R. If no BCNF violator has its right side contained in a key of R, you can achieve a lossless-join, dependency-preserving decomposition that satisfies BCNF.

An algorithm for checking dependency preservation

You can test a decomposition to determine if it's dependency-preserving. Using this test, you can check a lossless, BCNF decomposition to see if you were lucky enough to preserve the dependencies.

Suppose $(R_1, R_2, \ldots, R_n)$ is a decomposition of R. Let $\mathcal{F}$ be the set of governing FDs, and let $\mathcal{G}$ be the union of the projections, $\pi_{R_i}(\mathcal{F})$. You want to determine if $\mathcal{F} \equiv \mathcal{G}$. You know that $\mathcal{F}$ is potentially stronger, so $\mathcal{F} \models \mathcal{G}$. The question is then whether $\mathcal{G} \models \mathcal{F}$. To answer affirmatively, you must verify that $X \longrightarrow Y \in \mathcal{G}^+$, for each $X \longrightarrow Y \in \mathcal{F}$. This operation appears to be a simple invocation of $\mathtt{maxRight}(X, \mathcal{G})$ for each such FD. However, the operation becomes complicated because $\mathcal{G}$ consists of the applicable FDs from $\mathcal{F}^+$, which isn't immediately available.

Recall that $\mathtt{maxRight}(X, \mathcal{G})$ grows $(X; \mathcal{G})$ in an ever-expanding variable Z. It initializes $Z = X$ and makes successive passes through $\mathcal{G}$, searching for an FD, $U \longrightarrow V$, with $U \subset Z$ and $V \not\subset Z$. When it finds such an FD, it replaces Z with $Z \cup V$. This operation maintains the loop invariant: $Z \subset (X; \mathcal{G})$. The problem is how to scan $\mathcal{G}$ for the qualifying $U \longrightarrow V$ FDs when you have only $\mathcal{F}$ and no explicit listing of $\mathcal{G}$.

If $Z \subset (X; \mathcal{G})$, a condition that is certainly true when the algorithm initializes Z, then for any component, R_i, the following operation preserves that invariant.

- Compute $Y = \mathtt{maxRight}(Z \cap R_i, \mathcal{F})$.

- Replace Z with $Z \cup (Y \cap R_i)$.

The first part uses $\mathcal{F}$, and you do have an explicit listing for $\mathcal{F}$. It computes the largest Y such that $(Z \cap R_i) \longrightarrow Y \in \mathcal{F}^+$. Then $(Z \cap R_i) \longrightarrow (Y \cap R_i) \in \mathcal{F}^+$ by decomposition because you are replacing the right side with a subset of the right side. Moreover, R_i contains both the right and left sides of this last FD, so it appears in the projection $\pi_{R_i}(\mathcal{F})$. It also appears, therefore, in $\mathcal{G}$, which is the union of these projections. Thus, if you construct a processing loop that implements this operation and if you have succeeded in maintaining $Z \subset (X; \mathcal{G})$ at the beginning of an iteration, then you can reason as follows.

$Z \cap R_i \subset Z \subset (X; \mathcal{G})$	assume loop invariant holds at start of an iteration
$X \longrightarrow (Z \cap R_i) \in \mathcal{G}^+$	property of $(X; \mathcal{G})$
$(Z \cap R_i) \longrightarrow (Y \cap R_i) \in \mathcal{G} \subset \mathcal{G}^+$	loop operation as described above
$X \longrightarrow (Y \cap R_i) \in \mathcal{G}^+$	transitivity
$(Y \cap R_i) \in (X; \mathcal{G})$	property of $(X; \mathcal{G})$
$Z \cup (Y \cap R_i) \subset (X; \mathcal{G})$	loop invariant holds at end of iteration.

This operation then grows $Z \subset (X; \mathcal{G})$. The only question is whether it culminates in all of $(X; \mathcal{G})$. Specifically, the algorithm operates as follows.

```
attributeSet maxRight1(attribute X, FDset F, decomposition D) {
    attributeSet Y, Z;
    boolean change;

    Z = X; change = true;
    while (change) {
        change = false;
        for each Rᵢ ∈ D {
            Y = maxRight(Z ∩ Rᵢ, F);
            if ((Y ∩ Rᵢ) − Z ≠ φ) {
                change = true;
                Z = Z ∪ (Y ∩ Rᵢ); } }
    }
    return Z; }
```

The new algorithm, $\mathtt{maxRight1}(X, \mathcal{F}, D)$, calculates the largest right side, W, such that $X \longrightarrow W \in \mathcal{G}^+$, where $\mathcal{G}$ is the union of the projections $\pi_{R_i}(\mathcal{F})$ for the components $R_i \in D$. $\mathtt{maxRight1}$ uses the old $\mathtt{maxRight}$ to calculate the largest Y such that $(Z \cap R_i) \longrightarrow Y \in \mathcal{F}^+$. The earlier analysis of the loop operation guarantees that it maintains the loop invariant $Z \subset (X; \mathcal{G})$. The loop must terminate because each iteration that flips the $\mathtt{change}$ variable back to true must add a new attribute to Z. Because there are only finitely many attributes, the algorithm must reach a point where it can make no further progress. The $\mathtt{change}$ variable remains false throughout that final iteration, and the loop terminates. Therefore, when $\mathtt{maxRight1}$ returns the value Z, you must have $Z \subset (X; \mathcal{G})$.

You still haven't proved that the return is exactly $(X; \mathcal{G})$. To this end, consider the relational body r below, where Z is the attribute set returned by $\mathtt{maxRight1}$.

R	
Z	R − Z
...000...	...000...
...000...	...111...

Relation r satisfies all the FDs in $\mathcal{G}$. To prove this, let $U \longrightarrow V \in \mathcal{G}$. Then $U \longrightarrow V \in \mathcal{F}^+$ and $UV \subset R_j$, for at least one of the components R_j of the decomposition D. If $U \not\subset Z$, no violation occurs because the two tuples can't agree on U. If $U \subset Z$, consider what happens when the algorithm computes $Y = \mathtt{maxRight}(Z \cap R_j, \mathcal{F})$ on the last pass before the loop terminates. Because $U \subset (Z \cap R_j)$, you have $U \subset Y$, which says that $(Z \cap R_j) \longrightarrow U \in \mathcal{F}^+$. Then, by transitivity, $(Z \cap R_i) \longrightarrow V \in \mathcal{F}^+$. Then $V \subset Y$. Because $V \subset R_j$, you have $V \subset Y \cap R_j$. However, the algorithm doesn't add any attributes to Z in the last iteration of the loop, so $V \subset (Y \cap R_j) \subset Z$. Therefore, if $U \subset Z$, then $V \subset Z$ also, and no violation of $U \longrightarrow V$ occurs.

Because r now satisfies every FD in $\mathcal{G}$, it must satisfy every FD in $\mathcal{G}^+$, including $X \longrightarrow (X; \mathcal{G})$. You have $X \subset Z$ because the algorithm initializes Z with X, and Z only grows thereafter. Therefore, $(X; \mathcal{G})$ is contained in Z, or else a violation would occur. This argument, together with the loop invariant, proves that $\mathtt{maxRight1}$ delivers precisely $(X; \mathcal{G})$.

You can trace the operation of $\mathtt{maxRight1}$ on the last example. To prove $\mathcal{F} \equiv \mathcal{G}$, you must show that each FD in $\mathcal{F}$ is contained in $\mathcal{G}^+$. Let D be the composition under consideration: $R_1 = BC$ and $R_2 = CA$. For $AB \longrightarrow C \in \mathcal{F}$, you compute maxRight1$(AB, \mathcal{F}, D)$ as follows. You initialize $Z = AB$. The first pass through the loop computes $Y = $ maxRight$(Z \cap R_1, \mathcal{F})$, growing just B. Because $B \cap R_1 = B$ is already in Z, no change to Z occurs. The same iteration then continues with R_2, computing $Y = $ maxRight$(Z \cap R_2, \mathcal{F})$ and growing just A. Again, $A \cap R_2 = A$ is already in Z, so no change occurs. The loop then terminates after one iteration and returns $Z = AB$. Because $C \not\subset AB$, you conclude that $AB \longrightarrow C \notin \mathcal{G}^+$ and $\mathcal{F} \not\equiv \mathcal{G}$. The test correctly determines that the decomposition isn't dependency-preserving.

In certain cases a simpler test suffices. Suppose $(R_1, R_2, \ldots, R_n)$ is a decomposition of R, and let $\mathcal{F}$ be the governing set of FDs. If each FD in $\mathcal{F}$ has both sides contained in one or more of the components, the decomposition is dependency-preserving. Again, let $\mathcal{G} = \pi_{R_1}(\mathcal{F}) \cup \pi_{R_2}(\mathcal{F}) \cup \ldots \cup \pi_{R_n}(\mathcal{F})$. You can reason as follows. If $X \longrightarrow Y \in \mathcal{F}$, then $XY \subset R_i$, for some i, which implies that $X \longrightarrow Y \in \pi_{R_i}(\mathcal{F}) \subset \mathcal{G} \subset \mathcal{G}^+$. Therefore, $\mathcal{G} \models (X \longrightarrow Y)$. Because this argument holds for all $X \longrightarrow Y \in \mathcal{F}$, you have $\mathcal{G} \models \mathcal{F}$, which implies that $\mathcal{F} \equiv \mathcal{G}$. So if the decomposition doesn't split any FDs in $\mathcal{F}$, it is dependency-preserving. If it does split one or more of the FDs in $\mathcal{F}$, it still may be dependency-preserving, but you must invoke algorithm maxRight1 to make the determination.

If a decomposition doesn't split an FD from $\mathcal{F}$ across two or more tables, it is dependency-preserving. If a split does occur, dependency preservation is still possible, but you must verify that $\mathcal{F}$ is in the closure of the union of $\mathcal{F}$'s projections.

Consider the BCNF, lossless-join decomposition of the aquarium universal relation derived earlier. The simpler test shows that it is dependency-preserving. The final BCNF decomposition appears below, and you can see that each component receives some of the FDs from the governing $\mathcal{F}'_{aq}$ of Figure 18.3. Because every FD in $\mathcal{F}'_{aq}$ associates with at least one component, the decomposition is dependency-preserving.

Relation	Attributes	FDs
Species	sno, sname, sfood	sno $\longrightarrow$ sname
		sno $\longrightarrow$ sfood
Tank	tno, tname, tvolume	tno $\longrightarrow$ tname
		tno $\longrightarrow$ tvolume
VolColor	tvolume, tcolor	tvolume $\longrightarrow$ tcolor
Fish	fno, fname, fcolor, fweight, sno, tno	fno $\longrightarrow$ fname
		fno $\longrightarrow$ fcolor
		fno $\longrightarrow$ fweight
		fno $\longrightarrow$ tno
		fno $\longrightarrow$ sno
Event	eno, edate, enote, fno	eno $\longrightarrow$ edate
		eno $\longrightarrow$ enote
		eno $\longrightarrow$ fno

You formed the BCNF decomposition of the aquarium using the minimal cover $\mathcal{F}'_{aq}$ of Figure 18.1. If you had worked with the original set of FDs, $\mathcal{F}_{aq}$ of Figure 18.1, you would have arrived at the same decomposition. However, one of the FDs, tno $\longrightarrow$ tcolor, would have split across two components. The decomposition would be dependency-preserving, but the simple test wouldn't be conclusive. You would have to use algorithm maxRight1 to prove dependency preservation.

The first three normal forms

A BCNF decomposition purges the database of any redundancy induced by the governing functional dependencies. BCNF accomplishes this feat by restructuring the tables so that the predictable cells no longer appear. In short, if $X \longrightarrow A$ lets you predict cell A in tuple t_1 by comparing it with cell A in another tuple, t_2, the BCNF rearrangement ensures that only one tuple with a given X value will appear in the table. Therefore, you can view BCNF as the ultimate arrangement of attributes into tables so as to rule out redundancies forced by FDs. (Other redundancies may still arise from constraints other than FDs.) Historically, BCNF format evolved through a sequence of steps, each improving on its predecessor in terms of reduced redundancy. BCNF is the fourth such step, and this section reviews the three normal forms that preceded BCNF. Although the first two aren't currently of great interest, the third remains valuable as a fall-back position if you can't obtain a lossless-join, dependency-preserving decomposition into BCNF.

First normal form

A relation R', a subset of the universal relation, is in **first normal form** (1NF) if each cell contains only atomic values. A decomposition $(R_1, R_2, \ldots, R_n)$ of R satisfies 1NF if each component satisfies first normal form. You must, of course, define atomic in application terms, but the general idea is to disallow repeating groups. In the aquarium example, if you define the fish table so that multiple values can occur under the fcolor attribute, the relation won't satisfy 1NF. However, you can't define the fish table this way because the definition of a relation disallows repeating groups. Therefore, any relation meeting the definition is automatically in 1NF. You may encounter multivalued attributes in ER and OMT diagrams, but you must export them to a related weak entity when you map the design to a relational schema.

First normal form then constrains a relation to single-valued attributes. Under the fcolor attributes, you expect to find entries such as blue or green but not (blue, green). You might quibble that blue isn't an atomic entry, but rather a repeating sequence of characters. The application, however, isn't concerned with the internal structure of the string blue. It treats the attribute value as an indivisible unit in operations that compare it with other values. In the final analysis, an understanding of the application underlies the meaning of atomic. Once that concept is in place, 1NF is unambiguously defined.

Second normal form

Let R' be a relation, and let $\mathcal{F}$ be the set of governing FDs. An attribute $A \in R'$ is **prime** if a key of R' contains A. In other words, A is prime in R' if there exists $K \subset R'$ such that (1) $K \longrightarrow R' \in \mathcal{F}^+$, (2) for all $B \in K, (K - B) \longrightarrow R' \notin \mathcal{F}^+$, and (3) $A \in K$.

A relation R', a subset of the universal relation, satisfies **second normal form** (2NF) when (1) it is already in 1NF and (2) if K a key of R' and A is non-prime, you can't find $X \subset K$ with $X \neq K$ and $X \longrightarrow A \in \mathcal{F}^+$. You can restate the definition as follows. A relation R' satisfies 2NF if it satisfies 1NF and if every non-prime attribute is *fully* dependent on every key. If K is a key for R', then all of K is necessary to determine a non-prime attribute. No proper subset of K can determine a non-prime attribute. Because you can depend on 1NF from the definition of a relation, you need only check for keys where a subset determines a non-prime attribute. In other words, to find a 2NF violator, you must find all the following features in R':

1. K a key of R'. Note that K must be a *key*—a minimal superkey.

2. An attribute A that is non-prime. Note that A must be excluded from *all* keys, not just from K.

3. A *proper* subset $B \subset K$, such that $B \longrightarrow A \in \mathcal{F}^+$. Note that B must be a proper subset of K, so $K - B \neq \varphi$.

If you can't find a violation, then R' is in 2NF. By extension, a decomposition scheme $(R_1, R_2, \ldots, R_n)$ satisfies 2NF if all its components satisfy 2NF.

Consider a part of the aquarium application consisting of the attributes tno, tname, tcolor, tvolume, fno, fname, fcolor, fweight. For this example, vary the meaning of the fno attribute to allow the reuse of fno values, provided that fish with the same fno value swim in different tanks. The fish swimming in a particular tank all have distinct fno values. With this new understanding, you need the (tno, fno) pair to identify a fish. You also have the constraint that tanks are color-coded according to volume. The governing FDs, $\mathcal{F}$, for the situation are as follows.

$\mathcal{F}$	
FD	Intended constraint
tno $\longrightarrow$ tname	A particular tank has a determined name
tno $\longrightarrow$ tcolor	A particular tank has a determined color
tno $\longrightarrow$ tvolume	A particular tank has a determined volume
tvolume $\longrightarrow$ tcolor	Tanks are color-coded by volume
tno fno $\longrightarrow$ fname	A particular fish has a determined name
tno fno $\longrightarrow$ fcolor	A particular fish has a determined color
tno fno $\longrightarrow$ fweight	A particular fish has a determined weight

Let R' contain the attributes tno, tname, tcolor, tvolume, fno, fname, fcolor, and fweight. You compute `maxRight(tno fno, ` $\mathcal{F}$ `) =` R' to verify that (tno, fno) is a key. By examining the other subsets, you conclude that no other keys exist in R'. The prime attributes are then tno and fno; the rest are non-prime. You can now begin searching for a 2NF violation. The first criterion requires that you locate a key of R', so you must choose (tno, fno). Next, you must find an FD where the left side is a proper subset of the key and the right side is non-prime. The only choices for a left side are tno or fno. Examining $\mathcal{F}$, you see that tno determines several non-prime attributes, so you choose tno $\longrightarrow$ tname, which proves that R' is not in 2NF. It isn't BCNF either because of the same violation: tno $\longrightarrow$ tname, holds, and tno isn't a superkey. The immediate concern, however, is 2NF, which is less restrictive than BCNF.

If a relation fails to satisfy 2NF, it suffers redundancies in certain cells. If $Y \longrightarrow A$ is the violator, Y must be a proper subset of a key, K. Many tuples, therefore, can have the same Y value. If that weren't possible, Y itself would be a superkey and would contradict the minimality of K. The relational body must duplicate the A value for each of the many tuples with the same Y value. In the example just considered, an excerpt from a possible R' relation appears below. The redundancy is obvious because tno, which is only part of the key, determines several non-prime attributes.

R'							
tno	tname	tcolor	tvolume	fno	fname	fcolor	fweight
$\vdots$	$\vdots$	$\vdots$	$\vdots$	$\vdots$	$\vdots$	$\vdots$	$\vdots$
35	lagoon	red	400	347	flipper	black	150
35	lagoon	red	400	388	cory	purple	52
35	lagoon	red	400	654	darron	white	79
$\vdots$	$\vdots$	$\vdots$	$\vdots$	$\vdots$	$\vdots$	$\vdots$	$\vdots$

A collection of **storage anomalies** classifies the negative consequences of this redundancy. An anomaly is simply an irregularity. The table R' exhibits an **insertion anomaly** because you can't enter a new fish unless you assign it to a tank. You could enter null values for the tno, tname, tcolor, and tvolume attributes, but that approach places a null value in part of the key and violates entity integrity. Similarly, you can't enter a new tank without first associating it with at least one fish. A **deletion anomaly** exists because removing the last fish for a given tank also removes all attributes of the tank. An **update anomaly** appears because you must enter a tname change in several tuples, which affords an opportunity for an inconsistent database state when the operation is only partially completed.

You can remove the redundancies by decomposing the table into the following two components, each accompanied by its relevant FDs.

R_1			
tno	tname	tcolor	tvolume

R_2				
tno	fno	fname	fcolor	fweight

tno $\longrightarrow$ tname
tno $\longrightarrow$ tcolor
tno $\longrightarrow$ tvolume
tvolume $\longrightarrow$ tcolor

tno fno $\longrightarrow$ fname
tno fno $\longrightarrow$ fcolor
tno fno $\longrightarrow$ fweight

Note that each FD in $\mathcal{F}$ falls completely in one of the components, and therefore the decomposition is dependency-preserving. Moreover, $(\text{tno}; \mathcal{F}'_{aq}) = R_1$, so the common column is a superkey of the first component, which implies that the decomposition is lossless. You can verify that tno is the only key in R_1, so you can't find a 2NF violation there. Generally, you can't generate a 2NF violation from a single-attribute key because you must find a proper subset of the key for the left side of the violator. In the second component, the pair (tno, fno) remains the only key, and you can't determine fname, fcolor, or fweight without both components. Consequently, this decomposition satisfies 2NF.

The storage anomalies described above no longer apply to the decomposition. You can insert and delete tank and fish tuples independently, and you don't have to propagate a tank attribute update across several tuples. Some redundancy does still exist in the first component because of the FD, tvolume $\longrightarrow$ tcolor. In particular, you can predict the value of the missing cell in the following excerpt.

R_1			
tno	tname	tcolor	tvolume
35	lagoon	red	400
27	newtub	–	400

Third normal form

As illustrated in the last example, a 2NF decomposition can still have redundancies arising from the governing FDs. This deficiency provided the motivation for developing the third normal form (3NF). Let R' be a relation, a subset of the universal relation, in the context of a set of FDs $\mathcal{F}$. R' satisfies **third normal form** if for every nontrivial $X \longrightarrow A \in \mathcal{F}^+$, either (1) X is superkey for R' or (2) A is a prime attribute in R'. 3NF is almost the same as BCNF. It is slightly weaker because a BCNF violator can escape being a 3NF violator if the right side is prime. Therefore, the search for a 3NF violator proceeds as for a BCNF violator. Some candidates, however, pass as non-violators because of a prime right side.

Consider tank component R_1 of the last example. It exhibits some redundancy even though it satisfies 2NF. Although tvolume $\longrightarrow$ tcolor $\in \mathcal{F}^+$, tvolume isn't a superkey of R_1. This FD is a BCNF violator. In this case, it is also a 3NF violator because tcolor isn't prime. You ascertain these facts about R_1 by using `maxRight` with $\mathcal{F}$ to compute the keys and superkeys for R_1.

To achieve 3NF, you decompose R_1 further into R_{11} and R_{12} as shown below.

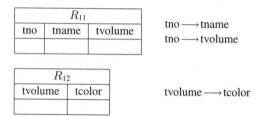

R_{11}		
tno	tname	tvolume

tno $\longrightarrow$ tname
tno $\longrightarrow$ tvolume

R_{12}	
tvolume	tcolor

tvolume $\longrightarrow$ tcolor

The constraint tvolume $\longrightarrow$ tcolor now applies in a meaningful way only to component R_{12}, where tvolume is a superkey. The superkey status of tvolume removes the 3NF violation. Moreover, the decomposition is lossless because the common attribute, tvolume, is a superkey in the second component. However, it isn't immediately obvious that the decomposition is dependency-preserving because the FD, tno $\longrightarrow$ tcolor, splits across the two components. If $\mathcal{G} = \pi_{R_{11}}(\mathcal{F}) \cup \pi_{R_{12}}(\mathcal{F}) \cup \pi_{R_2}(\mathcal{F})$, then tno $\longrightarrow$ tvolume $\in \mathcal{G}$ because it is one of the $\mathcal{F}$ elements that remains attached to R_{11}. Furthermore, tvolume $\longrightarrow$ tcolor $\in \mathcal{G}$ because it remains attached to R_{12}. Therefore, by transitivity, tno $\longrightarrow$ tcolor $\in \mathcal{G}^+$. Because this FD is the only one in question, you have $\mathcal{G} \equiv \mathcal{F}$, and the decomposition is dependency-preserving. In this particular case, the 3NF decomposition happens to be a BCNF decomposition. This frequently occurs in practice because a distinction can arise between the two normal forms only when $X \longrightarrow A$, X isn't a superkey, and A is prime.

Consider again the counterexample of the last section, which exhibited a relation that you can't decompose into BCNF while maintaining the lossless-join and dependency-preserving properties. The tables below repeat that relation and its decomposition. $\mathcal{F} = (AB \longrightarrow C, C \longrightarrow A)$, and the discussion showed that $\mathcal{F}^+$ contains only these two FDs plus trivial FDs. In this context, $C \longrightarrow A$ provides a BCNF violation because C isn't a superkey. But it doesn't provide a 3NF violation because A is prime. A is a constituent of the only key, AB. So the original relation is in 3NF but not yet in BCNF.

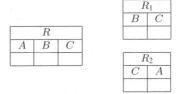

In this example, the governing FDs are interweaved so that a determined attribute subsequently determines part of a key. This condition does occur in practice, but it isn't frequent. Ideally, each application entity should have a single-attribute key even if you must artificially introduce an attribute for the purpose. Therefore, you initially expect that each application entity will appear in a separate relation and that the only other relations in the database will be intersection tables, which reflect relationships among the entities. In the simplest case, an intersection relation merely tabulates the relationship groupings. Further constraints, such as multiplicity ratios or participation limits, disallow certain entries. A later section will deal with these complications. As a first approximation, you expect to find a relation for each application entity and intersection entities involving the keys from the application entities.

An intersection relation tabulates the corresponding relationship groupings, and if no constraints prevent certain groupings, the intersection attribute scheme is all key. In other words, no nontrivial FDs establish constraints among its attributes. Therefore, the intersection tables can have no BCNF violators. As for the other relations, each represents some application entity. With single-attribute keys for such entities, you can't have $X \longrightarrow A$, with A prime, unless $X \longrightarrow K$ for a key, K. The only way that A can be part of a key is to be the whole key. However, because $K \longrightarrow R'$, the entire relation, you have $X \longrightarrow R'$. This means that X is a superkey, and no violation occurs. So with unconstrained intersection relations and single-attribute keys for all the application relations, a BCNF violator will also be a 3NF violator. Under this condition, a 3NF decomposition is equivalent to a BCNF decomposition.

Consider the situation in the ER diagram of Figure 18.4, where a ternary relationship exists among the entities: Developer, Workstation, and Project. The participation limit $(1, 1)$ near the project entity means that a given project can enter at most once in a relationship grouping, which implies that (dno wsno) $\longrightarrow$ pno is part of the governing set of FDs. When a given developer works at a given workstation, he works on a determined project. Other FDs arise naturally to associate the descriptive attributes with the entity keys. These FDs account for the rest of the entries in the list below—except the last one. The last entry, pno $\longrightarrow$ wsno constrains the application such that a given project always associates with a particular workstation—perhaps the project requires the workstation's special capabilities. You can't, however, place a participation limit of $(1, 1)$ near the workstation entity of Figure 18.4. A given workstation can indeed enter into multiple relationship groupings, corresponding to multiple developers using the workstation on the same project. You can't capture this constraint with ER symbols although you can note it in a comments section of the diagram. By computing maxRight for the various attribute subsets, you can verify that the only key in R is (dno, wsno). Then, the standard decomposition technique identifies the BCNF violators, dno $\longrightarrow$ dname, wsno $\longrightarrow$ wsname, and pno $\longrightarrow$ pname. The violators lead to the following decomposition.

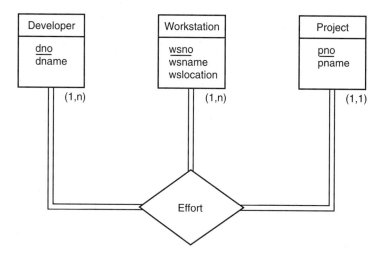

Figure 18.4   A ternary relationship that distinguishes between 3NF and BCNF

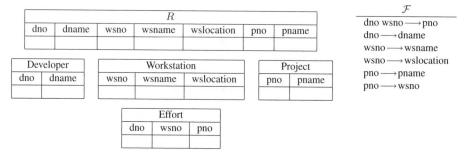

When you split off Developer, dno is the common attribute that joins it back to the remaining attributes. Because dno is a superkey of Developer, the decomposition possesses the lossless-join property. Similar observations apply to the remaining splits, so the entire decomposition has this property. Because each of the governing FDs falls completely inside at least one of the components, the final decomposition is dependency-preserving. Finally, it satisfies 3NF because the only left side that isn't a superkey in a table is pno in Effort. There, you have pno $\longrightarrow$ wsno. Although pno isn't a superkey in that table, wsno is prime, so no 3NF violation occurs. This FD does, however, constitute a BCNF violation. Therefore, you have a situation where the BCNF-3NF distinction arises naturally.

Here you can identify each of the three application entities with a singleton key: dno, wsno, and pno. The decomposition arrives at the same tabular arrangement as would result from the mapping of the last chapter, which translates an ER diagram into a relational schema. Effort appears as an intersection entity to tabulate the relationship groupings. If the intersection attributes weren't constrained, the only key to the Effort would contain all the attributes: dno, wsno, pno. However, Project has a participation limit of $(1, 1)$, so (dno wsno) $\longrightarrow$ pno. However, this constraint doesn't induce a BCNF violation because (dno, wsno) is a superkey of Effort.

The application, however, does have another constraint, pno $\longrightarrow$ wsno. This constraint is reasonable in the application context, but you can't express it with participation limits. Nevertheless, it further restricts the valid relationship groupings and introduces some redundancy. In particular, it's a BCNF violator because pno isn't a superkey. The BCNF decomposition of Effort produces Effort_1 = (pno, wsno) and Effort_2 = (pno, dno). This decomposition isn't dependency-preserving because (dno wsno) $\longrightarrow$ pno splits across two tables and you can't recover it from the projections of $\mathcal{F}$. You must decide which format is more important in the application: the BCNF decomposition, which purges the last vestige of redundancy at the expense of requiring a join operation to verify one of the FDs, or the 3NF decomposition, which suffers some redundancy while retaining a simple mechanism for checking the FD constraints.

The normal forms studied to this point form a sequence of increasingly restrictive formats, which remove more and more of a relation's FD-generated redundancy. If R' is in 2NF, it is by definition already in 1NF. If R' is in 3NF, it must already be in 2NF. You can prove this as follows. Suppose R' is in 3NF, but a 2NF violator $X \longrightarrow A \in \mathcal{F}^+$ exists. You must then have K, a key for R', with $X \subset K, X \neq K, A \notin X$, and A non-prime. However, $X \longrightarrow A$ is then a 3NF violator because X, a proper subset of a minimal superkey K, can't itself be a superkey. This contradiction establishes that R' must already be in 2NF. Finally, if R' is in BCNF, it is already in 3NF. Indeed, if $X \longrightarrow A$ is a 3NF violator, then $A \notin X$, X isn't a superkey, and A isn't prime. Therefore, it is a BCNF violator as well.

 The normal forms, 1NF, 2NF, 3NF, BCNF, specify increasingly restrictive formats, which result in decreasing data redundancy. BCNF removes all redundancy associated with FD constraints.

Because of its position in this sequence and because fourth normal form is reserved to deal with a different kind of constraint, Boyce-Codd normal form is sometimes called *3*$^+$ **normal form**.

An algorithm for a 3NF, lossless-join, dependency-preserving decomposition

Although you can't always achieve a lossless-join, dependency-preserving BCNF decomposition, you can always find a 3NF decomposition with both of these properties. This section develops an algorithm for this type of decomposition. Suppose R' is the relation to be decomposed. You start by replacing the governing set of FDs with a minimal cover. Assume, therefore, without loss of generality, that $\mathcal{F}$ is minimal. You then partition $\mathcal{F}$ into subsets such that all the FDs in a given subset have the same left side. Suppose m subsets, $\mathcal{F}_1, \mathcal{F}_2, \ldots, \mathcal{F}_m$, arise from this partition and the n_i FDs in $\mathcal{F}_i$ are of the form $X_i \longrightarrow A_{i1}, X_i \longrightarrow A_{i2}, \ldots, X_i \longrightarrow A_{in_i}$. Each subset, $\mathcal{F}_i$, gives rise to a component of the decomposition, R_i, and you add one further component, R_0. The attributes of R_0 are an arbitrarily chosen key, K, for R'. The decomposition $(R_0, R_1, \ldots, R_m)$, followed by the algorithm that produces it, appears below.

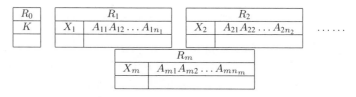

```
decomposition 3NFdecomp(attributeSet R, FDset F) {
    partition F into the m subsets F₁, F₂, ..., Fₘ based on the left sides of the FDs;
    set Rᵢ equal to the attributes mentioned in Fᵢ, for 1 ≤ i ≤ m;
    set R₀ equal to an arbitrarily chosen key of R;
    return (R₀, R₁, R₂, ..., Rₘ); }
```

The algorithm doesn't locate 3NF violators and export the closure of their left sides to new relations. Nevertheless, it does produce a lossless-join, dependency-preserving decomposition into 3NF. The proof follows. First, each FD in $\mathcal{F}$ applies to one of the components, so the decomposition is dependency-preserving. Proving the other properties is somewhat more difficult.

As for 3NF, you first check out R_0. R_0 contains a key of R, say $B_1 B_2 \ldots B_p$. If a nontrivial $X \longrightarrow B_j \in \mathcal{F}^+$ applies meaningfully to R_0, then $B_j \notin X$ and $X \subset R_0 - \{B_j\}$. Therefore, $(R_0 - \{B_j\}) \longrightarrow B_j$ holds, which implies that you have $(R_0 - \{B_j\}) \longrightarrow R_0$. Because R_0, in turn, determines all the attributes of R, you establish that $(R_0 - \{B_j\})$ is a superkey for R, which contradicts the fact that R_0 is a key (i.e., a minimal superkey). So no nontrivial FD in $\mathcal{F}^+$ applies meaningfully to R_0, which prevents a 3NF violator for R_0.

You must still show that no 3NF violators exist for the other components: $R_1, R_2, \ldots, R_m$. Suppose $X \longrightarrow A \in \mathcal{F}^+$ and $A \notin X$ and $XA \subset R_i$. $X \longrightarrow A$ is then a potential 3NF violator for R_i, but you can reason that it can't actually be a violator. R_i arose from $X_i \longrightarrow A_{ik} \in \mathcal{F}, 1 \le k \le n_i$, and this forces X_i to be a key for R_i. To see this, note that X_i is a superkey for R_i because $X_i \longrightarrow B \in \mathcal{F}^+$, for every $B \in R_i$. If a proper subset $W \subset X_i$ is a superkey, then $W \longrightarrow A_{ik} \in \mathcal{F}^+$, for $1 \le k \le n_i$. Choosing one of these A_{ik} as A', you see that $X_i \longrightarrow A'$ doesn't have a minimal left side, and you can replace it with $W \longrightarrow A'$. This contradicts the fact that $\mathcal{F}$ is minimal. So X_i is a key for R_i. Therefore, for the potential 3NF violator, $X \longrightarrow A$, you must have that A is one of the $A_{ik}, 1 \le k \le n_i$. Otherwise, A would be prime and no violation would occur.

Now consider just how $X \longrightarrow A$ arrived in $\mathcal{F}^+$. This occurs when algorithm maxRight finds $A \in (X; \mathcal{F})$ as it grows $(X; \mathcal{F})$ from X using the FDs in $\mathcal{F}$. Algorithm maxRight grows $(X; \mathcal{F})$ by initializing the approximation $Z = X$ and then searching for an FD, $X_j \longrightarrow A_{jk} \in \mathcal{F}$ with $X_j \subset Z$ and $A_{jk} \notin Z$. Each time it uses an FD, it observes that some $X_j \subset Z$. Because $Z \subset (X; \mathcal{F})$ is an invariant for the search loop, the algorithm continues to find more and more of the X_j in $(X; \mathcal{F})$. This means that $X \longrightarrow X_j \in \mathcal{F}^+$, for each X_j so used by the algorithm. By transitivity, each of the $X \longrightarrow A_{jk} \in \mathcal{F}^+$, for $1 \le k \le n_j$. Because each R_j is composed of X_j and its dependent $A_{j1} A_{j2} \ldots A_{jn_j}$, you have that $X \longrightarrow R_j \in \mathcal{F}^+$, for each $X_j \longrightarrow A_{jk}$ used by the algorithm.

Because $X \longrightarrow A \in \mathcal{F}^+$, the algorithm eventually includes A in the expanding Z. At the point where A is included, either the algorithm has used an FD of the form $X_i \longrightarrow A_{ik}$ or it hasn't. Recall that R_i is the component where you are investigating a possible 3NF violator, $X \longrightarrow A$. If the algorithm expands Z to include A *without* using an FD of the form $X_i \longrightarrow A_{ik}$, then $X_i \longrightarrow A$ is a redundant element in $\mathcal{F}$. (Remember that A is one of the A_{ik} components of R_i.) To see that $\mathcal{F} \equiv \mathcal{F} - \{X_i \longrightarrow A\} = \mathcal{G}$, you proceed as follows. Because $A \notin X$, you have $X_i \longrightarrow X \in \mathcal{G}^+$. Remember, because $X \subset R_i$, X can contain only portions of X_i and some of the components, $A_{i1}, A_{i2}, \ldots$. Moreover, X can include only A_{ik} elements other than A, and all those $X_i \longrightarrow A_{ik}$ have been retained in $\mathcal{G}$. This branch of the argument also assumes that maxRight can grow Z from X to include A without using any FD with left side X_i. So, in particular, it doesn't use the excluded member, $X_i \longrightarrow A$. Therefore, maxRight can grow Z from X to include A using only FDs from $\mathcal{G}$, which implies that $X \longrightarrow A \in \mathcal{G}^+$. By transitivity, you then have $X_i \longrightarrow A \in \mathcal{G}^+$, which proves that $X_i \longrightarrow A$ is redundant in $\mathcal{F}$. However, because $\mathcal{F}$ is minimal, this conclusion is a contradiction.

Therefore, the algorithm *must* use an FD with X_i on the left side, which implies that $X \longrightarrow R_i \in \mathcal{F}^+$ and that X is a superkey for R_i. Thus, $X \longrightarrow A$ can't be a 3NF violator for R_i. With this last loose end wrapped up, you can conclude that the decomposition is 3NF.

Only the proof of the lossless-join property remains. Suppose r is a valid database state for R, and let $r_i = \pi_{R_i}(r), 0 \le i \le m$. Therefore, r_i is the content of component R_i of the decomposition. You know that r is always contained in $r' = r_0 * r_1 * r_2 * \ldots * r_m$. So to prove that the join is lossless, you need only show that $r' \subset r$. Accordingly, let $\mu \in r'$. Then μ arises from a concatenation of segments $\mu_i \in r_i$ assembled by the preliminary Cartesian product. To survive the subsequent selection operation, all these segments must agree on overlapping attributes. So $\mu(R_i) = \mu_i$, for $0 \le i \le m$. Because R_0 is a key for R, there is a single tuple, $\nu \in R$ with $\mu_0 = \nu(R_0)$. Consequently, $\mu(R_0) = \mu_0 = \nu(R_0)$.

Now watch how algorithm maxRight$(R_0, \mathcal{F})$ adds attributes to its expanding Z variable. Recall that it initializes Z to R_0 and continues to expand it using the FDs of $\mathcal{F}$. Because R_0 is a key of R, $R_0 \longrightarrow R \in \mathcal{F}^+$, and therefore every attribute of R must eventually enter the expanding Z. It turns out that $\mu(Z) = \nu(Z)$ is an invariant for the loop where the algorithm enlarges Z. You can prove this as follows. Because $\mu(R_0) = \nu(R_0)$ from above, this condition is true when the loop starts. Assuming the invariant holds through the first k iterations, you need to show that it remains true after iteration $k + 1$. So you have $\mu(Z) = \nu(Z)$ at the start of iteration $k + 1$, and you have an FD $X_i \longrightarrow A_{ij} \in \mathcal{F}$ such that $X_i \subset Z$ and $A_{ij} \notin Z$. However, $X_i \subset Z$ implies that $\mu(X_i) = \nu(X_i)$. Because μ is μ_i on attributes R_i and because $X_i \subset R_i$, you have $\mu_i(X_i) = \nu(X_i)$. Being in r_i, μ_i had to come from the projection on R_i of some tuple $\rho \in r$: $\mu_i = \rho(R_i)$. So $\rho(X_i) = \nu(X_i)$. Because r is a valid database state, it must satisfy $X_i \longrightarrow A_{ij} \in \mathcal{F}$. Thus, $\nu(A_{ij}) = \rho(A_{ij})$. Because $A_{ij} \in R_i$ also, you can continue the chain: $\nu(A_{ij}) = \rho(A_{ij}) = \mu_i(A_{ij}) = \mu(A_{ij})$. Therefore, after adding A_{ij} to Z, the loop invariant remains true. By induction, the loop invariant is true throughout the execution of the algorithm, including when the loop terminates with $Z = R$. Then $\mu(R) = \nu(R)$, which implies $\mu = \nu \in r$. So $r' \subset r$, and the decomposition possesses the lossless-join property.

Although this argument proves that the algorithm produces the desired result, the decomposition is sometimes redundant: it can create tables that are completely contained in other tables. If $R_i \subset R_j$ when the algorithm concludes, you can simply eliminate R_i. The lossless join of two tables where one is a subset of the other always results in the larger table. For example, suppose you apply the algorithm to the aquarium universal relation, in the context of minimal cover $\mathcal{F}'_{aq}$ of Figure 18.3. The algorithm partitions the FDs as shown below. The first component, R_0, contains a key, which is simply eno. $R_0 \subset R_5$, so you can remove R_0. With that adjustment, you arrive at the same decomposition developed earlier, which happens to be BCNF as well as 3NF.

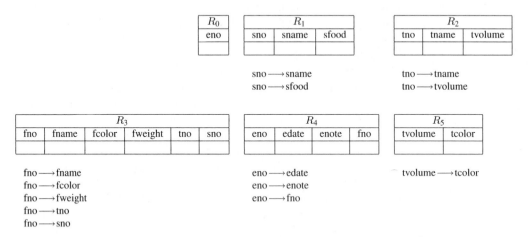

Consider again the counterexample that showed a BCNF decomposition isn't always dependency-preserving. You have $R = ABC$ in the context of $\mathcal{F} = (AB \longrightarrow C, C \longrightarrow A)$. The algorithm produces the decomposition below, where R_0 is the key AB. Since R_1 contains both R_0 and R_2, you retain only R_1, which is the original relation. So R_1 is 3NF, but it isn't BCNF.

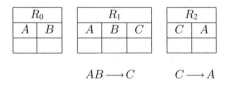

 You can algorithmically create a lossless-join, dependency-preserving, 3NF decomposition of any relation in the context of any set of FDs. The algorithm may produce extraneous tables that you should remove.

Algorithm 3NFdecomp doesn't actually proceed by successively splitting a relation into components. Instead, it synthesizes the components directly from the partition induced by the governing set of FDs. For this reason, the approach is called **normalization by synthesis**.

Limitations and extensions of FD analysis

You can remove all redundancy associated with functional dependency constraints by decomposing the universal relation into BCNF. However, you may not be able to preserve a representative set of the dependencies within the individual tables. If the decomposition isn't dependency-preserving, the procedures that enforce an FD must use joins to construct an intermediate table that contains both left and right sides of the FD. Earlier examples illustrated this operation using the create-assertion facility of SQL. If these advanced facilities aren't available, the application interface code must assume the burden of controlling all insertions, deletions, and updates in a manner to avoid FD violations. Ideally, you have a lossless-join, dependency-preserving, BCNF design, so all FDs assume a form where the left side is a superkey of one of the components. You can then enforce all FDs with primary-key clauses in the SQL schema.

A second problem arises because the decomposition process can go too far, and certain algorithms that deal with the attribute sets in a formal way can generate excessive decompositions. For example, an earlier section developed a BCNF decomposition of the aquarium application. Responding to BCNF violators in $\mathcal{F}^+$, it split off attribute groups from the universal relation. From your understanding of the application, you expected certain natural entities to emerge. The BCNF decomposition obtained the tables on the left below. With the possible exception of the VolColor table, each corresponds to one of the intuitive entities.

Relation	Attributes	FDs
Species	sno, sname, sfood	sno $\longrightarrow$ sname sno $\longrightarrow$ sfood
Tank	tno, tname, tvolume	tno $\longrightarrow$ tname tno $\longrightarrow$ tvolume
VolColor	tvolume, tcolor	tvolume $\longrightarrow$ tcolor
Fish	fno, fname, fcolor, fweight, sno, tno	fno $\longrightarrow$ fname fno $\longrightarrow$ fcolor fno $\longrightarrow$ fweight fno $\longrightarrow$ tno fno $\longrightarrow$ sno
Event	eno, edate, enote, fno	eno $\longrightarrow$ edate eno $\longrightarrow$ enote eno $\longrightarrow$ fno

Species$_1$		sno $\longrightarrow$ sname
sno	sname	

Species$_2$		sno $\longrightarrow$ sfood
sno	sfood	

However, you could decompose further and still maintain all the desired properties: BCNF, lossless join, and dependency preservation. For example, you can decompose the species relation as shown on the right above. Each component retains one of the FDs now associated with Species. Similarly, you can further decompose the tank relation into two components, the fish relation into five components, and the event table into three components. This arrangement, however, is less efficient than the original decomposition. Although it requires no joins to enforce any of the FD constraints, it needs a great many more joins to respond to queries. The general idea is that decomposition should result in a collection of tables, each representing an application entity, plus whatever additional decomposition you need to accommodate non-relationship constraints among the FDs. In the aquarium example, the FDs with sno on the left naturally isolate a species entity, and similar observations hold for the tank, fish, and event entities. The FDs, eno $\longrightarrow$ fno, fno $\longrightarrow$ tno, and fno $\longrightarrow$ sno, constrain the universal relation to contain tuples where the various segments relate to each other in a natural way. Beyond these constraints, the tvolume $\longrightarrow$ tcolor FD further restricts certain attribute values, which leads to one more split to export some of the tank attributes to a new table, VolColor.

Another limitation of functional dependency analysis is that even BCNF doesn't remove all redundancy: it removes only those redundancies that originate with FD constraints. For example, consider the somewhat whimsical constraint that the sum of the weights of the fish in a tank must be exactly 1000 pounds. Suppose the fish table contains the excerpt to the left below, and assume that it shows all the fish in tno 35.

Fish					
fno	fname	fcolor	fweight	tno	sno
384	alpha	blue	200	35	17
496	beta	green	300	35	26
571	gamma	purple	200	35	17
682	delta	red	250	35	34
766	epsilon	white	—	35	22

```
create assertion fweightBalance check (not exists
    (select * from
        (select Fish.tno, sum(Fish.fweight) as totalWeight
        from Fish
        groupby tno) as R
    where R.totalWeight ≠ 1000))).
```

You can predict the weight of fish epsilon to be 50 pounds, so the blank in the table is a redundant cell. This redundancy arises from a constraint that you can't express as a functional dependency. You can, however, create an SQL assertion to enforce it, as shown on the right above.

Another kind of redundancy occurs when a relation mixes two attribute sets, but no dependencies link the two sets. The following example arose in the discussion of minimal covers. The universal relation $R = ABCDEFGHJKL$ and the final FDs repeated here constitute a minimal cover of the original functional dependencies. The display below partitions the FDs by their left sides and produces the 3NF decomposition indicated above the FDs. The first component, R_0, contains a key to R: AEF.

R_0		
A	E	F

R_1		
A	C	D

R_2	
C	B

R_3				
E	F	H	J	L

R_4		
F	L	G

R_5		
H	J	K

$$A \longrightarrow D$$
$$A \longrightarrow C$$

$$C \longrightarrow B$$

$$EF \longrightarrow H$$
$$EF \longrightarrow J$$
$$EF \longrightarrow L$$

$$FL \longrightarrow G$$

$$HJ \longrightarrow K$$

Although the 3NFdecomp algorithm produced this decomposition, it is actually a BCNF decomposition. However, careful inspection shows that it involves two disconnected databases. The attributes $ABCD$ are clustered through several interconnecting FDs, as are the attributes $EFGHJKL$. Refer to the first cluster as the A database and the second as the EF database because the indicated attributes are keys of the clusters. You can regard the original relation as a collection of pairs of the form $(a_i, (ef)_j)$. Each tuple combines an $ABCD$ segment with an $EFGHJKL$ segment. The component, $R_0 = (AEF)$, keeps track of which elements from the A database appear in conjunction with which elements of the EF database. In particular, R_0 exhibits a tuple over AEF for each such pairing. The tuple records the A value of the a_i segment and the EF value of the $(ef)_j$ segment. This table isn't redundant because the pairing information can be important in terms of the application. So the contents of R_0 exhibit no particular pattern that would allow you to predict any of its entries.

However, it could also happen that the two databases are completely independent and no significance attaches to a particular a_i tuple from the A database appearing with a particular $(ef)_j$ tuple from the EF database. In that case, you expect R_0 to exhibit a pattern, where every A value pairs with every EF value. Any less symmetric pattern carries some information that certain a_i elements preferentially pair with certain $(ef)_j$ elements. In this case, the entire table R_0 is redundant: you can predict every entry. You simply note the A values from R_1 and the EF values from R_3. R_0 then contains all possible combinations. In other words, if r_i is the body of R_i, you have $r_0 = \pi_A(r_1) \times \pi_{EF}(r_3)$.

Although it leads to redundancies in the relations, the constraint that A and EF must not appear in preferential combinations can't be expressed as a functional dependency. However, you can express this constraint as a multivalued dependency. The next chapter will discuss multivalued dependencies.

 Some disadvantages of functional dependency analysis are (1) compromise tradeoffs between full redundancy suppression and dependency preservation, (2) remaining redundancies forced by non-FD constraints, (3) the possibility of decomposing beyond the optimal table arrangement, and (4) the danger that disjoint, unrelated attribute sets may occupy the same universal relation.

SUMMARY

Functional dependencies (FDs) are application constraints of the form $X \longrightarrow Y$. $X \longrightarrow Y$ means that two tuples agreeing on attributes X must also agree on attributes Y. When $X \longrightarrow Y$ holds, you say X is a determinant and X determines Y. These constraints are initially intended to hold for the universal relation R, the collection of all application attributes. A body, $r(R)$, that satisfies all such constraints is a valid or consistent database state. You obtain the body of a component relation, $R' \subset R$, as a projection of the universal relation: $r(R') = \pi_{R'}(r(R))$. An FD, $X \longrightarrow Y$, applies to a component relation R' if $X \subset R'$. If the FD, $X \longrightarrow Y$, constrains the universal relation, then $X \longrightarrow (Y \cap R')$ constrains every component relation, R', to which the original FD applies.

You can express many naturally occurring application constraints as FDs, including key or superkey constraints. Once you establish the initial set, $\mathcal{F}$, through an analysis of the application, a larger group, the closure of $\mathcal{F}$, follows by logical implication. The closure $\mathcal{F}^+$ is the set of FDs that must hold for any valid database state. If an FD, $X \longrightarrow Y \in \mathcal{F}^+$, you say that $\mathcal{F}$ models the FD and write it as $\mathcal{F} \models (X \longrightarrow Y)$. If $\mathcal{F}$ models every FD in a set $\mathcal{G}$, you write $\mathcal{F} \models \mathcal{G}$ and say that $\mathcal{F}$ covers $\mathcal{G}$. In addition to substantive FDs arising as consequences of $\mathcal{F}$, $\mathcal{F}^+$ also contains all FDs of the form $X \longrightarrow Y$, where $Y \subset X$. These FDs are reflexive or trivial FDs.

Armstrong's axioms are rules that generates new FDs in $\mathcal{F}^+$ from FDs already known to be there. Three of these rules—reflexivity, augmentation, and transitivity—are sufficient to generate all of $\mathcal{F}^+$. $\mathcal{F}^+$ is exponentially large in terms of the number of attributes mentioned in $\mathcal{F}$. This chapter developed two algorithms to manipulate $\mathcal{F}^+$ without actually constructing all of it. The first, `maxRight`, generates the largest right side, $(X; \mathcal{F})$, such that $X \longrightarrow (X; \mathcal{F}) \in \mathcal{F}^+$. The second checks to determine if a given FD is a member of $\mathcal{F}^+$.

Although the algorithm for determining membership in $\mathcal{F}^+$ uses only the FDs in the much smaller $\mathcal{F}$, an incentive remains for reducing $\mathcal{F}$ to a nonredundant set while maintaining equivalence with the original FDs. Two sets of FDs, $\mathcal{F}$ and G, are equivalent if their closures are equal. Given a set of FDs, $\mathcal{F}$, a minimal cover for $\mathcal{F}$ is a set G, such that $G \equiv \mathcal{F}$ and G is "small" in the following sense: (1) every FD in G has a single attribute on the right side, (2) you can't remove an FD in G without destroying the equivalence between G and $\mathcal{F}$, and (3) you can't remove an attribute from the left side of an FD in G without destroying the equivalence between G and $\mathcal{F}$. $\mathcal{F}$ is minimal if it's a minimal cover for itself. You can convert any set of FDs into a minimal equivalent set.

A decomposition of a relation is a set of relations, such that the union of the component attributes equals the attribute set of the original relation. In other words, $R = R_1 \cup R_2 \cup \ldots R_n$. When you project a relational body $r(R)$ onto the components, you always have $r \subset \pi_{R_1}(r) * \pi_{R_2}(r) * \ldots * \pi_{R_n}(r)$. If $r = \pi_{R_1}(r) * \pi_{R_2}(r) * \ldots * \pi_{R_n}(r)$ for each valid database state $r(R)$, the decomposition is a lossless-join decomposition. A decomposition into two components is lossless if and only if the common attributes form a superkey of one of the components. The lossless-join property is important because it guarantees that a join operation will faithfully reconstruct the original relation. Therefore, queries that use joins on the components will return the same results as queries that operate from a valid database state of the original undecomposed table.

A component, R_i, contains an FD, $X \longrightarrow Y \in \mathcal{F}^+$, if both left and right side attributes lie in R_i. $\pi_{R_i}(\mathcal{F})$ consists of all the FDs from $\mathcal{F}^+$ that are contained in R_i. The decomposition is dependency-preserving if $(\pi_{R_1}(\mathcal{F}) \cup \pi_{R_2}(\mathcal{F}) \cup \ldots \cup \pi_{R_n}(\mathcal{F})) \equiv \mathcal{F}$. Dependency preservation is important because it allows a check for a potential FD violation without using the expensive join operation.

A decomposition satisfies Boyce-Codd normal form (BCNF) if, for every nontrivial $X \longrightarrow A \in \mathcal{F}^+$ that applies meaningfully to a component, R_i, you have that X is a superkey of R_i. Every relation admits a lossless-join decomposition into BCNF although it may not admit a BCNF, lossless-join, dependency-preserving decomposition. BCNF removes all redundancy induced by FD constraints.

A relation is in first normal form (1NF) if every cell holds atomic entries. In other words, 1NF disallows repeating groups. Because a relation, by definition, already excludes repeating groups, every relation satisfies 1NF. An attribute is prime if it is a component of some key. A relation is in second normal form (2NF) if it is in 1NF and if every non-prime attribute is fully dependent on every key (i.e., a partial key can't determine a non-prime attribute). A relation that isn't in 2NF exhibits redundancies and allows you to predict certain cell contents from other entries. These redundancies lead to certain storage difficulties: insertion, deletion, and update anomalies. A relation is in 3NF if for every $X \longrightarrow A \in \mathcal{F}^+$, you have either X is a superkey or A is prime. 3NF is almost the same as BCNF, but in some cases a distinction arises so that 3NF leaves some redundancy that BCNF eliminates. Every relation admits a lossless-join, dependency-preserving decomposition into 3NF. The sequence 1NF, 2NF, 3NF, BCNF is increasingly restrictive, and in this context, BCNF is sometimes called 3^+ normal form.

BCNF and 3NF decompositions represent desirable database designs because they minimize redundancy and thus reduce opportunities for an inconsistent database state. However, BCNF can remove only redundancies forced by FDs. Other constraints may introduce re-

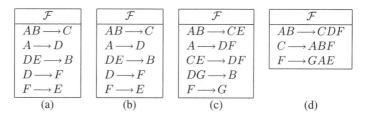

Figure 18.5 Functional dependency sets for exercises

dundancy that remains even with a BCNF decomposition. Moreover, a BCNF design may violate the dependency-preserving property and lead to potentially expensive operations to ensure that the governing FDs aren't violated. Decomposition beyond that necessary for the BCNF (or 3NF) properties can be detrimental because queries may then need unnecessary join operations. An extreme form of redundancy occurs when two unrelated attribute sets are merged in the same initial table. You can't express as a functional dependency the constraint that the attribute sets be independent. Instead, you need a multivalued dependency.

EXERCISES

Sources of functional dependency constraints

1. For the $\mathcal{F}$ of Figure 18.5(a), prove directly that $A \longrightarrow C \in \mathcal{F}^+$. In other words, assume a valid database state where $\mu(A) = \nu(A)$ and show that $\mu(C) = \nu(C)$ must follow.

2. For the $\mathcal{F}$ of Figure 18.5(a), prove that $A \longrightarrow C \in \mathcal{F}^+$ by applying Armstrong's axioms to $\mathcal{F}$.

3. For the $\mathcal{F}$ of Figure 18.5(a), determine $(A; \mathcal{F})$. A later section developed the algorithm for this computation. However, the FDs involve only six attributes. You can include an attribute with an argument similar to the preceding exercise; you can exclude an attribute with a counterexample.

Minimal covers

4. Compute a minimal cover for the $\mathcal{F}$ in Figure 18.5(b).

5. Compute a minimal cover for the $\mathcal{F}$ in Figure 18.5(c).

6. Find two distinct minimal covers for Figure 18.5(d).

Lossless joins

Let $R = ABCDEF$ and $\mathcal{F} = \begin{array}{l} A \longrightarrow CD \\ D \longrightarrow BF \\ F \longrightarrow E \end{array}$.

7. Prove that the decomposition in Figure 18.6(a) is lossless.

8. Prove that the decomposition in Figure 18.6(b) is lossless.

9. Prove that the decomposition in Figure 18.6(c) is lossless.

10. Prove that the decomposition in Figure 18.6(d) isn't lossless by showing that neither $B \longrightarrow R_1$ nor $B \longrightarrow R_2$ is a member of $\mathcal{F}^+$.

11. Prove that the decomposition of the preceding exercise isn't lossless by directly exhibiting a valid database state where the join of the components doesn't recover the database state.

12. Prove that the decomposition in Figure 18.6(e) is lossless.

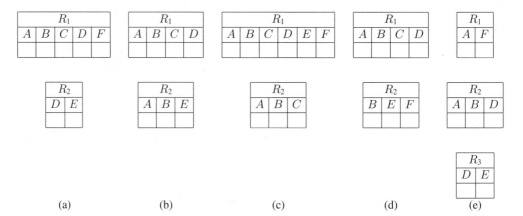

Figure 18.6   Decompositions for the exercises

Boyce-Codd normal form

Let $R = ABCDEF$, subject to

$\mathcal{F}$
$AB \longrightarrow CD$
$CE \longrightarrow AD$
$CF \longrightarrow EB$
$E \longrightarrow F$
$CD \longrightarrow E$

13. Find a minimal cover $\mathcal{F}'$ for $\mathcal{F}$.

14. Find a lossless BCNF decomposition of R.

Suppose the library system database is subject to the following rules. A library is described by a unique libno key plus libname and location values. An author is a (authno, authname) pair, and authno is unique across authors. A book is a (bookno, title, pages) triple, and bookno is unique across books. A patron is described by a unique patno key plus patname and patweight values. A copy associates with a particular book and resides in a particular library. A loan associates with a particular patron and notes that the patron has borrowed a particular copy. A copy is further described by a cost value, and a loan is further described by a duedate value. Each book has a single author. Each copy has a copyno key value, and each loan has a loanno key value. This context is familiar from other exercises in the library setting. However, add one additional constraint: a patron always uses the same library for all his loans.

15. Construct FDs to force the universal relation to conform to the constraints.

16. Derive a minimal cover, $\mathcal{F}$, for the FDs.

17. Derive a BCNF decomposition of the library universal relation that results in the five relations that have been used in previous examples: Library = (libno, libname, location), Author = (authno, authname), Book = (bookno, title, pages, authno), Copy = (copyno, cost, bookno, libno), Patron = (patno, patname, patweight), and Loan = (loanno, duedate, patno, copyno).

18. The BCNF decomposition of the preceding exercise is deficient because the DBMS can't easily enforce the constraint patno $\longrightarrow$ libno. The FD applies to the patron and loan tables, but it doesn't meaningfully constrain them because libno appears in neither table. Provide a second BCNF decomposition such that the right and left sides of each FD in $\mathcal{F}$ lie within a single table.

Dependency preservation

19. Show that the decomposition of the universal relation below isn't dependency-preserving in the context of the given constraints, $\mathcal{F}$.

R_1				
A	B	C	D	E

R_2	
E	F

$\mathcal{F}$
$AB \longrightarrow CD$
$CE \longrightarrow AD$
$CF \longrightarrow EB$
$E \longrightarrow F$
$CD \longrightarrow E$

20. Provide an example of a minimal set of FD constraints, $\mathcal{F}$, and a two-way decomposition of the universal relation such that (1) some FD from $\mathcal{F}$ splits across the two components, and (2) the decomposition is still dependency-preserving.

The first three normal forms

Let $R = ABCDE$, subject to the following constraints:

$\mathcal{F}$
$AB \longrightarrow E$
$E \longrightarrow B$
$BE \longrightarrow C$
$B \longrightarrow D$

21. Find a lossless-join, dependency-preserving decomposition of R that satisfies 2NF but violates 3NF.

22. Find a lossless-join, dependency-preserving decomposition of R that satisfies 3NF but violates BCNF.

23. Find a lossless-join decomposition of R that satisfies BCNF.

24. Determine if the final decomposition of the preceding exercise is dependency-preserving.

Health club records are 7-tuples of the form (club#, location, manager, facility, size, rate, priority). The location is a city, such as Seattle, and several clubs can have the same location. The club# value is unique within a given city although duplicates may exist in different cities. The combination of club# and location determine a unique tuple. A manager is a person assigned to a particular location, and he manages all clubs in that city. A facility is a subunit of a club, such as a swimming pool, a sauna, or a tennis court. Size describes a facility in the appropriate units, such as volume for a swimming pool, area for a tennis court, or seats for a sauna. The rate is the charge per hour for using a particular facility. The rate is constant for a given facility across all clubs in the same city. The priority is a ranking scheme that the enterprise uses to measure the economic importance of clubs. It is location-based. Rankings in the range 1–10 are reserved for Seattle clubs, where the enterprise has its headquarters. The range 11–20 pertains to Spokane, and so forth. Each city commands a distinct range of priority values.

25. Create a collection of FDs, $\mathcal{F}$, to capture the constraints of the health club database.

26. Reduce $\mathcal{F}$ of the preceding exercise to a minimal set, $\mathcal{F}'$.

27. Find a lossless-join, dependency-preserving decomposition of the health club universal relation that satisfies 2NF but violates 3NF.

28. Find a lossless-join, dependency-preserving decomposition of the health club universal relation that satisfies 3NF but violates BCNF.

29. Find a lossless-join decomposition of the health club universal relation that satisfies BCNF.

30. Determine if the decomposition of the preceding exercise is dependency-preserving.

19 Join Dependency Analysis

THIS CHAPTER DISCUSSES A NEW KIND OF CONSTRAINT—A MULTIVALUED dependency (MVD). Although you can't express an MVD in functional dependency (FD) notation, you can resolve MVD-induced redundancies with decompositions similar to those used to resolve FD-induced redundancies.

Suppose a set of FDs, $\mathcal{F}$, constrains the universal relation, R. As described in Chapter 18, you can eliminate FD-induced redundancy with a lossless decomposition into components, $R_1, R_2, \ldots, R_n$. You can exactly recover any valid state, $r(R)$, from a natural join of the projections onto its components. In other words, if r is a valid database state of R with respect to $\mathcal{F}$, then $r = \pi_{R_1}(r) * \pi_{R_2}(r) * \ldots * \pi_{R_n}(r)$. The lossless-join property of a particular decomposition is *not* one of the constraints on r. Instead, you restrict the decompositions to those where the lossless-join property follows from other constraints in $\mathcal{F}$.

However, independently of the other constraints in $\mathcal{F}$, you can insist from the beginning that a certain decomposition always remain lossless. In this case, the lossless-join requirement is a further constraint on the database state, $r(R)$, rather than a consequence of other constraints. For example, you can decree that the decomposition (R_1, R_2) will always be lossless, regardless of whether the common attributes form a superkey of one of the components. This restriction now acts as a new constraint on $r(R)$. If the common attributes are a superkey of one of the components, the new restriction doesn't constrain $r(R)$ any more than it was already constrained by $\mathcal{F}$. But if the common attributes aren't a superkey of either component, the join of the projections may introduce extraneous tuples that aren't present in $r(R)$. The new restriction then states that such tuples can't be extraneous. A valid database state, $r(R)$, must always include any tuples that can be reassembled in the join of the component projections. This new restriction does indeed constrain $r(R)$ beyond the FDs of $\mathcal{F}$. A constraint of this form is a multivalued dependency, and a generalization to more than two components is a join dependency. This chapter discusses redundancies associated with such dependencies and decompositions that minimize that redundancy.

Multivalued dependencies

Let R' be a subset of the universal relation R, and let $XY \subset R'$. A **multivalued dependency** (MVD) $X \longrightarrow\!\!\!\!\!\rightarrow Y$ constrains $r(R')$ as follows. If tuples μ and ν are in R' with $\mu(X) = \nu(X)$, then there exist tuples μ' and ν' in R' such that (1) $\mu'(X) = \nu'(X) = \mu(X) = \nu(X)$, (2) $\mu'(Y) = \mu(Y)$ and $\mu'(R' - XY) = \nu(R' - XY)$, and (3) $\nu'(Y) = \nu(Y)$ and $\nu'(R' - XY) = \mu(R' - XY)$. In plain English, any two tuples that agree on X must be accompanied by two other tuples with interchanged $R' - XY$ values. The tuple μ' is the tuple μ with its $R' - XY$ values replaced with the $R' - XY$ values of ν. Similarly, the tuple ν' is the tuple ν with its $R' - XY$ values replaced with the $R' - XY$ values of μ.

The table excerpt below illustrates the MVD $X \longrightarrow\!\!\!\!\!\rightarrow Y$. The first two tuples agree on X. The constraint then requires that two additional tuples appear, similar to the original tuples but with the $R' - XY$ attributes interchanged. These two tuples appear in the lower part of the table. The condition constrains the table because the second pair of tuples *must* appear. This restriction clearly constrains $r(R')$, but in a different manner than a functional dependency. An FD, $X \longrightarrow Y$, keeps certain tuples *out* of a relation. In particular, it excludes any tuple whose X value duplicates that of an existing tuple but whose Y value doesn't. An MVD, $X \longrightarrow\!\!\!\!\!\rightarrow Y$, forces certain tuples *into* a relation. It forces the appearance of tuples necessary to swap the Y and $R' - XY$ values in two existing tuples.

	R'			
	X			
			Y	
	$X - (X \cap Y)$	$X \cap Y$	$Y - (X \cap Y)$	$R' - XY$
	$\vdots$	$\vdots$	$\vdots$	$\vdots$
μ	x	v	y_1	z_1
ν	x	v	y_2	z_2
	$\vdots$	$\vdots$	$\vdots$	$\vdots$
μ'	x	v	y_1	z_2
ν'	x	v	y_2	z_1
	$\vdots$	$\vdots$	$\vdots$	$\vdots$

Suppose, for the moment, that the second pair of tuples isn't present in R', as shown in the upper part of Figure 19.1. You can decompose R' as indicated and populate the components with the projections from $r(R')$. You then notice that the natural join of the components generates the last two tuples even though they weren't present in the original body. Therefore, the MVD $X \longrightarrow\!\!\!\!\!\rightarrow Y$ constrains the body $r(R')$ to contain the "extraneous" tuples introduced by the join of its projections. In other words, the constraint forces the decomposition to be a lossless-join decomposition even though the common attributes, X, aren't a superkey of either component.

You should reconcile this observation with the result proved in Chapter 18: a decomposition is lossless if and only if the common attributes are a superkey of one of the components. A careful review of the lossless-join definition reveals that it requires the following condition to hold. If you project a *valid* database state, $r(R)$, onto the components, $\pi_{R_1}(r)$ and $\pi_{R_2}(r)$, then the natural join of these projections must exactly recover the state $r(R)$. Moreover, a valid database state, as defined in Chapter 18, was a state that satisfied all the constraints in $\mathcal{F}$. However, the database state is now further constrained

R'				
X				
		Y		
$X - (X \cap Y)$	$X \cap Y$	$Y - (X \cap Y)$	$R' - XY$	
	$\vdots$	$\vdots$	$\vdots$	$\vdots$
μ	x	v	y_1	z_1
ν	x	v	y_2	z_2
	$\vdots$	$\vdots$	$\vdots$	$\vdots$

R_1			
X			
		Y	
$X - (X \cap Y)$	$X \cap Y$	$Y - (X \cap Y)$	
	$\vdots$	$\vdots$	$\vdots$
x	v	y_1	
x	v	y_2	
	$\vdots$	$\vdots$	$\vdots$

R_2		
X		
$X - (X \cap Y)$	$X \cap Y$	$R' - XY$
$\vdots$	$\vdots$	$\vdots$
x	v	z_1
x	v	z_2
$\vdots$	$\vdots$	$\vdots$

Natural join of components				
X				
		Y		
$X - (X \cap Y)$	$X \cap Y$	$Y - (X \cap Y)$	$R' - XY$	
	$\vdots$	$\vdots$	$\vdots$	$\vdots$
μ	x	v	y_1	z_1
ν	x	v	y_2	z_2
μ'	x	v	y_1	z_2
ν'	x	v	y_2	z_1
	$\vdots$	$\vdots$	$\vdots$	$\vdots$

Figure 19.1   Illustrating the introduction of extraneous tuples with a join

by the MVD, $X \longrightarrow Y$. So some states that were legal under $\mathcal{F}$ alone are no longer valid states. Chapter 18's lossless-join definition still holds when the valid database states are determined only by the FDs in $\mathcal{F}$. However, in the presence of further constraints, you can have a lossless-join decomposition even if the common attributes aren't a superkey of either component. A later section will discuss this matter more thoroughly.

When an MVD, $X \longrightarrow Y$, constrains $r(R)$, it imposes a condition on any two tuples agreeing on X. For brevity, this condition is called the **MVD interchange condition**. The MVD, $X \longrightarrow Y$, **applies** to a relation R' if $X \subset R'$. Suppose the MVD, $X \longrightarrow Y$, constrains $r(R)$ and applies to R'. The MVD, $X \longrightarrow (Y \cap R')$, then constrains $r(R')$. Figure 19.2 illustrates the situation. Because $r(R')$ must be a projection of $r(R)$, the tuples in $r(R')$ must be segments of longer tuples in $r(R)$. For convenience, the figure groups all the R' attributes on the left. It then shows the $R - XY$ attributes as two segments: those inside R' and those outside it.

Because $R' - XY \subset R - XY$, the interchange of the $R - XY$ values in R produces an interchange of the $R' - XY$ values in R'. Therefore, as in the case with FDs, you can speak

R				
$(R - XY)_1$	X	$Y - X$		$(R - XY)_2$
R'				$R - R'$
$R' - XY$	X	$Y - X$		
$\vdots$	$\vdots$	$\vdots$	$\vdots$	$\vdots$
w_1	x	y_{11}	y_{12}	z_1
w_2	x	y_{21}	y_{22}	z_2
$\vdots$	$\vdots$	$\vdots$	$\vdots$	$\vdots$
w_2	x	y_{11}	y_{12}	z_2
w_1	x	y_{21}	y_{22}	z_1
$\vdots$	$\vdots$	$\vdots$	$\vdots$	$\vdots$

Figure 19.2   Illustrating the MVD interchange condition in a component of the universal relation

of an MVD constraining the application without mentioning the specific relation that must observe the interchange condition. In other words, when an application MVD, $X \longrightarrow\!\!\!\!\!\rightarrow Y$, constrains the universal relation $r(R)$ with an interchange condition on the $R - XY$ values, it necessarily constrains any component $r(R')$ with an interchange condition on the $R' - XY$ values, provided the MVD applies to R'. The reverse direction isn't true for MVDs. Unlike an FD, if an MVD constrains a component $r(R')$, it doesn't necessarily constrain the universal relation $r(R)$ with a similar MVD interchange condition.

For $X \subset R', r(R')$ **satisfies** an MVD, $X \longrightarrow\!\!\!\!\!\rightarrow Y$, if two tuples in R' agreeing on X are always accompanied by two tuples with the same structure except for interchanged values under the $R' - XY$ attributes. If an MVD doesn't apply to R', it's convenient to extend the definition to say that R' satisfies the MVD by default. If $r(R')$ doesn't satisfy an MVD, it **violates** the MVD.

 An MVD, $X \longrightarrow\!\!\!\!\!\rightarrow Y$, constrains $r(R')$ such that any two tuples agreeing on X must be accompanied by two similar tuples with the $R' - XY$ values interchanged. The MVD, $X \longrightarrow\!\!\!\!\!\rightarrow Y$, constrains $r(R')$ by requiring that $r(R')$ contain all tuples from the join of the XY and $X(R' - Y)$ projections.

MVD-induced redundancy

Consider the following example. You have workstations, developers, and projects, each with a few descriptive attributes. The first tier below shows the universal relation; the tables that follow constitute a BCNF decomposition, which removes any redundancies associated with the FDs. The intersection table, Effort, contains keys from the dispersed entities of the BCNF decomposition. In terms of the governing FDs, $\mathcal{F}$, no functional dependencies exist among the intersection attributes, so the only key for the intersection table is the set of all its attributes.

R						
dno	dname	wsno	wsname	wslocation	pno	pname

$$\mathcal{F}$$
$$\text{dno} \longrightarrow \text{dname}$$
$$\text{wsno} \longrightarrow \text{wsname}$$
$$\text{wsno} \longrightarrow \text{wslocation}$$
$$\text{pno} \longrightarrow \text{pname}$$

Developer	
dno	dname

Workstation		
wsno	wsname	wslocation

Project	
pno	pname

Effort		
dno	wsno	pno

Now add a new constraint, dno $\longrightarrow\!\!\!\!\rightarrow$ wsno, which applies to the intersection entity, Effort. With the tools of Chapter 18, you can easily check that (dno, wsno, pno) is the only key of Effort. In other words, `maxRight` can expand these attributes to include all of Effort, but it can't expand any proper subset of them to the full complement of Effort attributes. For example, (dno; $\mathcal{F}$) = (dno, dname), which doesn't include all the attributes of Effort. So dno isn't a superkey. You can check the other subsets in a similar fashion. However, some redundancy remains in Effort because dno $\longrightarrow\!\!\!\!\rightarrow$ wsno. In particular, you can predict the contents of both tuples marked with a star in the excerpt on the left below. Once the first two tuples are present, the starred tuples must appear to satisfy the multivalued dependency.

Effort		
dno	wsno	pno
⋮	⋮	⋮
6	4	7
6	3	8
6	4	8	*
6	3	7	*
⋮	⋮	⋮

Effort		
dno	wsno	pno

Effort$_1$	
dno	wsno

Effort$_2$	
dno	pno

Effort$_1$		
dno	wsno	φ
⋮	⋮	⋮
6	3	—
6	4	—
⋮	⋮	⋮

The constraint captures the idea that the workstations and projects associated with a particular developer aren't correlated in any way. If the first two tuples of the excerpt above appear without the starred tuples, they disclose information that developer 6 uses workstation 4 when dealing with project 7 and workstation 3 when dealing with project 8. You don't intend such an interpretation. Instead, you intend that the developer use certain workstations and work on certain projects, but he can use any of his workstations to deal with any of his projects. By adding the starred tuples, you restore the symmetry needed to convey the latter interpretation. The developer uses several workstations, the set $w = \pi_{q_1}\sigma_b$ (Effort), and works on several projects, the set $p = \pi_{q_2}\sigma_b$ (Effort). Here $q_1 = $ wsno, $q_2 = $ pno, and $b = $ (dno = 6). When arrayed in a single table, all possible (wsno, pno) pairs from $w \times p$ must appear with developer 6.

Therefore, when you see the first two tuples of the excerpt above, you know that the starred tuples must also appear. You can remove the redundancy by decomposing the Effort relation as shown in the center above. You populate the component bodies with projections from the effort table. Effort$_1$ now contains all the wsno values for a given developer; Effort$_2$

contains all the pno values for a given developer. Developer 6, for example, associates with a set of wsno values, w, and separately with a set of pno values, p. The join of the two components associates developer 6 with each (wsno, pno) pair such that the wsno value comes from w and the pno value comes from p. In other words, the join associates developer 6 with each (wsno, pno) from $w \times p$.

Note that dno $\longrightarrow\!\!\!\!\!\longrightarrow$ wsno applies to the first component. Moreover, dno isn't a superkey for that component, so multiple tuples can appear with the same dno value. However, there are no attributes in $Effort_1 - (dno\ wsno)$ to serve in the mixing role demanded by the definition. If you find two tuples, μ and ν, with the same dno value, you must also find two tuples, μ' and ν', with the same dno value and interchanged $Effort_1 - (dno\ wsno)$ values. However, the attribute set $Effort_1 - (dno\ wsno)$ is empty, so the swap simply regenerates μ and ν. In response to the demand to find μ' and ν' with the appropriate properties, you simply choose $\mu' = \mu$ and $\nu' = \nu$. The table to the right of the Effort decomposition above illustrates the situation. The heading φ is the empty set.

As illustrated in this example, a table with less than three attributes can't contain an MVD violation. A violation requires at least three attributes to fill the roles for a meaningful interchange situation: one attribute for the left side of an MVD, another for the right side, and a third where the interchange takes place. An exception occurs if the MVD is of the form $\varphi \longrightarrow\!\!\!\!\!\longrightarrow Y$ because a violation in this case can occur with just two attributes. Stated more accurately, a table with less than three attributes satisfies all MVDs, except possibly those of the form $\varphi \longrightarrow\!\!\!\!\!\longrightarrow Y$.

Because the example contains no MVDs of the form $\varphi \longrightarrow\!\!\!\!\!\longrightarrow Y$, $Effort_1$ and $Effort_2$ satisfy MVD dno $\longrightarrow\!\!\!\!\!\longrightarrow$ wsno. Note that you can't predict the value of any cells in either component. Because no attributes occur outside (dno, wsno) in $Effort_1$, no opportunity arises to generate new tuples by interchanging values under the $Effort_1 - (dno, wsno)$ attributes. Recall that FD-related decompositions remove redundancy by preventing any opportunity to find two tuples where you can copy a cell in the second from the corresponding cell in the first. Similarly, MVD-related decompositions remove redundancy by preventing any meaningful swapping opportunities. An MVD, $X \longrightarrow\!\!\!\!\!\longrightarrow Y$, applicable to relation R' provides an opportunity to predict cell values by interchanging $R' - XY$ values from other tuples. However, as illustrated in the last example, if $R' - XY = \varphi$, no swapping opportunities appear, and the redundancy vanishes.

Interactions among MVDs and FDs

Just as with FD analysis, you start with a core of MVD constraints that arise from the application. You then find that additional MVDs are automatically satisfied by any database state that satisfies the core MVDs. However, the situation is more complicated because FDs and MVDs can work together to force new FDs or MVDs to hold. Therefore, you should view the pool of FDs and MVDs as a unified set of constraints. $\mathcal{F}$ will continue to denote the FDs that arise from the application; $\mathcal{M}$ will denote the MVDs. A **valid** or **consistent** database state with respect to $\mathcal{F} \cup \mathcal{M}$ is now a body $r(R)$ that satisfies all the FDs and MVDs in $\mathcal{F} \cup \mathcal{M}$. Earlier discussion has shown that any component relation R' contains a projection of $r(R)$ and that an applicable FD, $X \longrightarrow Y$, or MVD, $X \longrightarrow\!\!\!\!\!\longrightarrow Y$, constrains $r(R')$ with $X \longrightarrow (Y \cap R')$ or $X \longrightarrow\!\!\!\!\!\longrightarrow (Y \cap R')$ as appropriate.

The closure of a set of FDs and MVDs

$\mathcal{F} \cup \mathcal{M}$ **implies** an FD or MVD constraint if that constraint must be satisfied by any valid database state with respect to $\mathcal{F} \cup \mathcal{M}$. When $\mathcal{F} \cup \mathcal{M}$ implies an FD, $X \longrightarrow Y$, or an MVD, $X \longrightarrow\!\!\!\!\!\rightarrow Y$, you write $\mathcal{F} \cup \mathcal{M} \models X \longrightarrow Y$ or $\mathcal{F} \cup \mathcal{M} \models X \longrightarrow\!\!\!\!\!\rightarrow Y$. Alternative expressions for "$\mathcal{F} \cup \mathcal{M}$ implies an FD or MVD" are "$\mathcal{F} \cup \mathcal{M}$ **models** the FD or MVD," or if the context of $\mathcal{F} \cup \mathcal{M}$ is clear, "the FD or MVD must hold," or even "you have the FD or MVD." The **closure** of $\mathcal{F} \cup \mathcal{M}$, denoted by $(\mathcal{F} \cup \mathcal{M})^+$, is the set of FDs and MVDs that must be satisfied by any valid database state with respect to $\mathcal{F} \cup \mathcal{M}$. In other words,

$$(\mathcal{F} \cup \mathcal{M})^+ = \{X \longrightarrow Y \mid \mathcal{F} \cup \mathcal{M} \models X \longrightarrow Y\} \cup \{X \longrightarrow\!\!\!\!\!\rightarrow Y \mid \mathcal{F} \cup \mathcal{M} \models X \longrightarrow\!\!\!\!\!\rightarrow Y\}. \tag{19.1}$$

You can generate $(\mathcal{F} \cup \mathcal{M})^+$ with certain rules, just as you can generate $\mathcal{F}^+$ with Armstrong's axioms. A later section will present these rules; for now, this section will continue a general discussion of MVDs and note from time to time that you can use a certain mechanism to create new members of $(\mathcal{F} \cup \mathcal{M})^+$.

Recall the earlier example where Effort_1 trivially satisfied dno $\longrightarrow\!\!\!\!\!\rightarrow$ wsno. It did so by not providing any attributes in the swapping columns. In other words, if $XY = R'$, then any $r(R')$ satisfies $X \longrightarrow\!\!\!\!\!\rightarrow Y$. The definition of an MVD requires that tuples, μ and ν, agreeing on X force the appearance of tuples μ' and ν' that swap the $R' - XY$ values of μ and ν. But if $R' = XY$, then $R' - XY$ is empty. This doesn't mean that $X \longrightarrow\!\!\!\!\!\rightarrow Y \in (\mathcal{F} \cup \mathcal{M})^+$. If $X \longrightarrow\!\!\!\!\!\rightarrow Y$ were in $(\mathcal{F} \cup \mathcal{M})^+$, it would have to constrain $r(R)$ with the same interchange condition. However, unless $R' = R$, you have $R - XY \neq \varphi$, and you can't guarantee that the interchanged tuples will appear in R.

Another trivial MVD is $X \longrightarrow\!\!\!\!\!\rightarrow \varphi$. Here, the swapping attributes are $R' - X$. If two tuples, μ and ν, agree on X, the swap gives $\mu' = \nu$ and $\nu' = \mu$. Of course, these two tuples are in the relation because they are the original tuples. In this case, however, $X \longrightarrow\!\!\!\!\!\rightarrow \varphi \in (\mathcal{F} \cup \mathcal{M})^+$ because the swapping argument regenerates the original tuples in the universal relation also.

In a similar manner, you can see that $X \longrightarrow\!\!\!\!\!\rightarrow Y$ always holds in R' or R, if $Y \subset X$. As in the preceding case, you have $R - XY = R - X$, so the swapping simply regenerates the original tuples. The following tables illustrate the operation. The tuples on the left require the appearance of those on the right. Because the tuples on the right duplicate those on the left, they certainly appear in the relation.

R'		
X		
$X - Y$	Y	$R' - XY$
$\vdots$	$\vdots$	$\vdots$
x	y	z_1
x	y	z_2
$\vdots$	$\vdots$	$\vdots$

R'		
X		
$X - Y$	Y	$R' - XY$
$\vdots$	$\vdots$	$\vdots$
x	y	z_2
x	y	z_1
$\vdots$	$\vdots$	$\vdots$

So you immediately find a large number of entries in $(\mathcal{F} \cup \mathcal{M})^+$ because all relational bodies satisfy these trivial MVDs. $X \longrightarrow\!\!\!\!\!\rightarrow Y \in (\mathcal{F} \cup \mathcal{M})^+$ whenever $Y \subset X$ (including $Y = \varphi$) or $XY = R$. These trivial MVDs introduce no opportunities for predicting values. The required new tuples are always equal to the original tuples. As a formal definition, an

MVD, $X \longrightarrow Y$, is **trivial** for R' if $XY = R'$ or if $Y \subset X$. The latter case includes $Y = \varphi$. A trivial MVD for R' introduces no redundancy into R'.

The closure of $\mathcal{F} \cup \mathcal{M}$ consists of all FDs and MVDs that must be satisfied by all valid database states, $r(R)$, with respect to $\mathcal{F} \cup \mathcal{M}$. $(\mathcal{F} \cup \mathcal{M})^{+}$ contains $X \longrightarrow Y$ whenever $Y \subset X$. An MVD, $X \longrightarrow Y$, is trivial for R' if $R' = XY$ or if $Y \subset X$. A trivial MVD introduces no redundancy into any relational body.

FDs can force certain MVDs into the closure

FDs and MVDs influence each other. FDs in $\mathcal{F} \cup \mathcal{M}$ can force new MVDs into $(\mathcal{F} \cup \mathcal{M})^{+}$ and combinations of FDs and MVDs can force new FDs into $(\mathcal{F} \cup \mathcal{M})^{+}$. Suppose $X \longrightarrow Y$ holds. $X \longrightarrow Y$ then also holds. To prove this, suppose you have two tuples, μ and ν in $r(R)$, that agree on X. From $X \longrightarrow Y$, you then deduce that they must also agree on Y. Therefore, when you construct μ' by replacing the $R - XY$ value from μ with the $R - XY$ value from ν, you simply regenerate the tuple ν because μ and ν are identical on XY. A similar comment applies to ν'. The table excerpts below illustrate this point. The left table contains the original tuples; the right shows the required tuples. Because the required tuples duplicate the original tuples, they certainly appear in R, and therefore R satisfies $X \longrightarrow Y$. This proves that $X \longrightarrow Y \in (\mathcal{F} \cup \mathcal{M})^{+}$ whenever $X \longrightarrow Y \in (\mathcal{F} \cup \mathcal{M})^{+}$.

R			
X			
		Y	
$X - X \cap Y$	$X \cap Y$	$Y - X \cap Y$	$R - XY$
$\vdots$	$\vdots$	$\vdots$	$\vdots$
x	v	y	z_1
x	v	y	z_2
$\vdots$	$\vdots$	$\vdots$	$\vdots$

R			
X			
		Y	
$X - X \cap Y$	$X \cap Y$	$Y - X \cap Y$	$R - XY$
$\vdots$	$\vdots$	$\vdots$	$\vdots$
x	v	y	z_2
x	v	y	z_1
$\vdots$	$\vdots$	$\vdots$	$\vdots$

FDs and MVDs can force new FDs into the closure

The argument above showed how an FD can force an MVD to hold. Is the reverse direction is possible? Consider the three-attribute relation on the left below in the context of $\mathcal{F} = (C \longrightarrow B)$ and $\mathcal{M} = (A \longrightarrow B)$. Suppose two tuples agree on A, as exemplified by the top two tuples. No violation of $C \longrightarrow B$ occurs because the two tuples don't agree on C. However, $A \longrightarrow B$ forces the lower pair of tuples to appear. The first tuple of the upper pair and the second tuple of the lower pair then agree on C but have B values b_1 and b_2. Therefore, b_1 must equal b_2, which implies that $A \longrightarrow B$ must hold.

Notice that $A \longrightarrow B$ is a new FD that wasn't present in $\mathcal{F}^{+}$. Indeed, you can compute $(A; \mathcal{F})$ by initializing the approximation Z to A and searching for an FD in $\mathcal{F}$ with a left side contained in Z. Finding none, you conclude that $(A; \mathcal{F}) = A$, and therefore $A \longrightarrow B \notin \mathcal{F}^{+}$.

R		
A	B	C
.	.	.
a	b_1	c_1
a	b_2	c_2
.	.	.
a	b_1	c_2
a	b_2	c_1
.	.	.

R			
A	B	B'	C
.	.	.	.
a	b_1	b'_1	c_1
a	b_2	b'_2	c_2
.	.	.	.
a	b_1	b'_1	c_2
a	b_2	b'_2	c_1
.	.	.	.

R							
	Z					W	
	Y			X			R' − XY
.	.	.	.	.	.	.	.
y_1	z_1	x_1	x_2	x_3	x_4	w_1	v_1
y_2	z_2	x_1	x_2	x_3	x_4	w_2	v_2
.	.	.	.	.	.	.	.
y_1	z_1	x_1	x_2	x_3	x_4	w_2	v_2
y_2	z_2	x_1	x_2	x_3	x_4	w_1	v_1
.	.	.	.	.	.	.	.

The argument also holds if C determines only part of the right side of the MVD. Suppose you have $\mathcal{F} = (C \longrightarrow B')$ and $\mathcal{M} = (A \longrightarrow\!\!\!\!\rightarrow BB')$, as shown in the center table above. When the bottom pair of tuples appears, as required by the MVD, you still get two tuples that agree on C and have B' values of b'_1 and b'_2. Therefore, $b'_1 = b'_2$, which implies that $A \longrightarrow B'$.

The left side of the FD must be disjoint from the right side of the MVD for this reasoning to apply. However, the left side of the FD need not be disjoint from the left side of the MVD. Therefore, the most general situation where an FD-MVD combination can force a new FD is as follows: if $X \longrightarrow\!\!\!\!\rightarrow Y$ and $W \longrightarrow\!\!\!\!\rightarrow Z$ with $Z \subset Y$ and $W \cap Y = \varphi$, then $X \longrightarrow Z$ holds.

To prove this, consider two tuples, μ and ν in R, that agree on X. The upper two tuples in the table to the far right above exemplify the most general form for two tuples agreeing on X. Because $X \longrightarrow\!\!\!\!\rightarrow Y$, the second pair of tuples must also appear; they swap the $R - XY$ values of the original tuples. Note that the first tuple of the upper pair and the second tuple of the lower pair agree on W. They must, therefore, agree on Z, which forces $z_1 = z_2$. With this adjustment, however, the original tuples agree on Z, which proves that $X \longrightarrow Z$ must hold. Consequently, you can assert an additional FD in $(\mathcal{F} \cup \mathcal{M})^+$ under these circumstances: if $X \longrightarrow\!\!\!\!\rightarrow Y, W \longrightarrow\!\!\!\!\rightarrow Z \in (\mathcal{F} \cup \mathcal{M})^+$, with $Z \subset Y$ and $Y \cap W = \varphi$, then $X \longrightarrow Z \in (\mathcal{F} \cup \mathcal{M})^+$.

 If $X \longrightarrow Y$ holds, then $X \longrightarrow\!\!\!\!\rightarrow Y$ also holds. If $X \longrightarrow\!\!\!\!\rightarrow Y$ and $W \longrightarrow Z$ hold for $Z \subset Y$ and W disjoint from Y, then $X \longrightarrow Z$ holds.

Complementation and augmentation

Each MVD in $(\mathcal{F} \cup \mathcal{M})^+$ gives rise to a complementary MVD in the universal relation. If $X \longrightarrow\!\!\!\!\rightarrow Y \in (\mathcal{F} \cup \mathcal{M})^+$, then $X \longrightarrow\!\!\!\!\rightarrow (R - XY) \in (\mathcal{F} \cup \mathcal{M})^+$ also. To prove this, suppose two tuples agree on X as exemplified by the two upper tuples in the leftmost table below. The constraint $X \longrightarrow\!\!\!\!\rightarrow Y$ then forces the lower tuples to appear. To prove the assertion, however, you need to interchange the $R - X(R - XY) = Y - (X \cap Y)$ portions of the original tuples. When you do so, you obtain exactly the two lower tuples. Therefore, if $X \longrightarrow\!\!\!\!\rightarrow Y \in (\mathcal{F} \cup \mathcal{M})^+$, then $X \longrightarrow\!\!\!\!\rightarrow (R - XY) \in (\mathcal{F} \cup \mathcal{M})^+$. Note that this result holds only in the universal relation R. If you have a proper subset $R' \subset R$ with $X \longrightarrow Y$ constraining R', you will also have $X \longrightarrow (R' - XY)$ constraining R'. The proof is similar to the one just given for R. But this doesn't enter $X \longrightarrow (R' - XY)$ into $(\mathcal{F} \cup \mathcal{M})^+$ because the attributes $R' - XY$ aren't the full complement of XY in R. You can't guarantee that the excess attributes will swap appropriately.

R				R											
$X - (X \cap Y)$	$X \cap Y$	$Y - (X \cap Y)$	$R - XY$	X						Y					$R - XY$
						W								W	
						Z								Z	
⋮	⋮	⋮	⋮	⋮	⋮	⋮	⋮	⋮	⋮	⋮	⋮	⋮	⋮	⋮	⋮
x	v	y_1	z_1	x_1	x_2	x_3	x_4	x_5	x_6	y_1	y_2	y_3	v_1	v_2	v_3
x	v	y_2	z_2	x_1	x_2	x_3	x_4	x_5	x_6	y_1'	y_2	y_3	v_1	v_2	v_3'
⋮	⋮	⋮	⋮	⋮	⋮	⋮	⋮	⋮	⋮	⋮	⋮	⋮	⋮	⋮	⋮
x	v	y_1	z_2	x_1	x_2	x_3	x_4	x_5	x_6	y_1	y_2	y_3	v_1	v_2	v_3'
x	v	y_2	z_1	x_1	x_2	x_3	x_4	x_5	x_6	y_1'	y_2	y_3	v_1	v_2	v_3
⋮	⋮	⋮	⋮	⋮	⋮	⋮	⋮	⋮	⋮	⋮	⋮	⋮	⋮	⋮	⋮

An augmentation activity, similar to the augmentation axiom in the FD case, can generate new MVDs that must hold in the context of existing MVDs. If $X \longrightarrow Y$ holds, then $WX \longrightarrow ZY$ whenever $Z \subset W$. In other words, you can strengthen both sides of an MVD, provided the left side receives at least the attributes added to the right side. The proof is as follows. Suppose you have two tuples agreeing on WX. The most general situation appears as the upper pair of tuples in the rightmost table above, which splits the W and Z segments to accommodate all the possibilities. W can reside partially in X alone, partially in $X \cap Y$, partially in Y alone, and partially in $R - XY$. Z can also reside in all these segments, provided it remains within W. The tuples certainly agree on X, and therefore the second pair of tuples must appear with interchanged $R - XY$ suffixes. You must show the existence of two tuples similar to the first but with the $R - WXZY$ portions interchanged. The only attributes in $R - WXZY$ are in the last column of the table, as displayed above. Note that the second pair of tuples agrees on WX, and it corresponds to first pair with the last column interchanged. The required tuples, therefore, exist in the table, and this proves $WX \longrightarrow ZY$.

If $X \longrightarrow Y$ holds, then $X \longrightarrow (R - XY)$ also holds. If $X \longrightarrow Y$ holds, then $WX \longrightarrow ZY$ holds for any $Z \subset W$.

The FD-MVD inference rules

As illustrated in the examples above, MVDs arise from various sources. The most significant MVDs arise from the application itself, where they express the intent that certain attributes be treated independently. Other MVDs arise from trivial situations where the right side is a subset of the left. Each FD in $(\mathcal{F} \cup \mathcal{M})^+$ generates a corresponding MVD, and under certain circumstances, an FD and MVD can conspire to generate a new FD. Each MVD generates a complementary MVD in the universal relation, and augmentation can create new MVDs from existing ones. These facts form part of the following **FD-MVD inference rules**, all of which generate new elements of $(\mathcal{F} \cup \mathcal{M})^+$.

1. **Reflexivity**

    - If $Y \subset X$, then $X \longrightarrow Y$.
    - If $Y \subset X$, then $X \longrightarrow\!\!\!\!\twoheadrightarrow Y$.

2. **Augmentation**

    - If $X \longrightarrow Y$ holds, then $XZ \longrightarrow YZ$ also holds.
    - If $X \longrightarrow\!\!\!\!\twoheadrightarrow Y$ holds, then $WX \longrightarrow\!\!\!\!\twoheadrightarrow ZY$ holds for $Z \subset W$.

3. **Transitivity**

    - If $X \longrightarrow Y$ and $Y \longrightarrow Z$ hold, then $X \longrightarrow Z$ holds.
    - If $X \longrightarrow\!\!\!\!\twoheadrightarrow Y$ and $Y \longrightarrow\!\!\!\!\twoheadrightarrow Z$ hold, then $X \longrightarrow\!\!\!\!\twoheadrightarrow (Z - Y)$ holds.

4. **Composition**

    - If $X \longrightarrow Y$ and $X \longrightarrow Z$ hold, then $X \longrightarrow YZ$ holds.
    - If $X \longrightarrow\!\!\!\!\twoheadrightarrow Y$ and $X \longrightarrow\!\!\!\!\twoheadrightarrow Z$ hold, then $X \longrightarrow\!\!\!\!\twoheadrightarrow YZ$ holds.

5. **Decomposition**

    - If $X \longrightarrow YZ$ holds, then $X \longrightarrow Y$ and $X \longrightarrow Z$ hold.
    - If $X \longrightarrow\!\!\!\!\twoheadrightarrow Y$ and $X \longrightarrow\!\!\!\!\twoheadrightarrow Z$ hold, then $X \longrightarrow\!\!\!\!\twoheadrightarrow (Y - Z), X \longrightarrow\!\!\!\!\twoheadrightarrow (Z - Y)$, and $X \longrightarrow\!\!\!\!\twoheadrightarrow (Y \cap Z)$ hold.

6. **Pseudotransitivity**

    - If $X \longrightarrow Y$ and $WY \longrightarrow Z$ hold, then $WX \longrightarrow Z$ holds.
    - If $X \longrightarrow\!\!\!\!\twoheadrightarrow Y$ and $WY \longrightarrow\!\!\!\!\twoheadrightarrow Z$ hold, then $WX \longrightarrow\!\!\!\!\twoheadrightarrow (Z - WY)$ holds.

7. **Complementation**

    - If $X \longrightarrow\!\!\!\!\twoheadrightarrow Y$ holds, then $X \longrightarrow\!\!\!\!\twoheadrightarrow (R - XY)$ holds.

8. **Replication**

    - If $X \longrightarrow Y$ holds, then $X \longrightarrow\!\!\!\!\twoheadrightarrow Y$ holds.

9. **Coalescence**

    - If $X \longrightarrow\!\!\!\!\twoheadrightarrow Y$ and $W \longrightarrow Z$ hold with $Z \subset Y$ and W disjoint from Y, then $X \longrightarrow Z$ holds.

The discussion so far has shown that the last three rules are valid. Furthermore, the first entry of each of the preceding pairs is one of Armstrong's axioms from Chapter 18. The arguments above have demonstrated that reflexivity and augmentation are valid for MVDs. Only the MVD-proofs for transitivity, composition, decomposition, and pseudotransitivity remain. The following approach is useful in proving the composition and decomposition rules, but in a circuitous fashion that reveals more consequences of MVDs.

Suppose you have $X \longrightarrow\!\!\!\!\!\rightarrow Y$ and $X \longrightarrow\!\!\!\!\!\rightarrow Z$. In the most general case, the attributes of X, Y, and Z intersect to produce eight segments. These segments, labeled $P_0, P_2, \ldots, P_7$, appear in the Venn diagram of Figure 19.3. In the left table below, the first two tuples, μ_{0000} and μ_{1111}, represent the most general case for two tuples that agree on X. From Figure 19.3, $R - XY = P_3 P_0$. So $X \longrightarrow\!\!\!\!\!\rightarrow Y$ requires that two more tuples appear with the P_3 and P_0 values interchanged. These tuples are μ_{1001} and μ_{0110}. Also, $R - XZ = P_1 P_0$, so the tuples μ_{0011} and μ_{1100} must appear. If you consider the possible entries under P_i to be a_i or b_i, for $0 \leq i \leq 3$, then six of the sixteen possibilities appear in the table—just from exercising the known MVDs.

Actually, the remaining ten possibilities must also appear because of the MVDs $X \longrightarrow\!\!\!\!\!\rightarrow Y$ and $X \longrightarrow\!\!\!\!\!\rightarrow Z$. The new table to the right below systematically lists all the possibilities and marks with an asterisk those already established from the left table. The naming pattern for the tuples should be clear by now. The four-bit subscript corresponds to the segments $P_3 P_2 P_1$ and P_0. A zero appears if the corresponding segment contains an a_i; a one appears if it contains a b_i. For example, μ_{1001} contains a-values in segments P_2 and P_1, and it contains b values in segments P_3 and P_0.

				R'				
	P_7	P_6	P_5	P_4	P_3	P_2	P_1	P_0
	$\vdots$	$\vdots$	$\vdots$	$\vdots$	$\vdots$	$\vdots$	$\vdots$	$\vdots$
μ_{0000}	x_7	x_6	x_5	x_4	a_3	a_2	a_1	a_0
μ_{1111}	x_7	x_6	x_5	x_4	b_3	b_2	b_1	b_0
μ_{1001}	x_7	x_6	x_5	x_4	b_3	a_2	a_1	b_0
μ_{0110}	x_7	x_6	x_5	x_4	a_3	b_2	b_1	a_0
μ_{0011}	x_7	x_6	x_5	x_4	a_3	a_2	b_1	b_0
μ_{1100}	x_7	x_6	x_5	x_4	b_3	b_2	a_1	a_0
	$\vdots$	$\vdots$	$\vdots$	$\vdots$	$\vdots$	$\vdots$	$\vdots$	$\vdots$

				R'					
	P_7	P_6	P_5	P_4	P_3	P_2	P_1	P_0	
	$\vdots$	$\vdots$	$\vdots$	$\vdots$	$\vdots$	$\vdots$	$\vdots$	$\vdots$	
μ_{0000}	x_7	x_6	x_5	x_4	a_3	a_2	a_1	a_0	*
μ_{0001}	x_7	x_6	x_5	x_4	a_3	a_2	a_1	b_0	
μ_{0010}	x_7	x_6	x_5	x_4	a_3	a_2	b_1	a_0	
μ_{0011}	x_7	x_6	x_5	x_4	a_3	a_2	b_1	b_0	*
μ_{0100}	x_7	x_6	x_5	x_4	a_3	b_2	a_1	a_0	
μ_{0101}	x_7	x_6	x_5	x_4	a_3	b_2	a_1	b_0	
μ_{0110}	x_7	x_6	x_5	x_4	a_3	b_2	b_1	a_0	*
μ_{0111}	x_7	x_6	x_5	x_4	a_3	b_2	b_1	b_0	
μ_{1000}	x_7	x_6	x_5	x_4	b_3	a_2	a_1	a_0	
μ_{1001}	x_7	x_6	x_5	x_4	b_3	a_2	a_1	b_0	*
μ_{1010}	x_7	x_6	x_5	x_4	b_3	a_2	b_1	a_0	
μ_{1011}	x_7	x_6	x_5	x_4	b_3	a_2	b_1	b_0	
μ_{1100}	x_7	x_6	x_5	x_4	b_3	b_2	a_1	a_0	*
μ_{1101}	x_7	x_6	x_5	x_4	b_3	b_2	a_1	b_0	
μ_{1110}	x_7	x_6	x_5	x_4	b_3	b_2	b_1	a_0	
μ_{1111}	x_7	x_6	x_5	x_4	b_3	b_2	b_1	b_0	*
	$\vdots$	$\vdots$	$\vdots$	$\vdots$	$\vdots$	$\vdots$	$\vdots$	$\vdots$	

Because $R - XZ = P_1 P_0$, you can obtain new tuples that must appear in the table by interchanging the $P_1 P_0$ values of two parent tuples that are known to reside in the table. The subscripts of these new tuples correspond to interchanging the last two bits of the subscripts

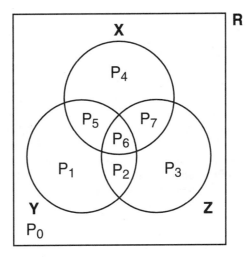

Figure 19.3   Segments produced by overlapping attributes X, Y, and $Z \subset R$

on the two parent tuples. So you can generate the remaining entries of the table above as shown below.

Obtained	From
μ_{0001}, μ_{1000}	μ_{0000}, μ_{1001}
μ_{0010}, μ_{0100}	μ_{0000}, μ_{0110}
μ_{0101}, μ_{1010}	μ_{0110}, μ_{1001}
μ_{0111}, μ_{1110}	μ_{0110}, μ_{1111}
μ_{1101}, μ_{1011}	μ_{1001}, μ_{1111}

This result shows that X multidetermines all the individual segments, P_0 through P_7, obtained by intersecting X, Y, Z, and the universal relation R. X also multidetermines any unions of the components P_0 through P_7. To prove this, suppose W is a union of components chosen from P_1 through P_7, and you want to establish $X \longrightarrow W$. Two generic tuples agreeing on X take the form μ_{0000} and μ_{1111}, and you must show that two further tuples appear with interchanged $R - WX$ values. However, $R - WX$ has components, P_j, that are missing from WX. Because X contains components P_4 through P_7, the missing components will always be in the set P_0 through P_3. So you must find the tuples where the 0s and 1s are interchanged in the subscripts that correspond to those P_j missing from W. For example, if $P_2 P_0$ are missing, you must find tuples μ_{0101} and μ_{1010}. But you know these tuples occur because $X \longrightarrow Y$ and $X \longrightarrow Z$ hold. Indeed, a tuple corresponding to *any* of the 16 patterns in the subscripts appears in the table. Therefore, $X \longrightarrow W$ holds whenever W is a union of selected components from P_0 through P_7.

Because $YZ = P_1 P_2 P_3 P_5 P_6 P_7$, the above argument shows that $X \longrightarrow YZ$ holds, which proves the composition rule for MVDs. Also, $Y - Z = P_1 P_5$, $Z - Y = P_3 P_7$, and $Y \cap Z = P_2 P_6$, so $X \longrightarrow Y - Z$, $X \longrightarrow Z - Y$, and $X \longrightarrow Y \cap Z$, which proves the decomposition rule for MVDs.

You can use the same arrangement of Figure 19.3 to prove the transitivity rule for MVDs. Suppose $X \longrightarrow\!\!\!\!\!\rightarrow Y$ and $Y \longrightarrow\!\!\!\!\!\rightarrow Z$ hold. You want to show that $X \longrightarrow\!\!\!\!\!\rightarrow Z - Y$ also holds. As before, μ_{0000} and μ_{1111} represent the most general tuples that agree on X. Then, $R - X(Z - Y) = P_2 P_1 P_0$. Therefore, you must show the existence of tuples μ_{0001} and μ_{1110} in the table. Note that $R - XY = P_3 P_0$, and therefore $X \longrightarrow\!\!\!\!\!\rightarrow Y$ requires that tuples μ_{1001} and μ_{0110} appear. $Y = P_6 P_5 P_2 P_1$, and $P_6 P_5 \subset X$, which implies that all the tuples agree on $P_5 P_6$. Looking for further agreement on $P_2 P_1$, you see that the pairs (μ_{0000}, μ_{1001}) and (μ_{1111}, μ_{0110}) match. Because $Y \longrightarrow\!\!\!\!\!\rightarrow Z$, you can interchange the $R - YZ = P_4 P_0$ portions of these tuples. Because $P_4 \subset X$, that part of the interchange goes unnoticed. However, swapping P_0 in the first pair gives μ_{0001} and μ_{1000}, which produces one of the required tuples. Interchanging the last bit in the second pair produces μ_{1110} and μ_{0111}, which yields the other tuple needed to prove that $X \longrightarrow\!\!\!\!\!\rightarrow Z - Y$.

Pseudotransitivity for MVDs follows as a consequence of transitivity and augmentation. Suppose $X \longrightarrow\!\!\!\!\!\rightarrow Y$, and $WY \longrightarrow\!\!\!\!\!\rightarrow Z$. Augmenting the first MVD with W gives $WX \longrightarrow\!\!\!\!\!\rightarrow WY$, and transitivity with the second MVD then gives $WX \longrightarrow\!\!\!\!\!\rightarrow (Z - WY)$, as required. At this point, you have shown that all the rules are sound in the sense that the application of a rule to FDs and MVDs in $(\mathcal{F} \cup \mathcal{M})^+$ yields other FDs or MVDs in $(\mathcal{F} \cup \mathcal{M})^+$.

The FD-MVD inference rules are sound. These rules operate on elements of $(\mathcal{F} \cup \mathcal{M})^+$ to produce new members through reflexivity, augmentation, transitivity, composition, decomposition, pseudotransitivity, complementation, replication, and coalescence.

A necessary condition for an attribute determinant

At this point, you may wonder how many new FDs you can introduce through the interaction of FDs and MVDs in the original $\mathcal{F} \cup \mathcal{M}$. A fact that will be useful later is that a nontrivial FD, $X \longrightarrow A$, can appear in $(\mathcal{F} \cup \mathcal{M})^+$ only if some $Y \longrightarrow AZ$, with $A \notin Y$, appears in the original $\mathcal{F}$. In other words, some attributes must nontrivially determine A in the original set of constraints, or else all the interplay between FDs and MVDs can never generate a determinant for A.

This observation is easy to prove. Suppose A never appears in the right side of an FD in $\mathcal{F}$. The relational body $r(R)$ below must then satisfy all the constraints in $\mathcal{F} \cup \mathcal{M}$. If $U \longrightarrow V \in \mathcal{F}$, then you know that $V \subset R - A$. So the two tuples agree on V, which implies that no violation occurs. Next, suppose $U \longrightarrow\!\!\!\!\!\rightarrow V \in \mathcal{M}$. If the two tuples agree on U, you must show that interchanging the $R - UV$ attributes produces tuples in the table. However, interchanging any set of attributes simply regenerates the same two tuples, so $U \longrightarrow\!\!\!\!\!\rightarrow V$ is satisfied.

R	
$R - A$	A
...000...	0
...000...	1

So $r(R)$ satisfies $\mathcal{F} \cup \mathcal{M}$ but violates $X \longrightarrow A$. ($A \notin X$ and $X \subset R - A$, so you have two tuples agreeing on X but differing on A.) Because $X \longrightarrow A \in (\mathcal{F} \cup \mathcal{M})^+$, this contradiction proves that A must appear as part of the right side of at least one FD in $\mathcal{F}$.

A nontrivial $X \longrightarrow A$ can appear in $(\mathcal{F} \cup \mathcal{M})^+$ only if $Y \longrightarrow AZ$ appears in $\mathcal{F}$, with $A \notin Y$. The interplay of FDs and MVDs in $\mathcal{F}$ and $\mathcal{M}$ can't materialize a new determinant for A unless some starting determinant already exists.

The dependency basis

A minimal basis for a collection of sets

If you have a group of MVDs with the same left side, $X \longrightarrow Y_1, X \longrightarrow Y_2, \ldots$, you can repeatedly apply the decomposition rule to show that X multidetermines all the disjoint components formed through intersections and set differences among the Y_i right sides. Calligraphic letters will denote sets whose elements are themselves attribute sets. Calligraphic letters will also denote sets of FDs and MVDs, but the distinction should clear from the context.

Let $\mathcal{C} = (S_1, S_2, \ldots, S_n)$ be a collection of non-empty attribute sets. A **basis** for $\mathcal{C}$ is a collection of sets, $\mathcal{D} = (T_1, T_2, \ldots, T_m)$, such that the T_j are pairwise disjoint and each $S_i \in \mathcal{C}$ is the union of selected components from $\mathcal{D}$. The basis sets $\mathcal{D}$ represent disjoint attribute segments that are exactly commensurate with the sets of $\mathcal{C}$. For each set $S_i \in \mathcal{C}$, a group of T_j sets in $\mathcal{D}$ can merge to equal S_i. For example, the collection $P_0, P_1, \ldots, P_7$ from Figure 19.3 is a basis for the collection X, Y, Z, R. Indeed, this basis is precisely the one that will prove useful in subsequent arguments because it is the group of sets that X individually multidetermines through the interaction of $X \longrightarrow Y$ and $X \longrightarrow Z$.

A problem with the basis is that other set collections also meet the definition but aren't multidetermined through transitivity-derived MVDs. For example, the collection of all singleton sets, each containing one attribute from the union of the sets in $\mathcal{C}$, is also a basis for $\mathcal{C}$. Moreover, a basis may contain some sets that are never used in the reconstruction of the sets in $\mathcal{C}$. Therefore, a **minimal basis** for $\mathcal{C}$ is a basis $\mathcal{D}$, such that $|\mathcal{D}| \leq |\mathcal{E}|$ for any basis $\mathcal{E}$ for $\mathcal{C}$. In other words, a minimal basis is a basis with a minimal number of components.

A basis for a collection of sets, $\mathcal{C}$, is another collection, $\mathcal{D}$, of potentially smaller sets, such that every member of $\mathcal{C}$ is a union of selected members of $\mathcal{D}$. A minimal basis for $\mathcal{C}$ is a basis such that no other basis has fewer members.

You can construct a minimal basis for a collection $\mathcal{C}$ as follows. Assume a data structure called `setCollection` for manipulating sets of attribute sets. A similar data structure appeared in Chapter 18, where it was used for handling decompositions. There it was called `decomposition`. This is the same structure, but a different name is better for the current context.

```
setCollection minBasis(setCollection C) {
  setCollection D;
  D = C;
  while (there exists X,Y ∈ D with X∩Y ≠ φ)
    replace X,Y in D with the non-empty parts of the sequence:  X − Y, Y − X, X ∩ Y;
  return D; }
```

Two invariants for the while-loop are: (1) any basis for C is a basis for D, and (2) any member of C is the union of selected members from D. The second invariant is easier to prove. It's certainly true when you enter the loop because $D = C$. When the loop operation replaces X and Y with $X − Y$, $Y − X$, and $X \cap Y$, you can still recover $X = (X − Y) \cup (X \cap Y)$ and $Y = (Y − X) \cup (X \cap Y)$. Therefore, any element of C expressible, at the beginning of the loop, as a union of D-members is still expressible, at the end of the loop, as a union of members from the new D. Where the union from the old D uses X, you simply substitute $(X − Y) \cup (X \cap Y)$; where the old D uses Y, you substitute $(Y − X) \cup (X \cap Y)$.

For the first invariant, note that it is also true when the loop is entered because $C = D$. Suppose any basis for C is a basis for D after k iterations of the loop. You must show that iteration $k + 1$ maintains the condition. To this end, suppose $\mathcal{E}$ is a basis for C. $\mathcal{E}$ is then a basis for D at the beginning of the iteration. Let $X \in D$ and $Y \in D$ be the overlapping sets that the loop intersects. Define

$$\mathcal{E}_X = \{E \in \mathcal{E} \mid E \subset X\} \qquad \mathcal{E}_{(X−Y)} = \mathcal{E}_X − \mathcal{E}_Y$$
$$\mathcal{E}_Y = \{E \in \mathcal{E} \mid E \subset Y\} \qquad \mathcal{E}_{(X\cap Y)} = \mathcal{E}_X \cap \mathcal{E}_Y$$
$$\mathcal{E}_{(Y−X)} = \mathcal{E}_Y − \mathcal{E}_X.$$

Because $\mathcal{E}$ is a basis for D, you must have $X = \cup \mathcal{E}_X$ and $Y = \cup \mathcal{E}_Y$. From its definition, $\cup \mathcal{E}_{(X \cap Y)} \subset (X \cap Y)$. Moreover, if $A \in X \cap Y$, then A must be in some $E \in \mathcal{E}_X$, and it must also be in some $E' \in \mathcal{E}_Y$. Because the elements of the basis $\mathcal{E}$ are disjoint, you must, however, have $E = E'$. Therefore, $A \in E \in \mathcal{E}_X \cap \mathcal{E}_Y$. So $X \cap Y \subset \cup \mathcal{E}_{(X \cap Y)}$. Combining this result with the reverse inclusion already established, you see that $X \cap Y = \cup \mathcal{E}_{(X \cap Y)}$. It then follows that $X − Y = \cup \mathcal{E}_{(X−Y)}$ and $Y − X = \cup \mathcal{E}_{(Y−X)}$. So when you substitute $X − Y, Y − X$, and $X \cap Y$ for X and Y in D, $\mathcal{E}$ remains a basis for the new D.

By induction, the invariant is then true when the loop terminates. When it terminates, however, D consists of disjoint sets, and it is therefore a basis for itself. If D contains n disjoint sets, then it can't have a basis with fewer than n members because at least one distinct basis member is required to cover each member of D. By the loop invariant, any basis for C is a basis for D. Therefore, any basis for C must contain at least as many members as D. Finally, by the second loop invariant, every member of C is expressible as a union of elements from D. So D, as delivered by the algorithm, is a minimal basis for C.

You can also argue that the minimal basis returned by the algorithm is unique. Suppose that $\mathcal{E}$ is another minimal basis for C. By the loop invariant, $\mathcal{E}$ must then be a basis for D, and because it's minimal, it must contain exactly the same number of members as D. Because the members of D are disjoint, $\mathcal{E}$ must dispatch a separate member for each of them. Because this allocation consumes all the members of $\mathcal{E}$, you can conclude that each member of D is the union of exactly one member of $\mathcal{E}$. This means, however, that each member of D is equal to a member of $\mathcal{E}$. Because the sets have the same number of members, this correspondence is one-to-one, and therefore $\mathcal{E} = D$. The algorithm `minBasis` then returns the unique minimal basis for a collection of attribute sets. In these terms, you can express the consequences of $X \longrightarrow\!\!\!\!\rightarrow Y$ and $X \longrightarrow\!\!\!\!\rightarrow Z$ as follows.

Suppose R is the universal relation, and $X \longrightarrow\!\!\!\!\rightarrow Y_1$, $X \longrightarrow\!\!\!\!\rightarrow Y_2$, ... $X \longrightarrow\!\!\!\!\rightarrow Y_n$ holds. $X \longrightarrow\!\!\!\!\rightarrow Z$ then holds for every Z that is a union of components from the minimal basis for $(X, Y_1, Y_2, \ldots, Y_n, R)$.

You can trace the operation of algorithm `minBasis` on the following collection, $\mathcal{C}$.

	$\mathcal{C}$	
ABC	CDGHIJ	B
ABCDEFGHIJKLM	BCDFGJ	C
ABCDEF	A	

The algorithm continually intersects overlapping components as follows and obtains the minimal basis as the final line. Because you have three singleton sets, the second line represents several steps, each of which strips a singleton from a composite attribute. The intersection operation between a singleton set and a composite set results in removing the singleton from the composite.

```
ABC          ABCDEF    CDGHIJ   BCDFGJ   A      B     C           ABCDEFGHIJKLM
DEFGHIJKLM   DEF       DGHIJ    DFGJ     A      B     C
DEF          GHIJKLM   DGHIJ    DFGJ     A      B     C
DEF          GHIJ      KLM      D        DFGJ   A     B    C
D            EF        GHIJ     KLM      DFGJ   A     B    C
D            FGJ       EF       GHIJ     KLM    A     B    C
D            F         GJ       E        GHIJ   KLM   A    B    C
D            F         GJ       HI       E      KLM   A    B    C
```

If you have $ABC \longrightarrow\!\!\!\!\rightarrow ABCDEF$, $ABC \longrightarrow\!\!\!\!\rightarrow CDGHIJ$, and $ABC \longrightarrow\!\!\!\!\rightarrow BCDFGJ$ in the context of the universal relation $R = ABCDEFGHIJKLM$, you can conclude that $ABC \longrightarrow\!\!\!\!\rightarrow A$, $ABC \longrightarrow\!\!\!\!\rightarrow B$, and $ABC \longrightarrow\!\!\!\!\rightarrow C$ by reflexivity. ABC then multidetermines all unions of elements from the minimal basis for $\mathcal{C}$, which is the last line of the calculation above. Some of these MVDs are trivial, but others constitute substantial constraints. In particular, they mean that the following decomposition must be lossless.

R										
ABC	D	E	F	G	H	I	J	K	L	M

R_1		R_2		R_3		R_4			R_5			R_6			
ABC	D	ABC	E	ABC	F	ABC	G	J	ABC	H	I	ABC	K	L	M

The dependency basis of a determinant

For a given set of constraints, $\mathcal{F} \cup \mathcal{M}$, and a given subset of attributes, X, let $\mathcal{C} = \{Y \mid X \longrightarrow\!\!\!\!\rightarrow Y \in (\mathcal{F} \cup \mathcal{M})^+\}$. The minimal basis for $\mathcal{C}$ is the **dependency basis** for X with respect to $\mathcal{F} \cup \mathcal{M}$, and it's denoted by $[X; \mathcal{F} \cup \mathcal{M}]$. It follows that $X \longrightarrow\!\!\!\!\rightarrow Y$ if and only if there is a subset $\mathcal{D} \subset [X; \mathcal{F} \cup \mathcal{M}]$ such that $Y = \cup \mathcal{D}$. In other words, $X \longrightarrow\!\!\!\!\rightarrow Y$ if and only if Y is the union of selected members of the dependency basis for X. This construction provides a method for determining if an MVD, $X \longrightarrow Y$, is in $(\mathcal{F} \cup \mathcal{M})^+$. You compute the dependency basis, $[X; \mathcal{F} \cup \mathcal{M}]$, and then check to see if there are elements of $[X; \mathcal{F} \cup \mathcal{M}]$ with union Y. The following algorithm computes the dependency basis. Assume a data type `constraintSet` that holds a collection of FDs and MVDs. As always, R is the universal relation.

```
setCollection depBasis(attributeSet X, attributeSet R, constraintSet F∪M) {
    boolean change;
    constraintSet G;
    setCollection C;
    G = F∪M∪{X ⟶ A | X ⟶AY ∈ F};
    change = true; C = {R − X};
    while (change)
        if (there exists V ∈ C and Y ⟶ Z ∈ G such that
            V∩Y = φ and V∩Z ≠ φ and V − Z ≠ φ)
            replace V with V∩Z and V − Z
        else
            change = false;
    return C ∪ {{A} | A ∈ X}; }
```

As a first step, the algorithm enlarges the constraints $\mathcal{F} \cup \mathcal{M}$ to include all the MVDs generated from the FDs through the decomposition and replication rules. Because these MVDs follow from the inference rules, the closure isn't changed. You must now show that depBasis$(X, R, \mathcal{F} \cup \mathcal{M})$ correctly computes $[X; \mathcal{F} \cup \mathcal{M}]$. The while-loop continually subdivides $R - X$, and you can show that it obtains the components of the dependency basis that lie outside of X. Because $X \longrightarrow A$, by reflexivity for every $A \in X$, you can then add a singleton set for each attribute contained in X, just before returning the result. The final return, therefore, is the full dependency basis.

$X \longrightarrow V$, for every $V \in \mathcal{C}$, is a loop invariant. The proof runs as follows. Before entering the loop, you initialize $\mathcal{C}$ to $R - X$. Because $X \longrightarrow X$ by reflexivity, you have $X \longrightarrow (R - X)$ by complementation. So the alleged invariant is true upon entry to the loop. Assuming that it's true at the start of an arbitrary iteration, you need to show that the loop operation leaves it true. When a splitting operation occurs, four sets take part: X, V, Y, and Z. You have $V \in \mathcal{C}$, and therefore $X \longrightarrow V$ because the loop invariant is true when the iteration begins. $Y \longrightarrow Z \in \mathcal{G}$, with $V \cap Y = \varphi, V \cap Z \neq \varphi$, and $V - Z \neq \varphi$. At this point, you replace V with $V \cap Z$ and $V - Z$.

Because the other sets of $\mathcal{C}$ aren't disturbed, the loop invariant will be preserved if $X \longrightarrow (V \cap Z)$ and $X \longrightarrow (V - Z)$. In the most general case, the four sets produce sixteen disjoint attribute segments. These correspond to the attributes that are outside all four sets, those that are outside the first three but inside the fourth, and so on. The following table organizes these sixteen segments and arrays them vertically. The segments carry the names 0000 through 1111, and the bits correspond to $XVYZ$ in a left-to-right order. For example, the segment 0101 comprises those attributes that aren't in X, are in V, aren't in Y, and are in Z. Certain segments are empty. Because V is part of a subdivision of $R - X$, V is disjoint from X. Therefore, the segments 1100, 1101, 1110, and 1111 are empty. You also have $V \cap Y = \varphi$, so the segments 0110, 0111, 1110, 1111 are empty. Some of these segments were already declared empty because X and V are disjoint, but in total you have six empty segments, shown by the dashes in the table.

X	V	Y	Z	μ_{000000}	μ_{111111}	μ_{001111}	μ_{110000}	μ_{010000}	μ_{100000}	μ_{101111}	μ_{011111}
0	0	0	0	a_0	b_0	b_0	a_0	a_0	a_0	b_0	b_0
0	0	0	1	a_1	b_1	b_1	a_1	a_1	a_1	b_1	b_1
0	0	1	0	a_2	b_2	b_2	a_2	a_2	a_2	b_2	b_2
0	0	1	1	a_3	b_3	b_3	a_3	a_3	a_3	b_3	b_3
0	1	0	0	a_4	b_4	a_4	b_4	b_4	b_4	a_4	b_4
0	1	0	1	a_5	b_5	a_5	b_5	a_5	b_5	b_5	a_5
0	1	1	0	—	—	—	—	—	—	—	—
0	1	1	1	—	—	—	—	—	—	—	—
1	0	0	0	x_8	x_8	x_8	x_8	x_8	x_8	x_8	x_8
1	0	0	1	x_9	x_9	x_9	x_9	x_9	x_9	x_9	x_9
1	0	1	0	x_a	x_a	x_a	x_a	x_a	x_a	x_a	x_a
1	0	1	1	x_b	x_b	x_b	x_b	x_b	x_b	x_b	x_b
1	1	0	0	—	—	—	—	—	—	—	—
1	1	0	1	—	—	—	—	—	—	—	—
1	1	1	0	—	—	—	—	—	—	—	—
1	1	1	1	—	—	—	—	—	—	—	—

The first two columns represent two generic tuples that agree on X. The names reflect the values in segments 0101, 0100, 0011, 0010, 0001, and 0000. Therefore, μ_{000000} has a_i values in these segments, and μ_{111111} has b_i values. The remaining segments are empty or contain the same values in both tuples. In either case, you don't need to be concerned with them. Because $X \longrightarrow\!\!\!\!\!\rightarrow V$ holds, you must have two more tuples that reflect the interchange of the $R - XV$ portions of the first two columns. Segments in $R - XV$ have a 0 in the X and V parts of their names. So among the first six rows where interchanges make a difference, these segments are 0000, 0001, 0010, and 0011. These segments correspond to the last four bits of the tuple names, so the interchange produces μ_{001111} and μ_{110000}. These tuples appear to the right of the original tuples. You also have $Y \longrightarrow\!\!\!\!\!\rightarrow Z$. To agree on Y, the segments with a 1 in the Y position must agree. In other words, segments 0010 and 0011 must agree. You see that the first and fourth agree, as do the second and third. The first pair is μ_{000000} and μ_{110000}. The $R - YZ$ segments are those with 0s in the YZ parts—0000 and 0100. Swapping these values on μ_{000000} and μ_{110000} gives μ_{010000} and μ_{100000}, which then appear as tuples five and six. The second pair is μ_{111111} and μ_{001111}. Swapping segments 0000 and 0100 gives μ_{101111} and μ_{011111}, which become the last two columns.

To prove that $X \longrightarrow\!\!\!\!\!\rightarrow (V \cap Z)$, you must show that two tuples appear that swap the $R - X(V \cap Z)$ portions of the first two tuples: μ_{000000} and μ_{111111}. The segments in $R - X(V \cap Z)$ are those that exhibit a 0 in the X position and anything other than a 11 in the VZ positions: 0000, 0001, 0010, 0011, 0100. The interchange then gives μ_{011111} and μ_{100000}. These tuples do indeed appear, which proves $X \longrightarrow\!\!\!\!\!\rightarrow (V \cap Z)$.

To prove that $X \longrightarrow\!\!\!\!\!\rightarrow (V - Z)$, you must exhibit two tuples that interchange the $R - X(V - Z)$ portions of μ_{000000} and μ_{111111}. The $R - X(V - Z)$ segments are those that have a 0 in the X position and anything other than a 10 in the VZ positions: 0000, 0001, 0010, 0011, 0101. Swapping these positions on tuples μ_{000000} and μ_{111111} gives μ_{101111} and μ_{010000}, which also appear in the table. Therefore, $X \longrightarrow\!\!\!\!\!\rightarrow (V - Z)$ is proved. This establishes the validity of the loop invariant.

Although the arguments above show directly that $X \longrightarrow\!\!\!\!\!\rightarrow (V \cap Z)$ and $X \longrightarrow\!\!\!\!\!\rightarrow (V - Z)$ hold, these facts also follow from the FD-MVD inference rules. Figure 19.4 shows the most general circumstances for the four sets. V is disjoint from X because it is part of the

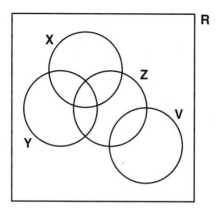

Figure 19.4   Set components manipulated by the depBasis algorithm

growing partition of $R - X$. Y and Z are arbitrarily positioned with respect to X. Finally, V intersects Z but not Y. You can then reason as follows from the rules.

(1) $X \longrightarrow\!\!\!\rightarrow V$	loop invariant holds at the beginning of the iteration
(2) $X \longrightarrow\!\!\!\rightarrow (R - XV)$	complementation of (1)
(3) $X \longrightarrow\!\!\!\rightarrow (R - V)$	augmentation of (2) with X
(4) $(R - V) \longrightarrow\!\!\!\rightarrow Y$	reflexivity
(5) $Y \longrightarrow\!\!\!\rightarrow Z$	qualifying MVD from $\mathcal{M}'$
(6) $(R - V) \longrightarrow\!\!\!\rightarrow Z - Y$	transitivity of (4) and (5)
(7) $X \longrightarrow\!\!\!\rightarrow (Z - Y) - (R - V) = V \cap Z$	transitivity of (3) and (6)
(8) $X \longrightarrow\!\!\!\rightarrow (V - (V \cap Z)) = (V - Z)$	decomposition with (1) and (7)

Returning to the main theme of the proof, you must show that the loop terminates. It does so because it continually subdivides the finite set $R - X$. When it terminates, the invariant states that $X \longrightarrow\!\!\!\rightarrow V$, for every $V \in \mathcal{C}$. This condition doesn't change when you add the singleton attributes of X before returning the result. Because the loop begins with just one set in $\mathcal{C}$ and because each operation replaces a member of $\mathcal{C}$ with two disjoint members whose union is the replaced set, you can conclude that the sets in $\mathcal{C}$ are disjoint and represent all of R.

So $\mathcal{C}$ is a disjoint collection of sets, and $X \longrightarrow\!\!\!\rightarrow Y$ for any Y that is a union of selected members of $\mathcal{C}$. The final value of $\mathcal{C}$ is, therefore, a good candidate for the dependency basis, $[X; \mathcal{F} \cup \mathcal{M}]$, but the proof isn't yet complete. The above derivation using the FD-MVD inference rules shows that you can obtain the MVD, $X \longrightarrow\!\!\!\rightarrow Y$, for any Y in the returned collection $\mathcal{C}$, by repeated application of the inference rules. Using the composition rule, you can then obtain $X \longrightarrow\!\!\!\rightarrow Y$, for any Y that is a union of elements from $\mathcal{C}$.

If Y is a union of selected members of $\mathcal{C}$ as returned by the algorithm `depBasis`$(X, R, \mathcal{F} \cup \mathcal{M}')$, *then* $X \longrightarrow\!\!\!\rightarrow Y$ *follows from* $\mathcal{F} \cup \mathcal{M}$ *by repeated application of the FD-MVD inference rules.*

A second loop invariant is the condition: $[X; \mathcal{F} \cup \mathcal{M}]$ is a basis for $\mathcal{C}$. From the definition of $[X; \mathcal{F} \cup \mathcal{M}]$, you know that any Y multidetermined by X must be the union of sets from $[X; \mathcal{F} \cup \mathcal{M}]$. Because you have just shown that $X \longrightarrow\!\!\!\!\!\rightarrow Y$, for any Y in $\mathcal{C}$, it follows that any $Y \in \mathcal{C}$ must be the union of sets from $[X; \mathcal{F} \cup \mathcal{M}]$. Therefore, $[X; \mathcal{F} \cup \mathcal{M}]$ is a basis for $\mathcal{C}$. Because $\mathcal{C}$ consists of disjoint sets at all times, the basis $[X; \mathcal{F} \cup \mathcal{M}]$ must dispatch separate elements to cover each set of $\mathcal{C}$ with a union. So the dependency basis must be at least as large as $\mathcal{C}$: $|\mathcal{C}| \leq |[X; \mathcal{F} \cup \mathcal{M}]|$. If $\mathcal{C}$ is a basis for $\{Y \mid X \longrightarrow\!\!\!\!\!\rightarrow Y\}$, then it must be the minimal basis. In other words, it must equal $[X; \mathcal{F} \cup \mathcal{M}]$. You are halfway to this goal because you know that if Y is a union of elements from $\mathcal{C}$, then $X \longrightarrow\!\!\!\!\!\rightarrow Y$.

In prepare for proving the reverse direction, compose a body $r(R)$ for the universal relation as follows. Let the components of the final value of $\mathcal{C}$ be $V_1, V_2, \ldots, V_n$, after removing the singleton sets containing the attributes of X. The V_i are then all disjoint from X. You then construct n tables with attributes X and V_i. If $V_i = A$, a singleton, and if there exists an FD, $U \longrightarrow AW \in \mathcal{F}$ with $A \notin U$, you install one tuple in the body, as illustrated with R_i. Otherwise you install two, as illustrated with R_j. The tuples all contain $\ldots x \ldots$ under the X attributes. Under V_i the value is $\ldots a_i \ldots$, and if there is a second tuple, $\ldots b_i \ldots$. The a_i, b_i and x values are all distinct. Referring to the body of component R_i as r_i, let $r = r_1 * r_2 * \ldots * r_n$.

	R_i			R_j			R_n	
	X	V_i		X	V_j		X	V_n
$\ldots\ldots$	$\ldots x \ldots$	a_i	$\ldots\ldots$	$\ldots x \ldots$	$\ldots a_j \ldots$	$\ldots\ldots$	$\ldots x \ldots$	$\ldots a_n \ldots$
				$\ldots x \ldots$	$\ldots b_j \ldots$		$\ldots x \ldots$	$\ldots b_n \ldots$

The join has attribute scheme R because the V_i partition $R - X$. The V_i are disjoint, and a tuple in r has the format $x : v_1 : v_2 : \ldots : v_n$ under the attributes $XV_1V_2\ldots V_n$. Under certain circumstances, a v_i corresponds to a V_i singleton, A, where $U \longrightarrow AW \in \mathcal{F}$ with $A \notin U$. In that case, the v_i segment is always a_i. Otherwise, v_i can be $\ldots a_i \ldots$ or $\ldots b_i \ldots$. Therefore, except when you must choose a single a_i corresponding to one of the special V_i, you can independently choose either $\ldots a_j \ldots$ or $\ldots b_j \ldots$ for the v_j segments. Whatever your choices may be, the join operation ensures that the tuple so constructed appears in the table.

The relational body r satisfies $\mathcal{F} \cup \mathcal{M}$, and the proof runs as follows. Suppose $U \longrightarrow W \in \mathcal{F}$. If $W = A_1 A_2 \ldots A_m$, then $U \longrightarrow\!\!\!\!\!\rightarrow A_i \in \mathcal{M}'$ as input to the algorithm. $U \longrightarrow W$ will be satisfied if each $U \longrightarrow A_i$ is satisfied when $A_i \notin U$. Accordingly, let $A \notin U$ be one of the $A_i \in W$. You must show that r satisfies $U \longrightarrow A$. Suppose $\mu \in r$ and $\nu \in r$ agree on U. If $A \in X$ or $A \in U$, then the two tuples also agree on A. The only other possibility is that $A \in V_j$, for some j, and $A \notin U$. If $U \cap V_j \neq \varphi$, then because μ and ν agree on U, both tuples must contain $\ldots a_j \ldots$ or both must contain $\ldots b_j \ldots$ under attributes V_j. In this case, the tuples agree on all of V_j, including the attribute A. So you can assume that $U \cap V_j = \varphi$. Now A is in V_j, and U is spread across X and the other V_i. $U \longrightarrow A$, therefore, meets the criterion for splitting V_j, provided that $V_j - A \neq \varphi$. Because the algorithm has terminated, you must have $V_j - A = \varphi$, which means $V_j = A$. So V_j is a singleton, and you have $U \longrightarrow W = AW' \in \mathcal{F}$ with $A \notin U$. The constituent table with schema (X, V_j) then contains the single tuple $\ldots a_j \ldots$. However, all tuples in r then contain $\ldots a_j \ldots$ in the $V_j = A$ attribute, which implies that μ and ν agree on

A. Therefore, you have that r satisfies $U \longrightarrow W$. This proves that r satisfies all the FDs in $\mathcal{F}$.

Suppose now that $U \longrightarrow\!\!\!\!\!\rightarrow W \in \mathcal{M}$ and two tuples, $\mu \in r$ and $\nu \in r$ agree on U. You must exhibit two tuples that interchange the values in the $R - UW$ attributes. Consider where the two tuples must agree. Obviously they agree on X because all tuples in r agree on X. For each V_i that intersects U, μ and ν must agree on all V_i. After all, the value under V_i is either $\ldots a_i \ldots$ or $\ldots b_i \ldots$, and these values have nothing in common. So to agree on part of V_i is to agree on all of it. Let T be the union of the V_i that have an attribute in common with U. You then have μ and ν agreeing on XT. Because the V_i that share attributes with U partition $R - X$, you must also have $U \subset XT$. Now consider the V_j that are outside of XT. If $W \cap V_j \neq \varphi$ for one of these sets, you must have $V_j - W = \varphi$, or the algorithm wouldn't have terminated. So $V_j \subset W$. You have demonstrated that W contains each V_j with which it shares a non-empty intersection. In other words, each V_j is either completely inside of W, or it is disjoint from W. So μ and ν must appear as follows.

		X	V_{i_1}	V_{i_2}	$\ldots$	V_{i_p}	V_{j_1}	V_{j_2}	$\ldots$	V_{j_q}	$\ldots$	V_{k_1}	V_{k_2}	$\ldots$	V_{k_t}
									R						
μ		x	v_{i_1}	v_{i_2}	$\ldots$	v_{i_p}	v_{j_1}	v_{j_2}	$\ldots$	v_{j_q}	$\ldots$	v_{k_1}	v_{k_2}	$\ldots$	v_{k_t}
ν		x	v_{i_1}	v_{i_2}	$\ldots$	v_{i_p}	w_{j_1}	w_{j_2}	$\ldots$	w_{j_q}	$\ldots$	w_{k_1}	w_{k_2}	$\ldots$	w_{k_t}

The first set of V_i, the $V_{i_1}, \ldots, V_{i_p}$, are the attribute packets where μ and ν must agree. These are the packets touched by U. The second set, the $V_{j_1}, \ldots, V_{j_q}$, are the attribute packets that are completely contained in W. Finally, the third set, the $V_{k_1}, \ldots, V_{k_t}$, are the packets that are disjoint from W, from X, and from the earlier packets. μ and ν can differ on the second and third sets of packets. A v or w value is either an $\ldots a \ldots$ or a $\ldots b \ldots$ for the packet where it occurs. Because the tuples differ only on entire packets, never on partial packets, you can interchange the packets where the tuples differ. This interchange simply produces another choice of $\ldots a \ldots$ or $\ldots b \ldots$ for the V_i segments, and you know the join that created r delivered all such choices. Therefore, the required tuples with the attributes of $R - UV$ interchanged are in the table, and $U \longrightarrow\!\!\!\!\!\rightarrow V$ is satisfied.

Now r satisfies all the constraints of $\mathcal{F} \cup \mathcal{M}$, so r satisfies all the constraints of the closure $(\mathcal{F} \cup \mathcal{M})'$. Recall the original goal: to prove that depBasis correctly computes the dependency basis, $[\mathcal{F} \cup \mathcal{M}]$. You know that $X \longrightarrow\!\!\!\!\!\rightarrow Y$ holds for any Y that is constructed as a union of members from $\mathcal{C}$ as returned by the algorithm. For the reverse direction, suppose that $X \longrightarrow\!\!\!\!\!\rightarrow Y$ holds. Because r must satisfy $X \longrightarrow\!\!\!\!\!\rightarrow Y$, the part of Y outside of X completely includes any V_i that it touches. Why? Consider the consequences if Y were to include only a part of a V_i. You can find two tuples in r that violate the MVD. You choose one tuple with value $\ldots a_i \ldots$ under the V_i attributes and a second with the value $\ldots b_i \ldots$ under the V_i. (Note that V_i can't be a singleton because there is no way to partially include a single attribute. Either Y includes the singleton, or it is disjoint from it. So both the $\ldots a_i \ldots$ and $\ldots b_i \ldots$ tuples are available in the join operand that contributes the V_i segment.) Now the $R - XY$ segments of the two tuples also include a fraction of the V_i, and the interchange produces two tuples that have a_i values in part of the V_i attributes and b_i values in the other part. No such tuples exist in r, and this violates the MVD. Because the MVD holds, you conclude that Y must include each V_i that it touches. So the part of Y outside of X is the union of V_i packets. Because you can construct the part of Y inside X

from the singleton packets in $\mathcal{C}$ that were added just before it was returned by the algorithm, you can conclude that Y is the union of members of $\mathcal{C}$.

Finally, you have established that the $\mathcal{C}$ returned by depBasis is a basis for $\{Y \mid X \longrightarrow\!\!\!\!\!\rightarrow Y \in (\mathcal{F} \cup \mathcal{M})^+\}$. An earlier argument noted that the minimal basis for this set can have no fewer members, so you conclude that the algorithm returns a minimal basis.

 depBasis *correctly calculates the dependency basis*, $[X; \mathcal{F} \cup \mathcal{M}]$, *by repeatedly subdividing* $R - X$ *using only the MVDs of* $\mathcal{M}$ *plus MVDs of the form* $U \longrightarrow\!\!\!\!\!\rightarrow A$ *arising from FDs of the form* $U \longrightarrow AW$ *in* $\mathcal{F}$.

Before leaving the laboriously constructed relational body, r, you can extract one more result. Because r satisfies all the constraints of $\mathcal{F} \cup \mathcal{M}$, it must satisfy all of $(\mathcal{F} \cup \mathcal{M})^+$ by definition of the closure. Suppose $X \longrightarrow A$ holds and $A \notin X$. Then A must be in one of the singleton V_i sections that was assigned a single tuple in the corresponding table, R_i. Otherwise, the join assembles two tuples that agree on X but have differing values, a_i and b_i, in A. Thus, you have shown that if $X \longrightarrow A \in (\mathcal{F} \cup \mathcal{M})^+$, for $A \notin X$, then the return value from algorithm depBasis includes A as a singleton set. Moreover, there must exist an FD, $U \longrightarrow AW \in \mathcal{F}$, with $A \notin U$. The reverse direction is clear. If $X \longrightarrow A$ holds, then so does $X \longrightarrow\!\!\!\!\!\rightarrow A$. But then $\{A\} \in \{Y \mid X \longrightarrow\!\!\!\!\!\rightarrow Y \in (\mathcal{F} \cup \mathcal{M})^+\}$, so the singleton $\{A\}$ must appear in the dependency basis. An earlier argument established that if $X \longrightarrow A$ holds, there must exist an FD, $U \longrightarrow AW \in \mathcal{F}$, with $A \notin U$. This shows that $X \longrightarrow A$ is equivalent to (1) A is determined by some attribute set disjoint from A and (2) A is a singleton member of the dependency basis, $[X; \mathcal{F} \cup \mathcal{M}]$.

 $X \longrightarrow A$ *holds if and only if the singleton* $\{A\}$ *is a member of the dependency basis,* $[X; \mathcal{F} \cup \mathcal{M}]$, *and there exists an FD,* $U \longrightarrow AW \in \mathcal{F}$ *with* $A \notin U$.

Completeness of the FD-MVD inference rules

You can now prove that the FD-MVD inference rules generate all of $(\mathcal{F} \cup \mathcal{M})^+$. Suppose $X \longrightarrow Y \in (\mathcal{F} \cup \mathcal{M})^+$, and let $Y = A_1 A_2 \ldots A_t$. You must show that you can reach $X \longrightarrow Y$ by using the inference rules on the starting collection $\mathcal{F} \cup \mathcal{M}$. If you can prove that you can obtain each $X \longrightarrow A_i$ by repeated application of the rules, you can then reach $X \longrightarrow Y$ by composition. Accordingly, let A be one of the A_i. You now know that the singleton $\{A\}$ appears in the dependency basis, $[X; \mathcal{F} \cup \mathcal{M}]$, and that there exists an FD, $U \longrightarrow AW \in \mathcal{F}$, with $A \notin U$. You also know you can reach $X \longrightarrow\!\!\!\!\!\rightarrow A$ by repeated application of the inference rules. This follows because A is in the dependency basis for X. However, $X \longrightarrow A$ then follows by coalescence. This proves that all the FDs in $(\mathcal{F} \cup \mathcal{M})^+$ follow from repeated application of the rules.

Now suppose $X \longrightarrow\!\!\!\!\!\rightarrow Y \in (\mathcal{F} \cup \mathcal{M})^+$. Y is then the union of elements from $[X; \mathcal{F} \cup \mathcal{M}]$. Moreover, if V is a member of $[X; \mathcal{F} \cup \mathcal{M}]$, you can reach it from $\mathcal{F} \cup \mathcal{M}$ by repeated application of the rules. $X \longrightarrow\!\!\!\!\!\rightarrow Y$ then follows from several applications of the composition rule. The FD-MVD inference rules, therefore, are both sound and complete.

The FD-MVD inference rules are sound and complete in the generation of $(\mathcal{F} \cup \mathcal{M})^+$. Using reflexivity, augmentation, transitivity, composition, decomposition, pseudotransitivity, complementation, replication, and coalescence, you can reach any member of $(\mathcal{F} \cup \mathcal{M})^+$ from the starting collection $\mathcal{F} \cup \mathcal{M}$.

Because $X \longrightarrow A$ if and only if $\{A\}$ appears as a singleton in the dependency basis $[X; \mathcal{F} \cup \mathcal{M}]$ and there exists $U \longrightarrow AW \in \mathcal{F}$ with $A \notin U$, you can express the largest attribute set determined by X as follows. Note that $\{A\}$ appearing as a singleton member of the dependency basis is equivalent to $X \longrightarrow\!\!\!\!\!\rightarrow A$.

$$(X; \mathcal{F} \cup \mathcal{M}) = X \cup \{A \mid X \longrightarrow\!\!\!\!\!\rightarrow A \text{ and } \exists U \longrightarrow AW \in \mathcal{F} \text{ with } A \notin U\}. \quad (19.2)$$

A new criterion for a lossless join in the presence of MVDs

The previous chapter proved that a two-way decomposition is lossless if and only if the common attributes are a superkey of at least one component. The situation changes slightly in the presence of MVDs. The lossless-join definition remains unchanged: a decomposition (R_1, R_2) of R is lossless if $r = \pi_{R_1}(r) * \pi_{R_2}(r)$ for every valid database state $r(R)$. In Chapter 18, however, $r(R)$ was valid if it satisfied all the constraints of $\mathcal{F}$. In the presence of MVDs, a valid database state must satisfy the more stringent constraints of $\mathcal{F} \cup \mathcal{M}$. In particular, assuming that $\mathcal{F}$ remains the same, some valid database states in the context of Chapter 18 are now invalid under the enlarged constraint set. For example, suppose $\mathcal{F}$ is empty and $\mathcal{M}$ contains the single MVD, $A \longrightarrow\!\!\!\!\!\rightarrow B$. Consider the following decomposition, where A isn't a superkey of either component.

R		
A	B	C
0	1	2
0	3	4

R_1	
A	B
0	1
0	3

R_2	
A	C
0	2
0	4

Join of components		
A	B	C
0	1	2
0	1	4
0	3	2
0	3	4

Under the constraints of $\mathcal{F}$, the database state is valid. However, the decomposition isn't lossless because A isn't a superkey of either component. Under the constraints $\mathcal{F} \cup \mathcal{M}$, the database state isn't valid because it lacks the tuples needed to complete the interchange of C values among the existing tuples. The decomposition is indeed a lossless-join decomposition, and if you present it with a valid database state, the computation will reflect that fact. The two missing tuples necessary to accommodate the interchange of the $R - AB = C$ values are precisely the two extraneous tuples introduced by the join operation.

The point of the example is as follows. Suppose you have a decomposition, and you use the governing FDs, $\mathcal{F}$, to determine that the common attributes are a superkey of neither component. You can then show that the decomposition is lossy by exhibiting a valid relational body, the appropriate projections, and the join showing extraneous tuples. However, if some further constraint forces all such counterexamples to involve invalid database states, you can't demonstrate the lossy nature of the decomposition. The MVD, $A \longrightarrow\!\!\!\!\!\rightarrow B$, performs precisely that function in the example. Every counterexample that you could bring forward to show that the join is lossy can be ruled out as an invalid database state.

In the presence of MVDs, the criteria for a lossless join are: if (R_1, R_2) is a decomposition of the universal relation, R, then it is lossless if and only if $(R_1 \cap R_2) \longrightarrow\!\!\!\!\!\rightarrow R_1$ and $(R_1 \cap R_2) \longrightarrow\!\!\!\!\!\rightarrow R_2$ are both in $(\mathcal{F} \cup \mathcal{M})^+$. The proof runs as follows. Suppose $(R_1 \cap R_2) \longrightarrow\!\!\!\!\!\rightarrow R_1$ and $r(R)$ is a valid database state. You can project r onto R_1 and R_2 and obtain r_1 and r_2 respectively. Suppose μ appears in $r_1 * r_2$. μ then arises from a combination in the underlying Cartesian product. So there must be a $\mu_1 \in r$ agreeing with μ on the attributes R_1 and a $\mu_2 \in r$ agreeing with μ on the attributes R_2. The general format for $\mu = x : a : d$, where the $R_1 \cap R_2$ values are x, the $R_1 - (R_1 \cap R_2)$ values are a, and the $R_2 - (R_1 \cap R_2)$ values are d. You must then have μ_1 and μ_2 as given in the first two tuples of the table below. The MVD $(R_1 \cap R_2) \longrightarrow\!\!\!\!\!\rightarrow R_1$ then forces the second pair of tuples to appear. $\mu = x : a : d$ appears among these tuples, so $\mu \in r$. Therefore, $r = r_1 * r_2$, and the join is lossless.

	R		
	$R_1 \cap R_2$	$R_1 - (R_1 \cap R_2)$	$R_2 - (R_1 \cap R_2)$
	$\vdots$	$\vdots$	$\vdots$
μ_1	x	a	b
μ_2	x	c	d
	$\vdots$	$\vdots$	$\vdots$
μ	x	a	d
	x	c	b
	$\vdots$	$\vdots$	$\vdots$

For the reverse direction, suppose two tuples agree on $R_1 \cap R_2$. The general format of the tuples appears as μ_1 and μ_2 in the table above. The patterns $(x : a)$ and $(x : c)$ then appear in r_1, and the patterns $(x : b)$ and $(x : d)$ appear in r_2. Besides the two original tuples, $r_1 * r_2$ exhibits the tuples $(x : a : d)$ and $(x : c : b)$. However, these new tuples represent the original tuples with the $R - R_1(R_1 \cap R_2) = R_2 - (R_1 \cap R_2)$ attributes interchanged. Therefore, $(R_1 \cap R_2) \longrightarrow\!\!\!\!\!\rightarrow R_1$ holds. The new tuples also represent the original tuples with the $R - R_2(R_1 \cap R_2) = R_1 - (R_1 \cap R_2)$ attributes interchanged. Therefore, $(R_1 \cap R_2) \longrightarrow\!\!\!\!\!\rightarrow R_2$ also holds, which completes the proof. The fact that both MVDs hold isn't significant because if one holds, the other must follow by the complementation rule.

 A decomposition of the universal relation R into (R_1, R_2) is lossless if and only if $(R_1 \cap R_2) \longrightarrow\!\!\!\!\!\rightarrow R_1$ and $(R_1 \cap R_2) \longrightarrow\!\!\!\!\!\rightarrow R_2$ hold under the constraints $\mathcal{F} \cup \mathcal{M}$.

The situation is somewhat different when you deal with a subset of R. Suppose $R' \subset R$, and let (R_1, R_2) be a decomposition of R'. The earlier result remains true in one direction. If $(R_1 \cap R_2) \longrightarrow\!\!\!\!\!\rightarrow R_1$ holds, the decomposition is lossless. All the relational bodies are projections of $r(R)$, and the interchange condition of an MVD holds in $r(R')$ if it holds in $r(R)$. So when $(R_1 \cap R_2) \longrightarrow\!\!\!\!\!\rightarrow R_1$ constrains $r(R)$, it also constrains $r(R')$. Any two tuples in R' agreeing on $R_1 \cap R_2$ must have neighboring tuples with the $R' - R_1(R_1 \cap R_2) = R_2 - (R_1 \cap R_2)$ values interchanged. This condition forces any tuples generated by the join to appear in the original relation. The decomposition, therefore, is lossless.

However, the other direction isn't true in the general case. If the decomposition $R' = R_1 \cup R_2$ is lossless, a constraint limits $r(R')$, but it isn't necessarily expressible as an MVD constraint on the universal relation. Any two tuples in $r(R')$ agreeing on $R_1 \cap R_2$ must have neighboring tuples in $r(R')$ with interchanged $R_2 - (R_1 \cap R_2)$ values. But this observation doesn't require $(R_1 \cap R_2) \longrightarrow\!\!\!\!\!\rightarrow R_1$ or $(R_1 \cap R_2) \longrightarrow\!\!\!\!\!\rightarrow R_2$ to hold in the universal relation $r(R)$. Indeed, the constraint on $r(R)$ insists only that two tuples that agree on $(R_1 \cap R_2)$ have neighboring tuples in $r(R)$ with interchanged values under $R_2 - (R_1 \cap R_2)$. The constraint doesn't mention attributes that aren't in R'.

This restriction is a **partial interchange constraint** involving attributes R'. If the first pair in the table below appears in $r(R)$, the partial interchange constraint forces the second pair to appear. This constraint isn't an MVD because a true MVD would require the pair specified below the table. The partial interchange constraint doesn't require the values under attributes outside R' to participate in the interchange.

| | R | | | |
| | R' | | | |
	$R_1 \cap R_2$	$R_1 - (R_1 \cap R_2)$	$R_2 - (R_1 \cap R_2)$	$R - R'$
	$\vdots$	$\vdots$	$\vdots$	$\vdots$
	x	a	b	z_1
	x	c	d	z_2
	$\vdots$	$\vdots$	$\vdots$	$\vdots$
partial	x	a	d	z_3
interchange	x	c	b	z_4
	$\vdots$	$\vdots$	$\vdots$	$\vdots$
MVD	x	a	d	z_2
interchange	x	c	b	z_1

Because you can't express this constraint on the universal relation as an FD or MVD, it doesn't appear in $\mathcal{F} \cup \mathcal{M}$. For a relation that is a subset of the universal relation, the result, therefore, should read as follows. A decomposition (R_1, R_2) of $R' \subset R$ is lossless if and only if $r(R)$ is constrained by the appropriate partial interchange constraint on R'. This nuance is frequently ignored in favor of the simpler statement: a lossless-join decomposition occurs when $(R_1 \cap R_2) \longrightarrow\!\!\!\!\!\rightarrow R_1$. You can usually use the latter condition because when you decompose R', you have already losslessly decomposed the universal relation into components. At that point, the important consideration is that $(R_1 \cap R_2) \longrightarrow\!\!\!\!\!\rightarrow R_1$ constrains R' because that constraint allows a lossless-join decomposition of R'. Just how that constraint descended on R' isn't important. It may have come from an MVD constraining $r(R)$ or from the more complicated partial interchange constraint on $r(R)$. In effect, subsequent analysis of potential decompositions of R' can proceed as though R' were the universal relation.

If *all* the application constraints are expressed as FDs and MVDs on the universal relation, no partial interchange constraints can arise. In this case, a lossless-join decomposition of R' into (R_1, R_2) means that the partial interchange constraint on $r(R)$, must actually be a stronger MVD restriction. But this MVD need not be either $(R_1 \cap R_2) \longrightarrow R_1$ or $(R_1 \cap R_2) \longrightarrow R_2$ because the decomposition might split elements of the dependency basis for $R_1 \cap R_2$. For example, suppose $V_1, V_2, \ldots, V_n$ constitute the dependency basis for $R_1 \cap R_1$, after removing the singleton attributes of $R_1 \cap R_2$. Suppose also that V_i and V_k each contain several attributes and that R' contains part of V_i and part of V_k as shown below. In particular, R_1 contains part of V_i and all of V_{i+1} through V_j. R_2 contains V_{j+1} through V_{k-1} and part of V_k. Because (R_1, R_2) is a lossless-join decomposition of R' and because the upper tuples are present, the lower two tuples of the table below must also appear. However, you must accomplish the required swap within R' by interchanging *complete* packets from the dependency basis.

R															
$(R-R')_1$				R'										$(R-R')_2$	
				$R_1 - (R_1 \cap R_2)$				$R_1 \cap R_2$	$R_2 - (R_1 \cap R_2)$						
V_1	V_2	$\cdots$	V_i		V_{i+1}	$\cdots$	V_j		V_{j+1}	$\cdots$	V_{k-1}	V_k		$\cdots$	V_n
$\vdots$	$\vdots$	$\vdots$	$\vdots$	$\vdots$	$\vdots$	$\vdots$	$\vdots$	$\vdots$	$\vdots$	$\vdots$	$\vdots$	$\vdots$	$\vdots$	$\vdots$	$\vdots$
v_1	v_2	$\cdots$	v_i	v'_i	v_{i+1}	$\cdots$	v_j	x	v_{j+1}	$\cdots$	v_{k-1}	v_k	v'_k	$\cdots$	v_n
w_1	w_2	$\cdots$	w_i	w'_i	w_{i+1}	$\cdots$	w_j	x	w_{j+1}	$\cdots$	w_{k-1}	w_k	w'_k	$\cdots$	w_n
$\vdots$	$\vdots$	$\vdots$	$\vdots$	$\vdots$	$\vdots$	$\vdots$	$\vdots$	$\vdots$	$\vdots$	$\vdots$	$\vdots$	$\vdots$	$\vdots$	$\vdots$	$\vdots$
w_1	w_2	$\cdots$	v_i	v'_i	v_{i+1}	$\cdots$	v_j	x	w_{j+1}	$\cdots$	w_{k-1}	w_k	w'_k	$\cdots$	w_n
v_1	v_2	$\cdots$	w_i	w'_i	w_{i+1}	$\cdots$	w_j	x	v_{j+1}	$\cdots$	v_{k-1}	v_k	v'_k	$\cdots$	v_n
$\vdots$	$\vdots$	$\vdots$	$\vdots$	$\vdots$	$\vdots$	$\vdots$	$\vdots$	$\vdots$	$\vdots$	$\vdots$	$\vdots$	$\vdots$	$\vdots$	$\vdots$	$\vdots$

So in this example, neither $(R_1 \cap R_2) \longrightarrow R_1$ nor $(R_1 \cap R_2) \longrightarrow R_2$ holds because neither R_1 nor R_2 is a union of members of the dependency basis for $R_1 \cap R_2$. As shown above, R_1 involves a fractional part of V_i, and R_2 partially includes V_k. However, if you write $Y = V_i \cup V_{i+1} \cup \ldots \cup V_j$, you must have $(R_1 \cap R_2) \longrightarrow Y$, and therefore the upper tuple pair forces the appearance of the lower pair. But this lower pair reverses the $R' - R_1(R_1 \cap R_2)$ values of the upper pair, which proves that $(R_1 \cap R_2) \longrightarrow R_1$ constrains $r(R')$. Consequently, even if you know that all constraints on $r(R)$ must be FDs and MVDs, you can only assert that some MVD of the form $(R_1 \cap R_2) \longrightarrow Y$ must constrain $r(R)$, with $Y \cap R' = R_1$.

 Let (R_1, R_2) be a decomposition of $R' \subseteq R$. If $(R_1 \cap R_2) \longrightarrow R_1$ or $(R_1 \cap R_2) \longrightarrow R_2$ is in $(\mathcal{F} \cup \mathcal{M})^+$, then the decomposition is lossless. Conversely, if the decomposition is lossless, then $(R_1 \cap R_2) \longrightarrow Y \in (\mathcal{F} \cup \mathcal{M})^+$ for some Y such that $Y \cap R' = R_1$ or $Y \cap R' = R_2$.

Fourth normal form

Redundancy induced by an MVD

The earlier example with workstations, projects, and developers involved the MVD constraint dno $\longrightarrow$ wsno. Consider again the intersection table, Effort, which contained keys from the primary entities. The MVD lets you predict the tuples shown by the dashes in the table below. You know that the missing values must copy the displayed tuples with the pno values interchanged. This redundancy occurs even though the table satisfies BCNF.

Effort		
dno	wsno	pno
⋮	⋮	⋮
1	2	3
1	4	5
—	—	—
—	—	—
⋮	⋮	⋮

In some cases, an MVD doesn't provide a context for prediction. The MVD, $X \longrightarrow\!\!\!\!\!\longrightarrow Y$, where $Y \subset X$ is an example. When you interchange the $R' - XY$ attributes in two tuples agreeing on X, you regenerate the same two tuples. This situation includes the case where $Y = \varphi$. Another example is the MVD, $X \longrightarrow\!\!\!\!\!\longrightarrow Y$, when $R' - XY = \varphi$. In this case, no attributes exist in the interchange columns. Therefore, the formal operation again generates the same two tuples, which preclude a prediction. These types of MVDs are trivial, and they present no redundancy problems.

Another circumstance also frustrates attribute prediction. Consider the MVD, $X \longrightarrow\!\!\!\!\!\longrightarrow Y$, applicable to R' where X is a superkey. In this case, you can't find two distinct tuples agreeing on X, so any interchange of the $R' - XY$ attributes takes place inside the same tuple. The operation, of course, simply regenerates that tuple, and it predicts no new attribute values.

Fourth normal form (4NF) evolves from these observations. A relation, R', is in **fourth normal form** with respect to a set of constraints $\mathcal{F} \cup \mathcal{M}$ if X is a superkey of R' for every nontrivial MVD, $X \longrightarrow\!\!\!\!\!\longrightarrow Y \in (\mathcal{F} \cup \mathcal{M})^+$, that applies to R'. In other words, you must have $X \longrightarrow\!\!\!\!\!\longrightarrow R'$ if X multidetermines any attribute set of R' in a nontrivial way. When $X \longrightarrow\!\!\!\!\!\longrightarrow Y$ applies to R', you have $X \subset R'$, and $X \longrightarrow\!\!\!\!\!\longrightarrow (Y \cap R')$ then constrains R'. The MVD is trivial for R' if $(Y \cap R') \subset X$ or if $X(Y \cap R') = R'$. The 4NF definition isn't concerned with such trivial MVDs. However, it does require all applicable, nontrivial MVDs to have a superkey on the left side. By extension, a group of relations satisfies 4NF if each relation in the group is in 4NF.

Removing a 4NF violator through decomposition

Consider the following example with the universal relation $R = ABCDEFGHIJK$. The constraints $\mathcal{F} \cup \mathcal{M}$ give rise to the enlarged version $\mathcal{F} \cup \mathcal{M}'$ as shown below. The second table rewrites the FDs in $\mathcal{F}$ with singleton right sides and refers to the new, equivalent set as $\mathcal{F}'$. Each $X \longrightarrow A$ in $\mathcal{F}'$ induces an entry $X \longrightarrow\!\!\!\!\!\longrightarrow A$ in $\mathcal{M}'$. Recall that the algorithm depBasis uses the larger set to calculate a dependency basis.

$\mathcal{M}$	$\mathcal{F}$	
$A \longrightarrow\!\!\!\!\!\longrightarrow J$	$AB \longrightarrow C$	$G \longrightarrow HIJ$
	$C \longrightarrow DE$	$IJ \longrightarrow K$
	$E \longrightarrow AF$	

$\mathcal{M}'$		$\mathcal{F}'$	
$AB \longrightarrow\!\!\!\!\!\longrightarrow C$	$C \longrightarrow\!\!\!\!\!\longrightarrow D$	$AB \longrightarrow C$	$C \longrightarrow D$
$C \longrightarrow\!\!\!\!\!\longrightarrow E$	$E \longrightarrow\!\!\!\!\!\longrightarrow F$	$C \longrightarrow E$	$E \longrightarrow F$
$E \longrightarrow\!\!\!\!\!\longrightarrow A$	$G \longrightarrow\!\!\!\!\!\longrightarrow H$	$E \longrightarrow A$	$G \longrightarrow H$
$G \longrightarrow\!\!\!\!\!\longrightarrow I$	$G \longrightarrow\!\!\!\!\!\longrightarrow J$	$G \longrightarrow I$	$G \longrightarrow J$
$IJ \longrightarrow\!\!\!\!\!\longrightarrow K$	$A \longrightarrow\!\!\!\!\!\longrightarrow J$	$IJ \longrightarrow K$	

You can compute the dependency basis for ABG by tracing the operation of algorithm depBasis$(ABG, R, \mathcal{F} \cup \mathcal{M})$. You first initialize an approximation of the basis, $\mathcal{C}$, as a collection with one member: $R - ABG = CDEFHIJK$. You then repeatedly look for $U \longrightarrow\!\!\!\!\!\rightarrow W$ MVDs in $\mathcal{M}'$, with W intersecting a member V of $\mathcal{C}$ but U disjoint from V. Upon finding a suitable MVD, you replace V with $V - W$ and $V \cap W$. In this case, $AB \longrightarrow\!\!\!\!\!\rightarrow C$ is applicable, and it splits $CDEFHIJK$ into C and $DEFHIJK$. $C \longrightarrow\!\!\!\!\!\rightarrow D$ then becomes applicable to split $DEFHIJK$ into D and $EFHIJK$. You continue this process as shown in the following table until you can induce no further splitting.

Applicable MVD	Basis approximation, $\mathcal{C}$							
								$CDEFHIJK$
$AB \longrightarrow\!\!\!\!\!\rightarrow C$							C	$DEFHIJK$
$C \longrightarrow\!\!\!\!\!\rightarrow D$						C	D	$EFHIJK$
$C \longrightarrow\!\!\!\!\!\rightarrow E$					C	D	E	$FHIJK$
$E \longrightarrow\!\!\!\!\!\rightarrow F$				C	D	E	F	$HIJK$
$G \longrightarrow\!\!\!\!\!\rightarrow H$			C	D	E	F	H	IJK
$G \longrightarrow\!\!\!\!\!\rightarrow I$		C	D	E	F	H	I	JK
$G \longrightarrow\!\!\!\!\!\rightarrow J$	C	D	E	F	H	I	J	K

Recall that ABG determines a singleton set from the dependency basis if there exists an FD in $\mathcal{F}'$ with the singleton attribute on the right side. Here, all the singleton sets qualify, so $ABG \longrightarrow\!\!\!\!\!\rightarrow CDEFHIJK$. In this case, algorithm maxRight of Chapter 18 delivers this same result: it grows $(ABG; \mathcal{F}') = ABGCDEFHIJK$ using only the FDs. In any case, you now know that ABG is a superkey of R, and you must compute the dependency basis for the subsets of ABG to see if a proper subset could also be a superkey. Algorithm depBasis computes as shown on the left below. Because the singleton attributes from the left side are always members of the dependency basis, the second column omits them. The third column lists those determined attributes that arise from singletons with an appropriate FD in $\mathcal{F}'$.

X	$[X; \mathcal{F}' \cup \mathcal{M}'] - X$	Determined attributes
A	$J, BCDEFGHIK$	J
B	$ACDEFGHIJK$	
G	$H, I, J, K, ABCDEF$	$HIJK$
AB	$C, D, E, F, J, GHIK$	$CDEFJ$
AG	$H, I, J, K, BCDEF$	$HIJK$
BG	$H, I, J, K, ACDEF$	$HIJK$

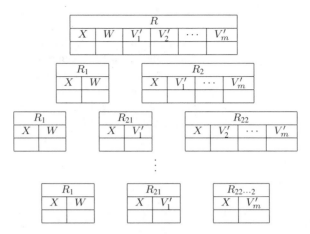

In these computations, you can see some interaction between the FDs and MVDs. In particular, algorithm maxRight can grow $(X; \mathcal{F}')$ only to A. However, $A \longrightarrow J$ holds, so J must also be in $(X; \mathcal{F}')$. Other differences also appear. In no case, however, does a proper subset of ABG determine all of R. Therefore, ABG is a key for R.

Because AB isn't a superkey of R, $AB \longrightarrow\!\!\!\!\!\rightarrow C$ is a 4NF violator. You can correct this problem by decomposing R into components corresponding to the dependency basis for AB. In general terms, the decomposition proceeds as shown to the right above. Suppose $X \longrightarrow\!\!\!\!\!\rightarrow Y$ is the 4NF violator, and the dependency basis for X contains the singletons from X plus the sets $V_1, V_2, \ldots, V_n$. Let W be the union of those singletons A among the V_i such that $X \longrightarrow A$. Let $V_1', V_2', \ldots, V_m'$ be the remaining V_i. You can decompose R with a succession of two-way splits, each lossless because X multidetermines one of the components.

For convenience in the following discussion, rename the components as follows.

R_0		R_1		R_2			R_m	
X	W	X	V_1'	X	V_2'	$\ldots\ldots$	X	V_m'

In the decomposition, $X \longrightarrow\!\!\!\!\!\rightarrow Y$ is no longer a 4NF violator for any components. Indeed, none of the final components can violate an MVD with X on the left. You can immediately exonerate the first component because X is a superkey of R_0. As for the others, suppose $X \longrightarrow\!\!\!\!\!\rightarrow Z \in (\mathcal{F} \cup \mathcal{M})^+$. Z is then the union of selected members of the dependency basis, $V_1, V_2, \ldots, V_n$. Therefore, $R_i \cap Z$, for $i > 0$, must be either empty or equal to V_i'. In the first case, $Z \cap R_i = \varphi \subset X$; in the second case, $X(Z \cap R_i) = R_i$. In either case, the MVD is trivial for R_i. So this decomposition removes any violations induced by MVDs with X on the left.

Moreover, if you further decompose a component, no violations can apply to the subcomponents. Assume a subcomponent of R_i, say R_i', contains X and is therefore vulnerable to an MVD, $X \longrightarrow\!\!\!\!\!\rightarrow Z \in (\mathcal{F} \cup \mathcal{M})^+$. If $i = 0$, then X remains a superkey of the subcomponent, so a violation isn't possible through this MVD. If $i > 0$, let U be the subset of V_i' included in the component. If $Z \cap U = \varphi$, then $(Z \cap R_i') \subset X$, and the MVD is trivial for R_i'. If $Z \cap U \neq \varphi$, then Z must include all of V_i' because Z must be a union of members of the dependency basis. Thus, $Z \cap R_i'$ includes all of U, and $X(Z \cap R_i') = R_i'$, which proves that the MVD is again trivial for R_i'. This decomposition, therefore, has completely cleared all MVDs with X on the left as a source of 4NF violations. No violations can arise from the immediate components of the decomposition or from the final components of any subsequent decomposition.

Applying this technique to the example, for the 4NF violator $AB \longrightarrow C$, you obtain the lossless-join decomposition of R as given in the first tier below. Noting the dependency basis for A, you see that A isn't a superkey of the first table, but $A \longrightarrow J$. From the dependency basis for G, you see that G isn't a superkey of the second table, but $G \longrightarrow HIK$. So you must further decompose the two components to arrive at the second tier below.

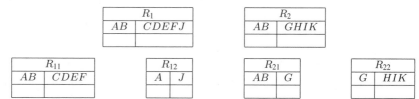

R_1	
AB	$CDEFJ$

R_2	
AB	$GHIK$

R_{11}	
AB	$CDEF$

R_{12}	
A	J

R_{21}	
AB	G

R_{22}	
G	HIK

In decomposing R_1 into R_{11} and R_{12}, you remove any possibility that A can be the left side of a 4NF violator. In R_{12}, you have that A is a superkey. In R_{11}, all attributes except A itself appear in a single member of the dependency basis for A. Therefore, following the argument given above for the general case, no subcomponent can ever violate an MVD with A on the left side. Similar comments apply to the role of G in the decomposition of R_2 into R_{12} and R_{22}.

Generally, only one route is available for an MVD with U on the left to induce a 4NF violation in a relation R'. First, the MVD must apply to R', so $U \subset R'$. Second, the attributes of R' outside U must contain portions of at least two distinct members of the dependency basis for U. If all the attributes outside U come from a single member of the dependency basis, the MVD is trivial for R'.

Continuing with the example, you can calculate the dependency basis for C to be A, D, E, F, J, and $BHIK$. Although C determines all the singletons, they don't comprise all of the $ABCDEF$ table. Instead, C determines only $CDEF$ in that table and fails to be a superkey. The table then splits losslessly into $CDEF$ and ABC.

When you decompose a component, you need to consider only the MVDs that apply to the component. Equivalently, only dependency basis elements that reside within the component can affect further decomposition. At this point, the dependency basis for C shows that although $C \longrightarrow A$, C isn't a superkey of ABC. The ABC component thus splits losslessly into AC and BC. Finally, you calculate the dependency basis for E as A, F, J, and $BCDGHIK$, where E determines all the singletons. So E isn't a superkey of the intermediate table $CDEF$ although $E \longrightarrow F$. The $CDEF$ table then splits into EF and CDE. With some harmless renaming, the final decomposition is then:

R_1	R_2	R_3	R_4	R_5	R_6	R_7
AJ	EF	CDE	AC	BC	ABG	$GHIK$

You can reason that no further 4NF violations exist. From a preceding section, you know that you need at least three disjoint attribute segments to constitute a nontrivial MVD. So all the two-attribute components are immediately cleared of further violation. Two components contain three attributes: CDE and ABG. In these cases, the only three disjoint segments that could comprise a nontrivial MVD must have one attribute per segment. To show that no violations occur, you need to eliminate only the MVDs with a single attribute on the left. Collecting the dependency bases for C and E from the decomposition above and adding the dependency basis for D, you obtain:

X	$[X; \mathcal{F}' \cup \mathcal{M}'] - X$	Determined attributes
C	$A, D, E, F, J, BHIK$	$ADEFJ$
E	$A, F, J, BCDGHIK$	AFJ
D	$ABCEFGHIJK$	

Looking at CDE, you note that C is a superkey, that the dependency basis for E places CD in a single member, and that the dependency basis for D places CE in a single member. No nontrivial MVDs, therefore, exist among the elements of CDE unless the left side is a superkey. A similar analysis pertains to the ABG table. Finally, you must exonerate the $GHIK$ table. You know that G is a superkey, as are any supersets of G. So any violations must involve MVDs with some subset of HIK on the left. You can use the depBasis algorithm to verify that the dependency basis of any such subset, X, contains the single member $R - X$ plus the individual attributes of X. This result always places attributes other than X in a single member of the dependency basis and precludes any nontrivial MVDs. Consequently, no further violations occur in the $GHIK$ table, and the final decomposition satisfies 4NF.

   Note that the depBasis algorithm always starts its calculation of the dependency basis for X with the single member $R - X$ in its approximation $\mathcal{C}$. At that point, the only attributes that don't intersect a member of $\mathcal{C}$ are subsets of X. So the only candidates for $U \longrightarrow V$ that allow the algorithm to progress must have X, or some subset of X, on the left side. In the argument above, you needed the dependency bases for various subsets of HIK. You can quickly calculate them by noting that the algorithm blocks immediately. For example, suppose you are computing the dependency basis for H. Because H doesn't appear on the left of any MVD in $\mathcal{M}'$, $\mathcal{C}$ can't grow from its initialized state. Therefore, it certainly doesn't contain any combination of GIK. Similar observations apply to the other possibilities for 4NF violators.

The set of 4NF relations is strictly contained in the set of BCNF relations

Having argued that the final decomposition of the example satisfies 4NF, you may wonder about possible 3NF or BCNF violations. Such violations aren't possible because any relation that satisfies 4NF will automatically satisfy BCNF. As proof, suppose R' satisfies 4NF and $X \longrightarrow A$ is a BCNF violator. Then $A \notin X$, and X isn't a superkey of R'. At least one other attribute, B, must then appear in R' with $B \in R' - AX$. Because $X \longrightarrow A$, you must have $X \longrightarrow\!\!\!\!\rightarrow A$. Because $AX \neq R'$, this MVD isn't trivial. Therefore, $X \longrightarrow\!\!\!\!\rightarrow A$ is a 4NF violator, which establishes a contradiction. You can conclude that R' satisfies BCNF. Chapter 18 showed that BCNF is a stronger condition than 3NF, which in turn is stronger than 2NF. So a 4NF decomposition automatically eliminates any redundancy associated with the lower normal forms.

Any relation satisfying 4NF automatically satisfies BCNF, 3NF, and 2NF.

If you use only the FD constraints to carry out a BCNF decomposition on the last example according to the methods of Chapter 18, you obtain the following decomposition.

R_1	R_2	R_3	R_4	R_5	R_6
AEF	CDE	BC	ABG	IJK	$GHIJ$

This BCNF decomposition also satisfies 4NF even though you didn't consider the MVD, $A \longrightarrow\!\!\!\!\!\rightarrow J$, in the process. The BCNF decomposition has fewer tables, but it is still similar to the 4NF decomposition. The only tables that haven't been cleared of 4NF violations by the preceding analysis are AEF, IJK, and $GHIJ$. The same techniques quickly demonstrate that no 4NF violations lurk in these tables.

A BCNF decomposition doesn't always satisfy 4NF. Suppose you change the example slightly so that the MVDs don't imply an FD through coalescence. Specifically, replace the MVD with $L \longrightarrow\!\!\!\!\!\rightarrow AB$ to obtain the following constraints.

$\mathcal{M}$	$\mathcal{F}$	
$L \longrightarrow\!\!\!\!\!\rightarrow AB$	$AB \longrightarrow C$	$G \longrightarrow HIJ$
	$C \longrightarrow DE$	$IJ \longrightarrow K$
	$E \longrightarrow AF$	

$\mathcal{M}'$		$\mathcal{F}'$	
$AB \longrightarrow\!\!\!\!\!\rightarrow C$	$C \longrightarrow D$	$AB \longrightarrow C$	$C \longrightarrow D$
$C \longrightarrow\!\!\!\!\!\rightarrow E$	$E \longrightarrow F$	$C \longrightarrow E$	$E \longrightarrow F$
$E \longrightarrow\!\!\!\!\!\rightarrow A$	$G \longrightarrow H$	$E \longrightarrow A$	$G \longrightarrow H$
$G \longrightarrow\!\!\!\!\!\rightarrow I$	$G \longrightarrow J$	$G \longrightarrow I$	$G \longrightarrow J$
$IJ \longrightarrow\!\!\!\!\!\rightarrow K$	$L \longrightarrow\!\!\!\!\!\rightarrow AB$	$IJ \longrightarrow K$	

Using the BCNF decomposition method of Chapter 18, you obtain the decomposition below. However, this decomposition doesn't satisfy 4NF. To verify this, you can compute the dependency basis for L to be L, A, B, C, D, E, F and $GHIJK$. L determines all the singletons except B. L, therefore, isn't a superkey of the $ABGL$ table, and $L \longrightarrow\!\!\!\!\!\rightarrow A$ is nontrivial in that table. So you need a further decomposition of the $ABGL$ table into LA, LB, and LG to satisfy 4NF.

R_1	R_2	R_3	R_4	R_5	R_6
AEF	CDE	BC	$GHIJ$	IJK	$ABGL$

MVDs in the context of the aquarium database

In practice, multivalued dependency constraints are less frequent than functional dependencies. The aquarium application, for example, exhibits no MVD constraints. In the absence of MVD constraints, the dependency basis approach produces a 4NF decomposition that is identical with the BCNF decomposition you get from the methods of Chapter 18.

You can use the dependency basis technique with the aquarium constraints of Figure 18.3. First, you compute the dependency basis for sno to be (sno, sname, sfood, —). The dash indicates that the rest of the attributes appear as one component. Because sno determines both singletons in the dependency basis, you break off (sno, sname, sfood) as the species table. This first level decomposition appears as the first two lines in the breakout below. The dependency basis for sname contains only (sname, —), so it introduces no further nontrivial MVDs into the species table. The same holds for sfood.

The dependency basis for tno is (tno, tname, tvolume, tcolor, —), and tno determines all the singletons. This provokes the decomposition given at the first indentation level below.

(sno, sname, sfood)
(sno, tno, tname, tvolume, tcolor, fno, fname, fcolor, fweight, eno, edate, enote)
  (tno, tname, tvolume, tcolor)
    (tno, tname, tvolume)
    (tvolume, tcolor)
  (sno, tno, fno, fname, fcolor, fweight, eno, edate, enote)
    (fno, fname, fcolor, fweight, sno, tno)
    (fno, eno, enote, edate).

The dependency basis for tvolume is (tvolume, tcolor, —), which forces a further decomposition as shown at the second indentation level. The two-attribute table can't harbor a 4NF violator, but you must still examine the other table. You find, however, that the dependency bases for tname and tvolume induce no further splits. Computing the dependency basis for fno gives (fno, fname, fcolor, fweight, sno, tno, —), and fno determines all the singletons. This leads to the final decomposition shown above. You now have a 4NF decomposition, where you can identify the tables Species, Fish, Tank, VolColor, and Event that you obtained with the BCNF decomposition of Chapter 18.

An MVD constraint with an empty left side

Consider again an example from Chapter 18, which mixed unrelated attribute segments in the same table. This situation is an extreme case of an MVD. The example developed the following BCNF decomposition of the universal relation $R = ABCDEFGHJKL$ and then noted that you could consider R as a collection of $(a_i, (ef)_j)$ pairs. In each pair, the a_i entry is a key to the more elaborate entity described by $ABCD$ in the other tables. Similarly, the $(ef)_j$ is a key to a longer tuple under $EFGHJKL$, also completed in other tables.

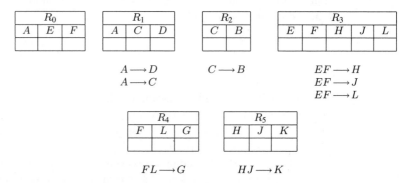

Without additional constraints, this decomposition satisfies 4NF. However, the application may attach no significance to the pairing of a particular a_i with a particular $(ef)_j$ in the AEF table. In this case, you can predict the entire AEF table as the Cartesian product of the A values from R_1 and the EF values from R_3. In the notation for multivalued dependencies, this constraint is simply $\varphi \longrightarrow\hspace{-0.6em}\rightarrow ABCD$. In other words, if two tuples agree on φ in a relation R', then R' must contain two more tuples with interchanged $R' - ABCD$

attributes. Of course, any two tuples agree on φ, so any table with contributions from both $ABCD$ and $EFGHJKL$ must exhibit the full Cartesian product of those contributions.

In the decomposition process, you can compute the dependency basis of φ with the normal depBasis loop. You initialize the approximation $\mathcal{C}$ to $R - \varphi = R$. The MVD, $\varphi \longrightarrow\!\!\!\!\!\rightarrow ABCD$, then applies to give $\mathcal{C} = \{ABCD, EFGHJKL\}$. Although $\varphi \longrightarrow\!\!\!\!\!\rightarrow ABCD$ applies to all components of the decomposition, it induces trivial MVDs in all tables except the first. In all tables except R_0, all attributes fall in a single component of the dependency basis for φ. However, $ABCD \cap R_0 = A$, and therefore $\varphi \longrightarrow\!\!\!\!\!\rightarrow A$ constrains R_0 nontrivially. The decomposition $(\varphi A, \varphi EF)$ ensues, which is, of course, simply A and EF. The A table is now a subset of R_1, and the EF table is a subset of R_3. You can, therefore, eliminate both subset tables as redundant. In the presence of the MVD, $\varphi \longrightarrow\!\!\!\!\!\rightarrow ABCD$, the decomposition is then as follows.

R_1		
A	C	D

R_2	
C	B

R_3				
E	F	H	J	L

R_4		
F	L	G

R_5		
H	J	K

The first two tables amount to the BCNF decomposition of the $ABCD$ attribute segment. The last three tables are a BCNF decomposition of the $EFGHJKL$ segment. The MVD, $\varphi \longrightarrow\!\!\!\!\!\rightarrow ABCD$, expresses the fact that the two segments must be independent. An equivalent condition is $\varphi \longrightarrow\!\!\!\!\!\rightarrow EFGHJKL$. Either MVD allows the formal process to undertake a final decomposition to remove the table where the keys from the two independent systems appear together.

General join dependencies

MVDs are a special case of a more general constraint involving lossless joins. To make a specified join lossless, an MVD forces certain tuples to appear in a relation. Generally, the join of two projections can introduce extraneous tuples that aren't present in the original relation. An MVD constraint forces these tuples into the relation, or else the database state is invalid. Under these circumstances, you can tautologically assert that the join is lossless because you have restricted the valid database states to those for which the statement is true.

Tuples arising from the join of multiple components

The extraneous tuples introduced by the join of three projections aren't necessarily the same as those introduced by the join of any two of the three projections. This is true even when the attribute schemas for the join results are identical. Consider the example on $R = ABC$ shown in Figure 19.5. You decompose R into (R_1, R_2, R_3) and project the body of the original R to populate the components. Refer to the body of R as r and to the component bodies as $r_1, r_2,$ and r_3. From these calculations, you see that you must insist on two additional tuples in the original relation if $(R_1 = AB, R_2 = BC)$ is to be a lossless-join decomposition. In the figure, these tuples are marked with an asterisk in the join $r_1 * r_2$. An equivalent constraint is $B \longrightarrow\!\!\!\!\!\rightarrow A$ or $B \longrightarrow\!\!\!\!\!\rightarrow C$.

A similar argument applies to the other possible decompositions. In each case, the join introduces two extraneous tuples. To render the join lossless, you must impose a constraint on the original relation such that the extra tuples appear there. For the decomposition

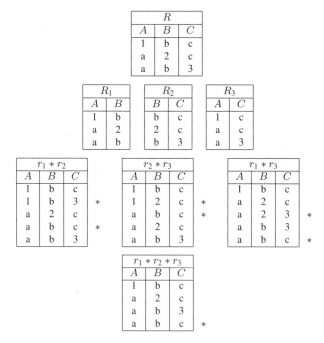

Figure 19.5　Different extraneous tuples from a three-way join than from pairwise joins

(BC, AC), this restriction is $C \longrightarrow\!\!\!\!\!\rightarrow A$ or $C \longrightarrow\!\!\!\!\!\rightarrow B$. For the decomposition (AB, AC), it's $A \longrightarrow\!\!\!\!\!\rightarrow B$ or $A \longrightarrow\!\!\!\!\!\rightarrow C$.

When you join all three components, however, only one extraneous tuple appears. Therefore, requiring the decomposition onto (R_1, R_2, R_3) to be lossless is different from any of the MVDs associated with the two-way decompositions. It constrains R less stringently than any of the MVDs: it requires only that the tuple (a, b, c) be present. Each of the MVDs requires this tuple plus one other.

The above example deals with the lossless decomposition of the universal relation into several components. A more general context uses a subset of the universal relation. Let R' be a subset of R, the universal relation, and let $(R_1, R_2, \ldots, R_n)$ be a decomposition of R'. A **join dependency** is a constraint on $r(R)$ that forces $\pi_{R'}(r) = \pi_{R_1}(r) * \pi_{R_2}(r) * \ldots * \pi_{R_n}(r)$ for every valid database $r(R)$. For join dependency, you can write JD or if you want to emphasize the components, $\mathrm{JD}(R_1, R_2, \ldots R_n)$. The set $S = R_1 \cup R_2 \cup \ldots \cup R_n$ is the **support** of the JD. If the support is the entire universal relation, you say that the JD has universal support. If the support isn't the entire universal relation, the JD is an **embedded join dependency** (EJD). This discussion will use the abbreviation JD for both cases.

 A join dependency $\mathrm{JD}(R_1, R_2, \ldots, R_n)$, where $(R_1, R_2, \ldots, R_n)$ is a decomposition of $R' \subset R$, constrains the body of R such that the projection onto R' is the lossless join of the projections onto the R_i. The support of the JD is the union of its component schemas.

Redundancy induced by a general join dependency

Consider again the preceding example, but with some additional attributes. Let $R = ABCX$. Suppose the JD(AB, BC, AC) holds. If you observe the three upper tuples shown to the left below, you can infer the existence of a fourth tuple of the form $(a, b, c, \ldots)$. However, the constraint doesn't involve the values under the attributes X because they are outside its support. A certain redundancy is apparent because you can predict the occurrence of the prefix $(a, b, c, \ldots)$ although you can't predict its x_4 suffix.

R			
R'			
A	B	C	X
1	b	c	x_1
a	2	c	x_2
a	b	3	x_3
a	b	c	x_4

R'		
A	B	C
1	b	c
a	2	c
a	b	3
—	—	—

R''	
Y	X

If you can losslessly isolate the support of the JD in a separate table, the redundancy becomes more apparent because you can then predict an entire tuple. Suppose Y is a subset of ABC that enables the decomposition to the right above. For example, you may have $Y \longrightarrow X$ or $Y \longrightarrow\!\!\!\!\rightarrow X$; either would permit the lossless decomposition into ABC and YX. You can now predict the blank tuple to be (a, b, c), and you don't need to worry about the location of the prefix in the larger table. You can eliminate the redundancy by decomposing R' into the components, AB, BC, and AC. From the definition of a JD, the decomposition must be lossless.

Inferring new JDs from existing ones

Consider two simple operations that create new JDs from a known JD. First, if JD$(R_1, R_2, \ldots, R_n)$ holds, then JD$((R_1 R_2), R_3, \ldots, R_n)$ also holds. Because the order of the components isn't significant, this means that you can replace any two components in a JD with their union and produce a new JD that must also hold. Moreover, by applying this construction repeatedly, you can merge any number of components with unions, and the new JD will still hold. Second, if $R_1 \subset R_2$, then JD$(R_1, R_2, \ldots, R_n)$ holds if and only if JD$(R_2, R_3, \ldots, R_n)$ holds. Because the order isn't significant, this construction lets you remove any component of a JD if it is a subset of another component. You can also introduce a new component, provided it's a subset of an existing component.

To prove the first assertion, you must show that the revised join is lossless. Equivalently, the join must not produce any extraneous tuples. Let $R' = R_1 \cup R_2 \cup \ldots \cup R_n$. Let r' be the content of R', $r_i = \pi_{R_i}(r')$, and $r'' = \pi_{R_1 R_2}(r')$. Because (R_1, R_2) is a decomposition of $R_1 R_2$, you have $r'' \subset r_1 * r_2$. The following inclusion then holds: $r'' * r_3 * \ldots * r_n \subset (r_1 * r_2) * r_3 * \ldots * r_n = r'$. It holds because the join on the left has potentially fewer tuples in its first component. The equality holds because of JD$(R_1, R_2, \ldots, R_n)$. Therefore, no tuples beyond the content r' appear in the join of the components of JD$((R_1 R_2), R_3, \ldots, R_n)$, which proves that the decomposition is lossless.

To prove the second assertion, note that $R_1 \subset R_2$ means that the content of R_1 is a further projection of the content of R_2. Continuing with the notation from the first proof, you have $r_1 = \pi_{R_1}(r_2)$ and, of course, $r_2 = \pi_{R_2}(r_2)$. The join appears below, where ν_1 and ν_2 are compatible tuples that join to produce μ. Obviously, $\mu = \nu_1$, which proves that $r_1 * r_2 \subset r_1$. Because the reverse inclusion is always true, you have shown that $r_1 = r_1 * r_2$. Therefore, you can remove the component R_1 from $JD(R_1, R_2, \ldots, R_n)$ or add it to $JD(R_2, R_3, \ldots, R_n)$ without changing the join of the components.

	R_2				R_2	
		R_1				R_1
ν_1	y	x	$\Longrightarrow$	μ	y	x
ν_2	$-$	x					

 If $JD(R_1, R_2, \ldots, R_n)$ holds, then so does the new JD obtained by replacing a subgroup of the components by their union. If $R_i \subset R_j$, then the JD with R_i included among the components holds if and only if the JD with R_i excluded from the components holds.

Conditions that admit JDs without redundancy

Under what conditions will a JD *not* introduce any redundancy in a relation? You can investigate the matter with the operations above, which manipulate the components in a JD. For the moment, assume that the support of the JD is the entire relation. First, consider the case where $JD(R_1, R_2, \ldots, R_n)$ holds and $R_i = S$ for some i, where S is the support of the JD. Then $R_j \subset R_i$, for $j \neq i$, and you can conclude that $JD(R_1, R_2, \ldots, R_n)$ holds precisely when $JD(R_i)$ holds. However, a JD with one component always holds, regardless of the relation's content, and therefore $JD(R_1, R_2, \ldots, R_n)$ doesn't constrain the content in any way. Stated differently, the constraint doesn't force any particular cell to assume a specific value based on a pattern of existing values. It introduces no redundancy. Naturally enough, a $JD(R_1, R_2, \ldots, R_n)$ is **trivial** if a component is equal to the support of the JD.

The components of a JD generally divide the support into a collection of overlapping segments. The projections of $r(R)$ onto each of these segments provide n sources of tuple segments that you can reassemble with a join operation. The join assembles a tuple by choosing a segment from each of the n sources such that the segments agree on their overlapping attributes. The leftmost table below illustrates the point. Note that the action takes place only under the support, S. It's difficult to visualize the most general situation in a two-dimensional format because n components usually have 2^n possible intersections and differences.

				R					
				S				X	
			R_1						
					R_2				
	R_3			R_4					

Segment	Tuples				New tuple
0000	—	—	—	—	—
0001	a_{0001}	b_{0001}	c_{0001}	d_{0001}	d_{0001}
0010	a_{0010}	b_{0010}	c_{0010}	d_{0010}	c_{0010}
0011	a_{0011}	b_{0011}	c_{0011}	c_{0011}	c_{0011}
0100	a_{0100}	b_{0100}	c_{0100}	d_{0100}	b_{0100}
0101	a_{0101}	b_{0101}	c_{0101}	b_{0101}	b_{0101}
0110	a_{0110}	b_{0110}	b_{0110}	d_{0110}	b_{0110}
0111	a_{0111}	b_{0111}	b_{0111}	b_{0111}	b_{0111}
1000	a_{1000}	b_{1000}	c_{1000}	d_{1000}	a_{1000}
1001	a_{1001}	b_{1001}	c_{1001}	a_{1001}	a_{1001}
1010	a_{1010}	b_{1010}	a_{1010}	d_{1010}	a_{1010}
1011	a_{1011}	b_{1011}	a_{1011}	a_{1011}	a_{1011}
1100	a_{1100}	a_{1100}	c_{1100}	d_{1100}	a_{1100}
1101	a_{1101}	a_{1101}	c_{1101}	a_{1101}	a_{1101}
1110	a_{1110}	a_{1110}	a_{1110}	d_{1110}	a_{1110}
1111	a_{1111}	a_{1111}	a_{1111}	a_{1111}	a_{1111}

You can obtain a more systematic visualization by organizing the tuples vertically as shown on the right above. The table accounts only for the attributes inside the support of the JD. Suppose you have four components. Order them as R_3, R_2, R_1, and R_0. Name each attribute segment formed by the intersections and differences of the components with a binary scheme that reflects whether the segment is inside or outside each component. For example, segment 0101 contains those attributes that are outside R_3, inside R_2, outside R_1, and inside R_0. The first bit of the segment name positions the segment inside R_3 if it's a one and outside R_3 if it's a zero. The next bit pertains to R_2, and so on. The 2^n disjoint segments appear along the left edge of the table. Segment 0000 is always empty because the scheme accounts only for attributes in the support of the JD, so no attributes lie outside all four components.

This table organizes the most general format for compatible tuples. In forming the join, a preliminary Cartesian product combines four segments—one from each component. A subsequent selection retains the combination only if the segments agree on all overlapping attributes. Suppose you choose the R_3 segment from the projection of the tuple in the leftmost column. You then take the R_2 segment from the projection of the next tuple to the right. In segments with a 0 in the R_2 place, the second bit from the left, the entry can be arbitrary because these attributes don't appear in the R_2 component. In segments with a 1 in the R_2 place, the entry can still be arbitrary unless a 1 also appears in the R_3 place. In the latter case, the entry must correspond to the value in the first tuple so that the segments agree on the overlapping attributes. The table shows that you must duplicate four of the first tuple's values in the second tuple, but you can still make many arbitrary entries.

Next, you choose the R_1 segment from the next tuple by applying similar rules. For segments with a 0 in the R_1 place, the entry can be arbitrary. If a 1 occurs in the R_1 place, the entry can still be arbitrary unless a 1 appears in the R_3 or R_2 place. In this case, the entry must agree with the value in the first or second tuple respectively. Note that if a 1 occurs in both places, the first and second tuple already agree on that segment, so no conflict arises in making the third tuple agree. Finally, you take the R_0 segment from the last tuple and maintain compatibility with the tuples already chosen. The final tuple introduced by the join then appears on the far right. If the relation satisfies the JD(R_3, R_2, R_1, R_0), this constructed tuple must appear in the table. The tuples used in the construction are the **antecedent tuples**. The new tuple is the **conclusion tuple**.

The join operation interchanges segments from compatible tuples in a relational body, r, to construct potentially new tuples. Because the JD constraint forces the body to contain these tuples beforehand, you can predict their values. One circumstance that frustrates these predictions occurs when the conclusion tuple duplicates one of the antecedent tuples. This situation occurs if one of the components of the JD, say R_3, is a superkey of the support, S. In the table above, the conclusion tuple must agree with the leftmost member of the antecedent set on those attributes contained in R_3. If R_3 is a support superkey, the conclusion tuple must then agree with that antecedent on all of S. The conclusion tuple, therefore, duplicates the antecedent, and no redundancy occurs. In fact, the apparently arbitrary entries in the other antecedent tuples must adjust their values so that the conclusion tuple duplicates the leftmost antecedent. Obviously, you can reach the same conclusion if any one of the components is a superkey of the support. If any of the components of a constraining JD is a superkey of the support, the join operation reconstructs one of the antecedent tuples.

However, this condition isn't strong enough to remove all redundancy associated with the JD. Assume that R_3 is a superkey of the support, and consider the pattern to the left below. The figure omits the 0000 segment; it's always empty. The conclusion tuple duplicates the leftmost antecedent because of the superkey constraint. Interpret a single question mark as a value that you can't see but which is the same across all instances of a single question mark. All instances of a double question mark stand for a single unknown value, and similarly for the triple and quadruple question marks. This pattern of antecedents combines to give the conclusion tuple because the projections onto R_3 through R_1 agree on overlapping attributes. Because you know the conclusion tuple must duplicate the leftmost antecedent, you can predict all the unknown values in the template. For example, the blank in the top row must be a_{0001} because the rightmost tuple provides the projection onto R_1, and R_1 contains the attributes of segment 0001. Similarly, all instances of the single question mark in row 7 must be a_{0111} because this common value occurs in attributes 0111 of the projections onto R_2, R_1, and R_0. In this manner, you can argue that the unknown values in any given row must be equal to the value of the conclusion tuple in that row.

Segment	Tuples				New tuple
0001	a_{0001}	b_{0001}	c_{0001}	—	a_{0001}
0010	a_{0010}	b_{0010}	—	d_{0010}	a_{0010}
0011	a_{0011}	b_{0011}	????	????	a_{0011}
0100	a_{0100}	—	c_{0100}	d_{0100}	a_{0100}
0101	a_{0101}	???	c_{0101}	???	a_{0101}
0110	a_{0110}	??	??	d_{0110}	a_{0110}
0111	a_{0111}	?	?	?	a_{0111}
1000	a_{1000}	b_{1000}	c_{1000}	d_{1000}	a_{1000}
1001	a_{1001}	b_{1001}	c_{1001}	a_{1001}	a_{1001}
1010	a_{1010}	b_{1010}	a_{1010}	d_{1010}	a_{1010}
1011	a_{1011}	b_{1011}	a_{1011}	a_{1011}	a_{1011}
1100	a_{1100}	a_{1100}	c_{1100}	d_{1100}	a_{1100}
1101	a_{1101}	a_{1101}	c_{1101}	a_{1101}	a_{1101}
1110	a_{1110}	a_{1110}	a_{1110}	d_{1110}	a_{1110}
1111	a_{1111}	a_{1111}	a_{1111}	a_{1111}	a_{1111}

Segment	Tuples				New tuple
0001	a_{0001}	b_{0001}	c_{0001}	a_{0001}	a_{0001}
0010	a_{0010}	b_{0010}	a_{0010}	d_{0010}	a_{0010}
0011	a_{0011}	b_{0011}	a_{0011}	a_{0011}	a_{0011}
0100	a_{0100}	a_{0100}	c_{0100}	d_{0100}	a_{0100}
0101	a_{0101}	a_{0101}	c_{0101}	a_{0101}	a_{0101}
0110	a_{0110}	a_{0110}	a_{0110}	d_{0110}	a_{0110}
0111	a_{0111}	a_{0111}	a_{0111}	a_{0111}	a_{0111}
1000	a_{1000}	b_{1000}	c_{1000}	d_{1000}	a_{1000}
1001	a_{1001}	b_{1001}	c_{1001}	a_{1001}	a_{1001}
1010	a_{1010}	b_{1010}	a_{1010}	d_{1010}	a_{1010}
1011	a_{1011}	b_{1011}	a_{1011}	a_{1011}	a_{1011}
1100	a_{1100}	a_{1100}	c_{1100}	d_{1100}	a_{1100}
1101	a_{1101}	a_{1101}	c_{1101}	a_{1101}	a_{1101}
1110	a_{1110}	a_{1110}	a_{1110}	d_{1110}	a_{1110}
1111	a_{1111}	a_{1111}	a_{1111}	a_{1111}	a_{1111}

So redundancy can still occur even if one of the components of the JD is a superkey of the support. However, this redundancy among the antecedent tuples doesn't appear if all the antecedents collapse into a single tuple. This situation occurs when *every* component, R_i, of the JD is a superkey of S, the support of the JD. The rightmost table above repeats the earlier prediction scenario with the predicted values in bold type. The second antecedent now agrees with the first on all of R_2, so it must agree with the first on all the support attributes. The remaining b entries, therefore, must revert to a values. The third antecedent now agrees with the first on all of R_1, so it must also coincide with the first on the entire support. A similar observation holds for the remaining antecedents, and you can conclude that all the antecedents must indeed derive from the same tuple. Therefore, if each component of the JD is a superkey of the support, any pattern of antecedents must in reality be a single tuple, and the conclusion tuple must also equal to that single antecedent.

 A JD($R_1, R_2, \ldots, R_n$) constraint introduces no redundancy into a relation if (1) one of the $R_i = S$, the support of the JD; or (2) every R_i is a superkey of S.

A small problem remains with this characterization. Suppose JD($R_1, R_2, \ldots, R_n$) holds, and each R_i is a superkey of the support. You can compose another component by randomly choosing attributes from the support, provided you don't assemble a superkey. Call this new component R_{n+1}. Then JD($R_1, R_2, \ldots, R_n, R_{n+1}$) surely holds. The join of the first n components losslessly recovers the relation's content, and a final join with R_{n+1} leaves that result unchanged. Because JD($R_1, R_2, \ldots, R_n$) introduces no redundancy, neither does $JD(R_1, R_2, \ldots, R_n, R_{n+1})$. Indeed, all $n + 1$ antecedents must collapse into a single tuple in the manner noted above.

You now have a JD where one component isn't a superkey, and it still doesn't force a redundancy. Therefore, the characterization derived so far isn't symmetric. You have shown that if one of the components equals the full support or if all components are superkeys, the JD introduces no redundancy. But the current example provides a case where neither condition holds, and still there is no redundancy. A superkey in each component is a sufficient, but not necessary, condition for a JD to exist without causing a data redundancy. So you must refine the conditions slightly to correspond exactly to nonredundancy in the relation.

JDs forced by FDs and MVDs

You find the necessary refinement of the nonredundancy condition in the interplay among FDs, MVDs, and JDs. First, note that $X \longrightarrow\!\!\!\!\rightarrow Y$ if and only if JD($XY, X(R - Y)$). The proof runs as follows. Recall that a decomposition $R = (R_1, R_2)$ is lossless if and only if $(R_1 \cap R_2) \longrightarrow\!\!\!\!\rightarrow R_1$ holds. Suppose JD($XY, X(R - Y)$) holds. The decomposition $R = (XY, X(R - Y))$ is then lossless, which implies that $(XY \cap X(R - Y)) = X \longrightarrow\!\!\!\!\rightarrow XY$. Because $X \longrightarrow\!\!\!\!\rightarrow X$ by reflexivity, you have $X \longrightarrow\!\!\!\!\rightarrow Y$ by decomposition. In the other direction, suppose $X \longrightarrow\!\!\!\!\rightarrow Y$. Then $X \longrightarrow\!\!\!\!\rightarrow XY$ by augmentation. Setting $R_1 = XY$ and $R_2 = X(R - Y)$, you see that $R_1 \cap R_2 = X$. So $X \longrightarrow\!\!\!\!\rightarrow XY$ translates to $(R_1 \cap R_2) \longrightarrow\!\!\!\!\rightarrow R_1$, which means that $R = (R_1, R_2) = (XY, X(R - Y))$ is a lossless-join decomposition. However, that is the definition of JD($XY, X(R - Y)$). So you have shown that an MVD is a special form of JD involving two complementary components of the universal relation.

Because an FD is a special form of MVD, you can conclude that an FD is also a special form of JD. In particular, if $X \longrightarrow Y$ holds, then $X \longrightarrow\!\!\!\!\!\rightarrow Y$ also holds. So $JD(XY, X(R - Y))$ must hold. This result isn't completely reversible. If $JD(XY, X(R - Y))$ holds, you have proved that $X \longrightarrow\!\!\!\!\!\rightarrow Y$ holds. But this doesn't imply that $X \longrightarrow Y$ necessarily holds.

The $JD(XY, X(R - Y))$ is equivalent to the MVD $X \longrightarrow\!\!\!\!\!\rightarrow Y$. If FD $X \longrightarrow Y$ holds, then MVD $X \longrightarrow\!\!\!\!\!\rightarrow Y$ and $JD(XY, X(R - Y))$ also hold.

This mechanism produces two-component JDs from FDs. More subtle connections also exist between FDs and JDs. Suppose $R = ABCD$, and the following FDs hold.

$$A \longrightarrow BCD \qquad B \longrightarrow ACD \qquad C \longrightarrow ABD \qquad D \longrightarrow ABC.$$

The $JD(AB, BC, CD, DA)$ must then hold. The join of the first two components losslessly recovers $\pi_{ABC}(r)$ because B is a superkey of the components. Further joins continue the lossless accumulation of the remaining attributes. If you let $\mathcal{F}$ denote the set of FDs, you can write $\mathcal{F} \models JD(AB, BC, CD, DA)$. In other words, any relation that satisfies the constraints of $\mathcal{F}$ must also satisfy the JD. In the tradition of previous chapters, you say that "the JD is implied by $\mathcal{F}$" or that "$\mathcal{F}$ models the JD."

A JD admits no redundancy if and only if it is implied by certain FDs

All the preliminary exploration is now complete. The long-awaited condition is: a JD introduces no redundancy if and only if the JD is implied by the superkey constraints on the support. Suppose $S = R_1 \cup R_2 \cup \ldots \cup R_n$ is the support of $JD(R_1, R_2, \ldots, R_n)$ and $S \subset R$, the universal relation. Suppose further that $\mathcal{F} \cup \mathcal{M}$ are the FDs and MVDs that constrain $r(R)$. Define the **superkey constraints on the JD support**, $\mathcal{K}_S$, as follows:

$$\mathcal{K}_S = \{K \longrightarrow S \mid K \subset S, K \longrightarrow S \in (\mathcal{F} \cup \mathcal{M})^+\}. \tag{19.3}$$

The following discussion will show that the $JD(R_1, R_2, \ldots, R_n)$ introduces no redundancy precisely when $\mathcal{K}_S \models JD(R_1, R_2, \ldots, R_n)$. First, an algorithm can determine when $\mathcal{K}_S \models JD(R_1, R_2, \ldots, R_n)$. The following procedure returns true if and only if $\mathcal{K}_S$ implies JD J.

```
boolean forcesJD(setCollection J, attributeSet S, constraintSet K_S) {
    setCollection X;

    X = J;
    while (S ∉ X and exists R_i, R_j ∈ X, K ⟶ S ∈ K_S with i ≠ j, K ⊂ R_i ∩ R_j)
        X = (X − {R_i, R_j}) ∪ {R_i ∪ R_j};
    if (S ∈ X)
        return true;
    else
        return false; }
```

The algorithm initializes X to the collection of JD components. If two components contain the same superkey of S, the algorithm replaces the two components by their union. Therefore, the number of sets in X continually decreases until no two members contain a K from $\mathcal{K}_S$ in common. This means the algorithm must terminate, and the union of the sets in X remains S throughout the execution. Moreover, the two components removed on a given iteration constitute a lossless join of the substituted component. So throughout the procedure you have: JD J holds if and only if JD, X, holds. If eventually X contains the component S, the support of the JD, you have that JD(S) holds if and only if JD, J, holds. Because JD(S) holds trivially, without further constraining the content of the relation, you can conclude that the JD, J, must also hold. So if the algorithm returns true, then $\mathcal{K}_S \models J$.

If the algorithm returns false, then $\mathcal{K}_S \not\models J$. Why? In this case, you can construct a relation that satisfies all the FDs of $\mathcal{K}_S$ but doesn't satisfy J. For specificity, assume that the algorithm terminates with three components in X, none equal to S. The argument for a larger number of components is similar. In particular, suppose $X = (R_2, R_1, R_0)$ at termination. You can again group the attributes of S into segments and use binary names to denote their relationships with R_2, R_1, R_0. For example, segment 011 contains the attributes that are outside R_2, inside R_1, and inside R_0. No S attributes appear in segment 000, and the table below arrays the rest of the segments.

001	a_1	b_1	c_1	c_1
010	a_2	b_2	c_2	b_2
011	a_3	b_3	b_3	b_3
100	a_4	b_4	c_4	a_4
101	a_5	b_5	a_5	a_5
110	a_6	a_6	c_6	a_6
111	a_7	a_7	a_7	a_7

The counterexample relation contains only the three antecedent tuples. For later discussion, the conclusion tuple appears on the right. The first two antecedents agree only on segments 110 and 111, which are contained in $R_2 \cap R_1$. Because the algorithm didn't merge R_2 and R_1, you can conclude that no K from $\mathcal{K}_S$ exists in these segments. The first two antecedents then can't agree on any left side from $\mathcal{K}_S$. Consequently, these two tuples can't violate any FDs of $\mathcal{K}_S$. Similarly, the first and third antecedents agree only on attributes in 101 and 111, which are contained in $R_2 \cap R_0$. Therefore, these two tuples can't violate an FD of $\mathcal{K}_S$. Finally, antecedents two and three agree on segments 011 and 111, which are contained in $R_1 \cap R_0$. So the relation consisting of the three antecedent tuples, plus an arbitrary extension into the attributes outside the support, satisfies $\mathcal{K}_S$.

But if it's to satisfy JD, J, it must satisfy JD, X, which forces the conclusion tuple to appear in the relation. If the conclusion tuple is to agree with the first antecedent, segments 001, 010, and 011 must be empty. However, these are the only segments that contain attributes outside R_2. If all these segments are empty, there are no S attributes outside R_2, which implies that $R_2 = S$. The algorithm terminated early, however, with no component of X equal to S. So at least one of the segments must be non-empty, and the conclusion tuple can't agree with the first antecedent. If the conclusion tuple is to coincide with the second antecedent, segments 001, 100, and 101 must be empty. Because these segments contain all the attributes outside R_1, that would imply that $R_1 = S$. Again, that's not possible, so they can't all be empty. Therefore, the conclusion tuple can't coincide with the second antecedent. A similar argument applies to the third antecedent, which finally implies that the conclusion tuple is distinct from all the antecedents. Because the conclusion tuple isn't in the relation, JD, X, doesn't hold, and thus JD, J, doesn't hold either.

So the algorithm is correct. If $\mathcal{K}_S \models \mathrm{JD}(R_1, R_2, \ldots, R_n)$, superkeys of the support, S, exist in enough of the components to recover S as a lossless join. If you join only the components containing superkeys of the support, the result will provide no opportunities for redundancy because all antecedents must collapse to a single tuple. Perhaps the remaining components don't contain superkeys, but they don't materially contribute to the join anyway.

If $\mathrm{JD}(R_1, R_2, \ldots, R_n)$ holds and if each component contains a superkey, the algorithm must return true, and $\mathcal{K}_S \models \mathrm{JD}(R_1, R_2, \ldots, R_n)$. If the algorithm returns false, you can construct a counterexample, as discussed above, that satisfies all the superkey constraints but the not the JD. That would establish a contradiction. Moreover, if one of the JD components is the full support, the algorithm immediately returns true. So the two earlier conditions for absolving a JD from redundancies are subsumed in the latest result.

 A JD$(R_1, R_2, \ldots, R_n)$ introduces no redundancy if and only if $\mathcal{K}_S \models$ JD$(R_1, R_2, \ldots, R_n)$, where $\mathcal{K}_S$ contains the FDs expressing the superkey constraints on the support $S = R_1 \cup R_2 \cup \ldots \cup R_n$.

Return to the example of $R = ABCD$ with $\mathcal{F} = \{A \longrightarrow BCD, B \longrightarrow ACD, C \longrightarrow ABD, D \longrightarrow ABC\}$. You can apply algorithm forceJD to establish that JD(AB, BC, CD, DA) must hold in this context. The algorithm initially sets $X = (AB, BC, CD, DA)$. Observing the superkey B common to the first two components, X becomes (ABC, CD, DA). A second pass gives $X = (ABCD, DA)$, and the algorithm terminates with a true return. Because the last component isn't used, you note that JD(AB, BC, CD) must also follow from the FDs.

Embedded join dependencies

Some JDs are embedded: the support isn't all of the constrained relation. A JD with support S constrains the body, $r(R)$, of the universal relation in the part that extends into S. In other words, if you observe certain antecedent tuples in $\pi_S(r)$, you can infer an additional conclusion tuple in $\pi_S(r)$. The constraint isn't concerned with the tuple values under the attributes outside the JD support. Sometimes you can't losslessly isolate the JD support as a separate table, and significant consequences follow when the decomposition process attempts to eliminate redundancy. In these cases, you must deal with the embedded nature of the JD. This discussion will use the proper abbreviation, EJD, for an embedded JD.

Consider again the $R = ABCX$ example with EJD(AB, BC, CA). Assume that no other constraints allow you to losslessly decompose R into $R_1 = ABC$ and $R_2 = YX$. You must then deal with the full table when investigating the consequences of the EJD. The table to the left below illustrates this situation. If the first three tuples appear, the fourth must also appear. The conditions on the parts of the tuples that extend into $R' = ABC$ remain as before. However, the constraint is indifferent as to the attribute values under $R - R'$.

You can now see that the earlier partial interchange constraint is a special case of an EJD. If the MVD interchange condition holds in a subset R' of R, then, in general, you can only assume a partial interchange restriction on the universal relation. The excerpts to the right below summarize this situation. The left column illustrates the consequences of an MVD interchange constraint on the body of R. You have $X \longrightarrow Y$ applicable to $R' \subset R$, and the $R' - XY$ attributes of R' are a subset of the $R - XY$ attributes of R. Therefore, when the second pair of tuples appear R, the effect is to interchange the $R' - XY$ attributes of R'. So if $X \longrightarrow Y$ holds, the corresponding interchange restriction also constrains any projection $R' \subset R$ that contains XY. The reverse direction is shown in the right column. If the MVD interchange condition holds in $R' \subset R$, the body of R must exhibit tuples that project to the required tuples in R' with the $R' - XY$ attributes interchanged. As the upper table shows, the condition is satisfied if the $EJD(XY, X(R' - Y))$ holds. In other words, the part of R that extends into R' must decompose losslessly onto the components associated with the MVD, $X \longrightarrow Y$. However, the condition $X \longrightarrow Y$ need not hold because the interchange condition need not apply to full tuples of R.

R			
R'			R − R'
A	B	C	X
·	·	·	·
α	b	c	x_1
a	β	c	x_2
a	b	γ	x_3
·	·	·	·
a	b	c	x_4
·	·	·	·

R			
R'			
		R − XY	
X	Y	R' − XY	R − R'
·	·	·	·
x	y_1	z_1	w_1
x	y_2	z_2	w_2
·	·	·	·
x	y_1	z_2	w_2
x	y_2	z_1	w_1
·	·	·	·

R			
R'			
		R − XY	
X	Y	R' − XY	R − R'
·	·	·	·
x	y_1	z_1	w_1
x	y_2	z_2	w_2
·	·	·	·
x	y_1	z_2	w_3
x	y_2	z_1	w_4
·	·	·	·

R'		
X	Y	R' − XY
·	·	·
x	y_1	z_1
x	y_2	z_2
·	·	·
x	y_1	z_2
x	y_2	z_1
·	·	·

R'		
X	Y	R' − XY
·	·	·
x	y_1	z_1
x	y_2	z_2
·	·	·
x	y_1	z_2
x	y_2	z_1
·	·	·

An example of a redundancy-inducing JD

Because each FD and MVD forces a JD to hold, you can say that JDs occur frequently as part of application constraints. But naturally occurring JDs that aren't actually FDs or MVDs are rare. You can, however, conjure up an example with the database of developers, workstations, and projects. As before, suppose that dno determines the descriptive characteristics of a developer, and wsno and pno play similar roles for workstation and project. Under these conditions, the earlier development produces the following 3NF decomposition.

R								$\mathcal{F}$
dno	dname	wsno	wsname	wslocation	pno	pname		dno $\longrightarrow$ dname
								wsno $\longrightarrow$ wsname
								wsno $\longrightarrow$ wslocation
								pno $\longrightarrow$ pname

Developer		Workstation			Project		Effort		
dno	dname	wsno	wsname	wslocation	pno	pname	dno	wsno	pno

Without further constraints, the only key to the Effort table is the entire schema, (dno, wsno, pno), and the decomposition satisfies both BCNF and 4NF. Earlier examples imposed additional constraints at this point to illustrate how you might need further decomposition to achieve BCNF or 4NF. For example, if you introduce the two FDs, (dno, wsno) $\longrightarrow$ pno and pno $\longrightarrow$ wsno, the decomposition satisfies 3NF but violates BCNF. Similarly, if you impose the MVD, dno $\longrightarrow\!\!\!\rightarrow$ wsno, you produce a 4NF violation.

In each case, the constraints have a natural meaning in the application. For the BCNF illustration, the restrictions can arise because a given developer, x, working on a given workstation, y, must always deal with the same project, z. Developer x can work on projects other than y, but only when using a workstation other than z. Also, workstation y can be used on projects other than z, but only when operated by a developer other than x. Moreover, the work on a particular project is conducted on a single workstation. Note that this last constraint does not contradict the fact that a workstation can be used with many projects. The relationship is one-to-many from workstation to project.

The second scenario is also grounded in a realistic application constraint. The MVD, dno $\longrightarrow\!\!\!\rightarrow$ wsno, states that no significance attaches to the pairing of particular workstations with particular projects in the context of a given developer. A developer simply owns a collection of workstations and, independently, a collection of projects. In order not to imply some preference for a particular workstation-project pairing, all such pairings must appear in the table. Admittedly, this constraint is somewhat more contrived than the previous one, but it is still credible. Imagine the manager of a software development shop instructing a newly hired developer on proper operating procedures. One rule states that a developer can show no preference in associating workstations with projects. Strict records register each time a developer uses a workstation for a project. Inspecting these records, you find that the developer has used workstations α, β, and γ and has worked on projects x and y. The condition now demands that he use each workstation on each project, or else he will be reprimanded for breaking the preference rule. The manager may have good reason for such a seemingly arbitrary rule. For example, he may be trying to evaluate the capabilities of several types of workstations, and he wants the developers to spread their assigned projects across their assigned workstations so that the evaluation will be unbiased. However, the contrived nature of this example shows that true MVDs (i.e., MVDs that don't arise from underlying FDs) aren't very common.

Let's now try to state a constraint that must be expressed as a true JD, a JD that doesn't arise from an underlying FD or MVD. Imagine that the rules concerning the use of workstations are as follows. If developer x uses workstation y for whatever project, and if workstation y is used for project z by whomever, and if developer x works on project z using whatever workstation, then you require that developer x use workstation y for project

z. In other words, if you know that developer x can operate workstation y, that developer x works project z, and that workstation y is used for project z, then you can conclude that x uses y for z. A table body for Effort that doesn't support this conclusion is then declared invalid.

You can summarize the various two-way connections by saying that you can make a case for (x, y, z). The constraint is then: if you can make a case for (x, y, z), then (x, y, z) must appear in the table. In terms of the tuples in the Effort table, to the left below, this constraint states: if the tuples shown appear in the table, then the tuple (x, y, z) must also appear. The three antecedent tuples constitute the case for (x, y, z). Comparing this situation with the example from the beginning of the section, you see that the required tuple is precisely the one introduced by the join of the projections to the right.

Effort		
dno	wsno	pno
x	y	α
β	y	z
x	γ	z

dno	wsno
x	y
β	y
x	γ

wsno	pno
y	α
y	z
γ	z

dno	pno
x	α
β	z
x	z

Therefore, the constraint is precisely JD(dno wsno), (wsno pno), (dno pno)). You can't express this constraint as an MVD interchange condition involving two of the components. The join of the first two projections introduces two extraneous tuples: the desired (x, y, z), and also (β, y, α). The required constraint isn't this strong. You don't insist that both these tuples appear as a consequence of the three original tuples, just that the first one appear. The required constraint isn't the same as stipulating a lossless join between the first two components. You can easily express the latter as wsno $\longrightarrow\!\!\!\rightarrow$ dno. A similar analysis shows that the constraint differs from that associated with a lossless join between any two components. So the JD((dno wsno), (wsno pno), (dno pno)) doesn't arise from an underlying MVD.

Because of the FDs in this example, the descriptive attributes must follow in lock step with the keys. If the decomposition ((dno wsno), (wsno pno), (pno dno)) is lossless, the decomposition ((dno dname wsno), (wsno wsname wslocation pno), (pno pname dno)) is also lossless. In other words, a tuple (dno dname wsno wsname wslocation pno pname) appears in the join of the latter three components if and only if a tuple (dno wsno pno) appears in the join of the former three components. Therefore, you can lift the JD developed above to R in the form JD((dno dname wsno), (wsno wsname wslocation pno), (pno pname)).

Fifth normal form

The universal relation is usually not the most convenient context to express a JD constraint. The example in the last section used a JD, JD((dno wsno), (wsno, pno), (pno, dno)), with less than universal support. After analyzing the situation, you found that you could bundle the descriptive attributes with their keys, which resulted in a JD with support equal to the entire universal relation. In the application analysis, you needed to capture the complex relationship among developers, workstations, and projects. A table of application entity keys provided the most natural context for formulating the constraint. Generally, this approach produces an EJD constraint for R, the universal relation. As the examples so far have shown, you can often then construct an equivalent JD with universal support. However, this doesn't always occur. The EJD doesn't always lift to an equivalent JD with universal support. Suppose, for example, you have the EJD(AB, BC, CA) in the context of a universal relation $ABCX$, as shown below.

\multicolumn{4}{c}{R'}			
A	B	C	X
$\vdots$	$\vdots$	$\vdots$	$\vdots$
a	b	α	x_1
a	β	c	x_2
γ	b	c	x_3
$\vdots$	$\vdots$	$\vdots$	$\vdots$
a	b	c	x_4
$\vdots$	$\vdots$	$\vdots$	$\vdots$

The first three tuples make a case for $(abc\ldots)$, so a fourth tuple must appear to materialize that prefix. However, the constraint is indifferent as to the content of the attributes outside the EJD support (i.e., the values under attributes X). At first glance, some redundancy seems to exist in the table because knowing the three antecedent tuples lets you predict that the abc prefix will occur. But you can't predict the tuple where the prefix will attach. Imagine that you can see the three antecedent tuples in their entirety and that the ABC values of the remaining tuples show only blanks. You know that the prefix abc must occur in one of these tuples, but you can't predict the exact location.

Consequently, you don't have a redundancy in the strictest sense. The fact that the abc prefix attaches to a particular X value does impart additional information. Of course, the ideal situation occurs if you can losslessly decompose the relation into $R_1 = ABC$ and $R_2 = YX$, where Y is a proper subset of ABC that provides common attributes to link R_1 and R_2. In this case, you can predict an entire tuple in R_1, and you can remove this true redundancy by further decomposing R_1 into $R_{11} = AB, R_{12} = BC$, and $R_{13} = CA$.

The opportunity to proceed further with the decomposition of R_1 hinges on the viability of the initial decomposition of R into R_1 and R_2. This first decomposition is possible if $Y \longrightarrow\!\!\!\!\rightarrow X$. Even if $Y = \varphi$, it's still possible that $\varphi \longrightarrow\!\!\!\!\rightarrow X$ if the ABC and X components represent disjoint clusters. Another possibility is that the attributes of X are descriptive features of the keys ABC. In this case, you can bundle each attribute of X with its key to produce a JD with universal support. Decomposition can then proceed from the larger JD.

The resulting components may undergo further decomposition. Suppose that $X = DEFGHIJKL$ and that you have the constraints shown adjacent to the table below. As in the preceding example, you can attach the attributes of X to their keys in the EJD support to imply that JD$((ADEF\ B), (BGHI\ C), (CJKL\ A))$ holds. The decomposition on the second level is then lossless, and you can use the FDs to further decompose the components as shown. Note that the tables AB, BC, and CA associated with the EJD appear in the final decomposition.

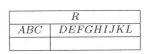

R	
ABC	$DEFGHIJKL$

$$A \longrightarrow DEF$$
$$E \longrightarrow F$$
$$B \longrightarrow GHI$$
$$C \longrightarrow JKL$$
$$\text{EJD}(AB, BC, CA)$$

R_1				R_2				R_3	
A	DEF	B		B	GHI	C		C	JKL	A

R_{11}		R_{12}		R_{13}		R_{21}		R_{22}		R_{31}		R_{32}	
A	DE	E	F	A	B	B	GHI	B	C	C	JKL	C	A

In this discussion, the decomposition evolves to a point where an EJD support is an entire component. At that point, you can losslessly decompose the component into the subcomponents mentioned in the EJD. However, if you can't exploit other constraints to isolate the support of the EJD in a single component, you can't remove the redundancy associated with that EJD through lossless decomposition.

In this case, the redundancy isn't as objectionable as the redundancies encountered in earlier situations. In particular, when a pattern of antecedent tuples presents a case for a conclusion pattern within the support attributes, you can't immediately predict where to attach the predicted prefix. Consequently, the association of the forced prefix with a particular set of values outside of S doesn't constitute completely wasted storage. Instead, the stored pattern registers the fact that the prefix relates to a particular suffix. This storage pattern, however, does present an opportunity for inconsistency because an update can change the table to leave the antecedent pattern intact while removing the required prefix.

You can exploit an EJD to reduce redundancy if you can first use other constraints to isolate the EJD support in a single table.

Let $\mathcal{G} = \mathcal{F} \cup \mathcal{M} \cup \mathcal{J}$ be a collection of constraints; FDs in $\mathcal{F}$, MVDs that don't arise from FDs in $\mathcal{M}$, and JDs that don't arise from MVDs in $\mathcal{J}$. You know that each FD gives rise to an MVD and that each MVD is a special case of a JD. Therefore, segregating the constraints in three categories is a convenience because all are JDs with certain side conditions. In particular, the MVD, $X \longrightarrow\!\!\!\!\rightarrow Y$, is equivalent to a JD with exactly two components: $\text{JD}(XY, X(R - Y))$. The FD, $X \longrightarrow Y$, is equivalent to the $\text{JD}(XY, X(R - Y))$ with the side condition that X is a superkey of the first component.

A $\text{JD}(R_1, R_2, \ldots, R_n)$ **applies** to a subset $R' \subset R$ if the JD support is equal to R'. Let R be the universal relation, with valid states constrained by $\mathcal{G}$. Let $R' \subset R$, and let $\mathcal{K}_{R'}$ be the superkey constraints on R'. $\mathcal{K}_{R'} = \{K \longrightarrow R' \mid K \subset R', K \longrightarrow R' \in \mathcal{G}^+\}$. R' satisfies **fifth normal form** (5NF) if for every $\text{JD}(R_1, R_2, \ldots, R_n)$ of $\mathcal{G}^+$ that applies to R', $\mathcal{K}_{R'} \models \text{JD}(R_1, R_2, \ldots, R_n)$. A collection of relations satisfies 5NF if each member of the collection satisfies 5NF. A $\text{JD}(R_1, R_2, \ldots, R_n)$ that applies to a relation R' but doesn't have $\mathcal{K}_{R'} \models \text{JD}(R_1, R_2, \ldots, R_n)$ is a 5NF **violator** for R'.

The definition allows a JD to escape the violator status if the JD is implied by the superkey constraints on its support. These exclusions comprise (1) the trivial JDs (i.e., JDs with a component equal to the support), (2) JDs where all components contain a superkey, and (3) JDs where some component doesn't contain a superkey, provided that a sufficient number of components contain superkeys to losslessly reconstruct the support with algorithm forceJD. All these excluded cases correspond to situations where the JD doesn't introduce any redundancies.

Revisiting the example with developers, workstations, and projects, suppose you start with all attributes in the universal relation, R. You then impose the following constraints.

$\mathcal{F}$	$\mathcal{M}$	$\mathcal{J}$
dno $\longrightarrow$ dname wsno $\longrightarrow$ wsname wsno $\longrightarrow$ wslocation pno $\longrightarrow$ pname		JD((dno wsno), (wsno pno), (pno dno))

The JD support is (dno wsno pno). Because no component appears on the right side of FDs in $\mathcal{F}$, any superkey of the support must contain all three of these attributes. In other words, the only superkey of the support is (dno wsno pno). Therefore, algorithm forceJD immediately returns false, which means that the JD isn't implied by the support superkeys.

Nevertheless, this JD isn't a 5NF violator because it doesn't apply to R. The FDs establish the remaining attributes as descriptive features associated with dno, wsno, and pno, so the JD((dno dname wsno), (wsno wsname wslocation pno), (pno pname dno)) must also hold. This JD has universal support, but the only superkeys remain supersets of (dno wsno pno). Algorithm forceJD then can make no progress in coalescing components and immediately returns false. At this point, you have a true 5NF violator.

There are other 5NF violators as well. For example, FD dno $\longrightarrow$ dname induces MVD dno $\longrightarrow\!\!\!\!\!\rightarrow$ dname, which, in turn, induces the JD((dno dname), (dno wsno wsname wslocation pno pname)). Because the superkeys all contain (dno wsno pno), algorithm forceJD is again unable to coalesce the components, and it returns false. Therefore, the JD isn't implied by the superkeys, and it is another 5NF violator.

5NF subsumes 4NF

This last observation above generalizes: any 3NF, BCNF, or 4NF violator will also be a 5NF violator. You already know that a relation in 4NF is already in BCNF, and so on back through the lower normal forms. So a BCNF violator must be a 4NF violator because when a violation removes a relation from the BCNF group, it certainly removes it from any subset of the BCNF group. In a similar spirit, suppose that $X \longrightarrow\!\!\!\!\!\rightarrow Y$ is a 4NF violator for $R' \subset R$. You can show that it is also a 5NF violator as follows. You must have that $Y - X$ and $R' - XY$ are non-empty and that X isn't a superkey of R'. Because $X \longrightarrow\!\!\!\!\!\rightarrow Y$, however, the decomposition $(XY, X(R' - Y))$ is lossless. In other words, JD$(XY, X(R' - Y))$ holds. The support of the JD is R'. Therefore, to show that this JD is a 5NF violator, you need to check only that it isn't implied by the superkey constraints on R'. To respond true in this situation, algorithm forceJD must find a K such that $K \longrightarrow R'$ and $K \subset XY \cap X(R' - Y)$. Suppose such a K exists. That is, both XY and $X(R' - Y) = X(R' - XY)$ are superkeys of R'. This situation implies that X is a superkey of R', which contradicts the assumption that $X \longrightarrow\!\!\!\!\!\rightarrow Y$ is a 4NF violator. Why? Consider two tuples that agree on X. Take, for example, the first two tuples in the leftmost excerpt below.

R			
R'			
X	Y − X	R' − XY	R − R'
⋮	⋮	⋮	⋮
x	y_1	z_1	w_1
x	y_2	z_2	w_2
⋮	⋮	⋮	⋮
x	y_1	z_2	w_3
x	y_2	z_1	w_4
⋮	⋮	⋮	⋮

R			
R'			
X	Y − X	R' − XY	R − R'
⋮	⋮	⋮	⋮
x	y_1	z_1	w_1
x	y_2	z_1	w_2
⋮	⋮	⋮	⋮
x	y_1	z_1	w_3
x	y_2	z_1	w_4
⋮	⋮	⋮	⋮

Because $X \longrightarrow\!\!\!\!\!\rightarrow Y$, the second two tuples must appear. Note that the values under $R − R'$ need not interchange because you are assuming that $X \longrightarrow\!\!\!\!\!\rightarrow Y$ constrains only R', not R. Because XY is a superkey of R', however, you have $XY \longrightarrow R' − XY$. Observing the first tuple of each pair, you then find two tuples agreeing on XY, so they must agree on $R' − XY$. This forces $z_1 = z_2$. The scenario then actually appears as the table to the right above.

You are also assuming that $X(R' − Y) = X(R' − XY)$ is a superkey of R', so $X(R' − XY) \longrightarrow Y − X$. All four tuples agree on $X(R' − XY)$, so they must agree on $Y − X$, which forces $y_1 = y_2$. Therefore, you can conclude that two tuples agreeing on X must agree on all of R', which implies that X is a superkey of R'. Because this is a contradiction, you must have that either XY isn't a superkey of R' or that $X(R' − Y)$ isn't a superkey of R'. In either case, algorithm forceJD returns false, and $JD(XY, X(R − Y))$ becomes a 5NF violator. Thus you have shown that any 4NF violator is also a 5NF violator. 5NF then joins the progression of normal forms as the strictest format so far.

If a relation satisfies 5NF, it satisfies 4NF, and therefore it also satisfies BCNF, 3NF, and 2NF. Conversely, a 2NF violator is a 3NF violator, a 3NF violator is a 4NF violator, a 4NF violator is a BCNF violator, and 4NF violator is a 5NF violator.

An example satisfying 4NF, but not 5NF

Returning to the example, you can conclude that all the BCNF violators, such as dno $\longrightarrow$ dname and wsno $\longrightarrow$ wslocation, are also 5NF violators. You can decompose the universal relation with the BCNF decomposition technique of Chapter 18 or with the dependency basis approach of this chapter. With either approach, you will obtain the following arrangement.

R						
dno	dname	wsno	wsname	wslocation	pno	pname

$\mathcal{F}$
dno $\longrightarrow$ dname
wsno $\longrightarrow$ wsname
wsno $\longrightarrow$ wslocation
pno $\longrightarrow$ pname
JD((dno wsno), (wsno pno), (pno dno))

Developer	
dno	dname

Workstation		
wsno	wsname	wslocation

Project	
pno	pname

Effort		
dno	wsno	pno

The decomposition now satisfies 4NF because no MVDs exist that don't arise from the FDs. However, the Effort table doesn't satisfy 5NF because the join dependency applies to it and no component contains a superkey. Therefore, algorithm forceJD returns false, and you conclude that the JD isn't implied by the superkey constraints on the support. To achieve 5NF, you must decompose the Effort table into the three components of the JD.

As this example illustrates, you must identify the violating JDs in $\mathcal{G}^+$ to guide the decomposition. JDs are complicated constraints, but algorithms exist to determine all the JDs that must follow from an initial set. Details on one such algorithm will be discussed shortly. In practice, however, you can best organize the situation by performing the decomposition into 4NF before considering any JDs. At that point, you have separated the application entities and represented the relationships among them with tables of keys. Any JDs that arise from underlying FDs or MVDs aren't 5NF violators because the JD components at this point are all superkeys of the tables where they apply.

For example, if $X \longrightarrow Y$ holds and XY appear together in a table, R', then X must be a superkey of R' or else a BCNF violation occurs. Because you have already decomposed into 4NF, no BCNF violations are present, so X is a superkey of R'. The induced JD is $JD(XY, X(R' - Y))$, and both components are superkeys of R'. So the JD can't be a 5NF violator. In the 4NF decomposition, moreover, a 5NF violator must be a JD that applies to one of the components. Therefore, any JD whose support isn't equal to one of the component tables can't be a violator. If there are cyclic constraints among the application entities, they will now appear among the key attributes of the relationship tables.

You can summarize the practical technique for achieving 5NF in two steps. First, perform a 4NF decomposition to fracture the universal relation into a number of tables, each representing an application entity or a relationship among such entities. Second, analyze the application for JDs that apply to these tables. For each such JD that is a 5NF violator, decompose the component into the subcomponents specified in the JD. Continue this process until the application yields no more JDs that apply to the component tables. At that point, the decomposition satisfies 5NF.

Although this method is effective in practice, as illustrated in the developer-workstation-project example, it isn't ironclad because you simply terminate the process when you can find no further JDs that violate 5NF. The question is, of course, how to be sure that you have found all the JDs. The method works in practice because JDs aren't typically found among the descriptive attributes of the tables corresponding to the application entities, and in a 4NF decomposition, the tables corresponding to relationships are usually small. You can easily visualize, in application terms, the consequences of a JD among a small set of attributes.

In this fashion, you can dismiss most possibilities. The few remaining possibilities might then result in further decomposition.

The chase algorithm for verifying that a JD is in the closure

Purists, however, can use the following algorithm to ferret out all JDs. Suppose $R' = A_1 A_2 \ldots A_n$ is one of the components of the 4NF decomposition. Only a finite number of JDs can apply to R'. You can systematically consider all JDs with two components, then those with three components, and so on, up through those with 2^n components. Because the n attributes have only 2^n subsets, this list will eventually capture any JDs that apply to R'. The JDs with two components number $(2^n)^2 = 2^{2n}$ because each component can be an arbitrary subset of the n attributes. Similarly, there are 2^{3n} possible JDs with three components, and so forth. The total list is very long, super-exponentially so in terms of n. Some of these JDs are trivial, and many others are redundant in the sense that you can eliminate a component that is completely contained in another. You can also eliminate a JD with the empty set, φ, as a component. Even with these exclusions, the list is very large. Nevertheless, you can systematically consider each JD$(R_m, R_{m-1}, \ldots, R_0)$ of the list to determine if it holds. You make this determination with an algorithm called the **chase**, which operates as follows.

You construct a table that includes the antecedent tuples that make a case for the tuple $\mu = (a_m : a_{m-1} : \ldots : a_0)$, where $a_i \in R_i$. Although the notation implies that common attributes can appear in the various segments, this isn't the case. The extra copies are suppressed in forming μ from the a_i segments. You then systematically $\mathcal{G}$, the initial collection of FDs, MVDs, and JDs that constrain the application. You are searching for a constraint that is violated. When you find one, you make changes to the table to remove the violation. These changes may involve replacing certain symbols with others when a constraint forces them to be equal, or they may involve introducing additional tuples as required by MVDs and JDs when the antecedent patterns are present. You stop when you have generated μ or when you can find no more violations among the constraints of $\mathcal{G}$. If you have generated μ upon termination, the JD$(R_1, R_2, \ldots, R_n) \in \mathcal{G}^+$. If the process terminates without generating μ, you have a table that satisfies all $\mathcal{G}$ constraints. By definition, therefore, it satisfies all $\mathcal{G}^+$ constraints. Because μ isn't in the table, the JD$(R_1, R_2, \ldots, R_n) \notin \mathcal{G}^+$. The chase thus determines if the given JD holds.

Consider again the example with $R = ABCDEFGHIJKL$, subject to the constraints:

$$\mathcal{G} = \{A \longrightarrow DEF, E \longrightarrow F, B \longrightarrow GHI, C \longrightarrow JKL, \text{JD}(AB, BC, CA)\}.$$

An earlier analysis asserted that JD$(ADEFB, BGHIC, CJKLA)$ holds because the descriptive attributes must follow in lock step with their keys. You can verify this with the chase. Start with three tuples that make a case for the tuple $(abcdefghijkl)$. You need a tuple agreeing with the target on the first component of the JD, another tuple agreeing on the second component, and a final tuple agreeing on the third component. If the JD holds, these three tuples will combine to generate the target. Initially, you place arbitrary symbols in all attributes that aren't constrained to agree with the target, as noted in the leftmost table below. The target symbols are $(abcdefghijkl)$.

R											
A	B	C	D	E	F	G	H	I	J	K	L
a	b	c_1	d	e	f	g_1	h_1	i_1	j_1	k_1	l_1
a_2	b	c	d_2	e_2	f_2	g	h	i	j_2	k_2	l_2
a	b_3	c	d_3	e_3	f_3	g_3	h_3	i_3	j	k	l

(a)

R											
A	B	C	D	E	F	G	H	I	J	K	L
a	b	c_1	d	e	f	g_1	h_1	i_1	j_1	k_1	l_1
a_2	b	c	d_2	e_2	f_2	g	h	i	j_2	k_2	l_2
a	b_3	c	d	e	f	g_3	h_3	i_3	j	k	l

(b)

Because the first and third tuples agree on A and $A \longrightarrow DEF \in \mathcal{G}$, you force the these tuples to agree on DEF by replacing d_3 with d, e_3 with e, and f_3 with f. This produces the table (a) above. When you replace a symbol because it must be equal to some other symbol, you always retain the symbol from the target—if the comparison is between a target symbol and an arbitrary symbol. If the comparison doesn't involve a target symbol, you can choose either of the arbitrary symbols to retain. The same is true if the comparison is between two target symbols.

Because $B \longrightarrow GHI$, an operation on the first two tuples acquires the values ghi in the first tuple. $C \longrightarrow JKL$ then allows a similar replacement between tuples 2 and 3. The result appears as the leftmost table below.

R											
A	B	C	D	E	F	G	H	I	J	K	L
a	b	c_1	d	e	f	g	h	i	j_1	k_1	l_1
a_2	b	c	d_2	e_2	f_2	g	h	i	j	k	l
a	b_3	c	d	e	f	g_3	h_3	i_3	j	k	l

(a)

R											
A	B	C	D	E	F	G	H	I	J	K	L
a	b	c_1	d	e	f	g	h	i	j_1	k_1	l_1
a_2	b	c	d_2	e_2	f_2	g	h	i	j	k	l
a	b_3	c	d	e	f	g_3	h_3	i_3	j	k	l
a	b	c	d_4	e_4	f_4	g_4	h_4	i_4	j_4	k_4	l_4

(b)

The JD(AB, BC, CA) now applies to the embedded segment ABC, which adds a tuple with abc in that portion but with arbitrary values in the remaining attributes. The new table appears (a) above. At this point, FD $A \longrightarrow DEF$ forces the $d_4 e_4 f_4$ values of the fourth tuple to equal the def values of the first. Similarly, FD $B \longrightarrow GHI$ forces the $g_4 h_4 i_4$ values of the fourth tuple to equal the ghi values of the first. Finally, $C \longrightarrow JKL$ forces the $j_4 k_4 l_4$ values of the fourth tuple to equal the jkl entries of the second. At this point, the target appears as the fourth tuple, which proves that the JD must hold.

Because you now have an algorithm for discovering all possible JDs in $\mathcal{G}^+$, you can construct an algorithm to systematically decompose the universal relation R into 5NF. If the chase algorithm reveals a JD$(R_1, R_2, \ldots, R_n)$ applicable to R that is a 5NF violator, you decompose R into $(R_1, R_2, \ldots, R_n)$. You then recursively apply the chase algorithm to determine any JDs applicable to the components. If it finds any 5NF violators, you decompose the components accordingly. This process continues until no further decomposition is commanded by violating JDs. By definition, the resulting decomposition satisfies 5NF.

 The chase algorithm determines if a JD must hold on a relation initially constrained by $\mathcal{G}$. Using this algorithm to tabulate the JDs of $\mathcal{G}^+$, you can losslessly decompose every relation into components, each satisfying 5NF.

Simplifications afforded by singleton keys

Singleton keys have some remarkable advantages in the normalization process. You learned earlier that a relation can't violate 2NF if all its keys are singletons. The reason is that a 2NF violation must exhibit a composite key, where a proper subset determines a non-prime attribute. If all keys are singletons, the only proper subsets are φ. So a 2NF violator would have to assume the form $\varphi \longrightarrow X$. This FD requires the relation to contain constant values under attributes X. Assuming such extreme constraints aren't applicable, no 2NF violations will occur when all keys are singletons.

The matter of singleton keys isn't relevant to 3NF, but once you get that far, all further normal forms, BCNF, 4NF, and 5NF, are automatically satisfied if the keys are all singletons. Given the lengthy development of these normal forms, this is truly remarkable. You can guarantee 5NF simply by guaranteeing 3NF and insisting on all singleton keys.

Assume R' is in 3NF and all keys are singleton attributes. The first task is to show that R' satisfies BCNF. To this end, let $X \longrightarrow A$ be an arbitrary FD applicable to R'. Because R' satisfies 3NF, either X is a superkey or A is prime. If X is a superkey, the FD can't be a BCNF violator. If A is prime, some key must contain A. However, because all keys are singletons, A must then be a key. So $A \longrightarrow B$ for every $B \in R'$. By transitivity, $X \longrightarrow B$ for every $B \in R'$. So X is a superkey, and again the FD isn't a BCNF violator. Therefore, R' satisfies BCNF.

To show that R' satisfies 4NF, suppose $X \longrightarrow\!\!\!\!\rightarrow Y$ is a 4NF violator. Then $R' - XY$ isn't empty, and X isn't a superkey. Because $X \longrightarrow\!\!\!\!\rightarrow X$ trivially, you have $X \longrightarrow\!\!\!\!\rightarrow Y - X$ by decomposition, and $X \longrightarrow\!\!\!\!\rightarrow R' - XY$ by complementation. (The latter holds only in R'.) Because R' must contain a key, some singleton $A \notin X$ is a key. Two cases now arise: either $A \in Y - X$ or $A \in R' - XY$. The argument is symmetric in either case, so consider only the case where $A \in R' - XY$, as suggested by the following table shell.

R'			
X	$Y - X$	$R' - XY$	
		$\ldots$ A $\ldots$	

Because $X \longrightarrow\!\!\!\!\rightarrow (Y - X), A \longrightarrow (Y - X)$, and $A \cap (Y - X) = \varphi$, you have $X \longrightarrow (Y - X)$ by coalescence. Because you have shown that R' satisfies BCNF, X must then be a superkey.

This contradiction means that $X \longrightarrow\!\!\!\!\!\rightarrow Y$ isn't a 4NF violator after all. Therefore, R' satisfies 4NF.

Finally, you must show that R' satisfies 5NF. Suppose $JD(R_1, R_2, \ldots, R_n)$ holds, where $R_1 \cup R_2 \cup \ldots \cup R_n = R'$. Algorithm forceJD must then return true. To see this, let $X = (T_1, T_2, \ldots, T_m)$ when the algorithm terminates. Because R' must have a key and because R' is the union of the T_i, one of the T_i must contain a key. Renumbering if necessary, assume T_1 contains the key A. Because JD, X, holds at all times during the execution of the algorithm, you have that $JD(T_1, T_2, \ldots, T_m)$ holds. However, $JD(T_1, V)$ then holds, where $V = T_2 \cup T_3 \cup \ldots \cup T_m$. That JD is equivalent to $(T_1 \cap V) \longrightarrow\!\!\!\!\!\rightarrow V$. Because you know that R' satisfies 4NF, either (1) this MVD is trivial or (2) $(T_1 \cap V)$ is a superkey of R'. The second possibility can't occur because if $(T_1 \cap V)$ contains a key, that key must be a singleton, say B. However, $B \in V$ then implies that $B \in T_i$, for some $2 \leq i \leq m$, and the algorithm would have merged T_1 and T_i. Because that merge didn't happen, $(T_i \cap V)$ can't be a superkey of R'. So $(T_1 \cap V) \longrightarrow\!\!\!\!\!\rightarrow V$ must be trivial. One way that an MVD can be trivial is for the union of its left and right sides to encompass all of R': $(T_1 \cap V) \cup V = R'$. However, this forces $V = R'$, and V contains the key A that you used to distinguish T_1. Then $A \in T_i$, for some $2 \leq i \leq m$, which forces the algorithm to merge T_1 and T_i. Because that merge didn't happen, you can conclude that $(T_1 \cap V) \cup V = R'$ isn't possible. In the only remaining case, the MVD is trivial because its left side contains its right: $V \subset (T_1 \cap V)$. However, then $V \subset T_1$, which implies that $T_1 = R'$, and forceJD returns true. Therefore, the original JD is implied by the superkey constraints on R', and R' satisfies 5NF.

 If a relation is in 3NF and all keys are singleton attributes, the relation is also in BCNF, 4NF, and 5NF.

This last observation provides a simple criterion for guaranteeing higher normal forms. If all the keys are singletons, you don't need to resort to the chase algorithm or to the intuitive mechanisms discussed earlier to discover JDs that might compromise 5NF. This simple route, however, isn't the panacea that it might appear to be. When you cast an application into a collection of relations, some represent the intersection entities associated with many-to-many relationships. In such a relation, the key won't be a singleton. Instead, it will be a composite, which contains the primary keys of the participating entities, say (K_1, K_2). You could introduce a new singleton attribute as a key to the intersection relation, but that doesn't diminish the key stature of the composite (K_1, K_2). To make use of the singleton-key simplification, you must have singletons for *all* keys. Consequently, the advantages of singleton keys are usually not available. Intersection relations typically have composite keys, and intersection relations are also the most likely tables to host JD constraints.

Beyond join dependencies

Although you can always achieve a lossless-join decomposition into 5NF, a component may remain constrained by an embedded join dependency. The EJD doesn't necessarily constitute a 5NF violation because its support may not include the entire component. In this case, it doesn't apply to the component, and the definitions exclude it from the 5NF violators. You should separate the EJD support into a separate relation, where you can further decompose it, but in the absence of other suitable constraints, that separation isn't always possible. The table to the left below summarizes this difficulty.

R			
R'			$R - R'$
A	B	C	X
$\vdots$	$\vdots$	$\vdots$	$\vdots$
α	b	c	x_1
a	β	c	x_2
a	b	γ	x_3
$\vdots$	$\vdots$	$\vdots$	$\vdots$
a	b	c	x_4
$\vdots$	$\vdots$	$\vdots$	$\vdots$

```
create assertion EJD check not exists (
    select A, B, C from
        ((select A, B from R) natural join
        (select B, C from R) natural join
        (select C, A from R))
    where (A, B, C) not in
        (select A, B, C from R)).
```

The EJD(AB, BC, CA) holds in R, but you can't losslessly isolate the support, R', from the rest of the attributes. This redundancy doesn't represent wasted storage because additional information is carried in the fact that the forced prefix, abc, associates with a particular X value, x_4. The situation, however, isn't ideal because an update could change some aspect of the forced tuple and violate the EJD.

You can't construct a lossless-join solution to this problem, but you can use the create-assertion features of SQL to enforce the EJD. Because you know the join of the projections onto AB, BC, and CA will always contain the projection onto ABC, you can tabulate the tuples that appear in the join but not in the ABC projection. If no such tuples exist, the constraint is satisfied. The SQL clause appears on the right above.

This solution guarantees the integrity of the database with respect to the EJD because it rejects any update that would result in a violation. However, it is less desirable than the structural solutions involving decompositions. When you use decompositions to remove redundancy, violations are impossible by the very structure of the tables and their interconnecting columns. It isn't necessary to use SQL assertions to watch for a violating pattern. But this example does show that there is a limit to the redundancy that you can remove with the decomposition process.

Template constraints

A common theme across this chapter and the last is that a constraint corresponds to a data pattern in a table. The table satisfies the constraint if another data pattern is present. Previous examples have often used table excerpts, such as the leftmost one below, to visualize the effects of a constraint. The upper tuples constitute a pattern, or template, and the lower tuples represent a conclusion. The conclusion is the second pattern that must appear to satisfy the constraint. MVDs and JDs certainly conform to this format, and you can also accommodate FDs if you view the entries as predicates rather than tuples.

R		
X	$Y-X$	$R-XY$
$\vdots$	$\vdots$	$\vdots$
x	y_1	z_1
x	y_2	z_2
$\vdots$	$\vdots$	$\vdots$
x	y_1	z_2
x	y_2	z_1
$\vdots$	$\vdots$	$\vdots$

$X \longrightarrow Y$

X	$Y-X$	$R-XY$
x	y_1	z_1
x	y_2	z_2
	$y_1 = y_2$	

$X \longrightarrow\!\!\!\!\rightarrow Y$

X	$Y-X$	$R-XY$
x	y_1	z_1
x	y_2	z_2
x	y_1	z_2
x	y_2	z_1

EJD(AB, BC, CA)

A	B	C	X
a_1	b	c	x_1
a	b_1	c	x_2
a	b	c_1	x_3
a	b	c	x_4

The patterns in the example tables present a sort of logical syllogism. A **syllogism** is a logical argument, where the truth of certain predicates, the **premises**, imply the truth of other predicates, the **conclusions.** You identify certain premises with the antecedent tuples and draw a conclusion. The conclusion can be the existence of another tuple, or several tuples, in the table, or it can be a different predicate, such as the equality of two values.

The notation continues with the tabular presentation, but you now interpret a row as a predicate. If the row is simply a vector of values, the predicate is true if the values constitute a tuple in the table; it is false if the values do not appear as a table row. The patterns for FD, MVD, and EJD appear on the right above in this new format. The leftmost syllogism states that if two tuples exist in the table with equal X values, the Y values are also equal. Similar interpretations apply to the MVD and JD cases, except that the conclusion stipulates the existence of tuples, rather than the equality of values.

You can use syllogisms to express constraints beyond the FD, MVD, and JD constraints that lead to lossless decompositions. For example, the last pattern above is an EJD, which may not have a decomposition solution. The pattern is still useful to guide the construction of an SQL create-assertion statement to enforce the constraint.

Constraints expressed through syllogisms are **template constraints**. As illustrated above, you can express FDs, MVDs, and JDs in template form. You can also express more general constraints in the template notation. The template on the left below, for example, asserts that if the A and B values of a tuple are equal, the C and D values must also be equal. The enforcing SQL create-assertion statement appears to the right.

A	B	C	D
a	a	c	d
	$c = d$		

```
create assertion ABCDbalance check not exists (
    select A, B, C, D
    from R
    where A = B and C ≠ D).
```

A close relationship exists between template constraints and the inference rules of a deductive database. In that context, constraints appear as inference rules with a false head. For example, if $R(A, B, C, D)$ is the database predicate that judges membership in table R, you can write the above constraint as follows.

$$\texttt{false} \vdash R(A, A, C, D), \ C \neq D.$$

The translation is direct because you introduce a clause for each premise and a final clause to negate the conclusion. You read the rule as precluding the case where $R(A, A, C, D)$ is true for some binding A, A, C, D while $C \neq D$. Chapters 9 and 10 used this kind of expression to enforce functional dependency constraints on a deductive database. But the method also applies to more general template constraints. For example, you can translate the $JD(AB, BC, CA)$ template as follows, assuming that $R(A, B, C)$ is the database predicate judging a binding (A, B, C) as a tuple of R.

$$\texttt{false} \vdash R(A, B, C_1), R(A, B_2, C), R(A_3, B, C), \neg R(A, B, C).$$

Although this constraint does enforce the JD, it presents some problems. First, the system rejects the third antecedent binding in the axiom table if the conclusion binding isn't already there. So to establish a consistent database, you must lift the constraint while you load the axioms. Second, you would prefer to arrange the structure so the constraint can't be violated, rather than to impose a check to filter each database update. The decomposition approach in the relational model reflects this preference. In the deductive setting, you can imitate the technique with a rule that materializes the required binding from the antecedent bindings. This solution avoids both problems. The required rules are:

$$R_1(A, B, C) \vdash R(A, B, C).$$
$$R_1(A, B, C) \vdash R(A_1, B, C), R(A, B_2, C), R(A, B, C_3).$$

You can now use the database predicate R_1 in place of R and rest assured that the JD will always be satisfied. If the conclusion binding isn't in the R axiom table, the second inference rule materializes it. Therefore, you don't need a constraint to keep the axiom table in compliance.

 Template constraints exhibit a collection of premise predicates followed by conclusion predicates. The interpretation is: when a pattern appears in the constrained relation that renders the premises true, the conclusions must also be true. You can express FDs, MVDs, JDs, and more general constraints in template format.

Mechanisms for expressing and enforcing constraints are at the forefront of database research. Constraints allow the database implementation to parallel the mini-world application being modeled. In general, the task of closely approximating the conditions that govern the real-world entities and their relationships is called **semantic modeling**. Semantic modeling, as its name implies, attempts to capture the semantics (meaning) of the application in the model. The ability to express intricate application constraints is critical in this process. The general tools considered in Chapter 17 (i.e., entity-relationship and object modeling techniques) are semantic modeling tools because they provide features for expressing many of the commonly occurring application constraints. Similarly, FD, MVD, and JD constraints, together with the normalization procedures for ensuring compliance with these restrictions, constitute other methods for capturing the application semantics in the database model.

Domain-key normal form

Is there a normal form beyond 5NF? The 3NF condition is: if a nontrivial FD, $X \longrightarrow A$, applies to a relation, X must be a superkey or A must be prime. BCNF goes further and insists that X be a superkey even if A is prime. 4NF states: if a nontrivial MVD, $X \longrightarrow\!\!\!\!\rightarrow Y$, applies to a relation, X must be a superkey. Finally, 5NF says: if a nontrivial

$JD(R_1, R_2, \ldots, R_n)$ applies to a relation, it must be implied by the superkeys of the relation. The common theme is that certain constraints are acceptable, without further decomposition, if they involve a superkey.

When you studied the details of the 3NF, BCNF, 4NF, and 5NF situations, you found that redundancy isn't actually present if the superkey property holds. In other words, the superkey frustrates prediction opportunities because you can't establish the required context. You can rephrase the definitions of the normal forms to emphasize the superkey aspect. A relation is in BCNF if the left side of every nontrivial FD is a superkey. In other words, a superkey implies every nontrivial FD. A relation is in 4NF if the left side of every nontrivial MVD is a superkey. In other words, a superkey implies every nontrivial MVD. Finally, a relation is in 5NF if every nontrivial JD is implied by superkeys.

In this spirit, define **domain-key normal form** (DK-NF) as follows. A relation satisfies DK-NF when the only constraints on the relation derive from two sources: (1) implications of the superkeys and (2) restriction of attributes values to specified domains. The attractive aspect of DK-NF is that you can enforce all application constraints with primary-key clauses and domain assignments in the SQL that creates the database schema. Moreover, the DBMS can pass the key-constraint enforcement task to the underlying operating system, for example, by maintaining the table as an indexed sequential file. However, as illustrated with the template constraints above, many constraints don't fit this format. Therefore, you usually can't achieve DK-NF with a complex application.

 A relation satisfies domain-key normal form if each constraint either (1) restricts attribute values to a specified domains or (2) is implied by the relation's superkeys.

SUMMARY

A multivalued dependency constraint forces certain tuple pairs to appear in conjunction with related pairs. If $X \longrightarrow Y$ and two tuples agree on X, two mirror tuples must appear, each reflecting the structure of the originals but with the $R - XY$ values interchanged. This constraint is philosophically different from an FD. Where an FD, $X \longrightarrow Y$, *excludes* tuples that agree on X but fail to agree on Y, an MVD, $X \longrightarrow Y$, forces the *inclusion* of tuples to achieve the interchange condition.

An MVD, $X \longrightarrow Y$, applies to a relation R', a subset of the universal relation, if $X \subset R'$. If an MVD applies to R', the interchange condition on $R' - XY$ must hold. But if the MVD interchange condition holds on a subset R', the universal relation is constrained only by a partial interchange restriction. If $X \longrightarrow Y$ applies to a relation, you can losslessly decompose it into $X(Y \cap R')$ and $X(R' - Y)$.

Analyzing the application provides an initial collection of FDs and MVDs. A valid database state satisfies all these constraints. Interaction among the constraints then produces new FDs and MVDs, which must hold for any valid database state. If $\mathcal{F}$ is the initial set of FDs and $\mathcal{M}$ is the initial set of MVDs, the collection of all FDs and MVDs that must be satisfied by any valid database state is the closure of $\mathcal{F} \cup \mathcal{M}$, denoted by $(\mathcal{F} \cup \mathcal{M})^+$. A set of axioms, or inference rules, are available for calculating the closure. These rules resemble Armstrong's axioms for calculating $\mathcal{F}^+$, and they include FD and MVD versions of reflexivity, augmentation, transitivity, composition, decomposition, and pseudotransitivity. Additional rules define complementation, replication, and coalescence. The rules are both sound and complete. When applied to elements of the closure, they always generate results in the closure. Furthermore, you can obtain every FD or MVD in the closure by the repeated application of these rules to the initial set, $\mathcal{F} \cup \mathcal{M}$.

A basis for a collection of sets, $\mathcal{A}$, is a disjoint collection of sets, $\mathcal{B}$, such that each member of $\mathcal{A}$ is a union of selected members of $\mathcal{B}$. A minimal basis is a basis with the property that no other basis contains fewer members. The dependency basis for an attribute set X is a minimal basis for the collection $\{Y \mid X \longrightarrow\!\!\!\!\!\twoheadrightarrow Y \in (\mathcal{F} \cup \mathcal{M})^+\}$. You can compute the dependency basis from the given set of constraints, $\mathcal{F} \cup \mathcal{M}$, as follows. First, augment $\mathcal{M}$ to $\mathcal{M}'$, which contains $U \longrightarrow\!\!\!\!\!\twoheadrightarrow A$ for every A such that $U \longrightarrow AW \in \mathcal{F}$ with $A \notin U$. You then initialize an approximation $\mathcal{C}$ to the single set $\{R - X\}$ and subdivide that set as follows. If an MVD, $U \longrightarrow\!\!\!\!\!\twoheadrightarrow W$, appears in $\mathcal{M}'$ with W intersecting a member of $V \in \mathcal{C}$ and U disjoint from V, you replace V with $V \cap W$ and $V - W$. When subdivision is no longer possible, you complete the construction by adding the individual attributes of X to $\mathcal{C}$ as singleton sets. As a further consequence of the construction, $X \longrightarrow\!\!\!\!\!\twoheadrightarrow A \in (\mathcal{F} \cup \mathcal{M})^+$ if and only if A appears as a singleton in the dependency basis and there exists some $U \longrightarrow AW \in \mathcal{F}$ with $A \notin U$. The dependency basis for X then identifies all attributes determined by X and also all attribute sets multidetermined by X. The latter are precisely those sets that can be expressed as unions of dependency basis elements.

A decomposition of R' into (R_1, R_2) is lossless if R' is constrained by either of the MVDs: $(R_1 \cap R_2) \longrightarrow\!\!\!\!\!\twoheadrightarrow R_1$ or $(R_1 \cap R_2) \longrightarrow\!\!\!\!\!\twoheadrightarrow R_2$. An MVD, $X \longrightarrow\!\!\!\!\!\twoheadrightarrow Y$, introduces redundancy into a relation R' unless it is trivial (i.e., $XY = R'$ or $Y \subset X$) or X is a superkey of R'. A relation R' satisfies fourth normal form (4NF) if every nontrivial MVD, $X \longrightarrow\!\!\!\!\!\twoheadrightarrow Y$, applying to R' has X as a superkey of R'. You can achieve a 4NF decomposition by computing the dependency basis for the left side of a 4NF violator, say X. You then place X, plus all attributes determined by X, in one component of a decomposition and construct an additional component for each remaining element of the dependency basis. In other words, if V is a remaining member of the dependency basis, the corresponding component is (X, V). In this manner, you can algorithmically decompose every relation into 4NF. The lossless-join property holds at each stage of the decomposition, but you can't necessarily guarantee the dependency-preserving property. Any relation satisfying 4NF automatically satisfies BCNF, 3NF, and 2NF.

A general join dependency (JD) specifies a number of components, $(R_1, R_2, \ldots, R_n)$, whose union is the support of the JD. The JD restricts the body of the universal relation such that the projection onto the support is always equal to the join of the projections onto the components. A JD applies to a relation R' when the support of the JD equals R'. A JD forces the inclusion of certain tuples in the universal relation in a more complex manner than that associated with MVDs. In particular, the extraneous tuples introduced by the join of three or more components may be fewer than those introduced by two-way joins. Such constraints do have real-world interpretations, but the context usually seems somewhat contrived. General join dependencies, therefore, don't occur frequently in practice. Nevertheless, JD constraints merit study because they represent the most general pattern where you can eliminate a constraint-induced redundancy through lossless decomposition.

A JD causes no redundancy if one of its components equals the support of the JD or if all its components are superkeys of the support. Actually, a JD might not introduce redundancy even if some of its components aren't superkeys of the support. The precise condition that a JD have no redundancy consequences is that the components contain enough superkeys to reassemble the support through a lossless join. A JD satisfies this criterion if and only if the JD is a logical consequence of the key constraints on the support. You can test the condition with the algorithm `forceJD`, which continually merges components that contain a common key. If algorithm `forceJD` can't recover the support relation, the constraint does cause redundancy, which you can then eliminate with a fifth normal form (5NF) decomposition.

A relation R' is in 5NF if every JD that applies to R' is logically implied by the key constraints on R'. In practice, you obtain a 5NF decomposition by performing a 4NF decomposition and then analyzing the application for those JDs that apply to the relationship tables. You can also use the chase algorithm to obtain all JDs that follow from the given set of FDs, MVDs, and JDs. Because you can discover all JDs in this manner, you can decompose any relation into 5NF. The method simply decomposes any relation into the subcomponents specified by a JD that is a 5NF violator for the relation. When no further 5NF violators apply, the decomposition must satisfy 5NF. If all relations of a decomposition satisfy 5NF, they satisfy 4NF as well. Abusing the notation somewhat, you can write 3NF for the relations that satisfy 3NF, and similarly for the other categories. Then 5NF $\subset$ 4NF $\subset$ BCNF $\subset$ 3NF $\subset$ 2NF $\subset$ 1NF.

A remarkable simplification occurs if all keys are singleton attributes. In this case, a relation that satisfies 3NF automatically satisfies BCNF, 4NF, and 5NF. Although this observation provides a simple mechanism for ensuring higher normal forms, it is difficult to use because relations that express many-to-many relationships inherently contain composite keys.

FDs, MVDs, and JDs are special cases of a more general class of constraints called template constraints. You express a template constraint as a logical syllogism, where one or more conclusion predicates follow a collection of premise predicates. You can express FDs, MVDs, and JDs in template format. This format also extends to constraints that you can't enforce with decomposition techniques. You can, however, construct SQL create-assertion clauses to maintain the more general template constraints.

R		
A	B	C
$\vdots$	$\vdots$	$\vdots$
1	2	3
1	4	5
1	6	7
$\vdots$	$\vdots$	$\vdots$

(a)

R			
A	B	C	D
$\vdots$	$\vdots$	$\vdots$	$\vdots$
1	2	3	4
1	5	6	7
$\vdots$	$\vdots$	$\vdots$	$\vdots$

(b)

$\mathcal{F} \cup \mathcal{M}$
$A \longrightarrow\!\!\!\rightarrow BCDF$
$A \longrightarrow\!\!\!\rightarrow CDE$
$E \longrightarrow\!\!\!\rightarrow B$
$BF \longrightarrow\!\!\!\rightarrow C$

(c)

$\mathcal{F}$	$\mathcal{M}$
$F \longrightarrow A$	$AB \longrightarrow\!\!\!\rightarrow CD$
$BF \longrightarrow CE$	$C \longrightarrow\!\!\!\rightarrow E$
$A \longrightarrow D$	
$E \longrightarrow B$	

(d)

Figure 19.6 Tables for MVD exercises

Multivalued dependencies

1. Suppose $A \longrightarrow\!\!\!\rightarrow B$ constrains the relation in Figure 19.6(a) and the indicated tuples appear in the body. What other tuples can you predict?

2. Suppose $A \longrightarrow\!\!\!\rightarrow B$ and $B \longrightarrow\!\!\!\rightarrow C$ constrain the relation in Figure 19.6(b) and the indicated tuples appear in the body. What other tuples can you predict?

Interactions among FDs and MVDs and the dependency basis

Find the minimal basis for the following collections.

3. $\{ACE, BDF, ADE, BFG\}$.

4. $\{AB, ABCD, ABCDEF, ABCDEFGH\}$.

5. $\{ABCDEF, CDFGHIJ, ABHI\}$.

   Suppose $R = ABCDEFG$, and $\mathcal{F} \cup \mathcal{M}$ is given by Figure 19.6(c).

6. Calculate the dependency basis for AG.

7. Identify $(AG; \mathcal{F} \cup \mathcal{M})$ from the dependency basis of the preceding exercise.

8. Verify that $(AG; \mathcal{F} \cup \mathcal{M})$ is strictly larger than $(AG; \mathcal{F})$.

   Prove the following statements by giving a table excerpt where the required tuples must appear.

9. If $X \longrightarrow\!\!\!\rightarrow Y$ and $WY \longrightarrow\!\!\!\rightarrow Z$ hold, then $WX \longrightarrow\!\!\!\rightarrow (Z - WY)$ holds. This is the pseudotransitivity rule for MVDs, and the text showed that it follows from transitivity and augmentation. Prove it in this exercise by assuming an excerpt where two tuples agree on WX and demonstrating the appearance of the required supplementary tuples.

10. If $X \longrightarrow\!\!\!\rightarrow Y$, $Y \longrightarrow\!\!\!\rightarrow Z$, and $Z \longrightarrow\!\!\!\rightarrow W$, then $X(Y \cap Z) \longrightarrow\!\!\!\rightarrow (W - Z)$.

11. Prove the result of the preceding exercise using the FD-MVD inference rules.

Fourth normal form

Let $R = ABCDEF$, subject to the constraints in Figure 19.6(d).

12. Find a lossless-join, dependency-preserving decomposition of R that satisfies 2NF but violates 3NF.

13. Find a lossless-join, dependency-preserving decomposition of R that satisfies 3NF but violates BCNF.

14. Find a lossless-join decomposition of R that satisfies BCNF but violates 4NF.

15. Determine if the decomposition of the preceding exercise is dependency-preserving.

16. Find a lossless-join decomposition of R that satisfies 4NF.

Suppose that flight legs are scheduled trips between specific cities. A flight leg is a (fno, fname, source, destination, time) tuple, where fno is a key. The source and destination values are the cities at the beginning and terminating airports, and the time is the departure day and hour (e.g., Monday—15:00). The flight repeats weekly. A pilot is a (pno, pname, rating) triple, and pno is a key. An airplane is a (ano, aname) pair, and ano is a key. The three entities participate in a ternary relationship. Each relationship instance records the involvement of a particular pilot and a particular airplane on a specified flight leg. A given tuple from any of the three entities can enter many times into relationship instances. A particular flight leg must be symmetrically represented with respect to its pilots and airplanes. In other words, if p is the group of pilots who have flown the flight leg and if a is the group of airplanes used on the flight leg, then relationship instances must exist that relate each pair from $(p \times a)$ with the flight leg.

17. Capture the constraints in a set of FDs and MVDs.

18. Exhibit a lossless BCNF decomposition that contains a 4NF violation.

19. Exhibit a lossless 4NF decomposition.

General join dependencies

20. Suppose JD(AB, BC, AC) constrains the relation on the left below. What other tuples can you predict?

21. Suppose EJD(AB, BC, AC) constrains the relation in the center below. What predictions can you make for the table?

22. Suppose JD(AB, BC, AC) constrains the relation on the right below. What other tuples can you predict?

R		
A	B	C
⋮	⋮	⋮
1	2	3
4	5	6
4	2	7
1	8	7
⋮	⋮	⋮

R			
A	B	C	D
⋮	⋮	⋮	⋮
1	2	3	9
4	5	6	10
4	2	7	11
1	8	7	12
⋮	⋮	⋮	⋮

R		
A	B	C
⋮	⋮	⋮
1	2	3
4	5	3
6	2	7
4	8	7
4	2	9
⋮	⋮	⋮

A preceding exercise described a ternary relationship among pilots, airplanes, and flight legs. The three primary entities are as follows. A flight leg is a (fno, fname, source, destination, time) tuple, a pilot is a (pno, pname, rating) triple, and an airplane is a (ano, aname) pair. Change the context from the preceding exercise as follows. Relationship instances are now quadruples of the form (fno, pno, ano, date), where the date value records the calendar date when the pilot and airplane cooperated to complete the flight leg. As before, a particular flight leg must be symmetrically represented with respect to its pilots and airplanes. If p is the group of pilots who have flown the flight leg and if a is the group of airplanes used on the flight leg, then relationship instances must exist that relate each pair from $(p \times a)$ with the flight leg.

23. Capture the constraints in a set of FDs, MVDs, JDs, and EJDs.

24. Exhibit a lossless 4NF decomposition.

25. What redundancy remains in the 4NF decomposition?

Fifth normal form

Let $R = ABCDEFGHIJKLM$ be constrained as follows:

$\mathcal{G}$
$AB \longrightarrow CD$
$D \longrightarrow EF$
$GH \longrightarrow IJ$
$J \longrightarrow G$
$K \longrightarrow LM$
$KLM \longrightarrow\!\!\!\!\rightarrow ABCDEF$
EJD(KA, AB, BK)

26. Reduce the FDs of $\mathcal{G}$ to a minimal cover.

27. Find a lossless-join decomposition of R that satisfies 2NF but violates 3NF.

28. Find a lossless-join decomposition of R that satisfies 3NF but violates BCNF.

29. Find a lossless-join decomposition of R that satisfies BCNF but violates 4NF.

30. Find a lossless-join decomposition of R that satisfies 4NF but violates 5NF.

31. Find a lossless-join decomposition of R that satisfies 5NF.

A company markets products for many manufacturers. The three primary entities are salesman, product, and manufacturer. A salesman is a (sno, sname, sphone) triple, and sno is a key. A product is a (pno, pname, pcolor) triple, and pno is a key. A manufacturer is a (mname, mcity, mstate, mzipcode, reliability) 5-tuple, and (mname, mcity) is a key. Several manufacturers can have the same name, but they must be located in different cities. A city, of course, remains fixed in a particular state. Although many zipcodes exist in each city, a particular zipcode always remains associated with one city. The reliability factor for a manufacturer is a function only of the state where the manufacturer is located. Some states provide adequate physical transportation systems and minimal paperwork obstacles to the movement of manufactured goods while other states are less generous in these respects. The ternary relationship among the three entities is such that any given entity instance can appear in many relationship groupings. For example, salesmen represent the products of many manufacturers, and different manufacturers can make the same products. In the face of such arbitrary groupings of salesman, product, and manufacturer, the company operates under the following rule, which it provides for its customers' convenience. If a customer knows that salesman S carries product P, and he knows that product P is available from manufacturer M, and he knows that salesman S represents manufacturer M, then he can be assured that the salesman S carries product P for manufacturer M.

32. Capture the constraints with FDs, MVDs, and JDs.

33. Reduce the FDs to a minimal collection.

34. Exhibit a lossless-join 2NF decomposition that violates 3NF.

35. Exhibit a lossless-join 3NF decomposition that violates BCNF.

36. Exhibit a lossless-join 4NF decomposition that violates 5NF.

37. Exhibit a lossless-join 5NF decomposition.

Consider the salesman-product-manufacturer situation from above, but add the attributes quantity and date to the ternary relationship. In other words, a specific interaction of a salesman, product, and manufacturer is further described with the quantity of product sold and the date of the sale.

38. Exhibit a lossless-join decomposition that satisfies 5NF.

Beyond join dependencies

39. Let $R = ABCD$. Express a template constraint equivalent to JD(AB, BC, CD, DA).

40. Let $R = ABCD$. Express a template constraint for the following restriction. If two tuples agree on their AB attributes, either their C attributes agree or their D attributes differ.

41. Compose an SQL assertion to enforce the constraint of the preceding exercise.

42. Assume that $R(A, B, C, D)$ is a predicate that is true when $ABCD$ bind to values such that the resulting tuple is in R. Exhibit an inference rule that enforces the constraint of the preceding exercise in a deductive database.

IV EPILOGUE

THIS TEXT HAS EXPLORED THREE MAJOR THEMES: DATABASE MODELS, access languages, and design. Part I introduced five models and investigated the associated query languages. The popular relational model received the most detailed treatment because it is currently the most widely used. Although the relational model continues to evolve, the object-oriented and deductive models provide new perspectives that are more suitable for modern applications, particularly those emphasizing non-textual data elements. The likely outcome is that some well-adapted combination of relational, object-oriented, and deductive concepts will appear in the near future. The older hierarchical and network models were also discussed in Part I. The presentations for these five models were parallel: each compared approaches to data representation, relationship linkages, constraints, and query facilities. Part II reviewed the physical disk file and indexing mechanisms that underlie the features on the database models. Part III covered selected aspects of database design, including two examples of semantic modeling tools and a detailed treatment of functional dependency analysis.

The database models, languages, and design aspects covered to this point are the basic components of database management systems. However, many advanced features build on these basic concepts. Part IV provides a single-chapter introduction to several advanced features: concurrency, recovery, security, and query optimization—all performance-related topics. Because of space considerations, the material is abbreviated. Indeed, each of these topics is the subject of entire textbooks, so you should consider the final chapter as a pointer toward further study. Unlike the preceding chapters, Chapter 20 presents most results without proofs.

20 Performance

THIS CHAPTER DISCUSSES SEVERAL PERFORMANCE TOPICS. So far, the text has concentrated on the expected functionality of a DBMS: storage mechanisms for data and relationships, query expressions, and semantic modeling constraints. Except for the chapters on files and indexes, the discussions haven't been concerned with the efficiency of the underlying processes. This chapter's goal, by contrast, is to provide an overview of selected performance issues.

One of the most pressing efficiency concerns is concurrency. If the database is to function as a central coordinated repository of information, many agents must be able to conduct simultaneous interchanges with the DBMS. Unfortunately, the competing agents' transactions can interfere with each other, so the first section explains the standard techniques of locking and timestamping that solve this problem. A second topic is failure recovery. The database typically retains some data in memory buffers, where it is vulnerable to power interruptions, programming errors, and a variety of other threats. The DBMS must be able to recover from failures that destroy memory buffers before they have been transferred to disk. It must also handle more catastrophic disasters where the disk storage itself is destroyed or corrupted. The third section deals with security issues, in particular with methods for restricting access to selected portions of the database to certain users or programs. Finally, the chapter concludes with a section on query optimization. It illustrates relational algebra transformations that can convert an inefficient query into an equivalent one with greatly enhanced execution speed.

The chapter uses a relational database context. You can use similar techniques with the other models. The topics are relatively independent of each other; they do, however, draw on material from the earlier chapters of the text. The section on failure recovery also assumes that you understand transaction concepts, which are introduced in the concurrency discussion.

867

Concurrency

Because the DBMS must respond to simultaneous requests from several users, conflicts arise when these users converge on the same data elements. Consider a banking application where a balance table records the funds available in each account. Suppose two agents, A and B, intend to reduce the balance of account 754 by $50.00 each. Presumably, the owner of account 754 has made two purchases, each in the amount of $50.00, and he has authorized the appropriate transfer of funds from his account. Referring to the table excerpt to the left below, you see that the net effect of this activity should reduce the account balance by $100.00 to $214.60. Each agent reads the account balance and updates the value by subtracting $50.00. Suppose the timing of these actions is as shown to the right below. You should read time as increasing in a downward direction. Agent B's update overwrites agent A's. This overwrite would be acceptable if agent B were working with the results produced by agent A. However, the DBMS interleaves the read-write activities of the two agents, so agent B actually works with the balance as it existed before the change performed by agent A. The net result is that the final balance figure is wrong.

Account	Balance
⋮	⋮
754	314.60
821	659.20
⋮	⋮

Agent A	Agent B
read account 754 ($314.60)	
	read account 754 ($314.60)
update account 754 ($264.60)	
	update account 754 ($264.60)

A number of scenarios illustrate the negative consequences of mutual interference between independent database activities. The problem just examined is the **lost-update scenario**.

Transactions

A **transaction** is an indivisible unit of work that the DBMS must accomplish in an all-or-nothing fashion. In other words, the DBMS completes all the database activity in the transaction in a consistent manner. It completes the transaction as though no other agents were simultaneously accessing the database, or it aborts the process and leaves no trace of the attempted execution. In the example above, each agent's task should be a transaction with two database accesses: one to read the account balance and the other to update it. If the DBMS recognizes transactions, it must disallow the scenario above because it doesn't treat either agent's activity as an indivisible unit. Agent A doesn't enjoy exclusive use of the database for the duration of his transaction. Instead, he shares the database with agent B, and harmful interference results.

A transaction is an application-level unit of activity, which specifies an explicit division of responsibility between the DBMS and the application. The application is responsible for defining the content of each transaction and for determining the submission order to the DBMS. The DBMS is responsible for executing each transaction in an atomic and consistent manner. It treats each transaction as though it were running in isolation from its competitors. The acronym ACID summarizes the contractual obligations of the DBMS in processing a transaction. ACID means atomic, consistent, isolated, and durable. The last property ensures that the DBMS permanently records a successful transaction's results in the database with appropriate safeguards to survive subsequent software or hardware failures.

Suppose you have a database command, begin transaction, to alert the DBMS that an indivisible unit of work is beginning. The unit will end in one of two ways. If the submitting agent, a person or a program, detects no irregularities in the processing, the last action of the transaction will be a commit command. This means the DBMS should establish a permanent record of the results in the database and make them available to any subsequent transaction. If the processing agent detects an error, it issues instead the rollback command. This means the DBMS should restore the database to the state that existed when the transaction started. In this case, the net result is as if the transaction were never attempted.

With these commands, the DBMS can adopt an obvious strategy to eliminate interference between transactions. If a transaction is in process when an agent issues a begin transaction, the DBMS blocks the new transaction until the existing one completes. With this disentanglement, the example above now appears as shown to the left below. This approach clearly eliminates interference, but it's unnecessarily pessimistic in assuming that any concurrent activity poses an interference threat. If agent B were operating on a different account, he could proceed in parallel and interleave his read-write activity with agent A. Both agents could still correctly complete their tasks. Moreover, even if both agents access the same data, the DBMS might still interleave some individual database calls without jeopardizing the final results. For example, suppose you expand the transactions to include a credit to another account. The owner of account 754 makes his purchases from the owner of account 821. When you reduce account 754, you must increase account 831 by the same amount. In each transaction, the DBMS should record the credits and debits as one indivisible unit of work. The final result of both transactions is that account 754 decreases by $100.00 to $214.60, and account 821 increases by $100.00 to $759.20. Consider the timing scenario to the right above, which operates without transaction control.

Both agents correctly install their updates, and the final balances in both accounts are correct. You can conclude, therefore, that complete exclusion of concurrent activity isn't necessary to guarantee the atomic nature of transactions. Indeed, the notion of a transaction is an application-level concept, which the DBMS can realize in many ways. When apprised of a transaction, the DBMS must process any concurrent activity so that the final result is as if the transaction were running in isolation. For performance reasons, it can interleave the database calls from competing transactions, provided the final result is as if one transaction completed before the other started.

Agent A	Agent B	Agent A	Agent B
⋮	⋮	⋮	⋮
begin transaction read account 754 ($314.60)		read account 754 ($314.60)	
⋮	⋮	⋮	⋮
	begin transaction wait	update account 754 ($264.60)	
⋮	⋮	⋮	⋮
update account 754 ($264.60)	wait		read account 754 ($264.60)
⋮	⋮	⋮	⋮
commit	wait read account 754 ($264.60)	read account 821 ($659.20)	
⋮	⋮	⋮	update account 754 ($214.60)
	update account 754 ($214.60)	⋮	⋮
⋮	⋮	update account 821 ($709.20)	
	commit	⋮	⋮
			read account 821 ($709.20)
		⋮	⋮
			update account 821 ($759.20)

 A transaction is an indivisible unit of work that can contain many database calls. The DBMS completes a transaction in its entirety, or it returns the database to a state as though the execution were never attempted.

Serializable schedules

Suppose you have n transactions, $T_1, T_2, \ldots, T_n$. The database calls of T_i are $c_{i1}, c_{i2}, \ldots, c_{im_i}$, listed in order of appearance. A **schedule** for $T_1, T_2, \ldots, T_n$ is a linear arrangement of the c_{ij} that preserves the order of the calls within any given transaction. In other words, if $d_1, d_2, \ldots$ is a schedule for the transactions, and $d_s = c_{ij}, d_t = c_{ik}$, with $j < k$, then $s < t$. A schedule can interleave the database calls from the transactions in any manner, provided the calls from a given transaction always appear in chronological order. In the example above, refer to the activity of agent A as transaction T_1 and to the work of agent B as T_2. The database calls for the two transactions then appear on the left below. The particular schedule followed in the processing scenario appears to the right.

T_1	T_2
c_{11}: read account 754	c_{21}: read account 754
c_{12}: update account 754	c_{22}: update account 754
c_{13}: read account 821	c_{23}: read account 821
c_{14}: update account 821	c_{24}: update account 821

c_{11}: read account 754
c_{12}: update account 754
c_{21}: read account 754
c_{13}: read account 821
c_{22}: update account 754
c_{14}: update account 821
c_{23}: read account 821
c_{24}: update account 821.

So a schedule can achieve the results of isolated transactions even though it interleaves the individual database calls from its constituent transactions. This type of schedule is a **serializable** schedule. The formal definition is as follows. A schedule for transactions $T_1, T_2, \ldots, T_n$ is serializable if there exists a permutation $(i_1, i_2, \ldots, i_n)$ of $(1, 2, \ldots, n)$, such that the database state resulting from performing the database calls in the schedule's sequence is the same as that achieved by running the transactions in isolation in the order $T_{i_1}, T_{i_2}, \ldots, T_{i_n}$. The property that a collection of transaction admits a serializable schedule is called **serializability**.

The schedule illustrated above is serializable because the net effect is as if T_1 were completed in its entirety before the start of T_2. In this particular example, the DBMS could achieve the same effect by first completing T_2 and then running T_1. However, the definition of serializability doesn't specify that the result must be the same as *all* possible orderings of the transactions. Indeed, it doesn't even require that the result correspond to some specified ordering, such as $T_1, T_2, \ldots, T_n$. It simply requires that the result must be the same as that achieved by one possible ordering. In other words, if the DBMS receives a group of transactions simultaneously, it only guarantees that the final result will reflect *some* ordering of the transactions. Therefore, the serializability guarantees that the final database state appears as if T_1 ran before T_2 or as if T_2 ran before T_1. Although both orderings produce the same database result in this example, this is a coincidence.

For a more informative example, suppose a database record contains an item X, whose current value is 5. Transaction T_1 doubles the value of X; transaction T_2 increments X by 1. If T_1 runs before T_2, X becomes $2(5) + 1 = 11$. If T_2 runs before T_1, X becomes $2(5 + 1) = 12$. The final database state is clearly different for these two scenarios. However, a DBMS that is enforcing serializable schedules can choose either of them. Serializablity means that the final results are as if the transactions were run in isolation in some order, but not in a particular order that you can specify beforehand. This is a reasonable responsibility for the DBMS. If you submit a number of simultaneous transactions, the DBMS can't infer any particular preferred order, but it can ensure some arbitrarily chosen order.

 A serializable schedule is a linear arrangement of the database calls from several transactions with the property: the final database state obtained by executing the calls in schedule order is the same as that obtained by running the transactions in some unspecified serial order.

Serializability through locks

Two standard approaches guarantee serializability: locks and timestamps. A **lock** is an access privilege on a database object, which the DBMS grants to a particular transaction.

New transaction requests	Existing transaction holds		
	None	Shared	Exclusive
Shared	Yes	Yes	No
Exclusive	Yes	No	No

Figure 20.1   Matrix of permissions for obtaining an exclusive or shared lock

To allow the privileged transaction to complete its work without undue interference, the lock restricts the access of competing transactions to the database object. You want to restrict the competing transactions no more than necessary to allow the privileged transaction to acquire the database objects that it needs. So you can invoke locks in varying strengths. A stronger lock gives more freedom to the privileged transaction but places tighter restrictions on its competitors. The exclusive lock and the shared lock represent two commonly used strength levels. The exclusive lock is the stronger: it prevents *any* access to the locked object by competing transactions. By contrast, the shared lock permits competing transactions to view the locked object but not to change it.

In the relational model, the locked object can be a field within a tuple, a tuple, a table, or the entire database. The **granularity** of the lock refers to the size of the locked object. When you lock a field within a tuple, the locking granularity is fine. When you lock the entire database, the granularity is coarse. Locks on objects of intermediate size represent granularity levels between these extremes.

A transaction must hold an exclusive lock on an object to modify it. A lock manager module within the DBMS grants such locks upon request by a transaction, but only if no other transaction currently holds a lock of either strength on the object. On the other hand, the lock manager grants a shared lock request even if another transaction holds a shared lock on the same object, provided no other transaction holds an exclusive lock on the object. Figure 20.1 summarizes the rules for obtaining a lock of a specified strength.

 Shared locks permit concurrent reads but no updates. Exclusive locks prevent any concurrent access. A shared or exclusive lock lets you read an object, but you need an exclusive lock to update it.

The **two-phase locking protocol** is a discipline that transactions can use to ensure serializability. The first phase is characterized by the monotonic acquisition of new locks or the strengthening of existing locks. During this growing phase, you can't release a lock or downgrade it in strength from exclusive to shared. The second phase involves the monotonic downgrade or release of existing locks. During this shrinking phase, you can't acquire a new lock or upgrade an existing lock's strength from shared to exclusive.

If all transactions obey the two-phase locking protocol, a serializable schedule always results. Rollbacks, however, can still cause interference problems. For example, suppose transaction A writes a data element, and then releases all its locks in the shrinking phase. Transaction B then acquires the proper lock in its growing phase and reads the data element. But transaction A now issues a rollback. Even though the schedule is serializable, with all of A's database activities preceding B's, the process leaves transaction B in an untenable situation. B has read a data element that was written by a transaction whose very existence is denied. In a sense, B has seen "unreal" data.

The DBMS must enforce a more restrictive discipline to prevent this problem. In the **strict two-phase locking protocol**, each transaction holds all its locks until it commits or rolls back. When the commit or rollback is secure, it releases all the locks. In other words, the shrinking phase occurs all at once, immediately after the transaction terminates. This more restrictive policy prevents the problem illustrated with transactions A and B.

 In the two-phase locking protocol, each transaction has two phases: a growing phase, when it acquires or upgrades locks, and a shrinking phase, when it releases or downgrades locks. Strict two-phase locking further restricts the shrinking phase to the moment after the transaction terminates.

Deadlock and the transaction dependency graph

Certain interference scenarios illustrate the effectiveness of the two-phase locking protocol. For this section, assume a locking granularity at the tuple level. First, reconsider the lost-update example. The timing now unfolds as follows and reveals an unexpected difficulty.

T_1	T_2
⋮	⋮
begin transaction	begin transaction
⋮	⋮
get shared lock on account 754 tuple	
lock granted	
read account 754 ($314.60)	
⋮	⋮
	get shared lock on account 754 tuple
	lock granted
	read account 754 ($314.60)
⋮	⋮
get exclusive lock on account 754 tuple	
wait	
⋮	⋮
wait	get exclusive lock on account 754 tuple
wait	wait
wait	wait

When transaction T_1 requests an exclusive lock on the target tuple, in preparation for updating the value, the lock manager denies the request because T_2 holds a shared lock on the same tuple. Therefore, T_1 blocks and waits for T_2 to release its lock. Unfortunately, T_2 then progresses to the point where it wants to update the tuple, and it seeks to upgrade its lock to the exclusive level. The DBMS, of course, denies the request because T_1 holds a shared lock on the tuple. This situation is a **deadlock**. Neither transaction can make progress because each is waiting on a resource that is locked by the other.

This example involves only two transactions, but deadlock can occur with more participants. You can have T_1 waiting for T_2 to release some lock. Meanwhile, T_2 is stalled, waiting for T_3 to release a lock. This mutual dependence propagates to a transaction T_n, which is holding until T_1 releases some object. Deadlock occurs when a cycle exists in these dependencies, so the first step toward a solution must detect the cycle. To this end, the DBMS maintains a graph, the **transaction dependency graph**, where each active transaction appears as a node. When a transaction, T_i, requests a lock that the DBMS can't grant, the DBMS blocks the transaction and installs an arc from node T_i to each conflicting transaction node in the transaction dependency graph. For example, if T_i requests an exclusive lock, and several other transactions currently hold shared locks on the target, the DBMS draws arcs from T_i to each of the conflicting transaction nodes. Of course, if a competing transaction holds an exclusive lock on the target, no other transaction can have locks of any kind. In this case, the DBMS draws a single arc.

When the DBMS detects a cycle in the dependency graph, it chooses a node in the cycle and issues a `rollback` command on behalf of that transaction. The affected transaction is the **victim**. The DBMS-commanded rollback reverses any changes that the victim has executed. Because the victim didn't complete, it must still hold an exclusive lock on any updated item, so no other transaction has seen the results of that update. The rollback also releases any locks held by the victim, which allows other transactions to proceed. After other transactions have made some progress, the DBMS restarts the victim.

With this safeguard in place, the lost-update scenario continues as shown in Figure 20.2. When T_2 restarts, T_1 hasn't yet committed, so T_2 must wait for a shared lock to read the account tuple. However, this wait doesn't cause a deadlock because T_1 isn't waiting on T_2. No cycle appears in the dependency graph, and both transactions then complete with the correct results.

When the DBMS must sacrifice a transaction to break a deadlock, it can choose an arbitrary node in the cycle, it can choose the transaction that has accrued the least amount of processing time, it can choose the transaction that started first, or the one that started last. The particular mechanism varies from one DBMS to another. But the DBMS must have some provision to ensure that it doesn't repeatedly sacrifice the same transaction. In other words, it must avoid the **livelock** situation, where a transaction T becomes the victim, achieves a restart, and then finds itself in another deadlock as the victim.

   A deadlock involves a chain of transactions that are cyclically waiting for each other to release a lock. The DBMS detects deadlock with a transaction dependency graph. It resolves the impasse by sacrificing one of the transactions in the cycle.

Dirty reads, unrepeatable reads, and phantoms

Another scenario is the **dirty read**. Transaction B reads an object that was previously updated by transaction A. Transaction A then terminates with a `rollback`, which retracts the update. The process leaves transaction B in possession of data that should never have existed. This scenario appeared earlier as justification for a strict two-phase locking protocol. In the absence of transaction locks, the dirty-read situation unfolds as shown to the left below. The result is now incorrect because the final balance should be $264.60, given that one of

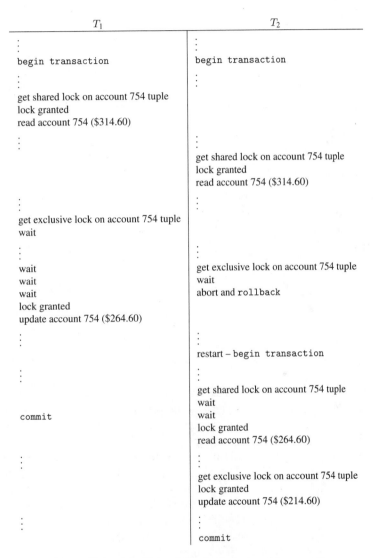

T_1	T_2
:	:
begin transaction	begin transaction
:	:
get shared lock on account 754 tuple	
lock granted	
read account 754 ($314.60)	
:	:
	get shared lock on account 754 tuple
	lock granted
	read account 754 ($314.60)
:	:
get exclusive lock on account 754 tuple	
wait	
:	:
wait	get exclusive lock on account 754 tuple
wait	wait
wait	abort and rollback
lock granted	
update account 754 ($264.60)	
:	:
	restart – begin transaction
:	:
	get shared lock on account 754 tuple
	wait
commit	wait
	lock granted
	read account 754 ($264.60)
:	:
	get exclusive lock on account 754 tuple
	lock granted
	update account 754 ($214.60)
:	:
	commit

Figure 20.2   A locking solution to the lost-update scenario

the $50.00 debits was canceled. With the strict two-phase locking protocol, this processing sequence can't occur. Instead, events proceed as in Figure 20.3.

T_1	T_2
⋮	⋮
begin transaction	
read account 754	
($314.60)	
⋮	⋮
update account 754	
($264.60)	
⋮	⋮
	begin transaction
	read account 754
	($264.60)
⋮	⋮
rollback	
⋮	⋮
	update account 754
	($214.60)
⋮	⋮
	commit

T_1	T_2
⋮	⋮
begin transaction	
read account 754	
($314.60)	
⋮	⋮
	begin transaction
	read account 754
	($314.60)
⋮	⋮
	update account 754
	($264.60)
⋮	⋮
	commit
⋮	⋮
read account 754	
($264.60)	
interference detected!	
⋮	⋮

Another problem is the **unrepeatable read**. In this case, a transaction reads an object that is then changed by a competing transaction. When the first transaction reads the object a second time, it encounters a new value. Obviously, the transaction now knows that it isn't the sole proprietor of the database. Consider the scenario to the right above, where the locking protocol isn't used. In this case, you might object that T_1 has no reason to reread the tuple because it has already transferred the account balance to memory. Nevertheless, if the DBMS guarantees serializability, the transaction shouldn't be able to perform operations that let it detect the presence of competing transactions. This would compromise the illusion of isolated execution. Moreover, in the general case, the transaction may read, on the first access, only selected attributes from the database record. After further processing, it may discover that it needs more of the record. In any case, a second read of the tuple should reveal no changes in the data that has already been acquired.

The locking protocol clears up the unrepeatable-read problem, as illustrated in Figure 20.4. The read operation is now repeatable in transaction T_1 because T_2 must have an exclusive lock to perform the update, and it can't upgrade its shared lock. T_1 can now read the locked object as often as desired with repeatable results. T_1 must terminate before the DBMS will grant T_2 the exclusive lock needed for the update.

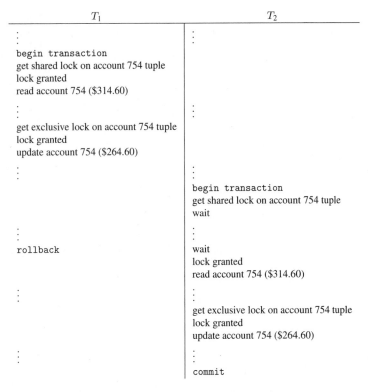

Figure 20.3   Locking solution to the dirty read scenario

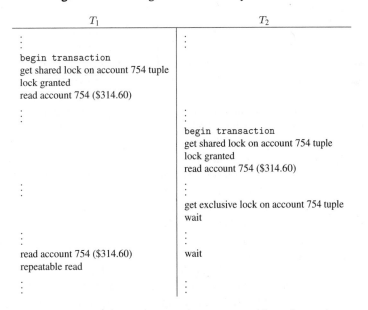

Figure 20.4   Locking solution to the non-repeatable read scenario

After termination, the unrepeatable-read problem can't occur because you can't expect the DBMS to provide repeatable reads across transactions. Serializability requires the final result to appear as though the DBMS performs the transactions in some serial order. Therefore, when a transaction closes, serializability allows the DBMS to interpose another transaction that updates a value observed in the closed transaction.

The last example noted that the DBMS can't guarantee serializability if a transaction can detect the concurrent presence of a competing transaction. You can easily concoct an example to prove this point. Suppose you have a numeric attribute X in some database table, and you have n transactions, $T_1, T_2, \ldots, T_n$, where T_i performs the following activity.

```
engage in activity to detect a competing transaction;
if (competitor is found)
   change the value of X to -1;
else if (X ≥ 0)
   change the value of X to i;
```

Suppose you initialize the value of X to 0 and then submit all n transactions simultaneously. Any serializable schedule corresponds to some ordering of the transactions, say $T_{i_1}, T_{i_2}, \ldots, T_{i_n}$, which results in a final X value of $i_n > 0$. But if any transaction detects the presence of another, it changes the value of X to -1. From that point on, no transaction makes any further change. When $X = -1$, the database's final state corresponds to no possible ordering of the transactions, and, therefore, represents the execution of a non-serializable schedule. So if the scheduling strategy doesn't prevent unrepeatable reads, transactions can defeat serializability. The locking protocol does prevent unrepeatable reads and thus blocks this particular method of detecting a concurrent transaction.

A more difficult scenario is the **phantom**. When a transaction observes a value, it must hold a shared lock on the containing object at some level of granularity. This shared lock prevents a competing transaction from acquiring the exclusive lock needed to modify the object. However, it doesn't prevent a competing transaction from creating a new object that can influence the observed values. For example, suppose T_1 observes a collection of values through some search condition, and T_2 subsequently creates a new object that satisfies the same search condition. If T_1 requeries on the search condition, it will obtain different results. The new object that appears in the second run of the query is a phantom. To illustrate the point, expand the example to include a "category" attribute. The account table now appears on the left below.

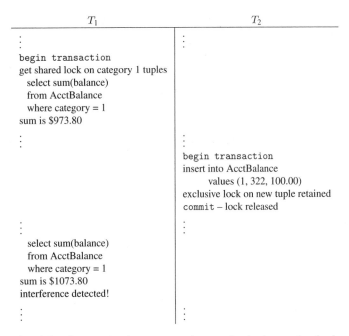

AcctBalance		
category	account	balance
⋮	⋮	⋮
1	754	314.60
1	821	659.20
2	438	246.10
⋮	⋮	⋮

T_1	T_2
⋮	⋮

`begin transaction`
get shared lock on category 1 tuples
   select sum(balance)
   from AcctBalance
   where category = 1
sum is $973.80	

⋮	⋮
	`begin transaction` insert into AcctBalance values (1, 322, 100.00) exclusive lock on new tuple retained `commit` – lock released
	⋮
select sum(balance) from AcctBalance where category = 1 sum is $1073.80 interference detected!	
⋮	⋮

Consider the schedule on the right above. An insert operation can't obtain a prior lock on the new tuple because it doesn't yet exist. However, when the DBMS completes the insertion, it gives the creating transaction an exclusive lock on the new tuple.

The phantom is a generalization of the non-repeatable read. Like the non-repeatable read, it reveals the existence of a competing transaction, which compromises serializability. You can use the two-phase locking strategy to prevent phantoms, but the DBMS must lock objects larger than the individual tuples that have been observed or updated by the transaction. When a transaction observes multiple related values with a search criterion, the DBMS must isolate the contributing tuples as a snapshot. It places a shared lock on the snapshot and requires any competing activity that would change the snapshot to have an exclusive lock on it. Because it defines the snapshot, the search criterion itself is the tangible object for locking. A transaction that wants to create a new tuple must first obtain an exclusive lock on any search criterion that admits the new tuple. Only search criteria used in existing transactions exist as lockable objects. This expansion of the locking capability resolves the phantom problem, as shown in Figure 20.5.

 The dirty-read, unrepeatable read, and phantom scenarios represent interference among competing transactions that can jeopardize serializability. The strict two-phase locking protocol resolves these problems.

Isolation levels

Although you can enforce serializability and correctness with the strict two-phase locking protocol, you may want to operate without a serializability guarantee. Suppose, for example,

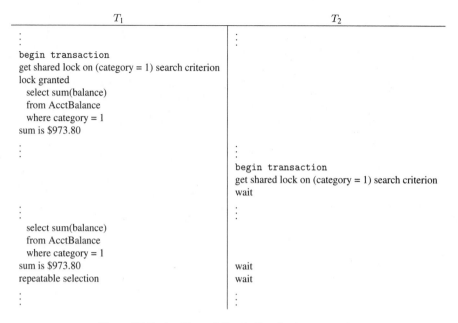

Figure 20.5   Locking solution to the phantom scenario

that all database updates take place during a special time (e.g., at night) when no other transactions compete for the system. The locking overhead unnecessarily decreases the database performance. To accommodate such special situations, SQL allows the user to set the **isolation level** for transactions issued from that user's session. The isolation level specifies the amount of tolerable interference from competing transactions. The user can choose from four levels, ranging from no protection to a full serializability guarantee. The levels are read-uncommitted, read-committed, repeatable read, and serializable.

The weakest level is read-uncommitted, which amounts to operation without any locks. With this level of isolation, all the interference scenarios are possible. The next level, read-committed, requires an exclusive lock to update an object but no locks for a read operation. Even so, the read is possible only if another transaction doesn't hold an exclusive lock. Recall that a dirty read occurs when a transaction modifies an object and then terminates with a rollback that retracts the update. A second transaction, however, manages to read the modified object during its brief existence. An exclusive lock on the updated object prevents the dirty read because the second transaction can't access the modified value until the first transaction terminates. When it terminates with a rollback, the DBMS returns the object to its initial state, and no dirty read is possible. An unrepeatable read, unfortunately, is still possible. Without shared locks for the read operations, a transaction can observe a value without locking it and then observe it again after an intervening transaction has locked it, changed it, and committed.

The repeatable-read isolation level prevents the unrepeatable-read scenario. It operates with the standard two-strength locks: a shared lock for reading and an exclusive lock for updating. But at this level of isolation, locks apply only to individual data objects, so the

Isolation level	Interference scenario		
	Dirty read	Non-repeatable read	Phantom
read uncommitted	Possible	Possible	Possible
read committed	Not possible	Possible	Possible
repeatable read	Not possible	Not possible	Possible
serializable	Not possible	Not possible	Not possible

Figure 20.6   Transaction interference associated with isolation levels

phantom scenario is still possible. The final isolation level, serializable, also locks search criteria and thus lays the phantom to rest.

Figure 20.6 shows the permissible interference effects of the various isolation levels as specified by SQL standard. You choose the desired isolation level with an SQL statement of the following form.

$$\text{set transaction isolation level} \left\{ \begin{array}{l} \texttt{read uncommitted} \\ \texttt{read committed} \\ \texttt{repeatable read} \\ \texttt{serializable} \end{array} \right\}.$$

 The isolation level sets the amount of interference that a transaction can tolerate from concurrent transactions. In order of decreasing interference, the levels are: read-uncommitted, read-committed, repeatable read, and serializable.

Serializability through timestamps

A second method for securing concurrency in the face of conflicting transactions is times-tamping. The transaction manager portion of the DBMS gives each transaction a time of origin, called a timestamp, when it starts. The DBMS can use the system clock for this purpose although it must ensure that no two transactions receive the same timestamp. If the system clock's resolution is smaller than the time interval needed to process a begin transaction statement, this constraint will be met. If not, the DBMS must add a few bits to the least significant end of the time value to distinguish among transactions that start on the same clock tick. In truth, the method only requires that transactions receive unique identifiers, which the DBMS can compare to determine which of two transactions is older. So instead of using the system clock, the DBMS can simply provide a central source of steadily increasing numbers, a mechanism similar to the take-a-number dispensers in retail stores.

The timestamping approach guarantees not only a serializable schedule but also a final result that is the same as a particular ordering of the competing transactions. The final result will appear as if the transactions had executed serially in isolation in timestamp order. Because each transaction has a different timestamp, you can use the timestamp to name it. So when the discussion refers to transaction t, it means the transaction with timestamp t.

A timestamp is a centrally dispensed number assigned to each transaction in strictly increasing order. The DBMS guarantees that the final result from competing transactions will appear as if the transactions had executed serially in timestamp order.

The database stores two timestamps for each tuple: t_r is the timestamp of the youngest transaction that has observed the tuple, and t_u is the timestamp of the youngest transaction that has updated or created the tuple. Without loss of generality, you can assume that a transaction always observes a tuple before modifying it, so an updating or creating transaction, t, sets both $t_u = t$ and $t_r = t$. Therefore, $t_u \leq t_r$. Refer to t_r as the read-time of the tuple and to t_u as the update-time. Now, all transactions simply proceed under the optimistic assumption that they won't interfere. Each transaction monitors the timestamps of the objects that it touches, and if the timestamps reveal that interference is occurring, the transaction issues a rollback and restarts with a new, larger timestamp.

Suppose transaction t wants to observe a tuple with update- and read-times $t_u \leq t_r$. If $t \geq t_u$, transaction t is observing a tuple that has been updated by an older transaction. Because the final result will appear as though older transactions finish before younger transactions begin, transaction t can safely read the tuple and replace t_r with $\max(t, t_r)$. However, if $t_u > t$, transaction t is attempting to read a value that won't be valid until some time in the future after transaction t has terminated. In this case, transaction t issues a rollback and restarts with a new, larger timestamp t'.

Because t_u represents the timestamp of the last transaction to update the troublesome tuple, you must have that $t' > t_u$ at this point. Therefore, if the restarted transaction can get back to the read operation immediately, it will succeed. Alas, t_u may have changed by then, and the transaction may be aborted again. This situation poses another livelock dilemma, where the same transaction is repeatedly sacrificed.

A similar argument applies when transaction t wants to update a tuple. Now, however, you must insist not only that a future transaction hasn't updated the tuple, but also that a future transaction hasn't even seen the tuple. In other words, you must have $t \geq t_r$ to update the tuple safely. This constraint ensures that no transaction younger than t has read the tuple. Because $t_u \leq t_r$ always, it follows that $t \geq t_u$, so no younger transaction has updated the tuple either. In other words, transaction t is operating on a proper value from the past, and the update is safe. It also advances both t_r and t_u to t. On the other hand, if $t < t_r$, transaction t issues a rollback and restarts with a new, larger timestamp.

If a rollback involves reinstating previous values, the rollback activity itself must have a new timestamp, which it uses to update the t_r and t_u values of the reinstated tuple. Otherwise, the read- and update-time values aren't changed. This provision is necessary for the protocol to deal with the conflict scenarios, as you can see by revisiting the previous examples.

The lost-update situation proceeds as shown in Figure 20.7. You can assume that $t_r = t_u = 0$ for the account 754 tuple when the action begins. Although one of the transactions suffers a restart, this schedule concludes successfully with the proper final balance. Trouble can develop, however, if the restarted transaction races to the read point and installs a larger t_r value before the surviving transaction performs the timestamp check for an update. In this case, the DBMS also restarts the surviving transaction, and it can

t_1	t_2
$\vdots$	$\vdots$
begin transaction ($t_1 = 1$)	
$\vdots$	$\vdots$
check for read: $t_1 = 1 \geq 0 = t_u$? ok	
read account 754 ($314.60)	
set $t_r = \max(t_r, t_1) = \max(0, 1) = 1$	
$\vdots$	$\vdots$
	begin transaction ($t_2 = 2$)
$\vdots$	$\vdots$
	check for read: $t_2 = 2 \geq 0 = t_u$? ok
	read account 754 ($314.60)
	set $t_r = \max(t_r, t_2) = \max(1, 2) = 2$
$\vdots$	$\vdots$
check for update: $t_1 = 1 \geq 2 = t_r$? No!	
rollback – no changes to undo	
begin transaction ($t_1 = 3$)	
$\vdots$	$\vdots$
	check for update: $t_2 = 2 \geq 2 = t_r$? ok
	update account 754 ($264.60)
	set $t_r = t_u = t_2 = 2$
$\vdots$	$\vdots$
check for read: $t_1 = 3 \geq 2 = t_u$? ok	
read account 754 ($264.60)	
set $t_r = \max(t_r, t_1) = \max(2, 3) = 3$	
$\vdots$	$\vdots$
	commit
$\vdots$	$\vdots$
check for update: $t_1 = 3 \geq 3 = t_r$? ok	
update account 754 ($214.60)	
set $t_r = t_u = t_1 = 3$	
$\vdots$	$\vdots$
commit	

Figure 20.7 Timestamp solution to the lost-update scenario

	t_1		t_2

t_1 column:

$\vdots$

begin transaction $(t_1 = 1)$

$\vdots$

check for read: $t_1 = 1 \geq 0 = t_u$? ok
read account 754 ($314.60)
set $t_r = \max(t_r, t_1) = \max(0, 1) = 1$

$\vdots$

t_2 column:

begin transaction $(t_2 = 2)$

$\vdots$

check for read: $t_2 = 2 \geq 0 = t_u$? ok
read account 754 ($314.60)
set $t_r = \max(t_r, t_2) = \max(1, 2) = 2$

t_1 column:

check for update: $t_1 = 1 \geq 2 = t_r$? No!
rollback – no changes to undo
begin transaction $(t_1 = 3)$

$\vdots$

check for read: $t_1 = 3 \geq 0 = t_u$? ok
read account 754 ($314.60)
set $t_r = \max(t_r, t_1) = \max(2, 3) = 3$

$\vdots$

t_2 column:

check for update: $t_2 = 2 \geq 3 = t_r$? No!
rollback – no changes to undo
begin transaction $(t_2 = 4)$

$\vdots$

check for read: $t_2 = 4 \geq 0 = t_u$? ok
read account 754 ($314.60)
set $t_r = \max(t_r, t_2) = \max(3, 4) = 4$

t_1 column:

check for update: $t_1 = 3 \geq 4 = t_r$? No!
rollback – no changes to undo
begin transaction $(t_1 = 5)$

$\vdots$

Figure 20.8 Livelock scenario with timestamps

then force out the first restart in a similar manner. This produces a livelock situation, where neither transaction can complete successfully. Figure 20.8 illustrates this development.

This behavior is disheartening because each transaction upon rebirth immediately kills the other. Whenever an older transaction accesses a tuple that has been touched in an interfering manner by a younger transaction, the older transaction aborts. You can prevent the above livelock situation by withholding the restart of an aborted transaction until its younger competitor has cleared the system. This approach reduces the concurrency somewhat because the restarted transaction may be able to interleave with its competitor to complete correctly. The outcome depends on the relative timing of the database calls. You can't predict the timing because the database usually operates in a timeshared fashion with other jobs on the same processor. Therefore, the amount of time between adjacent commands in a transaction isn't predictable: it depends on the largess of the operating system. Moreover, even if you withhold the restart of an aborted transaction until its triumphant competitor has cleared the system, you can't guarantee that another competitor won't choke off the new restart. The original winner could even suffer a rollback in some later confrontation and appear again under a new timestamp. In that case, the original battle could be fought again. These problems do have solutions. One possibility is for the DBMS to keep a queue of transactions that have been aborted more than some fixed number of times (e.g., three). The DBMS periodically halts the normal transaction flow and clears the queue by processing the troublesome transactions in a true serial fashion.

The dirty-read scenario, which unfolds as shown in Figure 20.9, provides an opportunity to observe a rollback where a change must be undone. Again assume that $t_r = t_u = 0$ for the target tuple when the transactions begin. The outcome is correct although the DBMS must give the next available timestamp to the rollback activity. Otherwise, the transaction in possession of the dirty read could update that incorrect data. The unrepeatable-read problem also resolves correctly, as shown in Figure 20.10. Again, $t_r = t_u = 0$ at the outset. Although the process avoids the unrepeatable read, the transaction making the probe aborts and restarts. The phantom scenario develops along the lines of Figure 20.11. Assume that the read- and update-timestamps of all involved records are initially 0. The second search detects the phantom as a tuple satisfying the search criterion with the update-timestamp of a younger transaction.

 Involving less overhead than locks, timestamps constitute an alternative concurrency control mechanism. Transactions proceed under the optimistic assumption that no conflict will arise. The DBMS detects conflict when a younger transaction influences an object that is subsequently accessed by an older transaction. The older transaction aborts and restarts with a new timestamp.

Recovery

The DBMS faces and must recover from a variety of failures. These range from errors in application programs or system software to hardware failures and power interruptions. The key to disaster recovery is storage redundancy, and the extent of replicated storage is determined by the risk exposure that can be tolerated. If you must reduce the risk to a very low value, you may have to maintain two or more complete copies of the entire database. This approach suffers the added overhead of executing transactions on all copies and maintaining continuous synchronization among the redundant systems. Most database systems take a less radical approach. They attempt to minimize the amount of lost data in a failure by restoring the correct database state to a point in time as close as possible to the point of failure. Moreover, the DBMS can restart certain transactions that were interrupted by the failure. This section gives an overview of the essential concepts of database recovery.

t_1	t_2
$\vdots$	$\vdots$
`begin transaction` $(t_1 = 1)$	
$\vdots$	$\vdots$
check for read: $t_1 = 1 \geq 0 = t_u$? ok	
read account 754 ($314.60)	
set $t_r = \max(t_r, t_1) = \max(0, 1) = 1$	
$\vdots$	
check for update: $t_1 = 1 \geq 1 = t_r$? ok	
update account 754 ($264.60)	
set $t_r = t_u = 1$	
$\vdots$	$\vdots$
	`begin transaction` $(t_2 = 2)$
	check for read: $t_2 = 2 \geq 0 = t_u$? ok
	read account 754 ($264.60)
	set $t_r = \max(t_r, t_2) = \max(1, 2) = 2$
$\vdots$	$\vdots$
`rollback` use $t' = 3$	
restore account 754 ($314.60)	
set $t_r = t_u = 3$	
$\vdots$	$\vdots$
	check for update: $t_2 = 2 \geq 3 = t_r$? No!
	`rollback` – no changes to undo
	`begin transaction` $(t_2 = 4)$
	check for read: $t_2 = 4 \geq 3 = t_u$? ok
	read account 754 ($314.60)
	set $t_r = \max(t_r, t_2) = \max(3, 4) = 4$
$\vdots$	$\vdots$
	check for update: $t_2 = 4 \geq 4 = t_r$? ok
	update account 754 ($264.60)
	set $t_r = t_u = 4$
$\vdots$	$\vdots$
	`commit`

Figure 20.9   Timestamp solution to the dirty-read scenario

The log file's role in rollbacks and failure recovery

The first line of defense is a **log file** that records the changes associated with each transaction. The log file entries represent a chronological trace of events that affected the database. The log notes each `begin transaction`, and at some later point, a `commit` or `rollback` entry confirms the transaction's conclusion. Between these two landmarks, **before-images** and **after-images** reflect the database changes made by the transaction. Of course, these events are interspersed with similar events from concurrent transactions, so the DBMS must flag each of them with the ID of the perpetrating transaction.

The log file's particular format varies with the database product, but it must be sufficiently detailed to identify the modified objects, their precise storage locations, and the

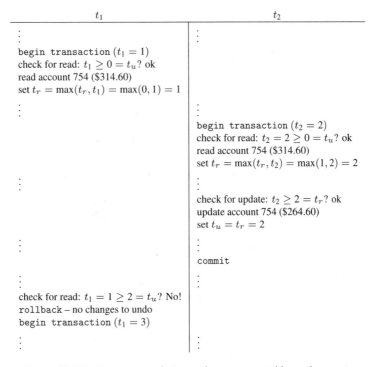

t_1	t_2
⋮	⋮
begin transaction ($t_1 = 1$) check for read: $t_1 \geq 0 = t_u$? ok read account 754 ($314.60) set $t_r = \max(t_r, t_1) = \max(0, 1) = 1$	
⋮	⋮
	begin transaction ($t_2 = 2$) check for read: $t_2 = 2 \geq 0 = t_u$? ok read account 754 ($314.60) set $t_r = \max(t_r, t_2) = \max(1, 2) = 2$
	⋮
	check for update: $t_2 \geq 2 = t_r$? ok update account 754 ($264.60) set $t_u = t_r = 2$
⋮	⋮
	commit
⋮	⋮
check for read: $t_1 = 1 \geq 2 = t_u$? No! rollback – no changes to undo begin transaction ($t_1 = 3$)	
⋮	⋮

Figure 20.10   Timestamp solution to the non-repeatable read scenario

structure before and after each change. To illustrate the concepts, consider an approach based on disk pages under a two-phase locking protocol. Keep in mind, however, that this mechanism is just one of many possibilities.

 A log file maintains a record of all changes to the database, including the ID of the perpetrating transaction, a before-image, and an after-image of each modified object.

Part II discussed the disk storage formats used by database systems and noted that a unit of storage, called a page or a block, serves as the smallest data segment that the DBMS can transfer between disk and computer memory. The recovery mechanism here will deal only with pages; it won't attempt to interpret the data on a page. To this end, consider a strategy where the locks apply to pages, rather than to tuples or objects. When a transaction wants to read an object, it acquires a shared lock on the page, or pages, occupied by the object. For update, the transaction must acquire an exclusive lock on the relevant pages. This approach reduces parallel activity somewhat because objects on the same page as a targeted object are restricted from full access by competing transactions. It does, however, simplify the recovery process because the bits corresponding to a particular modified object need not be specifically identified and manipulated. Assume also that the conservative approach of the preceding section is in effect. In other words, the DBMS acquires shared or exclusive locks on behalf of a transaction when it initiates a read or update operation.

t_1	t_2
$\vdots$	$\vdots$

begin transaction $(t_1 = 1)$
  select sum(balance)
  from AcctBalance
  where category = 1
succeeds because $t_1 = 1 \geq 0 = t_u$
for every tuple with category = 1
t_r is set to max$(0, 1) = 1$ for
all such tuples
sum is \$973.80	

$\vdots$	$\vdots$

	begin transaction $(t_2 = 2)$
	  insert into AcctBalance (category, account, balance)
	  values (1, 322, 100.00)
	set $t_r = t_u = 2$ for new tuple
	commit

$\vdots$	$\vdots$

select sum(balance)
  from AcctBalance
  where category = 1
fails because $t_u = 2 > 1 = t_1$
for the new tuple
rollback – no changes to undo
begin transaction $(t_1 = 3)$	

$\vdots$	$\vdots$

Figure 20.11   Timestamp solution to the phantom scenario

The transaction then retains all locks until after its commit or rollback, when it releases all of them simultaneously.

The DBMS caches many pages in its memory buffers to reduce the data transfer traffic with the disk. As a transaction progresses, the buffer pages accumulate the updates until an event occurs that forces a modified page to the disk. The DBMS uses some strategy to determine which page to rewrite to disk when it must bring a new page into a buffer with no more free space. This strategy can replace the least frequently accessed page, the oldest page, or the youngest page. Or it can favor pages associated with particular application entities or indexes by replacing them only as a last resort. In any case, at some point the pages modified by the transaction become replacement targets, and the DBMS physically writes them to the disk.

Typically, the replacement strategy is such that a page remains in the buffer, if at all possible, while a transaction holds an exclusive lock on it. This constraint may be difficult to enforce because a transaction doesn't release any locks until it concludes with a commit or rollback. Therefore, a long transaction can accumulate a large number of locked pages and monopolize the buffer. So the DBMS may have to transfer a locked page to disk with appropriate precautions. The DBMS also maintains the log records in a buffer that it periodically flushes to disk.

When the DBMS writes a data or log record, it modifies the appropriate page in the buffer, and some unpredictable amount of time passes before it physically transfers the page to disk storage. The term **forced to disk** means that the DBMS modifies the proper buffer page and then immediately writes the page to disk. The database's normal functioning involves an autonomous buffer manager that writes modified pages to disk according to some space management strategy. This activity isn't necessarily aligned with the beginning or conclusion of a transactions. Although you can assume that the buffer manager tries to retain a locked page, you can't assume that the DBMS will flush it to disk when the transaction concludes. The page may remain in the buffer for some time before it becomes a replacement target. Indeed, it might become locked by another transaction, which would make it a low probability replacement candidate until the new lock is released. Despite these complications, the buffer manager must be capable of forcing certain records to disk on command.

When a transaction wants to modify a page, it obtains an exclusive lock on the page. Before installing the modifications, however, it writes a log record containing the transaction ID and the page's before- and after-image. The before-image is available in the buffer, and the after-image is the before-image with the modification installed. After successfully writing the log record, the DBMS writes the modified page. The write action merely installs the new data in the buffer, where it waits for a transfer to disk.

While the modified data page and the log records remain in the buffers, they are especially vulnerable to failure. If a failure occurs before they transfer to disk, their contents are lost. The buffer manager must never transfer a page to disk while log records for the page remain in the buffer. Because the DBMS writes the log records sequentially, this constraint means that the buffer manager must first transfer all log records through the last one that pertains to the page in question.

The particular order of events described above is the **write-ahead log protocol**. It guards against a failure that may occur between writing the log and flushing the page to disk. If the DBMS flushes the disk page first and a failure occurs before it writes the log record, no record exists of the page's before-image, and the DBMS can't undo the transaction. Consequently, while executing a transaction, the DBMS always writes the log records before writing the data page for any update, insertion, or deletion. Furthermore, the buffer manager never replaces a modified page without first flushing all log records pertaining to it. Because the DBMS wrote the log records first, any log records pertaining to the modified page will be in the buffer, or they will have already been transferred to disk.

With the help of the log file, the DBMS can easily perform a `rollback` commanded by either a transaction or the system. The DBMS first writes a rollback record to the log. As far as the page replacement strategy of the buffer manager is concerned, the rollback record pertains to all pages of the transaction. Therefore, all log records for the transaction transfer to disk before the DBMS considers any data page involved in the transaction. The DBMS then scans the log backward, starting with any tail portion still in the buffer, and rewrites each before-image page associated with the transaction. In truth, only the earliest before-image of a given page needs to be reinstated, and the algorithm can defer writing a before-image until it encounters the earliest. This information becomes available only when the DBMS reaches the `begin transaction` record in the backward log scan. To some extent, the buffer manager handles this optimization because it doesn't replace the rewritten page in the buffer unless the space is needed for other pages. In any case, because the transaction holds an exclusive lock on a modified page at the time of the rollback, other transactions haven't observed any of the after-images although they may have seen the earliest before-image. So the restored page is exactly as any competing transaction believes it to be.

The DBMS writes the restored pages into the buffer and produces no additional log records. So an unpredictable amount of time may pass before the rollback appears on disk. This latency presents no problems in the absence of other failures because another transaction requesting one of the restored pages receives it from the buffer copy in the normal manner. Indeed, the reason for caching pages is to reduce disk traffic by frequently finding a required page already in memory. But just as the modified pages of a committed transaction may reside in the buffers for some indeterminate amount of time, so may the restored pages of a transaction that concludes with a rollback. You can be sure, however, that if any of the restored pages have transferred to disk, the log record of the rollback is also safely on disk.

When a transaction concludes with a commit, the DBMS writes a commit record to the log, but it doesn't need to revisit the data pages associated with the transaction. With either transaction conclusion, commit or rollback, the DBMS removes the locks from all pages used by the transaction.

 Using the write-ahead log protocol, the DBMS writes the log records associated with a modified object before it writes the new value of the object. The buffer manager must cooperate by transferring the relevant log records to disk before replacing a data page in its buffers.

Some failures lose the buffers' contents but leave the disk intact. These problems include power interruptions, most application program or system software errors that require a machine restart, and hardware malfunctions that don't involve the disk storage unit. Consider how you can recover from one of these failures by using the log file. At the time of failure, some transactions have completed; others are in progress. A difficulty arises because you can't know which completed transactions have actually transferred to disk. If the commit or rollback record appears in the log, you know that the transaction concluded before the failure. However, you still don't know if the results are safely on disk or if they were lost in the buffers. This uncertainty means that you must scan the entire log. Because the log can be very long, this process isn't efficient, and you can use checkpoints to reduce the log segment that you must examine. A later section will discuss checkpoints. For the moment, assume you must scan the full log.

You maintain three lists: a redo list, an undo list, and a restart list. Scanning backward in the log, you reinstall each before-image, which reverses all the transactions. When you encounter a commit record, you place the corresponding transaction on the redo list. When you encounter a rollback, you place the transaction on the undo list. The successive rewriting of the before-images simply reverses the transaction a second time. If the restored images have transferred to disk, rewriting the before-images produces no change. If they haven't transferred before the failure, the proper rollback now takes place. When you encounter a `begin transaction`, you check the redo and undo lists. If the transaction appears on neither list, it must have been in progress when the failure occurred, and you place it on the restart list. When you reach the beginning of the log, you've undone all transactions, and you now scan forward to redo all transactions on the redo list. You redo a transaction by rewriting its after-images in the order encountered. You don't have to execute the transaction a second time. When you encounter the end of the log, you have redone all transactions that `committed` before the failure. All transactions that concluded with a `rollback` remain undone from the backward pass. Finally, you resubmit the restart list to the DBMS as new transactions.

 The log file enables recovery from a failure that loses the memory buffers' contents but doesn't corrupt the database. You scan the log backward and reverse transactions by rewriting their before-images. You then scan it forward to redo committed transactions by rewriting their after-images.

Checkpoints to limit extensive log file searching

A database can exist for years and accumulate an enormous record of changes. Therefore, the DBMS must have some provision for an ever-growing log file. Because the log file is sequential, you can periodically transfer the older portion of the on-line log to backup storage, which may be tape or another disk unit. You can also postprocess the log to reduce its size. Some transactions are read-only, and they appear in the log as a `begin transaction` followed at some later point by a `commit`, but with no intervening records of before- and after-images. You can simply purge these transactions from the log. You can also remove any transaction that concludes with a rollback. Finally, you can compress transactions that commit with multiple changes by retaining only the first before-image and the last after-image of each affected page. Although these considerations reduce the log's volume somewhat, a problem remains because the log experiences never-ending growth.

A **checkpoint** is a synchronization record written into the log. It guarantees that all transactions that have concluded at that point are fully represented on disk. You can instruct the DBMS to take a checkpoint at some periodic interval, say every 15 minutes, or when it accumulates a certain number of log records since the last checkpoint. To take a checkpoint, the DBMS forces all log records and all modified database pages to disk. It then writes a checkpoint record, which contains the IDs of all transactions currently in progress, and forces that log record to disk also.

The checkpoint bounds the portion of the log needed for a recovery. Suppose a failure occurs and the system restarts. The DBMS scans the log backward, and until it locates a checkpoint record, the activity is as described above. It rewrites before-images to reverse the transactions and maintains redo, undo, and restart lists. If it encounters a `commit`, it places the corresponding transaction on the redo list. If it encounters a `rollback`, it places the transaction on the undo list. If it encounters a `begin transaction` and the transaction isn't on the redo or undo list, it places the transaction on the restart list. But if the transaction is on the undo list when `begin transaction` is encountered, the DBMS simply removes it from that list.

Eventually, the scan reaches the log's last checkpoint or its beginning. At that point, all transactions that were in progress at the time of the checkpoint have been examined. Some are on the redo or undo list because a `commit` or `rollback` appeared earlier in the backward scan. Any transactions that were in progress at the time of the checkpoint but are not on the redo or undo list must have been in progress at the time of the failure. The DBMS adds this last collection to the undo list. Their IDs are available from the checkpoint record.

The scan then continues backward, past the checkpoint, but it now installs before-images only for the transactions that are on the undo list. Therefore, the backward scan continues to reverse any transactions that were in progress at the time of the failure. It also reverses any transactions that concluded with a `rollback` after the checkpoint but before the failure. The DBMS now ignores `commit` and `rollback` records because it doesn't need to redo or undo transactions that concluded before the checkpoint. Any such transactions were safely on disk at the time of the checkpoint. When it encounters a `begin transaction` record, it compares the transaction ID with the undo list. If a match occurs, it removes the transaction from the undo list.

When the undo list is empty, the backward scan terminates. Under normal circumstances, the backward scan examines only a small portion of the most recent log entries. After the abbreviated backward excursion, the scan proceeds forward again in the normal fashion and installs after-images to redo any transactions on the redo list. This list is now much smaller than in the non-checkpoint situation because it contains only transactions that have concluded with a `commit` between the checkpoint and the failure. When the scan reaches the end of the log, the DBMS restarts the transactions on the restart list.

 A checkpoint is a synchronization record placed in the log to note a point when all concluded transactions are safely on disk. It limits the log segment needed to recover from a failure.

Recovery from a backup copy of the database

If a more catastrophic failure occurs, such as a head crash on the disk unit, the supposedly safe records on the disk are destroyed. To guard against this problem, you must periodically archive the database to a second disk unit or to magnetic tape. You can record all disk pages in each archival copy, or you can use an incremental scheme that copies only pages with changes since the last backup. You take backups when no transaction activity is in progress and after all buffers are flushed to disk. So the backup copy reflects a consistent database state between transactions. Finally, the DBMS writes a log record noting the backup activity. Usually, you can then discard the portion of the log before the backup record.

When a failure occurs that corrupts the database, you can restore the database state from the backup copy. You then scan any portion of the log that remains intact in a reverse direction, but only as far as the log record for the backup. When you encounter a `commit` or `rollback` entry, you add the transaction to the redo or undo list respectively. The backward scan, however, doesn't write before-images. The scan operates only on the log segment that was generated after the backup. Therefore, none of the database activity associated with completed transactions appears in the restored state. As before, a `begin` `transaction` entry for which the corresponding transaction is in neither the redo nor the undo list represents a transaction that was in progress at the time of the failure or that was in progress at the time the last available log record was written. Such a transaction may indeed have concluded, but the log record of the conclusion was lost with the database. You place all such transactions in a restart list. When it reaches the log record of the backup, the backward scan terminates. A forward scan then writes after-images to redo the transactions on the redo list. When it reaches the end of the log, the DBMS begins to reexecute the transactions of the restart list.

If the entire log is intact, this procedure will recover or restart all the transactions and completely restore the database. For this reason, good practice maintains the log file on a separate disk device from the database. If the disk unit containing the database fails, complete recovery is possible from the log and a backup. Depending on the frequency of backups, some parts of the log may exist as archived media, but in any case, these segments should remain available. On the other hand, if the disk unit containing the log file fails, the operator can immediately perform a database backup. The log before the backup record isn't needed anyway.

If the log segment after the backup is completely or partially destroyed, there may be transactions that started after the last available log record. These transactions won't appear in any of the lists accumulated by the recovery process, so you must identify and resubmit such transactions manually. To avoid this inconvenience, you should do frequent backups and pay careful attention to the log file.

If a failure corrupts the database, you can reinstate a previous state from a backup copy. If some portion of the log remains intact, you can recover certain transactions that committed subsequent to the backup.

Special provisions for restarting a long transaction

Many variations and improvements in the general recovery process are available in commercial database products. For example, you can add pointers to the sequential log file entries to access records for a particular transaction without reading through the intervening records from other transactions. You could also make a special case for rolling back a transaction when all its affected pages remain in the buffer. You simply release the buffer space. You don't need to rewrite the before-images of the log because the before-images correspond to the pages as they exist on disk.

What about the messages, files, and reports that many transactions generate? These items convey knowledge about the transaction to the external world beyond the database. When the recovery process restores the database state associated with a committed transaction, it shouldn't regenerate the external messages because they are already available. It should only reinstall the updated database objects. This problem also occurs in normal, failure-free processing because a transaction that terminates with a `rollback` should retract all traces of its existence. Of course, this retraction is impossible in the case of messages sent to the external world. So a more sophisticated approach retains control of all messages, files, and reports until the transaction's fate is known. If the transaction concludes with a rollback, the messages are destroyed, and the external world is unaware that they ever existed. If the transaction commits successfully, the messages are made available in the order that they were produced. In any case, a subsequent recovery from a failure shouldn't regenerate these materials.

One particular enhancement concerns the provisions a transaction can take to anticipate a restart. The most prudent advice, of course, is to break the processing into several transactions, if possible, by issuing periodic `commit` commands to make permanent the work performed to a certain point. In the event of a recovery, the DBMS will redo these subtransactions by reinstalling the after-images. Suppose, for example, you are calculating some function of the fish weights in the aquarium application, some function that is beyond the simple aggregates of SQL. Suppose you want to report for each fish whether its weight exceeds $w_{\mathrm{rms}} = \sqrt{(\sum f_i^2)/N}$, where the f_i are the fish weights in the fish table and N is the number of fish tuples. The ideal situation is to acquire a shared lock on all fish tuples, so that no updates can occur while the computation is in progress. So you might design the transaction as follows, using the embedded SQL of Chapter 5.

```
exec sql set transaction isolation level serializable, diagnostics size 10;
exec sql begin transaction;
exec sql prepare getFish from "select fno, fname, fweight from Fish";
exec sql declare fishCursor cursor for getFish;
exec sql open cursor fishCursor;
w = 0; n = 0;
exec sql fetch fishCursor into :fno, :fname, :fweight;
exec sql get diagnostics :code = number;
while (code == 0) {
  w = w + fweight * fweight;
  n++;
  exec sql fetch fishCursor into :fno, :fname, :fweight;
  exec sql get diagnostics :code = number; }
exec sql close cursor fishCursor;
w = sqrt(w/n);
exec sql open cursor fishCursor;
exec sql fetch fishCursor into :fno, :fname, :fweight;
exec sql get diagnostics :code = number;
while (code == 0) {
  if (fweight > w)
    printf("%d %s exceeds rms weight\n", fno, fname);
  else
    printf("%d %s does not exceed rms weight\n", fno, fname);
  exec sql fetch fishCursor into :fno, :fname, :fweight;
  exec sql get diagnostics :code = number; }
exec sql close cursor fishCursor;
exec sql commit;
```

When the cursor opens, the prepared select-statement executes, and the transaction acquires a shared lock on the search condition. In this case, the search condition covers the entire fish relation. The DBMS will allow no concurrent updates, insertions, or deletions on this relation by competitors until the transaction releases the lock with the final `commit`. This precaution ensures that the set of fish weight values doesn't change as the computation progresses. If the number of fish tuples is very large, this computation could be lengthy, and a restart would force it to start over at the beginning. The transaction can't issue a `commit` after it absorbs each fish weight into the growing sum-of-squares, w, because a commit operation closes all cursors. The DBMS must close the cursor because the commit

releases the shared lock and allows concurrent transactions to update the tuples where the
search condition operates. You can reopen the cursor, but you must then position the fetch
after the fish tuples that have already been processed. Because a commit releases the locks,
another transaction can update, delete, or insert fish tuples and compromise the condition
that the computation take place on a fixed set of tuples. You might be willing to accept
that possibility if activity of the competing transactions resulted in very little change in the
root-mean-square weight calculation. A slightly inaccurate result might be preferable to
a forced restart from the beginning of the computation. So the goal now is to maintain
the isolation of the computation set, if possible, but to salvage any computation performed
before a restart, if necessary.

The transaction can keep track of its progress by writing an external record, which
notes the result at the time a particular fish was processed. It then updates the external
record periodically to reflect progress through the fish tuples. In the event of a restart, it
uses the last value to avoid reprocessing most of the previously accessed fish tuples. The
tentative code might appear as follows.

```
exec sql set transaction isolation level serializable, diagnostics size 10;
exec sql begin transaction;
exec sql prepare getFish from
   "select fno, fname, fweight from Fish where fno > ?  orderby fno";
f = fopen("placeset", "r+"); /* open with read/write privileges */
if (f == NULL) { /* no file */
   w = 0; n = 0; lastfno = 0;
   f = fopen("placeset", "w+"); } /* create external read/write file */
else {
   fscanf(f, "%d%d%d", &lastfno, &w, &n); /* get last fno prior to restart */
   reset(f); } /* return to beginning to prepare for new record */
exec sql declare fishCursor cursor for getFish;
exec sql open cursor fishCursor using :lastfno;
exec sql fetch fishCursor into :fno, :fname, :fweight;
exec sql get diagnostics :code = number;
while (code == 0) {
   w = w + fweight * fweight;
   n++;
   if (n % 100 == 0) { /* update placeset record every 100 fish */
      fprintf(f, "%d %d %d", fno, w, n);
      fclose(f); f = fopen("placeset", "r+"); }
   exec sql fetch fishCursor into :fno, :fname, :fweight;
   exec sql get diagnostics :code = number; }
exec sql close cursor fishCursor;
w = sqrt(w/n);
   .
   .
   .
   /* produce report comparing each fish with rms weight as before */
   .
   .
   .
exec sql commit;
unlink(f); /* delete placeset file */
```

This transaction checks for a placeset file, which would have been created if the transaction
had previously been interrupted and restarted. If such a file exists, it provides a lastfno
value, reflecting the largest fno (within 100 tuples) processed before the interruption. It
also provides a corresponding value of w and n. If the file doesn't exist, the transaction

initializes w, n, and lastfno to zero. The code passes lastfno as a parameter when it opens the cursor. This leads to a selection of those tuples with larger fno values. The omitted tuples have already contributed to the w and n values that were recovered from the placeset record. In the processing loop, the transaction writes a new placeset record every 100 fish tuples to protect itself against another interruption. It also closes the file after each such write so that it survives any unexpected demise of the program.

The approach seems to be a clever circumvention of the restart mechanism of the recovery process. If a failure catches the transaction while the computation is in progress, the DBMS will roll it back and restart it. The placeset record allows the new reincarnation to salvage the earlier computation, to within 100 tuples, and then to proceed from that point. This approach, however, contains two flaws. First, closing the placeset file after every fish access is an expensive operation and may slow the processing to an unacceptable pace. Second, a more serious drawback lies in the way the DBMS handles external messages, files, and reports during a rollback. A rollback should retract any external products. In practice, this means that they shouldn't be released until the transaction's successful termination is assured. A rollback should restore a state that makes it appear that the transaction never began. Therefore, a recovery system that withholds all external signs of processing until successful conclusion must discard the placeset file that was so carefully constructed.

Some database systems do recognize that a transaction should be able to prepare for the possibility of a failure, and they provide a special restart table that isn't destroyed when the DBMS rolls back a transaction. This table contains one row for each transaction that was in progress at the time of failure, assuming that the transaction has taken the trouble to write data into its restart tuple. The restart tuple for a given transaction can only be read by that transaction, and you must assume that a restarted transaction retains its original ID. This restart information doesn't violate the principle that a rolled back transaction should leave no visible trace to the external world. The only way the restart tuple can be observed is by rerunning the same transaction with the same ID. Because the DBMS centrally dispenses transaction IDs with no duplication, only a system restart can cause the same transaction to execute a second time.

The restart tuple contains a single string of formatted data, which saves whatever values the transaction needs to facilitate a restart. The details of the operation are similar to those illustrated above, except that the transaction uses SQL select and insert statements to read and write the restart information, and the DBMS retains only the most recently inserted tuple for a given transaction. When the transaction finally concludes, either with a commit or with a rollback, the DBMS destroys the restart tuple. Although the syntax is usually more complicate, the code segment of Figure 20.12 illustrates this general idea.

Security

Because an application database offers a centralized service to a potentially large collection of users, the DBMS must provide a mechanism to protect the information from abuse. Certain data are confidential and should be seen only by privileged persons or programs. Other data may be more generally available on a read-only basis but should be protected from update.

```
exec sql set transaction isolation level serializable, diagnostics size 10;
exec sql begin transaction;
exec sql prepare getFish from
    "select fno, fname, fweight from Fish where fno > ?  orderby fno";
exec sql prepare startData from "select * from restart";
exec sql prepare newStart from "insert into restart values (?)";
exec sql execute startData into :buffer;
exec sql get diagnostics :code = number;
if (code != 0) { /* no restart data */
    w = 0; n = 0; lastfno = 0; }
else /* restart data in string buffer */
    sscanf(buffer, "%d%d%d", &lastfno, &w, &n);
exec sql declare fishCursor cursor for getFish;
exec sql open cursor fishCursor using :lastfno;
exec sql fetch fishCursor into :fno, :fname, :fweight;
exec sql get diagnostics :code = number;
while (code == 0) {
    w = w + fweight * fweight;
    n++;
    if (n % 100 == 0) { /* update restart record every 100 fish */
        sprintf(buffer, "%d %d %d", fno, w, n); /* format restart data into buffer */
        exec sql execute newStart using :buffer; }
    exec sql fetch fishCursor into :fno, :fname, :fweight;
    exec sql get diagnostics :code = number; }
exec sql close cursor fishCursor;
w = sqrt(w/n);
    .
    .
    .
    /* produce report comparing each fish with rms weight as before */
    .
    .
    .
exec sql commit;
```

Figure 20.12   Illustrating the use of application-specific restart information

In a relational database, SQL provides several features to customize the database's access profile to the application. The SQL view offers one such approach. A view is a virtual table, and the DBMS materializes the view contents on demand from underlying base tables. Earlier chapters used views to match the database's data formats with the application programs' expectations. You can also use a view to conceal sensitive information. In the aquarium application, for example, suppose the database administrator (DBA) decides that the color information on fish and tanks shouldn't be accessed by certain personnel. The DBA can enforce this policy with a special view for those individuals. The view simply omits the sensitive attributes as shown below.

```
create view monochromeAqua as
    (select F.fno as fishno, F.fname as fishname, S.sno as specno, S.sname as specname,
        S.sfood as specfood, T.tno as tankno, T.tname as tankname, T.tvolume as tankvolume
    from Species S, Fish F, Tank T
    where S.sno = F.sno and F.tno = T.tno).
```

Although an SQL view can conceal sensitive information, this precaution isn't sufficient by itself because the user can directly query the tank and fish tables after detecting their existence through the system catalog.

Privilege descriptors

The SQL standard includes a process for associating users with privileged operations on database objects. As far as the DBMS is concerned, the user is an authorization ID (authID), and the operating system assumes the responsibility of correlating authIDs with real persons or programs. Each executing SQL session then identifies with the authID of the agent that opened the session. An initial session executes a create-schema command, as described in Chapter 2, to create the database. At that time, the DBMS creates the table shells, domains, constraint assertions, and views. It also records the authID of the controlling session as the owner of the schema and all objects created within the schema. The owner retains all privileges concerning the schema and any data that may later inhabit the table shells. The owner can alter the schema by adding new tables, adding attributes to existing tables, dropping attributes from tables, dropping complete tables, or dropping the entire schema. Any views, constraint assertions, or domains defined within the create-schema statement are also considered part of the database structure, as distinguished from data that will eventually reside within the structure. Only the owner can command changes to the database structure although other users can receive varying levels of privileges that relate to the data stored within the structure.

In particular, the owner can authorize other users to observe or modify the tables' content. Moreover, another user can, under certain conditions, create a dependent schema, which contains domains, tables, constraints, and views based on the original schema definitions but external to it. The subsidiary user then becomes the owner of these secondary assets and enjoys any privileges needed to modify or destroy them. This section's goal is to describe how the SQL standard controls these privileges.

SQL supports six privileges. Five apply to tables: select, insert, update, delete, and references. One applies to domains: usage. In any case, a privilege always associates with a particular named object on behalf of a particular user (i.e., authID). The standard speaks of privilege descriptors, which contain five primary values: object, grantor, grantee, action, grantable. The DBMS stores privilege descriptors in the tables of the system catalog. Some privileges apply to a table as a whole; others apply to specified columns. Such differences make it convenient to distribute the descriptors across several system tables. For purposes of this discussion, however, you can envision the privilege descriptors as residing in a single table, as illustrated in the following excerpt.

Privilege descriptors				
Object	Grantor	Grantee	Action	Grantable
⋮	⋮	⋮	⋮	⋮
Table: Fish	_SYSTEM	34572	select	yes
Table: Fish	34572	54177	select	no
Table: Fish, Columns: fcolor, fname	34572	68146	update	yes
⋮	⋮	⋮	⋮	⋮

The first entry notes that user 34572 can select tuples from the fish table. The grantor is the special authID, _SYSTEM. The system is the grantor of initial privileges when the DBMS first creates an object. The last column indicates that user 34572 has the authority to extend this privilege to other users. The second line specifies that user 54177 can observe tuples from the fish table and that this privilege has been extended by user 34572. The object of a privilege descriptor can be an entire table, or it can be particular columns, as illustrated by the third entry.

 SQL allows a schema's owner to grant certain privileges to other users pertaining to reference-update rights on data in the table shells. The six privileges are select, insert, delete, update, references, and usage. The grantor specifies whether the grantee can extend acquired privileges to third parties.

When the DBMS creates the database, it grants all privileges by _SYSTEM to the owning authID and records the corresponding descriptors in the system tables. The privilege descriptors deal only with the six actions: select, insert, update, delete, references, and usage because actions associated with the database structure, such as the creation and dropping of tables, domains, columns, constraint assertions, and views remain at all times with the owner. Therefore, the six actions in privilege descriptors are **non-structural privileges**. The owner delegates a non-structural privilege as follows.

grant *<privilege-list>* on *<object>* to *<user-list>* [with grant option].

The *<privilege-list>* can be the phrase *all privileges*, taken to mean all the non-structural privileges currently held by the executing authID with a grantable attribute of "yes." The *<privilege-list>* can also be a comma-separated list of elements selected from the entries of Figure 20.13. The figure also includes a brief summary of the effect and context of each privilege. If the description states that the object must be a table, either a base table or a view qualifies. A privilege doesn't relieve the grantee of the obligation to conform to other constraints. For example, if a user receives the privilege of updating tuples in a view, the view must be updatable for this privilege to be exercised. Also, the right to insert tuples in a table, specifying values in any column, doesn't override a schema-imposed requirement that the value in a particular column not be null or that it be drawn from some specified domain.

Note from Figure 20.13 that the grantee can use certain non-structural privileges to construct a new schema. For example, the grantee can design a new database using the domains inherited from the first database and specifying certain columns from the first database in referential integrity constraints. The grantee is then the owner of the new schema, and as owner, he retains sole rights to modify or destroy the new structure. He can now delegate non-structural privileges associated with the new structure. Certain complications develop if a grantor revokes a privilege after the grantee has used it to build new structures. A later discussion will address this problem.

The *<object>* of the grant-statement must be compatible with the *<privilege-list>*, as noted in Figure 20.13. Therefore, in most cases, the object is a table or a view. The *<user-list>* is a comma-separated list of authIDs with each member receiving the specified privileges. Finally, if you specify the with-grant-option clause, the privilege descriptor records the fact that the grantee can grant the same privileges on the same objects to other users.

Because the DBMS assumes the grantor is the user that submitted the grant-statement, all the information needed for a privilege descriptor appears in the statement. The DBMS processes the statement by installing the appropriate privilege descriptors, provided that it's

select	The object must be a table. The grantee may select all table columns, including any columns that might be added at some later time.
insert	The object must be a table. The grantee may insert tuples into the table and specify a value for any column, including any column that might be added at some later time.
insert$(c_1, c_2, \ldots)$	The object must be a table. The grantee may insert tuples in the table, specifying values only for columns chosen from $c_1, c_2, \ldots$. Other columns assume their default values as specified in the schema.
delete	The object must be a table. The grantee may delete tuples from the table.
update	The object must be a table. The grantee may update tuples in the table and specify a new value for any column, including any column that might be added at some later time.
update$(c_1, c_2, \ldots)$	The object must be a table. The grantee may update tuples in the table, specifying new values only for columns chosen from $c_1, c_2, \ldots$.
references	The object must be a table. The grantee may reference any column of the table in an integrity constraint, such as a referential-integrity clause or a check constraint.
references$(c_1, c_2, \ldots)$	The object must be a table. The grantee may reference the columns $c_1, c_2, \ldots$ in an integrity constraint.
usage	For the purposes here, the object must be a domain although the standard allows other possibilities, such as character sets and collations, that haven't been discussed in the text. The grantee may use the domain. For example, the domain can appear in a column definition in a table in a new schema, or it can appear in the definition of another domain.

Figure 20.13   Non-structural privileges that can be granted and revoked

legal to do so. If the grantor doesn't possess one of the privileges of the *<privilege-list>* or if the grantor doesn't have the authority to extend that privilege to additional users, the corresponding privilege descriptor isn't installed.

All privileges ultimately derive from _SYSTEM. Initial privileges on any new structure may descend from a combination of _SYSTEM and other authIDs. For example, a secondary user can create a view over tables from a different schema only if he holds select privileges on all the tables used in the view. To control the dispersion of privileges among users and the grantor-grantee interactions among privileges, the DBMS maintains a directed graph, the **privilege dependency graph**. The nodes of the graph are the privilege descriptors, and an arc extends from n_1 to n_2 if a grant extended by n_1 enabled n_2. Suppose grantee u of node n_1 is the grantor of a second node, n_2. Also assume the action (i.e., privilege) and the object are the same in both descriptors. This condition appears in Figure 20.14, where u passes on to a third party a privilege that was granted to u by an antecedent party (_SYSTEM). When a grant-statement creates a privilege descriptor, the grantor must possess the privilege, and therefore an antecedent privilege descriptor must exist. The new privilege descriptor

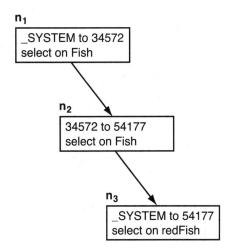

Figure 20.14 Connecting privilege descriptors in the privilege dependency graph

will appear in the dependency graph with an arc entering from the corresponding privilege descriptor for the grantor.

There are, however, other ways for nodes and arcs to appear in the graph. Referring again to Figure 20.14, you see that user 54177 has select privileges on the fish table. Therefore, user 54177 can create a view over this table as follows.

```
create view redFish as
    (select fno as fishno, fname as fishname, fweight as fishweight
    from Fish
    where fcolor = "red").
```

Various privilege descriptors come into existence at this point, including one that proclaims user 54177 as having select privileges on the redFish table. This privilege is granted by _SYSTEM, but it couldn't be granted if user 54177 didn't have the select privilege on the underlying fish table. Therefore, an arc appears from the descriptor that establishes this prerequisite. Similar dependencies occur if a secondary user creates a table that uses an inherited domain or an integrity constraint based on an inherited table. The nodes with no incoming arcs are the **independent nodes**, and they correspond to privileges granted by _SYSTEM that are independent of any other privileges. All nodes in the graph must belong to a path extending from one of these independent nodes. As the DBMS dispenses and revokes privileges, it must always maintain this condition.

As shown in Figure 20.15, a user can acquire a privilege from two or more sources. The corresponding privilege descriptors are distinct, and if one of the sources withdraws the privilege, the user retains the right to perform the action, as long as at least one of the remaining sources is connected. In the figure, you see that user 54177 holds select privileges on the fish table from two sources. Consequently, when user 54177 creates the redFish view, incoming arcs connects the new privilege descriptor to both of its progenitors. Both parent nodes satisfy the criterion that the DBMS can't grant the select privilege on the redFish table in the absence of the privilege extended by the parent. In this case, an

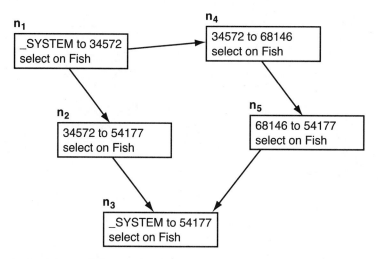

Figure 20.15   Multiple sources of a privilege in the privilege dependency graph

earlier grantor can revoke one of the select privileges on the underlying fish table, and the new descriptor will still belong to a path extending from an independent node.

 A privilege dependency graph relates privileges that are prerequisites to other privileges. Revoking a privilege can result in an abandoned privilege, a privilege with a withdrawn but needed prerequisite.

Privilege revocation and the problem of abandoned privileges

With the help of the privilege dependency graph, you can now understand how to revoke privileges. A successful revocation removes the specified privilege descriptor and the corresponding node from the privilege dependency graph. It also removes all arcs extending to or from the excised node. Without the deleted arcs, some descriptor node may lose its last inbound arc delivering a needed prerequisite. Such a node is an **abandoned privilege**. Further abandonment is now possible because the abandoned node may be the sole source of a needed prerequisite for a third node. Therefore, the child of an abandoned node may itself become abandoned. However, this propagation isn't inevitable because the child may have a second source for the prerequisite that was redundantly supplied by the abandoned parent. In any case, the governing rule for the `revoke` statement is that revoking privileges must not leave any abandoned privileges. The general format of a revocation is as follows.

```
revoke [grant option for] <privilege-list> on <object> from <user-list> { cascade
                                                                          restrict }.
```

If the phrase *grant option for* appears, the privilege descriptor isn't deleted, but the grantable value is changed to "no." In the privilege graph, this operation removes arcs that extend certain privileges: users in <*user-list*> can no longer serve as grantors for the privileges in <*privilege-list*>, *except* for any privileges in the list for which they have a second source

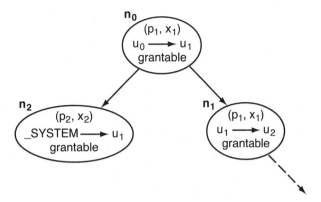

Figure 20.16   A delegated privilege that is vulnerable to an indirect revocation

that still allows the freedom to extend the privilege to third parties. For example, suppose n_1 establishes the fact that u_1 extends privilege p_1 on object x_1 to user u_2. If u_1 isn't _SYSTEM, u_1 must possess p_1 on x_1 in order to delegate it, so an inbound arc must reach n_1 from a descriptor n_0 that establishes this fact. This arrangement appears in the upper portion of Figure 20.16. Now, if u_0 issues the command revoke grant option for p_1 on x_1 from $u_1 \ldots$, the corresponding node, n_0, remains because the command doesn't revoke the privilege itself, only the authority to extend the privilege to third parties. However, the grantable value of n_0 becomes "no," which affects arcs leaving n_0. Any arc leaving n_0 that represents the transfer of p_1 on x_1 must vanish. In particular, the arc to n_1 disappears, rendering n_1 an abandoned privilege. Other arcs may leave n_0 that aren't deleted. For example, the privilege may involve select rights on some table, and there may be an arc from n_0 to a privilege descriptor associated with a view defined over that table, as created by u_1. This possibility is illustrated in the figure with the node n_2. There may also be other abandoned privileges on the paths leading from n_1, depending on whether n_1 is the sole supplier of some prerequisite privilege. In any case, the DBMS can determine if the revocation leaves any abandoned privileges, and it will always conclude the operation so that no abandonments exist.

If the revoke command doesn't include the *grant option for* phrase, the DBMS tentatively removes every targeted descriptor. A descriptor is targeted if the grantor field is the authID executing the command, the grantee field matches an entry in the *<user-list>*, the action field matches an entry in the *<privilege-list>*, and the object field matches *<object>*. When the DBMS removes a descriptor, it also removes the corresponding node, and any arcs impinging on that node, in the privilege dependency graph. The possibility of abandoned privileges again appears. Consider again Figure 20.16. The command revoke p_1 on x_1 from $u_1 \ldots$, issued by u_0, removes node n_0 and again renders n_1 an abandoned privilege. As before, this raises the possibility of other abandoned privileges among the descendants of n_1. Moreover, n_2 is now endangered as well. Although _SYSTEM granted the privilege associated with n_2, the incoming arc indicates that the possession of p_1 on x_1 is a prerequisite privilege. Perhaps u_1 has a second source for that privilege, in which case a second incoming arc to n_2 would save it from abandonment.

Resolving these dependencies consistently is a recursive process, and the SQL standard provides a long and complicated mechanism for achieving the final result. The important point is that the DBMS can identify the nodes to remove, the nodes to downgrade to *not grantable*, and the nodes to abandon. Having established a tentative update of the dependency graph by removing certain nodes and arcs, the DBMS then makes its decision based on abandoned privileges. If the suggested changes leave no abandoned privileges in the graph, the DBMS carries out the modification. It removes the affected arcs and nodes, which deprives the specified users of the enumerated privileges on the objects (or of the authority to grant these privileges to other users), unless they have second sources for the rights. If the change would result in abandoned privileges, the DBMS consults the cascade-restrict clause. If restrict appears there, the revocation fails. The privilege dependency graph and the privilege descriptor table remain unchanged, and the DBMS returns an error code. If the command chooses the cascade option, the DBMS removes both the specified and all abandoned privileges. In either case, the net result is that no abandoned privileges appear in the final dependency graph.

Referring to Figure 20.14, suppose user 34572 issues the command `revoke select on Fish from 54177 cascade`. The DBMS tentatively removes node n_2, which results in the abandoned privilege n_3. The cascade phrase then forces the removal of n_3 as well. This is an example of an abandoned privilege that affects a view. The cascade follow-up then drops the view because the creator no longer possesses the necessary privileges on the underlying base table. If other views are defined over this view, the DBMS drops them also. Removing a privilege may also remove access to an integrity constraint, a constraint assertion, or a domain. In these cases, the DBMS alters tables, if possible, or drops them, if necessary, to accommodate the new situation. The DBMS also drops assertions and domain definitions that depend on the now unavailable resources. All this activity cascades because the demise of these structures can result in the removal of objects needed in the definition of other structures. If the revocation uses the restrict option, `revoke select on Fish from 54177 restrict`, the operation simply fails in the presence of the abandoned privilege n_3.

In Figure 20.15, where second sources are available, the command `revoke select on Fish from 54177 cascade` from user 34572 removes node n_2, but it generates no abandoned privileges because n_3 enjoys a second incoming arc that supplies the necessary prerequisite. Therefore, the cascade proceeds no further, and the redFish view remains intact.

Suppose user 34572 issues the command `revoke grant option for select on Fish from 54177 cascade` in the context of Figure 20.14. The dependency graph shows that user 54177 hasn't passed on the privilege to another user, so the DBMS removes no arcs or nodes from the dependency graph. It does change the grantable field of n_2 to "no," if necessary. The operation changes no existing privileges although it curtails the future evolution of privileges.

Finally, suppose user 34572 issues `revoke grant option for select on Fish from 68146 cascade` in the context of Figure 20.15. You see that 68146 has used its authority to extend a privilege by passing the same privilege on to user 54177. Because this authority is now to be revoked, the DBMS removes the arc from n_4 to n_5, which leaves n_5 as an abandoned privilege. In keeping with the cascade requirement, the DBMS also removes

n_5, together with the arc to n_3. However, n_3 remains viable because it has a second source through n_2 to readability rights on the fish table. Because n_3 survives, the redFish view remains defined over resources to which the owner has access, and no further cascading ensues.

 A cascade option in a privilege revocation results in the revocation of any abandoned privileges, together with alterations to any tables, constraints, or views that have been constructed from the withdrawn resources. A restrict option causes the revocation to fail in the presence of abandoned privileges.

Query optimization

Chapter 5 presented a straightforward but inefficient algorithm for translating an SQL query into relational algebra. The intent there was to show the theoretical equivalence of the two languages and not to offer the relational algebra expression as a viable candidate for execution. Many techniques are available to construct an efficient execution plan. For example, Chapters 14 and 15 provided some examples of the performance improvements you can achieve with indexes to guide the searches. The research literature on query optimization is extensive, and an entire book, or more, would be necessary to investigate the topic in detail. This section adopts the more modest goal of illustrating two traditional optimization techniques: transforming a relational algebra expression into a more efficiently executable equivalent and choosing an appropriate strategy for evaluating a join operation.

Reordering operations in a relational algebra expression tree

As an initial example, consider the following query against the aquarium database. It requests the names of species represented by a red fish. The algorithm, $\mathcal{A}$, of Chapter 5 produces the relational algebra solution to the right, where Q represents the query.

```
select S.sname
from Species S, Fish F
where S.sno = F.sno and F.fcolor = "red".
```

$X = \breve{\rho}(S = \text{Species}) \times \breve{\rho}(F = \text{Fish})$
$R_h = \sigma_{b_1}(X) \cap \sigma_{b_2}(X)$
$\mathcal{A}(Q, \varphi) = \pi_q(R_h)$
where b_1 = $(S.\text{sno} = F.\text{sno})$
            b_2 = $(F.\text{fcolor} = \text{"red"})$
            q = $(S.\text{sname})$.

Back-substituting, you can express the solution in terms of the base tables as follows. This approach leads to the evaluation tree of Figure 20.17.

$$\pi_q(\sigma_{b_1}(\breve{\rho}(S = \text{Species}) \times \breve{\rho}(F = \text{Fish})) \cap \sigma_{b_1}(\breve{\rho}(S = \text{Species}) \times \breve{\rho}(F = \text{Fish}))).$$

You can apply certain transformations to the evaluation tree with the goal of obtaining an equivalent but more efficient computation. The general idea is that binary operations, particularly Cartesian products and joins, are more expensive, in terms of disk transfers, than unary operations. Select and project operations produce results that are usually much smaller than their operands. Therefore, you should perform these operations before the Cartesian products and joins. This will reduce the size of the operands to the more expensive operations.

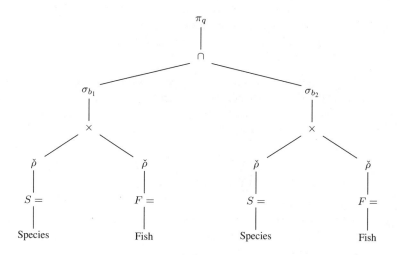

Figure 20.17　Initial expression tree for a relational algebra query solution

Consider the tree of Figure 20.17. The most glaring inefficiency is the repetition of the Cartesian products that feed the σ_{b_1} and σ_{b_2} operators. You can obviously express the intersection of two selections on the same relation as a single selection with a conjunctive predicate. In other words, $\sigma_{b_1}(X) \cap \sigma_{b_2}(X) = \sigma_{b_1 \wedge b_2}(X)$. Moreover, you can express $\sigma_{b_1 \wedge b_2}(X)$ as $\sigma_{b_1}\sigma_{b_2}(X)$, if that decomposition is helpful. In this case, the decomposition is useful because $b_2 = (F.\text{fcolor} = \text{"red"})$ deals only with the fish table, so you can move it ahead of the Cartesian product. Generally, if the boolean b involves only attributes of X, then $\sigma_b(X \times Y) = \sigma_b(X) \times Y$. These two transformations result in parts (a) and (b) of Figure 20.18.

Moving the selection operations ahead of the Cartesian product reduces the number of tuples in the operands. You can further increase efficiency by reducing the number of attributes in those operands. Recall from earlier examples that a large portion of the disk transfer traffic for a join operation deals with writing the output. If you don't trim unnecessary attributes, the length of the output tuples is approximately the sum of the lengths of the input tuples. Long tuples mean fewer tuples per block and consequently more blocks to write.

The last projection of Figure 20.18(b) involves a single attribute, $S.\text{sname}$. However, you can't move this projection ahead of the selection σ_{b_1} because that would remove attributes needed for that selection. But you can augment the projection to include the attributes needed for the selection, producing $\pi_{q'}$, where $q' = (S.\text{sname}, S.\text{sno}, F.\text{sno})$. You can now place this projection ahead of σ_{b_1}, but the original projection must remain at the top of the tree to remove the $S.\text{sno}$ and $F.\text{sno}$ values that aren't part of the answer set. The operator sequence at the top of the tree of Figure 20.18(b) is then $\pi_q \sigma_{b_1} \pi_{q'}$.

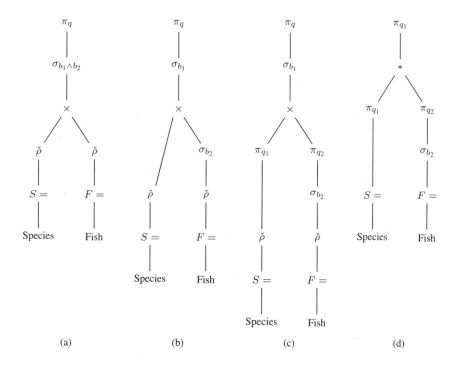

Figure 20.18 Transformed expression tree for a relational algebra query solution

In general, you can move a projection past a Cartesian product by interposing a projection in each leg of the product. You must tailor each projection to its leg by retaining only those attributes that pertain to the leg's operand. For example, suppose you have $\pi_s(X \times Y)$, where s contains attributes from both X and Y. You can replace the expression with $\pi_{s_1}(X) \times \pi_{s_2}(Y)$, where s_1 contains the attributes from s that apply to X and s_2 contains the attributes of s that apply to Y. The sets s_1 and s_2 need not be disjoint. Therefore, if you let $q_1 = (S.\text{sname}, S.\text{sno})$ and $q_2 = (F.\text{sno})$, you can transform the evaluation tree to the version of Figure 20.18(c).

Finally, you recognize that the Cartesian product followed by σ_{b_1} is actually a natural join. Join operations are usually more efficient than Cartesian products, if only because the output tuple size is smaller. Further efficiencies are also possible if you can access the operand blocks in sorted order on the common attributes. Converting the Cartesian product and subsequent selection to a natural join requires renaming operators and thus some modification of the selection and projection operators to reflect the new names. In particular, you drop the $\breve{\rho}$ operators, modify b_2 to refer to the fcolor attribute rather than to F.fcolor, and change q_1, q_2, and q to refer to sno and sname as appropriate. The final evaluation tree then appears in Figure 20.18(d), where now

$$
\begin{aligned}
q &= \text{(sname)} \\
b_2 &= \text{(fcolor = "red")} \\
q_1 &= \text{(sno, sname)} \\
q_2 &= \text{(sno)}.
\end{aligned}
$$

A heuristic for transforming the evaluation tree

In general, after transforming an expression tree as illustrated in the preceding example, you divide it into islands around the binary operations. These operations are typically natural joins although they can include Cartesian products, unions, intersections, and set differences. Any unary operators that reside on the path out of a operator act as a final filter on the result stream of the binary operation.

In the example, the final configuration of Figure 20.18(d) represents just one island, and it is organized around a natural join. There are a variety of methods for performing the natural join; they differ only in the strategies for assembling the tuples that combine successfully. All the algorithms emit a stream of result tuples that are accumulated in an output block and written to disk as necessary. If unary operators appear on the join's output arm, the process imposes them on the output tuple stream before writing it into the output block. In the example, a single operator, π_q, reduces the number of attributes in the output stream. In turn, this allows more tuples per block and, therefore, fewer blocks. Generally, a collection of selections, projections, and renaming operations can appear on the join's output arm. In this case, you combine the selections and projections into a single selection followed by a single projection. Renaming operators modify the attribute schema of the output relation but don't affect the data itself.

In the general case, an island accepts its operands from other islands lower in the evaluation tree. Typically, no unary operators appear on the input streams because they are absorbed into the final stages of the binary operations of the previous islands. However, a special case occurs when the inputs arise from the leaf nodes. In this case, the unary operators serve as input filters on the incoming operands. In Figure 20.18(d), π_{q_1} reduces the tuples flowing from the species relation, and $\pi_{q_2}\sigma_{b_2}$ perform a similar function on the tuple stream from the fish relation. A reducer on the input stream usually permits the DBMS to pack several input blocks in a single buffer block. Even if this savings isn't significant, incorporating the unary operators on the input streams from the leaf nodes removes the need for separate passes across the relations for the unary operators.

The heuristic for transforming the evaluation tree is to migrate the selection and projection operators as far down the tree as possible, thus reducing the size of the operands to the expensive binary operations. Each pair of relational algebra operators has a different set of circumstances that permit a transposition. You can reverse the pair $\pi_q\sigma_b$, for example, if the projection list q contains the attributes used in the boolean list b. The following list offers some useful rules, which supplement the commutative and associative properties of the relational algebra operators established in Chapter 3.

- $\pi_q(X) = \pi_q\pi_{q,p}(X)$. This rule augments a projection, which enables it to move past a selection involving additional attributes, p. The next rule illustrates an application.

- $\pi_q\sigma_b(X) = \sigma_b\pi_{q,p}(X)$, where b involves attributes p that aren't among those in the list q.

- $\sigma_{b_1}\sigma_{b_2}(X) = \sigma_{b_1 \wedge b_2}(X) = \sigma_{b_1}(X) \cap \sigma_{b_2}(X)$.

- $\sigma_{b_1 \vee b_2}(X) = \sigma_{b_1}(X) \cup \sigma_{b_2}(X)$.

- $\sigma_{b_1 \wedge b_2}(X \times Y) = \sigma_{b_1}(X) \times \sigma_{b_2}(Y)$, if b_1 involves only attributes of X and b_2 involves only attributes of Y.

- $\sigma_{b_1 \wedge b_2}(X \times Y) = \sigma_{b_1}\sigma_{b_2}(X \times Y) = \sigma_{b_2}(\sigma_{b_1}(X) \times Y)$, if b_1 involves only attributes of X.

- $\sigma_b(X * Y) = \sigma_b(X) * Y$, if b involves only attributes of X.

- $\pi_q(X \times Y) = \pi_{q_1}(X) \times \pi_{q_2}(Y)$, where q_1 contains the elements of q that are among the attributes of X, and q_2 is similarly constructed with respect to Y.

- $\pi_q(X * Y) = \pi_{q_1}(X) * \pi_{q_2}(Y)$, where q_1 contains the elements of q that are among the attributes of X, plus any common attributes of X and Y that aren't already included in q. q_2 is similarly constructed with respect to Y.

Algebraic query optimization proceeds by migrating selection and projection operators down the evaluation tree as far as possible, thus reducing the size of operands to the expensive binary operations.

A comprehensive example

For a second example, consider the following query that determines for each species the average volume of the tanks where it's represented. Recall that a subquery is necessary to prevent overcounting a tank when it connects to a given species through more than one fish. The algorithm of Chapter 5 delivers the relational algebra solution to the right below.

```
select S.sno, S.sname,
    average(T.tvolume) as volume
from Species S, Tank T
where exists
    (select *
    from Fish F
    where S.sno = F.sno and F.tno = T.tno)
groupby S.sno.
```

$X_1 = \check{\rho}(S = \text{Species}) \times \check{\rho}(T = \text{Tank})$
$X_2 = X_1 \times \check{\rho}(F = \text{Fish})$
$X_3 = \sigma_{b_1}(X_2) \cap \sigma_{b_2}(X_2)$
$X_4 = \pi_q \Psi^f_\gamma \pi_{X_1}(X_3)$
where $b_1 = (S.\text{sno} = F.\text{sno})$
$\quad\quad b_2 = (F.\text{tno} = T.\text{tno})$
$\quad\quad f = (\text{volume} = \text{average}(T.\text{tvolume}))$
$\quad\quad \gamma = (S.\text{sno})$
$\quad\quad q = (S.\text{sno}, S.\text{sname}, \text{volume})$.

π_{X_1} means the projection on all the attributes of X_1 (i.e., on S.sno, S.sname, S.sfood, T.tno, T.tname, T.tcolor, and T.tvolume). Figure 20.19 illustrates the initial evaluation tree. In this case, the Cartesian product involves more than two operands, which reduces the number of islands in the final tree and therefore the number of passes over the intermediate relations. Moreover, Cartesian products frequently evolve to natural joins, and the simultaneous natural join of three input streams is more efficient than a pairwise approach. Because both the Cartesian product and the natural join are associative operations, the rearrangement is valid.

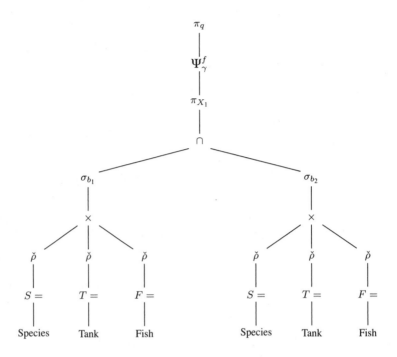

Figure 20.19   Initial relational algebra from SQL with a subquery

Again, you see the pattern $\sigma_{b_1}(Y) \cap \sigma_{b_2}(Y)$, which you can reduce to $\sigma_{b_1 \wedge b_2}(Y)$. At this point, you recognize the selection following the Cartesian product as a natural join, and you introduce the appropriate changes into the expression tree. These changes require attention to the attribute names and the proper parameter adjustments in subsequent operations to reflect the correct names. The parameters in this case must now read as follows.

$$
\begin{aligned}
f &= \text{(volume = average(tvolume))} \\
\gamma &= \text{(sno)} \\
q &= \text{(sno, sname, volume).}
\end{aligned}
$$

The transformation gives the arrangement of Figure 20.20(a). The optimization process recovers the natural join even though the SQL had to separate the components by placing one of them in a subquery. After the join, the projection π_{X_1} retains only the attributes of Species and Tank and therefore eliminates duplicates corresponding to a multifish connection between a species and a tank. You can manipulate the projections to reduce the size of the operands to the natural join, as shown in part (b) of Figure 20.20. The projection after the join must remain to remove the duplicates associated with many fish connecting a (species, tank) pair, but it needs to retain only enough attributes to enable the following aggregate to function properly. The projections pushed onto the legs of the join must also

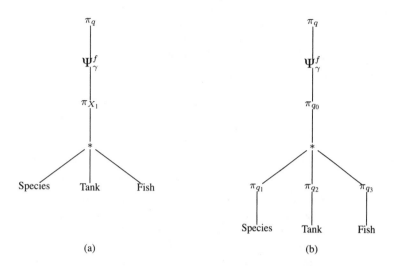

Figure 20.20   Optimized configuration for the subquery example

maintain these attributes plus any common attributes among the components. Therefore, you have the following parameters.

q_0 = (sno, sname, tvolume) q_2 = (tno, tvolume)
q_1 = (sno, sname) q_3 = (tno, sno).

Estimating the cost of a join operation: writing the output

These examples illustrate algebraic transformations to increase execution efficiency, independent of the circumstances that prevail during the actual processing. The processing of each island in the tree hinges on a binary operation or on an extended binary operation in the case of joins or Cartesian products with more than two inputs. At that point, a number of factors influence the choice of join method: the size of the operands, the number of distinct values expected in the common attributes, the availability of indexes, the packing scheme of the tuples, and the amount of memory available. So you need a second optimization phase to choose a particular approach to feed the input streams to the central operation of the island. This phase is illustrated here with a discussion of several competing methods for performing a join.

Suppose you want to join relation R_1, containing attributes X and A, with relation R_2, containing attributes Y and A. The common attribute in this case is the single attribute A, but in general, a collection of common attributes is possible. Suppose you know the number of tuples in each relation, T_1 and T_2, and the number of blocks, B_1 and B_2, where they are packed. Assume the tuples of each relation are packed by themselves on separate blocks. Let $I_1(A)$ and $I_2(A)$ be the images of the common attribute in each relation. The image is the number of distinct values of the attribute in the relation. Subsequent discussion will refer to them simply as I_1 and I_2. The images of A are probably available because the DBMS can easily accumulate these values as it inserts and deletes tuples.

Another useful parameter is J, the total number of distinct values of A across both relations. You can use J to estimate the output size of the join $r(R_1) * r(R_2)$ as follows. Let K be the number of distinct values of A that are common to $r(R_1)$ and (R_2). Then

$$I_1 = I_1' + K,$$ where I_1' is the number of A values in R_1, but not in R_2
$$I_2 = I_2' + K,$$ where I_2' is the number of A values in R_2, but not in R_1
$$J = I_1' + I_2' + K$$
$$J = I_1 - K + I_2 - K + K$$
$$J = I_1 + I_2 - K$$
$$K = I_1 + I_2 - J.$$

Knowing K, you can infer that the fraction K/I_1 of the tuples from R_1 will successfully join with tuples from R_2. This estimate assumes that the distinct A values are uniformly represented among the R_1 tuples. Although this condition may not be strictly true, it isn't likely that more detailed information on the distribution profile is available. Each of the $(K/I_1)T_1$ participating tuples in R_1 contains a single A value, and you can predict that A value will occur T_2/I_2 times in R_2, assuming that the distribution of tuples across the distinct A values of R_2 is uniform. Therefore, the number of tuples expected from the join is

$$T = \frac{KT_1T_2}{I_1I_2}. \tag{20.1}$$

The tuples of R_1 occupy B_1 blocks, which implies that there are T_1/B_1 tuples per block. Equivalently, each tuple occupies the fraction B_1/T_1 of a block. Similarly, each tuple from R_2 occupies B_2/T_2 of a block. The tuples of the join include all the attributes from both relations, without the extra copy of A. Assuming that dropping the extra A value doesn't significantly affect the length of the join tuples, a join tuple then occupies the fraction $(B_1/T_1 + B_2/T_2)$ of a block. The number of tuples per block is the reciprocal of this value, which you can equate to T/B, where B is the number of blocks needed to write the output of the join.

$$\frac{T_1T_2}{B_1T_2 + B_2T_1} = \frac{T}{B}. \tag{20.2}$$

Using the calculation for T above, you calculate the number of output blocks as

$$B = \frac{K(B_1T_2 + B_2T_1)}{I_1I_2}. \tag{20.3}$$

Because the process must write each of the B blocks, this value constitutes a common cost, regardless of the method used to compute the join. This information is useful because if it turns out to be the dominant term in the total cost, all the methods are roughly equal in cost, and you must make a choice on some criterion other than minimal disk traffic.

If the value J isn't available, you can't calculate K, and consequently you can't evaluate Equation 20.3. In this case, you assume that *all* the tuples in the relation with the smaller image successfully join with tuples of the other relation. This assumption is certainly true if the join is working with the components of a one-to-many relationship under a referential integrity constraint, as is often the case. The "many" side of the relationship will have the smaller image, and each tuple will join with exactly one tuple from the dominant side. In any case, if the assumption is erroneous, you will overestimate the cost of writing the output because in reality, some tuples from the relation with the smaller image may not participate in the join. The true cost in this case would be smaller than predicted. With this assumption, you can estimate the cost of writing the output as follows, where $I = \max(I_1, I_2)$.

$$B = \frac{B_1 T_2 + B_2 T_1}{I}. \tag{20.4}$$

Estimating the cost of a join operation: organizing the input streams

All join methods bear the cost derived above, but from this point different approaches encounter different costs associated with paging the input streams through memory to create the join. To better appreciate the differences involved, assume the following values for the problem parameters. The available memory size, M, is strictly for block caching. You can assume that additional space is reserved to accumulate an output block, to store a few transient blocks, and to hold the processing logic.

$T_1 = T_2 = 10000$	number of tuples in each relation
$B_1 = B_2 = 1000$	number of blocks used in storing each relation
$I_1 = 1000$	image of A in R_1
$I_2 = 100$	image of A in R_2
$M = 10$	memory size available.

Equation 20.4 then gives the cost of writing the output as 20,000 block accesses. To that you must add the cost of streaming the operands through the join process. The first possibility is to read M blocks of R_1 and then page R_2 through the memory working area one block at a time. When you have emitted all join tuples from these combinations, you bring a second sequence of M blocks of R_1 into the buffers and rescan the entire R_2 relation. There will be B_1/M such passes. Each will require you to read all B_2 blocks of R_2. Therefore, the cost of streaming the input operands through the processing loop is $B_1 M/B_2$. For the given parameters, this cost is 100,000 block accesses. This method is an **unordered join** because it arranges for every pair of blocks, one from R_1 and one from R_2, to reside simultaneously in memory at some point in the process. That approach clearly captures all possible tuples that participate in the join, but it can be wasteful when the blocks under consideration are filled with incompatible tuples.

If you have the tuples from the two relations available in sorted order on attribute A, you can avoid this waste. For example, if indexes are available on A for both relations, an ordered approach is possible. The most efficient arrangement occurs when both indexes are sparse. In other words, the data records appear in index order, and the index holds one entry per data block. Under these conditions, an index for 1000 blocks occupies only 5 or 6 blocks. The index is so small in relation to the data blocks and the common cost of writing the join output that you can ignore it. Indeed, because the data blocks are in sorted order, you can read them directly without using the index.

The join process then streams the tuples from both operands through a matching process as follows. As long as a mismatch persists between the current tuples from the two streams, you advance the stream with the smaller A value. When a match occurs, you bring into memory all tuples from both streams with the common A value and emit the appropriate join results. You can expect that memory will accommodate the blocks from both relations corresponding to a particular value of the common attribute. In the example, you expect $T_1/I_1 = 10$ tuples from R_1 and $T_2/I_2 = 100$ tuples from R_2. These represent about one block of R_1 and 10 blocks of R_2. This volume is marginally large for the memory capacity, $M = 10$, but to illustrate the most common case, assume that you can accommodate it anyway. (You use the M blocks for R_2 and store the matching 10 tuples of R_1 in the working area.) If you don't have enough memory for the task, you must use a paging loop similar to the unordered join, but only for the relatively small number of blocks containing the matching tuples. In any case, when you have accommodated the matching tuples, the process continues through the indexes, always advancing the index with the smallest A value, until it finds another match. Therefore, if memory is sufficient to hold all tuples corresponding to a particular value of the common attribute, you can complete the join process by reading each data block just once.

A **clustering index** is an index that can recover targeted tuples by reading a number of blocks roughly equal to the number of blocks where the target tuples reside. Therefore, if clustering indexes using the A value are available on both R_1 and R_2, you can access both relations in order and emit join tuples as the scans progress. The cost of streaming the input through the computational loop is then $B_1 + B_2$, which for the example is 1000 + 1000 = 2000. This method is the **clustering-index join**, and it is obviously significantly better than the unordered join.

If M isn't large enough to accommodate matching tuples on a specific common value, you incur an added expense for a small paging loop to process the matching values. In general, you expect B_1/I_1 blocks of tuples from the R_1 relation to join with the B_2/I_2 blocks from R_2 with the same common value. You can use the M buffer blocks to process the segments from the relation with the smaller image, which you choose here to be R_2. You will then have $B_2/(MI_2)$ passes, and each will reread the B_1/I_1 related blocks of R_1 sequentially through a single block in the working area. You don't need to reread any block of R_2 because these are passing through the buffer in groups of M. Because you are already charging $B_1 + B_2$ block reads, even in the absence of this memory complication, you levy no additional charge against R_2. Furthermore, the first pass of R_1 is also free because its charge already appears in the $B_1 + B_2$ expression. So you can calculate the additional charge to process each matching situation as follows, where you again assume that all tuples from the relation with the smaller image participate in the join.

$$\left[\frac{B_2}{I_2 M} - 1\right] \cdot \frac{B_1}{I_1} \cdot I_2.$$

In the example, the additional cost is zero because you can accommodate the 10 blocks of R_2 with the same A value in the $M = 10$ buffer blocks. If M were reduced to 5, the added expense would be 100 block accesses.

If non-clustering (e.g., dense) indexes are available, you must assume a separate block read for each tuple, from either relation, in order to acquire them in order. The number of index entries is now larger by the factor T_i/B_i, which is 10 in our example. However, this number is still negligible in comparison with the number of data blocks that must be read because that value is now $T_1 + T_2$, or 20,000 in the example. The index blocks number only 50 to 60. This approach is the **non-clustering-index join**.

A **sort join** absorbs the cost of sorting the relations. After the sort, the computation proceeds as in the case of clustering indexes, requiring $B_1 + B_2$ block accesses to process the input. You can use a multiway-merge sort. In that algorithm, you first use the M memory blocks to produce a collection of runs, each of length M blocks. You use an internal sorting algorithm, such as the quicksort, to produce the runs. The second pass groups M of these runs together and uses the M memory blocks to maintain a current block from each of the runs in the group. The pass starts by reading the first block from each run into memory. The tuples in each memory block are then in order, but there is no order across the M memory blocks because their contents come from different runs. However, a merge process can continually pick off the tuple with the smallest common attribute value across all M blocks and transfer it to an output block. When you transfer a tuple, a pointer moves forward through the contributing block to consider the next tuple. The blocks empty at different rates, and you replenish each from its particular run. Eventually all the runs flow through the M blocks, which results in a single long run of M^2 blocks on the output. You then process a second group of M runs in the same way, and the pattern continues until all runs are reorganized. You now have fewer runs, but each is of length M^2. Subsequent passes result in fewer and fewer runs of longer lengths, $M^3, M^4, \ldots$. At some point M^n exceeds the number of blocks in the relation to be sorted, which means that a single sorted run exists. Therefore, the number of passes is n, where M^n first equals or exceeds the number of blocks, B_i. Solving for n, you have $n = \log_M B_i$. Each pass reads and writes the entire relation, suffering a cost of $2B_i$ block accesses. The cost of the sort is then $2B_i \log_M B_i$.

If you sort both relations in this manner, you must add the cost of the sort to the cost of scanning the results in the join loop. This gives a total cost of $B_1 + B_2 + 2B_1 \log_M B_1 + 2B_2 \log_M B_2$. In the example, this value is 14,000 block accesses.

The table below summarizes the relative costs of the different join methods. In the example, you see that the availability of clustering indexes gives the lowest cost, only 10% of the common output cost. If the clustering indexes aren't available, the next best option sorts the relations before scanning them to emit the join tuples. In this particular case, sorting is even preferable to using an existing non-clustering index.

Cost of streaming the operands through the join process		
Join type	General Cost	Cost in the example
unordered join	$B_1 B_2 / M$	100,000
clustering-index join	$B_1 + B_2$	2,000
non-clustering-index join	$T_1 + T_2$	20,000
sort join	$B_1(1 + \log_M B_1) + B_2(1 + \log_M B_2)$	14,000

 In addition to algebraic optimizations on the evaluation tree, you must choose an efficient method for processing the central binary operation of each island in the tree. Options for a natural join include an unordered join, a join on either a clustering or non-clustering index, and a sort join.

SUMMARY

Database concurrency refers to the simultaneous use of the database by several agents, persons, or programs. Concurrency leads to interference problems when multiple users compete for the same resources, but these problems are minimized when the users cooperate by using transactions. A transaction is a unit of work, possibly comprising many database calls, that the DBMS must complete on an all-or-nothing basis. An interface session must be able to signal the beginning of a transaction with a `begin transaction` statement or some implicit convention. For example, many database systems implicitly begin a transaction when an SQL session initiates a database read or write activity. The transaction ends with a `commit`, which implies a successful execution, or with a `rollback`, which indicates an error. In the case of a `rollback`, the DBMS restores the database state so that no evidence remains to suggest that the transaction was ever attempted.

A schedule for a group of transactions is a sequential list of the database calls from the transactions so that the calls associated with any given transaction remain in order. A schedule can, however, interleave calls from different transactions. A schedule is serializable if the final database state that results from executing the schedule is the same as that obtained by a serial execution of the transactions in some unspecified order. Locking and timestamps are two protocols that can achieve serializability.

A lock is a temporary access privilege given to a transaction on some specific database resource, such as a field, a tuple, a relation, or the entire database. The DBMS restricts competing transactions in their use of the locked asset to allow the privileged transaction to complete its work without interference. An exclusive lock prevents any concurrent access; a shared lock allows simultaneous observation of an object but not update. A transaction must obtain a shared lock to read an object and an exclusive lock to update or delete an object. The two-phase locking protocol guarantees serializability. It involves a growth phase, when the transaction acquire locks, followed by a shrinking phase, when it releases locks. The strict two-phase locking protocol holds all locks until the transaction terminates.

Timestamps allow concurrent transactions to proceed under the optimistic assumption that they won't interfere with each other. Timestamps can be related to the system clock, but such precision isn't necessary. However, the DBMS must implement a centralized resource that dispenses timestamps in a strictly increasing fashion so that no two transactions receive the same timestamp. The DBMS stamps each object with the timestamp of the last transaction that observed the object (i.e., the read timestamp) and the last transaction that created or updated the object (i.e., the update timestamp). If a transaction observes an object with a younger update-time, it is observing the future, and therefore it must abort and restart with a larger timestamp. If a transaction wishes to update an object with a younger read-time, a future transaction has already seen the current value, and therefore the transaction must abort and restart.

Both locks and timestamps successfully avoid the standard interference scenarios: lost-update, dirty-read, unrepeatable-read, and phantom. On lock-based systems, SQL allows the user to set an isolation level, which specifies the amount of tolerable interference from concurrent transactions. The most protective isolation level is serializable. Other options are read-uncommitted, which allows the dirty-read scenario; read-committed, which allows the unrepeatable-read scenario; and repeatable-read, which allows only the phantom.

The DBMS accomplishes failure recovery through a log file and periodic backups. The log retains a record of each transaction, noting its beginning, conclusion, before-images of affected pages, and after-images. The DBMS uses the before-images to undo a transaction that terminates with a `rollback`. A checkpoint is a log record that guarantees that the DBMS has successfully flushed all buffer pages to disk. The checkpoint includes the identity of all transactions that are in progress at the time the DBMS writes the checkpoint record. The write-ahead log protocol specifies that the DBMS must write all relevant log records before writing the corresponding modifications to the data pages. This precaution protects against a failure between the log output and the data output.

Some failures lose data in the memory buffers but don't corrupt the physical database as stored on disk. Recovery from such a failure involves a backward scan of the log file, which undoes transactions by installing before-images until it reaches a checkpoint. The backward scan then continues only as far as necessary to undo the transactions that were in progress at the time of the checkpoint. A forward scan then reinstates, by rewriting the after-images, transactions that successfully committed before the failure. If a failure does corrupt the physical database, you must restore the database state from a backup copy. You can use any surviving portion of the log to recover some transactions that committed successfully after the backup but before the failure. However, you may still need to resubmit some transactions manually.

The DBMS handles security by associating the rights to observe or update database objects with privilege descriptors. The creator (i.e., the owner) of a schema receives all rights to the structures and to any data that might inhabit the structures. The owner can grant certain non-structural rights to other users. These include select, insert, delete, update, and references privileges on tables, and usage privileges on domains. The grant statement contains a phrase that enables the receiver (i.e., the grantee) to pass the privileges on to third parties.

The DBMS maintains a privilege dependency graph that connects each privilege descriptor to other descriptors that provide prerequisite rights. A prerequisite privilege may be available from several sources. In that case, the dependency graph reflects all the sources. If revoking a privilege removes the last source of a prerequisite from a privilege descriptor, the descriptor is abandoned. The DBMS processes privilege revocations so that the final dependency graph contains no abandoned privileges. The cascade option of the revocation statement removes any abandoned privileges along with those that are actually targeted for revocation. Further alterations are made in any tables, constraints, or views that depend on the withdrawn rights. The restrict option simply fails in the presence of abandoned privileges.

Query optimization is a large topic, and only two aspects were discussed here: transformations of the relational algebra evaluation tree and competing methods for processing a natural join. You can transform the evaluation tree into a more efficient equivalent by migrating selection and projection operators as far toward the leaves as possible. This reduces the size of the operands to the binary operators, such as joins and products. You evaluate the tree as a collection of islands, each centered around a binary operation. Any unary operations on the output leg act as a final filter on the output stream from the binary operation. This typically reduces the size of output tuples and the number of output blocks generated.

The unordered join, clustering-index join, non-clustering-index join, and the sort join represent some possibilities for streaming the input operands through the loop where matching tuples meet to create an output tuple for the join. Choosing the best method depends on the prevailing circumstances, including the size of the operands, the existence and types of indexes, and the memory resources available for buffering disk pages.

Despite its length, this text has provided only an introduction to database systems. Further study can take several directions. In a theoretical vein, more advanced books develop mathematical models to explore the abstract problem of data storage and recovery. On the applied side, books are available to explain the features of a given commercial database product. Both these approaches examine databases from the outside. A third option for continued study looks at the construction of the DBMS itself. In any case, whether you continue or not, you must by now have a different, and more complete, impression of databases.

References

Abiteboul, S.; Hull, R. "IFO: a formal semantic database model," ACM Trans. Database Systems 12:4, pp. 525–565, 1987.

Aho, A.; Beeri, C.; Ullman, J.D. "The theory of joins in relational databases," ACM Trans. Database Systems 4:3, pp. 297–314, 1979.

Aho, A.; Sagiv, Y.; Ullman, J.D. "Efficient Optimization of a class of relational expressions," ACM Trans. Database Systems 4:4, pp. 435–454, 1979.

American National Standards Institute. *The Database Language SQL*, Document ANSI X3.135-1992, 1992.

Association of Computing Machinery. *Computing Curricula 1991: Report of the ACM/IEEE–CS Joint Curriculum Task Force*, ACM Order No. 201910, 1991.

Astrahan, M.; Chamberlin, D.D. "Implementation of a structured English query language," Comm. ACM 18:10, pp. 580–588, 1975.

Atre, S. *Database: Structured Techniques for Design, Performance, and Management*, John Wiley & Sons, 1980.

Austing, R.H.; Cassel, L.N. *File Organization and Access: From Data to Information*, D. C. Heath and Company, 1988.

Bachman, C. "The programmer as navigator," Comm. ACM 16:11, pp. 653–658, 1973.

Bachman, C. "Data structure diagrams," Data Base 1:2, pp. 4–16, 1969.

Bancilhon, F.; Ferran, G. "Object databases and the ODMG standard," Object Magazine 4:9, pp. 30–40, 1995.

Batini, C.; Ceri, S.; Navathe, S. *Conceptual Database Design*, Benjamin Cummings, 1992.

Bayer, F.; McCreight, E.M. "Organization and maintenance of large ordered indexes," Acta Informatica 1:3, pp. 173–189, 1972.

Beeri, C.; Bernstein, P.A. "Computational problems related to the design of normal form relational schemes," ACM Trans. Database Systems 4:1, pp. 30–59, 1979.

Beeri, C. "On the membership problem for functional and multivalued dependencies in relational databases," ACM Trans. Database Systems 5:3, pp. 241–259, 1980.

Bell, D.; Grimson, J. *Distributed Database Systems*, Addison–Wesley, 1992.

Bernstein, P.A.; Hadzilacos, V.; Goodman, N. *Concurrency Control and Recovery in Database Systems*, Addison-Wesley, 1987.

Bernstein, P.A. "Synthesizing third normal form relations from functional dependencies," ACM Trans. Database Systems 1:4, pp. 277–298, 1976.

Bertino, E.; Martino, L. "Object–oriented database management systems: concepts and issues," IEEE Computer 24:4, pp. 33–47, 1991.

Bertino, E.; Martino, L. *Object–Oriented Database Systems*, Addison–Wesley, 1993.

Biskup, J. "A foundation of Codd's maybe–operations," ACM Trans. Database Systems 8:4, pp. 608–636, 1983.

Blaha, M.R.; Premerlani, W.J.; Rumbaugh, J.E. "Relational database design using an object–oriented methodology," Comm. ACM 31:4, pp. 414–427, 1988.

Boyce, R.F.; Chamberlin, D.D.; King, W.F.; Hammer, M.M. "Specifying queries as relational expressions," Comm. ACM 18:11, pp. 621–628, 1975.

Bradley, J. "An extended owner–coupled set data model and predicate calculus for database management," ACM Trans. Database Systems 3:4, pp. 385–416, 1978.

Bradley, J. *File and Data Base Techniques*, Holt, Rinehart, and Winston, 1982.

Bradley, J. *Introduction to Data Base Management in Business*, Holt, Rinehart, and Winston, 1987.

Braithwaite, K.S. *Data Administration*, John Wiley & Sons, 1985.

Brosda, V; Vossen, G. "Update and retrieval through a universal schema interface," ACM Trans. Database Systems 13:4, pp. 449–485, 1988.

Cardenas, A.F. *Data Base Management Systems*, Allyn and Bacon, 1985.

Cattell, R. G. G. (Editor) *The Object Database Standard: ODMG-93*, Morgan Kaufman Publishers, 1994.

Chamberlin, D.D.; Boyce, R.F. "SEQUEL: A structured English query language," Proc. ACM SIGMOD Workshop on Data Description, Access, and Control, pp. 249–264, Ann Arbor, MI, May, 1974.

Chen, P.P. "The entity–relationship model – toward a unified view of data," ACM Trans. Database Systems 1:1, pp. 9–36, 1976.

Clocksin, W.F.; Mellish, C.S. *Programming in Prolog, Second Edition*, Springer–Verlag, 1984.

CODASYL Data Base Task Group. *April 1971 Report*, ACM, 1971.

Codd, E.F. "Relational database: a practical foundation for productivity," Comm. ACM 25:2, pp. 109–117, 1982.

Codd, E.F. "A relational model for large shared data banks," Comm. ACM 13:6, pp. 377–387, 1979.

Codd, E.F. "Extending the database relational model to capture more meaning," ACM Trans. Database Systems 4:4, pp. 397–434, 1979.

Cohen, J. "A view of the origins and development of Prolog," Comm. ACM 31:1, pp. 26–36, 1988.

Copeland, G.; Maier, D. "Making Smalltalk a database system," ACM SIGMOD Intl. Conf. on Management of Data, Boston, MA, June, 1984.

Czejdo, B.; Elmasri, R.; Rusinkiewicz, M.; Embley, D.W. "A graphical data manipulation language for an extended entity–relationship model," IEEE Computer 23:3, pp. 26–36, 1990.

Date, C.J. *An Introduction to Database Systems, Sixth Edition*, Addison–Wesley, 1995.

Date, C.J. *Relational Database: Selected Writings*, Addison–Wesley, 1986.

Date, C.J. *An Introduction to Database Systems, Vol. II*, Addison–Wesley, 1984.

Date, C.J.; Fagin, R. "Simple conditions for guaranteeing higher normal forms in relational databases," ACM Trans. Database Systems 17:3, pp. 465–476, 1992.

Date, C.J.; Darwen, H. *A Guide to the SQL Standard, Third Edition*, Addison–Wesley, 1993.

Davis, W.S. *Business Systems Analysis and Design*, Wadsworth, 1994.

Diederich, J.; Milton, J. "New methods and fast Algorithms for database normalization," ACM Trans. Database Systems 13:3, pp. 339–365, 1988.

Diehr, G. *Database Management*, Scott, Foresman and Company, 1989.

Digitalk, Inc. *Smalltalk V, Object–Oriented Programming System: Tutorial and Programming Handbook*, Digitalk Corp., 9841 Airport Blvd., Los Angeles, Calif., 1992.

Digitalk, Inc. *Smalltalk V, Object–Oriented Programming System: Encyclopedia of Classes*, Digitalk Corp., 9841 Airport Blvd., Los Angeles, Calif., 1992.

Eckols, S. *IMS for the COBOL Programmer*, Mike Murach & Associates, 1985.

Elmasri, R; Navathe, S.B. *Fundamentals of Database Systems*, Benjamin Cummings, 1989.

Fagin, R. "A normal form for relational databases that is based on domains and keys," ACM Trans. Database Systems 6:3, pp. 387–415, 1981.

Fagin, R.; Nievergelt, J.; Pippenger, N.; Strong, H.R. "Extendible hashing–a fast access method for dynamic files," ACM Trans. Database Systems 4:3, pp. 315–344, 1979.

Fagin, R. "Multivalued dependencies and a new normal form for relational databases," ACM Trans. Database Systems 2:3, pp. 262–278, 1977.

Folk, M.J.; Zoellick, B. *File Structures, Second Edition*, Addison–Wesley, 1992.

Freundlich, Y. "Knowledge bases and databases: Converging technologies, diverging interests," IEEE Computer 23:11, pp. 51–57, 1990.

Garg, A.K.; Gotlieb, C.C. "Order–preserving key transformations," ACM Trans. Database Systems 11:2, pp. 213–234, 1986.

Goldberg, A. *Smalltalk–80: The Language and its Application*, Addison–Wesley, 1983.

Gray, J.; Reuter, A. *Transaction Processing: Concepts and Techniques*, Morgan Kaufmann, 1993.

Gupta, G.K. "A self–assessment procedure dealing with binary search trees and B–trees," Comm. ACM 27:5, pp. 435–443, 1984.

Hammer, M.; McLeod, D. "Database description with SDM: a semantic database model," ACM Trans. Database Systems 6:3, pp. 351–386, 1981.

Hansen, J.V.; Messier, W.F. "A relational approach to decision support for EDP auditing," Comm. ACM 27:11, pp. 1129–1133, 1984.

Hawryszkiewycz, I.T. *Database Analysis and Design*, Science Research Associates, 1984.

Howe, D.R. *Data Analysis for Data Base Design*, Edward Arnold, Ltd., 1983.

Hurson, A.R.; Pakzad, S.H.; Cheng, J. "Object–oriented database management systems: evolution and performance issues," IEEE Computer 26:2, pp. 48–60, 1993.

Informix Software, Inc. *Informix–SQL, Version 2.10: Relational Database Management System Reference Manual*, Part No. 200–404–2020–0, Rev. A, 1987.

Jacobs, B.E. *Applied Database Logic, Vol. I: Fundamental Database Issues*, Prentice–Hall, 1985.

Johnson, T.; Shasha, D. "The performance of current B–tree algorithms," ACM Trans. Database Systems 18:1, pp. 51–101, 1993.

Kent, W. "A simple guide to five normal forms in relational database theory," Comm. ACM 26:2, pp. 120–125, 1983.

Kent, W. "The universal relation revisited," ACM Trans. Database Systems 8:4, pp. 644–648, 1983.

Kent, W. "Consequences of assuming a universal relation," ACM Trans. Database Systems 6:4, pp. 539–556, 1981.

Kim, W. "Object–oriented database systems: strengths and weaknesses," J. Object–Oriented Programming 4:4, pp. 21–29, 1991.

Knuth, D. *The Art of Computer Programming, Volume 3, Sorting and Searching*, Addison–Wesley, 1973.

Korth, H.F.; Silberschatz, A. *Database System Concepts*, McGraw–Hill, 1986.

Kroenke, D.M.; Dolan, K.A. *Database Processing, Third Edition*, Science Research Associates, 1988.

Kuper, G.M.; Vardi, M.Y. "The logical data model," ACM Trans. Database Systems 18:3, pp. 379–413, 1993.

Larson, P.A. "Linear hashing with separators – a dynamic hashing scheme achieving one–access retrieval," ACM Trans. Database Systems 13:3, pp. 366–388, 1988.

Larson, P.A. "Linear hashing with overflow handling by linear probing," ACM Trans. Database Systems 10:1, pp. 75–89, 1985.

Larson, P.A. "Dynamic Hashing," BIT 18, pp. 184–201, 1978.

Lien, Y.E. "Hierarchical schemata for relational databases," ACM Trans. Database Systems 6:1, pp. 48–69, 1981.

Lindgren, B.W. *Statistical Theory*, Macmillan, 1968.

Loomis, M.E.S. *Object Databases: The Essentials*, Addison–Wesley, 1995.

Loomis, M.E.S. "Objects and SQL: accessing relational databases," Object Magazine, pp. 68–78, Sept/Oct, 1991.

Loomis, M.E.S. *The Database Book*, Macmillan, 1987.

Loomis, M.E.S. *Data Management and File Processing*, Prentice–Hall, 1983.

Maier, D.; Ullman, J.D.; Vardi, M.Y. "On the foundations of the universal relation model," ACM Trans. Database Systems 9:2, pp. 283–308, 1984.

Maier, D. *The Theory of Relational Databases*, Computer Science Press, 1983.

Maier, D.; Mendelzon, A.O.; Sagiv, Y. "Testing implications of data dependencies," ACM Trans. Database Systems 4:4, pp. 455–469, 1979.

Malpas, J. *Prolog: A Relational Language and its Applications*, Prentice–Hall, 1987.

Markowitz, V.M.; Shoshani, A. "Representing extended entity–relationship structures in relational databases: a modular approach," ACM Trans. Database Systems 17:3, pp. 423–464, 1992.

McFadden, F.R.; Hoffer, J.A. *Data Base Management*, Benjamin Cummings, 1985.

Mendelson, H. "Analysis of extendible hashing," IEEE Trans. Software Engineering SE–8:6, pp. 611–619, 1982.

Microsoft Corporaton. *Microsoft Access User's Guide*, Microsoft Corporation, 1992.

Mittra, S.S. *Principles of Relational Database Systems*, Prentice–Hall, 1991.

Navathe, S.B. "Evolution of data modeling for databases," Comm. ACM 35:9, pp. 112–123, 1992.

Negri, M.; Pelagatti, G. "Distributive join: a new algorithm for joining relations," ACM Trans. Database Systems 16:4, pp. 655–559, 1991.

Ozkarahan, E. *Database Management: Concepts, Design, and Practice*, Prentice–Hall, 1990.

Özsoyoğlu, G.; Wang, H. "Example–based graphical database query languages," IEEE Computer 26:5, pp. 25–38, 1993.

Özsoyoğlu, G.; Özsoyoğlu, Z.M.; Matos, V. "Extending relational algebra and relational calculus with set–valued attributes and aggregate functions," ACM Trans. Database Systems 12:4, pp. 566-592, 1987.

Pizano, A.; Klinger, A.; Cardenas, A. "Specification of spatial integrity constraints in pictorial databases," IEEE Computer 22:12, pp. 59–71, 1989.

Premeriani, W.J.; Blaha, M.R.; Rumbaugh, J.E.; Varwig, T.A. "An object–oriented relational database," Comm. ACM, 33:11, pp. 99–109, 1990.

Ricardo, C. *Database Systems: Principles, Design, & Implementation*, Macmillen, 1990.

Rob, P.; Coronel, C. *Database Systems: Design, Implementation, and Management*, Wadsworth, 1993.

Rothnie Jr., J.B. "An approach to implementing a relational data management system," Proc. ACM SIGMOD Workshop on Data Description, Access, and Control, pp. 277–294, Ann Arbor, MI, 1974.

Rumbaugh, J.E.; Blaha, M.; Premerlani, W.; Eddy, F.; Lorensen, W. *Object–Oriented Modeling and Design*, Prentice–Hall, 1991.

Sacco, G.M. "Fragmentation: a technique for efficient query processing," ACM Trans. Database Systems 11:2, pp. 113–133, 1986.

Salem, K.; Gracia–Molina, H.; Shands, J. "Altruistic locking," ACM Trans. Database Systems 19:1, pp. 117–165, 1994.

Scholl, M. "New file organizations based on dynamic hashing," ACM Trans. Database Systems 6:1, pp. 194–211, 1981.

Servio Corporation. *Programming in Opal, Opal Kernel Classes, Topaz Opal Programming Environment*, Servio Corp., Alameda, Calif., 1990.

Shapiro, L.D. "Join processing in database systems with large main memories," ACM Trans. Database Systems 11:3, pp. 239–264, 1986.

Shipman, D.W. "The functional data model and the data language DAPLEX," ACM Trans. Database Systems 6:1, pp. 140–173, 1981.

Smith, H.C. "Database design: composing fully normalized tables from a rigorous dependency diagram," Comm. ACM 28:8, pp. 826–838, 1985.

Smith, J.M.; Chang, P.Y. "Optimizing the performance of a relational algebra interface," Comm. ACM 18:10, pp. 568–579, 1975.

Smith, J.R.; Monarchi, D.E. "Using Smalltalk/V objects as rows in relational tables," J. Object–Oriented Programming 5:8, pp. 37–41, 1993.

Smith, P.D.; Barnes, G.M. *Files & Databases: An Introduction*, Addison–Wesley, 1987.

Sowa, J.F. *Conceptual Structures: Information Processing in Mind and Machine*, Addison–Wesley, 1984.

Stonebraker, M. "A functional view of data independence," Proc. ACM SIGMOD Workshop on Data Description, Access, and Control, pp. 63–81, Ann Arbor, MI, May, 1974.

Ullman, J.D. "Implementation of logical query languages for databases," ACM Trans. Database Systems 10:3, pp. 289–321, 1985.

Ullman, J.D. *Principles of Database and Knowledge–Base Systems, Vols. I–II*, Computer Science Press, 1988.

Valduriez, P. "Join indices," ACM Trans. on Database Systems 12:2, pp. 218–246, 1987.

Van Gelder, A.; Topor, R.W. "Safety and translation of relational calculus queries," ACM Trans. Database Systems 16:2, pp. 235–278, 1991.

Vasta, J.A. *Understanding Data Base Management Systems*, Wadsworth, 1985.

Veklerov, E. "Analysis of dynamic hashing with deferred splitting," ACM Trans. Database Systems 10:1, pp. 90–96, 1985.

Walsh, M.E. *Information Management Systems / Virtual Storage*, Prentice–Hall (Reston), 1979.

Wells, D.L.; Blakeley, J.A.; Thompson, C.W. "Architecture of an open object–oriented database management system," IEEE Computer 25:10, pp. 74–82, 1992.

Wilmot, R.B. "Foreign keys decrease adaptability of database designs," Comm. ACM 27:12, pp. 1237–1243, 1984.

Zaniolo, C.; Malkanoff, M.A. "On the design of relational database schemata," ACM Trans. Database Systems 6:1, pp. 1–47, 1981.

Zaniolo, C. "A new normal form for the design of relational database schemata," ACM Trans. Database Systems 7:3, pp. 489–499, 1982.

Index